M000164587

# Collins

## ENGLISH
### DICTIONARY
#### POCKET EDITION

Published by Collins
An imprint of HarperCollins Publishers
Westerhill Road
Bishopbriggs
Glasgow G64 2QT

Tenth edition 2016

ISBN 978-0-00-814180-6

10 9 8 7 6 5 4 3 2 1

© HarperCollins Publishers 1992, 1996, 2000, 2004, 2006, 2008, 2010, 2012, 2016

Collins® is a registered trademark of HarperCollins Publishers Limited

www.collinsdictionary.com
www.collins.co.uk/languagesupport

Typeset by Davidson Publishing Solutions, Glasgow

Printed in Italy by GRAFICA VENETA S.p.A.

If you would like to comment on any aspect of this book, please contact us at the given address or online.
E-mail: dictionaries@harpercollins.co.uk
 facebook.com/collinsdictionary
 @collinsdict

Acknowledgements
We would like to thank those authors and publishers who kindly gave permission for copyright material to be used in the Collins Corpus. We would also like to thank Times Newspapers Ltd for providing valuable data.

# Contents

# Editorial Staff

**Editors**
Ian Brookes
Mary O'Neill

**Supplement**
Martin and Simon Toseland

**For the publisher**
Gerry Breslin
Hannah Dove
Kerry Ferguson

# Using this Dictionary

**Main entry words** are printed in blue, in large bold type:

**abbey**

All main entry words, including abbreviations and combining forms, are listed in strict alphabetical sequence:

**abbot**
**abbreviate**
**ABC**
**abdicate**

**Variant spellings** are shown in full:

**adrenalin, adrenaline**

*Note*: where the spellings *-ize* and *-ization* are used at the end of a word, the alternative forms *-ise* and *-isation* are equally acceptable.

**Pronunciations** are given in square brackets for words that are difficult or confusing; the word is respelt as it is pronounced, with the stressed syllable in bold type:

**antipodes** [an-**tip**-pod-deez]

**Parts of speech** are shown in italics as an abbreviation:

**ablaze** *adj*

When a word can be used as more than one part of speech, the change of part of speech is shown after an arrow:

> **mock** *v* make fun of; mimic
> ▷ *adj* sham or imitation

Parts of speech may be combined for some words, eg

> **alone** *adj*, *adv* without anyone or
> anything else

**Cross references** are shown in bold type:

> **doner kebab** *n* see **kebab**

**Irregular parts** or confusing forms of verbs, nouns, adjectives, and adverbs shown in bold type:

> **begin** *v* **-ginning, -gan, -gun**
> **regret** *v* **-gretting, -gretted**
> **anniversary** *n, pl* **-ries**
> **angry** *adj* **-grier, -griest**
> **well** *adv* **better, best**

**Meanings** are separated by semicolons:

> **casual** *adj* careless, nonchalant;
> (of work or workers) occasional or
> not permanent; for informal wear;
> happening by chance

**Phrases and idioms** are included in the meanings of the main entry word:

> **hand** *n* ... *v* ... **have a hand
> in** be involved in **lend a hand**
> help...

**Related words** are shown in the same paragraph as the main entry word after an arrow:

> **absurd** *adj* incongruous or
> ridiculous ▶ **absurdly** *adv*
> ▶ **absurdity** *n*

*Note:* where the meaning of a related word is not given, it may be understood from the main entry word, or from another related word.

**Compounds** are shown in alphabetical order at the end of the paragraph after an arrow:

> **ash** *n* ...
> ▶ **ashtray** *n* receptacle for tobacco
> ash and cigarette butts ▶ **Ash
> Wednesday** first day of Lent

# Abbreviations

| | | | |
|---|---|---|---|
| *AD* | anno Domini | *meteorol* | meteorology |
| *adj* | adjective | *mil* | military |
| *adv* | adverb | *n* | noun |
| *anat* | anatomy | *N* | North |
| *archit* | architecture | *naut* | nautical |
| *astrol* | astrology | *NZ* | New Zealand |
| *Austral* | Australia(n) | *obs* | obsolete |
| *BC* | before Christ | *offens* | offensive |
| *biol* | biology | *orig* | originally |
| *Brit* | British | *photog* | photography |
| *chem* | chemistry | *pl* | plural |
| *C of E* | Church of England | *prep* | preposition |
| *conj* | conjuction | *pron* | pronoun |
| *E* | East | *psychol* | psychology |
| *e.g.* | for example | ® | trademark |
| *esp.* | especially | *RC* | Roman Catholic |
| *etc.* | et cetera | *S* | South |
| *fem* | feminine | *S Afr* | South Africa(n) |
| *foll* | followed | *Scot* | Scottish |
| *geom* | geometry | *sing* | singular |
| *hist* | history | *US* | United States |
| *interj* | interjection | *usu.* | usually |
| *lit* | literary | *vb* | verb |
| *masc* | masculine | *W* | West |
| *med* | medicine | *zool* | zoology |

# Aa

**a** *adj* indefinite article, used before a noun being mentioned for the first time

**AA** Alcoholics Anonymous; Automobile Association

**aardvark** *n* S African anteater with long ears and snout

**AB** able-bodied seaman

**aback** *adv* **taken aback** startled or disconcerted

**abacus** *n* beads on a wire frame, used for doing calculations

**abalone** [ab-a-**lone**-ee] *n* edible sea creature with a shell lined with mother of pearl

**abandon** *v* desert or leave (one's wife, children, etc.); give up (hope etc.) altogether ▷ *n* lack of inhibition ▶ **abandoned** *adj* deserted; uninhibited ▶ **abandonment** *n*

**abase** *v* humiliate or degrade (oneself) ▶ **abasement** *n*

**abashed** *adj* embarrassed and ashamed

**abate** *v* make or become less strong ▶ **abatement** *n*

**abattoir** [**ab**-a-twahr] *n* place where animals are killed for food

**abbess** *n* nun in charge of a convent

**abbey** *n* dwelling place of, or a church belonging to, a community of monks or nuns

**abbot** *n* head of an abbey of monks

**abbreviate** *v* shorten (a word) by leaving out some letters ▶ **abbreviation** *n* shortened form of a word or words

**ABC**[1] *n* alphabet; basics of a subject

**ABC**[2] Australian Broadcasting Corporation

**abdicate** *v* give up (the throne or a responsibility) ▶ **abdication** *n*

**abdomen** *n* part of the body containing the stomach and intestines ▶ **abdominal** *adj*

**abduct** *v* carry off, kidnap ▶ **abduction** *n* ▶ **abductor** *n*

**aberration** *n* sudden change from what is normal, accurate, or correct; brief lapse in control of one's thoughts or feelings ▶ **aberrant** *adj* showing aberration

**abet** *v* **abetting, abetted** help or encourage in wrongdoing ▶ **abettor** *n*

**abeyance** *n* **in abeyance** not in use

**abhor** *v* **-horring, -horred** detest utterly ▶ **abhorrent** *adj* hateful, loathsome ▶ **abhorrence** *n*

**abide** *v* endure, put up with; (*obs*) stay or dwell e.g. *abide with me* ▶ **abide by** *v* obey (the law, rules, etc.) ▶ **abiding** *adj* lasting

**ability** *n*, *pl* **-ties** competence, power; talent

**abject** *adj* utterly miserable; lacking all self-respect ▶ **abjectly** *adv*

**abjure** *v* deny or renounce on oath

**ablative** *n* case of nouns in Latin and other languages, indicating source, agent, or instrument of action

**ablaze** *adj* burning fiercely

**able** *adj* capable, competent ▶ **ably** *adv* ▶ **able-bodied** *adj* strong and healthy

**ablutions** *pl n* act of washing

**abnormal** *adj* not normal or usual ▶ **abnormally** *adv* ▶ **abnormality** *n*

**aboard** *adv*, *prep* on, in, onto, or into (a ship, train, or plane)

**abode** *n* home, dwelling

**abolish** v do away with ▸ **abolition** n ▸ **abolitionist** n person who wishes to do away with something, esp. slavery

**abominable** adj detestable, very bad ▸ **abominable snowman** large apelike creature said to live in the Himalayas ▸ **abominably** adv

**abomination** n someone or something that is detestable

**aborigine** [ab-or-**rij**-in-ee], **aboriginal** n original inhabitant of a country or region; (**A-**) original inhabitant of Australia ▸ **aboriginal** adj

**abort** v have an abortion or perform an abortion on; have a miscarriage; end a plan or process before completion ▸ **abortive** adj unsuccessful

**abortion** n operation to end a pregnancy; (informal) something grotesque ▸ **abortionist** n person who performs abortions, esp. illegally

**abound** v be plentiful ▸ **abounding** adj

**about** prep concerning, on the subject of; in or near (a place) ▷ adv nearly, approximately; nearby **about to** shortly going to **not about to** determined not to ▸ **about-turn** n complete change of attitude

**above** adv, prep over or higher (than); greater (than); superior (to) ▸ **above board** in the open, without dishonesty

**abracadabra** n supposedly magic word

**abrasion** n scraped area on the skin

**abrasive** adj harsh and unpleasant in manner; tending to rub or scrape ▷ n substance for cleaning or polishing by rubbing

**abreast** adv, adj side by side **abreast of** up to date with

**abridge** v shorten by using fewer words ▸ **abridgment, abridgement** n

**abroad** adv to or in a foreign country; at large

**abrogate** v cancel (a law or agreement) formally ▸ **abrogation** n

**abrupt** adj sudden, unexpected; blunt and rude ▸ **abruptly** adv ▸ **abruptness** n

**abs** pl n (informal) abdominal muscles

**abscess** n inflamed swelling containing pus

> **SPELLING TIP**
> There is a silent c in the middle of **abscess**

**abscond** v leave secretly

**abseil** [ab-sale] v go down a steep drop by a rope fastened at the top and tied around one's body

**absent** adj not present; lacking; inattentive ▷ v stay away ▸ **absently** adv ▸ **absence** n being away; lack ▸ **absentee** n person who should be present but is not ▸ **absenteeism** n persistent absence from work or school ▸ **absent-minded** adj inattentive or forgetful ▸ **absent-mindedly** adv

**absinthe** n strong green aniseed-flavoured liqueur

**absolute** adj complete, perfect; not limited, unconditional; pure e.g. absolute alcohol ▸ **absolutely** adv completely ▷ interj certainly, yes ▸ **absolutism** n government by a ruler with unrestricted power

**absolve** v declare to be free from blame or sin ▸ **absolution** n

**absorb** v soak up (a liquid); take in; engage the interest of (someone) ▸ **absorption** n ▸ **absorbent** adj able to absorb liquid ▸ **absorbency** n

**abstain** v choose not to do something; choose not to vote ▶ **abstainer** n ▶ **abstention** n abstaining, esp. from voting ▶ **abstinence** n abstaining, esp. from drinking alcohol ▶ **abstinent** adj

**abstemious** adj taking very little alcohol or food ▶ **abstemiousness** n

**abstract** adj existing as a quality or idea rather than a material object; theoretical; (of art) using patterns of shapes and colours rather than realistic likenesses ▷ n summary; abstract work of art; abstract word or idea ▷ v summarize; remove ▶ **abstracted** adj lost in thought ▶ **abstraction** n

**abstruse** adj not easy to understand

**absurd** adj incongruous or ridiculous ▶ **absurdly** adv ▶ **absurdity** n

**abundant** adj plentiful ▶ **abundantly** adv ▶ **abundance** n

**abuse** v use wrongly; ill-treat violently; speak harshly and rudely to ▷ n prolonged ill-treatment; harsh and vulgar comments; wrong use ▶ **abuser** n ▶ **abusive** adj ▶ **abusively** adv ▶ **abusiveness** n

**abut** v **abutting, abutted** be next to or touching

**abysmal** adj (informal) extremely bad, awful ▶ **abysmally** adv

**abyss** n very deep hole or chasm

**AC** alternating current

**a/c** account

**acacia** [a-**kay**-sha] n tree or shrub with yellow or white flowers

**academy** n, pl -**mies** society to advance arts or sciences; institution for training in a particular skill; (Scot) secondary school ▶ **academic** adj of an academy or university; of theoretical interest only ▷ n lecturer or researcher at a university ▶ **academically** adv ▶ **academician** n member of an academy

**acanthus** n prickly plant

**ACAS** (in Britain) Advisory Conciliation and Arbitration Service

**ACC** (in New Zealand) Accident Compensation Corporation

**accede** v consent or agree (to); take up (an office or position)

**accelerate** v (cause to) move faster ▶ **acceleration** n ▶ **accelerator** n pedal in a motor vehicle to increase speed

> **SPELLING TIP**
> There is a double c in **accelerate**, but only one l

**accent** n distinctive style of pronunciation of a local, national, or social group; mark over a letter to show how it is pronounced; stress on a syllable or musical note ▷ v place emphasis on

**accentuate** v stress, emphasize ▶ **accentuation** n

**accept** v receive willingly; agree to; consider to be true ▶ **acceptance** n ▶ **acceptable** adj tolerable; satisfactory ▶ **acceptably** adv ▶ **acceptability** n

**access** n means of or right to approach or enter ▷ v obtain (data) from a computer ▶ **accessible** adj easy to reach ▶ **accessibility** n

**accession** n taking up of an office or position

**accessory** n, pl -**ries** supplementary part or object; person involved in a crime although not present when it is committed

**accident** n mishap, often causing injury; event happening by chance

**a**

▶ **accidental** *adj* happening by chance or unintentionally ▷ *n* (*Music*) symbol indicating that a sharp, flat, or natural note is not a part of the key signature ▶ **accidentally** *adv*

**acclaim** *v* applaud, praise ▷ *n* enthusiastic approval ▶ **acclamation** *n*

**acclimatize** *v* adapt to a new climate or environment ▶ **acclimatization** *n*

**accolade** *n* award, honour, or praise; award of knighthood

**accommodate** *v* provide with lodgings; have room for; oblige, do a favour for; adapt or adjust (to something) ▶ **accommodation** *n* house or room for living in ▶ **accommodating** *adj* obliging

> **SPELLING TIP**
> **Accommodation** and **accommodate** have two *c*s, but remember they have two *m*s as well

**accompany** *v* **-nying, -nied** go along with; occur with; provide a musical accompaniment for ▶ **accompaniment** *n* something that accompanies; (*Music*) supporting part that goes with a solo ▶ **accompanist** *n*

**accomplice** *n* person who helps another to commit a crime

**accomplish** *v* manage to do; finish ▶ **accomplishment** *n* completion; personal ability or skill ▶ **accomplished** *adj* expert, proficient

**accord** *n* agreement, harmony ▷ *v* fit in with **of one's own accord** voluntarily

> **USAGE NOTE**
> Do not confuse *of one's own accord* with *on one's own account* 'for one's own benefit'

**accordance** *n* **in accordance with** conforming to or according to

**according** *adv* **according to** as stated by; in conformity with ▶ **accordingly** *adv* in an appropriate manner; consequently

**accordion** *n* portable musical instrument played by moving the two sides apart and together, and pressing a keyboard or buttons to produce the notes ▶ **accordionist** *n*

**accost** *v* approach and speak to, often aggressively

**account** *n* report, description; business arrangement making credit available; record of money received and paid out with the resulting balance; person's money held in a bank; importance, value ▷ *v* judge to be **on account of** because of ▶ **accountable** *adj* responsible to someone or for something ▶ **accountability** *n*

**accounting** *n* skill or practice of maintaining and auditing business accounts ▶ **accountant** *n* person who maintains and audits business accounts ▶ **accountancy** *n*

**accoutrements** *pl n* clothing and equipment for a particular activity

**accredited** *adj* authorized, officially recognized

**accretion** [ak-**kree**-shun] *n* gradual growth; something added

**accrue** *v* **-cruing, -crued** increase gradually ▶ **accrual** *n*

**accumulate** *v* gather together in increasing quantity ▶ **accumulation** *n* ▶ **accumulative** *adj* ▶ **accumulator** *n* (*Brit & Aust*) rechargeable electric battery

**accurate** *adj* exact, correct ▶ **accurately** *adv* ▶ **accuracy** *n*

**accursed** *adj* under a curse; detestable

**accusative** *n* grammatical case indicating the direct object

**accuse** v charge with wrongdoing
▸ **accused** n ▸ **accuser** n
▸ **accusing** adj ▸ **accusation** n
▸ **accusatory** adj

**accustom** v make used to
▸ **accustomed** adj usual; used (to);
in the habit (of)

**ace** n playing card with one symbol
on it; (informal) expert; (Tennis)
unreturnable serve ▷ adj (informal)
excellent

**acerbic** [ass-**sir**-bik] adj harsh or
bitter ▸ **acerbity** n

**acetate** [**ass**-it-tate] n (Chem)
salt or ester of acetic acid; (also
**acetate rayon**) synthetic textile
fibre

**acetic** [ass-**see**-tik] adj of or
involving vinegar ▸ **acetic acid**
colourless liquid used to make
vinegar

**acetone** [**ass**-it-tone] n colourless
liquid used as a solvent

**acetylene** [ass-**set**-ill-een] n
colourless flammable gas used in
welding metals

**ache** n dull continuous pain ▷ v be in
or cause continuous dull pain

**achieve** v gain by hard work
or ability ▸ **achievement** n
something accomplished

**Achilles heel** [ak-**kill**-eez] n small
but fatal weakness

**Achilles tendon** n cord
connecting the calf muscle to the
heel bone

**achromatic** adj colourless; (Music)
with no sharps or flats

**acid** n (Chem) one of a class of
compounds, corrosive and sour
when dissolved in water, that
combine with a base to form a
salt; (slang) LSD ▷ adj containing
acid; sour-tasting; sharp or sour
in manner ▸ **acidic** adj ▸ **acidify**
v ▸ **acidity** n ▸ **Acid (House)** n
type of funk-based electronically

edited disco music with hypnotic
sound effects ▸ **acid rain** rain
containing acid from atmospheric
pollution ▸ **acid test** conclusive
test of value

**acknowledge** v admit,
recognize; indicate recognition
of (a person); say one has
received ▸ **acknowledgment,
acknowledgement** n

**acme** [**ak**-mee] n highest point of
achievement or excellence

**acne** [**ak**-nee] n pimply skin disease

**acolyte** n follower or attendant;
(Christianity) person who assists
a priest

**aconite** n poisonous plant with
hoodlike flowers; poison obtained
from this plant

**acorn** n nut of the oak tree

**acoustic** adj of sound and
hearing; (of a musical instrument)
not electronically amplified
▸ **acoustics** n science of sounds
▷ pl features of a room or building
determining how sound is heard
within it ▸ **acoustically** adv

**acquaint** v make familiar, inform
▸ **acquainted** adj ▸ **acquaintance**
n person known; personal
knowledge

**acquiesce** [ak-wee-**ess**] v
agree to what someone
wants ▸ **acquiescence** n
▸ **acquiescent** adj

> **USAGE NOTE**
> The use of to after acquiesce was
> formerly regarded as incorrect,
> with in being preferred, but
> either is now acceptable

**acquire** v gain, get ▸ **acquisition** n
thing acquired; act of getting

**acquisitive** adj eager to
gain material possessions
▸ **acquisitiveness** n

**acquit** v **-quitting, -quitted**
pronounce (someone) innocent;

**a**

behave in a particular way
▶ **acquittal** n

**acre** n measure of land, 4840 square yards (4046.86 square metres)
▶ **acreage** [ake-er-rij] n land area in acres

**acrid** [ak-rid] adj pungent, bitter

**acrimonious** adj bitter in speech or manner ▶ **acrimony** n

**acrobat** n person skilled in gymnastic feats requiring agility and balance ▶ **acrobatic** adj
▶ **acrobatics** pl n acrobatic feats

**acronym** n word formed from the initial letters of other words, such as NASA

**across** adv, prep from side to side (of); on or to the other side (of)
▶ **across the board** applying equally to all

**acrostic** n lines of writing in which the first or last letters of each line spell a word or saying

**acrylic** n, adj (synthetic fibre, paint, etc.) made from acrylic acid
▶ **acrylic acid** strong-smelling corrosive liquid

**ACT** Australian Capital Territory

**act** n thing done; law or decree; section of a play or opera; one of several short performances in a show; pretended attitude ▷ v do something; behave in a particular way; perform in a play, film, etc. ▶ **act of God** unpredictable natural event ▶ **acting** n art of an actor ▷ adj temporarily performing the duties of ▶ **actor, actress** n person who acts in a play, film, etc.

**actinium** n (Chem) radioactive chemical element

**action** n process of doing something; thing done; lawsuit; operating mechanism; minor battle ▶ **actionable** adj giving grounds for a lawsuit ▶ **action**

**replay** rerun of an event on a television recording

**active** adj moving, working; busy, energetic; (Grammar) (of a verb) in a form indicating that the subject is performing the action, e.g. threw in Kim threw the ball ▶ **actively** adv ▶ **activity** n state of being active; (pl **-ties**) leisure pursuit ▶ **activate** v make active ▶ **activation** n ▶ **activator** n ▶ **activist** n person who works energetically to achieve political or social goals ▶ **activism** n

**actual** adj existing in reality ▶ **actually** adv really, indeed ▶ **actuality** n

**actuary** n, pl **-aries** statistician who calculates insurance risks ▶ **actuarial** adj

**actuate** v start up (a device)

**acuity** [ak-**kew**-it-ee] n keenness of vision or thought

**acumen** [ak-yew-men] n ability to make good judgments

**acupuncture** n medical treatment involving the insertion of needles at various points on the body ▶ **acupuncturist** n

**acute** adj severe; keen, shrewd; sharp, sensitive; (of an angle) less than 90° ▷ n accent (´) over a letter to indicate the quality or length of its sound, as in café ▶ **acutely** adv ▶ **acuteness** n

**AD** anno Domini

**ad** n (informal) advertisement

**adage** n wise saying, proverb

**adagio** adv, n, pl **-gios** (Music) (piece to be played) slowly and gracefully

**adamant** adj unshakable in determination or purpose ▶ **adamantly** adv

**Adam's apple** n projecting lump of thyroid cartilage at the front of the throat

**adapt** v alter for new use or new conditions ▶ **adaptable** adj ▶ **adaptability** n ▶ **adaptation** n thing produced by adapting something; adapting ▶ **adaptor, adapter** n device for connecting several electrical appliances to a single socket

**add** v combine (numbers or quantities); join (to something); say or write further

**addendum** n, pl **-da** addition; appendix to a book etc.

**adder** n small poisonous snake

**addict** n person who is unable to stop taking drugs; (informal) person devoted to something ▶ **addicted** adj ▶ **addiction** n ▶ **addictive** adj causing addiction

**addition** n adding; thing added **in addition** besides, as well ▶ **additional** adj ▶ **additionally** adv ▶ **additive** n something added, esp. to a foodstuff, to improve it or prevent deterioration

**addled** adj confused or unable to think clearly

**address** n place where a person lives; direction on a letter; location; formal public speech ▷ v mark the destination, as on an envelope; make a speech; give attention to (a problem, task, etc.) ▶ **addressee** n person addressed

**SPELLING TIP**
Remember to double the d and the s in **address**

**adduce** v mention something as evidence or proof

**adenoids** [ad-in-oidz] pl n mass of tissue at the back of the throat ▶ **adenoidal** adj having a nasal voice caused by swollen adenoids

**adept** adj, n very skilful (person)

**adequate** adj sufficient, enough; not outstanding ▶ **adequately** adv ▶ **adequacy** n

**adhere** v stick (to); be devoted (to) ▶ **adherence** n ▶ **adherent** n devotee, follower ▶ **adhesion** n sticking (to); joining together of parts of the body that are normally separate, as after surgery

**adhesive** n substance used to stick things together ▷ adj able to stick to things

**ad hoc** adj, adv (Latin) for a particular purpose only

**adieu** [a-**dew**] interj (lit) farewell, goodbye

**ad infinitum** [ad in-fin-**eye**-tum] adv (Latin) endlessly

**adipose** adj of or containing fat

**adj** adjective

**adjacent** adj near or next (to); having a common boundary; (Geom) (of a side in a right-angled triangle) lying between a specified angle and the right angle

**adjective** n word that adds information about a noun or pronoun ▶ **adjectival** adj

**adjoin** v be next to ▶ **adjoining** adj

**adjourn** v close (a court) at the end of a session; postpone temporarily; (informal) go elsewhere ▶ **adjournment** n

**adjudge** v declare (to be)

**adjudicate** v give a formal decision on (a dispute); judge (a competition) ▶ **adjudication** n ▶ **adjudicator** n

**adjunct** n subordinate or additional person or thing

**adjure** v command (to do); appeal earnestly

**adjust** v adapt to new conditions; alter slightly so as to be suitable ▶ **adjustable** adj ▶ **adjuster** n ▶ **adjustment** n

**adjutant** [aj-oo-tant] n army officer in charge of routine administration

**ad-lib** v **-libbing, -libbed** improvise a speech etc. without preparation ▷ *n* improvised remark

**admin** *n* (*informal*) administration

**administer** *v* manage (business affairs); organize and put into practice; give (medicine or treatment)

**administrate** *v* manage (an organization) ▶ **administrator** *n*

**administration** *n* management of an organization; people who manage an organization; government e.g. *the Bush administration*

**administrative** *adj* of the management of an organization

**admiral** *n* highest naval rank ▶ **Admiralty** *n* (in Britain) former government department in charge of the Royal Navy

**admire** *v* regard with esteem and approval ▶ **admirable** *adj* ▶ **admirably** *adv* ▶ **admiration** *n* ▶ **admirer** *n* ▶ **admiring** *adj* ▶ **admiringly** *adv*

**admissible** *adj* allowed to be brought in as evidence in court ▶ **admissibility** *n*

**admission** *n* permission to enter; entrance fee; confession

**admit** *v* -**mitting**, -**mitted** confess, acknowledge; concede the truth of; allow in ▶ **admittance** *n* permission to enter ▶ **admittedly** *adv* it must be agreed

**admixture** *n* mixture; ingredient

**admonish** *v* reprove sternly ▶ **admonition** *n*

**ad nauseam** [ad **naw**-zee-am] *adv* (*Latin*) to a boring or sickening extent

**ado** *n* (*lit*) fuss, trouble

**adobe** [ad-**oh**-bee] *n* sun-dried brick

**adolescence** *n* period between puberty and adulthood ▶ **adolescent** *n*, *adj* (person) between puberty and adulthood

**adopt** *v* take (someone else's child) as one's own; take up (a plan or principle) ▶ **adopter, adoptor** *n* ▶ **adoption** *n* ▶ **adoptive** *adj* related by adoption

**adore** *v* love intensely; worship ▶ **adorable** *adj* ▶ **adoration** *n* ▶ **adoring** *adj* ▶ **adoringly** *adv*

**adorn** *v* decorate, embellish ▶ **adornment** *n*

**adrenal** [ad-**reen**-al] *adj* near the kidneys ▶ **adrenal glands** glands covering the top of the kidneys

**adrenalin, adrenaline** *n* hormone secreted by the adrenal glands in response to stress

**adrift** *adj*, *adv* drifting; without a clear purpose

**adroit** *adj* quick and skilful ▶ **adroitly** *adv* ▶ **adroitness** *n*

**adsorb** *v* (of a gas or vapour) condense and form a thin film on a surface ▶ **adsorption** *n*

**adulation** *n* uncritical admiration

**adult** *adj* fully grown, mature ▷ *n* adult person or animal ▶ **adulthood** *n*

**adulterate** *v* spoil something by adding inferior material ▶ **adulteration** *n*

**adultery** *n*, *pl* -**teries** sexual unfaithfulness of a husband or wife ▶ **adulterer, adulteress** *n* ▶ **adulterous** *adj*

**adv** adverb

**advance** *v* go or bring forward; further (a cause); propose (an idea); lend (a sum of money) ▷ *n* forward movement; improvement; loan ▷ *pl* approaches to a person with the hope of starting a romantic or sexual relationship ▷ *adj* done or happening before an event **in advance** ahead ▶ **advanced** *adj* at a late stage in development; not elementary ▶ **advancement** *n* promotion

**advantage** n more favourable position or state; benefit or profit; (Tennis) point scored after deuce **take advantage of** use (a person) unfairly; use (an opportunity) ▶ **advantageous** adj ▶ **advantageously** adv

**advent** n arrival; (**A-**) season of four weeks before Christmas ▶ **Adventist** n member of a Christian sect that believes in the imminent return of Christ (also **Seventh Day Adventist**)

**adventitious** adj added or appearing accidentally

**adventure** n exciting and risky undertaking or exploit ▶ **adventurer, adventuress** n person who unscrupulously seeks money or power; person who seeks adventures ▶ **adventurous** adj

**adverb** n word that adds information about a verb, adjective, or other adverb ▶ **adverbial** adj

**adversary** [ad-**verse**-er-ree] n, pl **-saries** opponent or enemy

**adverse** adj unfavourable; antagonistic or hostile ▶ **adversely** adv ▶ **adversity** n very difficult or hard circumstances

**advert** n (informal) advertisement

**advertise** v present or praise (goods or services) to the public in order to encourage sales; make (a vacancy, event, etc.) known publicly ▶ **advertisement** n public announcement to sell goods or publicize an event ▶ **advertiser** n ▶ **advertising** adj, n

**SPELLING TIP**
Some verbs can be spelt ending in either -ise or -ize, but **advertise** and **advise** always have an s

**advice** n recommendation as to what to do ▶ **advise** v offer advice to; notify (someone) ▶ **advisable** adj prudent, sensible ▶ **advisability** n ▶ **advisory** adj giving advice ▶ **advised** adj considered, thought-out e.g. ill-advised ▶ **advisedly** adv deliberately

**SPELLING TIP**
The verb is **advise** with an s and the noun is **advice** with a c

**adviser, advisor** n person who offers advice, e.g. on careers to students or school pupils

**advocaat** n liqueur with a raw egg base

**advocate** v propose or recommend ▷ n person who publicly supports a cause; (Scot & S Afr) barrister ▶ **advocacy** n

**adze** n tool with an arched blade at right angles to the handle

**aegis** [ee-jiss] n sponsorship, protection

**aeolian harp** [ee-oh-lee-an] n musical instrument that produces sounds when the wind passes over its strings

**aeon** [ee-on] n immeasurably long period of time

**aerate** v put gas into (a liquid), as when making a fizzy drink ▶ **aeration** n

**aerial** adj in, from, or operating in the air; relating to aircraft ▷ n metal pole, wire, etc., for receiving or transmitting radio or TV signals ▶ **aerial top dressing** spreading of fertilizer from an aeroplane onto remote areas

**aerobatics** pl n stunt flying ▶ **aerobatic** adj

**aerobics** n exercises designed to increase the amount of oxygen in the blood ▶ **aerobic** adj

**aerodrome** n small airport

**aerodynamics** n study of how air flows around moving solid objects ▶ **aerodynamic** adj

**aerofoil** n part of an aircraft, such as the wing, designed to give lift

**aerogram** n airmail letter on a single sheet of paper that seals to form an envelope

**aeronautics** n study or practice of aircraft flight ▸ **aeronautical** adj

**aeroplane** n powered flying vehicle with fixed wings

**aerosol** n pressurized can from which a substance can be dispensed as a fine spray

> **SPELLING TIP**
>
> Be careful not to confuse the spelling aer- with air-

**aerospace** n earth's atmosphere and space beyond

**aesthetic** [iss-**thet**-ik] adj relating to the appreciation of art and beauty ▸ **aesthetics** n study of art, beauty, and good taste ▸ **aesthetically** adv ▸ **aesthete** [**eess**-theet] n person who has or affects an extravagant love of art ▸ **aestheticism** n

**aether** n same as **ether**

**aetiology** [ee-tee-**ol**-a-jee] n same as **etiology**

**afar** adv from afar from or at a great distance

**affable** adj friendly and easy to talk to ▸ **affably** adv ▸ **affability** n

**affair** n event or happening; sexual relationship outside marriage; thing to be done or attended to ▹ pl personal or business interests; matters of public interest

**affect¹** v act on, influence; move (someone) emotionally

> **USAGE NOTE**
>
> Do not confuse affect meaning 'influence' with effect meaning 'accomplish'

**affect²** v put on a show of; wear or use by preference ▸ **affectation** n attitude or manner put on to impress ▸ **affected** adj displaying affectation; pretended

**affection** n fondness or love ▸ **affectionate** adj loving ▸ **affectionately** adv

**affianced** [af-**fie**-anst] adj (old-fashioned) engaged to be married

**affidavit** [af-fid-**dave**-it] n written statement made on oath

**affiliate** v (of a group) link up with a larger group ▸ **affiliation** n

**affinity** n, pl -ties close connection or liking; close resemblance; chemical attraction

**affirm** v declare to be true; uphold or confirm (an idea or belief) ▸ **affirmation** n ▸ **affirmative** n, adj (word or phrase) indicating agreement

**affix** v attach or fasten ▹ n word or syllable added to a word to change its meaning

**afflict** v give pain or grief to ▸ **affliction** n

**affluent** adj having plenty of money ▸ **affluence** n wealth

**afford** v have enough money to buy; be able to spare (the time etc.); give or supply ▸ **affordable** adj

**afforest** v plant trees on ▸ **afforestation** n

**affray** n (Brit, Aust & NZ Law) noisy fight, brawl

**affront** v, n insult

**Afghan** adj of Afghanistan or its language ▸ **Afghan hound** large slim dog with long silky hair

**aficionado** [af-fish-yo-**nah**-do] n, pl -dos enthusiastic fan of something or someone

**afield** adv far afield far away

**aflame** adj burning

**afloat** adv, adj floating; at sea

**afoot** adv, adj happening, in operation

**aforesaid, aforementioned** adj referred to previously

**aforethought** *adj* premeditated e.g. *with malice aforethought*

**Afr** Africa(n)

**afraid** *adj* frightened; regretful

**afresh** *adv* again, anew

**African** *adj* of Africa ▷ *n* person from Africa ▶ **African violet** house plant with pink or purple flowers and hairy leaves

**Afrikaans** *n* language used in S Africa, descended from Dutch

**Afrikaner** *n* White S African whose mother tongue is Afrikaans

**Afro-** *combining form* African e.g. *Afro-Caribbean*

**aft** *adv* at or towards the rear of a ship or aircraft

**after** *prep* following in time or place; in pursuit of; in imitation of ▷ *conj* at a later time than ▷ *adv* at a later time ▶ **afters** *pl n* (*Brit informal*) dessert

**afterbirth** *n* material expelled from the womb after childbirth

**aftercare** *n* support given to a person discharged from a hospital or prison; regular care required to keep something in good condition

**aftereffect** *n* result occurring some time after its cause

**afterglow** *n* glow left after a source of light has gone; pleasant feeling left after an enjoyable experience

**afterlife** *n* life after death

**aftermath** *n* results of an event considered together

**afternoon** *n* time between noon and evening

**aftershave** *n* lotion applied to the face after shaving

**afterthought** *n* idea occurring later; something added later

**afterwards, afterward** *adv* later

**Ag** (*Chem*) silver

**again** *adv* once more; in addition

**against** *prep* in opposition or contrast to; in contact with; as a protection from

**agape** *adj* (of the mouth) wide open; (of a person) very surprised

**agaric** *n* fungus with gills on the underside of the cap, such as a mushroom

**agate** [**ag**-git] *n* semiprecious form of quartz with striped colouring

**age** *n* length of time a person or thing has existed; time of life; latter part of human life; period of history; long time ▷ *v* **ageing** *or* **aging, aged** make or grow old ▶ **aged** *adj* [**ay**-jid] old; [rhymes with **raged**] being at the age of ▶ **ageing, aging** *n, adj* ▶ **ageless** *adj* apparently never growing old; seeming to have existed for ever ▶ **age-old** *adj* very old

**agency** *n, pl* **-cies** organization providing a service; business or function of an agent; (*old-fashioned*) power or action by which something happens

**agenda** *n* list of things to be dealt with, esp. at a meeting

**agent** *n* person acting on behalf of another; person or thing producing an effect

**agent provocateur** [**azh**-on prov-vok-at-**tur**] *n, pl* **agents provocateurs** [**azh**-on prov-vok-at-**tur**] person employed by the authorities to tempt people to commit illegal acts and so be discredited or punished

**agglomeration** *n* confused mass or cluster

**aggrandize** *v* make greater in size, power, or rank ▶ **aggrandizement** *n*

**aggravate** *v* make worse; (*chiefly informal*) annoy ▶ **aggravating** *adj* ▶ **aggravation** *n*

**a**

**SPELLING TIP**
Remember that there is an *a* (not an *e*) in the middle of **aggravate**

**aggregate** *n* total; rock consisting of a mixture of minerals; sand or gravel used to make concrete ▷ *adj* gathered into a mass; total or final ▷ *v* combine into a whole ▶ **aggregation** *n*

**aggression** *n* hostile behaviour; unprovoked attack ▶ **aggressive** *adj* showing aggression; forceful ▶ **aggressively** *adv* ▶ **aggressiveness** *n* ▶ **aggressor** *n*

**SPELLING TIP**
Note the double *g* and double *s* in **aggressive**

**aggrieved** *adj* upset and angry

**aggro** (*slang*) *n* (*Brit, Aust & NZ*) aggressive behaviour ▷ *adj* (*Aust & NZ*) aggressive

**aghast** *adj* overcome with amazement or horror

**agile** *adj* nimble, quick-moving; mentally quick ▶ **agility** *n*

**agitate** *v* disturb or excite; stir or shake (a liquid); stir up public opinion for or against something ▶ **agitation** *n* ▶ **agitator** *n*

**aglow** *adj* glowing

**AGM** annual general meeting

**agnostic** *n* person who believes that it is impossible to know whether God exists ▷ *adj* of agnostics ▶ **agnosticism** *n*

**ago** *adv* in the past

**agog** *adj* eager or curious

**agony** *n*, *pl* **-nies** extreme physical or mental pain ▶ **agonize** *v* worry greatly; (cause to) suffer agony ▶ **agonizing** *adj* ▶ **agony aunt** journalist who gives advice in an agony column ▶ **agony column** newspaper or magazine feature offering advice on personal problems

**agoraphobia** *n* fear of open spaces ▶ **agoraphobic** *n*, *adj*

**agrarian** *adj* of land or agriculture

**agree** *v* **agreeing, agreed** be of the same opinion; consent; reach a joint decision; be consistent; (foll by *with*) be suitable to (one's health or digestion) ▶ **agreeable** *adj* pleasant and enjoyable; prepared to consent ▶ **agreeably** *adv* ▶ **agreement** *n* agreeing; contract

**agriculture** *n* raising of crops and livestock ▶ **agricultural** *adj* ▶ **agriculturalist** *n*

**agronomy** [ag-**ron**-om-mee] *n* science of soil management and crop production ▶ **agronomist** *n*

**aground** *adv* onto the bottom of shallow water

**ague** [**aig**-yew] *n* (*old-fashioned*) periodic fever with shivering

**ahead** *adv* in front; forwards

**ahoy** *interj* shout used at sea to attract attention

**AI** artificial insemination; artificial intelligence

**aid** *v*, *n* (give) assistance or support

**aide** *n* assistant

**aide-de-camp** [aid-de-**kom**] *n*, *pl* **aides-de-camp** [aid-de-**kom**] military officer serving as personal assistant to a senior

**AIDS** acquired immunodeficiency syndrome: a viral disease that destroys the body's ability to fight infection

**AIH** artificial insemination by husband

**ail** *v* trouble, afflict; be ill ▶ **ailing** *adj* sickly ▶ **ailment** *n* illness

**aileron** *n* movable flap on an aircraft wing which controls rolling

**aim** *v* point (a weapon or missile) or direct (a blow or remark) at a target; propose or intend ▷ *n* aiming; intention, purpose ▶ **aimless** *adj* having no purpose ▶ **aimlessly** *adv*

**ain't** (*not standard*) am not; is not; are not; has not; have not

**air** *n* mixture of gases forming the earth's atmosphere; space above the ground, sky; breeze; quality or manner; tune ▷ *pl* affected manners ▷ *v* make known publicly; expose to air to dry or ventilate **on the air** in the act of broadcasting on radio or television ▸ **airless** *adj* stuffy ▸ **air bag** vehicle safety device which inflates automatically in a crash to protect the driver or passenger when he or she is thrown forward ▸ **airborne** *adj* carried by air; (of aircraft) flying ▸ **airbrush** *n* atomizer spraying paint by compressed air ▸ **airfield** *n* place where aircraft can land and take off ▸ **air force** branch of the armed forces responsible for air warfare ▸ **air gun** gun fired by compressed air ▸ **air hostess** female flight attendant ▸ **airlift** *n* transport of troops or cargo by aircraft when other routes are blocked ▷ *v* transport by airlift ▸ **airlock** *n* air bubble blocking the flow of liquid in a pipe; airtight chamber ▸ **airmail** *n* system of sending mail by aircraft; mail sent in this way ▸ **airman** *n* member of the air force ▸ **air miles** miles of free air travel that can be earned by buying airline tickets and various other products ▸ **airplay** *n* broadcast performances of a record on radio ▸ **airport** *n* airfield for civilian aircraft, with facilities for aircraft maintenance and passengers ▸ **air raid** attack by aircraft ▸ **airship** *n* lighter-than-air self-propelled aircraft ▸ **airspace** *n* atmosphere above a country, regarded as its territory ▸ **airstrip** *n* cleared area where aircraft can take off and land ▸ **airtight** *adj* sealed so that air cannot enter

**air conditioning** *n* system that controls the temperature and humidity of the air in a building ▸ **air conditioner**

**aircraft** *n* any machine that flies, such as an aeroplane ▸ **aircraft carrier** warship for the launching and landing of aircraft

**airing** *n* exposure to air for drying or ventilation; exposure to public debate

**airline** *n* company providing scheduled flights for passengers and cargo ▸ **airliner** *n* large passenger aircraft

**airworthy** *adj* (of aircraft) fit to fly ▸ **airworthiness** *n*

**airy** *adj* **airier, airiest** well-ventilated; light-hearted and casual ▸ **airily** *adv*

**aisle** [rhymes with **mile**] *n* passageway separating seating areas in a church, theatre, etc., or row of shelves in a supermarket

**ajar** *adj*, *adv* (of a door) partly open

**akimbo** *adv* **with arms akimbo** with hands on hips and elbows outwards

**akin** *adj* **akin to** similar, related

**alabaster** *n* soft white translucent stone

**à la carte** *adj*, *adv* (of a menu) having dishes individually priced

**alacrity** *n* speed, eagerness

**à la mode** *adj* fashionable

**alarm** *n* sudden fear caused by awareness of danger; warning sound; device that gives this; alarm clock ▷ *v* fill with fear ▸ **alarming** *adj* ▸ **alarmist** *n* person who alarms others needlessly ▸ **alarm clock** clock which sounds at a set time to wake someone up

**alas** *adv* unfortunately, regrettably

**a**

**albatross** *n* large sea bird with very long wings

**albeit** *conj* even though

**albino** *n, pl* **-nos** person or animal with white skin and hair and pink eyes

**album** *n* book with blank pages for keeping photographs or stamps in; long-playing record

**albumen** *n* egg white

**albumin, albumen** *n* protein found in blood plasma, egg white, milk, and muscle

**alchemy** *n* medieval form of chemistry concerned with trying to turn base metals into gold and to find the elixir of life ▶ **alchemist** *n*

**alcohol** *n* colourless flammable liquid present in intoxicating drinks; intoxicating drinks generally ▶ **alcoholic** *adj* of alcohol ▷ *n* person addicted to alcohol ▶ **alcoholism** *n* addiction to alcohol

**alcopop** *n* (*Brit, Aust & S Afr informal*) alcoholic drink that tastes like a soft drink

**alcove** *n* recess in the wall of a room

**aldehyde** *n* one of a group of chemical compounds derived from alcohol by oxidation

**alder** *n* tree related to the birch

**alderman** *n* formerly, senior member of a local council

**ale** *n* kind of beer

**alert** *adj* watchful, attentive ▷ *n* warning of danger ▷ *v* warn of danger; make (someone) aware of (a fact) **on the alert** watchful ▶ **alertness** *n*

**A level** *n* (*Brit*) (pass in a subject at) the advanced level of the GCE

**alfalfa** *n* kind of plant used to feed livestock

**alfresco** *adv, adj* in the open air

**algae** [**al**-jee] *pl n* plants which live in or near water and have no true stems, leaves, or roots

**algebra** *n* branch of mathematics using symbols to represent numbers ▶ **algebraic** *adj*

**ALGOL** *n* (*Computing*) programming language for mathematical and scientific purposes

**algorithm** *n* logical arithmetical or computational procedure for solving a problem

**alias** *adv* also known as ▷ *n* false name

**alibi** *n* plea of being somewhere else when a crime was committed; (*informal*) excuse

**alien** *adj* foreign; repugnant (to); from another world ▷ *n* foreigner; being from another world ▶ **alienate** *v* cause to become hostile ▶ **alienation** *n*

**alight**[1] *v* step out of (a vehicle); land

**alight**[2] *adj* on fire; lit up

**align** [a-**line**] *v* bring (a person or group) into agreement with the policy of another; place in a line ▶ **alignment** *n*

**alike** *adj* like, similar ▷ *adv* in the same way

**alimentary** *adj* of nutrition ▶ **alimentary canal** food passage in the body

**alimony** *n* allowance paid under a court order to a separated or divorced spouse

**A-line** *adj* (of a skirt) slightly flared

**aliquot** (*Maths*) *adj* of or denoting an exact divisor of a number ▷ *n* exact divisor

**alive** *adj* living, in existence; lively **alive to** aware of **alive with** swarming with

**alkali** [**alk**-a-lie] *n* substance which combines with acid and neutralizes it to form a salt ▶ **alkaline** *adj* ▶ **alkalinity** *n* ▶ **alkaloid** *n* any of a group of organic compounds containing nitrogen

**all** *adj* whole quantity or number (of) ▷ *adv* wholly, entirely; (in the score of games) each **give one's all** make the greatest possible effort ▶ **all in** *adj* exhausted; (of wrestling) with no style forbidden ▷ *adv* with all expenses included ▶ **all right** *adj* adequate, satisfactory; unharmed ▷ *interj* expression of approval or agreement ▶ **all-rounder** *n* person with ability in many fields

**Allah** *n* name of God in Islam

**allay** *v* reduce (fear or anger)

**allege** *v* state without proof ▶ **alleged** *adj* ▶ **allegedly** *adv* ▶ **allegation** *n* unproved accusation

**allegiance** *n* loyalty to a person, country, or cause

**allegory** *n, pl* **-ries** story with an underlying meaning as well as the literal one ▶ **allegorical** *adj*

**allegretto** *adv, n, pl* **-tos** (*Music*) (piece to be played) fairly quickly or briskly

**allegro** *adv, n, pl* **-gros** (*Music*) (piece to be played) in a brisk lively manner

**alleluia** *interj* same as **hallelujah**

**allergy** *n, pl* **-gies** extreme sensitivity to a substance, which causes the body to react to it ▶ **allergic** *adj* having or caused by an allergy ▶ **allergen** *n* substance capable of causing an allergic reaction

**alleviate** *v* lessen (pain or suffering) ▶ **alleviation** *n*

**alley** *n* narrow street or path; long narrow enclosure in which tenpin bowling or skittles is played

**alliance** *n* state of being allied; formal relationship between countries or groups for a shared purpose

**alligator** *n* reptile of the crocodile family, found in the southern US and China

**alliteration** *n* use of the same sound at the start of words occurring together, e.g. *moody music* ▶ **alliterative** *adj*

**allocate** *v* assign to someone or for a particular purpose ▶ **allocation** *n*

**allot** *v* **-lotting, -lotted** assign as a share or for a particular purpose ▶ **allotment** *n* distribution; portion allotted; small piece of public land rented to grow vegetables on

**allotrope** *n* any of two or more physical forms in which an element can exist

**allow** *v* permit; set aside; acknowledge (a point or claim) ▶ **allow for** *v* take into account ▶ **allowable** *adj* ▶ **allowance** *n* amount of money given at regular intervals; amount permitted **make allowances for** treat or judge (someone) less severely because he or she has special problems; take into account

**alloy** *n* mixture of two or more metals ▷ *v* mix (metals)

**allspice** *n* spice made from the berries of a tropical American tree

**allude** *v* (foll by *to*) refer indirectly to ▶ **allusion** *n* indirect reference ▶ **allusive** *adj*

> **USAGE NOTE**
> *Allude* is followed by *to*. Be careful not to confuse this word with *elude* meaning 'escape'. Also be careful not to confuse *allusion* with *illusion* meaning 'fallacy' or 'fantasy'

**allure** *n* attractiveness ▷ *v* entice or attract ▶ **alluring** *adj*

**alluvium** *n* fertile soil deposited by flowing water ▶ **alluvial** *adj*

**ally** *n, pl* **-lies** country, person, or group with an agreement to support another ▷ *v* **-lying, -lied** ▶ **ally oneself with** join as an ally ▶ **allied** *adj*

**alma mater** n school, university, or college that one attended

**almanac** n yearly calendar with detailed information on anniversaries, phases of the moon, etc.

**almighty** adj having absolute power; (informal) very great ▷ n **the Almighty** God

**almond** n edible oval-shaped nut which grows on a small tree

**almoner** n (Brit) formerly, a hospital social worker

**almost** adv very nearly

**alms** [ahmz] pl n (old-fashioned) gifts to the poor

**aloe** n plant with fleshy spiny leaves ▷ pl bitter drug made from aloe leaves

**aloft** adv in the air; in a ship's rigging

**alone** adj, adv without anyone or anything else

**along** prep over part or all the length of ▷ adv forward; in company with others ▶ **alongside** prep, adv beside (something)

> **USAGE NOTE**
> Avoid following alongside with of. Its use is unnecessary

**aloof** adj distant or haughty in manner ▶ **aloofness** n

**alopecia** [al-loh-**pee**-sha] n loss of hair

**aloud** adv in an audible voice

**alpaca** n Peruvian llama; wool or cloth made from its hair

**alpenstock** n iron-tipped stick used by climbers

**alpha** n first letter in the Greek alphabet ▶ **alpha male** dominant male animal or person in a group

**alphabet** n set of letters used in writing a language ▶ **alphabetical** adj in the conventional order of the letters of an alphabet ▶ **alphabetically** adv

▶ **alphabetize** v put in alphabetical order

**alpine** adj of high mountains; (**A-**) of the Alps ▷ n mountain plant

**already** adv before the present time; sooner than expected

**alright** adj, interj all right

> **USAGE NOTE**
> The form alright, though very common, is still considered by many people to be wrong or less acceptable than all right

**Alsatian** n large wolflike dog

**also** adv in addition, too ▶ **also-ran** n loser in a race, competition, or election

**alt.** combining form (informal) alternative e.g. alt.rock

**altar** n table used for Communion in Christian churches; raised structure on which sacrifices are offered and religious rites are performed ▶ **altarpiece** n work of art above and behind the altar in some Christian churches

**alter** v make or become different ▶ **alteration** n

**altercation** n heated argument

**alter ego** n second self; very close friend

**alternate** v (cause to) occur by turns ▷ adj occurring by turns; every second (one) of a series ▶ **alternately** adv ▶ **alternation** n ▶ **alternator** n electric generator for producing alternating current ▶ **alternating current** electric current that reverses direction at frequent regular intervals

**alternative** n one of two choices ▷ adj able to be done or used instead of something else; (of medicine, lifestyle, etc.) not conventional ▶ **alternatively** adv

**although** conj despite the fact that

**altimeter** [al-**tim**-it-er] n instrument that measures altitude

**altitude** *n* height above sea level

**alto** *n*, *pl* **-tos** (*Music*) short for **contralto**; (singer with) the highest adult male voice; instrument with the second-highest pitch in its group

**altogether** *adv* entirely; on the whole; in total

**altruism** *n* unselfish concern for the welfare of others ▶ **altruistic** *adj* ▶ **altruistically** *adv*

**aluminium** *n* (*Chem*) light silvery-white metal that does not rust

**alumnus** [al-**lumm**-nuss] *n*, *pl* **-ni** [-nie] graduate of a college ▶ **alumna** [al-**lumm**-na] *n fem*, *pl* **-nae** [-nee]

**always** *adv* at all times; for ever

**alyssum** *n* garden plant with small yellow or white flowers

**AM** amplitude modulation; (in Britain) Member of the National Assembly for Wales

**am** *v* see **be**

**a.m.** ante meridiem: before noon

**amakhosi** *n* plural of **inkhosi**

**amalgam** *n* blend or combination; alloy of mercury and another metal

**amalgamate** *v* combine or unite ▶ **amalgamation** *n*

**amandla** [ah-**mand**-lah] *n* (*SAfr*) political slogan calling for power to the Black population

**amanuensis** [am-man-yew-**en**-siss] *n*, *pl* **-ses** [-seez] person who writes from dictation

**amaranth** *n* imaginary flower that never fades; lily-like plant with red, green, or purple flowers

**amaryllis** *n* lily-like plant with large red, pink, or white flowers

**amass** *v* collect or accumulate

**amateur** *n* person who engages in a sport or activity as a pastime rather than as a profession; person unskilled in something ▷ *adj* not professional ▶ **amateurish** *adj* lacking skill ▶ **amateurishly** *adv*

**amatory** *adj* relating to romantic or sexual love

**amaze** *v* surprise greatly, astound ▶ **amazing** *adj* ▶ **amazingly** *adv* ▶ **amazement** *n*

**Amazon** *n* strong and powerful woman; legendary female warrior ▶ **Amazonian** *adj*

**ambassador** *n* senior diplomat who represents his or her country in another country ▶ **ambassadorial** *adj*

**amber** *n* clear yellowish fossil resin ▷ *adj* brownish-yellow

**ambergris** [**am**-ber-greece] *n* waxy substance secreted by the sperm whale, used in making perfumes

**ambidextrous** *adj* able to use both hands with equal ease

**ambience** *n* atmosphere of a place

**ambient** *adj* surrounding

**ambiguous** *adj* having more than one possible meaning ▶ **ambiguously** *adv* ▶ **ambiguity** *n*

**ambit** *n* limits or boundary

**ambition** *n* desire for success; something so desired, goal ▶ **ambitious** *adj* ▶ **ambitiously** *adv*

**ambivalence** *n* state of feeling two conflicting emotions at the same time ▶ **ambivalent** *adj* ▶ **ambivalently** *adv*

**amble** *v* walk at a leisurely pace ▷ *n* leisurely walk or pace

**ambrosia** *n* (*Myth*) food of the gods ▶ **ambrosial** *adj*

**ambulance** *n* motor vehicle designed to carry sick or injured people

**ambush** *n* act of waiting in a concealed position to make a surprise attack; attack from a concealed position ▷ *v* attack from a concealed position

**ameliorate** [am-**meal**-yor-rate] *v* make (something) better ▶ **amelioration** *n*

**amen** *interj* so be it: used at the end of a prayer

**amenable** *adj* likely or willing to cooperate

**amend** *v* make small changes to correct or improve (something)
▶ **amendment** *n*

**amends** *pl n* **make amends for** compensate for

**amenity** *n, pl* **-ties** useful or enjoyable feature

**American** *adj* of the United States of America or the American continent ▷ *n* person from America or the American continent
▶ **Americanism** *n* expression or custom characteristic of Americans

**Americano** *n, pl* **-nos** espresso coffee diluted with hot water

**amethyst** [**am**-myth-ist] *n* bluish-violet variety of quartz used as a gemstone

**amiable** *adj* friendly, pleasant-natured ▶ **amiably** *adv*
▶ **amiability** *n*

**amicable** *adj* friendly
▶ **amicably** *adv*

**amid, amidst** *prep* in the middle of, among ▶ **amidships** *adv* at or towards the middle of a ship

> **USAGE NOTE**
> The form *amidst* is old-fashioned. Nowadays use *amid* or *among*

**amino acid** [am-**mean**-oh] *n* organic compound found in protein

**amiss** *adv* wrongly, badly ▷ *adj* wrong, faulty **take something amiss** be offended by something

**amity** *n* friendship

**ammeter** *n* instrument for measuring electric current

**ammonia** *n* strong-smelling alkaline gas containing hydrogen and nitrogen; solution of this in water

**ammonite** *n* fossilized spiral shell of an extinct sea creature

**ammunition** *n* bullets, bombs, and shells that can be fired from or as a weapon; facts that can be used in an argument

**amnesia** *n* loss of memory
▶ **amnesiac** *adj, n*

**amnesty** *n, pl* **-ties** general pardon for offences against a government

**amniocentesis** *n, pl* **-ses** removal of some amniotic fluid to test for possible abnormalities in a fetus

**amniotic fluid** *n* fluid surrounding a fetus in the womb

**amoeba** [am-**mee**-ba] *n, pl* **-bae, -bas** microscopic single-celled animal able to change its shape

**amok** [a-**muck**, a-**mock**] *adv* **run amok** run about in a violent frenzy

**among, amongst** *prep* in the midst of; in the group or number of; to each of e.g. *divide it among yourselves*

> **USAGE NOTE**
> *Among* is generally used when more than two things are mentioned: *It's hard to choose among friends*. The form *amongst* is rather old-fashioned

**amoral** [aim-**mor**-ral] *adj* without moral standards ▶ **amorality** *n*

**amorous** *adj* feeling, showing, or relating to sexual love
▶ **amorously** *adv*

**amorphous** *adj* without distinct shape

**amortize** *v* pay off (a debt) gradually by periodic transfers to a sinking fund

**amount** *n* extent or quantity ▷ *v* (foll by *to*) be equal or add up to

**amour** *n* (secret) love affair

**amp** *n* ampere; (*informal*) amplifier

**ampere** [**am**-pair] *n* basic unit of electric current

**ampersand** *n* the character (&), meaning *and*

**amphetamine** [am-**fet**-am-mean] *n* drug used as a stimulant

**amphibian** *n* animal that lives on land but breeds in water; vehicle that can travel on both land and water ▶ **amphibious** *adj* living or operating both on land and in water

**amphitheatre** *n* open oval or circular building with tiers of seats rising round an arena

**amphora** [am-for-ra] *n*, *pl* -**phorae** two-handled ancient Greek or Roman jar

**ample** *adj* more than sufficient; large ▶ **amply** *adv*

**amplifier** *n* device used to amplify a current or sound signal

**amplify** *v* -**fying, -fied** increase the strength of (a current or sound signal); explain in more detail; increase the size or effect of ▶ **amplification** *n*

**amplitude** *n* greatness of extent

**ampoule** *n* small sealed glass vessel containing liquid for injection

**amputate** *v* cut off (a limb or part of a limb) for medical reasons ▶ **amputation** *n*

**amuck** *adv* same as **amok**

**amulet** *n* something carried or worn as a protection against evil

**amuse** *v* cause to laugh or smile; entertain or divert ▶ **amusing** *adj* ▶ **amusement** *n* state of being amused; something that amuses

**an** *adj* form of **a** used before vowels, and sometimes before h

> **USAGE NOTE**
> This form of the indefinite article is also used with abbreviations which have a vowel sound when read aloud: *an MA*. It is old-fashioned to use *an* before words like *hotel* or *historic*.

**anabolic steroid** *n* synthetic steroid hormone used to stimulate muscle and bone growth

**anachronism** [an-**nak**-kron-iz-zum] *n* person or thing placed in the wrong historical period or seeming to belong to another time ▶ **anachronistic** *adj*

**anaconda** *n* large S American snake which kills by constriction

**anaemia** [an-**neem**-ee-a] *n* deficiency in the number of red blood cells ▶ **anaemic** *adj* having anaemia; pale and sickly; lacking vitality

**anaesthetic** [an-niss-**thet**-ik] *n*, *adj* (substance) causing loss of bodily feeling ▶ **anaesthesia** [an-niss-**theez**-ee-a] *n* loss of bodily feeling ▶ **anaesthetist** [an-**neess**-thet-ist] *n* doctor trained to administer anaesthetics ▶ **anaesthetize** *v*

**anagram** *n* word or phrase made by rearranging the letters of another word or phrase

**anal** [**ain**-al] *adj* of the anus

**analgesic** [an-nal-**jeez**-ik] *n*, *adj* (drug) relieving pain ▶ **analgesia** *n* absence of pain

**analogous** *adj* similar in some respects

**analogue** *n* something that is similar in some respects to something else ▷ *adj* displaying information by means of a dial

**analogy** *n*, *pl* -**gies** similarity in some respects; comparison made to show such a similarity ▶ **analogical** *adj*

**analysis** *n*, *pl* -**ses** separation of a whole into its parts for study and interpretation; psychoanalysis ▶ **analyse** *v* make an analysis of (something); psychoanalyse ▶ **analyst** *n* person skilled in analysis ▶ **analytical, analytic** *adj* ▶ **analytically** *adv*

**anarchism** *n* doctrine advocating the abolition of government

**a**

**anarchist** n person who advocates the abolition of government; person who causes disorder ▶ **anarchistic** adj

**anarchy** [an-ark-ee] n lawlessness and disorder; lack of government in a state ▶ **anarchic** adj

**anathema** [an-**nath**-im-a] n detested person or thing

**anatomy** n, pl **-mies** science of the structure of the body; physical structure; person's body; detailed analysis ▶ **anatomical** adj ▶ **anatomically** adv ▶ **anatomist** n expert in anatomy

**ANC** African National Congress

**ancestor** n person from whom one is descended; forerunner ▶ **ancestral** adj ▶ **ancestry** n lineage or descent

**anchor** n heavy hooked device attached to a boat by a cable and dropped overboard to fasten the ship to the sea bottom ▷ v fasten with or as if with an anchor ▶ **anchorage** n place where boats can be anchored ▶ **anchorman, anchorwoman** n broadcaster in a central studio who links up and presents items from outside camera units and other studios; last person to compete in a relay team

**anchorite** n religious recluse

**anchovy** [an-**chov**-ee] n, pl **-vies** small strong-tasting fish

**ancient** adj dating from very long ago; very old ▶ **ancients** pl n people who lived very long ago

**ancillary** adj supporting the main work of an organization; used as an extra or supplement

**and** conj in addition to; as a consequence; then, afterwards

**andante** [an-**dan**-tay] n, adv (Music) (piece to be played) moderately slowly

**andiron** n iron stand for supporting logs in a fireplace

**androgynous** adj having both male and female characteristics

**android** n robot resembling a human; Android® software package for smartphones; smartphone that uses this software

**anecdote** n short amusing account of an incident ▶ **anecdotal** adj

**anemometer** n instrument for recording wind speed

**anemone** [an-**nem**-on-ee] n plant with white, purple, or red flowers

**aneroid barometer** n device for measuring air pressure, consisting of a partially evacuated chamber in which variations in pressure cause a pointer on the lid to move

**aneurysm, aneurism** [an-new-riz-zum] n permanent swelling of a blood vessel

**anew** adv once more; in a different way

**angel** n spiritual being believed to be an attendant or messenger of God; person who is kind, pure, or beautiful ▶ **angelic** adj ▶ **angelically** adv

**angelica** n aromatic plant; its candied stalks, used in cookery

**Angelus** [an-jell-uss] n (in the Roman Catholic Church) prayers recited in the morning, at midday, and in the evening; bell signalling the times of these prayers

**anger** n fierce displeasure or extreme annoyance ▷ v make (someone) angry

**angina** [an-**jine**-a] n heart disorder causing sudden severe chest pains (also **angina pectoris**)

**angle¹** n space between or shape formed by two lines or surfaces that meet; divergence between these, measured in degrees;

corner; point of view ▷ *v* bend or place (something) at an angle

**angle²** *v* fish with a hook and line; (foll by *for*) try to get by hinting ▶ **angling** *n*

**angler** *n* person who fishes with a hook and line

**Anglican** *n*, *adj* (member) of the Church of England ▶ **Anglicanism** *n*

**anglicize** *v* make or become English in outlook, form, etc.

**Anglo-** *combining form* English e.g. *Anglo-Scottish*; British e.g. *Anglo-American*

**Anglo-Saxon** *n* member of any of the W Germanic tribes that settled in England from the fifth century AD; language of the Anglo-Saxons ▷ *adj* of the Anglo-Saxons or their language

**angophora** *n* Australian tree related to the eucalyptus

**angora** *n* variety of goat, cat, or rabbit with long silky hair; hair of the angora goat or rabbit; cloth made from this hair

**Angostura Bitters**® *pl n* bitter tonic, used as a flavouring in alcoholic drinks

**angry** *adj* **-grier, -griest** full of anger; inflamed e.g. *an angry wound* ▶ **angrily** *adv*

**angst** *n* feeling of anxiety

**angstrom** *n* unit of length used to measure wavelengths

**anguish** *n* great mental pain ▶ **anguished** *adj*

**angular** *adj* (of a person) lean and bony; having angles; measured by an angle ▶ **angularity** *n*

**anhydrous** *adj* (*Chem*) containing no water

**aniline** *n* colourless oily liquid obtained from coal tar and used for making dyes, plastics, and explosives

**animal** *n* living creature with specialized sense organs and capable of voluntary motion, esp. one other than a human being; quadruped ▷ *adj* of animals; sensual, physical

**animate** *v* give life to; make lively; make a cartoon film of ▷ *adj* having life ▶ **animated** *adj* ▶ **animation** *n* technique of making cartoon films; liveliness and enthusiasm ▶ **animator** *n*

**animism** *n* belief that natural objects possess souls ▶ **animist** *n*, *adj* ▶ **animistic** *adj*

**animosity** *n*, *pl* **-ties** hostility, hatred

**animus** *n* hatred, animosity

**anion** [an-eye-on] *n* ion with negative charge

**anise** [an-niss] *n* plant with liquorice-flavoured seeds

**aniseed** *n* liquorice-flavoured seeds of the anise plant

**ankle** *n* joint between the foot and leg ▶ **anklet** *n* ornamental chain worn round the ankle

**annals** *pl n* yearly records of events

**anneal** *v* toughen (metal or glass) by heating and slow cooling

**annelid** *n* worm with a segmented body, such as an earthworm

**annex** *v* seize (territory); take (something) without permission; join or add (something) to something larger ▶ **annexation** *n*

**annexe** *n* extension to a building; nearby building used as an extension

**annihilate** *v* destroy utterly ▶ **annihilation** *n*

**anniversary** *n*, *pl* **-ries** date on which something occurred in a previous year; celebration of this

**anno Domini** [an-no **dom**-in-eye] *adv* (*Latin*) (indicating years numbered from the supposed year of the birth of Christ) in the year of our Lord

**annotate** v add notes to (a written work) ▶ **annotation** n

**announce** v make known publicly; proclaim ▶ **announcement** n ▶ **announcer** n person who introduces radio or television programmes

**annoy** v irritate or displease ▶ **annoyance** n

**annual** adj happening once a year; lasting for a year ▷ n plant that completes its life cycle in a year; book published once every year ▶ **annually** adv

**annuity** n, pl **-ties** fixed sum paid every year

**annul** v **-nulling, -nulled** declare (something, esp. a marriage) invalid ▶ **annulment** n

**annular** [an-new-lar] adj ring-shaped

**Annunciation** n (Christianity) angel Gabriel's announcement to the Virgin Mary of her conception of Christ

**anode** n (Electricity) positive electrode in a battery, valve, etc. ▶ **anodize** v coat (metal) with a protective oxide film by electrolysis

**anodyne** n something that relieves pain or distress ▷ adj relieving pain or distress

**anoint** v smear with oil as a sign of consecration

**anomaly** [an-nom-a-lee] n, pl **-lies** something that deviates from the normal, irregularity ▶ **anomalous** adj

**anon** adv (obs) in a short time, soon

**anon.** anonymous

**anonymous** adj by someone whose name is unknown or withheld; having no known name ▶ **anonymously** adv ▶ **anonymity** n

**anorak** n light waterproof hooded jacket

**anorexia** n psychological disorder characterized by fear of becoming fat and refusal to eat (also **anorexia nervosa**) ▶ **anorexic** adj, n

**another** adj, pron one more; different (one)

**answer** n reply to a question, request, letter, etc.; solution to a problem; reaction or response ▷ v give an answer (to); be responsible to (a person); respond or react ▶ **answerable** adj (foll by for or to) responsible for or accountable to ▶ **answering machine** device for answering a telephone automatically and recording messages

**ant** n small insect living in highly organized colonies ▶ **anteater** n mammal which feeds on ants by means of a long snout; same as **echidna**; same as **numbat** ▶ **ant hill** mound built by ants around their nest

**antacid** n substance that counteracts acidity, esp. in the stomach

**antagonist** n opponent or adversary ▶ **antagonism** n open opposition or hostility ▶ **antagonistic** adj ▶ **antagonize** v arouse hostility in, annoy

**Antarctic** n the Antarctic area around the South Pole ▷ adj of this region

> **SPELLING TIP**
> Note there is a c after the r in **Antarctic**

**ante** n player's stake in poker ▷ v **-teing, -ted** or **-teed** place (one's stake) in poker

**ante-** prefix before in time or position e.g. antedate; antechamber

**antecedent** n event or circumstance happening or

existing before another ▷ *adj* preceding, prior

**antedate** *v* precede in time

**antediluvian** *adj* of the time before the biblical Flood; old-fashioned

**antelope** *n* deerlike mammal with long legs and horns

**antenatal** *adj* during pregnancy, before birth

**antenna** *n* (*pl* **-nae**) insect's feeler; (*pl* **-nas**) aerial

**anterior** *adj* to the front; earlier

**anteroom** *n* small room leading into a larger one, often used as a waiting room

**anthem** *n* song of loyalty, esp. to a country; piece of choral music, usu. set to words from the Bible

**anther** *n* part of a flower's stamen containing pollen

**anthology** *n*, *pl* **-gies** collection of poems or other literary pieces by various authors ▶ **anthologist** *n*

**anthracite** *n* hard coal burning slowly with little smoke or flame but intense heat

**anthrax** *n* dangerous disease of cattle and sheep, communicable to humans

**anthropoid** *adj* like a human ▷ *n* ape, such as a chimpanzee, that resembles a human

**anthropology** *n* study of human origins, institutions, and beliefs ▶ **anthropological** *adj* ▶ **anthropologist** *n*

**anthropomorphic** *adj* attributing human form or personality to a god, animal, or object ▶ **anthropomorphism** *n*

**anti-** *prefix* against, opposed to e.g. *anti-war*; opposite to e.g. *anticlimax*; counteracting e.g. *antifreeze*

**anti-aircraft** *adj* for defence against aircraft attack

**antibiotic** *n* chemical substance capable of destroying bacteria ▷ *adj* of antibiotics

**antibody** *n*, *pl* **-bodies** protein produced in the blood, which destroys bacteria

**anticipate** *v* foresee and act in advance of; look forward to ▶ **anticipation** *n* ▶ **anticipatory** *adj*

**anticlimax** *n* disappointing conclusion to a series of events

**anticlockwise** *adv*, *adj* in the opposite direction to the rotation of the hands of a clock

**antics** *pl n* absurd acts or postures

**anticyclone** *n* area of moving air of high pressure in which the winds rotate outwards

**antidote** *n* substance that counteracts a poison

**antifreeze** *n* liquid added to water to lower its freezing point, used esp. in car radiators

**antigen** [**an**-tee-jen] *n* substance, usu. a toxin, causing the blood to produce antibodies

**anti-globalization** *n* opposition to globalization

**antihero** *n*, *pl* **-roes** central character in a book, film, etc., who lacks the traditional heroic virtues

**antihistamine** *n* drug used to treat allergies

**antimacassar** *n* cloth put over a chair-back to prevent soiling

**antimony** *n* (*Chem*) brittle silvery-white metallic element

**antipasto** *n*, *pl* **-tos** appetizer in an Italian meal

**antipathy** [an-**tip**-a-thee] *n* dislike, hostility ▶ **antipathetic** *adj*

**antiperspirant** *n* substance used to reduce or prevent sweating

**antiphon** *n* hymn sung in alternate parts by two groups of singers ▶ **antiphonal** *adj*

**antipodes** [an-**tip**-pod-deez] *pl n* any two places diametrically opposite one another on the earth's surface **the Antipodes** Australia and New Zealand ▸ **antipodean** *adj*

**antipyretic** *adj* reducing fever ▹ *n* drug that reduces fever

**antiquary** *n, pl* -**quaries** student or collector of antiques or ancient works of art ▸ **antiquarian** *adj* of or relating to antiquities or rare books ▹ *n* antiquary

**antiquated** *adj* out-of-date

**antique** *n* object of an earlier period, valued for its beauty, workmanship, or age ▹ *adj* made in an earlier period; old-fashioned

**antiquity** *n* great age; ancient times ▸ **antiquities** *pl n* objects dating from ancient times

**antiracism** *n* policy of challenging racism and promoting racial tolerance

**antirrhinum** *n* two-lipped flower of various colours

**anti-Semitism** *n* discrimination against Jews ▸ **anti-Semitic** *adj*

**antiseptic** *adj* preventing infection by killing germs ▹ *n* antiseptic substance

**anti-social** *adj* avoiding the company of other people; (of behaviour) harmful to society

**antistatic** *adj* reducing the effects of static electricity

**antithesis** [an-**tith**-iss-iss] *n, pl* -**ses** [-seez] exact opposite; placing together of contrasting ideas or words to produce an effect of balance ▸ **antithetical** *adj*

**antitoxin** *n* (serum containing) an antibody that acts against a toxin

**antitrust** *adj* (*Aust & S Afr*) (of laws) opposing business monopolies

**antivirus** *n, adj* (software) protecting computers from viruses

**antler** *n* branched horn of male deer

**antonym** *n* word that means the opposite of another

**anus** [**ain**-uss] *n* opening at the end of the alimentary canal, through which faeces are discharged

**anvil** *n* heavy iron block on which metals are hammered into particular shapes

**anxiety** *n, pl* -**ties** state of being anxious

**anxious** *adj* worried and tense; intensely desiring ▸ **anxiously** *adv*

**any** *adj, pron* one or some, no matter which ▹ *adv* at all e.g. *it isn't any worse* ▸ **anybody** *pron* anyone ▸ **anyhow** *adv* anyway ▸ **anyone** *pron* any person; person of any importance ▸ **anything** *pron* ▸ **anyway** *adv* at any rate, nevertheless; in any manner ▸ **anywhere** *adv* in, at, or to any place

**Anzac** *n* (in World War 1) a soldier serving with the Australian and New Zealand Army Corps ▸ **Anzac Day** 25 April, a public holiday in Australia and New Zealand commemorating the Anzac landing at Gallipoli in 1915

**AOB** (on the agenda for a meeting) any other business

**aorta** [eh-**or**-ta] *n* main artery of the body, carrying oxygen-rich blood from the heart

**apace** *adv* (*lit*) swiftly

**apart** *adv* to or in pieces; to or at a distance; individual, distinct

**apartheid** *n* former official government policy of racial segregation in S Africa

**apartment** *n* room in a building; flat

**apathy** *n* lack of interest or enthusiasm ▸ **apathetic** *adj*

**ape** *n* tailless monkey such as the chimpanzee or gorilla; stupid, clumsy, or ugly man ▹ *v* imitate

**aperient** [ap-**peer**-ee-ent] *adj* having a mild laxative effect ▷ *n* mild laxative

**aperitif** [ap-per-rit-**teef**] *n* alcoholic drink taken before a meal

**aperture** *n* opening or hole

**APEX** (*Brit, NZ & S Afr*) Advance Purchase Excursion: reduced fare for journeys booked a specified period in advance

**apex** *n* highest point

**aphasia** *n* disorder of the central nervous system that affects the ability to speak and understand words

**aphid** [eh-fid], **aphis** [eh-fiss] *n* small insect which sucks the sap from plants

**aphorism** *n* short clever saying expressing a general truth

**aphrodisiac** [af-roh-**diz**-zee-ak] *n* substance that arouses sexual desire ▷ *adj* arousing sexual desire

**apiary** *n, pl* **-ries** place where bees are kept

**apiculture** *n* breeding and care of bees

**apiece** *adv* each

**aplomb** *n* calm self-possession

**apocalypse** *n* end of the world; event of great destruction **the Apocalypse** book of Revelation, the last book of the New Testament ▶ **apocalyptic** *adj*

**Apocrypha** [ap-**pok**-rif-fa] *pl n* **the Apocrypha** collective name for the 14 books of the Old Testament which are not accepted as part of the Hebrew scriptures

**apocryphal** [ap-**pok**-rif-al] *adj* (of a story) of questionable authenticity

**apogee** [ap-oh-jee] *n* point of the moon's or a satellite's orbit that is farthest from the earth; highest point

**apology** *n, pl* **-gies** expression of regret for wrongdoing; (foll by *for*) poor example (of); ▶ **apologetic** *adj* showing or expressing regret ▶ **apologetically** *adv* ▶ **apologetics** *n* branch of theology concerned with the reasoned defence of Christianity ▶ **apologist** *n* person who formally defends a cause ▶ **apologize** *v* make an apology

SPELLING TIP
Remember that there is one *p* and one *l* in **apology**

**apoplexy** *n* (*Med*) stroke ▶ **apoplectic** *adj* of apoplexy; (*informal*) furious

**apostasy** [ap-**poss**-stass-ee] *n, pl* **-sies** abandonment of one's religious faith or other belief ▶ **apostate** *n, adj*

**a posteriori** [eh poss-steer-ee-or-rye] *adj* involving reasoning from effect to cause

**Apostle** *n* one of the twelve disciples chosen by Christ to preach his gospel; (**a-**) ardent supporter of a cause or movement ▶ **apostolic** *adj*

**apostrophe** [ap-**poss**-trof-fee] *n* punctuation mark (') showing the omission of a letter or letters in a word, e.g. *don't*, or forming the possessive, e.g. *Jill's car*; digression from a speech to address an imaginary or absent person or thing

**apothecary** *n, pl* **-caries** (*obs*) chemist

**apotheosis** [ap-poth-ee-**oh**-siss] *n, pl* **-ses** [-seez] perfect example; elevation to the rank of a god

**app** *n* computer program designed for a particular purpose

**appal** *v* **-palling, -palled** dismay, terrify ▶ **appalling** *adj* dreadful, terrible

SPELLING TIP
The verb **appal** has two *p*s, but only one *l*. If you extend it with an ending beginning with a

vowel, you must add another *l*, as in **appalling**

**apparatus** *n* equipment for a particular purpose

**apparel** *n* (*old-fashioned*) clothing

**apparent** *adj* readily seen, obvious; seeming as opposed to real
▶ **apparently** *adv*

**SPELLING TIP**
**Apparently** is spelt with two *a*s - and then an *e*

**apparition** *n* ghost or ghostlike figure

**appeal** *v* make an earnest request; attract, please, or interest; request a review of a lower court's decision by a higher court ▷ *n* earnest request; attractiveness; request for a review of a lower court's decision by a higher court
▶ **appealing** *adj*

**appear** *v* become visible or present; seem; be seen in public
▶ **appearance** *n* appearing; outward aspect

**appease** *v* pacify (a person) by yielding to his or her demands; satisfy or relieve (a feeling)
▶ **appeasement** *n*

**appellant** *n* person who makes an appeal to a higher court

**appellation** *n* (*formal*) name, title

**append** *v* join on, add
▶ **appendage** *n* thing joined on or added

**appendicitis** *n* inflammation of the appendix

**appendix** *n*, *pl* -**dices** *or* -**dixes** separate additional material at the end of a book; (*Anat*) short closed tube attached to the large intestine

**USAGE NOTE**
Extra sections at the end of a book are *appendices*. The plural *appendixes* is used in medicine

**appertain** *v* (*foll by to*) belong to; be connected with

**appetite** *n* desire for food or drink; liking or willingness
▶ **appetizer** *n* thing eaten or drunk to stimulate the appetite
▶ **appetizing** *adj* stimulating the appetite

**applaud** *v* show approval of by clapping one's hands; approve strongly ▶ **applause** *n* approval shown by clapping one's hands

**apple** *n* round firm fleshy fruit that grows on trees **in apple-pie order** (*informal*) very tidy

**appliance** *n* device with a specific function

**applicable** *adj* relevant, appropriate ▶ **applicability** *n*

**applicant** *n* person who applies for something

**application** *n* formal request; act of applying something to a particular use; diligent effort; act of putting something onto a surface

**appliqué** [ap-**plee**-kay] *n* kind of decoration in which one material is cut out and attached to another

**apply** *v* -**plying, -plied** make a formal request; put to practical use; put onto a surface; be relevant or appropriate **apply oneself** concentrate one's efforts
▶ **applied** *adj* (of a skill, science, etc.) put to practical use

**appoint** *v* assign to a job or position; fix or decide e.g. *appoint a time*; equip or furnish
▶ **appointment** *n* arrangement to meet a person; act of placing someone in a job; the job itself ▷ *pl* fixtures or fittings

**apportion** *v* divide out in shares

**apposite** *adj* suitable, apt
▶ **apposition** *n* grammatical construction in which two nouns or phrases referring to the same thing are placed one after another

without a conjunction e.g. *my son
the doctor*

**appraise** *v* estimate the value or
quality of ▸ **appraisal** *n*

**appreciate** *v* value highly;
be aware of and understand;
be grateful for; rise in value
▸ **appreciable** *adj* enough to
be noticed ▸ **appreciably** *adv*
▸ **appreciation** *n* ▸ **appreciative**
*adj* feeling or showing appreciation

**apprehend** *v* arrest and take
into custody; grasp (something)
mentally ▸ **apprehension** *n* dread,
anxiety; arrest; understanding
▸ **apprehensive** *adj* fearful or
anxious

**apprentice** *n* someone working for
a skilled person for a fixed period
in order to learn his or her trade
▷ *v* take or place (someone) as an
apprentice ▸ **apprenticeship** *n*

**apprise** *v* make aware (of)

**appro** *n* **on appro** (*Brit, Aust, NZ & S
Afr informal*) on approval

**approach** *v* come near or nearer
(to); make a proposal or suggestion
to; begin to deal with (a matter)
▷ *n* approaching or means of
approaching; approximation
▸ **approachable** *adj* ▸ **approach
road** smaller road leading into a
major road

**approbation** *n* approval

**appropriate** *adj* suitable,
fitting ▷ *v* take for oneself;
put aside for a particular
purpose ▸ **appropriately**
*adv* ▸ **appropriateness** *n*
▸ **appropriation** *n*

**approve** *v* consider good or right;
authorize, agree to ▸ **approval** *n*
consent; favourable opinion ▸ **on
approval** (of goods) with an option
to be returned without payment if
unsatisfactory

**approx.** approximate(ly)

**approximate** *adj* almost but
not quite exact ▷ *v* (foll by *to*)
come close to; be almost the
same as ▸ **approximately** *adv*
▸ **approximation** *n*

**appurtenances** *pl n* minor or
additional features

**Apr** April

**après-ski** [ap-ray-**skee**] *n* social
activities after a day's skiing

**apricot** *n* yellowish-orange juicy
fruit like a small peach ▷ *adj*
yellowish-orange

**April** *n* fourth month of the year
▸ **April fool** victim of a practical
joke played on April 1 (**April Fools'
Day**)

**a priori** [eh pry-**or**-rye] *adj* involving
reasoning from cause to effect

**apron** *n* garment worn over the
front of the body to protect the
clothes; area at an airport or
hangar for manoeuvring and
loading aircraft; part of a stage in
front of the curtain

**apropos** [ap-prop-**poh**] *adj, adv*
appropriate(ly) **apropos of** with
regard to

**apse** *n* arched or domed recess, esp.
in a church

**apt** *adj* having a specified tendency;
suitable; quick to learn ▸ **aptly** *adv*
▸ **aptness** *n* ▸ **aptitude** *n* natural
ability

**aqualung** *n* mouthpiece
attached to air cylinders, worn for
underwater swimming

**aquamarine** *n* greenish-blue
gemstone ▷ *adj* greenish-blue

**aquaplane** *n* board on which
a person stands to be towed
by a motorboat ▷ *v* ride on an
aquaplane; (of a motor vehicle)
skim uncontrollably on a thin film
of water

**aquarium** *n, pl* **aquariums** or
**aquaria** tank in which fish and

other underwater creatures are kept; building containing such tanks

**aquatic** *adj* living in or near water; done in or on water ▷ **aquatics** *pl n* water sports

**aquatint** *n* print like a watercolour, produced by etching copper

**aqua vitae** [ak-wa **vee**-tie] *n (obs)* brandy

**aqueduct** *n* structure carrying water across a valley or river

**aqueous** *adj* of, like, or containing water

**aquiline** *adj* (of a nose) curved like an eagle's beak; of or like an eagle

**Arab** *n* member of a Semitic people originally from Arabia ▷ *adj* of the Arabs ▶ **Arabian** *adj* of Arabia or the Arabs ▶ **Arabic** *n* language of the Arabs ▷ *adj* of Arabic, Arabs, or Arabia

**arabesque** [ar-ab-**besk**] *n* ballet position in which one leg is raised behind and the arms are extended; elaborate ornamental design

**arable** *adj* suitable for growing crops on

**arachnid** [ar-**rak**-nid] *n* eight-legged invertebrate, such as a spider, scorpion, tick, or mite

**Aran** *adj* (of sweaters etc.) knitted in a complicated pattern traditional to the Aran Islands, usu. with natural unbleached wool

**arbiter** *n* person empowered to judge in a dispute; person with influential opinions about something

**arbitrary** *adj* based on personal choice or chance, rather than reason ▶ **arbitrarily** *adv*

> **SPELLING TIP**
> Don't forget the second of the three *r*s in **arbitrary**

**arbitration** *n* hearing and settling of a dispute by an impartial referee

chosen by both sides ▶ **arbitrate** *v* ▶ **arbitrator** *n*

**arboreal** *adj* of or living in trees

**arboretum** [ahr-bore-**ee**-tum] *n, pl* **-ta** place where rare trees or shrubs are cultivated

**arboriculture** *n* cultivation of trees or shrubs

**arbour** *n* glade sheltered by trees

**arc** *n* part of a circle or other curve; luminous discharge of electricity across a small gap between two electrodes ▷ *v* form an arc

**arcade** *n* covered passageway lined with shops; set of arches and their supporting columns

**arcane** *adj* mysterious and secret

**arch$^1$** *n* curved structure supporting a bridge or roof; something curved; curved lower part of the foot ▷ *v* (cause to) form an arch ▶ **archway** *n* passageway under an arch

**arch$^2$** *adj* superior, knowing; coyly playful ▶ **archly** *adv* ▶ **archness** *n*

**arch-** *combining form* chief, principal e.g. *archenemy*

**archaeology** *n* study of ancient cultures from their physical remains ▶ **archaeological** *adj* ▶ **archaeologist** *n*

**archaic** [ark-**kay**-ik] *adj* ancient; out-of-date ▶ **archaism** [**ark**-kay-iz-zum] *n* archaic word or phrase

**archangel** [**ark**-ain-jell] *n* chief angel

**archbishop** *n* chief bishop

**archdeacon** *n* priest ranking just below a bishop

**archdiocese** *n* diocese of an archbishop

**archer** *n* person who shoots with a bow and arrow ▶ **archery** *n*

**archetype** [**ark**-ee-type] *n* perfect specimen; original model ▶ **archetypal** *adj*

**archipelago** [ark-ee-**pel**-a-go] *n, pl* **-gos** group of islands; sea full of small islands

**architect** n person qualified to design and supervise the construction of buildings
▶ **architecture** n style in which a building is designed and built; designing and construction of buildings ▶ **architectural** adj

**architrave** n (Archit) beam that rests on columns; moulding round a doorway or window

**archive** [ark-ive] n (often pl) collection of records or documents; place where these are kept
▶ **archival** adj ▶ **archivist** [ark-iv-ist] n person in charge of archives

**Arctic** n **the Arctic** area around the North Pole ▷ adj of this region; (**a-**) (informal) very cold

**ardent** adj passionate; eager, zealous ▶ **ardently** adv ▶ **ardour** n passion; enthusiasm, zeal

**arduous** adj hard to accomplish, strenuous ▶ **arduously** adv

**are**¹ v see **be**

**are**² n unit of measure, 100 square metres

**area** n part or region; size of a two-dimensional surface; subject field

**arena** n seated enclosure for sports events; area of a Roman amphitheatre where gladiators fought; sphere of intense activity

**aren't** are not

**areola** n, pl **-lae** or **-las** small circular area, such as the coloured ring around the human nipple

**argon** n (Chem) inert gas found in the air

**argot** [ahr-go] n slang or jargon

**argue** v **-guing, -gued** try to prove by giving reasons; debate; quarrel, dispute ▶ **arguable** adj
▶ **arguably** adv ▶ **argument** n quarrel; discussion; point presented for or against something
▶ **argumentation** n process of reasoning methodically

▶ **argumentative** adj given to arguing

**SPELLING TIP**
There is an e at the end of **argue**, but you should leave it out when you write **argument**

**argy-bargy** n, pl **-bargies** (informal) squabbling argument

**aria** [ah-ree-a] n elaborate song for solo voice, esp. one from an opera

**arid** adj parched, dry; uninteresting
▶ **aridity** n

**aright** adv rightly

**arise** v **arising, arose, arisen** come about; come into notice; get up

**aristocracy** n, pl **-cies** highest social class ▶ **aristocrat** n member of the aristocracy
▶ **aristocratic** adj

**arithmetic** n calculation by or of numbers ▷ adj of arithmetic ▶ **arithmetical** adj
▶ **arithmetically** adv

**ark** n (Old Testament) boat built by Noah, which survived the Flood; (**A-**) (Judaism) chest containing the writings of Jewish Law

**arm**¹ n either of the upper limbs from the shoulder to the wrist; sleeve of a garment; side of a chair ▶ **armful** n as much as can be held in the arms ▶ **armchair** n upholstered chair with side supports for the arms ▶ **armhole** n opening in a garment through which the arm passes ▶ **armpit** n hollow under the arm at the shoulder

**arm**² v supply with weapons; prepare (a bomb etc.) for use
▶ **arms** pl n weapons; military exploits; heraldic emblem

**armada** n large number of warships

**armadillo** n, pl **-los** small S American mammal covered in strong bony plates

**a**

**Armageddon** n (New Testament) final battle between good and evil at the end of the world; catastrophic conflict

**armament** n military weapons; preparation for war

**armature** n revolving structure in an electric motor or generator, wound with coils carrying the current

**armistice** [arm-miss-stiss] n agreed suspension of fighting

**armour** n metal clothing formerly worn to protect the body in battle; metal plating of tanks, warships, etc. ▶ **armourer** n maker, repairer, or keeper of arms or armour ▶ **armoury** n place where weapons are stored

**army** n, pl **armies** military land forces of a nation; great number

**aroma** n pleasant smell ▶ **aromatic** adj ▶ **aromatherapy** n massage with fragrant oils to relieve tension

**arose** v past tense of **arise**

**around** prep, adv on all sides (of); from place to place (in); somewhere in or near; approximately

**arouse** v stimulate, make active; awaken

**arpeggio** [arp-**pej**-ee-oh] n, pl **-gios** (Music) notes of a chord played or sung in quick succession

**arr.** arranged (by); arrival; arrive(d)

**arraign** [ar-**rain**] v bring (a prisoner) before a court to answer a charge; accuse ▶ **arraignment** n

**arrange** v plan; agree; put in order; adapt (music) for performance in a certain way ▶ **arrangement** n

**arrant** adj utter, downright

**arras** n tapestry wall-hanging

**array** n impressive display or collection; orderly arrangement, esp. of troops; (poetic) rich clothing ▷ v arrange in order; dress in rich clothing

**arrears** pl n money owed **in arrears** late in paying a debt

**arrest** v take (a person) into custody; stop the movement or development of; catch and hold (the attention) ▷ n act of taking a person into custody; slowing or stopping ▶ **arresting** adj attracting attention, striking

**arrive** v reach a place or destination; happen, come; (informal) be born; (informal) attain success ▶ **arrival** n arriving; person or thing that has just arrived

**arrogant** adj proud and overbearing ▶ **arrogantly** adv ▶ **arrogance** n

**arrogate** v claim or seize without justification

**arrow** n pointed shaft shot from a bow; arrow-shaped sign or symbol used to show direction ▶ **arrowhead** n pointed tip of an arrow

**arrowroot** n nutritious starch obtained from the root of a W Indian plant

**arse** n (vulgar slang) buttocks or anus ▶ **arsehole** n (vulgar slang) anus; stupid or annoying person

**arsenal** n place where arms and ammunition are made or stored

**arsenic** n toxic grey element; highly poisonous compound of this ▶ **arsenical** adj

**arson** n crime of intentionally setting property on fire ▶ **arsonist** n

**art** n creation of works of beauty, esp. paintings or sculpture; works of art collectively; skill ▷ pl nonscientific branches of knowledge ▶ **artist** n person who produces works of art, esp. paintings or sculpture; person skilled at something; artiste ▶ **artiste** n professional entertainer such as a singer or dancer ▶ **artistic** adj ▶ **artistically** adv ▶ **artistry** n artistic skill ▶ **arty** adj (informal) having an affected interest in art

**artefact** n something made by human beings

**arteriosclerosis** [art-ear-ee-oh-skler-**oh**-siss] n hardening of the arteries

**artery** n, pl -**teries** one of the tubes carrying blood from the heart; major road or means of communication ▶ **arterial** adj of an artery; (of a route) major

**artesian well** [art-**teez**-yan] n well bored vertically so that the water is forced to the surface by natural pressure

**Artex**® n (Brit) textured covering for ceilings and walls

**artful** adj cunning, wily ▶ **artfully** adv ▶ **artfulness** n

**arthritis** n painful inflammation of a joint or joints ▶ **arthritic** adj, n

**arthropod** n animal, such as a spider or insect, with jointed limbs and a segmented body

**artichoke** n flower head of a thistle-like plant, cooked as a vegetable

**article** n written piece in a magazine or newspaper; item or object; clause in a document; (Grammar) any of the words the, a, or an

**articled** adj bound (as an apprentice) by a written contract

**articulate** adj able to express oneself clearly and coherently; (of speech) clear, distinct; (Zool) having joints ▷ v speak or say clearly and coherently ▶ **articulately** adv ▶ **articulated** adj jointed

▶ **articulated vehicle** large vehicle in two separate sections joined by a pivoted bar ▶ **articulation** n

**artifice** n clever trick; cleverness, skill ▶ **artificer** [art-**tiff**-iss-er] n craftsman

**artificial** adj man-made, not occurring naturally; made in imitation of something natural; not sincere ▶ **artificial insemination** introduction of semen into the womb by means other than sexual intercourse

▶ **artificial intelligence** branch of computer science aiming to produce machines which can imitate intelligent human behaviour ▶ **artificial respiration** method of restarting a person's breathing after it has stopped

▶ **artificially** adv ▶ **artificiality** n

**artillery** n large-calibre guns; branch of the army who use these

**artisan** n skilled worker, craftsman

**artless** adj free from deceit or cunning; natural, unpretentious ▶ **artlessly** adv

**arum lily** [**air**-rum] n plant with a white funnel-shaped leaf surrounding a spike of flowers

**arvie** n (S Afr informal) afternoon

**as** conj while, when; in the way that; that which e.g. do as you are told; since, seeing that; for instance ▷ adv, conj used to indicate amount or extent in comparisons e.g. he is as tall as you ▷ prep in the role of, being e.g. as a mother, I am concerned

**asafoetida** n strong-smelling plant resin used as a spice in Eastern cookery

**a.s.a.p.** as soon as possible

**asbestos** n fibrous mineral which does not burn ▶ **asbestosis** n lung disease caused by inhalation of asbestos fibre

**ASBO** (*Brit*) anti-social behaviour order: a civil order made against a persistently anti-social person

**ascend** *v* go or move up ▸ **ascent** *n* ascending; upward slope ▸ **ascendant** *adj* dominant or influential ▷ *n* **in the ascendant** increasing in power or influence ▸ **ascendancy** *n* condition of being dominant **the Ascension** (*Christianity*) passing of Jesus Christ from earth into heaven

**ascertain** *v* find out definitely ▸ **ascertainable** *adj* ▸ **ascertainment** *n*

**ascetic** [ass-**set**-tik] *n, adj* (person) abstaining from worldly pleasures and comforts ▸ **asceticism** *n*

**ascorbic acid** [ass-**core**-bik] *n* vitamin C

**ascribe** *v* attribute, as to a particular origin ▸ **ascription** *n*

**aseptic** [eh-**sep**-tik] *adj* free from harmful bacteria

**asexual** [eh-**sex**-yew-al] *adj* without sex ▸ **asexually** *adv*

**ash¹** *n* powdery remains left when something is burnt ▷ *pl* remains after burning, esp. of a human body after cremation **the Ashes** cricket trophy competed for in test matches by England and Australia ▸ **ashen** *adj* pale with shock ▸ **ashtray** *n* receptacle for tobacco ash and cigarette butts ▸ **Ash Wednesday** first day of Lent

**ash²** *n* tree with grey bark

**ashamed** *adj* feeling shame

**ashlar** *n* square block of hewn stone used in building

**ashore** *adv* towards or on land

**ashram** *n* religious retreat where a Hindu holy man lives

**Asian** *adj* of the continent of Asia or any of its peoples or languages ▷ *n* person from Asia or a descendant of one; person from the Indian subcontinent or a descendant of one ▸ **Asian pear** apple-shaped pear with crisp flesh

**aside** *adv* to one side; out of other people's hearing e.g. *he took me aside to tell me his plans* ▷ *n* remark not meant to be heard by everyone present

**asinine** *adj* stupid, idiotic

**ask** *v* say or write (something) in a form that requires an answer; make a request or demand; invite

**askance** [ass-**kanss**] *adv* **look askance at** look at with an oblique glance; regard with suspicion

**askew** *adv, adj* to one side, crooked

**aslant** *adv, prep* at a slant (to), slanting (across)

**asleep** *adj* sleeping; (of limbs) numb

**asp** *n* small poisonous snake

**asparagus** *n* plant whose shoots are cooked as a vegetable

**aspect** *n* feature or element; position facing a particular direction; appearance or look

**aspen** *n* kind of poplar tree

**asperity** *n* roughness of temper

**aspersion** *n* **cast aspersions on** make derogatory remarks about

**asphalt** *n* black hard tarlike substance used for road surfaces etc.

**asphodel** *n* plant with clusters of yellow or white flowers

**asphyxia** [ass-**fix**-ee-a] *n* suffocation ▸ **asphyxiate** *v* suffocate ▸ **asphyxiation** *n*

**aspic** *n* savoury jelly used to coat meat, eggs, fish, etc.

**aspidistra** *n* plant with long tapered leaves

**aspirate** (*Phonetics*) *v* pronounce with an *h* sound ▷ *n* *h* sound

**aspire** *v* (foll by *to*) yearn (for), hope (to do or be) ▸ **aspirant** *n* person who aspires ▸ **aspiration** *n* strong desire or aim

**aspirin** n drug used to relieve pain and fever; tablet of this

**ass** n donkey; stupid person

**assagai** n same as **assegai**

**assail** v attack violently ▶ **assailant** n

**assassin** n person who murders a prominent person ▶ **assassinate** v murder (a prominent person) ▶ **assassination** n

**assault** n violent attack ▷ v attack violently ▶ **assault course** series of obstacles used in military training

**assay** n analysis of a substance, esp. a metal, to ascertain its purity ▷ v make such an analysis

**assegai** [ass-a-guy] n slender spear used in S Africa

**assemble** v collect or congregate; put together the parts of (a machine) ▶ **assemblage** n collection or group; assembling ▶ **assembly** n (pl **-blies**) assembled group; assembling ▶ **assembly line** sequence of machines and workers in a factory assembling a product

**assent** n agreement or consent ▷ v agree or consent

**assert** v declare forcefully; insist upon (one's rights etc.) **assert oneself** put oneself forward forcefully ▶ **assertion** n ▶ **assertive** adj ▶ **assertively** adv

**assess** v judge the worth or importance of; estimate the value of (income or property) for taxation purposes ▶ **assessment** n ▶ **assessor** n

**asset** n valuable or useful person or thing ▷ pl property that a person or firm can sell, esp. to pay debts

**asseverate** v declare solemnly

**assiduous** adj hard-working ▶ **assiduously** adv ▶ **assiduity** n

**assign** v appoint (someone) to a job or task; allot (a task); attribute

▶ **assignation** n assigning; secret arrangement to meet

▶ **assignment** n task assigned; assigning

**assimilate** v learn and understand (information); absorb or be absorbed or incorporated ▶ **assimilable** adj ▶ **assimilation** n

**assist** v give help or support ▶ **assistance** n ▶ **assistant** n helper ▷ adj junior or deputy

**assizes** pl n (Brit) court sessions formerly held in each county of England and Wales

**associate** v connect in the mind; mix socially ▷ n partner in business; friend or companion ▷ adj having partial rights or subordinate status e.g. associate member ▶ **association** n society or club; associating

**assonance** n rhyming of vowel sounds but not consonants, as in time and light

**assorted** adj consisting of various types mixed together ▶ **assortment** n assorted mixture

**assuage** [ass-**wage**] v relieve (pain, grief, thirst, etc.)

**assume** v take to be true without proof; take upon oneself e.g. he assumed command; pretend e.g. I assumed indifference ▶ **assumption** n thing assumed; assuming

**assure** v promise or guarantee; convince; make (something) certain; insure against loss of life ▶ **assured** adj confident; certain to happen ▶ **assuredly** adv definitely ▶ **assurance** n assuring or being assured

**USAGE NOTE**
When used in the context of business, assurance and insurance have the same meaning

**astatine** n (Chem) radioactive nonmetallic element

**aster** n plant with daisy-like flowers

**asterisk** n star-shaped symbol (*) used in printing or writing to indicate a footnote etc. ▷ v mark with an asterisk

**astern** adv at or towards the stern of a ship; backwards

**asteroid** n any of the small planets that orbit the sun between Mars and Jupiter

**asthma** [ass-ma] n illness causing difficulty in breathing ▶ **asthmatic** adj, n

**astigmatism** [eh-stig-mat-tiz-zum] n inability of a lens, esp. of the eye, to focus properly

**astir** adj (old-fashioned) out of bed; in motion

**astonish** v surprise greatly ▶ **astonishment** n

**astound** v overwhelm with amazement ▶ **astounding** adj

**astrakhan** n dark curly fleece of lambs from Astrakhan in Russia; fabric resembling this

**astral** adj of stars; of the spirit world

**astray** adv off the right path

**astride** adv, prep with a leg on either side (of)

**astringent** adj causing contraction of body tissue; checking the flow of blood from a cut; severe or harsh ▷ n astringent substance ▶ **astringency** n

**astrolabe** n instrument formerly used to measure the altitude of stars and planets

**astrology** n study of the alleged influence of the stars, planets, and moon on human affairs ▶ **astrologer** n ▶ **astrological** adj

**astronaut** n person trained for travelling in space

**astronautics** n science and technology of space flight ▶ **astronautical** adj

**astronomy** n scientific study of heavenly bodies ▶ **astronomer** n ▶ **astronomical** adj very large; of astronomy ▶ **astronomically** adv

**astrophysics** n science of the physical and chemical properties of stars, planets, etc. ▶ **astrophysical** adj ▶ **astrophysicist** n

**Astroturf** ® n artificial grass

**astute** adj perceptive or shrewd ▶ **astutely** adv ▶ **astuteness** n

**asunder** adv (obs or poetic) into parts or pieces

**asylum** n refuge or sanctuary; old name for a mental hospital

**asymmetry** n lack of symmetry ▶ **asymmetrical, asymmetric** adj

**asymptote** [ass-im-tote] n straight line closely approached but never met by a curve

**at** prep indicating position in space or time, movement towards an object, etc. e.g. at midnight; throwing stones at windows

**atavism** [at-a-viz-zum] n recurrence of a trait present in distant ancestors ▶ **atavistic** adj

**ate** v past tense of **eat**

**atheism** [aith-ee-iz-zum] n belief that there is no God ▶ **atheist** n ▶ **atheistic** adj

**atherosclerosis** n, pl -ses disease in which deposits of fat cause the walls of the arteries to thicken

**athlete** n person trained in or good at athletics ▶ **athletic** adj physically fit or strong; of an athlete or athletics ▶ **athletics** pl n track-and-field sports such as running, jumping, throwing, etc. ▶ **athletically** adv ▶ **athleticism** n

**athwart** prep across ▷ adv transversely

**atlas** n book of maps

**atmosphere** n mass of gases surrounding a heavenly body,

esp. the earth; prevailing tone or mood (of a place etc.); unit of pressure ▶ **atmospheric** *adj* ▶ **atmospherics** *pl n* radio interference due to electrical disturbance in the atmosphere

**atoll** *n* ring-shaped coral reef enclosing a lagoon

**atom** *n* smallest unit of matter which can take part in a chemical reaction; very small amount ▶ **atom bomb** same as **atomic bomb**

**atomic** *adj* of or using atomic bombs or atomic energy; of atoms ▶ **atomic bomb** bomb in which the energy is provided by nuclear fission ▶ **atomic energy** nuclear energy ▶ **atomic number** number of protons in the nucleus of an atom ▶ **atomic weight** ratio of the mass per atom of an element to one twelfth of the mass of a carbon atom

**atomize** *v* reduce to atoms or small particles

**atomizer** *n* device for discharging a liquid in a fine spray

**atonal** [eh-**tone**-al] *adj* (of music) not written in an established key

**atone** *v* make amends (for sin or wrongdoing) ▶ **atonement** *n*

**atop** *prep* (*lit*) on top of

**atrium** *n*, *pl* **atria** upper chamber of either half of the heart; central hall extending through several storeys of a modern building; main courtyard of an ancient Roman house

**atrocious** *adj* extremely cruel or wicked; horrifying or shocking; (*informal*) very bad ▶ **atrociously** *adv* ▶ **atrocity** *n* wickedness; (*pl* **-ties**) act of cruelty

**atrophy** [**at**-trof-fee] *n*, *pl* **-phies** wasting away of an organ or part ▷ *v* **-phying, -phied** (cause to) waste away

**attach** *v* join, fasten, or connect; attribute or ascribe ▶ **attached** *adj* (foll by *to*) fond of ▶ **attachment** *n* affection; accessory that can be fitted to a device; computer file sent with an e-mail

**attaché** [at-**tash**-shay] *n* specialist attached to a diplomatic mission ▶ **attaché case** flat rectangular briefcase for papers

**attack** *v* launch a physical assault (against); criticize; set about (a job or problem) with vigour; affect adversely ▷ *n* act of attacking; sudden bout of illness ▶ **attacker** *n*

**attain** *v* achieve or accomplish (a task or aim); reach ▶ **attainable** *adj* ▶ **attainment** *n* accomplishment

**attar** *n* fragrant oil made from roses

**attempt** *v* try, make an effort ▷ *n* effort or endeavour

**attend** *v* be present at; go regularly to a school, college, etc.; look after; pay attention; apply oneself (to) ▶ **attendance** *n* attending; number attending ▶ **attendant** *n* person who assists, guides, or provides a service ▷ *adj* accompanying ▶ **attention** *n* concentrated direction of the mind; consideration; care; alert position in military drill ▶ **attentive** *adj* giving attention; considerately helpful ▶ **attentively** *adv* ▶ **attentiveness** *n*

**attenuated** *adj* weakened; thin and extended ▶ **attenuation** *n*

**attest** *v* affirm the truth of, be proof of ▶ **attestation** *n*

**attic** *n* space or room within the roof of a house

**attire** *n* (*formal*) fine or formal clothes

**attired** *adj* dressed in a specified way

**attitude** *n* way of thinking and behaving; posture of the body

**attorney** *n* person legally appointed to act for another; (*US & S Afr*) lawyer

**a**

**attract** v arouse the interest or admiration of; draw (something) closer by exerting a force on it ▸ **attraction** n power to attract; something that attracts ▸ **attractive** adj ▸ **attractively** adv ▸ **attractiveness** n

**attribute** v (usu. foll by to) regard as belonging to or produced by ▷ n quality or feature representative of a person or thing ▸ **attributable** adj ▸ **attribution** n ▸ **attributive** adj (Grammar) (of an adjective) preceding the noun modified

**attrition** n constant wearing down to weaken or destroy

**attune** v adjust or accustom (a person or thing)

**atypical** [eh-**tip**-ik-al] adj not typical

**Au** (Chem) gold

**aubergine** [**oh**-bur-zheen] n (Brit) dark purple tropical fruit, cooked and eaten as a vegetable

**aubrietia** [aw-**bree**-sha] n trailing plant with purple flowers

**auburn** adj (of hair) reddish-brown

**auction** n public sale in which articles are sold to the highest bidder ▷ v sell by auction ▸ **auctioneer** n person who conducts an auction

**audacious** adj recklessly bold or daring; impudent ▸ **audaciously** adv ▸ **audacity** n

**audible** adj loud enough to be heard ▸ **audibly** adv ▸ **audibility** n

**audience** n group of spectators or listeners; formal interview

**audio** adj of sound or hearing; of or for the transmission or reproduction of sound ▸ **audio typist** typist trained to type from a dictating machine ▸ **audiovisual** adj (esp. of teaching aids) involving both sight and hearing

**audit** n official examination of business accounts ▷ v **auditing,**

**audited** examine (business accounts) officially ▸ **auditor** n

**audition** n test of a performer's ability for a particular role or job ▷ v test or be tested in an audition

**auditorium** n, pl **-toriums** or **-toria** area of a concert hall or theatre where the audience sits

**auditory** adj of or relating to hearing

**au fait** [oh **fay**] adj (French) fully informed; expert

**Aug** August

**auger** n tool for boring holes

**aught** pron (obs) anything whatever

**augment** v increase or enlarge ▸ **augmentation** n

**au gratin** [oh **grat**-tan] adj covered and cooked with breadcrumbs and sometimes cheese

**augur** v be a sign of (future events) ▸ **augury** n foretelling of the future; (pl **-ries**) omen

**August** n eighth month of the year

**august** [aw-**gust**] adj dignified and imposing

**auk** n northern sea bird with short wings and black-and-white plumage

**aunt** n father's or mother's sister; wife of parent's sibling ▸ **auntie, aunty** n, pl **aunties** (informal) aunt ▸ **Aunt Sally** (Brit, NZ & S Afr) figure used in fairgrounds as a target; target of abuse or criticism

**au pair** n young foreign woman who does housework in return for board and lodging

**aura** n distinctive air or quality of a person or thing

**aural** adj of or using the ears or hearing

**aureole, aureola** n halo

**au revoir** [oh riv-**vwahr**] interj (French) goodbye

**auricle** n upper chamber of the heart; outer part of the ear ▸ **auricular** adj

**aurochs** *n, pl* **aurochs** recently extinct European wild ox

**aurora** *n, pl* **-ras** *or* **-rae** bands of light sometimes seen in the sky in polar regions ▶ **aurora australis** aurora seen near the South Pole ▶ **aurora borealis** aurora seen near the North Pole

**auscultation** *n* listening to the internal sounds of the body, usu. with a stethoscope, to help with diagnosis

**auspices** [**aw**-spiss-siz] *pl n* **under the auspices of** with the support and approval of

**auspicious** *adj* showing signs of future success, favourable ▶ **auspiciously** *adv*

**Aussie** *n, adj* (*informal*) Australian

**Aust** Australia(n)

**austere** *adj* stern or severe; ascetic or self-disciplined; severely simple or plain ▶ **austerely** *adv* ▶ **austerity** *n*

**Australasian** *n, adj* (person) from Australia, New Zealand, and neighbouring islands

**Australia Day** *n* (*Aust*) public holiday on 26 January

**Australian** *n, adj* (person) from Australia **Indigenous Australian** same as **aborigine**

**autarchy** [**aw**-tar-kee] *n* absolute power or autocracy

**autarky** [**aw**-tar-kee] *n* policy of economic self-sufficiency

**authentic** *adj* known to be real, genuine ▶ **authentically** *adv* ▶ **authenticity** *n* ▶ **authenticate** *v* establish as genuine ▶ **authentication** *n*

**author** *n* writer of a book etc.; originator or creator ▶ **authorship** *n*

**authority** *n, pl* **-ties** power to command or control others; (often *pl*) person or group having this power; expert in a particular field ▶ **authoritarian** *n, adj* (person) insisting on strict obedience to authority ▶ **authoritative** *adj* recognized as being reliable; possessing authority ▶ **authoritatively** *adv* ▶ **authorize** *v* give authority to; give permission for ▶ **authorization** *n*

**autism** *n* (*Psychiatry*) disorder, usu. of children, characterized by lack of response to people and limited ability to communicate ▶ **autistic** *adj*

**auto-** *combining form* self- e.g. *autobiography*

**autobiography** *n, pl* **-phies** account of a person's life written by that person ▶ **autobiographical** *adj* ▶ **autobiographically** *adv*

**autocrat** *n* ruler with absolute authority; dictatorial person ▶ **autocratic** *adj* ▶ **autocratically** *adv* ▶ **autocracy** *n* government by an autocrat

**autocross** *n* motor-racing over a rough course

**Autocue**® *n* electronic television prompting device displaying a speaker's script, unseen by the audience

**autogiro, autogyro** *n, pl* **-ros** self-propelled aircraft resembling a helicopter but with an unpowered rotor

**autograph** *n* handwritten signature of a (famous) person ▷ *v* write one's signature on or in

**automat** *n* (*US*) vending machine

**automate** *v* make (a manufacturing process) automatic ▶ **automation** *n*

**automatic** *adj* (of a device) operating mechanically by itself; (of a process) performed by automatic equipment; done

without conscious thought;
(of a firearm) self-loading ▷ *n*
self-loading firearm; vehicle
with automatic transmission
▶ **automatically** *adv*
**automaton** *n* robot; person who
acts mechanically
**automobile** *n* (*US*) motor car
**autonomy** *n* self-government
▶ **autonomous** *adj*
**autopsy** *n, pl* **-sies** examination of
a corpse to determine the cause
of death
**autosuggestion** *n* process in
which a person unconsciously
influences his or her own behaviour
or beliefs
**autumn** *n* season between
summer and winter
▶ **autumnal** *adj*
**auxiliary** *adj* secondary or
supplementary; supporting
▷ *n, pl* **-ries** person or thing
that supplements or supports
▶ **auxiliary verb** verb used to
form the tense, voice, or mood of
another, such as *will* in *I will go*
**avail** *v* be of use or advantage (to)
▷ *n* use or advantage e.g. *to no avail*
**avail oneself of** make use of
**available** *adj* obtainable or
accessible ▶ **availability** *n*
**avalanche** *n* mass of snow or
ice falling down a mountain;
sudden overwhelming quantity
of anything
**avant-garde** [av-ong-**gard**] *n*
group of innovators, esp. in
the arts ▷ *adj* innovative and
progressive
**avarice** [av-a-riss] *n* greed for
wealth ▶ **avaricious** *adj*
**avast** *interj* (*Naut*) stop
**avatar** *n* (*Hinduism*) appearance
of a god in animal or human
form; (*Computing*) graphical
representation of a person in a

virtual environment, such as an
online role-playing game
**Ave** Avenue
**avenge** *v* take revenge in
retaliation for (harm done) or
on behalf of (a person harmed)
▶ **avenger** *n*
**avenue** *n* wide street; road
between two rows of trees; way
of approach
**aver** [av-**vur**] *v* **averring, averred**
state to be true
**average** *n* typical or normal
amount or quality; result obtained
by adding quantities together and
dividing the total by the number
of quantities ▷ *adj* usual or typical;
calculated as an average ▷ *v*
calculate the average of; amount
to as an average
**averse** *adj* (usu. foll by *to*) disinclined
or unwilling ▶ **aversion** *n* strong
dislike; person or thing disliked
**avert** *v* turn away; ward off
**avian** *adj* relating to birds ▶ **avian
flu** same as **bird flu**
**aviary** *n, pl* **aviaries** large cage or
enclosure for birds
**aviation** *n* art of flying aircraft
▶ **aviator** *n*
**avid** *adj* keen or enthusiastic;
greedy (for) ▶ **avidly** *adv*
▶ **avidity** *n*
**avocado** *n, pl* **-dos** pear-shaped
tropical fruit with a leathery green
skin and yellowish-green flesh
**avocation** *n* (*old-fashioned*)
occupation; hobby
**avocet** *n* long-legged wading bird
with a long slender upward-
curving bill
**avoid** *v* prevent from happening;
refrain from; keep away from
▶ **avoidable** *adj* ▶ **avoidance** *n*
**avoirdupois** [av-er-de-**poise**]
*n* system of weights based on
pounds and ounces

**avow** v state or affirm; admit openly ▶ **avowal** n ▶ **avowed** adj ▶ **avowedly** adv

**avuncular** adj (of a man) friendly, helpful, and caring towards someone younger

**await** v wait for; be in store for

**awake** v **awaking, awoke, awoken** emerge or rouse from sleep; (cause to) become alert ▷ adj not sleeping; alert

**awaken** v awake

**award** v give (something, such as a prize) formally ▷ n something awarded, such as a prize

**aware** adj having knowledge, informed ▶ **awareness** n

**awash** adv washed over by water

**away** adv from a place e.g. go away; to another place e.g. put that gun away; out of existence e.g. fade away; continuously e.g. laughing away ▷ adj not present; distant e.g. two miles away; (Sport) played on an opponent's ground

**awe** n wonder and respect mixed with dread ▷ v fill with awe ▶ **awesome** adj inspiring awe; (slang) excellent or outstanding ▶ **awestruck** adj filled with awe

**awful** adj very bad or unpleasant; (informal) very great; (obs) inspiring awe ▶ **awfully** adv in an unpleasant way; (informal) very

**awhile** adv for a brief time

**awkward** adj clumsy or ungainly; embarrassed; difficult to use or handle; inconvenient ▶ **awkwardly** adv ▶ **awkwardness** n

**awl** n pointed tool for piercing wood, leather, etc.

**awning** n canvas roof supported by a frame to give protection against the weather

**awoke** v past tense of **awake** ▶ **awoken** v past participle of **awake**

**AWOL** adj (Mil) absent without leave

**awry** [a-**rye**] adv, adj with a twist to one side, askew; amiss

**axe** n tool with a sharp blade for felling trees or chopping wood; (informal) dismissal from employment etc. ▷ v (informal) dismiss (employees), restrict (expenditure), or terminate (a project)

**axil** n angle where the stalk of a leaf joins a stem

**axiom** n generally accepted principle; self-evident statement ▶ **axiomatic** adj self-evident

**axis** n, pl **axes** (imaginary) line round which a body can rotate or about which an object or geometrical figure is symmetrical; one of two fixed lines on a graph, against which quantities or positions are measured ▶ **axial** adj

**axle** n shaft on which a wheel or pair of wheels turns

**axolotl** n aquatic salamander of central America

**ayatollah** n Islamic religious leader in Iran

**aye, ay** interj yes ▷ n affirmative vote or voter

**azalea** [az-**zale**-ya] n garden shrub grown for its showy flowers

**azimuth** n arc of the sky between the zenith and the horizon; horizontal angle of a bearing measured clockwise from the north

**Aztec** n, adj (person) of the race ruling Mexico before the Spanish conquest in the 16th century

**azure** adj, n (of) the colour of a clear blue sky

# Bb

**BA** Bachelor of Arts

**baa** v **baaing, baaed** make the characteristic bleating sound of a sheep ▷ n cry made by a sheep

**baas** n (SAfr) boss

**babble** v talk excitedly or foolishly; (of streams) make a low murmuring sound ▷ n muddled or foolish speech

**babe** n baby

**babel** n confused mixture of noises or voices

**baboon** n large monkey with a pointed face and a long tail

**baby** n, pl -**bies** very young child or animal; (slang) sweetheart ▷ adj comparatively small of its type ▶ **babyish** adj ▶ **baby-sit** v take care of a child while the parents are out ▶ **baby-sitter** n

**baccarat** [**back**-a-rah] n card game involving gambling

**bacchanalia** [back-a-**nail**-ee-a] n wild drunken party or orgy

**bach** [**batch**] (NZ) n small holiday cottage ▷ v look after oneself when one's spouse is away

**bachelor** n unmarried man; person who holds the lowest university or college degree

> **SPELLING TIP**
> Not **batchelor**, but **bachelor**: the correct spelling has no t

**bacillus** [bass-**ill**-luss] n, pl -**li** [-lie] rod-shaped bacterium

**back** n rear part of the human body, from the neck to the pelvis; part or side of an object opposite the front; part of anything less often seen or used; (Ball games) defensive player or position ▷ v (cause to) move backwards; provide money for (a person or enterprise); bet on the success of; (foll by onto) have the back facing towards ▷ adj situated behind; owing from an earlier date ▷ adv at, to, or towards the rear; to or towards the original starting point or condition ▶ **backer** n person who gives financial support ▶ **backing** n support; musical accompaniment for a pop singer ▶ **backward** adj directed towards the rear; retarded in physical, material, or intellectual development ▶ **backwardness** n ▶ **backwards** adv towards the rear; with the back foremost; in the reverse of the usual direction ▶ **back up** v support ▶ **backup** n support or reinforcement; reserve or substitute

**backbencher** n Member of Parliament who does not hold office in the government or opposition

**backbiting** n spiteful talk about an absent person

**backbone** n spinal column; strength of character

**backchat** n (informal) impudent replies

**backcloth, backdrop** n painted curtain at the back of a stage set

**backdate** v make (a document) effective from a date earlier than its completion

**backfire** v (of a plan) fail to have the desired effect; (of an engine) make a loud noise like an explosion

**backgammon** n game played with counters and dice

**background** n events or circumstances that help to explain something; person's social class, education, or experience; part of a scene or picture furthest from the viewer

**backhand** n (Tennis etc.) stroke played with the back of the hand facing the direction of the stroke ▸ **backhanded** adj ambiguous or implying criticism e.g. a backhanded compliment ▸ **backhander** n (slang) bribe

**backlash** n sudden and adverse reaction

**backlog** n accumulation of things to be dealt with

**backpack** n large pack carried on the back ▹ v go travelling or hiking with a backpack ▸ **backpacker** n

**backside** n (informal) buttocks

**backslide** v relapse into former bad habits ▸ **backslider** n

**backstage** adv, adj behind the stage in a theatre

**backstroke** n swimming stroke performed on the back

**backtrack** v return by the same route by which one has come; retract or reverse one's opinion or policy

**backwash** n water washed backwards by the motion of a boat; repercussion

**backwater** n isolated or backward place or condition

**backwoods** pl n remote sparsely populated area

**bacon** n salted or smoked pig meat

**bacteria** pl n, sing **-rium** large group of microorganisms, many of which cause disease ▸ **bacterial** adj ▸ **bacteriology** n study of bacteria ▸ **bacteriologist** n

> **USAGE NOTE**
> Note that the word bacteria is already plural and does not need an '-s'. The singular form is bacterium

**bad** adj **worse, worst** of poor quality; lacking skill or talent; harmful; immoral or evil; naughty or mischievous; rotten or decayed; unpleasant ▸ **badly** adv ▸ **badness** n ▸ **bad bank** financial institution set up to manage underperforming assets owned by other banks ▸ **bad debt** n debt that is not collectible and therefore worthless to the creditor

**bade** v a past tense of **bid**

**badge** n emblem worn to show membership, rank, etc.

**badger** n nocturnal burrowing mammal of Europe, Asia, and N America with a black and white head ▹ v pester or harass

**badinage** [bad-in-nahzh] n playful and witty conversation

**badminton** n game played with rackets and a shuttlecock, which is hit back and forth over a high net

**Bafana Bafana** [bah-**fan**-na] pl n (S Afr) South African national soccer team

**baffle** v perplex or puzzle ▹ n device to limit or regulate the flow of fluid, light, or sound ▸ **bafflement** n

**bag** n flexible container with an opening at one end; handbag or piece of luggage; (offens) ugly or bad-tempered woman ▹ v **bagging, bagged** put into a bag; succeed in capturing, killing or scoring ▸ **baggy** adj (of clothes) hanging loosely

**bagatelle** n something of little value; board game in which balls are struck into holes

**bagel** n hard ring-shaped bread roll

**baggage** n suitcases packed for a journey

**bagpipes** pl n musical wind instrument with reed pipes and an inflatable bag

**bail**[1] n (Law) money deposited with a court as security for a person's reappearance in court ▷ v pay bail for (a person)

**bail²**, **bale** v (foll by out) remove (water) from (a boat); (informal) help (a person or organization) out of a predicament; make an emergency parachute jump from an aircraft

**bail³** n (Cricket) either of two wooden bars across the tops of the stumps

**bailey** n outermost wall or court of a castle

**bailiff** n sheriff's officer who serves writs and summonses; landlord's agent

**bairn** n (Scot) child

**bait** n piece of food on a hook or in a trap to attract fish or animals ▷ v put a piece of food on or in (a hook or trap); persecute or tease

> **SPELLING TIP**
> The phrase with bated breath is sometimes wrongly spelled with baited breath

**baize** n woollen fabric used to cover billiard and card tables

**bake** v cook by dry heat as in an oven; make or become hardened by heat ▸ **bakeoff** n baking competition ▸ **baking powder** powdered mixture containing sodium bicarbonate, used as a raising agent in baking

**baker** n person whose business is to make or sell bread, cakes, etc. ▸ **baker's dozen** thirteen ▸ **bakery** n, pl **-eries** place where bread, cakes, etc. are baked or sold

**bakkie** n (S Afr) small truck

**Balaclava**, **Balaclava helmet** n close-fitting woollen hood that covers the ears and neck

**balalaika** n guitar-like musical instrument with a triangular body

**balance** n state in which a weight or amount is evenly distributed; amount that remains e.g. the balance of what you owe; weighing device; difference between the credits and debits of an account ▷ v weigh in a balance; make or remain steady; consider or compare; compare or equalize the money going into or coming out of an account

**balcony** n, pl **-nies** platform on the outside of a building with a rail along the outer edge; upper tier of seats in a theatre or cinema

**bald** adj having little or no hair on the scalp; plain or blunt; (of a tyre) having a worn tread ▸ **balding** adj becoming bald ▸ **baldness** n

**balderdash** n stupid talk

**bale¹** n large bundle of hay or goods tightly bound together ▷ v make or put into bales

**bale²** v same as **bail²**

**baleful** adj vindictive or menacing ▸ **balefully** adv

**balk**, **baulk** v be reluctant to (do something); thwart or hinder

**Balkan** adj of any of the countries of the Balkan Peninsula: Romania, Bulgaria, Albania, Greece, the former Yugoslavia, and the European part of Turkey

**ball¹** n round or nearly round object, esp. one used in games; single delivery of the ball in a game ▷ pl (vulgar slang) testicles; nonsense ▷ v form into a ball ▸ **ball bearings** steel balls between moving parts of a machine to reduce friction ▸ **ball cock** device with a floating ball and a valve for regulating the flow of water ▸ **ballpoint, ballpoint pen** n pen with a tiny ball bearing as a writing point

**ball²** n formal social function for dancing ▸ **ballroom** n

**ballad** n narrative poem or song; slow sentimental song

**ballast** *n* substance, such as sand, used to stabilize a ship when it is not carrying cargo

**ballet** *n* classical style of expressive dancing based on conventional steps; theatrical performance of this ▸ **ballerina** *n* female ballet dancer

**ballistics** *n* study of the flight of projectiles, such as bullets ▸ **ballistic missile** missile guided automatically in flight but which falls freely at its target

**balloon** *n* inflatable rubber bag used as a plaything or decoration; large bag inflated with air or gas, designed to float in the atmosphere with passengers in a basket underneath ▷ *v* fly in a balloon; swell or increase rapidly in size ▸ **balloonist** *n*

**ballot** *n* method of voting; actual vote or paper indicating a person's choice ▷ *v* **-loting, -loted** vote or ask for a vote from

**ballyhoo** *n* exaggerated fuss

**balm** *n* aromatic substance used for healing and soothing; anything that comforts or soothes

**Balmain bug** *n* edible Australian shellfish

**balmy** *adj* **balmier, balmiest** (of weather) mild and pleasant

**baloney** *n* (*informal*) nonsense

**balsa** [**bawl**-sa] *n* very light wood from a tropical American tree

**balsam** *n* soothing ointment; flowering plant

**baluster** *n* set of posts supporting a rail

**balustrade** *n* ornamental rail supported by balusters

**bamboo** *n* tall treelike tropical grass with hollow stems

**bamboozle** *v* (*informal*) cheat or mislead; confuse, puzzle

**ban** *v* **banning, banned** prohibit or forbid officially ▷ *n* official prohibition

**banal** [ban-**nahl**] *adj* ordinary and unoriginal ▸ **banality** *n*

**banana** *n* yellow crescent-shaped fruit

**band¹** *n* group of musicians playing together; group of people having a common purpose ▸ **bandsman** *n* ▸ **bandstand** *n* roofed outdoor platform for a band ▸ **band together** *v* unite

**band²** *n* strip of some material, used to hold objects; (*Physics*) range of frequencies or wavelengths between two limits

**bandage** *n* piece of material used to cover a wound or wrap an injured limb ▷ *v* cover with a bandage

**bandanna, bandana** *n* large brightly coloured handkerchief or neckerchief

**B & B** bed and breakfast

**bandicoot** *n* ratlike Australian marsupial

**bandit** *n* robber, esp. a member of an armed gang ▸ **banditry** *n*

**bandolier** *n* shoulder belt for holding cartridges

**bandwagon** *n* **jump, climb on the bandwagon** join a party or movement that seems assured of success

**bandwidth** *n* the range of frequencies used in a telecommunications signal

**bandy** *adj* **-dier, -diest** (also **bandy-legged**) having legs curved outwards at the knees ▷ *v* **-dying, -died** exchange (words) in a heated manner; use (a name, term, etc.) frequently

**bane** *n* person or thing that causes misery or distress ▸ **baneful** *adj*

**bang** *n* short loud explosive noise; hard blow or loud knock ▷ *v* hit or knock, esp. with a loud noise; close (a door) noisily ▷ *adv* precisely; with a sudden impact

**banger** *n* (*Brit & Aust informal*) old decrepit car; (*slang*) sausage; firework that explodes loudly

**bangle** *n* bracelet worn round the arm or the ankle

**banish** *v* send (someone) into exile; drive away ▶ **banishment** *n*

**banisters** *pl n* railing supported by posts on a staircase

**banjo** *n, pl* **-jos** *or* **-joes** guitar-like musical instrument with a circular body

**bank¹** *n* institution offering services such as the safekeeping and lending of money; any supply, store, or reserve ▷ *v* deposit (cash or cheques) in a bank ▶ **banking** *n* ▶ **banknote** *n* piece of paper money ▶ **bank on** *v* rely on

**bank²** *n* raised mass, esp. of earth; sloping ground at the side of a river ▷ *v* form into a bank; cause (an aircraft) or (of an aircraft) to tip to one side on turning

**bank³** *n* arrangement of switches, keys, oars, etc. in a row or in tiers

**banker** *n* manager or owner of a bank

**bankrupt** *n* person declared by a court to be unable to pay his or her debts ▷ *adj* financially ruined ▷ *v* make bankrupt ▶ **bankruptcy** *n*

**banksia** *n* Australian evergreen tree or shrub

**banner** *n* long strip of cloth displaying a slogan, advertisement, etc.; placard carried in a demonstration or procession; advert that extends across the top of a web page

**bannisters** *pl n* same as **banisters**

**banns** *pl n* public declaration, esp. in a church, of an intended marriage

**banquet** *n* elaborate formal dinner

**banshee** *n* (in Irish folklore) female spirit whose wailing warns of a coming death

**bantam** *n* small breed of chicken ▶ **bantamweight** *n* boxer weighing up to 118lb (professional) or 54kg (amateur)

**banter** *v* tease jokingly ▷ *n* teasing or joking conversation

**Bantu** *n* group of languages of Africa; (*offens*) Black speaker of a Bantu language

**baobab** [**bay**-oh-bab] *n* African tree with a thick trunk and angular branches

**baptism** *n* Christian religious ceremony in which a person is immersed in or sprinkled with water as a sign of being cleansed from sin and accepted into the Church ▶ **baptismal** *adj* ▶ **baptize** *v* perform baptism on

**Baptist** *n* member of a Protestant denomination that believes in adult baptism by immersion

**bar¹** *n* rigid length of metal, wood, etc.; solid, usu. rectangular block, of any material; anything that obstructs or prevents; counter or room where drinks are served; heating element in an electric fire; (*Music*) group of beats repeated throughout a piece of music ▷ *v* **barring, barred** secure with a bar; obstruct; ban or forbid ▷ *prep* (also **barring**) except for **the Bar** barristers collectively ▶ **barman, barmaid** *n*

**bar²** *n* unit of atmospheric pressure

**barb** *n* cutting remark; point facing in the opposite direction to the main point of a fish-hook etc. ▶ **barbed** *adj* ▶ **barbed wire** strong wire with protruding sharp points

**barbarian** *n* member of a primitive or uncivilized people ▶ **barbaric**

*adj* cruel or brutal ▶ **barbarism** *n* condition of being backward or ignorant ▶ **barbarity** *n* state of being barbaric or barbarous; (*pl* **-ties**) vicious act ▶ **barbarous** *adj* uncivilized; brutal or cruel

**barbecue** *n* grill on which food is cooked over hot charcoal, usu. outdoors; outdoor party at which barbecued food is served ▷ *v* cook (food) on a barbecue

**barber** *n* person who cuts men's hair and shaves beards

**barbiturate** *n* drug used as a sedative

**bar code** *n* arrangement of numbers and parallel lines on a package, which can be electronically scanned at a checkout to give the price of the goods

**bard** *n* (*lit*) poet

**bare** *adj* unclothed, naked; without the natural or usual covering; unembellished, simple; just sufficient ▷ *v* uncover ▶ **barely** *adv* only just ▶ **bareness** *n* ▶ **barebones** *adj* basic, containing only the essential elements e.g. *a barebones summary*

**bareback** *adj, adv* (of horse-riding) without a saddle

**barefaced** *adj* shameless or obvious

**barefoot, barefooted** *adj, adv* with the feet uncovered

**bargain** *n* agreement establishing what each party will give, receive, or perform in a transaction; something bought or offered at a low price ▷ *v* negotiate the terms of an agreement ▶ **bargain for** *v* anticipate or take into account

**barge** *n* flat-bottomed boat used to transport freight ▷ *v* (*informal*) push violently ▶ **barge in, barge into** *v* interrupt rudely

**barista** [bar-**ee**-sta] *n* person who makes and sells coffee in a coffee bar

**baritone** *n* (singer with) the second lowest adult male voice

**barium** *n* (*Chem*) soft white metallic element

**bark¹** *n* loud harsh cry of a dog ▷ *v* (of a dog) make its typical cry; shout in an angry tone

**bark²** *n* tough outer layer of a tree

**barley** *n* tall grasslike plant cultivated for grain

**barmy** *adj* **-mier, -miest** (*slang*) insane

**barn** *n* large building on a farm used for storing grain

**barnacle** *n* shellfish that lives attached to rocks, ship bottoms, etc.

**barney** *n* (*informal*) noisy fight or argument

**barometer** *n* instrument for measuring atmospheric pressure ▶ **barometric** *adj*

**baron** *n* member of the lowest rank of nobility; powerful businessman ▶ **baroness** *n* ▶ **baronial** *adj*

**baronet** *n* commoner who holds the lowest hereditary British title

**baroque** [bar-**rock**] *n* highly ornate style of art, architecture, or music from the late 16th to the early 18th century ▷ *adj* ornate in style

**barque** [bark] *n* sailing ship, esp. one with three masts

**barra** *n* (*Aust informal*) short for **barramundi**

**barrack** *v* criticize loudly or shout against (a team or speaker)

**barracks** *pl n* building used to accommodate military personnel

**barracouta** *n* large Pacific fish with a protruding lower jaw and strong teeth

**barracuda** *n* tropical sea fish

**barrage** [bar-**rahzh**] *n* continuous delivery of questions, complaints, etc.; continuous artillery fire; artificial barrier across a river to control the water level

**barramundi** n edible Australian fish

**barrel** n cylindrical container with rounded sides and flat ends; tube in a firearm through which the bullet is fired ▶ **barrel organ** musical instrument played by turning a handle

**barren** adj (of a woman or female animal) incapable of producing offspring; (of land) unable to support the growth of crops, fruit, etc. ▶ **barrenness** n

**barricade** n barrier, esp. one erected hastily for defence ▷ v erect a barricade across (an entrance)

**barrier** n anything that prevents access, progress, or union

**barrister** n (Brit, Aust & NZ) lawyer qualified to plead in a higher court

**barrow¹** n wheelbarrow; movable stall used by street traders

**barrow²** n mound of earth over a prehistoric tomb

**barter** v trade (goods) in exchange for other goods ▷ n trade by the exchange of goods

**basalt** [bass-awlt] n dark volcanic rock ▶ **basaltic** adj

**base¹** n bottom or supporting part of anything; fundamental part; centre of operations, organization, or supply; starting point ▷ v (foll by on or upon) use as a basis (for); (foll by at or in) to station or place ▶ **baseless** adj

**base²** adj dishonourable or immoral; of inferior quality or value ▶ **baseness** n

**baseball** n team game in which runs are scored by hitting a ball with a bat then running round four bases; ball used for this

**basement** n partly or wholly underground storey of a building

**bash** (informal) v hit violently or forcefully ▷ n heavy blow; party

**bashful** adj shy or modest ▶ **bashfully** adv ▶ **bashfulness** n

**BASIC** n computer programming language that uses common English words

**basic** adj of or forming a base or basis; elementary or simple ▶ **basics** pl n fundamental principles, facts, etc. ▶ **basically** adv

**basil** n aromatic herb used in cooking

**basilica** n rectangular church with a rounded end and two aisles

**basilisk** n legendary serpent said to kill by its breath or glance

**basin** n round open container; sink for washing the hands and face; sheltered area of water where boats may be moored; catchment area of a particular river

**basis** n, pl **-ses** fundamental principles etc. from which something is started or developed

**bask** v lie in or be exposed to something, esp. pleasant warmth

**basket** n container made of interwoven strips of wood or cane ▶ **basketwork** n

**basketball** n team game in which points are scored by throwing the ball through a high horizontal hoop; ball used for this

**Basque** n, adj (member or language) of a people living in the W Pyrenees in France and Spain

**basque** n tight-fitting bodice for women

**bas-relief** n sculpture in which the figures project slightly from the background

**bass¹** [base] n (singer with) the lowest adult male voice ▷ adj of the lowest range of musical notes

**bass²** n edible sea fish

**basset hound** n smooth-haired dog with short legs and long ears

**bassoon** n low-pitched woodwind instrument

**bastard** n (offens) obnoxious or despicable person; person born of parents not married to each other

**baste¹** v moisten (meat) during cooking with hot fat

**baste²** v sew with loose temporary stitches

**bastion** n projecting part of a fortification; thing or person regarded as defending a principle

**bat¹** n any of various types of club used to hit the ball in certain sports ▷ v **batting, batted** strike with or as if with a bat ▶ **batsman** n (Cricket) person who bats or specializes in batting

**bat²** n nocturnal mouse-like flying animal

**batch** n group of people or things dealt with at the same time

**bated** adj **with bated breath** in suspense or fear

**bath** n large container in which to wash the body; act of washing in such a container ▷ pl public swimming pool ▷ v wash in a bath ▶ **bathroom** n room with a bath, sink, and usu. a toilet

**Bath chair** n wheelchair for an invalid

**bathe** v swim in open water for pleasure; apply liquid to (the skin or a wound) in order to cleanse or soothe; (foll by in) fill (with) e.g. bathed in sunlight ▶ **bather** n

**bathos** [bay-thoss] n sudden ludicrous change in speech or writing from a serious subject to a trivial one

**batik** [bat-**teek**] n process of printing fabric using wax to cover areas not to be dyed; fabric printed in this way

**batman** n officer's servant in the armed forces

**baton** n thin stick used by the conductor of an orchestra; short bar transferred in a relay race; police officer's truncheon

**battalion** n army unit consisting of three or more companies

**batten** n strip of wood fixed to something, esp. to hold it in place ▶ **batten down** v secure with battens

**batter¹** v hit repeatedly ▶ **battering ram** large beam used to break down fortifications

**batter²** n mixture of flour, eggs, and milk, used in cooking

**battery** n, pl **-teries** device that produces electricity in a torch, radio, etc.; group of heavy guns operating as a single unit ▷ adj kept in series of cages for intensive rearing

**battle** n fight between large armed forces; conflict or struggle ▷ v struggle

**battle-axe** n (informal) domineering woman; (formerly) large heavy axe

**battlement** n wall with gaps along the top for firing through

**battleship** n large heavily armoured warship

**batty** adj **-tier, -tiest** (slang) eccentric or crazy

**bauble** n trinket of little value

**bauera** n small evergreen Australian shrub

**baulk** v same as **balk**

**bauxite** n claylike substance that is the chief source of aluminium

**bawdy** adj **bawdier, bawdiest** (of writing etc.) containing humorous references to sex

**bawl** v shout or weep noisily

**bay¹** n stretch of coastline that curves inwards

**bay²** n recess in a wall; area set aside for a particular purpose e.g. *loading bay*

**bay³** v howl in deep prolonged tones

**bay⁴** n Mediterranean laurel tree ▶ **bay leaf** its dried leaf, used in cooking

**bay⁵** adj, n reddish-brown (horse)

**bayonet** n sharp blade that can be fixed to the end of a rifle ▷ v **-neting, -neted** stab with a bayonet

**bazaar** n sale in aid of charity; market area, esp. in Eastern countries

**bazooka** n portable rocket launcher that fires an armour-piercing projectile

**BBC** British Broadcasting Corporation

**BC** before Christ

**BCE** before Common Era

**BCG**® antituberculosis vaccine

**be** v, *present sing 1st person* **am,** *2nd person* **are,** *3rd person* **is,** *present pl* **are,** *past sing 1st person* **was,** *2nd person* **were,** *3rd person* **was,** *past pl* **were,** *present participle* **being,** *past participle* **been** exist or live; used as a linking between the subject of a sentence and its complement e.g. *John is a musician;* forms the progressive present tense e.g. *the man is running;* forms the passive voice of all transitive verbs e.g. *a good film is being shown on television tonight*

**beach** n area of sand or pebbles on a shore ▷ v run or haul (a boat) onto a beach ▶ **beachhead** n beach captured by an attacking army on which troops can be landed

**beacon** n fire or light on a hill or tower, used as a warning

**bead** n small piece of plastic, wood, etc., pierced for threading on a string to form a necklace etc.; small drop of moisture ▶ **beaded**

*adj* ▶ **beading** n strip of moulding used for edging furniture ▶ **beady** adj small, round, and glittering e.g. *beady eyes*

**beagle** n small hound with short legs and drooping ears

**beak¹** n projecting horny jaws of a bird; (*slang*) nose ▶ **beaky** adj

**beak²** n (*Brit, Aust & NZ slang*) judge, magistrate, or headmaster

**beaker** n large drinking cup; lipped glass container used in laboratories

**beam** n broad smile; ray of light; narrow flow of electromagnetic radiation or particles; long thick piece of wood, metal, etc., used in building ▷ v smile broadly; divert or aim (a radio signal, light, etc.) in a certain direction

**bean** n seed or pod of various plants, eaten as a vegetable or used to make coffee etc.

**beanie** n close-fitting woollen hat

**bear¹** v **bearing, bore, borne** support or hold up; bring e.g. *to bear gifts;* (*past participle* (passive) **born**) give birth to; tolerate or endure; hold in the mind ▶ **bearable** adj ▶ **bear out** v show to be truthful

**bear²** n large heavy mammal with a shaggy coat ▶ **bearskin** n tall fur helmet worn by some British soldiers

**beard** n hair growing on the lower parts of a man's face ▶ **bearded** adj

**bearer** n person who carries, presents, or upholds something

**bearing** n relevance (to); person's general social conduct; part of a machine that supports another part, esp. one that reduces friction ▷ pl sense of one's own relative position

**beast** n large wild animal; brutal or uncivilized person ▶ **beastly** adj unpleasant or disagreeable

**beat** v **beating, beat, beaten**
or **beat** hit hard and repeatedly;
move (wings) up and down; throb
rhythmically; stir or mix vigorously;
overcome or defeat ▷ n regular
throb; assigned route, as of a
policeman; basic rhythmic unit
in a piece of music ▶ **beatbox** n
machine that produces musical
beats ▶ **beat up** v injure (someone)
by repeated blows or kicks

**beatify** [bee-**at**-if-fie] v **-fying, -fied**
(RC Church) declare (a dead person)
to be among the blessed in heaven:
the first step towards canonization
▶ **beatific** adj displaying great
happiness ▶ **beatification** n
▶ **beatitude** n (Christianity) any of
the blessings on the poor, meek,
etc., in the Sermon on the Mount

**beau** [boh] n, pl **beaux** or **beaus**
boyfriend or admirer; man greatly
concerned with his appearance

**Beaufort scale** n scale for
measuring wind speeds

**beautician** n person who gives
beauty treatments professionally

**beautiful** adj very attractive to look
at; very pleasant ▶ **beautifully** adv

**beautify** v **-fying, -fied** make
beautiful ▶ **beautification** n

**beauty** n, pl **-ties** combination of
all the qualities of a person or thing
that delight the senses and mind;
very attractive woman; (informal)
something outstanding of its kind

**beaver** n amphibious rodent with a
big flat tail ▶ **beaver away** v work
industriously

**becalmed** adj (of a sailing ship)
motionless through lack of wind

**became** v past tense of **become**

**because** conj on account of the fact
that **because of** on account of

**beck¹** n **at someone's beck and
call** having to be constantly
available to do as someone asks

**beck²** n (N English) stream

**beckon** v summon with a gesture

**become** v **-coming, -came, -come**
come to be; (foll by of) happen to;
suit ▶ **becoming** adj attractive or
pleasing; appropriate or proper

**bed** n piece of furniture on which
to sleep; garden plot; bottom
of a river, lake, or sea; layer of
rock **go to bed with** have sexual
intercourse with ▶ **bed down** v
go to or put into a place to sleep
or rest ▶ **bedpan** n shallow bowl
used as a toilet by bedridden
people ▶ **bedridden** adj confined
to bed because of illness or old age
▶ **bedrock** n solid rock beneath
the surface soil; basic facts or
principles ▶ **bedroom** n ▶ **bedsit,
bedsitter** n furnished sitting room
with a bed

**bedding** n sheets and covers that
are used on a bed

**bedevil** v **-illing, -illed** harass,
confuse, or torment

**bedlam** n noisy confused situation

**bedraggled** adj untidy, wet, or
dirty

**bee¹** n insect that makes wax and
honey ▶ **beehive** n structure
in which bees live ▶ **beeswax**
n wax secreted by bees, used in
polishes etc.

**bee²** n social gathering to carry out
a communal task e.g. quilting bee
▶ **spelling bee** contest in which
players are required to spell words
▶ **working bee** voluntary group
doing a job for charity

**beech** n tree with a smooth greyish
bark

**beef** n flesh of a cow, bull, or ox
▶ **beefy** adj like beef; (informal)
strong and muscular ▶ **beefburger**
n flat grilled or fried cake of minced
beef ▶ **beefeater** n yeoman warder
at the Tower of London

**been** v past participle of **be**

**beep** n high-pitched sound, like that of a car horn ▷ v (cause to) make this noise

**beer** n alcoholic drink brewed from malt and hops ▶ **beery** adj

**beet** n plant with an edible root and leaves ▶ **beetroot** n type of beet plant with a dark red root

**beetle** n insect with a hard wing cover on its back

**befall** v (old-fashioned) happen to (someone)

**befit** v be appropriate or suitable for ▶ **befitting** adj

**before** conj, prep, adv indicating something earlier in time, in front of, or preferred to e.g. before the war; brought before a judge; death before dishonour ▶ **beforehand** adv in advance

**befriend** v become friends with

**beg** v **begging, begged** solicit (for money or food), esp. in the street; ask formally or humbly

**began** v past tense of **begin**

**beget** v **-getting, -got** or **-gat, -gotten** or **-got** (old-fashioned) cause or create; father

**beggar** n person who lives by begging ▶ **beggarly** adj

**begin** v **-ginning, -gan, -gun** start; bring or come into being ▶ **beginner** n person who has just started learning to do something ▶ **beginning** n

**begonia** n tropical plant with waxy flowers

**begrudge** v envy (someone) the possession of something; give or allow unwillingly

**beguile** [big-**gile**] v cheat or mislead; charm or amuse ▶ **beguiling** adj

**begun** v past participle of **begin**

**behalf** n **on behalf of** in the interest of or for the benefit of

**behave** v act or function in a particular way; conduct (oneself) properly

**behaviour** n manner of behaving

**behead** v remove the head from

**beheld** v past of **behold**

**behest** n order or earnest request

**behind** prep, adv indicating position to the rear, lateness, responsibility, etc. e.g. behind the wall; behind schedule; the reasons behind her departure ▷ n (informal) buttocks

**behold** v **-holding, -held** (old-fashioned) look (at) ▶ **beholder** n

**beholden** adj indebted or obliged

**behove** v (old-fashioned) be necessary or fitting for

**beige** adj pale brown

**being** n state or fact of existing; something that exists or is thought to exist; human being ▷ v present participle of **be**

**belabour** v attack verbally or physically

**belated** adj late or too late ▶ **belatedly** adv

**belch** v expel wind from the stomach noisily through the mouth; expel or be expelled forcefully e.g. smoke belched from the factory ▷ n act of belching

**beleaguered** adj struggling against difficulties or criticism; besieged by an enemy

**belfry** n, pl **-fries** part of a tower where bells are hung

**Belgium sausage** n (NZ) large smooth bland sausage

**belie** v show to be untrue

**belief** n faith or confidence; opinion; principle accepted as true, often without proof

**believe** v accept as true or real; think, assume, or suppose **believe in** be convinced of the truth or existence of ▶ **believable** adj ▶ **believer** n

**Belisha beacon** [bill-**lee**-sha] n (Brit) flashing orange globe mounted on a post, marking a pedestrian crossing

**belittle** v treat as having little value or importance

**bell** n hollow, usu. metal, cup-shaped instrument that emits a ringing sound when struck; device that rings or buzzes as a signal

**belladonna** n (drug obtained from) deadly nightshade

**bellbird** n Australasian bird with bell-like call

**belle** n beautiful woman, esp. the most attractive woman at a function

**bellicose** adj warlike and aggressive

**belligerent** adj hostile and aggressive; engaged in war ▷ n person or country engaged in war ▶ **belligerence** n

**bellow** v make a low deep cry like that of a bull; shout in anger ▷ n loud deep roar

**bellows** pl n instrument for pumping a stream of air into something

**belly** n, pl -**lies** part of the body of a vertebrate which contains the intestines; stomach; front, lower, or inner part of something ▷ v -**lying, -lied** (cause to) swell out ▶ **bellyful** n (slang) more than one can tolerate

**belong** v (foll by to) be the property of; (foll by to) be a part or member of ▶ **belongings** pl n personal possessions

**beloved** adj dearly loved ▷ n person dearly loved

**below** prep, adv at or to a position lower than, under

**belt** n band of cloth, leather, etc., worn usu. around the waist; long narrow area e.g. a belt of trees;

circular strip of rubber that drives moving parts in a machine ▷ v fasten with a belt; (slang) hit very hard; (slang) move very fast

**bemoan** v express sorrow or dissatisfaction about

**bemused** adj puzzled or confused

**bench** n long seat; long narrow work table **the bench** judge or magistrate sitting in court, or judges and magistrates collectively ▶ **benchmark** n criterion by which to measure something

**bend** v **bending, bent** (cause to) form a curve; (often foll by down) incline the body ▷ n curved part **the bends** (informal) decompression sickness ▶ **bendy** adj

**beneath** adv, prep below; not worthy of

**Benedictine** adj of an order of Christian monks and nuns founded by Saint Benedict

**benediction** n prayer for divine blessing

**benefactor, benefactress** n someone who supports a person or institution by giving money ▶ **benefaction** n

**beneficent** [bin-**eff**-iss-ent] adj charitable or generous ▶ **beneficence** n

**beneficial** adj helpful or advantageous

**beneficiary** n, pl -**ciaries** person who gains or benefits

**benefit** n something that improves or promotes; advantage or sake e.g. I'm doing this for your benefit; payment made by a government to a poor, ill, or unemployed person ▷ v -**fiting, -fited** do or receive good

**benevolence** n inclination to do good; act of

kindness ▸ **benevolent** adj
▸ **benevolently** adv

**benighted** adj ignorant or
uncultured

**benign** [bin-**nine**] adj showing
kindliness; (of a tumour)
not threatening to life
▸ **benignly** adv

**bent** v past of **bend** ▷ adj curved;
(slang) dishonest or corrupt; (Brit &
Aust offens slang) homosexual ▷ n
personal inclination or aptitude
**bent on** determined to pursue (a
course of action)

**bento, bento box** n thin
lightweight box divided into
compartments, which contain
small separate dishes comprising a
Japanese meal

**benzene** n flammable poisonous
liquid used as a solvent, insecticide,
etc.

**bequeath** v dispose of (property)
as in a will ▸ **bequest** n legal gift
of money or property by someone
who has died

**berate** v scold harshly

**bereaved** adj having recently lost
a close friend or relative through
death ▸ **bereavement** n

**bereft** adj (foll by of) deprived

**beret** [**ber**-ray] n round flat close-
fitting brimless cap

**berg¹** n iceberg

**berg²** n (SAfr) mountain

**bergamot** n small Asian tree, the
fruit of which yields an oil used in
perfumery

**beri-beri** n disease caused by
vitamin B deficiency

**berk** n (Brit, Aust & NZ slang) stupid
person

**berm** n (NZ) narrow grass strip
between the road and the footpath
in a residential area

**berry** n, pl **-ries** small soft
stoneless fruit

**berserk** adj **go berserk** become
violent or destructive

**berth** n bunk in a ship or train; place
assigned to a ship at a mooring ▷ v
dock (a ship)

**beryl** n hard transparent mineral

**beryllium** n (Chem) toxic silvery-
white metallic element

**beseech** v **-seeching, -sought** or
**-seeched** ask earnestly; beg

**beset** v trouble or harass constantly

**beside** prep at, by, or to the side of;
as compared with **beside oneself**
overwhelmed or overwrought
▸ **besides** adv, prep in addition

**besiege** v surround with military
forces; overwhelm, as with
requests

**besotted** adj infatuated

**besought** v a past of **beseech**

**bespeak** v indicate or suggest
▸ **bespoke** adj (esp. of a suit)
made to the customer's
specifications

**best** adj most excellent of a
particular group etc. ▷ adv
in a manner surpassing all
others ▷ n most outstanding
or excellent person, thing, or
group in a category ▸ **best man**
groom's attendant at a wedding
▸ **bestseller** n book or other
product that has sold in great
numbers

**bestial** adj brutal or savage; of or
like a beast ▸ **bestiality** n

**bestir** v cause (oneself) to become
active

**bestow** v present (a gift) or confer
(an honour) ▸ **bestowal** n

**bestride** v have or put a leg on
either side of

**bet** n the act of staking a sum
of money or other stake on the
outcome of an event; stake risked
▷ v **betting, bet** or **betted** make or
place (a bet); (informal) predict

**betel** [bee-tl] *n* Asian climbing plant, the leaves and nuts of which can be chewed

**bête noire** [bet nwahr] *n*, *pl* **bêtes noires** person or thing that one particularly dislikes

**betide** *v* happen (to)

**betoken** *v* indicate or signify

**betray** *v* hand over or expose (one's nation, friend, etc.) treacherously to an enemy; disclose (a secret or confidence) treacherously; reveal unintentionally ▷ **betrayal** *n* ▶ **betrayer** *n*

**betrothed** *adj* engaged to be married ▶ **betrothal** *n*

**better** *adj* more excellent than others; improved or fully recovered in health ▷ *adv* in a more excellent manner; in or to a greater degree ▷ *pl n* one's superiors ▷ *v* improve upon

**bettong** *n* short-nosed rat kangaroo

**between** *prep*, *adv* indicating position in the middle, alternatives, etc.

**USAGE NOTE**
*Between* is used when two people or things are mentioned: *the trade war between Europe and America*. Otherwise use *among*

**betwixt** *prep*, *adv* (*old-fashioned*) between

**bevel** *n* slanting edge ▷ *v* **-elling, -elled** cut a bevel on (a piece of timber etc.)

**beverage** *n* drink

**bevy** *n*, *pl* **bevies** flock or group

**bewail** *v* express great sorrow over

**beware** *v* be on one's guard (against)

**bewilder** *v* confuse utterly ▶ **bewildering** *adj* ▶ **bewilderment** *n*

**bewitch** *v* attract and fascinate; cast a spell over ▶ **bewitching** *adj*

**beyond** *prep* at or to a point on the other side of; outside the limits or scope of ▷ *adv* at or to the far side of something

**bi-** *combining form* two or twice e.g. *bifocal*; *biweekly*

**biannual** *adj* occurring twice a year ▶ **biannually** *adv*

**bias** *n* mental tendency, esp. prejudice; diagonal cut across the weave of a fabric; (*Bowls*) bulge or weight on one side of a bowl that causes it to roll in a curve ▷ *v* **-asing, -ased** or **-assing, -assed** cause to have a bias ▶ **biased, biassed** *adj*

**bib** *n* piece of cloth or plastic worn to protect a young child's clothes when eating; upper front part of dungarees etc.

**Bible** *n* sacred writings of the Christian religion; (**b-**) book regarded as authoritative ▶ **biblical** *adj*

**bibliography** *n*, *pl* **-phies** list of books on a subject; list of sources used in a book etc. ▶ **bibliographer** *n*

**bibliophile** *n* person who collects or is fond of books

**bibulous** *adj* addicted to alcohol

**bicarbonate** *n* salt of carbonic acid ▶ **bicarbonate of soda** powder used in baking or as medicine

**bicentenary** *n*, *pl* **-naries** 200th anniversary

**biceps** *n* muscle with two origins, esp. the muscle that flexes the forearm

**bicker** *v* argue over petty matters

**bicycle** *n* vehicle with two wheels, one behind the other, pedalled by the rider

**bid** *v* **bidding, bade, bidden** say (a greeting); command; (*past tense* **bid**) offer (an amount) in an attempt to buy something ▷ *n* offer

of a specified amount; attempt
▸ **bidder** n ▸ **biddable** adj obedient
▸ **bidding** n command

**biddy-bid, biddy-biddy** n, pl
**-bids** or **-biddies** (NZ) low-growing
plant with hooked burrs

**bide** v **bide one's time** wait
patiently for an opportunity

**bidet** [bee-day] n low basin for
washing the genital area

**biennial** adj occurring every two
years ▷ n plant that completes its
life cycle in two years

**bier** n stand on which a corpse or
coffin rests before burial

**bifocals** pl n spectacles with lenses
permitting near and distant vision

**big** adj **bigger, biggest** of
considerable size, height, number,
or capacity; important through
having power, wealth, etc.;
elder; generous ▷ adv on a grand
scale ▸ **bighead** n (informal)
conceited person ▸ **big-headed**
adj ▸ **big shot, bigwig** n (informal)
important person

**bigamy** n crime of marrying a
person while still legally married
to someone else ▸ **bigamist** n
▸ **bigamous** adj

**bigot** n person who is intolerant,
esp. regarding religion or race
▸ **bigoted** adj ▸ **bigotry** n

**bijou** [bee-zhoo] adj (of a house)
small and elegant

**bike** n (informal) bicycle or
motorcycle

**bikini** n woman's brief two-piece
swimming costume

**bilateral** adj affecting or
undertaken by two parties

**bilberry** n bluish-black edible berry

**bilby** n, pl -**bies** Australian
marsupial with long pointed ears
and grey fur

**bile** n bitter yellow fluid secreted
by the liver

**bilge** n (informal) nonsense; ship's
bottom

**bilingual** adj involving or using two
languages

**bilious** adj sick, nauseous

**bill¹** n statement of money owed for
goods or services supplied; draft
of a proposed new law; poster;
(chiefly US & Canadian) piece of
paper money; list of events, such
as a theatre programme ▷ v send
or present a bill to; advertise by
posters

**bill²** n bird's beak

**billabong** n (Aust) stagnant pool in
an intermittent stream

**billboard** n large outdoor board for
displaying advertisements

**billet** v -**leting, -leted** assign
a lodging to (a soldier) ▷ n
accommodation for a soldier in
civil lodgings

**billet-doux** [bill-ee-**doo**] n, pl
**billets-doux** love letter

**billhook** n tool with a hooked
blade, used for chopping etc.

**billiards** n game played on a table
with balls and a cue

**billion** n one thousand million;
formerly, one million million
▸ **billionth** adj

**billow** n large sea wave ▷ v
rise up or swell out ▸ **billowy,
billowing** adj

**billy, billycan** n, pl -**lies** or -**lycans**
metal can or pot for cooking on a
camp fire

**biltong** n (SAfr) strips of dried meat

**bimbo** n (slang) attractive but
empty-headed young person, esp.
a woman

**bin** n container for rubbish or for
storing grain, coal, etc.

**binary** adj composed of two
parts; (Maths, Computing) of or in
a counting system with only two
digits, 0 and 1

**bind** v **binding, bound** make secure with or as if with a rope; place (someone) under obligation; enclose and fasten (the pages of a book) between covers ▷ n (informal) annoying situation ▸ **binder** n firm cover for holding loose sheets of paper together ▸ **binding** n anything that binds or fastens; book cover

**bindi-eye** n small Australian plant with burlike fruit

**bindweed** n plant that twines around a support

**binge** n (informal) bout of excessive indulgence, esp. in drink

**bingo** n gambling game in which numbers are called out and covered by the players on their individual cards

**binoculars** pl n optical instrument consisting of two small telescopes joined together

**binomial** n, adj (mathematical expression) consisting of two terms

**bio-** combining form life or living organisms e.g. biology

**bioactive** adj having an effect on living tissue

**biochemistry** n study of the chemistry of living things ▸ **biochemist** n

**biodegradable** adj capable of being decomposed by natural means

**biodiesel** n biofuel for use in diesel engines

**biodiversity** n existence of a wide variety of species in their natural environment

**biofuel** n fuel derived from renewable biological resources

**biographer** n person who writes an account of another person's life

**biography** n, pl **-phies** account of a person's life by another person ▸ **biographical** adj

**biological** adj of or relating to biology

**biology** n study of living organisms ▸ **biologist** n

**biometric** adj of any automated system using physiological or behavioural traits as a means of identification

**bionic** adj having a part of the body that is operated electronically

**biopsy** n, pl **-sies** examination of tissue from a living body

**BIOS** n (Computing) built-in software that controls main functions of a computer

**biosphere** n part of the earth's surface and atmosphere inhabited by living things

**biotechnology** n use of microorganisms, such as cells or bacteria, in industry and technology

**bioterrorism** n use of viruses, bacteria, etc., by terrorists ▸ **bioterrorist** n

**biped** [**bye-ped**] n animal with two feet

**biplane** n aeroplane with two sets of wings, one above the other

**bipolar** adj having two poles; having two extremes; (Psychiatry) (of a person) manic-depressive

**birch** n tree with peeling bark; birch rod or twigs used, esp. formerly, for flogging offenders

**bird** n creature with feathers and wings, most types of which can fly; (slang) young woman ▸ **bird flu** form of flu occurring in poultry in SE Asia, capable of spreading to humans (also **avian flu**)

**birdie** n (Golf) score of one stroke under par for a hole

**biretta** n stiff square cap worn by the Catholic clergy

**Biro**® n ballpoint pen

**birth** n process of bearing young; childbirth; act of being born; ancestry **give birth to** bear (offspring) ▸ **birth control**

any method of contraception
▶ **birthday** n anniversary of the day of one's birth ▶ **birthmark** n blemish on the skin formed before birth ▶ **birthright** n privileges or possessions that someone is entitled to at birth

**biscuit** n small flat dry sweet or plain cake

**bisect** v divide into two equal parts

**bisexual** adj sexually attracted to both men and women ▶ **bisexuality** n

**bishop** n clergyman who governs a diocese; chessman which is moved diagonally ▶ **bishopric** n diocese or office of a bishop

**bismuth** n (Chem) pinkish-white metallic element

**bison** n, pl -**son** large hairy animal of the cattle family, native to N America and Europe

**bisque** n thick rich soup made from shellfish

**bistro** n, pl -**tros** small restaurant

**bit**¹ n small piece, portion, or quantity **a bit** rather, somewhat **bit by bit** gradually

**bit**² n metal mouthpiece on a bridle; drilling part of a tool

**bit**³ v past tense of **bite**

**bit**⁴ n (Maths, Computing) single digit of binary notation, either 0 or 1

**bitch** n female dog, fox, or wolf; (offens) spiteful woman ▷ v (informal) complain or grumble ▶ **bitchy** adj ▶ **bitchiness** n

**bite** v **biting, bit, bitten** grip, tear, or puncture the skin, as with the teeth or jaws; take firm hold of or act effectively upon ▷ n act of biting; wound or sting inflicted by biting; snack ▶ **biter** n ▶ **biting** adj piercing or keen; sarcastic

**bitter** adj having a sharp unpleasant taste; showing or caused by hostility or resentment; extremely cold ▷ n beer with a slightly bitter taste ▷ pl bitter-tasting alcoholic drink ▶ **bitterly** adv ▶ **bitterness** n

**bittern** n wading marsh bird with a booming call

**bitumen** n black sticky substance obtained from tar or petrol

**bivalve** n, adj (marine mollusc) with two hinged segments to its shell

**bivouac** n temporary camp in the open air ▷ v -**acking, -acked** camp in a bivouac

**bizarre** adj odd or unusual

**blab** v **blabbing, blabbed** reveal (secrets) indiscreetly

**black** adj of the darkest colour, like coal; (**B-**) (of a person) dark-skinned; without hope; angry or resentful e.g. black looks; unpleasant in a macabre manner e.g. black comedy ▷ n darkest colour; (**B-**) member of a dark-skinned race; complete darkness ▷ v make black; (of trade unionists) boycott (goods or people) ▶ **blackness** n ▶ **blacken** v make or become black; defame or slander ▶ **black magic** magic used for evil purposes ▶ **black market** illegal trade in goods or currencies ▶ **black sheep** person who is regarded as a disgrace by his or her family ▶ **black spot** place on a road where accidents frequently occur

**blackball** v exclude from a group ▷ n (NZ) hard boiled sweet with black-and-white stripes

**BlackBerry®** n hand-held wireless device incorporating e-mail, browser and mobile-phone functions

**blackberry** n small blackish edible fruit

**blackbird** n common European thrush

**blackboard** n hard black surface used for writing on with chalk

**blackboy** n Australian plant with grasslike leaves and a spike of small white flowers

**blackbutt** n Australian eucalyptus tree with hard wood used as timber

**blackcurrant** n very small blackish edible fruit that grows in bunches

**blackfish** n small dark Australian estuary fish

**blackguard** [**blag**-gard] n unprincipled person

**blackhead** n black-tipped plug of fatty matter clogging a skin pore

**blackleg** n person who continues to work during a strike

**blacklist** n list of people or organizations considered untrustworthy etc.

**blackmail** n act of attempting to extort money by threats ▷ v (attempt to) obtain money by blackmail

**blackout** n extinguishing of all light as a precaution against an air attack; momentary loss of consciousness or memory ▶ **black out** v extinguish (lights); lose consciousness or memory temporarily

**blacksmith** n person who works iron with a furnace, anvil, etc.

**black snake** n venomous Australian snake

**black swan** n black Australian swan with a red beak

**bladder** n sac in the body where urine is held; hollow bag which may be filled with air or liquid

**blade** n cutting edge of a weapon or tool; thin flattish part of a propeller, oar, etc.; leaf of grass

**blame** v consider (someone) responsible for ▷ n responsibility for something that is wrong

▶ **blameless** adj ▶ **blameworthy** adj deserving blame

**blanch** v become white or pale; prepare (vegetables etc.) by plunging them in boiling water

**blancmange** [blam-**monzh**] n jelly-like dessert made with milk

**bland** adj dull and uninteresting ▶ **blandly** adv

**blandishments** pl n flattery intended to coax or persuade

**blank** adj not written on; showing no interest or expression ▷ n empty space; cartridge containing no bullet ▶ **blankly** adv ▶ **blank verse** unrhymed verse

**blanket** n large thick cloth used as covering for a bed; concealing cover, as of snow ▷ v cover as with a blanket

**blare** v sound loudly and harshly ▷ n loud harsh noise

**blarney** n flattering talk

**blasé** [**blah**-zay] adj indifferent or bored through familiarity

**blaspheme** v speak disrespectfully of (God or sacred things) ▶ **blasphemy** n ▶ **blasphemous** adj ▶ **blasphemer** n

**blast** n explosion; sudden strong gust of air or wind; sudden loud sound, as of a trumpet ▷ v blow up (a rock etc.) with explosives ▶ **blastoff** n launching of a rocket

**blatant** adj glaringly obvious ▶ **blatantly** adv

**blaze**¹ n strong fire or flame; very bright light ▷ v burn or shine brightly

**blaze**² n mark made on a tree to indicate a route

**blazer** n lightweight jacket, often in the colours of a school etc.

**blazon** v proclaim publicly

**bleach** v make or become white or colourless ▷ n bleaching agent

**bleak** adj exposed and barren; offering little hope

**b**

**bleary** *adj* **-rier, -riest** with eyes dimmed, as by tears or tiredness ▸ **blearily** *adv*

**bleat** *v* (of a sheep, goat, or calf) utter its plaintive cry ▷ *n* cry of sheep, goats, and calves

**bleed** *v* **bleeding, bled** lose or emit blood; draw blood from (a person or animal); (*informal*) obtain money by extortion

**bleep** *n* short high-pitched sound made by an electrical device ▷ *v* make a bleeping sound ▸ **bleeper** *n* small portable radio receiver that makes a bleeping signal

**blemish** *n* defect or stain ▷ *v* spoil or tarnish

**blench** *v* shy away, as in fear

**blend** *v* mix or mingle (components or ingredients); look good together ▷ *n* mixture ▸ **blender** *n* electrical appliance for puréeing vegetables etc.

**bless** *v* make holy by means of a religious rite; call upon God to protect; endow with health, talent, etc. ▸ **blessed** *adj* holy ▸ **blessing** *n* invoking of divine aid; approval; happy event

**blether** (*Scot*) *v* talk, esp. foolishly or at length ▷ *n* conversation

**blew** *v* past tense of **blow**¹

**blight** *n* person or thing that spoils or prevents growth; withering plant disease ▷ *v* frustrate or disappoint

**blighter** *n* (*informal*) irritating person

**blimp** *n* small airship

**blind** *adj* unable to see; unable or unwilling to understand; not determined by reason e.g. *blind hatred* ▷ *v* deprive of sight; deprive of good sense, reason, or judgment ▷ *n* covering for a window; something that serves to conceal the truth ▸ **blindly** *adv* ▸ **blindness** *n*

**blindfold** *v* prevent (a person) from seeing by covering the eyes ▷ *n* piece of cloth used to cover the eyes

**blink** *v* close and immediately reopen (the eyes); shine intermittently ▷ *n* act of blinking **on the blink** (*slang*) not working properly

**blinkers** *pl n* leather flaps on a horse's bridle to prevent sideways vision

**blip** *n* spot of light on a radar screen indicating the position of an object

**bliss** *n* perfect happiness ▸ **blissful** *adj* ▸ **blissfully** *adv*

**blister** *n* small bubble on the skin; swelling, as on a painted surface ▷ *v* (cause to) have blisters ▸ **blistering** *adj* (of weather) very hot; (of criticism) extremely harsh

**blithe** *adj* casual and indifferent ▸ **blithely** *adv*

**blitz** *n* violent and sustained attack by aircraft; intensive attack or concerted effort ▷ *v* attack suddenly and intensively

**blizzard** *n* blinding storm of wind and snow

**bloat** *v* cause to swell, as with liquid or air

**bloater** *n* (*Brit*) salted smoked herring

**blob** *n* soft mass or drop; indistinct or shapeless form

**bloc** *n* people or countries combined by a common interest

**block** *n* large solid piece of wood, stone, etc.; large building of offices, flats, etc.; group of buildings enclosed by intersecting streets; obstruction or hindrance; (*slang*) person's head ▷ *v* obstruct or impede by introducing an obstacle ▸ **blockage** *n* ▸ **blockhead** *n* stupid person ▸ **block letter** plain capital letter

**blockade** n sealing off of a place to prevent the passage of goods ▷ v impose a blockade on

**blockie** n (Aust) owner of a small property, esp. a farm

**blog** n person's online journal (also **weblog**)

**blogosphere** n (informal) blogs on the internet as a whole

**bloke** n (informal) man

**blonde,** (masc) **blond** adj, n fair-haired (person)

**blood** n red fluid that flows around the body; race or kinship **in cold blood** done deliberately ▶ **bloodless** adj ▶ **blood bath** massacre ▶ **bloodhound** n large dog formerly used for tracking ▶ **bloodshed** n slaughter or killing ▶ **bloodshot** adj (of an eye) inflamed ▶ **blood sport** sport involving the killing of animals ▶ **bloodstream** n flow of blood round the body ▶ **bloodsucker** n animal that sucks blood; (informal) person who extorts money from other people ▶ **bloodthirsty** adj taking pleasure in violence

**bloody** adj covered with blood; marked by much killing ▷ adj, adv (slang) extreme or extremely ▷ v stain with blood ▶ **bloody-minded** adj deliberately unhelpful

**bloom** n blossom on a flowering plant; youthful or healthy glow ▷ v bear flowers; be in a healthy, glowing condition

**bloomer** n (Brit informal) stupid mistake

**bloomers** pl n woman's baggy knickers

**blooper** n (chiefly US informal) stupid mistake

**blossom** n flowers of a plant ▷ v (of plants) flower; come to a promising stage

**blot** n spot or stain; something that spoils ▷ v **blotting, blotted** cause a blemish in or on; soak up (ink) by using blotting paper ▶ **blotter** n ▶ **blot out** v darken or hide completely ▶ **blotting paper** soft absorbent paper for soaking up ink

**blotch** n discoloured area or stain ▶ **blotchy** adj

**blotto** adj (Brit, Aust & NZ slang) extremely drunk

**blouse** n woman's shirtlike garment

**blow¹** v **blowing, blew, blown** (of air, the wind, etc.) move; move or be carried as if by the wind; expel (air etc.) through the mouth or nose; cause (a musical instrument) to sound by forcing air into it; burn out (a fuse etc.); (slang) spend (money) freely ▶ **blower** n ▶ **blowy** adj windy ▶ **blow-dry** v style (the hair) with a hand-held dryer ▶ **blowout** n sudden loss of air in a tyre; escape of oil or gas from a well; (slang) filling meal; (Aust informal) large financial deficit ▶ **blow up** v explode; fill with air; (informal) lose one's temper; (informal) enlarge (a photograph)

**blow²** n hard hit; sudden setback; attacking action

**blowie** n (Aust informal) bluebottle

**blown** v past participle of **blow¹**

**blowsy** adj fat, untidy, and red-faced

**blubber** n fat of whales, seals, etc. ▷ v sob without restraint

**bludge** v (Aust informal) (Aust & NZ) evade work; (Aust & NZ) scrounge ▷ n (Aust) easy task ▶ **bludger** ▷ n person who scrounges

**bludgeon** n short thick club ▷ v hit with a bludgeon; force or bully

**blue** n colour of a clear unclouded sky ▷ pl feeling of depression; type of folk music of Black American origin ▷ adj **bluer, bluest** of the colour blue; depressed; pornographic **out of the blue** unexpectedly ▶ **bluish** adj ▶ **bluebell** n flower with blue bell-shaped flowers ▶ **bluebottle** n large fly with a dark-blue body ▶ **blue-collar** adj denoting manual industrial workers ▶ **blue heeler** (Aust & NZ informal) dog that controls cattle by biting their heels ▶ **blueprint** n photographic print of a plan; description of how a plan is expected to work ▶ **bluetongue** n Australian lizard with a blue tongue ▶ **Bluetooth®** n technology allowing short-range wireless communication

**bluff¹** v pretend to be confident in order to influence (someone) ▷ n act of bluffing

**bluff²** n steep cliff or bank ▷ adj good-naturedly frank and hearty

**blunder** n clumsy mistake ▷ v make a blunder; act clumsily

**blunderbuss** n obsolete gun with a wide flared muzzle

**blunt** adj not having a sharp edge or point; (of people, speech, etc.) straightforward or uncomplicated ▷ v make less sharp ▶ **bluntly** adv

**blur** v **blurring, blurred** make or become vague or less distinct ▷ n something vague, hazy, or indistinct ▶ **blurry** adj

**blurb** n promotional description, as on the jacket of a book

**blurt** v (foll by out) utter suddenly and involuntarily

**blush** v become red in the face, esp. from embarrassment or shame ▷ n reddening of the face

**bluster** v speak loudly or in a bullying way ▷ n empty threats or protests ▶ **blustery** adj (of weather) rough and windy

**BMA** British Medical Association

**BO** (informal) body odour

**boa** n large nonvenomous snake; long scarf of fur or feathers ▶ **boa constrictor** large snake that kills its prey by crushing

**boab** [boh-ab] n (Aust informal) short for **baobab**

**boar** n uncastrated male pig; wild pig

**board** n long flat piece of sawn timber; smaller flat piece of rigid material for a specific purpose e.g. ironing board; chess board; group of people who administer a company, trust, etc.; meals provided for money ▷ v go aboard (a train, aeroplane, etc.); cover with boards; receive meals and lodgings in return for money **on board** on or in a ship, aeroplane, etc. ▶ **boarder** n person who pays rent in return for accommodation in someone else's home; (Brit) pupil who lives at school during the school term ▶ **boarding house** private house that provides meals and accommodation for paying guests ▶ **boardroom** n room where the board of a company meets

**boast** v speak too proudly about one's talents etc.; possess (something to be proud of) ▷ n bragging statement ▶ **boastful** adj

**boat** n small vehicle for travelling across water ▶ **boater** n flat straw hat ▶ **boating** n

**boatswain** n same as **bosun**

**bob¹** v **bobbing, bobbed** move up and down repeatedly ▷ n short abrupt movement

**bob²** n hairstyle in which the hair is cut short evenly all round the head ▷ v **bobbing, bobbed** cut (the hair) in a bob

**bobbin** n reel on which thread is wound

**bobble** n small ball of material, usu. for decoration

**bobby** n, pl -**bies** (Brit informal) policeman

**bobotie** [ba-**boot**-ee] n (SAfr) dish of curried mince

**bobsleigh** n sledge for racing down an icy track ▷ v ride on a bobsleigh

**bode** v be an omen of (good or ill)

**bodice** n upper part of a dress

**bodkin** n blunt large-eyed needle

**body** n, pl **bodies** entire physical structure of an animal or human; trunk or torso; corpse; group regarded as a single entity; main part of anything; woman's one-piece undergarment ▶ **bodily** adj relating to the body ▷ adv by taking hold of the body ▶ **body-board** n small polystyrene surfboard ▶ **body-boarder** n ▶ **bodyguard** n person or group of people employed to protect someone ▶ **body mass index** measure used to gauge whether a person is overweight: a person's weight in kilograms divided by the square of his or her height in metres ▶ **bodywork** n outer shell of a motor vehicle

**Boer** n descendant of the Dutch settlers in S Africa ▶ **boerewors** n (SAfr) spiced sausage

**boffin** n (Brit, Aust, NZ & SAfr informal) scientist or expert

**bog** n wet spongy ground; (slang) toilet ▶ **boggy** adj ▶ **bog down** v **bogging, bogged** impede physically or mentally

**bogan** n (Aust & NZ slang) youth who dresses and behaves rebelliously

**bogey, bogy** n something that worries or annoys; (Golf) score of one stroke over par on a hole

**boggle** v be surprised, confused, or alarmed

**bogong, bugong** n large nocturnal Australian moth

**bogus** adj not genuine

**bogy** n, pl -**gies** same as **bogey**

**bohemian** n, adj (person) leading an unconventional life

**boil**[1] v (cause to) change from a liquid to a vapour so quickly that bubbles are formed; cook by the process of boiling ▷ n state or action of boiling ▶ **boiler** n piece of equipment which provides hot water

**boil**[2] n red pus-filled swelling on the skin

**boisterous** adj noisy and lively ▶ **boisterously** adv

**bold** adj confident and fearless; immodest or impudent ▶ **boldly** adv ▶ **boldness** n

**bole** n tree trunk

**bolero** n, pl -**ros** (music for) traditional Spanish dance; short open jacket

**bollard** n short thick post used to prevent the passage of motor vehicles

**boloney** n same as **baloney**

**Bolshevik** n (formerly) Russian Communist ▶ **bolshie, bolshy** adj (informal) difficult or rebellious

**bolster** v support or strengthen ▷ n long narrow pillow

**bolt** n sliding metal bar for fastening a door etc.; metal pin which screws into a nut; flash (of lightning) ▷ v run away suddenly; fasten with a bolt; eat hurriedly **bolt upright** stiff and rigid ▶ **bolt hole** place of escape

**bomb** n container fitted with explosive material; (slang) large amount of money ▷ v attack with bombs; move very quickly **the bomb** nuclear bomb ▶ **bomber** n aircraft that drops bombs; person who throws or puts a bomb in a particular place ▶ **bomb out** v (Aust, NZ & SAfr informal) fail disastrously ▸ **bombshell** *n* shocking or unwelcome surprise

**bombard** *v* attack with heavy gunfire or bombs; attack verbally, esp. with questions ▸ **bombardment** *n*

**bombast** *n* pompous language ▸ **bombastic** *adj*

**bona fide** [bone-a **fide**-ee] *adj* genuine

**bonanza** *n* sudden good luck or wealth

**bond** *n* something that binds, fastens or holds together; something that unites people; written or spoken agreement; (*Finance*) certificate of debt issued to raise funds; (*S Afr*) conditional pledging of property, esp. a house, as security for the repayment of a loan ▹ *pl* something that restrains or imprisons ▹ *v* bind ▸ **bonded** *adj*

**bondage** *n* slavery

**bone** *n* any of the hard parts in the body that form the skeleton ▹ *v* remove the bones from (meat for cooking etc.) ▸ **boneless** *adj* ▸ **bony** *adj* having many bones; thin or emaciated ▸ **bone-dry** *adj* completely dry ▸ **bone-idle** *adj* extremely lazy

**bonfire** *n* large outdoor fire

**bongo** *n, pl* **-gos** *or* **-goes** small drum played with the fingers

**bonhomie** [bon-om-**ee**] *n* cheerful friendliness

**bonito** [ba-**nee**-toh] *n, pl* **-os** small tunny-like marine food fish; related fish, whose flesh is dried and flaked and used in Japanese cookery

**bonk** *v* (*informal*) have sex with; hit

**bonnet** *n* metal cover over a vehicle's engine; hat which ties under the chin

**bonny** *adj* **-nier, -niest** (*Scot*) beautiful

**bonsai** *n, pl* **-sai** ornamental miniature tree or shrub

**bonus** *n* something given, paid, or received above what is due or expected

**boo** *interj* shout of disapproval ▹ *v* **booing, booed** shout 'boo' to show disapproval

**boob** (*slang*) *n* foolish mistake; female breast; (*Aust*) prison

**boobook** [**boo**-book] *n* small spotted Australian brown owl

**booby** *n, pl* **-bies** foolish person ▸ **booby prize** prize given for the lowest score in a competition ▸ **booby trap** hidden bomb primed to be set off by an unsuspecting victim; trap for an unsuspecting person, intended as a joke

**boogie** *v* (*informal*) dance to fast pop music

**book** *n* number of pages bound together between covers; long written work; number of tickets, stamps, etc. fastened together ▹ *pl* record of transactions of a business or society ▹ *v* reserve (a place, passage, etc.) in advance; record the name of (a person) who has committed an offence ▸ **booklet** *n* thin book with paper covers

**bookie** *n* (*informal*) short for **bookmaker**

**book-keeping** *n* systematic recording of business transactions

**bookmaker** *n* person whose occupation is taking bets

**bookmark** *n* person whose occupation is taking bets; (*Computing*) marker on a website that enables the user to return to it quickly and easily ▹ *v* (*Computing*) identify and store (a website) so that one can return to it quickly and easily

**bookworm** *n* person devoted to reading

**boom**[1] v make a loud deep echoing sound; prosper vigorously and rapidly ▷ n loud deep echoing sound; period of high economic growth ▶ **boomer** n (Aust) large male kangaroo

**boom**[2] n pole to which the foot of a sail is attached; pole carrying an overhead microphone; barrier across a waterway

**boomerang** n curved wooden missile which can be made to return to the thrower ▷ v (of a plan) recoil unexpectedly

**boon** n something helpful or beneficial

**boongary** [boong-gar-ree] n, pl **-garies** tree kangaroo of NE Queensland, Australia

**boor** n rude or insensitive person ▶ **boorish** adj

**boost** n encouragement or help; increase ▷ v improve; increase ▶ **booster** n small additional injection of a vaccine

**boot**[1] n outer covering for the foot that extends above the ankle; space in a car for luggage; (informal) kick ▷ v (informal) kick; start up (a computer) ▶ **bootee** n baby's soft shoe ▶ **boot camp** centre for young offenders, with strict discipline and hard physical exercise ▶ **boot-cut** adj (of trousers) slightly flared at the bottom of the legs

**boot**[2] n **to boot** in addition

**booth** n small partly enclosed cubicle; stall at a fair or market

**bootleg** adj produced, distributed, or sold illicitly ▷ v **-legging, -legged** make, carry, or sell (illicit goods) ▶ **bootlegger** n

**booty** n, pl **-ties** valuable articles obtained as plunder

**booze** v, n (informal) (consume) alcoholic drink ▶ **boozy** adj ▶ **boozer** n (informal) person who is fond of drinking; (Brit, Aust & NZ)

pub ▶ **booze bus** (Aust informal) mobile police unit for drug and alcohol testing ▶ **booze-up** n (informal) drinking spree

**bop** v **bopping, bopped** (informal) dance to pop music

**bora** n (Aust) Aboriginal ceremony

**borax** n white mineral used in making glass

**border** n dividing line between political or geographical regions; band around or along the edge of something ▷ v provide with a border; be nearly the same as e.g. resentment that borders on hatred

**bore**[1] v make (a hole) with a drill etc. ▷ n (diameter of) the hollow of a gun barrel or other tube

**bore**[2] v make weary by being dull or repetitious ▷ n dull or repetitious person or thing ▶ **bored** adj ▶ **boredom** n

**bore**[3] n high wave in a narrow estuary, caused by the tide

**bore**[4] v past tense of **bear**[1]

**boree** [baw-ree] n (Aust) same as **myall**

**born** v a past participle of **bear**[1] ▷ adj possessing certain qualities from birth e.g. a born musician

**borne** v a past participle of **bear**[1]

**boron** n (Chem) element used in hardening steel

**boronia** n Australian aromatic flowering shrub

**borough** n (chiefly Brit) town or district with its own council

**borrow** v obtain (something) temporarily; adopt (ideas etc.) from another source ▶ **borrower** n

> **USAGE NOTE**
> Borrow is followed by from: Borrow a pound from Frank. The use of borrow followed by off of is nonstandard

**borscht, borsch** n Russian soup based on beetroot

**borstal** n (formerly in Britain) prison for young criminals

**borzoi** n tall dog with a long silky coat

**bosh** n (Brit, Aust & NZ informal) empty talk, nonsense

**Bosnian** n, adj (person) from Bosnia

**bosom** n chest of a person, esp. the female breasts ▷ adj very dear e.g. *a bosom friend*

**boss**[1] n person in charge of or employing others ▷ v **boss around, about** be domineering towards ▶ **bossy** adj

**boss**[2] n raised knob or stud

**bosun** n officer responsible for the maintenance of a ship

**botany** n study of plants ▶ **botanical, botanic** adj ▶ **botanist** n

**botch** v spoil through clumsiness ▷ n (also **botch-up**) badly done piece of work or repair

**both** adj, pron two considered together

**bother** v take the time or trouble; give annoyance or trouble to; pester ▷ n trouble, fuss, or difficulty ▶ **bothersome** adj

**Botox**® n drug used to treat muscle spasms and to reduce wrinkles ▷ v apply Botox to (a person or a body part)

**bottle** n container for holding liquids; (Brit informal) courage ▷ v put in a bottle ▶ **bottleneck** n narrow stretch of road where traffic is held up ▶ **bottle shop** (Aust & NZ) shop licensed to sell alcohol for drinking elsewhere ▶ **bottle store** (S Afr) shop licensed to sell alcohol for drinking elsewhere ▶ **bottle tree** Australian tree with a bottle-shaped swollen trunk ▶ **bottle up** v restrain (powerful emotion)

**bottom** n lowest, deepest, or farthest removed part of a thing; buttocks ▷ adj lowest or last ▶ **bottomless** adj

**botulism** n severe food poisoning

**boudoir** [boo-dwahr] n woman's bedroom or private sitting room

**bougainvillea** n climbing plant with red or purple flowers

**bough** n large branch of a tree

**bought** v past of **buy**

**boulder** n large rounded rock

**boulevard** n wide, usu. tree-lined, street

**bounce** v (of a ball etc.) rebound from an impact; (slang) (of a cheque) be returned uncashed owing to a lack of funds in the account ▷ n act of rebounding; springiness; (informal) vitality or vigour ▶ **bouncer** n person employed at a disco etc. to remove unwanted people ▶ **bouncing** adj vigorous and robust

**bound**[1] v past of **bind** ▷ adj destined or certain; compelled or obliged

**bound**[2] v move forwards by jumps ▷ n jump upwards or forwards

**bound**[3] v form a boundary of ▷ pl n limit ▶ **boundary** n dividing line that indicates the farthest limit

**bound**[4] adj going or intending to go towards e.g. *homeward bound*

**bounty** n, pl **-ties** generosity; generous gift or reward ▶ **bountiful, bounteous** adj

**bouquet** n bunch of flowers; aroma of wine

**bourbon** [bur-bn] n whiskey made from maize

**bourgeois** [boor-zhwah] adj, n (offens) middle-class (person)

**bout** n period of activity or illness; boxing or wrestling match

**boutique** n small clothes shop

**bovine** adj relating to cattle; rather slow and stupid

**bow¹** [rhymes with **now**] v lower (one's head) or bend (one's knee or body) as a sign of respect or shame; comply or accept ▷ n movement made when bowing

**bow²** [rhymes with **go**] n knot with two loops and loose ends; weapon for shooting arrows; long stick stretched with horsehair for playing stringed instruments ▸ **bow-legged** adj having legs that curve outwards at the knees

**bow³** [rhymes with **now**] n front end of a ship

**bowdlerize** v remove words regarded as indecent from (a play, novel, etc.)

**bowel** n intestine, esp. the large intestine ▷ pl innermost part

**bower** n shady leafy shelter ▸ **bowerbird** n songbird of Australia and New Guinea, the males of which build bower-like display grounds to attract females

**bowl¹** n round container with an open top; hollow part of an object

**bowl²** n large heavy ball ▷ pl game played on smooth grass with wooden bowls ▷ v (Cricket) send (a ball) towards the batsman ▸ **bowling** n game in which bowls are rolled at a group of pins

**bowler¹** n (Cricket) player who sends (a ball) towards the batsman; person who plays bowls or bowling

**bowler²** n stiff felt hat with a rounded crown

**box¹** n container with a firm flat base and sides; separate compartment in a theatre, stable, etc. ▷ v put into a box **the box** (informal) television ▸ **box jellyfish** highly venomous jellyfish with a cuboidal body that lives in Australian tropical waters ▸ **box office** place where theatre or cinema tickets are sold

**box²** v fight (an opponent) in a boxing match ▸ **boxer** n person who participates in the sport of boxing; medium-sized dog with smooth hair and a short nose ▸ **boxer shorts, boxers** pl n men's underpants shaped like shorts but with a front opening ▸ **boxing** n sport of fighting with the fists

**box³** n evergreen tree with shiny leaves; eucalyptus with similar timber and foliage, and with rough bark

**boy** n male child ▸ **boyish** adj ▸ **boyhood** n ▸ **boyfriend** n male friend with whom a person is romantically or sexually involved

**boycott** v refuse to deal with (an organization or country) ▷ n instance of boycotting

**SPELLING TIP**
The word **boycott** has two ts, whether or not it has an ending such as in **boycotting**

**boykie** n (S Afr informal) chap or fellow

**bra** n woman's undergarment for supporting the breasts

**braaivleis** [brye-flayss], **braai** (S Afr) n grill on which food is cooked over hot charcoal, usu. outdoors; outdoor party at which food like this is served ▷ v cook (food) in this way

**brace** n object fastened to something to straighten or support it; pair, esp. of game birds ▷ pl straps worn over the shoulders to hold up trousers ▷ v steady or prepare (oneself) for something unpleasant; strengthen or fit with a brace ▸ **bracing** adj refreshing and invigorating

**bracelet** n ornamental chain or band for the wrist

**bracken** n large fern

**bracket** n pair of characters used to enclose a section of writing; group falling within certain defined limits; support fixed to a wall ▷ v **-eting, -eted** put in brackets; class together

**brackish** adj (of water) slightly salty

**bract** n leaf at the base of a flower

**brag** v **bragging, bragged** speak arrogantly and boastfully ▶ **braggart** n

**braid** v interweave (hair, thread, etc.) ▷ n length of hair etc. that has been braided; narrow ornamental tape of woven silk etc.

**Braille** n system of writing for the blind, consisting of raised dots interpreted by touch

**brain** n soft mass of nervous tissue in the head; intellectual ability ▷ v hit (someone) hard on the head ▶ **brainless** adj stupid ▶ **brainy** adj (informal) clever ▶ **brainchild** n idea produced by creative thought ▶ **brainfood** n food thought to promote brain function ▶ **brain up** v (Brit) make (something) more intellectually demanding or sophisticated ▶ **brainwash** v cause (a person) to alter his or her beliefs, esp. by methods based on isolation, sleeplessness, etc. ▶ **brainwave** n sudden idea

**braise** v cook slowly in a covered pan with a little liquid

**brake** n device for slowing or stopping a vehicle ▷ v slow down or stop by using a brake

**bramble** n prickly shrub that produces blackberries

**bran** n husks of cereal grain

**branch** n secondary stem of a tree; offshoot or subsidiary part of something larger or more complex ▷ v (of stems, roots, etc.) divide, then develop in different directions ▶ **branch out** v expand one's interests

**brand** n particular product; particular kind or variety; identifying mark burnt onto the skin of an animal ▷ v mark with a brand; denounce as being e.g. he was branded a fascist ▶ **brand-new** adj absolutely new

**brandish** v wave (a weapon etc.) in a threatening way

**brandy** n, pl **-dies** alcoholic spirit distilled from wine

**brash** adj offensively loud, showy, or self-confident ▶ **brashness** n

**brass** n alloy of copper and zinc; family of wind instruments made of brass; (N English dialect) money ▶ **brassy** adj brazen or flashy; like brass, esp. in colour

**brasserie** n restaurant serving drinks and cheap meals

**brassiere** n bra

**brat** n unruly child

**bravado** n showy display of self-confidence

**brave** adj having or showing courage, resolution, and daring ▷ n Native American warrior ▷ v confront with resolution or courage ▶ **bravery** n

**bravo** interj well done!

**brawl** n noisy fight ▷ v fight noisily

**brawn** n physical strength; pressed meat from the head of a pig or calf ▶ **brawny** adj

**bray** v (of a donkey) utter its loud harsh sound ▷ n donkey's loud harsh sound

**brazen** adj shameless and bold ▶ **brazenly** adv

**brazier** [bray-zee-er] n portable container for burning charcoal or coal

**breach** n breaking of a promise, obligation, etc.; gap or break

▷ *v* break (a promise, law, etc.); make a gap in

**bread** *n* food made by baking a mixture of flour and water or milk; (*slang*) money ▸ **breadwinner** *n* person whose earnings support a family

**breadth** *n* extent of something from side to side

**break** *v* **breaking, broke, broken** separate or become separated into two or more pieces; damage or become damaged so as to be inoperative; fail to observe (an agreement etc.); disclose or be disclosed e.g. *he broke the news*; bring or come to an end e.g. *the good weather broke at last*; weaken or be weakened, as in spirit; improve on or surpass e.g. *break a record*; (of the male voice) become permanently deeper at puberty ▷ *n* act or result of breaking; gap or interruption in continuity; (*informal*) fortunate opportunity ▸ **break even** make neither a profit nor a loss ▸ **breakable** *adj* ▸ **breakage** *n* ▸ **breaker** *n* large wave ▸ **break down** *v* cease to function; yield to strong emotion ▸ **breakdown** *n* act or instance of breaking down; nervous breakdown ▸ **break-in** *n* illegal entering of a building, esp. by thieves ▸ **breakneck** *adj* fast and dangerous ▸ **break off** *v* sever or detach; end (a relationship etc.) ▸ **break out** *v* begin or arise suddenly ▸ **breakthrough** *n* important development or discovery ▸ **break up** *v* (cause to) separate; come to an end; (of a school) close for the holidays; (of a caller) to become inaudible on the telephone ▸ **breakwater** *n* wall that extends into the sea to protect a harbour or beach from the force of waves

**breakfast** *v, n* (eat) the first meal of the day

**bream** *n* freshwater fish with silvery scales; food fish of European seas

**breast** *n* either of the two soft fleshy milk-secreting glands on a woman's chest; chest ▸ **breastbone** *n* long flat bone in the front of the body, to which most of the ribs are attached ▸ **breaststroke** *n* swimming stroke in which the arms are extended in front of the head and swept back on either side

**breath** *n* taking in and letting out of air during breathing; air taken in and let out during breathing ▸ **breathless** *adj* ▸ **breathtaking** *adj* causing awe or excitement ▸ **breathe** *v* take in oxygen and give out carbon dioxide; whisper ▸ **breather** *n* (*informal*) short rest ▸ **breathing** *n*

**Breathalyser**® *n* device for estimating the amount of alcohol in the breath ▸ **breathalyse** *v*

**bred** *v* past of **breed**

**breech** *n* buttocks; back part of gun where bullet or shell is loaded ▸ **breech birth** birth of a baby with the feet or buttocks appearing first

**breeches** *pl n* trousers extending to just below the knee

**breed** *v* **breeding, bred** produce new or improved strains of (domestic animals or plants); bear (offspring); produce or be produced e.g. *breed trouble* ▷ *n* group of animals etc. within a species that have certain clearly defined characteristics; kind or sort ▸ **breeder** *n* ▸ **breeding** *n* result of good upbringing or training

**breeze** *n* gentle wind ▷ *v* move quickly or casually ▸ **breezy** *adj* windy; casual or carefree

**brethren** pl n (old-fashioned) (used in religious contexts) brothers

**Breton** adj of Brittany ▷ n person from Brittany; language of Brittany

**brevity** n shortness

**brew** v make (beer etc.) by steeping, boiling, and fermentation; prepare (a drink) by infusing; be about to happen or forming ▷ n beverage produced by brewing

**brewer** n person or company that brews beer ▶ **brewery** n, pl **-eries** place where beer etc. is brewed

**briar¹**, **brier** n European shrub with a hard woody root; tobacco pipe made from this root

**briar²** n same as **brier¹**

**bribe** v offer or give something to someone to gain favour, influence, etc. ▷ n something given or offered as a bribe ▶ **bribery** n

**bric-a-brac** n miscellaneous small ornamental objects

**brick** n (rectangular block of) baked clay used in building ▷ v (foll by up or over) build, enclose, or fill with bricks ▶ **bricklayer** n person who builds with bricks

**bride** n woman who has just been or is about to be married ▶ **bridal** adj ▶ **bridegroom** n man who has just been or is about to be married ▶ **bridesmaid** n girl or woman who attends a bride at her wedding

**bridge¹** n structure for crossing a river etc.; platform from which a ship is steered or controlled; upper part of the nose; piece of wood supporting the strings of a violin etc. ▷ v build a bridge over (something) ▶ **bridgehead** n fortified position at the end of a bridge nearest the enemy

**bridge²** n card game based on whist, played between two pairs

**bridle** n headgear for controlling a horse ▷ v show anger or indignation ▶ **bridle path** path suitable for riding horses

**Brie** [bree] n soft creamy white cheese

**brief** adj short in duration ▷ n condensed statement or written synopsis; (also **briefing**) set of instructions ▷ pl men's or women's underpants ▷ v give information and instructions to (a person) ▶ **briefly** adv ▶ **briefcase** n small flat case for carrying papers, books, etc.

**brier¹**, **briar** n wild rose with long thorny stems

**brier²** n same as **briar¹**

**brig** n two-masted square-rigged ship

**brigade** n army unit smaller than a division; group of people organized for a certain task

**brigadier** n high-ranking army officer

**brigalow** n (Aust) type of acacia tree

**brigand** n (lit) bandit

**brigantine** n two-masted sailing ship

**bright** adj emitting or reflecting much light; (of colours) intense; clever ▶ **brightly** adv ▶ **brightness** n ▶ **brighten** v

**brilliant** adj shining with light; splendid; extremely clever ▶ **brilliance, brilliancy** n

**brim** n upper rim of a cup etc.; projecting edge of a hat ▷ v **brimming, brimmed** be full to the brim

**brimstone** n (obs) sulphur

**brine** n salt water ▶ **briny** adj very salty **the briny** (informal) the sea

**bring** v **bringing, brought** carry, convey, or take to a designated place or person; cause to happen; (Law) put forward (charges) officially ▶ **bring about** v cause to happen ▶ **bring off** v succeed in achieving ▶ **bring out** v publish or have (a book) published; reveal or cause to be seen ▶ **bring up** v rear (a child); mention; vomit (food)

**brinjal** n (SAfr) dark purple tropical fruit, cooked and eaten as a vegetable

**brink** n edge of a steep place

**brisk** adj lively and quick ▶ **briskly** adv

**brisket** n beef from the breast of a cow

**bristle** n short stiff hair ▷ v (cause to) stand up like bristles; show anger ▶ **bristly** adj

**Brit** n (informal) British person

**British** adj of Great Britain or the British Commonwealth ▷ pl n **the British** people of Great Britain

**Briton** n native or inhabitant of Britain

**brittle** adj hard but easily broken ▶ **brittleness** n

**broach** v introduce (a topic) for discussion; open (a bottle or barrel)

**broad** adj having great breadth or width; not detailed; extensive e.g. broad support; strongly marked e.g. a broad American accent ▶ **broadly** adv ▶ **broaden** v ▶ **broadband** n telecommunication transmission technique using a wide range of frequencies ▶ **broad bean** thick flat edible bean ▶ **broad-minded** adj tolerant ▶ **broadside** n strong verbal or written attack; (Naval) firing of all the guns on one side of a ship at once

**broadcast** n programme or announcement on radio or television ▷ v transmit (a programme or announcement) on radio or television; make widely known ▶ **broadcaster** n ▶ **broadcasting** n

**brocade** n rich fabric woven with a raised design

**broccoli** n type of cabbage with greenish flower heads

> **SPELLING TIP**
> Remember **broccoli** has two cs and one l

**brochure** n booklet that contains information about a product or service

**broekies** [brook-eez] pl n (SAfr informal) underpants

**brogue**¹ n sturdy walking shoe

**brogue**² n strong accent, esp. Irish

**broil** v (Aust, NZ, US & Canadian) cook by direct heat under a grill

**broke** v past tense of **break** ▷ adj (informal) having no money

**broken** v past participle of **break** ▷ adj fractured or smashed; (of the speech of a foreigner) noticeably imperfect e.g. broken English ▶ **brokenhearted** adj overwhelmed by grief

**broker** n agent who buys or sells goods, securities, etc.

**brolga** n large grey Australian crane with a trumpeting call (also **native companion**)

**brolly** n, pl **-lies** (informal) umbrella

**bromance** n (informal) close, non-sexual friendship between two men

**bromide** n chemical compound used in medicine and photography

**bromine** n (Chem) dark red liquid element that gives off a pungent vapour

**bronchial** [bronk-ee-al] adj of the bronchi

**bronchitis** [bronk-**eye**-tiss] n inflammation of the bronchi

**bronchus** [bronk-uss] n, pl **bronchi** [bronk-eye] either of the two branches of the windpipe

**bronco** n, pl **-cos** (in the US) wild or partially tamed pony

**brontosaurus** n very large plant-eating four-footed dinosaur

**bronze** n alloy of copper and tin; statue, medal, etc. made of bronze ▷ adj made of, or coloured like, bronze ▷ v (esp. of the skin) make or become brown ▶ **Bronze Age** era when bronze tools and weapons were used

**brooch** n ornament with a pin, worn fastened to clothes

**brood** n number of birds produced at one hatching; all the children of a family ▷ v think long and unhappily ▶ **broody** adj moody and sullen; (informal) (of a woman) wishing to have a baby

**brook**¹ n small stream

**brook**² v bear or tolerate

**broom** n long-handled sweeping brush; yellow-flowered shrub ▶ **broomstick** n handle of a broom

**broth** n soup, usu. containing vegetables

**brothel** n house where men pay to have sex with prostitutes

**brother** n boy or man with the same parents as another person; member of a male religious order ▶ **brotherly** adj ▶ **brotherhood** n fellowship; association, such as a trade union ▶ **brother-in-law** n, pl **brothers-in-law** brother of one's husband or wife; husband of one's sibling

**brought** v past of **bring**

**brow** n part of the face from the eyes to the hairline; eyebrow; top of a hill

**browbeat** v frighten (someone) with threats

**brown** n colour of earth or wood ▷ adj of the colour brown ▷ v make or become brown ▶ **brownish** adj ▶ **browned-off** adj (informal) bored and depressed

**Brownie Guide, Brownie** n junior Guide

**browse** v look through (a book or articles for sale) in a casual manner; nibble on young shoots or leaves ▷ n instance of browsing ▶ **browser** n (Computing) software package that enables a user to read hypertext, esp. on the internet

**bruise** n discoloured area on the skin caused by an injury ▷ v cause a bruise on ▶ **bruiser** n strong tough person

**brumby** n, pl **-bies** (Aust) wild horse; unruly person

**brunch** n (informal) breakfast and lunch combined

**brunette** n girl or woman with dark brown hair

**brunt** n main force or shock of a blow, attack, etc.

**brush**¹ n device made of bristles, wires, etc. used for cleaning, painting, etc.; brief unpleasant encounter; fox's tail ▷ v clean, scrub, or paint with a brush; touch lightly and briefly ▶ **brush off** v (slang) dismiss or ignore (someone) ▶ **brush up** v refresh one's knowledge of (a subject)

**brush**² n thick growth of shrubs

**brush turkey** n bird of New Guinea and Australia resembling the domestic fowl, with black plumage

**brusque** adj blunt or curt in manner or speech ▶ **brusquely** adv ▶ **brusqueness** n

**Brussels sprout** n vegetable like a tiny cabbage

**brute** n brutal person; animal other than man ▷ adj wholly instinctive or physical, like an animal; without reason ▶ **brutish** adj of or like an animal ▶ **brutal** adj cruel and vicious; extremely honest in speech or manner ▶ **brutally** adv ▶ **brutality** n ▶ **brutalize** v

**BSc** Bachelor of Science

**BSE** bovine spongiform encephalopathy: fatal virus disease of cattle

**BST** British Summer Time

**bubble** n ball of air in a liquid or solid ▷ v form bubbles; move or flow with a gurgling sound ▶ **bubbly** adj excited and lively; full of bubbles ▶ **bubble over** v express an emotion freely

**bubonic plague** [bew-**bonn**-ik] n acute infectious disease characterized by swellings

**buccaneer** n (Hist) pirate

**buck¹** n male of the goat, hare, kangaroo, rabbit, and reindeer ▷ v (of a horse etc.) jump with legs stiff and back arched ▶ **buck up** v make or become more cheerful

**buck²** n (US, Canadian, Aust & NZ slang) dollar; (S Afr) rand

**buck³** n **pass the buck** (informal) shift blame or responsibility onto someone else

**bucket** n open-topped round container with a handle ▷ v -**eting**, -**eted** rain heavily ▶ **bucketful** n ▶ **bucket list** (informal) list of things wanted to be experienced before one dies

**buckle** n clasp for fastening a belt or strap ▷ v fasten or be fastened with a buckle; (cause to) bend out of shape through pressure or heat ▶ **buckle down** v (informal) apply oneself with determination

**buckshee** adj (slang) free

**buckteeth** pl n projecting upper front teeth ▶ **buck-toothed** adj

**buckwheat** n small black grain used for making flour

**bucolic** [bew-**koll**-ik] adj of the countryside or country life

**bud** n swelling on a tree or plant that develops into a leaf or flower ▷ v **budding**, **budded** produce buds ▶ **budding** adj beginning to develop or grow

**Buddhism** n eastern religion founded by Buddha ▶ **Buddhist** n, adj

**buddleia** n shrub with long spikes of purple flowers

**buddy** n, pl -**dies** (informal) friend

**budge** v move slightly

**budgerigar** n small cage bird bred in many different-coloured varieties

**budget** n financial plan for a period of time; money allocated for a specific purpose ▷ v -**eting**, -**eted** plan the expenditure of (money or time) ▷ adj cheap ▶ **budgetary** adj

> **SPELLING TIP**
> Many verbs ending in et, have two ts when you add an ending like -ing, but **budget** is not one of them: **budgeting** and **budgeted** have one t

**budgie** n (informal) short for **budgerigar**

**buff¹** adj dull yellowish-brown ▷ v clean or polish with soft material

**buff²** n (informal) expert on or devotee of a given subject

**buffalo** n type of cattle; (US) bison

**buffer** n something that lessens shock or protects from damaging impact, circumstances, etc.

**buffet¹** [**boof**-ay, **buff**-ay] n counter where drinks and snacks are served

**buffet²** [**buff**-it] v -**feting**, -**feted** knock against or about

**buffoon** n clown or fool ▶ **buffoonery** n

**bug** n small insect; (informal) minor illness; small mistake in a computer program; concealed microphone; (Aust) flattish edible shellfish ▷ v **bugging**, **bugged** (informal) irritate (someone); conceal a microphone in (a room or phone)

**bugbear** n thing that causes obsessive anxiety

**bugger** (slang) n unpleasant or difficult person or thing; person who practises buggery ▷ v tire; practise buggery with ▶ **buggery** ▷ n anal intercourse

**bugle** n instrument like a small trumpet ▶ **bugler** n

**build** v **building, built** make, construct, or form by joining parts or materials ▷ n shape of the body ▶ **builder** n ▶ **building** n structure with walls and a roof ▶ **building society** organization where money can be borrowed or invested ▶ **build-up** n gradual increase

**built** v past of **build** ▶ **built-up** adj having many buildings

**bulb** n same as **light bulb**; onion-shaped root which grows into a flower or plant ▶ **bulbous** adj round and fat

**bulge** n swelling on a normally flat surface; sudden increase in number ▷ v swell outwards ▶ **bulging** adj

**bulimia** n disorder characterized by compulsive overeating followed by vomiting ▶ **bulimic** adj, n

**bulk** n size or volume, esp. when great; main part **in bulk** in large quantities ▶ **bulky** adj

**bulkhead** n partition in a ship or aeroplane

**bull¹** n male of some animals, such as cattle, elephants, and whales ▶ **bullock** n castrated bull ▶ **bulldog** n thickset dog with a broad head and a muscular body ▶ **bulldozer** n powerful tractor for moving earth ▶ **bulldoze** v ▶ **bullfight** n public show in which a matador kills a bull ▶ **bull's-eye** n central disc of a target ▶ **bullswool** n (Aust & NZ slang) nonsense

**bull²** n (informal) complete nonsense

**bull³** n papal decree

**bullet** n small piece of metal fired from a gun

**bulletin** n short official report or announcement

**bullion** n gold or silver in the form of bars

**bully** n, pl **-lies** person who hurts, persecutes, or intimidates a weaker person ▷ v **-lying, -lied** hurt, intimidate, or persecute (a weaker person)

**bulrush** n tall stiff reed

**bulwark** n wall used as a fortification; person or thing acting as a defence

**bum¹** n (slang) buttocks or anus

**bum²** (informal) n disreputable idler ▷ adj of poor quality

**bumble** v speak, do, or move in a clumsy way ▶ **bumbling** adj, n

**bumblebee** n large hairy bee

**bumf, bumph** n (informal) official documents or forms

**bump** v knock or strike with a jolt; travel in jerks and jolts ▷ n dull thud from an impact or collision; raised uneven part ▶ **bumpy** adj ▶ **bump off** v (informal) murder

**bumper¹** n bar on the front and back of a vehicle to protect against damage

**bumper²** adj unusually large or abundant

**bumph** n same as **bumf**

**bumpkin** n awkward simple country person

**bumptious** adj offensively self-assertive

**bun** n small sweet bread roll or cake; hair gathered into a bun shape at the back of the head

**bunch** n number of things growing, fastened, or grouped together ▷ v group or be grouped together in a bunch

**bundle** n number of things gathered loosely together ▷ v cause to go roughly or unceremoniously ▶ **bundle up** v make into a bundle

**bung** n stopper for a cask etc. ▷ v (foll by up) (informal) close with a bung; (Brit slang) throw (something) somewhere in a careless manner

**bungalow** n one-storey house

**bungee jumping, bungy jumping** n sport of leaping from a high bridge, tower, etc., to which one is connected by a rubber rope

**bungle** v spoil through incompetence ▸ **bungler** n ▸ **bungling** adj, n

**bunion** n inflamed swelling on the big toe

**bunk¹** n narrow shelflike bed ▸ **bunk bed** one of a pair of beds constructed one above the other

**bunk²** n same as **bunkum**

**bunk³** (slang) n (Brit) **do a bunk** make a hurried and secret departure ▷ v (Brit, NZ & S Afr) be absent without permission

**bunker** n sand-filled hollow forming an obstacle on a golf course; underground shelter; large storage container for coal etc.

**bunkum** n nonsense

**bunny** n, pl -nies child's word for a rabbit

**Bunsen burner** n gas burner used in laboratories

**bunting** n decorative flags

**bunya** n tall dome-shaped Australian coniferous tree (also **bunya-bunya**)

**bunyip** n (Aust) legendary monster said to live in swamps and lakes

**buoy** n floating marker anchored in the sea ▷ v prevent from sinking; encourage or hearten ▸ **buoyant** adj able to float; cheerful or resilient ▸ **buoyancy** n

**bur** n same as **burr¹**

**burble** v make a bubbling sound; talk quickly and excitedly

**burden¹** n heavy load; something difficult to cope with ▷ v put a burden on; oppress ▸ **burdensome** adj

**burden²** n theme of a speech etc.

**bureau** n, pl **-reaus** or **-reaux** office that provides a service; writing desk with shelves and drawers ▸ **bureau de change** place where foreign currencies can be exchanged

**bureaucracy** n, pl **-cies** administrative system based on complex rules and procedures; excessive adherence to complex procedures ▸ **bureaucrat** n ▸ **bureaucratic** adj

**burgeon** v develop or grow rapidly

**burgh** n Scottish borough

**burglar** n person who enters a building to commit a crime, esp. theft ▸ **burglary** n ▸ **burgle** v

**Burgundy** n type of French wine ▸ **burgundy** adj dark-purplish red

**burial** n burying of a dead body

**burlesque** n artistic work which satirises a subject by caricature

**burly** adj **-lier, -liest** (of a person) broad and strong

**burn¹** v **burning, burnt** or **burned** be or set on fire; destroy or be destroyed by fire; damage, injure, or mark by heat; feel strong emotion; record data on (a compact disc) ▷ n injury or mark caused by fire or exposure to heat ▸ **burning** adj intense; urgent or crucial

**USAGE NOTE**

Either burnt or burned may be used as a past form

**burn²** n (Scot) small stream

**burnish** v make smooth and shiny by rubbing

**burp** v, n (informal) belch

**burr¹** n head of a plant with prickles or hooks

**burr²** n soft trilling sound given to the letter r in some dialects; whirring sound

**burrawang** n Australian plant with fernlike leaves and an edible nut

**burrow** n hole dug in the ground by a rabbit etc. ▷ v dig holes in the ground

**bursar** n treasurer of a school, college, or university ▶ **bursary** n scholarship

**burst** v **bursting, burst** (cause to) break open or apart noisily and suddenly; come or go suddenly and forcibly; be full to the point of breaking open ▷ n instance of breaking open suddenly; sudden outbreak or occurrence ▶ **burst into** v give vent to (an emotion) suddenly

**bury** v **burying, buried** place in a grave; place in the earth and cover with soil; conceal or hide

**bus** n large motor vehicle for carrying passengers ▷ v **bussing, bussed** travel or transport by bus

**busby** n, pl **-bies** tall fur hat worn by some soldiers

**bush** n dense woody plant, smaller than a tree; wild uncultivated part of a country ▶ **bushy** adj (of hair) thick and shaggy ▶ **bushbaby** n small African tree-living mammal with large eyes ▶ **bushfire** n uncontrolled scrub or forest fire

**bushel** n obsolete unit of measure equal to 8 gallons (36.4 litres)

**business** n purchase and sale of goods and services; commercial establishment; trade or profession; proper concern or responsibility; affair e.g. *it's a dreadful business* ▶ **businesslike** adj efficient and methodical ▶ **businessman, businesswoman** n

**busker** n street entertainer ▶ **busk** v act as a busker

**bust¹** n woman's bosom; sculpture of the head and shoulders

**bust²** (*informal*) v **busting, bust** or **busted** burst or break; (of the police) raid (a place) or arrest

(someone) ▷ adj broken **go bust** become bankrupt

**bustard** n bird with long strong legs, a heavy body, a long neck, and speckled plumage

**bustle¹** v hurry with a show of activity or energy ▷ n energetic and noisy activity ▶ **bustling** adj

**bustle²** n cushion or framework formerly worn under the back of a woman's skirt to hold it out

**busy** adj **busier, busiest** actively employed; crowded or full of activity ▷ v **busying, busied** keep (someone, esp. oneself) busy ▶ **busily** adv ▶ **busybody** n meddlesome or nosy person

**but** conj contrary to expectation; in contrast; other than; without it happening ▷ prep except ▷ adv only **but for** were it not for

**butane** n gas used for fuel

**butch** adj (*slang*) markedly or aggressively masculine

**butcher** n person who slaughters animals or sells their meat; brutal murderer ▷ v kill and prepare (animals) for meat; kill (people) brutally or indiscriminately ▶ **butchery** n ▶ **butcherbird** n Australian magpie that impales its prey on thorns

**butler** n chief male servant

**butt¹** n thicker end of something; unused end of a cigar or cigarette; (*slang*) buttocks

**butt²** n person or thing that is the target of ridicule

**butt³** v strike with the head or horns ▶ **butt in** v interrupt a conversation

**butt⁴** n large cask

**butter** n edible fatty solid made by churning cream ▷ v put butter on ▶ **buttery** adj ▶ **butter up** v flatter

**butter bean** n large pale flat edible bean

**buttercup** n small yellow flower

**butterfingers** n (informal) person who drops things by mistake

**butterfly** n insect with brightly coloured wings; swimming stroke in which both arms move together in a forward circular action

**buttermilk** n sourish milk that remains after the butter has been separated from milk

**butterscotch** n kind of hard brittle toffee

**buttock** n either of the two fleshy masses that form the human rump

**button** n small disc or knob sewn to clothing, which can be passed through a slit in another piece of fabric to fasten them; knob that operates a piece of equipment when pressed ▷ v fasten with buttons ▸ **buttonhole** n slit in a garment through which a button is passed; flower worn on a lapel ▷ v detain (someone) in conversation

**buttress** n structure to support a wall ▷ v support with, or as if with, a buttress

**buxom** adj (of a woman) healthily plump and full-bosomed

**buy** v **buying, bought** acquire by paying money for; (slang) accept as true ▷ n thing acquired through payment ▸ **buyer** n customer; person employed to buy merchandise

**buzz** n rapidly vibrating humming sound; (informal) sense of excitement ▷ v make a humming sound; be filled with an air of excitement ▸ **buzzer** n ▸ **buzz around** v move around quickly and busily ▸ **buzz word** jargon word which becomes fashionably popular

**buzzard** n bird of prey of the hawk family

**by** prep indicating the doer of an action, nearness, movement past, time before or during which, etc. e.g. bitten by a dog; down by the river; driving by the school; in bed by midnight ▷ adv near; past **by and by** eventually **by and large** in general

**bye, bye-bye** interj (informal) goodbye

**by-election** n election held during parliament to fill a vacant seat

**bygone** adj past or former

**bylaw, bye-law** n rule made by a local authority

**BYO, BYOG** n (Aust & NZ) unlicensed restaurant at which diners may bring their own alcoholic drink

**bypass** n main road built to avoid a city; operation to divert blood flow away from a damaged part of the heart ▷ v go round or avoid

**by-product** n secondary or incidental product of a process

**byre** n (Brit) shelter for cows

**bystander** n person present but not involved

**byte** n (Computing) group of bits processed as one unit of data

**byway** n minor road

**byword** n person or thing regarded as a perfect example of something

# Cc

**C** (*Chem*) carbon; Celsius; centigrade; century

**c.** circa

**cab** *n* taxi; enclosed driver's compartment on a train, truck, etc. ▸ **cabbie, cabby** *n, pl* **-bies** (*informal*) taxi driver

**cabal** [kab-**bal**] *n* small group of political plotters; secret plot

**cabaret** [**kab**-a-ray] *n* dancing and singing show in a nightclub

**cabbage** *n* vegetable with a large head of green leaves ▸ **cabbage tree** (*NZ*) palm-like tree with a bare trunk and spiky leaves

**caber** *n* tree trunk tossed in competition at Highland games

**cabin** *n* compartment in a ship or aircraft; small hut ▸ **cabin cruiser** motorboat with a cabin

**cabinet** *n* piece of furniture with drawers or shelves; (**C-**) committee of senior government ministers ▸ **cabinet-maker** *n* person who makes fine furniture

**cable** *n* strong thick rope; bundle of wires that carries electricity or electronic signals; telegram sent abroad ▷ *v* send (someone) a message by cable ▸ **cable car** vehicle pulled up a steep slope by a moving cable ▸ **cable television** television service conveyed by cable to subscribers

**caboodle** *n* **the whole caboodle** (*informal*) the whole lot

**cabriolet** [kab-ree-oh-**lay**] *n* small horse-drawn carriage with a folding hood

**cacao** [kak-**kah**-oh] *n* tropical tree with seed pods from which chocolate and cocoa are made

**cache** [**kash**] *n* hidden store of weapons or treasure

**cachet** [**kash**-shay] *n* prestige, distinction

**cack-handed** *adj* (*informal*) clumsy

**cackle** *v* laugh shrilly; (of a hen) squawk with shrill broken notes ▷ *n* cackling noise

**cacophony** [kak-**koff**-on-ee] *n* harsh discordant sound ▸ **cacophonous** *adj*

**cactus** *n, pl* **-tuses** or **-ti** fleshy desert plant with spines but no leaves

**cad** *n* (*old-fashioned*) dishonourable man ▸ **caddish** *adj*

**cadaver** [kad-**dav**-ver] *n* corpse ▸ **cadaverous** *adj* pale, thin, and haggard

**caddie, caddy** *n, pl* **-dies** person who carries a golfer's clubs ▷ *v* **-dying, -died** act as a caddie

**caddis fly** *n* insect whose larva (**caddis worm**) lives underwater in a protective case of sand and stones

**caddy** *n, pl* **-dies** small container for tea

**cadence** [**kade**-enss] *n* rise and fall in the pitch of the voice; close of a musical phrase

**cadenza** *n* complex solo passage in a piece of music

**cadet** *n* young person training for the armed forces or police

**cadge** *v* (*informal*) get (something) by taking advantage of someone's generosity ▸ **cadger** *n*

**cadmium** *n* (*Chem*) bluish-white metallic element used in alloys

**cadre** [**kah**-der] *n* small group of people selected and trained to form the core of a political organization or military unit

**caecum** [**seek**-um] *n, pl* **-ca** [-ka] pouch at the beginning of the large intestine

**Caesar** [**seez**-ar] *n* title of Roman emperors ▸ **Caesar salad** salad of lettuce, cheese, and croutons, with olive oil, garlic, and lemon juice

**Caesarean section** [see-**zair**-ee-an] *n* surgical incision into the womb to deliver a baby

**caesium** *n* (*Chem*) silvery-white metallic element used in photocells

**café** *n* small or inexpensive restaurant serving light refreshments; (*SAfr*) corner shop or grocer ▸ **cafeteria** *n* self-service restaurant

**caffeine** *n* stimulant found in tea and coffee

**caftan** *n* same as **kaftan**

**cage** *n* enclosure of bars or wires, for keeping animals or birds; enclosed platform of a lift in a mine ▸ **caged** *adj* kept in a cage

**cagey** *adj* **cagier, cagiest** (*informal*) reluctant to go into details

**cagoule** *n* (*Brit*) lightweight hooded waterproof jacket

**cahoots** *pl n* **in cahoots** (*informal*) conspiring together

**cairn** *n* mound of stones erected as a memorial or marker

**cajole** *v* persuade by flattery ▸ **cajolery** *n*

**cake** *n* sweet food baked from a mixture of flour, eggs, etc.; flat compact mass of something, such as soap ▸ *v* form into a hardened mass or crust

**calamine** *n* pink powder consisting chiefly of zinc oxide, used in skin lotions and ointments

**calamity** *n, pl* **-ties** disaster ▸ **calamitous** *adj*

**calcify** *v* **-fying, -fied** harden by the depositing of calcium salts ▸ **calcification** *n*

**calcium** *n* (*Chem*) silvery-white metallic element found in bones, teeth, limestone, and chalk

**calculate** *v* solve or find out by a mathematical procedure or by reasoning; aim to have a particular effect ▸ **calculable** *adj* ▸ **calculating** *adj* selfishly scheming ▸ **calculation** *n* ▸ **calculator** *n* small electronic device for making calculations

**calculus** *n* branch of mathematics dealing with infinitesimal changes to a variable number or quantity; (*pl* **-li**) (*Pathology*) hard deposit in kidney or bladder

**Caledonian** *adj* Scottish

**calendar** *n* chart showing a year divided up into months, weeks, and days; system for determining the beginning, length, and division of years; schedule of events or appointments

**calendula** *n* marigold

**calf**[1] *n, pl* **calves** young cow, bull, elephant, whale, or seal; leather made from calf skin ▸ **calve** *v* give birth to a calf

**calf**[2] *n, pl* **calves** back of the leg between the ankle and knee

**calibre** *n* person's ability or worth; diameter of the bore of a gun or of a shell or bullet ▸ **calibrate** *v* mark the scale or check the accuracy of (a measuring instrument) ▸ **calibration** *n*

**calico** *n, pl* **-coes** or **-cos** white cotton fabric

**caliph** *n* (*Hist*) Muslim ruler

**call** *v* name; shout to attract attention; telephone; summon; (often foll by *on*) visit; arrange (a meeting, strike, etc.) ▸ *n* cry, shout; animal's or bird's cry; telephone communication; short visit; summons, invitation; need, demand ▸ **caller** *n* ▸ **calling** *n* vocation, profession ▸ **call box** kiosk for a public telephone ▸ **call centre** office where staff carry out an organization's telephone transactions ▸ **call for** v require ▸ **call off** v cancel ▸ **call up** v summon to serve in the armed forces; cause one to remember

**calligraphy** n (art of) beautiful handwriting ▸ **calligrapher** n

**calliper** n metal splint for supporting the leg; instrument for measuring diameters

**callisthenics** pl n light keep-fit exercises

**callous** adj showing no concern for other people's feelings ▸ **calloused** adj (of skin) thickened and hardened ▸ **callously** adv ▸ **callousness** n

**callow** adj young and inexperienced

**callus** n, pl **-luses** area of thick hardened skin

**calm** adj not agitated or excited; not ruffled by the wind; windless ▹ n peaceful state ▹ v (often foll by *down*) make or become calm ▸ **calmly** adv ▸ **calmness** n

**calorie** n unit of measurement for the energy value of food; unit of heat ▸ **calorific** adj of calories or heat

**calumny** n, pl **-nies** false or malicious statement

**calypso** n, pl **-sos** West Indian song with improvised topical lyrics

**calyx** n, pl **calyxes** or **calyces** outer leaves that protect a flower bud

**cam** n device that converts a circular motion to a to-and-fro motion ▸ **camshaft** n part of an engine consisting of a rod to which cams are fixed

**camaraderie** n comradeship

**camber** n slight upward curve to the centre of a surface

**cambric** n fine white linen fabric

**camcorder** n combined portable video camera and recorder

**came** v past tense of **come**

**camel** n humped mammal that can survive long periods without food or water in desert regions

**camellia** [kam-**meal**-ya] n evergreen ornamental shrub with white, pink, or red flowers

**Camembert** [**kam**-mem-bare] n soft creamy French cheese

**cameo** n, pl **cameos** brooch or ring with a profile head carved in relief; small part in a film or play performed by a well-known actor or actress

**camera** n apparatus used for taking photographs or pictures for television or cinema **in camera** in private session ▸ **cameraman** n man who operates a camera for television or cinema ▸ **camera phone** mobile phone incorporating a camera

**camiknickers** pl n (Brit) woman's undergarment consisting of knickers attached to a camisole

**camisole** n woman's bodice-like garment

**camomile** n aromatic plant, used to make herbal tea

**camouflage** [**kam**-moo-flahzh] n use of natural surroundings or artificial aids to conceal or disguise something ▹ v conceal by camouflage

**camp¹** n (place for) temporary lodgings consisting of tents, huts, or cabins; group supporting a particular doctrine ▹ v stay in a camp ▸ **camper** n

**camp²** adj (informal) effeminate or homosexual; consciously artificial or affected **camp it up** (informal) behave in a camp way

**campaign** n series of coordinated activities designed to achieve a goal ▹ v take part in a campaign

**campanology** n art of ringing bells

**campanula** n plant with blue or white bell-shaped flowers

**camphor** n aromatic crystalline substance used medicinally and in mothballs

**campion** n red, pink, or white wild flower

**campus** n, pl **-puses** grounds of a university or college

**can¹** v, past tense **could** be able to; be allowed to

**can²** n metal container for food or liquids ▷ v **canning, canned** put (something) into a can ▷ **canned** adj preserved in a can; (of music) prerecorded ▷ **cannery** n, pl **-neries** factory where food is canned

**Canadian** n, adj (person) from Canada

**canal** n artificial waterway; passage in the body

**canapé** [kan-nap-pay] n small piece of bread or toast with a savoury topping

**canary** n, pl **-ries** small yellow songbird often kept as a pet

**canasta** n card game like rummy, played with two packs

**cancan** n lively high-kicking dance performed by a female group

**cancel** v **-celling, -celled** stop (something that has been arranged) from taking place; mark (a cheque or stamp) with an official stamp to prevent further use ▷ **cancellation** n ▷ **cancel out** v counterbalance, neutralize

**cancer** n serious disease resulting from a malignant growth or tumour; malignant growth or tumour ▷ **cancerous** adj

**candela** [kan-**dee**-la] n unit of luminous intensity

**candelabrum** n, pl **-bra** large branched candle holder

**candid** adj honest and straightforward ▷ **candidly** adv

**candidate** n person seeking a job or position; person taking an examination ▷ **candidacy, candidature** n

**candle** n stick of wax enclosing a wick, which is burned to produce light ▷ **candlestick** n holder for a candle ▷ **candlewick** n cotton fabric with a tufted surface

**candour** n honesty and straightforwardness

**candy** n, pl **-dies** (US) sweet or sweets ▷ **candied** adj coated with sugar ▷ **candyfloss** n light fluffy mass of spun sugar on a stick ▷ **candy-striped** adj having coloured stripes on a white background

**cane** n stem of the bamboo or similar plant; flexible rod used to beat someone; slender walking stick ▷ v beat with a cane ▷ **cane toad** large toad used to control insects and other pests of sugar-cane plantations

**canine** adj of or like a dog ▷ n sharp pointed tooth between the incisors and the molars

**canister** n metal container

**canker** n ulceration, ulcerous disease; something evil that spreads and corrupts

**cannabis** n Asian plant with tough fibres; drug obtained from the dried leaves and flowers of this plant, which can be smoked or chewed

**cannelloni** pl n tubular pieces of pasta filled with meat etc.

**cannibal** n person who eats human flesh; animal that eats others of its own kind ▷ **cannibalism** n ▷ **cannibalize** v use parts from (one machine) to repair another

**cannon** n large gun on wheels; billiard stroke in which the cue ball hits two balls successively ▶ **cannonade** n continuous heavy gunfire ▶ **cannonball** n heavy metal ball fired from a cannon ▶ **cannon into** v collide with

**cannot** can not

**canny** adj **-nier, -niest** shrewd, cautious ▶ **cannily** adv

**canoe** n light narrow open boat propelled by a paddle or paddles ▶ **canoeing** n sport of rowing in a canoe ▶ **canoeist** n

**canon**¹ n priest serving in a cathedral

**canon**² n Church decree regulating morals or religious practices; general rule or standard; list of the works of an author that are accepted as authentic ▶ **canonical** adj ▶ **canonize** v declare (a person) officially to be a saint ▶ **canonization** n

**canoodle** v (slang) kiss and cuddle

**canopy** n, pl **-pies** covering above a bed, door, etc; any large or wide covering ▶ **canopied** adj covered with a canopy

**cant**¹ n insincere talk; specialized vocabulary of a particular group

**cant**² n tilted position ▷ v tilt, overturn

**can't** can not

**cantaloupe, cantaloup** n kind of melon with sweet orange flesh

**cantankerous** adj quarrelsome, bad-tempered

**cantata** n musical work consisting of arias, duets, and choruses

**canteen** n restaurant attached to a workplace or school; box containing a set of cutlery

**canter** n horse's gait between a trot and a gallop ▷ v move at a canter

**canticle** n short hymn with words from the Bible

**cantilever** n beam or girder fixed at one end only

**canto** n, pl **-tos** main division of a long poem

**canton** n political division of a country, esp. Switzerland

**cantor** n man employed to lead services in a synagogue

**canvas** n heavy coarse cloth used for sails and tents, and for oil painting; oil painting on canvas

**canvass** v try to get votes or support (from); find out the opinions of (people) by conducting a survey ▷ n canvassing

**canyon** n deep narrow valley ▶ **canyoning** n sport of swimming, scrambling, and abseiling through a canyon

**cap** n soft close-fitting covering for the head; small lid; small explosive device used in a toy gun ▷ v **capping, capped** cover or top with something; select (a player) for a national team; impose an upper limit on (a tax); outdo, excel

**capable** adj (foll by of) having the ability (for); competent and efficient ▶ **capably** adv ▶ **capability** n, pl **-ties**

**capacity** n, pl **-ties** ability to contain, absorb, or hold; maximum amount that can be contained or produced; physical or mental ability; position, function ▶ **capacious** adj roomy ▶ **capacitance** n (measure of) the ability of a system to store electrical charge ▶ **capacitor** n device for storing electrical charge

**caparisoned** adj magnificently decorated

**cape**¹ n short cloak

**cape**² n large piece of land that juts out into the sea

**caper** n high-spirited prank ▷ v skip about

**capercaillie, capercailzie**
[kap-per-**kale**-yee] n large black
European grouse

**capers** pl n pickled flower buds of a
Mediterranean shrub used in sauces

**capillary** n, pl -**laries** very fine
blood vessel

**capital**[1] n chief city of a country;
accumulated wealth; wealth used
to produce more wealth; large
letter, as used at the beginning of a
name or sentence ▷ adj involving or
punishable by death; (old-fashioned)
excellent ▶ **capitalize** v write or
print (words) in capitals; convert
into or provide with capital
▶ **capitalize on** v take advantage
of (a situation)

**capital**[2] n top part of a pillar

**capitalism** n economic system
based on the private ownership
of industry ▶ **capitalist** adj
of capitalists or capitalism;
supporting capitalism ▷ n
supporter of capitalism; person
who owns a business

**capitation** n tax of a fixed amount
per person

**capitulate** v surrender on agreed
terms ▶ **capitulation** n

**capon** n castrated cock fowl
fattened for eating

**cappuccino** [kap-poo-**cheen**-oh]
n, pl -**nos** coffee with steamed
milk, sprinkled with powdered
chocolate

**caprice** [kap-**reess**] n
sudden change of attitude
▶ **capricious** adj tending to have
sudden changes of attitude
▶ **capriciously** adv

**capsicum** n kind of pepper used as
a vegetable or as a spice

**capsize** v (of a boat) overturn
accidentally

**capstan** n rotating cylinder round
which a ship's rope is wound

**capsule** n soluble gelatine case
containing a dose of medicine;
plant's seed case; detachable crew
compartment of a spacecraft

**captain** n commander of a ship or
civil aircraft; middle-ranking naval
officer; junior officer in the army;
leader of a team or group ▷ v be
captain of ▶ **captaincy** n

**caption** n title or explanation
accompanying an illustration ▷ v
provide with a caption

**captious** adj tending to make
trivial criticisms

**captivate** v attract and hold the
attention of ▶ **captivating** adj

**captive** n person kept in
confinement ▷ adj kept in
confinement; (of an audience)
unable to leave ▶ **captivity** n

**captor** n person who captures a
person or animal

**capture** v take by force; succeed in
representing (something elusive)
artistically ▷ n **capturing**

**car** n motor vehicle designed to
carry a small number of people;
passenger compartment of a cable
car, lift, etc.; (US) railway carriage
▶ **car park** area or building
reserved for parking cars

**carafe** [kar-**raff**] n glass bottle for
serving water or wine

**caramel** n chewy sweet made
from sugar and milk; burnt sugar,
used for colouring and flavouring
food ▶ **caramelize** v turn into
caramel

**carapace** n hard upper shell of
tortoises and crustaceans

**carat** n unit of weight of precious
stones; measure of the purity of
gold in an alloy

**caravan** n large enclosed vehicle
for living in, designed to be towed
by a car or horse; group travelling
together in Eastern countries

C

**caraway** n plant whose seeds are used as a spice

**carb** n short for **carbohydrate**, **carburettor**

**carbide** n compound of carbon with a metal

**carbine** n light automatic rifle

**carbohydrate** n any of a large group of energy-producing compounds in food, such as sugars and starches

**carbolic acid** n disinfectant derived from coal tar

**carbon** n nonmetallic element occurring as charcoal, graphite, and diamond, found in all organic matter ▶ **carbonate** n salt or ester of carbonic acid ▶ **carbonated** adj (of a drink) containing carbon dioxide ▶ **carbonize** v turn into carbon as a result of heating; coat with carbon ▶ **carbon copy** copy made with carbon paper; very similar person or thing ▶ **carbon dioxide** colourless gas exhaled by people and animals ▶ **carbon footprint** measure of the carbon dioxide produced by an individual or company ▶ **carbonic acid** weak acid formed from carbon dioxide and water ▶ **carbon-neutral** adj not affecting the overall volume of carbon dioxide in the atmosphere ▶ **carbon offset** act which compensates for carbon emissions of an individual or company ▶ **carbon paper** paper coated on one side with a dark waxy pigment, used to make a copy of something as it is typed or written

**Carborundum**® n compound of silicon and carbon, used for grinding and polishing

**carbuncle** n inflamed boil

**carburettor** n device which mixes petrol and air in an internal-combustion engine

**carcass, carcase** n dead body of an animal

**carcinogen** n substance that produces cancer ▶ **carcinogenic** adj ▶ **carcinoma** n malignant tumour

**card** n piece of thick stiff paper or cardboard used for identification, reference, or sending greetings or messages; one of a set of cards with a printed pattern, used for playing games; small rectangle of stiff plastic with identifying numbers for use as a credit card, cheque card, or charge card; (old-fashioned) witty or eccentric person ▷ pl any card game, or card games in general ▶ **cardboard** n thin stiff board made from paper pulp ▶ **cardholder** n person who owns a credit or debit card ▶ **cardsharp** n professional card player who cheats

**cardamom** n spice obtained from the seeds of a tropical plant

**cardiac** adj of the heart ▶ **cardiogram** n electrocardiogram ▶ **cardiograph** n electrocardiograph ▶ **cardiology** n study of the heart and its diseases ▶ **cardiologist** n ▶ **cardiovascular** adj of the heart and the blood vessels

**cardigan** n knitted jacket

**cardinal** n any of the high-ranking clergymen of the RC Church who elect the Pope and act as his counsellors ▷ adj fundamentally important ▶ **cardinal number** number denoting quantity but not order in a group, for example four as distinct from fourth ▶ **cardinal points** the four main points of the compass

**care** v be concerned; like (to do something); (foll by for) like, be fond of; (foll by for) look after

▷ *n* careful attention, caution; protection, charge; trouble, worry ▶ **careful** *adj* ▶ **carefully** *adv* ▶ **carefulness** *n* ▶ **careless** *adj* ▶ **carelessly** *adv* ▶ **carelessness** *n*

**careen** *v* tilt over to one side

**USAGE NOTE**
Be careful not to confuse *careen*, 'tilt', with *career*, 'rush headlong'

**career** *n* series of jobs in a profession or occupation that a person has through their life; part of a person's life spent in a particular occupation ▷ *v* rush in an uncontrolled way ▶ **careerist** *n* person who seeks advancement by any possible means

**carefree** *adj* without worry or responsibility

**caress** *n* gentle affectionate touch or embrace ▷ *v* touch gently and affectionately

**caret** [kar-rett] *n* symbol (∧) indicating a place in written or printed matter where something is to be inserted

**caretaker** *n* person employed to look after a place

**careworn** *adj* showing signs of worry

**cargo** *n, pl* **-goes** goods carried by a ship, aircraft, etc. ▶ **cargo pants, cargo trousers** loose trousers with a large pocket on the outside of each leg

**caribou** *n, pl* **-bou** *or* **-bous** large N American reindeer

**caricature** *n* drawing or description of a person that exaggerates features for comic effect ▷ *v* make a caricature of

**caries** [care-reez] *n* tooth decay

**carillon** [kar-**rill**-yon] *n* set of bells played by keyboard or mechanically; tune played on such bells

**cark** *v* **cark it** (*Aust & NZ slang*) die

**carmine** *adj* vivid red

**carnage** *n* extensive slaughter of people

**carnal** *adj* of a sexual or sensual nature ▶ **carnal knowledge** sexual intercourse

**carnation** *n* cultivated plant with fragrant white, pink, or red flowers

**carnival** *n* festive period with processions, music, and dancing in the street

**carnivore** *n* meat-eating animal ▶ **carnivorous** *adj*

**carob** *n* pod of a Mediterranean tree, used as a chocolate substitute

**carol** *n* joyful Christmas hymn ▷ *v* **-olling, -olled** sing carols; sing joyfully

**carotid** *adj, n* (of) either of the two arteries supplying blood to the head

**carouse** *v* have a merry drinking party

**carousel** [kar-roo-**sell**] *n* revolving conveyor belt for luggage or photographic slides; (*US*) merry-go-round

**carp**¹ *n* large freshwater fish

**carp**² *v* complain, find fault

**carpel** *n* female reproductive organ of a flowering plant

**carpenter** *n* person who makes or repairs wooden structures ▶ **carpentry** *n*

**carpet** *n* heavy fabric for covering floors ▷ *v* **carpeting, carpeted** cover with a carpet **on the carpet** (*informal*) being reprimanded ▶ **carpet snake, carpet python** large nonvenomous Australian snake with a carpet-like pattern on its back

**carpus** *n, pl* **-pi** set of eight bones of the wrist

**carriage** *n* one of the sections of a train for passengers; way a person holds his or her head and body;

C

four-wheeled horse-drawn vehicle; moving part of a machine that supports and shifts another part; charge made for conveying goods ▶ **carriageway** n (*Brit*) part of a road along which traffic passes in one direction

**carrier** n person or thing that carries something; person or animal that does not suffer from a disease but can transmit it to others ▶ **carrier pigeon** homing pigeon used for carrying messages

**carrion** n dead and rotting flesh

**carrot** n long tapering orange root vegetable; something offered as an incentive ▶ **carroty** adj (of hair) reddish-orange

**carry** v **-rying, -ried** take from one place to another; have with one habitually, in one's pocket etc.; transmit (a disease); have as a factor or result; hold (one's head or body) in a specified manner; secure the adoption of (a bill or motion); (of sound) travel a certain distance ▶ **carry on** v continue; (*informal*) cause a fuss ▶ **carry out** v follow, accomplish

**cart** n open two-wheeled horse-drawn vehicle for carrying goods or passengers ▷ v carry, usu. with some effort ▶ **carthorse** n large heavily built horse ▶ **cartwheel** n sideways somersault supported by the hands with legs outstretched; large spoked wheel of a cart

**carte blanche** [kaht **blahntsh**] n (*French*) complete authority

**cartel** n association of competing firms formed to fix prices

**cartilage** n strong flexible tissue forming part of the skeleton ▶ **cartilaginous** adj

**cartography** n map making ▶ **cartographer** n ▶ **cartographic** adj

**carton** n container made of cardboard or waxed paper

**cartoon** n humorous or satirical drawing; sequence of these telling a story; film made by photographing a series of drawings which give the illusion of movement when projected ▶ **cartoonist** n

**cartridge** n casing containing an explosive charge and bullet for a gun; sealed container of film, tape, ink, etc. ▶ **cartridge paper** strong thick drawing paper

**carve** v cut to form an object; form (an object or design) by cutting; slice (cooked meat) ▶ **carving** n

**caryatid** [kar-ree-**at**-id] n supporting column in the shape of a female figure

**Casanova** n promiscuous man

**casbah** n citadel of a N African city

**cascade** n waterfall; something flowing or falling like a waterfall ▷ v flow or fall in a cascade

**case¹** n instance, example; condition, state of affairs; set of arguments supporting an action or cause; person or problem dealt with by a doctor, social worker, or solicitor; action, lawsuit; (*Grammar*) form of a noun, pronoun, or adjective showing its relation to other words in the sentence **in case** so as to allow for the possibility that

**case²** n container, protective covering ▷ v (*slang*) inspect (a building) with the intention of burgling it ▶ **case-hardened** adj having been made callous by experience

**casement** n window that is hinged on one side

**cash** n banknotes and coins ▷ v obtain cash for ▶ **cash in on** v (*informal*) gain profit or advantage

from ▶ **cash register** till that
displays and adds the prices of the
goods sold ▶ **cash-strapped** *adj*
short of money

**cashew** *n* edible kidney-shaped nut

**cashier**¹ *n* person responsible for
handling cash in a bank, shop, etc.

**cashier**² *v* dismiss with dishonour
from the armed forces

**cashmere** *n* fine soft wool obtained
from goats

**casing** *n* protective case, covering

**casino** *n*, *pl* **-nos** public building
where gambling games are played

**cask** *n* barrel used to hold alcoholic
drink; (*Aust*) cubic carton
containing wine, with a tap for
dispensing

**casket** *n* small box for valuables;
(*US*) coffin

**cassava** *n* starch obtained from the
roots of a tropical American plant,
used to make tapioca

**casserole** *n* covered dish in which
food is cooked slowly, usu. in an
oven; dish cooked in this way ▷ *v*
cook in a casserole

**cassette** *n* plastic case containing a
reel of film or magnetic tape

**cassock** *n* long tunic, usu. black,
worn by priests

**cassowary** *n*, *pl* **-waries** large
flightless bird of Australia and
New Guinea

**cast** *n* actors in a play or film
collectively; object shaped by a
mould while molten; mould used to
shape such an object; rigid plaster-
of-Paris casing for immobilizing
broken bones while they heal; sort,
kind; slight squint in the eye ▷ *v*
**casting, cast** select (an actor) to
play a part in a play or film; give (a
vote); let fall, shed; shape (molten
material) in a mould; throw with
force; direct (a glance) ▶ **castaway**
*n* shipwrecked person ▶ **casting**

**vote** deciding vote used by the
chairperson of a meeting when
the votes on each side are equal
▶ **cast-iron** *adj* made of a hard
but brittle type of iron; definite,
unchallengeable ▶ **cast-off** *adj*, *n*
discarded (person or thing)

**castanets** *pl n* musical instrument,
used by Spanish dancers,
consisting of curved pieces of
hollow wood clicked together in
the hand

**caste** *n* any of the hereditary classes
into which Hindu society is divided;
social rank

**castellated** *adj* having
battlements

**caster sugar** *n* finely ground
white sugar

**castigate** *v* reprimand severely
▶ **castigation** *n*

**castle** *n* large fortified building,
often built as a ruler's residence;
rook in chess

**castor** *n* small swivelling wheel
fixed to the bottom of a piece of
furniture for easy moving

**castor oil** *n* oil obtained from an
Indian plant, used as a lubricant
and purgative

**castrate** *v* remove the testicles of;
deprive of vigour or masculinity
▶ **castration** *n*

**casual** *adj* careless, nonchalant;
(of work or workers) occasional or
not permanent; for informal wear;
happening by chance ▶ **casually**
*adv*

**casualty** *n*, *pl* **-ties** person killed
or injured in an accident or war;
person or thing that has suffered as
the result of something

**casuarina** [kass-yew-a-**reen**-a] *n*
Australian tree with jointed green
branches

**casuistry** *n* reasoning that is
misleading or oversubtle

**cat** n small domesticated furry mammal; related wild mammal, such as the lion or tiger ▸ **catty** adj (informal) spiteful ▸ **catcall** n derisive whistle or cry ▸ **catfish** n fish with whisker-like barbels round the mouth ▸ **catgut** n strong cord used to string musical instruments and sports rackets ▸ **catkin** n drooping flower spike of certain trees ▸ **catnap** n, v doze ▸ **Catseyes**® pl n glass reflectors set in the road to indicate traffic lanes ▸ **cat's paw** person used by another to do unpleasant things for him or her ▸ **catwalk** n narrow platform where models display clothes in a fashion show

**cataclysm** [kat-a-kliz-zum] n violent upheaval; disaster, such as an earthquake ▸ **cataclysmic** adj

**catacombs** [kat-a-koomz] pl n underground burial place consisting of tunnels with recesses for tombs

**catafalque** [kat-a-falk] n raised platform on which a body lies in state before or during a funeral

**catalepsy** n trancelike state in which the body is rigid ▸ **cataleptic** adj

**catalogue** n book containing details of items for sale; systematic list of items ▸ v make a systematic list of

**catalyst** n substance that speeds up a chemical reaction without itself changing ▸ **catalyse** v speed up (a chemical reaction) by a catalyst ▸ **catalysis** n ▸ **catalytic** adj

**catamaran** n boat with twin parallel hulls

**catapult** n Y-shaped device with a loop of elastic, used by children for firing stones ▸ v shoot forwards or upwards violently

**cataract** n eye disease in which the lens becomes opaque; opaque area of an eye; large waterfall

**catarrh** [kat-tar] n excessive mucus in the nose and throat, during or following a cold ▸ **catarrhal** adj

**catastrophe** [kat-ass-trof-fee] n great and sudden disaster ▸ **catastrophic** adj

**catch** v catching, caught seize, capture; surprise in an act e.g. two boys were caught stealing; hit unexpectedly; be in time for (a bus, train, etc.); see or hear; be infected with (an illness); entangle; understand, make out ▸ n device for fastening a door, window, etc.; (informal) concealed or unforeseen drawback **catch it** (informal) be punished ▸ **catching** adj infectious ▸ **catchy** adj (of a tune) pleasant and easily remembered ▸ **catchcry** n (Aust) well-known phrase associated with a person, group, etc. ▸ **catchment area** area served by a particular school or hospital; area of land draining into a river, basin, or reservoir ▸ **catch on** v (informal) become popular; understand ▸ **catch out** v (informal) trap (someone) in an error or lie ▸ **catch phrase** well-known phrase associated with a particular entertainer ▸ **catch 22** inescapable dilemma ▸ **catchword** n well-known and frequently used phrase

**catechism** [kat-ti-kiz-zum] n instruction on the doctrine of a Christian Church in a series of questions and answers

**category** n, pl -ries class, group ▸ **categorical** adj absolutely clear and certain ▸ **categorically** adv ▸ **categorize** v put in a category ▸ **categorization** n

**cater** v provide what is needed or wanted, esp. food or services ▷ **caterer** n

**caterpillar** n wormlike larva of a moth or butterfly; (**C-**)® endless track, driven by cogged wheels, used to propel a heavy vehicle

**caterwaul** v wail, yowl

**catharsis** [kath-**thar**-siss] n, pl **-ses** relief of strong suppressed emotions ▷ **cathartic** adj

**cathedral** n principal church of a diocese

**Catherine wheel** n rotating firework

**catheter** [**kath**-it-er] n tube inserted into a body cavity to drain fluid

**cathode** n negative electrode, by which electrons leave a circuit ▷ **cathode rays** stream of electrons from a cathode in a vacuum tube

**catholic** adj (of tastes or interests) covering a wide range ▷ n, adj (**C-**) (member) of the Roman Catholic Church ▷ **Catholicism** n

**cation** [**kat**-eye-on] n positively charged ion

**cattle** pl n domesticated cows and bulls

**Caucasian** n, adj (member) of the light-skinned racial group of humankind

**caucus** n, pl **-cuses** local committee or faction of a political party; political meeting to decide future plans

**caught** v past of **catch**

**cauldron** n large pot used for boiling

**cauliflower** n vegetable with a large head of white flower buds surrounded by green leaves

**caulk** v fill in (cracks) with paste

**causal** adj of or being a cause ▷ **causally** adv ▷ **causation**,

**causality** n relationship of cause and effect

**cause** n something that produces a particular effect; (foll by for) reason, motive; aim or principle supported by a person or group ▷ v be the cause of

**cause célèbre** [kawz sill-**leb**-ra] n, pl **causes célèbres** [kawz sill-**leb**-ra] controversial legal case or issue

**causeway** n raised path or road across water or marshland

**caustic** adj capable of burning by chemical action; bitter and sarcastic ▷ **caustically** adv

**cauterize** v burn (a wound) with heat or a caustic agent to prevent infection

**caution** n care, esp. in the face of danger; warning ▷ v warn, advise ▷ **cautionary** adj warning ▷ **cautious** adj showing caution ▷ **cautiously** adv

**cavalcade** n procession of people on horseback or in cars

**cavalier** adj showing haughty disregard ▷ n (**C-**) supporter of Charles I in the English Civil War

**cavalry** n, pl **-ries** part of the army orig. on horseback, but now often using fast armoured vehicles

**cave** n hollow in the side of a hill or cliff ▷ **caving** n sport of exploring caves ▷ **cave in** v collapse inwards; (informal) yield under pressure ▷ **caveman** n prehistoric cave dweller

**caveat** [**kav**-vee-at] n warning

**cavern** n large cave ▷ **cavernous** adj

**caviar, caviare** n salted sturgeon roe, regarded as a delicacy

**cavil** v **-illing, -illed** make petty objections ▷ n petty objection

**cavity** n, pl **-ties** hollow space; decayed area on a tooth

**cavort** v skip about

**caw** n cry of a crow, rook, or raven ▷ v make this cry

**cayenne pepper, cayenne** n hot red spice made from capsicum seeds

**cayman** n, pl **-mans** S American reptile similar to an alligator

**CB** Citizens' Band

**CBE** (in Britain) Commander of the Order of the British Empire

**CBI** Confederation of British Industry

**cc** cubic centimetre; carbon copy; (in South Africa) closed corporation

**CD** compact disc

**CD-ROM** compact disc read-only memory

**CE** Common Era

**cease** v bring or come to an end ▶ **ceaseless** adj ▶ **ceaselessly** adv ▶ **ceasefire** n temporary truce

**cedar** n evergreen coniferous tree; its wood

**cede** v surrender (territory or legal rights)

**cedilla** n character ( ˌ ) placed under a c in some languages, to show that it is pronounced s, not k

**ceilidh** [**kay**-lee] n informal social gathering for singing and dancing, esp. in Scotland

**ceiling** n inner upper surface of a room; upper limit set on something

**celandine** n wild plant with yellow flowers

**celebrate** v hold festivities to mark (a happy event, anniversary, etc.); perform (a religious ceremony) ▶ **celebrated** adj well known ▶ **celebration** n ▶ **celebrant** n person who performs a religious ceremony ▶ **celebrity** n, pl **-rities** famous person; state of being famous

**celeriac** [sill-**ler**-ee-ak] n variety of celery with a large turnip-like root

**celerity** [sill-**ler**-rit-tee] n swiftness

**celery** n vegetable with long green crisp edible stalks

**celestial** adj heavenly, divine; of the sky

**celibate** adj unmarried or abstaining from sex, esp. because of a religious vow of chastity ▷ n celibate person ▶ **celibacy** n

**cell** n smallest unit of an organism that is able to function independently; small room for a prisoner, monk, or nun; small compartment of a honeycomb etc.; small group operating as the core of a larger organization; device that produces electrical energy by chemical reaction ▶ **cellular** adj of or consisting of cells

**cellar** n underground room for storage; stock of wine

**cello** [**chell**-oh] n, pl **-los** large low-pitched instrument of the violin family ▶ **cellist** n

**Cellophane**® n thin transparent cellulose sheeting used as wrapping

**cellulite** n fat deposits under the skin alleged to resist dieting

**celluloid** n kind of plastic used to make toys and, formerly, photographic film

**cellulose** n main constituent of plant cell walls, used in making paper, plastics, etc.

**Celsius** adj of the temperature scale in which water freezes at 0° and boils at 100°

**Celt** [kelt, selt] n person from Scotland, Ireland, Wales, Cornwall, or Brittany

**Celtic** [**kel**-tik, **sel**-tik] n group of languages including Gaelic and Welsh ▷ adj of the Celts or the Celtic languages

**cement** n fine grey powder mixed with water and sand to make mortar or concrete; something that unites, binds, or joins;

material used to fill teeth ▷ v join, bind, or cover with cement; make (a relationship) stronger

**cemetery** n, pl **-teries** place where dead people are buried

**cenotaph** n monument honouring soldiers who died in a war

**censer** n container for burning incense

**censor** n person authorized to examine films, books, etc., to ban or cut anything considered obscene or objectionable ▷ v ban or cut parts of (a film, book, etc.) ▶ **censorship** n ▶ **censorious** adj harshly critical

**censure** n severe disapproval ▷ v criticize severely

**census** n, pl **-suses** official count of a population

**cent** n hundredth part of a monetary unit such as the dollar or euro

**centaur** n mythical creature with the head, arms, and torso of a man, and the lower body and legs of a horse

**centenary** [sen-**teen**-a-ree] n, pl **-naries** (chiefly Brit) 100th anniversary or its celebration ▶ **centenarian** n person at least 100 years old

**centennial** n 100th anniversary or its celebration

**centi-** prefix one hundredth

**centigrade** adj same as **Celsius**

> **USAGE NOTE**
> Scientists now use Celsius in preference to centigrade

**centigram, centigramme** n one hundredth of a gram

**centilitre** n one hundredth of a litre

**centimetre** n one hundredth of a metre

**centipede** n small wormlike creature with many legs

**central** adj of, at, or forming the centre; main, principal ▶ **centrally**

adv ▶ **centrality** n ▶ **centralism** n principle of central control of a country or organization ▶ **centralize** v bring under central control ▶ **centralization** n ▶ **central heating** system for heating a building from one central source of heat

**centre** n middle point or part; place for a specified activity; political party or group favouring moderation; (Sport) player who plays in the middle of the field ▷ v put in the centre of something ▶ **centred** adj emotionally stable and confident ▶ **centrist** n person favouring political moderation ▶ **centre on** v have as a centre or main theme

**centrifugal** adj moving away from a centre ▶ **centrifuge** n machine that separates substances by centrifugal force

**centripetal** adj moving towards a centre

**centurion** n (in ancient Rome) officer commanding 100 men

**century** n, pl **-ries** period of 100 years; cricket score of 100 runs

**CEO** chief executive officer

**cephalopod** [**seff**-a-loh-pod] n sea mollusc with a head and tentacles, such as the octopus

**ceramic** n hard brittle material made by heating clay to a very high temperature; object made of this ▷ pl art of producing ceramic objects ▷ adj made of ceramic

**cereal** n grass plant with edible grain, such as oat or wheat; this grain; breakfast food made from this grain, eaten mixed with milk

**cerebral** [ser-**rib**-ral, ser-**reeb**-ral] adj of the brain; intellectual

**cerebrum** [**serr**-rib-rum] n, pl **-brums** or **-bra** main part of the brain

**ceremony** *n, pl* **-nies** formal act or ritual; formally polite behaviour ▶ **ceremonial** *adj, n* ▶ **ceremonially** *adv* ▶ **ceremonious** *adj* excessively polite or formal ▶ **ceremoniously** *adv*

**cerise** [ser-**reess**] *adj* cherry-red

**certain** *adj* positive and confident; definite; some but not much ▶ **certainly** *adv* ▶ **certainty** *n* state of being sure; (*pl* **-ties**) something that is inevitable

**certificate** *n* official document stating the details of a birth, academic course, etc.

**certify** *v* **-fying, -fied** confirm, attest to; guarantee; declare legally insane ▶ **certifiable** *adj* considered legally insane ▶ **certification** *n*

**certitude** *n* confidence, certainty

**cervix** *n, pl* **cervixes** or **cervices** narrow entrance of the womb; neck ▶ **cervical** *adj*

**cessation** *n* ceasing

**cesspit, cesspool** *n* covered tank or pit for sewage

**cetacean** [sit-**tay**-shun] *n* fish-shaped sea mammal such as a whale or dolphin

**cf** compare

**CFC** chlorofluorocarbon

**CGI** computer-generated image(s)

**ch.** chapter; church

**chafe** *v* make sore or worn by rubbing; be annoyed or impatient

**chaff**[1] *n* grain husks

**chaff**[2] *v* (*old-fashioned*) tease good-naturedly

**chaffinch** *n* small European songbird

**chagrin** [**shag**-grin] *n* annoyance and disappointment ▶ **chagrined** *adj* annoyed and disappointed

**chain** *n* flexible length of connected metal links; series of connected

facts or events; group of shops, hotels, etc. owned by one firm ▷ *v* restrict or fasten with or as if with a chain ▶ **chain reaction** series of events, each of which causes the next ▶ **chain-smoke** *v* smoke (cigarettes) continuously ▶ **chain smoker**

**chair** *n* seat with a back, for one person; official position of authority; person holding this; professorship ▷ *v* preside over (a meeting) ▶ **chairlift** *n* series of chairs suspended from a moving cable for carrying people up a slope ▶ **chairman, chairwoman** *n* person in charge of a company's board of directors or a meeting (also **chairperson**)

**chaise** [**shaze**] *n* (*Hist*) light horse-drawn carriage

**chaise longue** [**long**] *n* couch with a back and a single armrest

**chalcedony** [kal-**sed**-don-ee] *n, pl* **-nies** variety of quartz

**chalet** *n* kind of Swiss wooden house with a steeply sloping roof; similar house, used as a holiday home

**chalice** *n* large goblet

**chalk** *n* soft white rock consisting of calcium carbonate; piece of chalk, often coloured, used for drawing and writing on blackboards ▷ *v* draw or mark with chalk ▶ **chalky** *adj*

**challenge** *n* demanding or stimulating situation; call to take part in a contest or fight; questioning of a statement of fact; demand by a sentry for identification or a password ▷ *v* issue a challenge to ▶ **challenged** *adj* disabled as specified e.g. *physically challenged* ▶ **challenger** *n*

**chamber** *n* hall used for formal meetings; legislative or judicial assembly; (*old-fashioned*) bedroom; compartment, cavity ▷ *pl* set of rooms used as offices by a barrister ▶ **chambermaid** *n* woman employed to clean bedrooms in a hotel ▶ **chamber music** classical music to be performed by a small group of musicians ▶ **chamber pot** bowl for urine, formerly used in bedrooms

**chamberlain** *n* (*Hist*) officer who managed the household of a king or nobleman

**chameleon** [kam-**meal**-yon] *n* small lizard that changes colour to blend in with its surroundings

**chamfer** [**cham**-fer] *v* bevel the edge of

**chamois** [**sham**-wah] *n*, *pl* **-ois** small mountain antelope; [**sham**-ee] soft suede leather; piece of this, used for cleaning or polishing

**chamomile** [**kam**-mo-mile] *n* same as **camomile**

**champ**[1] *v* chew noisily **champ at the bit** (*informal*) be impatient to do something

**champ**[2] *n* short for **champion**

**champagne** *n* sparkling white French wine

**champion** *n* overall winner of a competition; (foll by *of*) someone who defends a person or cause ▷ *v* support ▷ *adj* (*dialect*) excellent ▶ **championship** *n*

**chance** *n* likelihood, probability; opportunity to do something; risk, gamble; unpredictable element that causes things to happen one way rather than another ▷ *v* risk, hazard ▶ **chancy** *adj* uncertain, risky

**chancel** *n* part of a church containing the altar and choir

**chancellor** *n* head of government in some European countries; honorary head of a university ▶ **chancellorship** *n*

**Chancery** *n* division of the British High Court of Justice

**chandelier** [shan-dill-**eer**] *n* ornamental light with branches and holders for several candles or bulbs

**chandler** *n* dealer, esp. in ships' supplies

**change** *n* becoming different; variety or novelty; different set, esp. of clothes; balance received when the amount paid is more than the cost of a purchase; coins of low value ▷ *v* make or become different; give and receive (something) in return; exchange (money) for its equivalent in a smaller denomination or different currency; put on other clothes; leave one vehicle and board another ▶ **changeable** *adj* changing often ▶ **changeling** *n* child believed to have been exchanged by fairies for another

**channel** *n* band of broadcasting frequencies; means of access or communication; broad strait connecting two areas of sea; bed or course of a river, stream, or canal; groove ▷ *v* **-nelling, -nelled** direct or convey through a channel

**chant** *v* utter or sing (a slogan or psalm) ▷ *n* rhythmic or repetitious slogan; psalm that has a short simple melody with several words sung on one note

**chanter** *n* (on bagpipes) pipe on which the melody is played

**chaos** *n* complete disorder or confusion ▶ **chaotic** *adj* ▶ **chaotically** *adv*

**chap** *n* (*informal*) man or boy

**chapati, chapatti** *n* (in Indian cookery) flat thin unleavened bread

**chapel** *n* place of worship with its own altar, within a church; similar place of worship in a large house or institution; Nonconformist place of worship

**chaperone** [**shap**-per-rone] n older person who accompanies and supervises a young person or young people on a social occasion ▷ v act as a chaperone to

**chaplain** n clergyman attached to a chapel, military body, or institution ▶ **chaplaincy** n, pl **-cies**

**chaplet** n garland for the head

**chapped** adj (of the skin) raw and cracked, through exposure to cold

**chapter** n division of a book; period in a life or history; branch of a society or club

**char¹** v **charring, charred** blacken by partial burning

**char²** (Brit informal) n charwoman ▷ v **charring, charred** clean other people's houses as a job

**char³** n (Brit old-fashioned slang) tea

**charabanc** [**shar**-rab-bang] n (old-fashioned) coach for sightseeing

**character** n combination of qualities distinguishing a person, group, or place; reputation, esp. good reputation; person represented in a play, film, or story; unusual or amusing person; letter, numeral, or symbol used in writing or printing ▶ **characteristic** n distinguishing feature or quality ▷ adj typical ▶ **characteristically** adv ▶ **characterize** v be a characteristic of; (foll by as) describe ▶ **characterization** n

**charade** [shar-**rahd**] n absurd pretence ▷ pl game in which one team acts out a word or phrase, which the other team has to guess

**charcoal** n black substance formed by partially burning wood

**charge** v ask as a price; enter a debit against a person's account for (a purchase); accuse formally; make a rush at or sudden attack upon; fill (a glass); fill (a battery) with electricity; command, assign ▷ n price charged; formal accusation; attack; command, exhortation; custody, guardianship; person or thing entrusted to someone's care; amount of electricity stored in a battery **in charge of** in control of ▶ **chargeable** adj ▶ **charger** n device for charging an accumulator; (in the Middle Ages) warhorse

**chargé d'affaires** [**shar**-zhay daf-**fair**] n, pl **chargés d'affaires** head of a diplomatic mission in the absence of an ambassador or in a small mission

**chariot** n two-wheeled horse-drawn vehicle used in ancient times in wars and races ▶ **charioteer** n chariot driver

**charisma** [kar-**rizz**-ma] n person's power to attract or influence people ▶ **charismatic** [kar-rizz-**mat**-ik] adj

**charity** n, pl **-ties** organization that gives help, such as money or food, to those in need; giving of help to those in need; help given to those in need; kindly attitude towards people ▶ **charitable** adj ▶ **charitably** adv

**charlady** n (Brit informal) same as **charwoman**

**charlatan** [**shar**-lat-tan] n person who claims expertise that he or she does not have

**charleston** n lively dance of the 1920s

**charm** n attractive quality; trinket worn on a bracelet; magic spell ▷ v attract, delight; influence by personal charm; protect or influence as if by magic ▶ **charmer** n ▶ **charming** adj attractive

**charnel house** n (Hist) building or vault for the bones of the dead

**chart** n graph, table, or diagram showing information; map of the sea or stars ▷ v plot the course of; make a chart of **the charts** (informal) weekly lists of the bestselling pop records

**charter** n document granting or demanding certain rights; fundamental principles of an organization; hire of transport for private use ▷ v hire by charter; grant a charter to ▶ **chartered** adj officially qualified to practise a profession

**chartreuse** [shar-**trerz**] n sweet-smelling green or yellow liqueur

**charwoman** n woman whose job is to clean other people's homes

**chary** [**chair**-ee] adj **-rier, -riest** wary, careful

**chase**¹ v run after quickly in order to catch or drive away; (informal) rush, run; (informal) try energetically to obtain ▷ n chasing, pursuit ▶ **chaser** n milder drink drunk after another stronger one

**chase**² v engrave or emboss (metal)

**chasm** [**kaz**-zum] n deep crack in the earth

**chassis** [**shass**-ee] n, pl **-sis** frame, wheels, and mechanical parts of a vehicle

**chaste** adj abstaining from sex outside marriage or altogether; (of style) simple ▶ **chastely** adv ▶ **chastity** n

**chasten** [**chase**-en] v subdue by criticism

**chastise** v scold severely; punish by beating ▶ **chastisement** n

**chat** n informal conversation ▷ v **chatting, chatted** have an informal conversation ▶ **chatty** adj ▶ **chatroom** n site on the internet where users have group discussions by e-mail

**chateau** [**shat**-toe] n, pl **-teaux** or **-teaus** French castle

**chatelaine** [**shat**-tell-lane] n (formerly) mistress of a large house or castle

**chattels** pl n possessions

**chatter** v speak quickly and continuously about unimportant things; (of the teeth) rattle with cold or fear ▷ n idle talk ▶ **chatterbox** n person who chatters a lot

**chauffeur** n person employed to drive a car for someone

**chauvinism** [**show**-vin-iz-zum] n irrational belief that one's own country, race, group, or sex is superior ▶ **chauvinist** n, adj ▶ **chauvinistic** adj

**chav** n (Brit derogatory informal) young working-class person considered to have vulgar tastes

**cheap** adj costing relatively little; of poor quality; not valued highly; mean, despicable ▶ **cheaply** adv ▶ **cheapen** v lower the reputation of; reduce the price of ▶ **cheapskate** n (informal) miserly person

**cheat** v act dishonestly to gain profit or advantage ▷ n person who cheats; fraud, deception

**check** v examine, investigate; slow the growth or progress of; correspond, agree ▷ n test to ensure accuracy or progress; break in progress; (US) cheque; pattern of squares or crossed lines; (Chess) position of a king under attack ▶ **check in** v register one's arrival ▶ **checkmate** n (Chess) winning position in which an opponent's king is under attack and unable to escape; utter defeat ▷ v (Chess) place the king of (one's opponent) in checkmate; thwart, defeat ▶ **check out** v pay the bill and leave a hotel; examine, investigate; (*informal*) have a look at ▸ **checkout** *n* counter in a supermarket, where customers pay ▸ **checkup** *n* thorough medical examination

**Cheddar** *n* firm orange or yellowy-white cheese

**cheek** *n* either side of the face below the eye; (*informal*) impudence, boldness ▸ *v* (*Brit, Aust & NZ informal*) speak impudently to ▸ **cheeky** *adj* impudent, disrespectful ▸ **cheekily** *adv* ▸ **cheekiness** *n*

**cheep** *n* young bird's high-pitched cry ▸ *v* utter a cheep

**cheer** *v* applaud or encourage with shouts; make or become happy ▸ *n* shout of applause or encouragement ▸ **cheerful** *adj* ▸ **cheerfully** *adv* ▸ **cheerfulness** *n* ▸ **cheerless** *adj* dreary, gloomy ▸ **cheery** *adj* ▸ **cheerily** *adv*

**cheerio** (*informal*) *interj* goodbye ▸ *n* (*Aust & NZ*) small red cocktail sausage

**cheese** *n* food made from coagulated milk curd; block of this ▸ **cheesy** *adj* ▸ **cheeseburger** *n* hamburger topped with melted cheese ▸ **cheesecake** *n* dessert with a biscuit-crumb base covered with a sweet cream-cheese mixture; (*slang*) photographs of naked or near-naked women ▸ **cheesecloth** *n* light cotton cloth ▸ **cheesed off** bored, annoyed

**cheetah** *n* large fast-running spotted African wild cat

**chef** *n* cook in a restaurant

**chef-d'oeuvre** [shay-**durv**] *n, pl* **chefs-d'oeuvre** masterpiece

**chemical** *n* substance used in or resulting from a reaction involving changes to atoms or molecules ▸ *adj* of chemistry or chemicals ▸ **chemically** *adv*

**chemise** [shem-**meez**] *n* (*old-fashioned*) woman's loose-fitting slip

**chemistry** *n* science of the composition, properties, and reactions of substances ▸ **chemist** *n* shop selling medicines and cosmetics; qualified dispenser of prescribed medicines; specialist in chemistry

**chemotherapy** *n* treatment of disease, often cancer, using chemicals

**chenille** [shen-**neel**] *n* (fabric of) thick tufty yarn

**cheque** *n* written order to one's bank to pay money from one's account ▸ **cheque card** (*Brit*) plastic card issued by a bank guaranteeing payment of a customer's cheques

**chequer** *n* piece used in Chinese chequers ▸ *pl* game of draughts

**chequered** *adj* marked by varied fortunes; having a pattern of squares

**cherish** *v* cling to (an idea or feeling); care for

**cheroot** [sher-**root**] *n* cigar with both ends cut flat

**cherry** *n, pl* **-ries** small red or black fruit with a stone; tree on which it grows ▸ *adj* deep red

**cherub** *n, pl* **-ubs** *or* **-ubim** angel, often represented as a winged child; sweet child ▸ **cherubic** [cher-**rew**-bik] *adj*

**chervil** *n* aniseed-flavoured herb

**chess** *n* game for two players with 16 pieces each, played on a chequered board of 64 squares ▸ **chessman** *n* piece used in chess

**chest** *n* front of the body, from neck to waist; large strong box ▸ **chest of drawers** piece of furniture consisting of drawers in a frame

**chesterfield** *n* couch with high padded sides and back

**chestnut** n reddish-brown edible nut; tree on which it grows; reddish-brown horse; (informal) old joke ▷ adj (of hair or a horse) reddish-brown

**chevron** [**shev**-ron] n V-shaped pattern, esp. on the sleeve of a military uniform to indicate rank

**chew** v grind (food) between the teeth ▶ **chewy** adj requiring a lot of chewing ▶ **chewing gum** flavoured gum to be chewed but not swallowed

**chianti** [kee-**ant**-ee] n dry red Italian wine

**chiaroscuro** [kee-ah-roh-**skew**-roh] n, pl -**ros** distribution of light and shade in a picture

**chic** [**sheek**] adj stylish, elegant ▷ n stylishness, elegance

**chicane** [shik-**kane**] n obstacle in a motor-racing circuit

**chicanery** n trickery, deception

**chick** n baby bird ▶ **chickpea** n edible yellow pealike seed ▶ **chickweed** n weed with small white flowers

**chicken** n domestic fowl; its flesh, used as food; (slang) coward ▷ adj (slang) cowardly ▶ **chicken feed** (slang) trifling amount of money ▶ **chicken out** v (informal) fail to do something through cowardice ▶ **chickenpox** n infectious disease with an itchy rash

**chicory** n, pl -**ries** plant whose leaves are used in salads; root of this plant, used as a coffee substitute

**chide** v **chiding, chided** or **chid, chid** or **chidden** rebuke, scold

**chief** n head of a group of people ▷ adj most important ▶ **chiefly** adv especially; mainly ▶ **chieftain** n leader of a tribe

**chiffon** [**shif**-fon] n fine see-through fabric

**chignon** [**sheen**-yon] n knot of hair pinned up at the back of the head

**chihuahua** [chee-**wah**-wah] n tiny short-haired dog

**chilblain** n inflammation of the fingers or toes, caused by exposure to cold

**child** n, pl **children** young human being, boy or girl; son or daughter ▶ **childhood** n ▶ **childish** adj immature, silly; of or like a child ▶ **childishly** adv ▶ **childless** adj ▶ **childlike** adj innocent, trustful ▶ **childbirth** n giving birth to a child ▶ **child's play** very easy task

**USAGE NOTE**
Note the difference between childish and childlike

**chill** n feverish cold; moderate coldness ▷ v make (something) cool or cold; cause (someone) to feel cold or frightened ▷ adj unpleasantly cold ▶ **chilly** adj moderately cold; unfriendly ▶ **chilly-bin** n (NZ informal) insulated container for carrying food and drink ▶ **chilliness** n ▶ **chill (out)** v (informal) relax ▶ **chill-out** adj (informal) suitable for relaxation, esp. after energetic activity

**chilli, chili** n small red or green hot-tasting capsicum pod, used in cooking; (also **chilli con carne**) hot-tasting Mexican dish of meat, onions, beans, and chilli powder

**chime** n musical ringing sound of a bell or clock ▷ v make a musical ringing sound; indicate (the time) by chiming; (foll by with) be consistent with

**chimera** [kime-**meer**-a] n unrealistic hope or idea; fabled monster with a lion's head, goat's body, and serpent's tail

**chimney** n hollow vertical structure for carrying away smoke from a fire ▶ **chimney pot** short pipe on the top of a chimney ▶ **chimney sweep** person who cleans soot from chimneys

**chimp** n (informal) short for **chimpanzee**

**chimpanzee** n intelligent black African ape

**chin** n part of the face below the mouth ▶ **chinwag** n (Brit, Aust & NZ informal) chat

**china** n fine earthenware or porcelain; dishes or ornaments made of this; (Brit, Aust, NZ & S Afr informal) friend

**chinchilla** n S American rodent bred for its soft grey fur; its fur

**chine** n cut of meat including part of the backbone

**Chinese** adj of China ▷ n (pl -nese) person from China; any of the languages of China

**chink**[1] n small narrow opening

**chink**[2] v, n (make) a light ringing sound

**chintz** n printed cotton fabric with a glazed finish

**chip** n strip of potato, fried in deep fat; tiny wafer of semiconductor material forming an integrated circuit; counter used to represent money in gambling games; small piece removed by chopping, breaking, etc.; mark left where a small piece has been broken off something ▷ v **chipping, chipped** break small pieces from **have a chip on one's shoulder** (informal) bear a grudge ▶ **chip in** v (informal) contribute (money); interrupt with a remark ▶ **chippie** n (Brit, Aust & NZ informal) carpenter ▶ **chip and PIN** system in which a credit- or debit-card payment is validated by a customer entering a unique identification number instead of a signature

**chipboard** n thin board made of compressed wood particles

**chipmunk** n small squirrel-like N American rodent with a striped back

**chiropodist** [kir-**rop**-pod-ist] n person who treats minor foot complaints ▶ **chiropody** n

**chiropractic** [kire-oh-**prak**-tik] n system of treating bodily disorders by manipulation of the spine ▶ **chiropractor** n

**chirp** v (of a bird or insect) make a short high-pitched sound ▷ n chirping sound ▶ **chirpy** adj (informal) lively and cheerful

**chisel** n metal tool with a sharp end for shaping wood or stone ▷ v **-elling, -elled** carve with a chisel

**chit**[1] n short official note, such as a receipt

**chit**[2] n (Brit, Aust & NZ old-fashioned) pert or impudent girl

**chitchat** n chat, gossip

**chitterlings** pl n pig's intestines cooked as food

**chivalry** n courteous behaviour, esp. by men towards women; medieval system and principles of knighthood ▶ **chivalrous** adj

**chives** pl n herbs with a mild onion flavour

**chivvy** v **-vying, -vied** (informal) harass, nag

**chlorine** n strong-smelling greenish-yellow gaseous element, used to disinfect water ▶ **chlorinate** v disinfect (water) with chlorine ▶ **chlorination** n ▶ **chloride** n compound of chlorine and another substance

**chlorofluorocarbon** n any of various gaseous compounds of carbon, hydrogen, chlorine, and fluorine, used in refrigerators and aerosol propellants, some of which break down the ozone in the atmosphere

**chloroform** n strong-smelling liquid formerly used as an anaesthetic

**chlorophyll** n green colouring matter of plants, which enables them to convert sunlight into energy

**chock** n block or wedge used to prevent a heavy object from moving ▸ **chock-full, chock-a-block** adj completely full

**chocolate** n sweet food made from cacao seeds; sweet or drink made from this ▷ adj dark brown

**choice** n choosing; opportunity or power of choosing; person or thing chosen or that may be chosen; alternative action or possibility ▷ adj of high quality

**choir** n organized group of singers, esp. in church; part of a church occupied by the choir

**choke** v hinder or stop the breathing of (a person) by strangling or smothering; have trouble in breathing; block, clog up ▷ n device controlling the amount of air that is mixed with the fuel in a petrol engine ▸ **choker** n tight-fitting necklace ▸ **choke back** v suppress (tears or anger)

**cholera** [kol-ler-a] n serious infectious disease causing severe vomiting and diarrhoea

**choleric** [kol-ler-ik] adj bad-tempered

**cholesterol** [kol-lest-er-oll] n fatty substance found in animal tissue, an excess of which can cause heart disease

**chomp** v chew noisily

**chook** n (Aust & NZ informal) hen or chicken ▸ **chook raffle** n raffle for which the main prize is a roast chicken **not be able to run a chook raffle** be totally incompetent

**choose** v **choosing, chose, chosen** select from a number of alternatives; decide (to do something) because one wants to ▸ **choosy** adj (informal) fussy

**chop**[1] v **chopping, chopped** cut with a blow from an axe or knife; cut into pieces; dispense with; (Boxing, Karate) hit (an opponent) with a short sharp blow ▷ n cutting or sharp blow; slice of lamb or pork, usu. with a rib ▸ **chopper** n (informal) helicopter; small axe ▸ **choppy** adj (of the sea) fairly rough

**chop**[2] v **chopping, chopped** ▸ **chop and change** change one's mind repeatedly

**chops** pl n (Brit, Aust & NZ informal) jaws, cheeks

**chopsticks** pl n pair of thin sticks used to eat Chinese food

**chop suey** n Chinese dish of chopped meat and vegetables in a sauce

**choral** adj of a choir

**chorale** [kor-rahl] n slow stately hymn tune

**chord**[1] n (Maths) straight line joining two points on a curve

**chord**[2] n simultaneous sounding of three or more musical notes

**chore** n routine task

**choreography** n composition of steps and movements for dancing ▸ **choreographer** n ▸ **choreographic** adj

**chorister** n singer in a choir

**chortle** v chuckle in amusement ▷ n amused chuckle

**chorus** n, pl **-ruses** large choir; part of a song repeated after each verse; something expressed by many people at once; group of singers or dancers who perform together in a show ▷ v **chorusing, chorused** sing or say together **in chorus** in unison

**chose** v past tense of **choose**
▶ **chosen** v past participle of **choose**

**choux pastry** [shoo] n very light pastry made with eggs

**chow** n thick-coated dog with a curled tail, orig. from China

**chowder** n thick soup containing clams or fish

**chow mein** n Chinese-American dish of chopped meat or vegetables fried with noodles

**Christ** n Jesus of Nazareth, regarded by Christians as the Messiah

**christen** v baptize; give a name to; (informal) use for the first time ▶ **christening** n

**Christendom** n all Christian people or countries

**Christian** n person who believes in and follows Christ ▷ adj of Christ or Christianity; kind, good
▶ **Christianity** n religion based on the life and teachings of Christ
▶ **Christian name** personal name given to Christians at baptism: loosely used to mean a person's first name ▶ **Christian Science** religious system which emphasizes spiritual healing

**Christmas** n annual festival on December 25 commemorating the birth of Christ; period around this time ▶ **Christmassy** adj
▶ **Christmas Day** December 25
▶ **Christmas Eve** December 24
▶ **Christmas tree** evergreen tree or imitation of one, decorated as part of Christmas celebrations

**chromatic** adj of colour or colours; (Music) (of a scale) proceeding by semitones

**chromatography** n separation and analysis of the components of a substance by slowly passing it through an adsorbing material

**chromium, chrome** n (Chem) grey metallic element used in steel alloys and for electroplating

**chromosome** n microscopic gene-carrying body in the nucleus of a cell

**chronic** adj (of an illness) lasting a long time; habitual e.g. chronic drinking; (Brit, Aust & NZ informal) of poor quality ▶ **chronically** adv

**chronicle** n record of events in order of occurrence ▷ v record in or as if in a chronicle ▶ **chronicler** n

**chronology** n, pl -gies arrangement or list of events in order of occurrence
▶ **chronological** adj
▶ **chronologically** adv

**chronometer** n timepiece designed to be accurate in all conditions

**chrysalis** [kriss-a-liss] n insect in the stage between larva and adult, when it is in a cocoon

**chrysanthemum** n flower with a large head made up of thin petals

**chub** n European freshwater fish

**chubby** adj -bier, -biest plump and round

**chuck¹** v (informal) throw; (informal) give up, reject; touch (someone) affectionately under the chin; (Aust & NZ informal) vomit

**chuck²** n cut of beef from the neck to the shoulder; device that holds a workpiece in a lathe or a tool in a drill

**chuckle** v laugh softly ▷ n soft laugh

**chuffed** adj (informal) very pleased

**chug** n short dull sound like the noise of an engine ▷ v **chugging, chugged** operate or move with this sound

**chukka** n period of play in polo

**chum** (informal) n close friend ▷ v **chumming, chummed** ▶ **chum**

**up with** form a close friendship with ▶ **chummy** ▷ adj

**chump** n (informal) stupid person; thick piece of meat

**chunk** n thick solid piece; considerable amount ▶ **chunky** adj (of a person) broad and heavy; (of an object) large and thick

**church** n building for public Christian worship; particular Christian denomination; (**C-**) Christians collectively; clergy ▶ **churchgoer** n person who attends church regularly ▶ **churchwarden** n member of a congregation who assists the vicar ▶ **churchyard** n grounds round a church, used as a graveyard

**churlish** adj surly and rude

**churn** n machine in which cream is shaken to make butter; large container for milk ▷ v stir (cream) vigorously to make butter; move about violently ▶ **churn out** v (informal) produce (things) rapidly in large numbers

**chute¹** [shoot] n steep slope down which things may be slid

**chute²** n (informal) short for **parachute**

**chutney** n pickle made from fruit, vinegar, spices, and sugar

**CIA** (in the US) Central Intelligence Agency

**cicada** [sik-**kah**-da] n large insect that makes a high-pitched drone

**cicatrix** [**sik**-a-trix] n, pl **-trices** scar

**CID** (in Britain) Criminal Investigation Department

**cider** n alcoholic drink made from fermented apple juice

**cigar** n roll of cured tobacco leaves for smoking

**cigarette** n thin roll of shredded tobacco in thin paper, for smoking

**cinch** [sinch] n (informal) easy task

**cinder** n piece of material that will not burn, left after burning coal

**cine camera** n camera for taking moving pictures

**cinema** n place for showing films; films collectively ▶ **cinematic** adj ▶ **cinematography** n technique of making films ▶ **cinematographer** n

**cineraria** n garden plant with daisy-like flowers

**cinnamon** n spice obtained from the bark of an Asian tree

> **SPELLING TIP**
> The correct spelling of **cinnamon** has two ns in the middle and only one m

**cipher** [**sife**-er] n system of secret writing; unimportant person

**circa** [**sir**-ka] prep (Latin) approximately, about

**circle** n perfectly round geometric figure, line, or shape; group of people sharing an interest or activity; (Theatre) section of seats above the main level of the auditorium ▷ v move in a circle (round); enclose in a circle

**circlet** n circular ornament worn on the head

**circuit** n complete route or course, esp. a circular one; complete path through which an electric current can flow; periodical journey round a district, as made by judges; motor-racing track ▶ **circuitous** [sir-**kew**-it-uss] adj indirect and lengthy ▶ **circuitry** [**sir**-kit-tree] n electrical circuit(s)

**circular** adj in the shape of a circle; moving in a circle ▷ n letter for general distribution ▶ **circularity** n

**circulate** v send, go, or pass from place to place or person to person ▶ **circulation** n flow of blood around the body; number of copies of a newspaper or magazine sold; sending or moving round ▸ **circulatory** adj

**circumcise** v remove the foreskin of ▸ **circumcision** n

**circumference** n boundary of a specified area or shape, esp. of a circle; distance round this

**circumflex** n mark (^) over a vowel to show that it is pronounced in a particular way

**circumlocution** n indirect way of saying something

**circumnavigate** v sail right round ▸ **circumnavigation** n

**circumscribe** v limit, restrict; draw a line round ▸ **circumscription** n

**circumspect** adj cautious and careful not to take risks ▸ **circumspectly** adv ▸ **circumspection** n

**circumstance** n (usu. pl) occurrence or condition that accompanies or influences a person or event ▸ **circumstantial** adj (of evidence) strongly suggesting something but not proving it; very detailed

**circumvent** v avoid or get round (a rule etc.) ▸ **circumvention** n

**circus** n, pl **-cuses** (performance given by) a travelling company of acrobats, clowns, performing animals, etc.

**cirrhosis** [sir-**roh**-siss] n serious liver disease, often caused by drinking too much alcohol

**cirrus** n, pl **-ri** high wispy cloud

**cistern** n water tank, esp. one that holds water for flushing a toilet

**citadel** n fortress in a city

**cite** v quote, refer to; bring forward as proof ▸ **citation** n

**citizen** n native or naturalized member of a state or nation; inhabitant of a city or town ▸ **citizenship** n ▸ **Citizens' Band** range of radio frequencies for

private communication by the public

**citric acid** n weak acid found in citrus fruits

**citrus fruit** n juicy sharp-tasting fruit such as an orange or lemon

**city** n, pl **-ties** large or important town **the City** (Brit) area of London as a financial centre

**civet** [**siv**-vit] n spotted catlike African mammal; musky fluid from its glands used in perfume

**civic** adj of a city or citizens ▸ **civics** n study of the rights and responsibilities of citizenship

**civil** adj relating to the citizens of a state as opposed to the armed forces or the Church; polite, courteous ▸ **civilly** adv ▸ **civility** n polite or courteous behaviour ▸ **civilian** n, adj (person) not belonging to the armed forces ▸ **civil servant** member of the civil service ▸ **civil service** service responsible for the administration of the government ▸ **civil war** war between people of the same country

**civilize** v refine or educate (a person); make (a place) more pleasant or more acceptable ▸ **civilization** n high level of human cultural and social development; particular society which has reached this level

**civvies** pl n (Brit, Aust & NZ slang) ordinary clothes that are not part of a uniform

**clack** n sound made by two hard objects striking each other ▷ v make this sound

**clad** v a past of **clothe**

**cladding** n material used to cover the outside of a building

**claim** v assert as a fact; demand as a right; need, require ▷ n assertion that something is true; assertion of a right; something claimed as a right ▶ **claimant** n

**clairvoyance** n power of perceiving things beyond the natural range of the senses ▶ **clairvoyant** n, adj

**clam** n edible shellfish with a hinged shell ▷ v **clamming, clammed** ▶ **clam up** (informal) stop talking, esp. through nervousness

**clamber** v climb awkwardly

**clammy** adj **-mier, -miest** unpleasantly moist and sticky

**clamour** n loud protest; loud persistent noise or outcry ▷ v make a loud noise or outcry ▶ **clamorous** adj ▶ **clamour for** v demand noisily

**clamp** n tool with movable jaws for holding things together tightly ▷ v fasten with a clamp ▶ **clamp down on** v become stricter about; suppress

**clan** n group of families with a common ancestor, esp. among Scottish Highlanders; close group ▶ **clannish** adj (of a group) tending to exclude outsiders

**clandestine** adj secret and concealed

**clang** v make a loud ringing metallic sound ▷ n ringing metallic sound

**clanger** n (informal) obvious mistake

**clangour** n loud continuous clanging sound

**clank** n harsh metallic sound ▷ v make such a sound

**clap**[1] v **clapping, clapped** applaud by hitting the palms of one's hands sharply together; put quickly or forcibly ▷ n act or sound of clapping; sudden loud noise e.g. a clap of thunder ▶ **clapped out** (slang) worn out, dilapidated

**clap**[2] n (slang) gonorrhoea

**clapper** n piece of metal inside a bell, which causes it to sound when struck against the side ▶ **clapperboard** n pair of hinged boards clapped together during filming to help in synchronizing sound and picture

**claptrap** n (informal) foolish or pretentious talk

**claret** [**klar**-rit] n dry red wine from Bordeaux

**clarify** v **-fying, -fied** make (a matter) clear and unambiguous ▶ **clarification** n

**clarinet** n keyed woodwind instrument with a single reed ▶ **clarinettist** n

**clarion** n obsolete high-pitched trumpet; its sound ▶ **clarion call** strong encouragement to do something

**clarity** n clearness

**clash** v come into conflict; (of events) happen at the same time; (of colours) look unattractive together; (of objects) make a loud harsh sound by being hit together ▷ n fight, argument; fact of two events happening at the same time

**clasp** n device for fastening things; firm grasp or embrace ▷ v grasp or embrace firmly; fasten with a clasp

**class** n group of people sharing a similar social position; system of dividing society into such groups; group of people or things sharing a common characteristic; group of pupils or students taught together; standard of quality; (informal) elegance or excellence e.g. a touch of class ▷ v place in a class

**classic** adj being a typical example of something; of lasting interest because of excellence; attractive because of simplicity of form ▷ n author, artist, or work of art of recognized excellence ▷ pl study of ancient Greek and Roman literature and culture ▸ **classical** adj of or in a restrained conservative style; denoting serious art music; of or influenced by ancient Greek and Roman culture ▸ **classically** adv ▸ **classicism** n artistic style showing emotional restraint and regularity of form ▸ **classicist** n

**classify** v -fying, -fied divide into groups with similar characteristics; declare (information) to be officially secret ▸ **classifiable** adj ▸ **classification** n

**classy** adj **classier, classiest** (informal) stylish and elegant

**clatter** v, n (make) a rattling noise

**clause** n section of a legal document; part of a sentence, containing a verb

**claustrophobia** n abnormal fear of confined spaces ▸ **claustrophobic** adj

**clavichord** n early keyboard instrument

**clavicle** n same as **collarbone**

**claw** n sharp hooked nail of a bird or beast; similar part, such as a crab's pincer ▷ v tear with claws or nails

**clay** n fine-grained earth, soft when moist and hardening when baked, used to make bricks and pottery ▸ **clayey** adj ▸ **clay pigeon** baked clay disc hurled into the air as a target for shooting

**claymore** n large two-edged sword formerly used by Scottish Highlanders

**clean** adj free from dirt or impurities; not yet used; morally acceptable, inoffensive; (of a reputation or record) free from dishonesty or corruption; complete e.g. a clean break; smooth and regular ▷ v make (something) free from dirt ▷ adv (not standard) completely e.g. I clean forgot **come clean** (informal) reveal or admit

something ▸ **cleaner** n ▸ **cleanly** adv ▸ **cleanliness** n

**cleanse** v make clean ▸ **cleanser** n

**clean technology, clean-tech** n manufacturing processes that minimize damage caused to the environment ▷ adj using clean technology

**clear** adj free from doubt or confusion; easy to see or hear; able to be seen through; free of obstruction; (of weather) free from clouds; (of skin) without blemish ▷ adv out of the way ▷ v make or become clear; pass by or over (something) without contact; prove (someone) innocent of a crime or mistake; make as profit ▸ **clearly** adv ▸ **clearance** n clearing; official permission ▸ **clearing** n treeless area in a wood ▸ **clear off** v (Brit, Aust & NZ informal) go away ▸ **clear out** v remove and sort the contents of; (Brit, Aust & NZ informal) go away ▸ **clear-sighted** adj having good judgment ▸ **clearway** n stretch of road on which motorists may stop in an emergency

**cleat** n wedge; piece of wood, metal, or plastic with two projecting ends round which ropes are fastened

**cleave**¹ v **cleaving, cleft, cleaved** or **clove, cleft, cleaved** or **cloven** split apart ▸ **cleavage** n space between a woman's breasts, as revealed by a low-cut dress; division, split

**cleave**² v cling or stick

**cleaver** n butcher's heavy knife with a square blade

**clef** n (Music) symbol at the beginning of a stave to show the pitch

**cleft** n narrow opening or crack ▷ v a past of **cleave**¹; **in a cleft stick** in a very difficult position

**clematis** n climbing plant with large colourful flowers

**clement** adj (of weather) mild ▶ **clemency** n kind or lenient treatment

**clementine** n small orange citrus fruit

**clench** v close or squeeze (one's teeth or fist) tightly; grasp firmly

**clerestory** [**clear**-store-ee] n, pl **-ries** row of windows at the top of a wall above an adjoining roof

**clergy** n priests and ministers as a group ▶ **clergyman** n

**cleric** n member of the clergy

**clerical** adj of clerks or office work; of the clergy

**clerk** n employee in an office, bank, or court who keeps records, files, and accounts

**clever** adj intelligent, quick at learning; showing skill ▶ **cleverly** adv ▶ **cleverness** n

**clianthus** [klee-**anth**-us] n Australian or NZ plant with slender scarlet flowers

**cliché** [**klee**-shay] n expression or idea that is no longer effective because of overuse ▶ **clichéd** adj

**click** n short sharp sound ▷ v make this sound; (informal) (of two people) get on well together; (informal) become suddenly clear; (Computing) press and release (a button on a mouse); (slang) be a success

**client** n person who uses the services of a professional person or company; (Computing) program or work station that requests data from a server ▶ **clientele** [klee-on-**tell**] n clients collectively

**cliff** n steep rock face, esp. along the sea shore ▶ **cliffhanger** n film, game, etc., that is tense and exciting because its outcome is uncertain

**climate** n typical weather conditions of an area ▶ **climatic** adj

**climax** n most intense point of an experience, series of events, or story ▶ **climactic** adj

**climb** v go up, ascend; rise to a higher point or intensity ▷ n climbing; place to be climbed ▶ **climber** n ▶ **climb down** v retreat from an opinion or position

**clime** n (poetic) place or its climate

**clinch** v settle (an argument or agreement) decisively ▶ **clincher** n (informal) something decisive

**cling** v **clinging**, **clung** hold tightly or stick closely ▶ **clingfilm** n thin polythene material for wrapping food

**clinic** n building where outpatients receive medical treatment or advice; private or specialized hospital ▶ **clinical** adj of a clinic; logical and unemotional ▶ **clinically** adv

**clink**¹ v, n (make) a light sharp metallic sound

**clink**² n (Brit, Aust & NZ slang) prison

**clinker** n fused coal left over in a fire or furnace

**clinker-built** adj (of a boat) made of overlapping planks

**clip**¹ v **clipping**, **clipped** cut with shears or scissors; (informal) hit sharply ▷ n short extract of a film; (informal) sharp blow ▶ **clippers** pl n tool for clipping ▶ **clipping** n something cut out, esp. an article from a newspaper

**clip**² n device for attaching or holding things together ▷ v **clipping**, **clipped** attach or hold together with a clip

**clipper** n fast commercial sailing ship

**clique** [kleek] n small exclusive group

**clitoris** [klit-or-iss] *n* small sexually sensitive organ at the front of the vulva ▶ **clitoral** *adj*

**cloak** *n* loose sleeveless outer garment ▷ *v* cover or conceal ▶ **cloakroom** *n* room where coats may be left temporarily

**clobber¹** *v* (*informal*) hit; defeat utterly

**clobber²** *n* (*Brit, Aust & NZ informal*) belongings, esp. clothes

**cloche** [klosh] *n* cover to protect young plants; woman's close-fitting hat

**clock** *n* instrument for showing the time; device with a dial for recording or measuring ▶ **clockwise** *adv, adj* in the direction in which the hands of a clock rotate ▶ **clock in, clock on** *v* register arrival at work on an automatic time recorder ▶ **clock off, clock out** *v* register departure from work ▶ **clock up** *v* reach (a total) ▶ **clockwork** *n* mechanism similar to the kind in a clock, used in wind-up toys

**clod** *n* lump of earth; (*Brit, Aust & NZ*) stupid person

**clog** *v* **clogging, clogged** obstruct ▷ *n* wooden or wooden-soled shoe

**cloister** *n* covered pillared arcade, usu. in a monastery ▶ **cloistered** *adj* sheltered

**clone** *n* animal or plant produced artificially from the cells of another animal or plant, and identical to the original; (*informal*) person who closely resembles another ▷ *v* produce as a clone

**close¹** *v* [rhymes with **nose**] shut; prevent access to; end, terminate; bring or come nearer together ▷ *n* end, conclusion; [rhymes with **dose**] street closed at one end; [rhymes with **dose**] (*Brit*)

courtyard, quadrangle ▶ **closed shop** place of work in which all workers must belong to a particular trade union

**close²** *adj* [rhymes with **dose**] near; intimate; careful, thorough; compact, dense; oppressive, stifling; secretive ▷ *adv* closely, tightly ▶ **closely** *adv* ▶ **closeness** *n* ▶ **close season** period when it is illegal to kill certain game or fish ▶ **close shave** (*informal*) narrow escape ▶ **close-up** *n* photograph or film taken at close range

**closet** *n* (*US*) cupboard; small private room ▷ *adj* private, secret ▷ *v* **closeting, closeted** shut (oneself) away in private

**closure** *n* closing

**clot** *n* soft thick lump formed from liquid; (*Brit, Aust & NZ informal*) stupid person ▷ *v* **clotting, clotted** form soft thick lumps

**cloth** *n* (piece of) woven fabric

**clothe** *v* **clothing, clothed** or **clad** put clothes on; provide with clothes ▶ **clothes** *pl n* articles of dress; bed coverings ▶ **clothing** *n* clothes collectively

**cloud** *n* mass of condensed water vapour floating in the sky; floating mass of smoke, dust, etc.; (*Computing*) internet server used to store data and services ▷ *v* (foll by *over*) become cloudy; confuse; make gloomy or depressed ▷ *adj* of or relating to cloud computing ▶ **cloudless** *adj* ▶ **cloudy** *adj* having a lot of clouds; (of liquid) not clear ▶ **cloudburst** *n* heavy fall of rain ▶ **cloud computing** *n* model of computer use in which internet services are provided to users on a temporary basis

**clout** (*informal*) *n* hard blow; power, influence ▷ *v* hit hard

**clove**[1] n dried flower bud of a tropical tree, used as a spice

**clove**[2] n segment of a bulb of garlic

**clove**[3] v a past tense of **cleave**[1]
▶ **clove hitch** knot used to fasten a rope to a spar

**cloven** v a past participle of **cleave**[1]
▶ **cloven hoof** divided hoof of a cow, goat, etc.

**clover** n plant with three-lobed leaves **in clover** in luxury

**clown** n comic entertainer in a circus; amusing person; stupid person ▷ v behave foolishly; perform as a clown ▶ **clownish** adj ▶ **clownfish** n brightly coloured striped fish

**club** n association of people with common interests; building used by such a group; thick stick used as a weapon; stick with a curved end used to hit the ball in golf; playing card with black three-leaved symbols ▷ v **clubbing, clubbed** hit with a club ▶ **club together** v combine resources for a common purpose

**club foot** n deformity of the foot causing inability to put the foot flat on the ground

**cluck** n low clicking noise made by a hen ▷ v make this noise

**clue** n something that helps to solve a mystery or puzzle **not have a clue** be completely baffled ▶ **clueless** adj stupid

**clump** n small group of things or people; dull heavy tread ▷ v walk heavily; form into clumps

**clumsy** adj **-sier, -siest** lacking skill or physical coordination; badly made or done ▶ **clumsily** adv ▶ **clumsiness** n

**clung** v past of **cling**

**clunk** n dull metallic sound ▷ v make such a sound

**cluster** n small close group ▷ v gather in clusters

**clutch**[1] v grasp tightly; (foll by at) try to get hold of ▷ n device enabling two revolving shafts to be connected and disconnected, esp. in a motor vehicle; tight grasp

**clutch**[2] n set of eggs laid at the same time

**clutter** v scatter objects about (a place) untidily ▷ n untidy mess

**cm** centimetre

**CND** Campaign for Nuclear Disarmament

**CO** Commanding Officer

**Co.** Company; County

**co-** prefix together, joint, or jointly e.g. coproduction

**c/o** care of; (Book-keeping) carried over

**coach** n long-distance bus; railway carriage; large four-wheeled horse-drawn carriage; trainer, instructor ▷ v train, teach

**coagulate** [koh-**ag**-yew-late] v change from a liquid to a semisolid mass ▶ **coagulation** n ▶ **coagulant** n substance causing coagulation

**coal** n black rock consisting mainly of carbon, used as fuel ▶ **coalfield** n area with coal under the ground

**coalesce** [koh-a-**less**] v come together, merge ▶ **coalescence** n

**coalition** [koh-a-**lish**-un] n temporary alliance, esp. between political parties

**coarse** adj rough in texture; unrefined, indecent ▶ **coarsely** adv ▶ **coarseness** n ▶ **coarsen** v ▶ **coarse fish** any freshwater fish not of the salmon family

**coast** n place where the land meets the sea ▷ v move by momentum, without the use of power ▶ **coastal** adj ▶ **coaster** n small mat placed under a glass ▶ **coastguard** n organization that aids ships and swimmers in trouble and prevents smuggling; member of this ▶ **coastline** n outline of a coast

**coat** n outer garment with long sleeves; animal's fur or hair; covering layer e.g. *a coat of paint* ▷ v cover with a layer ▶ **coating** n covering layer ▶ **coat of arms** heraldic emblem of a family or institution

**coax** v persuade gently; obtain by persistent coaxing

**coaxial** [koh-**ax**-ee-al] *adj* (of a cable) transmitting by means of two concentric conductors separated by an insulator

**cob** n stalk of an ear of maize; thickset type of horse; round loaf of bread; male swan

**cobalt** n (*Chem*) brittle silvery-white metallic element

**cobber** n (*Aust & NZ, old-fashioned informal*) friend

**cobble** n cobblestone ▶ **cobblestone** n rounded stone used for paving ▶ **cobble together** v put together clumsily

**cobbler** n shoe mender

**cobia** [**koh**-bee-a] n large dark-striped game fish of tropical and subtropical seas

**cobra** n venomous hooded snake of Asia and Africa

**cobweb** n spider's web

**cocaine** n addictive drug used as a narcotic and as an anaesthetic

**coccyx** [**kok**-six] n, *pl* **coccyges** [kok-**sije**-eez] bone at the base of the spinal column

**cochineal** n red dye obtained from a Mexican insect, used for food colouring

**cock** n male bird, esp. of domestic fowl; stopcock ▷ v draw back (the hammer of a gun) to firing position; lift and turn (part of the body) ▶ **cockerel** n young

domestic cock ▶ **cock-a-hoop** *adj* (*Brit, Aust & NZ*) in high spirits ▶ **cock-and-bull story** highly improbable story

**cockade** n feather or rosette worn on a hat as a badge

**cockatiel, cockateel** n crested Australian parrot with a greyish-brown and yellow plumage

**cockatoo** n crested parrot of Australia or the East Indies

**cocker spaniel** n small spaniel

**cockeyed** *adj* (*informal*) crooked, askew; foolish, absurd

**cockie, cocky** n, *pl* **-kies** (*Aust & NZ informal*) farmer

**cockle** n edible shellfish

**Cockney** n native of the East End of London; London dialect

**cockpit** n pilot's compartment in an aircraft; driver's compartment in a racing car

**cockroach** n beetle-like insect which is a household pest

**cocksure** *adj* overconfident, arrogant

**cocktail** n mixed alcoholic drink; appetizer of seafood or mixed fruits

**cocky** *adj* **cockier, cockiest** conceited and overconfident ▶ **cockily** *adv* ▶ **cockiness** n

**cocoa** n powder made from the seed of the cacao tree; drink made from this powder

**coconut** n large hard fruit of a type of palm tree; edible flesh of this fruit

**cocoon** n silky protective covering of a silkworm; protective covering ▷ v wrap up tightly for protection

**COD** cash on delivery

**cod** n large food fish of the North Atlantic; any other Australian fish of the same family

**coda** n final part of a musical composition

**coddle** v pamper, overprotect

**code** n system of letters, symbols, or prearranged signals by which messages can be communicated secretly or briefly; set of principles or rules ▷ v put into code; write computer programs ▶ **codify** v **-fying, -fied** organize (rules or procedures) systematically ▶ **codification** n

**codeine** [**kode**-een] n drug used as a painkiller

**codex** n, pl **codices** volume of manuscripts of an ancient text

**codger** n (Brit, Aust & NZ informal) old man

**codicil** [**kode**-iss-ill] n addition to a will

**coeducation** n education of boys and girls together ▶ **coeducational** adj

**coefficient** n (Maths) number or constant placed before and multiplying a quantity

**coelacanth** [**seel**-a-kanth] n primitive marine fish

**coeliac disease** [**seel**-ee-ak] n disease which hampers the digestion of food containing gluten

**coerce** [koh-**urss**] v compel, force ▶ **coercion** n ▶ **coercive** adj

**coeval** [koh-**eev**-al] adj, n contemporary

**coexist** v exist together, esp. peacefully despite differences ▶ **coexistence** n

**C of E** Church of England

**coffee** n drink made from the roasted and ground seeds of a tropical shrub; beanlike seeds of this shrub ▷ adj medium-brown ▶ **coffee bar** café, snack bar ▶ **coffee table** small low table

**coffer** n chest for valuables ▷ pl store of money

**coffin** n box in which a corpse is buried or cremated

**cog** n one of the teeth on the rim of a gearwheel; unimportant person in a big organization

**cogent** [**koh**-jent] adj forcefully convincing ▶ **cogency** n

**cogitate** [**koj**-it-tate] v think deeply about ▶ **cogitation** n

**cognac** [**kon**-yak] n French brandy

**cognate** adj derived from a common original form

**cognition** n act or experience of knowing or acquiring knowledge ▶ **cognitive** adj

**cognizance** n knowledge, understanding ▶ **cognizant** adj

**cognoscenti** [kon-yo-**shen**-tee] pl n connoisseurs

**cohabit** v live together without being married ▶ **cohabitation** n

**cohere** v hold or stick together; be logically connected or consistent

**coherent** adj logical and consistent; capable of intelligible speech ▶ **coherence** n ▶ **coherently** adv

**cohesion** n sticking together

**cohesive** adj sticking together to form a whole

**cohort** n band of associates; tenth part of an ancient Roman legion

**coiffure** n hairstyle ▶ **coiffeur, coiffeuse** n hairdresser

**coil** v wind in loops; move in a winding course ▷ n something coiled; single loop of this; coil-shaped contraceptive device inserted in the womb

**coin** n piece of metal money; metal currency collectively ▷ v invent (a word or phrase) **coin it in** (informal) earn money quickly ▶ **coinage** n coins collectively; word or phrase coined; coining

**coincide** v happen at the same time; agree or correspond exactly ▶ **coincidence** n occurrence of simultaneous or apparently connected events; coinciding ▶ **coincident** *adj* in agreement ▶ **coincidental** *adj* resulting from coincidence ▶ **coincidentally** *adv*

**coir** *n* coconut fibre, used for matting

**coitus** [**koh**-it-uss], **coition** [koh-**ish**-un] *n* sexual intercourse ▶ **coital** *adj*

**coke¹** *n* solid fuel left after gas has been distilled from coal

**coke²** *n* (*slang*) cocaine

**col** *n* high mountain pass

**cola** *n* dark brown fizzy soft drink

**colander** *n* perforated bowl for straining or rinsing foods

**cold** *adj* lacking heat; lacking affection or enthusiasm; (of a colour) giving an impression of coldness; (*slang*) unconscious e.g. *out cold* ▷ *n* lack of heat; mild illness causing a runny nose, sneezing, and coughing ▶ **coldly** *adv* ▶ **coldness** *n* ▶ **cold-blooded** *adj* cruel, unfeeling; having a body temperature that varies according to the surrounding temperature ▶ **cold cream** creamy preparation for softening and cleansing the skin ▶ **cold feet** (*slang*) nervousness, fear ▶ **cold-shoulder** *v* treat with indifference ▶ **cold war** political hostility between countries without actual warfare

**coleslaw** *n* salad dish of shredded raw cabbage in a dressing

**coley** *n* codlike food fish of the N Atlantic

**colic** *n* severe pains in the stomach and bowels ▶ **colicky** *adj*

**colitis** [kol-**lie**-tiss] *n* inflammation of the colon

**collaborate** *v* work with another on a project; cooperate with an enemy invader ▶ **collaboration** *n* ▶ **collaborative** *adj* ▶ **collaborator** *n*

**collage** [kol-**lahzh**] *n* art form in which various materials or objects are glued onto a surface; picture made in this way

**collapse** *v* fall down suddenly; fail completely; fold compactly ▷ *n* collapsing; sudden failure or breakdown ▶ **collapsible** *adj*

**collar** *n* part of a garment round the neck; band put round an animal's neck; cut of meat from an animal's neck ▷ *v* (*Brit, Aust & NZ informal*) seize, arrest; catch in order to speak to ▶ **collarbone** *n* bone joining the shoulder blade to the breastbone

**collate** *v* gather together, examine, and put in order ▶ **collation** *n* collating; light meal

**collateral** *n* security pledged for the repayment of a loan

**colleague** *n* fellow worker, esp. in a profession

**collect¹** *v* gather together; accumulate (stamps etc.) as a hobby; fetch ▶ **collected** *adj* calm and controlled ▶ **collection** *n* things collected; collecting; sum of money collected ▶ **collector** *n*

**collect²** *n* short prayer

**collective** *adj* of or done by a group ▷ *n* group of people working together on an enterprise and sharing the benefits from it ▶ **collectively** *adv*

**colleen** *n* (*Irish*) girl

**college** *n* place of higher education; group of people of the same profession or with special duties ▶ **collegiate** *adj*

**collide** *v* crash together violently; have an argument ▶ **collision** *n*

**collie** *n* silky-haired sheepdog

**collier** *n* coal miner; coal ship

**colliery** *n*, *pl* **-lieries** coal mine

**collocate** *v* (of words) occur together regularly ▶ **collocation** *n*

**colloid** *n* suspension of particles in a solution

**colloquial** *adj* suitable for informal speech or writing ▶ **colloquialism** *n* colloquial word or phrase

**collusion** *n* secret or illegal cooperation ▶ **collude** *v* act in collusion

**collywobbles** *pl n* (*slang*) nervousness

**cologne** *n* mild perfume

**colon**¹ *n* punctuation mark (:)

**colon**² *n* part of the large intestine connected to the rectum

**colonel** *n* senior commissioned army or air-force officer

**colonnade** *n* row of columns

**colony** *n*, *pl* **-nies** group of people who settle in a new country but remain under the rule of their homeland; territory occupied by a colony; group of people or animals of the same kind living together ▶ **colonial** *adj*, *n* (inhabitant) of a colony ▶ **colonialism** *n* policy of acquiring and maintaining colonies ▶ **colonist** *n* settler in a colony ▶ **colonize** *v* make into a colony ▶ **colonization** *n*

**Colorado beetle** *n* black-and-yellow beetle that is a serious pest of potatoes

**coloration** *n* arrangement of colours

**colossal** *adj* very large

**colossus** *n*, *pl* **-si** or **-suses** huge statue; huge or important person or thing

**colostomy** *n*, *pl* **-mies** operation to form an opening from the colon onto the surface of the body, for emptying the bowel

**colour** *n* appearance of things as a result of reflecting light; substance that gives colour; complexion ▷ *pl* flag of a country or regiment; (*Sport*) badge or symbol denoting membership of a team ▷ *v* apply colour to; influence (someone's judgment); blush ▶ **coloured** *adj* having colour; (**C-**) (in S Africa) of mixed White and non-White parentage ▶ **colourful** *adj* with bright or varied colours; vivid, distinctive ▶ **colourfully** *adv* ▶ **colourless** *adj* ▶ **colour-blind** *adj* unable to distinguish between certain colours

**colt** *n* young male horse

**columbine** *n* garden flower with five petals

**column** *n* pillar; vertical division of a newspaper page; regular feature in a newspaper; vertical arrangement of numbers; narrow formation of troops ▶ **columnist** *n* journalist who writes a regular feature in a newspaper

**coma** *n* state of deep unconsciousness ▶ **comatose** *adj* in a coma; sound asleep

**comb** *n* toothed implement for arranging the hair; cock's crest; honeycomb ▷ *v* use a comb on; search with great care

**combat** *n*, *v* **-bating, -bated** fight, struggle ▶ **combatant** *n* ▶ **combative** *adj* ▶ **combat trousers, combats** loose casual trousers with large pockets on the legs

**combine** *v* join together ▷ *n* association of people or firms for a common purpose ▶ **combination** *n* combining; people or things combined; set of numbers that opens a special lock ▷ *pl* (*Brit*) old-fashioned undergarment with long sleeves and long legs ▶ **combine harvester** machine that reaps and threshes grain in one process

**combustion** *n* process of burning ▶ **combustible** *adj* burning easily

**come** v **coming, came, come**
move towards a place, arrive;
occur; reach a specified point or
condition; be produced; (foll by
*from*) be born in; become e.g. *a
dream come true* ▸ **come across** v
meet or find by accident; (often
foll by *as*) give an impression of
(being) ▸ **comeback** n (*informal*)
return to a former position; retort
▸ **comedown** n decline in status;
disappointment ▸ **comeuppance**
n (*informal*) deserved punishment

**comedy** n, pl **-dies** humorous play,
film, or programme ▸ **comedian,
comedienne** n entertainer who
tells jokes; person who performs
in comedy

**comely** adj **-lier, -liest** (*old-
fashioned*) nice-looking

**comestibles** pl n (*formal*) food

**comet** n heavenly body with a long
luminous tail

**comfit** n (*old-fashioned*) sugar-
coated sweet

**comfort** n physical ease or
wellbeing; consolation; means of
consolation ▹ v soothe, console
▸ **comfortable** adj giving comfort;
free from pain; (*informal*) well-off
financially ▸ **comfortably** adv
▸ **comforter** n ▸ **comfort food**
simple food that makes the eater
feel better emotionally

**comfrey** n tall plant with bell-
shaped flowers

**comfy** adj **-fier, -fiest** (*informal*)
comfortable

**comic** adj humorous, funny;
of comedy ▹ n comedian;
magazine containing strip
cartoons ▸ **comical** adj amusing
▸ **comically** adv

**comma** n punctuation mark (,)

**command** v order; have authority
over; deserve and get; look
down over ▹ n authoritative
instruction that something
must be done; authority to
command; knowledge; military
or naval unit with a specific
function ▸ **commandant** n officer
commanding a military group
▸ **commandeer** v seize for military
use ▸ **commandment** n command
from God

**commander** n military officer in
command of a group or operation;
middle-ranking naval officer
▸ **commander-in-chief** n, pl
**commanders-in-chief** supreme
commander of a nation's armed
forces

**commando** n, pl **-dos** or **-does**
(member of) a military unit trained
for swift raids in enemy territory

**commemorate** v honour the
memory of ▸ **commemoration** n
▸ **commemorative** adj

> **SPELLING TIP**
> Remember that **commemorate**
> has only three *m*s; a double *m*
> shortly followed by a single

**commence** v begin
▸ **commencement** n

**commend** v praise;
recommend ▸ **commendable**
adj ▸ **commendably** adv
▸ **commendation** n

**commensurable** adj measurable
by the same standards

**commensurate** adj
corresponding in degree, size,
or value

**comment** n remark; talk, gossip;
explanatory note ▹ v make a
comment ▸ **commentary** n, pl
**-taries** spoken accompaniment
to a broadcast or film; explanatory
notes ▸ **commentate** v provide a
commentary ▸ **commentator** n

**commerce** n buying and selling,
trade ▸ **commercial** adj of
commerce; (of television or

radio) paid for by advertisers; having profit as the main aim ▷ *n* television or radio advertisement ▶ **commercialize** *v* make commercial ▶ **commercialization** *n*

**commiserate** *v* (foll by *with*) express sympathy (for) ▶ **commiseration** *n*

**SPELLING TIP**
There are two *m*s in **commiserate**, but only one *s*

**commissar** *n* (formerly) official responsible for political education in Communist countries

**commissariat** *n* (*Brit, Aust & NZ*) military department in charge of food supplies

**commission** *n* piece of work that an artist is asked to do; duty, task; percentage paid to a salesperson for each sale made; group of people appointed to perform certain duties; committing of a crime; (*Mil*) rank or authority officially given to an officer ▷ *v* place an order for; (*Mil*) give a commission to; grant authority to **out of commission** not in working order ▶ **commissioner** *n* appointed official in a government department; member of a commission

**commissionaire** *n* uniformed doorman at a hotel, theatre, etc.

**commit** *v* -**mitting, -mitted** perform (a crime or error); pledge (oneself) to a course of action; send (someone) to prison or hospital ▶ **committal** *n* sending someone to prison or hospital ▶ **commitment** *n* dedication to a cause; responsibility that restricts freedom of action

**SPELLING TIP**
The correct spelling of **commitment** has three *m*s

altogether, but only two *t*s (which are not next to each other)

**committee** *n* group of people appointed to perform a specified service or function

**SPELLING TIP**
Remember **committee** has two *m*s and two *t*s

**commode** *n* seat with a hinged flap concealing a chamber pot; chest of drawers

**commodious** *adj* roomy

**commodity** *n, pl* -**ities** something that can be bought or sold

**commodore** *n* senior commissioned officer in the navy

**common** *adj* occurring often; belonging to two or more people; public, general; lacking in taste or manners ▷ *n* area of grassy land belonging to a community **House of Commons, the Commons** lower chamber of the British parliament ▶ **commonly** *adv* ▶ **commoner** *n* person who does not belong to the nobility ▶ **common-law** *adj* (of a relationship) regarded as a marriage through being long-standing ▶ **Common Market** former name for **European Union** ▶ **commonplace** *adj* ordinary, everyday ▷ *n* trite remark ▶ **common sense** good practical understanding

**commonwealth** *n* state or nation viewed politically; (**C-**) association of independent states that used to be ruled by Britain

**commotion** *n* noisy disturbance

**commune¹** *n* group of people who live together and share everything ▶ **communal** *adj* shared ▶ **communally** *adv*

**commune²** *v* (foll by *with*) feel very close (to) e.g. *communing with* nature ▶ **communion** n sharing of thoughts or feelings; (**C-**) Christian ritual of sharing consecrated bread and wine; religious group with shared beliefs and practices

**communicate** v make known or share (information, thoughts, or feelings) ▶ **communicable** adj (of a disease) able to be passed on ▶ **communicant** n person who receives Communion ▶ **communicating** adj (of a door) joining two rooms ▶ **communication** n communicating; thing communicated ▷ pl means of travelling or sending messages ▶ **communicative** adj talking freely

**communiqué** [kom-**mune**-ik-kay] n official announcement

**communism** n belief that all property and means of production should be shared by the community; (**C-**) system of state control of the economy and society in some countries ▶ **communist** n, adj

**community** n, pl -**ties** all the people living in one district; group with shared origins or interests; the public, society ▶ **community centre** building used by a community for activities

**commute** v travel daily to and from work; reduce (a sentence) to a less severe one ▶ **commutator** n device used to change alternating electric current into direct current

**commuter** n person who commutes to and from work

**compact**¹ adj closely packed; neatly arranged; concise, brief ▷ n small flat case containing a mirror and face powder ▷ v pack closely together ▶ **compactly** adv ▶ **compactness** n ▶ **compact disc** small digital audio disc on which the sound is read by an optical laser system

**compact**² n contract, agreement

**companion** n person who associates with or accompanies someone ▶ **companionable** adj friendly ▶ **companionship** n

**companionway** n ladder linking the decks of a ship

**company** n, pl -**nies** business organization; group of actors; fact of being with someone; guest or guests

**compare** v examine (things) and point out the resemblances or differences; (foll by to) declare to be (like); (foll by with) be worthy of comparison ▶ **comparable** adj ▶ **comparability** n ▶ **comparative** adj relative; involving comparison; (Grammar) denoting the form of an adjective or adverb indicating more ▷ n (Grammar) comparative form of a word ▶ **comparatively** adv ▶ **comparison** n comparing; similarity or equivalence

**compartment** n section of a railway carriage; separate section

**compass** n instrument for showing direction, with a needle that points north; limits, range ▷ pl hinged instrument for drawing circles

**compassion** n pity, sympathy ▶ **compassionate** adj

**compatible** adj able to exist, work, or be used together ▶ **compatibility** n

**compatriot** n fellow countryman or countrywoman

**compel** v -**pelling**, -**pelled** force (to be or do)

**compendium** n, pl -**diums** or -**dia** selection of board games in one box ▶ **compendious** adj brief but comprehensive

**compensate** v make amends to (someone), esp. for injury or loss;

(foll by *for*) cancel out (a bad effect) ▶ **compensation** *n* payment to make up for loss or injury ▶ **compensatory** *adj*

**compere** *n* person who presents a stage, radio, or television show ▷ *v* be the compere of

**compete** *v* try to win or achieve (a prize, profit, etc.) ▶ **competition** *n* competing; event in which people compete; people against whom one competes ▶ **competitive** *adj* ▶ **competitor** *n*

**competent** *adj* having the skill or knowledge to do something well ▶ **competently** *adv* ▶ **competence** *n*

**compile** *v* collect and arrange (information), esp. to make a book ▶ **compilation** *n* ▶ **compiler** *n*

**complacent** *adj* self-satisfied ▶ **complacently** *adv* ▶ **complacency** *n*

**complain** *v* express resentment or displeasure; (foll by *of*) say that one is suffering from (an illness) ▶ **complaint** *n* complaining; mild illness ▶ **complainant** *n* (*Law*) plaintiff

**complaisant** [kom-**play**-zant] *adj* willing to please ▶ **complaisance** *n*

**complement** *n* thing that completes something; complete amount or number; (*Grammar*) word or words added to a verb to complete the meaning ▷ *v* make complete ▶ **complementary** *adj*

> **USAGE NOTE**
> Avoid confusing this word with *compliment*

**complete** *adj* thorough, absolute; finished; having all the necessary parts ▷ *v* finish; make whole or perfect ▶ **completely** *adv* ▶ **completeness** *n* ▶ **completion** *n* finishing

**complex** *adj* made up of parts; complicated ▷ *n* whole made up of parts; group of unconscious feelings that influences behaviour ▶ **complexity** *n*

**complexion** *n* skin of the face; character, nature

**compliance** *n* complying; tendency to do what others want ▶ **compliant** *adj*

**complicate** *v* make or become complex or difficult to deal with ▶ **complication** *n*

**complicity** *n* fact of being an accomplice in a crime

**compliment** *n* expression of praise ▷ *pl* formal greetings ▷ *v* praise ▶ **complimentary** *adj* expressing praise; free of charge

> **USAGE NOTE**
> Avoid confusing this word with *complement*

**compline** *n* last service of the day in the Roman Catholic Church

**comply** *v* -**plying**, -**plied** (foll by *with*) act in accordance (with)

**component** *n*, *adj* (being) part of a whole

**comport** *v* (*formal*) behave (oneself) in a specified way

**compose** *v* put together; be the component parts of; create (a piece of music or writing); calm (oneself); arrange artistically

**composer** *n* person who writes music

**composite** *n*, *adj* (something) made up of separate parts

**composition** *n* way that something is put together or arranged; work of art, esp. a musical one; essay; composing

**compositor** *n* person who arranges type for printing

**compos mentis** *adj* (*Latin*) sane

**compost** *n* decayed plants used as a fertilizer

**composure** n calmness

**compote** n fruit stewed with sugar

**compound**[1] n, adj (thing, esp. chemical) made up of two or more combined parts or elements ▷ v combine or make by combining; intensify, make worse

**compound**[2] n fenced enclosure containing buildings

**comprehend** v understand
▶ **comprehensible** adj
▶ **comprehension** n
▶ **comprehensive** adj of broad scope, fully inclusive ▷ n (Brit) comprehensive school
▶ **comprehensive school** (Brit) secondary school for children of all abilities

**compress** v [kum-**press**] squeeze together; make shorter ▷ n [**kom**-press] pad applied to stop bleeding or cool inflammation
▶ **compression** n ▶ **compressor** n machine that compresses gas or air

**comprise** v be made up of or make up

**USAGE NOTE**
Comprise is not followed by of but directly by its object

**compromise** [kom-prom-mize] n settlement reached by concessions on each side ▷ v settle a dispute by making concessions; put in a dishonourable position

**comptroller** n (in titles) financial controller

**compulsion** n irresistible urge; forcing by threats or violence ▶ **compulsive** adj
▶ **compulsively** adv
▶ **compulsory** adj required by rules or laws

**compunction** n feeling of guilt or shame

**compute** v calculate, esp. using a computer ▶ **computation** n

**computer** n electronic machine that stores and processes data

▶ **computerize** v adapt (a system) to be handled by computer; store or process in a computer
▶ **computerization** n

**comrade** n fellow member of a union or socialist political party; companion ▶ **comradeship** n

**con**[1] (informal) n short for **confidence trick** ▷ v **conning, conned** deceive, swindle

**con**[2] n pros and cons see **pro**[1]

**concatenation** n series of linked events

**concave** adj curving inwards

**conceal** v cover and hide; keep secret ▶ **concealment** n

**concede** v admit to be true; acknowledge defeat in (a contest or argument); grant as a right

**conceit** n too high an opinion of oneself; far-fetched or clever comparison ▶ **conceited** adj

**conceive** v imagine, think; form in the mind; become pregnant
▶ **conceivable** adj imaginable, possible ▶ **conceivably** adv

**concentrate** v fix one's attention or efforts on something; bring or come together in large numbers in one place; make (a liquid) stronger by removing water from it ▷ n concentrated liquid ▶ **concentration** n concentrating; proportion of a substance in a mixture or solution
▶ **concentration camp** prison camp for civilian prisoners, esp. in Nazi Germany

**concentric** adj having the same centre

**concept** n abstract or general idea ▶ **conceptual** adj of or based on concepts
▶ **conceptualize** v form a concept of

**conception** n general idea; becoming pregnant

**concern** *n* anxiety, worry; something that is of importance to someone; business, firm ▷ *v* worry (someone); involve (oneself); be relevant or important to ▶ **concerned** *adj* interested, involved; anxious, worried ▶ **concerning** *prep* about, regarding

**concert** *n* musical entertainment **in concert** working together; (of musicians) performing live ▶ **concerted** *adj* done together

**concertina** *n* small musical instrument similar to an accordion ▷ *v* **-naing, -naed** collapse or fold up like a concertina

**concerto** [kon-**chair**-toe] *n, pl* **-tos** *or* **-ti** large-scale composition for a solo instrument and orchestra

**concession** *n* grant of rights, land, or property; reduction in price for a specified category of people; conceding; thing conceded ▶ **concessionary** *adj*

**conch** *n* shellfish with a large spiral shell; its shell

**concierge** [kon-see-**airzh**] *n* (in France) caretaker in a block of flats

**conciliate** *v* try to end a disagreement (with) ▶ **conciliation** *n* ▶ **conciliator** *n*

**conciliatory** *adj* intended to end a disagreement

**concise** *adj* brief and to the point ▶ **concisely** *adv* ▶ **concision, conciseness** *n*

**conclave** *n* secret meeting; private meeting of cardinals to elect a new pope

**conclude** *v* decide by reasoning; end, finish; arrange or settle finally ▶ **conclusion** *n* decision based on reasoning; ending; final arrangement or settlement ▶ **conclusive** *adj* ending doubt, convincing ▶ **conclusively** *adv*

**concoct** *v* make up (a story or plan); make by combining ingredients ▶ **concoction** *n*

**concomitant** *adj* existing along with something else

**concord** *n* state of peaceful agreement, harmony ▶ **concordance** *n* similarity or consistency; index of words in a book ▶ **concordant** *adj* agreeing

**concourse** *n* large open public place where people can gather; large crowd

**concrete** *n* mixture of cement, sand, stone, and water, used in building ▷ *adj* made of concrete; particular, specific; real or solid, not abstract

**concubine** [kon-kew-bine] *n* (*Hist*) woman living in a man's house but not married to him and kept for his sexual pleasure

**concupiscence** [kon-**kew**-piss-enss] *n* (*formal*) lust

**concur** *v* **-curring, -curred** agree ▶ **concurrence** *n* ▶ **concurrent** *adj* happening at the same time or place ▶ **concurrently** *adv* at the same time

**concussion** *n* period of unconsciousness caused by a blow to the head ▶ **concussed** *adj* having concussion

**condemn** *v* express disapproval of; sentence e.g. *he was condemned to death*; force into an unpleasant situation; declare unfit for use ▶ **condemnation** *n* ▶ **condemnatory** *adj*

**condense** *v* make shorter; turn from gas into liquid ▶ **condensation** *n* ▶ **condenser** *n* (*Electricity*) capacitor

**condescend** *v* behave patronizingly towards someone; agree to do something, but as if doing someone a favour ▶ **condescension** *n*

c

**condiment** n seasoning for food, such as salt or pepper

**condition** n particular state of being; necessary requirement for something else to happen; restriction, qualification; state of health, physical fitness; medical problem ▷ pl circumstances ▷ v train or influence to behave in a particular way; treat with conditioner; control **on condition that** only if ▶ **conditional** adj depending on circumstances ▶ **conditioner** n thick liquid used when washing to make hair or clothes feel softer

**condolence** n sympathy ▷ pl expression of sympathy

**condom** n rubber sheath worn on the penis or in the vagina during sexual intercourse to prevent conception or infection

**condominium** n (Aust, US & Canadian) block of flats in which each flat is owned by the occupant

**condone** v overlook or forgive (wrongdoing)

**condor** n large vulture of S America

**conducive** adj (foll by to) likely to lead (to)

**conduct** n management of an activity; behaviour ▷ v carry out (a task); behave (oneself); direct (musicians) by moving the hands or a baton; lead, guide; transmit (heat or electricity) ▶ **conduction** n transmission of heat or electricity ▶ **conductivity** n ability to transmit heat or electricity ▶ **conductive** adj ▶ **conductor** n person who conducts musicians; (fem **conductress**) official on a bus who collects fares; something that conducts heat or electricity

**conduit** [kon-dew-it] n channel or tube for fluid or cables

**cone** n object with a circular base, tapering to a point; cone-shaped ice-cream wafer; (Brit, Aust & NZ) plastic cone used as a traffic marker on the roads; scaly fruit of a conifer tree

**coney** n same as **cony**

**confab** n (informal) conversation (also **confabulation**)

**confection** n any sweet food; (old-fashioned) elaborate article of clothing

**confectioner** n maker or seller of confectionery ▶ **confectionery** n sweets

**confederate** n member of a confederacy; accomplice ▷ adj united, allied ▷ v unite in a confederacy ▶ **confederacy** n, pl **-cies** union of states or people for a common purpose ▶ **confederation** n alliance of political units

**confer** v **-ferring, -ferred** discuss together; grant, give ▶ **conferment** n granting, giving

**conference** n meeting for discussion

**confess** v admit (a fault or crime); admit to be true; declare (one's sins) to God or a priest, in hope of forgiveness ▶ **confession** n something confessed; confessing ▶ **confessional** n small stall in which a priest hears confessions ▶ **confessor** n priest who hears confessions

**confetti** n small pieces of coloured paper thrown at weddings

**confidant** n person confided in ▶ **confidante** n fem

**confide** v tell someone (a secret); entrust

**confidence** n trust; self-assurance; something confided **in confidence** as a secret ▶ **confidence trick** swindle involving gaining a person's trust in order to cheat him or her

**confident** *adj* sure, esp. of oneself ▶ **confidently** *adv* ▶ **confidential** *adj* private, secret; entrusted with someone's secret affairs ▶ **confidentially** *adv* ▶ **confidentiality** *n*

**configuration** *n* arrangement of parts

**confine** *v* keep within bounds; restrict the free movement of ▶ **confines** *pl n* boundaries, limits ▶ **confinement** *n* being confined; period of childbirth

**confirm** *v* prove to be true; reaffirm, strengthen; administer the rite of confirmation to ▶ **confirmation** *n* confirming; something that confirms; (*Christianity*) rite that admits a baptized person to full church membership ▶ **confirmed** *adj* firmly established in a habit or condition

**confiscate** *v* seize (property) by authority ▶ **confiscation** *n*

**conflagration** *n* large destructive fire

**conflate** *v* combine or blend into a whole ▶ **conflation** *n*

**conflict** *n* disagreement; struggle or fight ▷ *v* be incompatible

**confluence** *n* place where two rivers join

**conform** *v* comply with accepted standards or customs; (foll by *to* or *with*) be like or in accordance with ▶ **conformist** *n, adj* (person) complying with accepted standards or customs ▶ **conformity** *n* compliance with accepted standards or customs

**confound** *v* astound, bewilder; confuse ▶ **confounded** *adj* (old-fashioned) damned

**confront** *v* come face to face with ▶ **confrontation** *n* serious argument

**confuse** *v* mix up; perplex, disconcert; make unclear ▶ **confusion** *n*

**confute** *v* prove wrong

**conga** *n* dance performed by a number of people in single file; large single-headed drum played with the hands

**congeal** *v* (of a liquid) become thick and sticky

**congenial** *adj* pleasant, agreeable; having similar interests and attitudes ▶ **congeniality** *n*

**congenital** *adj* (of a condition) existing from birth ▶ **congenitally** *adv*

**conger** *n* large sea eel

**congested** *adj* crowded to excess ▶ **congestion** *n*

**conglomerate** *n* large corporation made up of many companies; thing made up of several different elements ▷ *v* form into a mass ▷ *adj* made up of several different elements ▶ **conglomeration** *n*

**congratulate** *v* express one's pleasure to (someone) at his or her good fortune or success ▶ **congratulations** *pl n, interj* ▶ **congratulatory** *adj*

**congregate** *v* gather together in a crowd ▶ **congregation** *n* people who attend a church ▶ **congregational** *adj* ▶ **Congregationalism** *n* Protestant denomination in which each church is self-governing ▶ **Congregationalist** *adj, n*

**congress** *n* formal meeting for discussion; (**C-**) federal parliament of the US ▶ **congressional** *adj* ▶ **Congressman, Congresswoman** *n* member of Congress

**congruent** *adj* similar, corresponding; (*Geom*) identical in shape and size ▶ **congruence** *n*

**conical** adj cone-shaped
**conifer** n cone-bearing tree, such as the fir or pine ▶ **coniferous** adj
**conjecture** n, v guess ▶ **conjectural** adj
**conjugal** adj of marriage
**conjugate** v give the inflections of (a verb) ▶ **conjugation** n complete set of inflections of a verb
**conjunction** n combination; simultaneous occurrence of events; part of speech joining words, phrases, or clauses
**conjunctivitis** n inflammation of the membrane covering the eyeball and inner eyelid ▶ **conjunctiva** n this membrane
**conjure** v perform tricks that appear to be magic ▶ **conjuror** n ▶ **conjure up** v produce as if by magic
**conk** n (*Brit, Aust & NZ slang*) nose
**conker** n (*informal*) nut of the horse chestnut
**conk out** v (*informal*) (of a machine) break down
**connect** v join together; associate in the mind ▶ **connection, connexion** n relationship, association; link or bond; opportunity to transfer from one public vehicle to another; influential acquaintance ▶ **connective** adj
**conning tower** n raised observation tower containing the periscope on a submarine
**connive** v (foll by *at*) allow (wrongdoing) by ignoring it; conspire ▶ **connivance** n
**connoisseur** [kon-noss-**sir**] n person with special knowledge of the arts, food, or drink
**connotation** n associated idea conveyed by a word ▶ **connote** v
**connubial** adj (*formal*) of marriage
**conquer** v defeat; overcome (a difficulty); take (a place) by force ▶ **conqueror** n ▶ **conquest** n conquering; person or thing conquered
**conscience** n sense of right or wrong as regards thoughts and actions
**conscientious** adj painstaking ▶ **conscientiously** adv ▶ **conscientious objector** person who refuses to serve in the armed forces on moral or religious grounds
**conscious** adj alert and awake; aware; deliberate, intentional ▶ **consciously** adv ▶ **consciousness** n
**conscript** n person enrolled for compulsory military service ▷ v enrol (someone) for compulsory military service ▶ **conscription** n
**consecrate** v make sacred; dedicate to a specific purpose ▶ **consecration** n
**consecutive** adj in unbroken succession ▶ **consecutively** adv
**consensus** n general agreement

> **SPELLING TIP**
> Note the spelling of this word; it is often misspelled *concensus*, perhaps because people think it is related to the word *census*

> **USAGE NOTE**
> In view of its meaning, it is redundant to say 'a consensus of opinion'

**consent** n agreement, permission ▷ v (foll by *to*) permit, agree to
**consequence** n result, effect; importance ▶ **consequent** adj resulting ▶ **consequently** adv as a result, therefore ▶ **consequential** adj important
**conservative** adj opposing change; moderate, cautious; conventional in style; (**C-**) of the Conservative Party, the British right-wing political party which

believes in private enterprise and capitalism ▷ *n* conservative person; (C-) supporter or member of the Conservative Party ▶ **conservatism** *n*

**conservatoire** [kon-**serv**-a-twahr] *n* school of music

**conservatory** *n, pl* **-ries** room with glass walls and a glass roof, attached to a house; (*chiefly US*) conservatoire

**conserve** *v* protect from harm, decay, or loss; preserve (fruit) with sugar ▷ *n* jam containing large pieces of fruit ▶ **conservancy** *n* environmental conservation ▶ **conservation** *n* protection of natural resources and the environment; conserving ▶ **conservationist** *n*

**consider** *v* regard as; think about; be considerate of; discuss; look at ▶ **considerable** *adj* large in amount or degree ▶ **considerably** *adv* ▶ **considerate** *adj* thoughtful towards others ▶ **considerately** *adv* ▶ **consideration** *n* careful thought; fact that should be considered; thoughtfulness; payment for a service ▶ **considering** *prep* taking (a specified fact) into account

**consign** *v* put somewhere; send (goods) ▶ **consignment** *n* shipment of goods

**consist** *v* **consist of** be made up of **consist in** have as its main or only feature

**consistent** *adj* unchanging, constant; (foll by *with*) in agreement ▶ **consistently** *adv* ▶ **consistency** *n, pl* **-cies** being consistent; degree of thickness or smoothness

**console¹** *v* comfort in distress ▶ **consolation** *n* consoling; person or thing that consoles

**console²** *n* panel of controls for electronic equipment; same as **games console**; cabinet for a television or audio equipment; ornamental wall bracket; part of an organ containing the pedals, stops, and keys

**consolidate** *v* make or become stronger or more stable; combine into a whole ▶ **consolidation** *n*

**consommé** [kon-**som**-may] *n* thin clear meat soup

**consonant** *n* speech sound made by partially or completely blocking the breath stream, such as *b* or *f*; letter representing this ▷ *adj* (foll by *with*) agreeing (with) ▶ **consonance** *n* agreement, harmony

**consort** *v* (foll by *with*) keep company (with) ▷ *n* husband or wife of a monarch

**consortium** *n, pl* **-tia** association of business firms

**conspectus** *n* (*formal*) survey or summary

**conspicuous** *adj* clearly visible; noteworthy, striking ▶ **conspicuously** *adv*

**conspire** *v* plan a crime together in secret; act together as if by design ▶ **conspiracy** *n, pl* **-cies** conspiring; plan made by conspiring ▶ **conspirator** *n* ▶ **conspiratorial** *adj*

**constable** *n* police officer of the lowest rank ▶ **constabulary** *n, pl* **-laries** police force of an area

**constant** *adj* continuous; unchanging; faithful ▷ *n* unvarying quantity; something that stays the same ▶ **constantly** *adv* ▶ **constancy** *n*

**constellation** *n* group of stars

**consternation** *n* anxiety or dismay

**constipation** n difficulty in defecating ▶ **constipated** adj having constipation

**constituent** n member of a constituency; component part ▷ adj forming part of a whole ▶ **constituency** n, pl -**cies** area represented by a Member of Parliament; voters in such an area

**constitute** v form, make up ▶ **constitution** n principles on which a state is governed; physical condition; structure ▶ **constitutional** adj of a constitution; in accordance with a political constitution ▷ n walk taken for exercise ▶ **constitutionally** adv

**constrain** v compel, force; limit, restrict ▶ **constraint** n

**constrict** v make narrower by squeezing ▶ **constriction** n ▶ **constrictive** adj ▶ **constrictor** n large snake that squeezes its prey to death; muscle that compresses an organ

**construct** v build or put together ▶ **construction** n constructing; thing constructed; interpretation; (Grammar) way in which words are arranged in a sentence, clause, or phrase ▶ **constructive** adj (of advice, criticism, etc.) useful and helpful ▶ **constructively** adv

**construe** v -**struing**, -**strued** interpret

**consul** n official representing a state in a foreign country; one of the two chief magistrates in ancient Rome ▶ **consular** adj ▶ **consulate** n workplace or position of a consul ▶ **consulship** n

**consult** v go to for advice or information ▶ **consultant** n specialist doctor with a senior position in a hospital; specialist who gives professional advice

▶ **consultancy** n, pl -**cies** work or position of a consultant ▶ **consultation** n (meeting for) consulting ▶ **consultative** adj giving advice

**consume** v eat or drink; use up; destroy; obsess ▶ **consumption** n amount consumed; consuming; (old-fashioned) tuberculosis ▶ **consumptive** n, adj (old-fashioned) (person) having tuberculosis

**consumer** n person who buys goods or uses services

**consummate** v [kon-sum-mate] make (a marriage) legal by sexual intercourse; complete or fulfil ▷ adj [kon-**sum**-mit] supremely skilled; complete, extreme ▶ **consummation** n

**cont.** continued

**contact** n communicating; touching; useful acquaintance; connection between two electrical conductors in a circuit ▷ v get in touch with ▶ **contact lens** lens placed on the eyeball to correct defective vision

**contagion** n passing on of disease by contact; disease spread by contact; spreading of a harmful influence ▶ **contagious** adj spreading by contact, catching

**contain** v hold or be capable of holding; consist of; control, restrain ▶ **container** n object used to hold or store things in; large standard-sized box for transporting cargo by truck or ship ▶ **containment** n prevention of the spread of something harmful

**contaminate** v make impure, pollute; make radioactive ▶ **contaminant** n contaminating substance ▶ **contamination** n

**contemplate** v think deeply; consider as a possibility;

gaze at ▷ **contemplation** n
▷ **contemplative** adj

**contemporary** adj present-day, modern; living or occurring at the same time ▷ n, pl **-raries** person or thing living or occurring at the same time as another ▷ **contemporaneous** adj happening at the same time

> **SPELLING TIP**
> It's easy to miss a syllable out when you say **contemporary**. Syllables get lost from spellings too - for example, *contempory* is a common mistake. But remember that the correct spelling ends in *orary*.

**contempt** n dislike and disregard; open disrespect for the authority of a court ▷ **contemptible** adj deserving contempt ▷ **contemptuous** adj showing contempt ▷ **contemptuously** adv

**contend** v (foll by *with*) deal with; state, assert; compete

**contender** n competitor, esp. a strong one

**content**¹ n meaning or substance of a piece of writing; amount of a substance in a mixture ▷ pl what something contains; list of chapters at the front of a book

**content**² adj satisfied with things as they are ▷ v make (someone) content ▷ n happiness and satisfaction ▷ **contented** adj ▷ **contentment** n

**contention** n disagreement or dispute; point asserted in argument ▷ **contentious** adj causing disagreement; quarrelsome

**contest** n competition or struggle ▷ v dispute, object to; fight or compete for ▷ **contestant** n

**context** n circumstances of an event or fact; words before and

after a word or sentence that help make its meaning clear ▷ **contextual** adj

**contiguous** adj very near or touching

**continent**¹ n one of the earth's large masses of land **the Continent** mainland of Europe ▷ **continental** adj ▷ **continental breakfast** light breakfast of coffee and rolls

**continent**² adj able to control one's bladder and bowels; sexually restrained ▷ **continence** n

**contingent** n group of people that represents or is part of a larger group ▷ adj (foll by *on*) dependent on (something uncertain) ▷ **contingency** n, pl **-cies** something that may happen

**continue** v **-tinuing, -tinued** (cause to) remain in a condition or place; carry on (doing something); resume ▷ **continual** adj constant; recurring frequently ▷ **continually** adv ▷ **continuance** n continuing ▷ **continuation** n continuing; part added ▷ **continuity** n, pl **-ties** smooth development or sequence ▷ **continuous** adj continuing uninterrupted ▷ **continuously** adv

**continuo** n, pl **-tinuos** (*Music*) continuous bass part, usu. played on a keyboard instrument

**continuum** n, pl **-tinua** or **-tinuums** continuous series

**contort** v twist out of shape ▷ **contortion** n ▷ **contortionist** n performer who contorts his or her body to entertain

**contour** n outline; (also **contour line**) line on a map joining places of the same height

**contra-** *prefix* against or contrasting e.g. *contraflow*

**contraband** n, adj smuggled (goods)

**contraception** n prevention of pregnancy by artificial means ▶ **contraceptive** n device used or pill taken to prevent pregnancy ▷ adj preventing pregnancy

**contract** n (document setting out) a formal agreement ▷ v make a formal agreement (to do something); make or become smaller or shorter; catch (an illness) ▶ **contraction** n ▶ **contractor** n firm that supplies materials or labour ▶ **contractual** adj

**contradict** v declare the opposite of (a statement) to be true; be at variance with ▶ **contradiction** n ▶ **contradictory** adj

**contraflow** n flow of traffic going alongside but in an opposite direction to the usual flow

**contralto** n, pl **-tos** (singer with) the lowest female voice

**contraption** n strange-looking device

**contrapuntal** adj (Music) of or in counterpoint

**contrary** n complete opposite ▷ adj opposed, completely different; perverse, obstinate ▷ adv in opposition ▶ **contrarily** adv ▶ **contrariness** n ▶ **contrariwise** adv

**contrast** n obvious difference; person or thing very different from another ▷ v compare in order to show differences; (foll by with) be very different (from)

**contravene** v break (a rule or law) ▶ **contravention** n

**contretemps** [**kon**-tra-tahn] n, pl **-temps** embarrassing minor disagreement

**contribute** v give for a common purpose or fund; (foll by to) be partly responsible (for) ▶ **contribution** n ▶ **contributor** n ▶ **contributory** adj

**contrite** adj sorry and apologetic ▶ **contritely** adv ▶ **contrition** n

**contrive** v make happen; devise or construct ▶ **contrivance** n device; plan; contriving ▶ **contrived** adj planned or artificial

**control** n power to direct something; curb or check ▷ pl instruments used to operate a machine ▷ v **-trolling, -trolled** have power over; limit, restrain; regulate, operate ▶ **controllable** adj ▶ **controller** n

**controversy** n, pl **-sies** fierce argument or debate ▶ **controversial** adj causing controversy

**contumely** [**kon**-tume-mill-ee] n (lit) scornful or insulting treatment

**contusion** n (formal) bruise

**conundrum** n riddle

**conurbation** n large urban area formed by the growth and merging of towns

**convalesce** v recover after an illness or operation ▶ **convalescence** n ▶ **convalescent** n, adj

**convection** n transmission of heat in liquids or gases by the circulation of currents ▶ **convector** n heater that gives out hot air

**convene** v gather or summon for a formal meeting ▶ **convener, convenor** n person who calls a meeting

**convenient** adj suitable or opportune; easy to use; nearby ▶ **conveniently** adv ▶ **convenience** n quality of being convenient; useful object; (euphemistic) public toilet

**convent** n building where nuns live; school run by nuns

**convention** n widely accepted view of proper behaviour; assembly or meeting; formal

agreement ▶ **conventional**
*adj* (unthinkingly) following the
accepted customs; customary;
(of weapons or warfare) not
nuclear ▶ **conventionally** *adv*
▶ **conventionality** *n*
**converge** *v* meet or join
▶ **convergence** *n*
**conversant** *adj* **conversant with**
having knowledge or experience of
**conversation** *n* informal
talk ▶ **conversational** *adj*
▶ **conversationalist** *n* person with
a specified ability at conversation
**converse¹** *v* have a conversation
**converse²** *adj, n* opposite or
contrary ▶ **conversely** *adv*
**convert** *v* change in form, character,
or function; cause to change in
opinion or belief ▷ *n* person who
has converted to a different belief
or religion ▶ **conversion** *n* (thing
resulting from) converting; (*Rugby*)
score made after a try by kicking the
ball over the crossbar ▶ **convertible**
*adj* capable of being converted ▷ *n*
car with a folding or removable roof
**convex** *adj* curving outwards
**convey** *v* communicate
(information); carry, transport
▶ **conveyance** *n* (*old-fashioned*)
vehicle; transfer of the legal title
to property ▶ **conveyancing** *n*
branch of law dealing with the
transfer of ownership of property
▶ **conveyor belt** continuous
moving belt for transporting
things, esp. in a factory
**convict** *v* declare guilty ▷ *n*
person serving a prison sentence
▶ **conviction** *n* firm belief; instance
of being convicted
**convince** *v* persuade by argument
or evidence ▶ **convincing** *adj*
▶ **convincingly** *adv*
**convivial** *adj* sociable, lively
▶ **conviviality** *n*

**convocation** *n* calling together;
large formal meeting ▶ **convoke** *v*
call together
**convoluted** *adj* coiled, twisted;
(of an argument or sentence)
complex and hard to understand
▶ **convolution** *n*
**convolvulus** *n* twining plant with
funnel-shaped flowers
**convoy** *n* group of vehicles or ships
travelling together
**convulse** *v* (of part of the body)
undergo violent spasms; (*informal*)
(be) overcome with laughter
▶ **convulsion** *n* violent muscular
spasm ▷ *pl* uncontrollable laughter
▶ **convulsive** *adj*
**cony** *n, pl* **conies** (*Brit*) rabbit;
rabbit fur
**coo** *v* **cooing, cooed** (of a dove or
pigeon) make a soft murmuring
sound
**cooee** *interj* (*Brit, Aust & NZ*) call to
attract attention
**cook** *v* prepare (food) by heating;
(of food) be cooked ▷ *n* person who
cooks food **cook the books** falsify
accounts ▶ **cooker** *n* (*chiefly Brit*)
apparatus for cooking heated by
gas or electricity; apple suitable for
cooking ▶ **cookery** *n* art of cooking
▶ **cookie** *n* (*US*) biscuit; (*Computing*)
item of data allowing user of a
website to be identified on future
visits ▶ **cook up** *v* (*informal*) devise
(a story or scheme)
**Cooktown orchid** *n* purple
Australian orchid
**cool** *adj* moderately cold; calm
and unemotional; indifferent or
unfriendly; (*informal*) sophisticated
or excellent; (*informal*) (of a
large sum of money) without
exaggeration e.g. *a cool million* ▷ *v*
make or become cool ▷ *n* coolness;
(*slang*) calmness, composure
▶ **coolly** *adv* ▶ **coolness** *n*

▶ **coolant** n fluid used to cool machinery while it is working
▶ **cool drink** (SAfr) nonalcoholic drink ▶ **cooler** n container for making or keeping things cool

**coolibah** n Australian eucalypt that grows beside rivers

**coolie** n (old-fashioned offens) unskilled Oriental labourer

**coomb, coombe** n (S English) short valley or deep hollow

**coon** n (SAfr offens) person of mixed race

**coop**[1] n cage or pen for poultry
▶ **coop up** v confine in a restricted place

**coop**[2] [koh-op] n (Brit, US & Aust) (shop run by) a cooperative society

**cooper** n person who makes or repairs barrels

**cooperate** v work or act together
▶ **cooperation** n ▶ **cooperative** adj willing to cooperate; (of an enterprise) owned and managed collectively ▷ n cooperative organization

**coopt** [koh-**opt**] v add (someone) to a group by the agreement of the existing members

**coordinate** v bring together and cause to work together efficiently ▷ n (Maths) any of a set of numbers defining the location of a point ▷ pl clothes designed to be worn together ▶ **coordination** n ▶ **coordinator** n

**coot** n small black water bird

**cop** (slang) n policeman ▷ v **copping, copped** take or seize **cop it** get into trouble or be punished ▶ **cop out** ▷ v avoid taking responsibility or committing oneself

**cope**[1] v (often foll by with) deal successfully (with)

**cope**[2] n large ceremonial cloak worn by some Christian priests

**coping** n sloping top row of a wall

**copious** [**kope**-ee-uss] adj abundant, plentiful
▶ **copiously** adv

**copper**[1] n soft reddish-brown metal; copper or bronze coin
▶ **copper-bottomed** adj financially reliable ▶ **copperplate** n fine handwriting style

**copper**[2] n (Brit slang) policeman

**coppice, copse** n small group of trees growing close together

**copra** n dried oil-yielding kernel of the coconut

**copulate** v have sexual intercourse
▶ **copulation** n

**copy** n, pl **copies** thing made to look exactly like another; single specimen of a book etc.; material for printing ▷ v **copying, copied** make a copy of; act or try to be like ▶ **copyright** n exclusive legal right to reproduce and control a book, work of art, etc. ▷ v take out a copyright on ▷ adj protected by copyright ▶ **copywriter** n person who writes advertising copy

**coquette** n woman who flirts
▶ **coquettish** adj

**coracle** n small round boat of wicker covered with skins

**coral** n hard substance formed from the skeletons of very small sea animals ▷ adj orange-pink

**cor anglais** n, pl **cors anglais** woodwind instrument similar to the oboe

**cord** n thin rope or thick string; cordlike structure in the body; corduroy ▷ pl corduroy trousers

**cordial** adj warm and friendly ▷ n drink with a fruit base ▶ **cordially** adv ▶ **cordiality** n

**cordite** n explosive used in guns and bombs

**cordon** n chain of police, soldiers, etc., guarding an area ▶ **cordon off** v form a cordon round

**cordon bleu** [bluh] adj (of cookery or cooks) of the highest standard

**corduroy** n cotton fabric with a velvety ribbed surface

**core** n central part of certain fruits, containing the seeds; essential part ▷ v remove the core from

**corella** n white Australian cockatoo

**co-respondent** n (Brit, Aust & NZ) person with whom someone being sued for divorce is claimed to have committed adultery

**corgi** n short-legged sturdy dog

**coriander** n plant grown for its aromatic seeds and leaves

**cork** n thick light bark of a Mediterranean oak; piece of this used as a stopper ▷ v seal with a cork ▸ **corkage** n restaurant's charge for serving wine bought elsewhere ▸ **corkscrew** n spiral metal tool for pulling corks from bottles

**corm** n bulblike underground stem of certain plants

**cormorant** n large dark-coloured long-necked sea bird

**corn**[1] n cereal plant such as wheat or oats; grain of such plants; (US, Canadian, Aust & NZ) maize; (slang) something unoriginal or oversentimental ▸ **corny** adj (slang) unoriginal or oversentimental ▸ **cornflakes** pl n breakfast cereal made from toasted maize ▸ **cornflour** n (chiefly Brit) fine maize flour; (NZ) fine wheat flour ▸ **cornflower** n plant with blue flowers

**corn**[2] n painful hard skin on the toe

**cornea** [korn-ee-a] n, pl **-neas** or **-neae** transparent membrane covering the eyeball ▸ **corneal** adj

**corned beef** n beef preserved in salt

**corner** n area or angle where two converging lines or surfaces meet; place where two streets meet; remote place; (Sport) free kick or shot from the corner of the field ▷ v force into a difficult or inescapable position; (of a vehicle) turn a corner; obtain a monopoly of ▸ **cornerstone** n indispensable part or basis

**cornet** n brass instrument similar to the trumpet; cone-shaped ice-cream wafer

**cornice** n decorative moulding round the top of a wall

**Cornish** pl n, adj (people) of Cornwall ▸ **Cornish pasty** pastry case with a filling of meat and vegetables

**corn on the cob** n corn cooked and eaten on the cob

**cornucopia** [korn-yew-kope-ee-a] n great abundance; symbol of plenty, consisting of a horn overflowing with fruit and flowers

**corolla** n petals of a flower collectively

**corollary** n, pl **-laries** idea, fact, or proposition which is the natural result of something else

**corona** n, pl **-nas** or **-nae** ring of light round the moon or sun

**coronary** [kor-ron-a-ree] adj of the arteries surrounding the heart ▷ n, pl **-naries** coronary thrombosis ▸ **coronary thrombosis** condition in which the flow of blood to the heart is blocked by a blood clot

**coronation** n ceremony of crowning a monarch

**coronavirus** n type of airborne virus that causes colds

**coroner** n (Brit, Aust & NZ) official responsible for the investigation of violent or sudden deaths

**coronet** n small crown

**corpora** n plural of **corpus**

**corporal**[1] n noncommissioned officer in an army

**corporal²** *adj* of the body
▶ **corporal punishment** physical punishment, such as caning

**corporation** *n* large business or company; city or town council
▶ **corporate** *adj* of business corporations; shared by a group

**corporeal** [kore-**pore**-ee-al] *adj* physical or tangible

**corps** [kore] *n, pl* **corps** military unit with a specific function; organized body of people

**corpse** *n* dead body

**corpulent** *adj* fat or plump
▶ **corpulence** *n*

**corpus** *n, pl* **corpora** collection of writings, esp. by a single author

**corpuscle** *n* red or white blood cell

**corral** (*US*) *n* enclosure for cattle or horses ▷ *v* **-ralling, -ralled** put in a corral

**correct** *adj* free from error, true; in accordance with accepted standards ▷ *v* put right; indicate the errors in; rebuke or punish
▶ **correctly** *adv* ▶ **correctness** *n* ▶ **correction** *n* correcting; alteration correcting something
▶ **corrective** *adj* intended to put right something wrong

**correlate** *v* place or be placed in a mutual relationship
▶ **correlation** *n*

**correspond** *v* be consistent or compatible (with); be the same or similar; communicate by letter ▶ **corresponding** *adj*
▶ **correspondingly** *adv*
▶ **correspondence** *n* communication by letters; letters so exchanged; relationship or similarity ▶ **correspondent** *n* person employed by a newspaper etc. to report on a special subject or from a foreign country; letter writer

**corridor** *n* passage in a building or train; strip of land or airspace providing access through foreign territory

**corrigendum** [kor-rij-**end**-um] *n, pl* **-da** error to be corrected

**corroborate** *v* support (a fact or opinion) by giving proof ▶ **corroboration** *n*
▶ **corroborative** *adj*

**corroboree** *n* (*Aust*) Aboriginal gathering or dance

**corrode** *v* eat or be eaten away by chemical action or rust
▶ **corrosion** *n* ▶ **corrosive** *adj*

**corrugated** *adj* folded into alternate grooves and ridges

**corrupt** *adj* open to or involving bribery; morally depraved; (of a text or data) unreliable through errors or alterations ▷ *v* make corrupt ▶ **corruptly** *adv*
▶ **corruption** *n* ▶ **corruptible** *adj*

**corsage** [kor-**sahzh**] *n* small bouquet worn on the bodice of a dress

**corsair** *n* pirate; pirate ship

**corset** *n* women's close-fitting undergarment worn to shape the torso

**cortege** [kor-**tayzh**] *n* funeral procession

**cortex** *n, pl* **-tices** (*Anat*) outer layer of the brain or other internal organ
▶ **cortical** *adj*

**cortisone** *n* steroid hormone used to treat various diseases

**corundum** *n* hard mineral used as an abrasive

**coruscate** *v* (*formal*) sparkle

**corvette** *n* lightly armed escort warship

**cos** (*Maths*) cosine

**cosh** *n* (*Brit*) heavy blunt weapon ▷ *v* hit with a cosh

**cosine** [**koh**-sine] *n* (in trigonometry) ratio of the length of the adjacent side to that of the hypotenuse in a right-angled triangle

**cosmetic** n preparation used to improve the appearance of a person's skin ▷ adj improving the appearance only

**cosmic** adj of the whole universe ▶ **cosmic rays** electromagnetic radiation from outer space

**cosmonaut** n Russian name for an astronaut

**cosmopolitan** adj composed of people or elements from many countries; having lived and travelled in many countries ▷ n cosmopolitan person ▶ **cosmopolitanism** n

**cosmos** n the universe ▶ **cosmology** n study of the origin and nature of the universe ▶ **cosmological** adj

**Cossack** n member of a S Russian people famous as horsemen and dancers

**cosset** v cosseting, cosseted pamper

**cost** n amount of money, time, labour, etc., required for something ▷ pl expenses of a lawsuit ▷ v **costing, cost** have as its cost; involve the loss or sacrifice of; (past tense **costed**) estimate the cost of ▶ **costly** adj expensive; involving great loss or sacrifice ▶ **costliness** n

**costermonger** n (Brit) person who sells fruit and vegetables from a street barrow

**costume** n style of dress of a particular place or time, or for a particular activity; clothes worn by an actor or performer ▶ **costumier** n maker or seller of costumes ▶ **costume jewellery** inexpensive artificial jewellery

**cosy** adj -sier, -siest warm and snug; intimate, friendly ▷ n cover for keeping things warm e.g. a tea cosy ▶ **cosily** adv ▶ **cosiness** n

**cot** n baby's bed with high sides; small portable bed ▶ **cot death** unexplained death of a baby while asleep

**cote** n shelter for birds or animals

**coterie** [kote-er-ee] n exclusive group, clique

**cotoneaster** [kot-tone-ee-ass-ter] n garden shrub with red berries

**cottage** n small house in the country ▶ **cottage cheese** soft mild white cheese ▶ **cottage industry** craft industry in which employees work at home ▶ **cottage pie** dish of minced meat topped with mashed potato

**cotter** n pin or wedge used to secure machine parts

**cotton** n white downy fibre covering the seeds of a tropical plant; cloth or thread made from this ▶ **cottony** adj ▶ **cotton on (to)** v (informal) understand ▶ **cotton wool** fluffy cotton used for surgical dressings etc.

**cotyledon** [kot-ill-ee-don] n first leaf of a plant embryo

**couch** n piece of upholstered furniture for seating more than one person ▷ v express in a particular way ▶ **couch potato** (slang) lazy person whose only hobby is watching television

**couchette** [koo-shett] n bed converted from seats on a train or ship

**couch grass** n quickly spreading grassy weed

**cougan** n (Aust slang) drunk and rowdy person

**cougar** n puma

**cough** v expel air from the lungs abruptly and noisily ▷ n act or sound of coughing; illness which causes coughing

**could** v past tense of **can¹**

**couldn't** could not

**coulomb** [koo-lom] *n* SI unit of electric charge

**coulter** *n* blade at the front of a ploughshare

**council** *n* group meeting for discussion or consultation; local governing body of a town or region ▷ *adj* of or by a council ▶ **councillor** *n* member of a council ▶ **council tax** (in Britain) tax based on the value of property, to fund local services

**counsel** *n* advice or guidance; barrister or barristers ▷ *v* **-selling, -selled** give guidance to; urge, recommend ▶ **counsellor** *n*

**count¹** *v* say numbers in order; find the total of; be important; regard as; take into account ▷ *n* counting; number reached by counting; (*Law*) one of a number of charges ▶ **countless** *adj* too many to count ▶ **count on** *v* rely or depend on

**count²** *n* European nobleman

**countdown** *n* counting backwards to zero of the seconds before an event

**countenance** *n* (expression of) the face ▷ *v* allow or tolerate

**counter¹** *n* long flat surface in a bank or shop, on which business is transacted; small flat disc used in board games

**counter²** *v* oppose, retaliate against ▷ *adv* in the opposite direction; in direct contrast ▷ *n* opposing or retaliatory action

**counter-** *prefix* opposite, against e.g. *counterattack*; complementary, corresponding e.g. *counterpart*

**counteract** *v* act against or neutralize ▶ **counteraction** *n*

**counterattack** *n*, *v* attack in response to an attack

**counterbalance** *n* weight or force balancing or neutralizing another ▷ *v* act as a counterbalance to

**counterblast** *n* aggressive response to a verbal attack

**counterfeit** *adj* fake, forged ▷ *n* fake, forgery ▷ *v* fake, forge

**counterfoil** *n* part of a cheque or receipt kept as a record

**countermand** *v* cancel (a previous order)

**counterpane** *n* bed covering

**counterpart** *n* person or thing complementary to or corresponding to another

**counterpoint** *n* (*Music*) technique of combining melodies

**counterpoise** *n*, *v* counterbalance

**counterproductive** *adj* having an effect opposite to the one intended

**countersign** *v* sign (a document already signed by someone) as confirmation

**countersink** *v* drive (a screw) into a shaped hole so that its head is below the surface

**countertenor** *n* male alto

**counterterrorism** *n* measures to prevent terrorist attacks or eradicate terrorist groups

**countess** *n* woman holding the rank of count or earl; wife or widow of a count or earl

**country** *n*, *pl* **-tries** nation; nation's territory; nation's people; part of the land away from cities ▶ **countrified** *adj* rustic in manner or appearance ▶ **country and western, country music** popular music based on American White folk music ▶ **countryman, countrywoman** *n* person from one's native land; (*Brit, Aust & NZ*) person who lives in the country ▶ **countryside** *n* land away from cities

**county** *n*, *pl* **-ties** (in some countries) division of a country

**coup** [koo] *n* successful action; coup d'état

**coup de grâce** [**koo** de **grahss**] *n*
final or decisive action

**coup d'état** [**koo** day-**tah**] *n*
sudden violent overthrow of a
government

**coupé** [**koo**-pay] *n* sports car with
two doors and a sloping fixed roof

**couple** *n* two people who are
married or romantically involved;
two partners in a dance or game
▷ *v* connect, associate **a couple**
pair; (*informal*) small number
▶ **couplet** *n* two consecutive lines
of verse, usu. rhyming and of the
same metre ▶ **coupling** *n* device
for connecting things, such as
railway carriages

**coupon** *n* piece of paper entitling
the holder to a discount or gift;
detachable order form; football
pools entry form

**courage** *n* ability to face danger or
pain without fear ▶ **courageous**
*adj* ▶ **courageously** *adv*

**courgette** *n* type of small
vegetable marrow

**courier** *n* person employed to
look after holiday-makers; person
employed to deliver urgent
messages

**course** *n* series of lessons or medical
treatment; route or direction
taken; area where golf is played or
a race is run; any of the successive
parts of a meal; mode of conduct
or action; natural development of
events ▷ *v* (of liquid) run swiftly **of
course** as expected, naturally

**court** *n* body which decides legal
cases; place where it meets;
marked area for playing a racket
game; courtyard; residence,
household, or retinue of a
sovereign ▷ *v* (*old-fashioned*) try
to gain the love of; try to win the
favour of; invite e.g. *to court disaster*
▶ **courtier** *n* attendant at a royal

court ▶ **courtly** *adj* ceremoniously
polite ▶ **courtliness** *n* ▶ **courtship**
*n* courting of an intended spouse or
mate ▶ **court martial** *n, pl* **courts
martial** court for trying naval or
military offences ▶ **court shoe**
woman's low-cut shoe without
straps or laces ▶ **courtyard** *n*
paved space enclosed by buildings
or walls

**courtesan** [kor-tiz-**zan**] *n* (*Hist*)
mistress or high-class prostitute

**courtesy** *n* politeness, good
manners; (*pl* **-sies**) courteous act
**(by) courtesy of** by permission
of ▶ **courteous** *adj* polite
▶ **courteously** *adv*

**cousin** *n* child of one's uncle or aunt

**couture** [koo-**toor**] *n* high-fashion
designing and dressmaking
▶ **couturier** *n* person who designs
women's fashion clothes

**cove** *n* small bay or inlet

**coven** [**kuv**-ven] *n* meeting of
witches

**covenant** [**kuv**-ven-ant] *n*
contract; (*chiefly Brit*) formal
agreement to make an annual
(charitable) payment ▷ *v* agree by
a covenant

**Coventry** *n* **send someone to
Coventry** punish someone by
refusing to speak to him or her

**cover** *v* cover something over, to
protect or conceal; extend over or
lie on the surface of; travel over;
insure against loss or risk; include;
report (an event) for a newspaper;
be enough to pay for ▷ *n* anything
that covers; outside of a book or
magazine; insurance; shelter or
protection ▶ **coverage** *n* amount
or extent covered ▶ **coverlet** *n*
bed cover

**covert** *adj* concealed, secret ▷ *n*
thicket giving shelter to game birds
or animals ▶ **covertly** *adv*

**covet** v **coveting, coveted** long to possess (what belongs to someone else) ▶ **covetous** adj ▶ **covetousness** n

**covey** [kuv-vee] n small flock of grouse or partridge

**cow¹** n mature female of cattle and of certain other mammals, such as the elephant or seal; (informal offens) disagreeable woman ▶ **cowboy** n (in the US) ranch worker who herds and tends cattle, usu. on horseback; (informal) irresponsible or unscrupulous worker

**cow²** v intimidate, subdue

**coward** n person who lacks courage ▶ **cowardly** adj ▶ **cowardice** n lack of courage

**cower** v cringe in fear

**cowl** n loose hood; monk's hooded robe; cover on a chimney to increase ventilation

**cowling** n cover on an engine

**cowrie** n brightly-marked sea shell

**cowslip** n small yellow wild European flower

**cox** n coxswain ▷ v act as cox of (a boat)

**coxswain** [kok-sn] n person who steers a rowing boat

**coy** adj affectedly shy or modest ▶ **coyly** adv ▶ **coyness** n

**coyote** [koy-ote-ee] n prairie wolf of N America

**coypu** n beaver-like aquatic rodent native to S America, bred for its fur

**cozen** v (lit) cheat, trick

**CPU** (Computing) central processing unit

**crab** n edible shellfish with ten legs, the first pair modified into pincers

**crab apple** n small sour apple

**crabbed** adj (of handwriting) hard to read; (also **crabby**) bad-tempered

**crack** v break or split partially; (cause to) make a sharp noise; break down or yield under strain; hit suddenly; solve (a code or problem); tell (a joke) ▷ n sudden sharp noise; narrow gap; sharp blow; (informal) gibe, joke; (slang) highly addictive form of cocaine ▷ adj (informal) first-rate, excellent e.g. a crack shot ▶ **cracking** adj very good ▶ **crackdown** n severe disciplinary measures ▶ **crack down on** v take severe measures against

**cracker** n thin dry biscuit; decorated cardboard tube, pulled apart with a bang, containing a paper hat and a joke or toy; small explosive firework; (slang) outstanding thing or person

**crackers** adj (slang) insane

**crackle** v make small sharp popping noises ▷ n crackling sound ▶ **crackling** n crackle; crisp skin of roast pork

**crackpot** n, adj (informal) eccentric (person)

**cradle** n baby's bed on rockers; place where something originates; supporting structure ▷ v hold gently as if in a cradle

**craft** n occupation requiring skill with the hands; skill or ability; (pl **craft**) boat, ship, aircraft, or spaceship ▶ **crafty** adj skilled in deception ▶ **craftily** adv ▶ **craftiness** n ▶ **craftsman, craftswoman** n skilled worker ▶ **craftsmanship** n

**crag** n steep rugged rock ▶ **craggy** adj

**cram** v **cramming, crammed** force into too small a space; fill too full; study hard just before an examination

**cramp¹** n painful muscular contraction; clamp for holding masonry or timber together

**cramp²** v confine, restrict

**crampon** n spiked plate strapped to a boot for climbing on ice

**cranberry** n sour edible red berry

**crane** n machine for lifting and moving heavy weights; large wading bird with a long neck and legs ▷ v stretch (one's neck) to see something

**crane fly** n long-legged insect with slender wings

**cranium** n, pl-niums or-nia (Anat) skull ▶ **cranial** adj

**crank** n arm projecting at right angles from a shaft, for transmitting or converting motion; (informal) eccentric person ▷ v start (an engine) with a crank ▶ **cranky** adj (informal) eccentric; bad-tempered ▶ **crankshaft** n shaft driven by a crank

**cranny** n, pl-nies narrow opening

**crape** n same as **crepe**

**craps** n gambling game played with two dice

**crash** n collision involving a vehicle or vehicles; sudden loud smashing noise; financial collapse ▷ v (cause to) collide violently with a vehicle, a stationary object, or the ground; (cause to) make a loud smashing noise; (cause to) fall with a crash; collapse or fail financially ▶ **crash course** short, very intensive course in a particular subject ▶ **crash helmet** protective helmet worn by a motorcyclist ▶ **crash-land** v (of an aircraft) land in an emergency, causing damage ▶ **crash-landing** n

**crass** adj stupid and insensitive ▶ **crassly** adv ▶ **crassness** n

**crate** n large wooden container for packing goods

**crater** n very large hole in the ground or in the surface of the moon

**cravat** n man's scarf worn like a tie

**crave** v desire intensely; beg or plead for ▶ **craving** n

**craven** adj cowardly

**crawfish** n same as **crayfish**

**crawl** v move on one's hands and knees; move slowly; (foll by to) flatter in order to gain some advantage; feel as if covered with crawling creatures ▷ n crawling motion or pace; overarm swimming stroke ▶ **crawler** n

**crayfish** n edible shellfish like a lobster; Australian freshwater crustacean

**crayon** v, n (draw or colour with) a stick or pencil of coloured wax or clay

**craze** n short-lived fashion or enthusiasm ▶ **crazed** adj wild and uncontrolled; (of porcelain) having fine cracks

**crazy** adj ridiculous; (foll by about) very fond (of); insane ▶ **craziness** n ▶ **crazy paving** paving made of irregularly shaped slabs of stone

**creak** v, n (make) a harsh squeaking sound ▶ **creaky** adj

**cream** n fatty part of milk; food or cosmetic resembling cream in consistency; best part (of something) ▷ adj yellowish-white ▷ v beat to a creamy consistency ▶ **creamy** adj ▶ **cream cheese** rich soft white cheese ▶ **cream off** v take the best part from

**crease** n line made by folding or pressing; (Cricket) line marking the bowler's and batsman's positions ▷ v crush or line

**create** v make, cause to exist; appoint to a new rank or position; (slang) make an angry fuss ▶ **creation** n ▶ **creationism** n doctrine that ascribes the origins of all things to God's acts of creation rather than to evolution ▶ **creationist** n ▶ **creative**

*adj* imaginative or inventive ▶ **creativity** *n* ▶ **creator** *n*

**creature** *n* animal, person, or other being

**crèche** *n* place where small children are looked after while their parents are working, shopping, etc.

**credence** *n* belief in the truth or accuracy of a statement

**credentials** *pl n* document giving evidence of a person's identity or qualifications

**credible** *adj* believable; trustworthy ▶ **credibly** *adv* ▶ **credibility** *n*

**credit** *n* system of allowing customers to receive goods and pay later; reputation for trustworthiness in paying debts; money at one's disposal in a bank account; side of an account book on which such sums are entered; (source or cause of) praise or approval; influence or reputation based on the good opinion of others; belief or trust ▷ *pl* list of people responsible for the production of a film, programme, or record ▷ *v* **crediting, credited** enter as a credit in an account; (foll by *with*) attribute (to); believe ▶ **creditable** *adj* praiseworthy ▶ **creditably** *adv* ▶ **creditor** *n* person to whom money is owed ▶ **credit card** card allowing a person to buy on credit ▶ **credit crunch** period during which there is a sudden reduction in the availability of credit from banks, mortgage lenders, etc.

**credo** *n, pl* **-dos** creed

**credulous** *adj* too willing to believe ▶ **credulity** *n*

**creed** *n* statement or system of (Christian) beliefs or principles

**creek** *n* narrow inlet or bay; (*Aust, NZ, US & Canadian*) small stream

**creel** *n* wicker basket used by anglers

**creep** *v* **creeping, crept** move quietly and cautiously; crawl with the body near to the ground; (of a plant) grow along the ground or over rocks ▷ *n* (*slang*) obnoxious or servile person **give one the creeps** (*informal*) make one feel fear or disgust ▶ **creeper** *n* creeping plant ▶ **creepy** *adj* (*informal*) causing a feeling of fear or disgust

**cremate** *v* burn (a corpse) to ash ▶ **cremation** *n* ▶ **crematorium** *n* building where corpses are cremated

**crenellated** *adj* having battlements

**creole** *n* language developed from a mixture of languages; (**C-**) native-born W Indian or Latin American of mixed European and African descent

**creosote** *n* dark oily liquid made from coal tar and used for preserving wood ▷ *v* treat with creosote

**crepe** [krayp] *n* fabric or rubber with a crinkled texture; very thin pancake ▶ **crepe paper** paper with a crinkled texture

**crept** *v* past of **creep**

**crepuscular** *adj* (*lit*) of or like twilight

**crescendo** [krish-**end**-oh] *n, pl* **-dos** gradual increase in loudness, esp. in music

**crescent** *n* (curved shape of) the moon as seen in its first or last quarter; crescent-shaped street

**cress** *n* plant with strong-tasting leaves, used in salads

**crest** *n* top of a mountain, hill, or wave; tuft or growth on a bird's or animal's head; heraldic design used on a coat of arms and elsewhere

▶ **crested** adj ▶ **crestfallen** adj disheartened

**cretin** n (informal offens) stupid person; (obs) person afflicted with physical and mental retardation caused by a thyroid deficiency ▶ **cretinous** adj

**crevasse** n deep open crack in a glacier

**crevice** n narrow crack or gap in rock

**crew** n people who work on a ship or aircraft; group of people working together; (informal) any group of people ▷ v serve as a crew member (on) ▶ **crew cut** man's closely cropped haircut

**crewel** n fine worsted yarn used in embroidery

**crib** n piece of writing stolen from elsewhere; translation or list of answers used by students, often illicitly; baby's cradle; rack for fodder; short for **cribbage** ▷ v **cribbing, cribbed** copy (someone's work) dishonestly ▶ **crib-wall** n (NZ) retaining wall built against an earth bank

**cribbage** n card game for two to four players

**crick** n muscle spasm or cramp in the back or neck ▷ v cause a crick in

**cricket**¹ n outdoor game played with bats, a ball, and wickets by two teams of eleven ▶ **cricketer** n

**cricket**² n chirping insect like a grasshopper

**crime** n unlawful act; unlawful acts collectively ▶ **criminal** n person guilty of a crime ▷ adj of crime; (informal) deplorable ▶ **criminally** adv ▶ **criminality** n ▶ **criminology** n study of crime ▶ **criminologist** n

**crimp** v fold or press into ridges

**crimson** adj deep purplish-red

**cringe** v flinch in fear; behave in a submissive or timid way

**crinkle** v, n wrinkle, crease, or fold

**crinoline** n hooped petticoat

**cripple** n (offens) person who is lame or disabled ▷ v make lame or disabled; damage (something)

**crisis** n, pl **-ses** crucial stage, turning point; time of extreme trouble

**crisp** adj fresh and firm; dry and brittle; clean and neat; (of weather) cold but invigorating; lively or brisk ▷ n (Brit) very thin slice of potato fried till crunchy ▶ **crisply** adv ▶ **crispness** n ▶ **crispy** adj hard and crunchy ▶ **crispbread** n thin dry biscuit

**crisscross** v move in or mark with a crosswise pattern ▷ adj (of lines) crossing in different directions

**criterion** n, pl **-ria** standard of judgment

**USAGE NOTE**
It is incorrect to use *criteria* as a singular, though this use is often found

**critic** n professional judge of any of the arts; person who finds fault ▶ **critical** adj very important or dangerous; fault-finding; able to examine and judge carefully; of a critic or criticism ▶ **critically** adv ▶ **criticism** n fault-finding; analysis of a book, work of art, etc. ▶ **criticize** v find fault with ▶ **critique** n critical essay

**croak** v (of a frog or crow) give a low hoarse cry; utter or speak with a croak ▷ n low hoarse sound ▶ **croaky** adj hoarse

**Croatian** [kroh-**ay**-shun], **Croat** adj of Croatia ▷ n person from Croatia; dialect of Serbo-Croat spoken in Croatia

**crochet** [**kroh**-shay] v **-cheting, -cheted** make by looping and intertwining yarn with a hooked needle ▷ n work made in this way

**crock**[1] n earthenware pot or jar
▶ **crockery** n dishes

**crock**[2] n (Brit, Aust & NZ informal) old or decrepit person or thing

**crocodile** n large amphibious tropical reptile; (Brit, Aust & NZ) line of people, esp. schoolchildren, walking two by two ▶ **crocodile tears** insincere show of grief

**crocus** n, pl **-cuses** small plant with yellow, white, or purple flowers in spring

**croft** n small farm worked by one family in Scotland ▶ **crofter** n

**croissant** [krwah-son] n rich flaky crescent-shaped roll

**cromlech** n (Brit) circle of prehistoric standing stones

**crone** n witchlike old woman

**crony** n, pl **-nies** close friend

**crook** n (informal) criminal; bent or curved part; hooked pole ▷ adj (Aust & NZ slang) unwell, injured **go crook** (Aust & NZ slang) become angry ▶ **crooked** adj bent or twisted; set at an angle; (informal) dishonest

**croon** v sing, hum, or speak in a soft low tone

**crooner** n male singer of sentimental ballads

**crop** n cultivated plant; season's total yield of produce; group of things appearing at one time; (handle of) a whip; pouch in a bird's gullet; very short haircut ▷ v **cropping, cropped** cut very short; produce or harvest as a crop; (of animals) feed on (grass) ▶ **cropper** n **come a cropper** (informal) have a disastrous failure or heavy fall ▶ **crop-top** n short T-shirt or vest that reveals the wearer's midriff ▶ **crop up** v (informal) happen unexpectedly

**croquet** [kroh-kay] n game played on a lawn in which balls are hit through hoops

**croquette** [kroh-kett] n fried cake of potato, meat, or fish

**crosier** n same as **crozier**

**cross** v move or go across (something); meet and pass; (foll by out) delete with a cross or lines; place (one's arms or legs) crosswise ▷ n structure, symbol, or mark of two intersecting lines; such a structure of wood as a means of execution; representation of the Cross as an emblem of Christianity; mixture of two things ▷ adj angry, annoyed **the Cross** (Christianity) the cross on which Christ was crucified ▶ **crossing** n place where a street may be crossed safely; place where one thing crosses another; journey across water ▶ **crossly** adv ▶ **crossbar** n horizontal bar across goalposts or on a bicycle ▶ **crossbow** n weapon consisting of a bow fixed across a wooden stock ▶ **crossbred** adj bred from two different types of animal or plant ▶ **crossbreed** n crossbred animal or plant ▶ **cross-check** v check using a different method ▶ **cross-country** adj, adv by way of open country or fields ▶ **cross-examine** v (Law) question (a witness for the opposing side) to check his or her testimony ▶ **cross-examination** n ▶ **cross-eyed** adj with eyes looking towards each other ▶ **cross-fertilize** v fertilize (an animal or plant) from one of a different kind ▶ **cross-fertilization** n ▶ **crossfire** n gunfire crossing another line of fire ▶ **cross-purposes** pl n **at cross-purposes** misunderstanding each other ▶ **cross-reference** n reference within a text to another part ▶ **crossroads** n place where roads intersect ▶ **cross section** (diagram of) a surface made by cutting across something; representative sample ▶ **crosswise** adj, adv across; in the shape of a cross ▶ **crossword puzzle, crossword** n puzzle in which words suggested by clues are written into a grid of squares

**crotch** n part of the body between the tops of the legs

**crotchet** n musical note half the length of a minim

**crotchety** adj (informal) bad-tempered

**crouch** v bend low with the legs and body close ▷ n this position

**croup**[1] [kroop] n throat disease of children, with a cough

**croup**[2] [kroop] n hind quarters of a horse

**croupier** [kroop-ee-ay] n person who collects bets and pays out winnings at a gambling table in a casino

**crouton** [kroot-on] n small piece of fried or toasted bread served in soup

**crow**[1] n large black bird with a harsh call **as the crow flies** in a straight line **stone the crows!** (Brit & Aust slang) expression of surprise, dismay, etc. ▶ **crow's feet** wrinkles at the corners of the eyes ▶ **crow's nest** lookout platform at the top of a ship's mast

**crow**[2] v (of a cock) make a shrill squawking sound; boast or gloat

**crowbar** n iron bar used as a lever

**crowd** n large group of people or things; particular group of people ▷ v gather together in large numbers; press together in a confined space; fill or occupy fully

**crown** n monarch's headdress of gold and jewels; wreath for the head, given as an honour; top of the head or of a hill; artificial cover for a broken or decayed tooth; former British coin worth 25 pence ▷ v put a crown on the head of (someone) to proclaim him or her monarch; put on or form the top of; put the finishing touch to (a series of events); (informal) hit on the head **the Crown** power of the monarchy ▶ **crown court** local criminal court in England and Wales ▶ **crown-of-thorns** n starfish with a spiny outer covering that feeds on living coral ▶ **crown prince, crown princess** heir to a throne

**crozier** n bishop's hooked staff

**crucial** adj very important ▶ **crucially** adv

**cruciate ligament** [kroo-shee-it] n either of a pair of ligaments in the knee, connecting the tibia and the femur

**crucible** n pot in which metals are melted

**crucify** v **-fying, -fied** put to death by fastening to a cross ▶ **crucifix** n model of Christ on the Cross ▶ **crucifixion** n crucifying **the Crucifixion** (Christianity) crucifying of Christ ▶ **cruciform** adj cross-shaped

**crude** adj rough and simple; tasteless, vulgar; in a natural or unrefined state ▶ **crudely** adv ▶ **crudity** n

**cruel** adj delighting in others' pain; causing pain or suffering ▶ **cruelly** adv ▶ **cruelty** n

**cruet** n small container for salt, pepper, etc., at table

**cruise** n sail for pleasure ▷ v sail from place to place for pleasure; (of a vehicle) travel at a moderate and economical speed ▶ **cruiser** n fast warship; motorboat with a cabin ▶ **cruise missile** low-flying guided missile

**crumb** n small fragment of bread or other dry food; small amount

**crumble** v break into fragments; fall apart or decay ▷ n pudding of stewed fruit with a crumbly topping ▶ **crumbly** adj

**crummy** adj **-mier, -miest** (slang) of poor quality

**crumpet** n round soft yeast cake, eaten buttered; (Brit, Aust & NZ slang) sexually attractive women collectively

**crumple** v crush, crease; collapse, esp. from shock ▶ **crumpled** adj

**crunch** v bite or chew with a noisy crushing sound; make a crisp or brittle sound ▷ n crunching sound; (informal) critical moment ▶ **crunchy** adj

**crupper** n strap that passes from the back of a saddle under a horse's tail

**crusade** n medieval Christian war to recover the Holy Land from the Muslims; vigorous campaign in favour of a cause ▷ v take part in a crusade

**crusader** n person who took part in the medieval Christian war to recover the Holy Land from the Muslims; person who campaigns vigorously in favour of a cause

**crush** v compress so as to injure, break, or crumple; break into small pieces; defeat or humiliate utterly ▷ n dense crowd; (informal) infatuation; drink made by crushing fruit

**crust** n hard outer part of something, esp. bread ▷ v cover with or form a crust ▶ **crusty** adj having a crust; irritable

**crustacean** n hard-shelled, usu. aquatic animal with several pairs of legs, such as the crab or lobster

**crutch** n long sticklike support with a rest for the armpit, used by a lame person; person or thing that gives support; crotch

**crux** n, pl **cruxes** crucial or decisive point

**cry** v **crying, cried** shed tears; call or utter loudly ▷ n, pl **cries** fit of weeping; loud utterance; urgent appeal e.g. a cry for help ▶ **crybaby** n person, esp. a child, who cries too readily ▶ **cry off** v (informal) withdraw from an arrangement ▶ **cry out for** v need urgently

**cryogenics** n branch of physics concerned with very low temperatures ▶ **cryogenic** adj

**crypt** n vault under a church, esp. one used as a burial place

**cryptic** adj obscure in meaning, secret ▶ **cryptically** adv ▶ **cryptography** n art of writing in and deciphering codes

**crystal** n (single grain of) a symmetrically shaped solid formed naturally by some substances; very clear and brilliant glass, usu. with the surface cut in many planes; tumblers, vases, etc., made of crystal ▷ adj bright and clear ▶ **crystalline** adj of or like crystal or crystals; clear ▶ **crystallize** v make or become definite; form into crystals ▶ **crystallization** n

**cu.** cubic

**cub** n young wild animal such as a bear or fox; (**C-**) Cub Scout ▷ v **cubbing, cubbed** give birth to cubs ▶ **Cub Scout** member of a junior branch of the Scout Association

**cubbyhole** n small enclosed space or room

**cube** n object with six equal square sides; number resulting from multiplying a number by itself twice ▷ v cut into cubes; find the cube of (a number) ▶ **cubic** adj having three dimensions; cube-shaped ▶ **cubism** n style of art in which objects are represented by geometrical shapes ▶ **cubist** adj, n ▶ **cube root** number whose cube is a given number

**cubicle** n enclosed part of a large room, screened for privacy

**cuckold** n man whose spouse has been unfaithful ▷ v be unfaithful to (one's spouse)

**cuckoo** n migratory bird with a characteristic two-note call, which lays its eggs in the nests of other birds ▷ adj (informal) insane or foolish

**cucumber** n long green-skinned fleshy fruit used in salads

**cud** n partially digested food which a ruminant brings back into its mouth to chew again **chew the cud** think deeply

**cuddle** v, n hug ▶ **cuddly** adj

**cudgel** n short thick stick used as a weapon

**cue¹** n signal to an actor or musician to begin speaking or playing; signal or reminder ▷ v **cueing, cued** give a cue to

**cue²** n long tapering stick used in billiards, snooker, or pool ▷ v **cueing, cued** hit (a ball) with a cue

**cuff¹** n end of a sleeve **off the cuff** (informal) without preparation ▶ **cuff link** one of a pair of decorative fastenings for shirt cuffs

**cuff²** (Brit, Aust & NZ) v hit with an open hand ▷ n blow with an open hand

**cuisine** [quiz-**zeen**] n style of cooking

**cul-de-sac** n road with one end blocked off

**culinary** adj of kitchens or cookery

**cull** v choose, gather; remove or kill (inferior or surplus animals) from a herd ▷ n culling

**culminate** v reach the highest point or climax ▶ **culmination** n

**culottes** pl n women's knee-length trousers cut to look like a skirt

**culpable** adj deserving blame ▶ **culpability** n

**culprit** n person guilty of an offence or misdeed

**cult** n specific system of worship; devotion to a person, idea, or activity; popular fashion

**cultivate** v prepare (land) to grow crops; grow (plants); develop or improve (something); try to develop a friendship with (someone) ▶ **cultivated** adj well-educated ▶ **cultivation** n

**culture** n ideas, customs, and art of a particular society; particular society; developed understanding of the arts; cultivation of plants or rearing of animals; growth of bacteria for study ▶ **cultural** adj ▶ **cultured** adj showing good taste or manners ▶ **cultured pearl** pearl artificially grown in an oyster shell

**culvert** n drain under a road or railway

**cumbersome** adj awkward because of size or shape

**cumin, cummin** n sweet-smelling seeds of a Mediterranean plant, used in cooking

**cummerbund** n wide sash worn round the waist

**cumulative** adj increasing steadily

**cumulus** [**kew**-myew-luss] n, pl -**li** thick white or dark grey cloud

**cuneiform** [**kew**-nif-form] n, adj (written in) an ancient system of writing using wedge-shaped characters

**cunjevoi** n (Aust) plant of tropical Asia and Australia with small flowers, cultivated for its edible rhizome; sea squirt

**cunning** adj clever at deceiving; ingenious ▷ n cleverness

at deceiving; ingenuity
▶ **cunningly** adv
**cup** n small bowl-shaped drinking container with a handle; contents of a cup; (competition with) a cup-shaped trophy given as a prize; hollow rounded shape ▷ v **cupping, cupped** form (one's hand) into the shape of a cup; hold in cupped hands ▶ **cupful** n
**cupboard** n piece of furniture or alcove with a door, for storage
**cupidity** [kew-**pid**-it-ee] n greed for money or possessions
**cupola** [**kew**-pol-la] n domed roof or ceiling
**cur** n (lit) mongrel dog; contemptible person
**curaçao** [**kew**-rah-so] n orange-flavoured liqueur
**curare** [kew-**rah**-ree] n poisonous resin of a S American tree, used as a muscle relaxant in medicine
**curate** n clergyman who assists a parish priest ▶ **curacy** [**kew**-rah-see] n, pl **-cies** work or position of a curate
**curative** n, adj (something) able to cure
**curator** n person in charge of a museum or art gallery ▶ **curatorship** n
**curb** n something that restrains ▷ v control, restrain
**curd** n coagulated milk, used to make cheese ▶ **curdle** v turn into curd, coagulate
**cure** v get rid of (an illness or problem); make (someone) well again; preserve by salting, smoking, or drying ▷ n (treatment causing) curing of an illness or person; remedy or solution ▶ **curable** adj
**curette** n surgical instrument for scraping tissue from body

cavities ▷ v scrape with a curette ▶ **curettage** n
**curfew** n law ordering people to stay inside their homes after a specific time at night; time set as a deadline by such a law
**curie** n standard unit of radioactivity
**curio** n, pl **-rios** rare or unusual object valued as a collector's item
**curious** adj eager to learn or know; eager to find out private details; unusual or peculiar ▶ **curiously** adv ▶ **curiosity** n eagerness to know or find out; (pl **-ties**) rare or unusual object
**curl** n curved piece of hair; curved spiral shape ▷ v make (hair) into curls or (of hair) grow in curls; make into a curved spiral shape ▶ **curly** adj ▶ **curling** n game like bowls, played with heavy stones on ice
**curlew** n long-billed wading bird
**curmudgeon** n bad-tempered person
**currajong** n same as **kurrajong**
**currant** n small dried grape; small round berry, such as a redcurrant
**currawong** n Australian songbird
**current** adj of the immediate present; most recent, up-to-date; commonly accepted ▷ n flow of water or air in one direction; flow of electricity; general trend ▶ **currently** adv ▶ **currency** n, pl **-cies** money in use in a particular country; general acceptance or use
**curriculum** n, pl **-la** or **-lums** all the courses of study offered by a school or college ▶ **curriculum vitae** [**vee**-tie] outline of someone's educational and professional history, prepared for job applications

> **SPELLING TIP**
> The only letter that is doubled in **curriculum** is the r in the middle

**curry**[1] *n, pl* **-ries** Indian dish of meat or vegetables in a hot spicy sauce ▷ *v* **-rying, -ried** prepare (food) with curry powder ▶ **curry powder** mixture of spices for making curry

**curry**[2] *v* **-rying, -ried** groom (a horse) **curry favour** ingratiate oneself with an important person ▶ **curry comb** ridged comb for grooming a horse

**curse** *v* swear (at); ask a supernatural power to cause harm to ▷ *n* swearword; (result of) a call to a supernatural power to cause harm to someone; something causing trouble or harm ▶ **cursed** *adj*

**cursive** *n, adj* (handwriting) done with joined letters

**cursor** *n* movable point of light that shows a specific position on a visual display unit

**cursory** *adj* quick and superficial ▶ **cursorily** *adv*

**curt** *adj* brief and rather rude ▶ **curtly** *adv* ▶ **curtness** *n*

**curtail** *v* cut short; restrict ▶ **curtailment** *n*

**curtain** *n* piece of cloth hung at a window or opening as a screen; hanging cloth separating the audience and the stage in a theatre; fall or closing of the curtain at the end, or the rise or opening of the curtain at the start of a theatrical performance; something forming a barrier or screen ▷ *v* provide with curtains; (foll by *off*) separate by a curtain

**curtsy, curtsey** *n, pl* **-sies** *or* **-seys** woman's gesture of respect made by bending the knees and bowing the head ▷ *v* **-sying, -sied** *or* **-seying, -seyed** make a curtsy

**curve** *n* continuously bending line with no straight parts ▷ *v* form or move in a curve ▶ **curvy** *adj* ▶ **curvaceous** *adj* (*informal*) (of a woman) having a shapely body ▶ **curvature** *n* curved shape ▶ **curved** *adj* curved shape ▶ **curvilinear** *adj* consisting of or bounded by a curve

**cuscus** *n, pl* **-cuses** large Australian nocturnal possum

**cushion** *n* bag filled with soft material, to make a seat more comfortable; something that provides comfort or absorbs shock ▷ *v* lessen the effects of; protect from injury or shock

**cushy** *adj* **cushier, cushiest** (*informal*) easy

**cusp** *n* pointed end, esp. on a tooth; (*Astrol*) division between houses or signs of the zodiac

**cuss** (*informal*) *n* curse, oath; annoying person ▷ *v* swear (at) ▶ **cussed** [**kuss**-id] ▷ *adj* (*informal*) obstinate

**custard** *n* sweet yellow sauce made from milk and eggs

**custody** *n* protective care; imprisonment prior to being tried ▶ **custodial** *adj* ▶ **custodian** *n* person in charge of a public building

**custom** *n* long-established activity or action; usual habit; regular use of a shop or business ▷ *pl* duty charged on imports or exports; government department which collects these; area at a port, airport, or border where baggage and freight are examined for dutiable goods ▶ **customary** *adj* usual; established by custom ▶ **customarily** *adv* ▶ **custom-built, custom-made** *adj* made to the specifications of an individual customer ▶ **customize** *v* modify (something) according to a customer's individual requirements ▶ **customization** *n*

**customer** n person who buys goods or services

**cut** v **cutting, cut** open up, penetrate, wound, or divide with a sharp instrument; divide; trim or shape by cutting; abridge, shorten; reduce, restrict; (informal) hurt the feelings of; pretend not to recognize ▷ n stroke or incision made by cutting; piece cut off; reduction; deletion in a text, film, or play; (informal) share, esp. of profits; style in which hair or a garment is cut ▸ **cut in** v interrupt; obstruct another vehicle in overtaking

**cutaneous** [kew-**tane**-ee-uss] adj of the skin

**cute** adj appealing or attractive; (informal) clever or shrewd ▸ **cutely** adv ▸ **cuteness** n

**cuticle** n skin at the base of a fingernail or toenail

**cutlass** n curved one-edged sword formerly used by sailors

**cutlery** n knives, forks, and spoons ▸ **cutler** n maker of cutlery

**cutlet** n small piece of meat like a chop; flat croquette of chopped meat or fish

**cutter** n person or tool that cuts; any of various small fast boats

**cut-throat** adj fierce or relentless ▷ n murderer

**cutting** n article cut from a newspaper or magazine; piece cut from a plant from which to grow a new plant; passage cut through high ground for a road or railway ▷ adj (of a remark) hurtful

**cuttlefish** n squidlike sea mollusc

**cuz** n (Aust & NZ informal) term of address for a male friend or family member

**CV** curriculum vitae

**cwt** hundredweight

**cyanide** n extremely poisonous chemical compound

**cyber-** combining form computers e.g. cyberspace

**cybernetics** n branch of science in which electronic and mechanical systems are studied and compared to biological systems

**cyberspace** n place said to contain all the data stored in computers

**cybersquatting** n registering an internet domain name belonging to another person in the hope of selling it to them for a profit ▸ **cybersquatter** n

**cyclamen** [**sik**-la-men] n plant with red, pink, or white flowers

**cycle** v ride a bicycle ▷ n (Brit, Aust & NZ) bicycle; (US) motorcycle; complete series of recurring events; time taken for one such series ▸ **cyclical, cyclic** adj occurring in cycles ▸ **cyclist** n person who rides a bicycle

**cyclone** n violent wind moving round a central area

**cyclotron** n apparatus that accelerates charged particles by means of a strong vertical magnetic field

**cygnet** n young swan

**cylinder** n solid or hollow body with straight sides and circular ends; chamber within which the piston moves in an internal-combustion engine ▸ **cylindrical** adj

**cymbal** n percussion instrument consisting of a brass plate which is struck against another or hit with a stick

**cynic** [**sin**-ik] n person who believes that people always act selfishly ▸ **cynical** adj ▸ **cynically** adv ▸ **cynicism** n

**cynosure** [**sin**-oh-zyure] n centre of attention

**cypher** n same as **cipher**

# Dd

**cypress** n evergreen tree with dark green leaves

**Cypriot** n, adj (person) from Cyprus

**cyst** [sist] n (abnormal) sac in the body containing fluid or soft matter ▶ **cystic** adj ▶ **cystitis** [siss-**tite**-iss] n inflammation of the bladder

**cytology** [site-**ol**-a-jee] n study of plant and animal cells ▶ **cytological** adj ▶ **cytologist** n

**czar** [zahr] n same as **tsar**

**Czech** n, adj (person) from the Czech Republic ▷ n language of the Czech Republic

**D** (Chem) deuterium

**d** (Physics) density

**d.** (Brit)(before decimalization) penny; died

**dab**[1] v **dabbing, dabbed** pat lightly; apply with short tapping strokes ▷ n small amount of something soft or moist; light stroke or tap ▶ **dab hand** (informal) person who is particularly good at something

**dab**[2] n small European flatfish with rough scales

**dabble** v be involved in something superficially; splash about ▶ **dabbler** n

**dace** n small European freshwater fish

**dachshund** n dog with a long body and short legs

**dad** n (informal) father

**daddy** n, pl **-dies** (informal) father

**daddy-longlegs** n (Brit) crane fly; (US & Canadian) small web-spinning spider with long legs

**dado** [**day**-doe] n, pl **-does** or **-dos** lower part of an interior wall, below a rail, decorated differently from the upper part

**daffodil** n yellow trumpet-shaped flower that blooms in spring

**daft** adj (informal) foolish or crazy

**dag** (NZ) n dried dung on a sheep's rear; (informal) amusing person ▷ pl n **rattle one's dags** (informal) hurry up ▷ v remove the dags from a sheep ▶ **daggy** ▷ adj (informal) amusing

**dagga** n (S Afr informal) cannabis

**dagger** n short knifelike weapon with a pointed blade

**daguerreotype** [dag-**gair**-oh-type] n type of early photograph produced on chemically treated silver

**dahlia** [**day**-lya] n brightly coloured garden flower

**daily** adj occurring every day or every weekday ▷ adv every day ▷ n, pl **-lies** daily newspaper; (Brit informal) person who cleans other people's houses

**dainty** adj **-tier, -tiest** delicate or elegant ▸ **daintily** adv

**daiquiri** [**dak**-eer-ee] n iced drink containing rum, lime juice, and sugar

**dairy** n, pl **dairies** place for the processing or sale of milk and its products; (NZ) small shop selling groceries and milk often outside normal trading hours; food containing milk or its products e.g. She can't eat dairy ▷ adj of milk or its products

**dais** [**day**-iss, **dayss**] n raised platform in a hall, used by a speaker

**daisy** n, pl **-sies** small wild flower with a yellow centre and white petals ▸ **daisy wheel** flat disc in a word processor with radiating spokes for printing letters

**Dalai Lama** n chief lama and (until 1959) ruler of Tibet

**dale** n (esp. in N England) valley

**dally** v **-lying, -lied** waste time; (foll by with) deal frivolously (with) ▸ **dalliance** n flirtation

**Dalmatian** n large dog with a white coat and black spots

**dam**[1] n barrier built across a river to create a lake; lake created by this ▷ v **damming, dammed** build a dam across (a river)

**dam**[2] n mother of an animal such as a sheep or horse

**damage** v harm, spoil ▷ n harm to a person or thing; (informal) cost e.g. what's the damage? ▷ pl money awarded as compensation for injury or loss

**damask** n fabric with a pattern woven into it, used for tablecloths etc.

**dame** n (chiefly US & Canadian slang) woman; (**D-**) title of a woman who has been awarded the OBE or another order of chivalry

**damn** interj (slang) exclamation of annoyance ▷ adv, adj (also **damned**) (slang) extreme(ly) ▷ v condemn as bad or worthless; (of God) condemn to hell ▸ **damnable** adj annoying ▸ **damnably** adv ▸ **damnation** interj, n ▸ **damning** adj proving or suggesting guilt e.g. a damning report

**damp** adj slightly wet ▷ n slight wetness, moisture ▷ v (also **dampen**) make damp; (foll by down) reduce the intensity of (feelings or actions) ▸ **damply** adv ▸ **dampness** n ▸ **damper** n movable plate to regulate the draught in a fire; pad in a piano that deadens the vibration of each string **put a damper on** have a depressing or inhibiting effect on

**damsel** n (old-fashioned) young woman

**damson** n small blue-black plumlike fruit

**dance** v move the feet and body rhythmically in time to music; perform (a particular dance); skip or leap; move rhythmically ▷ n series of steps and movements in time to music; social meeting arranged for dancing ▸ **dancer** n

**D and C** n (Med) dilatation and curettage: a minor operation in which the neck of the womb is stretched and the lining of the womb scraped, to clear the womb or remove tissue for diagnosis

**dandelion** n yellow-flowered wild plant

**dander** n **get one's dander up** (*slang*) become angry

**dandle** v move (a child) up and down on one's knee

**dandruff** n loose scales of dry dead skin shed from the scalp

**dandy** n, pl **-dies** man who is overconcerned with the elegance of his appearance ▷ adj **-dier, -diest** (*informal*) very good ▶ **dandified** adj

**Dane** n person from Denmark ▶ **Danish** n, adj (language) of Denmark ▶ **Danish blue** strong white cheese with blue veins ▶ **Danish pastry** iced puff pastry filled with fruit, almond paste, etc.

**danger** n possibility of being injured or killed; person or thing that may cause injury or harm; likelihood that something unpleasant will happen ▶ **dangerous** adj ▶ **dangerously** adv

**dangle** v hang loosely; display as an enticement

**dank** adj unpleasantly damp and chilly

**dapper** adj (of a man) neat in appearance

**dappled** adj marked with spots of a different colour ▶ **dapple-grey** n horse with a grey coat and darker coloured spots

**dare** v be courageous enough to try (to do something); challenge to do something risky ▷ n challenge to do something risky ▶ **daring** adj willing to take risks ▷ n courage to do dangerous things ▶ **daringly** adv ▶ **daredevil** adj, n recklessly bold (person)

▌ **USAGE NOTE**
▌ When *dare* is used in a question

or as a negative, it does not take an -s: *He dare not come*

**dark** adj having little or no light; (of a colour) reflecting little light; (of hair or skin) brown or black; gloomy, sad; sinister, evil; secret e.g. *keep it dark* ▷ n absence of light; night ▶ **darkly** adv ▶ **darkness** n ▶ **darken** v ▶ **dark horse** person about whom little is known ▶ **darkroom** n darkened room for processing photographic film

**darling** n much-loved person; favourite ▷ adj much-loved

**darn**¹ v mend (a garment) with a series of interwoven stitches ▷ n patch of darned work

**darn**² interj, adv, adj, v (*euphemistic*) damn

**dart** n small narrow pointed missile that is thrown or shot, esp. in the game of darts; sudden quick movement; tapered tuck made in dressmaking ▷ pl game in which darts are thrown at a circular numbered board ▷ v move or direct quickly and suddenly

**Darwinism** n theory of the origin of animal and plant species by evolution ▶ **Darwinian, Darwinist** adj, n

**dash** v move quickly; hurl or crash; frustrate (someone's hopes) ▷ n sudden quick movement; small amount; mixture of style and courage; punctuation mark (–) indicating a change of subject; longer symbol used in Morse code ▶ **dashing** adj stylish and attractive ▶ **dashboard** n instrument panel in a vehicle

**dassie** n (*SAfr*) type of hoofed rodent-like animal (also **hyrax**)

**dastardly** adj wicked and cowardly

**dasyure** [**dass**-ee-your] n small marsupial of Australia, New Guinea, and adjacent islands

**data** n information consisting of observations, measurements, or facts; numbers, digits, etc., stored by a computer ▶ **data base** store of information that can be easily handled by a computer ▶ **data capture** process for converting information into a form that can be handled by a computer ▶ **data processing** series of operations performed on data, esp. by a computer, to extract or interpret information

**date¹** n specified day of the month; particular day or year when an event happened; (*informal*) appointment, esp. with a person to whom one is sexually attracted; (*informal*) person with whom one has a date ▷ v mark with the date; (*informal*) go on a date (with); assign a date of occurrence to; become old-fashioned; (foll by *from*) originate from ▶ **dated** adj old-fashioned

**date²** n dark-brown sweet-tasting fruit of the date palm ▶ **date palm** tall palm grown in tropical regions for its fruit

**dative** n (in certain languages) the form of the noun that expresses the indirect object

**datum** n, pl **data** single piece of information in the form of a fact or statistic

**daub** v smear or spread quickly or clumsily

**daughter** n female offspring; woman who comes from a certain place or is connected with a certain thing ▶ **daughterly** adj ▶ **daughter-in-law** n, pl **daughters-in-law** wife of one's child

**daunting** adj intimidating or worrying ▶ **dauntless** adj fearless

**dauphin** [doe-fan] n (formerly) eldest son of the king of France

**davenport** n (*chiefly Brit*) small writing table with drawers; (*Aust, US & Canadian*) large couch

**davit** [**dav**-vit] n crane, usu. one of a pair, at a ship's side, for lowering and hoisting a lifeboat

**Davy lamp** n miner's lamp designed to prevent it from igniting gas

**dawdle** v walk slowly, lag behind

**dawn** n daybreak; beginning (of something) ▷ v begin to grow light; begin to develop or appear; (foll by *on*) become apparent (to)

**day** n period of 24 hours; period of light between sunrise and sunset; part of a day occupied with regular activity, esp. work; period or point in time; time of success ▶ **daybreak** n time in the morning when light first appears ▶ **daydream** n pleasant fantasy indulged in while awake ▷ v indulge in idle fantasy ▶ **daydreamer** n ▶ **daylight** n light from the sun ▶ **day release** (*Brit*) system in which workers go to college one day a week ▶ **day-to-day** adj routine

**daze** v stun, by a blow or shock ▷ n state of confusion or shock

**dazzle** v impress greatly; blind temporarily by sudden excessive light ▷ n bright light that dazzles ▶ **dazzling** adj ▶ **dazzlingly** adv

**dB, db** decibel(s)

**DC** direct current

**DD** Doctor of Divinity

**D-day** n day selected for the start of some operation, orig. the Allied invasion of Europe in 1944

**DDT** n kind of insecticide

**de-** prefix indicating removal e.g. dethrone; indicating reversal e.g. declassify; indicating departure e.g. decamp

**deacon** n (*Christianity*) ordained minister ranking immediately below a priest; (in some Protestant churches) lay official who assists the minister

**dead** *adj* no longer alive; no longer in use; numb e.g. *my leg has gone dead*; complete, absolute e.g. *dead silence*; (*informal*) very tired; (of a place) lacking activity ▷ *n* period during which coldness or darkness is most intense e.g. *in the dead of night* ▷ *adv* extremely; suddenly e.g. *I stopped dead* **the dead** dead people ▶ **dead set** firmly decided ▶ **deadbeat** *n* (*informal*) lazy useless person ▶ **dead beat** (*informal*) exhausted ▶ **dead end** road with one end blocked off; situation in which further progress is impossible ▶ **dead heat** tie for first place between two participants in a contest ▶ **deadline** *n* time limit ▶ **deadlock** *n* point in a dispute at which no agreement can be reached ▶ **deadlocked** *adj* ▶ **deadpan** *adj, adv* showing no emotion or expression ▶ **dead reckoning** method of establishing one's position using the distance and direction travelled ▶ **dead zone** area where a mobile phone does not receive a signal; area where something does not exist or prosper ▶ **dead weight** heavy weight

**deaden** *v* make less intense

**deadly** *adj* -lier, -liest likely to cause death; (*informal*) extremely boring ▷ *adv* extremely ▶ **deadly nightshade** plant with poisonous black berries

**deaf** *adj* unable to hear **deaf to** refusing to listen to or take notice of ▶ **deafen** *v* make deaf, esp. temporarily ▶ **deafness** *n*

**deal¹** *n* agreement or transaction; kind of treatment e.g. *a fair deal*; large amount ▷ *v* **dealing,**

**dealt** [delt] inflict (a blow) on; (*Cards*) give out (cards) to the players ▶ **dealer** *n* ▶ **dealings** *pl n* transactions or business relations ▶ **deal in** *v* buy or sell (goods) ▶ **deal out** *v* distribute ▶ **deal with** *v* take action on; be concerned with

**deal²** *n* plank of fir or pine wood

**dean** *n* chief administrative official of a college or university faculty; chief administrator of a cathedral ▶ **deanery** *n*, *pl* -eries office or residence of a dean; parishes of a dean

**dear** *n* someone regarded with affection ▷ *adj* much-loved; costly ▶ **dearly** *adv* ▶ **dearness** *n*

**dearth** [dirth] *n* inadequate amount, scarcity

**death** *n* permanent end of life in a person or animal; instance of this; ending, destruction ▶ **deathly** *adj, adv* like death e.g. *a deathly silence*; deathly pale ▶ **death duty** (in Britain) former name for **inheritance tax** ▶ **death's-head** *n* human skull or a representation of one ▶ **death trap** place or vehicle considered very unsafe ▶ **deathwatch beetle** beetle that bores into wood and makes a tapping sound

**deb** *n* (*informal*) debutante

**debacle** [day-**bah**-kl] *n* disastrous failure

**debar** *v* prevent, bar

**debase** *v* lower in value, quality, or character ▶ **debasement** *n*

**debate** *n* discussion ▷ *v* discuss formally; consider (a course of action) ▶ **debatable** *adj* not absolutely certain

**debauch** [dib-**bawch**] *v* make (someone) bad or corrupt, esp. sexually ▶ **debauched** *adj* immoral, sexually corrupt ▶ **debauchery** *n*

**debenture** n long-term bond bearing fixed interest, issued by a company or a government agency

**debilitate** v weaken, make feeble
▶ **debilitation** n ▶ **debility** n weakness, infirmity

**debit** n acknowledgment of a sum owing by entry on the left side of an account ▷ v **debiting, debited** charge (an account) with a debt

**debonair** adj (of a man) charming and refined

**debouch** v move out from a narrow place to a wider one

**debrief** v receive a report from (a soldier, diplomat, etc.) after an event ▶ **debriefing** n

**debris** [**deb**-ree] n fragments of something destroyed

**debt** n something owed, esp. money **in debt** owing money
▶ **debtor** n

**debug** v (informal) find and remove defects in (a computer program); remove concealed microphones from (a room or telephone)

**debunk** v (informal) expose the falseness of

**debut** [**day**-byoo] n first public appearance of a performer
▶ **debutante** [**day**-byoo-tont] n young upper-class woman being formally presented to society

**Dec** December

**decade** n period of ten years

**decadence** n deterioration in morality or culture
▶ **decadent** adj

**decaffeinated** [dee-**kaf**-fin-ate-id] adj (of coffee, tea, or cola) with caffeine removed

**decagon** n geometric figure with ten sides

**decahedron** [deck-a-**heed**-ron] n solid figure with ten faces

**Decalogue** n the Ten Commandments

**decamp** v depart secretly or suddenly

**decant** v pour (a liquid) from one container to another; (chiefly Brit) rehouse (people) while their homes are being renovated

**decanter** n stoppered bottle for wine or spirits

**decapitate** v behead
▶ **decapitation** n

**decathlon** n athletic contest with ten events

**decay** v become weaker or more corrupt; rot ▷ n process of decaying; state brought about by this process

**decease** n (formal) death

**deceased** adj (formal) dead **the deceased** dead person

**deceive** v mislead by lying; be unfaithful to (one's sexual partner)
▶ **deceiver** n ▶ **deceit** n behaviour intended to deceive ▶ **deceitful** adj

**decelerate** v slow down
▶ **deceleration** n

**December** n twelfth month of the year

**decent** adj (of a person) polite and morally acceptable; fitting or proper; conforming to conventions of sexual behaviour; (informal) kind
▶ **decently** adv ▶ **decency** n

**decentralize** v reorganize into smaller local units
▶ **decentralization** n

**deception** n deceiving; something that deceives, trick
▶ **deceptive** adj likely or designed to deceive ▶ **deceptively** adv
▶ **deceptiveness** n

**deci-** combining form one tenth

**decibel** n unit for measuring the intensity of sound

**decide** v (cause to) reach a decision; settle (a contest or question)
▶ **decided** adj unmistakable; determined ▶ **decidedly** adv

**deciduous** adj (of a tree) shedding its leaves annually

**decimal** n fraction written in the form of a dot followed by one or more numbers ▷ adj relating to or using powers of ten; expressed as a decimal ▶ **decimalization** n ▶ **decimal currency** system of currency in which the units are parts or powers of ten ▶ **decimal point** dot between the unit and the fraction of a number in the decimal system ▶ **decimal system** number system with a base of ten, in which numbers are expressed by combinations of the digits 0 to 9

**decimate** v destroy or kill a large proportion of ▶ **decimation** n

**decipher** v work out the meaning of (something illegible or in code) ▶ **decipherable** adj

**decision** n judgment, conclusion, or resolution; act of making up one's mind; firmness of purpose ▶ **decisive** adj having a definite influence; having the ability to make quick decisions ▶ **decisively** adv ▶ **decisiveness** n

**deck** n area of a ship that forms a floor; similar area in a bus; platform that supports the turntable and pick-up of a record player ▶ **deck chair** folding chair made of canvas over a wooden frame ▶ **decking** n wooden platform in a garden ▶ **deck out** v decorate

**declaim** v speak loudly and dramatically; protest loudly ▶ **declamation** n ▶ **declamatory** adj

**declare** v state firmly and forcefully; announce officially; acknowledge for tax purposes ▶ **declaration** n ▶ **declaratory** adj

**declension** n (Grammar) changes in the form of nouns, pronouns, or adjectives to show case, number, and gender

**decline** v become smaller, weaker, or less important; refuse politely to accept or do; (Grammar) list the inflections of (a noun, pronoun, or adjective) ▷ n gradual weakening or loss

**declivity** n, pl -ties downward slope

**declutch** v disengage the clutch of a motor vehicle

**decoct** v extract the essence from (a substance) by boiling ▶ **decoction** n

**decode** v convert from code into ordinary language ▶ **decoder** n

**décolleté** [day-**kol**-tay] adj (of a woman's garment) low-cut

**decommission** v dismantle (a nuclear reactor, weapon, etc.) which is no longer needed

**decompose** v be broken down through chemical or bacterial action ▶ **decomposition** n

**decompress** v free from pressure; return (a diver) to normal atmospheric pressure ▶ **decompression** n ▶ **decompression sickness** severe pain and difficulty in breathing, caused by a sudden change in atmospheric pressure

**decongestant** n medicine that relieves nasal congestion

**decontaminate** v make safe by removing poisons, radioactivity, etc. ▶ **decontamination** n

**decor** [**day**-core] n style in which a room or house is decorated

**decorate** v make more attractive by adding something ornamental; paint or wallpaper; award a (military) medal to ▶ **decoration** n ▶ **decorative** adj ▶ **decorator** n

**decorous** [**dek**-a-russ] adj polite, calm, and sensible in behaviour ▶ **decorously** adv

**d**

**decorum** [dik-**core**-um] n polite
and socially correct behaviour

**decoy** n person or thing used to lure
someone into danger; dummy bird
or animal, used to lure game within
shooting range ▷ v lure away by
means of a trick

**decrease** v make or become less
▷ n lessening, reduction; amount
by which something has decreased

**decree** n law made by someone
in authority; court judgment ▷ v
order by decree

**decrepit** adj weakened or worn out
by age or long use ▶ **decrepitude** n

**decry** v **-crying, -cried** express
disapproval of

**decrypt** v decode (a message) with
or without previous knowledge
of its key; make intelligible (a
television or other signal) that has
been deliberately distorted for
transmission

**dedicate** v commit (oneself or one's
time) wholly to a special purpose
or cause; inscribe or address
(a book etc.) to someone as a
tribute ▶ **dedicated** adj devoted
to a particular purpose or cause
▶ **dedication** n

**deduce** v reach (a conclusion)
by reasoning from evidence
▶ **deducible** adj

**deduct** v subtract

**deduction** n deducting; something
that is deducted; deducing;
conclusion reached by deducing
▶ **deductive** adj

**deduplicate** v remove (duplicated
material) from a system

**deed** n something that is done;
legal document

**deem** v consider, judge

**deep** adj extending or situated far
down, inwards, backwards, or
sideways; of a specified dimension
downwards, inwards, or

backwards; difficult to understand;
of great intensity; (foll by in)
absorbed in (an activity); (of a
colour) strong or dark; low in pitch
**the deep** (poetic) the sea ▶ **deeply**
adv profoundly or intensely (also
**deep down**) ▶ **deepen** v ▶ **deep-
freeze** n same as **freezer**

**deer** n, pl **deer** large wild animal,
the male of which has antlers
▶ **deerstalker** n cloth hat with peaks
at the back and front and earflaps

**deface** v deliberately spoil the
appearance of ▶ **defacement** n

**de facto** adv in fact ▷ adj existing
in fact, whether legally recognized
or not

**defame** v attack the good
reputation of ▶ **defamation** n
▶ **defamatory** [dif-**fam**-a-tree] adj

**default** n failure to do something;
(Computing) instruction to a
computer to select a particular
option unless the user specifies
otherwise ▷ v fail to fulfil an
obligation **in default of** in the
absence of ▶ **defaulter** n

**defeat** v win a victory over;
thwart, frustrate ▷ n defeating
▶ **defeatism** n ready acceptance
or expectation of defeat
▶ **defeatist** adj, n

**defecate** v discharge waste
from the body through the anus
▶ **defecation** n

**defect** n imperfection, blemish
▷ v desert one's cause or country
to join the opposing forces
▶ **defective** adj imperfect, faulty
▶ **defection** n ▶ **defector** n

**defence** n resistance against
attack; argument in support of
something; country's military
resources; defendant's case in a
court of law ▶ **defenceless** adj

**defend** v protect from harm or
danger; support in the face of

criticism; represent (a defendant) in court ▶ **defendant** n person accused of a crime ▶ **defensible** adj capable of being defended because believed to be right ▶ **defensibility** n ▶ **defensive** adj intended for defence; overanxious to protect oneself against (threatened) criticism ▶ **defensively** adv

**defender** n person who supports someone or something in the face of criticism; player whose chief task is to stop the opposition scoring

**defer¹** v -ferring, -ferred delay (something) until a future time ▶ **deferment, deferral** n

**defer²** v -ferring, -ferred (foll by to) comply with the wishes (of) ▶ **deference** n polite and respectful behaviour ▶ **deferential** adj ▶ **deferentially** adv

**defiance** n see **defy**

**defibrillator** n apparatus for stopping fibrillation of the heart by application of an electric current to the chest wall or directly to the heart

**deficient** adj lacking some essential thing or quality; inadequate in quality or quantity ▶ **deficiency** n state of being deficient; lack, shortage

**deficit** n amount by which a sum of money is too small

**defile¹** v treat (something sacred or important) without respect ▶ **defilement** n

**defile²** n narrow valley or pass

**define** v state precisely the meaning of; show clearly the outline of ▶ **definable** adj ▶ **definite** adj firm, clear, and precise; having precise limits; known for certain ▶ **definitely** adv ▶ **definition** n statement of the meaning of a word or phrase;

quality of being clear and distinct ▶ **definitive** adj providing an unquestionable conclusion; being the best example of something

**deflate** v (cause to) collapse through the release of air; take away the self-esteem or conceit from; (Economics) cause deflation of (an economy) ▶ **deflation** n (Economics) reduction in economic activity resulting in lower output and investment; feeling of sadness following excitement ▶ **deflationary** adj

**deflect** v (cause to) turn aside from a course ▶ **deflection** n ▶ **deflector** n

**deflower** v (lit) deprive (a woman) of her virginity

**defoliate** v deprive (a plant) of its leaves ▶ **defoliant** n ▶ **defoliation** n

**deforestation** n destruction of all the trees in an area

**deform** v put out of shape or spoil the appearance of ▶ **deformation** n ▶ **deformity** n

**defraud** v cheat out of money, property, etc.

**defray** v provide money for (costs or expenses)

**defriend** v remove (a person) from the list of one's friends on a social networking website

**defrock** v deprive (a priest) of priestly status

**defrost** v make or become free of ice; thaw (frozen food) by removing it from a freezer

**deft** adj quick and skilful in movement ▶ **deftly** adv ▶ **deftness** n

**defunct** adj no longer existing or operative

**defuse** v remove the fuse of (an explosive device); remove the tension from (a situation)

**defy** v **-fying, -fied** resist openly and boldly; make impossible e.g. *the condition of the refugees defied description* ▸ **defiance** n ▸ **defiant** adj

**degenerate** adj having deteriorated to a lower mental, moral, or physical level ▸ n degenerate person ▸ v become degenerate ▸ **degeneracy** n degenerate behaviour ▸ **degeneration** n

**degrade** v reduce to dishonour or disgrace; reduce in status or quality; (*Chem*) decompose into smaller molecules ▸ **degradation** n

**degree** n stage in a scale of relative amount or intensity; academic award given by a university or college on successful completion of a course; unit of measurement for temperature, angles, or latitude and longitude

**dehumanize** v deprive of human qualities; make (an activity) mechanical or routine ▸ **dehumanization** n

**dehydrate** v remove water from (food) to preserve it **be dehydrated** become weak through losing too much water from the body ▸ **dehydration** n

**de-ice** v free of ice ▸ **de-icer** n

**deify** [**day**-if-fie] v **-fying, -fied** treat or worship as a god ▸ **deification** n

**deign** [**dane**] v agree (to do something), but as if doing someone a favour

**deity** [**dee**-it-ee, **day**-it-ee] n, pl **-ties** god or goddess; state of being divine

**déjà vu** [**day**-zhah **voo**] n feeling of having experienced before something that is actually happening now

**dejected** adj unhappy ▸ **dejectedly** adv ▸ **dejection** n

**de jure** adv, adj according to law

**dekko** n (*Brit, Aust & NZ slang*) **have a dekko** have a look

**delay** v put off to a later time; slow up or cause to be late ▸ n act of delaying; interval of time between events

**delectable** adj delightful, very attractive ▸ **delectation** n (*formal*) great pleasure

**delegate** n person chosen to represent others, esp. at a meeting ▸ v entrust (duties or powers) to someone; appoint as a delegate ▸ **delegation** n group chosen to represent others; delegating

**delete** v remove (something written or printed) ▸ **deletion** n

**deleterious** [del-lit-**eer**-ee-uss] adj harmful, injurious

**deli** n (*informal*) delicatessen

**deliberate** adj planned in advance, intentional; careful and unhurried ▸ v think something over ▸ **deliberately** adv ▸ **deliberation** n ▸ **deliberative** adj

**delicate** adj fine or subtle in quality or workmanship; having a fragile beauty; (of a taste etc.) pleasantly subtle; easily damaged; requiring tact ▸ **delicately** adv ▸ **delicacy** n being delicate; (pl **-cies**) something particularly good to eat

**delicatessen** n shop selling imported or unusual foods, often already cooked or prepared

**delicious** adj very appealing to taste or smell ▸ **deliciously** adv

**delight** n (source of) great pleasure ▸ v please greatly; (foll by in) take great pleasure (in) ▸ **delightful** adj ▸ **delightfully** adv

**delimit** v mark or lay down the limits of ▸ **delimitation** n

**delineate** [dill-**lin**-ee-ate] v show by drawing; describe in words ▶ **delineation** n

**delinquent** n someone, esp. a young person, who repeatedly breaks the law ▷ adj repeatedly breaking the law ▶ **delinquency** n

**delirium** n state of excitement and mental confusion, often with hallucinations; great excitement ▶ **delirious** adj ▶ **deliriously** adv

**deliver** v carry (goods etc.) to a destination; hand over; aid in the birth of; present (a lecture or speech); release or rescue; strike (a blow) ▶ **deliverance** n rescue from captivity or evil ▶ **delivery** n, pl **-eries** delivering; something that is delivered; act of giving birth to a baby; style in public speaking

**dell** n (chiefly Brit) small wooded hollow

**Delphic** adj ambiguous, like the ancient Greek oracle at Delphi

**delphinium** n large garden plant with blue flowers

**delta** n fourth letter in the Greek alphabet; flat area at the mouth of some rivers where the main stream splits up into several branches

**delude** v deceive

**deluge** [**del**-lyooj] n great flood; torrential rain; overwhelming number ▷ v flood; overwhelm

**delusion** n mistaken idea or belief; state of being deluded ▶ **delusive** adj

**de luxe** adj rich or sumptuous, superior in quality

**delve** v research deeply (for information)

**demagogue** n political agitator who appeals to the prejudice and passions of the mob ▶ **demagogic** adj ▶ **demagogy** n

**demand** v request forcefully; require as just, urgent, etc.; claim

as a right ▷ n forceful request; (Economics) willingness and ability to purchase goods and services; something that requires special effort or sacrifice ▶ **demanding** adj requiring a lot of time or effort

**demarcation** n (formal) establishing limits or boundaries, esp. between the work performed by different trade unions

**demean** v **demean oneself** do something unworthy of one's status or character

**demeanour** n way a person behaves

**demented** adj mad ▶ **dementedly** adv ▶ **dementia** [dim-**men**-sha] n state of serious mental deterioration

**demerara sugar** n brown crystallized cane sugar

**demerit** n fault, disadvantage

**demesne** [dim-**mane**] n land surrounding a house; (Law) possession of one's own property or land

**demi-** combining form half

**demijohn** n large bottle with a short neck, often encased in wicker

**demilitarize** v remove the military forces from ▶ **demilitarization** n

**demimonde** n (esp. in the 19th century) class of women considered to be outside respectable society because of promiscuity; group considered not wholly respectable

**demise** n eventual failure (of something successful); (formal) death

**demo** n, pl **demos** (informal) demonstration, organized expression of public opinion

**demob** v (Brit, Aust & NZ informal) demobilize

**demobilize** v release from the armed forces ▶ **demobilization** n

**democracy** *n*, *pl* **-cies** government by the people or their elected representatives; state governed in this way ▶ **democrat** *n* advocate of democracy; (**D-**) member or supporter of the Democratic Party in the US ▶ **democratic** *adj* of democracy; upholding democracy; (**D-**) of the Democratic Party, the more liberal of the two main political parties in the US ▶ **democratically** *adv*

**demography** *n* study of population statistics, such as births and deaths ▶ **demographer** *n* ▶ **demographic** *adj*

**demolish** *v* knock down or destroy (a building); disprove (an argument) ▶ **demolition** *n*

**demon** *n* evil spirit; person who does something with great energy or skill ▶ **demonic** *adj* evil ▶ **demoniac, demoniacal** *adj* appearing to be possessed by a devil; frenzied ▶ **demonology** *n* study of demons

**demonstrate** *v* show or prove by reasoning or evidence; display and explain the workings of; reveal the existence of; show support or opposition by public parades or rallies ▶ **demonstrable** *adj* able to be proved ▶ **demonstrably** *adv* ▶ **demonstration** *n* organized expression of public opinion; explanation or display of how something works; proof ▶ **demonstrative** *adj* tending to show one's feelings unreservedly ▶ **demonstratively** *adv* ▶ **demonstrator** *n* person who demonstrates how a device or machine works; person who takes part in a public demonstration

**demoralize** *v* undermine the morale of ▶ **demoralization** *n*

**demote** *v* reduce in status or rank ▶ **demotion** *n*

**demur** *v* **-murring, -murred** show reluctance ▷ *n* **without demur** without objecting

**demure** *adj* quiet, reserved, and rather shy ▶ **demurely** *adv*

**den** *n* home of a wild animal; small secluded room in a home; place where people indulge in criminal or immoral activities

**denationalize** *v* transfer (an industry) from public to private ownership ▶ **denationalization** *n*

**denature** *v* change the nature of; make (alcohol) unfit to drink

**denier** [**den**-yer] *n* unit of weight used to measure the fineness of nylon or silk

**denigrate** *v* criticize unfairly ▶ **denigration** *n*

**denim** *n* hard-wearing cotton fabric, usu. blue ▷ *pl* jeans made of denim

**denizen** *n* inhabitant

**denominate** *v* give a specific name to

**denomination** *n* group having a distinctive interpretation of a religious faith; unit in a system of weights, values, or measures ▶ **denominational** *adj*

**denominator** *n* number below the line in a fraction

**denote** *v* be a sign of; have as a literal meaning ▶ **denotation** *n*

**denouement** [day-**noo**-mon] *n* final outcome or solution in a play or book

**denounce** *v* speak vehemently against; give information against ▶ **denunciation** *n* open condemnation

**dense** *adj* closely packed; difficult to see through; stupid ▶ **densely** *adv* ▶ **density** *n*, *pl* **-ties** degree to which something is filled or occupied; measure of the compactness of a substance,

**dent** n hollow in the surface of something, made by hitting it ▷ v make a dent in

**dental** adj of teeth or dentistry ▶ **dental floss** waxed thread used to remove food particles from between the teeth ▶ **dentine** [den-teen] n hard dense tissue forming the bulk of a tooth ▶ **denture** n false tooth

**dentist** n person qualified to practise dentistry ▶ **dentistry** n branch of medicine concerned with the teeth and gums

**denude** v remove the covering or protection from

**deny** v **-nying, -nied** declare to be untrue; refuse to give or allow; refuse to acknowledge ▶ **deniable** adj ▶ **denial** n statement that something is not true; rejection of a request

**deodorant** n substance applied to the body to mask the smell of perspiration

**deodorize** v remove or disguise the smell of

**depart** v leave; differ, deviate ▶ **departed** adj (euphemistic) dead **the departed** (euphemistic) dead person ▶ **departure** n

**department** n specialized division of a large organization; major subdivision of the administration of a government ▶ **departmental** adj ▶ **department store** large shop selling many kinds of goods

**depend** v (foll by **on**) put trust (in); be influenced or determined (by); rely (on) for income or support ▶ **dependable** adj ▶ **dependably** adv ▶ **dependability** n ▶ **dependant** n person who depends on another for financial

support ▶ **dependence** n state of being dependent ▶ **dependency** n, pl **-cies** country controlled by another country; overreliance on another person or on a drug ▶ **dependent** adj depending on someone or something

**SPELLING TIP**

The words **dependant** and **dependent** are easy to confuse. The first, ending in -ant, is a noun meaning a person who is dependent (adjective ending in -ent) on someone else

**depict** v produce a picture of; describe in words ▶ **depiction** n

**depilatory** [dip-**pill**-a-tree] n, pl **-tories** ▷ adj (substance) designed to remove unwanted hair

**deplete** v use up; reduce in number ▶ **depletion** n

**deplore** v condemn strongly ▶ **deplorable** adj very bad or unpleasant

**deploy** v organize (troops or resources) into a position ready for immediate action ▶ **deployment** n

**depopulate** v reduce the population of ▶ **depopulation** n

**deport** v remove forcibly from a country **deport oneself** behave in a specified way ▶ **deportation** n ▶ **deportee** n

**deportment** n way in which a person moves or stands

**depose** v remove from an office or position of power; (Law) testify on oath

**deposit** v put down; entrust for safekeeping, esp. to a bank; lay down naturally ▷ n sum of money paid into a bank account; money given in part payment for goods or services; accumulation of sediments, minerals, etc. ▶ **depositary** n person to whom something is entrusted for safety

▶ **depositor** n ▶ **depository** n store for furniture etc.

**deposition** n (Law) sworn statement of a witness used in court in his or her absence; deposing; depositing; something deposited

**depot** [dep-oh] n building where goods or vehicles are kept when not in use; (NZ & US) bus or railway station

**depraved** adj morally bad ▶ **depravity** n

**deprecate** v express disapproval of ▶ **deprecation** n ▶ **deprecatory** adj

**depreciate** v decline in value or price; criticize ▶ **depreciation** n

**depredation** n plundering

**depress** v make sad; lower (prices or wages); push down ▶ **depressing** adj ▶ **depressingly** adv ▶ **depressant** n, adj (drug) able to reduce nervous activity ▶ **depression** n mental state in which a person has feelings of gloom and inadequacy; economic condition in which there is high unemployment and low output and investment; area of low air pressure; sunken place ▶ **depressive** adj tending to cause depression ▷ n person who suffers from depression

**deprive** v (foll by of) prevent from (having or enjoying) ▶ **deprivation** n ▶ **deprived** adj lacking adequate living conditions, education, etc.

**dept** department

**depth** n distance downwards, backwards, or inwards; intensity of emotion; profundity of character or thought ▶ **depth charge** bomb used to attack submarines by exploding at a preset depth of water

**depute** v appoint (someone) to act on one's behalf ▶ **deputation** n body of people appointed to represent others

**deputy** n, pl -**ties** person appointed to act on behalf of another ▶ **deputize** v act as deputy

**derail** v cause (a train) to go off the rails ▶ **derailment** n

**deranged** adj insane or uncontrolled; in a state of disorder ▶ **derangement** n

**derby** [dah-bee] n, pl -**bies** sporting event between teams from the same area ▷ n any of various horse races

**deregulate** v remove regulations or controls from ▶ **deregulation** n

**derelict** adj unused and falling into ruins ▷ n social outcast, vagrant ▶ **dereliction** n state of being abandoned **dereliction of duty** failure to do one's duty

**deride** v treat with contempt or ridicule ▶ **derision** n ▶ **derisive** adj mocking, scornful ▶ **derisory** adj too small or inadequate to be considered seriously

**de rigueur** [de rig-gur] adj required by fashion

**derive** v (foll by from) take or develop (from) ▶ **derivation** n ▶ **derivative** adj ▷ n word, idea, etc., derived from another; (Maths) rate of change of one quantity in relation to another

**dermatitis** n inflammation of the skin

**dermatology** n branch of medicine concerned with the skin ▶ **dermatologist** n

**derogatory** [dir-**rog**-a-tree] adj intentionally offensive

**derrick** n simple crane; framework erected over an oil well

**derv** n (Brit) diesel oil, when used for road transport

**dervish** n member of a Muslim religious order noted for a frenzied whirling dance

**descant** n (Music) tune played or sung above a basic melody

**descend** v move down (a slope etc.); move to a lower level, pitch, etc.; (foll by to) stoop to (unworthy behaviour); (foll by on) visit unexpectedly **be descended from** be connected by a blood relationship to ▶ **descendant** n person or animal descended from an individual, race, or species ▶ **descendent** adj descending ▶ **descent** n descending; downward slope; derivation from an ancestor

**describe** v give an account of (something or someone) in words; trace the outline of (a circle etc.) ▶ **description** n statement that describes something or someone; sort e.g. *flowers of every description* ▶ **descriptive** adj ▶ **descriptively** adv

**descry** v -**scrying**, -**scried** catch sight of; discover by looking carefully

**desecrate** v damage or insult (something sacred) ▶ **desecration** n

**desegregate** v end racial segregation in ▶ **desegregation** n

**deselect** v (Brit Politics) refuse to select (an MP) for re-election ▶ **deselection** n

**desert**¹ n region with little or no vegetation because of low rainfall

**desert**² v abandon (a person or place) without intending to return; (Mil) leave (a post or duty) with no intention of returning ▶ **deserter** n ▶ **desertion** n

**deserts** pl n **get one's just deserts** get the punishment one deserves

**deserve** v be entitled to or worthy of ▶ **deserved** adj rightfully earned

▶ **deservedly** adv ▶ **deserving** adj worthy of help, praise, or reward

**deshabille** [day-zab-**beel**] n state of being partly dressed

**desiccate** v remove most of the water from ▶ **desiccation** n

> **SPELLING TIP**
> The word **desiccate** has two cs because it comes from the Latin word *siccus*, which means 'dry'

**design** v work out the structure or form of (something), by making a sketch or plans; plan and make artistically; intend for a specific purpose ▷ n preliminary drawing; arrangement or features of an artistic or decorative nature; art of designing; intention e.g. *by design* ▶ **designedly** [dee-**zine**-id-lee] adv intentionally ▶ **designer** n person who draws up original sketches or plans from which things are made ▷ adj designed by a well-known designer ▶ **designing** adj cunning and scheming

**designate** [**dez**-zig-nate] v give a name to; select (someone) for an office or duty ▷ adj appointed but not yet in office ▶ **designation** n name

**desire** v want very much ▷ n wish, longing; sexual appetite; person or thing desired ▶ **desirable** adj worth having; arousing sexual desire ▶ **desirability** n **desirous of** having a desire for

**desist** v (foll by from) stop (doing something)

**desk** n piece of furniture with a writing surface and drawers; service counter in a public building; section of a newspaper covering a specific subject e.g. *the sports desk* ▶ **desktop** adj (of a computer) small enough to use at a desk ▷ n main screen display on computer

**desolate** adj uninhabited and bleak; very sad ▷ v deprive of inhabitants; make (someone) very sad ▶ **desolation** n

**despair** n total loss of hope ▷ v lose hope

**despatch** v, n same as **dispatch**

**desperado** n, pl **-does** or **-dos** reckless person ready to commit any violent illegal act

**desperate** adj in despair and reckless; (of an action) undertaken as a last resort; having a strong need or desire ▶ **desperately** adv ▶ **desperation** n

> **SPELLING TIP**
> Spelling **desperate** as *desparate* (with an *a* in its second syllable) is a common mistake

**despise** v regard with contempt ▶ **despicable** adj deserving contempt ▶ **despicably** adv

**despite** prep in spite of

**despoil** v (formal) plunder ▶ **despoliation** n

**despondent** adj unhappy ▶ **despondently** adv ▶ **despondency** n

**despot** n person in power who acts unfairly or cruelly ▶ **despotic** adj ▶ **despotism** n unfair or cruel government or behaviour

**dessert** n sweet course served at the end of a meal ▶ **dessertspoon** n spoon between a tablespoon and a teaspoon in size

**destination** n place to which someone or something is going

**destined** [**dess**-tind] adj certain to be or to do something

**destiny** n, pl **-nies** future marked out for a person or thing; the power that predetermines the course of events

**destitute** adj having no money or possessions ▶ **destitution** n

**destroy** v ruin, demolish; put an end to; kill (an animal) ▶ **destroyer** n small heavily armed warship; person or thing that destroys

**destruction** n destroying; cause of ruin ▶ **destructive** adj (capable of) causing destruction ▶ **destructively** adv

**desuetude** [diss-**syoo**-it-tude] n condition of not being in use

**desultory** [**dez**-zl-tree] adj jumping from one thing to another, disconnected; random ▶ **desultorily** adv

**detach** v disengage and separate ▶ **detachable** adj ▶ **detached** adj (Brit, Aust & SAfr) (of a house) not joined to another house; showing no emotional involvement ▶ **detachment** n lack of emotional involvement; small group of soldiers

**detail** n individual piece of information; unimportant item; small individual features of something, considered collectively; (chiefly Mil) (personnel assigned) a specific duty ▷ v list fully

**detain** v delay (someone); hold (someone) in custody ▶ **detainee** n

**detect** v notice; discover, find ▶ **detectable** adj ▶ **detection** n ▶ **detective** n policeman or private agent who investigates crime ▶ **detector** n instrument used to find something

**detente** [day-**tont**] n easing of tension between nations

**detention** n imprisonment; form of punishment in which a pupil is detained after school

**deter** v **-terring, -terred** discourage (someone) from doing something by instilling fear or doubt ▶ **deterrent** n something that deters; weapon, esp. nuclear, intended to deter attack ▷ adj tending to deter

**detergent** n chemical substance for washing clothes or dishes

**deteriorate** v become worse
▸ **deterioration** n

**determine** v settle (an argument or a question) conclusively; find out the facts about; make a firm decision (to do something) ▸ **determinant** n factor that determines ▸ **determinate** adj definitely limited or fixed ▸ **determination** n being determined or resolute ▸ **determined** adj firmly decided, unable to be dissuaded ▸ **determinedly** adv ▸ **determiner** n (Grammar) word that determines the object to which a noun phrase refers e.g. all ▸ **determinism** n theory that human choice is not free, but decided by past events ▸ **determinist** n, adj

**detest** v dislike intensely ▸ **detestable** adj ▸ **detestation** n

**dethrone** v remove from a throne or position of power

**detonate** v explode ▸ **detonation** n ▸ **detonator** n small amount of explosive, or a device, used to set off an explosion

**detour** n route that is not the most direct one

**detox** v, n (informal) (undergo) treatment to rid the body of poisonous substances, esp. alcohol or drugs

**detract** v (foll by from) make (something) seem less good ▸ **detractor** n

**detriment** n disadvantage or damage ▸ **detrimental** adj ▸ **detrimentally** adv

**detritus** [dit-**trite**-uss] n loose mass of stones and silt worn away from rocks; debris

**de trop** [de **troh**] adj (French) unwanted, unwelcome

**deuce** [**dyooss**] n (Tennis) score of forty all; playing card with two symbols or dice with two spots

**deuterium** n isotope of hydrogen twice as heavy as the normal atom

**Deutschmark** [**doytch**-mark], **Deutsche Mark** [**doytch**-a] n former monetary unit of Germany

**devalue** v -**valuing**, -**valued** reduce the exchange value of (a currency); reduce the value of (something or someone) ▸ **devaluation** n

**devastate** v destroy ▸ **devastated** adj shocked and extremely upset ▸ **devastation** n

**develop** v grow or bring to a later, more elaborate, or more advanced stage; come or bring into existence; build houses or factories on (an area of land); produce (photographs) by making negatives or prints from a film ▸ **developer** n person who develops property; chemical used to develop photographs or films ▸ **development** n ▸ **developing country** poor or nonindustrial country that is trying to develop its resources by industrialization

**deviate** v differ from others in belief or thought; depart from one's previous behaviour ▸ **deviation** n ▸ **deviant** n, adj (person) deviating from what is considered acceptable behaviour ▸ **deviance** n

**device** n machine or tool used for a specific task; scheme or plan

**devil** n evil spirit; evil person; person e.g. poor devil; daring person e.g. be a devil!; (informal) something difficult or annoying e.g. a devil of a long time ▸ v -**illing**, -**illed** prepare (food) with a highly flavoured spiced mixture **the Devil** (Theology) chief spirit of evil and enemy of God ▸ **devilish** adj cruel or unpleasant ▷ *adv* (also **devilishly**) (*informal*) extremely ▶ **devilment** *n* mischievous conduct ▶ **devilry** *n* mischievousness ▶ **devil-may-care** *adj* carefree and cheerful ▶ **devil's advocate** person who takes an opposing or unpopular point of view for the sake of argument

**devious** *adj* insincere and dishonest; indirect ▶ **deviously** *adv* ▶ **deviousness** *n*

**devise** *v* work out (something) in one's mind

**devoid** *adj* (foll by *of*) completely lacking (in)

**devolve** *v* (foll by *on* or *to*) pass (power or duties) or (of power or duties) be passed to a successor or substitute ▶ **devolution** *n* transfer of authority from a central government to regional governments

**devote** *v* apply or dedicate to a particular purpose ▶ **devoted** *adj* showing loyalty or devotion ▶ **devotedly** *adv* ▶ **devotee** *n* person who is very enthusiastic about something; zealous follower of a religion ▶ **devotion** *n* strong affection for or loyalty to someone or something; religious zeal ▷ *pl* prayers ▶ **devotional** *adj*

**devour** *v* eat greedily; (of an emotion) engulf and destroy; read eagerly

**devout** *adj* deeply religious ▶ **devoutly** *adv*

**dew** *n* drops of water that form on the ground at night from vapour in the air ▶ **dewy** *adj*

**dewlap** *n* loose fold of skin hanging under the throat in dogs, cattle, etc.

**dexterity** *n* skill in using one's hands; mental quickness ▶ **dexterous** *adj* ▶ **dexterously** *adv*

**dextrose** *n* glucose occurring in fruit, honey, and the blood of animals

**DH** (in Britain) Department of Health

**DI** donor insemination: method of making a woman pregnant by transferring sperm from a man other than her regular partner using artificial means: method of making a woman pregnant by transferring sperm from a man other than her regular partner using artificial means

**diabetes** [die-a-**beet**-eez] *n* disorder in which an abnormal amount of urine containing an excess of sugar is excreted ▶ **diabetic** *n* ▷ *adj*

**diabolic** *adj* of the Devil ▶ **diabolism** *n* witchcraft, devil worship

**diabolical** *adj* (*informal*) extremely bad ▶ **diabolically** *adv*

**diaconate** *n* position or period of office of a deacon

**diacritic** *n* sign above or below a character to indicate phonetic value or stress

**diadem** *n* (*old-fashioned*) crown

**diaeresis** *n*, *pl* **-ses** mark (¨) placed over a vowel to show that it is pronounced separately from the preceding one, for example in *Noël*

**diagnosis** [die-ag-**no**-siss] *n*, *pl* **-ses** [-seez] discovery and identification of diseases from the examination of symptoms ▶ **diagnose** *v* ▶ **diagnostic** *adj*

**diagonal** *adj* from corner to corner; slanting ▷ *n* diagonal line ▶ **diagonally** *adv*

**diagram** *n* sketch showing the form or workings of something ▶ **diagrammatic** *adj*

**dial** *n* face of a clock or watch; graduated disc on a measuring instrument; control on a radio or television set used to change the station; numbered disc on the front of some telephones ▷ v **dialling, dialled** operate the dial or buttons on a telephone in order to contact (a number)

**dialect** n form of a language spoken in a particular area ▶ **dialectal** adj

**dialectic** n logical debate by question and answer to resolve differences between two views ▶ **dialectical** adj

**dialogue** n conversation between two people, esp. in a book, film, or play; discussion between representatives of two nations or groups ▶ **dialogue box** small window that may open on a computer screen to prompt the user to enter information or select an option

**dialysis** [die-**al**-iss-iss] n (Med) filtering of blood through a membrane to remove waste products

**diamanté** [die-a-**man**-tee] adj decorated with artificial jewels or sequins

**diameter** n (length of) a straight line through the centre of a circle or sphere ▶ **diametric, diametrical** adj of a diameter; completely opposed e.g. the diametric opposite ▶ **diametrically** adv

**diamond** n exceptionally hard, usu. colourless, precious stone; (Geom) figure with four sides of equal length forming two acute and two obtuse angles; playing card marked with red diamond-shaped symbols ▶ **diamond wedding** sixtieth anniversary of a wedding

**diaper** n (US) nappy

**diaphanous** [die-**af**-fan-ous] adj fine and almost transparent

**diaphragm** [die-a-fram] n muscular partition that separates the abdominal cavity and chest cavity; contraceptive device placed over the neck of the womb

**diarrhoea** [die-a-**ree**-a] n frequent discharge of abnormally liquid faeces

| **SPELLING TIP**
The word **diarrhoea** has two rs and one h

**diary** n, pl -**ries** (book for) a record of daily events, appointments, or observations ▶ **diarist** n

**diatribe** n bitter critical attack

**dibble** n small hand tool used to make holes in the ground for seeds or plants

**dice** n, pl **dice** small cube each of whose sides has a different number of spots (1 to 6), used in games of chance ▷ v cut (food) into small cubes **dice with death** take a risk ▶ **dicey** adj (informal) dangerous or risky

**dichotomy** [die-**kot**-a-mee] n, pl -**mies** division into two opposed groups or parts

**dicky**[1] n, pl **dickies** false shirt front ▶ **dicky-bird** n child's word for a bird

**dicky**[2] adj **dickier, dickiest** (informal) shaky or weak

**Dictaphone**® n tape recorder for recording dictation for subsequent typing

**dictate** v say aloud for someone else to write down; (foll by to) seek to impose one's will on (other people) ▷ n authoritative command; guiding principle ▶ **dictation** n ▶ **dictator** n ruler who has complete power; person in power who acts unfairly or cruelly ▶ **dictatorship** n ▶ **dictatorial** adj like a dictator

**diction** n manner of pronouncing words and sounds

**dictionary** n, pl **-aries** book consisting of an alphabetical list of words with their meanings; alphabetically ordered reference book of terms relating to a particular subject

**dictum** n, pl **-tums** or **-ta** formal statement; popular saying

**did** v past tense of **do¹**

**didactic** adj intended to instruct ▶ **didactically** adv

**diddle** v (informal) swindle

**didgeridoo** n Australian musical instrument made from a long hollow piece of wood

**didn't** did not

**die¹** v **dying, died** (of a person, animal, or plant) cease all biological activity permanently; (of something inanimate) cease to exist or function **be dying for something, be dying to do something** (informal) be eager for or to do something ▶ **die-hard** n person who resists change

**die²** n shaped block used to cut or form metal

**dieresis** [die-**air**-iss-iss] n, pl **-ses** [-seez] same as **diaeresis**

**diesel** n diesel engine; vehicle driven by a diesel engine; diesel oil ▶ **diesel engine** internal-combustion engine in which oil is ignited by compression ▶ **diesel oil** fuel obtained from petroleum distillation

**diet¹** n food that a person or animal regularly eats; specific range of foods, to control weight or for health reasons ▷ v follow a special diet so as to lose weight ▷ adj (of food) suitable for a weight-reduction diet ▶ **dietary** adj ▶ **dietary fibre** fibrous substances in fruit and vegetables that aid digestion ▶ **dieter** n ▶ **dietetic** adj prepared for special dietary requirements ▶ **dietetics** n study of diet and nutrition ▶ **dietician** n person who specializes in dietetics

**diet²** n parliament of some countries

**differ** v be unlike; disagree

**different** adj unlike; unusual ▶ **difference** n state of being unlike; disagreement; remainder left after subtraction ▶ **differently** adv

**USAGE NOTE**
The accepted idiom is different from but different to is also used. Different than is used in America

**differential** adj of or using a difference; (Maths) involving differentials ▷ n factor that differentiates between two comparable things; (Maths) tiny difference between values in a scale; difference between rates of pay for different types of work ▶ **differential calculus** branch of calculus concerned with derivatives and differentials ▶ **differentiate** v perceive or show the difference (between); make (one thing) distinct from other such things ▶ **differentiation** n

**difficult** adj requiring effort or skill to do or understand; not easily pleased ▶ **difficulty** n

**diffident** adj lacking self-confidence ▶ **diffidence** n ▶ **diffidently** adv

**diffraction** n (Physics) deviation in the direction of a wave at the edge of an obstacle in its path; formation of light and dark fringes by the passage of light through a small aperture

**diffuse** v spread over a wide area ▷ adj widely spread; lacking concision ▶ **diffusion** n

**dig** v **digging, dug** cut into, break up, and turn over or remove (earth), esp. with a spade; (foll by *out* or *up*) find by effort or searching; (foll by *in* or *into*) thrust or jab ▷ n digging; archaeological excavation; thrust or poke; spiteful remark ▷ pl (*Brit, Aust & S Afr informal*) lodgings ▶ **digger** n machine used for digging

**digest** v subject to a process of digestion; absorb mentally ▷ n shortened version of a book, report, or article ▶ **digestible** adj ▶ **digestion** n (body's system for) breaking down food into easily absorbed substances ▶ **digestive** adj ▶ **digestive biscuit** biscuit made from wholemeal flour

**digicam** n digital camera

**digit** [**dij**-it] n finger or toe; numeral from 0 to 9 ▶ **digital** adj displaying information as numbers rather than with hands and a dial e.g. *a digital clock* ▶ **digital recording** sound-recording process that converts audio or analogue signals into a series of pulses ▶ **digital television** television in which the picture is transmitted in digital form and then decoded ▶ **digitally** adv

**digitalis** n drug made from foxglove leaves, used as a heart stimulant

**dignity** n, pl -ties serious, calm, and controlled behaviour or manner; quality of being worthy of respect; sense of self-importance ▶ **dignify** v add distinction to ▶ **dignitary** n person of high official position

**digress** v depart from the main subject in speech or writing ▶ **digression** n

**dike** n same as **dyke¹, dyke²**

**dilapidated** adj (of a building) having fallen into ruin ▶ **dilapidation** n

**dilate** v make or become wider or larger ▶ **dilation, dilatation** n

**dilatory** [**dill**-a-tree] adj tending or intended to waste time

**dildo** n, pl **-dos** object used as a substitute for an erect penis

**dilemma** n situation offering a choice between two equally undesirable alternatives

> **USAGE NOTE**
> If a difficult choice involves more than two courses of action, it is preferable to speak of a *problem* or *difficulty*

**dilettante** [dill-it-**tan**-tee] n, pl -tantes or -tanti person whose interest in a subject is superficial rather than serious ▶ **dilettantism** n

**diligent** adj careful and persevering in carrying out duties; carried out with care and perseverance ▶ **diligently** adv ▶ **diligence** n

**dill** n sweet-smelling herb

**dilly-dally** v -lying, -lied (*Brit, Aust & NZ informal*) dawdle, waste time

**dilute** v make (a liquid) less concentrated, esp. by adding water; make (a quality etc.) weaker in force ▶ **dilution** n

**diluvial, diluvian** adj of a flood, esp. the great Flood described in the Old Testament

**dim** adj **dimmer, dimmest** badly lit; not clearly seen; unintelligent ▷ v **dimming, dimmed** make or become dim **take a dim view of** disapprove of ▶ **dimly** adv ▶ **dimness** n ▶ **dimmer** n device for dimming an electric light

**dime** n coin of the US and Canada, worth ten cents

**dimension** n measurement of the size of something in a particular direction; aspect, factor

**diminish** v make or become smaller, fewer, or less ▶ **diminution** n ▶ **diminutive** adj very small ▷ n word or affix which implies smallness or unimportance

**diminuendo** n (Music) gradual decrease in loudness

**dimple** n small natural dent, esp. in the cheeks or chin ▷ v produce dimples by smiling

**din** n loud unpleasant confused noise ▷ v **dinning, dinned** (foll by into) instil (something) into someone by constant repetition

**dinar** [dee-**nahr**] n monetary unit of various Balkan, Middle Eastern, and North African countries

**dine** v eat dinner ▶ **diner** n person eating a meal; (chiefly US) small cheap restaurant ▶ **dining car** railway coach where meals are served ▶ **dining room** room where meals are eaten

**ding** n (Aust & NZ, old-fashioned informal) small dent in a vehicle

**ding-dong** n sound of a bell; (informal) lively quarrel or fight

**dinghy** [**ding**-ee] n, pl **-ghies** small boat, powered by sails, oars, or a motor

**dingo** n, pl **-goes** Australian wild dog

**dingy** [**din**-jee] adj **-gier, -giest** (Brit, Aust & NZ) dull and drab ▶ **dinginess** n

**dinkum** adj (Aust & NZ informal) genuine or right

**dinky** adj **-kier, -kiest** (Brit, Aust & NZ informal) small and neat

**dinky-di** adj (Aust informal) typical

**dinner** n main meal of the day, eaten either in the evening or at midday ▶ **dinner jacket** man's semiformal black evening jacket

**dinosaur** n type of extinct prehistoric reptile, many of which were of gigantic size

**dint** n **by dint of** by means of

**diocese** [**die**-a-siss] n district over which a bishop has control ▶ **diocesan** adj

**diode** n semiconductor device for converting alternating current to direct current

**dioptre** [die-**op**-ter] n unit for measuring the refractive power of a lens

**dioxide** n oxide containing two oxygen atoms per molecule

**dip** v **dipping, dipped** plunge quickly or briefly into a liquid; slope downwards; switch (car headlights) from the main to the lower beam; lower briefly ▷ n dipping; brief swim; liquid chemical in which farm animals are dipped to rid them of insects; depression in a landscape; creamy mixture into which pieces of food are dipped before being eaten ▶ **dip into** v read passages at random from (a book or journal)

**diphtheria** [dif-**theer**-ya] n contagious disease producing fever and difficulty in breathing and swallowing

**diphthong** n union of two vowel sounds in a single compound sound

**diploma** n qualification awarded by a college on successful completion of a course

**diplomacy** n conduct of the relations between nations by peaceful means; tact or skill in dealing with people ▶ **diplomat** n official engaged in diplomacy ▶ **diplomatic** adj of diplomacy; tactful in dealing with people ▶ **diplomatically** adv

**dipper** n ladle used for dipping; (also **ousel, ouzel**) European songbird that lives by a river

**diprotodont** [die-**pro**-toe-dont] n marsupial with fewer than three upper incisor teeth on each side of the jaw

**dipsomania** *n* compulsive craving for alcohol ▸ **dipsomaniac** *n, adj*

**diptych** [**dip**-tik] *n* painting on two hinged panels

**dire** *adj* disastrous, urgent, or terrible

**direct** *adj* (of a route) shortest, straight; without anyone or anything intervening; likely to have an immediate effect; honest, frank ▷ *adv* in a direct manner ▷ *v* lead and organize; tell (someone) to do something; tell (someone) the way to a place; address (a letter, package, remark, etc.); provide guidance to (actors, cameramen, etc.) in (a play or film) ▸ **directly** *adv* in a direct manner; at once ▷ *conj* as soon as ▸ **directness** *n* ▸ **direct current** electric current that flows in one direction only

**direction** *n* course or line along which a person or thing moves, points, or lies; management or guidance ▷ *pl* instructions for doing something or for reaching a place ▸ **directional** *adj*

**directive** *n* instruction, order

**director** *n* person or thing that directs or controls; member of the governing board of a business etc.; person responsible for the artistic and technical aspects of the making of a film etc.
▸ **directorial** *adj* ▸ **directorship** *n* ▸ **directorate** *n* board of directors; position of director

**directory** *n, pl* **-tories** book listing names, addresses, and telephone numbers; (*Computing*) area of a disk containing the names and locations of the files it currently holds

**dirge** *n* slow sad song of mourning

**dirigible** [**dir**-rij-jib-bl] *adj* able to be steered ▷ *n* airship

**dirk** *n* dagger, formerly worn by Scottish Highlanders

**dirndl** *n* full gathered skirt originating from Tyrolean peasant wear

**dirt** *n* unclean substance, filth; earth, soil; obscene speech or writing; (*informal*) harmful gossip ▸ **dirt track** racetrack made of packed earth or cinders

**dirty** *adj* **dirtier, dirtiest** covered or marked with dirt; unfair or dishonest; obscene; displaying dislike or anger e.g. *a dirty look* ▷ *v* **dirtying, dirtied** make dirty ▸ **dirtiness** *n*

**dis-** *prefix* indicating reversal e.g. *disconnect*; indicating negation or lack e.g. *dissimilar*; *disgrace*; indicating removal or release e.g. *disembowel*

**disable** *v* make ineffective, unfit, or incapable ▸ **disabled** *adj* lacking a physical power, such as the ability to walk ▸ **disablement** *n* ▸ **disability** *n, pl* **-ties** condition of being disabled; something that disables someone

**disabuse** *v* (foll by *of*) rid (someone) of a mistaken idea

**disadvantage** *n* unfavourable or harmful circumstance ▸ **disadvantageous** *adj* ▸ **disadvantaged** *adj* socially or economically deprived

**disaffected** *adj* having lost loyalty to or affection for someone or something ▸ **disaffection** *n*

**disagree** *v* **-greeing, -greed** argue or have different opinions; be different, conflict; (foll by *with*) cause physical discomfort (to) e.g. *curry disagrees with me* ▸ **disagreement** *n* ▸ **disagreeable** *adj* unpleasant; (of a person) unfriendly or unhelpful ▸ **disagreeably** *adv*

**disallow** v reject as untrue or invalid

**disappear** v cease to be visible; cease to exist ▶ **disappearance** n

**disappoint** v fail to meet the expectations or hopes of ▶ **disappointment** n feeling of being disappointed; person or thing that disappoints

> **SPELLING TIP**
> Remember there is only one s in **disappointment**, but two ps

**disapprobation** n disapproval

**disapprove** v (foll by of) consider wrong or bad ▶ **disapproval** n

**disarm** v deprive of weapons; win the confidence or affection of; (of a country) decrease the size of one's armed forces ▶ **disarmament** n ▶ **disarming** adj removing hostility or suspicion ▶ **disarmingly** adv

**disarrange** v throw into disorder

**disarray** n confusion and lack of discipline; extreme untidiness

**disaster** n occurrence that causes great distress or destruction; project etc. that fails ▶ **disastrous** adj ▶ **disastrously** adv

**disavow** v deny connection with or responsibility for ▶ **disavowal** n

**disband** v (cause to) cease to function as a group

**disbelieve** v reject as false; (foll by in) have no faith (in) ▶ **disbelief** n

**disburse** v pay out ▶ **disbursement** n

**disc** n flat circular object; gramophone record; (*Anat*) circular flat structure in the body, esp. between the vertebrae; (*Computing*) same as **disk** ▶ **disc jockey** person who introduces and plays pop records on a radio programme or at a disco

**discard** v get rid of (something or someone) as useless or undesirable

**discern** v see or be aware of (something) clearly ▶ **discernible** adj ▶ **discerning** adj having good judgment ▶ **discernment** n

**discharge** v release, allow to go; dismiss (someone) from duty or employment; fire (a gun); pour forth, send out; meet the demands of (a duty or responsibility); relieve oneself of (a debt) ▷ n substance that comes out from a place; discharging

**disciple** [diss-**sipe**-pl] n follower of the doctrines of a teacher, esp. Jesus Christ

**discipline** n practice of imposing strict rules of behaviour; area of academic study ▷ v attempt to improve the behaviour of (oneself or another) by training or rules; punish ▶ **disciplined** adj able to behave and work in a controlled way ▶ **disciplinarian** n person who practises strict discipline ▶ **disciplinary** adj

**disclaimer** n statement denying responsibility ▶ **disclaim** v

**disclose** v make known; allow to be seen ▶ **disclosure** n

**disco** n, pl **-cos** nightclub where people dance to amplified pop records; occasion at which people dance to amplified pop records; mobile equipment for providing music for a disco

**discolour** v change in colour, fade ▶ **discoloration** n

**discomfit** v make uneasy or confused ▶ **discomfiture** n

**discomfort** n inconvenience, distress, or mild pain

**discommode** v cause inconvenience to

**disconcert** v embarrass or upset

**disconnect** v undo or break the connection between (two things); stop the supply of electricity or gas of ▶ **disconnected** adj (of speech or ideas) not logically connected ▶ **disconnection** n

**disconsolate** adj sad beyond comfort ▶ **disconsolately** adv

**discontent** n lack of contentment ▶ **discontented** adj

**discontinue** v come or bring to an end ▶ **discontinuous** adj characterized by interruptions ▶ **discontinuity** n

**discord** n lack of agreement or harmony between people; harsh confused sounds ▶ **discordant** adj ▶ **discordance** n

**discotheque** n same as **disco**

**discount** v take no account of (something) because it is considered to be unreliable, prejudiced, or irrelevant; deduct (an amount) from the price of something ▷ n deduction from the full price of something

**discourage** v deprive of the will to persist in something; oppose by expressing disapproval ▶ **discouragement** n

**discourse** n conversation; formal treatment of a subject in speech or writing ▷ v (foll by on) speak or write (about) at length

**discourteous** adj showing bad manners ▶ **discourtesy** n

**discover** v be the first to find or to find out about; learn about for the first time; find after study or search ▶ **discoverer** n ▶ **discovery** n, pl -**eries** discovering; person, place, or thing that has been discovered

**discredit** v damage the reputation of; cause (an idea) to be disbelieved or distrusted ▷ n damage to someone's reputation ▶ **discreditable** adj bringing shame

**discreet** adj careful to avoid embarrassment, esp. by keeping

confidences secret; unobtrusive ▶ **discreetly** adv

**discrepancy** n, pl -**cies** conflict or variation between facts, figures, or claims

**discrete** adj separate, distinct

**discretion** n quality of behaving in a discreet way; freedom or authority to make judgments and decide what to do ▶ **discretionary** adj

**discriminate** v (foll by against or in favour of) single out (a particular person or group) for worse or better treatment than others; (foll by between) recognize or understand the difference (between) ▶ **discriminating** adj showing good taste and judgment ▶ **discrimination** n ▶ **discriminatory** adj based on prejudice

**discursive** adj passing from one topic to another

**discus** n heavy disc-shaped object thrown in sports competitions

**discuss** v consider (something) by talking it over; treat (a subject) in speech or writing ▶ **discussion** n

**disdain** n feeling of superiority and dislike ▷ v refuse with disdain ▶ **disdainful** adj ▶ **disdainfully** adv

**disease** n illness, sickness ▶ **diseased** adj

**disembark** v get off a ship, aircraft, or bus ▶ **disembarkation** n

**disembodied** adj lacking a body; seeming not to be attached to or coming from anyone

**disembowel** v -**elling**, -**elled** remove the entrails of

**disenchanted** adj disappointed and disillusioned ▶ **disenchantment** n

**disenfranchise** v deprive (someone) of the right to vote or of other rights of citizenship

**disengage** v release from a connection ▶ **disengagement** n

**disentangle** v release from entanglement or confusion

**disfavour** n disapproval or dislike

**disfigure** v spoil the appearance of ▶ **disfigurement** n

**disfranchise** v same as **disenfranchise**

**disgorge** v empty out, discharge

**disgrace** n condition of shame, loss of reputation, or dishonour; shameful person or thing ▷ v bring shame upon (oneself or others) ▶ **disgraceful** adj ▶ **disgracefully** adv

**disgruntled** adj sulky or discontented ▶ **disgruntlement** n

**disguise** v change the appearance or manner in order to conceal the identity of (someone or something); misrepresent (something) in order to obscure its actual nature or meaning ▷ n mask, costume, or manner that disguises; state of being disguised

**disgust** n great loathing or distaste ▷ v sicken, fill with loathing

**dish** n shallow container used for holding or serving food; particular kind of food; short for **dish aerial**; (informal) attractive person ▶ **dish aerial** aerial consisting of a concave disc-shaped reflector, used esp. for satellite television ▶ **dishcloth** n cloth for washing dishes ▶ **dish out** v (informal) distribute ▶ **dish up** v (informal) serve (food)

**dishabille** [diss-a-**beel**] n same as **deshabille**

**dishearten** v weaken or destroy the hope, courage, or enthusiasm of

**dishevelled** adj (of a person's hair, clothes, or general appearance) disordered and untidy

**dishonest** adj not honest or fair ▶ **dishonestly** adv ▶ **dishonesty** n

**dishonour** v treat with disrespect ▷ n lack of respect; state of shame or disgrace; something that causes a loss of honour ▶ **dishonourable** adj ▶ **dishonourably** adv

**disillusion** v destroy the illusions or false ideas of ▷ n (also **disillusionment**) state of being disillusioned

**disincentive** n something that acts as a deterrent

**disinclined** adj unwilling, reluctant ▶ **disinclination** n

**disinfect** v rid of harmful germs, chemically ▶ **disinfectant** n substance that destroys harmful germs ▶ **disinfection** n

**disinformation** n false information intended to mislead

**disingenuous** adj not sincere ▶ **disingenuously** adv

**disinherit** v (Law) deprive (an heir) of inheritance ▶ **disinheritance** n

**disintegrate** v break up ▶ **disintegration** n

**disinter** v **-terring, -terred** dig up; reveal, make known

**disinterested** adj free from bias or involvement ▶ **disinterest** n

> **USAGE NOTE**
> People sometimes use *disinterested* where they mean *uninterested*. If you want to say that someone shows a lack of interest, use *uninterested*. *Disinterested* would be used in a sentence such as *We asked him to decide because he was a disinterested observer*

**disjointed** adj having no coherence, disconnected

**disk** n (Computing) storage device, consisting of a stack of plates coated with a magnetic layer, which rotates rapidly as a single unit

**dislike** v consider unpleasant or disagreeable ▷ n feeling of not liking something or someone

**dislocate** v displace (a bone or joint) from its normal position; disrupt or shift out of place ▸ **dislocation** n

**dislodge** v remove (something) from a previously fixed position

**disloyal** adj not loyal, deserting one's allegiance ▸ **disloyalty** n

**dismal** adj gloomy and depressing; (informal) of poor quality ▸ **dismally** adv

**dismantle** v take apart piece by piece

**dismay** v fill with alarm or depression ▷ n alarm mixed with sadness

**dismember** v remove the limbs of; cut to pieces ▸ **dismemberment** n

**dismiss** v remove (an employee) from a job; allow (someone) to leave; put out of one's mind; (of a judge) state that (a case) will not be brought to trial ▸ **dismissal** n ▸ **dismissive** adj scornful, contemptuous

**dismount** v get off a horse or bicycle

**disobey** v neglect or refuse to obey ▸ **disobedient** adj ▸ **disobedience** n

**disobliging** adj unwilling to help

**disorder** n state of untidiness and disorganization; public violence or rioting; illness ▸ **disordered** adj untidy ▸ **disorderly** adj untidy and disorganized; uncontrolled, unruly

**disorganize** v disrupt the arrangement or system of ▸ **disorganization** n

**disorientate, disorient** v cause (someone) to lose his or her bearings ▸ **disorientation** n

**disown** v deny any connection with (someone)

**disparage** v speak contemptuously of ▸ **disparagement** n

**disparate** adj completely different ▸ **disparity** n

**dispassionate** adj not influenced by emotion ▸ **dispassionately** adv

**dispatch** v send off to a destination or to perform a task; carry out (a duty or a task) with speed; (old-fashioned) kill ▷ n official communication or report, sent in haste; report sent to a newspaper by a correspondent ▸ **dispatch rider** (Brit, Aust & NZ) motorcyclist who carries dispatches

**dispel** v -pelling, -pelled destroy or remove

**dispense** v distribute in portions; prepare and distribute (medicine); administer (the law etc.) ▸ **dispensable** adj not essential ▸ **dispensation** n dispensing; exemption from an obligation ▸ **dispenser** n ▸ **dispensary** n, pl -saries place where medicine is dispensed ▸ **dispense with** v do away with, manage without

**disperse** v scatter over a wide area; (cause to) leave a gathering ▸ **dispersal, dispersion** n

**dispirit** v make downhearted

**displace** v move from the usual location; remove from office ▸ **displacement** n ▸ **displaced person** person forced from his or her home or country, esp. by war

**display** v make visible or noticeable ▷ n displaying; something displayed; exhibition

**displease** v annoy or upset ▸ **displeasure** n

**disport** v **disport oneself** indulge oneself in pleasure

**dispose** v place in a certain order ▸ **disposed** adj willing

**d**

or eager; having an attitude as specified e.g. *he felt well disposed towards her* ▶ **disposable** *adj* designed to be thrown away after use; available for use e.g. *disposable income* ▶ **disposal** *n* getting rid of something **at one's disposal** available for use ▶ **disposition** *n* person's usual temperament; desire or tendency to do something; arrangement ▶ **dispose of** *v* throw away, get rid of; deal with (a problem etc.); kill

**dispossess** *v* (foll by *of*) deprive (someone) of (a possession) ▶ **dispossession** *n*

**disproportion** *n* lack of proportion or equality

**disproportionate** *adj* out of proportion ▶ **disproportionately** *adv*

**disprove** *v* show (an assertion or claim) to be incorrect

**dispute** *n* disagreement, argument ▷ *v* argue about (something); doubt the validity of; fight over possession of

**disqualify** *v* stop (someone) officially from taking part in something for wrongdoing ▶ **disqualification** *n*

**disquiet** *n* feeling of anxiety ▷ *v* make (someone) anxious ▶ **disquietude** *n*

**disregard** *v* give little or no attention to ▷ *n* lack of attention or respect

**disrepair** *n* condition of being worn out or in poor working order

**disrepute** *n* loss or lack of good reputation ▶ **disreputable** *adj* having or causing a bad reputation

**disrespect** *n* lack of respect ▶ **disrespectful** *adj* ▶ **disrespectfully** *adv*

**disrobe** *v* undress

**disrupt** *v* interrupt the progress of ▶ **disruption** *n* ▶ **disruptive** *adj*

**dissatisfied** *adj* not pleased or contented ▶ **dissatisfaction** *n*

**dissect** *v* cut open (a corpse) to examine it; examine critically and minutely ▶ **dissection** *n*

**dissemble** *v* conceal one's real motives or emotions by pretence

**disseminate** *v* spread (information) ▶ **dissemination** *n*

**dissent** *v* disagree; (*Christianity*) reject the doctrines of an established church ▷ *n* disagreement; (*Christianity*) separation from an established church ▶ **dissension** *n* ▶ **dissenter** *n*

**dissertation** *n* written thesis, usu. required for a higher university degree; long formal speech

**disservice** *n* harmful action

**dissident** *n* person who disagrees with and criticizes the government ▷ *adj* disagreeing with the government ▶ **dissidence** *n*

**dissimilar** *adj* not alike, different ▶ **dissimilarity** *n*

**dissimulate** *v* conceal one's real feelings by pretence ▶ **dissimulation** *n*

**dissipate** *v* waste or squander; scatter, disappear ▶ **dissipated** *adj* showing signs of overindulgence in alcohol and other physical pleasures ▶ **dissipation** *n*

**dissociate** *v* regard or treat as separate **dissociate oneself from** deny or break an association with ▶ **dissociation** *n*

**dissolute** *adj* leading an immoral life

**dissolution** *n* official breaking up of an organization or institution, such as Parliament; official ending of a formal agreement, such as a marriage

**dissolve** v (cause to) become liquid; break up or end officially; break down emotionally e.g. *she dissolved into tears*

**dissonance** n lack of agreement or harmony ▶ **dissonant** adj

**dissuade** v deter (someone) by persuasion from doing something ▶ **dissuasion** n

**distaff** n rod on which wool etc. is wound for spinning ▶ **distaff side** female side of a family

**distance** n space between two points; state of being apart; remoteness in manner **the distance** most distant part of the visible scene **distance oneself from** separate oneself mentally from ▶ **distant** adj far apart; separated by a specified distance; remote in manner ▶ **distantly** adv

**distaste** n dislike, disgust ▶ **distasteful** adj unpleasant, offensive

**distemper¹** n highly contagious viral disease of dogs

**distemper²** n paint mixed with water, glue, etc., used for painting walls

**distend** v (of part of the body) swell ▶ **distension** n

**distil** v **-tilling, -tilled** subject to or obtain by distillation; give off (a substance) in drops; extract the essence of ▶ **distillation** n process of evaporating a liquid and condensing its vapour; (also **distillate**) concentrated essence

**distiller** n person or company that makes strong alcoholic drink, esp. whisky ▶ **distillery** n, pl **-leries** place where a strong alcoholic drink, esp. whisky, is made

**distinct** adj not the same; easily sensed or understood; clear and definite ▶ **distinctly**

adv ▶ **distinction** n act of distinguishing; distinguishing feature; state of being different; special honour, recognition, or fame ▶ **distinctive** adj easily recognizable ▶ **distinctively** adv ▶ **distinctiveness** n

**distinguish** v (usu. foll by *between*) make, show, or recognize a difference (between); be a distinctive feature of; make out by hearing, seeing, etc. ▶ **distinguishable** adj ▶ **distinguished** adj dignified in appearance; highly respected

**distort** v misrepresent (the truth or facts); twist out of shape ▶ **distortion** n

**distract** v draw the attention of (a person) away from something; entertain ▶ **distracted** adj unable to concentrate, preoccupied ▶ **distraction** n

**distrait** [diss-**tray**] adj absent-minded or preoccupied

**distraught** [diss-**trawt**] adj extremely anxious or agitated

**distress** n extreme unhappiness; great physical pain; poverty ▷ v upset badly ▶ **distressed** adj extremely upset; in financial difficulties ▶ **distressing** adj ▶ **distressingly** adv

**distribute** v hand out or deliver; share out ▶ **distribution** n distributing; arrangement or spread ▶ **distributor** n wholesaler who distributes goods to retailers in a specific area; device in a petrol engine that sends the electric current to the spark plugs ▶ **distributive** adj

**district** n area of land regarded as an administrative or geographical unit ▶ **district court judge** (*Aust & NZ*) judge presiding over a lower court

**distrust** v regard as untrustworthy ▷ n feeling of suspicion or doubt ▶ **distrustful** adj

**disturb** v intrude on; worry, make anxious; change the position or shape of ▶ **disturbance** n ▶ **disturbing** adj ▶ **disturbingly** adv ▶ **disturbed** adj (Psychiatry) emotionally upset or maladjusted

**disunite** v cause disagreement among ▶ **disunity** n

**disuse** n state of being no longer used ▶ **disused** adj

**ditch** n narrow channel dug in the earth for drainage or irrigation ▷ v (slang) abandon

**dither** v be uncertain or indecisive ▷ n state of indecision or agitation ▶ **ditherer** n ▶ **dithery** adj

**ditto** n, pl -tos the same ▷ adv in the same way

**ditty** n, pl -ties short simple poem or song

**diuretic** [die-yoor-et-ik] n drug that increases the flow of urine

**diurnal** [die-urn-al] adj happening during the day or daily

**diva** n distinguished female singer

**divan** n low backless bed; backless sofa or couch

**dive** v diving, dived plunge headfirst into water; (of a submarine or bird) submerge under water; fly in a steep nose-down descending path; move quickly in a specified direction; (foll by in or into) start doing (something) enthusiastically ▷ n diving; steep nose-down descent; (slang) disreputable bar or club ▶ **diver** n person who works or explores underwater; person who dives for sport ▶ **dive bomber** military aircraft designed to release bombs during a dive

**diverge** v separate and go in different directions; deviate (from a

prescribed course) ▶ **divergence** n ▶ **divergent** adj

**divers** adj (old-fashioned) various

**diverse** adj having variety, assorted; different in kind ▶ **diversity** n, pl -ties quality of being different or varied; range of difference ▶ **diversify** v -fying, -fied ▶ **diversification** n

**divert** v change the direction of; entertain, distract the attention of ▶ **diversion** n official detour used by traffic when a main route is closed; something that distracts someone's attention; diverting; amusing pastime ▶ **diversionary** adj

**divest** v strip (of clothes); deprive (of a role or function)

**divide** v separate into parts; share or be shared out in parts; (cause to) disagree; keep apart, be a boundary between; calculate how many times (one number) can be contained in (another) ▷ n division, split ▶ **dividend** n sum of money representing part of the profit made, paid by a company to its shareholders; extra benefit ▶ **divider** n screen used to divide a room into separate areas ▷ pl compasses with two pointed arms, used for measuring or dividing lines

**divine** adj of God or a god; godlike; (informal) splendid ▷ v discover (something) by intuition or guessing ▶ **divinely** adv ▶ **divination** n art of discovering future events, as though by supernatural powers ▶ **divinity** n study of religion; (pl -ties) god; state of being divine ▶ **divining rod** forked twig said to move when held over ground in which water or metal is to be found

**division** n dividing, sharing out; one of the parts into

which something is divided;
mathematical operation of
dividing; difference of opinion
▶ **divisional** adj of a division in
an organization ▶ **divisible** adj
▶ **divisibility** n ▶ **divisive** adj
tending to cause disagreement
▶ **divisor** n number to be divided
into another number

**divorce** n legal ending of a marriage;
any separation, esp. a permanent
one ▷ v legally end one's marriage
(to); separate, consider separately
▶ **divorcée,** (masc) **divorcé** n person
who is divorced

**divulge** v make known, disclose
▶ **divulgence** n

**Dixie** n southern states of the US
(also **Dixieland**)

**DIY** (Brit, Aust & NZ) do-it-yourself

**dizzy** adj **-zier, -ziest** having or
causing a whirling sensation;
mentally confused ▷ v **-zying,**
**-zied** make dizzy ▶ **dizzily** adv
▶ **dizziness** n

**DJ** disc jockey; (Brit) dinner jacket

**DNA** n deoxyribonucleic acid,
the main constituent of the
chromosomes of all living things

**do** v **does, doing, did, done**
perform or complete (a deed or
action); be adequate e.g. that one
will do; suit or improve e.g. that
style does nothing for you; find the
answer to (a problem or puzzle);
cause, produce e.g. it does no
harm to think ahead; give, grant
e.g. do me a favour; work at, as a
course of study or a job; used to
form questions e.g. how do you
know?; used to intensify positive
statements and commands e.g.
I do like port; do go on; used to
form negative statements and
commands e.g. I do not know her
well; do not get up; used to replace
an earlier verb e.g. he gets paid more

than I do ▷ n, pl **dos** or **do's** (informal)
party, celebration ▶ **do away**
**with** v get rid of ▶ **do-it-yourself** n
constructing and repairing things
oneself ▶ **do up** v fasten; decorate
and repair ▶ **do with** v find useful
or benefit from e.g. I could do with
a rest ▶ **do without** v manage
without

**Doberman pinscher,**
**Doberman** n large dog with a
black-and-tan coat

**dob in** v **dobbing, dobbed** (Aust
& NZ informal) inform against;
contribute to a fund

**DOC** (in New Zealand) Department
of Conservation

**docile** adj (of a person or animal)
easily controlled ▶ **docilely** adv
▶ **docility** n

**dock¹** n enclosed area of water
where ships are loaded, unloaded,
or repaired ▷ v bring or be brought
into dock; link (two spacecraft)
or (of two spacecraft) be linked
together in space ▶ **docker** n
(Brit) person employed to load and
unload ships ▶ **dockyard** n place
where ships are built or repaired

**dock²** v deduct money from (a
person's wages); remove part
of (an animal's tail) by cutting
through the bone

**dock³** n enclosed space in a court
of law where the accused person
sits or stands

**dock⁴** n weed with broad leaves

**docket** n label on a package or
other delivery, stating contents,
delivery instructions, etc.

**doctor** n person licensed to
practise medicine; person who
has been awarded a doctorate
▷ v alter in order to deceive; poison
or drug (food or drink); (informal)
castrate (an animal) ▶ **doctoral**
adj ▶ **doctorate** n highest

academic degree in any field of knowledge

**doctrine** n body of teachings of a religious, political, or philosophical group; principle or body of principles that is taught or advocated ▷ **doctrinal** adj of doctrines ▷ **doctrinaire** adj stubbornly insistent on the application of a theory without regard to practicality

**document** n piece of paper providing an official record of something ▷ v record or report (something) in detail; support (a claim) with evidence ▷ **documentation** n

**documentary** n, pl **-ries** film or television programme presenting the facts about a particular subject ▷ adj (of evidence) based on documents

**docu-soap** n television documentary series presenting the lives of the people filmed as entertainment

**dodder** v move unsteadily ▷ **doddery** adj

**dodecagon** [doe-**deck**-a-gon] n geometric figure with twelve sides

**dodge** v avoid (a blow, being seen, etc.) by moving suddenly; evade by cleverness or trickery ▷ n cunning or deceitful trick ▷ **dodgy** adj **dodgier, dodgiest** (informal) dangerous, risky; untrustworthy

**Dodgem**® n small electric car driven and bumped against similar cars in a rink at a funfair

**dodger** n person who evades by a responsibility or duty

**dodo** n, pl **dodos** or **dodoes** large flightless extinct bird

**doe** n female deer, hare, or rabbit

**does** v third person singular of the present tense of **do¹**

**doesn't** does not

**doff** v take off or lift (one's hat) in polite greeting

**dog** n domesticated four-legged mammal of many different breeds; related wild mammal, such as the dingo or coyote; male animal of the dog family; (informal) person e.g. you lucky dog! ▷ v **dogging, dogged** follow (someone) closely; trouble, plague **go to the dogs** (informal) go to ruin physically or morally **let sleeping dogs lie** leave things undisturbed ▷ **dogging** n (Brit slang) exhibitionist sex in parked cars, often with strangers ▷ **doggy, doggie** n, pl **-gies** child's word for a dog ▷ **dogcart** n light horse-drawn two-wheeled cart ▷ **dog collar** collar for a dog; (informal) white collar fastened at the back, worn by members of the clergy ▷ **dog-eared** adj (of a book) having pages folded down at the corner; shabby, worn ▷ **dogfight** n close-quarters combat between fighter aircraft ▷ **dogfish** n small shark ▷ **doghouse** n (US) kennel **in the doghouse** (informal) in disgrace ▷ **dogleg** n sharp bend ▷ **dog-roll** n (NZ) sausage-shaped roll of meat processed as dog food ▷ **dog rose** wild rose with pink or white flowers ▷ **dog-tired** adj (informal) exhausted

**doge** [**doje**] n (formerly) chief magistrate of Venice or Genoa

**dogged** [**dog**-gid] adj obstinately determined ▷ **doggedly** adv ▷ **doggedness** n

**doggerel** n poorly written poetry, usu. comic

**doggo** adv **lie doggo** (informal) hide and keep quiet

**dogma** n doctrine or system of doctrines proclaimed by authority as true ▷ **dogmatic** adj habitually stating one's opinions forcefully

or arrogantly ▶ **dogmatically** adv
▶ **dogmatism** n

**dogsbody** n, pl **-bodies** (informal)
person who carries out boring
tasks for others

**doily** n, pl **-lies** decorative lacy
paper mat, laid on a plate

**doldrums** pl n depressed state of
mind; state of inactivity

**dole** n (Brit, Aust & NZ informal)
money received from the state
while unemployed ▷ v (foll by out)
distribute in small quantities

**doleful** adj dreary, unhappy
▶ **dolefully** adv

**doll** n small model of a human
being, used as a toy; (slang) pretty
girl or young woman

**dollar** n standard monetary unit of
many countries

**dollop** n (informal) lump (of food)

**dolly** n, pl **-lies** child's word for a
doll; wheeled support on which a
camera may be moved

**dolman sleeve** n sleeve that is
very wide at the armhole, tapering
to a tight wrist

**dolmen** n prehistoric monument
consisting of a horizontal stone
supported by vertical stones

**dolomite** n mineral consisting of
calcium magnesium carbonate

**dolorous** adj sad, mournful

**dolphin** n sea mammal of the
whale family, with a beaklike snout
▶ **dolphinarium** n aquarium for
dolphins

**dolt** n stupid person ▶ **doltish** adj

**domain** n field of knowledge or
activity; land under one ruler
or government; (Computing)
group of computers with the
same name on the internet; (NZ)
public park

**dome** n rounded roof built on a
circular base; something shaped
like this ▶ **domed** adj

**domestic** adj of one's own
country or a specific country;
of the home or family; enjoying
running a home; (of an animal)
kept as a pet or to produce food
▷ n person whose job is to do
housework in someone else's
house ▶ **domestically** adv
▶ **domesticity** n ▶ **domesticate**
v bring or keep (a wild animal or
plant) under control or cultivation;
accustom (someone) to home life
▶ **domestication** n ▶ **domestic
science** study of household skills

**domicile** [dom-miss-ile] n place
where one lives

**dominant** adj having authority
or influence; main, chief
▶ **dominance** n

**dominate** v control or govern;
tower above (surroundings); be
very significant in ▶ **domination** n

**domineering** adj forceful and
arrogant

**Dominican** n, adj (friar or nun) of
an order founded by Saint Dominic

**dominion** n control or authority;
land governed by one ruler or
government; (formerly) self-
governing division of the British
Empire

**domino** n, pl **-noes** small
rectangular block marked with
dots, used in dominoes ▷ pl game
in which dominoes with matching
halves are laid together

**don¹** v **donning, donned** put on
(clothing)

**don²** n (Brit) member of the
teaching staff at a university or
college; Spanish gentleman or
nobleman ▶ **donnish** adj serious
and academic

**donate** v give, esp. to a charity
or organization ▶ **donation** n
donating; thing donated ▶ **donor**
n (Med) person who gives blood or

organs for use in the treatment of another person; person who makes a donation

**done** v past participle of **do¹**

**doner kebab** n see **kebab**

**donga** [dong-ga] n (S Afr, Aust & NZ) steep-sided gully created by soil erosion

**dongle** n (Computing) device that allows a computer user to access the internet via mobile broadband

**donkey** n long-eared member of the horse family ▶ **donkey jacket** (Brit, Aust & NZ) man's long thick jacket with a waterproof panel across the shoulders ▶ **donkey's years** (informal) long time ▶ **donkey-work** n tedious hard work

**don't** do not

**doodle** v scribble or draw aimlessly ▷ n shape or picture drawn aimlessly

**doom** n death or a terrible fate ▷ v destine or condemn to death or a terrible fate ▶ **doomsday** n (Christianity) day on which the Last Judgment will occur; any dreaded day

**door** n hinged or sliding panel for closing the entrance to a building, room, etc.; entrance ▶ **doormat** n mat for wiping dirt from shoes before going indoors; (informal) person who offers little resistance to ill-treatment ▶ **doorway** n opening into a building or room

**dope** n (slang) illegal drug, usu. cannabis; medicine, drug; (informal) stupid person ▷ v give a drug to, esp. in order to improve performance in a race ▶ **dopey, dopy** adj half-asleep, drowsy; (slang) silly

**dorba** n (Aust slang) stupid, inept, or clumsy person (also **dorb**)

**dork** n (slang) stupid person

**dormant** adj temporarily quiet, inactive, or not being used ▶ **dormancy** n

**dormer, dormer window** n window that sticks out from a sloping roof

**dormitory** n, pl -ries large room, esp. at a school, containing several beds

**dormouse** n, pl -mice small mouselike rodent with a furry tail

**dorp** n (S Afr) small town

**dorsal** adj of or on the back

**dory, John Dory** n, pl -ries spiny-finned edible sea fish

**dose** n specific quantity of a medicine taken at one time; (informal) something unpleasant to experience ▷ v give a dose to ▶ **dosage** n size of a dose

**doss** v doss down (slang) sleep in an uncomfortable place ▶ **dosshouse** n (Brit & S Afr slang) cheap lodging house for homeless people

**dossier** [doss-ee-ay] n collection of documents about a subject or person

**dot** n small round mark; shorter symbol used in Morse code ▷ v **dotting, dotted** mark with a dot; scatter, spread around **on the dot** at exactly the arranged time ▶ **dotty** adj (slang) rather eccentric ▶ **dotcom, dot.com** n company that does most of its business on the internet

**dote** v dote on love to an excessive degree ▶ **dotage** n weakness as a result of old age

**double** adj as much again in number, amount, size, etc.; composed of two equal or similar parts; designed for two users e.g. double room; folded in two ▷ adv twice over ▷ n twice the number, amount, size, etc.; person who looks almost exactly like another ▷ pl game between two pairs of players ▷ v make or become twice as much or as many; bend or fold (material etc.); play two parts; turn sharply **at the double, on the double** quickly or immediately ▶ **doubly** adv ▶ **double agent** spy employed by two enemy countries at the same time ▶ **double bass** stringed instrument, largest and lowest member of the violin family ▶ **double chin** fold of fat under the chin ▶ **double cream** (Brit) thick cream with a high fat content ▶ **double-cross** v cheat or betray ▷ n double-crossing ▶ **double-dealing** n treacherous or deceitful behaviour ▶ **double-decker** n bus with two passenger decks one on top of the other ▶ **double Dutch** (informal) incomprehensible talk, gibberish ▶ **double glazing** two panes of glass in a window, fitted to reduce heat loss ▶ **double talk** deceptive or ambiguous talk ▶ **double whammy** (informal) devastating setback made up of two elements

**double entendre** [doob-bl on-tond-ra] n word or phrase that can be interpreted in two ways, one of which is rude

**doublet** [dub-lit] n (Hist) man's close-fitting jacket, with or without sleeves

**doubloon** n former Spanish gold coin

**doubt** n uncertainty about the truth, facts, or existence of something; unresolved difficulty or point ▷ v question the truth of; distrust or be suspicious of (someone) ▶ **doubter** n ▶ **doubtful** adj unlikely; feeling doubt ▶ **doubtfully** adv ▶ **doubtless** adv probably or certainly

**USAGE NOTE**
If doubt is followed by a clause it is connected by whether: I doubt

whether she means it. If it is used with a negative it is followed by that: I don't doubt that he is sincere

**douche** [doosh] n (instrument for applying) a stream of water directed onto or into the body for cleansing or medical purposes ▷ v cleanse or treat by means of a douche

**dough** n thick mixture of flour and water or milk, used for making bread etc.; (slang) money ▶ **doughnut** n small cake of sweetened dough fried in deep fat

**doughty** [dowt-ee] adj **-tier, -tiest** (old-fashioned) brave and determined

**dour** [doo-er] adj sullen and unfriendly ▶ **dourness** n

**douse** [rhymes with **mouse**] v drench with water or other liquid; put out (a light)

**dove** n bird with a heavy body, small head, and short legs; (Politics) person opposed to war ▶ **dovecote, dovecot** n structure for housing pigeons ▶ **dovetail** n joint containing wedge-shaped tenons ▷ v fit together neatly

**dowager** n widow possessing property or a title obtained from her husband

**dowdy** adj **-dier, -diest** dull and old-fashioned ▶ **dowdiness** n

**dowel** n wooden or metal peg that fits into two corresponding holes to join two adjacent parts

**dower** n life interest in a part of her husband's estate allotted to a widow by law

**down**[1] prep, adv indicating movement to or position in a lower place ▷ adv indicating completion of an action, lessening of intensity, etc. e.g. calm down ▷ adj depressed, unhappy ▷ v (informal) drink quickly **have a down on** (informal) feel

hostile towards ▶ **down under**
(*informal*) (in or to) Australia or
New Zealand ▶ **downward** *adj,*
*adv* (descending) from a higher
to a lower level, condition, or
position ▶ **downwards** *adv* from a
higher to a lower level, condition,
or position ▶ **down-and-out**
*n* person who is homeless and
destitute ▷ *adj* without any means
of support ▶ **down-to-earth** *adj*
sensible or practical

**down²** *n* soft fine feathers
▶ **downy** *adj*

**downbeat** *adj* (*informal*) gloomy;
(*Brit, Aust & NZ*) relaxed

**downcast** *adj* sad, dejected; (of
the eyes) directed downwards

**downfall** *n* (cause of) a sudden
loss of position or reputation

**downgrade** *v* reduce in
importance or value

**downhearted** *adj* sad and
discouraged

**downhill** *adj* going or sloping
down ▷ *adv* towards the bottom
of a hill

**download** *v* transfer (data) from
the memory of one computer to
that of another, especially over
the internet ▷ *n* file transferred in
such a way

**downpour** *n* heavy fall of rain

**downright** *adj, adv* extreme(ly)

**downs** *pl n* low grassy hills, esp. in
S England

**Down's syndrome** *n* genetic
disorder characterized by a flat
face, slanting eyes, and mental
retardation

**downstairs** *adv* to or on a lower
floor ▷ *n* lower or ground floor

**downtrodden** *adj* oppressed and
lacking the will to resist

**dowry** *n, pl* **-ries** property brought
by a woman to her husband
at marriage

**dowse** [rhymes with **cows**] *v* search
for underground water or minerals
using a divining rod

**doxology** *n, pl* **-gies** short hymn of
praise to God

**doyen** [doy-en] *n* senior member
of a group, profession, or society
▶ **doyenne** [doy-en] *n fem*

**doze** *v* sleep lightly or briefly ▷ *n*
short sleep ▶ **dozy** *adj* **dozier,
doziest** feeling sleepy; (*informal*)
stupid ▶ **doze off** *v* fall into a
light sleep

**dozen** *adj, n* twelve ▶ **dozenth** *adj*

**DPB** (in New Zealand) Domestic
Purposes Benefit

**DPP** (in Britain) Director of Public
Prosecutions

**Dr** Doctor; Drive

**drab** *adj* **drabber, drabbest** dull
and dreary ▶ **drabness** *n*

**drachm** [dram] *n* (*Brit*) one eighth
of a fluid ounce

**drachma** *n, pl* **-mas** *or* **-mae** former
monetary unit of Greece

**draconian** *adj* severe, harsh

**draft** *n* plan, sketch, or drawing of
something; preliminary outline
of a book, speech, etc.; written
order for payment of money by
a bank; (*US & Aust*) selection for
compulsory military service ▷ *v*
draw up an outline or plan of;
send (people) from one place to
another to do a specific job; (*US &
Aust*) select for compulsory military
service

**drag** *v* **dragging, dragged** pull
with force, esp. along the ground;
trail on the ground; persuade or
force (oneself or someone else) to
go somewhere; (foll by *on* or *out*)
last or be prolonged tediously;
search (a river) with a dragnet or
hook; (*Computing*) move (an image)
on the screen by use of the mouse
▷ *n* person or thing that slows up

progress; (*informal*) tedious thing or person; (*slang*) women's clothes worn by a man ▶ **dragnet** *n* net used to scour the bottom of a pond or river to search for something ▶ **drag race** race in which specially built cars or motorcycles are timed over a measured course

**dragon** *n* mythical fire-breathing monster like a huge lizard; (*informal*) fierce woman ▶ **dragonfly** *n* brightly coloured insect with a long slender body and two pairs of wings

**dragoon** *n* heavily armed cavalryman ▷ *v* coerce, force

**drain** *n* pipe or channel that carries off water or sewage; cause of a continuous reduction in energy or resources ▷ *v* draw off or remove liquid from; flow away or filter off; drink the entire contents of (a glass or cup); make constant demands on (energy or resources), exhaust ▶ **drainage** *n* system of drains; process or method of draining

**drake** *n* male duck

**dram** *n* small amount of a strong alcoholic drink, esp. whisky; one sixteenth of an ounce

**drama** *n* serious play for theatre, television, or radio; writing, producing, or acting in plays; situation that is exciting or highly emotional ▶ **dramatic** *adj* of or like drama; behaving flamboyantly ▶ **dramatically** *adv* ▶ **dramatist** *n* person who writes plays ▶ **dramatize** *v* rewrite (a book) in the form of a play; express (something) in a dramatic or exaggerated way ▶ **dramatization** *n*

**drank** *v* past tense of **drink**

**drape** *v* cover with material, usu. in folds; place casually ▷ *n* (*Aust, US & Canadian*) piece of cloth hung at a window or opening as a screen ▶ **drapery** *n*, *pl* **-peries** fabric or clothing arranged and draped; fabrics and cloth collectively

**draper** *n* (*Brit*) person who sells fabrics and sewing materials

**drastic** *adj* strong and severe

**draught** *n* current of cold air, esp. in an enclosed space; portion of liquid to be drunk, esp. medicine; gulp or swallow; one of the flat discs used in the game of draughts ▷ *pl* game for two players using a chessboard and twelve draughts each ▷ *adj* (of an animal) used for pulling heavy loads ▶ **draughty** *adj* exposed to draughts of air ▶ **draughtsman** *n* person employed to prepare detailed scale drawings of machinery, buildings, etc. ▶ **draughtsmanship** *n* ▶ **draught beer** beer stored in a cask

**draw** *v* **drawing, drew, drawn** sketch (a figure, picture, etc.) with a pencil or pen; pull (a person or thing) closer to or further away from a place; move in a specified direction e.g. *the car drew near*; take from a source e.g. *draw money from bank accounts*; attract, interest; formulate or decide e.g. *to draw conclusions*; (of two teams or contestants) finish a game with an equal number of points ▷ *n* raffle or lottery; contest or game ending in a tie; event, act, etc., that attracts a large audience ▶ **drawing** *n* picture or plan made by means of lines on a surface; art of making drawings ▶ **drawing pin** short tack with a broad smooth head ▶ **drawing room** (*old-fashioned*) room where visitors are received and entertained ▶ **drawback** *n* disadvantage ▶ **drawbridge** *n* bridge that may be raised to prevent access or to enable vessels to pass ▸ **draw out** v encourage (someone) to talk freely; make longer ▸ **drawstring** n cord run through a hem around an opening, so that when it is pulled tighter, the opening closes ▸ **draw up** v prepare and write out (a contract); (of a vehicle) come to a stop

**drawer** n sliding box-shaped part of a piece of furniture, used for storage ▷ pl (old-fashioned) undergarment worn on the lower part of the body

**drawl** v speak slowly, with long vowel sounds ▷ n drawling manner of speech

**drawn** v past participle of **draw** ▷ adj haggard, tired, or tense in appearance

**dray** n low cart used for carrying heavy loads

**dread** v anticipate with apprehension or fear ▷ n great fear ▸ **dreadful** adj very disagreeable or shocking; extreme ▸ **dreadfully** adv

**dreadlocks** pl n hair worn in the Rastafarian style of tightly twisted strands

**dream** n imagined series of events experienced in the mind while asleep; cherished hope; (informal) wonderful person or thing ▷ v **dreaming, dreamed** or **dreamt** see imaginary pictures in the mind while asleep; (often foll by of or about) have an image (of) or fantasy (about); (foll by of) consider the possibility (of) ▷ adj ideal e.g. a dream house ▸ **dreamer** n ▸ **dreamy** adj vague or impractical; (informal) wonderful ▸ **dreamily** adv

**dreary** adj **drearier, dreariest** dull, boring ▸ **drearily** adv ▸ **dreariness** n

**dredge**[1] v clear or search (a river bed or harbour) by removing silt or mud ▸ **dredger** n boat fitted with machinery for dredging

**dredge**[2] v sprinkle (food) with flour etc.

**dregs** pl n solid particles that settle at the bottom of some liquids; most despised elements

**drench** v make completely wet

**dress** n one-piece garment for a woman or girl, consisting of a skirt and bodice and sometimes sleeves; complete style of clothing ▷ v put clothes on; put on formal clothes; apply a protective covering to (a wound); arrange or prepare ▸ **dressing** n sauce for salad; covering for a wound ▸ **dressing-down** n (informal) severe scolding ▸ **dressing gown** coat-shaped garment worn over pyjamas or nightdress ▸ **dressing room** room used for changing clothes, esp. backstage in a theatre ▸ **dressy** adj (of clothes) elegant ▸ **dress circle** first gallery in a theatre ▸ **dressmaker** n person who makes women's clothes ▸ **dressmaking** n ▸ **dress rehearsal** last rehearsal of a play or show, using costumes, lighting, etc.

**dressage** [dress-ahzh] n training of a horse to perform manoeuvres in response to the rider's body signals

**dresser**[1] n piece of furniture with shelves and cupboards, for storing or displaying dishes

**dresser**[2] n (Theatre) person employed to assist actors with their costumes

**drew** v past tense of **draw**

**drey** n squirrel's nest

**dribble** v (allow to) flow in drops; allow saliva to trickle from the mouth; (*Sport*) propel (a ball) by repeatedly tapping it with the foot, hand, or a stick ▷ *n* small quantity of liquid falling in drops ▶ **dribbler** *n*

**dried** *v* past of **dry**

**drier**[1] *adj* a comparative of **dry**

**drier**[2] *n* same as **dryer**

**driest** *adj* a superlative of **dry**

**drift** *v* be carried along by currents of air or water; move aimlessly from one place or activity to another ▷ *n* something piled up by the wind or current, such as a snowdrift; general movement or development; point, meaning e.g. *catch my drift?* ▶ **drifter** *n* person who moves aimlessly from place to place or job to job ▶ **driftwood** *n* wood floating on or washed ashore by the sea

**drill**[1] *n* tool or machine for boring holes; strict and often repetitive training; (*informal*) correct procedure ▷ *v* bore a hole in (something) with or as if with a drill; teach by rigorous exercises or training

**drill**[2] *n* machine for sowing seed in rows; small furrow for seed

**drill**[3] *n* hard-wearing cotton cloth

**drily** *adv* see **dry**

**drink** *v* **drinking, drank, drunk** swallow (a liquid); consume alcohol, esp. to excess ▷ *n* (portion of) a liquid suitable for drinking; alcohol, or its habitual or excessive consumption ▶ **drinkable** *adj* ▶ **drinker** *n* ▶ **drink in** *v* pay close attention to ▶ **drink to** *v* drink a toast to

**drip** *v* **dripping, dripped** (let) fall in drops ▷ *n* falling of drops of liquid; sound made by falling drops; (*informal*) weak dull person; (*Med*) device by which a solution is passed in small drops through

a tube into a vein ▶ **drip-dry** *adj* denoting clothing that will dry free of creases if hung up when wet

**dripping** *n* fat that comes from meat while it is being roasted or fried

**drive** *v* **driving, drove, driven** guide the movement of (a vehicle); transport in a vehicle; goad into a specified state; push or propel; (*Sport*) hit (a ball) very hard and straight ▷ *n* journey by car, van, etc.; (also **driveway**) path for vehicles connecting a building to a public road; united effort towards a common goal; energy and ambition; (*Psychol*) motive or interest e.g. *sex drive*; means by which power is transmitted in a mechanism ▶ **drive at** *v* (*informal*) intend or mean e.g. *what was he driving at?* ▶ **drive-in** *adj*, *n* (denoting) a cinema, restaurant, etc., used by people in their cars

**drivel** *n* foolish talk ▷ *v* **-elling, -elled** speak foolishly

**driver** *n* person who drives a vehicle

**drizzle** *n* very light rain ▷ *v* rain lightly ▶ **drizzly** *adj*

**droll** *adj* quaintly amusing ▶ **drolly** *adv* ▶ **drollery** *n*

**dromedary** [drom-mid-er-ee] *n*, *pl* **-daries** camel with a single hump

**drone**[1] *n* male bee

**drone**[2] *v*, *n* (make) a monotonous low dull sound ▶ **drone on** *v* talk for a long time in a monotonous tone

**drongo** *n*, *pl* **-gos** tropical songbird with a glossy black plumage, a forked tail, and a stout bill

**drool** *v* (foll by *over*) show excessive enthusiasm (for); allow saliva to flow from the mouth

**droop** *v* hang downwards loosely ▶ **droopy** *adj*

**drop** *v* **dropping, dropped** (allow to) fall vertically; decrease in amount, strength, or value; mention (a hint or name) casually; discontinue ▷ *n* small quantity of liquid forming a round shape; any small quantity of liquid; decrease in amount, strength, or value; vertical distance that something may fall ▷ *pl* liquid medication applied in small drops ▶ **droplet** *n* ▶ **droppings** *pl n* faeces of certain animals, such as rabbits or birds ▶ **drop in, drop by** *v* pay someone a casual visit ▶ **drop off** *v* (*informal*) fall asleep; grow smaller or less ▶ **dropout** *n* person who rejects conventional society; person who does not complete a course of study ▶ **drop out (of)** *v* abandon or withdraw from (a school, job, etc.)

**dropsy** *n* illness in which watery fluid collects in the body

**dross** *n* scum formed on the surfaces of molten metals; anything worthless

**drought** *n* prolonged shortage of rainfall

**drove¹** *v* past tense of **drive**

**drove²** *n* very large group, esp. of people ▶ **drover** *n* person who drives sheep or cattle

**drown** *v* die or kill by immersion in liquid; forget (one's sorrows) temporarily by drinking alcohol; drench thoroughly; make (a sound) inaudible by being louder

**drowse** *v* be sleepy, dull, or sluggish ▶ **drowsy** *adj* ▶ **drowsily** *adv* ▶ **drowsiness** *n*

**drubbing** *n* utter defeat in a contest etc.

**drudge** *n* person who works hard at uninteresting tasks ▶ **drudgery** *n*

**drug** *n* substance used in the treatment or prevention of disease; chemical substance, esp. a narcotic, taken for the effects it produces ▷ *v* **drugging,**

**drugged** give a drug to (a person or animal) to cause sleepiness or unconsciousness; mix a drug with (food or drink) ▶ **drugstore** *n* (*US*) pharmacy where a wide range of goods are available

**Druid** *n* member of an ancient order of Celtic priests ▶ **Druidic, Druidical** *adj*

**drum** *n* percussion instrument sounded by striking a membrane stretched across the opening of a hollow cylinder; cylindrical object or container ▷ *v* **drumming, drummed** play (music) on a drum; tap rhythmically or regularly ▶ **drum into** *v* instil into (someone) by constant repetition ▶ **drumstick** *n* stick used for playing a drum; lower joint of the leg of a cooked chicken etc. ▶ **drum up** *v* obtain (support or business) by making requests or canvassing

**drummer** *n* person who plays a drum or drums

**drunk** *v* past participle of **drink** ▷ *adj* intoxicated with alcohol to the extent of losing control over normal functions; overwhelmed by a strong influence or emotion ▷ *n* person who is drunk or who frequently gets drunk ▶ **drunkard** *n* person who frequently gets drunk ▶ **drunken** *adj* drunk or frequently drunk; caused by or relating to alcoholic intoxication ▶ **drunkenly** *adv* ▶ **drunkenness** *n*

**dry** *adj* **drier, driest** *or* **dryer, dryest** lacking moisture; having little or no rainfall; (*informal*) thirsty; (of wine) not sweet; uninteresting; (of humour) subtle and sarcastic; prohibiting the sale of alcohol e.g. *a dry town* ▷ *v* **drying, dried** make or become dry; preserve (food) by removing the moisture ▶ **drily,**

**dryly** *adv* ▶ **dryness** *n* ▶ **dryer** *n* apparatus for removing moisture ▶ **dry-clean** *v* clean (clothes etc.) with chemicals rather than water ▶ **dry-cleaner** *n* ▶ **dry-cleaning** *n* ▶ **dry out** *v* make or become dry; (cause to) undergo treatment for alcoholism ▶ **dry rot** crumbling and drying of timber, caused by certain fungi ▶ **dry run** (*informal*) rehearsal ▶ **dry stock** (*NZ*) cattle raised for meat

**dryad** *n* wood nymph

**DSS** (in Britain) Department of Social Security

**dual** *adj* having two parts, functions, or aspects ▶ **duality** *n* ▶ **dual carriageway** (*Brit*, *Aust & NZ*) road on which traffic travelling in opposite directions is separated by a central strip of grass or concrete

**dub¹** *v* **dubbing, dubbed** give (a person or place) a name or nickname

**dub²** *v* **dubbing, dubbed** provide (a film) with a new soundtrack, esp. in a different language; provide (a film or tape) with a soundtrack

**dubbin** *n* (*Brit*) thick grease applied to leather to soften and waterproof it

**dubious** [dew-bee-uss] *adj* feeling or causing doubt ▶ **dubiously** *adv* ▶ **dubiety** [dew-by-it-ee] *n*

**ducal** [duke-al] *adj* of a duke

**ducat** [duck-it] *n* former European gold or silver coin

**duchess** *n* woman who holds the rank of duke; wife or widow of a duke

**duchesse** *n* (*NZ*) dressing table with a mirror

**duchy** *n*, *pl* **duchies** territory of a duke or duchess

**duck¹** *n* water bird with short legs, webbed feet, and a broad blunt bill; its flesh, used as food; female of this bird; (*Cricket*) score of nothing ▶ **duckling** *n* baby duck

**duck²** *v* move (the head or body) quickly downwards, to avoid being seen or to dodge a blow; plunge suddenly under water; (*informal*) dodge (a duty or responsibility)

**duct** *n* tube, pipe, or channel through which liquid or gas is conveyed; bodily passage conveying secretions or excretions

**ductile** *adj* (of a metal) able to be shaped into sheets or wires

**dud** (*informal*) *n* ineffectual person or thing ▷ *adj* bad or useless

**dude** *n* (*US informal*) man; (*old-fashioned*) dandy; any person

**dudgeon** *n* **in high dudgeon** angry, resentful

**due** *adj* expected or scheduled to be present or arrive; owed as a debt; fitting, proper ▷ *n* something that is owed or required ▷ *pl* charges for membership of a club or organization ▷ *adv* directly or exactly e.g. *due south* **due to** attributable to or caused by

> **USAGE NOTE**
> The use of *due to* as a compound preposition as in *the performance has been cancelled due to bad weather* was formerly considered incorrect, but is now acceptable

**duel** *n* formal fight with deadly weapons between two people, to settle a quarrel ▷ *v* **duelling, duelled** fight in a duel ▶ **duellist** *n*

**duet** *n* piece of music for two performers

**duff** *adj* (*chiefly Brit*) broken or useless ▶ **duff up** *v* (*Brit informal*) beat (someone) severely

**duffel, duffle** *n* short for **duffel coat** ▶ **duffel bag** cylindrical canvas bag fastened with a drawstring ▶ **duffel coat** wool coat with toggle fastenings, usu. with a hood

**duffer** n (*informal*) dull or incompetent person

**dug**[1] v past of **dig**

**dug**[2] n teat or udder

**dugite** [doo-gyte] n medium-sized Australian venomous snake

**dugong** n whalelike mammal of tropical waters

**dugout** n (*Brit*) (at a sports ground) covered bench where managers and substitutes sit; canoe made by hollowing out a log; (*Mil*) covered excavation to provide shelter

**duke** n nobleman of the highest rank; prince or ruler of a small principality or duchy ▸ **dukedom** n

**dulcet** [dull-sit] adj (of a sound) soothing or pleasant

**dulcimer** n tuned percussion instrument consisting of a set of strings stretched over a sounding board and struck with hammers

**dull** adj not interesting; (of an ache) not acute; (of weather) not bright or clear; lacking in spirit; not very intelligent; (of a blade) not sharp ▸ v make or become dull ▸ **dullness** n ▸ **dully** adv ▸ **dullard** n dull or stupid person

**duly** adv in a proper manner; at the proper time

**dumb** adj (*offens*) lacking the power to speak; silent; (*informal*) stupid ▸ **dumbly** adv ▸ **dumbness** n ▸ **dumbbell** n short bar with a heavy ball or disc at each end, used for physical exercise ▸ **dumbfounded** adj speechless with astonishment ▸ **dumb down** make less intellectually demanding or sophisticated ▸ **dumb show** meaningful gestures without speech

**dumdum** n soft-nosed bullet that expands on impact and causes serious wounds

**dummy** n, pl **-mies** figure representing the human form, used for displaying clothes etc.; copy of an object, often lacking some essential feature of the original; rubber teat for a baby to suck; (*slang*) stupid person ▷ adj imitation, substitute ▸ **dummy run** rehearsal

**dump** v drop or let fall in a careless manner; (*informal*) get rid of (someone or something no longer wanted) ▷ n place where waste materials are left; (*informal*) dirty unattractive place; (*Mil*) place where weapons or supplies are stored **down in the dumps** (*informal*) depressed and miserable

**dumpling** n small ball of dough cooked and served with stew; round pastry case filled with fruit

**dumpy** adj **dumpier, dumpiest** short and plump

**dun** adj brownish-grey

**dunce** n person who is stupid or slow to learn

**dunderhead** n slow-witted person

**dune** n mound or ridge of drifted sand

**dung** n faeces from animals such as cattle

**dungarees** pl n trousers with a bib attached

**dungeon** n underground prison cell

**dunk** v dip (a biscuit or bread) in a drink or soup before eating it; put (something) in liquid

**dunny** n, pl **-nies** (*Aust & NZ informal*) toilet

**duo** n, pl **duos** pair of performers; (*informal*) pair of closely connected people

**duodenum** [dew-oh-**deen**-um] n, pl **-na** or **-nums** first part of the small intestine, just below the stomach ▷ **duodenal** adj

**dupe** v deceive or cheat ▷ n person who is easily deceived

**duple** adj (Music) having two beats in a bar

**duplex** n (chiefly US) apartment on two floors

**duplicate** adj copied exactly from an original ▷ n exact copy ▷ v make an exact copy of; do again (something that has already been done) ▷ **duplication** n ▷ **duplicator** n

**duplicity** n deceitful behaviour

**durable** adj long-lasting ▷ **durability** n ▷ **durable goods, durables** pl n goods that require infrequent replacement

**duration** n length of time that something lasts

**duress** n compulsion by use of force or threats

**during** prep throughout or within the limit of (a period of time)

**dusk** n time just before nightfall, when it is almost dark ▷ **dusky** adj dark in colour; shadowy

**dust** n small dry particles of earth, sand, or dirt ▷ v remove dust from (furniture) by wiping; sprinkle (something) with a powdery substance ▷ **duster** n cloth used for dusting ▷ **dusty** adj covered with dust ▷ **dustbin** n large container for household rubbish ▷ **dust bowl** dry area in which the surface soil is exposed to wind erosion ▷ **dust jacket** removable paper cover used to protect a book ▷ **dustman** n (Brit) man whose job is to collect household rubbish ▷ **dustpan** n short-handled shovel into which dust is swept from floors

**Dutch** adj of the Netherlands **go Dutch** (informal) share the expenses on an outing ▷ **Dutch courage** false courage gained from drinking alcohol

**duty** n, pl **-ties** work or a task performed as part of one's job; task that a person feels morally bound to do; government tax on imports **on duty** at work ▷ **dutiable** adj (of goods) requiring payment of duty ▷ **dutiful** adj doing what is expected ▷ **dutifully** adv

**duvet** [**doo**-vay] n kind of quilt used in bed instead of a top sheet and blankets

**DVD** Digital Versatile (or Video) Disk

**DVT** deep-vein thrombosis

**dwang** n (NZ & S Afr) short piece of wood inserted in a timber-framed wall

**dwarf** n, pl **dwarfs** or **dwarves** person who is smaller than average; (in folklore) small ugly manlike creature, often possessing magical powers ▷ adj (of an animal or plant) much smaller than the usual size for the species ▷ v cause (someone or something) to seem small by being much larger

**dwell** v **dwelling, dwelt** or **dwelled** live, reside ▷ **dwelling** n place of residence ▷ **dwell on, dwell upon** v think, speak, or write at length about

**dweller** n person who lives in a specified place e.g. city dweller

**dwindle** v grow less in size, strength, or number

**dye** n colouring substance; colour produced by dyeing ▷ v **dyeing, dyed** colour (hair or fabric) by applying a dye ▷ **dyer** n ▷ **dyed-in-the-wool** adj uncompromising or unchanging in opinion

**dying** v present participle of **die¹**

**dyke¹** n wall built to prevent flooding

**dyke²** n (offens slang) lesbian

**dynamic** *adj* full of energy, ambition, and new ideas; (*Physics*) of energy or forces that produce motion ▸ **dynamically** *adv* ▸ **dynamism** *n* great energy and enthusiasm

**dynamics** *n* branch of mechanics concerned with the forces that change or produce the motions of bodies ▷ *pl n* forces that produce change in a system

**dynamite** *n* explosive made of nitroglycerine; (*informal*) dangerous or exciting person or thing ▷ *v* blow (something) up with dynamite

**dynamo** *n, pl* **-mos** device for converting mechanical energy into electrical energy

**dynasty** *n, pl* **-ties** sequence of hereditary rulers ▸ **dynastic** *adj*

**dysentery** *n* infection of the intestine causing severe diarrhoea

**dysfunction** *n* (*Med*) disturbance or abnormality in the function of an organ or part ▸ **dysfunctional** *adj*

**dyslexia** *n* disorder causing impaired ability to read ▸ **dyslexic** *adj*

**dysmenorrhoea** *n* painful menstruation

**dyspepsia** *n* indigestion ▸ **dyspeptic** *adj*

**dystrophy** [**diss**-trof-fee] *n* see **muscular dystrophy**

# Ee

**E** East(ern) *n, pl* **Es** or **E's** (*slang*) ecstasy (the drug)

**e-** *prefix* electronic e.g. *e-mail*

**each** *adj, pron* every (one) taken separately

**eager** *adj* showing or feeling great desire, keen ▸ **eagerly** *adv* ▸ **eagerness** *n*

**eagle** *n* large bird of prey with keen eyesight; (*Golf*) score of two strokes under par for a hole ▸ **eaglet** *n* young eagle

**ear**[1] *n* organ of hearing, esp. the external part of it; sensitivity to musical or other sounds ▸ **earache** *n* pain in the ear ▸ **earbash** *v* (*Aust & NZ informal*) talk incessantly ▸ **earbashing** *n* ▸ **eardrum** *n* thin piece of skin inside the ear which enables one to hear sounds ▸ **earmark** *v* set (something) aside for a specific purpose ▸ **earphone** *n* receiver for a radio etc., held to or put in the ear ▸ **earring** *n* ornament for the lobe of the ear ▸ **earshot** *n* hearing range

**ear**[2] *n* head of corn

**earl** *n* British nobleman ranking next below a marquess ▸ **earldom** *n*

**early** *adj, adv* **-lier, -liest** before the expected or usual time; in the first part of a period; in a period far back in time

**early adopter** *n* one of the first people or organizations to make use of a new technology

**earn** v obtain by work or merit; (of investments etc.) gain (interest) ▶ **earnings** pl n money earned

**earnest¹** adj serious and sincere **in earnest** ▶ **earnestly** adv

**earnest²** n part payment given in advance, esp. to confirm a contract

**earth** n planet that we live on; land, the ground; soil; fox's hole; wire connecting an electrical apparatus with the earth ▷ v connect (a circuit) to earth ▶ **earthen** adj made of baked clay or earth ▶ **earthenware** n pottery made of baked clay ▶ **earthly** adj conceivable or possible ▶ **earthy** adj coarse or crude; of or like earth ▶ **earthquake** n violent vibration of the earth's surface ▶ **earthwork** n fortification made of earth ▶ **earthworm** n worm which burrows in the soil

**earwig** n small insect with a pincer-like tail

**ease** n freedom from difficulty, discomfort, or worry; rest or leisure ▷ v give bodily or mental ease to; lessen (severity, tension, pain, etc.); move carefully or gradually

**easel** n frame to support an artist's canvas or a blackboard

**east** n (direction towards) the part of the horizon where the sun rises; region lying in this direction ▷ adj to or in the east; (of a wind) from the east ▷ adv in, to, or towards the east ▶ **easterly** adj ▶ **eastern** adj ▶ **eastward** adj, adv ▶ **eastwards** adv

**Easter** n Christian spring festival commemorating the Resurrection of Jesus Christ ▶ **Easter egg** chocolate egg given at Easter

**easy** adj **easier, easiest** not needing much work or effort; free from pain, care, or anxiety; easy-going ▶ **easily** adv ▶ **easiness**

n ▶ **easy chair** comfortable armchair ▶ **easy-going** adj relaxed in attitude, tolerant

**eat** v **eating, ate, eaten** take (food) into the mouth and swallow it; have a meal; (foll by away or up) destroy ▶ **eatable** adj fit or suitable for eating

**eau de Cologne** [oh de kol-**lone**] n (French) light perfume

**eaves** pl n overhanging edges of a roof

**eavesdrop** v **-dropping, -dropped** listen secretly to a private conversation ▶ **eavesdropper** n ▶ **eavesdropping** n

**ebb** v (of tide water) flow back; fall away or decline ▷ n flowing back of the tide **at a low ebb** in a state of weakness

**Ebola virus** n virus that causes severe infectious disease

**ebony** n, pl **-onies** hard black wood ▷ adj deep black

**e-book** n electronic book ▷ v book (airline tickets, appointments, etc.) on the internet

**ebullient** adj full of enthusiasm or excitement ▶ **ebullience** n

**EC** European Commission; European Community: a former name for the European Union

**e-card, eCard** n greetings card created and sent electronically

**eccentric** adj odd or unconventional; (of circles) not having the same centre ▷ n eccentric person ▶ **eccentrically** adv ▶ **eccentricity** n

**ecclesiastic** n member of the clergy ▷ adj (also **ecclesiastical**) of the Christian Church or clergy

**ECG** electrocardiogram

**echelon** [esh-a-lon] n level of power or responsibility; (Mil) formation in which units follow one another but are spaced out sideways to allow each a line of fire ahead

**echidna** [ik-**kid**-na] *n*, *pl* **-nas** or **-nae** Australian spiny egg-laying mammal (also **spiny anteater**)

**echo** *n*, *pl* **-oes** repetition of sounds by reflection of sound waves off a surface; close imitation ▷ *v* **-oing, -oed** repeat or be repeated as an echo; imitate (what someone else has said) ▶ **echo sounder** sonar

**e-cigarette** *n* electronic vaporizer that simulates the effect of smoking

**éclair** *n* finger-shaped pastry filled with cream and covered with chocolate

**éclat** [ake-**lah**] *n* brilliant success; splendour

**eclectic** *adj* selecting from various styles, ideas, or sources ▶ **eclecticism** *n*

**eclipse** *n* temporary obscuring of one star or planet by another ▷ *v* surpass or outclass ▶ **ecliptic** *n* apparent path of the sun

**ecological** *adj* of ecology; intended to protect the environment ▶ **ecologically** *adv* ▶ **ecology** *n* study of the relationships between living things and their environment ▶ **ecologist** *n*

**e-commerce, ecommerce** *n* business transactions done on the internet

**economy** *n*, *pl* **-mies** system of interrelationship of money, industry, and employment in a country; careful use of money or resources to avoid waste ▶ **economic** *adj* of economics; profitable; (*informal*) inexpensive or cheap ▶ **economics** *n* social science concerned with the production and consumption of goods and services ▷ *pl n* financial aspects ▶ **economical** *adj* not wasteful, thrifty ▶ **economically** *adv* ▶ **economist** *n* specialist in economics ▶ **economize** *v* reduce

expense or waste ▶ **economic migrant** person emigrating to improve his or her standard of living

**ecosystem** *n* system involving interactions between a community and its environment

**ecru** *adj* pale creamy-brown

**ecstasy** *n* state of intense delight; (*slang*) powerful drug that can produce hallucinations ▶ **ecstatic** *adj* ▶ **ecstatically** *adv*

> **SPELLING TIP**
> Spelling **ecstasy** with an extra *c*, as *ecstacy*, is a common mistake

**ectoplasm** *n* (*Spiritualism*) substance that supposedly is emitted from the body of a medium during a trance

**ecumenical** *adj* of the Christian Church throughout the world, esp. with regard to its unity

**eczema** [ek-sim-a, ig-**zeem**-a] *n* skin disease causing intense itching

**Edam** *n* round Dutch cheese with a red waxy cover

**eddy** *n*, *pl* **eddies** circular movement of air, water, etc. ▷ *v* **eddying, eddied** move with a circular motion

**edelweiss** [**ade**-el-vice] *n* alpine plant with white flowers

**Eden** *n* (*Bible*) garden in which Adam and Eve were placed at the Creation

**edge** *n* border or line where something ends or begins; cutting side of a blade; sharpness of tone ▷ *v* provide an edge or border for; push (one's way) gradually **have the edge on** have an advantage over **on edge** nervous or irritable ▶ **edgeways** *adv* with the edge forwards or uppermost ▶ **edging** *n* anything placed along an edge to finish it ▶ **edgy** *adj* nervous or irritable

**edible** *adj* fit to be eaten ▶ **edibility** *n*

**edict** [ee-dikt] n order issued by an authority

**edifice** [ed-if-iss] n large building

**edify** [ed-if-fie] v **-fying, -fied** improve morally by instruction ▶ **edification** n

**edit** v prepare (a book, film, etc.) for publication or broadcast ▶ **edition** n number of copies of a new publication printed at one time ▶ **editor** n person who edits; person in charge of one section of a newspaper or magazine ▶ **editorial** n newspaper article stating the opinion of the editor ▷ adj of editing or editors

**educate** v teach; provide schooling for ▶ **education** n ▶ **educational** adj ▶ **educationally** adv ▶ **educationalist** n expert in the theory of education ▶ **educative** adj educating

**Edwardian** adj of the reign of King Edward VII of Great Britain and Ireland (1901–10)

**EEG** electroencephalogram

**eel** n snakelike fish

**eerie** adj **eerier, eeriest** uncannily frightening or disturbing ▶ **eerily** adv

**efface** v remove by rubbing; make (oneself) inconspicuous ▶ **effacement** n

**effect** n change or result caused by someone or something; condition of being operative e.g. *the law comes into effect next month*; overall impression ▷ pl personal belongings; lighting, sounds, etc. to accompany a film or a broadcast ▷ v cause to happen, accomplish ▶ **effective** adj producing a desired result; operative; impressive ▶ **effectively** adv ▶ **effectual** adj producing the intended result ▶ **effectually** adv

**USAGE NOTE**
Note the difference between *effect* meaning 'accomplish' and *affect* meaning 'influence'

**effeminate** adj (of a man) displaying characteristics thought to be typical of a woman ▶ **effeminacy** n

**effervescent** adj (of a liquid) giving off bubbles of gas; (of a person) lively and enthusiastic ▶ **effervescence** n

**effete** [if-feet] adj powerless, feeble

**efficacious** adj producing the intended result ▶ **efficacy** n

**efficient** adj functioning effectively with little waste of effort ▶ **efficiently** adv ▶ **efficiency** n

**effigy** [ef-fij-ee] n, pl **-gies** image or likeness of a person

**efflorescence** n flowering

**effluent** n liquid discharged as waste

**effluvium** n, pl **-via** unpleasant smell, as of decaying matter or gaseous waste

**effort** n physical or mental exertion; attempt ▶ **effortless** adj

**effrontery** n brazen impudence

**effusion** n unrestrained outburst ▶ **effusive** adj openly emotional, demonstrative ▶ **effusively** adv

**EFTA** European Free Trade Association

**e.g.** for example

**egalitarian** adj upholding the equality of all people ▷ n person who holds egalitarian beliefs ▶ **egalitarianism** n

**egg**[1] n oval or round object laid by the females of birds and other creatures, containing a developing embryo; hen's egg used as food; (also **egg cell**) ovum ▶ **egghead** n (*informal*) intellectual person ▶ **eggplant** n (*US, Canadian, Aust & NZ*) dark purple tropical fruit, cooked and eaten as a vegetable

**egg**² v **egg on** encourage or incite, esp. to do wrong

**ego** n, pl **egos** the conscious mind of an individual; self-esteem ▶ **egoism, egotism** n excessive concern for one's own interests; excessively high opinion of oneself ▶ **egotist, egoist** n ▶ **egotistic, egoistic** adj ▶ **egocentric** adj self-centred

**egregious** [ig-**greej**-uss] adj outstandingly bad

**egress** [**ee**-gress] n departure; way out

**egret** [**ee**-grit] n lesser white heron

**Egyptian** adj relating to Egypt ▷ n person from Egypt

**Egyptology** n study of the culture of ancient Egypt

**eider** n Arctic duck ▶ **eiderdown** n quilt (orig. stuffed with eider feathers)

**eight** adj, n one more than seven ▷ n eight-oared boat; its crew ▶ **eighth** adj, n (of) number eight in a series ▶ **eighteen** adj, n eight and ten ▶ **eighteenth** adj, n ▶ **eighty** adj, n eight times ten ▶ **eightieth** adj, n

**eisteddfod** [ice-**sted**-fod] n Welsh festival with competitions in music and other performing arts

**either** adj, pron one or the other (of two); each of two ▷ conj used preceding two or more possibilities joined by or ▷ adv likewise e.g. I don't eat meat and he doesn't either

**ejaculate** v eject (semen); utter abruptly ▶ **ejaculation** n

**eject** v force out, expel ▶ **ejection** n ▶ **ejector** n

**eke out** v make (a supply) last by frugal use; make (a living) with difficulty

**elaborate** adj with a lot of fine detail ▷ v expand upon ▶ **elaboration** n

**élan** [ale-**an**] n style and vigour

**eland** [**eel**-and] n large antelope of southern Africa

**elapse** v (of time) pass by

**elastic** adj resuming normal shape after distortion; adapting easily to change ▷ n tape or fabric containing interwoven strands of flexible rubber ▶ **elasticity** n

**elated** v extremely happy and excited ▶ **elation** n

**elbow** n joint between the upper arm and the forearm ▷ v shove or strike with the elbow ▶ **elbow grease** vigorous physical labour ▶ **elbow room** sufficient room to move freely

**elder**¹ adj older ▷ n older person; (in certain Protestant Churches) lay officer ▶ **elderly** adj (fairly) old ▶ **eldest** adj oldest

**USAGE NOTE**
Elder (eldest) is used for age comparison in families, older for other age comparisons

**elder**² n small tree with white flowers and black berries

**El Dorado** [el dor-**rah**-doe] n fictitious country rich in gold

**eldritch** adj (Scot) weird, uncanny

**elect** v choose by voting; decide (to do something) ▷ adj appointed but not yet in office e.g. president elect ▶ **election** n choosing of representatives by voting; act of choosing ▶ **electioneering** n active participation in a political campaign ▶ **elective** adj chosen by election; optional ▶ **elector** n someone who has the right to vote in an election ▶ **electoral** adj ▶ **electorate** n people who have the right to vote

**electricity** n form of energy associated with stationary or moving electrons or other charged particles; electric current or charge ▶ **electric** *adj* produced by, transmitting, or powered by electricity; exciting or tense ▶ **electrical** *adj* using or concerning electricity ▶ **electrician** *n* person trained to install and repair electrical equipment ▶ **electrics** *pl n* (*Brit*) electric appliances ▶ **electric chair** (*US*) chair in which criminals who have been sentenced to death are electrocuted

**electrify** *v* **-fying, -fied** adapt for operation by electric power; charge with electricity; startle or excite intensely ▶ **electrification** *n*

**electro-** *combining form* operated by or caused by electricity

**electrocardiograph** *n* instrument for recording the electrical activity of the heart ▶ **electrocardiogram** *n* tracing produced by this

**electrocute** *v* kill or injure by electricity ▶ **electrocution** *n*

**electrode** *n* conductor through which an electric current enters or leaves a battery, vacuum tube, etc.

**electrodynamics** *n* branch of physics concerned with the interactions between electrical and mechanical forces

**electroencephalograph** [ill-lek-tro-en-**sef**-a-loh-graf] *n* instrument for recording the electrical activity of the brain ▶ **electroencephalogram** *n* tracing produced by this

**electrolysis** [ill-lek-**troll**-iss-iss] *n* conduction of electricity by an electrolyte, esp. to induce chemical change; destruction of living tissue such as hair roots by an electric current

**electrolyte** *n* solution or molten substance that conducts electricity ▶ **electrolytic** *adj*

**electromagnet** *n* magnet containing a coil of wire through which an electric current is passed

**electromagnetic** *adj* of or operated by an electromagnet ▶ **electromagnetism** *n*

**electron** *n* elementary particle in all atoms that has a negative electrical charge ▶ **electron microscope** microscope that uses electrons, rather than light, to produce a magnified image ▶ **electronvolt** *n* unit of energy used in nuclear physics

**electronic** *adj* (of a device) dependent on the action of electrons; (of a process) using electronic devices ▶ **electronic mail** see **e-mail** ▶ **electronics** *n* technology concerned with the development of electronic devices and circuits

**electroplate** *v* coat with silver etc. by electrolysis

**elegant** *adj* pleasing or graceful in dress, style, or design ▶ **elegance** *n*

**elegy** [**el**-lij-ee] *n, pl* **-egies** mournful poem, esp. a lament for the dead ▶ **elegiac** *adj* mournful or plaintive

**element** *n* component part; substance which cannot be separated into other substances by ordinary chemical techniques; section of people within a larger group e.g. *the rowdy element*; heating wire in an electric kettle, stove, etc. ▷ *pl* basic principles of something; weather conditions, esp. wind, rain, and cold **in one's element** in a situation where one is happiest ▶ **elemental** *adj* of primitive natural forces or passions ▶ **elementary** *adj* simple and straightforward

**elephant** *n* huge four-footed thick-skinned animal with ivory tusks

and a long trunk ▶ **elephantine** adj
unwieldy, clumsy ▶ **elephantiasis**
[el-lee-fan-**tie**-a-siss] n disease
with hardening of the skin and
enlargement of the legs etc.

**elevate** v raise in rank or status; lift
up ▶ **elevation** n raising; height
above sea level; scale drawing of
one side of a building ▶ **elevator**
n (Aust, US & Canadian) lift for
carrying people

**eleven** adj, n one more than ten
▷ n (Sport) team of eleven people
▶ **eleventh** adj, n (of) number
eleven in a series ▶ **elevenses** n
(Brit & S Afr informal) mid-morning
snack

**elf** n, pl **elves** (in folklore) small
mischievous fairy ▶ **elfin** adj small
and delicate

**elicit** v bring about (a response or
reaction); find out (information)
by careful questioning

**elide** v omit (a vowel or syllable)
from a spoken word ▶ **elision** n

**eligible** adj meeting the
requirements or qualifications
needed; desirable as a spouse
▶ **eligibility** n

**eliminate** v get rid of
▶ **elimination** n

**elite** [ill-**eet**] n most powerful,
rich, or gifted members of a group
▶ **elitism** n belief that society
should be governed by a small group
of superior people ▶ **elitist** n, adj

**elixir** [ill-**ix**-er] n imaginary liquid
that can prolong life or turn base
metals into gold

**Elizabethan** adj of the reign of
Elizabeth I of England (1558–1603)

**elk** n large deer of N Europe and Asia

**ellipse** n oval shape ▶ **elliptical** adj
oval-shaped; (of speech or writing)
obscure or ambiguous

**ellipsis** n, pl **-ses** omission of letters
or words in a sentence

**elm** n tree with serrated leaves

**elocution** n art of speaking clearly
in public

**elongate** [eel-long-gate] v make or
become longer ▶ **elongation** n

**elope** v (of two people) run
away secretly to get married
▶ **elopement** n

**eloquence** n fluent powerful
use of language ▶ **eloquent** adj
▶ **eloquently** adv

**else** adv in addition or more e.g.
what else can I do?; other or different
e.g. it was unlike anything else that
had happened ▶ **elsewhere** adv in or
to another place

**elucidate** v make (something
difficult) clear ▶ **elucidation** n

**elude** v escape from by cleverness
or quickness; baffle ▶ **elusive** adj
difficult to catch or remember

**elver** n young eel

**elves** n plural of **elf**

**emaciated** [im-**mace**-ee-
ate-id] adj abnormally thin
▶ **emaciation** n

**e-mail, email** n (also **electronic
mail**) sending of messages
between computer terminals ▷ v
communicate in this way

**emanate** [em-a-nate] v
issue, proceed from a source
▶ **emanation** n

**emancipate** v free from social,
political, or legal restraints
▶ **emancipation** n

**emasculate** v deprive of power
▶ **emasculation** n

**embalm** v preserve (a corpse) from
decay by the use of chemicals etc.

**embankment** n man-made ridge
that carries a road or railway or
holds back water

**embargo** n, pl **-goes** order by a
government prohibiting trade with
a country ▷ v **-going, -goed** put
an embargo on

**embark** v board a ship or aircraft; (foll by *on*) begin (a new project)
▶ **embarkation** n

**embarrass** v cause to feel self-conscious or ashamed
▶ **embarrassed** adj
▶ **embarrassing** adj
▶ **embarrassment** n

**SPELLING TIP**
Remember **embarrass** and all the other words in this family should each have two rs and two ss

**embassy** n, pl **-sies** offices or official residence of an ambassador; ambassador and his staff

**embattled** adj having a lot of difficulties

**embed** v **-bedding, -bedded** fix firmly in something solid
▶ **embedded** adj (of a journalist) assigned to accompany an active military unit

**embellish** v decorate; embroider (a story) ▶ **embellishment** n

**ember** n glowing piece of wood or coal in a dying fire

**embezzle** v steal money that has been entrusted to one
▶ **embezzlement** n ▶ **embezzler** n

**embittered** adj feeling anger as a result of misfortune

**emblazon** v decorate with bright colours; proclaim or publicize

**emblem** n object or design that symbolizes a quality, type, or group
▶ **emblematic** adj

**embody** v **-bodying, -bodied** be an example or expression of; comprise, include
▶ **embodiment** n

**embolden** v encourage (someone)

**embolism** n blocking of a blood vessel by a blood clot or air bubble

**embossed** adj (of a design or pattern) standing out from a surface

**embrace** v clasp in the arms, hug; accept (an idea) eagerly; comprise ▷ n act of embracing

**embrasure** n door or window having splayed sides so that the opening is larger on the inside; opening like this in a fortified wall, for shooting through

**embrocation** n lotion for rubbing into the skin to relieve pain

**embroider** v decorate with needlework; make (a story) more interesting with fictitious detail
▶ **embroidery** n

**embroil** v involve (a person) in problems

**embryo** [**em**-bree-oh] n, pl **-bryos** unborn creature in the early stages of development; something at an undeveloped stage
▶ **embryonic** adj at an early stage
▶ **embryology** n

**emend** v remove errors from
▶ **emendation** n

**emerald** n bright green precious stone ▷ adj bright green

**emerge** v come into view; (foll by *from*) come out of; become known
▶ **emergence** n ▶ **emergent** adj

**emergency** n, pl **-cies** sudden unforeseen occurrence needing immediate action

**emeritus** [im-**mer**-rit-uss] adj retired, but retaining an honorary title e.g. *emeritus professor*

**emery** n hard mineral used for smoothing and polishing
▶ **emery board** cardboard strip coated with crushed emery, for filing the nails

**emetic** [im-**met**-ik] n substance that causes vomiting ▷ adj causing vomiting

**emigrate** v go and settle in another country ▶ **emigrant** n
▶ **emigration** n

e

**émigré** [**em**-mig-gray] n someone who has left his native country for political reasons

**eminent** adj distinguished, well-known ▸ **eminently** adv
▸ **eminence** n position of superiority or fame; (**E-**) title of a cardinal

**emir** [em-**meer**] n Muslim ruler
▸ **emirate** n his country

**emissary** n, pl **-saries** agent sent on a mission by a government

**emit** v **emitting, emitted** give out (heat, light, or a smell); utter
▸ **emission** n

**emollient** adj softening, soothing
▷ n substance which softens or soothes the skin

**emolument** n (formal) fees or wages from employment

**emoji** [im-**moh**-jee] n image used in electronic messages

**emoticon** [i-**mote**-i-kon] n (Computing) same as **smiley**

**emotion** n strong feeling
▸ **emotional** adj readily affected by or appealing to the emotions
▸ **emotionally** adv ▸ **emotive** adj tending to arouse emotion

**empathy** n ability to understand someone else's feelings as if they were one's own

**emperor** n ruler of an empire
▸ **empress** n fem

**emphasis** n, pl **-ses** special importance or significance; stress on a word or phrase in speech ▸ **emphasize** v
▸ **emphatic** adj showing emphasis
▸ **emphatically** adv

**emphysema** [em-fiss-**see**-ma] n condition in which the air sacs of the lungs are grossly enlarged, causing breathlessness

**empire** n group of territories under the rule of one state or person; large organization that is directed by one person or group

**empirical** adj relying on experiment or experience, not on theory
▸ **empirically** adv ▸ **empiricism** n doctrine that all knowledge derives from experience ▸ **empiricist** n

**emplacement** n prepared position for a gun

**employ** v hire (a person); provide work or occupation for; use ▷ n **in the employ of** doing regular paid work for ▸ **employee** n
▸ **employment** n state of being employed; work done by a person to earn money

**employer** n person or organization that employs someone

**emporium** n, pl **-riums** or **-ria** (old-fashioned) large general shop

**empower** v enable, authorize

**empress** n see **emperor**

**empty** adj **-tier, -tiest** containing nothing; unoccupied; without purpose or value; (of words) insincere ▷ v **-tying, -tied** make or become empty ▸ **empties** pl n empty boxes, bottles, etc.
▸ **emptiness** n

**emu** n large Australian flightless bird with long legs ▸ **emu oil** oil derived from emu fat, used as a liniment by native Australians

**emulate** v attempt to equal or surpass by imitating ▸ **emulation** n

**emulsion** n light-sensitive coating on photographic film; type of water-based paint ▷ v paint with emulsion paint ▸ **emulsify** v (of two liquids) join together or join (two liquids) together ▸ **emulsifier** n

**enable** v provide (a person) with the means, opportunity, or authority (to do something)

**enact** v establish by law; perform (a story or play) by acting
▸ **enactment** n

**enamel** n glasslike coating applied to metal etc. to preserve the surface; hard white coating on a tooth ▷ v **-elling, -elled** cover with enamel

**enamoured** adj inspired with love

**en bloc** adv (French) as a whole, all together

**encamp** v set up in a camp ▶ **encampment** n

**encapsulate** v summarize; enclose as in a capsule

**encephalitis** [en-sef-a-**lite**-iss] n inflammation of the brain

**encephalogram** n short for **electroencephalogram**

**enchant** v delight and fascinate ▶ **enchantment** n ▶ **enchanter** n ▶ **enchantress** n fem

**encircle** v form a circle around ▶ **encirclement** n

**enclave** n part of a country entirely surrounded by foreign territory

**enclose** v surround completely; include along with something else ▶ **enclosure** n

**encomium** n, pl **-miums** or **-mia** formal expression of praise

**encompass** v surround; include comprehensively

**encore** interj again, once more ▷ n extra performance due to enthusiastic demand

**encounter** v meet unexpectedly; be faced with ▷ n unexpected meeting; game or battle

**encourage** v inspire with confidence; spur on ▶ **encouragement** n

**encroach** v intrude gradually on a person's rights or land ▶ **encroachment** n

**encrust** v cover with a layer of something

**encrypt** v put (a message) into code; distort (a television or other signal) so that it cannot be viewed or understood without decryption equipment

**encumber** v hinder or impede ▶ **encumbrance** n something that impedes or is burdensome

**encyclical** [en-**sik**-lik-kl] n letter sent by the Pope to all bishops

**encyclopedia, encyclopaedia** n book or set of books containing facts about many subjects, usu. in alphabetical order ▶ **encyclopedic, encyclopaedic** adj

**end** n furthest point or part; limit; last part of something; fragment; death or destruction; purpose; (Sport) either of the two defended areas of a playing field ▷ v bring or come to a finish **make ends meet** have just enough money for one's needs ▶ **ending** n ▶ **endless** adj ▶ **endways** adv having the end forwards or upwards

**endanger** v put in danger

**endear** v cause to be liked ▶ **endearing** adj ▶ **endearment** n affectionate word or phrase

**endeavour** v try ▷ n effort

**endemic** adj present within a localized area or peculiar to a particular group of people

**endive** n curly-leaved plant used in salads

**endocrine** adj relating to the glands which secrete hormones directly into the bloodstream

**endogenous** [en-**dodge**-in-uss] adj originating from within

**endorse** v give approval to; sign the back of (a cheque); record a conviction on (a driving licence) ▶ **endorsement** n

**endow** v provide permanent income for **endowed with** provided with ▶ **endowment** n

**endure** v bear (hardship) patiently; last for a long time ▶ **endurable** adj ▶ **endurance** n act or power of enduring

**enema** [en-im-a] *n* medicine injected into the rectum to empty the bowels

**enemy** *n*, *pl* **-mies** hostile person or nation, opponent

**energy** *n*, *pl* **-gies** capacity for intense activity; capacity to do work and overcome resistance; source of power, such as electricity ▶ **energetic** *adj* ▶ **energetically** *adv* ▶ **energize** *v* give vigour to ▶ **energy drink** soft drink supposed to boost the drinker's energy levels

**enervate** *v* deprive of strength or vitality ▶ **enervation** *n*

**enfant terrible** [on-fon ter-**reeb**-la] *n*, *pl* **enfants terribles** (*French*) clever but unconventional or indiscreet person

**enfeeble** *v* weaken

**enfold** *v* cover by wrapping something around; embrace

**enforce** *v* impose obedience (to a law etc.); impose (a condition) ▶ **enforceable** *adj* ▶ **enforcement** *n*

**enfranchise** *v* grant (a person) the right to vote ▶ **enfranchisement** *n*

**engage** *v* take part, participate; involve (a person or his or her attention) intensely; employ (a person); begin a battle with; bring (a mechanism) into operation ▶ **engaged** *adj* pledged to be married; in use ▶ **engagement** *n* ▶ **engaging** *adj* charming

**engender** *v* produce, cause to occur

**engine** *n* any machine which converts energy into mechanical work; railway locomotive

**engineer** *n* person trained in any branch of engineering ▷ *v* plan in a clever manner; design or construct as an engineer

**engineering** *n* profession of applying scientific principles to the design and construction of engines, cars, buildings, or machines

**English** *n* official language of Britain, Ireland, Australia, New Zealand, South Africa, Canada, the US, and several other countries ▷ *adj* relating to England **the English** the people of England

**engrave** *v* carve (a design) onto a hard surface; fix deeply in the mind ▶ **engraver** *n* ▶ **engraving** *n* print made from an engraved plate

**engross** [en-**groce**] *v* occupy the attention of (a person) completely

**engulf** *v* cover or surround completely

**enhance** *v* increase in quality, value, or attractiveness ▶ **enhancement** *n*

**enigma** *n* puzzling thing or person ▶ **enigmatic** *adj* ▶ **enigmatically** *adv*

**enjoin** *v* order (someone) to do something

**enjoy** *v* take joy in; have the benefit of; experience ▶ **enjoyable** *adj* ▶ **enjoyment** *n*

**enlarge** *v* make or grow larger; (foll by *on*) speak or write about in greater detail ▶ **enlargement** *n*

**enlighten** *v* give information to ▶ **enlightenment** *n*

**enlist** *v* enter the armed forces; obtain the support of ▶ **enlistment** *n*

**enliven** *v* make lively or cheerful

**en masse** [on **mass**] *adv* (*French*) in a group, all together

**enmeshed** *adj* deeply involved

**enmity** *n*, *pl* **-ties** ill will, hatred

**ennoble** *v* make noble, elevate

**ennui** [on-**nwee**] *n* boredom, dissatisfaction

**enormous** *adj* very big, vast ▶ **enormity** *n*, *pl* **-ties** great wickedness; gross offence; (*informal*) great size

**enough** adj as much or as many as necessary ▷ n sufficient quantity ▷ adv sufficiently; fairly or quite e.g. *that's a common enough experience*

**en passant** [on pass-on] adv (French) in passing, by the way

**enquire** v same as **inquire** ▸ **enquiry** n

**enraptured** adj filled with delight and fascination

**enrich** v improve in quality; make wealthy or wealthier

**enrol** v **-rolling, -rolled** (cause to) become a member ▸ **enrolment** n

**en route** adv (French) on the way

**ensconce** v settle firmly or comfortably

**ensemble** [on-**som**-bl] n all the parts of something taken together; complete outfit of clothes; company of actors or musicians; (Music) group of musicians playing together

**enshrine** v cherish or treasure

**ensign** n naval flag; banner; (US) naval officer

**enslave** v make a slave of (someone) ▸ **enslavement** n

**ensnare** v catch in or as if in a snare

**ensue** v come next, result

**en suite** adv (French) connected to a bedroom and entered directly from it

**ensure** v make certain or sure; make safe or protect

**entail** v bring about or impose inevitably

**entangle** v catch or involve in or as if in a tangle ▸ **entanglement** n

**entente** [on-**tont**] n friendly understanding between nations

**enter** v come or go in; join; become involved in, take part in; record (an item) in a journal etc.; begin ▸ **entrance** n way into a place; act of entering; right of entering ▸ **entrant** n person who enters a university, contest, etc. ▸ **entry** n,

pl **-tries** entrance; entering; item entered in a journal etc.

**enteric** [en-**ter**-ik] adj intestinal ▸ **enteritis** [en-ter-**rite**-iss] n inflammation of the intestine, causing diarrhoea

**enterprise** n company or firm; bold or difficult undertaking; boldness and energy ▸ **enterprising** adj full of boldness and initiative

**entertain** v amuse; receive as a guest; consider (an idea) ▸ **entertainer** n ▸ **entertainment** n

**enthral** [en-**thrawl**] v **-thralling, -thralled** hold the attention of ▸ **enthralling** adj

**enthusiasm** n ardent interest, eagerness ▸ **enthuse** v (cause to) show enthusiasm ▸ **enthusiast** n ardent supporter of something ▸ **enthusiastic** adj ▸ **enthusiastically** adv

**entice** v attract by exciting hope or desire, tempt ▸ **enticement** n

**entire** adj including every detail, part, or aspect of something ▸ **entirely** adv ▸ **entirety** n

**entitle** v give a right to; give a title to ▸ **entitlement** n

**entity** n, pl **-ties** separate distinct thing

**entomology** n study of insects ▸ **entomological** adj ▸ **entomologist** n

**entourage** [on-toor-**ahzh**] n group of people who assist an important person

**entrails** pl n intestines; innermost parts of something

**entrance**¹ n see **enter**

**entrance**² v delight; put into a trance

**entreat** v ask earnestly ▸ **entreaty** n, pl **-ties** earnest request

**entrée** [on-**tray**] n dish served before a main course; main course; right of admission

**entrench** v establish firmly; establish in a fortified position with trenches ▶ **entrenchment** n

**entrepreneur** n business person who attempts to make a profit by risk and initiative

**entropy** [en-trop-ee] n lack of organization

**entrust** v put into the care or protection of

**entwine** v twist together or around

**E number** n any of a series of numbers with the prefix E indicating a specific food additive recognized by the EU

**enumerate** v name one by one ▶ **enumeration** n

**enunciate** v pronounce clearly; state precisely or formally ▶ **enunciation** n

**envelop** v **enveloping, enveloped** wrap up, enclose ▶ **envelopment** n

**envelope** n folded gummed paper cover for a letter

**environment** [en-**vire**-on-ment] n external conditions and surroundings in which people, animals, or plants live ▶ **environmental** adj ▶ **environmentalist** n person concerned with the protection of the natural environment

> **SPELLING TIP**
> Note the n before the m in the spelling of environment

**environs** pl n surrounding area, esp. of a town

**envisage** v conceive of as a possibility

**envoy** n messenger; diplomat ranking below an ambassador

**envy** n feeling of discontent aroused by another's good fortune ▷ v **-vying, -vied** grudge (another's good fortune, success, or qualities) ▶ **enviable** adj arousing envy, fortunate ▶ **envious** adj full of envy

**enzyme** n any of a group of complex proteins that act as catalysts in specific biochemical reactions

**Eolithic** adj of the early part of the Stone Age

**epaulette** n shoulder ornament on a uniform

**ephemeral** adj short-lived

**epic** n long poem, book, or film about heroic events or actions ▷ adj very impressive or ambitious

**epicentre** n point on the earth's surface immediately above the origin of an earthquake

**epicure** n person who enjoys good food and drink ▶ **epicurean** adj devoted to sensual pleasures, esp. food and drink ▷ n epicure

**epidemic** n widespread occurrence of a disease; rapid spread of something

**epidermis** n outer layer of the skin

**epidural** [ep-pid-**dure**-al] adj, n (of) spinal anaesthetic injected to relieve pain during childbirth

**epiglottis** n thin flap that covers the opening of the larynx during swallowing

**epigram** n short witty remark or poem ▶ **epigrammatic** adj

**epigraph** n quotation at the start of a book; inscription

**epilepsy** n disorder of the nervous system causing loss of consciousness and sometimes convulsions ▶ **epileptic** adj of or having epilepsy ▷ n (offens) person who has epilepsy

**epilogue** n short speech or poem at the end of a literary work, esp. a play

**Epiphany** n Christian festival held on January 6 commemorating the manifestation of Christ to the Magi

**episcopal** [ip-**piss**-kop-al] adj of or governed by bishops ▶ **episcopalian** adj advocating

Church government by bishops
▷ *n* advocate of such Church
government

**episode** *n* incident in a series of
incidents; section of a serialized
book, television programme,
etc. ▶ **episodic** *adj* occurring at
irregular intervals

**epistemology** [ip-iss-stem-**ol**-a-
jee] *n* study of the source, nature,
and limitations of knowledge
▶ **epistemological** *adj*

**epistle** *n* letter, esp. of an apostle
▶ **epistolary** *adj*

**epitaph** *n* commemorative
inscription on a tomb;
commemorative speech or
passage

**epithet** *n* descriptive word or name

**epitome** [ip-**pit**-a-mee] *n* typical
example ▶ **epitomize** *v* be the
epitome of

**USAGE NOTE**
Avoid the use of *epitome* to mean
'the peak' of something

**epoch** [**ee**-pok] *n* period of notable
events ▶ **epoch-making** *adj*
extremely important

**eponymous** [ip-**pon**-im-uss] *adj*
after whom a book, play, etc. is
named

**equable** [**ek**-wab-bl] *adj* even-
tempered ▶ **equably** *adv*

**equal** *adj* identical in size, quantity,
degree, etc.; having identical
rights or status; evenly balanced;
(foll by *to*) having the necessary
ability (for) ▷ *n* person or thing
equal to another ▷ *v* **equalling,
equalled** be equal to ▶ **equally** *adv*
▶ **equality** *n* state of being equal
▶ **equalize** *v* make or become
equal; reach the same score as
one's opponent ▶ **equalization** *n*
▶ **equal opportunity**
nondiscrimination as to sex, race,
etc. in employment

**equanimity** *n* calmness of mind

**equate** *v* make or regard as
equivalent ▶ **equation** *n*
mathematical statement that
two expressions are equal; act of
equating

**equator** *n* imaginary circle round
the earth, equidistant from the
poles ▶ **equatorial** *adj*

**equerry** [**ek**-kwer-ee] *n, pl*
**-ries** (*Brit*) officer who acts as an
attendant to a member of a royal
family

**equestrian** *adj* of horses and riding

**equidistant** *adj* equally distant

**equilateral** *adj* having equal sides

**equilibrium** *n, pl* **-ria** steadiness
or stability

**equine** *adj* of or like a horse

**equinox** *n* time of year when day
and night are of equal length
▶ **equinoctial** *adj*

**equip** *v* **equipping, equipped**
provide with supplies,
components, etc. ▶ **equipment**
*n* set of tools or devices used
for a particular purpose; act of
equipping

**equipoise** *n* perfect balance

**equity** *n, pl* **-ties** fairness;
legal system, founded on the
principles of natural justice, that
supplements common law ▷ *pl*
interest of ordinary shareholders in
a company ▶ **equitable** *adj* fair and
reasonable ▶ **equitably** *adv*

**equivalent** *adj* equal in value;
having the same meaning or result
▷ *n* something that is equivalent
▶ **equivalence** *n*

**equivocal** *adj* ambiguous;
deliberately misleading; of
doubtful character or sincerity
▶ **equivocally** *adv* ▶ **equivocate**
*v* use vague or ambiguous
language to mislead people
▶ **equivocation** *n*

**ER** Queen Elizabeth

**era** n period of time considered as distinctive

**eradicate** v destroy completely ▶ **eradication** n

**erase** v rub out; remove sound or information from (a magnetic tape or disk) ▶ **eraser** n object for erasing something written ▶ **erasure** n erasing; place or mark where something has been erased

**ere** prep, conj (poetic) before

**e-reader, eReader** n portable device that allows users to download and read texts in electronic form

**erect** v build; found or form ▷ adj upright; (of the penis, clitoris, or nipples) rigid as a result of sexual excitement ▶ **erectile** adj capable of becoming erect from sexual excitement ▶ **erection** n

**erg** n unit of work or energy

**ergonomics** n study of the relationship between workers and their environment ▶ **ergonomic** adj

**ergot** n fungal disease of cereal; dried fungus used in medicine

**ermine** n stoat in northern regions; its white winter fur

**erode** v wear away ▶ **erosion** n

**erogenous** [ir-**roj**-in-uss] adj sensitive to sexual stimulation

**erotic** adj relating to sexual pleasure or desire ▶ **eroticism** n ▶ **erotica** n sexual literature or art

**err** v make a mistake ▶ **erratum** n, pl **-ta** error in writing or printing ▶ **erroneous** adj incorrect, mistaken

**errand** n short trip to do something for someone

**errant** adj behaving in a manner considered to be unacceptable

**erratic** adj irregular or unpredictable ▶ **erratically** adv

**error** n mistake, inaccuracy, or misjudgment

**ersatz** [**air**-zats] adj made in imitation e.g. ersatz coffee

**erstwhile** adj former

**erudite** adj having great academic knowledge ▶ **erudition** n

**erupt** v eject (steam, water, or volcanic material) violently; burst forth suddenly and violently; (of a blemish) appear on the skin ▶ **eruption** n

**erysipelas** [err-riss-**sip**-pel-ass] n acute skin infection causing purplish patches

**escalate** v increase in extent or intensity ▶ **escalation** n

**escalator** n moving staircase

**escalope** [ess-kal-lop] n thin slice of meat, esp. veal

**escapade** n mischievous adventure

**escape** v get free (of); avoid e.g. escape attention; (of a gas, liquid, etc.) leak gradually ▷ n act of escaping; means of relaxation ▶ **escapee** n person who has escaped ▶ **escapism** n taking refuge in fantasy to avoid unpleasant reality ▶ **escapologist** n entertainer who specializes in freeing himself from confinement ▶ **escapology** n

**escarpment** n steep face of a ridge or mountain

**eschew** [iss-**chew**] v abstain from, avoid

**escort** n people or vehicles accompanying another person for protection or as an honour; person who accompanies a person of the opposite sex to a social event ▷ v act as an escort to

**escudo** [ess-**kyoo**-doe] n, pl **-dos** former monetary unit of Portugal

**escutcheon** n shield with a coat of arms **blot on one's escutcheon** stain on one's honour

**Eskimo** n member of the aboriginal race inhabiting N Canada, Greenland, Alaska, and E Siberia; their language

**USAGE NOTE**
*Eskimo* is considered by many people to be offensive, and in North America the term *Inuit* is often used

**esoteric** [ee-so-**ter**-rik] adj understood by only a small number of people with special knowledge

**ESP** extrasensory perception

**esp.** especially

**espadrille** [ess-pad-drill] n light canvas shoe with a braided cord sole

**espalier** [ess-**pal**-yer] n shrub or fruit tree trained to grow flat; trellis for this

**esparto** n, pl **-tos** grass of S Europe and N Africa used for making rope etc.

**especial** adj (formal) special

**especially** adv particularly

**Esperanto** n universal artificial language

**espionage** [ess-pyon-ahzh] n spying

**esplanade** n wide open road used as a public promenade

**espouse** v adopt or give support to (a cause etc.) ▶ **espousal** n

**espresso** n, pl **-sos** strong coffee made by forcing steam or boiling water through ground coffee beans

**SPELLING TIP**
Note that the second letter is s not x

**esprit** [ess-**pree**] n spirit, liveliness, or wit ▶ **esprit de corps** [de **core**] pride in and loyalty to a group

**espy** v **espying, espied** catch sight of

**Esq.** esquire

**esquire** n courtesy title placed after a man's name

**essay** n short literary composition; short piece of writing on a subject done as an exercise by a student ▷ v attempt ▶ **essayist** n

**essence** n most important feature of a thing which determines its identity; concentrated liquid used to flavour food ▶ **essential** adj vitally important; basic or fundamental ▷ n something fundamental or indispensable ▶ **essentially** adv

**establish** v set up on a permanent basis; make secure or permanent in a certain place, job, etc.; prove; cause to be accepted ▶ **establishment** n act of establishing; commercial or other institution **the Establishment** group of people having authority within a society

**estate** n landed property; large area of property development, esp. of new houses or factories; property of a deceased person ▶ **estate agent** agent concerned with the valuation, lease, and sale of property ▶ **estate car** car with a rear door and luggage space behind the rear seats

**esteem** n high regard ▷ v think highly of; judge or consider

**ester** n (Chem) compound produced by the reaction between an acid and an alcohol

**estimate** v calculate roughly; form an opinion about ▷ n approximate calculation; statement from a workman etc. of the likely charge for a job; opinion ▶ **estimable** adj worthy of respect ▶ **estimation** n considered opinion

**estranged** adj no longer living with one's spouse ▶ **estrangement** n

**estuary** n, pl **-aries** mouth of a river

**ETA** estimated time of arrival

**et al.** and elsewhere

**etc.** et cetera

**et cetera** [et **set**-ra] (*Latin*) and the rest, and others; or the like ▶ **etceteras** ▷ *pl n* miscellaneous extra things or people

**etch** *v* wear away or cut the surface of (metal, glass, etc.) with acid; imprint vividly (on someone's mind) ▶ **etching** *n*

**eternal** *adj* without beginning or end; unchanging ▶ **eternally** *adv* ▶ **eternity** *n* infinite time; timeless existence after death ▶ **eternity ring** ring given as a token of lasting affection

**ether** *n* colourless sweet-smelling liquid used as an anaesthetic; region above the clouds ▶ **ethereal** [eth-**eer**-ee-al] *adj* extremely delicate

**ethic** *n* moral principle ▶ **ethical** *adj* ▶ **ethically** *adv* ▶ **ethics** *n* code of behaviour; study of morals

**ethnic** *adj* relating to a people or group that shares a culture, religion, or language; belonging or relating to such a group, esp. one that is a minority group in a particular place ▶ **ethnic cleansing** practice, by the dominant ethnic group in an area, of removing other ethnic groups by expulsion or extermination ▶ **ethnology** *n* study of human races ▶ **ethnological** *adj* ▶ **ethnologist** *n*

**ethos** [**eeth**-oss] *n* distinctive spirit and attitudes of a people, culture, etc.

**ethyl** [**eeth**-ile] *adj* of, consisting of, or containing the hydrocarbon group C2H5 ▶ **ethylene** *n* poisonous gas used as an anaesthetic and as fuel

**etiolate** [ee-tee-oh-late] *v* become pale and weak; (*Botany*) whiten through lack of sunlight

**etiology** *n* study of the causes of diseases

**etiquette** *n* conventional code of conduct

**étude** [ay-tewd] *n* short musical composition for a solo instrument, esp. intended as a technical exercise

**etymology** *n*, *pl* **-gies** study of the sources and development of words ▶ **etymological** *adj*

**EU** European Union

**eucalyptus, eucalypt** *n* tree, mainly grown in Australia, that provides timber, gum, and medicinal oil from the leaves

**Eucharist** [**yew**-kar-ist] *n* Christian sacrament commemorating Christ's Last Supper; consecrated elements of bread and wine ▶ **Eucharistic** *adj*

**eugenics** [yew-**jen**-iks] *n* study of methods of improving the human race

**eulogy** *n*, *pl* **-gies** speech or writing in praise of a person ▶ **eulogize** *v* praise (a person or thing) highly in speech or writing ▶ **eulogistic** *adj*

**eunuch** *n* castrated man, esp. (formerly) a guard in a harem

**euphemism** *n* inoffensive word or phrase substituted for one considered offensive or upsetting ▶ **euphemistic** *adj* ▶ **euphemistically** *adv*

**euphony** *n*, *pl* **-nies** pleasing sound ▶ **euphonious** *adj* pleasing to the ear ▶ **euphonium** *n* brass musical instrument, tenor tuba

**euphoria** *n* sense of elation ▶ **euphoric** *adj*

**Eurasian** *adj* of Europe and Asia; of mixed European and Asian parentage ▷ *n* person of Eurasian parentage

**eureka** [yew-**reek**-a] *interj* exclamation of triumph at finding something

**euro** n, pl **euros** unit of the single currency of the European Union

**European** n, adj (person) from Europe ▶ **European Union** economic and political association of a number of European nations

**Eustachian tube** n passage leading from the ear to the throat

**euthanasia** n act of killing someone painlessly, esp. to relieve his or her suffering

**evacuate** v send (someone) away from a place of danger; empty ▶ **evacuation** n ▶ **evacuee** n

**evade** v get away from or avoid; elude ▶ **evasion** n ▶ **evasive** adj not straightforward ▶ **evasively** adv

**evaluate** v find or judge the value of ▶ **evaluation** n

**evanescent** adj quickly fading away ▶ **evanescence** n

**evangelical** adj of or according to gospel teaching; of certain Protestant sects which maintain the doctrine of salvation by faith ▷ n member of an evangelical sect ▶ **evangelicalism** n

**evangelist** n writer of one of the four gospels; travelling preacher ▶ **evangelism** n teaching and spreading of the Christian gospel ▶ **evangelize** v preach the gospel ▶ **evangelization** n

**evaporate** v change from a liquid or solid to a vapour; disappear ▶ **evaporation** n ▶ **evaporated milk** thick unsweetened tinned milk

**eve** n evening or day before some special event; period immediately before an event ▶ **evensong** n evening prayer

**even** adj flat or smooth; (foll by with) on the same level (as); constant; calm; equally balanced; divisible by two ▷ adv equally; simply; nevertheless ▷ v make even

**evening** n end of the day or early part of the night ▷ adj of or in the evening

**event** n anything that takes place; planned and organized occasion; contest in a sporting programme ▶ **eventful** adj full of exciting incidents

**eventing** n (Brit, Aust & NZ) riding competitions, usu. involving cross-country, jumping, and dressage

**eventual** adj ultimate ▶ **eventuality** n possible event

**eventually** adv at the end of a situation or process

**ever** adv at any time; always ▶ **evergreen** n, adj (tree or shrub) having leaves throughout the year ▶ **everlasting** adj ▶ **evermore** adv for all time to come

**every** adj each without exception; all possible ▶ **everybody** pron every person ▶ **everyday** adj usual or ordinary ▶ **everyone** pron every person ▶ **everything** pron ▶ **everywhere** adv in all places

**evict** v legally expel (someone) from his or her home ▶ **eviction** n

**evidence** n ground for belief; matter produced before a law court to prove or disprove a point; sign, indication ▷ v demonstrate, prove **in evidence** conspicuous ▶ **evident** adj easily seen or understood ▶ **evidently** adv ▶ **evidential** adj of, serving as, or based on evidence

**evil** n wickedness; wicked deed ▷ adj harmful; morally bad; very unpleasant ▶ **evilly** adv ▶ **evildoer** n wicked person

**evince** v make evident

**eviscerate** v disembowel ▶ **evisceration** n

**evoke** v call or summon up (a memory, feeling, etc.) ▶ **evocation** n ▶ **evocative** adj

**evolve** v develop gradually; (of an animal or plant species) undergo evolution ▶ **evolution** n gradual change in the characteristics of living things over successive generations, esp. to a more complex form ▶ **evolutionary** adj

**ewe** n female sheep

**ewer** n large jug with a wide mouth

**ex** n (informal) former wife or husband

**ex-** prefix out of, outside, from e.g. exodus; former e.g. ex-wife

**exacerbate** [ig-**zass**-er-bate] v make (pain, emotion, or a situation) worse ▶ **exacerbation** n

**exact** adj correct and complete in every detail; precise, as opposed to approximate ▷ v demand (payment or obedience) ▶ **exactly** adv precisely, in every respect ▶ **exactness, exactitude** n ▶ **exacting** adj making rigorous or excessive demands

**exaggerate** v regard or represent as greater than is true; make greater or more noticeable ▶ **exaggeratedly** adv ▶ **exaggeration** n

| SPELLING TIP
Note that **exaggerate** has a double g but only one r

**exalt** v praise highly; raise to a higher rank ▶ **exalted** adj ▶ **exaltation** n

**exam** n short for **examination**

**examine** v look at closely; test the knowledge of; ask questions of ▶ **examination** n examining; test of a candidate's knowledge or skill ▶ **examinee** n ▶ **examiner** n

**example** n specimen typical of its group; person or thing worthy of imitation; punishment regarded as a warning to others

**exasperate** v cause great irritation to ▶ **exasperation** n

**excavate** v unearth buried objects from (a piece of land) methodically to learn about the past; make (a hole) in solid matter by digging ▶ **excavation** n ▶ **excavator** n large machine used for digging

**exceed** v be greater than; go beyond (a limit) ▶ **exceedingly** adv very

**excel** v -celling, -celled be superior to; be outstandingly good at something

**Excellency** n title used to address a high-ranking official, such as an ambassador

**excellent** adj exceptionally good ▶ **excellence** n

**except** prep (sometimes foll by for) other than, not including ▷ v not include **except that** but for the fact that **excepting** prep except ▶ **exception** n excepting; thing that is excluded from or does not conform to the general rule ▶ **exceptional** adj not ordinary; much above the average

**excerpt** n passage taken from a book, speech, etc.

**excess** n state or act of exceeding the permitted limits; immoderate amount; amount by which a thing exceeds the permitted limits ▶ **excessive** adj ▶ **excessively** adv

**exchange** v give or receive (something) in return for something else ▷ n act of exchanging; thing given or received in place of another; centre in which telephone lines are interconnected; (Finance) place where securities or commodities are traded; transfer of sums of money of equal value between different currencies ▶ **exchangeable** adj

**Exchequer** n (Brit) government department in charge of state money

**excise¹** n tax on goods produced for the home market

**excise²** v cut out or away ▸ **excision** n

**excite** v arouse to strong emotion; arouse or evoke (an emotion); arouse sexually ▸ **excitement** n ▸ **excitable** adj easily excited ▸ **excitability** n

**exclaim** v speak suddenly, cry out ▸ **exclamation** n ▸ **exclamation mark** punctuation mark (!) used after exclamations ▸ **exclamatory** adj

**exclude** v keep out, leave out; leave out of consideration ▸ **exclusion** n ▸ **exclusive** adj excluding everything else; not shared; catering for a privileged minority ▷ n story reported in only one newspaper ▸ **exclusively** adv ▸ **exclusivity, exclusiveness** n

**excommunicate** v exclude from membership and the sacraments of the Church ▸ **excommunication** n

**excoriate** v censure severely; strip skin from ▸ **excoriation** n

**excrement** n waste matter discharged from the body

**excrescence** n lump or growth on the surface of an animal or plant

**excrete** v discharge (waste matter) from the body ▸ **excretion** n ▸ **excreta** [ik-**skree**-ta] n excrement ▸ **excretory** adj

**excruciating** adj agonizing; hard to bear ▸ **excruciatingly** adv

**exculpate** v free from blame or guilt

**excursion** n short journey, esp. for pleasure

**excuse** n explanation offered to justify (a fault etc.) ▷ v put forward a reason or justification for (a fault etc.); forgive (a person) or overlook (a fault etc.); make allowances

for; exempt; allow to leave ▸ **excusable** adj

**ex-directory** adj not listed in a telephone directory by request

**execrable** [**eks**-sik-rab-bl] adj of very poor quality

**execute** v put (a condemned person) to death; carry out or accomplish; produce (a work of art); render (a legal document) effective, as by signing ▸ **execution** n ▸ **executioner** n

**executive** n person or group in an administrative position; branch of government responsible for carrying out laws etc. ▷ adj having the function of carrying out plans, orders, laws, etc.

**executor,** (fem) **executrix** n person appointed to perform the instructions of a will

**exegesis** [eks-sij-**jee**-siss] n, pl **-ses** [-seez] explanation of a text, esp. of the Bible

**exemplar** n person or thing to be copied, model; example ▸ **exemplary** adj being a good example; serving as a warning

**exemplify** v **-fying, -fied** show an example of; be an example of ▸ **exemplification** n

**exempt** adj not subject to an obligation etc. ▷ v release from an obligation etc. ▸ **exemption** n

**exequies** [**eks**-sik-wiz] pl n funeral rites

**exercise** n activity to train the body or mind; set of movements or tasks designed to improve or test a person's ability; performance of a function ▷ v make use of e.g. to exercise one's rights; take exercise or perform exercises

**exert** v use (influence, authority, etc.) forcefully or effectively **exert oneself** make a special effort ▸ **exertion** n

**exeunt** [eks-see-unt] (*Latin*) they go out: used as a stage direction

**exfoliate** *v* scrub away dead skin cells, esp by washing with abrasive lotion

**ex gratia** [eks gray-sha] *adj* given as a favour where no legal obligation exists

**exhale** *v* breathe out ▸ **exhalation** *n*

**exhaust** *v* tire out; use up; discuss (a subject) thoroughly ▹ *n* gases ejected from an engine as waste products; pipe through which an engine's exhaust fumes pass ▸ **exhaustion** *n* extreme tiredness; exhausting ▸ **exhaustive** *adj* comprehensive ▸ **exhaustively** *adv*

**exhibit** *v* display to the public; show (a quality or feeling) ▹ *n* object exhibited to the public; (*Law*) document or object produced in court as evidence ▸ **exhibitor** *n* ▸ **exhibition** *n* public display of art, skills, etc.; exhibiting ▸ **exhibitionism** *n* compulsive desire to draw attention to oneself; compulsive desire to display one's genitals in public ▸ **exhibitionist** *n*

**exhilarate** *v* make lively and cheerful ▸ **exhilaration** *n*

> **SPELLING TIP**
> A common error is to spell the third syllable of **exhilarate**, **exhilaration**, etc. with an *e* rather than the correct *a*

**exhort** *v* urge earnestly ▸ **exhortation** *n*

**exhume** [ig-zyume] *v* dig up (something buried, esp. a corpse) ▸ **exhumation** *n*

**exigency** *n*, *pl* **-cies** urgent demand or need ▸ **exigent** *adj*

**exiguous** *adj* scanty or meagre

**exile** *n* prolonged, usu. enforced, absence from one's country; person banished or living away from his or her country ▹ *v* expel from one's country

**exist** *v* have being or reality; eke out a living; live ▸ **existence** *n* ▸ **existent** *adj*

> **SPELLING TIP**
> There is much confusion about whether certain words end with *-ance* or with *-ence*: **existence** is one that ends with the latter

**existential** *adj* of or relating to existence, esp. human existence ▸ **existentialism** *n* philosophical movement stressing the personal experience and responsibility of the individual, who is seen as a free agent ▸ **existentialist** *adj*, *n*

**exit** *n* way out; going out; actor's going off stage ▹ *v* go out; go offstage: used as a stage direction

**exocrine** *adj* relating to a gland, such as the sweat gland, that secretes externally through a duct

**exodus** [eks-so-duss] *n* departure of a large number of people

**ex officio** [eks off-fish-ee-oh] *adv*, *adj* (*Latin*) by right of position or office

**exonerate** *v* free from blame or a criminal charge ▸ **exoneration** *n*

**exorbitant** *adj* (of prices, demands, etc.) excessive, immoderate ▸ **exorbitantly** *adv*

**exorcize** *v* expel (evil spirits) by prayers and religious rites ▸ **exorcism** *n* ▸ **exorcist** *n*

**exotic** *adj* having a strange allure or beauty; originating in a foreign country ▹ *n* non-native plant ▸ **exotically** *adv* ▸ **exotica** *pl n* (collection of) exotic objects

**expand** *v* make or become larger; spread out; (foll by *on*) enlarge (on); become more relaxed, friendly, and talkative ▸ **expansion** *n* ▸ **expanse** *n* uninterrupted wide area ▶ **expansive** adj wide or extensive; friendly and talkative

**expat** adj, n short for **expatriate**

**expatiate** [iks-**pay**-shee-ate] v (foll by on) speak or write at great length (on)

**expatriate** [eks-**pat**-ree-it] adj living outside one's native country ▷ n person living outside his or her native country ▶ **expatriation** n

**expect** v regard as probable; look forward to, await; require as an obligation ▶ **expectancy** n something expected on the basis of an average e.g. *life expectancy*; feeling of anticipation ▶ **expectant** adj expecting or hopeful; pregnant ▶ **expectantly** adv ▶ **expectation** n act or state of expecting; something looked forward to; attitude of anticipation or hope

**expectorant** n medicine that helps to bring up phlegm from the respiratory passages

**expectorate** v spit out (phlegm etc.) ▶ **expectoration** n

**expedient** n something that achieves a particular purpose ▷ adj suitable to the circumstances, appropriate ▶ **expediency** n

**expedite** v hasten the progress of ▶ **expedition** n organized journey, esp. for exploration; people and equipment comprising an expedition; pleasure trip or excursion ▶ **expeditionary** adj relating to an expedition, esp. a military one ▶ **expeditious** adj done quickly and efficiently

**expel** v **-pelling, -pelled** drive out with force; dismiss from a school etc. permanently ▶ **expulsion** n

**expend** v spend, use up ▶ **expendable** adj able to be sacrificed to achieve an objective ▶ **expenditure** n something

expended, esp. money; amount expended

**expense** n cost; (cause of) spending ▷ pl charges, outlay incurred

**expensive** adj high-priced

**experience** n direct personal participation; particular incident, feeling, etc. that a person has undergone; accumulated knowledge ▷ v participate in; be affected by (an emotion) ▶ **experienced** adj skilful from extensive participation

**experiment** n test to provide evidence to prove or disprove a theory; attempt at something new ▷ v carry out an experiment ▶ **experimental** adj ▶ **experimentally** adv ▶ **experimentation** n

**expert** n person with extensive skill or knowledge in a particular field ▷ adj skilful or knowledgeable ▶ **expertise** [eks-per-**teez**] n special skill or knowledge

**expiate** v make amends for ▶ **expiation** n

**expire** v finish or run out; breathe out; (lit) die ▶ **expiration** n ▶ **expiry** n end, esp. of a contract period

**explain** v make clear and intelligible; account for ▶ **explanation** n ▶ **explanatory** adj

**expletive** n swearword

**explicable** adj able to be explained ▶ **explicate** v (formal) explain ▶ **explication** n

**explicit** adj precisely and clearly expressed; shown in realistic detail ▶ **explicitly** adv

**explode** v burst with great violence, blow up; react suddenly with emotion; increase rapidly; show (a theory etc.) to be baseless

▶ **explosion** n ▶ **explosive** adj tending to explode ▷ n substance that causes explosions

**exploit** v take advantage of for one's own purposes; make the best use of ▷ n notable feat or deed ▶ **exploitation** n ▶ **exploiter** n

**explore** v investigate; travel into (unfamiliar regions), esp. for scientific purposes ▶ **exploration** n ▶ **exploratory** adj ▶ **explorer** n

**expo** n, pl **expos** (informal) exposition, large public exhibition

**exponent** n person who advocates an idea, cause, etc.; skilful performer, esp. a musician

**exponential** adj (informal) very rapid ▶ **exponentially** adv

**export** n selling or shipping of goods to a foreign country; product shipped or sold to a foreign country ▷ v sell or ship (goods) to a foreign country ▶ **exporter** n

**expose** v uncover or reveal; make vulnerable, leave unprotected; subject (a photographic film) to light **expose oneself** display one's sexual organs in public ▶ **exposure** n exposing; lack of shelter from the weather, esp. the cold; appearance before the public, as on television

**exposé** [iks-**pose**-ay] n bringing of a crime, scandal, etc. to public notice

**exposition** n see **expound**

**expostulate** v (foll by with) reason (with), esp. to dissuade

**expound** v explain in detail ▶ **exposition** n explanation; large public exhibition

**express** v put into words; show (an emotion); indicate by a symbol or formula; squeeze out (juice etc.) ▷ adj explicitly stated; (of a purpose) particular; of or for rapid transportation of people, mail, etc. ▷ n fast train or bus stopping at only a few stations ▷ adv by express delivery ▶ **expression** n expressing; word or phrase; showing or communication of emotion; look on the face that indicates mood; (Maths) variable, function, or some combination of these ▶ **expressionless** adj ▶ **expressive** adj

**expressionism** n early 20th-century artistic movement which sought to express emotions rather than represent the physical world ▶ **expressionist** n, adj

**expropriate** v deprive an owner of (property) ▶ **expropriation** n

**expunge** v delete, erase, blot out

**expurgate** v remove objectionable parts from (a book etc.)

**exquisite** adj of extreme beauty or delicacy; intense in feeling ▶ **exquisitely** adv

**extant** adj still existing

**extemporize** v speak, perform, or compose without preparation

**extend** v draw out or be drawn out, stretch; last for a certain time; (foll by to) include; increase in size or scope; offer e.g. extend one's sympathy ▶ **extendable** adj ▶ **extension** n room or rooms added to an existing building; additional telephone connected to the same line as another; extending ▶ **extensive** adj having a large extent, widespread ▶ **extensor** n muscle that extends a part of the body ▶ **extent** n range over which something extends, area

**SPELLING TIP**

Lots of nouns in English end with -tion, but **extension** is not one of them

**extenuate** v make (an offence or fault) less blameworthy ▶ **extenuation** n

**exterior** n part or surface on the outside; outward appearance ▷ adj of, on, or coming from the outside

**exterminate** v destroy (animals or people) completely ▶ **extermination** n ▶ **exterminator** n

**external** adj of, situated on, or coming from the outside ▶ **externally** adv

**extinct** adj having died out; (of a volcano) no longer liable to erupt ▶ **extinction** n

**extinguish** v put out (a fire or light); remove or destroy entirely

**extinguisher** n device for extinguishing a fire or light

**extirpate** v destroy utterly

**extol** v **-tolling, -tolled** praise highly

**extort** v get (something) by force or threats ▶ **extortion** n ▶ **extortionate** adj (of prices) excessive

**extra** adj more than is usual, expected or needed ▷ n additional person or thing; something for which an additional charge is made; (Films) actor hired for crowd scenes ▷ adv unusually or exceptionally

**extra-** prefix outside or beyond an area or scope e.g. extrasensory; extraterritorial

**extract** v pull out by force; remove; derive; copy out (an article, passage, etc.) from a publication ▷ n something extracted, such as a passage from a book etc.; preparation containing the concentrated essence of a substance e.g. beef extract ▶ **extraction** n ▶ **extractor** n

**extradite** v send (an accused person) back to his or her own country for trial ▶ **extradition** n

**extramural** adj connected with but outside the normal courses of a university or college

**extraneous** [iks-**train**-ee-uss] adj irrelevant

**extraordinary** adj very unusual; (of a meeting) specially arranged to deal with a particular subject ▶ **extraordinarily** adv

**extraordinary rendition** n process by which a country seizes a suspected terrorist and transports them for interrogation to a country where due process of law is unlikely to be respected

**extrapolate** v infer (something not known) from the known facts; (Maths) estimate (a value of a function or measurement) beyond the known values by the extension of a curve ▶ **extrapolation** n

**extrasensory** adj ▶ **extrasensory perception** supposed ability to obtain information other than through the normal senses

**extravagant** adj spending money excessively; going beyond reasonable limits ▶ **extravagance** n ▶ **extravaganza** n elaborate and lavish entertainment, display, etc.

> **SPELLING TIP**
> Make sure that **extravagant** ends in -ant, even though -ent sounds like a possibility

**extreme** adj of a high or the highest degree or intensity; severe; immoderate; farthest or outermost ▷ n either of the two limits of a scale or range ▶ **extremely** adv ▶ **extreme sport** sport with a high risk of injury or death ▶ **extremist** n person who favours immoderate methods ▷ adj holding extreme opinions ▶ **extremity** n, pl **-ties** farthest point; extreme condition, as of misfortune ▷ pl hands and feet

e

**extricate** v free from complication or difficulty ▶ **extrication** n

**extrovert** adj lively and outgoing; concerned more with external reality than inner feelings ▷ n extrovert person

**extrude** v squeeze or force out ▶ **extrusion** n

**exuberant** adj high-spirited; growing luxuriantly ▶ **exuberance** n

**exude** v (of a liquid or smell) seep or flow out slowly and steadily; make apparent by mood or behaviour e.g. exude confidence

**exult** v be joyful or jubilant ▶ **exultation** n ▶ **exultant** adj

**eye** n organ of sight; ability to judge or appreciate e.g. a good eye for detail; one end of a sewing needle; dark spot on a potato from which a stem grows ▷ v **eyeing** or **eying, eyed** look at carefully or warily ▶ **eyeless** adj ▶ **eyelet** n small hole for a lace or cord to be passed through; ring that strengthens this ▶ **eyeball** n ball-shaped part of the eye ▶ **eyebrow** n line of hair on the bony ridge above the eye ▶ **eyeglass** n lens for aiding defective vision ▶ **eyelash** n short hair that grows out from the eyelid ▶ **eyelid** n fold of skin that covers the eye when it is closed ▶ **eyeliner** n cosmetic used to outline the eyes ▶ **eye-opener** n (informal) something startling or revealing ▶ **eye shadow** coloured cosmetic worn on the upper eyelids ▶ **eyesight** n ability to see ▶ **eyesore** n ugly object ▶ **eye tooth** canine tooth ▶ **eyewitness** n person who is present at an event and can describe what happened

**eyrie** n nest of an eagle; high isolated place

**Ff**

**F** Fahrenheit; farad

**f** (Music) forte

**FA** Football Association (of England)

**fable** n story with a moral; false or fictitious account; legend ▶ **fabled** adj made famous in legend

**fabric** n knitted or woven cloth; framework or structure

**fabricate** v make up (a story or lie); make or build ▶ **fabrication** n

**fabulous** adj (informal) excellent; astounding; told of in fables ▶ **fabulously** adv

**facade** [fas-sahd] n front of a building; (false) outward appearance

**face** n front of the head; facial expression; distorted expression; outward appearance; front or main side; dial of a clock; dignity, self-respect ▷ v look or turn towards; be opposite; be confronted by; provide with a surface ▶ **faceless** adj impersonal, anonymous ▶ **face-lift** n operation to tighten facial skin, to remove wrinkles ▶ **face-saving** adj maintaining dignity or self-respect ▶ **face up to** v accept (an unpleasant fact or reality) ▶ **face value** apparent worth or meaning

**facet** n aspect; surface of a cut gem

**facetious** [fas-see-shuss] adj funny or trying to be funny, esp. at inappropriate times

**facia** n, pl -**ciae** same as **fascia**

**facial** adj of the face ▷ n beauty treatment for the face

**facile** [**fas**-sile] *adj* (of a remark, argument, etc.) superficial and showing lack of real thought

**facilitate** *v* make easy ▶ **facilitation** *n*

**facility** *n, pl* **-ties** skill; easiness ▷ *pl* means or equipment for an activity

**facing** *n* lining or covering for decoration or reinforcement ▷ *pl* contrasting collar and cuffs on a jacket

**facsimile** [fak-**sim**-ill-ee] *n* exact copy

**fact** *n* event or thing known to have happened or existed; provable truth **facts of life** details of sex and reproduction ▶ **factual** *adj*

**faction** *n* (dissenting) minority group within a larger body; dissension ▶ **factious** *adj* of or producing factions

**factitious** *adj* artificial

**factor** *n* element contributing to a result; (*Maths*) one of the integers multiplied together to give a given number; (*Scot*) property manager ▶ **factorial** *n* product of all the integers from one to a given number ▶ **factorize** *v* calculate the factors of (a number)

**factory** *n, pl* **-ries** building where goods are manufactured

**factotum** *n* person employed to do all sorts of work

**faculty** *n, pl* **-ties** physical or mental ability; department in a university or college

**fad** *n* short-lived fashion; whim ▶ **faddy, faddish** *adj*

**fade** *v* (cause to) lose brightness, colour, or strength; vanish slowly

**faeces** [**fee**-seez] *pl n* waste matter discharged from the anus ▶ **faecal** [**fee**-kl] *adj*

**fag**¹ *n* (*informal*) boring task; (*Brit*) young public schoolboy who does menial chores for a senior boy ▷ *v*

(*Brit*) do menial chores in a public school

**fag**² *n* (*Brit slang*) cigarette ▶ **fag end** last and worst part; (*slang*) cigarette stub

**faggot**¹ *n* (*Brit, Aust & NZ*) ball of chopped liver, herbs, and bread; bundle of sticks for fuel

**faggot**² *n* (*offens*) male homosexual

**Fahrenheit** [**far**-ren-hite] *adj* of a temperature scale with the freezing point of water at 32° and the boiling point at 212°

**faïence** [**fie**-ence] *n* tin-glazed earthenware

**fail** *v* be unsuccessful; stop operating; be or judge to be below the required standard in a test; disappoint or be useless to (someone); neglect or be unable to do (something); go bankrupt ▷ *n* instance of not passing an exam or test **without fail** regularly; definitely ▶ **failing** *n* weak point ▷ *prep* in the absence of ▶ **failure** *n* act or instance of failing; unsuccessful person or thing

**fain** *adv* (*obs*) gladly

**faint** *adj* lacking clarity, brightness, or volume; feeling dizzy or weak; lacking conviction or force ▷ *v* lose consciousness temporarily ▷ *n* temporary loss of consciousness

**fair**¹ *adj* unbiased and reasonable; light in colour; beautiful; quite good e.g. *a fair attempt*; quite large e.g. *a fair amount of money*; (of weather) fine ▷ *adv* fairly ▶ **fairly** *adv* moderately; to a great degree or extent; as deserved, reasonably ▶ **fairness** *n* ▶ **fairway** *n* (*Golf*) smooth area between the tee and the green

**fair**² *n* travelling entertainment with sideshows, rides, and amusements; exhibition of commercial or industrial products

▶**fairground** n open space used for a fair

**Fair Isle** n intricate multicoloured knitted pattern

**fair trade** n practice of directly benefiting producers in the developing world by buying straight from them at a guaranteed price

**fairy** n, pl **fairies** imaginary small creature with magic powers; (offens) male homosexual ▶**fairy godmother** person who helps in time of trouble ▶**fairyland** n ▶**fairy lights** small coloured electric bulbs used as decoration ▶**fairy penguin** small penguin with a bluish head and back, found on the Australian coast ▶**fairy tale, fairy story** story about fairies or magic; unbelievable story or explanation

**fait accompli** [fate ak-kom-plee] n (French) something already done that cannot be altered

**faith** n strong belief, esp. without proof; religion; complete confidence or trust; allegiance to a person or cause ▶**faithful** adj loyal; consistently reliable; accurate in detail ▶**faithfully** adv ▶**faithless** adj disloyal or dishonest ▶**faith school** (Brit) school that provides a general education within a framework of a specific religious belief

**fake** v cause something not genuine to appear real or more valuable by fraud; pretend to have (an illness, emotion, etc.) ▷ n person, thing, or act that is not genuine ▷ adj not genuine

**fakir** [fay-keer] n Muslim who spurns worldly possessions; Hindu holy man

**falcon** n small bird of prey ▶**falconry** n art of training falcons;

sport of hunting with falcons ▶**falconer** n

**fall** v **falling, fell, fallen** drop from a higher to a lower place through the force of gravity; collapse to the ground; decrease in number or quality; pass into a specified condition; occur ▷ n falling; thing or amount that falls; decrease in value or number; decline in power or influence; (US) autumn ▷ pl waterfall ▶**fall for** v (informal) fall in love with; be deceived by (a lie or trick) ▶**fall guy** (informal) victim of a confidence trick; scapegoat ▶**fallout** n radioactive particles spread as a result of a nuclear explosion

**fallacy** n, pl **-cies** false belief; unsound reasoning ▶**fallacious** adj

**fallible** adj (of a person) liable to make mistakes ▶**fallibility** n

**Fallopian tube** n either of a pair of tubes through which egg cells pass from the ovary to the womb

**fallow** adj (of land) ploughed but left unseeded to regain fertility

**false** adj not true or correct; artificial, fake; deceptive e.g. false promises ▶**falsely** adv ▶**falseness** n ▶**falsity** n ▶**falsehood** n quality of being untrue; lie

**falsetto** n, pl **-tos** voice pitched higher than one's natural range

**falsify** v **-fying, -fied** alter fraudulently ▶**falsification** n

**falter** v be hesitant, weak, or unsure; lose power momentarily; utter hesitantly; move unsteadily

**fame** n state of being widely known or recognized ▶**famed** adj famous

**familiar** adj well-known; intimate, friendly; too friendly ▷ n demon supposed to attend a witch; friend ▶**familiarly** adv ▶**familiarity** n ▶**familiarize** v acquaint

fully with a particular subject
▶ **familiarization** n

**family** n, pl **-lies** group of parents and their children; one's spouse and children; group descended from a common ancestor; group of related objects or beings ▷ adj suitable for parents and children together ▶ **familial** adj ▶ **family planning** control of the number of children in a family by the use of contraception

**famine** n severe shortage of food

**famished** adj very hungry

**famous** adj very well-known
▶ **famously** adv (informal) excellently

**fan**¹ n hand-held or mechanical object used to create a current of air for ventilation or cooling ▷ v **fanning, fanned** blow or cool with a fan; spread out like a fan
▶ **fanbase** n body of admirers of a particular pop singer, sports team, etc. ▶ **fan belt** belt that drives a cooling fan in a car engine ▶ **fantail** n small New Zealand bird with a tail like a fan

**fan**² n (informal) devotee of a pop star, sport, or hobby

**fanatic** n person who is excessively enthusiastic about something
▶ **fanatical** adj ▶ **fanatically** adv
▶ **fanaticism** n

**fancy** adj **-cier, -ciest** elaborate, not plain; (of prices) higher than usual ▷ n, pl **-cies** sudden irrational liking or desire; uncontrolled imagination ▷ v **-cying, -cied** (informal) be sexually attracted to; (informal) have a wish for; picture in the imagination; suppose **fancy oneself** (informal) have a high opinion of oneself ▶ **fanciful** adj not based on fact; excessively elaborate ▶ **fancifully** adv ▶ **fancy dress** party costume representing

a historical figure, animal, etc.
▶ **fancy-free** adj not in love

**fandango** n, pl **-gos** lively Spanish dance

**fanfare** n short loud tune played on brass instruments

**fang** n snake's tooth which injects poison; long pointed tooth

**fantasia** n musical composition of an improvised nature

**fantastic** adj (informal) very good; unrealistic or absurd; strange or difficult to believe ▶ **fantastically** adv

**fantasy** n, pl **-sies** far-fetched notion; imagination unrestricted by reality; daydream; fiction with a large fantasy content ▶ **fantasize** v indulge in daydreams

**FAQ** (Computing) frequently asked question or questions

**far** adv **farther** or **further, farthest** or **furthest** at, to, or from a great distance; at or to a remote time; very much ▷ adj remote in space or time **the Far East** East Asia ▶ **far-fetched** adj hard to believe

> **USAGE NOTE**
> Farther is often used, rather than further, when distance, not time or effort, is involved

**farad** n unit of electrical capacitance

**farce** n boisterous comedy; ludicrous situation ▶ **farcical** adj ludicrous ▶ **farcically** adv

**fare** n charge for a passenger's journey; passenger; food provided ▷ v get on (as specified) e.g. we fared badly

**farewell** interj goodbye ▷ n act of saying goodbye and leaving ▷ v (NZ) say goodbye

**farinaceous** adj containing starch or having a starchy texture

**farm** n area of land for growing crops or rearing livestock; area of land or water for growing or rearing a specified animal or plant e.g. *fish farm* ▷ v cultivate (land); rear (stock) ▶ **farmhouse** n ▶ **farm out** v send (work) to be done by others ▶ **farmstead** n farm and its buildings ▶ **farmyard** n

**farmer** n person who owns or runs a farm ▶ **farmers' market** market at which farm produce is sold directly to the public by the producer

**farrago** [far-**rah**-go] n, pl **-gos** or **-goes** jumbled mixture of things

**farrier** n person who shoes horses

**farrow** n litter of piglets ▷ v (of a sow) give birth

**fart** (*vulgar slang*) n emission of gas from the anus ▷ v emit gas from the anus

**farther, farthest** adv, adj see **far**

**farthing** n former British coin equivalent to a quarter of a penny

**fascia** [**fay**-shya] n, pl **-ciae** or **-cias** outer surface of a dashboard; flat surface above a shop window; mobile phone casing with spaces for the buttons

**fascinate** v attract and interest strongly; make motionless from fear or awe ▶ **fascinating** adj ▶ **fascination** n

> **SPELLING TIP**
> Remember that there is a silent c after the s in **fascinate**, **fascinated**, and **fascinating**

**fascism** [**fash**-iz-zum] n right-wing totalitarian political system characterized by state control and extreme nationalism ▶ **fascist** adj, n

**fashion** n style in clothes, hairstyle, etc., popular at a particular time; way something happens or is done ▷ v form or make into a particular shape ▶ **fashionable** adj currently popular ▶ **fashionably** adv

**fast**[1] adj (capable of) acting or moving quickly; done in or lasting a short time; adapted to or allowing rapid movement; (of a clock or watch) showing a time later than the correct time; dissipated; firmly fixed, fastened, or shut ▷ adv quickly; soundly, deeply e.g. *fast asleep*; tightly and firmly ▶ **fast food** food, such as hamburgers, prepared and served very quickly ▶ **fast-track** adj taking the quickest but most competitive route to success e.g. *fast-track executives* ▷ v speed up the progress of (a project or person)

**fast**[2] v go without food, esp. for religious reasons ▷ n period of fasting

**fasten** v make or become firmly fixed or joined; close by fixing in place or locking; (foll by on) direct (one's attention) towards ▶ **fastener, fastening** n device that fastens

**fastidious** adj very fussy about details; excessively concerned with cleanliness ▶ **fastidiously** adv ▶ **fastidiousness** n

**fastness** n fortress, safe place

**fat** adj **fatter, fattest** having excess flesh on the body; (of meat) containing a lot of fat; thick; profitable ▷ n extra flesh on the body; oily substance obtained from animals or plants ▶ **fatness** n ▶ **fatten** v (cause to) become fat ▶ **fatty** adj containing fat ▶ **fathead** n (*informal*) stupid person ▶ **fat-headed** adj

**fatal** adj causing death or ruin ▶ **fatally** adv ▶ **fatality** n, pl **-ties** death caused by an accident or disaster

**fatalism** n belief that all events are predetermined and people are powerless to change their destinies ▶ **fatalist** n ▶ **fatalistic** adj

**fate** n power supposed to predetermine events; inevitable fortune that befalls a person or thing ▷ **fated** adj destined; doomed to death or destruction ▷ **fateful** adj having important, usu. disastrous, consequences

**father** n male parent; person who founds a line or family; man who starts, creates, or invents something; (**F-**) God; (**F-**) title of some priests ▷ v be the father of (offspring) ▷ **fatherhood** n ▷ **fatherless** adj ▷ **fatherly** adj ▷ **father-in-law** n, pl **fathers-in-law** father of one's husband or wife ▷ **fatherland** n one's native country

**fathom** n unit of length, used in navigation, equal to six feet (1.83 metres) ▷ v understand ▷ **fathomable** adj ▷ **fathomless** adj too deep or difficult to fathom

**fatigue** [fat-**eeg**] n extreme physical or mental tiredness; weakening of a material due to stress; soldier's nonmilitary duty ▷ v tire out

**fatuous** adj foolish ▷ **fatuously** adv ▷ **fatuity** n

**faucet** [**faw**-set] n (US) tap

**fault** n responsibility for something wrong; defect or flaw; mistake or error; (Geology) break in layers of rock; (Tennis, squash etc.) invalid serve ▷ v criticize or blame **at fault** guilty of error **find fault with** seek out minor imperfections in **to a fault** excessively ▷ **faulty** adj ▷ **faultless** adj ▷ **faultlessly** adv

**faun** n (in Roman legend) creature with a human face and torso and a goat's horns and legs

**fauna** n, pl **-nas** or **-nae** animals of a given place or time

**faux pas** [foe **pah**] n, pl **faux pas** social blunder

**favicon** n (Computing) small icon associated with a particular website, usu displayed before the URL in a web browser

**favour** n approving attitude; act of goodwill or generosity; partiality ▷ v prefer; regard or treat with especial kindness; support or advocate

**favourable** adj encouraging or advantageous; giving consent; useful or beneficial ▷ **favourably** adv

**favourite** adj most liked ▷ n preferred person or thing; (Sport) competitor expected to win ▷ **favouritism** n practice of giving special treatment to a person or group

**fawn¹** n young deer ▷ adj light yellowish-brown

**fawn²** v (foll by on) seek attention from (someone) by insincere flattery; (of a dog) try to please by a show of extreme affection

**fax** n electronic system for sending facsimiles of documents by telephone; document sent by this system ▷ v send (a document) by this system

**FBI** (US) Federal Bureau of Investigation

**FC** (in Britain) Football Club

**Fe** (Chem) iron

**fealty** n (in feudal society) subordinate's loyalty to his ruler or lord

**fear** n distress or alarm caused by impending danger or pain; something that causes distress ▷ v be afraid of (something or someone) **fear for** feel anxiety about something ▷ **fearful** adj feeling fear; causing fear; (informal) very unpleasant ▷ **fearfully** adv ▷ **fearless** adj ▷ **fearlessly** adv ▷ **fearsome** adj terrifying

**feasible** *adj* able to be done, possible ▶ **feasibly** *adv* ▶ **feasibility** *n*

**feast** *n* lavish meal; something extremely pleasing; annual religious celebration ▷ *v* eat a feast; give a feast to; (foll by *on*) eat a large amount of

**feat** *n* remarkable, skilful, or daring action

**feather** *n* one of the barbed shafts forming the plumage of birds ▷ *v* fit or cover with feathers; turn (an oar) edgeways **feather in one's cap** achievement one can be pleased with **feather one's nest** make one's life comfortable ▶ **feathered** *adj* ▶ **feathery** *adj* ▶ **featherweight** *n* boxer weighing up to 126lb (professional) or 57kg (amateur); insignificant person or thing

**feature** *n* part of the face, such as the eyes; prominent or distinctive part; special article in a newspaper or magazine; main film in a cinema programme ▷ *v* have as a feature or be a feature in; give prominence to ▶ **featureless** *adj*

**Feb.** February

**febrile** [**fee**-brile] *adj* feverish

**February** *n* second month of the year

**feckless** *adj* ineffectual or irresponsible

**fecund** *adj* fertile ▶ **fecundity** *n*

**fed** *v* past of **feed** ▶ **fed up** (*informal*) bored, dissatisfied

**federal** *adj* of a system in which power is divided between one central government and several regional governments; of the central government of a federation ▶ **federalism** *n* ▶ **federalist** *n* ▶ **federate** *v* unite in a federation ▶ **federation** *n* union of several states, provinces, etc.; association

**fedora** [fid-**or**-a] *n* man's soft hat with a brim

**fee** *n* charge paid to be allowed to do something; payment for professional services

**feeble** *adj* lacking physical or mental power; unconvincing ▶ **feebleness** *n* ▶ **feebly** *adv* ▶ **feeble-minded** *adj* unable to think or understand effectively

**feed** *v* **feeding, fed** give food to; give (something) as food; eat; supply or prepare food for; supply (what is needed) ▷ *n* act of feeding; food, esp. for babies or animals; (*informal*) meal ▶ **feeder** *n* road or railway line linking outlying areas to the main traffic network ▶ **feedback** *n* information received in response to something done; return of part of the output of an electrical circuit or loudspeaker to its source

**feel** *v* **feeling, felt** have a physical or emotional sensation of; become aware of or examine by touch; believe ▷ *n* act of feeling; impression; way something feels; sense of touch; instinctive aptitude **feel like** wish for, want ▶ **feeler** *n* organ of touch in some animals; remark made to test others' opinion ▶ **feeling** *n* emotional reaction; intuitive understanding; opinion; sympathy, understanding; ability to experience physical sensations; sensation experienced ▷ *pl* emotional sensitivities

**feet** *n* plural of **foot**

**feign** [**fane**] *v* pretend

**feint¹** [**faint**] *n* sham attack or blow meant to distract an opponent ▷ *v* make a feint

**feint²** [**faint**] *n* narrow lines on ruled paper

**feldspar** *n* hard mineral that is the main constituent of igneous rocks

**felicity** n happiness; (pl -**ties**) appropriate expression or style
▶ **felicitations** pl n congratulations
▶ **felicitous** adj

**feline** adj of cats; catlike ▷ n member of the cat family

**fell¹** v past tense of **fall**

**fell²** v cut down (a tree); knock down

**fell³** adj **in one fell swoop** in a single action or occurrence

**fell⁴** n (Scot & N English) mountain, hill, or moor

**felloe** n (segment of) the rim of a wheel

**fellow** n man or boy; comrade or associate; person in the same group or condition; member of a learned society or the governing body of a college ▷ adj in the same group or condition ▶ **fellowship** n sharing of aims or interests; group with shared aims or interests; feeling of friendliness; paid research post in a college or university

**felon** n (Criminal law) (formerly) person guilty of a felony
▶ **felony** n, pl -**nies** serious crime
▶ **felonious** adj

**felspar** n same as **feldspar**

**felt¹** v past of **feel**

**felt²** n matted fabric made by bonding fibres by pressure ▶ **felt-tip pen** n pen with a writing point made from pressed fibres

**fem.** feminine

**female** adj of the sex which bears offspring; (of plants) producing fruits ▷ n female person or animal

**feminine** adj having qualities traditionally regarded as suitable for, or typical of, women; of women; belonging to a particular class of grammatical inflection in some languages ▶ **femininity** n
▶ **feminism** n advocacy of equal rights for women ▶ **feminist** n, adj

**femme fatale** [fam fat-**tahl**] n, pl **femmes fatales** alluring woman who leads men into dangerous situations by her charm

**femur** [fee-mer] n thighbone
▶ **femoral** adj of the thigh

**fen** n (Brit) low-lying flat marshy land

**fence** n barrier of posts linked by wire or wood, enclosing an area; (slang) dealer in stolen property ▷ v enclose with or as if with a fence; fight with swords as a sport; avoid a question ▶ **fencing** n sport of fighting with swords; material for making fences ▶ **fencer** n

**fend** v **fend for oneself** provide for oneself ▶ **fend off** v defend oneself against (verbal or physical attack)

**fender** n low metal frame in front of a fireplace; soft but solid object hung over a ship's side to prevent damage when docking; (chiefly US) wing of a car

**feng shui** [fung **shway**] n Chinese art of deciding the best design of a building, etc., in order to bring good luck

**fennel** n fragrant plant whose seeds, leaves, and root are used in cookery

**fenugreek** n Mediterranean plant grown for its heavily scented seeds

**feral** adj wild

**ferment** n commotion, unrest ▷ v undergo or cause to undergo fermentation ▶ **fermentation** n reaction in which an organic molecule splits into simpler substances, esp. the conversion of sugar to alcohol

**fern** n flowerless plant with fine fronds

**ferocious** adj savagely fierce or cruel ▶ **ferocity** n

**ferret** n tamed polecat used to catch rabbits or rats ▷ v **ferreting,**

**ferreted** hunt with ferrets; search around ▸ **ferret out** v find by searching

**ferric, ferrous** adj of or containing iron

**Ferris wheel** n large vertical fairground wheel with hanging seats for riding in

**ferry** n, pl **-ries** boat for transporting people and vehicles ▷ v **-rying, -ried** carry by ferry; convey (goods or people) ▸ **ferryman** n

**fertile** adj capable of producing young, crops, or vegetation; highly productive e.g. *a fertile mind* ▸ **fertility** n ▸ **fertilize** v provide (an animal or plant) with sperm or pollen to bring about fertilization; supply (soil) with nutrients ▸ **fertilization** n

**fertilizer** n substance added to the soil to increase its productivity

**fervent, fervid** adj intensely passionate and sincere ▸ **fervently** adv ▸ **fervour** n intensity of feeling

**fescue** n pasture and lawn grass with stiff narrow leaves

**fester** v grow worse and increasingly hostile; (of a wound) form pus; rot and decay

**festival** n organized series of special events or performances; day or period of celebration ▸ **festive** adj of or like a celebration ▸ **festivity** n, pl **-ties** happy celebration ▷ pl celebrations

**festoon** v hang decorations in loops

**feta** n white salty Greek cheese

**fetch** v go after and bring back; be sold for; (*informal*) deal (a blow) ▸ **fetching** adj attractive ▸ **fetch up** v (*informal*) arrive or end up

**fete** [**fate**] n gala, bazaar, etc., usu. held outdoors ▷ v honour or entertain regally

**fetid** adj stinking

**fetish** n form of behaviour in which sexual pleasure is derived from looking at or handling an inanimate object; thing with which one is excessively concerned; object believed to have magical powers ▸ **fetishism** n ▸ **fetishist** n

**fetlock** n projection behind and above a horse's hoof

**fetter** n chain or shackle for the foot ▷ pl restrictions ▷ v restrict; bind in fetters

**fettle** n state of health or spirits

**fetus** [**fee-tuss**] n, pl **-tuses** embryo of a mammal in the later stages of development ▸ **fetal** adj

**feu** n (in Scotland) right of use of land in return for a fixed annual payment

**feud** n long bitter hostility between two people or groups ▷ v carry on a feud

**feudalism** n medieval system in which people held land from a lord, and in return worked and fought for him ▸ **feudal** adj of or like feudalism

**fever** n (illness causing) high body temperature; nervous excitement ▸ **fevered** adj ▸ **feverish** adj suffering from fever; in a state of nervous excitement ▸ **feverishly** adv

**few** adj not many **a few** small number **quite a few, a good few** several

> **USAGE NOTE**
> *Few(er)* is used of things that can be counted: *Fewer than five visits.* Compare *less*, which is used for quantity: *It uses less sugar*

**fey** adj whimsically strange; having the ability to look into the future

**fez** n, pl **fezzes** brimless tasselled cap, orig. from Turkey

**ff** (*Music*) fortissimo

**fiancé** [fee-**on**-say] *n* man engaged to be married ▸ **fiancée** *n fem*

**fiasco** *n, pl* **-cos** *or* **-coes** ridiculous or humiliating failure

**fiat** [fee-at] *n* arbitrary order; official permission

**fib** *n* trivial lie ▸ *v* **fibbing, fibbed** tell a lie ▸ **fibber** *n*

**fibre** *n* thread that can be spun into yarn; threadlike animal or plant tissue; fibrous material in food; strength of character; essential substance or nature ▸ **fibrous** *adj* ▸ **fibreglass** *n* material made of fine glass fibres ▸ **fibre optics** transmission of information by light along very thin flexible fibres of glass

**fibrillation** *n* uncontrollable twitching of muscles, esp. those in the heart

**fibro** *n* (*Aust*) mixture of cement and asbestos fibre, used in sheets for building (also **fibrocement**)

**fibroid** [fibe-royd] *n* benign tumour composed of fibrous connective tissue ▸ **fibrositis** [fibe-roh-**site**-iss] *n* inflammation of the tissues of muscle sheaths

**fibula** *n, pl* **-lae** *or* **-las** slender outer bone of the lower leg

**fiche** [feesh] *n* sheet of film for storing publications in miniaturized form

**fickle** *adj* changeable, inconstant ▸ **fickleness** *n*

**fiction** *n* literary works of the imagination, such as novels; invented story ▸ **fictional** *adj* ▸ **fictionalize** *v* turn into fiction ▸ **fictitious** *adj* not genuine; of or in fiction

**fiddle** *n* violin; (*informal*) dishonest action or scheme ▸ *v* play the violin; falsify (accounts); move or touch something restlessly ▸ **fiddling** *adj* trivial ▸ **fiddly** *adj* awkward to do or use

▸ **fiddlesticks** *interj* expression of annoyance or disagreement

**fidelity** *n* faithfulness; accuracy in detail; quality of sound reproduction

**fidget** *v* move about restlessly ▸ *n* person who fidgets ▸ *pl* restlessness ▸ **fidgety** *adj*

**fiduciary** [fid-**yew**-she-er-ee] (*Law*) *n, pl* **-aries** person bound to act for someone else's benefit, as a trustee ▸ *adj* of a trust or trustee

**fief** [feef] *n* (*Hist*) land granted by a lord in return for war service

**field** *n* enclosed piece of agricultural land; marked off area for sports; area rich in a specified natural resource; sphere of knowledge or activity; place away from the laboratory or classroom where practical work is done ▸ *v* (*Sport*) catch and return (a ball); deal with (a question) successfully ▸ **fielder** *n* (*Sport*) player whose task is to field the ball ▸ **field day** day or time of exciting activity ▸ **field events** throwing and jumping events in athletics ▸ **fieldfare** *n* type of large Old World thrush ▸ **field glasses** binoculars ▸ **field marshal** army officer of the highest rank ▸ **field sports** hunting, shooting, and fishing ▸ **fieldwork** *n* investigation made in the field as opposed to the classroom or the laboratory

**fiend** [feend] *n* evil spirit; cruel or wicked person; (*informal*) person devoted to something e.g. *fitness fiend* ▸ **fiendish** *adj* ▸ **fiendishly** *adv*

**fierce** *adj* wild or aggressive; intense or strong ▸ **fiercely** *adv* ▸ **fierceness** *n*

**fiery** *adj* **fierier, fieriest** consisting of or like fire; easily angered; (of food) very spicy

**fiesta** n religious festival, carnival

**FIFA** [**fee**-fa] Fédération Internationale de Football Association (International Association Football Federation)

**fife** n small high-pitched flute

**fifteen** adj, n five and ten ▶ **fifteenth** adj, n

**fifth** adj, n (of) number five in a series ▶ **fifth column** group secretly helping the enemy

**fifty** adj, n, pl **-ties** five times ten ▶ **fiftieth** adj, n

**fig** n soft pear-shaped fruit; tree bearing it

**fight** v **fighting, fought** struggle (against) in battle or physical combat; struggle to overcome someone or obtain something; carry on (a battle or contest); make (one's way) somewhere with difficulty ▷ n aggressive conflict between two (groups of) people; quarrel or contest; resistance; boxing match ▶ **fighter** n boxer; determined person; aircraft designed to destroy other aircraft ▶ **fight off** v drive away (an attacker); struggle to avoid

**figment** n **figment of one's imagination** imaginary thing

**figure** n numerical symbol; amount expressed in numbers; bodily shape; well-known person; representation in painting or sculpture of a human form; (Maths) any combination of lines, planes, points, or curves ▷ v consider, conclude; (usu. foll by in) be included (in) ▶ **figure of speech** expression in which words do not have their literal meaning ▶ **figurative** adj (of language) abstract, imaginative, or symbolic ▶ **figuratively** adv ▶ **figurine** n statuette ▶ **figurehead** n nominal leader; carved bust at the bow

of a ship ▶ **figure out** v solve or understand

**filament** n fine wire in a light bulb that gives out light; fine thread

**filbert** n hazelnut

**filch** v steal (small amounts)

**file¹** n box or folder used to keep documents in order; documents in a file; information about a person or subject; line of people one behind the other; (Computing) organized collection of related material ▷ v place (a document) in a file; place (a legal document) on official record; bring a lawsuit, esp. for divorce; walk or march in a line ▶ **file sharing** sharing computer data on a network, esp. the internet

**file²** n tool with a roughened blade for smoothing or shaping ▷ v shape or smooth with a file ▶ **filings** pl n shavings removed by a file

**filial** adj of or befitting a son or daughter

**filibuster** n obstruction of legislation by making long speeches; person who filibusters ▷ v obstruct (legislation) with such delaying tactics

**filigree** n delicate ornamental work of gold or silver wire ▷ adj made of filigree

**Filipino** [fill-lip-**pee**-no] adj of the Philippines ▷ n (fem **Filipina**) person from the Philippines

**fill** v make or become full; occupy completely; plug (a gap); satisfy (a need); hold and perform the duties of (a position); appoint to (a job or position) **one's fill** sufficient for one's needs or wants ▶ **filler** n substance that fills a gap or increases bulk ▶ **filling** n substance that fills a gap or cavity, esp. in a tooth ▷ adj (of food) substantial and satisfying ▶ **filling station**

(*chiefly Brit*) garage selling petrol, oil, etc.

**fillet** *n* boneless piece of meat or fish ▷ *v* **filleting, filleted** remove the bones from

**fillip** *n* something that adds stimulation or enjoyment

**filly** *n*, *pl* **-lies** young female horse

**film** *n* sequence of images projected on a screen, creating the illusion of movement; story told in such a sequence of images; thin strip of light-sensitive cellulose used to make photographic negatives and transparencies; thin sheet or layer ▷ *v* photograph with a movie or video camera; make a film of (a scene, story, etc.); cover or become covered with a thin layer ▷ *adj* connected with films or the cinema ▶ **filmy** *adj* very thin, delicate ▶ **film strip** set of pictures on a strip of film, projected separately as slides

**filter** *n* material or device permitting fluid to pass but retaining solid particles; device that blocks certain frequencies of sound or light; (*Brit*) traffic signal that allows vehicles to turn either left or right while the main signals are at red ▷ *v* remove impurities from (a substance) with a filter; pass slowly or faintly

**filth** *n* disgusting dirt; offensive material or language ▶ **filthy** *adj* ▶ **filthiness** *n*

**filtrate** *n* filtered gas or liquid ▷ *v* remove impurities with a filter ▶ **filtration** *n*

**fin** *n* projection from a fish's body enabling it to balance and swim; vertical tailplane of an aircraft

**finagle** [fin-**nay**-gl] *v* get or achieve by craftiness or trickery

**final** *adj* at the end; having no possibility of further change, action, or discussion ▷ *n* deciding contest between winners of previous rounds in a competition ▷ *pl* (*Brit & S Afr*) last examinations in an educational course ▶ **finally** *adv* ▶ **finality** *n* ▶ **finalist** *n* competitor in a final ▶ **finalize** *v* put into final form ▶ **finale** [fin-**nah**-lee] *n* concluding part of a dramatic performance or musical work

**finance** *v* provide or obtain funds for ▷ *n* management of money, loans, or credits; (provision of) funds ▷ *pl* money resources ▶ **financial** *adj* ▶ **financially** *adv* ▶ **financier** *n* person involved in large-scale financial business ▶ **financial year** twelve-month period used for financial calculations

**finch** *n*, *pl* **finches** small songbird with a short strong beak

**find** *v* **finding, found** discover by chance; discover by search or effort; become aware of; consider to have a particular quality; experience (a particular feeling); (*Law*) pronounce (the defendant) guilty or not guilty; provide, esp. with difficulty ▷ *n* person or thing found, esp. when valuable ▶ **finder** *n* ▶ **finding** *n* conclusion from an investigation ▶ **find out** *v* gain knowledge of; detect (a crime, deception, etc.)

**fine¹** *adj* very good; (of weather) clear and dry; in good health; satisfactory; of delicate workmanship; thin or slender; subtle or abstruse e.g. *a fine distinction* ▶ **finely** *adv* ▶ **fineness** *n* ▶ **finery** *n* showy clothing ▶ **fine art** art produced to appeal to the sense of beauty ▶ **fine-tune** *v* make small adjustments to (something) so that it works really well

**fine²** n payment imposed as a penalty ▷ v impose a fine on

**finesse** [fin-**ness**] n delicate skill; subtlety and tact

**finger** n one of the four long jointed parts of the hand; part of a glove that covers a finger; quantity of liquid in a glass as deep as a finger is wide ▷ v touch or handle with the fingers ▸ **fingering** n technique of using the fingers in playing a musical instrument ▸ **fingerboard** n part of a stringed instrument against which the strings are pressed ▸ **fingerprint** n impression of the ridges on the tip of the finger ▷ v take the fingerprints of (someone) ▸ **finger stall** cover to protect an injured finger

**finicky** adj excessively particular, fussy; overelaborate

**finish** v bring to an end, stop; use up; bring to a desired or completed condition; put a surface texture on (wood, cloth, or metal); defeat or destroy ▷ n end, last part; death or defeat; surface texture

**finite** adj having limits in space, time, or size

**Finn** n native of Finland ▸ **Finnish** adj of Finland ▷ n official language of Finland

**fiord** n same as **fjord**

**fir** n pyramid-shaped tree with needle-like leaves and erect cones

**fire** n state of combustion producing heat, flames, and smoke; (Brit) burning coal or wood, or a gas or electric device, used to heat a room; uncontrolled destructive burning; shooting of guns; intense passion, ardour ▷ v operate (a weapon) so that a bullet or missile is released; (informal) dismiss from employment; bake (ceramics etc.) in a kiln; excite ▸ **firearm** n rifle, pistol, or shotgun ▸ **firebrand** n person who causes

unrest ▸ **firebreak** n strip of cleared land to stop the advance of a fire ▸ **fire brigade** organized body of people whose job is to put out fires ▸ **firedamp** n explosive gas, composed mainly of methane, formed in mines ▸ **fire drill** rehearsal of procedures for escape from a fire ▸ **fire engine** vehicle with apparatus for extinguishing fires ▸ **fire escape** metal staircase or ladder down the outside of a building for escape in the event of fire ▸ **firefighter** n member of a fire brigade ▸ **firefly** n, pl **-flies** beetle that glows in the dark ▸ **fireguard** n protective grating in front of a fire ▸ **fire irons** tongs, poker, and shovel for tending a domestic fire ▸ **fireplace** n recess in a room for a fire ▸ **fire power** (Mil) amount a weapon or unit can fire ▸ **fire station** building where firefighters are stationed ▸ **firewall** n (Computing) computer that prevents unauthorized access to a computer network from the internet ▸ **firework** n device containing chemicals that is ignited to produce spectacular explosions and coloured sparks ▷ pl show of fireworks; (informal) outburst of temper ▸ **firing squad** group of soldiers ordered to execute an offender by shooting

**firie** n (Aust informal) firefighter

**firm¹** adj not soft or yielding; securely in position; definite; having determination or strength ▷ adv in an unyielding manner e.g. hold firm ▷ v make or become firm ▸ **firmly** adv ▸ **firmness** n

**firm²** n business company

**firmament** n (lit) sky or the heavens

**first** adj earliest in time or order; graded or ranked above all others ▷ n person or thing coming before all others; outset or beginning; first-class honours degree at university; lowest forward gear in a motor vehicle ▷ *adv* before anything else; for the first time ▶ **firstly** *adv* ▶ **first aid** immediate medical assistance given in an emergency ▶ **first-class** *adj* of the highest quality or grade; excellent ▶ **first-hand** *adj*, *adv* (obtained) directly from the original source ▶ **first mate** officer of a merchant ship second in command to the captain ▶ **first person** (*Grammar*) category of verbs and pronouns used by a speaker to refer to himself or herself ▶ **first-rate** *adj* excellent ▶ **first-strike** *adj* (of a nuclear missile) for use in an opening attack to destroy enemy weapons

**firth** *n* narrow inlet of the sea, esp. in Scotland

**fiscal** *adj* of government finances, esp. taxes

**fish** *n*, *pl* **fish** or **fishes** cold-blooded vertebrate with gills, that lives in water; its flesh as food ▷ *v* try to catch fish; fish in (a particular area of water); (foll by *for*) grope for and find with difficulty; (foll by *for*) seek indirectly ▶ **fisherman** *n* person who catches fish for a living or for pleasure ▶ **fishery** *n*, *pl* **-eries** area of the sea used for fishing ▶ **fishy** *adj* of or like fish; (*informal*) suspicious or questionable ▶ **fishfinger** *n* oblong piece of fish covered in breadcrumbs ▶ **fishmeal** *n* dried ground fish used as animal feed or fertilizer ▶ **fishmonger** *n* seller of fish ▶ **fishnet** *n* open mesh fabric resembling netting ▶ **fishwife** *n*, *pl* **-wives** coarse scolding woman

**fishplate** *n* metal plate holding rails together

**fission** *n* splitting; (*Biol*) asexual reproduction involving a division into two or more equal parts; splitting of an atomic nucleus with the release of a large amount of energy ▶ **fissionable** *adj* ▶ **fissile** *adj* capable of undergoing nuclear fission; tending to split

**fissure** [**fish**-er] *n* long narrow cleft or crack

**fist** *n* clenched hand ▶ **fisticuffs** *pl n* fighting with the fists

**fit**[1] *v* **fitting, fitted** be appropriate or suitable for; be of the correct size or shape (for); adjust so as to make appropriate; try (clothes) on and note any adjustments needed; make competent or ready; correspond with the facts or circumstances ▷ *adj* appropriate; in good health; worthy or deserving ▷ *n* way in which something fits ▶ **fitness** *n* ▶ **fitter** *n* person skilled in the installation and adjustment of machinery; person who fits garments ▶ **fitting** *adj* appropriate, suitable ▷ *n* accessory or part; trying on of clothes for size ▷ *pl* furnishings and accessories in a building ▶ **fitment** *n* detachable part of the furnishings of a room ▶ **fit in** *v* give a place or time to; belong or conform ▶ **fit out** *v* provide with the necessary equipment

**fit**[2] *n* sudden attack or convulsion, such as an epileptic seizure; sudden short burst or spell

**fitful** *adj* occurring in irregular spells ▶ **fitfully** *adv*

**five** *adj*, *n* one more than four ▶ **fiver** *n* (*informal*) five-pound note ▶ **fives** *n* ball game resembling squash but played with bats or the hands

**fix** *v* make or become firm, stable, or secure; repair; place permanently; settle definitely; direct (the eyes etc.) steadily; (*informal*) unfairly influence the outcome of ▷ *n* (*informal*) difficult situation; ascertaining the position of a ship by radar etc.; (*slang*) injection of a narcotic drug ▶ **fixed** *adj* ▶ **fixedly** *adv* steadily ▶ **fixer** *n* solution used to make a photographic image permanent; (*slang*) person who arranges things ▶ **fix up** *v* arrange; provide (with)

**fixation** *n* obsessive interest in something ▶ **fixated** *adj* obsessed

**fixative** *n* liquid used to preserve or hold things in place

**fixture** *n* permanently fitted piece of household equipment; person whose presence seems permanent; sports match or the date fixed for it

**fizz** *v* make a hissing or bubbling noise; give off small bubbles ▷ *n* hissing or bubbling noise; releasing of small bubbles of gas by a liquid; effervescent drink ▶ **fizzy** *adj*

**fizzle** *v* make a weak hissing or bubbling sound ▶ **fizzle out** *v* (*informal*) come to nothing, fail

**fjord** [fee-**ord**] *n* long narrow inlet of the sea between cliffs, esp. in Norway

**flab** *n* (*informal*) unsightly body fat

**flabbergasted** *adj* completely astonished

**flabby** *adj* -**bier**, -**biest** having flabby flesh; loose or limp

**flaccid** [**flas**-sid] *adj* soft and limp

**flag**¹ *n* piece of cloth attached to a pole as an emblem or signal ▷ *v* **flagging, flagged** mark with a flag or sticker; (often foll by *down*) signal (a vehicle) to stop by waving the arm ▶ **flag day** (*Brit*) day on which small stickers are sold in the streets for charity ▶ **flagpole, flagstaff** *n* pole for a flag ▶ **flagship** *n*

admiral's ship; most important product of an organization ▶ **flag up** *v* bring (something) to someone's attention

**flag**² *v* **flagging, flagged** lose enthusiasm or vigour

**flag**³, **flagstone** *n* flat paving-stone ▶ **flagged** *adj* paved with flagstones

**flagellate** [**flaj**-a-late] *v* whip, esp. in religious penance or for sexual pleasure ▶ **flagellation** *n* ▶ **flagellant** *n* person who whips himself or herself

**flageolet** [flaj-a-**let**] *n* small instrument like a recorder

**flagon** *n* wide bottle for wine or cider; narrow-necked jug for liquid

**flagrant** [**flayg**-rant] *adj* openly outrageous ▶ **flagrantly** *adv*

**flail** *v* wave about wildly; beat or thrash ▷ *n* tool formerly used for threshing grain by hand

**flair** *n* natural ability; stylishness

**flak** *n* anti-aircraft fire; (*informal*) severe criticism

**flake**¹ *n* small thin piece, esp. chipped off something; (*Aust & NZ informal*) unreliable person ▷ *v* peel off in flakes ▶ **flaky** *adj* ▶ **flake out** *v* (*informal*) collapse or fall asleep from exhaustion

**flake**² *n* (in Australia) the commercial name for the meat of the gummy shark

**flambé** [**flahm**-bay] *v* **flambéing, flambéed** cook or serve (food) in flaming brandy

**flamboyant** *adj* behaving in a very noticeable, extravagant way; very bright and showy ▶ **flamboyance** *n*

**flame** *n* luminous burning gas coming from burning material; (*informal*) abusive e-mail message ▷ *v* burn brightly; become bright red; (*informal*) send an abusive

e-mail message **old flame**
(*informal*) former sweetheart

**flamenco** *n, pl* **-cos** rhythmical
Spanish dance accompanied by
a guitar and vocalist; music for
this dance

**flamingo** *n, pl* **-gos** *or* **-goes** large
pink wading bird with a long neck
and legs

**flammable** *adj* easily set on fire
▸ **flammability** *n*

> **USAGE NOTE**
> This now replaces *inflammable* in
> labelling and packaging because
> *inflammable* was often mistaken
> to mean 'not flammable'

**flan** *n* open sweet or savoury tart

**flange** *n* projecting rim or collar

**flank** *n* part of the side between
the hips and ribs; side of a body
of troops ▸ *v* be at or move along
the side of

**flannel** *n* (*Brit*) small piece of
cloth for washing the face; soft
woollen fabric for clothing;
(*informal*) evasive talk ▸ *pl* trousers
made of flannel ▸ *v* **-nelling,**
**-nelled** (*informal*) talk evasively
▸ **flannelette** *n* cotton imitation of
flannel ▸ **flanny, flannie** *n* (*Aust*)
shirt made of flannel or flannelette

**flap** *v* **flapping, flapped** move back
and forwards or up and down ▸ *n*
action or sound of flapping; piece
of something attached by one edge
only; (*informal*) state of panic

**flapjack** *n* chewy biscuit made
with oats

**flare** *v* blaze with a sudden
unsteady flame; (*informal*) (of
temper, violence, or trouble) break
out suddenly; (of a skirt or trousers)
become wider towards the hem
▸ *n* sudden unsteady flame; signal
light ▸ *pl* flared trousers ▸ **flared**
*adj* (of a skirt or trousers) becoming
wider towards the hem

**flash** *n* sudden burst of light or
flame; sudden occurrence (of
intuition or emotion); very short
time; brief unscheduled news
announcement; (*Photog*) small
bulb that produces an intense
flash of light ▸ *adj* (also **flashy**)
vulgarly showy ▸ *v* (cause to)
burst into flame; (cause to) emit
light suddenly or intermittently;
move very fast; come rapidly (to
mind or view); (*informal*) display
ostentatiously; (*slang*) expose
oneself indecently ▸ **flasher** *n*
(*slang*) man who exposes himself
indecently ▸ **flashback** *n* scene in
a book, play, or film, that shows
earlier events ▸ **flash drive**
portable computer hard drive
and data storage device ▸ **flash**
**flood** sudden short-lived flood
▸ **flashlight** *n* (*US*) torch ▸ **flash**
**point** critical point beyond which a
situation will inevitably erupt into
violence; lowest temperature at
which vapour given off by a liquid
can ignite

**flashing** *n* watertight material
used to cover joins in a roof

**flask** *n* same as **vacuum flask**; flat
bottle for carrying alcoholic drink
in the pocket; narrow-necked
bottle

**flat¹** *adj* **flatter, flattest** level and
horizontal; even and smooth; (of
a tyre) deflated; outright; fixed;
without variation or emotion; (of
a drink) no longer fizzy; (of a battery)
with no electrical charge; (*Music*)
below the true pitch ▸ *adv* in or
into a flat position; completely or
absolutely; exactly; (*Music*) too
low in pitch ▸ *n* (*Music*) symbol
lowering the pitch of a note by a
semitone; mud bank exposed at
low tide **flat out** with maximum
speed or effort ▸ **flatly** *adv*

▶ **flatness** *n* ▶ **flatten** *v* ▶ **flatfish** *n* sea fish, such as the sole, which has a flat body ▶ **flat-pack** *adj* (of furniture, etc.) supplied in pieces in a flat box for assembly by the buyer ▶ **flatscreen** *n* slim lightweight TV set or computer with a flat screen ▶ **flat racing** horse racing over level ground with no jumps

**flat²** *n* set of rooms for living in which are part of a larger building ▷ *v* **flatting, flatted** (*Aust & NZ*) live in a flat ▶ **flatlet** *n* (*Brit, Aust & S Afr*) small flat ▶ **flatmate** *n* person with whom one shares a flat

**flatter** *v* praise insincerely; show to advantage; make (a person) appear more attractive in a picture than in reality ▶ **flatterer** *n* ▶ **flattery** *n*

**flattie** *n* (*NZ & S Afr informal*) flat tyre

**flatulent** *adj* suffering from or caused by too much gas in the intestines ▶ **flatulence** *n*

**flaunt** *v* display (oneself or one's possessions) arrogantly

> **USAGE NOTE**
> Be careful not to confuse this with *flout* meaning 'disobey'

**flautist** *n* flute player

**flavour** *n* distinctive taste; distinctive characteristic or quality ▷ *v* give flavour to ▶ **flavouring** *n* substance used to flavour food ▶ **flavourless** *adj*

**flaw** *n* imperfection or blemish; mistake that makes a plan or argument invalid ▶ **flawed** *adj* ▶ **flawless** *adj*

**flax** *n* plant grown for its stem fibres and seeds; its fibres, spun into linen thread ▶ **flaxen** *adj* (of hair) pale yellow

**flay** *v* strip the skin off; criticize severely

**flea** *n* small wingless jumping bloodsucking insect ▶ **flea market**

market for cheap goods ▶ **fleapit** *n* (*informal*) shabby cinema or theatre

**fleck** *n* small mark, streak, or speck ▷ *v* speckle

**fled** *v* past of **flee**

**fledged** *adj* (of young birds) able to fly; (of people) fully trained ▶ **fledgling, fledgeling** *n* young bird ▷ *adj* new or inexperienced

**flee** *v* **fleeing, fled** run away (from)

**fleece** *n* sheep's coat of wool; sheepskin used as a lining for coats etc.; warm polyester fabric; (*Brit*) jacket or top made of this fabric ▷ *v* defraud or overcharge ▶ **fleecy** *adj* made of or like fleece

**fleet¹** *n* number of warships organized as a unit; number of vehicles under the same ownership

**fleet²** *adj* swift in movement ▶ **fleeting** *adj* rapid and soon passing ▶ **fleetingly** *adv*

**Flemish** *n* one of two official languages of Belgium ▷ *adj* of Flanders, in Belgium

**flesh** *n* soft part of a human or animal body; (*informal*) excess fat; meat of animals as opposed to fish or fowl; thick soft part of a fruit or vegetable; human body as opposed to the soul **in the flesh** in person, actually present **one's own flesh and blood** one's family ▶ **flesh-coloured** *adj* yellowish-pink ▶ **fleshly** *adj* carnal; worldly ▶ **fleshy** *adj* plump; like flesh ▶ **flesh wound** wound affecting only superficial tissue

**fleur-de-lys, fleur-de-lis** [flur-de-**lee**] *n, pl* **fleurs-de-lys** *or* **fleurs-de-lis** heraldic lily with three petals

**flew** *v* past tense of **fly¹**

**flex** *n* flexible insulated electric cable ▷ *v* bend ▶ **flexible** *adj* easily bent; adaptable ▶ **flexibly** *adv* ▶ **flexibility** *n* ▶ **flexitime,**

**flextime** n system permitting variation in starting and finishing times of work

**flick** v touch or move with the finger or hand in a quick movement; move with a short sudden movement, often repeatedly ▷ n tap or quick stroke ▷ pl (slang) the cinema ▸ **flick knife** knife with a spring-loaded blade which shoots out when a button is pressed ▸ **flick through** v look at (a book or magazine) quickly or idly

**flicker** v shine unsteadily or intermittently; move quickly to and fro ▷ n unsteady brief light; brief faint indication

**flier** n see **fly¹**

**flight¹** n journey by air; act or manner of flying through the air; group of birds or aircraft flying together; aircraft flying on a scheduled journey; set of stairs between two landings; stabilizing feathers or plastic fins on an arrow or dart ▸ **flightless** adj (of certain birds or insects) unable to fly ▸ **flight attendant** person who looks after passengers on an aircraft ▸ **flight deck** crew compartment in an airliner; runway deck on an aircraft carrier ▸ **flight recorder** electronic device in an aircraft storing information about its flight

**flight²** n act of running away

**flighty** adj **flightier, flightiest** frivolous and fickle

**flimsy** adj **-sier, -siest** not strong or substantial; thin; not very convincing ▸ **flimsily** adv ▸ **flimsiness** n

**flinch** v draw back or wince, as from pain ▸ **flinch from** v shrink from or avoid

**fling** v **flinging, flung** throw, send, or move forcefully or hurriedly ▷ n

spell of self-indulgent enjoyment; brief romantic or sexual relationship **fling oneself into** (start to) do with great vigour

**flint** n hard grey stone; piece of this; small piece of an iron alloy, used in cigarette lighters ▸ **flinty** adj cruel; of or like flint

**flip** v **flipping, flipped** throw (something small or light) carelessly; turn (something) over; (also **flip one's lid**) (slang) fly into an emotional state ▷ n snap or tap ▷ adj (informal) flippant ▸ **flipper** n limb of a sea animal adapted for swimming; one of a pair of paddle-like rubber devices worn on the feet to help in swimming ▸ **flip-flop** n (Brit & S Afr) rubber-soled sandal held on by a thong between the big toe and the next toe ▸ **flip through** v look at (a book or magazine) quickly or idly

**flippant** adj treating serious things lightly ▸ **flippancy** n

**flirt** v behave as if sexually attracted to someone; consider lightly, toy (with) ▷ n person who flirts ▸ **flirtation** n ▸ **flirtatious** adj

**flit** v **flitting, flitted** move lightly and rapidly; (Scot) move house; (informal) depart hurriedly and secretly ▷ n act of flitting

**float** v rest on the surface of a liquid; move lightly and freely; move about aimlessly; launch (a company); offer for sale on the stock market; allow (a currency) to fluctuate against other currencies ▷ n light object used to help someone or something float; indicator on a fishing line that moves when a fish bites; decorated truck in a procession; (Brit) small delivery vehicle; sum of money used for minor expenses or to provide change ▸ **floating**

*adj* moving about, changing e.g. *floating population*; (of a voter) not committed to one party

**flock**¹ *n* number of animals of one kind together; large group of people; (*Christianity*) congregation ▷ *v* gather in a crowd

**flock**² *n* wool or cotton waste used as stuffing ▷ *adj* (of wallpaper) with a velvety raised pattern

**floe** *n* sheet of floating ice

**flog** *v* **flogging, flogged** beat with a whip or stick; (sometimes foll by *off*) (*Brit, NZ & S Afr informal*) sell; (*NZ informal*) steal ▶ **flogging** *n*

**flood** *n* overflow of water onto a normally dry area; large amount of water; rising of the tide ▷ *v* cover or become covered with water; fill to overflowing; come in large numbers or quantities ▶ **floodgate** *n* gate used to control the flow of water ▶ **floodlight** *n* lamp that casts a broad intense beam of light ▷ *v* **-lighting, -lit** illuminate by floodlight

**floor** *n* lower surface of a room; level of a building; flat bottom surface; (right to speak in) a legislative hall ▷ *v* knock down; (*informal*) disconcert or defeat ▶ **floored** *adj* covered with a floor ▶ **flooring** *n* material for floors ▶ **floor show** entertainment in a nightclub

**floozy** *n, pl* **-zies** (*old-fashioned slang*) disreputable woman

**flop** *v* **flopping, flopped** bend, fall, or collapse loosely or carelessly; (*informal*) fail ▷ *n* (*informal*) failure; flopping movement ▶ **floppy** *adj* hanging downwards, loose ▶ **floppy disk** (*Computing*) flexible magnetic disk that stores information

**flora** *n* plants of a given place or time

**floral** *adj* consisting of or decorated with flowers

**floret** *n* small flower forming part of a composite flower head

**floribunda** *n* type of rose whose flowers grow in large clusters

**florid** *adj* with a red or flushed complexion; ornate

**florin** *n* former British and Australian coin

**florist** *n* seller of flowers

**floss** *n* fine silky fibres

**flotation** *n* launching or financing of a business enterprise

**flotilla** *n* small fleet or fleet of small ships

**flotsam** *n* floating wreckage **flotsam and jetsam** odds and ends; (*Brit*) homeless or vagrant people

**flounce**¹ *v* go with emphatic movements ▷ *n* flouncing movement

**flounce**² *n* ornamental frill on a garment

**flounder**¹ *v* move with difficulty, as in mud; behave or speak in a bungling or hesitating manner

**flounder**² *n* edible flatfish

**flour** *n* powder made by grinding grain, esp. wheat ▷ *v* sprinkle with flour ▶ **floury** *adj*

**flourish** *v* be active, successful, or widespread; be at the peak of development; wave (something) dramatically ▷ *n* dramatic waving motion; ornamental curly line in writing ▶ **flourishing** *adj*

**flout** *v* deliberately disobey (a rule, law, etc.)

▎**USAGE NOTE**
Be careful not to confuse this with *flaunt* meaning 'display'

**flow** *v* (of liquid) move in a stream; (of blood or electricity) circulate; proceed smoothly; hang loosely; be abundant ▷ *n* act, rate, or manner of flowing; continuous stream or discharge ▶ **flow chart** diagram showing a sequence of operations in a process

**flower** n part of a plant that produces seeds; plant grown for its colourful flowers; best or finest part ▷ v produce flowers, bloom; reach full growth or maturity **in flower** with flowers open ▶ **flowered** adj decorated with a floral design ▶ **flowery** adj decorated with a floral design; (of language or style) elaborate ▶ **flowerbed** n piece of ground for growing flowers

**flown** v past participle of **fly¹**

**fl. oz.** fluid ounce(s)

**flu** n short for **influenza**

**fluctuate** v change frequently and erratically ▶ **fluctuation** n

**flue** n passage or pipe for smoke or hot air

**fluent** adj able to speak or write with ease; spoken or written with ease ▶ **fluently** adv ▶ **fluency** n

**fluff** n soft fibres; (Brit, Aust & NZ informal) mistake ▷ v make or become soft and puffy; (informal) make a mistake ▶ **fluffy** adj

**fluid** n substance able to flow and change its shape; a liquid or a gas ▷ adj able to flow or change shape easily ▶ **fluidity** n ▶ **fluid ounce** (Brit) one twentieth of a pint (28.4 ml)

**fluke¹** n accidental stroke of luck

**fluke²** n flat triangular point of an anchor; lobe of a whale's tail

**fluke³** n parasitic worm

**flume** n narrow sloping channel for water; enclosed water slide at a swimming pool

**flummox** v puzzle or confuse

**flung** v past of **fling**

**flunk** v (US, Aust, NZ & S Afr informal) fail

**flunky, flunkey** n, pl **flunkies** or **flunkeys** servile person; manservant who wears a livery

**fluorescence** n emission of light from a substance bombarded by particles, such as electrons, or by radiation ▶ **fluoresce** v exhibit fluorescence

**fluorescent** adj of or resembling fluorescence

**fluoride** n compound containing fluorine ▶ **fluoridate** v add fluoride to (water) as protection against tooth decay ▶ **fluoridation** n

**fluorine** n (Chem) toxic yellow gas, most reactive of all the elements

**flurry** n, pl **-ries** sudden commotion; gust of rain or wind or fall of snow ▷ v **-rying, -ried** confuse

**flush¹** v blush or cause to blush; send water through (a toilet or pipe) so as to clean it; elate ▷ n blush; rush of water; excitement or elation

**flush²** adj level with the surrounding surface; (informal) having plenty of money

**flush³** v drive out of a hiding place

**flush⁴** n (in card games) hand all of one suit

**fluster** v make nervous or upset ▷ n nervous or upset state

**flute** n wind instrument consisting of a tube with sound holes and a mouth hole in the side; tall narrow wineglass ▶ **fluted** adj having decorative grooves

**flutter** v wave rapidly; flap the wings; move quickly and irregularly; (of the heart) beat abnormally quickly ▷ n flapping movement; nervous agitation; (informal) small bet; abnormally fast heartbeat

**fluvial** adj of rivers

**flux** n constant change or instability; flow or discharge; substance mixed with metal to assist in fusion

**fly¹** v **flying, flew, flown** move through the air on wings or in an aircraft; control the flight of; float, flutter, display, or be displayed in the air; transport or be transported by air; move quickly or suddenly; (of time) pass rapidly; flee ▷ n, pl **flies** (often pl) (Brit) fastening at the front of trousers; flap forming the entrance to a tent ▷ pl space above a stage, used for storage ▶ **flyer, flier** n small advertising leaflet; aviator ▶ **flyleaf** n blank leaf at the beginning or end of a book ▶ **flyover** n road passing over another by a bridge ▶ **flywheel** n heavy wheel regulating the speed of a machine

**fly²** n, pl **flies** two-winged insect ▶ **flycatcher** n small insect-eating songbird ▶ **fly-fishing** n fishing with an artificial fly as a lure ▶ **flypaper** n paper with a sticky poisonous coating, used to kill flies ▶ **flyweight** n boxer weighing up to 112lb (professional) or 51kg (amateur)

**fly³** adj (slang) sharp and cunning

**flying** adj hurried and brief ▶ **flying boat** aircraft fitted with floats instead of landing wheels ▶ **flying colours** conspicuous success ▶ **flying fish** fish with winglike fins used for gliding above the water ▶ **flying fox** large fruit-eating bat; (Aust & NZ) platform suspended from an overhead cable, used for transporting people or materials ▶ **flying phalanger** phalanger with black-striped greyish fur, which moves with gliding leaps ▶ **flying saucer** unidentified disc-shaped flying object, supposedly from outer space ▶ **flying squad** small group of police, soldiers, etc., ready to act quickly ▶ **flying start** very good start

**FM** (in Scotland) First Minister; frequency modulation

**foal** n young of a horse or related animal ▷ v give birth to a foal

**foam** n mass of small bubbles on a liquid; frothy saliva; light spongelike solid used for insulation, packing, etc. ▷ v produce foam ▶ **foamy** adj

**fob** n short watch chain; small pocket in a waistcoat

**fob off** v **fobbing, fobbed** pretend to satisfy (a person) with lies or excuses; sell or pass off (inferior goods) as valuable

**fo'c's'le** n same as **forecastle**

**focus** n, pl **-cuses** or **-ci** point at which light or sound waves converge; state of an optical image when it is clearly defined; state of an instrument producing such an image; centre of interest or activity ▷ v **-cusing, -cused** or **-cussing, -cussed** bring or come into focus; concentrate (on) ▶ **focal** adj of or at a focus ▶ **focus group** group of people gathered by a market-research company to discuss and assess a product or service

**fodder** n feed for livestock

**foe** n enemy, opponent

**foefie slide** n (S Afr) rope, fixed at an incline, along which a person suspended on a pulley may cross a river, esp a river

**foetid** adj same as **fetid**

**foetus** n, pl **-tuses** same as **fetus**

**fog** n mass of condensed water vapour in the lower air, often greatly reducing visibility ▷ v **fogging, fogged** cover with steam ▶ **foggy** adj ▶ **foghorn** n large horn sounded to warn ships in fog

**fogey, fogy** n, pl **-geys** or **-gies** old-fashioned person

**foible** n minor weakness or slight peculiarity

**foil¹** v ruin (someone's plan)

**foil²** n metal in a thin sheet, esp. for wrapping food; anything which sets off another thing to advantage

**foil³** n light slender flexible sword tipped with a button

**foist** v (foll by on or upon) force or impose on

**fold¹** v bend so that one part covers another; interlace (the arms); clasp (in the arms); (Cooking) mix gently; (informal) fail or go bankrupt ▷ n folded piece or part; mark, crease, or hollow made by folding ▶ **folder** n piece of folded cardboard for holding loose papers

**fold²** n (Brit, Aust & S Afr) enclosure for sheep; church or its members

**foliage** n leaves ▶ **foliation** n process of producing leaves

**folio** n, pl **-lios** sheet of paper folded in half to make two leaves of a book; book made up of such sheets; page number

**folk** n people in general; race of people ▷ pl relatives ▶ **folksy** adj simple and unpretentious ▶ **folk dance** traditional country dance ▶ **folklore** n traditional beliefs and stories of a people ▶ **folk song** song handed down among the common people; modern song like this ▶ **folk singer**

**follicle** n small cavity in the body, esp. one from which a hair grows

**follow** v go or come after; be a logical or natural consequence of; keep to the course or track of; act in accordance with; accept the ideas or beliefs of; understand; have a keen interest in; (Computing) choose to receive messages posted by (a blogger or microblogger) ▶ **follower** n disciple or supporter ▶ **following** adj about to be mentioned; next in time ▷ n group of supporters ▷ prep as a result of ▶ **follow up** v investigate; do a second, often similar, thing after (a first) ▶ **follow-up** n something done to reinforce an initial action

**folly** n, pl **-lies** foolishness; foolish action or idea; useless extravagant building

**foment** [foam-**ent**] v encourage or stir up (trouble)

**fond** adj tender, loving; unlikely to be realized e.g. a fond hope **fond of** having a liking for ▶ **fondly** adv ▶ **fondness** n

**fondant** n (sweet made from) flavoured paste of sugar and water

**fondle** v caress

**fondue** n Swiss dish of a hot melted cheese sauce into which pieces of bread are dipped

**font¹** n bowl in a church for baptismal water

**font²** n set of printing type of one style and size

**fontanelle** n soft membranous gap between the bones of a baby's skull

**food** n what one eats, solid nourishment ▶ **foodie** n (informal) gourmet ▶ **food group** category of food based on its nutritional content ▶ **foodstuff** n substance used as food

**fool¹** n person lacking sense or judgment; person made to appear ridiculous; (Hist) jester, clown ▷ v deceive (someone) ▶ **foolish** adj unwise, silly, or absurd ▶ **foolishly** adv ▶ **foolishness** n ▶ **foolery** n foolish behaviour ▶ **fool around** v act or play irresponsibly or aimlessly ▶ **foolproof** adj unable to fail

**fool²** n dessert of puréed fruit mixed with cream

**foolhardy** adj recklessly adventurous ▶ **foolhardiness** n

**foolscap** n size of paper, 34.3 × 43.2 centimetres

**foosball** n (US & Canadian) same as **table football**

**foot** n, pl **feet** part of the leg below the ankle; unit of length of twelve inches (0.3048 metre); lowest part of anything; unit of poetic rhythm **foot it** (informal) walk **foot the bill** pay the entire cost ▸ **footage** n amount of film used ▸ **foot-and-mouth disease** infectious viral disease of sheep, cattle, etc. ▸ **footbridge** n bridge for pedestrians ▸ **footfall** n sound of a footstep ▸ **foothills** pl n hills at the foot of a mountain ▸ **foothold** n secure position from which progress may be made; small place giving a secure grip for the foot ▸ **footlights** pl n lights across the front of a stage ▸ **footloose** adj free from ties ▸ **footman** n male servant in uniform ▸ **footnote** n note printed at the foot of a page ▸ **footpath** n narrow path for walkers only; (Aust) raised space alongside a road, for pedestrians ▸ **footplate** n platform in the cab of a locomotive for the driver ▸ **footprint** n mark left by a foot ▸ **footstep** n step in walking; sound made by walking ▸ **footstool** n low stool used to rest the feet on while sitting ▸ **footwear** n anything worn to cover the feet ▸ **footwork** n skilful use of the feet, as in sport or dancing

**football** n game played by two teams of eleven players kicking a ball in an attempt to score goals; any of various similar games, such as rugby; ball used for this ▸ **footballer** n ▸ **football pools** form of gambling on the results of soccer matches

**footing** n basis or foundation; relationship between people; secure grip by or for the feet

**footling** adj (chiefly Brit informal) trivial

**footsie** n (informal) flirtation involving the touching together of feet

**fop** n man excessively concerned with fashion ▸ **foppery** n ▸ **foppish** adj

**for** prep indicating a person intended to benefit from or receive something, span of time or distance, person or thing represented by someone, etc. e.g. a gift for you; for five miles; playing for his country ▷ conj because **for it** (informal) liable for punishment or blame

**forage** v search about (for) ▷ n food for cattle or horses

**foray** n brief raid or attack; first attempt or new undertaking

**forbear** v cease or refrain (from doing something) ▸ **forbearance** n tolerance, patience

**forbid** v prohibit, refuse to allow ▸ **forbidden** adj ▸ **forbidding** adj severe, threatening

**force** n strength or power; compulsion; (Physics) influence tending to produce a change in a physical system; mental or moral strength; person or thing with strength or influence; vehemence or intensity; group of people organized for a particular task or duty ▷ v compel, make (someone) do something; acquire or produce through effort, strength, etc.; propel or drive; break open; impose or inflict; cause to grow at an increased rate **in force** having legal validity; in great numbers ▸ **forced** adj compulsory; false or unnatural; due to an emergency ▸ **forceful** adj emphatic and confident; effective ▸ **forcefully** adv ▸ **forcible** adj involving physical force or violence; strong and emphatic ▸ **forcibly** adv

**forceps** pl n surgical pincers

**ford** n shallow place where a river may be crossed ▷ v cross (a river) at a ford

**fore** adj in, at, or towards the front ▷ n front part **to the fore** in a conspicuous position

**fore-** prefix before in time or rank e.g. forefather; at the front e.g. forecourt

**fore-and-aft** adj located at both ends of a ship

**forearm¹** n arm from the wrist to the elbow

**forearm²** v prepare beforehand

**forebear** n ancestor

**foreboding** n feeling that something bad is about to happen

**forecast** v -casting, -cast or -casted predict (weather, events, etc.) ▷ n prediction

**forecastle** [foke-sl] n raised front part of a ship

**foreclose** v take possession of (property bought with borrowed money which has not been repaid) ▸ **foreclosure** n

**forecourt** n courtyard or open space in front of a building

**forefather** n ancestor

**forefinger** n finger next to the thumb

**forefront** n most active or prominent position; very front

**foregather** v meet together or assemble

**forego** v same as **forgo**

**foregoing** adj going before, preceding ▸ **foregone conclusion** inevitable result

**foreground** n part of a view, esp. in a picture, nearest the observer

**forehand** n (Tennis etc.) stroke played with the palm of the hand facing forward

**forehead** n part of the face above the eyebrows

**foreign** adj not of, or in, one's own country; relating to or connected with other countries; unfamiliar, strange; in an abnormal place or position e.g. foreign matter ▸ **foreigner** n

**foreleg** n either of the front legs of an animal

**forelock** n lock of hair over the forehead

**foreman** n person in charge of a group of workers; leader of a jury

**foremast** n mast nearest the bow of a ship

**foremost** adj, adv first in time, place, or importance

**forename** n first name

**forenoon** n (chiefly US & Canadian) morning

**forensic** adj used in or connected with courts of law ▸ **forensic medicine** use of medical knowledge for the purposes of the law

**foreplay** n sexual stimulation before intercourse

**forerunner** n person or thing that goes before, precursor

**foresail** n main sail on the foremast of a ship

**foresee** v see or know beforehand ▸ **foreseeable** adj

**SPELLING TIP**
According to the Collins Corpus, the word **unforeseen** is misspelled as unforseen once for every eight occurrences

**foreshadow** v show or indicate beforehand

**foreshore** n part of the shore between high- and low-tide marks

**foreshorten** v represent (an object) in a picture as shorter than it really is, in accordance with perspective

**foresight** n ability to anticipate and provide for future needs

**foreskin** n fold of skin covering the tip of the penis

**forest** n large area with a thick growth of trees ▶ **forested** adj ▶ **forestry** n science of planting and caring for trees; management of forests ▶ **forester** n person skilled in forestry

**forestall** v prevent or guard against in advance

**foretaste** n early limited experience of something to come

**foretell** v tell or indicate beforehand

**forethought** n thoughtful planning for future events

**forever, for ever** adv without end; at all times; (informal) for a long time

**forewarn** v warn beforehand

**foreword** n introduction to a book

**forfeit** [for-fit] n thing lost or given up as a penalty for a fault or mistake ▷ v lose as a forfeit ▷ adj lost as a forfeit ▶ **forfeiture** n

**forge¹** n place where metal is worked, smithy; furnace for melting metal ▷ v make a fraudulent imitation of (something); shape (metal) by heating and hammering it; create (an alliance etc.)

**forge²** v advance steadily **forge ahead** increase speed or take the lead

**forger** n person who makes an illegal copy of something

**forgery** n, pl -ries illegal copy of something; crime of making an illegal copy

**forget** v -getting, -got, -gotten fail to remember; neglect; leave behind by mistake ▶ **forgetful** adj tending to forget ▶ **forgetfulness** n ▶ **forget-me-not** n plant with clusters of small blue flowers

**forgive** v -giving, -gave, -given cease to blame or hold resentment against, pardon ▶ **forgiveness** n

**forgo** v do without or give up

**forgot** v past tense of **forget** ▶ **forgotten** v past participle of **forget**

**fork** n tool for eating food, with prongs and a handle; large similarly-shaped tool for digging or lifting; point where a road, river, etc. divides into branches; one of the branches ▷ v pick up, dig, etc. with a fork; branch; take one or other branch at a fork in the road ▶ **forked** adj ▶ **fork-lift truck** vehicle with a forklike device at the front which can be raised or lowered to move loads ▶ **fork out** v (informal) pay

**forlorn** adj lonely and unhappy ▶ **forlorn hope** hopeless enterprise ▶ **forlornly** adv

**form** n shape or appearance; mode in which something appears; type or kind; printed document with spaces for details; physical or mental condition; previous record of an athlete, racehorse, etc.; class in school ▷ v give a (particular) shape to or take a (particular) shape; come or bring into existence; make or be made; train; acquire or develop ▶ **formless** adj

**formal** adj of or characterized by established conventions of ceremony and behaviour; of or for formal occasions; stiff in manner; organized; symmetrical ▶ **formally** adv ▶ **formality** n, pl -ties requirement of custom or etiquette; necessary procedure without real importance ▶ **formalize** v make official or formal

**formaldehyde** [for-mal-de-hide] n colourless pungent gas used to make formalin ▶ **formalin** n solution of formaldehyde in water, used as a disinfectant or a preservative for biological specimens

**format** *n* style in which something is arranged ▷ *v* **-matting, -matted** arrange in a format

**formation** *n* forming; thing formed; structure or shape; arrangement of people or things acting as a unit

**formative** *adj* of or relating to development; shaping

**former** *adj* of an earlier time, previous **the former** first mentioned of two ▶ **formerly** *adv*

**Formica®** *n* kind of laminated sheet used to make heat-resistant surfaces

**formic acid** *n* acid derived from ants

**formidable** *adj* frightening because difficult to overcome or manage; extremely impressive ▶ **formidably** *adv*

**formula** *n, pl* **-las** *or* **-lae** group of numbers, letters, or symbols expressing a scientific or mathematical rule; method or rule for doing or producing something; set form of words used in religion, law, etc.; specific category of car in motor racing ▶ **formulaic** *adj* ▶ **formulate** *v* plan or describe precisely and clearly ▶ **formulation** *n*

**fornicate** *v* have sexual intercourse without being married ▶ **fornication** *n* ▶ **fornicator** *n*

**forsake** *v* **-saking, -sook, -saken** withdraw support or friendship from; give up, renounce

**forsooth** *adv* (*obs*) indeed

**forswear** *v* **-swearing, -swore, -sworn** renounce or reject

**forsythia** [for-**syth**-ee-a] *n* shrub with yellow flowers in spring

**fort** *n* fortified building or place **hold the fort** (*informal*) keep things going during someone's absence

**forte¹** [**for**-tay] *n* thing at which a person excels

**forte²** [**for**-tay] *adv* (*Music*) loudly

**forth** *adv* forwards, out, or away

**forthcoming** *adj* about to appear or happen; available; (of a person) communicative

**forthright** *adj* direct and outspoken

**forthwith** *adv* at once

**fortieth** *adj, n* see **forty**

**fortify** *v* **-fying, -fied** make (a place) defensible, as by building walls; strengthen; add vitamins etc. to (food); add alcohol to (wine) to make sherry or port ▶ **fortification** *n*

**fortissimo** *adv* (*Music*) very loudly

**fortitude** *n* courage in adversity or pain

**fortnight** *n* two weeks ▶ **fortnightly** *adv, adj*

**FORTRAN** *n* (*Computing*) programming language for mathematical and scientific purposes

**fortress** *n* large fort or fortified town

**fortuitous** [for-**tyew**-it-uss] *adj* happening by (lucky) chance ▶ **fortuitously** *adv*

**fortunate** *adj* having good luck; occurring by good luck ▶ **fortunately** *adv*

**fortune** *n* luck, esp. when favourable; power regarded as influencing human destiny; wealth, large sum of money ▷ *pl* person's destiny ▶ **fortune-teller** *n* person who claims to predict the future of others

**forty** *adj, n, pl* **-ties** four times ten ▶ **fortieth** *adj, n*

**forum** n meeting or medium for open discussion or debate

**forward** adj directed or moving ahead; in, at, or near the front; presumptuous; well developed or advanced; relating to the future ▷ n attacking player in various team games, such as soccer or hockey ▷ adv forwards ▷ v send (a letter etc.) on to an ultimate destination; advance or promote ▶ **forwards** adv towards or at a place further ahead in space or time; towards the front

**fossick** v (Aust & NZ) search, esp. for gold or precious stones

**fossil** n hardened remains of a prehistoric animal or plant preserved in rock ▶ **fossilize** v turn into a fossil; become out-of-date or inflexible

**foster** v promote the growth or development of; bring up (a child not one's own) ▷ adj of or involved in fostering a child e.g. foster parents

**fought** v past of **fight**

**foul** adj loathsome or offensive; stinking or dirty; (of language) obscene or vulgar; unfair ▷ n (Sport) violation of the rules ▷ v make dirty or polluted; make or become entangled or clogged; (Sport) commit a foul against (an opponent) **fall foul of** come into conflict with ▶ **foul-mouthed** adj habitually using foul language ▶ **foul play** unfair conduct, esp. involving violence

**found¹** v past of **find**

**found²** v establish or bring into being; lay the foundation of; (foll by on or upon) have a basis (in) ▶ **founder** n

**found³** v cast (metal or glass) by melting and setting in a mould; make (articles) by this method

**foundation** n basis or base; part of a building or wall below the ground; act of founding; institution supported by an endowment; cosmetic used as a base for make-up

**founder** v break down or fail; (of a ship) sink; stumble or fall

**foundling** n (chiefly Brit) abandoned baby

**foundry** n, pl -**ries** place where metal is melted and cast

**fount¹** n (lit) fountain; source

**fount²** n set of printing type of one style and size

**fountain** n jet of water; structure from which such a jet spurts; source ▶ **fountainhead** n original source ▶ **fountain pen** pen supplied with ink from a container inside it

**four** adj, n one more than three ▷ n (crew of) four-oared rowing boat **on all fours** on hands and knees ▶ **four-letter word** short obscene word referring to sex or excrement ▶ **four-poster** n bed with four posts supporting a canopy ▶ **foursome** n group of four people

**fourteen** adj, n four and ten ▶ **fourteenth** adj, n

**fourth** adj, n (of) number four in a series ▷ n quarter ▶ **fourth dimension** time ▶ **fourth estate** the press

**fowl** n domestic cock or hen; any bird used for food or hunted as game

**fox** n reddish-brown bushy-tailed animal of the dog family; its fur; cunning person ▷ v (informal) perplex or deceive ▶ **foxy** adj of or like a fox, esp. in craftiness ▶ **foxglove** n tall plant with purple or white flowers ▶ **foxhole** n (Mil) small pit dug for protection

▶ **foxhound** n dog bred for hunting foxes ▶ **fox terrier** small short-haired terrier ▶ **foxtrot** n ballroom dance with slow and quick steps; music for this

**foyer** [**foy**-ay] n entrance hall in a theatre, cinema, or hotel

**fracas** [**frak**-ah] n, pl **-cas** noisy quarrel

**fracking** n extraction of oil or gas by forcing liquid into rock at high pressure

**fraction** n numerical quantity that is not a whole number; fragment, piece; (*Chem*) substance separated by distillation ▶ **fractional** adj ▶ **fractionally** adv

**fractious** adj easily upset and angered

**fracture** n breaking, esp. of a bone ▷ v break

**fragile** adj easily broken or damaged; in a weakened physical state ▶ **fragility** n

**fragment** n piece broken off; incomplete piece ▷ v break into pieces ▶ **fragmentary** adj ▶ **fragmentation** n

**fragrant** adj sweet-smelling ▶ **fragrance** n pleasant smell; perfume; scent

**frail** adj physically weak; easily damaged ▶ **frailty** n, pl **-ties** physical or moral weakness

**frame** n structure giving shape or support; enclosing case or border, as round a picture; person's build; individual exposure on a strip of film; individual game of snooker in a match ▷ v put together, construct; put into words; put into a frame; (*slang*) incriminate (a person) on a false charge **frame of mind** mood or attitude ▶ **frame-up** n (*slang*) false incrimination ▶ **framework** n supporting structure

**franc** n monetary unit of Switzerland, various African

countries, and formerly of France and Belgium

**franchise** n right to vote; authorization to sell a company's goods

**Franciscan** n, adj (friar or nun) of the order founded by St. Francis of Assisi

**francium** n (*Chem*) radioactive metallic element

**Franco-** combining form of France or the French

**frangipani** [fran-jee-**pah**-nee] n Australian evergreen tree with large yellow fragrant flowers; tropical shrub with fragrant white or pink flowers

**frank** adj honest and straightforward in speech or attitude ▷ n official mark on a letter permitting delivery ▷ v put such a mark on (a letter) ▶ **frankly** adv ▶ **frankness** n

**frankfurter** n smoked sausage

**frankincense** n aromatic gum resin burned as incense

**frantic** adj distracted with rage, grief, joy, etc.; hurried and disorganized ▶ **frantically** adv

**fraternal** adj of a brother, brotherly ▶ **fraternally** adv ▶ **fraternity** n group of people with shared interests, aims, etc.; brotherhood; (*US*) male social club at college ▶ **fraternize** v associate on friendly terms ▶ **fraternization** n ▶ **fratricide** n crime of killing one's brother; person who does this

**Frau** [rhymes with **how**] n, pl **Fraus** or **Frauen** German title, equivalent to *Mrs* ▶ **Fräulein** [**froy**-line] n, pl **-leins** or **-lein** German title, equivalent to *Miss*

**fraud** n (criminal) deception, swindle; person who acts in a deceitful way ▶ **fraudulent** adj ▶ **fraudulence** n

**fraught** [frawt] adj tense or anxious **fraught with** involving, filled with

**fray**[1] n (Brit, Aust & NZ) noisy quarrel or conflict

**fray**[2] v make or become ragged at the edge; become strained

**frazzle** n (informal) exhausted state

**freak** n abnormal person or thing; person who is excessively enthusiastic about something ▷ adj abnormal ▶ **freakish** adj ▶ **freak out** v (informal) (cause to) be in a heightened emotional state

**freckle** n small brown spot on the skin ▶ **freckled** adj marked with freckles

**free** adj **freer, freest** able to act at will, not compelled or restrained; not subject (to); provided without charge; not in use; (of a person) not busy; not fixed or joined ▷ v **freeing, freed** release, liberate; remove (obstacles, pain, etc.) from; make available or usable **a free hand** unrestricted freedom to act ▶ **freely** adv ▶ **Freecycle** n ® informal network of citizens who promote recycling by offering one another unwanted items free of charge ▷ v (**f-**) recycle (an unwanted item) by offering it to someone free of charge ▶ **free fall** part of a parachute descent before the parachute opens ▶ **free-for-all** n (informal) brawl ▶ **freehand** adj drawn without guiding instruments ▶ **freehold** n tenure of land for life without restrictions ▶ **freeholder** n ▶ **free house** (Brit) public house not bound to sell only one brewer's products ▶ **freelance** adj, n (of) a self-employed person doing specific pieces of work for various employers ▶ **freeloader** n (slang) habitual scrounger ▶ **free-range** adj kept or produced in natural conditions ▶ **Freeview**® n (in Britain) free service providing digital terrestrial television

▶ **freeway** n (US & Aust) motorway

▶ **freewheel** v travel downhill on a bicycle without pedalling

**-free** combining form without e.g. a trouble-free journey

**freedom** n being free; right or privilege of unlimited access e.g. the freedom of the city

**Freemason** n member of a secret fraternity pledged to help each other

**freesia** n plant with fragrant tubular flowers

**freeze** v **freezing, froze, frozen** change from a liquid to a solid by the reduction of temperature, as water to ice; preserve (food etc.) by extreme cold; (cause to) be very cold; become motionless with fear, shock, etc.; fix (prices or wages) at a particular level; ban the exchange or collection of (loans, assets, etc.) ▷ n period of very cold weather; freezing of prices or wages ▶ **freezer** n insulated cabinet for cold-storage of perishable foods ▶ **freeze-dry** v preserve (food) by rapid freezing and drying in a vacuum ▶ **freezing** adj (informal) very cold

**freight** [**frate**] n commercial transport of goods; cargo transported; cost of this ▷ v send by freight ▶ **freighter** n ship or aircraft for transporting goods

**French** n language of France, also spoken in parts of Belgium, Canada, and Switzerland ▷ adj of France, its people, or their language ▶ **French bread** white bread in a long thin crusty loaf ▶ **French dressing** salad dressing of oil and vinegar ▶ **French fries** potato chips ▶ **French horn** brass wind instrument with a coiled tube ▶ **French letter** (slang) condom ▶ **French polish** shellac varnish for wood ▶ **French**

**window** window extending to floor level, used as a door

**frenetic** [frin-**net**-ik] *adj* uncontrolled, excited ▶ **frenetically** *adv*

**frenzy** *n, pl* **-zies** violent mental derangement; wild excitement ▶ **frenzied** *adj* ▶ **frenziedly** *adv*

**frequent** *adj* happening often; habitual ▷ *v* visit habitually ▶ **frequently** *adv* ▶ **frequency** *n, pl* **-cies** rate of occurrence; (*Physics*) number of times a wave repeats itself in a given time

**fresco** *n, pl* **-coes** *or* **-cos** watercolour painting done on wet plaster on a wall

**fresh** *adj* newly made, acquired, etc.; novel, original; further, additional; (of food) not preserved; (of water) not salty; (of weather) brisk or invigorating; not tired ▶ **freshly** *adv* ▶ **freshness** *n* ▶ **freshen** *v* make or become fresh or fresher ▶ **fresher,** (*US*) **freshman** *n* (*Brit & US*) first-year student

**fret**[1] *v* **fretting, fretted** be worried ▶ **fretful** *adj* irritable

**fret**[2] *n* small bar on the fingerboard of a guitar etc.

**fretwork** *n* decorative carving in wood ▶ **fretsaw** *n* fine saw with a narrow blade, used for fretwork

**Freudian** [**froy**-dee-an] *adj* of or relating to the psychoanalyst Sigmund Freud or his theories

**friable** *adj* easily crumbled

**friar** *n* member of a male Roman Catholic religious order ▶ **friary** *n, pl* **-ries** house of friars

**fricassee** *n* stewed meat served in a thick white sauce

**friction** *n* resistance met with by a body moving over another; rubbing; clash of wills or personalities ▶ **frictional** *adj*

**Friday** *n* sixth day of the week **Good Friday** Friday before Easter

**fridge** *n* apparatus in which food and drinks are kept cool

**fried** *v* past of **fry**[1]

**friend** *n* person whom one knows well and likes; supporter or ally; (**F-**) Quaker ▶ **friendly** *adj* showing or expressing liking; not hostile, on the same side ▷ *n, pl* **-lies** (*Sport*) match played for its own sake and not as part of a competition ▶ **-friendly** *combining form* good or easy for the person or thing specified e.g. *user-friendly* ▶ **friendly society** (in Britain) association of people who pay regular dues in return for pensions, sickness benefits, etc. ▶ **friendliness** *n* ▶ **friendless** *adj* ▶ **friendship** *n*

**Friesian** [**free**-zhan] *n* breed of black-and-white dairy cattle

**frieze** [**freeze**] *n* ornamental band on a wall

**frigate** [**frig**-it] *n* medium-sized fast warship

**fright** *n* sudden fear or alarm; sudden alarming shock ▶ **frightful** *adj* horrifying; (*informal*) very great ▶ **frightfully** *adv*

**frighten** *v* scare or terrify; force (someone) to do something from fear ▶ **frightening** *adj*

**frigid** [**frij**-id] *adj* (of a woman) sexually unresponsive; very cold; excessively formal ▶ **frigidity** *n*

**frill** *n* gathered strip of fabric attached at one edge ▷ *pl* superfluous decorations or details ▶ **frilled** *adj* ▶ **frilled lizard** large tree-living Australian lizard with an erectile fold of skin round the neck ▶ **frilly** *adj*

**fringe** *n* hair cut short and hanging over the forehead; ornamental edge of hanging threads, tassels, etc.; outer edge; less important parts of an activity or group ▷ v decorate with a fringe ▷ adj (of theatre) unofficial or unconventional ▶ **fringed** adj ▶ **fringe benefit** benefit given in addition to a regular salary

**frippery** n, pl -peries useless ornamentation; trivia

**frisk** v move or leap playfully; (informal) search (a person) for concealed weapons etc. ▶ **frisky** adj lively or high-spirited

**frisson** [frees-sonn] n shiver of fear or excitement

**fritter** n piece of food fried in batter

**fritter away** v waste

**frivolous** adj not serious or sensible; enjoyable but trivial ▶ **frivolity** n

**frizz** v form (hair) into stiff wiry curls ▶ **frizzy** adj

**frizzle** v cook or heat until crisp and shrivelled

**frock** n dress ▶ **frock coat** man's skirted coat as worn in the 19th century

**frog** n smooth-skinned tailless amphibian with long back legs used for jumping **frog in one's throat** phlegm on the vocal cords, hindering speech ▶ **frogman** n swimmer with a rubber suit and breathing equipment for working underwater ▶ **frogspawn** n jelly-like substance containing frog's eggs

**frolic** v -icking, -icked run and play in a lively way ▷ n lively and merry behaviour ▶ **frolicsome** adj playful

**from** prep indicating the point of departure, source, distance, cause, change of state, etc.

**USAGE NOTE**
The use of *off* to mean *from* is very informal: *They bought milk from* (rather than *off*) *a farmer*

**frond** n long leaf or leaflike part of a fern, palm, or seaweed

**front** n fore part; position directly before or ahead; battle line or area; (Meteorol) dividing line between two different air masses; outward appearance; (informal) cover for another, usu. criminal, activity; particular field of activity e.g. *on the economic front* ▷ adj of or at the front ▷ v face (onto); be the presenter of (a television show) ▶ **frontal** adj ▶ **frontage** n facade of a building ▶ **front bench** (in Britain) parliamentary leaders of the government or opposition ▶ **front-bencher** n ▶ **frontrunner** n (informal) person regarded as most likely to win a race, election, etc.

**frontier** n area of a country bordering on another

**frontispiece** n illustration facing the title page of a book

**frost** n white frozen dew or mist; atmospheric temperature below freezing point ▷ v become covered with frost ▶ **frosted** adj (of glass) having a rough surface to make it opaque ▶ **frosting** n (chiefly US) sugar icing ▶ **frosty** adj characterized or covered by frost; unfriendly ▶ **frostily** adv ▶ **frostiness** n ▶ **frostbite** n destruction of tissue, esp. of the fingers or ears, by cold ▶ **frostbitten** adj

**froth** n mass of small bubbles ▷ v foam ▶ **frothy** adj

**frown** v wrinkle one's brows in worry, anger, or thought; look disapprovingly (on) ▷ n frowning expression

**frowsty** adj (Brit) stale or musty

**frowzy, frowsy** adj -zier, -ziest or -sier, -siest dirty or unkempt

**froze** v past tense of **freeze** ▶ **frozen** v past participle of **freeze**

**frugal** adj thrifty, sparing; meagre and inexpensive ▶ **frugally** adv ▶ **frugality** n

**fruit** n part of a plant containing seeds, esp. if edible; any plant product useful to humans; (often pl) result of an action or effort ▷ v bear fruit ▶ **fruiterer** n person who sells fruit ▶ **fruit fly** small fly that feeds on and lays its eggs in plant tissues; similar fly that feeds on plant sap, decaying fruit, etc., and is widely used in genetics experiments ▶ **fruitful** adj useful or productive ▶ **fruitfully** adv ▶ **fruitless** adj useless or unproductive ▶ **fruitlessly** adv ▶ **fruity** adj of or like fruit; (of a voice) mellow; (Brit informal) mildly bawdy ▶ **fruit machine** coin-operated gambling machine

**fruition** [froo-**ish**-on] n fulfilment of something worked for or desired

**frump** n dowdy woman ▶ **frumpy** adj

**frustrate** v upset or anger; hinder or prevent ▶ **frustrated** adj ▶ **frustrating** adj ▶ **frustration** n

**fry¹** v **frying, fried** cook or be cooked in fat or oil ▷ n, pl **fries** (also **fry-up**) dish of fried food ▷ pl potato chips

**fry²** pl n young fishes **small fry** young or insignificant people

**ft.** foot; feet

**ftp** file transfer protocol: standard protocol for transferring files across a network, esp. the internet

**fuchsia** [**fyew**-sha] n ornamental shrub with hanging flowers

**fuddle** v cause to be intoxicated or confused ▶ **fuddled** adj

**fuddy-duddy** adj, n, pl **-dies** (informal) old-fashioned (person)

**fudge¹** n soft caramel-like sweet

**fudge²** v avoid making a firm statement or decision

**fuel** n substance burned or treated to produce heat or power; something that intensifies (a feeling etc.) ▷ v **fuelling, fuelled** provide with fuel

**fug** n hot stale atmosphere ▶ **fuggy** adj

**fugitive** [**fyew**-jit-iv] n person who flees, esp. from arrest or pursuit ▷ adj fleeing; transient

**fugue** [fyewg] n musical composition in which a theme is repeated in different parts

**fulcrum** n, pl **-crums** or **-cra** pivot about which a lever turns

**fulfil** v **-filling, -filled** bring about the achievement of (a desire or promise); carry out (a request or order); do what is required ▶ **fulfilment** n ▶ **fulfil oneself** v achieve one's potential

**full** adj containing as much or as many as possible; abundant in supply; having had enough to eat; plump; complete, whole; (of a garment) of ample cut; (of a sound or flavour) rich and strong ▷ adv completely; directly; very ▶ **fully** adv ▶ **fullness** n **in full** without shortening ▶ **full-blooded** adj vigorous or enthusiastic ▶ **full-blown** adj fully developed ▶ **full moon** phase of the moon when it is visible as a fully illuminated disc ▶ **full-scale** adj (of a plan) of actual size; using all resources ▶ **full stop** punctuation mark (.) at the end of a sentence and after abbreviations

**fulmar** n Arctic sea bird

**fulminate** v (foll by against) criticize or denounce angrily

**fulsome** adj distastefully excessive or insincere

**fumble** v handle awkwardly; say awkwardly ▷ n act of fumbling

**fume** v be very angry; give out smoke or vapour ▷ pl n pungent smoke or vapour

**fumigate** [**fyew**-mig-gate] v disinfect with fumes ▶ **fumigation** n

**fun** n enjoyment or amusement **make fun of** mock or tease ▶ **funny** adj comical, humorous; odd ▶ **funny bone** part of the elbow where the nerve is near the surface ▶ **funnily** adv

**function** n purpose something exists for; way something works; large or formal social event; (Maths) quantity whose value depends on the varying value of another; sequence of operations performed by a computer at a key stroke ▷ v operate or work; (foll by as) fill the role of ▶ **functional** adj of or as a function; practical rather than decorative; in working order ▶ **functionally** adv ▶ **functionary** n, pl **-aries** official

**fund** n stock of money for a special purpose; supply or store ▷ pl money resources ▷ v provide money to ▶ **funding** n

**fundamental** adj essential or primary; basic ▷ n basic rule or fact ▶ **fundamentally** adv ▶ **fundamentalism** n literal or strict interpretation of a religion ▶ **fundamentalist** n, adj

**fundi** n (SAfr) expert or boffin

**funeral** n ceremony of burying or cremating a dead person

**funerary** adj of or for a funeral

**funereal** [fyew-**neer**-ee-al] adj gloomy or sombre

**funfair** n entertainment with machines to ride on and stalls

**fungus** n, pl **-gi** or **-guses** plant without leaves, flowers, or roots, such as a mushroom or mould ▶ **fungal, fungous** adj

▶ **fungicide** n substance that destroys fungi

**funicular** n cable railway on a mountainside or cliff

**funk¹** n style of dance music with a strong beat ▶ **funky** adj (of music) having a strong beat

**funk²** (informal) n nervous or fearful state ▷ v avoid (doing something) through fear

**funnel** n cone-shaped tube for pouring liquids into a narrow opening; chimney of a ship or locomotive ▷ v **-nelling, -nelled** (cause to) move through or as if through a funnel ▶ **funnel-web** n large poisonous black spider that builds funnel-shaped webs

**fur** n soft hair of a mammal; animal skin with the fur left on; garment made of this; whitish coating on the tongue or inside a kettle ▷ v cover or become covered with fur ▶ **furry** adj ▶ **furrier** n dealer in furs

**furbish** v smarten up

**furious** adj very angry; violent or unrestrained ▶ **furiously** adv

**furl** v roll up and fasten (a sail, umbrella, or flag)

**furlong** n unit of length equal to 220 yards (201.168 metres)

**furlough** [**fur**-loh] n leave of absence

**furnace** n enclosed chamber containing a very hot fire

**furnish** v provide (a house or room) with furniture; supply, provide ▶ **furnishings** pl n furniture, carpets, and fittings ▶ **furniture** n large movable articles such as chairs and wardrobes

**furore** [fyew-**ror**-ee] n very excited or angry reaction

**furrow** n trench made by a plough; groove, esp. a wrinkle on the forehead ▷ v make or become wrinkled; make furrows in

**further** adv in addition; to a greater distance or extent ▷ adj additional; more distant ▷ v assist the progress of ▶ **further education** (Brit) education beyond school other than at a university ▶ **furthest** adv to the greatest distance or extent ▷ adj most distant ▶ **furtherance** n ▶ **furthermore** adv besides ▶ **furthermost** adj most distant

**furtive** adj sly and secretive ▶ **furtively** adv

**fury** n, pl **-ries** wild anger; uncontrolled violence

**furze** n gorse

**fuse¹** n cord containing an explosive for detonating a bomb

**fuse²** n safety device for electric circuits, containing a wire that melts and breaks the connection when the circuit is overloaded ▷ v (cause to) fail as a result of a blown fuse; join or combine; unite by melting; melt with heat

**fuselage** [**fyew**-zill-lahzh] n body of an aircraft

**fusilier** [fyew-zill-**leer**] n soldier of certain regiments

**fusillade** [fyew-zill-**lade**] n continuous discharge of firearms; outburst of criticism, questions, etc.

**fusion** n melting; product of fusing; combination of the nucleus of two atoms with the release of energy; something new created by a mixture of qualities, ideas, or things; popular music blending styles, esp. jazz and funk ▷ adj of a style of cooking that combines traditional Western techniques and ingredients with those used in Eastern cuisine

**fuss** n needless activity or worry; complaint or objection; great display of attention ▷ v make a fuss ▶ **fussy** adj inclined to fuss;

overparticular; overelaborate ▶ **fussily** adv ▶ **fussiness** n

**fusty** adj **-tier, -tiest** stale-smelling; behind the times ▶ **fustiness** n

**futile** adj unsuccessful or useless ▶ **futility** n

**futon** [**foo**-tonn] n Japanese-style bed

**futsal** [**foot**-sal] n form of soccer played indoors with five players on each side

**future** n time to come; what will happen; prospects ▷ adj yet to come or be; of or relating to time to come; (of a verb tense) indicating that the action specified has not yet taken place ▶ **futuristic** adj of a design appearing to belong to some future time

**fuzz¹** n mass of fine or curly hairs or fibres ▶ **fuzzy** adj of, like, or covered with fuzz; blurred or indistinct; (of hair) tightly curled ▶ **fuzzily** adv ▶ **fuzziness** n

**fuzz²** n (slang) police

# Gg

**g** gram(s); (acceleration due to) gravity

**gab** *n, v* **gabbing, gabbed** (*informal*) talk or chatter **gift of the gab** eloquence ▸ **gabby** *adj* **-bier, -biest** (*informal*) talkative

**gabardine, gaberdine** *n* strong twill cloth used esp. for raincoats

**gabble** *v* speak rapidly and indistinctly ▷ *n* rapid indistinct speech

**gable** *n* triangular upper part of a wall between sloping roofs ▸ **gabled** *adj*

**gad** *v* **gadding, gadded** ▸ **gad about, around** go around in search of pleasure ▸ **gadabout** *n* pleasure-seeker

**gadfly** *n* fly that bites cattle; constantly annoying person

**gadget** *n* small mechanical device or appliance ▸ **gadgetry** *n* gadgets

**Gael** [gayl] *n* speaker of Gaelic ▸ **Gaelic** [**gal**-lik, **gay**-lik] *n* any of the Celtic languages of Ireland and the Scottish Highlands ▷ *adj* of the Gaels or their language

**gaff** *n* stick with an iron hook for landing large fish

**gaff** *n* **blow the gaff** (*slang*) divulge a secret

**gaffe** *n* social blunder

**gaffer** *n* (*Brit informal*) foreman or boss; (*informal*) old man; senior electrician on a TV or film set

**gag** *v* **gagging, gagged** choke or retch; stop up the mouth of (a person) with cloth etc.; deprive of free speech ▷ *n* cloth etc. put into or tied across the mouth

**gag** *n* (*informal*) joke

**gaga** [**gah**-gah] *adj* (*slang*) senile

**gaggle** *n* (*informal*) disorderly crowd; flock of geese

**gaiety** *n* cheerfulness; merrymaking ▸ **gaily** *adv* merrily; colourfully

**gain** *v* acquire or obtain; increase or improve; reach; (of a watch or clock) be or become too fast ▷ *n* profit or advantage; increase or improvement ▸ **gainful** *adj* useful or profitable ▸ **gainfully** *adv* ▸ **gain on, gain upon** *v* get nearer to or catch up with

**gainsay** *v* **-saying, -said** deny or contradict

**gait** *n* manner of walking

**gaiter** *n* cloth or leather covering for the lower leg

**gala** [**gah**-la] *n* festival; competitive sporting event

**galaxy** *n, pl* **-axies** system of stars; gathering of famous people ▸ **galactic** *adj*

**gale** *n* strong wind; (*informal*) loud outburst

**gall** [gawl] *n* (*informal*) impudence; bitter feeling ▸ **gall bladder** sac attached to the liver, storing bile ▸ **gallstone** *n* hard mass formed in the gall bladder or its ducts

**gall** [gawl] *v* annoy; make sore by rubbing

**gall** [gawl] *n* abnormal outgrowth on a tree or plant

**gallant** *adj* brave and noble; (of a man) attentive to women ▸ **gallantly** *adv* ▸ **gallantry** *n* showy, attentive treatment of women; bravery

**galleon** *n* large three-masted sailing ship of the 15th–17th centuries

**gallery** *n, pl* **-ries** room or building for displaying works of art; balcony in a church, theatre, etc.; passage in a mine; long narrow room for a specific purpose e.g. *shooting gallery*

**galley** *n* kitchen of a ship or aircraft; (*Hist*) ship propelled by oars, usu. rowed by slaves ▶ **galley slave** (*Hist*) slave forced to row in a galley; (*informal*) drudge

**Gallic** *adj* French; of ancient Gaul

**gallium** *n* (*Chem*) soft grey metallic element used in semiconductors

**gallivant** *v* go about in search of pleasure

**gallon** *n* liquid measure of eight pints, equal to 4.55 litres

**gallop** *n* horse's fastest pace; galloping ▶ *v* **galloping, galloped** go or ride at a gallop; move or progress rapidly

> **SPELLING TIP**
> Although **gallop** has two ls, remember that **galloping** and **galloped** have only one p.

**gallows** *n* wooden structure used for hanging criminals

**Gallup poll** *n* public opinion poll carried out by questioning a cross section of the population

**galore** *adv* in abundance

**galoshes** *pl n* (*Brit, Aust & NZ*) waterproof overshoes

**galumph** *v* (*Brit, Aust & NZ informal*) leap or move about clumsily

**galvanic** *adj* of or producing an electric current generated by chemical means; (*informal*) stimulating or startling ▶ **galvanize** *v* stimulate into action; coat (metal) with zinc

**gambit** *n* opening line or move intended to secure an advantage; (*Chess*) opening move involving the sacrifice of a pawn

**gamble** *v* play games of chance to win money; act on the expectation of something ▶ *n* risky undertaking; bet or wager ▶ **gambler** *n* ▶ **gambling** *n*

**gamboge** [gam-**boje**] *n* gum resin used as a yellow pigment and purgative

**gambol** *v* **-bolling, -bolled** jump about playfully, frolic ▶ *n* frolic

> **SPELLING TIP**
> Although the pronunciation is the same as 'gamble', both the verb and the noun **gambol** must always contain an *o*.

**game¹** *n* amusement or pastime; contest for amusement; single period of play in a contest; animals or birds hunted for sport or food; their flesh; scheme or trick ▶ *v* gamble ▶ *adj* brave; willing ▶ **gamely** *adv* ▶ **gaming** *n* gambling ▶ **gamekeeper** *n* (*Brit, Aust & S Afr*) person employed to breed game and prevent poaching ▶ **gamer** *n* person who plays computer games ▶ **games console** *n* electronic device enabling computer games to be played on a TV screen ▶ **gamesmanship** *n* art of winning by cunning practices without actually cheating

**game²** *adj* (*Brit, Aust & NZ*) lame, crippled

**gamete** *n* (*Biol*) reproductive cell

**gamine** [gam-**een**] *n* slim boyish young woman

**gamma** *n* third letter of the Greek alphabet ▶ **gamma ray** electromagnetic ray of shorter wavelength and higher energy than an x-ray

**gammon** *n* cured or smoked ham

**gammy** *adj* **-mier, -miest** same as **game²**

**gamut** *n* whole range or scale (of music, emotions, etc.)

**gander** *n* male goose; (*informal*) quick look

**gang** *n* (criminal) group; organized group of workmen ▶ **gangland** *n* criminal underworld ▸ **gang up** v form an alliance (against)

**gangling** adj lanky and awkward

**ganglion** n group of nerve cells; small harmless tumour

**gangplank** n portable bridge for boarding or leaving a ship

**gangrene** n decay of body tissue as a result of disease or injury ▸ **gangrenous** adj

**gangsta rap** n style of rap music originating from US Black street culture

**gangster** n member of a criminal gang

**gangway** n passage between rows of seats; gangplank

**gannet** n large sea bird; (Brit slang) greedy person

**gantry** n, pl **-tries** structure supporting something such as a crane or rocket

**gaol** [jayl] n same as **jail**

**gap** n break or opening; interruption or interval; divergence or difference ▸ **gappy** adj

**gape** v stare in wonder; open the mouth wide; be or become wide open ▸ **gaping** adj

**garage** n building used to house cars; place for the refuelling, sale, and repair of cars ▸ v put or keep a car in a garage

**garb** n clothes ▸ v clothe

**garbage** n rubbish

**garbled** adj (of a story etc.) jumbled and confused

**garden** n piece of land for growing flowers, fruit, or vegetables ▸ pl ornamental park ▸ v cultivate a garden ▸ **gardener** n ▸ **gardening** n ▸ **garden centre** place selling plants and gardening equipment

**gardenia** [gar-**deen**-ya] n large fragrant white waxy flower; shrub bearing this

**garfish** n freshwater fish with a long body and very long toothed jaws; sea fish with similar characteristics

**gargantuan** adj huge

**gargle** v wash the throat with (a liquid) by breathing out slowly through the liquid ▸ n liquid used for gargling

**gargoyle** n waterspout carved in the form of a grotesque face, esp. on a church

**garish** adj crudely bright or colourful ▸ **garishly** adv ▸ **garishness** n

**garland** n wreath of flowers worn or hung as a decoration ▸ v decorate with garlands

**garlic** n pungent bulb of a plant of the onion family, used in cooking

**garment** n article of clothing ▸ pl clothes

**garner** v collect or store

**garnet** n red semiprecious stone

**garnish** v decorate (food) ▸ n decoration for food

**garret** n attic in a house

**garrison** n troops stationed in a town or fort; fortified place ▸ v station troops in

**garrotte, garotte** n Spanish method of execution by strangling; cord or wire used for this ▸ v kill by this method

**garrulous** adj talkative

**garter** n band worn round the leg to hold up a sock or stocking

**gas** n, pl **gases** or **gasses** airlike substance that is not liquid or solid; fossil fuel in the form of a gas, used for heating; gaseous anaesthetic; (chiefly US) petrol ▸ v **gassing, gassed** poison or render unconscious with gas; (informal) talk idly or boastfully ▸ **gassy** adj filled with gas ▸ **gaseous** adj of or like gas ▸ **gasbag** n (informal) person who talks too much ▶ **gas chamber** airtight room which is filled with poison gas to kill people or animals ▶ **gasholder, gasometer** [gas-**som**-it-er] n large tank for storing gas ▶ **gas mask** mask with a chemical filter to protect the wearer against poison gas

**gash** v make a long deep cut in ▷ n long deep cut

**gasket** n piece of rubber etc. placed between the faces of a metal joint to act as a seal

**gasoline** n (US) petrol

**gasp** v draw in breath sharply or with difficulty; utter breathlessly ▷ n convulsive intake of breath

**gastric** adj of the stomach ▶ **gastritis** n inflammation of the stomach lining

**gastroenteritis** n inflammation of the stomach and intestines

**gastronomy** n art of good eating ▶ **gastronomic** adj

**gastropod** n mollusc, such as a snail, with a single flattened muscular foot

**gate** n movable barrier, usu. hinged, in a wall or fence; opening with a gate; any entrance or way in; (entrance money paid by) those attending a sporting event ▶ **gate-crash** v enter (a party) uninvited ▶ **gatehouse** n building at or above a gateway ▶ **gateway** n entrance with a gate; means of access e.g. *London's gateway to Scotland*

**gâteau** [gat-toe] n, pl **-teaux** [-toes] rich elaborate cake

**gather** v assemble; collect gradually; increase gradually; learn from information given; pick or harvest; draw (material) into small tucks or folds ▶ **gathers** pl n gathered folds in material ▶ **gathering** n assembly

**gatvol** [**hhut**-fol] adj (S Afr slang) disenchanted; fed up

**gauche** [**gohsh**] adj socially awkward ▶ **gaucheness** n

**gaucho** [**gow**-choh] n, pl **-chos** S American cowboy

**gaudy** adj **gaudier, gaudiest** vulgarly bright or colourful ▶ **gaudily** adv ▶ **gaudiness** n

**gauge** [**gayj**] v estimate or judge; measure the amount or condition of ▷ n measuring instrument; scale or standard of measurement; distance between the rails of a railway track

> **SPELLING TIP**
> The vowels in **gauge** are often confused so that the misspelling *guage* is common in the Collins Corpus

**gaunt** adj lean and haggard ▶ **gauntness** n

**gauntlet**[1] n heavy glove with a long cuff **throw down the gauntlet** offer a challenge

**gauntlet**[2] n **run the gauntlet** be exposed to criticism or unpleasant treatment

**gauze** n transparent loosely-woven fabric, often used for surgical dressings ▶ **gauzy** adj

**gave** v past tense of **give**

**gavel** [**gav**-el] n small hammer banged on a table by a judge, auctioneer, or chairman to call for attention

**gavotte** n old formal dance; music for this

**gawk** v stare stupidly ▶ **gawky** adj clumsy or awkward ▶ **gawkiness** n

**gawp** v (slang) stare stupidly

**gay** adj homosexual; carefree and merry; colourful ▷ n homosexual ▶ **gayness** n homosexuality

**gaze** v look fixedly ▷ n fixed look

**gazebo** [gaz-**zee**-boh] n, pl **-bos** or **-boes** summerhouse with a good view

**gazelle** n small graceful antelope

**gazette** n official publication containing announcements
▸ **gazetteer** n (part of) a book that lists and describes places

**gazillion** n (informal) extremely large, unspecified amount
▸ **gazillionaire** n (informal) enormously rich person

**gazump** v (Brit & Aust) raise the price of a property after verbally agreeing it with (a prospective buyer)

**GB** Great Britain; (also **Gb**) gigabyte

**GBH** (in Britain) grievous bodily harm

**GCE** (in Britain) General Certificate of Education

**GCSE** (in Britain) General Certificate of Secondary Education

**GDP** Gross Domestic Product

**gear** n set of toothed wheels connecting with another or with a rack to change the direction or speed of transmitted motion; mechanism for transmitting motion by gears; setting of a gear to suit engine speed e.g. first gear; clothing or belongings; equipment ▸ v prepare or organize for something **in gear, out of gear** with the gear mechanism engaged or disengaged ▸ **gearbox** n case enclosing a set of gears in a motor vehicle ▸ **gear up** v prepare for an activity

**gecko** n, pl **geckos** or **geckoes** small tropical lizard

**geebung** [gee-bung] n Australian tree or shrub with an edible but tasteless fruit; fruit of this tree

**geek** n (informal) person who is knowledgeable and enthusiastic about a subject; boring, unattractive person ▸ **geeky** adj

**geelbek** n (SAfr) edible marine fish

**geese** n plural of **goose**

**geezer** n (Brit, Aust & NZ informal) man

**Geiger counter** [guy-ger] n instrument for detecting and measuring radiation

**geisha** [gay-sha] n, pl -**sha** or -**shas** (in Japan) professional female companion for men

**gel** [jell] n jelly-like substance, esp. one used to secure a hairstyle ▹ v **gelling, gelled** form a gel; (informal) take on a definite form

**gelatine** [jel-at-teen], **gelatin** n substance made by boiling animal bones; edible jelly made of this ▸ **gelatinous** [jel-**at**-in-uss] adj of or like jelly

**geld** v castrate

**gelding** n castrated horse

**gelignite** n type of dynamite used for blasting

**gem** n precious stone or jewel; highly valued person or thing ▸ **gemfish** n Australian food fish with a delicate flavour

**gen** n (informal) information ▸ **gen up on** v **genning, genned** (Brit informal) make or become fully informed about

**gendarme** [zhohn-darm] n member of the French police force

**gender** n state of being male or female; (Grammar) classification of nouns in certain languages as masculine, feminine, or neuter

**gene** [jean] n part of a cell which determines inherited characteristics ▸ **gene therapy** n (Med) replacement or alteration of defective genes to prevent inherited diseases

**genealogy** [jean-ee-**al**-a-gee] n, pl -**gies** (study of) the history and descent of a family or families ▸ **genealogical** adj ▸ **genealogist** n

**genera** [jen-er-a] n plural of **genus**

**general** adj common or widespread; of or affecting all or most; not specific; including or dealing with various or miscellaneous items; highest in authority or rank e.g. *general manager* ▷ *n* very senior army officer **in general** mostly or usually ▶ **generally** *adv* ▶ **generality** *n*, *pl* **-ties** general principle; state of being general ▶ **generalize** *v* draw general conclusions; speak in generalities; make widely known or used ▶ **generalization** *n* ▶ **general election** election in which representatives are chosen for every constituency ▶ **general practitioner** nonspecialist doctor serving a local area

**generate** *v* produce or bring into being ▶ **generative** *adj* capable of producing ▶ **generator** *n* machine for converting mechanical energy into electrical energy

**generation** *n* all the people born about the same time; average time between two generations (about 30 years); generating

**generic** [jin-**ner**-ik] *adj* of a class, group, or genus ▶ **generically** *adv*

**generous** *adj* free in giving; free from pettiness; plentiful ▶ **generously** *adv* ▶ **generosity** *n*

**genesis** [jen-iss-iss] *n*, *pl* **-eses** [-iss-eez] beginning or origin

**genetic** [jin-**net**-tik] *adj* of genes or genetics ▶ **genetics** *n* study of heredity and variation in organisms ▶ **geneticist** *n* ▶ **genetic engineering** alteration of the genetic structure of an organism for a particular purpose ▶ **genetic fingerprinting** use of a person's unique DNA pattern as a means of identification

**genial** [**jean**-ee-al] *adj* cheerful and friendly ▶ **genially** *adv* ▶ **geniality** *n*

**genie** [**jean**-ee] *n* (in fairy tales) servant who appears by magic and grants wishes

**genital** *adj* of the sexual organs or reproduction ▶ **genitals, genitalia** [jen-it-**ail**-ya] *pl n* external sexual organs

**genitive** *n* grammatical case indicating possession or association

**genius** [**jean**-yuss] *n* (person with) exceptional ability in a particular field

**genocide** [jen-no-side] *n* murder of a race of people

**genome** *n* (Biol) full complement of genetic material within an organism

**genre** [**zhohn**-ra] *n* style of literary, musical, or artistic work

**gent** *n* (Brit, Aust & NZ informal) gentleman ▶ **gents** *n* men's public toilet

**genteel** *adj* affectedly proper and polite ▶ **genteelly** *adv*

**gentian** [jen-shun] *n* mountain plant with deep blue flowers

**gentile** *adj*, *n* non-Jewish (person)

**gentle** *adj* mild or kindly; not rough or severe; gradual; easily controlled, tame ▶ **gentleness** *n* ▶ **gently** *adv* ▶ **gentleman** *n* polite well-bred man; man of high social position; polite name for a man ▶ **gentlemanly** *adj* ▶ **gentlewoman** *n fem*

**gentry** *n* people just below the nobility in social rank ▶ **gentrification** *n* taking-over of a traditionally working-class area by middle-class incomers ▶ **gentrify** *v*

**genuflect** *v* bend the knee as a sign of reverence or deference ▶ **genuflection, genuflexion** *n*

**genuine** *adj* not fake, authentic; sincere ▶ **genuinely** *adv* ▶ **genuineness** *n*

**genus** [**jean**-uss] *n*, *pl* **genera** group into which a family of animals or plants is divided; kind, type

g

**geocentric** adj having the earth as a centre; measured as from the earth's centre

**geography** n study of the earth's physical features, climate, population, etc. ▶ **geographer** n ▶ **geographical, geographic** adj ▶ **geographically** adv

**geology** n study of the earth's origin, structure, and composition ▶ **geological** adj ▶ **geologically** adv ▶ **geologist** n

**geometry** n branch of mathematics dealing with points, lines, curves, and surfaces ▶ **geometric, geometrical** adj ▶ **geometrically** adv

**Geordie** n person from, or dialect of, Tyneside, an area of NE England

**Georgian** adj of the time of any of the four kings of Britain called George who ruled from 1714 to 1830

**geostationary** adj (of a satellite) orbiting so as to remain over the same point of the earth's surface

**geothermal** adj of or using the heat in the earth's interior

**geranium** n cultivated plant with red, pink, or white flowers

**gerbil** [jer-bill] n burrowing desert rodent of Asia and Africa

**geriatrics** n branch of medicine dealing with old age and its diseases ▶ **geriatric** adj, n old (person)

**germ** n microbe, esp. one causing disease; beginning from which something may develop; simple structure that can develop into a complete organism

**German** n language of Germany, Austria, and part of Switzerland; person from Germany ▷ adj of Germany or its language ▶ **Germanic** adj ▶ **German measles** contagious disease accompanied by a cough, sore throat, and red spots ▶ **German shepherd dog** Alsatian

**germane** adj **germane to** relevant to

**germanium** n (Chem) brittle grey element that is a semiconductor

**germinate** v (cause to) sprout or begin to grow ▶ **germination** n ▶ **germinal** adj of or in the earliest stage of development

**gerrymandering** n alteration of voting constituencies in order to give an unfair advantage to one party

**gerund** [jer-rund] n noun formed from a verb e.g. living

**Gestapo** n secret state police of Nazi Germany

**gestation** n (period of) carrying of young in the womb between conception and birth; developing of a plan or idea in the mind

**gesticulate** v make expressive movements with the hands and arms ▶ **gesticulation** n

**gesture** n movement to convey meaning; thing said or done to show one's feelings ▷ v gesticulate

**get** v **getting, got** obtain or receive; bring or fetch; contract (an illness); (cause to) become as specified e.g. get wet; understand; (often foll by to) come (to) or arrive (at); go on board (a plane, bus, etc.); persuade; (informal) annoy ▶ **get across** v (cause to) be understood ▶ **get at** v gain access to; imply or mean; criticize ▶ **getaway** adj, n (used in) escape ▶ **get by** v manage in spite of difficulties ▶ **get off** v (cause to) avoid the consequences of, or punishment for, an action ▶ **get off with** v (informal) start a romantic or sexual relationship with ▶ **get over** v recover from ▶ **get through** v (cause to) succeed; use up (money or supplies) ▸ **get through to** v make (a person) understand; contact by telephone ▸ **get-up** n (informal) costume ▸ **get up to** v be involved in

**geyser** [**geez**-er] n spring that discharges steam and hot water; (Brit & S Afr) domestic gas water heater

**ghastly** adj **-lier**, **-liest** (informal) unpleasant; deathly pale; (informal) unwell; (informal) horrible ▸ **ghastliness** n

**ghat** n (in India) steps leading down to a river; mountain pass

**ghee** [**gee**] n (in Indian cookery) clarified butter

**gherkin** n small pickled cucumber

**ghetto** n, pl **-tos** or **-toes** slum area inhabited by a deprived minority ▸ **ghetto-blaster** n (informal) large portable cassette recorder or CD player

**ghillie** n same as **gillie**

**ghost** n disembodied spirit of a dead person; faint trace ▷ v ghostwrite ▸ **ghost gum** (Aust) eucalyptus with white trunk and branches ▸ **ghostly** adj ▸ **ghost town** deserted town ▸ **ghostwriter** n writer of a book or article on behalf of another person who is credited as the author

**ghoul** [**gool**] n person with morbid interests; demon that eats corpses ▸ **ghoulish** adj

**GI** n (informal) US soldier; glycaemic index: index showing the effects of various foods on blood sugar

**giant** n mythical being of superhuman size; very large person or thing ▷ adj huge

**gibber**[1] [**jib**-ber] v speak rapidly and unintelligibly ▸ **gibberish** n rapid unintelligible talk

**gibber**[2] [**gib**-ber] n (Aust) boulder; barren land covered with stones

**gibbet** [**jib**-bit] n gallows for displaying executed criminals

**gibbon** [**gib**-bon] n agile tree-dwelling ape of S Asia

**gibbous** adj (of the moon) more than half but less than fully illuminated

**gibe** [**jibe**] v, n same as **jibe**[1]

**giblets** [**jib**-lets] pl n gizzard, liver, heart, and neck of a fowl

**gidday, g'day** interj (Aust & NZ) expression of greeting

**giddy** adj **-dier**, **-diest** having or causing a feeling of dizziness ▸ **giddily** adv ▸ **giddiness** n

**gift** n present; natural talent ▷ v make a present of ▸ **gifted** adj talented

**gig**[1] n single performance by pop or jazz musicians ▷ v **gigging**, **gigged** play a gig or gigs

**gig**[2] n light two-wheeled horse-drawn carriage

**gig**[3] n (informal) short for **gigabyte**

**gigabyte** n (Computing) 1024 megabytes

**gigantic** adj enormous

**giggle** v laugh nervously ▷ n such a laugh ▸ **giggly** adj

**gigolo** [**jig**-a-lo] n, pl **-los** man paid by an older woman to be her escort or lover

**gigot** n (chiefly Brit) leg of lamb or mutton

**gild** v **gilding**, **gilded** or **gilt** put a thin layer of gold on; make falsely attractive

**gill** [**jill**] n liquid measure of quarter of a pint, equal to 0.142 litres

**gillie** n (in Scotland) attendant for hunting or fishing

**gills** [**gillz**] pl n breathing organs in fish and other water creatures

**gilt** adj covered with a thin layer of gold ▷ n thin layer of gold used as decoration ▸ **gilt-edged** adj denoting government stocks on which interest payments and final repayments are guaranteed

**gimbals** *pl n* set of pivoted rings which allow nautical instruments to remain horizontal at sea

**gimcrack** [jim-krak] *adj* showy but cheap; shoddy

**gimlet** [gim-let] *n* small tool with a screwlike tip for boring holes in wood ▸ **gimlet-eyed** *adj* having a piercing glance

**gimmick** *n* something designed to attract attention or publicity ▸ **gimmickry** *n* ▸ **gimmicky** *adj*

**gin¹** *n* spirit flavoured with juniper berries

**gin²** *n* wire noose used to trap small animals; machine for separating seeds from raw cotton

**gin³** *n* (*Aust offens*) Aboriginal woman

**ginger** *n* root of a tropical plant, used as a spice; light orange-brown colour ▸ **gingery** *adj* ▸ **ginger ale, ginger beer** fizzy ginger-flavoured soft drink ▸ **gingerbread** *n* moist cake flavoured with ginger ▸ **ginger group** (*Brit, Aust & NZ*) group within a larger group that agitates for a more active policy ▸ **ginger nut, ginger snap** crisp ginger-flavoured biscuit

**gingerly** *adv* cautiously

**gingham** *n* cotton cloth, usu. checked or striped

**gingivitis** [jin-jiv-**vite**-iss] *n* inflammation of the gums

**ginkgo** [gink-go] *n, pl* -**goes** ornamental Chinese tree

**ginseng** [jin-seng] *n* (root of) a plant believed to have tonic and energy-giving properties

**Gipsy** *n, pl* -**sies** same as **Gypsy**

**giraffe** *n* African ruminant mammal with a spotted yellow skin and long neck and legs

**gird** *v* **girding, girded** *or* **girt** put a belt round; secure with or as if with a belt; surround **gird (up) one's loins** prepare for action

**girder** *n* large metal beam

**girdle¹** *n* woman's elastic corset; belt; (*Anat*) encircling structure or part ▷ *v* surround or encircle

**girdle²** *n* (*Scot*) griddle

**girl** *n* female child; young woman; girlfriend; (*informal*) any woman ▸ **girlhood** *n* ▸ **girlish** *adj* ▸ **girlie, girly** *adj* (*informal*) featuring photographs of naked or scantily clad women ▸ **girlfriend** *n* girl or woman with whom a person is romantically or sexually involved; female friend

**giro** [jire-oh] *n, pl* -**ros** (in some countries) system of transferring money within a post office or bank directly from one account to another; (*Brit informal*) social security payment by giro cheque

**girt** *v* a past of **gird**

**girth** *n* measurement round something; band round a horse to hold the saddle in position

**gist** [jist] *n* substance or main point of a matter

**give** *v* **giving, gave, given** present (something) to another person; impart; administer; utter or emit; sacrifice or devote; organize or host; yield or break under pressure ▷ *n* resilience or elasticity ▸ **give away** *v* donate as a gift; reveal ▸ **giveaway** *n* something that reveals hidden feelings or intentions ▷ *adj* very cheap or free ▸ **give in** *v* admit defeat ▸ **give off** *v* emit ▸ **give out** *v* distribute; emit; come to an end or fail ▸ **give over** *v* set aside for a specific purpose; (*informal*) cease ▸ **give up** *v* abandon; acknowledge defeat

**gizzard** *n* part of a bird's stomach

**GL** glycaemic load: index showing the amount of carbohydrate contained in a specified serving of a particular food

**glacé** [glass-say] *adj* preserved in a thick sugary syrup

**glacier** *n* slow-moving mass of ice formed by accumulated snow ▶ **glacial** *adj* of ice or glaciers; very cold; unfriendly ▶ **glaciated** *adj* covered with or affected by glaciers ▶ **glaciation** *n*

**glad** *adj* **gladder, gladdest** pleased and happy; causing happiness **glad to** very willing to (do something) **the glad eye** (*chiefly Brit informal*) seductive glance ▶ **gladly** *adv* ▶ **gladness** *n* ▶ **gladden** *v* make glad ▶ **glad rags** (*informal*) best clothes

**glade** *n* open space in a forest

**gladiator** *n* (in ancient Rome) man trained to fight in arenas to provide entertainment

**gladiolus** *n*, *pl* **-lus** *or* **-li, -luses** garden plant with sword-shaped leaves

**gladwrap**® (*Aust, NZ & S Afr*) *n* thin polythene material for wrapping food ▷ *v* wrap in gladwrap

**glamour** *n* alluring charm or fascination ▶ **glamorous** *adj* alluring ▶ **glamorize** *v*

> **SPELLING TIP**
> People often forget to drop the *u* in **glamour** when they add *ous*, writing *glamourous* instead of the correct **glamorous**

**glance** *v* look rapidly or briefly; glint or gleam ▷ *n* brief look ▶ **glancing** *adj* hitting at an oblique angle ▶ **glance off** *v* strike and be deflected off (an object) at an oblique angle

**gland** *n* organ that produces and secretes substances in the body ▶ **glandular** *adj*

**glare** *v* stare angrily; be unpleasantly bright ▷ *n* angry stare; unpleasant brightness ▶ **glaring** *adj* conspicuous; unpleasantly bright ▶ **glaringly** *adv*

**glass** *n* hard brittle, usu. transparent substance consisting of metal silicates or similar compounds; tumbler; its contents; objects made of glass; mirror; barometer ▷ *pl* spectacles ▶ **glassy** *adj* like glass; expressionless ▶ **glasshouse** *n* greenhouse; (*Brit informal*) army prison

**glaucoma** *n* eye disease

**glaze** *v* fit or cover with glass; cover with a protective shiny coating ▷ *n* transparent coating; substance used for this ▶ **glazier** *n* person who fits windows with glass

**gleam** *n* small beam or glow of light; brief or faint indication ▷ *v* emit a gleam ▶ **gleaming** *adj*

**glean** *v* gather (facts etc.) bit by bit; gather (the useful remnants of a crop) after harvesting ▶ **gleaner** *n*

**glee** *n* triumph and delight ▶ **gleeful** *adj* ▶ **gleefully** *adv*

**glen** *n* deep narrow valley, esp. in Scotland

**glib** *adj* **glibber, glibbest** fluent but insincere or superficial ▶ **glibly** *adv* ▶ **glibness** *n*

**glide** *v* move easily and smoothly; (of an aircraft) move without the use of engines ▷ *n* smooth easy movement ▶ **glider** *n* plane without an engine; (*Aust*) flying phalanger ▶ **gliding** *n* sport of flying gliders

**glimmer** *v* shine faintly, flicker ▷ *n* faint gleam; faint indication

**glimpse** *n* brief or incomplete view ▷ *v* catch a glimpse of

**glint** *v* gleam brightly ▷ *n* bright gleam

**glissando** *n* (*Music*) slide between two notes in which all intermediate notes are played

**glisten** v gleam by reflecting light

**glitch** n small problem that stops something from working properly

**glitter** v shine with bright flashes; be showy ▷ n sparkle or brilliance; tiny pieces of shiny decorative material

**glitzy** adj **glitzier, glitziest** (slang) showily attractive

**gloaming** n (Scot poetic) twilight

**gloat** v (often foll by over) regard one's own good fortune or the misfortune of others with smug or malicious pleasure

**glob** n rounded mass of thick fluid

**globe** n sphere with a map of the earth on it; spherical object; (S Afr) light bulb **the globe** the earth ▸ **global** adj worldwide; total or comprehensive ▸ **globalization** n process by which a company, etc., expands to operate internationally ▸ **global warming** increase in the overall temperature worldwide believed to be caused by the greenhouse effect ▸ **globally** adv ▸ **globetrotter** n habitual worldwide traveller ▸ **globetrotting** n, adj

**globule** n small round drop ▸ **globular** adj

**glockenspiel** n percussion instrument consisting of small metal bars played with hammers

**gloom** n melancholy or depression; darkness ▸ **gloomy** adj ▸ **gloomily** adv

**glory** n, pl **-ries** praise or honour; splendour; praiseworthy thing ▷ v **-rying, -ried** (foll by in) triumph or exalt ▸ **glorify** v make (something) seem more worthy than it is; praise ▸ **glorification** n ▸ **glorious** adj brilliantly beautiful; delightful; full of or conferring glory ▸ **gloriously** adv ▸ **glory hole** (informal) untidy cupboard or storeroom

**gloss**¹ n surface shine or lustre; paint or cosmetic giving a shiny finish ▸ **glossy** adj **-sier, -siest** smooth and shiny; (of a magazine) printed on shiny paper ▸ **glossily** adv ▸ **glossiness** n ▸ **gloss over** v (try to) cover up (a fault or error)

**gloss**² n explanatory comment added to the text of a book ▷ v add glosses to

**glossary** n, pl **-ries** list of special or technical words with definitions

**glottal** adj of the glottis

**glottis** n, pl **-tises** or **-tides** vocal cords and the space between them

**glove** n covering for the hand with individual sheaths for each finger and the thumb ▸ **gloved** adj covered by a glove or gloves ▸ **glove compartment, glove box** small storage area in the dashboard of a car

**glow** v emit light and heat without flames; shine; have a feeling of wellbeing or satisfaction; (of a colour) look warm; be hot ▷ n glowing light; warmth of colour; feeling of wellbeing ▸ **glow-worm** n insect giving out a green light

**glower** [rhymes with **power**] v, n scowl

**gloxinia** n tropical plant with large bell-shaped flowers

**glucose** n kind of sugar found in fruit

**glue** n natural or synthetic sticky substance used as an adhesive ▷ v **gluing** or **glueing, glued** fasten with glue; (foll by to) pay full attention to e.g. her eyes were glued to the TV ▸ **gluey** adj ▸ **glue-sniffing** n inhaling of glue fumes for intoxicating or hallucinatory effects

**glum** adj **glummer, glummest** sullen or gloomy ▸ **glumly** adv

**glut** n excessive supply ▷ v **glutting, glutted** oversupply

**gluten** [gloo-ten] n protein found in cereal grain

**glutinous** [gloo-tin-uss] adj sticky or gluey

**glutton** n greedy person; person with a great capacity for something ▶ **gluttonous** adj ▶ **gluttony** n

**glycerine, glycerin** n colourless sweet liquid used widely in chemistry and industry

**glycerol** [gliss-ser-ol] n technical name for **glycerine**

**GM** genetically modified

**gm** gram

**GMO** genetically modified organism

**GMT** Greenwich Mean Time

**gnarled** adj rough, twisted, and knobbly

**gnash** v grind (the teeth) together in anger or pain

**gnat** n small biting two-winged fly

**gnaw** v **gnawing, gnawed, gnawed** or **gnawn** bite or chew steadily; (foll by at) cause constant distress (to)

**gneiss** n coarse-grained metamorphic rock

**gnome** n imaginary creature like a little old man

**gnomic** [no-mik] adj of pithy sayings

**Gnosticism** n religious movement believing in intuitive spiritual knowledge ▶ **Gnostic** n, adj

**gnu** [noo] n oxlike S African antelope

**go** v **going, went, gone** move to or from a place; be in regular attendance at; depart; be, do, or become as specified; be allotted to a specific purpose or recipient; blend or harmonize; fail or break down; elapse; be got rid of; attend; be acceptable ▷ n attempt; verbal attack; turn **make a go of** be successful at ▶ **go back on** v break (a promise etc.) ▶ **go-between** n intermediary ▶ **go for** v (informal)

choose; attack; apply to equally ▶ **go-getter** n energetically ambitious person ▶ **go-go dancer** scantily dressed erotic dancer ▶ **go off** v explode; ring or sound; (informal) become stale or rotten; (informal) stop liking ▶ **go out** v go to entertainments or social functions; be romantically involved (with); be extinguished ▶ **go over** v examine or check ▶ **go-slow** n deliberate slowing of work-rate as an industrial protest ▶ **go through** v suffer or undergo; examine or search

**goad** v provoke (someone) to take some kind of action, usu. in anger ▷ n spur or provocation; spiked stick for driving cattle

**goal** n (Sport) posts through which the ball or puck has to be propelled to score; score made in this way; aim or purpose ▶ **goalie** n (informal) goalkeeper ▶ **goalkeeper** n player whose task is to stop shots entering the goal ▶ **goalpost** n one of the two posts marking the limit of a goal **move the goalposts** change the aims of an activity to ensure the desired result

**goanna** n large Australian lizard

**goat** n sure-footed ruminant animal with horns **get someone's goat** (slang) annoy someone ▶ **goatee** n pointed tuftlike beard

**gob** n lump of a soft substance; (Brit, Aust & NZ slang) mouth

**gobbet** n lump, esp. of food

**gobble**[1] v eat hastily and greedily

**gobble**[2] n rapid gurgling cry of the male turkey ▷ v make this noise

**gobbledegook, gobbledygook** n unintelligible (official) language or jargon

**goblet** n drinking cup without handles

**goblin** n (in folklore) small malevolent creature

**goby** n, pl **-by** or **-bies** small spiny-finned fish

**god** n spirit or being worshipped as having supernatural power; object of worship, idol; (**G-**) (in monotheistic religions) the Supreme Being, creator and ruler of the universe **the gods** top balcony in a theatre ▶ **goddess** n fem ▶ **godlike** adj ▶ **godly** adj devout or pious ▶ **godliness** n ▶ **god-fearing** adj pious and devout ▶ **godforsaken** adj desolate or dismal ▶ **godsend** n something unexpected but welcome

**godetia** n plant with showy flowers

**godparent** n person who promises at a child's baptism to bring the child up as a Christian ▶ **godchild** n child for whom a person stands as godparent ▶ **goddaughter** n ▶ **godfather** n male godparent; head of a criminal, esp. Mafia, organization ▶ **godmother** n ▶ **godson** n

**gogga** n (S Afr informal) any small insect

**goggle** v (of the eyes) bulge; stare ▶ **goggles** pl n protective spectacles

**going** n condition of the ground for walking or riding over; speed or progress; departure ▷ adj thriving; current or accepted ▶ **going-over** n, pl **goings-over** (informal) investigation or examination; scolding or thrashing ▶ **goings-on** pl n mysterious or unacceptable events

**goitre** [goy-ter] n swelling of the thyroid gland in the neck

**go-kart** n small low-powered racing car

**gold** n yellow precious metal; coins or articles made of this; colour of gold ▷ adj made of gold; gold-coloured ▶ **goldcrest** n small bird with a yellow crown ▶ **gold-digger** n (informal) woman who uses her sexual attractions to get money from a man ▶ **goldfinch** n kind of finch, the male of which has yellow-and-black wings ▶ **goldfish** n orange fish kept in ponds or aquariums ▶ **gold leaf** thin gold sheet used for gilding ▶ **gold medal** medal given to the winner of a competition or race

**golden** adj made of gold; gold-coloured; very successful or promising ▶ **golden eagle** large mountain eagle of the N hemisphere ▶ **golden handshake** (informal) payment to a departing employee ▶ **golden rule** important principle ▶ **golden wattle** Australian plant with yellow flowers that yields a useful gum and bark ▶ **golden wedding** fiftieth wedding anniversary

**golf** n outdoor game in which a ball is struck with clubs into a series of holes ▷ v play golf ▶ **golfer** n

**golliwog** n soft black-faced doll

**gonad** n organ producing reproductive cells, such as a testicle or ovary

**gondola** n long narrow boat used in Venice; suspended cabin of a cable car, airship, etc. ▶ **gondolier** n person who propels a gondola

**gone** v past participle of **go** ▶ **goner** n (informal) person or thing beyond help or recovery

**gong** n rimmed metal disc that produces a note when struck; (slang) medal

**gonorrhoea** [gon-or-**ree**-a] n venereal disease with a discharge from the genitals

**good** adj **better, best** giving pleasure; morally excellent;

beneficial; kindly; talented; well-behaved; valid; reliable; complete or full ▷ *n* benefit; positive moral qualities ▷ *pl* merchandise; property; **as good as** virtually **for good** permanently ▶ **goodness** *n* ▶ **goodly** *adj* considerable

▶ **goody** *n* (*informal*) hero in a book or film; enjoyable thing ▶ **goody-goody** *adj, n* smugly virtuous (person) ▶ **good-for-nothing** *adj, n* irresponsible or worthless (person)

▶ **Good Samaritan** person who helps another in distress

▶ **goodwill** *n* kindly feeling; value of a business in reputation etc. over and above its tangible assets

| **USAGE NOTE**
Note that *good* is an adjective. To modify a verb, use *well*: *She did well*

**goodbye** *interj, n* expression used on parting

**gooey** *adj* **gooier, gooiest** (*informal*) sticky and soft

**goof** (*informal*) *n* mistake ▷ *v* make a mistake

**Google**® *n* popular internet search engine ▷ *v* (**g-**) search for (something on the internet) using a search engine

**googly** *n, pl* **-lies** (*Cricket*) ball that spins unexpectedly from off to leg on the bounce

**goon** *n* (*informal*) stupid person; (*chiefly US*) hired thug ▶ **goon bag** *n* (*Aust informal*) plastic bladder inside a box of (usu cheap) wine

**goose** *n, pl* **geese** web-footed bird like a large duck; female of this bird ▶ **goose flesh, goose pimples** bumpy condition of the skin and bristling of the hair due to cold or fright ▶ **goose step** march step in which the leg is raised rigidly

**gooseberry** *n* edible yellowy-green berry; (*Brit informal*) unwanted

third person accompanying a couple

**gopher** [**go**-fer] *n* American burrowing rodent

**gore**[1] *n* blood from a wound

**gore**[2] *v* pierce with horns

**gorge** *n* deep narrow valley ▷ *v* eat greedily **make one's gorge rise** cause feelings of disgust or nausea

**gorgeous** *adj* strikingly beautiful or attractive; (*informal*) very pleasant ▶ **gorgeously** *adv*

**gorgon** *n* terrifying or repulsive woman

**Gorgonzola** *n* sharp-flavoured blue-veined Italian cheese

**gorilla** *n* largest of the apes, found in Africa

**gormless** *adj* (*informal*) stupid

**gorse** *n* prickly yellow-flowered shrub

**gory** *adj* **gorier, goriest** horrific or bloodthirsty; involving bloodshed

**goshawk** *n* large hawk

**gosling** *n* young goose

**gospel** *n* (**G-**) any of the first four books of the New Testament; unquestionable truth; Black religious music originating in the churches of the Southern US

**gossamer** *n* very fine fabric; filmy cobweb

**gossip** *n* idle talk, esp. about other people; person who engages in gossip ▷ *v* **gossiping, gossiped** engage in gossip ▶ **gossipy** *adj*

**got** *v* past of **get**; **have got** possess **have got to** need or be required to

**Goth** *n* member of an East Germanic people who invaded the Roman Empire

**Gothic** *adj* (of architecture) of or in the style common in Europe from the 12th–16th centuries, with pointed arches; of or in an 18th-century literary style characterized by gloom and the supernatural;

g

(of print) using a heavy ornate typeface

**gouache** n (painting using) watercolours mixed with glue

**Gouda** n mild-flavoured Dutch cheese

**gouge** [gowj] v scoop or force out; cut (a hole or groove) in (something) ▷ n hole or groove; chisel with a curved cutting edge

**goulash** [goo-lash] n rich stew seasoned with paprika

**gourd** [goord] n fleshy fruit of a climbing plant; its dried shell, used as a container

**gourmand** [goor-mand] n person who is very keen on food and drink

**gourmet** [goor-may] n connoisseur of food and drink

**gout** [gowt] n disease causing inflammation of the joints

**govern** v rule, direct, or control; exercise restraint over (temper etc.) ▶ **governable** adj ▶ **governance** n governing ▶ **governess** n woman teacher in a private household ▶ **governor** n official governing a province or state; senior administrator of a society, institution, or prison ▶ **governor general** representative of the Crown in a Commonwealth country

**government** n executive policy-making body of a state; exercise of political authority over a country or state; system by which a country or state is ruled ▶ **governmental** adj

**SPELLING TIP**
Note the n between the r and the m in **government**

**gown** n woman's long formal dress; surgeon's overall; official robe worn by judges, clergymen, etc.

**goy** n, pl **goyim** or **goys** (slang) Jewish word for a non-Jew

**GP** general practitioner

**GPS** Global Positioning System: a satellite-based navigation system: a satellite-based navigation system

**grab** v **grabbing**, **grabbed** grasp suddenly, snatch ▷ n sudden snatch; mechanical device for gripping

**grace** n beauty and elegance; polite, kind behaviour; goodwill or favour; delay granted; short prayer of thanks for a meal; (**G-**) title of a duke, duchess, or archbishop ▷ v add grace to ▶ **graceful** adj ▶ **gracefully** adv ▶ **graceless** adj ▶ **gracious** adj kind and courteous; condescendingly polite; elegant ▶ **graciously** adv ▶ **grace note** (Music) note ornamenting a melody

**grade** n place on a scale of quality, rank, or size; mark or rating; (US, Aust & S Afr) class in school ▷ v arrange in grades; assign a grade to **make the grade** succeed ▶ **gradation** n (stage in) a series of degrees or steps; arrangement in stages

**gradient** n (degree of) slope

**gradual** adj occurring, developing, or moving in small stages ▶ **gradually** adv

**graduate** v receive a degree or diploma; group by type or quality; mark (a container etc.) with units of measurement ▷ n holder of a degree ▶ **graduation** n

**graffiti** [graf-**fee**-tee] pl n words or drawings scribbled or sprayed on walls etc.

**SPELLING TIP**
Remember that the correct spelling of **graffiti** has two fs and only one t

**graft¹** n surgical transplant of skin or tissue; shoot of a plant set in the stalk of another ▷ v transplant (living tissue) surgically; insert (a plant shoot) in another stalk

**graft²** (*Brit informal*) n hard work; obtaining of money by misusing one's position ▷ v work hard ▶ **grafter** n

**grail** n same as **Holy Grail**

**grain** n seedlike fruit of a cereal plant; cereal plants in general; small hard particle; very small amount; arrangement of fibres, as in wood; texture or pattern resulting from this **go against the grain** be contrary to one's natural inclination ▶ **grainy** adj

**gram, gramme** n metric unit of mass equal to one thousandth of a kilogram

**grammar** n branch of linguistics dealing with the form, function, and order of words; use of words; book on the rules of grammar ▶ **grammarian** n ▶ **grammatical** adj according to the rules of grammar ▶ **grammatically** adv ▶ **grammar school** (*Brit*) esp. formerly, a secondary school providing an education with a strong academic bias

**gramophone** n old-fashioned type of record player

**grampus** n, pl **-puses** dolphin-like mammal

**gran** n (*Brit, Aust & NZ informal*) grandmother

**granary** n, pl **-ries** storehouse for grain

**grand** adj large or impressive, imposing; dignified or haughty; (*informal*) excellent; (of a total) final ▷ n (*slang*) thousand pounds or dollars; grand piano ▶ **grandchild** n child of one's child ▶ **granddaughter** n female grandchild ▶ **grandfather** n male grandparent ▶ **grandfather clock** tall standing clock with

a pendulum and wooden case ▶ **grandmother** n female grandparent ▶ **grandparent** n parent of one's parent ▶ **grand piano** large harp-shaped piano with the strings set horizontally ▶ **grand slam** winning of all the games or major tournaments in a sport in one season ▶ **grandson** n male grandchild ▶ **grandstand** n terraced block of seats giving the best view at a sports ground

**grandee** n person of high station

**grandeur** n magnificence; nobility or dignity

**grandiloquent** adj using pompous language ▶ **grandiloquence** n

**grandiose** adj imposing; pretentiously grand ▶ **grandiosity** n

**grange** n (*Brit*) country house with farm buildings

**granite** [gran-nit] n very hard igneous rock often used in building

**granny, grannie** n, pl **-nies** (*informal*) grandmother ▶ **granny flat** flat in or added to a house, suitable for an elderly parent

**grant** v consent to fulfil (a request); give formally; admit ▷ n sum of money provided by a government for a specific purpose, such as education **take for granted** accept as true without proof; take advantage of without due appreciation

**granule** n small grain ▶ **granular** adj of or like grains ▶ **granulated** adj (of sugar) in the form of coarse grains

**grape** n small juicy green or purple berry, eaten raw or used to produce wine, raisins, currants, or sultanas ▶ **grapevine** n grape-bearing vine; (*informal*) unofficial way of spreading news

**grapefruit** n large round yellow citrus fruit

**graph** n drawing showing the relation of different numbers or quantities plotted against a set of axes

**graphic** adj vividly descriptive; of or using drawing, painting, etc. ▶ **graphics** pl n diagrams, graphs, etc., esp. as used on a television programme or computer screen ▶ **graphically** adv

**graphite** n soft black form of carbon, used in pencil leads

**graphology** n study of handwriting ▶ **graphologist** n

**grapnel** n device with several hooks, used to grasp or secure things

**grapple** v try to cope with (something difficult); come to grips with (a person) ▶ **grappling iron** grapnel

**grasp** v grip something firmly; understand; try to seize ▷ n grip or clasp; understanding; total rule or possession ▶ **grasping** adj greedy or avaricious

**grass** n common type of plant with jointed stems and long narrow leaves, including cereals and bamboo; lawn; pasture land; (slang) marijuana; (Brit slang) person who informs, esp. on criminals ▷ v cover with grass; (often foll by on) (Brit slang) inform on ▶ **grassy** adj **-sier, -siest** ▶ **grasshopper** n jumping insect with long hind legs ▶ **grass roots** ordinary members of a group, as distinct from its leaders; essentials ▶ **grassroots** adj ▶ **grass tree** Australian plant with stiff grasslike leaves and small white flowers

**grate¹** v rub into small bits on a rough surface; scrape with a harsh rasping noise; annoy ▶ **grater** n

▶ **grating** adj harsh or rasping; annoying

**grate²** n framework of metal bars for holding fuel in a fireplace ▶ **grating** n framework of metal bars covering an opening

**grateful** adj feeling or showing gratitude ▶ **gratefully** adv

**gratify** v **-fying, -fied** satisfy or please; indulge (a desire or whim) ▶ **gratification** n

**gratis** adv, adj free, for nothing

**gratitude** n feeling of being thankful for a favour or gift

**gratuitous** adj unjustified e.g. gratuitous violence; given free ▶ **gratuitously** adv

**gratuity** n, pl **-ties** money given for services rendered, tip

**grave¹** n hole for burying a corpse ▶ **gravestone** n stone marking a grave ▶ **graveyard** n cemetery

**grave²** adj causing concern; serious and solemn ▶ **gravely** adv

**grave³** [rhymes with **halve**] n accent (´) over a vowel to indicate a special pronunciation

**gravel** n mixture of small stones and coarse sand ▶ **gravelled** adj covered with gravel ▶ **gravelly** adj covered with gravel; rough-sounding

**graven** adj carved or engraved

**gravid** [**grav**-id] adj (Med) pregnant

**gravitate** v be influenced or drawn towards; (Physics) move by gravity ▶ **gravitation** n ▶ **gravitational** adj

**gravity** n, pl **-ties** force of attraction of one object for another, esp. of objects to the earth; seriousness or importance; solemnity

**gravy** n, pl **-vies** juices from meat in cooking; sauce made from these

**gray** adj (chiefly US) grey

**grayling** n fish of the salmon family

**graze**[1] *v* feed on grass

**graze**[2] *v* scratch or scrape the skin; touch lightly in passing ▷ *n* slight scratch or scrape

**grease** *n* soft melted animal fat; any thick oily substance ▷ *v* apply grease to ▶ **greasy** *adj* **greasier, greasiest** covered with or containing grease ▶ **greasiness** *n* ▶ **greasepaint** *n* theatrical make-up

**great** *adj* large in size or number; important; pre-eminent; (*informal*) excellent ▶ **great-** *prefix* one generation older or younger than e.g. *great-grandfather* ▶ **greatly** *adv* ▶ **greatness** *n* ▶ **greatcoat** *n* heavy overcoat ▶ **Great Dane** very large dog with short smooth hair

**greave** *n* piece of armour for the shin

**grebe** *n* diving water bird

**Grecian** [**gree**-shan] *adj* of ancient Greece

**greed** *n* excessive desire for food, wealth, etc. ▶ **greedy** *adj* ▶ **greedily** *adv* ▶ **greediness** *n*

**Greek** *n* language of Greece; person from Greece ▷ *adj* of Greece, the Greeks, or the Greek language

**green** *adj* of a colour between blue and yellow; characterized by green plants or foliage; (**G-**) of or concerned with environmental issues; unripe; envious or jealous; immature or gullible ▷ *n* colour between blue and yellow; area of grass kept for a special purpose; (**G-**) person concerned with environmental issues ▷ *pl* green vegetables ▷ *v* make or become green ▶ **greenness** *n* ▶ **greenish, greeny** *adj* ▶ **greenery** *n* vegetation ▶ **green belt** protected area of open country around a town ▶ **greenfinch** *n* European finch with dull green plumage in

the male ▶ **green fingers** skill in gardening ▶ **greenfly** *n* green aphid, a common garden pest ▶ **greengage** *n* sweet green plum ▶ **greengrocer** *n* (*Brit*) shopkeeper selling vegetables and fruit ▶ **greenhorn** *n* (*chiefly US*) novice ▶ **greenhouse** *n* glass building for rearing plants ▶ **greenhouse effect** rise in the temperature of the earth caused by heat absorbed from the sun being unable to leave the atmosphere ▶ **greenhouse gas** any gas that contributes to the greenhouse effect ▶ **green light** signal to go; permission to proceed with something ▶ **greenshank** *n* large European sandpiper ▶ **greenstone** *n* (*NZ*) type of green jade used for Māori ornaments ▶ **green tax** tax imposed with the aim of regulating activity in a way that benefits the environment

**greet** *v* meet with expressions of welcome; receive in a specified manner; be immediately noticeable to ▶ **greeting** *n*

**gregarious** *adj* fond of company; (of animals) living in flocks or herds

**gremlin** *n* imaginary being blamed for mechanical malfunctions

**grenade** *n* small bomb thrown by hand or fired from a rifle ▶ **grenadier** *n* soldier of a regiment formerly trained to throw grenades

**grenadine** [gren-a-**deen**] *n* syrup made from pomegranates

**grevillea** *n* any of various Australian evergreen trees and shrubs

**grew** *v* past tense of **grow**

**grey** *adj* of a colour between black and white; (of hair) partly turned white; dismal or dark; dull or boring ▷ *n* grey colour; grey or white horse ▶ **greyed out** *adj* (of an item on a computer screen) unavailable ▶ **greying** adj (of hair) turning grey ▶ **greyish** adj ▶ **greyness** n ▶ **grey matter** (informal) brains

**greyhound** n swift slender dog used in racing

**grid** n network of horizontal and vertical lines, bars, etc.; national network of electricity supply cables

**griddle** n flat iron plate for cooking

**gridiron** n frame of metal bars for grilling food; American football pitch

**gridlock** n situation where traffic is not moving; point in a dispute at which no agreement can be reached ▶ **gridlocked** adj

**grief** n deep sadness ▶ **grieve** v (cause to) feel grief ▶ **grievance** n real or imaginary cause for complaint ▶ **grievous** adj very severe or painful; very serious

**griffin** n mythical monster with an eagle's head and wings and a lion's body

**grill** n device on a cooker that radiates heat downwards; grilled food; gridiron ▷ v cook under a grill; question relentlessly ▶ **grilling** n relentless questioning

**grille, grill** n grating over an opening

**grilse** [grillss] n salmon on its first return from the sea to fresh water

**grim** adj **grimmer, grimmest** stern; harsh or forbidding; very unpleasant ▶ **grimly** adv ▶ **grimness** n

**grimace** n ugly or distorted facial expression of pain, disgust, etc. ▷ v make a grimace

**grime** n ingrained dirt ▷ v make very dirty ▶ **grimy** adj

**grin** v **grinning, grinned** smile broadly, showing the teeth ▷ n broad smile

**grind** v **grinding, ground** crush or rub to a powder; smooth or sharpen by friction; scrape together with a harsh noise; oppress ▷ n (informal) hard work; act or sound of grinding ▶ **grind out** v produce in a routine or uninspired manner ▶ **grindstone** n stone used for grinding

**grip** n firm hold or grasp; way in which something is grasped; mastery or understanding; (US) travelling bag; handle ▷ v **gripping, gripped** grasp or hold tightly; hold the interest or attention of ▶ **gripping** adj

**gripe** v (informal) complain persistently ▷ n (informal) complaint; sudden intense bowel pain

**grisly** adj **-lier, -liest** horrifying or ghastly

**grist** n grain for grinding **grist to one's mill** something which can be turned to advantage

**gristle** n tough stringy animal tissue found in meat ▶ **gristly** adj

**grit** n rough particles of sand; courage ▷ pl coarsely ground grain ▷ v **gritting, gritted** spread grit on (an icy road etc.); clench or grind (the teeth) ▶ **gritty** adj **-tier, -tiest** ▶ **grittiness** n

**grizzle** v (Brit, Aust & NZ informal) whine or complain

**grizzled** adj grey-haired

**grizzly** n, pl **-zlies** large American bear (also **grizzly bear**)

**groan** n deep sound of grief or pain; (informal) complaint ▷ v utter a groan; (informal) complain

**groat** n (Hist) fourpenny piece

**grocer** n shopkeeper selling foodstuffs ▶ **grocery** n, pl **-ceries** business or premises of a grocer ▷ pl goods sold by a grocer

**grog** n (Brit, Aust & NZ) spirit, usu. rum, and water

**groggy** adj -**gier**, -**giest** (informal) faint, shaky, or dizzy

**groin** n place where the legs join the abdomen

**grommet** n ring or eyelet; (Med) tube inserted in the ear to drain fluid from the middle ear

**groom** n person who looks after horses; bridegroom; officer in a royal household ▷ v make or keep one's clothes and appearance neat and tidy; brush or clean a horse; train (someone) for a future role

**groove** n long narrow channel in a surface

**grope** v feel about or search uncertainly; (slang) fondle (someone) in a rough sexual way ▸ **groping** n

**gross** adj flagrant; vulgar; (slang) disgusting or repulsive; repulsively fat; total, without deductions ▷ n twelve dozen ▷ v make as total revenue before deductions ▸ **grossly** adv ▸ **grossness** n

**grotesque** [grow-**tesk**] adj strangely distorted; absurd ▷ n grotesque person or thing; artistic style mixing distorted human, animal, and plant forms ▸ **grotesquely** adv

**grotto** n, pl -**toes** or -**tos** small picturesque cave

**grotty** adj -**tier**, -**tiest** (informal) nasty or in bad condition

**grouch** (informal) v grumble or complain ▷ n person who is always complaining; persistent complaint ▸ **grouchy** ▷ adj

**ground¹** n surface of the earth; soil; area used for a specific purpose e.g. rugby ground; position in an argument or controversy ▷ pl enclosed land round a house; reason or motive; coffee dregs

▷ v base or establish; instruct in the basics; ban an aircraft or pilot from flying; run (a ship) aground ▸ **groundless** adj without reason ▸ **grounding** n basic knowledge of a subject ▸ **ground-breaking** adj innovative ▸ **ground floor** floor of a building level with the ground ▸ **groundnut** n (Brit) peanut ▸ **groundsheet** n waterproof sheet put on the ground under a tent ▸ **groundsman** n person employed to maintain a sports ground or park ▸ **groundswell** n rapidly developing general feeling or opinion ▸ **groundwork** n preliminary work

**ground²** v past of **grind**

**group** n number of people or things regarded as a unit; small band of musicians or singers ▷ v place or form into a group

**grouse¹** n stocky game bird; its flesh

**grouse²** v grumble or complain ▷ n complaint

**grout** n thin mortar ▷ v fill up with grout

**grove** n small group of trees

**grovel** [**grov**-el] v -**elling**, -**elled** behave humbly in order to win a superior's favour; crawl on the floor

**grow** v **growing**, **grew**, **grown** develop physically; (of a plant) exist; cultivate (plants); increase in size or degree; originate; become gradually e.g. it was growing dark ▸ **growth** n growing; increase; something grown or growing; tumour ▸ **grown-up** adj, n adult ▸ **grow up** v mature

**growl** v make a low rumbling sound; utter with a growl ▷ n growling sound

**groyne** n wall built out from the shore to control erosion

**grub** n legless insect larva; (slang) food ▷ v **grubbing**, **grubbed**

**g**

search carefully for something by digging or by moving things about; dig up the surface of (soil)

**grubby** adj **-bier, -biest** dirty
▶ **grubbiness** n

**grudge** v be unwilling to give or allow ▷ n resentment

**gruel** n thin porridge

**gruelling** adj exhausting or severe

**gruesome** adj causing horror and disgust

**gruff** adj rough or surly in manner or voice ▶ **gruffly** adv
▶ **gruffness** n

**grumble** v complain; rumble ▷ n complaint; rumble ▶ **grumbler** n
▶ **grumbling** adj, n

**grumpy** adj **grumpier, grumpiest** bad-tempered ▶ **grumpily** adv
▶ **grumpiness** n

**grunge** n style of rock music with a fuzzy guitar sound; deliberately untidy and uncoordinated fashion style

**grunt** v make a low short gruff sound, like a pig ▷ n pig's sound; gruff noise

**Gruyère** [grew-yair] n hard yellow Swiss cheese with holes

**gryphon** n same as **griffin**

**GST** (in Australia, New Zealand, and Canada) Goods and Services Tax

**G-string** n small strip of cloth covering the genitals and attached to a waistband

**GT** (of a sports car) gran turismo

**guano** [gwah-no] n dried sea-bird manure, used as fertilizer

**guarantee** n formal assurance, esp. in writing, that a product will meet certain standards; something that makes a specified condition or outcome certain ▷ v **-teeing, -teed** give a guarantee; secure against risk etc.; ensure
▶ **guarantor** n person who gives or is bound by a guarantee

**guard** v watch over to protect or to prevent escape ▷ n person or group that guards; official in charge of a train; protection; screen for enclosing anything dangerous; posture of defence in sports such as boxing or fencing ▷ pl (**G-**) regiment with ceremonial duties ▶ **guarded** adj cautious or noncommittal
▶ **guardedly** adv ▶ **guard against** v take precautions against
▶ **guardsman** n member of the Guards

**guardian** n keeper or protector; person legally responsible for a child, mentally ill person, etc.
▶ **guardianship** n

**guava** [gwah-va] n yellow-skinned tropical American fruit

**gudgeon** n small freshwater fish

**Guernsey** [gurn-zee] n breed of dairy cattle

**guerrilla, guerilla** n member of an unofficial armed force fighting regular forces

**guess** v estimate or draw a conclusion without proper knowledge; estimate correctly by guessing; suppose ▷ n estimate or conclusion reached by guessing
▶ **guesswork** n process or results of guessing

**guest** n person entertained at another's house or at another's expense; invited performer or speaker; customer at a hotel or restaurant ▷ v appear as a visiting player or performer ▶ **guesthouse** n boarding house

**guff** n (Brit, Aust & NZ slang) nonsense

**guffaw** n crude noisy laugh ▷ v laugh in this way

**guide** n person who conducts tour expeditions; person who shows the way; book of instruction or information; model for behaviour;

something used to gauge
something or to help in planning
one's actions; (**G-**) member of an
organization for girls equivalent
to the Scouts ▷ *v* act as a guide for;
control, supervise, or influence
▶ **guidance** *n* leadership,
instruction, or advice ▶ **guided
missile** missile whose flight is
controlled electronically ▶ **guide
dog** dog trained to lead a blind
person ▶ **guideline** *n* set principle
for doing something

**guild** *n* organization or club; (*Hist*)
society of men in the same trade
or craft

**guilder** *n* former monetary unit of
the Netherlands

**guile** [**gile**] *n* cunning or deceit
▶ **guileful** *adj* ▶ **guileless** *adj*

**guillemot** [**gil-lee-mot**] *n* black-
and-white diving sea bird of N
hemisphere

**guillotine** *n* machine for
beheading people; device for
cutting paper or sheet metal;
method of preventing lengthy
debate in parliament by fixing a
time for taking the vote ▷ *v* behead
by guillotine; limit debate by the
guillotine

**guilt** *n* fact or state of having done
wrong; remorse for wrongdoing
▶ **guiltless** *adj* innocent ▶ **guilty**
*adj* responsible for an offence or
misdeed; feeling or showing guilt
▶ **guiltily** *adv*

**guinea** *n* former British monetary
unit worth 21 shillings (1.05
pounds); former gold coin of this
value ▶ **guinea fowl** wild bird
related to the pheasant ▶ **guinea
pig** tailless S American rodent,
commonly kept as a pet; (*informal*)
person used for experimentation

**guise** [rhymes with **size**] *n* false
appearance; external appearance

**guitar** *n* stringed instrument
with a flat back and a long neck,
played by plucking or strumming
▶ **guitarist** *n*

**gulch** *n* (*US*) deep narrow valley

**gulf** *n* large deep bay; chasm;
large difference in opinion or
understanding

**gull** *n* long-winged sea bird

**gullet** *n* muscular tube through
which food passes from the mouth
to the stomach

**gullible** *adj* easily tricked
▶ **gullibility** *n*

**gully** *n*, *pl* **-lies** channel cut by
running water

**gulp** *v* swallow hastily; gasp ▷ *n*
gulping; thing gulped

**gum¹** *n* firm flesh in which the teeth
are set ▶ **gummy** *adj* **-mier, -miest**
toothless

**gum²** *n* sticky substance obtained
from certain trees; adhesive;
chewing gum; gumdrop; gum
tree ▷ *v* **gumming, gummed** stick
with gum ▶ **gummy** *adj* **-mier,
-miest** ▶ **gumboots** *pl n* (*chiefly
Brit*) Wellington boots ▶ **gumdrop**
*n* hard jelly-like sweet ▶ **gum tree**
eucalyptus tree

**gumption** *n* (*informal*)
resourcefulness; courage

**gun** *n* weapon with a metal tube
from which missiles are fired by
explosion; device from which a
substance is ejected under pressure
▷ *v* **gunning, gunned** cause (an
engine) to run at high speed **jump
the gun** act prematurely ▶ **gunner**
*n* artillery soldier ▶ **gunnery** *n* use
or science of large guns ▶ **gunboat**
*n* small warship ▶ **gun dog** dog
used to retrieve game ▶ **gun down**
*v* shoot (a person) ▶ **gun for** *v* seek
or pursue vigorously ▶ **gunman**
*n* armed criminal ▶ **gunmetal**
*n* alloy of copper, tin, and zinc

g

▷ adj dark grey ▶ **gunpowder** n explosive mixture of potassium nitrate, sulphur, and charcoal
▶ **gunrunning** n smuggling of guns and ammunition
▶ **gunrunner** n ▶ **gunshot** n shot or range of a gun

**gunge** n (informal) sticky unpleasant substance ▶ **gungy** adj **-gier, -giest**

**gunny** n strong coarse fabric used for sacks

**gunwale, gunnel** [gun-nel] n top of a ship's side

**gunyah** n (Aust) hut or shelter in the bush

**guppy** n, pl **-pies** small colourful aquarium fish

**gurgle** v, n (make) a bubbling noise

**Gurkha** n person, esp. a soldier, belonging to a Hindu people of Nepal

**guru** n Hindu or Sikh religious teacher or leader; leader, adviser, or expert

**gush** v flow out suddenly and profusely; express admiration effusively ▷ n sudden copious flow; sudden surge of strong feeling
▶ **gusher** n spurting oil well

**gusset** n piece of material sewn into a garment to strengthen it

**gust** n sudden blast of wind ▷ v blow in gusts ▶ **gusty** adj

**gusto** n enjoyment or zest

**gut** n intestine; (informal) fat stomach; short for **catgut** ▷ pl internal organs; (informal) courage ▷ v **gutting, gutted** remove the guts from; (of a fire) destroy the inside of (a building) ▷ adj basic or instinctive e.g. a gut reaction
▶ **gutsy** adj **-sier, -siest** (informal) courageous; vigorous or robust e.g. a gutsy performance ▶ **gutted** adj (Brit, Aust & NZ informal) disappointed and upset

**gutta-percha** n whitish rubbery substance obtained from an Asian tree

**gutter** n shallow channel for carrying away water from a roof or roadside ▷ v (of a candle) burn unsteadily, with wax running down the sides **the gutter** degraded or criminal environment ▶ **guttering** n material for gutters ▶ **gutter press** newspapers that rely on sensationalism ▶ **guttersnipe** n (Brit) neglected slum child

**guttural** adj (of a sound) produced at the back of the throat; (of a voice) harsh-sounding

**guy¹** n (informal) man or boy; effigy of Guy Fawkes burnt on November 5 (**Guy Fawkes Day**)

**guy²** n rope or chain to steady or secure something ▶ **guy rope**

**guzzle** v eat or drink greedily

**gybe** [jibe] v (of a fore-and-aft sail) swing suddenly from one side to the other; (of a boat) change course by letting the sail gybe

**gym** n gymnasium; gymnastics

**gymkhana** [jim-kah-na] n horse-riding competition

**gymnasium** n large room with equipment for physical training
▶ **gymnast** n expert in gymnastics
▶ **gymnastic** adj ▶ **gymnastics** pl n exercises to develop strength and agility

**gynaecology** [guy-nee-kol-la-jee] n branch of medicine dealing with diseases and conditions specific to women ▶ **gynaecological** adj
▶ **gynaecologist** n

**gypsophila** n garden plant with small white flowers

**gypsum** n chalklike mineral used to make plaster of Paris

**Gypsy** n, pl **-sies** member of a travelling people found throughout Europe

**gyrate** [jire-**rate**] v rotate or spiral about a point or axis ▶ **gyration** n ▶ **gyratory** adj gyrating

**gyrocompass** n compass using a gyroscope

**gyroscope** [**jire**-oh-skohp] n disc rotating on an axis that can turn in any direction, so the disc maintains the same position regardless of the movement of the surrounding structure ▶ **gyroscopic** adj

**H** (Chem) hydrogen

**habeas corpus** [hay-bee-ass **kor**-puss] n writ ordering a prisoner to be brought before a court

**haberdasher** n (Brit, Aust & NZ) dealer in small articles used for sewing ▶ **haberdashery** n

**habit** n established way of behaving; addiction to a drug; costume of a monk or nun

**habitable** adj fit to be lived in ▶ **habitation** n (occupation of) a dwelling place

**habitat** n natural home of an animal or plant

**habitual** adj done regularly and repeatedly ▶ **habitually** adv

**habituate** v accustom ▶ **habituation** n ▶ **habitué** [hab-**it**-yew-ay] n frequent visitor to a place

**hacienda** [hass-ee-**end**-a] n ranch or large estate in Latin America

**hack**[1] v cut or chop violently; (Brit & NZ informal) tolerate

**hack**[2] n (inferior) writer or journalist; horse kept for riding

**hacker** n (slang) computer enthusiast, esp. one who breaks into the computer system of a company or government

**hackles** pl n **make one's hackles rise** make one feel angry or hostile

**hackney** n (Brit) taxi

**hackneyed** adj (of a word or phrase) unoriginal and overused

**hacksaw** n small saw for cutting metal

**had** v past of **have**

**haddock** n edible sea fish of N Atlantic

**Hades** [hay-deez] n (Greek myth) underworld home of the dead

**hadj** n same as **hajj**

**haematology** n study of blood and its diseases

**haemoglobin** [hee-moh-**globe**-in] n protein found in red blood cells which carries oxygen

**haemophilia** [hee-moh-**fill**-lee-a] n hereditary illness in which the blood does not clot ▶ **haemophiliac** n

**haemorrhage** [hem-or-ij] n heavy bleeding ▷ v bleed heavily

> ▌ **SPELLING TIP**
> The Collins Corpus shows that the most usual mistake in spelling **haemorrhage** is to miss out the second h, which is silent

**haemorrhoids** [hem-or-oydz] pl n swollen veins in the anus (also **piles**)

**hafnium** n (Chem) metallic element found in zirconium ores

**haft** n handle of an axe, knife, or dagger

**hag** n ugly old woman ▶ **hag-ridden** adj distressed or worried

**haggard** adj looking tired and ill

**haggis** n Scottish dish made from sheep's offal, oatmeal, suet, and seasonings, boiled in a bag made from the sheep's stomach

**haggle** v bargain or wrangle over a price

**hagiography** n, pl -**phies** writing about the lives of the saints

**hail**¹ n (shower of) small pellets of ice; large number of insults, missiles, blows, etc. ▷ v fall as or like hail ▶ **hailstone** n

**hail**² v call out to, greet; stop (a taxi) by waving; acknowledge publicly ▶ **hail from** v come originally from

**hair** n threadlike growth on the skin; such growths collectively, esp. on the head ▶ **hairy** adj covered with hair; (slang) dangerous or exciting ▶ **hairiness** n ▶ **hairclip** n small bent metal hairpin ▶ **hairdo** n (informal) hairstyle ▶ **hairdresser** n person who cuts and styles hair ▶ **hairgrip** n (Brit) same as **hairclip** ▶ **hairline** n edge of hair at the top of the forehead ▷ adj very fine or narrow ▶ **hairpin** n U-shaped wire used to hold the hair in place ▶ **hairpin bend** very sharp bend in a road ▶ **hair-raising** adj frightening or exciting ▶ **hair-splitting** n, adj making petty distinctions ▶ **hairstyle** n cut and arrangement of a person's hair

**hajj** n pilgrimage a Muslim makes to Mecca

**haka** n (NZ) ceremonial Māori dance with chanting; similar dance performed by a sports team before a match

**hake** n edible sea fish of N hemisphere; (Aust) same as **barracouta**

**hakea** [hah-kee-a] n Australian tree or shrub with hard woody fruit

**halal** n meat from animals slaughtered according to Muslim law

**halberd** n (Hist) spear with an axe blade

**halcyon** [hal-see-on] adj peaceful and happy ▶ **halcyon days** time of peace and happiness

**hale** adj healthy, robust

**half** n, pl **halves** either of two equal parts; (informal) half-pint of beer etc.; half-price ticket ▷ adj denoting one of two equal parts ▷ adv to the extent of half; partially ▶ **half-baked** adj (informal) not properly thought out ▶ **half-brother,**

**half-sister** n brother or sister related through one parent only
▶ **half-caste** n (offens) person with parents of different races
▶ **half-cocked** adj **go off half-cocked, go off at half-cock** fail because of inadequate preparation
▶ **half-hearted** adj unenthusiastic
▶ **half-life** n time taken for half the atoms in radioactive material to decay ▶ **half-nelson** n wrestling hold in which one wrestler's arm is pinned behind his back by his opponent ▶ **half-pie** adj (NZ informal) incomplete ▶ **half-pipe** n large U-shaped ramp used for skateboarding, snowboarding, etc.
▶ **half-timbered** adj (of a house) having an exposed wooden frame filled in with plaster ▶ **half-time** n (Sport) short rest period between two halves of a game ▶ **halftone** n illustration showing lights and shadows by means of very small dots ▶ **halfway** adv, adj at or to half the distance ▶ **halfwit** n foolish or stupid person

**halfpenny** [**hayp**-nee] n former British coin worth half an old penny

**halibut** n large edible flatfish of N Atlantic

**halitosis** n unpleasant-smelling breath

**hall** n (also **hallway**) entrance passage; large room or building for public meetings, dances, etc.; (Brit) large country house

**hallelujah** [hal-ee-**loo**-ya] interj exclamation of praise to God

**hallmark** n typical feature; mark indicating the standard of tested gold and silver ▷ v stamp with a hallmark

**hallo** interj same as **hello**

**hallowed** adj regarded as holy

**Halloween, Hallowe'en** n October 31, celebrated by children

by dressing up as ghosts, witches, etc.

**hallucinate** v seem to see something that is not really there ▶ **hallucination** n
▶ **hallucinatory** adj
▶ **hallucinogen** n drug that causes hallucinations ▶ **hallucinogenic** adj

**halo** [**hay**-loh] n, pl **-loes** or **-los** ring of light round the head of a sacred figure; circle of refracted light round the sun or moon

**halogen** [**hal**-oh-jen] n (Chem) any of a group of nonmetallic elements including chlorine and iodine

**halt** v come or bring to a stop ▷ n temporary stop; minor railway station without a building
▶ **halting** adj hesitant, uncertain

**halter** n strap round a horse's head with a rope to lead it with
▶ **halterneck** n woman's top or dress with a strap fastened at the back of the neck

**halve** v divide in half; reduce by half

**halves** n plural of **half**

**halyard** n rope for raising a ship's sail or flag

**ham¹** n smoked or salted meat from a pig's thigh ▶ **ham-fisted** adj clumsy

**ham²** (informal) n amateur radio operator; actor who overacts ▷ v **hamming, hammed** ▶ **ham it up** overact

**hamburger** n minced beef shaped into a flat disc, cooked and usu. served in a bread roll

**hamlet** n small village

**hammer** n tool with a heavy metal head and a wooden handle, used to drive in nails etc.; part of a gun which causes the bullet to be fired; heavy metal ball on a wire, thrown as a sport; auctioneer's mallet; striking mechanism in a piano ▷ v hit (as if) with a hammer;

**h**

(*informal*) punish or defeat utterly
**go at it hammer and tongs**
do something, esp. argue, very
vigorously ▶ **hammerhead** *n*
shark with a wide flattened head
▶ **hammer toe** condition in
which a toe is permanently bent
at the joint

**hammock** *n* hanging bed made of
canvas or net

**hamper**[1] *v* make it difficult for
(someone or something) to move
or progress

**hamper**[2] *n* large basket with a lid;
selection of food and drink packed
as a gift

**hamster** *n* small rodent with a
short tail and cheek pouches

> **SPELLING TIP**
> Spelling **hamster** as **hampster**
> is a common mistake. There
> is no *p*

**hamstring** *n* tendon at the back
of the knee ▷ *v* make it difficult for
(someone) to take any action

**hand** *n* part of the body at the end
of the arm, consisting of a palm,
four fingers, and a thumb; style of
handwriting; round of applause;
manual worker; pointer on a
dial, esp. on a clock; cards dealt
to a player in a card game; unit
of length of four inches (10.16
centimetres) used to measure
horses ▷ *v* pass, give **have a hand
in** be involved in **lend a hand**
help **out of hand** beyond control;
definitely and finally; **to hand, at
hand, on hand** nearby **win hands
down** win easily ▶ **handbag** *n*
woman's small bag for carrying
personal articles in ▶ **handbill** *n*
small printed notice ▶ **handbook**
*n* small reference or instruction
book ▶ **handcuff** *n* one of a linked
pair of metal rings designed to be
locked round a prisoner's wrists

by the police ▷ *v* put handcuffs on
▶ **hand-held** *adj* (of a film camera)
held rather than mounted, as
in close-up action shots; (of a
computer) able to be held in the
hand ▷ *n* computer that can be
held in the hand ▶ **hand-out** *n*
clothing, food, or money given to a
needy person; written information
given out at a talk etc. ▶ **hands-
free** *adj, n* (of) a device allowing
the user to make and receive
phonecalls without holding the
handset ▶ **hands-on** *adj* involving
practical experience of equipment
▶ **handstand** *n* act of supporting
the body on the hands in an upside-
down position ▶ **handwriting** *n*
(style of) writing by hand

**handful** *n* amount that can be
held in the hand; small number;
(*informal*) person or animal that is
difficult to control

**handicap** *n* physical or mental
disability; something that makes
progress difficult; contest in
which the competitors are given
advantages or disadvantages in an
attempt to equalize their chances;
advantage or disadvantage given
▷ *v* make it difficult for (someone)
to do something

**handicraft** *n* objects made by hand

**handiwork** *n* result of someone's
work or activity

**handkerchief** *n* small square of
fabric used to wipe the nose

> **SPELLING TIP**
> People often forget to write a
> *d* in **handkerchief**, probably
> because they don't say it or hear
> it either

**handle** *n* part of an object that
is held so that it can be used ▷ *v*
hold, feel, or move with the hands;
control or deal with ▶ **handler** *n*
person who controls an animal

▶ **handlebars** pl n curved metal bar used to steer a cycle

**handsome** adj (esp. of a man) good-looking; large or generous e.g. a handsome profit

**handy** adj **handier, handiest** convenient, useful; good at manual work ▶ **handily** adv ▶ **handyman** n man who is good at making or repairing things

**hang** v **hanging, hung** attach or be attached at the top with the lower part free; (past tense **hanged**) suspend or be suspended by the neck until dead; fasten to a wall **get the hang of** (informal) begin to understand ▶ **hanger** n curved piece of wood, wire, or plastic, with a hook, for hanging up clothes (also **coat hanger**) ▶ **hang back** v hesitate, be reluctant ▶ **hangman** n man who executes people by hanging ▶ **hangover** n headache and nausea as a result of drinking too much alcohol ▶ **hang-up** n (informal) emotional or psychological problem

**hangar** n large shed for storing aircraft

**hangdog** adj guilty, ashamed e.g. a hangdog look

**hang-glider** n glider with a light framework from which the pilot hangs in a harness ▶ **hang-gliding** n

**hangi** n, pl **-gi** or **-gis** (NZ) Māori oven consisting of a hole in the ground filled with hot stones

**hank** n coil, esp. of yarn

**hanker** v (foll by after or for) desire intensely

**hanky, hankie** n, pl **hankies** (informal) handkerchief

**hanky-panky** n (informal) illicit sexual relations

**hansom cab** n (formerly) two-wheeled horse-drawn carriage for hire

**haphazard** adj not organized or planned ▶ **haphazardly** adv

**hapless** adj unlucky

**happen** v take place, occur; chance (to be or do something) ▶ **happening** n event, occurrence

**happy** adj **-pier, -piest** feeling or causing joy; lucky, fortunate ▶ **happily** adv ▶ **happiness** n ▶ **happy-go-lucky** adj carefree and cheerful

**hara-kiri** n (formerly, in Japan) ritual suicide by disembowelling

**harangue** v address angrily or forcefully ▷ n angry or forceful speech

**harass** v annoy or trouble constantly ▶ **harassed** adj ▶ **harassment** n

> **SPELLING TIP**
> Note there is only one r but two ss in **harass** and its derivatives

**harbinger** [har-binj-a] n someone or something that announces the approach of something

**harbour** n sheltered port ▷ v maintain secretly in the mind; give shelter or protection to

**hard** adj firm, solid, or rigid; difficult; requiring a lot of effort; unkind, unfeeling; causing pain, sorrow, or hardship; (of water) containing calcium salts which stop soap lathering freely; (of a drug) strong and addictive ▷ adv with great energy or effort; with great intensity **hard of hearing** unable to hear properly **hard up** (informal) short of money ▶ **harden** v ▶ **hardness** n ▶ **hardship** n suffering; difficult circumstances ▶ **hard-bitten** adj tough and determined ▶ **hard-boiled** adj (of an egg) boiled until solid; (informal) tough, unemotional ▶ **hard copy** computer output printed on paper ▶ **hardfill** n (NZ & S Afr) stone waste

material used for landscaping
▶ **hard-headed** adj shrewd,
practical ▶ **hardhearted** adj
unsympathetic, uncaring ▶ **hard
sell** aggressive sales technique
▶ **hard shoulder** surfaced verge
at the edge of a motorway for
emergency stops

**hardback** n book with a stiff cover

**hardboard** n thin stiff board made
of compressed sawdust and wood
chips

**hard drive** n (Computing)
mechanism that handles the
reading, writing, and storage of
data on the hard disk of a computer

**hardly** adv scarcely or not at all;
with difficulty

**hardware** n metal tools or
implements; machinery used in a
computer system; heavy military
equipment, such as tanks and
missiles

**hardwood** n wood of a
broadleaved tree such as oak or ash

**hardy** adj **hardier, hardiest** able
to stand difficult conditions
▶ **hardiness** n

**hare** n animal like a large rabbit,
with longer ears and legs ▷ v
(usu. foll by off) run (away) quickly
▶ **harebell** n blue bell-shaped
flower ▶ **harebrained** adj foolish or
impractical ▶ **harelip** n slight split
in the upper lip

**harem** n (apartments of) a Muslim
man's wives and concubines

**haricot bean** [har-rik-oh] n small
pale edible bean, usu. sold dried

**harissa** n (in North African cuisine)
hot sauce made from chilli peppers,
spices, and olive oil

**hark** v (old-fashioned) listen ▶ **hark
back** v return (to an earlier subject)

**harlequin** n stock comic character
with a diamond-patterned costume
and mask ▷ adj in many colours

**harlot** n (lit) prostitute

**harm** v injure physically, mentally,
or morally ▷ n physical, mental,
or moral injury ▶ **harmful** adj
▶ **harmless** adj

**harmonica** n small wind instrument
played by sucking and blowing

**harmonium** n keyboard
instrument like a small organ

**harmony** n, pl **-nies** peaceful
agreement and cooperation;
pleasant combination of
notes sounded at the same
time ▶ **harmonious** adj
▶ **harmoniously** adv
▶ **harmonic** adj of harmony
▶ **harmonics** n science of musical
sounds ▶ **harmonize** v blend well
together ▶ **harmonization** n

**harness** n arrangement of straps
for attaching a horse to a cart or
plough; set of straps fastened
round someone's body to attach
something e.g. a safety harness
▷ v put a harness on; control
(something) in order to make
use of it

**harp** n large triangular stringed
instrument played with the fingers
▶ **harpist** n ▶ **harp on about** v talk
about continuously

**harpoon** n barbed spear attached
to a rope used for hunting whales
▷ v spear with a harpoon

**harpsichord** n stringed keyboard
instrument

**harpy** n, pl **-pies** nasty or bad-
tempered woman

**harridan** n nagging or vicious
woman

**harrier** n cross-country runner

**harrow** n implement used to
break up lumps of soil ▷ v draw a
harrow over

**harrowing** adj very distressing

**harry** v **-rying, -ried** keep asking
(someone) to do something, pester

**harsh** adj severe and difficult to cope with; unkind, unsympathetic; extremely hard, bright, or rough ▶ **harshly** adv ▶ **harshness** n

**hart** n adult male deer

**harum-scarum** adj reckless

**harvest** n (season for) the gathering of crops; crops gathered ▷ v gather (a ripened crop) ▶ **harvester** n

**has** v third person singular of the present tense of **have** ▶ **has-been** n (informal) person who is no longer popular or successful

**hash¹** n dish of diced cooked meat and vegetables reheated **make a hash of** (informal) spoil, do badly

**hash²** n (informal) hashish

**hashish** [hash-eesh] n drug made from the cannabis plant, smoked for its intoxicating effects

**hashtag** n (Computing) (on the Twitter website) word or phrase preceded by a hash mark, used to denote the topic of a post

**hasp** n clasp that fits over a staple and is secured by a bolt or padlock, used as a fastening

**hassle** (informal) n trouble, bother ▷ v bother or annoy

**hassock** n cushion for kneeling on in church

**haste** n (excessive) quickness **make haste** hurry, rush ▶ **hasten** v (cause to) hurry ▶ **hasty** adj (too) quick ▶ **hastily** adv

**hat** n covering for the head, often with a brim, usu. worn to give protection from the weather **keep something under one's hat** keep something secret ▶ **hat trick** any three successive achievements, esp. in sport

**hatch¹** v (cause to) emerge from an egg; devise (a plot)

**hatch²** n hinged door covering an opening in a floor or wall; opening in the wall between a kitchen and a dining area; door in an aircraft or spacecraft ▶ **hatchback** n car with a lifting door at the back ▶ **hatchway** n opening in the deck of a ship

**hatchet** n small axe **bury the hatchet** become reconciled ▶ **hatchet job** malicious verbal or written attack ▶ **hatchet man** (informal) person carrying out unpleasant tasks for an employer

**hate** v dislike intensely; be unwilling (to do something) ▷ n intense dislike; person or thing hated ▶ **hateful** adj causing or deserving hate ▶ **hater** n ▶ **hatred** n intense dislike

**haughty** adj -tier, -tiest proud, arrogant ▶ **haughtily** adv ▶ **haughtiness** n

**haul** v pull or drag with effort ▷ n amount gained by effort or theft **long haul** something that takes a lot of time and effort ▶ **haulage** n (charge for) transporting goods ▶ **haulier** n firm or person that transports goods by road

**haunch** n human hip or fleshy hindquarter of an animal

**haunt** v visit in the form of a ghost; remain in the memory or thoughts of ▷ n place visited frequently ▶ **haunted** adj frequented by ghosts; worried ▶ **haunting** adj memorably beautiful or sad

**haute couture** [oat koo-ture] n (French) high fashion

**hauteur** [oat-ur] n haughtiness

**have** v **has, having, had** possess, hold; receive, take, or obtain; experience or be affected by; (foll by to) be obliged, must e.g. I had to go; cause to be done; give birth to; used to form past tenses (with a past participle) e.g. we have looked; she had done enough **have**

**it out** (*informal*) settle a matter by argument ▶ **have on** *v* wear; (*informal*) tease or trick ▶ **have up** *v* bring to trial

**haven** *n* place of safety

**haversack** *n* canvas bag carried on the back or shoulder

**havoc** *n* disorder and confusion

**haw** *n* hawthorn berry

**hawk¹** *n* bird of prey with a short hooked bill and very good eyesight; (*Politics*) supporter or advocate of warlike policies ▶ **hawkish, hawklike** *adj* ▶ **hawk-eyed** *adj* having very good eyesight

**hawk²** *v* offer (goods) for sale in the street or door-to-door ▶ **hawker** *n*

**hawk³** *v* cough noisily

**hawser** *n* large rope used on a ship

**hawthorn** *n* thorny shrub or tree

**hay** *n* grass cut and dried as fodder ▶ **hay fever** allergy to pollen, causing sneezing and watery eyes ▶ **haystack** *n* large pile of stored hay ▶ **haywire** *adj* **go haywire** (*informal*) not function properly

**hazard** *n* something that could be dangerous ▷ *v* put in danger; make (a guess) ▶ **hazardous** *adj*

**haze** *n* mist, often caused by heat ▶ **hazy** *adj* not clear, misty; confused or vague

**hazel** *n* small tree producing edible nuts ▷ *adj* (of eyes) greenish-brown ▶ **hazelnut** *n*

**H-bomb** *n* hydrogen bomb

**he** *pron* referring to male person or animal ▷ *n* male person or animal e.g. *a he-goat*

**head** *n* upper or front part of the body, containing the sense organs and the brain; mind and mental abilities; upper or most forward part of anything; person in charge of a group, organization, or school; pus-filled tip of a spot or boil; white froth on beer; (*pl* **head**) person or animal considered as a unit ▷ *adj* chief, principal ▷ *v* be at the top or front of; be in charge of; move (in a particular direction); hit (a ball) with the head; provide with a heading **go to one's head** make one drunk or conceited **head over heels (in love)** very much in love **not make head nor tail of** not understand **off one's head** (*slang*) foolish or insane ▶ **heads** *adv* (*informal*) with the side of a coin which has a portrait of a head on it uppermost ▶ **header** *n* striking a ball with the head; headlong fall ▶ **heading** *n* title written or printed at the top of a page ▶ **heady** *adj* intoxicating or exciting ▶ **headache** *n* continuous pain in the head; cause of worry or annoyance ▶ **headboard** *n* vertical board at the top end of a bed ▶ **headdress** *n* decorative head covering ▶ **head-hunt** *v* (of a company) approach and offer a job to (a person working for a rival company) ▶ **head-hunter** *n* ▶ **headland** *n* area of land jutting out into the sea ▶ **headlight** *n* powerful light on the front of a vehicle ▶ **headline** *n* title at the top of a newspaper article, esp. on the front page ▷ *pl* main points of a news broadcast ▶ **headlong** *adv, adj* with the head first; hastily ▶ **headphones** *pl n* two small loudspeakers held against the ears ▶ **headquarters** *pl n* centre from which operations are directed ▶ **head start** advantage in a competition ▶ **headstone** *n* memorial stone on a grave ▶ **headstrong** *adj* self-willed, obstinate ▶ **headway** *n* progress ▶ **headwind** *n* wind blowing against the course of an aircraft or ship

**heal** v make or become well
▶ **healer** n

**health** n normal (good) condition of someone's body ▶ **health food** natural food, organically grown and free from additives
▶ **healthy** adj having good health; of or producing good health; functioning well, sound
▶ **healthily** adv

**heap** n pile of things one on top of another; (also **heaps**) large number or quantity ▷ v gather into a pile; (foll by on) give liberally (to)

**hear** v **hearing, heard** perceive (a sound) by ear; listen to; learn or be informed; (Law) try (a case) **hear! hear!** exclamation of approval or agreement ▶ **hearer** n ▶ **hearing** n ability to hear; trial of a case **within hearing** close enough to be heard

**hearsay** n gossip, rumour

**hearse** n funeral car used to carry a coffin

**heart** n organ that pumps blood round the body; centre of emotions, esp. love; courage, spirit; central or most important part; figure representing a heart; playing card with red heart-shaped symbols **break someone's heart** cause someone great grief **by heart** from memory **set one's heart on something** greatly desire something **take something to heart** be upset about something
▶ **hearten** v encourage, make cheerful ▶ **heartless** adj cruel, unkind ▶ **hearty** adj substantial, nourishing; friendly, enthusiastic
▶ **heartily** adv ▶ **heart attack** sudden severe malfunction of the heart ▶ **heart failure** sudden stopping of the heartbeat
▶ **heart-rending** adj causing great sorrow ▶ **heart-throb** n (slang)

very attractive man, esp. a film or pop star

**heartache** n intense anguish

**heartbeat** n one complete pulsation of the heart

**heartbreak** n intense grief

**heartburn** n burning sensation in the chest caused by indigestion

**heartfelt** adj felt sincerely or strongly

**hearth** n floor of a fireplace

**heat** v make or become hot ▷ n state of being hot; energy transferred as a result of a difference in temperature; hot weather; intensity of feeling; preliminary eliminating contest in a competition **on heat, in heat** (of some female animals) ready for mating ▶ **heated** adj angry and excited ▶ **heatedly** adv ▶ **heater** n

**heath** n (Brit) area of open uncultivated land

**heathen** adj, n (of) a person who does not believe in an established religion

**heather** n low-growing plant with small purple, pinkish, or white flowers, growing on heaths and mountains

**heave** v lift with effort; throw (something heavy); utter (a sigh); rise and fall; vomit ▷ n heaving

**heaven** n place believed to be the home of God, where good people go when they die; place or state of bliss **the heavens** sky ▶ **heavenly** adj of or like heaven; of or occurring in space; wonderful or beautiful

**heavy** adj **heavier, heaviest** of great weight; having a high density; great in degree or amount; (informal) (of a situation) serious
▶ **heavily** adv ▶ **heaviness** n
▶ **heavy industry** large-scale production of raw material or machinery ▶ **heavy metal** very

loud rock music featuring guitar riffs ▶ **heavyweight** n boxer weighing over 175lb (professional) or 81kg (amateur)

**Hebrew** n member of an ancient Semitic people; ancient language of the Hebrews; its modern form, used in Israel ▷ adj of the Hebrews

**heckle** v interrupt (a public speaker) with comments, questions, or taunts ▶ **heckler** n

**hectare** n one hundred ares or 10 000 square metres (2.471 acres)

**hectic** adj rushed or busy

**hector** v bully

**hedge** n row of bushes forming a barrier or boundary ▷ v be evasive or noncommittal; (foll by against) protect oneself (from) ▶ **hedgerow** n bushes forming a hedge

**hedgehog** n small mammal with a protective covering of spines

**hedonism** n doctrine that pleasure is the most important thing in life ▶ **hedonist** n ▶ **hedonistic** adj

**heed** n careful attention ▷ v pay careful attention to ▶ **heedless** adj **heedless of** taking no notice of

**heel**[1] n back part of the foot; part of a shoe supporting the heel; (old-fashioned) contemptible person ▷ v repair the heel of (a shoe) ▶ **heeler** n (Aust & NZ) dog that herds cattle by biting at their heels

**heel**[2] v (foll by over) lean to one side

**hefty** adj **heftier, heftiest** large, heavy, or strong

**hegemony** [hig-**em**-on-ee] n political domination

**Hegira** n Mohammed's flight from Mecca to Medina in 622 AD

**heifer** [**hef**-fer] n young cow

**height** n distance from base to top; distance above sea level; highest degree or topmost point ▶ **heighten** v make or become higher or more intense

**heinous** adj evil and shocking

**heir** n person entitled to inherit property or rank ▶ **heiress** n fem ▶ **heirloom** n object that has belonged to a family for generations

**held** v past of **hold**[1]

**helical** adj spiral

**helicopter** n aircraft lifted and propelled by rotating overhead blades ▶ **heliport** n airport for helicopters

**heliotrope** n plant with purple flowers ▷ adj light purple

**helium** [**heel**-ee-um] n (Chem) very light colourless odourless gas

**helix** [**heel**-iks] n, pl **helices** or **helixes** continuous curve winding as if around the surface of a cone or cylinder, as on a corkscrew

**hell** n place believed to be where wicked people go when they die; place or state of wickedness, suffering, or punishment **hell for leather** at great speed ▶ **hellish** adj ▶ **hellbent** adj (foll by on) intent

**Hellenic** adj of the (ancient) Greeks or their language

**hello** interj expression of greeting or surprise

**helm** n tiller or wheel for steering a ship

**helmet** n hard hat worn for protection

**help** v make something easier, better, or quicker for (someone); improve (a situation); refrain from e.g. I can't help smiling ▷ n assistance or support **help oneself** take something, esp. food or drink, without being served; (informal) steal something ▶ **helper** n ▶ **helpful** adj ▶ **helping** n single portion of food ▶ **helpless** adj weak or incapable ▶ **helplessly** adv ▶ **helpline** n telephone line set aside for callers to contact an organization for help with a problem ▶ **helpmate** n companion and helper, esp. a husband or wife

**helter-skelter** adj haphazard and careless ▷ adv in a haphazard and careless manner ▷ n high spiral slide at a fairground

**hem** n bottom edge of a garment, folded under and stitched down ▷ v **hemming, hemmed** provide with a hem ▶ **hem in** v surround and prevent from moving ▶ **hemline** n level to which the hem of a skirt hangs

**hemisphere** n half of a sphere, esp. the earth ▶ **hemispherical** adj

**hemlock** n poison made from a plant with spotted stems and small white flowers

**hemp** n (also **cannabis**) Asian plant with tough fibres; its fibre, used to make canvas and rope; narcotic drug obtained from hemp

**hen** n female domestic fowl; female of any bird ▶ **hen night, hen party** party for women only ▶ **henpecked** adj (of a man) dominated by his wife

**hence** conj for this reason ▷ adv from this time ▶ **henceforth** adv from now on

**henchman** n person employed by someone powerful to carry out orders

**henna** n reddish dye made from a shrub or tree ▷ v dye (the hair) with henna

**henry** n, pl **-ry** or **-ries** or **-rys** unit of electrical inductance

**hepatitis** n inflammation of the liver

**heptagon** n geometric figure with seven sides

**heptathlon** n athletic contest for women, involving seven events

**her** pron refers to a female person or animal or anything personified

as feminine when the object of a sentence or clause ▷ adj belonging to her

**herald** n person who announces important news; forerunner ▷ v signal the approach of ▶ **heraldry** n study of coats of arms and family trees ▶ **heraldic** adj

**herb** n plant used for flavouring in cookery, and in medicine ▶ **herbal** adj ▶ **herbalist** n person who grows or specializes in the use of medicinal herbs ▶ **herbaceous** adj (of a plant) soft-stemmed ▶ **herbicide** n chemical used to destroy plants, esp. weeds ▶ **herbivore** n animal that eats only plants ▶ **herbivorous** [her-**biv**-or-uss] adj

**herculean** [her-kew-**lee**-an] adj requiring great strength or effort

**herd** n group of animals feeding and living together; large crowd of people ▷ v collect into a herd ▶ **herdsman** n man who looks after a herd of animals

**Here** interj (SAfr) exclamation of surprise or dismay

**here** adv in, at, or to this place or point ▶ **hereabouts** adv near here ▶ **hereafter** adv after this point or time **the hereafter** life after death ▶ **hereby** adv by means of or as a result of this ▶ **herein** adv in this place, matter, or document ▶ **herewith** adv with this

**heredity** [hir-**red**-it-ee] n passing on of characteristics from one generation to another ▶ **hereditary** adj passed on genetically from one generation to another; passed on by inheritance

**SPELLING TIP**
Remember there are three letters after the t in **hereditary**

**heresy** [**herr**-iss-ee] n, pl **-sies** opinion contrary to accepted opinion or belief ▶ **heretic** [**herr**-it-ik] n person who holds unorthodox opinions ▶ **heretical** [hir-**ret**-ik-al] adj

**heritage** n something inherited; anything from the past, considered as the inheritance of present-day society

**hermaphrodite** [her-**maf**-roe-dite] n animal, plant, or person with both male and female reproductive organs

**hermetic** adj sealed so as to be airtight ▶ **hermetically** adv

**hermit** n person living in solitude, esp. for religious reasons ▶ **hermitage** n home of a hermit

**hernia** n protrusion of an organ or part through the lining of the surrounding body cavity

**hero** n, pl **heroes** principal character in a film, book, etc.; man greatly admired for his exceptional qualities or achievements ▶ **heroine** n fem ▶ **heroic** adj courageous; of or like a hero ▶ **heroics** pl n extravagant behaviour ▶ **heroically** adv ▶ **heroism** [**herr**-oh-izz-um] n

**heroin** n highly addictive drug derived from morphine

**heron** n long-legged wading bird

**herpes** [**her**-peez] n any of several inflammatory skin diseases, including shingles and cold sores

**Herr** [hair] n, pl **Herren** German term of address equivalent to Mr

**herring** n important food fish of northern seas ▶ **herringbone** n pattern of zigzag lines

**herself** pron emphatic or reflexive form of **she, her**

**hertz** n, pl **hertz** (Physics) unit of frequency

**hesitate** v be slow or uncertain in doing something; be reluctant (to do something) ▶ **hesitation** n

▶ **hesitant** adj undecided or wavering ▶ **hesitantly** adv ▶ **hesitancy** n

**hessian** n coarse jute fabric

**heterodox** adj differing from accepted doctrines or beliefs ▶ **heterodoxy** n

**heterogeneous** [het-er-oh-**jean**-ee-uss] adj composed of diverse elements ▶ **heterogeneity** n

**heterosexual** n, adj (person) sexually attracted to members of the opposite sex ▶ **heterosexuality** n

**heuristic** [hew-rist-ik] adj involving learning by investigation

**hew** v **hewing, hewed, hewed** or **hewn** cut with an axe; carve from a substance

**hexagon** n geometrical figure with six sides ▶ **hexagonal** adj

**hey** interj expression of surprise or for catching attention

**heyday** n time of greatest success, prime

**hiatus** [hie-**ay**-tuss] n, pl **-tuses** or **-tus** pause or interruption in continuity

**hibernate** v (of an animal) pass the winter as if in a deep sleep ▶ **hibernation** n

**Hibernian** adj (poetic) Irish

**hibiscus** n, pl **-cuses** tropical plant with large brightly coloured flowers

**hiccup, hiccough** n spasm of the breathing organs with a sharp coughlike sound; (informal) small problem, hitch ▷ v make a hiccup

**hick** n (US, Aust & NZ informal) unsophisticated country person

**hickory** n, pl **-ries** N American nut-bearing tree; its wood

**hide¹** v **hiding, hid, hidden** put (oneself or an object) somewhere difficult to see or find; keep secret ▷ n place of concealment, esp. for a bird-watcher ▸ **hiding** n state of concealment e.g. *in hiding* ▸ **hide-out** n place to hide in

**hide²** n skin of an animal ▸ **hiding** n (*slang*) severe beating ▸ **hidebound** *adj* unwilling to accept new ideas

**hideous** [hid-ee-uss] *adj* ugly, revolting ▸ **hideously** *adv*

**hierarchy** [hire-ark-ee] n, pl **-chies** system of people or things arranged in a graded order ▸ **hierarchical** *adj*

**hieroglyphic** [hire-oh-**gliff**-ik] *adj* of a form of writing using picture symbols, as used in ancient Egypt ▷ n symbol that is difficult to decipher; (also **hieroglyph**) symbol representing an object, idea, or sound

**hi-fi** n set of high-quality sound-reproducing equipment ▷ *adj* high-fidelity

**higgledy-piggledy** *adv, adj* in a muddle

**high** *adj* of a great height; far above ground or sea level; being at its peak; greater than usual in intensity or amount; (of a sound) acute in pitch; of great importance, quality, or rank; (*informal*) under the influence of alcohol or drugs ▷ *adv* at or to a high level ▸ **highly** *adv* ▸ **highly strung** nervous and easily upset ▸ **Highness** n title used to address or refer to a royal person ▸ **High-Church** *adj* belonging to a section within the Church of England stressing the importance of ceremony and ritual ▸ **higher education** education at colleges and universities ▸ **high-fidelity** *adj* able to reproduce sound with little or no distortion ▸ **high-flown** *adj* (of language) extravagant or pretentious ▸ **high-handed** *adj* excessively forceful ▸ **high-maintenance** *adj* (of a piece of equipment, vehicle etc.)

requiring regular maintenance; (*informal*) (of a person) requiring a high level of care and attention ▸ **high-rise** *adj* (of a building) having many storeys ▸ **high tea** early evening meal consisting of a cooked dish, bread, cakes, and tea ▸ **high time** latest possible time

**highbrow** *adj, n* intellectual and serious (person)

**Highland** *adj* of the Highlands, a mountainous region of N Scotland ▸ **Highlander** n

**highlands** pl n area of high ground

**highlight** n outstanding part or feature; light-toned area in a painting or photograph; lightened streak in the hair ▷ v give emphasis to

**highway** n (US, Aust & NZ) main road ▸ **Highway Code** regulations and recommendations applying to all road users ▸ **highwayman** n (formerly) robber, usu. on horseback, who robbed travellers at gunpoint

**hijab** n head covering worn by Muslim women

**hijack** v seize control of (an aircraft or other vehicle) while travelling ▸ **hijacker** n

**hike** n long walk in the country, esp. for pleasure ▷ v go for a long walk; (foll by *up*) pull (up) or raise ▸ **hiker** n

**hilarious** *adj* very funny ▸ **hilariously** *adv* ▸ **hilarity** n

**hill** n raised part of the earth's surface, less high than a mountain ▸ **hilly** *adj* ▸ **hillock** n small hill ▸ **hillbilly** n (US) unsophisticated country person

**Hills Hoist**® n Australian brand of rotary clothesline

**hilt** n handle of a sword or knife

**him** *pron* refers to a male person or animal when the object of a

sentence or clause ▶ **himself**
*pron* emphatic or reflexive form
of **he, him**

**hind¹** *adj* **hinder, hindmost**
situated at the back

**hind²** *n* female deer

**hinder** *v* get in the way of
▶ **hindrance** *n*

**Hindu** *n* person who practises
Hinduism ▷ *adj* of Hinduism
▶ **Hindi** *n* language of N central
India ▶ **Hinduism** *n* dominant
religion of India, which involves the
worship of many gods and a belief
in reincarnation

**hinge** *n* device for holding together
two parts so that one can swing
freely ▷ *v* (foll by *on*) depend (on);
fit a hinge to

**hint** *n* indirect suggestion; piece of
advice; small amount ▷ *v* suggest
indirectly

**hinterland** *n* land lying behind a
coast or near a city, esp. a port

**hip¹** *n* either side of the body
between the pelvis and the thigh

**hip²** *n* rosehip

**hip-hop** *n* pop-culture movement
originating in the 1980s, comprising
rap music, graffiti, and break dancing

**hippie** *adj, n* same as **hippy**

**hippo** *n, pl* **-pos** (*informal*)
hippopotamus

**hippodrome** *n* music hall, variety
theatre, or circus

**hippopotamus** *n, pl* **-muses** *or* **-mi**
large African mammal with thick
wrinkled skin, living near rivers

**hippy** *adj, n, pl* **-pies** (esp. in
the 1960s) (of) a person whose
behaviour and dress imply a
rejection of conventional values

**hipster** *n* (*informal*) person pursuing
non-mainstream cultural trends

**hire** *v* pay to have temporary use of;
employ for wages ▷ *n* hiring **for
hire** available to be hired

▶ **hireling** *n* person who works only
for wages ▶ **hire-purchase** *n*
system of purchase by which the
buyer pays for goods by instalments

**hirsute** [her-suit] *adj* hairy

**his** *pron, adj* (something) belonging
to him

**Hispanic** *adj* Spanish or Latin-
American

**hiss** *n* sound like that of a long *s* (as
an expression of contempt) ▷ *v*
utter a hiss; show derision or anger
towards

**histamine** [hiss-ta-meen] *n*
substance released by the body
tissues in allergic reactions

**histogram** *n* statistical graph in
which the frequency of values is
represented by vertical bars of
varying heights and widths

**histology** *n* study of the tissues of
an animal or plant

**history** *n, pl* **-ries** (record or
account of) past events and
developments; study of these;
record of someone's past
▶ **historian** *n* writer of history
▶ **historic** *adj* famous or significant
in history ▶ **historical** *adj*
occurring in the past; based on
history ▶ **historically** *adv*

**histrionic** *adj* excessively dramatic
▶ **histrionics** *pl n* excessively
dramatic behaviour

**hit** *v* **hitting, hit** strike, touch
forcefully; come into violent
contact with; affect badly; reach
(a point or place) ▷ *n* hitting;
successful record, film, etc.;
(*Computing*) single visit to a website
**hit it off** (*informal*) get on well
together **hit the road** (*informal*)
start a journey ▶ **hit-and-miss**
*adj* sometimes successful and
sometimes not ▶ **hit man**
hired assassin ▶ **hit on** *v* think
of (an idea)

**hitch** n minor problem ▷ v (informal) obtain (a lift) by hitchhiking; fasten with a knot or tie; (foll by up) pull up with a jerk ▶ **hitchhike** v travel by obtaining free lifts ▶ **hitchhiker** n

**hi-tech** adj using sophisticated technology

**hither** adv (old-fashioned) to or towards this place

**hitherto** adv until this time

**HIV** human immunodeficiency virus: the cause of AIDS

**hive** n same as **beehive**; **hive of activity** place where people are very busy ▶ **hive off** v separate from a larger group

**hives** n allergic reaction in which itchy red or whitish patches appear on the skin

**HM** (in Britain) Her (or His) Majesty

**HMS** (in Britain) Her (or His) Majesty's Ship

**HNC** (in Britain) Higher National Certificate

**HND** (in Britain) Higher National Diploma

**hoard** n store hidden away for future use ▷ v save or store ▶ **hoarder** n

**USAGE NOTE**
Do not confuse hoard with horde, which means 'a large group'

**hoarding** n large board for displaying advertisements

**hoarfrost** n white ground frost

**hoarse** adj (of a voice) rough and unclear; having a rough and unclear voice ▶ **hoarsely** adv ▶ **hoarseness** n

**hoary** adj **hoarier, hoariest** grey or white(-haired); very old

**hoax** n deception or trick ▷ v deceive or play a trick upon ▶ **hoaxer** n

**hob** n (Brit) flat top part of a cooker, or a separate flat surface, containing gas or electric rings for cooking on

**hobble** v walk lamely; tie the legs of (a horse) together

**hobby** n, pl **-bies** activity pursued in one's spare time ▶ **hobbyhorse** n favourite topic; toy horse

**hobgoblin** n mischievous goblin

**hobnail boots** pl n heavy boots with short nails in the soles

**hobnob** v **-nobbing, -nobbed** (foll by with) be on friendly terms (with)

**hobo** n, pl **-bos** (US, Aust & NZ) tramp or vagrant

**hock**¹ n joint in the back leg of an animal such as a horse that corresponds to the human ankle

**hock**² n white German wine

**hock**³ v (informal) pawn **in hock** (informal) in debt

**hockey** n team game played on a field with a ball and curved sticks; (US) ice hockey

**hocus-pocus** n trickery

**hod** n open wooden box attached to a pole, for carrying bricks or mortar

**hoe** n long-handled tool used for loosening soil or weeding ▷ v scrape or weed with a hoe

**hog** n castrated male pig; (informal) greedy person ▷ v **hogging, hogged** (informal) take more than one's share of ▶ **hogshead** n large cask ▶ **hogwash** n (informal) nonsense

**Hogmanay** n (in Scotland) New Year's Eve

**hoick** v raise abruptly and sharply

**hoi polloi** n the ordinary people

**hoisin** n sweet spicy sauce of soya beans, sugar, garlic, and vinegar, used in Chinese cookery

**hoist** v raise or lift up ▷ n device for lifting things

**hoity-toity** adj (informal) arrogant or haughty

**hokey-pokey** n (NZ) brittle toffee sold in lumps

**hold**[1] *v* **holding, held** keep or support in or with the hands or arms; arrange for (a meeting, party, etc.) to take place; consider to be as specified e.g. *who are you holding responsible?*; maintain in a specified position or state; have the capacity for; (*informal*) wait, esp. on the telephone; restrain or keep back; own, possess ▷ *n* act or way of holding; controlling influence ▶ **holder** *n* ▶ **holding** *n* property, such as land or stocks and shares ▶ **holdall** *n* large strong travelling bag ▶ **hold-up** *n* armed robbery; delay

**hold**[2] *n* cargo compartment in a ship or aircraft

**hole** *n* area hollowed out in a solid; opening or hollow; animal's burrow; (*informal*) unattractive place; (*informal*) difficult situation ▷ *v* make holes in; hit (a golf ball) into the target hole

**holiday** *n* time spent away from home for rest or recreation; day or other period of rest from work or studies

**holiness** *n* state of being holy; (**H-**) title used to address or refer to the Pope

**holistic** *adj* considering the complete person, physically and mentally, in the treatment of an illness ▶ **holism** *n*

**hollow** *adj* having a hole or space inside; (of a sound) as if echoing in a hollow place; without any real value or worth ▷ *n* cavity or space; dip in the land ▷ *v* form a hollow in

**holly** *n* evergreen tree with prickly leaves and red berries

**hollyhock** *n* tall garden plant with spikes of colourful flowers

**holocaust** *n* destruction or loss of life on a massive scale

**hologram** *n* three-dimensional photographic image

**holograph** *n* document handwritten by the author

**holster** *n* leather case for a pistol, hung from a belt

**holy** *adj* **-lier, -liest** of God or a god; devout or virtuous ▶ **holier-than-thou** *adj* self-righteous ▶ **Holy Communion** (*Christianity*) service in which people take bread and wine in remembrance of the death and resurrection of Jesus Christ ▶ **Holy Grail** (in medieval legend) the bowl used by Jesus Christ at the Last Supper ▶ **Holy Spirit, Holy Ghost** (*Christianity*) one of the three aspects of God ▶ **Holy Week** (*Christianity*) week before Easter

**homage** *n* show of respect or honour towards someone or something

**home** *n* place where one lives; institution for the care of the elderly, orphans, etc. ▷ *adj* of one's home, birthplace, or native country; (*Sport*) played on one's own ground ▷ *adv* to or at home ▷ *v* (foll by *in* or *in on*) direct towards (a point or target) **at home** at ease **bring home to** make clear to **home and dry** (*informal*) safe or successful ▶ **homeless** *adj* having nowhere to live ▷ *pl n* people who have nowhere to live ▶ **homelessness** *n* ▶ **homely** *adj* simple, ordinary, and comfortable; (*US*) unattractive ▶ **homeward** *adj, adv* ▶ **homewards** *adv* ▶ **home-brew** *n* beer made at home ▶ **home-made** *adj* made at home or on the premises ▶ **home page** (*Computing*) introductory information about a website with links to the information or services provided ▶ **home truths** unpleasant facts told to a person about himself or herself

**homeland** n country from which a person's ancestors came

**homeopathy** [home-ee-**op**-ath-ee] n treatment of disease by small doses of a drug that produces symptoms of the disease in healthy people ▶ **homeopath** n person who practises homeopathy ▶ **homeopathic** adj

**homesick** adj sad because missing one's home and family ▶ **homesickness** n

**homestead** n farmhouse plus the adjoining land

**homework** n school work done at home

**homicide** n killing of a human being; person who kills someone ▶ **homicidal** adj

**homily** n, pl **-lies** speech telling people how they should behave

**hominid** n man or any extinct forerunner of man

**homo-** combining form same, like e.g. homosexual

**homogeneous** [home-oh-**jean**-ee-uss] adj formed of similar parts ▶ **homogeneity** n ▶ **homogenize** v break up fat globules in (milk or cream) to distribute them evenly; make homogeneous

**homograph** n word spelt the same as another, but with a different meaning

**homologous** [hom-**ol**-log-uss] adj having a related or similar position or structure

**homonym** n word spelt or pronounced the same as another, but with a different meaning

**homophobia** n hatred or fear of homosexuals ▶ **homophobic** adj

**homophone** n word pronounced the same as another, but with a different meaning or spelling

**Homo sapiens** [**hoe**-moh **sap**-ee-enz] n human beings as a species

**homosexual** n, adj (person) sexually attracted to members of the same sex ▶ **homosexuality** n

**Hon.** Honourable

**hone** v sharpen

**honest** adj truthful and moral; open and sincere ▶ **honestly** adv ▶ **honesty** n quality of being honest; plant with silvery seed pods

**honey** n sweet edible sticky substance made by bees from nectar; term of endearment ▶ **honeycomb** n waxy structure of six-sided cells in which honey is stored by bees in a beehive ▶ **honeydew melon** melon with a yellow skin and sweet pale flesh ▶ **honeymoon** n holiday taken by a newly married couple ▶ **honeysuckle** n climbing shrub with sweet-smelling flowers; Australian tree or shrub with nectar-rich flowers

**hongi** [**hong**-jee] n (NZ) Māori greeting in which people touch noses

**honk** n sound made by a car horn; sound made by a goose ▷ v (cause to) make this sound

**honour** n sense of honesty and fairness; (award given out of) respect; pleasure or privilege ▷ pl university degree of a higher standard than an ordinary degree ▷ v give praise and attention to; give an award to (someone) out of respect; accept or pay (a cheque or bill); keep (a promise) **do the honours** act as host or hostess by pouring drinks or giving out food ▶ **honourable** adj worthy of respect or esteem ▶ **honourably** adv ▶ **honorary** adj held or given only as an honour; unpaid ▶ **honorific** adj showing respect

**hood**[1] n head covering, often attached to a coat or jacket; folding roof of a convertible car or a pram; (US & Aust) car bonnet ▶ **hooded** adj (of a garment) having a hood; (of eyes) having heavy eyelids that appear to be half-closed ▶ **hoodie** n (informal) hooded sweatshirt; person who wears a hooded sweatshirt

**hood²** n (chiefly US slang) hoodlum

**hoodlum** n (slang) violent criminal, gangster

**hoodoo** n, pl **-doos** (cause of) bad luck

**hoodwink** v trick, deceive

**hoof** n, pl **hooves** or **hoofs** horny covering of the foot of a horse, deer, etc. **hoof it** (slang) walk

**hoo-ha** n fuss or commotion

**hook** n curved piece of metal, plastic, etc., used to hang, hold, or pull something; short swinging punch ▷ v fasten or catch (as if) with a hook ▶ **hooked** adj bent like a hook; (foll by on) (slang) addicted (to) or obsessed (with) ▶ **hooker** n (chiefly US slang) prostitute; (Rugby) player who uses his feet to get the ball in a scrum ▶ **hook-up** n linking of radio or television stations ▶ **hookworm** n blood-sucking worm with hooked mouthparts

**hookah** n oriental pipe in which smoke is drawn through water and a long tube

**hooligan** n rowdy young person ▶ **hooliganism** n

**hoon** n (Aust & NZ slang) loutish youth who drives irresponsibly

**hoop** n rigid circular band, used esp. as a child's toy or for animals to jump through in the circus **jump through the hoops, be put through the hoops** go through an ordeal or test ▶ **hoop pine** Australian tree or shrub with flowers in dense spikes

**hoopla** n fairground game in which hoops are thrown over objects in an attempt to win them

**hooray** interj same as **hurrah**

**hoot** n sound of a car horn; cry of an owl; cry of derision; (informal) amusing person or thing ▷ v sound (a car horn); jeer or yell contemptuously (at someone) ▶ **hooter** n device that hoots; (chiefly Brit slang) nose

**Hoover®** n vacuum cleaner ▷ v (**h-**) clean with a vacuum cleaner

**hooves** n a plural of **hoof**

**hop¹** v **hopping, hopped** jump on one foot; move in short jumps; (informal) move quickly ▷ n instance of hopping; (informal) dance; short journey, esp. by air **catch someone on the hop** (informal) catch someone unprepared

**hop²** n (often pl) climbing plant, the dried flowers of which are used to make beer

**hope** v want (something) to happen or be true ▷ n expectation of something desired; thing that gives cause for hope or is desired ▶ **hopeful** adj having, expressing, or inspiring hope ▷ n person considered to be on the brink of success ▶ **hopefully** adv in a hopeful manner; it is hoped ▶ **hopeless** adj

**hopper** n container for storing substances such as grain or sand

**hopscotch** n children's game of hopping in a pattern drawn on the ground

**horde** n large crowd

> **USAGE NOTE**
> Do not confuse horde with hoard, which means 'to store hidden away for future use'

**horizon** n apparent line that divides the earth and the sky

▷ *pl* limits of scope, interest, or knowledge

**horizontal** *adj* parallel to the horizon, level, flat
▶ **horizontally** *adv*

**hormone** *n* substance secreted by certain glands which stimulates certain organs of the body; synthetic substance with the same effect ▶ **hormonal** *adj*

**horn** *n* one of a pair of bony growths sticking out of the heads of cattle, sheep, etc.; substance of which horns are made; musical instrument with a tube or pipe of brass fitted with a mouthpiece; device on a vehicle sounded as a warning ▶ **horned** *adj* ▶ **horny** *adj* of or like horn; (*slang*) (easily) sexually aroused
▶ **hornbeam** *n* tree with smooth grey bark ▶ **hornbill** *n* bird with a bony growth on its large beak
▶ **hornpipe** *n* (music for) a solo dance, traditionally performed by sailors

**hornblende** *n* mineral containing aluminium, calcium, sodium, magnesium, and iron

**hornet** *n* large wasp with a severe sting

**horoscope** *n* prediction of a person's future based on the positions of the planets, sun, and moon at his or her birth

**horrendous** *adj* very unpleasant and shocking

**horrible** *adj* disagreeable, unpleasant; causing horror
▶ **horribly** *adv*

**horrid** *adj* disagreeable, unpleasant; (*informal*) nasty

**horrify** *v* **-fying, -fied** cause to feel horror or shock ▶ **horrific** *adj* causing horror

**horror** *n* (thing or person causing) terror or hatred

**hors d'oeuvre** [**or durv**] *n* appetizer served before a main meal

**horse** *n* large animal with hooves, a mane, and a tail, used for riding and pulling carts etc.; piece of gymnastic equipment used for vaulting over **(straight) from the horse's mouth** from the original source ▶ **horsey, horsy** *adj* very keen on horses; of or like a horse
▶ **horse around** *v* (*informal*) play roughly or boisterously ▶ **horse chestnut** tree with broad leaves and inedible large brown shiny nuts in spiky cases ▶ **horsefly** *n* large bloodsucking fly ▶ **horsehair** *n* hair from the tail or mane of a horse ▶ **horse laugh** loud coarse laugh ▶ **horseman, horsewoman** *n* person riding a horse
▶ **horseplay** *n* rough or rowdy play
▶ **horsepower** *n* unit of power (equivalent to 745.7 watts), used to measure the power of an engine
▶ **horseradish** *n* strong-tasting root of a plant, usu. made into a sauce ▶ **horseshoe** *n* protective U-shaped piece of iron nailed to a horse's hoof, regarded as a symbol of good luck

**horticulture** *n* art or science of cultivating gardens ▶ **horticultural** *adj*
▶ **horticulturalist, horticulturist** *n*

**hosanna** *interj* exclamation of praise to God

**hose**[1] *n* flexible pipe for conveying liquid ▷ *v* water with a hose

**hose**[2] *n* stockings, socks, and tights
▶ **hosiery** *n* stockings, socks, and tights collectively

**hospice** [**hoss**-piss] *n* nursing home for the terminally ill

**hospital** *n* place where people who are ill are looked after and treated

▶ **hospitalize** v send or admit to hospital ▶ **hospitalization** n

**hospitality** n kindness in welcoming strangers or guests ▶ **hospitable** adj welcoming to strangers or guests

**host¹** n (fem **hostess**) person who entertains guests, esp. in his own home; place or country providing the facilities for an event; compere of a show; animal or plant on which a parasite lives ▷ v be the host of

**host²** n large number

**Host** n (Christianity) bread used in Holy Communion

**hostage** n person who is illegally held prisoner until certain demands are met by other people

**hostel** n building providing accommodation at a low cost for a specific group of people such as students, travellers, homeless people, etc.

**hostelry** n, pl -ries (old-fashioned or facetious) inn, pub

**hostile** adj unfriendly; (foll by to) opposed (to); of an enemy ▶ **hostility** n, pl -ties unfriendly and aggressive feelings or behaviour ▷ pl acts of warfare

**hot** adj **hotter, hottest** having a high temperature; strong, spicy; (of news) very recent; (of a contest) fiercely fought; (of a temper) quick to rouse; liked very much e.g. a hot favourite; (slang) stolen **in hot water** (informal) in trouble ▶ **hotly** adv ▶ **hot air** (informal) empty talk ▶ **hot-blooded** adj passionate or excitable ▶ **hot dog** long roll split lengthways with a hot frankfurter inside ▶ **hot-headed** adj rash, having a hot temper ▶ **hotline** n direct telephone link for emergency use ▶ **hot pool** (NZ) geothermally heated pool ▶ **hot**

**spot** place where there is a lot of exciting activity; area where there is a concentration of violence or political unrest; (Computing) place (esp. a public building or commercial premises) offering a Wi-Fi connection

**hotbed** n any place encouraging a particular activity e.g. hotbeds of unrest

**hotchpotch** n jumbled mixture

**hotel** n commercial establishment providing lodging and meals ▶ **hotelier** n owner or manager of a hotel

**hotfoot** adv (informal) quickly and eagerly **hotfoot it** (informal) go quickly and eagerly

**hothouse** n greenhouse

**hotplate** n heated metal surface on an electric cooker; portable device for keeping food warm

**hound** n hunting dog ▷ v pursue relentlessly

**hour** n twenty-fourth part of a day, sixty minutes; time of day ▷ pl period regularly appointed for work or business ▶ **hourly** adj, adv (happening) every hour; frequent(ly) ▶ **hourglass** n device with two glass compartments, containing a quantity of sand that takes an hour to trickle from the top section to the bottom one

**houri** n (Islam) any of the nymphs of paradise

**house** n building used as a home; building used for some specific purpose e.g. the opera house; business firm; law-making body or the hall where it meets; family or dynasty; theatre or cinema audience **get on like a house on fire** (informal) get on very well together **on the house** (informal) provided free by the management ▷ v give accommodation to;

contain or cover ▶ **housing** n
(providing of) houses; protective
case or covering of a machine
▶ **house arrest** confinement to
one's home rather than in prison
▶ **houseboat** n stationary boat
used as a home ▶ **housebreaker**
n burglar ▶ **housecoat** n woman's
long loose coat-shaped garment
for wearing at home ▶ **household**
n all the people living in a house
▶ **householder** n person who owns
or rents a house ▶ **housekeeper** n
person employed to run someone
else's household ▶ **housekeeping**
n (money for) running a household
▶ **housemaid** n female servant
employed to do housework
▶ **house-train** v train (a pet) to
urinate and defecate outside
▶ **house-warming** n party to
celebrate moving into a new home
▶ **housewife** n woman who runs
her own household and does not
have a job ▶ **housework** n work of
running a home, such as cleaning,
cooking, and shopping
**House music, House** n electronic
funk-based disco music with
samples of other recordings edited in
**hovea** n Australian plant with
purple flowers
**hovel** n small dirty house or hut
**hover** v (of a bird etc.) remain
suspended in one place in the air;
loiter; be in a state of indecision
▶ **hovercraft** n vehicle which can
travel over both land and sea on a
cushion of air
**how** adv in what way, by what
means; to what degree e.g. I
know how hard it is ▶ **however** adv
nevertheless; by whatever means;
no matter how e.g. however much it
hurt, he could do it
**howdah** n canopied seat on an
elephant's back

**howitzer** n large gun firing shells at
a steep angle
**howl** n loud wailing cry; loud
burst of laughter ▷ v utter a
howl ▶ **howler** n (informal) stupid
mistake
**hoyden** n (old-fashioned) wild or
boisterous girl
**HP, h.p.** hire-purchase;
horsepower
**HQ** headquarters
**HR** human resources
**HRH** Her (or His) Royal Highness
**HRT** hormone replacement
therapy
**HSDPA** high-speed download
packet access
**HTML** hypertext markup language:
text description language used on
the internet
**hub** n centre of a wheel, through
which the axle passes; central
point of activity
**hubbub** n confused noise of many
voices
**hubby** n, pl **-bies** (informal) husband
**hubris** [hew-briss] n (formal) pride,
arrogance
**huckster** n person using aggressive
methods of selling
**huddle** v hunch (oneself) through
cold or fear; crowd closely
together ▷ n small group; (informal)
impromptu conference
**hue** n colour, shade
**hue and cry** n public outcry
**huff** n passing mood of anger or
resentment ▷ v blow or puff heavily
▶ **huffy** adj ▶ **huffily** adv
**hug** v **hugging, hugged** clasp
tightly in the arms, usu. with
affection; keep close to (the
ground, kerb, etc.) ▷ n tight or fond
embrace
**huge** adj very big ▶ **hugely** adv
**huh** interj exclamation of derision,
bewilderment, or inquiry

h

**hui** [**hoo**-ee] n (NZ) meeting of
Māori people; meeting to discuss
Māori matters

**hula** n swaying Hawaiian dance
▶ **Hula Hoop**® plastic hoop
twirled round the body by gyrating
the hips

**hulk** n body of an abandoned ship;
(offens) large heavy person or thing
▶ **hulking** adj bulky, unwieldy

**hull** n main body of a boat; leaves
round the stem of a strawberry,
raspberry, etc. ▷ v remove the
hulls from

**hullabaloo** n, pl -loos loud
confused noise or clamour

**hum** v humming, hummed
make a low continuous vibrating
sound; sing with the lips closed;
(slang) (of a place) be very busy ▷ n
humming sound ▶ **hummingbird**
n very small American bird whose
powerful wings make a humming
noise as they vibrate

**human** adj of or typical of people
▷ n human being ▶ **humanly**
adv by human powers or means
▶ **human being** man, woman,
or child

**humane** adj kind or merciful
▶ **humanely** adv

**humanism** n belief in human effort
rather than religion ▶ **humanist** n

**humanitarian** n, adj (person)
having the interests of humankind
at heart

**humanity** n, pl -ties human
race; the quality of being human;
kindness or mercy ▷ pl study of
literature, philosophy, and the arts

**humanize** v make human or
humane

**humankind** n human race

**humble** adj conscious of one's
failings; modest, unpretentious;
unimportant ▷ v cause to feel
humble, humiliate ▶ **humbly** adv

**humbug** n (Brit) hard striped
peppermint sweet; nonsense;
dishonest person

**humdinger** n (slang) excellent
person or thing

**humdrum** adj ordinary, dull

**humerus** [**hew**-mer-uss] n, pl -meri
[-mer-rye] bone from the shoulder
to the elbow

**humid** adj damp and hot
▶ **humidity** n ▶ **humidify** v -fying,
-fied make humid ▶ **humidifier** n
device for increasing the amount of
water vapour in the air in a room

**humiliate** v lower the dignity or
hurt the pride of ▶ **humiliating** adj
▶ **humiliation** n

**humility** n quality of being humble

**hummock** n very small hill

**humour** n ability to say or perceive
things that are amusing; amusing
quality in a situation, film, etc.;
state of mind, mood; (old-fashioned)
fluid in the body ▷ v be kind and
indulgent to ▶ **humorous** adj
▶ **humorously** adv ▶ **humorist**
n writer or entertainer who uses
humour in his or her work

> **SPELLING TIP**
> Don't forget to drop the second
> u in **humour** when forming
> the derivatives **humorous** and
> **humorist**

**hump** n raised piece of ground;
large lump on the back of an
animal or person ▷ v (slang) carry
or heave **get the hump, take
the hump** (informal) be annoyed,
sulk ▶ **hump-back bridge,
humpbacked bridge** road bridge
with a sharp slope on each side

**humus** [**hew**-muss] n decomposing
vegetable and animal mould in
the soil

**hunch** n feeling or suspicion
not based on facts ▷ v draw
(one's shoulders) up or together

▶ **hunchback** n (offens) person with an abnormal curvature of the spine

**hundred** adj, n ten times ten ▷ n (often pl) large but unspecified number ▶ **hundredth** adj, n ▶ **hundredweight** n (Brit) unit of weight of 112 pounds (50.8 kilograms)

**hung** v past of **hang** ▷ adj (of a parliament or jury) with no side having a clear majority **hung over** (informal) suffering the effects of a hangover

**Hungarian** adj of Hungary ▷ n person from Hungary; language of Hungary

**hunger** n discomfort or weakness from lack of food; desire or craving ▷ v (foll by for) want very much ▶ **hunger strike** refusal of all food, as a means of protest

**hungry** adj **hungrier**, **hungriest** desiring food; (foll by for) having a desire or craving (for) ▶ **hungrily** adv

**hunk** n large piece; (slang) sexually attractive man

**hunt** v seek out and kill (wild animals) for food or sport; (foll by for) search (for) ▷ n hunting; (party organized for) hunting wild animals for sport ▶ **huntaway** n (NZ) sheepdog trained to drive sheep by barking ▶ **huntsman** n man who hunts wild animals, esp. foxes

**hunter** n person or animal that hunts wild animals for food or sport

**hurdle** n (Sport) light barrier for jumping over in some races; problem or difficulty ▷ pl race involving hurdles ▷ v jump over (something) ▶ **hurdler** n

**hurdy-gurdy** n, pl **-dies** mechanical musical instrument, such as a barrel organ

**hurl** v throw or utter forcefully

**hurling**, **hurley** n Irish game like hockey

**hurly-burly** n loud confusion

**hurrah**, **hurray** interj exclamation of joy or applause

**hurricane** n very strong, often destructive, wind or storm ▶ **hurricane lamp** paraffin lamp with a glass covering

**hurry** v **-rying**, **-ried** (cause to) move or act very quickly ▷ n doing something quickly or the need to do something quickly ▶ **hurriedly** adv

**hurt** v **hurting**, **hurt** cause physical or mental pain to; be painful; (informal) feel pain ▷ n physical or mental pain ▶ **hurtful** adj unkind

**hurtle** v move quickly or violently

**husband** n male partner in marriage ▷ v use economically ▶ **husbandry** n farming; management of resources

**hush** v make or be silent ▷ n stillness or silence ▶ **hush-hush** adj (informal) secret ▶ **hush up** v suppress information about

**husk** n outer covering of certain seeds and fruits ▷ v remove the husk from

**husky**[1] adj **huskier**, **huskiest** slightly hoarse; (informal) big and strong ▶ **huskily** adv

**husky**[2] n, pl **huskies** Arctic sledge dog with thick hair and a curled tail

**hussar** [hoo-**zar**] n (Hist) lightly armed cavalry soldier

**hussy** n, pl **-sies** immodest or promiscuous woman

**hustings** pl n political campaigns and speeches before an election

**hustle** v push about, jostle ▷ n lively activity or bustle

**hut** n small house, shelter, or shed

**hutch** n cage for pet rabbits etc.

**hyacinth** n sweet-smelling spring flower that grows from a bulb

**h**

**hyaena** n same as **hyena**

**hybrid** n offspring of two plants or animals of different species; anything of mixed origin ▷ adj of mixed origin

**hydra** n mythical many-headed water serpent

**hydrangea** n ornamental shrub with clusters of pink, blue, or white flowers

**hydrant** n outlet from a water main with a nozzle for a hose

**hydrate** n chemical compound of water with another substance

**hydraulic** adj operated by pressure forced through a pipe by a liquid such as water or oil ▶ **hydraulics** n study of the mechanical properties of fluids as they apply to practical engineering ▶ **hydraulically** adv

**hydro¹** n, pl **hydros** hotel offering facilities for hydropathy

**hydro²** adj short for **hydroelectric**

**hydro-** combining form water e.g. hydroelectric; hydrogen e.g. hydrochloric acid

**hydrocarbon** n compound of hydrogen and carbon

**hydrochloric acid** n strong colourless acid used in many industrial and laboratory processes

**hydroelectric** adj of the generation of electricity by water pressure

**hydrofoil** n fast light boat with its hull raised out of the water on one or more pairs of fins

**hydrogen** n (Chem) light flammable colourless gas that combines with oxygen to form water ▶ **hydrogen bomb** extremely powerful bomb in which energy is released by fusion of hydrogen nuclei to give helium nuclei ▶ **hydrogen peroxide** colourless liquid used as a hair bleach and as an antiseptic

**hydrolysis** [hie-**drol**-iss-iss] n decomposition of a chemical compound reacting with water

**hydrometer** [hie-**drom**-it-er] n instrument for measuring the density of a liquid

**hydropathy** n method of treating disease by the use of large quantities of water both internally and externally

**hydrophobia** n rabies; fear of water

**hydroplane** n light motorboat that skims the water

**hydroponics** n method of growing plants in water rather than soil

**hydrotherapy** n (Med) treatment of certain diseases by exercise in water

**hyena** n scavenging doglike mammal of Africa and S Asia

**hygiene** n principles and practice of health and cleanliness ▶ **hygienic** adj ▶ **hygienically** adv

**hymen** n membrane partly covering the opening of a girl's vagina, which breaks before puberty or at the first occurrence of sexual intercourse

**hymn** n Christian song of praise sung to God or a saint ▶ **hymnal** n book of hymns (also **hymn book**)

**hype** n intensive or exaggerated publicity or sales promotion ▷ v promote (a product) using intensive or exaggerated publicity

**hyper** adj (informal) overactive or overexcited

**hyper-** prefix over, above, excessively e.g. hyperactive

**hyperbola** [hie-**per**-bol-a] n (Geom) curve produced when a cone is cut by a plane at a steeper angle to its base than its side

**hyperbole** [hie-**per**-bol-ee] n deliberate exaggeration for effect ▶ **hyperbolic** adj

**hyperlink** (*Computing*) *n* link from a hypertext file that gives users instant access to related material in another file ▷ *v* link (files) in this way

**hypermarket** *n* huge self-service store

**hypersensitive** *adj* extremely sensitive to certain drugs, extremes of temperature, etc.; very easily upset

**hypersonic** *adj* having a speed of at least five times the speed of sound

**hypertension** *n* very high blood pressure

**hypertext** *n* computer software and hardware that allows users to store and view text and move between related items easily

**hyphen** *n* punctuation mark (-) indicating that two words or syllables are connected ▶ **hyphenated** *adj* (of two words or syllables) having a hyphen between them ▶ **hyphenation** *n*

**hypnosis** *n* artificially induced state of relaxation in which the mind is more than usually receptive to suggestion ▶ **hypnotic** *adj* of or (as if) producing hypnosis ▶ **hypnotism** *n* inducing hypnosis in someone ▶ **hypnotist** *n* ▶ **hypnotize** *v*

**hypo-** *prefix* beneath, less than e.g. *hypothermia*

**hypoallergenic** *adj* (of cosmetics) not likely to cause an allergic reaction

**hypochondria** *n* undue preoccupation with one's health ▶ **hypochondriac** *n*

**hypocrisy** [hip-**ok**-rass-ee] *n*, *pl* **-sies** (instance of) pretence of having standards or beliefs that are contrary to one's real character or actual behaviour

▶ **hypocrite** [**hip**-oh-krit] *n* person who pretends to be what he or she is not ▶ **hypocritical** *adj* ▶ **hypocritically** *adv*

**hypodermic** *adj*, *n* (denoting) a syringe or needle used to inject a drug beneath the skin

**hypotension** *n* very low blood pressure

**hypotenuse** [hie-**pot**-a-news] *n* side of a right-angled triangle opposite the right angle

**hypothalamus** *n* area at the base of the brain, which controls hunger, thirst, etc.

**hypothermia** *n* condition in which a person's body temperature is dangerously low as a result of prolonged exposure to severe cold

**hypothesis** [hie-**poth**-iss-iss] *n*, *pl* **-ses** [-seez] suggested but unproved explanation of something ▶ **hypothetical** *adj* based on assumption rather than fact or reality ▶ **hypothetically** *adv*

**hyrax** *n*, *pl* **-raxes** *or* **-races** type of hoofed rodent-like animal of Africa and Asia

**hysterectomy** *n*, *pl* **-mies** surgical removal of the womb

**hysteria** *n* state of uncontrolled excitement, anger, or panic ▶ **hysterical** *adj* ▶ **hysterically** *adv* ▶ **hysterics** *pl n* attack of hysteria; (*informal*) uncontrollable laughter

**Hz** hertz

# Ii

**I** *pron* used by a speaker or writer to refer to himself or herself as the subject of a verb

**Iberian** *adj* of Iberia, the peninsula comprising Spain and Portugal

**ibex** [ibe-eks] *n* wild goat of N Africa with large backward-curving horns

**ibid.** (referring to a book, page, or passage already mentioned) in the same place

**ibis** [ibe-iss] *n* large wading bird with long legs

**ice** *n* frozen water; (*chiefly Brit*) portion of ice cream **the Ice** (*NZ informal*) Antarctica ▷ *v* (foll by *up* or *over*) become covered with ice; cover with icing **break the ice** create a relaxed atmosphere, esp. between people meeting for the first time ▶ **iced** *adj* covered with icing; (of a drink) containing ice ▶ **icy** *adj* **icier, iciest** very cold; covered with ice; aloof and unfriendly ▶ **icily** *adv* ▶ **iciness** *n* ▶ **Ice Age** period when much of the earth's surface was covered in glaciers ▶ **iceberg** *n* large floating mass of ice ▶ **icebox** *n* (*US*) refrigerator ▶ **icecap** *n* mass of ice permanently covering an area ▶ **ice cream** sweet creamy frozen food ▶ **ice cube** small square block of ice added to a drink to cool it ▶ **ice floe** sheet of ice floating in the sea ▶ **ice hockey** team game like hockey played on ice with a puck ▶ **ice lolly** flavoured ice on a stick ▶ **ice pick** pointed tool for breaking ice ▶ **ice skate** boot with a steel blade fixed to the sole, to enable the wearer to glide over ice ▶ **ice-skate** *v* ▶ **ice-skater** *n*

**Icelandic** *adj* of Iceland ▷ *n* language of Iceland ▶ **Icelander** *n*

**ichthyology** [ik-thi-ol-a-jee] *n* scientific study of fish

**icicle** *n* tapering spike of ice hanging where water has dripped

**icing** *n* mixture of sugar and water etc., used to cover and decorate cakes ▶ **icing sugar** finely ground sugar for making icing

**icon** *n* picture of Christ or another religious figure, regarded as holy in the Orthodox Church; picture on a computer screen representing a function that can be activated by moving the cursor over it

**iconoclast** *n* person who attacks established ideas or principles ▶ **iconoclastic** *adj*

**ICT** Information and Communications Technology

**ID** identification

**id** *n* (*Psychoanalysis*) the mind's instinctive unconscious energies

**idea** *n* plan or thought formed in the mind; thought of something; belief or opinion

**ideal** *adj* most suitable; perfect ▷ *n* conception of something that is perfect; perfect person or thing ▶ **ideally** *adv* ▶ **idealism** *n* tendency to seek perfection in everything ▶ **idealist** *n* ▶ **idealistic** *adj* ▶ **idealize** *v* regard or portray as perfect or nearly perfect ▶ **idealization** *n*

**idem** *pron, adj* (*Latin*) the same: used to refer to an article, chapter, or book already quoted

**identical** *adj* exactly the same ▶ **identically** *adv*

**identify** *v* **-fying, -fied** prove or recognize as being a certain person or thing; (foll by *with*) understand and sympathize with (a person or group that one regards as being similar or similarly situated); treat as being the same ▶ **identifiable** *adj* ▶ **identification** *n*

**Identikit**® *n* composite picture, assembled from descriptions given, of a person wanted by the police

**identity** *n*, *pl* **-ties** state of being a specified person or thing; individuality or personality; state of being the same ▶ **identity theft** crime of using financial accounts fraudulently in another person's name without their knowledge

**ideology** *n*, *pl* **-gies** body of ideas and beliefs of a group, nation, etc. ▶ **ideological** *adj* ▶ **ideologist** *n*

**idiocy** *n* utter stupidity

**idiom** *n* group of words which when used together have a different meaning from the words individually e.g. *raining cats and dogs*; way of expression natural or peculiar to a language or group ▶ **idiomatic** *adj* ▶ **idiomatically** *adv*

**idiosyncrasy** *n*, *pl* **-sies** personal peculiarity of mind, habit, or behaviour

**idiot** *n* foolish or stupid person; (*offens*) mentally retarded person ▶ **idiotic** *adj* ▶ **idiotically** *adv*

**idle** *adj* not doing anything; not willing to work, lazy; not being used; useless or meaningless e.g. *an idle threat* ▷ *v* (usu. foll by *away*) spend (time) doing very little; (of an engine) run slowly with the gears disengaged ▶ **idleness** *n* ▶ **idler** *n* ▶ **idly** *adv*

**idol** *n* object of excessive devotion; image of a god as an object of worship ▶ **idolatry** *n* worship of idols ▶ **idolatrous** *adj* ▶ **idolize** *v* love or admire excessively

**idyll** [**id**-ill] *n* scene or time of great peace and happiness ▶ **idyllic** *adj* ▶ **idyllically** *adv*

**i.e.** that is to say

**IED** improvised explosive device

**if** *conj* on the condition or supposition that; whether; even though ▷ *n* uncertainty or doubt e.g. *no ifs, ands, or buts* ▶ **iffy** *adj* (*informal*) doubtful, uncertain

**igloo** *n*, *pl* **-loos** dome-shaped Inuit house made of snow and ice

**igneous** [**ig**-nee-uss] *adj* (of rock) formed as molten rock cools and hardens

**ignite** *v* catch fire or set fire to

**ignition** *n* system that ignites the fuel-and-air mixture to start an engine; igniting

**ignoble** *adj* dishonourable

**ignominy** [**ig**-nom-in-ee] *n* humiliating disgrace ▶ **ignominious** *adj* ▶ **ignominiously** *adv*

**ignoramus** *n*, *pl* **-muses** ignorant person

**ignorant** *adj* lacking knowledge; rude through lack of knowledge of good manners ▶ **ignorance** *n*

**ignore** *v* refuse to notice, disregard deliberately

**iguana** *n* large tropical American lizard

**ileum** *n* lowest part of the small intestine

**ilk** *n* type e.g. *others of his ilk*

**ill** *adj* not in good health; harmful or unpleasant e.g. *ill effects* ▷ *n* evil, harm ▷ *adv* badly; hardly, with difficulty e.g. *I can ill afford to lose him* **ill at ease** uncomfortable, unable to relax ▶ **illness** *n* ▶ **ill-advised** *adj* badly thought out; unwise ▶ **ill-disposed** *adj* (often foll by *towards*) unfriendly, unsympathetic ▶ **ill-fated** *adj* doomed to end unhappily

▶ **ill-gotten** adj obtained dishonestly ▶ **ill-health** n condition of being unwell ▶ **ill-mannered** adj having bad manners ▶ **ill-treat** v treat cruelly ▶ **ill will** unkind feeling, hostility

**illegal** adj against the law ▶ **illegally** adv ▶ **illegality** n, pl **-ties**

**illegible** adj unable to be read or deciphered

**illegitimate** adj born of parents not married to each other; not lawful ▶ **illegitimacy** n

**illicit** adj illegal; forbidden or disapproved of by society

**illiterate** n, adj (person) unable to read or write ▶ **illiteracy** n

**illogical** adj unreasonable; not logical ▶ **illogicality** n

**illuminate** v light up; make clear, explain; decorate with lights; (Hist) decorate (a manuscript) with designs of gold and bright colours ▶ **illumination** n ▶ **illuminating** adj

**illusion** n deceptive appearance or belief ▶ **illusionist** n conjuror ▶ **illusory** adj seeming to be true, but actually false

**illustrate** v explain by use of examples; provide (a book or text) with pictures; be an example of ▶ **illustration** n picture or diagram; example ▶ **illustrative** adj ▶ **illustrator** n

**illustrious** adj famous and distinguished

**IM** (Computing) instant messaging

**image** n mental picture of someone or something; impression people have of a person, organization, etc.; representation of a person or thing in a work of art; optical reproduction of someone or something, for example in a mirror; person or thing that looks almost

exactly like another; figure of speech, esp. a metaphor or simile ▶ **imagery** n images collectively, esp. in the arts

**imagine** v form a mental image of; think, believe, or guess ▶ **imaginable** adj ▶ **imaginary** adj existing only in the imagination ▶ **imagination** n ability to make mental images of things that may not exist in real life; creative mental ability ▶ **imaginative** adj having or showing a lot of creative mental ability ▶ **imaginatively** adv

> **SPELLING TIP**
> Remembering that an e changes to an a to form **imagination** is a good way of getting **imaginary** right, because it has an a instead of an e too

**imago** [im-**may**-go] n, pl **imagoes** or **imagines** sexually mature adult insect

**imam** n leader of prayers in a mosque; title of some Islamic leaders

**IMAX®** [**eye**-max] n film projection process which produces an image ten times larger than standard

**imbalance** n lack of balance or proportion

**imbecile** [imb-ess-eel] n stupid person ▷ adj (also **imbecilic**) stupid or senseless ▶ **imbecility** n

**imbibe** v drink (alcoholic drinks); (lit) absorb (ideas etc.)

**imbroglio** [imb-**role**-ee-oh] n, pl **-ios** confusing and complicated situation

**imbue** v **-buing**, **-bued** (usu. foll by with) fill or inspire with (ideals or principles)

**IMF** International Monetary Fund

**imitate** v take as a model; copy the voice and mannerisms of, esp. for entertainment ▶ **imitation**

*n* copy of an original; imitating ▶ **imitative** *adj* ▶ **imitator** *n*

**immaculate** *adj* completely clean or tidy; completely flawless ▶ **immaculately** *adv*

**immanent** *adj* present within and throughout something ▶ **immanence** *n*

**immaterial** *adj* not important, not relevant

**immature** *adj* not fully developed; lacking wisdom or stability because of youth ▶ **immaturity** *n*

**immediate** *adj* occurring at once; next or nearest in time, space, or relationship ▶ **immediately** *adv* ▶ **immediacy** *n*

**immemorial** *adj* **since, from time immemorial** longer than anyone can remember

**immense** *adj* extremely large ▶ **immensely** *adv* to a very great degree ▶ **immensity** *n*

**immerse** *v* involve deeply, engross; plunge (something or someone) into liquid ▶ **immersion** *n* ▶ **immersion heater** electrical device in a domestic hot-water tank for heating water

**immigration** *n* coming to a foreign country in order to settle there ▶ **immigrant** *n*

**imminent** *adj* about to happen ▶ **imminently** *adv* ▶ **imminence** *n*

**immobile** *adj* not moving; unable to move ▶ **immobility** *n* ▶ **immobilize** *v* make unable to move or work

**immoderate** *adj* excessive or unreasonable

**immolate** *v* kill as a sacrifice ▶ **immolation** *n*

**immoral** *adj* morally wrong, corrupt; sexually depraved or promiscuous ▶ **immorality** *n*

**USAGE NOTE**
Do not confuse *immoral* with *amoral*, which means 'having no moral standards'

**immortal** *adj* living forever; famous for all time ▷ *n* person whose fame will last for all time; immortal being ▶ **immortality** *n* ▶ **immortalize** *v*

**immune** *adj* protected against a specific disease; (foll by *to*) secure (against); (foll by *from*) exempt (from) ▶ **immunity** *n*, *pl* **-ties** ability to resist disease; freedom from prosecution, tax, etc. ▶ **immunize** *v* make immune to a disease ▶ **immunization** *n*

**immunodeficiency** *n* deficiency in or breakdown of a person's ability to fight diseases

**immunology** *n* branch of medicine concerned with the study of immunity ▶ **immunological** *adj* ▶ **immunologist** *n*

**immutable** [im-**mute**-a-bl] *adj* unchangeable ▶ **immutability** *n*

**imp** *n* (in folklore) mischievous small creature with magical powers; mischievous child

**impact** *n* strong effect; (force of) a collision ▷ *v* press firmly into something

**impair** *v* weaken or damage ▶ **impairment** *n*

**impala** [imp-**ah**-la] *n* southern African antelope

**impale** *v* pierce with a sharp object

**impalpable** *adj* difficult to define or understand

**impart** *v* communicate (information); give

**impartial** *adj* not favouring one side or the other ▶ **impartially** *adv* ▶ **impartiality** *n*

**impassable** *adj* (of a road etc.) impossible to travel through or over

**impasse** [**am**-pass] *n* situation in which progress is impossible

**impassioned** adj full of emotion

**impassive** adj showing no emotion, calm

**impatient** adj irritable at any delay or difficulty; restless (to have or do something) ▶ **impatiently** adv ▶ **impatience** n

**impeach** v charge with a serious crime against the state ▶ **impeachment** n

**impeccable** adj without fault, excellent ▶ **impeccably** adv

**impecunious** adj penniless, poor

**impedance** [imp-**eed**-anss] n (Electricity) measure of the opposition to the flow of an alternating current

**impede** v hinder in action or progress ▶ **impediment** n something that makes action, speech, or progress difficult ▶ **impedimenta** pl n objects impeding progress, esp. baggage or equipment

**impel** v -pelling, -pelled push or force (someone) to do something

**impending** adj (esp. of something bad) about to happen

**impenetrable** adj impossible to get through; impossible to understand

**imperative** adj extremely urgent, vital; (Grammar) denoting a mood of verbs used in commands ▷ n (Grammar) imperative mood

**imperceptible** adj too slight or gradual to be noticed ▶ **imperceptibly** adv

**imperfect** adj having faults or mistakes; not complete; (Grammar) denoting a tense of verbs describing continuous, incomplete, or repeated past actions ▷ n (Grammar) imperfect tense ▶ **imperfection** n

**imperial** adj of or like an empire or emperor; denoting a system of

weights and measures formerly used in Britain ▶ **imperialism** n rule by one country over many others ▶ **imperialist** adj, n

**imperil** v -illing, -illed put in danger

**imperious** adj proud and domineering

**impersonal** adj not relating to any particular person, objective; lacking human warmth or sympathy; (Grammar) (of a verb) without a personal subject e.g. it is snowing ▶ **impersonality** n

**impersonate** v pretend to be (another person); copy the voice and mannerisms of, esp. for entertainment ▶ **impersonation** n ▶ **impersonator** n

**impertinent** adj disrespectful or rude ▶ **impertinently** adv ▶ **impertinence** n

**imperturbable** adj calm, not excitable

**impervious** adj (foll by to) not letting (water etc.) through; not influenced by (a feeling, argument, etc.)

**impetigo** [imp-it-**tie**-go] n contagious skin disease

**impetuous** adj done or acting without thought, rash ▶ **impetuously** adv ▶ **impetuosity** n

**impetus** [**imp**-it-uss] n, pl -tuses incentive, impulse; force that starts a body moving

**impinge** v (foll by on) affect or restrict

**impious** [**imp**-ee-uss] adj showing a lack of respect or reverence

**impish** adj mischievous

**implacable** adj not prepared to be appeased, unyielding ▶ **implacably** adv ▶ **implacability** n

**implant** n (*Med*) something put into someone's body, usu. by surgical operation ▷ v put (something) into someone's body, usu. by surgical operation; fix firmly in someone's mind ▸ **implantation** n

**implement** v carry out (instructions etc.) ▷ n tool, instrument ▸ **implementation** n

**implicate** v show to be involved, esp. in a crime ▸ **implication** n something implied

**implicit** adj expressed indirectly; absolute and unquestioning e.g. *implicit support* ▸ **implicitly** adv

**implode** v collapse inwards

**implore** v beg earnestly

**imply** v -**plying**, -**plied** indicate by hinting, suggest; involve as a necessary consequence

**impolitic** adj unwise or inadvisable

**imponderable** n, adj (something) impossible to assess

**import** v bring in (goods) from another country ▷ n something imported; importance; meaning ▸ **importation** n ▸ **importer** n

**important** adj of great significance or value; having influence or power ▸ **importance** n

**importunate** adj persistent or demanding ▸ **importune** v harass with persistent requests ▸ **importunity** n, pl -**ties**

**impose** v force the acceptance of; (foll by *on*) take unfair advantage (of) ▸ **imposing** adj grand, impressive ▸ **imposition** n unreasonable demand

**impossible** adj not able to be done or to happen; absurd or unreasonable ▸ **impossibly** adv ▸ **impossibility** n, pl -**ties**

**imposter, impostor** n person who cheats or swindles by pretending to be someone else

**impotent** [**imp**-a-tent] adj powerless; (of a man) incapable of sexual intercourse ▸ **impotence** n ▸ **impotently** adv

**impound** v take legal possession of, confiscate

**impoverish** v make poor or weak ▸ **impoverishment** n

**impracticable** adj incapable of being put into practice

**impractical** adj not sensible

**imprecation** n curse

**impregnable** adj impossible to break into ▸ **impregnability** n

**impregnate** v saturate, spread all through; make pregnant ▸ **impregnation** n

**impresario** n, pl -**ios** person who runs theatre performances, concerts, etc.

> **SPELLING TIP**
> Note that **impresario** has only one s

**impress** v affect strongly, usu. favourably; stress, emphasize; imprint, stamp ▸ **impression** n effect, esp. a strong or favourable one; vague idea; impersonation for entertainment; mark made by pressing ▸ **impressionable** adj easily impressed or influenced

**Impressionism** n art style that gives a general effect or mood rather than form or structure ▸ **Impressionist** n ▸ **Impressionistic** adj

**impressive** adj making a strong impression, esp. through size, importance, or quality

**imprimatur** [imp-rim-**ah**-ter] n official approval to print a book

**imprint** n mark made by printing or stamping; publisher's name and address on a book ▷ v produce (a mark) by printing or stamping

**imprison** v put in prison ▸ **imprisonment** n

**improbable** *adj* not likely to be true or to happen ▸ **improbability** *n*, *pl* **-ties**

**impromptu** *adj* without planning or preparation

**improper** *adj* indecent; incorrect or irregular ▸ **improper fraction** fraction in which the numerator is larger than the denominator, as in 5/3

**impropriety** [imp-roe-**pry**-a-tee] *n*, *pl* **-ties** unsuitable or slightly improper behaviour

**improve** *v* make or become better ▸ **improvement** *n*

**improvident** *adj* not planning for future needs ▸ **improvidence** *n*

**improvise** *v* make use of whatever materials are available; make up (a piece of music, speech, etc.) as one goes along ▸ **improvisation** *n*

**impudent** *adj* cheeky, disrespectful ▸ **impudently** *adv* ▸ **impudence** *n*

**impugn** [imp-**yoon**] *v* challenge the truth or validity of

**impulse** *n* sudden urge to do something; short electrical signal passing along a wire or nerve or through the air **on impulse** suddenly and without planning ▸ **impulsive** *adj* acting or done without careful consideration ▸ **impulsively** *adv*

**impunity** [imp-**yoon**-it-ee] *n* **with impunity** without punishment

**impure** *adj* having dirty or unwanted substances mixed in; immoral, obscene ▸ **impurity** *n*

**impute** *v* attribute responsibility to ▸ **imputation** *n*

**in** *prep* indicating position inside, state or situation, etc. e.g. *in the net; in tears* ▷ *adv* indicating position inside, entry into, etc. e.g. *she stayed in; come in* ▷ *adj* fashionable ▸ **inward** *adj* directed towards the middle; situated within; spiritual or mental ▷ *adv* (also **inwards**) towards the inside or middle ▸ **inwardly** *adv*

**inability** *n* lack of means or skill to do something

**inaccessible** *adj* impossible or very difficult to reach ▸ **inaccessibility** *n*

**inaccurate** *adj* not correct ▸ **inaccuracy** *n*, *pl* **-cies**

**inadequate** *adj* not enough; not good enough ▸ **inadequacy** *n*

**inadvertent** *adj* unintentional ▸ **inadvertently** *adv*

**inalienable** *adj* not able to be taken away e.g. *an inalienable right*

**inane** *adj* senseless, silly ▸ **inanity** *n*

**inanimate** *adj* not living

**inappropriate** *adj* not suitable

**inarticulate** *adj* unable to express oneself clearly or well

**inasmuch as** *conj* because or in so far as

**inaugurate** *v* open or begin the use of, esp. with ceremony; formally establish (a new leader) in office ▸ **inaugural** *adj* ▸ **inauguration** *n*

**inauspicious** *adj* unlucky, likely to have an unfavourable outcome

**inauthentic** *adj* not authentic, false

**inboard** *adj* (of a boat's engine) inside the hull

**inborn** *adj* existing from birth, natural

**inbox** *n* (on a computer) folder in a mailbox in which incoming messages are stored and displayed

**inbred** *adj* produced as a result of inbreeding; inborn or ingrained

**inbreeding** *n* breeding of animals or people that are closely related

**inbuilt** *adj* present from the start

**Inc.** (*US & Aust*) (of a company) incorporated

**incalculable** *adj* too great to be estimated

**in camera** *adv* see **camera**

**incandescent** *adj* glowing with heat ▸ **incandescence** *n*

**incantation** *n* ritual chanting of magic words or sounds

**incapable** *adj* (foll by *of*) unable (to do something); incompetent

**incapacitate** *v* deprive of strength or ability ▸ **incapacity** *n*

**incarcerate** *v* imprison ▸ **incarceration** *n*

**incarnate** *adj* in human form ▸ **incarnation** *n* ▸ **Incarnation** *n* (*Christianity*) God's coming to earth in human form as Jesus Christ

**incendiary** [in-**send**-ya-ree] *adj* (of a bomb, attack, etc.) designed to cause fires ▷ *n*, *pl* -**aries** bomb designed to cause fires

**incense¹** *v* make very angry

**incense²** *n* substance that gives off a sweet perfume when burned

**incentive** *n* something that encourages effort or action

**inception** *n* beginning

**incessant** *adj* never stopping ▸ **incessantly** *adv*

**incest** *n* sexual intercourse between two people too closely related to marry ▸ **incestuous** *adj*

**inch** *n* unit of length equal to one twelfth of a foot or 2.54 centimetres ▷ *v* move slowly and gradually

**inchoate** [in-**koe**-ate] *adj* just begun and not yet properly developed

**incidence** *n* extent or frequency of occurrence

**incident** *n* something that happens; event involving violence

**incidental** *adj* occurring in connection with or resulting from something more important ▸ **incidentally** *adv* ▸ **incidental music** background music for a film or play

**incinerate** *v* burn to ashes ▸ **incineration** *n* ▸ **incinerator** *n* furnace for burning rubbish

**incipient** *adj* just starting to appear or happen

**incise** *v* cut into with a sharp tool ▸ **incision** *n* ▸ **incisor** *n* front tooth, used for biting into food

**incisive** *adj* direct and forceful

**incite** *v* stir up, provoke ▸ **incitement** *n*

**incivility** *n*, *pl* -**ties** rudeness or a rude remark

**inclement** *adj* (of weather) stormy or severe

**incline** *v* lean, slope; (cause to) have a certain disposition or tendency ▷ *n* slope ▸ **inclination** *n* liking, tendency, or preference; slope

**include** *v* have as part of the whole; put in as part of a set or group ▸ **inclusion** *n* ▸ **inclusive** *adj* including everything (specified) ▸ **inclusively** *adv*

**incognito** [in-kog-**nee**-toe] *adj*, *adv* having adopted a false identity ▷ *n*, *pl* -**tos** false identity

**incoherent** *adj* unclear and impossible to understand ▸ **incoherence** *n* ▸ **incoherently** *adv*

**income** *n* amount of money earned from work, investments, etc. ▸ **income support** (in New Zealand) allowance paid by the government to people with a very low income ▸ **income tax** personal tax levied on annual income

**incoming** *adj* coming in; about to come into office

**incommode** *v* cause inconvenience to

**incommunicado** *adj*, *adv* deprived of communication with other people

**incomparable** *adj* beyond comparison, unequalled ▶ **incomparably** *adv*

**incompatible** *adj* inconsistent or conflicting ▶ **incompatibility** *n*

**incompetent** *adj* not having the necessary ability or skill to do something ▶ **incompetence** *n*

**inconceivable** *adj* extremely unlikely, unimaginable

**inconclusive** *adj* not giving a final decision or result

**incongruous** *adj* inappropriate or out of place ▶ **incongruously** *adv* ▶ **incongruity** *n, pl* **-ties**

**inconsequential** *adj* unimportant, insignificant

**inconsiderable** *adj* **not inconsiderable** fairly large

**inconstant** *adj* liable to change one's loyalties or opinions

**incontinent** *adj* unable to control one's bladder or bowels ▶ **incontinence** *n*

**incontrovertible** *adj* impossible to deny or disprove

**inconvenience** *n* trouble or difficulty ▷ *v* cause trouble or difficulty to ▶ **inconvenient** *adj*

**incorporate** *v* include or be included as part of a larger unit

**incorporeal** *adj* without material form

**incorrigible** *adj* beyond correction or reform

**incorruptible** *adj* too honest to be bribed or corrupted; not subject to decay

**increase** *v* make or become greater in size, number, etc. ▷ *n* rise in number, size, etc.; amount by which something increases ▶ **increasingly** *adv*

**incredible** *adj* hard to believe or imagine; (*informal*) marvellous, amazing ▶ **incredibly** *adv*

**incredulous** *adj* not willing to believe something ▶ **incredulity** *n*

**increment** *n* increase in money or value, esp. a regular salary increase ▶ **incremental** *adj*

**incriminate** *v* make (someone) seem guilty of a crime ▶ **incriminating** *adj*

**incubate** [in-cube-ate] *v* (of a bird) hatch (eggs) by sitting on them; grow (bacteria); (of bacteria) remain inactive in an animal or person before causing disease ▶ **incubation** *n* ▶ **incubator** *n* heated enclosed apparatus for rearing premature babies; apparatus for artificially hatching birds' eggs

**incubus** [in-cube-uss] *n, pl* **-bi** or **-buses** (in folklore) demon believed to have sex with sleeping women; nightmarish burden or worry

**inculcate** *v* fix in someone's mind by constant repetition ▶ **inculcation** *n*

**incumbent** *n* person holding a particular office or position ▷ *adj* **it is incumbent on** it is the duty of ▶ **incumbency** *n, pl* **-cies**

**incur** *v* **-curring, -curred** cause (something unpleasant) to happen

**incurable** *adj* not able to be cured ▶ **incurably** *adv*

**incurious** *adj* showing no curiosity or interest

**incursion** *n* sudden brief invasion

**indebted** *adj* owing gratitude for help or favours; owing money ▶ **indebtedness** *n*

**indecent** *adj* morally or sexually offensive; unsuitable or unseemly e.g. *indecent haste* ▶ **indecently** *adv* ▶ **indecency** *n* ▶ **indecent assault** sexual attack which does not include rape ▶ **indecent exposure** showing of one's genitals in public

**indecipherable** *adj* impossible to read

**indeed** *adv* really, certainly ▷ *interj* expression of indignation or surprise

**indefatigable** *adj* never getting tired ▸ **indefatigably** *adv*

**indefensible** *adj* unable to be justified; impossible to defend

**indefinite** *adj* without exact limits e.g. *for an indefinite period*; vague, unclear ▸ **indefinite article** (*Grammar*) the word *a* or *an* ▸ **indefinitely** *adv*

**indelible** *adj* impossible to erase or remove; making indelible marks ▸ **indelibly** *adv*

**indelicate** *adj* offensive or embarrassing

**indemnify** *v* **-ifying, -ified** secure against loss, damage, or liability; compensate for loss or damage

**indemnity** *n*, *pl* **-ties** insurance against loss or damage; compensation for loss or damage

**indent** *v* start (a line of writing) further from the margin than the other lines; order (goods) using a special order form ▸ **indentation** *n* dent in a surface or edge

**indenture** *n* contract, esp. one binding an apprentice to his or her employer

**independent** *adj* free from the control or influence of others; separate; financially self-reliant; capable of acting for oneself or on one's own ▷ *n* politician who does not represent any political party ▸ **independently** *adv* ▸ **independence** *n*

> **SPELLING TIP**
> **Independent** should be spelt with an *e* at the end in the same way as the noun it is related to: **independence**

**in-depth** *adj* detailed, thorough

**indescribable** *adj* too intense or extreme for words ▸ **indescribably** *adv*

**indeterminate** *adj* uncertain in extent, amount, or nature ▸ **indeterminacy** *n*

**index** *n*, *pl* **indices** [in-diss-eez] alphabetical list of names or subjects dealt with in a book; file or catalogue used to find things ▷ *v* provide (a book) with an index; enter in an index; make index-linked ▸ **index finger** finger next to the thumb ▸ **index-linked** *adj* (of pensions, wages, etc.) rising or falling in line with the cost of living

**Indian** *n*, *adj* (person) from India; Native American ▸ **Indian summer** period of warm sunny weather in autumn

**indicate** *v* be a sign or symptom of; point out; state briefly; (of a measuring instrument) show a reading of ▸ **indication** *n* ▸ **indicative** *adj* (foll by *of*) suggesting; (*Grammar*) denoting a mood of verbs used to make a statement ▷ *n* (*Grammar*) indicative mood ▸ **indicator** *n* something acting as a sign or indication; flashing light on a vehicle showing the driver's intention to turn; dial or gauge

**indict** [in-**dite**] *v* formally charge with a crime ▸ **indictable** *adj* ▸ **indictment** *n*

**indie** *adj* (*informal*) (of rock music) released by an independent record company

**indifferent** *adj* showing no interest or concern; of poor quality ▸ **indifference** *n* ▸ **indifferently** *adv*

**indigenous** [in-**dij**-in-uss] *adj* born in or natural to a country

**indigent** *adj* extremely poor ▸ **indigence** *n*

**indigestion** n (discomfort or pain caused by) difficulty in digesting food ▶ **indigestible** adj

**indignation** n anger at something unfair or wrong ▶ **indignant** adj feeling or showing indignation ▶ **indignantly** adv

**indignity** n, pl **-ties** embarrassing or humiliating treatment

**indigo** adj deep violet-blue ▷ n dye of this colour

**indirect** adj done or caused by someone or something else; not by a straight route ▶ **indirect object** (Grammar) person or thing indirectly affected by the action of a verb, e.g. Amy in I bought Amy a bag ▶ **indirect tax** tax added to the price of something

**indiscreet** adj incautious or tactless in revealing secrets ▶ **indiscreetly** adv ▶ **indiscretion** n

**indiscriminate** adj showing lack of careful thought

**indispensable** adj absolutely essential

> **SPELLING TIP**
> For every twenty examples of the word **indispensable** in the Collins Corpus, there is one example of the misspelling indispensible

**indisposed** adj unwell, ill ▶ **indisposition** n

**indisputable** adj beyond doubt ▶ **indisputably** adv

**indissoluble** adj permanent

**indium** n (Chem) soft silvery-white metallic element

**individual** adj characteristic of or meant for a single person or thing; separate, distinct; distinctive, unusual ▷ n single person or thing ▶ **individually** adv ▶ **individuality** n ▶ **individualism** n principle of living one's life in one's own way ▶ **individualist** n ▶ **individualistic** adj

**indoctrinate** v teach (someone) to accept a doctrine or belief uncritically ▶ **indoctrination** n

**Indo-European** adj, n (of) a family of languages spoken in most of Europe and much of Asia, including English, Russian, and Hindi

**indolent** adj lazy ▶ **indolence** n

**indomitable** adj too strong to be defeated or discouraged ▶ **indomitably** adv

**indoor** adj inside a building ▶ **indoors** adv

**indubitable** adj beyond doubt, certain ▶ **indubitably** adv

**induce** v persuade or influence; cause; (Med) cause (a woman) to go into labour or bring on (labour) by the use of drugs etc. ▶ **inducement** n something used to persuade someone to do something

**induct** v formally install (someone, esp. a clergyman) in office

**inductance** n property of an electric circuit creating voltage by a change of current

**induction** n reasoning process by which general conclusions are drawn from particular instances; process by which electrical or magnetic properties are produced by the proximity of an electrified or magnetic object; formal introduction into an office or position ▶ **inductive** adj ▶ **induction coil** transformer for producing a high voltage from a low voltage ▶ **induction course** training course to help familiarize someone with a new job

**indulge** v allow oneself pleasure; allow (someone) to have or do everything he or she wants ▶ **indulgence** n something allowed because it gives pleasure; act of indulging oneself or someone else; liberal or tolerant treatment ▶ **indulgent** adj ▶ **indulgently** adv

**industrial** adj of, used in, or employed in industry ▶ **industrialize** v develop large-scale industry in (a country or region) ▶ **industrialization** n ▶ **industrial action** ways in which workers can protest about their conditions, e.g. by striking or working to rule ▶ **industrial estate** area of land set aside for factories and warehouses ▶ **industrial relations** relations between management and workers

**industry** n, pl **-tries** manufacture of goods; branch of this e.g. *the music industry*; quality of working hard ▶ **industrious** adj hard-working

**inebriate** n, adj (person who is) habitually drunk ▶ **inebriated** adj drunk ▶ **inebriation** n

**inedible** adj not fit to be eaten

**ineffable** adj too great for words ▶ **ineffably** adv

**ineffectual** adj having very little effect

**ineligible** adj not qualified for or entitled to something

**ineluctable** adj impossible to avoid

**inept** adj clumsy, lacking skill ▶ **ineptitude** n

**inequitable** adj unfair

**ineradicable** adj impossible to remove

**inert** adj without the power of motion or resistance; chemically unreactive ▶ **inertness** n

**inertia** n feeling of unwillingness to do anything; (*Physics*) tendency of a body to remain still or continue moving unless a force is applied to it

**inescapable** adj unavoidable

**inestimable** adj too great to be estimated ▶ **inestimably** adv

**inevitable** adj unavoidable, sure to happen **the inevitable** something that cannot be prevented ▶ **inevitably** adv ▶ **inevitability** n

**inexorable** adj unable to be prevented from continuing or progressing ▶ **inexorably** adv

**inexpert** adj lacking skill

**inexplicable** adj impossible to explain ▶ **inexplicably** adv

**in extremis** adv (*Latin*) in great difficulty; on the point of death

**inextricable** adj impossible to escape from; impossible to disentangle or separate

**infallible** adj never wrong ▶ **infallibly** adv ▶ **infallibility** n

**infamous** [in-fam-uss] adj well-known for something bad ▶ **infamously** adv ▶ **infamy** n

**infant** n very young child ▶ **infancy** n early childhood; early stage of development ▶ **infantile** adj childish

**infanticide** n murder of an infant; person guilty of this

**infantry** n soldiers who fight on foot

**infatuated** adj feeling intense unreasoning passion

**infatuation** n intense unreasoning passion

**infect** v affect with a disease; affect with a feeling ▶ **infection** n ▶ **infectious** adj (of a disease) spreading without actual contact; spreading from person to person e.g. *infectious enthusiasm*

**infer** v **-ferring, -ferred** work out from evidence ▶ **inference** n

**USAGE NOTE**
Someone *infers* something by 'reading between the lines' of a remark. Do not confuse with *imply*, which means 'to hint'

**inferior** adj lower in quality, position, or status ▷ n person of lower position or status ▸ **inferiority** n

**infernal** adj of hell; (informal) irritating ▸ **infernally** adv

**inferno** n, pl **-nos** intense raging fire

**infertile** adj unable to produce offspring; (of soil) barren, not productive ▸ **infertility** n

**infest** v inhabit or overrun in unpleasantly large numbers ▸ **infestation** n

**infidel** n person with no religion; person who rejects a particular religion, esp. Christianity or Islam

**infidelity** n, pl **-ties** (act of) sexual unfaithfulness to one's husband, wife, or lover

**infighting** n quarrelling within a group

**infiltrate** v enter gradually and secretly ▸ **infiltration** n ▸ **infiltrator** n

**infinite** [in-fin-it] adj without any limit or end ▸ **infinitely** adv

**infinitesimal** adj extremely small

**infinitive** n (Grammar) form of a verb not showing tense, person, or number e.g. to sleep

**infinity** n endless space, time, or number

**infirm** adj physically or mentally weak ▸ **infirmity** n, pl **-ties**

**infirmary** n, pl **-ries** hospital

**inflame** v make angry or excited ▸ **inflamed** adj (of part of the body) red, swollen, and painful because of infection ▸ **inflammation** n

**inflammable** adj easily set on fire

> **USAGE NOTE**
> Inflammable means the same as flammable but is falling out of general use as it was often mistaken to mean 'not flammable'

**inflammatory** adj likely to provoke anger

**inflate** v expand by filling with air or gas; cause economic inflation in ▸ **inflatable** adj able to be inflated ▷ n plastic or rubber object which can be inflated

**inflation** n inflating; increase in prices and fall in the value of money ▸ **inflationary** adj

**inflection, inflexion** n change in the pitch of the voice; (Grammar) change in the form of a word to show grammatical use

**inflexible** adj unwilling to be persuaded, obstinate; (of a policy etc.) firmly fixed, unalterable ▸ **inflexibly** adv ▸ **inflexibility** n

**inflict** v impose (something unpleasant) on ▸ **infliction** n

**inflorescence** n (Botany) arrangement of flowers on a stem

**influence** n effect of one person or thing on another; (person with) the power to have such an effect ▷ v have an effect on ▸ **influential** adj

**influenza** n contagious viral disease causing headaches, muscle pains, and fever

**influx** n arrival or entry of many people or things

**info** n (informal) information

**inform** v tell; give incriminating information to the police ▸ **informant** n person who gives information ▸ **information** n knowledge or facts ▸ **informative** adj giving useful information ▸ **information superhighway** worldwide network of computers transferring information at high speed ▸ **information technology** use of computers and electronic technology to store and communicate information ▸ **informer** n person who informs to the police

**informal** adj relaxed and friendly; appropriate for everyday life or use ▶ **informally** adv ▶ **informality** n

**infra dig** adj (informal) beneath one's dignity

**infrared** adj of or using rays below the red end of the visible spectrum

**infrastructure** n basic facilities, services, and equipment needed for a country or organization to function properly

**infringe** v break (a law or agreement) ▶ **infringement** n

**infuriate** v make very angry

**infuse** v fill (with an emotion or quality); soak to extract flavour ▶ **infusion** n infusing; liquid obtained by infusing

**ingenious** [in-**jean**-ee-uss] adj showing cleverness and originality ▶ **ingeniously** adv ▶ **ingenuity** [in-jen-**new**-it-ee] n

**ingénue** [**an**-jay-new] n naive young woman, esp. as a role played by an actress

**ingenuous** [in-**jen**-new-uss] adj unsophisticated and trusting ▶ **ingenuously** adv

**ingest** v take (food or liquid) into the body ▶ **ingestion** n

**inglorious** adj dishonourable, shameful

**ingot** n oblong block of cast metal

**ingrained** adj firmly fixed

**ingratiate** v try to make (oneself) popular with someone ▶ **ingratiating** adj ▶ **ingratiatingly** adv

**ingredient** n component of a mixture or compound

**ingress** n act or right of entering

**ingrowing** adj (of a toenail) growing abnormally into the flesh

**inhabit** v -habiting, -habited live in ▶ **inhabitable** adj ▶ **inhabitant** n

**inhale** v breathe in (air, smoke, etc.) ▶ **inhalation** n ▶ **inhalant**

n medical preparation inhaled to help breathing problems ▶ **inhaler** n container for an inhalant

**inherent** adj existing as an inseparable part ▶ **inherently** adv

**inherit** v -heriting, -herited receive (money etc.) from someone who has died; receive (a characteristic) from an earlier generation; receive from a predecessor ▶ **inheritance** n ▶ **inheritance tax** tax paid on property left at death ▶ **inheritor** n

**inhibit** v -hibiting, -hibited restrain (an impulse or desire); hinder or prevent (action) ▶ **inhibited** adj ▶ **inhibition** n feeling of fear or embarrassment that stops one from behaving naturally

**inhospitable** adj not welcoming, unfriendly; difficult to live in, harsh

**inhuman** adj cruel or brutal; not human

**inhumane** adj cruel or brutal ▶ **inhumanity** n

**inimical** adj unfavourable or hostile

**inimitable** adj impossible to imitate, unique

**iniquity** n, pl -ties injustice or wickedness; wicked act ▶ **iniquitous** adj

**initial** adj first, at the beginning ▶ n first letter, esp. of a person's name ▶ v -tialling, -tialled sign with one's initials ▶ **initially** adv

**initiate** v begin or set going; admit (someone) into a closed group; instruct in the basics of something ▶ n recently initiated person ▶ **initiation** n ▶ **initiator** n

**initiative** n first step, commencing move; ability to act independently

**inject** v put (a fluid) into the body with a syringe; introduce (a new element) e.g. *try to inject a bit of humour* ▶ **injection** n

**injudicious** adj showing poor judgment, unwise

**injunction** n court order not to do something

**injure** v hurt physically or mentally ▸ **injury** n, pl **-ries** ▸ **injury time** (Sport) playing time added at the end of a match to compensate for time spent treating injured players ▸ **injurious** adj

**injustice** n unfairness; unfair action

**ink** n coloured liquid used for writing or printing ▸ v (foll by in) mark in ink (something already marked in pencil) ▸ **inky** adj dark or black; covered in ink

**inkhosi** [in-**koh**-see] n, pl **amakhosi** (SAfr) tribal chief

**inkling** n slight idea or suspicion

**inlaid** adj set in another material so that the surface is smooth; made like this e.g. an inlaid table

**inland** adj, adv in or towards the interior of a country, away from the sea ▸ **Inland Revenue** (in Britain) government department that collects taxes

**in-laws** pl n one's husband's or wife's family

**inlay** n inlaid substance or pattern

**inlet** n narrow strip of water extending from the sea into the land; valve etc. through which liquid or gas enters

**in loco parentis** (Latin) in place of a parent

**inmate** n person living in an institution such as a prison

**inmost** adj innermost

**inn** n pub or small hotel, esp. in the country ▸ **innkeeper** n

**innards** pl n (informal) internal organs; working parts of a machine

**innate** adj being part of someone's nature, inborn

**inner** adj happening or located inside; relating to private feelings

e.g. the inner self ▸ **innermost** adj furthest inside ▸ **inner city** parts of a city near the centre, esp. having severe social and economic problems

**innings** n (Sport) player's or side's turn of batting; period of opportunity

**innocent** adj not guilty of a crime; without experience of evil; without malicious intent ▸ n innocent person, esp. a child ▸ **innocently** adv ▸ **innocence** n

**innocuous** adj not harmful ▸ **innocuously** adv

> **SPELLING TIP**
> Note there are two ns in **innocuous**, and only one c

**innovation** n new idea or method; introduction of new ideas or methods ▸ **innovate** v ▸ **innovative** adj ▸ **innovator** n

**innuendo** n, pl **-does** (remark making) an indirect reference to something rude or unpleasant

**innumerable** adj too many to be counted

**innumerate** adj having no understanding of mathematics or science ▸ **innumeracy** n

**inoculate** v protect against disease by injecting with a vaccine ▸ **inoculation** n

> **SPELLING TIP**
> It is tempting to spell **inoculate** with two ns but remember there is only one n, and only one c

**inoperable** adj (of a tumour or cancer) unable to be surgically removed

**inopportune** adj badly timed, unsuitable

**inordinate** adj excessive

**inorganic** adj not having the characteristics of living organisms; of chemical substances that do not contain carbon

**inpatient** n patient who stays in a hospital for treatment

**input** *n* resources put into a project etc.; data fed into a computer. ▷ *v* **-putting, -put** enter (data) in a computer

**inquest** *n* official inquiry into a sudden death

**inquire** *v* seek information or ask (about) ▸ **inquirer** *n*

**inquiry** *n, pl* **-ries** question; investigation

**inquisition** *n* thorough investigation; (**I-**) (*Hist*) organization within the Catholic Church for suppressing heresy ▸ **inquisitor** *n* ▸ **inquisitorial** *adj*

**inquisitive** *adj* excessively curious about other people's affairs ▸ **inquisitively** *adv*

**inquorate** *adj* without enough people present to make a quorum

**inroads** *pl n* **make inroads into** start affecting or reducing

**insalubrious** *adj* unpleasant, unhealthy, or sordid

**insane** *adj* mentally ill; stupidly irresponsible ▸ **insanely** *adv* ▸ **insanity** *n*

**insanitary** *adj* dirty or unhealthy

**insatiable** [in-**saysh**-a-bl] *adj* unable to be satisfied

**inscribe** *v* write or carve words on ▸ **inscription** *n* words inscribed

**inscrutable** *adj* mysterious, enigmatic ▸ **inscrutably** *adv*

**insect** *n* small animal with six legs and usu. wings, such as an ant or fly ▸ **insecticide** *n* substance for killing insects ▸ **insectivorous** *adj* insect-eating

**insecure** *adj* anxious, not confident; not safe or well-protected

**insemination** *n* putting semen into a woman's or female animal's body to try to make her pregnant ▸ **inseminate** *v*

**insensate** *adj* without sensation, unconscious; unfeeling

**insensible** *adj* unconscious, without feeling; (foll by *to* or *of*) not aware (of) or affected (by)

**insensitive** *adj* unaware of or ignoring other people's feelings ▸ **insensitivity** *n*

**inseparable** *adj* (of two people) spending most of the time together; (of two things) impossible to separate

> **SPELLING TIP**
> Note that the third syllable of the word **inseparable** is spelt with an *a* rather than an *e*

**insert** *v* put inside or include ▷ *n* something inserted ▸ **insertion** *n*

**inset** *n* small picture inserted within a larger one

**inshore** *adj* close to the shore ▷ *adj, adv* towards the shore

**inside** *prep* in or to the interior of ▷ *adj* on or of the inside; by or from someone within an organization e.g. *inside information* ▷ *adv* on, in, or to the inside, indoors; (*Brit, Aust & NZ slang*) in(to) prison ▷ *n* inner side, surface, or part ▷ *pl* (*informal*) stomach and bowels **inside out** with the inside facing outwards **know inside out** know thoroughly ▸ **insider** *n* member of a group who has privileged knowledge about it

> **USAGE NOTE**
> Avoid using the expression *inside of*, as the second preposition *of* is superfluous

**insidious** *adj* subtle or unseen but dangerous ▸ **insidiously** *adv*

**insight** *n* deep understanding

**insignia** *n, pl* **-nias** *or* **-nia** badge or emblem of honour or office

**insignificant** *adj* not important ▸ **insignificance** *n*

**insincere** *adj* showing false feelings, not genuine ▸ **insincerely** *adv* ▸ **insincerity** *n, pl* **-ties**

**insinuate** v suggest indirectly; work (oneself) into a position by gradual manoeuvres
▶ **insinuation** n

**insipid** adj lacking interest, spirit, or flavour

**insist** v demand or state firmly
▶ **insistent** adj making persistent demands; demanding attention
▶ **insistently** adv ▶ **insistence** n

**in situ** adv, adj (Latin) in its original position

**in so far as, insofar as** prep to the extent that

**insole** n inner sole of a shoe or boot

**insolent** adj rude and disrespectful
▶ **insolence** n ▶ **insolently** adv

**insoluble** adj incapable of being solved; incapable of being dissolved

**insolvent** adj unable to pay one's debts ▶ **insolvency** n

**insomnia** n inability to sleep
▶ **insomniac** n

**insouciant** adj carefree and unconcerned ▶ **insouciance** n

**inspect** v check closely or officially
▶ **inspection** n ▶ **inspector** n person who inspects; high-ranking police officer

**inspire** v fill with enthusiasm, stimulate; arouse (an emotion)
▶ **inspiration** n creative influence or stimulus; brilliant idea
▶ **inspirational** adj

**instability** n lack of steadiness or reliability

**install** v put in and prepare (equipment) for use; place (a person) formally in a position or rank ▶ **installation** n installing; equipment installed; place containing equipment for a particular purpose e.g. *oil installations*

**instalment** n any of the portions of a thing presented or a debt paid in successive parts

**instance** n particular example
▷ v mention as an example **for instance** as an example

**instant** n very brief time; particular moment ▷ adj happening at once; (of foods) requiring little preparation ▶ **instantly** adv

**instantaneous** adj happening at once ▶ **instantaneously** adv

**instead** adv as a replacement or substitute

**instep** n part of the foot forming the arch between the ankle and toes; part of a shoe or boot covering this

**instigate** v cause to happen
▶ **instigation** n ▶ **instigator** n

**instil** v -stilling, -stilled introduce (an idea etc.) gradually into someone's mind

**instinct** n inborn tendency to behave in a certain way ▶ **instinctive** adj
▶ **instinctively** adv

**institute** n organization set up for a specific purpose, esp. research or teaching ▷ v start or establish

**institution** n large important organization such as a university or bank; hospital etc. for people with special needs; long-established custom ▶ **institutional** adj
▶ **institutionalize** v

**instruct** v order to do something; teach (someone) how to do something ▶ **instruction** n order to do something; teaching ▷ pl information on how to do or use something ▶ **instructive** adj informative or helpful
▶ **instructor** n

**instrument** n tool used for particular work; object played to produce a musical sound; measuring device to show height, speed, etc.; (*informal*) someone or something used to achieve an aim ▶ **instrumental** *adj* (foll by *in*) having an important function (in); played by or composed for musical instruments ▶ **instrumentalist** *n* player of a musical instrument ▶ **instrumentation** *n* set of instruments in a car etc.; arrangement of music for instruments

**insubordinate** *adj* not submissive to authority ▶ **insubordination** *n*

**insufferable** *adj* unbearable

**insular** *adj* not open to new ideas, narrow-minded ▶ **insularity** *n*

**insulate** *v* prevent or reduce the transfer of electricity, heat, or sound by surrounding or lining with a nonconducting material; isolate or set apart ▶ **insulation** *n* ▶ **insulator** *n*

**insulin** *n* hormone produced in the pancreas that controls the amount of sugar in the blood

**insult** *v* behave rudely to, offend ▷ *n* insulting remark or action ▶ **insulting** *adj*

**insuperable** *adj* impossible to overcome

**insupportable** *adj* impossible to tolerate; impossible to justify

**insurance** *n* agreement by which one makes regular payments to a company who pay an agreed sum if damage, loss, or death occurs; money paid to or by an insurance company; means of protection ▶ **insure** *v* protect by insurance ▶ **insurance policy** contract of insurance

**insurgent** *n, adj* (person) in revolt against an established authority ▶ **insurgency** *n*

**insurmountable** *adj* impossible to overcome e.g. *an insurmountable problem*

**insurrection** *n* rebellion

**intact** *adj* not changed in any way

**intaglio** [in-**tah**-lee-oh] *n, pl* -**lios** (gem carved with) an engraved design

**intake** *n* amount or number taken in

**intangible** *adj* not clear or definite enough to be seen or felt easily e.g. *an intangible quality*

**integer** *n* positive or negative whole number or zero

**integral** *adj* being an essential part of a whole; ▷ *n* (*Maths*) sum of a large number of very small quantities

**integrate** *v* combine into a whole; amalgamate (a religious or racial group) into a community ▶ **integration** *n* ▶ **integrated circuit** tiny electronic circuit on a chip of semiconducting material

**integrity** *n* quality of having high moral principles; quality of being united

**intellect** *n* power of thinking and reasoning

**intellectual** *adj* of or appealing to the intellect; clever ▷ *n* intellectual person ▶ **intellectually** *adv*

**intelligent** *adj* able to understand, learn, and think things out quickly; (of a computerized device) able to initiate or modify action in the light of ongoing events ▶ **intelligently** *adv* ▶ **intelligent design** theory that a sentient being designed and created the universe and all life ▶ **intelligence** *n* quality of being intelligent; secret government or military information; people or department collecting such information

**intelligentsia** *n* intellectual or cultured people in a society

**intelligible** *adj* able to be understood ▶ **intelligibility** *n*

**intemperate** *adj* unrestrained, uncontrolled; drinking alcohol to excess ▶ **intemperance** *n*

**intend** v propose or plan (to do something); have as one's purpose

**intense** adj of great strength or degree; deeply emotional ▶ **intensity** n ▶ **intensify** v **-fying, -fied** make or become more intense ▶ **intensification** n

**intensive** adj using or needing concentrated effort or resources ▶ **intensively** adv

**intent** n intention ▷ adj paying close attention **intent on doing something** determined to do something ▶ **intently** adv ▶ **intentness** n

**intention** n something intended ▶ **intentional** adj deliberate, planned in advance ▶ **intentionally** adv

**inter** [in-**ter**] v **-terring, -terred** bury (a corpse) ▶ **interment** n

**inter-** prefix between or among e.g. international

**interact** v act on or in close relation with each other ▶ **interaction** n ▶ **interactive** adj

**interbreed** v breed within a related group

**intercede** v try to end a dispute between two people or groups ▶ **intercession** n

**intercept** v seize or stop in transit ▶ **interception** n

**interchange** v (cause to) exchange places ▷ n motorway junction ▶ **interchangeable** adj

**Intercity®** adj (in Britain) denoting a fast train (service) travelling between cities

**intercom** n internal communication system with loudspeakers

**intercontinental** adj travelling between or linking continents

**intercourse** n sexual intercourse; communication or dealings between people or groups

**interdiction, interdict** n formal order forbidding something

**interdisciplinary** adj involving more than one branch of learning

**interest** n desire to know or hear more about something; something in which one is interested; (often pl) advantage, benefit; sum paid for the use of borrowed money; (often pl) right or share ▷ v arouse the interest of ▶ **interested** adj feeling or showing interest; involved in or affected by something ▶ **interesting** adj ▶ **interestingly** adv

**interface** n area where two things interact or link; circuit linking a computer and another device

**interfaith** adj relating to or involving different religions

**interfere** v try to influence other people's affairs where one is not involved or wanted; (foll by with) clash (with); (foll by with) (Brit, Aust & NZ euphemistic) abuse (a child) sexually ▶ **interfering** adj ▶ **interference** n interfering; (Radio) interruption of reception by atmospherics or unwanted signals

**interferon** n protein that stops the development of an invading virus

**interim** adj temporary or provisional

**interior** n inside; inland region ▷ adj inside, inner; mental or spiritual

**interject** v make (a remark) suddenly or as an interruption ▶ **interjection** n

**interlace** v join together as if by weaving

**interlink** v connect together

**interlock** v join firmly together

**interlocutor** [in-ter-**lok**-yew-ter] n person who takes part in a conversation

**interloper** [in-ter-lope-er] n person in a place or situation where he or she has no right to be

**interlude** n short rest or break in an activity or event

**intermarry** v (of families, races, or religions) become linked by marriage ▸ **intermarriage** n

**intermediary** n, pl -ries person trying to create agreement between others

**intermediate** adj coming between two points or extremes

**intermezzo** [in-ter-**met**-so] n, pl -zos short piece of music, esp. one performed between the acts of an opera

**interminable** adj seemingly endless because boring ▸ **interminably** adv

**intermingle** v mix together

**intermission** n interval between parts of a play, film, etc.

**intermittent** adj occurring at intervals ▸ **intermittently** adv

**intern** v imprison, esp. during a war ▷ n trainee doctor in a hospital ▸ **internment** n ▸ **internee** n person who is interned

**internal** adj of or on the inside; within a country or organization; spiritual or mental ▸ **internally** adv ▸ **internal-combustion engine** engine powered by the explosion of a fuel-and-air mixture within the cylinders

**international** adj of or involving two or more countries ▷ n game or match between teams of different countries; player in such a match ▸ **internationally** adv

**internecine** adj mutually destructive

**internet, Internet** n large international computer network

**interplanetary** adj of or linking planets

**interplay** n action and reaction of two things upon each other

**interpolate** [in-**ter**-pole-ate] v insert (a comment or passage) into (a conversation or text) ▸ **interpolation** n

**interpose** v insert between or among things; say as an interruption

**interpret** v explain the meaning of; translate orally from one language into another; convey the meaning of (a poem, song, etc.) in performance ▸ **interpretation** n

**interpreter** n person who translates orally from one language into another

**interregnum** n, pl -nums or -na interval between reigns

**interrogate** v question closely ▸ **interrogation** n ▸ **interrogative** adj questioning ▷ n word used in asking a question, such as how or why ▸ **interrogator** n

**interrupt** v break into (a conversation etc.); stop (a process or activity) temporarily ▸ **interruption** n

**intersect** v (of roads) meet and cross; divide by passing across or through ▸ **intersection** n

**intersex** n condition of having physiological characteristics beween those of a male and a female

**interspersed** adj scattered (among, between, or on)

**interstellar** adj between or among stars

**interstice** [in-**ter**-stiss] n small crack or gap between things

**intertwine** v twist together

**interval** n time between two particular moments or events; break between parts of a play, concert, etc.; difference in pitch between musical notes **at**

**intervals** repeatedly; with spaces left between

**intervene** v involve oneself in a situation, esp. to prevent conflict; happen so as to stop something ▶ **intervention** n

**interview** n formal discussion, esp. between a job-seeker and an employer; questioning of a well-known person about his or her career, views, etc., by a reporter ▷ v conduct an interview with ▶ **interviewee** n ▶ **interviewer** n

**interweave** v weave together

**intestate** adj not having made a will ▶ **intestacy** n

**intestine** n (often pl) lower part of the alimentary canal between the stomach and the anus ▶ **intestinal** adj ▶ **intestinally** adv

**intimate¹** adj having a close personal relationship; personal or private; (of knowledge) extensive and detailed; (foll by with) (euphemistic) having a sexual relationship (with); having a friendly quiet atmosphere ▷ n close friend ▶ **intimately** adv ▶ **intimacy** n

**intimate²** v hint at or suggest; announce ▶ **intimation** n

**intimidate** v subdue or influence by fear ▶ **intimidating** adj ▶ **intimidation** n

**into** prep indicating motion towards the centre, result of a change, division, etc. e.g. into the valley; turned into a madman; cut into pieces; (informal) interested in

**intolerable** adj more than can be endured ▶ **intolerably** adv

**intolerant** adj refusing to accept practices and beliefs different from one's own ▶ **intolerance** n

**intonation** n sound pattern produced by variations in the voice

**intone** v speak or recite in an unvarying tone of voice

**intoxicate** v make drunk; excite to excess ▶ **intoxicant** n intoxicating drink

**intoxication** n state of being drunk; overexcited state

**intractable** adj (of a person) difficult to control; (of a problem or issue) difficult to deal with

**intranet** n (Computing) internal network that makes use of internet technology

**intransigent** adj refusing to change one's attitude ▶ **intransigence** n

**intransitive** adj (of a verb) not taking a direct object

**intrauterine** [in-tra-yoo-ter-rine] adj within the womb

**intravenous** [in-tra-vee-nuss] adj into a vein ▶ **intravenously** adv

**intrepid** adj fearless, bold ▶ **intrepidity** n

**intricate** adj involved or complicated; full of fine detail ▶ **intricately** adv ▶ **intricacy** n, pl -**cies**

**intrigue** v make interested or curious; plot secretly ▷ n secret plotting; secret love affair ▶ **intriguing** adj

**intrinsic** adj essential to the basic nature of something ▶ **intrinsically** adv

**introduce** v present (someone) by name (to another person); present (a radio or television programme); bring forward for discussion; bring into use; insert ▶ **introduction** n presentation of one person to another; preliminary part or treatment ▶ **introductory** adj

**introspection** n examination of one's own thoughts and feelings ▶ **introspective** adj

**introvert** n person concerned more with his or her thoughts and feelings than with the

outside world ▶ **introverted** adj
▶ **introversion** n

**intrude** v come in or join in without
being invited ▶ **intrusion** n
▶ **intrusive** adj

**intruder** n person who enters a
place without permission

**intuition** n instinctive knowledge or
insight without conscious reasoning
▶ **intuitive** adj ▶ **intuitively** adv

**Inuit** n indigenous inhabitant of
North America or Greenland

**inundate** v flood; overwhelm
▶ **inundation** n

**inured** adj accustomed, esp. to
hardship or danger

**invade** v enter (a country) by
military force; enter in large
numbers; disturb (someone's
privacy) ▶ **invader** n

**invalid**[1] adj, n disabled or
chronically ill (person) ▷ v (often
foll by out) dismiss from active
service because of illness or injury
▶ **invalidity** n

**invalid**[2] adj having no legal force;
(of an argument etc.) not valid
because based on a mistake
▶ **invalidate** v make or show to
be invalid

**invaluable** adj of very great value
or worth

**invasion** n invading; intrusion e.g.
an invasion of privacy

**invective** n abusive speech or
writing

**inveigh** [in-**vay**] v (foll by against)
criticize strongly

**inveigle** v coax by cunning or
trickery

**invent** v think up or create
(something new); make up (a
story, excuse, etc.) ▶ **invention**
n something invented; ability to
invent ▶ **inventive** adj creative
and resourceful ▶ **inventiveness** n
▶ **inventor** n

**inventory** n, pl -**tories** detailed list
of goods or furnishings

**inverse** adj reversed in effect,
sequence, direction, etc.; (Maths)
linking two variables in such a way
that one increases as the other
decreases ▶ **inversely** adv

**invert** v turn upside down or inside
out ▶ **inversion** n ▶ **inverted
commas** quotation marks

**invertebrate** n animal with no
backbone

**invest** v spend (money, time, etc.)
on something with the expectation
of profit; (foll by with) give (power
or rights) to ▶ **investment** n
money invested; something
invested in ▶ **investor** n ▶ **invest
in** v buy

**investigate** v inquire into,
examine ▶ **investigation** n
▶ **investigative** adj
▶ **investigator** n

**investiture** n formal installation of
a person in an office or rank

**inveterate** adj firmly established in
a habit or condition

**invidious** adj likely to cause
resentment

**invigilate** v supervise people
sitting an examination
▶ **invigilator** n

**invigorate** v give energy to, refresh

**invincible** adj impossible to defeat
▶ **invincibility** n

**inviolable** adj unable to be broken
or violated

**inviolate** adj unharmed,
unaffected

**invisible** adj not able to be seen
▶ **invisibly** adv ▶ **invisibility** n

**invite** v request the company of;
ask politely for; encourage or
provoke e.g. the two works inevitably
invite comparison ▷ n (informal)
invitation ▶ **inviting** adj tempting,
attractive ▶ **invitation** n

**in-vitro** *adj* happening outside the body in an artificial environment

**invoice** *v, n* (present with) a bill for goods or services supplied

**invoke** *v* put (a law or penalty) into operation; prompt or cause (a certain feeling); call on (a god or spirit) for help, inspiration, etc. ▶ **invocation** *n*

**involuntary** *adj* not done consciously, unintentional ▶ **involuntarily** *adv*

**involve** *v* include as a necessary part; affect, concern; implicate (a person) ▶ **involved** *adj* complicated; concerned, taking part ▶ **involvement** *n*

**invulnerable** *adj* not able to be wounded or harmed

**inward** *adj, adv* see **in**

**iodine** *n* (*Chem*) bluish-black element used in medicine and photography ▶ **iodize** *v* treat with iodine

**ion** *n* electrically charged atom ▶ **ionic** *adj* ▶ **ionize** *v* change into ions ▶ **ionization** *n* ▶ **ionosphere** *n* region of ionized air in the upper atmosphere that reflects radio waves

**iota** *n* very small amount

**IOU** *n* signed paper acknowledging debt

**IPA** International Phonetic Alphabet

**iPad**® *n* type of small portable computer activitated by touching the screen

**IP address** (*Computing*) internet protocol address: unique code that identifies each computer connected to the internet

**iPhone**® *n* type of mobile phone which includes a music player and internet browser

**i-Player**® *n* (in Britain) service provided by the BBC, allowing its recently broadcast television programmes to be viewed over the internet

**iPod**® *n* small portable digital audio player able to store thousands of tracks downloaded from the internet or transferred from CD

**ipso facto** *adv* (*Latin*) by that very fact

**IQ** intelligence quotient

**IRA** Irish Republican Army

**Iranian** *n, adj* (person) from Iran

**Iraqi** *n, adj* (person) from Iraq

**irascible** *adj* easily angered ▶ **irascibility** *n*

**irate** *adj* very angry

**ire** *n* (*lit*) anger

**iridescent** *adj* having shimmering changing colours like a rainbow ▶ **iridescence** *n*

**iridium** *n* (*Chem*) very hard corrosion-resistant metal

**iris** *n* coloured circular membrane of the eye containing the pupil; tall plant with purple, yellow, or white flowers

**Irish** *adj* of Ireland

**irk** *v* irritate, annoy ▶ **irksome** *adj* irritating, annoying

**iron** *n* strong silvery-white metallic element, widely used for structural and engineering purposes; appliance used, when heated, to press clothes; metal-headed golf club ▷ *pl* chains, restraints ▷ *adj* made of iron; strong, inflexible e.g. *iron will* ▷ *v* smooth (clothes or fabric) with an iron ▶ **ironbark** *n* Australian eucalyptus with hard rough bark ▶ **ironing** *n* clothes to be ironed ▶ **ironing board** long cloth-covered board with folding legs, for ironing clothes on ▶ **Iron Age** era when iron tools were used ▶ **iron out** *v* settle (a problem) through discussion

**ironic, ironical** *adj* using irony; odd or amusing because the

opposite of what one would expect
▶ **ironically** adv

**ironmonger** n shopkeeper or shop dealing in hardware ▶ **ironmongery** n

**ironstone** n rock consisting mainly of iron ore

**irony** n, pl **-nies** mildly sarcastic use of words to imply the opposite of what is said; aspect of a situation that is odd or amusing because the opposite of what one would expect

**irradiate** v subject to or treat with radiation ▶ **irradiation** n

**irrational** adj not based on or not using logical reasoning

**irredeemable** adj not able to be reformed or corrected

**irreducible** adj impossible to put in a simpler form

**irrefutable** adj impossible to deny or disprove

**irregular** adj not regular or even; not conforming to accepted practice; (of a word) not following the typical pattern of formation in a language ▶ **irregularly** adv ▶ **irregularity** n, pl **-ties**

**irrelevant** adj not connected with the matter in hand ▶ **irrelevantly** adv ▶ **irrelevance** n

**irreparable** adj not able to be repaired or put right ▶ **irreparably** adv

**irreplaceable** adj impossible to replace

**irrepressible** adj lively and jolly ▶ **irrepressibly** adv

**irreproachable** adj blameless, faultless

**irresistible** adj too attractive or strong to resist ▶ **irresistibly** adv

**irrespective** of prep without taking account of

**irresponsible** adj not showing or not done with due care for the consequences of one's

actions or attitudes; not capable of accepting responsibility ▶ **irresponsibility** n

**irreverent** adj not showing due respect ▶ **irreverence** n

**irreversible** adj not able to be reversed or put right again e.g. irreversible change ▶ **irreversibly** adv

**irrevocable** adj not possible to change or undo ▶ **irrevocably** adv

**irrigate** v supply (land) with water by artificial channels or pipes ▶ **irrigation** n

**irritate** v annoy, anger; cause (a body part) to itch or become inflamed ▶ **irritable** adj easily annoyed ▶ **irritably** adv ▶ **irritant** n, adj (person or thing) causing irritation ▶ **irritation** n

**is** v third person singular present tense of **be**

**ISA** (in Britain) Individual Savings Account

**isinglass** [ize-ing-glass] n kind of gelatine obtained from some freshwater fish

**Islam** n Muslim religion teaching that there is one God and that Mohammed is his prophet; Muslim countries and civilization ▶ **Islamic** adj

**island** n piece of land surrounded by water ▶ **islander** n person who lives on an island; (**I-**) (NZ) Pacific Islander

**isle** n (poetic) island ▶ **islet** n small island

**isobar** [ice-oh-bar] n line on a map connecting places of equal atmospheric pressure

**isolate** v place apart or alone; (Chem) obtain (a substance) in uncombined form ▶ **isolation** n ▶ **isolationism** n policy of not participating in international affairs ▶ **isolationist** n, adj

**isomer** [ice-oh-mer] *n* substance whose molecules contain the same atoms as another but in a different arrangement

**isometric** *adj* relating to muscular contraction without shortening of the muscle ▶ **isometrics** *pl n* isometric exercises

**isosceles triangle** [ice-**soss**-ill-eez] *n* triangle with two sides of equal length

**isotherm** [ice-oh-therm] *n* line on a map connecting points of equal temperature

**isotope** [ice-oh-tope] *n* one of two or more atoms with the same number of protons in the nucleus but a different number of neutrons

**ISP** internet service provider

**Israeli** *n, pl* -**lis** *or* -**li** *adj* (person) from Israel

**issue** *n* topic of interest or discussion; reason for quarrelling; particular edition of a magazine or newspaper; outcome or result; (*Law*) child or children ▷ *v* make (a statement etc.) publicly; supply officially (with); produce and make available **take issue with** disagree with

**isthmus** [**iss**-muss] *n, pl* -**muses** narrow strip of land connecting two areas of land

**IT** information technology

**it** *pron* refers to a nonhuman, animal, plant, or inanimate object; refers to a thing mentioned or being discussed; used as the subject of impersonal verbs e.g. *it's windy*; (*informal*) crucial or ultimate point ▶ **its** *adj, pron* belonging to it ▶ **it's** it is; it has ▶ **itself** *pron* emphatic form of **it**

> **USAGE NOTE**
> Beware of mistaking the possessive *its* (no apostrophe) as in *The cat has hurt its paw*, for the

abbreviation *it's* meaning *it is* or *it has: It's been a long time*

**Italian** *n* language of Italy and one of the languages of Switzerland; person from Italy ▷ *adj* of Italy

**italic** *adj* (of printing type) sloping to the right ▶ **italics** *pl n* this type, used for emphasis ▶ **italicize** *v* put in italics

**itch** *n* skin irritation causing a desire to scratch; restless desire ▷ *v* have an itch ▶ **itchy** *adj*

**item** *n* single thing in a list or collection; piece of information ▶ **itemize** *v* make a list of

**iterate** *v* repeat ▶ **iteration** *n*

**itinerant** *adj* travelling from place to place

**itinerary** *n, pl* -**aries** detailed plan of a journey

**ITV** (in Britain) Independent Television

**IUD** intrauterine device: a coil-shaped contraceptive fitted into the womb

**IVF** in-vitro fertilization

**ivory** *n* hard white bony substance forming the tusks of elephants ▷ *adj* yellowish-white ▶ **ivory tower** remoteness from the realities of everyday life

**ivy** *n, pl* **ivies** evergreen climbing plant

**iwi** [**ee**-wee] *n* (*NZ*) Māori tribe

**jab** v **jabbing, jabbed** poke sharply
▷ n quick punch or poke; (*informal*)
injection

**jabber** v talk rapidly or
incoherently

**jabiru** n large white-and-black
Australian stork

**jacaranda** n tropical tree with
sweet-smelling wood

**jack** n device for raising a motor
vehicle or other heavy object;
playing card with a picture of a
pageboy; (*Bowls*) small white bowl
aimed at by the players; socket in
electrical equipment into which a
plug fits; flag flown at the bow of a
ship, showing nationality ▶ **jack-
up** n (*NZ informal*) something
achieved dishonestly ▶ **jack up**
v raise with a jack; (*NZ informal*)
organize by dishonest means

**jackal** n dog-like wild animal of
Africa and Asia

**jackaroo, jackeroo** n, pl -**roos**
(*Aust*) trainee on a sheep station

**jackass** n fool; male of the ass
**laughing jackass** same as
**kookaburra**

**jackboot** n high military boot

**jackdaw** n black-and-grey Eurasian
bird of the crow family

**jacket** n short coat; skin of a baked
potato; outer paper cover on a
hardback book

**jackknife** v (of an articulated truck)
go out of control so that the trailer
swings round at a sharp angle to
the cab ▷ n large clasp knife

**jackpot** n largest prize that may be
won in a game **hit the jackpot** be
very successful through luck

**Jacobean** [jak-a-**bee**-an] adj of the
reign of James I of England

**Jacobite** n supporter of James II of
England and his descendants

**Jacquard** [**jak**-ard] n fabric in which
the design is incorporated into
the weave

**Jacuzzi®** [jak-**oo**-zee] n circular
bath with a device that swirls
the water

**jade** n ornamental semiprecious
stone, usu. dark green ▷ adj
bluish-green

**jaded** adj tired and unenthusiastic

**jagged** [**jag**-gid] adj having an
uneven edge with sharp points

**jaguar** n large S American spotted
cat

**jail** n prison ▷ v send to prison
▶ **jailer** n ▶ **jailbird** n (*informal*)
person who has often been in
prison

**jalopy** [jal-**lop**-ee] n, pl -**lopies**
(*informal*) old car

**jam**¹ v **jamming, jammed** pack
tightly into a place; crowd or
congest; make or become stuck;
(*Radio*) block (another station)
with impulses of equal wavelength
▷ n hold-up of traffic; (*informal*)
awkward situation **jam on the
brakes** apply brakes fiercely
▶ **jam-packed** adj filled to capacity
▶ **jam session** informal rock or jazz
performance

**jam²** n food made from fruit boiled
with sugar

**jamb** n side post of a door or
window frame

**jamboree** n large gathering or
celebration

**Jan.** January

**jandal** n (*NZ*) sandal with a strap
between the toes

**jangle** v (cause to) make a harsh ringing noise; (of nerves) be upset or irritated

**janitor** n caretaker of a school or other building

**January** n first month of the year

**japan** n very hard varnish, usu. black ▷ v **-panning, -panned** cover with this varnish

**Japanese** n, adj (native or language) of Japan

**jape** n (old-fashioned) joke or prank

**japonica** n shrub with red flowers

**jar¹** n wide-mouthed container, usu. round and made of glass

**jar²** v **jarring, jarred** have a disturbing or unpleasant effect; jolt or bump ▷ n jolt or shock

**jargon** n specialized technical language of a particular subject

**jarrah** n Australian eucalyptus yielding valuable timber

**jasmine** n shrub with sweet-smelling yellow or white flowers

**jasper** n red, yellow, dark green, or brown variety of quartz

**jaundice** n disease marked by yellowness of the skin ▶**jaundiced** adj (of an attitude or opinion) bitter or cynical; having jaundice

**jaunt** n short journey for pleasure

**jaunty** adj **-tier, -tiest** sprightly and cheerful; smart ▶**jauntily** adv

**javelin** n light spear thrown in sports competitions

**jaw** n one of the bones in which the teeth are set ▷ pl mouth; gripping part of a tool; narrow opening of a gorge or valley ▷ v (slang) talk lengthily

**jay** n bird with a pinkish body and blue-and-black wings

**jaywalker** n person who crosses the road in a careless or dangerous manner ▶**jaywalking** n

**jazz** n kind of music with an exciting rhythm, usu. involving improvisation ▶**jazzy** adj flashy or showy ▶**jazz up** v make more lively

**JCB®** n (Brit) construction machine with a shovel at the front and an excavator at the rear

**jealous** adj fearful of losing a partner or possession to a rival; envious; suspiciously watchful ▶**jealously** adv ▶**jealousy** n, pl **-sies**

**jeans** pl n casual denim trousers

**Jeep®** n four-wheel-drive motor vehicle

**jeer** v scoff or deride ▷ n cry of derision

**Jehovah** n God

**jejune** adj simple or naive; dull or boring

**jell** v form into a jelly-like substance; take on a definite form

**jelly** n, pl **-lies** soft food made of liquid set with gelatine; jam made from fruit juice and sugar ▶**jellied** adj prepared in a jelly

**jellyfish** n small jelly-like sea animal

**jemmy** n, pl **-mies** short steel crowbar used by burglars

**jenny** n, pl **-nies** female ass or wren

**jeopardy** n danger ▶**jeopardize** v place in danger

**jerboa** n small mouse-like rodent with long hind legs

**jerk** v move or throw abruptly ▷ n sharp or abruptly stopped movement; (slang) contemptible person ▶**jerky** adj sudden or abrupt ▶**jerkily** adv ▶**jerkiness** n

**jerkin** n sleeveless jacket

**jerry-built** adj built badly using flimsy materials

**jerry can** n flat-sided can for carrying petrol etc.

**jersey** n knitted jumper; machine-knitted fabric; (J-) breed of cow

**Jerusalem artichoke** n small yellowish-white root vegetable

**jest** n, v joke

**jester** n (Hist) professional clown at court

**Jesuit** [jezz-yoo-it] n member of the Society of Jesus, a Roman Catholic order

**jet**[1] n aircraft driven by jet propulsion; stream of liquid or gas, esp. one forced from a small hole; nozzle from which gas or liquid is forced ▷ v **jetting, jetted** fly by jet aircraft ▶ **jetboat** n motorboat propelled by a jet of water ▶ **jet lag** fatigue caused by crossing time zones in an aircraft ▶ **jet propulsion** propulsion by thrust provided by a jet of gas or liquid ▶ **jet-propelled** adj ▶ **jet set** rich and fashionable people who travel the world for pleasure

**jet**[2] n hard black mineral ▶ **jet-black** adj glossy black

**jetsam** n goods thrown overboard to lighten a ship

**jettison** v -soning, -soned abandon; throw overboard

**jetty** n, pl -ties small pier

**Jew** n person whose religion is Judaism; descendant of the ancient Hebrews ▶ **Jewish** adj ▶ **Jewry** n Jews collectively ▶ **jew's-harp** n musical instrument held between the teeth and played by plucking a metal strip with one's finger

**jewel** n precious stone; special person or thing ▶ **jeweller** n dealer in jewels ▶ **jewellery** n objects decorated with precious stones

**jewfish** n (Aust) freshwater catfish

**jib**[1] n triangular sail set in front of a mast

**jib**[2] v **jibbing, jibbed** (of a horse, person, etc.) stop and refuse to go on ▶ **jib at** v object to (a proposal etc.)

**jib**[3] n projecting arm of a crane or derrick

**jibe**[1] n, v taunt or jeer

**jibe**[2] v same as **gybe**

**jiffy** n, pl -**fies** (informal) very short period of time

**jig** n type of lively dance; music for it; device that holds a component in place for cutting etc. ▷ v **jigging, jigged** make jerky up-and-down movements

**jiggery-pokery** n (informal) trickery or mischief

**jiggle** v move up and down with short jerky movements

**jigsaw** n (also **jigsaw puzzle**) picture cut into interlocking pieces, which the user tries to fit together again; mechanical saw for cutting along curved lines

**jihad** n Islamic holy war against unbelievers

**jilt** v leave or reject (one's lover)

**jingle** n catchy verse or song used in a radio or television advert; gentle ringing noise ▷ v (cause to) make a gentle ringing sound

**jingoism** n aggressive nationalism ▶ **jingoistic** adj

**jinks** pl n **high jinks** boisterous merrymaking

**jinni** n, pl **jinn** spirit in Muslim mythology

**jinx** n person or thing bringing bad luck ▷ v be or put a jinx on

**jitters** pl n worried nervousness ▶ **jittery** adj nervous

**jive** n lively dance of the 1940s and 1950s ▷ v dance the jive

**job** n occupation or paid employment; task to be done; (informal) difficult task; (Brit, Aust & NZ informal) crime, esp. robbery ▶ **jobbing** adj doing individual jobs for payment ▶ **jobless** adj, pl n unemployed (people) ▶ **job lot** assortment sold together ▶ **job sharing** splitting of one post between two people working part-time

**jockey** n (professional) rider of racehorses ▷ v **jockey for position** manoeuvre to obtain an advantage

**jockstrap** n belt with a pouch to support the genitals, worn by male athletes

**jocose** [joke-**kohss**] adj playful or humorous

**jocular** adj fond of joking; meant as a joke ▸ **jocularity** n ▸ **jocularly** adv

**jocund** [jok-kund] adj (lit) merry or cheerful

**jodhpurs** pl n riding trousers, loose-fitting above the knee but tight below

**joey** n (Aust) young kangaroo

**jog** v **jogging, jogged** run at a gentle pace, esp. for exercise; nudge slightly ▷ n slow run ▸ **jogger** n ▸ **jogging** n

**joggle** v shake or move jerkily

**joie de vivre** [jwah de **veev**-ra] n (French) enjoyment of life

**join** v become a member (of); come into someone's company; take part (in); come or bring together ▷ n place where two things are joined ▸ **join up** v enlist in the armed services ▸ **joined-up** adj integrated by an overall strategy e.g. *joined-up government*

**joiner** n maker of finished woodwork ▸ **joinery** n joiner's work

**joint** adj shared by two or more ▷ n place where bones meet but can move; junction of two or more parts or objects; piece of meat for roasting; (slang) house or place, esp. a disreputable bar or nightclub; (slang) marijuana cigarette ▷ v divide meat into joints **out of joint** disorganized; dislocated ▸ **jointed** adj ▸ **jointly** adv

**joist** n horizontal beam that helps support a floor or ceiling

**jojoba** [hoe-**hoe**-ba] n shrub of SW North America whose seeds yield oil used in cosmetics

**joke** n thing said or done to cause laughter; amusing or ridiculous person or thing ▷ v make jokes ▸ **jokey** adj ▸ **jokingly** adv ▸ **joker** n person who jokes; (slang) fellow; extra card in a pack, counted as any other in some games

**jolly** adj **-lier, -liest** (of a person) happy and cheerful; (of an occasion) merry and festive ▷ v **-lying, -lied** ▸ **jolly along** try to keep (someone) cheerful by flattery or coaxing ▸ **jollity** n ▸ **jollification** n merrymaking

**jolt** n unpleasant surprise or shock; sudden jerk or bump ▷ v surprise or shock; move or shake with a jerk

**jonquil** n fragrant narcissus

**josh** v (chiefly US slang) tease

**joss stick** n stick of incense giving off a sweet smell when burnt

**jostle** v knock or push against

**jot** v **jotting, jotted** write briefly ▷ n very small amount ▸ **jotter** n notebook ▸ **jottings** pl n notes jotted down

**joule** [jool] n (Physics) unit of work or energy

**journal** n daily newspaper or magazine; daily record of events ▸ **journalese** n superficial style of writing, found in some newspapers ▸ **journalism** n writing in or editing of newspapers and magazines ▸ **journalist** n ▸ **journalistic** adj

**journey** n act or process of travelling from one place to another ▷ v travel

**journeyman** n qualified craftsman employed by another

**joust** (*Hist*) *n* combat with lances between two mounted knights ▷ *v* fight on horseback using lances

**jovial** *adj* happy and cheerful
▶ **jovially** *adv* ▶ **joviality** *n*

**jowl**[1] *n* lower jaw ▷ *pl* cheeks

**jowl**[2] *n* fatty flesh hanging from the lower jaw

**joy** *n* feeling of great delight or pleasure; cause of this feeling
▶ **joyful** *adj* ▶ **joyless** *adj*
▶ **joyous** *adj* extremely happy and enthusiastic ▶ **joyriding** *n* driving for pleasure, esp. in a stolen car
▶ **joyride** *n* ▶ **joyrider** *n* ▶ **joystick** *n* control device for an aircraft or computer

**JP** (in Britain) Justice of the Peace

**JPEG** [**jay**-peg] (*Computing*) *n* standard compressed file format used for pictures; picture held in this file format

**Jr** Junior

**JSA** jobseeker's allowance: (in Britain) a payment made to unemployed people

**jubilant** *adj* feeling or expressing great joy ▶ **jubilantly** *adv*
▶ **jubilation** *n*

**jubilee** *n* special anniversary, esp. 25th (**silver jubilee**) or 50th (**golden jubilee**)

**Judaism** *n* religion of the Jews, based on the Old Testament and the Talmud ▶ **Judaic** *adj*

**judder** *v* vibrate violently ▷ *n* violent vibration ▶ **judder bar** (*NZ*) raised strip across a road designed to slow down vehicles

**judge** *n* public official who tries cases and passes sentence in a court of law; person who decides the outcome of a contest ▷ *v* act as a judge; appraise critically; consider something to be the case ▶ **judgment, judgement** *n* opinion reached after careful

thought; verdict of a judge; ability to appraise critically
▶ **judgmental, judgemental** *adj*
**USAGE NOTE**
The alternative spellings with or without an 'e' between 'g' and 'm' are equally acceptable

**judicial** *adj* of or by a court or judge; showing or using judgment
▶ **judicially** *adv*

**judiciary** *n* system of courts and judges

**judicious** *adj* well-judged and sensible ▶ **judiciously** *adv*

**judo** *n* sport in which two opponents try to throw each other to the ground

**jug** *n* container for liquids, with a handle and small spout
▶ **jugged hare** hare stewed in an earthenware pot

**juggernaut** *n* (*Brit*) large heavy truck; any irresistible destructive force

**juggle** *v* throw and catch (several objects) so that most are in the air at the same time; manipulate (figures, situations, etc.) to suit one's purposes ▶ **juggler** *n*

**jugular, jugular vein** *n* one of three large veins of the neck that return blood from the head to the heart

**juice** *n* liquid part of vegetables, fruit, or meat; (*Brit, Aust & NZ informal*) petrol ▷ *pl* fluids secreted by an organ of the body ▶ **juicy** *adj* full of juice; interesting

**jujitsu** *n* Japanese art of wrestling and self-defence

**juju** *n* W African magic charm or fetish

**jukebox** *n* coin-operated machine on which records, CDs, or videos can be played

**Jul.** July

**julep** *n* sweet alcoholic drink

**July** n seventh month of the year

**jumble** n confused heap or state; articles for a jumble sale ▷ v mix in a disordered way ▶ **jumble sale** sale of miscellaneous second-hand items

**jumbo** adj (informal) very large ▷ n (also **jumbo jet**) large jet airliner

**jumbuck** n (Aust, old-fashioned slang) sheep

**jump** v leap or spring into the air using the leg muscles; move quickly and suddenly; jerk with surprise; increase suddenly; change the subject abruptly; (informal) attack without warning; pass over or miss out (intervening material) ▷ n act of jumping; sudden rise; break in continuity **jump the gun** act prematurely **jump the queue** not wait one's turn ▶ **jumpy** adj nervous ▶ **jump at** v accept (a chance etc.) gladly ▶ **jumped-up** adj arrogant because of recent promotion ▶ **jump jet** fixed-wing jet that can take off and land vertically ▶ **jump leads** electric cables to connect a flat car battery to an external battery to aid starting an engine ▶ **jump on** v attack suddenly and forcefully ▶ **jump suit** one-piece garment of trousers and top

**jumper** n sweater or pullover

**Jun.** June; Junior

**junction** n place where routes, railway lines, or roads meet

**juncture** n point in time, esp. a critical one

**June** n sixth month of the year

**jungle** n tropical forest of dense tangled vegetation; confusion or mess; place of intense struggle for survival

**junior** adj of lower standing; younger ▷ n junior person

**juniper** n evergreen shrub with purple berries

**junk¹** n discarded or useless objects; (informal) rubbish; (slang) narcotic drug, esp. heroin ▶ **junkie, junky** n, pl **junkies** (slang) drug addict ▶ **junk food** snack food of low nutritional value ▶ **junk mail** unwanted mail advertising goods or services

**junk²** n flat-bottomed Chinese sailing boat

**junket** n excursion by public officials paid for from public funds; sweetened milk set with rennet

**junta** n group of military officers holding power in a country, esp. after a coup

**Jupiter** n king of the Roman gods; largest of the planets

**juridical** adj of law or the administration of justice

**jurisdiction** n right or power to administer justice and apply laws; extent of this right or power

**jurisprudence** n science or philosophy of law

**jurist** n expert in law

**jury** n, pl **-ries** group of people sworn to deliver a verdict in a court of law ▶ **juror** n member of a jury

**just** adv very recently; at this instant; merely, only; exactly; barely; really ▷ adj fair or impartial in action or judgment; proper or right ▶ **justly** adv ▶ **justness** n

**justice** n quality of being just; judicial proceedings; judge or magistrate ▶ **Justice of the Peace** (in Britain) person who is authorized to act as a judge in a local court of law

**justify** v **-fying, -fied** prove right or reasonable; explain the reasons for an action; align (text) so the margins are straight

▶**justifiable** adj ▶**justifiably** adv
▶**justification** n
**jut** v**jutting, jutted** project or
stick out
**jute** n plant fibre, used for rope,
canvas, etc.
**juvenile** adj young; of or suitable
for young people; immature and
rather silly ▷ n young person
or child ▶**juvenilia** pl n works
produced in an author's youth
▶**juvenile delinquent** young
person guilty of a crime
**juxtapose** v put side by side
▶**juxtaposition** n

# Kk

**K** (informal) thousand(s)
**Kaffir** [**kaf**-fer] n (S Afr offens) Black
African
**kaftan** n long loose Eastern
garment; woman's dress
resembling this
**kai** n (NZ informal) food
**kaiser** [**kize**-er] n (Hist) German or
Austro-Hungarian emperor
**kak** n (S Afr slang) faeces; rubbish
**Kalashnikov** n Russian-made
automatic rifle
**kale** n cabbage with crinkled leaves
**kaleidoscope** n tube-shaped
toy containing loose coloured
pieces reflected by mirrors so
that intricate patterns form
when the tube is twisted
▶**kaleidoscopic** adj
**kamikaze** [kam-mee-**kah**-zee] n
(in World War II) Japanese pilot who
performed a suicide mission ▷ adj
(of an action) undertaken in the
knowledge that it will kill or injure
the person performing it
**kangaroo** n, pl -**roos** Australian
marsupial which moves by
jumping with its powerful hind
legs ▶**kangaroo court** unofficial
court set up by a group to discipline
its members ▶**kangaroo paw**
Australian plant with green-and-
red flowers
**kaolin** n fine white clay used to
make porcelain and also used in
some medicines
**kapok** n fluffy fibre from a tropical
tree, used to stuff cushions etc.

k

**kaput** [kap-**poot**] adj (informal) ruined or broken

**karaoke** n form of entertainment in which people sing over a prerecorded backing tape

**karate** n Japanese system of unarmed combat using blows with the feet, hands, elbows, and legs

**karma** n (Buddhism, Hinduism) person's actions affecting his or her fate in the next reincarnation

**karoo** n (SAfr) high arid plateau

**karri** n, pl **-ris** Australian eucalyptus; its wood, used for building

**katipo** n small poisonous New Zealand spider

**kauri** n large NZ conifer that yields valuable timber and resin

**kayak** n Inuit canoe made of sealskins stretched over a frame; fibreglass or canvas-covered canoe of this design

**kbps** (Computing) kilobits per second: measure of the rate of data transfer

**kbyte** (Computing) kilobyte

**kebab** n dish of small pieces of meat grilled on skewers; (also **doner kebab**) grilled minced lamb served in a split slice of unleavened bread

**kedgeree** n dish of fish with rice and eggs

**keel** n main lengthways timber or steel support along the base of a ship ▶ **keel over** v turn upside down; (informal) collapse suddenly

**keen**[1] adj eager or enthusiastic; intense or strong; intellectually acute; (of the senses) capable of recognizing small distinctions; sharp; cold and penetrating; competitive ▶ **keenly** adv ▶ **keenness** n

**keen**[2] v wail over the dead

**keep** v **keeping, kept** have or retain possession of; store; stay or cause to stay (in, on, or at a place

or position); continue or persist; detain (someone); look after or maintain ▷ n cost of food and everyday expenses ▶ **keeper** n person who looks after animals in a zoo; person in charge of a museum or collection; short for **goalkeeper** ▶ **keeping** n care or charge **in keeping with, out of keeping with** appropriate or inappropriate for ▶ **keep fit** exercises designed to promote physical fitness ▶ **keepsake** n gift treasured for the sake of the giver ▶ **keep up** v maintain at the current level ▶ **keep up with** v maintain a pace set by (someone)

**keg** n small metal beer barrel

**kelp** n large brown seaweed

**kelpie** n Australian sheepdog with a smooth coat and upright ears

**kelvin** n SI unit of temperature ▶ **Kelvin scale** temperature scale starting at absolute zero (-273.15° Celsius)

**ken** v **kenning, kenned** or **kent** (Scot) know **beyond one's ken** beyond one's range of knowledge

**kendo** n Japanese sport of fencing using wooden staves

**kennel** n hutlike shelter for a dog ▷ pl place for breeding, boarding, or training dogs

**kept** v past of **keep**

**keratin** n fibrous protein found in the hair and nails

**kerb** n edging to a footpath ▶ **kerb crawling** (Brit) act of driving slowly beside a pavement to pick up a prostitute

**kerchief** n piece of cloth worn over the head or round the neck

**kerfuffle** n (informal) commotion or disorder

**kernel** n seed of a nut, cereal, or fruit stone; central and essential part of something

k

**kerosene** n (US, Canadian, Aust & NZ) liquid mixture distilled from petroleum and used as a fuel or solvent

**kestrel** n type of small falcon

**ketch** n two-masted sailing ship

**ketchup** n thick cold sauce, usu. made of tomatoes

**kettle** n container with a spout and handle used for boiling water ▷ v (Brit informal) (of a police force) to contain (people involved in a public demonstration) in an enclosed space ▶ **kettledrum** n large bowl-shaped metal drum

**key** n device for operating a lock by moving a bolt; device turned to wind a clock, operate a machine, etc.; any of a set of levers or buttons pressed to operate a typewriter, computer, or musical keyboard instrument; (Music) set of related notes; something crucial in providing an explanation or interpretation; means of achieving a desired end; list of explanations of codes, symbols, etc. ▷ adj of great importance ▷ v (also **key in**) enter (text) using a keyboard **keyed up** very excited or nervous ▶ **key worker** (in Britain) worker in a public sector profession considered to be essential to society

**keyboard** n set of keys on a piano, computer, etc.; musical instrument played using a keyboard ▷ v enter (text) using a keyboard

**keyhole** n opening for inserting a key into a lock

**keynote** n dominant idea of a speech etc.; basic note of a musical key

**keypad** n panel with a set of buttons for operating an electronic device

**keystone** n most important part of a process, organization, etc.; central stone of an arch which locks the others in position

**kg** kilogram(s)

**KGB** n (formerly) Soviet secret police

**khaki** adj dull yellowish-brown ▷ n hard-wearing fabric of this colour used for military uniforms

**kHz** kilohertz

**kia ora** [kee-a **aw**-ra] interj (NZ) Māori greeting

**kibbutz** n, pl **kibbutzim** communal farm or factory in Israel

**kibosh** n **put the kibosh on** (slang) put a stop to

**kick** v drive, push, or strike with the foot; (of a gun) recoil when fired; (informal) object or resist; (informal) free oneself of (an addiction); (Rugby) score with a kick ▷ n thrust or blow with the foot; recoil of a gun; (informal) excitement or thrill ▶ **kickback** n money paid illegally for favours done ▶ **kick off** v start a game of soccer; (informal) begin ▶ **kick out** v dismiss or expel forcibly ▶ **kick-start** v start (a motorcycle) by kicking a pedal ▶ **kick up** v (informal) create (a fuss)

**kid¹** n (informal) child; young goat; leather made from the skin of a young goat

**kid²** v **kidding, kidded** (informal) tease or deceive (someone)

**kidnap** v **-napping, -napped** seize and hold (a person) to ransom ▶ **kidnapper** n

**kidney** n either of the pair of organs that filter waste products from the blood to produce urine; animal kidney used as food ▶ **kidney bean** reddish-brown kidney-shaped bean, edible when cooked

**kill** v cause the death of; (informal) cause (someone) pain or discomfort; put an end to; pass (time) ▷ n act of killing; animals

or birds killed in a hunt ▶ **killer** n
▶ **killing** (*informal*) adj very tiring;
very funny ▶ n sudden financial
success ▶ n person who
spoils others' pleasure

**killer whale** n predatory black-
and-white toothed whale with a
large erect dorsal fin

**kiln** n oven for baking, drying, or
processing pottery, bricks, etc.

**kilo** n short for **kilogram**

**kilo-** *combining form* one thousand
e.g. *kilometre*

**kilobyte** n (*Computing*) 1024 units of
information

**kilogram, kilogramme** n one
thousand grams

**kilohertz** n one thousand hertz

**kilometre** n one thousand metres

**kilowatt** n (*Electricity*) one
thousand watts

**kilt** n knee-length pleated tartan
skirt-like garment worn orig. by
Scottish Highlanders ▶ **kilted** adj

**kimono** n, pl **-nos** loose wide-
sleeved Japanese robe, fastened
with a sash; European dressing
gown resembling this

**kin, kinsfolk** n person's relatives
collectively ▶ **kinship** n

**kind¹** adj considerate, friendly, and
helpful ▶ **kindness** n ▶ **kindly** adj
having a warm-hearted nature;
pleasant or agreeable ▷ adv in a
considerate way; please e.g. *will
you kindly be quiet!* ▶ **kindliness** n
▶ **kind-hearted** adj

**kind²** n class or group with common
characteristics; essential nature
or character **in kind** (of payment)
in goods rather than money; with
something similar **kind of** to a
certain extent

**USAGE NOTE**
Note the singular/plural usage:
*this* (or *that*) *kind of dog*; *these* (or
*those*) *kinds of dog*. In the second,

plural example, you can also say
*these kinds of dogs*

**kindergarten** n class or school for
children under six years old

**kindle** v set (a fire) alight; (of a fire)
start to burn; arouse or be aroused
▷ n (**K-**)® portable electronic device
for downloading and reading
books ▶ **kindling** n dry wood or
straw for starting fires

**kindred** adj having similar qualities;
related by blood or marriage ▷ n
same as **kin**

**kindy, kindie** n, pl **-dies** (*Aust & NZ
informal*) kindergarten

**kinetic** [kin-**net**-ik] adj relating to
or caused by motion

**king** n male ruler of a monarchy;
ruler or chief; best or most
important of its kind; piece in chess
that must be defended; playing
card with a picture of a king on it
▶ **kingdom** n state ruled by a king
or queen; division of the natural
world ▶ **king prawn** large prawn,
fished commercially in Australian
waters ▶ **kingship** n ▶ **king-size,
king-sized** adj larger than standard
size

**kingfisher** n small bird, often with
a bright-coloured plumage, that
dives for fish

**kingpin** n most important person
in an organization

**kink** n twist or bend in rope, wire,
hair, etc.; (*informal*) quirk in
someone's personality ▶ **kinky**
adj (*slang*) given to unusual sexual
practices; full of kinks

**kiosk** n small booth selling drinks,
cigarettes, newspapers, etc.;
public telephone box

**kip** n, v **kipping, kipped** (*informal*)
sleep

**kipper** n cleaned, salted, and
smoked herring

**kirk** n (*Scot*) church

**Kirsch** n brandy made from cherries

**kismet** n fate or destiny

**kiss** v touch with the lips in affection or greeting; join lips with a person in love or desire ▷ n touch with the lips **kiss of life** mouth-to-mouth resuscitation ▶ **kisser** n (slang) mouth or face ▶ **kissagram** n greetings service in which a messenger kisses the person celebrating ▶ **kissing crust** (NZ & S Afr) soft end of a loaf of bread where two loaves have been separated

**kist** n (S Afr) large wooden chest

**kit** n outfit or equipment for a specific purpose; set of pieces of equipment sold ready to be assembled; (NZ) flax basket ▶ **kitbag** n bag for a soldier's or traveller's belongings ▶ **kit out** v **kitting, kitted** provide with clothes or equipment needed for a particular activity ▶ **kitset** n (NZ) unassembled pieces for constructing a piece of furniture

**kitchen** n room used for cooking ▶ **kitchenette** n small kitchen ▶ **kitchen garden** garden for growing vegetables, herbs, etc.

**kite** n light frame covered with a thin material flown on a string in the wind; large hawk with a forked tail ▶ **Kite mark** (Brit) official mark on articles approved by the British Standards Institution

**kith** n **kith and kin** friends and relatives

**kitsch** n art or literature with popular sentimental appeal

**kitten** n young cat ▶ **kittenish** adj lively and flirtatious

**kittiwake** n type of seagull

**kitty** n, pl **-ties** communal fund; total amount wagered in certain gambling games

**kiwi** n New Zealand flightless bird with a long beak and no tail; (informal) New Zealander ▶ **kiwi fruit** edible fruit with a fuzzy brownish skin and green flesh

**klaxon** n loud horn used on emergency vehicles as a warning signal

**kleptomania** n compulsive tendency to steal ▶ **kleptomaniac** n

**kloof** n (S Afr) mountain pass or gorge

**km** kilometre(s)

**knack** n skilful way of doing something; innate ability

**knacker** n (Brit) buyer of old horses for killing

**knackered** adj (slang) extremely tired; no longer functioning

**knapsack** n soldier's or traveller's bag worn strapped on the back

**knave** n jack at cards; (obs) dishonest man

**knead** v work (dough) into a smooth mixture with the hands; squeeze or press with the hands

**knee** n joint between thigh and lower leg; lap; part of a garment covering the knee ▷ v **kneeing, kneed** strike or push with the knee ▶ **kneecap** n bone in front of the knee ▷ v shoot in the kneecap ▶ **kneejerk** adj (of a reply or reaction) automatic and predictable ▶ **knees-up** n (Brit informal) party

**kneel** v **kneeling, kneeled** or **knelt** fall or rest on one's knees

**knell** n sound of a bell, esp. at a funeral or death; portent of doom

**knew** v past tense of **know**

**knickerbockers** pl n loose-fitting short trousers gathered in at the knee

**knickers** pl n woman's or girl's undergarment covering the lower trunk and having legs or legholes

k

**knick-knack** n trifle or trinket

**knife** n, pl **knives** cutting tool or weapon consisting of a sharp-edged blade with a handle ▷ v cut or stab with a knife

**knight** n man who has been given a knighthood; (Hist) man who served his lord as a mounted armoured soldier; chess piece shaped like a horse's head ▷ v award a knighthood to ▶ **knighthood** n honorary title given to a man by the British sovereign ▶ **knightly** adj

**knit** v **knitting, knitted** or **knit** make (a garment) by interlocking a series of loops in wool or other yarn; join closely together; draw (one's eyebrows) together ▶ **knitting** n ▶ **knitwear** n knitted clothes, such as sweaters

**knob** n rounded projection, such as a switch on a radio; rounded handle on a door or drawer; small amount of butter ▶ **knobbly** adj covered with small bumps

**knobkerrie** n (SAfr) club with a rounded end

**knock** v give a blow or push to; rap audibly with the knuckles; make or drive by striking; (informal) criticize adversely; (of an engine) make a regular banging noise as a result of a fault ▷ n blow or rap; knocking sound ▶ **knocker** n metal fitting for knocking on a door ▶ **knock about, knock around** v wander or spend time aimlessly; hit or kick brutally ▶ **knockabout** adj (of comedy) boisterous ▶ **knock back** v (informal) drink quickly; cost; reject or refuse ▶ **knock down** v demolish; reduce the price of ▶ **knockdown** adj (of a price) very low ▶ **knock-knees** pl n legs that curve in at the knees ▶ **knock off** v (informal) cease work; (informal) make or do

(something) hurriedly or easily; take (a specified amount) off a price; (Brit, Aust & NZ informal) steal ▶ **knock out** v render (someone) unconscious; (informal) overwhelm or amaze; defeat in a knockout competition ▶ **knockout** n blow that renders an opponent unconscious; competition from which competitors are progressively eliminated; (informal) overwhelmingly attractive person or thing ▶ **knock up** v (informal) assemble (something) quickly; (informal) waken ▶ **knock-up** n practice session at tennis, squash, or badminton

**knoll** n small rounded hill

**knot** n fastening made by looping and pulling tight strands of string, cord, or rope; tangle (of hair); small cluster or huddled group; round lump or spot in timber; feeling of tightness, caused by tension or nervousness; unit of speed used by ships, equal to one nautical mile (1.85 kilometres) per hour ▷ v **knotting, knotted** tie with or into a knot ▶ **knotty** adj full of knots; puzzling or difficult

**know** v **knowing, knew, known** be or feel certain of the truth of (information etc.); be acquainted with; have a grasp of or understand (a skill or language); be aware of **in the know** (informal) informed or aware ▶ **knowable** adj ▶ **knowing** adj suggesting secret knowledge ▶ **knowingly** adv deliberately; in a way that suggests secret knowledge ▶ **know-all** n (derogatory) person who acts as if knowing more than other people ▶ **know-how** n (informal) ingenuity, aptitude, or skill

**knowledge** n facts or experiences known by a person; state of knowing; specific information on a subject ▶ **knowledgeable, knowledgable** *adj* intelligent or well-informed

**knuckle** *n* bone at the finger joint; knee joint of a calf or pig **near the knuckle** (*informal*) rather rude or offensive ▶ **knuckle-duster** *n* metal appliance worn on the knuckles to add force to a blow ▶ **knuckle under** *v* yield or submit

**KO** knockout

**koala** *n* tree-dwelling Australian marsupial with dense grey fur

**kohanga reo, kohanga** *n* (*NZ*) infant class where children are taught in Māori

**kohl** *n* cosmetic powder used to darken the edges of the eyelids

**kookaburra** *n* large Australian kingfisher with a cackling cry

**koori** *n*, *pl* **-ris** Australian Aborigine

**kopje, koppie** *n* (*SAfr*) small hill

**Koran** *n* sacred book of Islam

**kosher** [koh-sher] *adj* conforming to Jewish religious law, esp. (of food) to Jewish dietary law; (*informal*) legitimate or authentic ▷ *n* kosher food

**kowhai** *n* New Zealand tree with clusters of yellow flowers

**kowtow** *v* be servile (towards)

**kph** kilometres per hour

**kraal** *n* S African village surrounded by a strong fence

**Kremlin** *n* central government of Russia and, formerly, the Soviet Union

**krill** *n*, *pl* **krill** small shrimplike sea creature

**krypton** *n* (*Chem*) colourless gas present in the atmosphere and used in fluorescent lights

**kryptonite** *n* imaginary substance said to render a person or thing powerless

**kudos** *n* fame or credit

**kugel** [koog-el] *n* (*SAfr*) rich, fashion-conscious, materialistic young woman

**kumara** *n* (*NZ*) tropical root vegetable with yellow flesh

**kumquat** [kumm-kwott] *n* citrus fruit resembling a tiny orange

**kung fu** *n* Chinese martial art combining hand, foot, and weapon techniques

**kura kaupapa Māori** *n* (*NZ*) primary school where the teaching is done in Māori

**kurrajong** *n* Australian tree or shrub with tough fibrous bark

**kW** kilowatt

**kwela** [kway-luh] *n* type of South African popular music using simple instruments

**kWh** kilowatt-hour

**k**

# Ll

**L** large; learner (driver)
**l** litre
**laat lammetjie** n (S Afr informal) a child born many years after its siblings
**lab** n (informal) short for **laboratory**
**label** n piece of card or other material fixed to an object to show its ownership, destination, etc. ▷ v **-elling, -elled** give a label to
**labia** pl n, sing **labium** four liplike folds of skin forming part of the female genitals ▶ **labial** [lay-bee-al] adj of the lips
**labor** n (US & Aust) same as **labour** ▶ **Labor Day** (in the US and Canada) public holiday in honour of labour, held on the first Monday in September; (in Australia) public holiday observed on different days in different states
**laboratory** n, pl **-ries** building or room designed for scientific research or for the teaching of practical science
**laborious** adj involving great prolonged effort ▶ **laboriously** adv
**Labor Party** n main left-wing political party in Australia
**labour,** (US & Aust) **labor** n physical work or exertion; workers in industry; final stage of pregnancy, leading to childbirth ▷ v work hard; stress to excess or too persistently; be at a disadvantage because of a mistake or false belief ▶ **laboured** adj uttered or done with difficulty ▶ **labourer** n person who labours,

esp. someone doing manual work for wages ▶ **Labour Day** (in Britain) a public holiday in honour of work, held on May 1; (in New Zealand) a public holiday commemorating the introduction of the eight-hour day, held on the fourth Monday in October ▶ **Labour Party** main left-wing political party in a number of countries including Britain and New Zealand
**labrador** n large retriever dog with a usu. gold or black coat
**laburnum** n ornamental tree with yellow hanging flowers
**labyrinth** [lab-er-inth] n complicated network of passages; interconnecting cavities in the internal ear ▶ **labyrinthine** adj
**lace** n delicate decorative fabric made from threads woven into an open weblike pattern; cord drawn through eyelets and tied ▷ v fasten with laces; thread a cord or string through holes in something; add a small amount of alcohol, a drug, etc. to (food or drink) ▶ **lacy** adj fine, like lace ▶ **lace-ups** pl n shoes which fasten with laces
**lacerate** [lass-er-rate] v tear (flesh) ▶ **laceration** n
**lachrymose** adj tearful; sad
**lack** n shortage or absence of something needed or wanted ▷ v need or be short of (something)
**lackadaisical** adj lazy and careless in a dreamy way
**lackey** n servile follower; uniformed male servant
**lacklustre** adj lacking brilliance or vitality
**laconic** adj using only a few words, terse ▶ **laconically** adv
**lacquer** n hard varnish for wood or metal; clear sticky substance sprayed onto the hair to hold it in place

**lacrimal** *adj* of tears or the glands which produce them

**lacrosse** *n* sport in which teams catch and throw a ball using long sticks with a pouched net at the end, in an attempt to score goals

**lactation** *n* secretion of milk by female mammals to feed young ▸ **lactic** *adj* of or derived from milk ▸ **lactose** *n* white crystalline sugar found in milk

**lacuna** [lak-**kew**-na] *n, pl* -**nae** gap or missing part, esp. in a document or series

**lad** *n* boy or young man

**ladder** *n* frame of two poles connected by horizontal steps used for climbing; line of stitches that have come undone in tights or stockings ▹ *v* have or cause to have such a line of undone stitches

**laden** *adj* loaded; burdened

**la-di-da, lah-di-dah** *adj* (*informal*) affected or pretentious

**ladle** *n* spoon with a long handle and a large bowl, used for serving soup etc. ▹ *v* serve out

**lady** *n, pl* -**dies** woman regarded as having characteristics of good breeding or high rank; pòlite term of address for a woman; (**L-**) title of some female members of the British nobility **Our Lady** the Virgin Mary ▸ **lady-in-waiting** *n, pl* **ladies-in-waiting** female servant of a queen or princess ▸ **ladykiller** *n* (*informal*) man who is or thinks he is irresistible to women ▸ **ladylike** *adj* polite and dignified

**ladybird** *n* small red beetle with black spots

**lag¹** *v* **lagging, lagged** go too slowly, fall behind ▹ *n* delay between events ▸ **laggard** *n* person who lags behind

**lag²** *v* **lagging, lagged** wrap (a boiler, pipes, etc.) with insulating material ▸ **lagging** *n* insulating material

**lag³** *n* **old lag** (*Brit, Aust & NZ slang*) convict

**lager** *n* light-bodied beer

**lagoon** *n* body of water cut off from the open sea by coral reefs or sand bars

**laid** *v* past of **lay¹** ▸ **laid-back** *adj* (*informal*) relaxed

**lain** *v* past participle of **lie²**

**lair** *n* resting place of an animal

**laird** *n* Scottish landowner

**laissez-faire** [less-ay-**fair**] *n* principle of nonintervention, esp. by a government in commercial affairs

**laity** [**lay**-it-ee] *n* people who are not members of the clergy

**lake¹** *n* expanse of water entirely surrounded by land ▸ **lakeside** *n*

**lake²** *n* red pigment

**lama** *n* Buddhist priest in Tibet or Mongolia

**lamb** *n* young sheep; its meat ▹ *v* (of sheep) give birth to a lamb or lambs ▸ **lamb's fry** (*Aust & NZ*) lamb's liver for cooking ▸ **lambskin** *n* ▸ **lambswool** *n*

**lambast, lambaste** *v* beat or thrash; reprimand severely

**lambent** *adj* (*lit*) (of a flame) flickering softly .

**lame** *adj* having an injured or disabled leg or foot; (of an excuse) unconvincing ▹ *v* make lame ▸ **lamely** *adv* ▸ **lameness** *n* ▸ **lame duck** person or thing unable to cope without help

**lamé** [**lah**-may] *n, adj* (fabric) interwoven with gold or silver thread

**lament** *v* feel or express sorrow (for) ▹ *n* passionate expression of grief ▸ **lamentable** *adj* very disappointing ▸ **lamentation** *n* ▸ **lamented** *adj* grieved for

**laminate** v make (a sheet of material) by sticking together thin sheets; cover with a thin sheet of material ▷ n laminated sheet ▸ **laminated** adj

**lamington** n (Aust & NZ) sponge cake coated with a sweet coating

**Lammas** n August 1, formerly a harvest festival

**lamp** n device which produces light from electricity, oil, or gas ▸ **lamppost** n post supporting a lamp in the street ▸ **lampshade** n

**lampoon** n humorous satire ridiculing someone ▷ v satirize or ridicule

**lamprey** n eel-like fish with a round sucking mouth

**LAN** (Computing) local area network

**lance** n long spear used by a mounted soldier ▷ v pierce (a boil or abscess) with a lancet ▸ **lancer** n formerly, cavalry soldier armed with a lance ▸ **lance corporal** noncommissioned army officer of the lowest rank

**lancet** n pointed two-edged surgical knife; narrow window in the shape of a pointed arch

**land** n solid part of the earth's surface; ground, esp. with reference to its type or use; rural or agricultural area; property consisting of land; country or region ▷ v come or bring to earth after a flight, jump, or fall; go or take from a ship at the end of a voyage; come to or touch shore; come or bring to some point or condition; (informal) obtain; take (a hooked fish) from the water; (informal) deliver (a punch) ▸ **landed** adj possessing or consisting of lands ▸ **landless** adj ▸ **landward** adj nearest to or facing the land ▷ adv (also **landwards**) towards land ▸ **landfall** n ship's first landing after a voyage

▸ **landlocked** adj completely surrounded by land ▸ **land up** v arrive at a final point or condition

**landau** [lan-daw] n four-wheeled carriage with two folding hoods

**landing** n floor area at the top of a flight of stairs; bringing or coming to land; (also **landing stage**) place where people or goods go onto or come off a boat

**landline** n fixed telephone communications cable

**landlord, landlady** n person who rents out land, houses, etc.; owner or manager of a pub or boarding house

**landlubber** n person who is not experienced at sea

**landmark** n prominent object in or feature of a landscape; event, decision, etc. considered as an important development

**landscape** n extensive piece of inland scenery seen from one place; picture of it ▷ v improve natural features of (a piece of land)

**landslide** n (also **landslip**) falling of soil, rock, etc. down the side of a mountain; overwhelming electoral victory

**lane** n narrow road; area of road for one stream of traffic; specified route followed by ships or aircraft; strip of a running track or swimming pool for use by one competitor

**language** n system of sounds, symbols, etc. for communicating thought; particular system used by a nation or people; system of words and symbols for computer programming

**languid** adj lacking energy or enthusiasm ▸ **languidly** adv

**languish** v suffer neglect or hardship; lose or diminish in strength or vigour; pine (for)

**languor** [**lang**-ger] *n* state of dreamy relaxation; laziness or weariness ▸ **languorous** *adj*

**lank** *adj* (of hair) straight and limp; thin or gaunt ▸ **lanky** *adj* ungracefully tall and thin

**lanolin** *n* grease from sheep's wool used in ointments etc.

**lantana** [lan-**tay**-na] *n* shrub with orange or yellow flowers, considered a weed in Australia

**lantern** *n* light in a transparent protective case ▸ **lantern jaw** long thin jaw ▸ **lantern-jawed** *adj*

**lanthanum** *n* (*Chem*) silvery-white metallic element ▸ **lanthanide series** class of 15 elements chemically related to lanthanum

**lanyard** *n* cord worn round the neck to hold a knife or whistle; (*Naut*) short rope

**lap**[1] *n* part between the waist and knees of a person when sitting ▸ **laptop** *adj* (of a computer) small enough to fit on a user's lap ▷ *n* computer small enough to fit on a user's lap

**lap**[2] *n* single circuit of a racecourse or track; stage of a journey ▷ *v* **lapping, lapped** overtake an opponent so as to be one or more circuits ahead

**lap**[3] *v* **lapping, lapped** (of waves) beat softly against (a shore etc.) ▸ **lap up** *v* drink by scooping up with the tongue; accept (information or attention) eagerly

**lapel** [lap-**pel**] *n* part of the front of a coat or jacket folded back towards the shoulders

**lapidary** *adj* of or relating to stones

**lapis lazuli** [**lap**-iss **lazz**-yoo-lie] *n* bright blue gemstone

**lapse** *n* temporary drop in a standard, esp. through forgetfulness or carelessness; instance of bad behaviour by someone usually well-behaved; break in occurrence or usage ▷ *v* drop in standard; end or become invalid, esp. through disuse; abandon religious faith; (of time) slip away ▸ **lapsed** *adj*

**lapwing** *n* plover with a tuft of feathers on the head

**larboard** *adj*, *n* (*old-fashioned*) port (side of a ship)

**larceny** *n*, *pl* **-nies** (*Law*) theft

**larch** *n* deciduous coniferous tree

**lard** *n* soft white fat obtained from a pig ▷ *v* insert strips of bacon in (meat) before cooking; decorate (speech or writing) with strange words unnecessarily

**larder** *n* storeroom for food

**large** *adj* great in size, number, or extent **at large** in general; free, not confined; fully ▸ **largely** *adv* ▸ **largish** *adj* ▸ **large-scale** *adj* wide-ranging or extensive

**largesse, largess** [lar-**jess**] *n* generous giving, esp. of money

**largo** *n*, *pl* **-gos** ▷ *adv* (*Music*) (piece to be played) in a slow and dignified manner

**lariat** *n* lasso

**lark**[1] *n* small brown songbird, skylark

**lark**[2] *n* (*informal*) harmless piece of mischief or fun; unnecessary activity or job ▸ **lark about** *v* play pranks

**larkspur** *n* plant with spikes of blue, pink, or white flowers with spurs

**larrikin** *n* (*Aust & NZ, old-fashioned slang*) mischievous or unruly person

**larva** *n*, *pl* **-vae** insect in an immature stage, often resembling a worm ▸ **larval** *adj*

**larynx** *n*, *pl* **larynges** part of the throat containing the vocal cords ▸ **laryngeal** *adj* ▸ **laryngitis** *n* inflammation of the larynx

**lasagne, lasagna** [laz-**zan**-ya] *n* pasta in wide flat sheets; dish made from layers of lasagne, meat, and cheese

**lascivious** [lass-**iv**-ee-uss] *adj* showing or producing sexual desire ▸ **lasciviously** *adv*

**laser** [**lay**-zer] *n* device that produces a very narrow intense beam of light, used for cutting very hard materials and in surgery etc. ▷ *v* remove by treating with a laser

**lash**[1] *n* eyelash; sharp blow with a whip ▷ *v* hit with a whip; (of rain or waves) beat forcefully against; attack verbally, scold; flick or wave sharply to and fro ▸ **lash out** *v* make a sudden physical or verbal attack; (*informal*) spend (money) extravagantly

**lash**[2] *v* fasten or bind tightly with cord etc.

**lashings** *pl n* (*old-fashioned*) large amounts

**lass, lassie** *n* (*Scot & N English*) girl

**lassitude** *n* physical or mental weariness

**lasso** [lass-**oo**] *n*, *pl* -**sos** or -**soes** rope with a noose for catching cattle and horses ▷ *v* -**soing, -soed** catch with a lasso

**last**[1] *adj, adv* coming at the end or after all others; most recent(ly) ▷ *adj* only remaining ▷ *n* last person or thing ▸ **lastly** *adv* ▸ **last-ditch** *adj* done as a final resort ▸ **last post** army bugle-call played at sunset or funerals ▸ **last straw** small irritation or setback that, coming after others, is too much to bear ▸ **last word** final comment in an argument; most recent or best example of something

**last**[2] *v* continue; be sufficient for (a specified amount of time); remain fresh, uninjured, or unaltered ▸ **lasting** *adj*

**last**[3] *n* model of a foot on which shoes and boots are made or repaired

**latch** *n* fastening for a door with a bar and lever; lock which can only be opened from the outside with a key ▷ *v* fasten with a latch ▸ **latch onto** *v* become attached to (a person or idea)

**late** *adj* after the normal or expected time; towards the end of a period; being at an advanced time; recently dead; recent; former ▷ *adv* after the normal or expected time; at a relatively advanced age; recently ▸ **lately** *adv* in recent times ▸ **lateness** *n*

**latent** *adj* hidden and not yet developed ▸ **latency** *n*

**lateral** [**lat**-ter-al] *adj* of or relating to the side or sides ▸ **laterally** *adv*

**latex** *n* milky fluid found in some plants, esp. the rubber tree, used in making rubber

**lath** *n* thin strip of wood used to support plaster, tiles, etc.

**lathe** *n* machine for turning wood or metal while it is being shaped

**lather** *n* froth of soap and water; frothy sweat; (*informal*) state of agitation ▷ *v* make frothy; rub with soap until lather appears

**Latin** *n* language of the ancient Romans ▷ *adj* of or in Latin; of a people whose language derives from Latin ▸ **Latin America** parts of South and Central America whose official language is Spanish or Portuguese ▸ **Latin American** *n, adj*

**latitude** *n* angular distance measured in degrees N or S of the equator; scope for freedom of action or thought ▷ *pl* regions considered in relation to their distance from the equator

**latrine** *n* toilet in a barracks or camp

**latter** adj second of two; later; recent ▸ **latterly** adv ▸ **latter-day** adj modern

> **USAGE NOTE**
> Latter is used for the last mentioned of two items. When there are more, use last-named

**lattice** [lat-iss] n framework of intersecting strips of wood, metal, etc.; gate, screen, etc. formed of such a framework ▸ **latticed** adj

**laud** v praise or glorify ▸ **laudable** adj praiseworthy ▸ **laudably** adv ▸ **laudatory** adj praising or glorifying

**laudanum** [lawd-a-num] n opium-based sedative

**laugh** v make inarticulate sounds with the voice expressing amusement, merriment, or scorn; utter or express with laughter ▷ n act or instance of laughing; (informal) person or thing causing amusement ▸ **laughable** adj ridiculously inadequate ▸ **laughter** n sound or action of laughing ▸ **laughing gas** nitrous oxide as an anaesthetic ▸ **laughing stock** object of general derision ▸ **laugh off** v treat (something serious or difficult) lightly

**launch¹** v put (a ship or boat) into the water, esp. for the first time; begin (a campaign, project, etc.); put a new product on the market; send (a missile or spacecraft) into space or the air ▷ n launching ▸ **launcher** n ▸ **launch into** v start doing something enthusiastically ▸ **launch out** v start doing something new

**launch²** n open motorboat

**launder** v wash and iron (clothes and linen); make (illegally obtained money) seem legal by passing it through foreign banks or legitimate businesses ▸ **laundry** n, pl **-dries** clothes etc. for washing or which have recently been washed; place for washing clothes and linen ▸ **Launderette**® n shop with coin-operated washing and drying machines

**laureate** [lor-ee-at] adj see **poet laureate**

**laurel** n glossy-leaved shrub, bay tree ▷ pl wreath of laurel, an emblem of victory or merit

**lava** n molten rock thrown out by volcanoes, which hardens as it cools

**lavatory** n, pl **-ries** toilet

**lavender** n shrub with fragrant flowers ▷ adj bluish-purple ▸ **lavender water** light perfume made from lavender

**lavish** adj great in quantity or richness; giving or spending generously; extravagant ▷ v give or spend generously ▸ **lavishly** adv

**law** n rule binding on a community; system of such rules; (informal) police; invariable sequence of events in nature; general principle deduced from facts ▸ **lawful** adj allowed by law ▸ **lawfully** adv ▸ **lawless** adj breaking the law, esp. in a violent way ▸ **lawlessness** n ▸ **law-abiding** adj obeying the laws ▸ **law-breaker** n ▸ **lawsuit** n court case brought by one person or group against another

**lawn¹** n area of tended and mown grass ▸ **lawn mower** machine for cutting grass ▸ **lawn tennis** tennis, esp. when played on a grass court

**lawn²** n fine linen or cotton fabric

**lawyer** n professionally qualified legal expert

**lax** adj not strict ▸ **laxity** n

**laxative** n, adj (medicine) inducing the emptying of the bowels

**lay¹** v **laying, laid** cause to lie; devise or prepare; set in a particular place or position; attribute (blame); put forward (a plan, argument, etc.); (of a bird or reptile) produce eggs; arrange (a table) for a meal **lay waste** devastate ▶ **lay-by** n stopping place for traffic beside a road ▶ **lay off** v dismiss staff during a slack period ▶ **lay-off** n ▶ **lay on** v provide or supply ▶ **lay out** v arrange or spread out; prepare (a corpse) for burial; (*informal*) spend money, esp. lavishly; (*informal*) knock unconscious ▶ **layout** n arrangement, esp. of matter for printing or of a building

**USAGE NOTE**
*Lay* and *lie* are often confused. The action of the verb *lay* is always done *to* a person or thing, for example *He laid down his weapon*, while the action of the verb *lie* is not: *I'm going to lie down*.

**lay²** v past tense of **lie²** ▶ **layabout** n lazy person

**lay³** adj of or involving people who are not clergymen; nonspecialist ▶ **layman** n person who is not a member of the clergy; person without specialist knowledge

**lay⁴** n short narrative poem designed to be sung

**layer** n single thickness of some substance, as a cover or coating on a surface; laying hen; shoot of a plant pegged down or partly covered with earth to encourage root growth ▷ v form a layer; propagate plants by layers ▶ **layered** adj

**layette** n clothes for a newborn baby

**laze** v be idle or lazy ▷ n time spent lazing

**lazy** adj **lazier, laziest** not inclined to work or exert oneself; done in a relaxed manner without much effort; (of movement) slow and gentle ▶ **lazily** adv ▶ **laziness** n

**lb** pound (weight)

**lbw** (*Cricket*) leg before wicket

**lea** n (*poetic*) meadow

**leach** v remove or be removed from a substance by a liquid passing through it

**lead¹** v **leading, led** guide or conduct; cause to feel, think, or behave in a certain way; be, go, or play first; (of a road, path, etc.) go towards; control or direct; (foll by to) result in; pass or spend (one's life) ▷ n first or most prominent place; amount by which a person or group is ahead of another; clue; length of leather or chain attached to a dog's collar to control it; principal role or actor in a film, play, etc.; cable bringing current to an electrical device ▷ adj acting as a leader or lead ▶ **leading** adj principal; in the first position ▶ **leading question** question worded to prompt the answer desired ▶ **lead-in** n introduction to a subject

**lead²** n soft heavy grey metal; (in a pencil) graphite; lead weight on a line, used for sounding depths of water ▶ **leaded** adj (of windows) made from many small panes of glass held together by lead strips ▶ **leaden** adj heavy or sluggish; dull grey; made from lead

**leader** n person who leads; article in a newspaper expressing editorial views ▶ **leadership** n

**leaf** n, pl **leaves** flat usu. green blade attached to the stem of a plant; single sheet of paper in a book; very thin sheet of metal; extending flap on a table ▶ **leafy** adj ▶ **leafless** adj ▶ **leaf mould** rich soil composed of decayed leaves ▶ **leaf through** v turn pages without reading them

**leaflet** n sheet of printed matter for distribution; small leaf

**league**¹ n association promoting the interests of its members; association of sports clubs organizing competitions between its members; (informal) class or level

**league**² n (obs) measure of distance, about three miles

**leak** n hole or defect that allows the escape or entrance of liquid, gas, radiation, etc.; liquid etc. that escapes or enters; disclosure of secrets ▷ v let liquid etc. in or out; (of liquid etc.) find its way through a leak; disclose secret information ▶ **leakage** n act or instance of leaking ▶ **leaky** adj

**lean**¹ v **leaning, leaned** or **leant** rest against; bend or slope from an upright position; tend (towards) ▶ **leaning** n tendency ▶ **lean on** v (informal) threaten or intimidate; depend on for help or advice ▶ **lean-to** n shed built against an existing wall

**lean**² adj thin but healthy-looking; (of meat) lacking fat; unproductive ▷ n lean part of meat ▶ **leanness** n

**leap** v **leaping, leapt** or **leaped** make a sudden powerful jump ▷ n sudden powerful jump; abrupt increase, as in costs or prices ▶ **leapfrog** n game in which a player vaults over another bending down ▶ **leap year** year with February 29 as an extra day

**learn** v **learning, learned** or **learnt** gain skill or knowledge by study, practice, or teaching; memorize (something); find out or discover ▶ **learned** adj erudite, deeply read; showing much learning ▶ **learner** n ▶ **learning** n knowledge got by study

**lease** n contract by which land or property is rented for a stated time by the owner to a tenant ▷ v let or rent by lease ▶ **leasehold** n, adj (land or property) held on lease ▶ **leaseholder** n

**leash** n lead for a dog

**least** adj superlative of **little**; smallest ▷ n smallest one ▷ adv in the smallest degree

**leather** n material made from specially treated animal skins ▷ adj made of leather ▷ v beat or thrash ▶ **leathery** adj like leather, tough

**leave**¹ v **leaving, left** go away from; allow to remain, accidentally or deliberately; cause to be or remain in a specified state; discontinue membership of; permit; entrust; bequeath ▶ **leave out** v exclude or omit

**leave**² n permission to be absent from work or duty; period of such absence; permission to do something; formal parting

**leaven** [lev-ven] n substance that causes dough to rise; influence that produces a gradual change ▷ v raise with leaven; spread through and influence (something)

**lecher** n man who has or shows excessive sexual desire ▶ **lechery** n

**lecherous** [letch-er-uss] adj (of a man) having or showing excessive sexual desire

**lectern** n sloping reading desk, esp. in a church

**lecture** n informative talk to an audience on a subject; lengthy rebuke or scolding ▷ v give a talk; scold

**lecturer** n person who lectures, esp. in a university or college ▶ **lectureship** n appointment as a lecturer

**LED** light-emitting diode

**ledge** n narrow shelf sticking out from a wall; shelflike projection from a cliff etc.

**ledger** n book of debit and credit accounts of a firm

**lee** n sheltered part or side ▶ **leeward** adj, n (on) the lee side ▷ adv towards this side ▶ **leeway** n room for free movement within limits

**leech** n species of bloodsucking worm; person who lives off others

**leek** n vegetable of the onion family with a long bulb and thick stem

**leer** v look or grin at in a sneering or suggestive manner ▷ n sneering or suggestive look or grin

**leery** adj (informal) suspicious or wary (of)

**lees** pl n sediment of wine

**left**[1] adj of the side that faces west when the front faces north ▷ adv on or towards the left ▷ n left hand or part; (Politics) people supporting socialism rather than capitalism ▶ **leftist** n, adj (person) of the political left ▶ **left-handed** adj more adept with the left hand than with the right ▶ **left-wing** adj socialist; belonging to the more radical part of a political party

**left**[2] v past of **leave**[1]

**leftover** n unused portion of food or material

**leg** n one of the limbs on which a person or animal walks, runs, or stands; part of a garment covering the leg; structure that supports, such as one of the legs of a table; stage of a journey; (Sport) (part of) one game or race in a series **pull someone's leg** tease someone ▶ **leggy** adj having long legs ▶ **legless** adj without legs; (slang) very drunk ▶ **leggings** pl n covering of leather or other material for the legs; close-fitting trousers for women or children

**legacy** n, pl **-cies** thing left in a will; thing handed down to a successor

**legal** adj established or permitted by law; relating to law or lawyers ▶ **legally** adv ▶ **legality** n ▶ **legalize** v make legal ▶ **legalization** n

**legate** n messenger or representative, esp. from the Pope ▶ **legation** n diplomatic minister and his staff; official residence of a diplomatic minister

**legatee** n recipient of a legacy

**legato** [leg-**ah**-toe] n, pl **-tos** ▷ adv (Music) (piece to be played) smoothly

**legend** n traditional story or myth; traditional literature; famous person or event; stories about such a person or event; inscription ▶ **legendary** adj famous; of or in legend

**legerdemain** [lej-er-de-**main**] n sleight of hand; cunning deception

**legible** adj easily read ▶ **legibility** n ▶ **legibly** adv

**legion** n large military force; large number; association of veterans; infantry unit in the Roman army ▶ **legionary** adj, n ▶ **legionnaire** n member of a legion ▶ **legionnaire's disease** serious bacterial disease similar to pneumonia

**legislate** v make laws ▶ **legislative** adj ▶ **legislator** n maker of laws ▶ **legislature** n body of people that makes, amends, or repeals laws

**legislation** n legislating; laws made

**legitimate** adj authorized by or in accordance with law; fairly deduced; born to parents married to each other ▷ v make legitimate

▶ **legitimacy** n ▶ **legitimately** adv
▶ **legitimize** v make legitimate, legalize ▶ **legitimization** n

**Lego**® n construction toy of plastic bricks fitted together by studs

**leguaan** [leg-oo-ahn] n large S African lizard

**legume** n pod of a plant of the pea or bean family ▷ pl peas or beans ▶ **leguminous** adj (of plants) pod-bearing

**lei** n (in Hawaii) garland of flowers

**leisure** n time for relaxation or hobbies **at one's leisure** when one has time ▶ **leisurely** adj deliberate, unhurried ▷ adv slowly ▶ **leisured** adj with plenty of spare time ▶ **leisure centre** building with facilities such as a swimming pool, gymnasium, and café

**leitmotif** [lite-mote-eef] n (Music) recurring theme associated with a person, situation, or thought

**lekker** adj (S Afr slang) attractive or nice; tasty

**lemming** n rodent of arctic regions, reputed to run into the sea and drown during mass migrations

**lemon** n yellow oval fruit that grows on trees; (slang) useless or defective person or thing ▷ adj pale-yellow ▶ **lemonade** n lemon-flavoured soft drink, often fizzy ▶ **lemon curd** creamy spread made of lemons, butter, etc. ▶ **lemon sole** edible flatfish

**lemur** n nocturnal animal like a small monkey, found in Madagascar

**lend** v **lending, lent** give the temporary use of; provide (money) temporarily, often for interest; add (a quality or effect) e.g. her presence lent beauty to the scene **lend itself to** be suitable for ▶ **lender** n

**length** n extent or measurement from end to end; period of time

for which something happens; quality of being long; piece of something narrow and long **at length** at last; in full detail.
▶ **lengthy** adj very long or tiresome
▶ **lengthily** adv ▶ **lengthen** v make or become longer ▶ **lengthways, lengthwise** adj, adv

**lenient** [lee-nee-ent] adj tolerant, not strict or severe ▶ **leniency** n
▶ **leniently** adv

**lens** n, pl **lenses** piece of glass or similar material with one or both sides curved, used to bring together or spread light rays in cameras, spectacles, telescopes, etc.; transparent structure in the eye that focuses light

**Lent** n period from Ash Wednesday to Easter Saturday ▶ **Lenten** adj of, in, or suitable to Lent

**lent** v past of **lend**

**lentil** n edible seed of a leguminous Asian plant

**lento** n, pl **-tos** ▷ adv (Music) (piece to be played) slowly

**leonine** adj like a lion

**leopard** n large spotted carnivorous animal of the cat family

**leotard** n tight-fitting garment covering the upper body, worn for dancing or exercise

**leper** n (offens) person suffering from leprosy; ignored or despised person

**lepidoptera** pl n order of insects with four wings covered with fine gossamer scales, as moths and butterflies ▶ **lepidopterist** n person who studies or collects butterflies or moths

**leprechaun** n mischievous elf of Irish folklore

**leprosy** n disease attacking the nerves and skin, resulting in loss of feeling in the affected parts ▶ **leprous** adj

**lesbian** n homosexual woman
▷ adj of homosexual women
▸ **lesbianism** n

**lese-majesty** [lezz-**maj**-est-ee] n
treason; taking of liberties against
people in authority

**lesion** n structural change in an
organ of the body caused by illness
or injury; injury or wound

**less** adj smaller in extent, degree,
or duration; not so much;
comparative of **little** ▷ pron
smaller part or quantity ▷ adv to
a smaller extent or degree ▷ prep
after deducting, minus ▸ **lessen** v
make or become smaller or not as
much ▸ **lesser** adj not as great in
quantity, size, or worth

> **USAGE NOTE**
> Avoid confusion with *few(er)*.
> *Less* is used with amounts that
> cannot be counted: *less time*; *less
> fuss*. *Few(er)* is used of things that
> can be counted

**lessee** n person to whom a lease
is granted

**lesson** n single period of instruction
in a subject; content of this;
experience that teaches; portion of
Scripture read in church

**lest** conj so as to prevent any
possibility that; for fear that

**let¹** v **letting, let** allow, enable,
or cause; used as an auxiliary to
express a proposal, command,
threat, or assumption; grant use
of for rent, lease; allow to escape
**let alone** not to mention ▸ **let
down** v disappoint; lower; deflate
▸ **letdown** n disappointment
▸ **let off** v excuse from (a duty
or punishment); fire or explode
(a weapon); emit (gas, steam,
etc.) ▸ **let on** v (*informal*) reveal
(a secret) ▸ **let out** v emit;
release ▸ **let up** v diminish or stop
▸ **let-up** n lessening

**let²** n (*Tennis*) minor infringement or
obstruction of the ball requiring a
replay of the point; hindrance

**lethal** adj deadly

**lethargy** n sluggishness or
dullness; abnormal lack of energy
▸ **lethargic** adj ▸ **lethargically** adv

**letter** n written message, usu.
sent by post; alphabetical
symbol; strict meaning (of a law
etc.) ▷ pl literary knowledge or
ability ▸ **lettered** adj learned
▸ **lettering** n ▸ **letter bomb**
explosive device in a parcel or
letter that explodes on opening
▸ **letter box** slot in a door through
which letters are delivered; box
in a street or post office where
letters are posted ▸ **letterhead** n
printed heading on stationery
giving the sender's name and
address

**lettuce** n plant with large green
leaves used in salads

**leucocyte** [**loo**-koh-site] n white
blood cell

**leukaemia** [loo-**kee**-mee-a] n
disease caused by uncontrolled
overproduction of white blood cells

**levee** n (*US*) natural or artificial river
embankment

**level** adj horizontal; having an even
surface; of the same height as
something else; equal to or even
with (someone or something else);
not going above the top edge of
(a spoon etc.) ▷ v **-elling, -elled**
make even or horizontal; make
equal in position or status; direct
(a gun, accusation, etc.) at; raze
to the ground ▷ n horizontal line
or surface; device for showing or
testing if something is horizontal;
position on a scale; standard or
grade; flat area of land **on the level**
(*informal*) honest or trustworthy
▸ **level crossing** point where a

railway line and road cross ▸ **level-headed** adj not apt to be carried away by emotion

**lever** n handle used to operate machinery; bar used to move a heavy object or to open something; rigid bar pivoted about a fulcrum to transfer a force to a load; means of exerting pressure to achieve an aim ▷ v prise or move with a lever ▸ **leverage** n action or power of a lever; influence or strategic advantage

**leveret** [lev-ver-it] n young hare

**leviathan** [lev-**vie**-ath-an] n sea monster; anything huge or formidable

**Levis®** pl n denim jeans

**levitation** n raising of a solid body into the air supernaturally ▸ **levitate** v rise or cause to rise into the air

**levity** n, pl **-ties** inclination to make a joke of serious matters

**levy** [**lev**-vee] v **levying, levied** impose and collect (a tax); raise (troops) ▷ n, pl **levies** imposition or collection of taxes; money levied

**lewd** adj lustful or indecent ▸ **lewdly** adv ▸ **lewdness** n

**lexicon** n dictionary; vocabulary of a language ▸ **lexical** adj relating to the vocabulary of a language ▸ **lexicographer** n writer of dictionaries ▸ **lexicography** n

**LGBT** lesbian, gay, bisexual, and transgender

**liable** adj legally obliged or responsible; given to or at risk from a condition ▸ **liability** n hindrance or disadvantage; state of being liable; financial obligation

> **USAGE NOTE**
> The use of *liable* to mean 'likely' is informal. It generally means 'responsible for': *He was liable for any damage*

**liaise** v establish and maintain communication (with) ▸ **liaison** n communication and contact between groups; secret or adulterous relationship

> **SPELLING TIP**
> Remember to include a second *i* in **liaise** and **liaison**

**liana** n climbing plant in tropical forests

**liar** n person who tells lies

**lib** n (informal) short for **liberation**

**libation** [lie-**bay**-shun] n drink poured as an offering to the gods

**libel** n published statement falsely damaging a person's reputation ▷ v **-belling, -belled** falsely damage the reputation of (someone) ▸ **libellous** adj

**liberal** adj having social and political views that favour progress and reform; generous in behaviour or temperament; tolerant; abundant; (of education) designed to develop general cultural interests ▷ n person who has liberal ideas or opinions ▸ **liberally** adv ▸ **liberalism** n belief in democratic reforms and individual freedom ▸ **liberality** n generosity ▸ **liberalize** v make (laws, a country, etc.) less restrictive ▸ **liberalization** n ▸ **Liberal Democrat, Lib Dem** member of the Liberal Democrats, a British political party favouring a mixed economy and individual freedom ▸ **Liberal Party** main right-wing political party in Australia

**liberate** v set free ▸ **liberation** n ▸ **liberator** n

**libertarian** n believer in freedom of thought and action ▷ adj having such a belief

**libertine** [**lib**-er-teen] n morally dissolute person

**liberty** n, pl **-ties** freedom; act or comment regarded as forward or socially unacceptable **at liberty** free; having the right; **take liberties** be presumptuous

**libido** [lib-**ee**-doe] *n, pl* -**dos** psychic energy; emotional drive, esp. of sexual origin ▶ **libidinous** *adj* lustful

**library** *n, pl* -**braries** room or building where books are kept; collection of books, records, etc. for consultation or borrowing ▶ **librarian** *n* keeper of or worker in a library ▶ **librarianship** *n*

**libretto** *n, pl* -**tos** *or* -**ti** words of an opera ▶ **librettist** *n*

**lice** *n* a plural of **louse**

**licence** *n* document giving official permission to do something; formal permission; disregard of conventions for effect e.g. *poetic licence*; excessive liberty ▶ **license** *v* grant a licence to ▶ **licensed** *adj* ▶ **licensee** *n* holder of a licence, esp. to sell alcohol

> **SPELLING TIP**
> Note the -*ce* ending for the noun *licence*, with -*se* for the verb *license*

**licentiate** *n* person licensed as competent to practise a profession

**licentious** *adj* sexually unrestrained or promiscuous

**lichen** *n* small flowerless plant forming a crust on rocks, trees, etc.

**licit** *adj* lawful, permitted

**lick** *v* pass the tongue over; touch lightly or flicker round; (*slang*) defeat ▷ *n* licking; small amount (of paint etc.); (*informal*) fast pace

**licorice** *n* same as **liquorice**

**lid** *n* movable cover; short for **eyelid**

**lido** [**lee**-doe] *n, pl* -**dos** open-air centre for swimming and water sports

**lie¹** *v* **lying**, **lied** make a deliberately false statement ▷ *n* deliberate falsehood **white lie** see **white**

**lie²** *v* **lying**, **lay**, **lain** place oneself or be in a horizontal position; be situated; be or remain in a certain state or position; exist or be found ▷ *n* way something lies ▶ **lie-down** *n* rest ▶ **lie in** *v* remain in bed late into the morning ▶ **lie-in** *n* long stay in bed in the morning

> **USAGE NOTE**
> Note that the past of *lie* is *lay*: *She lay on the beach all day.* Do not confuse with the main verb *lay* meaning 'put'

**lied** [leed] *n, pl* **lieder** (*Music*) song for voice and piano of a romantic poem

**liege** [leej] *adj* bound to give or receive feudal service ▷ *n* lord

**lien** *n* (*Law*) right to hold another's property until a debt is paid

**lieu** [lyew] *n* **in lieu of** instead of

**lieutenant** [lef-**ten**-ant] *n* junior officer in the army or navy; main assistant

**life** *n, pl* **lives** state of living beings, characterized by growth, reproduction, and response to stimuli; period between birth and death or between birth and the present time; way of living; amount of time something is active or functions; biography; liveliness or high spirits; living beings collectively ▶ **lifeless** *adj* dead; not lively or exciting; unconscious ▶ **lifelike** *adj* ▶ **lifelong** *adj* lasting all of a person's life ▶ **life belt, life jacket** buoyant device to keep afloat a person in danger of drowning ▶ **lifeboat** *n* boat used for rescuing people at sea ▶ **life cycle** series of changes undergone by each generation of an animal or plant ▶ **lifeline** *n* means of contact or support; rope used in rescuing a person in danger ▶ **life science** any science concerned with living organisms, such as biology, botany, or zoology ▸ **lifestyle** *n* particular attitudes, habits, etc. ▸ **life-support** *adj* (of equipment or treatment) necessary to keep a person alive ▸ **lifetime** *n* length of time a person is alive

**lift** *v* move upwards in position, status, volume, etc.; revoke or cancel; take (plants) out of the ground for harvesting; (of fog, etc.) disappear; make or become more cheerful ▹ *n* cage raised and lowered in a vertical shaft to transport people or goods; ride in a car etc. as a passenger; (*informal*) feeling of cheerfulness; lifting ▸ **liftoff** *n* moment a rocket leaves the ground

**ligament** *n* band of tissue joining bones

**ligature** *n* link, bond, or tie

**light**[1] *n* electromagnetic radiation by which things are visible; source of this, lamp; anything that lets in light, such as a window; aspect or view; mental vision; means of setting fire to ▹ *pl* traffic lights ▹ *adj* bright; (of a colour) pale ▹ *v* **lighting, lighted** *or* **lit** ignite; illuminate or cause to illuminate ▸ **lighten** *v* make less dark ▸ **lighting** *n* apparatus for and use of artificial light in theatres, films, etc. ▸ **light bulb** glass part of an electric lamp ▸ **lighthouse** *n* tower with a light to guide ships ▸ **light year** (*Astronomy*) distance light travels in one year, about six million million miles

**light**[2] *adj* not heavy, weighing relatively little; relatively low in strength, amount, density, etc.; not clumsy; not serious or profound; easily digested ▹ *adv* with little equipment or luggage ▹ *v* **lighting, lighted, lit** (esp. of birds) settle after flight; come

(upon) by chance ▸ **lightly** *adv* ▸ **lightness** *n* ▸ **lighten** *v* make less heavy or burdensome; make more cheerful or lively ▸ **light-fingered** *adj* skilful at stealing ▸ **light-headed** *adj* feeling faint, dizzy ▸ **light-hearted** *adj* carefree ▸ **lightweight** *n*, *adj* (person) of little importance ▹ *n* boxer weighing up to 135lb (professional) or 60kg (amateur)

**lighter**[1] *n* device for lighting cigarettes etc.

**lighter**[2] *n* flat-bottomed boat for unloading ships

**lightning** *n* visible discharge of electricity in the atmosphere ▹ *adj* fast and sudden

> **SPELLING TIP**
> Do not confuse the noun **lightning**, which doesn't have an *e* in the middle, with the verb *lighten*, which has the form *lightening*

**lights** *pl n* lungs of animals as animal food

**ligneous** *adj* of or like wood

**lignite** [**lig**-nite] *n* woody textured rock used as fuel

**like**[1] *prep, conj, adj, pron* indicating similarity, comparison, etc. ▸ **liken** *v* compare ▸ **likeness** *n* resemblance; portrait ▸ **likewise** *adv* similarly

**like**[2] *v* find enjoyable; be fond of; prefer, choose, or wish ▸ **likeable, likable** *adj* ▸ **liking** *n* fondness; preference

**likely** *adj* tending or inclined; probable; hopeful, promising ▹ *adv* probably **not likely** (*informal*) definitely not ▸ **likelihood** *n* probability

**lilac** *n* shrub with pale mauve or white flowers ▹ *adj* light-purple

**Lilliputian** [lil-lip-**pew**-shun] *adj* tiny

**Lilo®** n, pl **-los** inflatable rubber mattress

**lilt** n pleasing musical quality in speaking; jaunty rhythm; graceful rhythmic motion ▶ **lilting** adj

**lily** n, pl **lilies** plant which grows from a bulb and has large, often white, flowers

**limb** n arm, leg, or wing; main branch of a tree

**limber** v (foll by up) loosen stiff muscles by exercising ▷ adj pliant or supple

**limbo¹** n **in limbo** not knowing the result or next stage of something and powerless to influence it

**limbo²** n, pl **-bos** West Indian dance in which dancers lean backwards to pass under a bar

**lime¹** n calcium compound used as a fertilizer or in making cement ▶ **limelight** n glare of publicity ▶ **limestone** n sedimentary rock used in building

**lime²** n small green citrus fruit ▶ **lime-green** adj greenish-yellow

**lime³** n deciduous tree with heart-shaped leaves and fragrant flowers

**limerick** [lim-mer-ik] n humorous verse of five lines

**limey** n (US slang) British person

**limit** n ultimate extent, degree, or amount of something; boundary or edge ▷ v **-iting, -ited** restrict or confine ▶ **limitation** n ▶ **limitless** adj ▶ **limited company** company whose shareholders' liability for debts is restricted

**limousine** n large luxurious car

**limp¹** v walk with an uneven step ▷ n limping walk

**limp²** adj without firmness or stiffness ▶ **limply** adv

**limpet** n shellfish which sticks tightly to rocks

**limpid** adj clear or transparent; easy to understand ▶ **limpidity** n

**linchpin, lynchpin** n pin to hold a wheel on its axle; essential person or thing

**linctus** n, pl **-tuses** syrupy cough medicine

**linden** n same as **lime³**

**line¹** n long narrow mark; indented mark or wrinkle; boundary or limit; edge or contour of a shape; string or wire for a particular use; telephone connection; wire or cable for transmitting electricity; shipping company; railway track; course or direction of movement; prescribed way of thinking; field of interest or activity; row or queue of people; class of goods; row of words ▷ pl words of a theatrical part; school punishment of writing out a sentence a specified number of times ▷ v mark with lines; be or form a border or edge **in line for** likely to receive **in line with** in accordance with ▶ **line dancing** form of dancing performed by rows of people to country and western music ▶ **line-up** n people or things assembled for a particular purpose

**line²** v give a lining to; cover the inside of

**lineage** [lin-ee-ij] n descent from an ancestor

**lineament** n facial feature

**linear** [lin-ee-er] adj of or in lines

**linen** n cloth or thread made from flax; sheets, tablecloths, etc.

**liner¹** n large passenger ship or aircraft

**liner²** n something used as a lining

**linesman** n (in some sports) an official who helps the referee or umpire; person who maintains railway, electricity, or telephone lines

**ling¹** n slender food fish

**ling²** n heather

**linger** v delay or prolong departure; continue in a weakened state for a long time before dying or disappearing; spend a long time doing something

**lingerie** [lan-zher-ee] n women's underwear or nightwear

**lingo** n, pl **-goes** (informal) foreign or unfamiliar language or jargon

**lingua franca** n language used for communication between people of different mother tongues

**lingual** adj of the tongue

**linguist** n person skilled in foreign languages; person who studies linguistics ▶ **linguistic** adj of languages ▶ **linguistics** n scientific study of language

**liniment** n medicated liquid rubbed on the skin to relieve pain or stiffness

**lining** n layer of cloth attached to the inside of a garment etc.; inner covering of anything

**link** n any of the rings forming a chain; person or thing forming a connection; type of communications connection e.g. a radio link ▷ v connect with or as if with links; connect by association ▶ **linkage** n ▶ **link-up** n joining together of two systems or groups

**links** pl n golf course, esp. one by the sea

**linnet** n songbird of the finch family

**lino** n short for **linoleum**

**linoleum** n floor covering of hessian or jute with a smooth decorative coating of powdered cork

**Linotype®** n typesetting machine which casts lines of words in one piece

**linseed** n seed of the flax plant

**lint** n soft material for dressing a wound

**lintel** n horizontal beam at the top of a door or window

**lion** n large animal of the cat family, the male of which has a shaggy mane **the lion's share** the biggest part ▶ **lioness** n fem ▶ **lion-hearted** adj brave

**lip** n either of the fleshy edges of the mouth; rim of a jug etc.; (slang) impudence ▶ **lip-reading** n method of understanding speech by interpreting lip movements ▶ **lip service** insincere tribute or respect ▶ **lipstick** n cosmetic in stick form, for colouring the lips

**lipo** n (informal) short for **liposuction**

**liposuction** n surgical operation in which body fat is removed

**liquefy** v **-fying, -fied** make or become liquid ▶ **liquefaction** n

**liqueur** [lik-**cure**] n flavoured and sweetened alcoholic spirit

**liquid** n substance in a physical state which can change shape but not size ▷ adj of or being a liquid; flowing smoothly; (of assets) in the form of money or easily converted into money ▶ **liquidize** v make or become liquid ▶ **liquidizer** n kitchen appliance that liquidizes food ▶ **liquidity** n state of being able to meet financial obligations

**liquidate** v pay (a debt); dissolve a company and share its assets among creditors; wipe out or kill ▶ **liquidation** n ▶ **liquidator** n official appointed to liquidate a business

**liquor** n alcoholic drink, esp. spirits; liquid in which food has been cooked

**liquorice** [lik-ker-iss] n black substance used in medicine and as a sweet

**lira** n, pl **-re** or **-ras** monetary unit of Turkey and formerly of Italy

**lisle** [rhymes with **mile**] n strong fine cotton thread or fabric

**lisp** n speech defect in which s and z are pronounced th ▷ v speak or utter with a lisp

**lissom, lissome** adj supple, agile

**list¹** n item-by-item record of names or things, usu. written one below another ▷ v make a list of; include in a list

**list²** v (of a ship) lean to one side ▷ n leaning to one side

**listen** v concentrate on hearing something; heed or pay attention to ▶ **listener** n ▶ **listen in** v listen secretly, eavesdrop

**listeriosis** n dangerous form of food poisoning

**listless** adj lacking interest or energy ▶ **listlessly** adv

**lit** v past of **light¹, light²**

**litany** n, pl -**nies** prayer with responses from the congregation; any tedious recital

**literacy** n ability to read and write

**literal** adj according to the explicit meaning of a word or text, not figurative; (of a translation) word for word; actual, true ▶ **literally** adv

**USAGE NOTE**
Note that *literally* means much the same as 'actually'. It is very loosely used to mean 'just about' but this can be ambiguous

**literary** adj of or knowledgeable about literature; (of a word) formal, not colloquial

**literate** adj able to read and write; educated ▶ **literati** pl n literary people

**literature** n written works such as novels, plays, and poetry; books and writings of a country, period, or subject

**lithe** adj flexible or supple, pliant

**lithium** n (Chem) chemical element, the lightest known metal

**litho** n, pl -**thos** short for **lithograph** ▷ adj short for **lithographic**

**lithography** [lith-**og**-ra-fee] n method of printing from a metal or stone surface in which the printing areas are made receptive to ink ▶ **lithograph** n print made by lithography ▷ v reproduce by lithography ▶ **lithographer** n ▶ **lithographic** adj

**litigant** n person involved in a lawsuit

**litigation** n legal action ▶ **litigate** v bring or contest a law suit; engage in legal action ▶ **litigious** [lit-**ij**-uss] adj frequently going to law

**litmus** n blue dye turned red by acids and restored to blue by alkalis ▶ **litmus test** something which is regarded as a simple and accurate test of a particular thing

**litotes** [lie-**toe**-teez] n ironical understatement used for effect

**litre** n unit of liquid measure equal to 1000 cubic centimetres or 1.76 pints

**litter** n untidy rubbish dropped in public places; group of young animals produced at one birth; straw etc. as bedding for an animal; dry material to absorb a cat's excrement; bed or seat on parallel sticks for carrying people ▷ v strew with litter; scatter or be scattered about untidily; give birth to young

**little** adj small or smaller than average; young ▷ adv not a lot; hardly; not much or often ▷ n small amount, extent, or duration

**littoral** adj of or by the seashore ▷ n coastal district

**liturgy** n, pl -**gies** prescribed form of public worship ▶ **liturgical** adj

**live¹** v be alive; remain in life or existence; exist in a specified way e.g. *we live well*; reside; continue or last; subsist; enjoy life to the full ▸ **liver** *n* person who lives in a specified way ▸ **live down** *v* wait till people forget a past mistake or misdeed ▸ **live-in** *adj* resident ▸ **live together** *v* (of an unmarried couple) share a house and have a sexual relationship ▸ **live up to** *v* meet (expectations) ▸ **live with** *v* tolerate

**live²** *adj* living, alive; (of a broadcast) transmitted during the actual performance; (of a performance) done in front of an audience; (of a wire, circuit, etc.) carrying an electric current; causing interest or controversy; capable of exploding; glowing or burning ▷ *adv* in the form of a live performance ▸ **lively** *adj* full of life or vigour; animated; vivid ▸ **liveliness** *n* ▸ **liven up** *v* make (more) lively

**livelihood** *n* occupation or employment

**liver** *n* organ secreting bile; animal liver as food ▸ **liverish** *adj* having a disorder of the liver; touchy or irritable

**livery** *n*, *pl* **-eries** distinctive dress, esp. of a servant or servants; distinctive design or colours of a company ▸ **liveried** *adj* ▸ **livery stable** stable where horses are kept at a charge or hired out

**livestock** *n* farm animals

**livid** *adj* (*informal*) angry or furious; bluish-grey

**living** *adj* possessing life, not dead or inanimate; currently in use or existing; of everyday life e.g. *living conditions* ▷ *n* condition of being alive; manner of life; financial means ▸ **living room** room in a house used for relaxation and entertainment

**lizard** *n* four-footed reptile with a long body and tail

**llama** *n* woolly animal of the camel family used as a beast of burden in S America

**LLB** Bachelor of Laws

**loach** *n* carplike freshwater fish

**load** *n* burden or weight; amount carried; source of worry; amount of electrical energy drawn from a source ▷ *pl* (*informal*) lots ▷ *v* put a load on or into; burden or oppress; cause to be biased; put ammunition into (a weapon); put film into (a camera); transfer (a program) into computer memory ▸ **loaded** *adj* (of a question) containing a hidden trap or implication; (of dice) dishonestly weighted; (*slang*) wealthy

**loaf¹** *n*, *pl* **loaves** shaped mass of baked bread; shaped mass of food; (*slang*) head, esp. as the source of common sense e.g. *use your loaf*

**loaf²** *v* idle, loiter ▸ **loafer** *n*

**loam** *n* fertile soil

**loan** *n* money lent at interest; lending; thing lent ▷ *v* lend ▸ **loan shark** person who lends money at an extremely high interest rate

**loath, loth** [rhymes with **both**] *adj* unwilling or reluctant (to)

**USAGE NOTE**
Distinguish between *loath* 'reluctant' and *loathe* 'be disgusted by'

**loathe** *v* hate, be disgusted by ▸ **loathing** *n* ▸ **loathsome** *adj*

**lob** (*Sport*) *n* ball struck or thrown in a high arc ▷ *v* **lobbing, lobbed** strike or throw (a ball) in a high arc

**lobby** *n*, *pl* **-bies** corridor into which rooms open; group which tries to influence legislators; hall in a legislative building to which the public has access ▷ *v* try to influence (legislators) in the formulation of policy ▸ **lobbyist** *n*

**lobe** n rounded projection; soft hanging part of the ear; subdivision of a body organ ▶ **lobed** adj

**lobelia** n garden plant with blue, red, or white flowers

**lobola** [law-**bawl**-a] n (SAfr) (in African custom) price paid by a bridegroom's family to his bride's family

**lobotomy** n, pl -**mies** surgical incision into a lobe of the brain to treat mental disorders

**lobster** n shellfish with a long tail and claws, which turns red when boiled; (Aust informal) $20 note

**local** adj of or existing in a particular place; confined to a particular place ▷ n person belonging to a particular district; (informal) pub close to one's home ▶ **locally** adv ▶ **locality** n neighbourhood or area ▶ **localize** v restrict to a particular place ▶ **locale** [loh-**kahl**] n scene of an event ▶ **localism** n policy of devolving power to local bodies ▶ **local anaesthetic** anaesthetic which produces loss of feeling in one part of the body ▶ **local authority** governing body of a county, district, or region ▶ **local government** government of towns, counties, and districts by locally elected political bodies

**locate** v discover the whereabouts of; situate or place ▶ **location** n site or position; act of discovering where something is; site of a film production away from the studio; (SAfr) Black African or coloured township

**loch** n (Scot) lake; long narrow bay

**lock**[1] n appliance for fastening a door, case, etc.; section of a canal shut off by gates between which the water level can be altered to aid boats moving from one level to another; extent to which a vehicle's front wheels will turn; interlocking of parts; mechanism for firing a gun;

wrestling hold ▷ v fasten or become fastened securely; become or cause to become fixed or united; become or cause to become immovable; embrace closely ▶ **lockout** n closing of a workplace by an employer to force workers to accept terms ▶ **locksmith** n person who makes and mends locks ▶ **lockup** n prison; garage or storage place away from the main premises

**lock**[2] n strand of hair

**locker** n small cupboard with a lock

**locket** n small hinged pendant for a portrait etc.

**lockjaw** n tetanus

**locomotive** n self-propelled engine for pulling trains ▷ adj of locomotion ▶ **locomotion** n action or power of moving

**locum** n temporary stand-in for a doctor or clergyman

**locus** [loh-kuss] n, pl **loci** [loh-sigh] area or place where something happens; (Maths) set of points or lines satisfying one or more specified conditions

**locust** n destructive African insect that flies in swarms and eats crops

**lode** n vein of ore ▶ **lodestar** n star used in navigation or astronomy as a point of reference ▶ **lodestone** n magnetic iron ore

**lodge** n (chiefly Brit) gatekeeper's house; house or cabin used occasionally by hunters, skiers, etc.; porters' room in a university or college; local branch of some societies ▷ v live in another's house at a fixed charge; stick or become stuck (in a place); make (a complaint etc.) formally ▶ **lodger** n ▶ **lodging** n temporary residence ▷ pl rented room or rooms in another person's house

**loft** n space between the top storey and roof of a building; gallery in a church etc. ▷ v (Sport) strike, throw, or kick (a ball) high into the air

**lofty** adj **loftier, loftiest** of great height; exalted or noble; haughty ▶ **loftily** adv haughtily

**log¹** n portion of a felled tree stripped of branches; detailed record of a journey of a ship, aircraft, etc. ▷ v **logging, logged** saw logs from a tree; record in a log ▶ **logging** n work of cutting and transporting logs ▶ **logbook** n book recording the details about a car or a ship's journeys ▶ **log in, log out** v gain entrance to or leave a computer system by keying in a special command

**log²** n short for **logarithm**

**loganberry** n purplish-red fruit, similar to a raspberry

**logarithm** n one of a series of arithmetical functions used to make certain calculations easier

**loggerheads** pl n **at loggerheads** quarrelling, disputing

**loggia** [loj-ya] n covered gallery at the side of a building

**logic** n philosophy of reasoning; reasoned thought or argument ▶ **logical** adj of logic; capable of or using clear valid reasoning; reasonable ▶ **logically** adv ▶ **logician** n

**logistics** n detailed planning and organization of a large, esp. military, operation ▶ **logistical, logistic** adj

**logo** [loh-go] n, pl **-os** emblem used by a company or other organization

**loin** n part of the body between the ribs and the hips; cut of meat from this part of an animal ▷ pl hips and inner thighs ▶ **loincloth** n piece of cloth covering the loins only

**loiter** v stand or wait aimlessly or idly

**loll** v lounge lazily; hang loosely

**lollipop** n boiled sweet on a small wooden stick ▶ **lollipop man, lollipop lady** (Brit informal) person holding a circular sign on a pole, who controls traffic so that children may cross the road safely

**lolly** n, pl **-ies** (informal) lollipop or ice lolly; (Aust & NZ informal) sweet; (slang) money ▶ **lolly scramble** (NZ) sweets scattered on the ground for children to collect

**lone** adj solitary ▶ **lonely** adj sad because alone; resulting from being alone; unfrequented ▶ **loneliness** n ▶ **loner** n (informal) person who prefers to be alone ▶ **lonesome** adj lonely

**long¹** adj having length, esp. great length, in space or time ▷ adv for an extensive period ▶ **long-distance** adj going between places far apart ▶ **long face** glum expression ▶ **longhand** n ordinary writing, not shorthand or typing ▶ **long johns** (informal) long underpants ▶ **long-life** adj (of milk, batteries, etc.) lasting longer than the regular kind ▶ **long-lived** adj living or lasting for a long time ▶ **long-range** adj extending into the future; (of vehicles, weapons, etc.) designed to cover great distances ▶ **long shot** competitor, undertaking, or bet with little chance of success ▶ **long-sighted** adj able to see distant objects in focus but not nearby ones ▶ **long-standing** adj existing for a long time ▶ **long-suffering** adj enduring trouble or unhappiness without complaint ▶ **long-term** adj lasting or effective for a long time ▶ **long wave** radio wave with a wavelength of over 1000 metres ▶ **long-winded** adj speaking or writing at tedious length

**long²** v have a strong desire (for) ▸ **longing** n yearning ▸ **longingly** adv

**longevity** [lon-**jev**-it-ee] n long life

**longitude** n distance east or west from a standard meridian ▸ **longitudinal** adj of length or longitude; lengthways

**longshoreman** n (US) docker

**loo** n (informal) toilet

**loofah** n sponge made from the dried pod of a gourd

**look** v direct the eyes or attention (towards); have the appearance of being; face in a particular direction; search (for); hope (for) ▸ n instance of looking; (often pl) appearance ▸ **look after** v take care of ▸ **lookalike** n person who is the double of another ▸ **look down on** v treat as inferior or unimportant ▸ **look forward to** v anticipate with pleasure ▸ **look on** v be a spectator; consider or regard ▸ **lookout** n guard; place for watching; (informal) worry or concern; chances or prospect ▸ **look out** v be careful ▸ **look up** v discover or confirm by checking in a book; improve; visit ▸ **look up to** v respect

**loom¹** n machine for weaving cloth

**loom²** v appear dimly; seem ominously close

**loony** (slang) adj **loonier, looniest** foolish or insane ▸ n, pl **loonies** foolish or insane person

**loop** n rounded shape made by a curved line or rope crossing itself ▸ v form or fasten with a loop **loop the loop** fly or be flown in a complete vertical circle ▸ **loophole** n means of evading a rule without breaking it

**loose** adj not tight, fastened, fixed, or tense; vague; dissolute or promiscuous ▸ adv in a loose manner ▸ v free; unfasten; slacken; let fly (an arrow, bullet, etc.) **at a loose end** bored, with nothing to do ▸ **loosely** adv ▸ **looseness** n ▸ **loosen** v make loose ▸ **loosen up** v relax, stop worrying ▸ **loose-leaf** adj allowing the addition or removal of pages

**loot** n, v plunder ▸ n (informal) money ▸ **looter** n ▸ **looting** n

**lop** v **lopping, lopped** cut away twigs and branches; chop off

**lope** v run with long easy strides

**lop-eared** adj having drooping ears

**lopsided** adj greater in height, weight, or size on one side

**loquacious** adj talkative ▸ **loquacity** n

**lord** n person with power over others, such as a monarch or master; male member of the British nobility; (Hist) feudal superior; (L-) God or Jesus; (L-) (in Britain) title given to certain male officials and peers **House of Lords** unelected upper chamber of the British parliament **lord it over** act in a superior manner towards **the Lord's Prayer** prayer taught by Christ to his disciples ▸ **lordly** adj imperious, proud ▸ **Lordship** n (in Britain) title of some male officials and peers

**lore** n body of traditions on a subject

**lorgnette** [lor-**nyet**] n pair of spectacles mounted on a long handle

**lorikeet** n small brightly coloured Australian parrot

**lorry** n, pl **-ries** (Brit & S Afr) large vehicle for transporting loads by road

**lose** v **losing, lost** come to be without, esp. by accident or carelessness; fail to keep or maintain; be deprived of; fail to get or make use of; be defeated in a competition etc.; be or become engrossed e.g. *lost in thought* ▸ **loser** *n* person or thing that loses; (*informal*) person who seems destined to fail

> **USAGE NOTE**
> Note the difference in spelling between the verb *lose* and the adjective *loose*

**loss** *n* losing; that which is lost; damage resulting from losing **at a loss** confused or bewildered; not earning enough to cover costs ▸ **loss leader** item sold at a loss to attract customers

**lost** *v* past of **lose** ▷ *adj* unable to find one's way; unable to be found

**lot** *pron* great number ▷ *n* collection of people or things; fate or destiny; one of a set of objects drawn at random to make a selection or choice; item at auction ▷ *pl* (*informal*) great numbers or quantities **a lot** (*informal*) great deal

**loth** *adj* same as **loath**

**lotion** *n* medical or cosmetic liquid for use on the skin

**lottery** *n*, *pl* **-teries** method of raising money by selling tickets that win prizes by chance; gamble

**lotto** *n* game of chance like bingo; (**L-**) national lottery

**lotus** *n* legendary plant whose fruit induces forgetfulness; Egyptian water lily

**loud** *adj* relatively great in volume; capable of making much noise; insistent and emphatic; unpleasantly patterned or colourful ▸ **loudly** *adv* ▸ **loudness** *n* ▸ **loudspeaker** *n* instrument for converting electrical signals into sound

**lough** *n* (*Irish*) loch

**lounge** *n* living room in a private house; more expensive bar in a pub; area for waiting in an airport ▷ *v* sit, lie, or stand in a relaxed manner ▸ **lounge suit** man's suit for daytime wear

**lour** *v* same as **lower²**

**louse** *n* (*pl* **lice**) wingless parasitic insect; (*pl* **louses**) unpleasant person ▸ **lousy** *adj* (*slang*) mean or unpleasant; bad, inferior; unwell

**lout** *n* crude, oafish, or aggressive person ▸ **loutish** *adj*

**louvre** [**loo**-ver] *n* one of a set of parallel slats slanted to admit air but not rain ▸ **louvred** *adj*

**love** *v* have a great affection for; feel sexual passion for; enjoy (something) very much ▷ *n* great affection; sexual passion; wholehearted liking for something; beloved person; (*Tennis, squash etc.*) score of nothing **fall in love** become in love **in love (with)** feeling a strong emotional (and sexual) attraction (for) **make love (to)** have sexual intercourse (with) ▸ **lovable, loveable** *adj* ▸ **loveless** *adj* ▸ **lovely** *adj* **-lier, -liest** very attractive; highly enjoyable ▸ **lover** *n* person having a sexual relationship outside marriage; person in love; someone who loves a specified person or thing ▸ **loving** *adj* affectionate, tender ▸ **lovingly** *adv* ▸ **love affair** romantic or sexual relationship between two people who are not married to each other ▸ **lovebird** *n* small parrot ▸ **love child** (*euphemistic*) child of an unmarried couple ▸ **love life** person's romantic or sexual relationships ▸ **lovelorn** *adj* miserable because of unhappiness in love ▸ **lovemaking** *n*

**low¹** *adj* not tall, high, or elevated; of little or less than the usual amount, degree, quality, or cost;

coarse or vulgar; dejected; not loud; deep in pitch ▷ *adv* in or to a low position, level, or degree ▷ *n* low position, level, or degree; area of low atmospheric pressure, depression ▸ **lowly** *adj* modest, humble ▸ **lowliness** *n* ▸ **lowbrow** *n, adj* (person) with nonintellectual tastes and interests ▸ **Low Church** section of the Anglican Church stressing evangelical beliefs and practices ▸ **lowdown** *n* (*informal*) inside information ▸ **low-down** *adj* (*informal*) mean, underhand, or dishonest ▸ **low-key** *adj* subdued, restrained, not intense ▸ **lowland** *n* low-lying country ▷ *pl* (**L-**) less mountainous parts of Scotland ▸ **low profile** position or attitude avoiding prominence or publicity ▸ **low-spirited** *adj* depressed

**low²** *n* cry of cattle, moo ▷ *v* moo

**lower¹** *adj* below one or more other things; smaller or reduced in amount or value ▷ *v* cause or allow to move down; lessen ▸ **lower case** small, as distinct from capital, letters

**lower²**, **lour** *v* (of the sky or weather) look gloomy or threatening ▸ **lowering** *adj*

**loyal** *adj* faithful to one's friends, country, or government ▸ **loyally** *adv* ▸ **loyalty** *n* ▸ **loyalty card** swipe card issued by a supermarket or chain store to a customer, used to record credit points awarded for money spent in the store ▸ **loyalist** *n*

**lozenge** *n* medicated tablet held in the mouth until it dissolves; four-sided diamond-shaped figure

**LP** *n* record playing approximately 20–25 minutes each side

**L-plate** *n* (*Brit & Aust*) sign on a car being driven by a learner driver

**LSD** lysergic acid diethylamide: a hallucinogenic drug

**Lt** Lieutenant

**Ltd** (*Brit*) Limited (Liability)

**lubricate** [loo-brik-ate] *v* oil or grease to lessen friction ▸ **lubricant** *n* lubricating substance, such as oil ▸ **lubrication** *n*

**lubricious** *adj* (*lit*) lewd

**lucerne** *n* fodder plant like clover, alfalfa

**lucid** *adj* clear and easily understood; able to think clearly; bright and clear ▸ **lucidly** *adv* ▸ **lucidity** *n*

**Lucifer** *n* Satan

**luck** *n* fortune, good or bad; good fortune ▸ **lucky** *adj* having or bringing good luck ▸ **lucky dip** game in which prizes are picked from a tub at random ▸ **luckily** *adv* fortunately ▸ **luckless** *adj* having bad luck

**lucrative** *adj* very profitable

**lucre** [loo-ker] *n* **filthy lucre** (*facetious*) money

**Luddite** *n* person opposed to change in industrial methods

**luderick** *n* Australian fish, usu. black or dark brown in colour

**ludicrous** *adj* absurd or ridiculous ▸ **ludicrously** *adv*

**ludo** *n* game played with dice and counters on a board

**lug¹** *v* **lugging, lugged** carry or drag with great effort

**lug²** *n* projection serving as a handle; (*Brit informal*) ear

**luggage** *n* traveller's cases, bags, etc.

**lugubrious** *adj* mournful, gloomy ▸ **lugubriously** *adv*

**lugworm** *n* large worm used as bait

**lukewarm** *adj* moderately warm, tepid; indifferent or half-hearted

**lull** *v* soothe (someone) by soft sounds or motions; calm (fears or suspicions) by deception ▷ *n* brief time of quiet in a storm etc.

**lullaby** *n, pl* **-bies** quiet song to send a child to sleep

**lumbago** [lum-**bay**-go] *n* pain in the lower back ▶ **lumbar** *adj* relating to the lower back

**lumber**¹ *n* (*Brit*) unwanted disused household articles; (*chiefly US*) sawn timber ▷ *v* (*informal*) burden with something unpleasant ▶ **lumberjack** *n* (*US*) man who fells trees and prepares logs for transport

**lumber**² *v* move heavily and awkwardly ▶ **lumbering** *adj*

**luminous** *adj* reflecting or giving off light ▶ **luminosity** *n* ▶ **luminary** *n* famous person; (*lit*) heavenly body giving off light ▶ **luminescence** *n* emission of light at low temperatures by any process other than burning ▶ **luminescent** *adj*

**lump**¹ *n* shapeless piece or mass; swelling; (*informal*) awkward or stupid person ▷ *v* consider as a single group **lump in one's throat** tight dry feeling in one's throat, usu. caused by great emotion ▶ **lumpy** *adj* ▶ **lump sum** relatively large sum of money paid at one time

**lump**² *v* **lump it** (*informal*) tolerate or put up with it

**lunar** *adj* relating to the moon

**lunatic** *adj* foolish and irresponsible ▷ *n* foolish or annoying person; (*old-fashioned*) insane person ▶ **lunacy** *n*

**lunch** *n* meal taken in the middle of the day ▷ *v* eat lunch ▶ **luncheon** *n* formal lunch ▶ **luncheon meat** tinned ground mixture of meat and cereal ▶ **luncheon voucher** (*Brit*) voucher for a certain amount, given to an employee and accepted

by some restaurants as payment for a meal

**lung** *n* organ that allows an animal or bird to breathe air: humans have two lungs in the chest ▶ **lungfish** *n* freshwater bony fish with an air-breathing lung of South America and Australia

**lunge** *n* sudden forward motion; thrust with a sword ▷ *v* move with or make a lunge

**lupin** *n* garden plant with tall spikes of flowers

**lupine** *adj* like a wolf

**lurch**¹ *v* tilt or lean suddenly to one side; stagger ▷ *n* lurching movement

**lurch**² *n* **leave someone in the lurch** abandon someone in difficulties

**lurcher** *n* crossbred dog trained to hunt silently

**lure** *v* tempt or attract by the promise of reward ▷ *n* person or thing that lures; brightly-coloured artificial angling bait

**lurid** *adj* vivid in shocking detail, sensational; glaring in colour ▶ **luridly** *adv*

**lurk** *v* lie hidden or move stealthily, esp. for sinister purposes; be latent

**luscious** [**lush**-uss] *adj* extremely pleasurable to taste or smell; very attractive

**lush**¹ *adj* (of grass etc.) growing thickly and healthily; opulent; (*slang*) very attractive

**lush**² *n* (*slang*) alcoholic

**lust** *n* strong sexual desire; any strong desire ▷ *v* have passionate desire (for) ▶ **lustful** *adj* ▶ **lusty** *adj* vigorous, healthy ▶ **lustily** *adv*

**lustre** *n* gloss, sheen; splendour or glory; metallic pottery glaze ▶ **lustrous** *adj* shining, luminous

**lute** *n* ancient guitar-like musical instrument with a body shaped like a half pear

**Lutheran** adj of Martin Luther (1483–1546), German Reformation leader, his doctrines, or a Church following these doctrines

**luxuriant** adj rich and abundant; very elaborate ▶ **luxuriance** n ▶ **luxuriantly** adv

**luxuriate** v take self-indulgent pleasure (in); flourish

**luxury** n, pl **-ries** enjoyment of rich, very comfortable living; enjoyable but not essential thing ▷ adj of or providing luxury ▶ **luxurious** adj full of luxury, sumptuous ▶ **luxuriously** adv

**lychee** [lie-**chee**] n Chinese fruit with a whitish juicy pulp

**lych gate** n roofed gate to a churchyard

**Lycra®** n elastic fabric used for tight-fitting garments, such as swimsuits

**lye** n caustic solution obtained by leaching wood ash

**lying** v present participle of **lie¹**, **lie²**

**lymph** n colourless bodily fluid consisting mainly of white blood cells ▶ **lymphatic** adj

**lymphocyte** n type of white blood cell

**lynch** v put to death without a trial

**lynx** n animal of the cat family with tufted ears and a short tail

**lyre** n ancient musical instrument like a U-shaped harp

**lyric** adj (of poetry) expressing personal emotion in song-like style; like a song ▷ n short poem in a song-like style ▷ pl words of a popular song ▶ **lyrical** adj lyric; enthusiastic ▶ **lyricist** n person who writes the words of songs or musicals

# Mm

**M** Motorway; Monsieur

**m** metre(s); mile(s); minute(s)

**m.** male; married; masculine; meridian; month

**MA** Master of Arts

**ma** n (informal) mother

**ma'am** n madam

**mac** n (Brit informal) mackintosh

**macabre** [mak-**kahb**-ra] adj strange and horrible, gruesome

**macadam** n road surface of pressed layers of small broken stones

**macadamia** [mack-ah-**day**-mee-ah] n Australian tree with edible nuts

**macaroni** n pasta in short tube shapes

**macaroon** n small biscuit or cake made with ground almonds

**macaw** n large tropical American parrot

**mace¹** n ceremonial staff of office; medieval weapon with a spiked metal head

**mace²** n spice made from the dried husk of the nutmeg

**macerate** [**mass**-er-ate] v soften by soaking ▶ **maceration** n

**machete** [mash-**ett**-ee] n broad heavy knife used for cutting or as a weapon

**Machiavellian** [mak-ee-a-**vel**-yan] adj unprincipled, crafty, and opportunist

**machinations** [mak-in-**nay**-shunz] pl n cunning plots and ploys

**machine** n apparatus, usu. powered by electricity, designed to perform a particular task; vehicle, such as a car or aircraft; controlling system of an organization ▷ v make or produce by machine ▶ **machinery** n machines or machine parts collectively ▶ **machinist** n person who operates a machine ▶ **machine gun** automatic gun that fires rapidly and continuously ▶ **machine-gun** v fire at with such a gun ▶ **machine-readable** adj (of data) in a form suitable for processing by a computer

**machismo** [mak-**izz**-moh] n exaggerated or strong masculinity

**Mach number** [mak] n ratio of the speed of a body in a particular medium to the speed of sound in that medium

**macho** [**match**-oh] adj strongly or exaggeratedly masculine

**mackerel** n edible sea fish

**mackintosh** n waterproof raincoat of rubberized cloth

**macramé** [mak-**rah**-mee] n ornamental work of knotted cord

**macrobiotics** n dietary system advocating whole grains and vegetables grown without chemical additives ▶ **macrobiotic** adj

**macrocosm** n the universe; any large complete system

**mad** adj **madder, maddest** mentally deranged, insane; very foolish; (informal) angry; frantic; (foll by about or on) very enthusiastic (about) **like mad** (informal) with great energy, enthusiasm, or haste ▶ **madly** adv ▶ **madness** n ▶ **madden** v infuriate or irritate ▶ **maddening** adj ▶ **madman, madwoman** n

**madam** n polite form of address to a woman; (informal) precocious or conceited girl

**madame** [mad-**dam**] n, pl **mesdames** [may-**dam**] French title equivalent to Mrs

**madcap** adj foolish or reckless

**madder** n climbing plant; red dye made from its root

**made** v past of **make**

**Madeira** [mad-**deer**-a] n fortified white wine ▶ **Madeira cake** rich sponge cake

**mademoiselle** [mad-mwah-**zel**] n, pl **mesdemoiselles** [maid-mwah-**zel**] French title equivalent to Miss

**Madiba generation** n (S Afr) generation born around 1994, when Nelson Mandela became the first president of a multiracial South Africa

**Madonna** n the Virgin Mary; picture or statue of her

**madrigal** n 16th–17th-century part song for unaccompanied voices

**maelstrom** [**male**-strom] n great whirlpool; turmoil

**maestro** [**my**-stroh] n, pl **-tri** or **-tros** outstanding musician or conductor; any master of an art

**Mafia** n international secret criminal organization founded in Sicily ▶ **mafioso** n, pl **-sos** or **-si** member of the Mafia

**magazine** n periodical publication with articles by different writers; television or radio programme made up of short nonfictional items; appliance for automatically supplying cartridges to a gun or slides to a projector; storehouse for explosives or arms

**magenta** [maj-**jen**-ta] adj deep purplish-red

**maggot** n larva of an insect ▶ **maggoty** adj

**Magi** [**maje**-eye] pl n wise men from the East who came to worship the infant Jesus

m

**magic** n supposed art of invoking supernatural powers to influence events; mysterious quality or power ▷ adj (also **magical**) of, using, or like magic; (informal) wonderful, marvellous ▶ **magically** adv ▶ **magician** n conjuror; person with magic powers

**magistrate** n public officer administering the law; (Brit) Justice of the Peace; (Aust & NZ) former name for **district court judge** ▶ **magisterial** adj commanding or authoritative; of a magistrate

**magma** n molten rock inside the earth's crust

**magnanimous** adj noble and generous ▶ **magnanimously** adv ▶ **magnanimity** n

**magnate** n influential or wealthy person, esp. in industry

**magnesia** n white tasteless substance used as an antacid and a laxative; magnesium oxide

**magnesium** n (Chem) silvery-white metallic element

**magnet** n piece of iron or steel capable of attracting iron and pointing north when suspended ▶ **magnetic** adj having the properties of a magnet; powerfully attractive ▶ **magnetically** adv ▶ **magnetism** n magnetic property; powerful personal charm; science of magnetic properties ▶ **magnetize** v make into a magnet; attract strongly ▶ **magnetic tape** plastic strip coated with a magnetic substance for recording sound or video signals

**magneto** [mag-**nee**-toe] n, pl -**tos** apparatus for ignition in an internal-combustion engine

**magnificent** adj splendid or impressive; excellent ▶ **magnificently** adv ▶ **magnificence** n

**magnify** v -**fying**, -**fied** increase in apparent size, as with a lens; exaggerate ▶ **magnification** n

**magnitude** n relative importance or size

**magnolia** n shrub or tree with showy white or pink flowers

**magnum** n large wine bottle holding about 1.5 litres

**magpie** n black-and-white bird; any of various similar Australian birds, e.g. the butcherbird

**maharajah** n former title of some Indian princes ▶ **maharani** n fem

**mah jong, mah-jongg** n Chinese table game for four, played with tiles bearing different designs

**mahogany** n hard reddish-brown wood of several tropical trees

**mahout** [ma-**howt**] n (in India and the East Indies) elephant driver or keeper

**maid** n (also **maidservant**) female servant; (lit) young unmarried woman

**maiden** n (lit) young unmarried woman ▷ adj unmarried; first e.g. maiden voyage ▶ **maidenly** adj modest ▶ **maidenhair** n fern with delicate fronds ▶ **maidenhead** n virginity ▶ **maiden name** woman's surname before marriage ▶ **maiden over** (Cricket) over in which no runs are scored

**mail¹** n letters and packages transported and delivered by the post office; postal system; single collection or delivery of mail; train, ship, or aircraft carrying mail; same as **e-mail** ▷ v send by mail ▶ **mailbox** n (US, Canadian & Aust) box into which letters and parcels are delivered ▶ **mail order** system of buying goods by post ▶ **mailshot** n (Brit) posting of advertising material to many selected people at once

**mail²** n flexible armour of interlaced rings or links

**maim** v cripple or mutilate

**main** adj chief or principal ▷ n principal pipe or line carrying water, gas, or electricity ▷ pl main distribution network for water, gas, or electricity **in the main** on the whole ▶ **mainly** adv for the most part, chiefly ▶ **mainframe** n, adj (Computing) (denoting) a high-speed general-purpose computer ▶ **mainland** n stretch of land which forms the main part of a country ▶ **mainmast** n chief mast of a ship ▶ **mainsail** n largest sail on a mainmast ▶ **mainspring** n chief cause or motive; chief spring of a watch or clock ▶ **mainstay** n chief support; rope securing a mainmast ▶ **mainstream** adj (of) a prevailing cultural trend

**maintain** v continue or keep in existence; keep up or preserve; support financially; assert ▶ **maintenance** n maintaining; upkeep of a building, car, etc.; provision of money for a separated or divorced spouse

**maisonette** n (Brit) flat with more than one floor

**maître d'hôtel** [met-ra dote-**tell**] n (French) head waiter

**maize** n type of corn with spikes of yellow grains

**majesty** n, pl -**ties** stateliness or grandeur; supreme power ▶ **majestic** adj ▶ **majestically** adv

**major** adj greater in number, quality, or extent; significant or serious ▷ n middle-ranking army officer; scale in music; (US, Canadian, S Afr, Aust & NZ) principal field of study at a university etc. ▷ v (foll by in) (US, Canadian, S Afr, Aust & NZ) do one's principal study in (a particular subject) ▶ **major-domo**

n, pl -**domos** chief steward of a great household

**majority** n, pl -**ties** greater number; number by which the votes on one side exceed those on the other; largest party voting together; state of being legally an adult

**make** v **making, made** create, construct, or establish; cause to do or be; bring about or produce; perform (an action); serve as or become; amount to; earn ▷ n brand, type, or style **make do** manage with an inferior alternative **make it** (informal) be successful **on the make** (informal) out for profit or conquest ▶ **maker** n ▶ **making** n creation or production ▷ pl necessary requirements or qualities ▶ **make-believe** n fantasy or pretence ▶ **make for** v head towards ▶ **make off with** v steal or abduct ▶ **makeshift** adj serving as a temporary substitute ▶ **make up** v form or constitute; prepare; invent; supply what is lacking, complete; (foll by for) compensate (for); settle a quarrel; apply cosmetics ▶ **make-up** n cosmetics; way something is made; mental or physical constitution ▶ **makeweight** n something unimportant added to make up a lack

**mal-** combining form bad or badly e.g. malformation

**malachite** [**mal**-a-kite] n green mineral

**maladjusted** adj (Psychol) unable to meet the demands of society ▶ **maladjustment** n

**maladministration** n inefficient or dishonest administration

**maladroit** adj clumsy or awkward

**malady** n, pl -**dies** disease or illness

**malaise** [mal-**laze**] n vague feeling of unease, illness, or depression

**malapropism** n comical misuse of a word by confusion with one which sounds similar, e.g. *I am not under the affluence of alcohol*

**malaria** n infectious disease caused by the bite of some mosquitoes ▶ **malarial** adj

**Malay** n member of a people of Malaysia or Indonesia; language of this people ▶ **Malayan** adj, n

**malcontent** n discontented person

**male** adj of the sex which can fertilize female reproductive cells ▷ n male person or animal

**malediction** [mal-lid-**dik**-shun] n curse

**malefactor** [**mal**-if-act-or] n criminal or wrongdoer

**malevolent** [mal-**lev**-a-lent] adj wishing evil to others ▶ **malevolently** adv ▶ **malevolence** n

**malfeasance** [mal-**fee**-zanss] n misconduct, esp. by a public official

**malformed** adj misshapen or deformed ▶ **malformation** n

**malfunction** v function imperfectly or fail to function ▷ n defective functioning or failure to function

**malice** [**mal**-iss] n desire to cause harm to others ▶ **malicious** adj ▶ **maliciously** adv

**malign** [mal-**line**] v slander or defame ▷ adj evil in influence or effect ▶ **malignity** n evil disposition

**malignant** [mal-**lig**-nant] adj seeking to harm others; (of a tumour) harmful and uncontrollable ▶ **malignancy** n

**malinger** v feign illness to avoid work ▶ **malingerer** n

**mall** [mawl] n street or shopping area closed to vehicles

**mallard** n wild duck

**malleable** [**mal**-lee-a-bl] adj capable of being hammered or pressed into shape; easily influenced ▶ **malleability** n

**mallee** n (Aust) low-growing eucalypt in dry regions

**mallet** n (wooden) hammer; stick with a head like a hammer, used in croquet or polo

**mallow** n plant with pink or purple flowers

**malnutrition** n inadequate nutrition

**malodorous** [mal-**lode**-or-uss] adj bad-smelling

**malpractice** n immoral, illegal, or unethical professional conduct

**malt** n grain, such as barley, prepared for use in making beer or whisky

**maltreat** v treat badly ▶ **maltreatment** n

**malware** n computer program, such as a virus, designed to damage or disrupt a system

**mama** n (old-fashioned) mother

**mamba** n deadly S African snake

**mamma** n same as **mama**

**mammal** n animal of the type that suckles its young ▶ **mammalian** adj

**mammary** adj of the breasts or milk-producing glands

**mammon** n wealth regarded as a source of evil

**mammoth** n extinct elephant-like mammal ▷ adj colossal

**mampara** [mum-**puh**-ruh] n (S Afr slang) incompetent fool

**man** n, pl **men** adult male; human being or person; mankind; manservant; piece used in chess etc. ▷ v **manning, manned** supply with sufficient people for operation or defence ▶ **manhood** n ▶ **mankind** n human beings collectively ▶ **manly** adj (possessing qualities) appropriate

to a man ▶ **manliness** n
▶ **mannish** adj (of a woman) like
a man ▶ **man-hour** n work done
by one person in one hour ▶ **man-
made** adj made artificially

**mana** n (NZ) authority, influence

**manacle** [man-a-kl] n, v handcuff
or fetter

**manage** v succeed in doing; be
in charge of, administer; handle
or control; cope with (financial)
difficulties ▶ **manageable** adj
▶ **management** n managers
collectively; administration or
organization

**manager, manageress** n
person in charge of a business,
institution, actor, sports team, etc.
▶ **managerial** adj

**manatee** n large tropical plant-
eating aquatic mammal

**mandarin** n high-ranking
government official; kind of small
orange

**Mandarin Chinese, Mandarin** n
official language of China

**mandate** n official or authoritative
command; authorization or
instruction from an electorate to
its representative or government
▷ v give authority to ▶ **mandatory**
adj compulsory

**mandible** n lower jawbone or
jawlike part

**mandolin** n musical instrument
with four pairs of strings

**mandrake** n plant with a forked
root, formerly used as a narcotic

**mandrel** n shaft on which work is
held in a lathe

**mandrill** n large blue-faced baboon

**mane** n long hair on the neck of a
horse, lion, etc.

**manful** adj determined and brave
▶ **manfully** adv

**manganese** n (Chem) brittle
greyish-white metallic element

**mange** n skin disease of domestic
animals

**mangelwurzel** n variety of beet
used as cattle food

**manger** n eating trough in a stable
or barn

**mangetout** [mawnzh-too] n
variety of pea with an edible pod

**mangle**[1] v destroy by crushing and
twisting; spoil

**mangle**[2] n machine with rollers
for squeezing water from washed
clothes ▷ v put through a mangle

**mango** n, pl **-goes** or **-gos** tropical
fruit with sweet juicy yellow flesh

**mangrove** n tropical tree with
exposed roots, which grows beside
water

**mangy** adj **mangier, mangiest**
having mange; scruffy or shabby

**manhandle** v treat roughly

**manhole** n hole with a cover,
through which a person can enter a
drain or sewer

**mania** n extreme enthusiasm;
madness ▶ **maniac** n mad person;
(informal) person who has an
extreme enthusiasm for something
▶ **maniacal** [man-**eye**-a-kl] adj

**manic** adj affected by mania
▶ **manic-depressive** adj, n
(Psychiatry) (person afflicted with) a
mental disorder that causes mood
swings from extreme euphoria to
deep depression

**manicure** n cosmetic care of the
fingernails and hands ▷ v care for
(the fingernails and hands) in this
way ▶ **manicurist** n

**manifest** adj easily noticed,
obvious ▷ v show plainly; be
evidence of ▷ n list of cargo
or passengers for customs
▶ **manifestation** n

**manifesto** n, pl **-tos** or **-toes**
declaration of policy as issued by
a political party

m

**manifold** adj numerous and varied ▷ n pipe with several outlets, esp. in an internal-combustion engine

**manikin** n little man or dwarf; model of the human body

**manila, manilla** n strong brown paper used for envelopes

**manipulate** v handle skilfully; control cleverly or deviously ▶ **manipulation** n ▶ **manipulative** adj ▶ **manipulator** n

**manna** n (Bible) miraculous food which sustained the Israelites in the wilderness; windfall

**mannequin** n life-size dummy of the human body used to fit or display clothes

**manner** n way a thing happens or is done; person's bearing or behaviour; type or kind; custom or style ▷ pl (polite) social behaviour ▶ **mannered** adj affected ▶ **mannerism** n person's distinctive habit or trait

**mannikin** n same as **manikin**

**manoeuvre** [man-noo-ver] n skilful movement; contrived, complicated, and possibly deceptive plan or action ▷ pl military or naval exercises ▷ v manipulate or contrive skilfully or cunningly; perform manoeuvres ▶ **manoeuvrable** adj

**manor** n (Brit) large country house and its lands ▶ **manorial** adj

**manpower** n available number of workers

**manqué** [mong-kay] adj would-be e.g. an actor manqué

**mansard roof** n roof with a break in its slope, the lower part being steeper than the upper

**manse** n house provided for a minister in some religious denominations

**manservant** n, pl **menservants** male servant, esp. a valet

**mansion** n large house

**manslaughter** n unlawful but unintentional killing of a person

**mantel** n structure round a fireplace ▶ **mantelpiece, mantel shelf** n shelf above a fireplace

**mantilla** n (in Spain) a lace scarf covering a woman's head and shoulders

**mantis** n, pl **-tises** or **-tes** carnivorous insect like a grasshopper

**mantle** n loose cloak; covering; responsibilities and duties which go with a particular job or position

**mantra** n (Hinduism, Buddhism) any sacred word or syllable used as an object of concentration

**manual** adj of or done with the hands; by human labour rather than automatic means ▷ n handbook; organ keyboard ▶ **manually** adv

**manufacture** v process or make (goods) on a large scale using machinery; invent or concoct (an excuse etc.) ▷ n process of manufacturing goods

**manufacturer** n company that manufactures goods

**manure** n animal excrement used as a fertilizer

**manuscript** n book or document, orig. one written by hand; copy for printing

**Manx** adj of the Isle of Man or its inhabitants ▷ n almost extinct language of the Isle of Man ▶ **Manx cat** tailless breed of cat

**many** adj **more, most** numerous ▷ n large number

**Maoism** n form of Marxism advanced by Mao Tse-tung in China ▶ **Maoist** n, adj

**Māori** n, pl **-ri** or **-ris** member of the indigenous race of New Zealand; language of the Māoris ▷ adj of the Māoris or their language

**map** n representation of the earth's surface or some part of it, showing geographical features ▷ v **mapping, mapped** make a map of ▶ **map out** v plan

**maple** n tree with broad leaves, a variety of which (**sugar maple**) yields sugar

**mar** v **marring, marred** spoil or impair

**Mar.** March

**marabou** n large black-and-white African stork; its soft white down, used to trim hats etc.

**maraca** [mar-**rak**-a] n shaken percussion instrument made from a gourd containing dried seeds etc.

**marae** n (NZ) enclosed space in front of a Māori meeting house; Māori meeting house and its buildings

**maraschino cherry** [mar-rass-**kee**-no] n cherry preserved in a cherry liqueur with a taste like bitter almonds

**marathon** n long-distance race of 26 miles 385 yards (42.195 kilometres); long or arduous task

**marauding** adj wandering or raiding in search of plunder ▶ **marauder** n

**marble** n kind of limestone with a mottled appearance, which can be highly polished; slab of or sculpture in this; small glass ball used in playing marbles ▷ pl game of rolling these at one another ▶ **marbled** adj having a mottled appearance like marble

**march**¹ v walk with a military step; make (a person or group) proceed; progress steadily ▷ n action of marching; steady progress; distance covered by marching; piece of music, as for a march ▶ **marcher** n ▶ **marching girl** (Aust & NZ) girl who does team formation marching as a sport

**march**² n border or frontier

**March** n third month of the year

**marchioness** [marsh-on-**ness**] n woman holding the rank of marquis; wife or widow of a marquis

**Mardi Gras** [**mar**-dee **grah**] n festival of Shrove Tuesday, celebrated in some cities with great revelry

**mare** n female horse or zebra ▶ **mare's nest** discovery which proves worthless

**margarine** n butter substitute made from animal or vegetable fats

**marge** n (informal) margarine

**margin** n edge or border; blank space round a printed page; additional amount or one greater than necessary; limit ▶ **marginal** adj insignificant, unimportant; near a limit; (Politics) (of a constituency) won by only a small margin ▷ n (Politics) marginal constituency ▶ **marginalize** v make or treat as insignificant ▶ **marginally** adv

**marguerite** n large daisy

**marigold** n plant with yellow or orange flowers

**marijuana** [mar-ree-**wah**-na] n dried flowers and leaves of the cannabis plant, used as a drug, esp. in cigarettes

**marina** n harbour for yachts and other pleasure boats

**marinade** n seasoned liquid in which fish or meat is soaked before cooking ▷ v same as **marinate** ▶ **marinate** v soak in marinade

**marine** adj of the sea or shipping ▷ n (esp. in Britain and the US) soldier trained for land and sea combat; country's shipping or fleet ▶ **mariner** n sailor

m

**marionette** n puppet worked with strings

**marital** adj relating to marriage

**maritime** adj relating to shipping; of, near, or living in the sea

**marjoram** n aromatic herb used for seasoning food and in salads

**mark¹** n line, dot, scar, etc. visible on a surface; distinguishing sign or symbol; written or printed symbol; letter or number used to grade academic work; indication of position; indication of some quality; target or goal ▷ v make a mark on; characterize or distinguish; indicate; pay attention to; notice or watch; grade (academic work); stay close to (a sporting opponent) to hamper his or her play ▶ **marked** adj noticeable ▶ **markedly** adv ▶ **marker** n

**mark²** n same as **Deutschmark**

**market** n assembly or place for buying and selling; demand for goods ▷ v -**keting, -keted** offer or produce for sale **on the market** for sale ▶ **marketable** adj ▶ **marketing** n part of a business that controls the way that goods or services are sold ▶ **market garden** place where fruit and vegetables are grown for sale ▶ **market maker** (in London Stock Exchange) person who uses a firm's money to create a market for a stock ▶ **marketplace** n market; commercial world ▶ **market research** research into consumers' needs and purchases

**marksman** n person skilled at shooting ▶ **marksmanship** n

**marl** n soil formed of clay and lime, used as fertilizer

**marlin** n large food and game fish of warm and tropical seas, with a very long upper jaw

**marlinespike, marlinspike** n pointed hook used to separate strands of rope

**marmalade** n jam made from citrus fruits

**marmoreal** adj of or like marble

**marmoset** n small bushy-tailed monkey

**marmot** n burrowing rodent

**maroon¹** adj reddish-purple

**maroon²** v abandon ashore, esp. on an island; isolate without resources

**marquee** n large tent used for a party or exhibition

**marquess** [mar-kwiss] n (Brit) nobleman of the rank below a duke

**marquetry** n ornamental inlaid work of wood

**marquis** n (in some European countries) nobleman of the rank above a count

**marram grass** n grass that grows on sandy shores

**marrow** n fatty substance inside bones; long thick striped green vegetable with whitish flesh

**marry** v -**rying, -ried** take as one's partner in marriage; join or give in marriage; unite closely ▶ **marriage** n state of being married; wedding ▶ **marriageable** adj

**Mars** n Roman god of war; fourth planet from the sun

**Marsala** [mar-sah-la] n dark sweet wine

**marsh** n low-lying wet land ▶ **marshy** adj

**marshal** n officer of the highest rank; official who organizes ceremonies or events; (US) law officer ▷ v -**shalling, -shalled** arrange in order; assemble; conduct with ceremony ▶ **marshalling yard** railway depot for goods trains

**marshmallow** n spongy pink or white sweet

**marsupial** [mar-**soop**-ee-al] n animal that carries its young in a pouch, such as a kangaroo

**mart** n market

**Martello tower** n round tower for coastal defence, formerly used in Europe

**marten** n weasel-like animal

**martial** adj of war, warlike ▸ **martial art** any of various philosophies and techniques of self-defence, orig. Eastern, such as karate ▸ **martial law** law enforced by military authorities in times of danger or emergency

**Martian** [**marsh**-an] adj of Mars ▷ n supposed inhabitant of Mars

**martin** n bird with a slightly forked tail

**martinet** n person who maintains strict discipline

**martini** n cocktail of vermouth and gin

**martyr** n person who dies or suffers for his or her beliefs ▷ v make a martyr of **be a martyr to** be constantly suffering from ▸ **martyrdom** n

**marvel** v **-velling, -velled** be filled with wonder ▷ n wonderful thing ▸ **marvellous** adj amazing; wonderful

**Marxism** n political philosophy of Karl Marx ▸ **Marxist** n, adj

**marzipan** n paste of ground almonds, sugar, and egg whites

**masala** n paste of ground spices, used in Indian cookery

**masc.** masculine

**mascara** n cosmetic for darkening the eyelashes

**mascot** n person, animal, or thing supposed to bring good luck

**masculine** adj relating to males; manly; (Grammar) of the gender of nouns that includes some male animate things ▸ **masculinity** n

**mash** n (informal) mashed potatoes; bran or meal mixed with warm water as food for horses etc. ▷ v crush into a soft mass

**mask** n covering for the face, as a disguise or protection; behaviour that hides one's true feelings ▷ v cover with a mask; hide or disguise

**masochism** [**mass**-oh-kiz-zum] n condition in which (sexual) pleasure is obtained from feeling pain or from being humiliated ▸ **masochist** n ▸ **masochistic** adj

**mason** n person who works with stone; (M-) Freemason ▸ **Masonic** adj of Freemasonry ▸ **masonry** n stonework; (M-) Freemasonry

**masque** [mask] n (Hist) 16th–17th-century form of dramatic entertainment

**masquerade** [mask-er-**aid**] n deceptive show or pretence; party at which masks and costumes are worn ▷ v pretend to be someone or something else

**Mass** n service of the Eucharist, esp. in the RC Church

**mass** n coherent body of matter; large quantity or number; (Physics) amount of matter in a body ▷ adj large-scale; involving many people ▷ v form into a mass **the masses** ordinary people ▸ **massive** adj large and heavy ▸ **mass-market** adj for or appealing to a large number of people ▸ **mass media** means of communication to many people, such as television and newspapers ▸ **mass-produce** v manufacture (standardized goods) in large quantities

**massacre** [**mass**-a-ker] n indiscriminate killing of large numbers of people ▷ v kill in large numbers

**massage** [mass-ahzh] n rubbing
and kneading of parts of the body
to reduce pain or stiffness ▷ v give
a massage to ▶ **masseur**, (fem)
**masseuse** n person who gives
massages

**massif** [mass-seef] n connected
group of mountains

**mast**[1] n tall pole for supporting
something, esp. a ship's sails

**mast**[2] n fruit of the beech, oak, etc.,
used as pig fodder

**mastectomy** [mass-tek-tom-ee] n,
pl-**mies** surgical removal of a breast

**master** n person in control, such
as an employer or an owner of
slaves or animals; expert; great
artist; original thing from which
copies are made; male teacher
▷ adj overall or controlling; main or
principal ▷ v acquire knowledge of
or skill in; overcome ▶ **masterful**
adj domineering; showing great
skill ▶ **masterly** adj showing
great skill ▶ **mastery** n expertise;
control or command ▶ **master
key** key that opens all the locks
of a set ▶ **mastermind** v plan
and direct (a complex task) ▷ n
person who plans and directs a
complex task ▶ **masterpiece** n
outstanding work of art

**mastic** n gum obtained from
certain trees; putty-like substance
used as a filler, adhesive, or seal

**masticate** v chew ▶ **mastication** n

**mastiff** n large dog

**mastitis** n inflammation of a breast
or udder

**mastodon** n extinct elephant-like
mammal

**mastoid** n projection of the bone
behind the ear

**masturbate** v fondle the genitals
(of) ▶ **masturbation** n

**mat** n piece of fabric used as a floor
covering or to protect a surface;

thick tangled mass ▷ v **matting,
matted** tangle or become tangled
into a dense mass

**matador** n man who kills the bull
in bullfights

**match**[1] n contest in a game or
sport; person or thing exactly
like, equal to, or in harmony with
another; marriage ▷ v be exactly
like, equal to, or in harmony with;
put in competition (with); find
a match for; join (in marriage)
▶ **matchless** adj unequalled
▶ **matchmaker** n person who
schemes to bring about a marriage
▶ **matchmaking** n, adj

**match**[2] n small stick with a tip
which ignites when scraped on
a rough surface ▶ **matchbox** n
▶ **matchstick** n wooden part of
a match ▷ adj (of drawn figures)
thin and straight ▶ **matchwood** n
small splinters

**mate**[1] n (informal) friend; associate
or colleague e.g. team-mate; sexual
partner of an animal; officer in
a merchant ship; tradesman's
assistant ▷ v pair (animals) or (of
animals) be paired for reproduction

**mate**[2] n, v (Chess) checkmate

**material** n substance of which a
thing is made; cloth; information
on which a piece of work may
be based ▷ pl things needed
for an activity ▷ adj of matter
or substance; not spiritual;
affecting physical wellbeing;
relevant ▶ **materially** adv
considerably ▶ **materialism** n
excessive interest in or desire
for money and possessions;
belief that only the material
world exists ▶ **materialist**
adj, n ▶ **materialistic** adj
▶ **materialize** v actually happen;
come into existence or view
▶ **materialization** n

**maternal** adj of a mother; related through one's mother ▶ **maternity** n motherhood ▷ adj of or for pregnant women

**matey** adj (Brit informal) friendly or intimate

**mathematics** n science of number, quantity, shape, and space ▶ **mathematical** adj ▶ **mathematically** adv ▶ **mathematician** n

**maths** n (informal) mathematics

**Matilda** n (Aust Hist) swagman's bundle of belongings **waltz Matilda** (Aust) travel about carrying one's bundle of belongings

**matinée** [**mat**-in-nay] n afternoon performance in a theatre or cinema

**matins** pl n early morning service in various Christian Churches

**matriarch** [**mate**-ree-ark] n female head of a tribe or family ▶ **matriarchal** adj ▶ **matriarchy** n society governed by a female, in which descent is traced through the female line

**matricide** n crime of killing one's mother; person who does this

**matriculate** v enrol or be enrolled in a college or university ▶ **matriculation** n

**matrimony** n marriage ▶ **matrimonial** adj

**matrix** [**may**-trix] n, pl **matrices** substance or situation in which something originates, takes form, or is enclosed; mould for casting; (Maths) rectangular array of numbers or elements

**matron** n staid or dignified married woman; woman who supervises the domestic or medical arrangements of an institution; former name for **nursing officer** ▶ **matronly** adj

**matt** adj dull, not shiny

**matter** n substance of which something is made; physical substance; event, situation, or subject; written material in general; pus ▷ v be of importance **what's the matter?** what is wrong?

**mattock** n large pick with one of its blade ends flattened for loosening soil

**mattress** n large stuffed flat case, often with springs, used on or as a bed

**mature** adj fully developed or grown-up; ripe ▷ v make or become mature; (of a bill or bond) become due for payment ▶ **maturity** n state of being mature ▶ **maturation** n

**maudlin** adj foolishly or tearfully sentimental

**maul** v handle roughly; beat or tear

**maunder** v talk or act aimlessly or idly

**mausoleum** [maw-so-**lee**-um] n stately tomb

**mauve** adj pale purple

**maverick** n, adj independent and unorthodox (person)

**maw** n animal's mouth, throat, or stomach

**mawkish** adj foolishly sentimental

**maxim** n general truth or principle

**maximum** adj, n, pl -**mums** or -**ma** greatest possible (amount or number) ▶ **maximal** adj ▶ **maximize** v increase to a maximum

**May** n fifth month of the year; (m-) same as **hawthorn** ▶ **mayfly** n short-lived aquatic insect ▶ **maypole** n pole set up for dancing round on the first day of May to celebrate spring

**may** v, past tense **might** used as an auxiliary to express possibility, permission, opportunity, etc.

**USAGE NOTE**
In very careful usage *may* is used in preference to *can* for asking permission. *Might* is used to express a more tentative request: *May/might I ask a favour?*

**maybe** *adv* perhaps, possibly

**Mayday** *n* international radio distress signal

**mayhem** *n* violent destruction or confusion

**mayonnaise** *n* creamy sauce of egg yolks, oil, and vinegar

**SPELLING TIP**
There are two *n*s in the middle of **mayonnaise**

**mayor** *n* head of a municipality ▶ **mayoress** *n* mayor's wife; female mayor ▶ **mayoralty** *n* (term of) office of a mayor

**maze** *n* complex network of paths or lines designed to puzzle; any confusing network or system

**mazurka** *n* lively Polish dance; music for this

**MB** Bachelor of Medicine

**MBE** (in Britain) Member of the Order of the British Empire

**MC** Master of Ceremonies

**MD** Doctor of Medicine

**me** *pron* objective form of **I**

**USAGE NOTE**
The use of *it's me* in preference to *it's I* is accepted as quite standard

**ME** myalgic encephalomyelitis: painful muscles and general weakness sometimes persisting long after a viral illness

**mead** *n* alcoholic drink made from honey

**meadow** *n* piece of grassland ▶ **meadowsweet** *n* plant with dense heads of small fragrant flowers

**meagre** *adj* scanty or insufficient

**meal¹** *n* occasion when food is served and eaten; the food itself

**meal²** *n* grain ground to powder ▶ **mealy** *adj* ▶ **mealy-mouthed** *adj* not outspoken enough

**mealie** *n* (SAfr) maize

**mean¹** *v* **meaning, meant** intend to convey or express; signify, denote, or portend; intend; have importance as specified ▶ **meaning** *n* sense, significance ▶ **meaningful** *adj* ▶ **meaningless** *adj*

**mean²** *adj* miserly, ungenerous, or petty; despicable or callous; (*chiefly US informal*) bad-tempered ▶ **meanly** *adv* ▶ **meanness** *n*

**mean³** *n* middle point between two extremes; average ▷ *pl* method by which something is done; money ▷ *adj* intermediate in size or quantity; average **by all means** certainly **by no means** in no way ▶ **means test** inquiry into a person's means to decide on eligibility for financial aid

**meander** [mee-**and**-er] *v* follow a winding course; wander aimlessly ▷ *n* winding course

**meantime** *n* intervening period ▷ *adv* meanwhile

**meanwhile** *adv* during the intervening period; at the same time

**measles** *n* infectious disease producing red spots ▶ **measly** *adj* (*informal*) meagre

**measure** *n* size or quantity; graduated scale etc. for measuring size or quantity; unit of size or quantity; extent; action taken; law; poetical rhythm ▷ *v* determine the size or quantity of; be (a specified amount) in size or quantity ▶ **measurable** *adj* ▶ **measured** *adj* slow and steady; carefully considered ▶ **measurement** *n* measuring; size ▶ **measure up to** *v* fulfil (expectations or requirements)

m

**meat** n animal flesh as food
▶ **meaty** adj (tasting) of or like meat; brawny; full of significance or interest

**Mecca** n holy city of Islam; place that attracts visitors

**mechanic** n person skilled in repairing or operating machinery
▶ **mechanics** n scientific study of motion and force ▶ **mechanical** adj of or done by machines; (of an action) without thought or feeling
▶ **mechanically** adv

**mechanism** n way a machine works; piece of machinery; process or technique e.g. *defence mechanism* ▶ **mechanize** v equip with machinery; make mechanical or automatic; (*Mil*) equip (an army) with armoured vehicles
▶ **mechanization** n

**med.** medical; medicine; medieval; medium

**medal** n piece of metal with an inscription etc., given as a reward or memento ▶ **medallion** n disc-shaped ornament worn on a chain round the neck; large medal; circular decorative device in architecture
▶ **medallist** n winner of a medal

**meddle** v interfere annoyingly
▶ **meddler** n ▶ **meddlesome** adj

**media** n a plural of **medium**; the mass media collectively

**mediaeval** adj same as **medieval**

**medial** adj of or in the middle

**median** adj, n middle (point or line)

**mediate** v intervene in a dispute to bring about agreement
▶ **mediation** n ▶ **mediator** n

**medic** n (*informal*) doctor or medical student

**medical** adj of the science of medicine ▷ n (*informal*) medical examination ▶ **medically** adv ▶ **medicate** v treat with a medicinal substance

▶ **medication** n (treatment with) a medicinal substance

**medicine** n substance used to treat disease; science of preventing, diagnosing, or curing disease
▶ **medicinal** [med-**diss**-in-al] adj having therapeutic properties
▶ **medicine man** witch doctor

**medieval** [med-ee-**eve**-al] adj of the Middle Ages

**mediocre** [mee-dee-**oak**-er] adj average in quality; second-rate
▶ **mediocrity** [mee-dee-**ok**-rit-ee] n

**meditate** v reflect deeply, esp. on spiritual matters; think about or plan
▶ **meditation** n ▶ **meditative** adj
▶ **meditatively** adv ▶ **meditator** n

**medium** adj midway between extremes, average ▷ n, pl **-dia** or **-diums** middle state, degree, or condition; intervening substance producing an effect; means of communicating news or information to the public, such as radio or newspapers; person who can supposedly communicate with the dead; surroundings or environment; category of art according to the material used
▶ **medium wave** radio wave with a wavelength between 100 and 1000 metres

**medlar** n apple-like fruit of a small tree, eaten when it begins to decay

**medley** n miscellaneous mixture; musical sequence of different tunes

**medulla** [mid-**dull**-la] n, pl **-las** or **-lae** marrow, pith, or inner tissue

**meek** adj submissive or humble
▶ **meekly** adv ▶ **meekness** n

**meerkat** n S African mongoose

**meerschaum** [**meer**-shum] n white substance like clay; tobacco pipe with a bowl made of this

m

**meet**[1] v **meeting, met** come together (with); come into contact (with); be at the place of arrival of; make the acquaintance of; satisfy (a need etc.); experience ▷ n meeting, esp. a sports meeting; assembly of a hunt ▶ **meeting** n coming together; assembly

> **USAGE NOTE**
> *Meet* is only followed by *with* in the context of misfortune: *I met his son; I met with an accident*

**meet**[2] adj (obs) fit or suitable

**meg** n (Computing informal) short for **megabyte**

**mega-** combining form denoting one million e.g. megawatt; very great e.g. megastar

**megabyte** n (Computing) 220 or 1 048 576 bytes

**megahertz** n, pl **-hertz** one million hertz

**megalith** n great stone, esp. as part of a prehistoric monument ▶ **megalithic** adj

**megalomania** n craving for or mental delusions of power ▶ **megalomaniac** adj, n

**megaphone** n cone-shaped instrument used to amplify the voice

**megapixel** n (Computing) one million pixels: used to describe the resolution of digital images

**megapode** n bird of Australia, New Guinea, and adjacent islands

**megaton** n explosive power equal to that of one million tons of TNT

**meh** interj expression of indifference or boredom

**melaleuca** [mel-a-loo-ka] n Australian shrub or tree with a white trunk and black branches

**melancholy** [mel-an-kol-lee] n sadness or gloom ▷ adj sad or gloomy ▶ **melancholia** [mel-an-kole-lee-a] n state of depression ▶ **melancholic** adj, n

**melange** [may-**lahnzh**] n mixture

**melanin** n dark pigment found in the hair, skin, and eyes of humans and animals

**mêlée** [**mel**-lay] n noisy confused fight or crowd

**mellifluous** [mel-**lif**-flew-uss] adj (of sound) smooth and sweet

**mellow** adj soft, not harsh; kind-hearted, esp. through maturity; (of fruit) ripe ▷ v make or become mellow

**melodrama** n play full of extravagant action and emotion; overdramatic behaviour or emotion ▶ **melodramatic** adj

**melody** n, pl **-dies** series of musical notes which make a tune; sweet sound ▶ **melodic** [mel-**lod**-ik] adj of melody; melodious ▶ **melodious** [mel-**lode**-ee-uss] adj pleasing to the ear; tuneful

**melon** n large round juicy fruit with a hard rind

**melt** v (cause to) become liquid by heat; dissolve; disappear; blend (into); soften through emotion ▶ **meltdown** n (in a nuclear reactor) melting of the fuel rods, with the possible release of radiation

**member** n individual making up a body or society; limb ▶ **membership** n ▶ **Member of Parliament** person elected to parliament

**membrane** n thin flexible tissue in a plant or animal body ▶ **membranous** adj

**meme** n video, photo, or story that is viewed by many internet users in a short time

**memento** n, pl **-tos** or **-toes** thing serving to remind, souvenir

**memo** n, pl **memos** short for **memorandum**

**memoir** [**mem**-wahr] n biography or historical account based on personal knowledge ▷ pl collection of these; autobiography

**memorable** adj worth remembering, noteworthy ▶ **memorably** adv

**memorandum** n, pl **-dums** or **-da** written record or communication within a business; note of things to be remembered

**memory** n, pl **-ries** ability to remember; sum of things remembered; particular recollection; length of time one can remember; commemoration; part of a computer which stores information ▶ **memorize** v commit to memory ▶ **memorial** n something serving to commemorate a person or thing ▷ adj serving as a memorial ▶ **memory card** small removable data storage device, used in mobile phones, digital cameras, etc. ▶ **Memory Stick**® (Computing) standard format for memory cards; (**m-**) (also **USB memory stick**) same as **USB drive**

**men** n plural of **man**

**menace** n threat; (informal) nuisance ▷ v threaten, endanger ▶ **menacing** adj

**ménage** [may-**nahzh**] n household

**menagerie** [min-**naj**-er-ee] n collection of wild animals for exhibition

**mend** v repair or patch; recover or heal; make or become better ▷ n mended area **on the mend** regaining health

**mendacity** n (tendency to) untruthfulness ▶ **mendacious** adj

**mendicant** adj begging ▷ n beggar

**menhir** [**men**-hear] n single upright prehistoric stone

**menial** [**mean**-nee-al] adj involving boring work of low status ▷ n person with a menial job

**meningitis** [men-in-**jite**-iss] n inflammation of the membranes of the brain

**meniscus** n curved surface of a liquid; crescent-shaped lens

**menopause** n time when a woman's menstrual cycle ceases ▶ **menopausal** adj

**menstruation** n approximately monthly discharge of blood and cellular debris from the womb of a nonpregnant woman ▶ **menstruate** v ▶ **menstrual** adj

**mensuration** n measuring, esp. in geometry

**mental** adj of, in, or done by the mind; of or for mental illness; (informal) insane ▶ **mentally** adv ▶ **mentality** n way of thinking

**menthol** n organic compound found in peppermint, used medicinally

**mention** v refer to briefly; acknowledge ▷ n brief reference to a person or thing; acknowledgment

**mentor** n adviser or guide

**menu** n list of dishes to be served, or from which to order; (Computing) list of options displayed on a screen

**MEP** Member of the European Parliament

**mercantile** adj of trade or traders

**mercenary** adj influenced by greed; working merely for reward ▷ n, pl **-aries** hired soldier

**merchandise** n commodities

**merchant** n person engaged in trade, wholesale trader ▶ **merchant bank** bank dealing mainly with businesses and investment ▶ **merchantman** n trading ship ▶ **merchant navy** ships or crew engaged in a nation's commercial shipping

**mercury** n (Chem) silvery liquid metal; (**M-**) (Roman myth) messenger of the gods; (**M-**) planet nearest the sun ▶ **mercurial** adj lively, changeable

**mercy** n, pl **-cies** compassionate treatment of an offender or enemy who is in one's power; merciful act ▶ **merciful** adj compassionate; giving relief ▶ **merciless** adj

**mere**[1] adj nothing more than e.g. mere chance ▶ **merely** adv

**mere**[2] n (Brit obs) lake

**meretricious** adj superficially or garishly attractive but of no real value

**merganser** [mer-**gan**-ser] n large crested diving duck

**merge** v combine or blend

**merger** n combination of business firms into one

**meridian** n imaginary circle of the earth passing through both poles

**meringue** [mer-**rang**] n baked mixture of egg whites and sugar; small cake of this

**merino** n, pl **-nos** breed of sheep with fine soft wool; this wool

**merit** n excellence or worth ▷ pl admirable qualities ▷ v **-iting**, **-ited** deserve ▶ **meritorious** adj deserving praise ▶ **meritocracy** [mer-it-**tok**-rass-ee] n rule by people of superior talent or intellect

**merlin** n small falcon

**mermaid** n imaginary sea creature with the upper part of a woman and the lower part of a fish

**merry** adj **-rier**, **-riest** cheerful or jolly; (informal) slightly drunk ▶ **merrily** adv ▶ **merriment** n ▶ **merry-go-round** n roundabout ▶ **merrymaking** n noisy, cheerful celebrations or fun

**mesdames** n plural of **madame**

**mesdemoiselles** n plural of **mademoiselle**

**mesh** n network or net; (open space between) strands forming a network ▷ v (of gear teeth) engage

**mesmerize** v hold spellbound; (obs) hypnotize

**meson** [**mee**-zon] n elementary atomic particle

**mess** n untidy or dirty confusion; trouble or difficulty; place where servicemen eat; group of servicemen who regularly eat together ▷ v muddle or dirty; (foll by about) potter about; (foll by with) interfere with; (Brit, Aust & NZ) (of servicemen) eat in a group

**message** n communication sent; meaning or moral ▶ **messaging** n sending and receiving of textual communications by mobile phone ▶ **message board** n internet discussion forum ▶ **messenger** n bearer of a message

**Messiah** n Jews' promised deliverer; Christ ▶ **Messianic** adj

**messieurs** n plural of **monsieur**

**Messrs** [**mess**-erz] n plural of **Mr**

**messy** adj **messier, messiest** dirty, confused, or untidy ▶ **messily** adv

**met** v past of **meet**[1]

**metabolism** [met-**tab**-oh-lizzum] n chemical processes of a living body ▶ **metabolic** adj ▶ **metabolize** v produce or be produced by metabolism

**metal** n chemical element, such as iron or copper, that is malleable and capable of conducting heat and electricity ▶ **metallic** adj ▶ **metallurgy** n scientific study of the structure, properties, extraction, and refining of metals ▶ **metallurgical** adj ▶ **metallurgist** n ▶ **metal road** (NZ) unsealed road covered in gravel

**metamorphosis** [met-a-**more**-foss-is] n, pl **-phoses** [-foss-eez] change of form or character ▶ **metamorphic** adj (of rocks) changed in texture or structure by heat and pressure ▶ **metamorphose** v transform

**metaphor** n figure of speech in which a term is applied to something it does not literally denote in order to imply a resemblance e.g. *he is a lion in battle* ▶ **metaphorical** adj ▶ **metaphorically** adv

**metaphysics** n branch of philosophy concerned with being and knowing ▶ **metaphysical** adj

**mete** v (usually foll by *out*) deal out as punishment

**meteor** n small fast-moving heavenly body, visible as a streak of incandescence if it enters the earth's atmosphere ▶ **meteoric** [meet-ee-**or**-rik] adj of a meteor; brilliant and very rapid ▶ **meteorite** n meteor that has fallen to earth

**meteorology** n study of the earth's atmosphere, esp. for weather forecasting ▶ **meteorological** adj ▶ **meteorologist** n

**meter** n instrument for measuring and recording something, such as the consumption of gas or electricity ▷ v measure by meter

**methane** n colourless inflammable gas

**methanol** n colourless poisonous liquid used as a solvent and fuel (also **methyl alcohol**)

**methinks** v, past tense **methought** (obs) it seems to me

**method** n way or manner; technique; orderliness ▶ **methodical** adj orderly ▶ **methodically** adv ▶ **methodology** n particular method or procedure

**Methodist** n member of any of the Protestant churches originated by John Wesley and his followers ▷ adj of Methodists or their Church ▶ **Methodism** n

**meths** n (informal) methylated spirits

**methyl** n (compound containing) a saturated hydrocarbon group of atoms ▶ **methylated spirits** alcohol with methanol added, used as a solvent and for heating

**meticulous** adj very careful about details ▶ **meticulously** adv

**métier** [met-ee-ay] n profession or trade; one's strong point

**metonymy** [mit-**on**-im-ee] n figure of speech in which one thing is replaced by another associated with it, such as 'the Crown' for 'the queen'

**metre** n basic unit of length equal to about 1.094 yards (100 centimetres); rhythm of poetry ▶ **metric** adj of the decimal system of weights and measures based on the metre ▶ **metrical** adj of measurement; of poetic metre ▶ **metrication** n conversion to the metric system

**metro** n, pl **metros** underground railway system, esp. in Paris

**metronome** n instrument which marks musical time by means of a ticking pendulum

**metropolis** [mit-**trop**-oh-liss] n chief city of a country or region

**metropolitan** adj of a metropolis

**metrosexual** adj, n (Aust) (of) a heterosexual man who is preoccupied with his appearance

**mettle** n courage or spirit

**mew** n cry of a cat ▷ v utter this cry

**mews** n yard or street orig. of stables, now often converted into houses

**Mexican** adj of Mexico ▷ n person from Mexico

**mezzanine** [mez-zan-een] n intermediate storey, esp. between the ground and first floor

**mezzo-soprano** [met-so-] n voice or singer between a soprano and contralto (also **mezzo**)

**mezzotint** [met-so-tint] n method of engraving by scraping the roughened surface of a metal plate; print so made

**mg** milligram(s)

**MHz** megahertz

**miaow** [mee-ow] n, v same as **mew**

**miasma** [mee-azz-ma] n unwholesome or foreboding atmosphere

**mica** [my-ka] n glasslike mineral used as an electrical insulator

**mice** n plural of **mouse**

**Michaelmas** [mik-kl-mass] n September 29, feast of St Michael the archangel ▸ **Michaelmas daisy** garden plant with small daisy-shaped flowers

**mickey** n **take the mickey (out of)** (informal) tease

**micro** n, pl -**cros** short for **microcomputer, microprocessor**

**microbe** n minute organism, esp. one causing disease ▸ **microbial** adj

**microblog** n blog in which there is a limitation on the length of individual postings ▸ **microblogger** n

**microchip** n small wafer of silicon containing electronic circuits

**microcomputer** n computer with a central processing unit contained in one or more silicon chips

**microcosm** n miniature representation of something

**microfiche** [my-kroh-feesh] n microfilm in sheet form

**microfilm** n miniaturized recording of books or documents on a roll of film

**microlight** n very small light private aircraft with large wings

**micrometer** [my-**krom**-it-er] n instrument for measuring very small distances or angles

**micron** [my-kron] n one millionth of a metre

**microorganism** n organism of microscopic size

**microphone** n instrument for amplifying or transmitting sounds

**microprocessor** n integrated circuit acting as the central processing unit in a small computer

**microscope** n instrument with lens(es) which produces a magnified image of a very small object ▸ **microscopic** adj too small to be seen except with a microscope; very small; of a microscope ▸ **microscopically** adv ▸ **microscopy** n use of a microscope

**microsurgery** n intricate surgery using a special microscope and miniature precision instruments

**microwave** n electromagnetic wave with a wavelength of a few centimetres, used in radar and cooking; microwave oven ▷ v cook in a microwave oven ▸ **microwave oven** oven using microwaves to cook food quickly

**mid** adj intermediate, middle

**midday** n noon

**midden** n (Brit & Aust) dunghill or rubbish heap

**middle** adj equidistant from two extremes; medium, intermediate ▷ n middle point or part ▸ **middle age** period of life between youth and old age ▸ **middle-aged** adj **Middle Ages** period from about 1000 AD to the 15th century ▸ **middle class** social class of business and professional people ▸ **middle-class** adj ▸ **Middle East** area around the eastern Mediterranean up to and including Iran ▸ **middleman** n trader who buys from the producer and sells to the consumer ▸ **middle-of-**

**the-road** *adj* politically moderate; (of music) generally popular
▶ **middleweight** *n* boxer weighing up to 160lb (professional) or 75kg (amateur)

**middling** *adj* mediocre; moderate

**midge** *n* small mosquito-like insect

**midget** *n* very small person or thing

**midland** *n* (*Brit, Aust & US*) middle part of a country ▷ *pl* (**M-**) central England

**midnight** *n* twelve o'clock at night

**midriff** *n* middle part of the body

**midshipman** *n* naval officer of the lowest commissioned rank

**midst** *n* **in the midst of** surrounded by; at a point during

**midsummer** *n* middle of summer; summer solstice ▶ **Midsummer's Day, Midsummer Day** (in Britain and Ireland) June 24th

**midway** *adj, adv* halfway

**midwife** *n* trained person who assists at childbirth ▶ **midwifery** *n*

**midwinter** *n* middle or depth of winter; winter solstice

**mien** [**mean**] *n* (*lit*) person's bearing, demeanour, or appearance

**miffed** *adj* (*informal*) offended or upset

**might**¹ *v* past tense of **may**

**might**² *n* power or strength **with might and main** energetically or forcefully ▶ **mighty** *adj* powerful; important ▷ *adv* (*US & Aust informal*) very ▶ **mightily** *adv*

**migraine** [**mee**-grain] *n* severe headache, often with nausea and visual disturbances

**migrate** *v* move from one place to settle in another; (of animals) journey between different habitats at specific seasons ▶ **migration** *n*
▶ **migrant** *n* person or animal that moves from one place to another ▷ *adj* moving from one place to

another ▶ **migratory** *adj* (of an animal) migrating every year

**mike** *n* (*informal*) microphone

**milch** *adj* (*chiefly Brit*) (of a cow) giving milk

**mild** *adj* not strongly flavoured; gentle; calm or temperate
▶ **mildly** *adv* ▶ **mildness** *n*

**mildew** *n* destructive fungus on plants or things exposed to damp
▶ **mildewed** *adj*

**mile** *n* unit of length equal to 1760 yards or 1.609 kilometres
▶ **mileage** *n* distance travelled in miles; miles travelled by a motor vehicle per gallon of petrol; (*informal*) usefulness of something
▶ **mileometer** *n* (*Brit*) device that records the number of miles a vehicle has travelled ▶ **milestone** *n* significant event; stone marker showing the distance to a certain place

**milieu** [meal-**yer**] *n*, *pl* **milieux** *or* **milieus** environment or surroundings

**militant** *adj* aggressive or vigorous in support of a cause ▶ **militancy** *n*

**military** *adj* of or for soldiers, armies, or war ▷ *n* armed services
▶ **militarism** *n* belief in the use of military force and methods
▶ **militarist** *n* ▶ **militarized** *adj*

**militate** *v* (usually foll by *against* or *for*) have a strong influence or effect

**USAGE NOTE**
Do not confuse *militate* with *mitigate* 'make less severe'

**militia** [mill-**ish**-a] *n* military force of trained citizens for use in emergency only

**milk** *n* white fluid produced by female mammals to feed their young; milk of cows, goats, etc., used by humans as food; fluid in some plants ▷ *v* draw milk from; exploit (a person or situation) ▸ **milky** *adj* ▸ **Milky Way** luminous band of stars stretching across the night sky ▸ **milk float** (*Brit*) small electrically powered vehicle used to deliver milk to houses ▸ **milkmaid** *n* (esp. in former times) woman who milks cows ▸ **milkman** *n* (*Brit, Aust & NZ*) man who delivers milk to people's houses ▸ **milkshake** *n* frothy flavoured cold milk drink ▸ **milksop** *n* feeble man ▸ **milk teeth** first set of teeth in young children

**mill** *n* factory; machine for grinding, processing, or rolling ▷ *v* grind, press, or process in or as if in a mill; cut fine grooves across the edges of (coins); (of a crowd) move in a confused manner

**millennium** *n, pl* **-nia, -niums** period of a thousand years; future period of peace and happiness

> **SPELLING TIP**
> **Millennium** is often misspelled with only one *n*: remember there are two *n*s and two *l*s

**miller** *n* person who works in a mill

**millet** *n* type of cereal grass

**milli-** *combining form* denoting a thousandth part e.g. *millisecond*

**millibar** *n* unit of atmospheric pressure

**millimetre** *n* thousandth part of a metre

**milliner** *n* maker or seller of women's hats ▸ **millinery** *n*

**million** *n* one thousand thousands ▸ **millionth** *adj, n* ▸ **millionaire** *n* person who owns at least a million pounds, dollars, etc.

> **SPELLING TIP**
> Note there is only one *n* in **millionaire**

**millipede** *n* small animal with a jointed body and many pairs of legs

**millstone** *n* flat circular stone for grinding corn

**millwheel** *n* waterwheel that drives a mill

**milometer** *n* (*Brit*) same as **mileometer**

**milt** *n* sperm of fish

**mime** *n* acting without the use of words; performer who does this ▷ *v* act in mime

**mimic** *v* **-icking, -icked** imitate (a person or manner), esp. for satirical effect ▷ *n* person or animal that is good at mimicking ▸ **mimicry** *n*

**min.** minimum; minute(s)

**minaret** *n* tall slender tower of a mosque

**mince** *v* cut or grind into very small pieces; walk or speak in an affected manner; soften or moderate (one's words) ▷ *n* minced meat ▸ **mincer** *n* machine for mincing meat ▸ **mincing** *adj* affected in manner ▸ **mincemeat** *n* sweet mixture of dried fruit and spices ▸ **mince pie** pie containing mincemeat

**mind** *n* thinking faculties; memory or attention; intention; sanity ▷ *v* take offence at; pay attention to; take care of; be cautious or careful about (something) ▸ **minded** *adj* having an inclination as specified e.g. *politically minded* ▸ **minder** *n* (*informal*) aide or bodyguard ▸ **mindful** *adj* heedful; keeping aware ▸ **mindless** *adj* stupid; requiring no thought; careless

**mine¹** *pron* belonging to me

**mine²** *n* deep hole for digging out coal, ores, etc.; bomb placed under the ground or in water; profitable source ▷ *v* dig for minerals; dig (minerals) from a mine; place explosive mines in or on ▸ **miner** *n* person who works in a mine ▸ **minefield** *n* area of land or water containing mines ▸ **minesweeper** *n* ship for clearing away mines

**mineral** n naturally occurring inorganic substance, such as metal ▷ adj of, containing, or like minerals ▶ **mineralogy** [min-er-**al**-a-jee] n study of minerals ▶ **mineral water** water containing dissolved mineral salts or gases

**minestrone** [min-ness-**strone**-ee] n soup containing vegetables and pasta

**minger** n (Brit informal) unattractive person ▶ **minging** adj (Brit informal) unattractive or unpleasant

**mingle** v mix or blend; come into association (with)

**mingy** adj **-gier, -giest** (informal) miserly

**mini** n, adj (something) small or miniature; short (skirt)

**miniature** n small portrait, model, or copy ▷ adj small-scale ▶ **miniaturist** n ▶ **miniaturize** v make to a very small scale

**minibar** n selection of drinks and confectionery provided in a hotel room

**minibus** n small bus

**minicab** n (Brit) ordinary car used as a taxi

**minicomputer** n computer smaller than a mainframe but more powerful than a microcomputer

**minidisc** n small recordable compact disc

**minim** n (Music) note half the length of a semibreve

**minimum** adj, n, pl **-mums** or **-ma** least possible (amount or number) ▶ **minimal** adj minimum ▶ **minimize** v reduce to a minimum; belittle

**minion** n servile assistant

**miniseries** n TV programme shown in several parts, often on consecutive days

**minister** n head of a government department; diplomatic representative; (in nonconformist churches) member of the clergy ▷ v (foll by to) attend to the needs of ▶ **ministerial** adj ▶ **ministration** n giving of help ▶ **ministry** n, pl **-tries** profession or duties of a clergyman; ministers collectively; government department

**mink** n stoatlike animal; its highly valued fur

**minnow** n small freshwater fish

**minor** adj lesser; (Music) (of a scale) having a semitone between the second and third notes ▷ n person regarded legally as a child; (Music) minor scale ▶ **minority** n lesser number; smaller party voting together; group in a minority in any state

**minster** n (Brit) cathedral or large church

**minstrel** n medieval singer or musician

**mint**¹ n plant with aromatic leaves used for seasoning and flavouring; sweet flavoured with this

**mint**² n place where money is coined ▷ v make (coins)

**minuet** [min-new-**wet**] n stately dance; music for this

**minus** prep, adj indicating subtraction ▷ adj less than zero ▷ n sign (-) denoting subtraction or a number less than zero

**minuscule** [**min**-niss-skyool] adj very small

> **SPELLING TIP**
> The pronunciation of **minuscule** often leads people to spell it *miniscule*, but it should have only one *i* and two *u*s

**minute**¹ [**min**-it] n 60th part of an hour or degree; moment ▷ pl record of the proceedings of a meeting ▷ v record in the minutes

**minute²** [my-**newt**] *adj* very
small; precise ▶ **minutely** *adv*
▶ **minutiae** [my-**new**-shee-eye] *pl*
*n* trifling or precise details

**minx** *n* bold or flirtatious girl

**miracle** *n* wonderful supernatural
event; marvel ▶ **miraculous** *adj*
▶ **miraculously** *adv* ▶ **miracle
play** medieval play based on a
sacred subject

**mirage** [mir-**rahzh**] *n* optical
illusion, esp. one caused by hot air

**mire** *n* swampy ground; mud

**mirror** *n* coated glass surface for
reflecting images ▷ *v* reflect in or
as if in a mirror

**mirth** *n* laughter, merriment, or
gaiety ▶ **mirthful** *adj* ▶ **mirthless** *adj*

**mis-** *prefix* wrong(ly), bad(ly)

**misadventure** *n* unlucky chance

**misanthrope** [**miz**-zan-thrope]
*n* person who dislikes people in
general ▶ **misanthropic** [miz-
zan-**throp**-ik] *adj* ▶ **misanthropy**
[miz-**zan**-throp-ee] *n*

**misapprehend** *v* misunderstand
▶ **misapprehension** *n*

**misappropriate** *v* take and
use (money) dishonestly
▶ **misappropriation** *n*

**miscarriage** *n* spontaneous
premature expulsion of a fetus
from the womb; failure e.g. *a
miscarriage of justice* ▶ **miscarry** *v*
have a miscarriage; fail

**miscast** *v* **-casting, -cast** cast
(a role or actor) in (a play or film)
inappropriately

**miscegenation** [miss-ij-in-**nay**-
shun] *n* interbreeding of races

**miscellaneous** [miss-sell-**lane**-
ee-uss] *adj* mixed or assorted
▶ **miscellany** [miss-**sell**-a-nee] *n*
mixed assortment

**mischance** *n* unlucky event

**mischief** *n* annoying but not
malicious behaviour; inclination

to tease; harm ▶ **mischievous** *adj*
full of mischief; intended to cause
harm ▶ **mischievously** *adv*

**miscible** [**miss**-sib-bl] *adj* able to
be mixed

**misconception** *n* wrong idea
or belief

**misconduct** *n* immoral or
unethical behaviour

**miscreant** [**miss**-kree-ant] *n*
wrongdoer

**misdeed** *n* wrongful act

**misdemeanour** *n* minor
wrongdoing

**miser** *n* person who hoards money
and hates spending it ▶ **miserly** *adj*

**miserable** *adj* very unhappy,
wretched; causing misery; squalid;
mean ▶ **misery** *n, pl* **-eries**
great unhappiness; (*informal*)
complaining person

**misfire** *v* (of a firearm or engine) fail
to fire correctly; (of a plan) fail to
turn out as intended

**misfit** *n* person not suited to his or
her social environment

**misfortune** *n* (piece of) bad luck

**misgiving** *n* feeling of fear or doubt

**misguided** *adj* mistaken or unwise

**mishandle** *v* handle badly or
inefficiently

**mishap** *n* minor accident

**misinform** *v* give incorrect
information to ▶ **misinformation** *n*

**misjudge** *v* judge wrongly
or unfairly ▶ **misjudgment,
misjudgement** *n*

**mislay** *v* lose (something)
temporarily

**mislead** *v* give false or confusing
information to ▶ **misleading** *adj*

**mismanage** *v* organize
or run (something) badly
▶ **mismanagement** *n*

**misnomer** [miss-**no**-mer] *n*
incorrect or unsuitable
name; use of this

**misogyny** [miss-**oj**-in-ee] *n* hatred of women ▶ **misogynist** *n*

**misplace** *v* mislay; put in the wrong place; give (trust or affection) inappropriately

**misprint** *n* printing error

**misrepresent** *v* represent wrongly or inaccurately

**Miss** *n* title of a girl or unmarried woman

**miss** *v* fail to notice, hear, hit, reach, find, or catch; not be in time for; notice or regret the absence of; avoid; (of an engine) misfire ▷ *n* fact or instance of missing ▶ **missing** *adj* lost or absent

**missal** *n* book containing the prayers and rites of the Mass

**misshapen** *adj* badly shaped, deformed

**missile** *n* object or weapon thrown, shot, or launched at a target

**mission** *n* specific task or duty; group of people sent on a mission; building in which missionaries work; (*SAfr*) long and difficult process ▶ **missionary** *n*, *pl* **-aries** person sent abroad to do religious and social work

**missive** *n* letter

**misspent** *adj* wasted or misused

**missus, missis** *n* (*informal*) one's wife or the wife of the person addressed or referred to

**mist** *n* thin fog; fine spray of liquid ▶ **misty** *adj* full of mist; dim or obscure

**mistake** *n* error or blunder ▷ *v* **-taking, -took, -taken** misunderstand; confuse (a person or thing) with another.

**Mister** *n* polite form of address to a man

**mistletoe** *n* evergreen plant with white berries growing as a parasite on trees

**mistral** *n* strong dry northerly wind of S France

**mistress** *n* woman who has a continuing sexual relationship with a married man; woman in control of people or animals; female teacher

**mistrial** *n* (*Law*) trial made void because of some error

**mistrust** *v* have doubts or suspicions about ▷ *n* lack of trust ▶ **mistrustful** *adj*

**misunderstand** *v* fail to understand properly ▶ **misunderstanding** *n*

**misuse** *n* incorrect, improper, or careless use ▷ *v* use wrongly; treat badly

**mite** *n* very small spider-like animal; very small thing or amount

**mitigate** *v* make less severe ▶ **mitigation** *n*

> **USAGE NOTE**
> *Mitigate* is often confused with *militate* 'have an influence on'

**mitre** [**my**-ter] *n* bishop's pointed headdress; joint between two pieces of wood bevelled to meet at right angles ▷ *v* join with a mitre joint

**mitt** *n* short for **mitten**; baseball catcher's glove

**mitten** *n* glove with one section for the thumb and one for the four fingers together

**mix** *v* combine or blend into one mass; form (something) by mixing; be sociable ▷ *n* mixture ▶ **mixed** *adj* ▶ **mix up** *v* confuse; make into a mixture ▶ **mixed up** *adj* ▶ **mix-up** *n* ▶ **mixer** *n* ▶ **mixture** *n* something mixed; combination

**mizzenmast** *n* (on a vessel with three or more masts) third mast from the bow

**mm** millimetre(s)

**mnemonic** [nim-**on**-ik] *n*, *adj* (something, such as a rhyme) intended to help the memory

**m**

**MO** Medical Officer

**mo** *n, pl* **mos** (*informal*) short for **moment**

**moa** *n* large extinct flightless New Zealand bird

**moan** *n* low cry of pain; (*informal*) grumble ▷ *v* make or utter with a moan; (*informal*) grumble

**moat** *n* deep wide ditch, esp. round a castle

**mob** *n* disorderly crowd; (*slang*) gang ▷ *v* **mobbing, mobbed** surround in a mob to acclaim or attack

**mobile** *adj* able to move ▷ *n* same as **mobile phone**; hanging structure designed to move in air currents ▶ **mobile phone** cordless phone powered by batteries ▶ **mobility** *n*

**mobilize** *v* (of the armed services) prepare for active service; organize for a purpose ▶ **mobilization** *n*

**moccasin** *n* soft leather shoe

> **SPELLING TIP**
> Note that **moccasin** has a double *c*, but only one *s*.

**mocha** [**mock**-a] *n* kind of strong dark coffee; flavouring made from coffee and chocolate

**mock** *v* make fun of; mimic ▷ *adj* sham or imitation ▶ **mocks** *pl n* (*informal*) (in England and Wales) practice exams taken before public exams **put the mockers on** (*Brit, Aust & NZ informal*) ruin the chances of success of ▶ **mockery** *n* derision; inadequate or worthless attempt ▶ **mockingbird** *n* N American bird which imitates other birds' songs ▶ **mock orange** shrub with white fragrant flowers ▶ **mock-up** *n* full-scale model for test or study

**MOD** (in Britain) Ministry of Defence

**mod.** moderate; modern

**mode** *n* method or manner; current fashion

**model** *n* (miniature) representation; pattern; person or thing worthy of imitation; person who poses for an artist or photographer; person who wears clothes to display them to prospective buyers ▷ *v* **-elling, -elled** make a model of; mould; display (clothing) as a model

**modem** [**mode**-em] *n* device for connecting two computers by a telephone line

**moderate** *adj* not extreme; self-restrained; average ▷ *n* person of moderate views ▷ *v* make or become less violent or extreme ▶ **moderately** *adv* ▶ **moderation** *n* ▶ **moderator** *n* (Presbyterian Church) minister appointed to preside over a Church court, general assembly, etc.; person who presides over a public or legislative assembly

**modern** *adj* of present or recent times; up-to-date ▶ **modernity** *n* ▶ **modernism** *n* (support of) modern tendencies, thoughts, or styles ▶ **modernist** *adj, n* ▶ **modernize** *v* bring up to date ▶ **modernization** *n*

**modest** *adj* not vain or boastful; not excessive; not showy; shy ▶ **modestly** *adv* ▶ **modesty** *n*

**modicum** *n* small quantity

**modify** *v* **-fying, -fied** change slightly; tone down; (of a word) qualify (another word) ▶ **modifier** *n* word that qualifies the sense of another ▶ **modification** *n*

**modish** [**mode**-ish] *adj* in fashion

**modulate** *v* vary in tone; adjust; change the key of (music) ▶ **modulation** *n* ▶ **modulator** *n*

**module** *n* self-contained unit, section, or component with a specific function

**modus operandi** [**mode**-uss op-er-**an**-die] *n* (*Latin*) method of operating

**mogul** [**moh**-gl] *n* important or powerful person

**mohair** *n* fine hair of the Angora goat; yarn or fabric made from this

**mohican** *n* punk hairstyle with shaved sides and a stiff central strip of hair, often brightly coloured

**moiety** [**moy**-it-ee] *n, pl* **-ties** half

**moist** *adj* slightly wet ▶ **moisten** *v* make or become moist ▶ **moisture** *n* liquid diffused as vapour or condensed in drops ▶ **moisturize** *v* add moisture to (the skin etc.)

**mojo** *n* (*slang*) uncanny power or influence

**moke** *n* (*Aust & NZ*) horse of inferior quality

**molar** *n* large back tooth used for grinding

**molasses** *n* dark syrup, a by-product of sugar refining

**mole¹** *n* small dark raised spot on the skin

**mole²** *n* small burrowing mammal; (*informal*) spy who has infiltrated and become a trusted member of an organization

**mole³** *n* unit of amount of substance

**mole⁴** *n* breakwater; harbour protected by this

**molecule** [**mol**-lik-kyool] *n* simplest freely existing chemical unit, composed of two or more atoms; very small particle ▶ **molecular** [mol-**lek**-yew-lar] *adj*

**molest** *v* interfere with sexually; annoy or injure ▶ **molester** *n* ▶ **molestation** *n*

**moll** *n* (*slang*) gangster's female accomplice

**mollify** *v* **-fying, -fied** pacify or soothe

**mollusc** *n* soft-bodied, usu. hard-shelled, animal, such as a snail or oyster

**mollycoddle** *v* pamper

**Molotov cocktail** *n* petrol bomb

**molten** *adj* liquefied or melted

**molybdenum** [mol-**lib**-din-um] *n* (*Chem*) hard silvery-white metallic element

**moment** *n* short space of time; (present) point in time ▶ **momentary** *adj* lasting only a moment ▶ **momentarily** *adv*

> **USAGE NOTE**
> Note that some American speakers use *momentarily* to mean 'soon' rather than 'for a moment'

**momentous** [moh-**men**-tuss] *adj* of great significance

**momentum** *n* impetus of a moving body; product of a body's mass and velocity

**monarch** *n* sovereign ruler of a state ▶ **monarchical** *adj* ▶ **monarchist** *n* supporter of monarchy ▶ **monarchy** *n* government by or a state ruled by a sovereign

**monastery** *n, pl* **-teries** residence of a community of monks ▶ **monastic** *adj* of monks, nuns, or monasteries; simple and austere ▶ **monasticism** *n*

**Monday** *n* second day of the week

**monetary** *adj* of money or currency ▶ **monetarism** *n* theory that inflation is caused by an increase in the money supply ▶ **monetarist** *n, adj*

**money** *n* medium of exchange, coins or banknotes ▶ **moneyed, monied** *adj* rich

**mongol** *n, adj* (*offens*) (person) affected by Down's syndrome ▶ **mongolism** *n*

**Mongolian** *n* person from Mongolia; language of Mongolia ▷ *adj* of Mongolia or its language

**mongoose** *n, pl* **-gooses** stoat-like mammal of Asia and Africa that kills snakes

**mongrel** *n* animal, esp. a dog, of mixed breed; something arising from a variety of sources ▷ *adj* of mixed breed or origin

**monitor** *n* person or device that checks, controls, warns, or keeps a record of something; (*Brit, Aust & NZ*) pupil assisting a teacher with duties; television set used in a studio to check what is being transmitted; large lizard of Africa, Asia, and Australia ▷ *v* watch and check on

**monk** *n* member of an all-male religious community bound by vows ▶ **monkish** *adj*

**monkey** *n* long-tailed primate; mischievous child ▷ *v* (usu. foll by *about* or *around*) meddle or fool ▶ **monkey nut** (*Brit*) peanut ▶ **monkey puzzle** coniferous tree with sharp stiff leaves ▶ **monkey wrench** wrench with adjustable jaws

**mono-** *combining form* single e.g. *monosyllable*

**monochrome** *adj* (*Photog*) black-and-white; in only one colour

**monocle** *n* eyeglass for one eye only

**monogamy** *n* custom of being married to one person at a time

**monogram** *n* design of combined letters, esp. a person's initials

**monograph** *n* book or paper on a single subject

**monolith** *n* large upright block of stone ▶ **monolithic** *adj*

**monologue** *n* long speech by one person; dramatic piece for one performer

**monomania** *n* obsession with one thing ▶ **monomaniac** *n*, *adj*

**monoplane** *n* aeroplane with one pair of wings

**monopoly** *n* (*pl* **-lies**) exclusive possession of or right to do something; (**M-**)® board game for four to six players who deal in

'property' as they move around the board ▶ **monopolize** *v* have or take exclusive possession of

**monorail** *n* single-rail railway

**monotheism** *n* belief in only one God ▶ **monotheistic** *adj*

**monotone** *n* unvaried pitch in speech or sound ▶ **monotonous** *adj* tedious due to lack of variety ▶ **monotonously** *adv* ▶ **monotony** *n*

**Monseigneur** [mon-sen-**nyur**] *n*, *pl* **Messeigneurs** [may-sen-**nyur**] title of French prelates

**monsieur** [muss-**syur**] *n*, *pl* **messieurs** [may-**syur**] French title of address equivalent to *sir* or *Mr*

**Monsignor** *n* (*RC Church*) title attached to certain offices

**monsoon** *n* seasonal wind of SE Asia; rainy season accompanying this

**monster** *n* imaginary, usu. frightening, beast; huge person, animal, or thing; very wicked person ▷ *adj* huge ▶ **monstrosity** *n* large ugly thing ▶ **monstrous** *adj* unnatural or ugly; outrageous or shocking; huge ▶ **monstrously** *adv*

**monstrance** *n* (*RC Church*) container in which the consecrated Host is exposed for adoration

**montage** [mon-**tahzh**] *n* (making of) a picture composed from pieces of others; method of film editing incorporating several shots to form a single image

**month** *n* one of the twelve divisions of the calendar year; period of four weeks ▶ **monthly** *adj* happening or payable once a month ▷ *adv* once a month ▷ *n* monthly magazine

**monument** *n* something, esp. a building or statue, that commemorates something ▶ **monumental** *adj* large, impressive, or lasting; of or being

a monument; (*informal*) extreme
▶ **monumentally** *adv*

**moo** *n* long deep cry of a cow ▷ *v* make this noise

**mooch** *v* (*slang*) loiter about aimlessly

**mood**¹ *n* temporary (gloomy) state of mind ▶ **moody** *adj* sullen or gloomy; changeable in mood ▶ **moodily** *adv*

**mood**² *n* (*Grammar*) form of a verb indicating whether it expresses a fact, wish, supposition, or command

**moon** *n* natural satellite of the earth; natural satellite of any planet ▷ *v* (foll by *about* or *around*) be idle in a listless or dreamy way ▶ **moonlight** *n* light from the moon ▷ *v* (*informal*) work at a secondary job, esp. illegally ▶ **moonshine** *n* (*US & Canadian*) illicitly distilled whisky; nonsense ▶ **moonstone** *n* translucent semiprecious stone ▶ **moonstruck** *adj* slightly mad or odd

**moor**¹ *n* (*Brit*) tract of open uncultivated ground covered with grass and heather ▶ **moorhen** *n* small black water bird

**moor**² *v* secure (a ship) with ropes etc. ▶ **mooring** *n* place for mooring a ship ▷ *pl* ropes etc. used in mooring a ship

**Moor** *n* member of a Muslim people of NW Africa who ruled Spain between the 8th and 15th centuries ▶ **Moorish** *adj*

**moose** *n* large N American deer

**moot** *adj* debatable e.g. *a moot point* ▷ *v* bring up for discussion

**mop** *n* long stick with twists of cotton or a sponge on the end, used for cleaning; thick mass of hair ▷ *v* **mopping, mopped** clean or soak up with or as if with a mop

**mope** *v* be gloomy and apathetic

**moped** *n* light motorized cycle

**mopoke** *n* small spotted owl of Australia and New Zealand

**moraine** *n* accumulated mass of debris deposited by a glacier

**moral** *adj* concerned with right and wrong conduct; based on a sense of right and wrong; (of support or a victory) psychological rather than practical ▷ *n* lesson to be obtained from a story or event ▷ *pl* principles of behaviour with respect to right and wrong ▶ **morally** *adv* ▶ **moralist** *n* person with a strong sense of right and wrong ▶ **morality** *n* good moral conduct; moral goodness or badness ▶ **morality play** medieval play with a moral lesson ▶ **moralize** *v* make moral pronouncements

**morale** [mor-**rahl**] *n* degree of confidence or hope of a person or group

**morass** *n* marsh; mess

**moratorium** *n, pl* -**ria** or -**riums** legally authorized ban or delay

**moray** *n* large voracious eel

**morbid** *adj* unduly interested in death or unpleasant events; gruesome

**mordant** *adj* sarcastic or scathing ▷ *n* substance used to fix dyes

**more** *adj* greater in amount or degree; comparative of **much, many**; additional or further ▷ *adv* to a greater extent; in addition ▷ *pron* greater or additional amount or number ▶ **moreover** *adv* in addition to what has already been said

**mores** [**more**-rayz] *pl n* customs and conventions embodying the fundamental values of a community

**Moreton Bay bug** *n* Australian flattish edible shellfish

**morganatic marriage** *n* marriage of a person of high rank to a lower-ranking person whose status remains unchanged

**morgue** n mortuary

**moribund** adj without force or vitality

**Mormon** n member of a religious sect founded in the USA

**morn** n (poetic or Aust) morning

**morning** n part of the day before noon ▸ **morning-glory** n plant with trumpet-shaped flowers which close in the late afternoon

**Moroccan** adj of Morocco ▷ n person from Morocco

**morocco** n goatskin leather

**moron** n (informal) foolish or stupid person; (formerly) person with a low intelligence quotient ▸ **moronic** adj

**morose** [mor-**rohss**] adj sullen or moody

**morphine, morphia** n drug extracted from opium, used as an anaesthetic and sedative

**morphology** n science of forms and structures of organisms or words ▸ **morphological** adj

**morris dance** n traditional English folk dance

**morrow** n (poetic) next day

**Morse** n former system of signalling in which letters of the alphabet are represented by combinations of short and long signals

**morsel** n small piece, esp. of food

**mortal** adj subject to death; causing death ▷ n human being ▸ **mortally** adv ▸ **mortality** n state of being mortal; great loss of life; death rate ▸ **mortal sin** (RC Church) sin meriting damnation

**mortar** n small cannon with a short range; mixture of lime, sand, and water for holding bricks and stones together; bowl in which substances are pounded ▸ **mortarboard** n black square academic cap

**mortgage** n conditional pledging of property, esp. a house, as security for the repayment of a loan; the loan itself ▷ v pledge (property) as security thus ▸ **mortgagee** n creditor in a mortgage ▸ **mortgagor** n debtor in a mortgage

**mortice, mortise** [**more**-tiss] n hole in a piece of wood or stone shaped to receive a matching projection on another piece ▸ **mortice lock** lock set into a door

**mortify** v -fying, -fied humiliate; subdue by self-denial; (of flesh) become gangrenous ▸ **mortification** n

**mortuary** n, pl -aries building where corpses are kept before burial or cremation

**Mosaic** adj of Moses

**mosaic** [mow-**zay**-ik] n design or decoration using small pieces of coloured stone or glass

**Moselle** n light white German wine

**Moslem** n, adj same as **Muslim**

**mosque** n Muslim temple

**mosquito** n, pl -toes or -tos blood-sucking flying insect

**moss** n small flowerless plant growing in masses on moist surfaces ▸ **mossy** adj

**most** n greatest number or degree ▷ adj greatest in number or degree; superlative of **much, many** ▷ adv in the greatest degree ▸ **mostly** adv for the most part, generally

**MOT, MOT test** n (in Britain) compulsory annual test of the roadworthiness of vehicles over a certain age

**motel** n roadside hotel for motorists

**motet** n short sacred choral song

**moth** n nocturnal insect like a butterfly ▸ **mothball** n small ball of camphor or naphthalene used to repel moths from stored clothes

▷ *v* store (something operational) for future use; postpone (a project etc.) ▸ **moth-eaten** *adj* decayed or scruffy; eaten or damaged by moth larvae

**mother** *n* female parent; head of a female religious community ▷ *adj* native or inborn e.g. *mother wit* ▷ *v* look after as a mother ▸ **motherhood** *n* ▸ **motherly** *adj* ▸ **motherless** *adj* ▸ **mother-in-law** *n* mother of one's husband or wife ▸ **mother of pearl** iridescent lining of certain shells ▸ **mother tongue** one's native language

**motif** [moh-**teef**] *n* (recurring) theme or design

**motion** *n* process, action, or way of moving; proposal in a meeting; evacuation of the bowels ▷ *v* direct (someone) by gesture ▸ **motionless** *adj* not moving ▸ **motion picture** cinema film

**motive** *n* reason for a course of action ▷ *adj* causing motion ▸ **motivate** *v* give incentive to ▸ **motivation** *n*

**motley** *adj* miscellaneous; multicoloured

**motocross** *n* motorcycle race over a rough course

**motor** *n* engine, esp. of a vehicle; machine that converts electrical energy into mechanical energy; (*chiefly Brit*) car ▷ *v* travel by car ▸ **motorist** *n* driver of a car ▸ **motorized** *adj* equipped with a motor or motor transport ▸ **motorbike** *n* ▸ **motorboat** *n* ▸ **motorcar** *n* ▸ **motorcycle** *n* ▸ **motorcyclist** *n* ▸ **motorhome** *n* large motor vehicle designed for living in while travelling ▸ **motor scooter** light motorcycle with small wheels and an enclosed engine ▸ **motorway** *n* main road for fast-moving traffic

**mottled** *adj* marked with blotches

**motto** *n, pl* **-toes** or **-tos** saying expressing an ideal or rule of conduct; verse or maxim in a paper cracker

**mould¹** *n* hollow container in which metal etc. is cast; shape, form, or pattern; nature or character ▷ *v* shape; influence or direct ▸ **moulding** *n* moulded ornamental edging

**mould²** *n* fungal growth caused by dampness ▸ **mouldy** *adj* stale or musty; dull or boring

**mould³** *n* loose soil ▸ **moulder** *v* decay into dust

**moult** *v* shed feathers, hair, or skin to make way for new growth ▷ *n* process of moulting

**mound** *n* heap, esp. of earth or stones; small hill

**mount** *v* climb or ascend; get up on (a horse etc.); increase or accumulate; fix on a support or backing; organize e.g. *mount a campaign* ▷ *n* backing or support on which something is fixed; horse for riding; hill

**mountain** *n* hill of great size; large heap ▸ **mountainous** *adj* full of mountains; huge ▸ **mountaineer** *n* person who climbs mountains ▸ **mountaineering** *n* ▸ **mountain bike** bicycle with straight handlebars and heavy-duty tyres, for cycling over rough terrain ▸ **mountain oyster** (*NZ informal*) sheep's testicle eaten as food

**mountebank** *n* charlatan or fake

**Mountie** *n* (*informal*) member of the Royal Canadian Mounted Police

**mourn** *v* feel or express sorrow for (a dead person or lost thing) ▸ **mournful** *adj* sad or dismal ▸ **mournfully** *adv* ▸ **mourning** *n* grieving; conventional symbols of

**m**

grief for death, such as the wearing of black

**mourner** n person attending a funeral

**mouse** n, pl **mice** small long-tailed rodent; timid person; (*Computing*) hand-held device for moving the cursor without keying ▶ **mouser** n cat used to catch mice ▶ **mousy** adj like a mouse, esp. in hair colour; meek and shy

**mousse** n dish of flavoured cream whipped and set

**moustache** n hair on the upper lip

**mouth** n opening in the head for eating and issuing sounds; entrance; point where a river enters the sea; opening ▷ v form (words) with the lips without speaking; speak or utter insincerely, esp. in public ▶ **mouthful** n amount of food or drink put into the mouth at any one time when eating or drinking ▶ **mouth organ** same as **harmonica** ▶ **mouthpiece** n part of a telephone into which a person speaks; part of a wind instrument into which the player blows; spokesperson

**move** v change in place or position; change (one's house etc.); take action; stir the emotions of; incite; suggest (a proposal) formally ▷ n moving; action towards some goal ▶ **movable, moveable** adj ▶ **movement** n action or process of moving; group with a common aim; division of a piece of music; moving parts of a machine

**movie** n (*informal*) cinema film

**mow** v **mowing, mowed, mowed** or **mown** cut (grass or crops) ▶ **mow down** v kill in large numbers

**mower** n machine for cutting grass

**mozzarella** [mot-sa-**rel**-la] n moist white cheese originally made in Italy from buffalo milk

**MP** Member of Parliament; Military Police(man)

**MP3** (*Computing*) Motion Picture Expert Group-1, Audio Layer-3: a digital compression format used to compress audio files to a fraction of their original size without loss of sound quality ▶ **MP3 player** small portable digital audio player capable of storing MP3 files downloaded from the internet or transferred from CD

**MP4** abbrev MPEG-4 Part 14: software for transmitting data streams to a receiving device in real time

**MPEG** [**em**-peg] (*Computing*) Motion Picture Experts Group: standard compressed file format used for audio and video files; file in this format

**mpg** miles per gallon

**mph** miles per hour

**Mr** Mister

**Mrs** n title of a married woman

**MS** manuscript; multiple sclerosis

**Ms** [**mizz**] n title used instead of Miss or Mrs

**MSc** Master of Science

**MSP** (in Britain) Member of the Scottish Parliament

**MSS** manuscripts

**Mt** Mount

**much** adj **more, most** large amount or degree of ▷ n large amount or degree ▷ adv **more, most** to a great degree; nearly

**mucilage** [**mew**-sill-ij] n gum or glue

**muck** n dirt, filth; manure ▶ **mucky** adj

**mucus** [**mew**-kuss] n slimy secretion of the mucous membranes ▶ **mucous**

**membrane** tissue lining body cavities or passages

**mud** n wet soft earth ▶ **muddy** adj ▶ **mudguard** n cover over a wheel to prevent mud or water being thrown up by it ▶ **mud pack** cosmetic paste to improve the complexion

**muddle** v (often foll by up) confuse; mix up ▷ n state of confusion

**muesli** [**mewz**-lee] n mixture of grain, nuts, and dried fruit, eaten with milk

**muezzin** [moo-**ezz**-in] n official who summons Muslims to prayer

**muff**¹ n tube-shaped covering to keep the hands warm

**muff**² v bungle (an action)

**muffin** n light round flat yeast cake

**muffle** v wrap up for warmth or to deaden sound ▶ **muffler** n (Brit) scarf; device to reduce the noise of an engine exhaust

**mufti** n civilian clothes worn by a person who usually wears a uniform

**mug**¹ n large drinking cup

**mug**² n (slang) face; (slang) gullible person ▷ v **mugging, mugged** (informal) attack in order to rob ▶ **mugger** n

**mug**³ v **mugging, mugged** (foll by up) (informal) study hard

**muggins** n (informal) stupid or gullible person

**muggy** adj -**gier, -giest** (of weather) damp and stifling

**mulatto** [mew-**lat**-toe] n, pl -**tos** -**toes** (offens) child of one Black and one White parent

**mulberry** n tree whose leaves are used to feed silkworms; purple fruit of this tree

**mulch** n mixture of wet straw, leaves, etc., used to protect the roots of plants ▷ v cover (land) with mulch

**mule**¹ n offspring of a horse and a donkey ▶ **mulish** adj obstinate

**mule**² n backless shoe or slipper

**mulga** n Australian acacia shrub growing in desert regions; (Aust) the outback

**mull** v think (over) or ponder ▶ **mulled** adj (of wine or ale) flavoured with sugar and spices and served hot

**mullah** n Muslim scholar, teacher, or religious leader

**mullet**¹ n edible sea fish

**mullet**² n haircut in which the hair is short at the top and sides and long at the back

**mulligatawny** n soup made with curry powder

**mullion** n vertical dividing bar in a window ▶ **mullioned** adj

**mulloway** n large Australian sea fish, valued for sport and food

**multi-** combining form many e.g. multicultural; multistorey

**multifarious** [mull-tee-**fare**-ee-uss] adj having many various parts

**multilateral** adj of or involving more than two nations or parties

**multiple** adj having many parts ▷ n quantity which contains another an exact number of times

**multiplex** n purpose-built complex containing several cinemas and usu. restaurants and bars ▷ adj having many elements, complex

**multiplicity** n, pl -**ties** large number or great variety

**multiply** v -**plying, -plied** (cause to) increase in number, quantity, or degree; add (a number or quantity) to itself a given number of times; increase in number by reproduction ▶ **multiplication** n ▶ **multiplicand** n (Maths) number to be multiplied

**multipurpose** adj having many uses e.g. a multipurpose tool

m

▸ **multipurpose vehicle** large vanlike car designed to carry up to eight passengers

**multitude** *n* great number; great crowd ▸ **multitudinous** *adj* very numerous

**mum**[1] *n* (*informal*) mother

**mum**[2] *adj* keep mum remain silent

**mumble** *v* speak indistinctly, mutter

**mumbo jumbo** *n* meaningless language; foolish religious ritual or incantation

**mummer** *n* actor in a traditional English folk play or mime

**mummy**[1] *n*, *pl* **-mies** body embalmed and wrapped for burial in ancient Egypt ▸ **mummified** *adj* (of a body) preserved as a mummy

**mummy**[2] *n*, *pl* **-mies** child's word for **mother**

**mumps** *n* infectious disease with swelling in the glands of the neck

**munch** *v* chew noisily and steadily

**mundane** *adj* everyday; earthly

**municipal** *adj* relating to a city or town ▸ **municipality** *n* city or town with local self-government; governing body of this

**munificent** [mew-**niff**-fiss-sent] *adj* very generous ▸ **munificence** *n*

**muniments** *pl n* title deeds or similar documents

**munitions** *pl n* military stores

**munted** *adj* (*NZ slang*) destroyed or ruined; abnormal or peculiar

**mural** *n* painting on a wall

**murder** *n* unlawful intentional killing of a human being ▷ *v* kill in this way ▸ **murderer, murderess** *n* ▸ **murderous** *adj*

**murky** *adj* dark or gloomy ▸ **murk** *n* thick darkness

**murmur** *v* **-muring, -mured** speak or say in a quiet indistinct way; complain ▷ *n* continuous low indistinct sound

**muscle** *n* tissue in the body which produces movement by contracting; strength or power ▸ **muscular** *adj* with well-developed muscles; of muscles ▸ **muscular dystrophy** disease with wasting of the muscles ▸ **muscle in** *v* (*informal*) force one's way in

**Muse** *n* (*Greek myth*) one of nine goddesses, each of whom inspired an art or science; (**m-**) force that inspires a creative artist

**muse** *v* ponder quietly

**museum** *n* building where natural, artistic, historical, or scientific objects are exhibited and preserved

**mush** *n* soft pulpy mass; (*informal*) cloying sentimentality ▸ **mushy** *adj*

**mushroom** *n* edible fungus with a stem and cap ▷ *v* grow rapidly

**music** *n* art form using a melodious and harmonious combination of notes; written or printed form of this ▸ **musical** *adj* of or like music; talented in or fond of music; pleasant-sounding ▷ *n* play or film with songs and dancing ▸ **musically** *adv* ▸ **musician** *n* ▸ **musicology** *n* scientific study of music ▸ **musicologist** *n* ▸ **music hall** variety theatre

**musk** *n* scent obtained from a gland of the musk deer or produced synthetically ▸ **musky** *adj* ▸ **muskrat** *n* N American beaver-like rodent; its fur

**musket** *n* (*Hist*) long-barrelled gun ▸ **musketeer** *n* ▸ **musketry** *n* (use of) muskets

**Muslim** *n* follower of the religion of Islam ▷ *adj* of or relating to Islam

**muslin** *n* fine cotton fabric

**mussel** *n* edible shellfish with a dark hinged shell

**must**[1] *v* used as an auxiliary to express obligation, certainty,

or resolution ▷ n essential or
necessary thing

**must²** n newly pressed grape juice

**mustang** n wild horse of SW USA

**mustard** n paste made from the
powdered seeds of a plant, used as
a condiment; the plant ▶ **mustard
gas** poisonous gas causing
blistering burns and blindness

**muster** v assemble ▷ n assembly of
military personnel

**musty** adj **mustier, mustiest**
smelling mouldy and stale
▶ **mustiness** n

**mutable** [mew-tab-bl] adj liable to
change ▶ **mutability** n

**mutation** n (genetic) change
▶ **mutate** v (cause to) undergo
mutation ▶ **mutant** n mutated
animal, plant, etc.

**mute** adj silent; (offens) unable to
speak ▷ n (offens) person who is
unable to speak; (Music) device to
soften the tone of an instrument
▶ **muted** adj (of sound or colour)
softened; (of a reaction) subdued
▶ **mutely** adv

**muti** [moo-ti] n (S Afr informal)
medicine, esp. herbal medicine

**mutilate** [mew-till-ate] v deprive
of a limb or other part; damage (a
book or text) ▶ **mutilation** n

**mutiny** [mew-tin-ee] n, pl -nies
rebellion against authority, esp.
by soldiers or sailors ▷ v -nying, -
nied commit mutiny ▶ **mutineer** n
▶ **mutinous** adj

**mutt** n (slang) mongrel dog; stupid
person

**mutter** v utter or speak indistinctly;
grumble ▷ n muttered sound or
grumble

**mutton** n flesh of sheep, used as food
▶ **mutton bird** (Aust) sea bird with
dark plumage; (NZ) any of a number
of migratory sea birds, the young of
which are a Māori delicacy

**mutual** [mew-chew-al] adj felt or
expressed by each of two people
about the other; common to both
or all ▶ **mutually** adv

**USAGE NOTE**

The objection that something
*mutual* has to do with two people
only is outdated; nowadays
*mutual* is equivalent to 'shared,
in common'

**Muzak**® n recorded light music
played in shops etc.

**muzzle** n animal's mouth and nose;
cover for these to prevent biting;
open end of a gun ▷ v prevent
from being heard or noticed; put
a muzzle on

**muzzy** adj -zier, -ziest confused or
muddled; blurred or hazy

**MW** megawatt(s)

**mW** milliwatt(s)

**my** adj belonging to me

**myall** n Australian acacia with hard
scented wood

**mycology** n study of fungi

**myna, mynah, mina** n Asian bird
which can mimic human speech

**myopia** [my-oh-pee-a] n
short-sightedness ▶ **myopic**
[my-op-ik] adj

**myriad** [mir-ree-ad] adj
innumerable ▷ n large indefinite
number

**myrrh** [mur] n aromatic gum used
in perfume, incense, and medicine

**myrtle** [mur-tl] n flowering
evergreen shrub

**myself** pron emphatic or reflexive
form of **I, me**

**mystery** n, pl -teries strange
or inexplicable event or
phenomenon; obscure or secret
thing; story or film that arouses
suspense ▶ **mysterious** adj
▶ **mysteriously** adv

**mystic** n person who seeks
spiritual knowledge ▷ adj

mystical ▶ **mystical** *adj* having a spiritual or religious significance beyond human understanding ▶ **mysticism** *n*

**mystify** *v* **-fying, -fied** bewilder or puzzle ▶ **mystification** *n*

**mystique** [miss-**steek**] *n* aura of mystery or power

**myth** *n* tale with supernatural characters, usu. of how the world and mankind began; untrue idea or explanation; imaginary person or object ▶ **mythical, mythic** *adj* ▶ **mythology** *n* myths collectively; study of myths ▶ **mythological** *adj*

**myxomatosis** [mix-a-mat-**oh**-siss] *n* contagious fatal viral disease of rabbits

# Nn

**N** (*Chem*) nitrogen; (*Physics*) newton(s); North(ern)

**n.** neuter; noun; number

**Na** (*Chem*) sodium

**Naafi** *n* (*Brit*) canteen or shop for military personnel

**naan** *n* same as **nan bread**

**naartjie** [**nahr**-chee] *n* (*S Afr*) tangerine

**nab** *v* **nabbing, nabbed** (*informal*) arrest (someone); catch (someone) in wrongdoing

**nadir** *n* point in the sky opposite the zenith; lowest point

**naevus** [**nee**-vuss] *n*, *pl* **-vi** birthmark or mole

**naff** *adj* (*Brit slang*) lacking quality or taste

**nag¹** *v* **nagging, nagged** scold or find fault constantly; be a constant source of discomfort or worry to ▷ *n* person who nags ▶ **nagging** *adj*, *n*

**nag²** *n* (*informal*) old horse

**naiad** [**nye**-ad] *n* (*Greek myth*) nymph living in a lake or river

**nail** *n* pointed piece of metal with a head, hit with a hammer to join two objects together; hard covering of the upper tips of the fingers and toes ▷ *v* attach (something) with nails; (*informal*) catch or arrest **hit the nail on the head** say something exactly correct ▶ **nail file** small metal file used to smooth or shape the finger or toe nails ▶ **nail varnish, nail polish** cosmetic lacquer applied to the finger or toe nails

n

**naive** [nye-**eev**] *adj* innocent and gullible; simple and lacking sophistication ▶ **naively** *adv* ▶ **naivety, naïveté** [nye-**eev**-tee] *n*

**naked** *adj* without clothes; without any covering **the naked eye** the eye unassisted by any optical instrument ▶ **nakedness** *n*

**namby-pamby** *adj* (*Brit, Aust & NZ*) sentimental or insipid

**name** *n* word by which a person or thing is known; reputation, esp. a good one ▶ *v* give a name to; refer to by name; fix or specify **call someone names, call someone a name** insult someone by using rude words to describe him or her ▶ **nameless** *adj* without a name; unspecified; too horrible to be mentioned ▶ **namely** *adv* that is to say ▶ **namesake** *n* person with the same name as another

**nan bread** *n* slightly leavened Indian bread in a large flat leaf shape

**nanny** *n, pl* **-nies** woman whose job is looking after young children ▶ **nanny goat** female goat

**nano-** *combining form* denoting one thousand millionth e.g. *nanosecond*

**nap**¹ *n* short sleep ▶ *v* **napping, napped** have a short sleep

**nap**² *n* raised fibres of velvet or similar cloth

**nap**³ *n* card game similar to whist

**napalm** *n* highly inflammable jellied petrol, used in bombs

**nape** *n* back of the neck

**naphtha** *n* liquid mixture distilled from coal tar or petroleum, used as a solvent and in petrol ▶ **naphthalene** *n* white crystalline product distilled from coal tar or petroleum, used in disinfectants, mothballs, and explosives

**napkin** *n* piece of cloth or paper for wiping the mouth or protecting the clothes while eating

**nappy** *n, pl* **-pies** piece of absorbent material fastened round a baby's lower torso to absorb urine and faeces

**narcissism** *n* exceptional interest in or admiration for oneself ▶ **narcissistic** *adj*

**narcissus** *n, pl* **-cissi** yellow, orange, or white flower related to the daffodil

**narcotic** *n, adj* (of) a drug, such as morphine or opium, which produces numbness and drowsiness, used medicinally but addictive ▶ **narcosis** *n* effect of a narcotic

**nark** (*slang*) *v* annoy ▶ *n* informer or spy; (*Brit*) someone who complains in an irritating manner ▶ **narky** *adj* (*slang*) irritable or complaining

**narrate** *v* tell (a story); speak the words accompanying and telling what is happening in a film or TV programme ▶ **narration** *n* ▶ **narrator** *n*

**narrative** *n* account, story

**narrow** *adj* small in breadth in comparison to length; limited in range, extent, or outlook; with little margin e.g. *a narrow escape* ▶ *v* make or become narrow; (often foll by *down*) limit or restrict ▶ **narrows** *pl n* narrow part of a strait, river, or current ▶ **narrowly** *adv* ▶ **narrowness** *n* ▶ **narrow boat** (*Brit*) long bargelike canal boat ▶ **narrow-minded** *adj* intolerant or bigoted

**narwhal** *n* arctic whale with a long spiral tusk

**NASA** (*US*) National Aeronautics and Space Administration

**nasal** *adj* of the nose; (of a sound) pronounced with air passing through the nose ▶ **nasally** *adv*

**nascent** *adj* starting to grow or develop

n

**NASDAQ** (*US*) National Association of Securities Dealers Automated Quotations (System)

**nasturtium** *n* plant with yellow, red, or orange trumpet-shaped flowers

**nasty** *adj* **-tier, -tiest** unpleasant; (of an injury) dangerous or painful; spiteful or unkind ▶ **nastily** *adv* ▶ **nastiness** *n*

**natal** *adj* of or relating to birth

**nation** *n* people of one or more cultures or races organized as a single state

**national** *adj* characteristic of a particular nation ▷ *n* citizen of a nation ▶ **nationally** *adv* ▶ **National Curriculum** curriculum of subjects taught in state schools in England and Wales since 1989 ▶ **National Health Service** (in Britain) system of national medical services financed mainly by taxation ▶ **national insurance** (in Britain) state insurance scheme providing payments to the unemployed, sick, and retired ▶ **national park** area of countryside protected by a government for its natural or environmental importance ▶ **national service** compulsory military service

**nationalism** *n* policy of national independence; patriotism, sometimes to an excessive degree ▶ **nationalist** *n, adj*

**nationality** *n, pl* **-ities** fact of being a citizen of a particular nation; group of people of the same race

**nationalize** *v* put (an industry or a company) under state control ▶ **nationalization** *n*

**native** *adj* relating to a place where a person was born; born in a specified place; (foll by *to*) originating (in); inborn ▷ *n* person born in a specified place;

indigenous animal or plant; member of the original race of a country ▶ **Native American** (person) descended from the original inhabitants of the American continent ▶ **native bear** (*Aust*) same as **koala** ▶ **native companion** (*Aust*) same as **brolga** ▶ **native dog** (*Aust*) dingo

**Nativity** *n* (*Christianity*) birth of Jesus Christ

**NATO** North Atlantic Treaty Organization

**natter** (*informal*) *v* talk idly or chatter ▷ *n* long idle chat

**natty** *adj* **-tier, -tiest** (*informal*) smart and spruce

**natural** *adj* normal or to be expected; genuine or spontaneous; of, according to, existing in, or produced by nature; not created by human beings; not synthetic ▷ *n* person with an inborn talent or skill ▶ **naturally** *adv* of course; in a natural or normal way; instinctively ▶ **natural gas** gas found below the ground, used mainly as a fuel ▶ **natural history** study of animals and plants in the wild ▶ **natural selection** process by which only creatures and plants well adapted to their environment survive

**naturalism** *n* movement in art and literature advocating detailed realism ▶ **naturalistic** *adj*

**naturalist** *n* student of natural history

**naturalize** *v* give citizenship to (a person born in another country) ▶ **naturalization** *n*

**nature** *n* whole system of the existence, forces, and events of the physical world that are not controlled by human beings; fundamental or essential qualities; kind or sort

**naturism** *n* nudism ▶ **naturist** *n*

**naught** n (lit) nothing

**naughty** adj **-tier, -tiest** disobedient or mischievous; mildly indecent ▶ **naughtily** adv ▶ **naughtiness** n

**nausea** [naw-zee-a] n feeling of being about to vomit ▶ **nauseate** v make (someone) feel sick; disgust ▶ **nauseous** adj as if about to vomit; sickening

**nautical** adj of the sea or ships ▶ **nautical mile** 1852 metres (6076.12 feet)

**nautilus** n, pl **-luses** or **-li** shellfish with many tentacles

**naval** adj see **navy**

**nave** n long central part of a church

**navel** n hollow in the middle of the abdomen where the umbilical cord was attached

**navigate** v direct or plot the path or position of a ship, aircraft, or car; travel over or through ▶ **navigation** n ▶ **navigator** n ▶ **navigable** adj wide, deep, or safe enough to be sailed through; able to be steered

**navvy** n, pl **-vies** (Brit) labourer employed on a road or a building site

**navy** n, pl **-vies** branch of a country's armed services comprising warships with their crews and organization; warships of a nation ▷ adj navy-blue ▶ **naval** adj of or relating to a navy or ships ▶ **navy-blue** adj very dark blue

**nay** interj (obs) no

**Nazi** n member of the fascist National Socialist Party, which came to power in Germany in 1933 under Adolf Hitler ▷ adj of or relating to the Nazis ▶ **Nazism** n

**NB** note well

**NCO** (Mil) noncommissioned officer

**NE** northeast(ern)

**Neanderthal** [nee-**ann**-der-tahl] adj of a type of primitive man that lived in Europe before 12 000 BC

**neap tide** n tide at the first and last quarters of the moon when there is the smallest rise and fall in tidal level

**near** prep, adv indicating a place or time not far away ▷ adj almost being the thing specified e.g. a near disaster ▷ v draw close (to) ▶ **nearly** adv almost ▶ **nearness** n ▶ **nearby** adj not far away ▶ **nearside** n side of a vehicle that is nearer the kerb

**neat** adj tidy and clean; smoothly or competently done; undiluted ▶ **neatly** adv ▶ **neatness** n

**nebula** n, pl **-lae** (Astronomy) hazy cloud of particles and gases ▶ **nebulous** adj vague and unclear e.g. a nebulous concept

**necessary** adj needed to obtain the desired result e.g. the necessary skills; certain or unavoidable e.g. the necessary consequences ▶ **necessarily** adv ▶ **necessitate** v compel or require ▶ **necessity** n circumstances that inevitably require a certain result; something needed

> **SPELLING TIP**
> The correct spelling of **necessary** has one c and two ss. When you add un- at the beginning, you end up with a double n too: **unnecessary**

**neck** n part of the body joining the head to the shoulders; part of a garment round the neck; long narrow part of a bottle or violin ▷ v (slang) kiss and cuddle **neck and neck** absolutely level in a race or competition ▶ **neckerchief** n piece of cloth worn tied round the neck ▶ **necklace** n decorative piece of jewellery worn around the neck

**necromancy** n communication with the dead; sorcery

n

**necropolis** [neck-**rop**-pol-liss] *n* cemetery

**nectar** *n* sweet liquid collected from flowers by bees; drink of the gods

**nectarine** *n* smooth-skinned peach

**ned** *n* (*Scot slang*) young working-class male who dresses in casual sports clothes

**née** [**nay**] *prep* indicating the maiden name of a married woman

**need** *v* require or be in want of; be obliged (to do something) ▷ *n* condition of lacking something; requirement or necessity; poverty ▶ **needs** *adv* (foll by *must*) necessarily ▶ **needy** *adj* poor, in need of financial support ▶ **needful** *adj* necessary or required ▶ **needless** *adj* unnecessary

**needle** *n* thin pointed piece of metal with an eye through which thread is passed for sewing; long pointed rod used in knitting; pointed part of a hypodermic syringe; small pointed part in a record player that touches the record and picks up the sound signals, stylus; pointer on a measuring instrument or compass; long narrow stiff leaf ▷ *v* (*informal*) goad or provoke ▶ **needlework** *n* sewing and embroidery

**ne'er** *adv* (*lit*) never ▶ **ne'er-do-well** *n* useless or lazy person

**nefarious** [nif-**fair**-ee-uss] *adj* wicked

**negate** *v* invalidate; deny the existence of ▶ **negation** *n*

**negative** *adj* expressing a denial or refusal; lacking positive qualities; (of an electrical charge) having the same electrical charge as an electron ▷ *n* negative word or statement; (*Photog*) image with a reversal of tones or colours from which positive prints are made

**neglect** *v* take no care of; fail (to do something) through carelessness; disregard ▷ *n* neglecting or being neglected ▶ **neglectful** *adj*

**negligee** [**neg**-lee-zhay] *n* woman's lightweight usu. lace-trimmed dressing gown

**negligence** *n* neglect or carelessness ▶ **negligent** *adj* ▶ **negligently** *adv*

**negligible** *adj* so small or unimportant as to be not worth considering

**negotiate** *v* discuss in order to reach (an agreement); succeed in passing round or over (a place or problem) ▶ **negotiation** *n* ▶ **negotiator** *n* ▶ **negotiable** *adj*

**Negro** *n*, *pl* **-groes** (*old-fashioned offens*) member of any of the Black peoples originating in Africa ▶ **Negroid** *adj* of or relating to the Black peoples originating in Africa

**neigh** *n* a loud high-pitched sound made by a horse ▷ *v* make this sound

**neighbour** *n* person who lives near another ▶ **neighbouring** *adj* situated nearby ▶ **neighbourhood** *n* district; surroundings; people of a district ▶ **neighbourly** *adj* kind, friendly, and helpful

**neither** *adj*, *pron* not one nor the other ▷ *conj* not

**nemesis** [**nem**-miss-iss] *n*, *pl* **-ses** retribution or vengeance

**neo-** *combining form* new, recent, or a modern form of e.g. *neoclassicism*

**neo-con** *adj*, *n* short for **neo-conservative**

**neo-conservatism** *n* (in the US) a right-wing tendency that originated amongst supporters of the political left ▶ **neo-conservative** *adj*, *n*

**Neolithic** *adj* of the later Stone Age

**neologism** [nee-**ol**-a-jiz-zum] *n* newly-coined word or an existing word used in a new sense

n

**neon** n (*Chem*) colourless odourless gaseous element used in illuminated signs and lights

**neonatal** adj relating to the first few weeks of a baby's life

**neophyte** n beginner or novice; new convert

**nephew** n son of one's sister or brother

**nephritis** [nif-**frite**-tiss] n inflammation of a kidney

**nepotism** [**nep**-a-tiz-zum] n favouritism in business shown to relatives and friends

**Neptune** n Roman god of the sea; eighth planet from the sun

**nerd** n (*slang*) boring person obsessed with a particular subject; stupid and feeble person ▶ **nerdic** n (*informal*) technical jargon used esp by computing enthusiasts

**nerve** n cordlike bundle of fibres that conducts impulses between the brain and other parts of the body; bravery and determination; impudence ▶ pl anxiety or tension; ability or inability to remain calm in a difficult situation; **get on someone's nerves** irritate someone **nerve oneself** prepare oneself (to do something difficult or unpleasant) ▶ **nerveless** adj numb, without feeling; fearless ▶ **nervy** adj excitable or nervous ▶ **nerve centre** place from which a system or organization is controlled ▶ **nerve-racking** adj very distressing or harrowing

**nervous** adj apprehensive or worried; of or relating to the nerves ▶ **nervously** adv ▶ **nervousness** n ▶ **nervous breakdown** mental illness in which the sufferer ceases to function properly

**nest** n place or structure in which birds or certain animals lay eggs or give birth to young; secluded place; set of things of graduated sizes designed to fit together ▶ v make or inhabit a nest ▶ **nest egg** fund of money kept in reserve

**nestle** v snuggle; be in a sheltered position

**nestling** n bird too young to leave the nest

**net**[1] n fabric of meshes of string, thread, or wire with many openings; piece of net used to protect or hold things or to trap animals ▶ v **netting, netted** catch (a fish or animal) in a net **the Net** internet ▶ **netting** n material made of net ▶ **netball** n team game in which a ball has to be thrown through a net hanging from a ring at the top of a pole ▶ **netbook** n type of small laptop computer

**net**[2], **nett** adj left after all deductions; (of weight) excluding the wrapping or container ▶ v **netting, netted** yield or earn as a clear profit

**nether** adj lower

**nettle** n plant with stinging hairs on the leaves ▶ **nettled** adj irritated

**network** n system of intersecting lines, roads, etc.; interconnecting group or system; (in broadcasting) group of stations that all transmit the same programmes simultaneously

**neural** adj of a nerve or the nervous system

**neuralgia** n severe pain along a nerve

**neuritis** [nyoor-**rite**-tiss] n inflammation of a nerve or nerves

**neurology** n scientific study of the nervous system ▶ **neurologist** n

**neurosis** n, pl **-ses** mental disorder producing hysteria, anxiety, depression, or obsessive behaviour

▶ **neurotic** adj emotionally unstable; suffering from neurosis ▷ n neurotic person

**neuter** adj belonging to a particular class of grammatical inflections in some languages ▷ v castrate (an animal)

**neutral** adj taking neither side in a war or dispute; of or belonging to a neutral party or country; (of a colour) not definite or striking ▷ n neutral person or nation; neutral gear ▶ **neutrality** n ▶ **neutralize** v make ineffective or neutral ▶ **neutral gear** position of the controls of a gearbox that leaves the gears unconnected to the engine

**neutrino** [new-**tree**-no] n, pl -**nos** elementary particle with no mass or electrical charge

**neutron** n electrically neutral elementary particle of about the same mass as a proton ▶ **neutron bomb** nuclear bomb designed to kill people and animals while leaving buildings virtually undamaged

**never** adv at no time ▶ **nevertheless** adv in spite of that

**USAGE NOTE**
Avoid the use of *never* with the past tense to mean *not: I didn't see her yesterday* (not *I never saw her yesterday*)

**never-never** n (informal) hire-purchase

**new** adj not existing before; recently acquired; having lately come into some state; additional; (foll by to) unfamiliar ▷ adv recently ▶ **newness** n ▶ **New Age** philosophy, originating in the late 1980s, characterized by a belief in alternative medicine and spiritualism ▶ **newbie** n (informal) person new to a job, club, etc.

▶ **newborn** adj recently or just born ▶ **newcomer** n recent arrival or participant ▶ **newfangled** adj objectionably or unnecessarily modern ▶ **newlyweds** pl n recently married couple ▶ **new moon** moon when it appears as a narrow crescent at the beginning of its cycle

**newel** n post at the top or bottom of a flight of stairs that supports the handrail

**news** n important or interesting new happenings; information about such events reported in the mass media ▶ **newsy** adj full of news ▶ **newsagent** n (Brit) shopkeeper who sells newspapers and magazines ▶ **newsflash** n brief important news item, which interrupts a radio or television programme ▶ **newsletter** n bulletin issued periodically to members of a group ▶ **newspaper** n weekly or daily publication containing news ▶ **newsprint** n inexpensive paper used for newspapers ▶ **newsreader, newscaster** n person who reads the news on the television or radio ▶ **newsreel** n short film giving news ▶ **newsroom** n room where news is received and prepared for publication or broadcasting ▶ **newsworthy** adj sufficiently interesting to be reported as news

**newt** n small amphibious creature with a long slender body and tail

**newton** n unit of force

**next** adj, adv immediately following; nearest ▶ **next-of-kin** n closest relative

**nexus** n, pl **nexus** connection or link

**NHS** (in Britain) National Health Service

**nib** n writing point of a pen

**nibble** v take little bites (of) ▷ n little bite

**nibs** n **his, her nibs** (slang) mock title of respect

**nice** adj pleasant; kind; good or satisfactory; subtle e.g. a nice distinction ▶ **nicely** adv ▶ **niceness** n

**nicety** n, pl **-ties** subtle point; refinement or delicacy

**niche** [**neesh**] n hollow area in a wall; suitable position for a particular person

**nick** v make a small cut in; (chiefly Brit slang) steal; (chiefly Brit slang) arrest ▷ n small cut; (slang) prison or police station **in good nick** (informal) in good condition **in the nick of time** just in time

**nickel** n (Chem) silvery-white metal often used in alloys; US coin worth five cents

**nickelodeon** n (US) early type of jukebox

**nickname** n familiar name given to a person or place ▷ v call by a nickname

**nicotine** n poisonous substance found in tobacco

**niece** n daughter of one's sister or brother

**nifty** adj **-tier, -tiest** (informal) neat or smart

**niggardly** adj stingy ▶ **niggard** n stingy person

**nigger** n (offens) Black person

**niggle** v worry slightly; continually find fault (with) ▷ n small worry or doubt

**nigh** adv, prep (lit) near

**night** n time of darkness between sunset and sunrise ▶ **nightly** adj, adv (happening) each night ▶ **nightcap** n drink taken just before bedtime; soft cap formerly worn in bed ▶ **nightclub** n establishment for dancing, music, etc., open late at night

▶ **nightdress** n woman's loose dress worn in bed ▶ **nightfall** n approach of darkness ▶ **nightie** n (informal) nightdress ▶ **nightingale** n small bird with a musical song usu. heard at night ▶ **nightjar** n nocturnal bird with a harsh cry ▶ **nightlife** n entertainment and social activities available at night in a town or city ▶ **nightmare** n very bad dream; very unpleasant experience ▶ **night school** place where adults can attend educational courses in the evenings ▶ **nightshade** n plant with bell-shaped flowers which are often poisonous ▶ **nightshirt** n long loose shirt worn in bed ▶ **night-time** n time from sunset to sunrise

**nihilism** [**nye**-ill-liz-zum] n rejection of all established authority and institutions ▶ **nihilist** n ▶ **nihilistic** adj

**nil** n nothing, zero

**nimble** adj agile and quick; mentally alert or acute ▶ **nimbly** adv

**nimbus** n, pl **-bi** or **-buses** dark grey rain cloud

**nincompoop** n (informal) stupid person

**nine** adj, n one more than eight ▶ **ninth** adj, n (of) number nine in a series ▶ **ninepins** n game of skittles

**nineteen** adj, n ten and nine ▶ **nineteenth** adj, n

**ninety** adj, n ten times nine ▶ **ninetieth** adj, n

**niobium** n (Chem) white superconductive metallic element

**nip¹** v **nipping, nipped** (informal) hurry; pinch or squeeze; bite lightly ▷ n pinch or light bite; sharp coldness ▶ **nipper** n (Brit, Aust & NZ informal) small child ▶ **nippy** adj frosty or chilly; (informal) quick or nimble

**nip²** n small alcoholic drink

**nipple** n projection in the centre of a breast

**niqab** n veil worn by Muslim women

**nirvana** [near-**vah**-na] n (Buddhism, Hinduism) absolute spiritual enlightenment and bliss

**nit** n egg or larva of a louse; (informal) short for **nitwit** ▶ **nit-picking** adj (informal) overconcerned with insignificant detail, esp. to find fault ▶ **nitwit** n (informal) stupid person

**nitrogen** [**nite**-roj-jen] n (Chem) colourless odourless gas that forms four fifths of the air ▶ **nitric, nitrous, nitrogenous** adj of or containing nitrogen ▶ **nitrate** n compound of nitric acid, used as a fertilizer ▶ **nitroglycerine, nitroglycerin** n explosive liquid

**nitty-gritty** n (informal) basic facts

**no** interj expresses denial, disagreement, or refusal ▷ adj not any, not a ▷ adv not at all ▷ n, pl **noes** or **nos** answer or vote of 'no'; person who answers or votes 'no' ▶ **no-go area** district barricaded off so that the police or army can enter only by force ▶ **no-man's-land** n land between boundaries, esp. contested land between two opposing forces ▶ **no-one, no one** pron nobody

**no.** number

**nob** n (chiefly Brit slang) person of wealth or social distinction

**nobble** v (Brit slang) attract the attention of (someone) in order to talk to him or her; bribe or threaten

**nobelium** n (Chem) artificially-produced radioactive element

**Nobel Prize** n prize awarded annually for outstanding achievement in various fields

**noble** adj showing or having high moral qualities; of the nobility; impressive and magnificent ▷ n member of the nobility ▶ **nobility** n quality of being noble; class of people holding titles and high social rank ▶ **nobly** adv ▶ **nobleman, noblewoman** n

**nobody** pron no person ▷ n, pl **-bodies** person of no importance

**no-brainer** n (slang) something that requires little or no mental effort

**nocturnal** adj of the night; active at night

**nocturne** n short dreamy piece of music

**nod** v **nodding, nodded** lower and raise (one's head) briefly in agreement or greeting; let one's head fall forward with sleep ▷ n act of nodding ▶ **nod off** v (informal) fall asleep

**noddle** n (chiefly Brit informal) the head

**node** n point on a plant stem from which leaves grow; point at which a curve crosses itself

**nodule** n small knot or lump; rounded mineral growth on the root of a plant

**Noel** n Christmas

**noggin** n (informal) head; small quantity of an alcoholic drink

**noise** n sound, usu. a loud or disturbing one ▶ **noisy** adj making a lot of noise; full of noise ▶ **noisily** adv ▶ **noiseless** adj

**noisome** adj (of smells) offensive; harmful or poisonous

**nomad** n member of a tribe with no fixed dwelling place, wanderer ▶ **nomadic** adj

**nom de plume** n, pl **noms de plume** pen name

**nomenclature** n system of names used in a particular subject

**nominal** adj in name only; very small in comparison with real worth ▶ **nominally** adv

**nominate** v suggest as a candidate; appoint to an office

or position ▸ **nomination** n
▸ **nominee** n candidate
▸ **nominative** n form of a noun
indicating the subject of a verb
**non-** prefix indicating negation
e.g. nonexistent; indicating refusal
or failure e.g. noncooperation;
indicating exclusion from a specified
class e.g. nonfiction; indicating lack
or absence e.g. nonevent
**nonagenarian** n person aged
between ninety and ninety-nine
**nonaggression** n policy of not
attacking other countries
**nonagon** n geometric figure with
nine sides
**nonalcoholic** adj containing no
alcohol
**nonaligned** adj (of a country) not
part of a major alliance or power bloc
**nonce** n **for the nonce** for the
present
**nonchalant** adj casually
unconcerned or indifferent
▸ **nonchalantly** adv
▸ **nonchalance** n
**noncombatant** n member of the
armed forces whose duties do not
include fighting
**noncommissioned officer** n (in
the armed forces) a subordinate
officer, risen from the ranks
**noncommittal** adj not
committing oneself to any
particular opinion
**non compos mentis** (Latin) adj of
unsound mind
**nonconductor** n substance
that is a poor conductor of heat,
electricity, or sound
**nonconformist** n person who
does not conform to generally
accepted patterns of behaviour
or thought; (**N-**) member of a
Protestant group separated
from the Church of England
▹ adj (of behaviour or ideas) not

conforming to accepted patterns
▸ **nonconformity** n
**noncontributory** adj (Brit)
denoting a pension scheme for
employees, the premiums of which
are paid entirely by the employer
**nondescript** adj lacking
outstanding features
**none** pron not any; no-one
▸ **nonetheless** adv despite that,
however
**nonentity** [non-**enn**-tit-tee] n, pl
**-ties** insignificant person or thing
**nonevent** n disappointing or
insignificant occurrence
**nonflammable** adj not easily
set on fire
**nonintervention** n refusal to
intervene in the affairs of others
**nonpareil** [non-par-**rail**] n person
or thing that is unsurpassed
**nonpayment** n failure to pay
money owed
**nonplussed** adj perplexed
**nonsense** n something that
has or makes no sense; absurd
language; foolish behaviour
▸ **nonsensical** adj
**non sequitur** [**sek**-wit-tur] n
statement with little or no relation
to what preceded it
**nonstandard** adj denoting
language that is not regarded as
correct by educated native speakers
**nonstarter** n person or idea that
has little chance of success
**nonstick** adj coated with a
substance that food will not stick
to when cooked
**nonstop** adj, adv without a stop
**nontoxic** adj not poisonous
**noob, noob** n (slang chiefly
Computing) same as **newbie**
**noodles** pl n long thin strips of pasta
**nook** n sheltered place
**noon** n twelve o'clock; midday
▸ **noonday** adj happening at noon

**n**

**noose** n loop in the end of a rope, tied with a slipknot

**nor** conj and not

**Nordic** adj of Scandinavia or its typically tall blond and blue-eyed people

**norm** n standard that is regarded as normal

**normal** adj usual, regular, or typical; free from mental or physical disorder ▶ **normally** adv ▶ **normality** n ▶ **normalize** v

**Norse** n, adj (language) of ancient and medieval Norway

**north** n direction towards the North Pole, opposite south; area lying in or towards the north ▷ adj to or in the north; (of a wind) from the north ▷ adv in, to, or towards the north ▶ **northerly** adj ▶ **northern** adj ▶ **northerner** n person from the north of a country or area ▶ **northward** adj, adv ▶ **northwards** adv ▶ **North Pole** northernmost point on the earth's axis

**nos.** numbers

**nose** n organ of smell, used also in breathing; front part of a vehicle ▷ v move forward slowly and carefully; pry or snoop ▶ **nose dive** sudden drop ▶ **nosegay** n small bunch of flowers ▶ **nosey, nosy** adj (informal) prying or inquisitive ▶ **nosiness** n

**nosh** (Brit, Aust & NZ slang) n food ▷ v eat

**nostalgia** n sentimental longing for the past ▶ **nostalgic** adj

**nostril** n one of the two openings at the end of the nose

**nostrum** n quack medicine; favourite remedy

**not** adv expressing negation, refusal, or denial

**notable** adj worthy of being noted, remarkable ▷ n person of distinction ▶ **notably** adv ▶ **notability** n

**notary** n, pl -**ries** person authorized to witness the signing of legal documents

**notation** n representation of numbers or quantities in a system by a series of symbols; set of such symbols

**notch** n V-shaped cut; (informal) step or level ▷ v make a notch in; (foll by up) score or achieve

**note** n short letter; brief comment or record; banknote; (symbol for) a musical sound; hint or mood ▷ v notice, pay attention to; record in writing; remark upon ▶ **noted** adj well-known ▶ **notebook** n book for writing in ▶ **noteworthy** adj worth noting, remarkable

**nothing** pron not anything; matter of no importance; figure o ▷ adv not at all ▶ **nothingness** n nonexistence; insignificance

> **USAGE NOTE**
> Nothing is usually followed by a singular verb but, if it comes before a plural noun, this can sound odd: Nothing but books was/were on the shelf. A solution is to rephrase the sentence: Only books were...

**notice** n observation or attention; sign giving warning or an announcement; advance notification of intention to end a contract of employment ▷ v observe, become aware of; point out or remark upon ▶ **noticeable** adj easily seen or detected, appreciable

**notify** v -**fying, -fied** inform ▶ **notification** n ▶ **notifiable** adj having to be reported to the authorities

**notion** n idea or opinion; whim ▶ **notional** adj speculative, imaginary, or unreal

**notorious** adj well known for something bad ▸ **notoriously** adv ▸ **notoriety** n

**notwithstanding** prep in spite of

**nougat** n chewy sweet containing nuts and fruit

**nought** n figure 0; nothing ▸ **noughties** pl n (informal) decade from 2000 to 2009

**noun** n word that refers to a person, place, or thing

**nourish** v feed; encourage or foster (an idea or feeling) ▸ **nourishment** n ▸ **nourishing** adj providing the food necessary for life and growth

**nouvelle cuisine** [noo-vell kwee-**zeen**] n style of preparing and presenting food with light sauces and unusual combinations of flavours

**Nov** November

**nova** n, pl -**vae** or -**vas** star that suddenly becomes brighter and then gradually decreases to its original brightness

**novel**¹ n long fictitious story in book form ▸ **novelist** n writer of novels ▸ **novella** n, pl -**las** or -**lae** short novel

**novel**² adj fresh, new, or original ▸ **novelty** n newness; something new or unusual

**November** n eleventh month of the year

**novena** [no-**vee**-na] n, pl -**nas** (RC Church) set of prayers or services on nine consecutive days

**novice** n beginner; person who has entered a religious order but has not yet taken vows

**now** adv at or for the present time; immediately ▷ conj seeing that, since **just now** very recently **now and again, now and then** occasionally ▸ **nowadays** adv in these times

**nowhere** adv not anywhere

**noxious** adj poisonous or harmful; extremely unpleasant

**nozzle** n projecting spout through which fluid is discharged

**NSPCC** (in Britain) National Society for the Prevention of Cruelty to Children

**NSW** New South Wales

**NT** (in Britain) National Trust; New Testament; Northern Territory

**nuance** [**new**-ahnss] n subtle difference in colour, meaning, or tone

**nub** n point or gist (of a story etc.)

**nubile** [**new**-bile] adj (of a young woman) sexually attractive; (of a young woman) old enough to get married

**nuclear** adj of nuclear weapons or energy; of a nucleus, esp. the nucleus of an atom ▸ **nuclear energy** energy released as a result of nuclear fission or fusion ▸ **nuclear fission** splitting of an atomic nucleus ▸ **nuclear fusion** combination of two nuclei to form a heavier nucleus with the release of energy ▸ **nuclear power** power produced by a nuclear reactor ▸ **nuclear reaction** change in structure and energy content of an atomic nucleus by interaction with another nucleus or particle ▸ **nuclear reactor** device in which a nuclear reaction is maintained and controlled to produce nuclear energy ▸ **nuclear weapon** weapon whose force is due to uncontrolled nuclear fusion or fission ▸ **nuclear winter** theoretical period of low temperatures and little light after a nuclear war

**nucleic acid** n complex compound, such as DNA or RNA, found in all living cells

**nucleus** n, pl -**clei** centre, esp. of an atom or cell; central thing around which others are grouped

**n**

**nude** *adj* naked ▷ *n* naked figure in painting, sculpture, or photography ▶ **nudity** *n* ▶ **nudism** *n* practice of not wearing clothes ▶ **nudist** *n*

**nudge** *v* push gently, esp. with the elbow ▷ *n* gentle push or touch

**nugatory** [**new**-gat-tree] *adj* of little value; not valid

**nugget** *n* small lump of gold in its natural state; something small but valuable ▷ *v* (*NZ & S Afr*) polish footwear

**nuisance** *n* something or someone that causes annoyance or bother

**nuke** (*slang*) *v* attack with nuclear weapons ▷ *n* nuclear weapon

**null** *adj* **null and void** not legally valid ▶ **nullity** *n* ▶ **nullify** *v* make ineffective; cancel

**nulla-nulla** *n* wooden club used by Australian Aborigines

**numb** *adj* without feeling, as through cold, shock, or fear ▷ *v* make numb ▶ **numbly** *adv* ▶ **numbness** *n* ▶ **numbskull** *n* stupid person

**numbat** *n* small Australian marsupial with a long snout and tongue

**number** *n* sum or quantity; word or symbol used to express a sum or quantity, numeral; numeral or string of numerals used to identify a person or thing; one of a series, such as a copy of a magazine; song or piece of music; group of people; (*Grammar*) classification of words depending on how many persons or things are referred to ▷ *v* count; give a number to; amount to; include in a group ▶ **numberless** *adj* too many to be counted ▶ **number crunching** (*Computing*) large-scale processing of numerical data ▶ **number one** *n* (*informal*) oneself; bestselling pop record in any one week ▷ *adj*

first in importance or quality ▶ **numberplate** *n* plate on a car showing the registration number

**numeral** *n* word or symbol used to express a sum or quantity

**numerate** *adj* able to do basic arithmetic ▶ **numeracy** *n*

**numeration** *n* act or process of numbering or counting

**numerator** *n* (*Maths*) number above the line in a fraction

**numerical** *adj* measured or expressed in numbers ▶ **numerically** *adv*

**numerous** *adj* existing or happening in large numbers

**numismatist** *n* coin collector

**numskull** *n* same as **numbskull**

**nun** *n* female member of a religious order ▶ **nunnery** *n* convent

**nuncio** *n* (*RC Church*) Pope's ambassador

**nuptial** *adj* relating to marriage ▶ **nuptials** *pl n* wedding

**nurse** *n* person employed to look after sick people, usu. in a hospital; woman employed to look after children ▷ *v* look after (a sick person); breast-feed (a baby); try to cure (an ailment); harbour or foster (a feeling) ▶ **nursing home** private hospital or home for old people ▶ **nursing officer** (in Britain) administrative head of the nursing staff of a hospital

**nursery** *n*, *pl* **-ries** room where children sleep or play; place where children are taken care of while their parents are at work; place where plants are grown for sale ▶ **nurseryman** *n* person who raises plants for sale ▶ **nursery school** school for children from 3 to 5 years old ▶ **nursery slopes** gentle ski slopes for beginners

**nurture** *n* act or process of promoting the development of a child or young plant ▷ *v* promote or encourage the development of

**nut** *n* fruit consisting of a hard shell and a kernel; small piece of metal that screws onto a bolt; (also **nutcase**) (*slang*) insane or eccentric person; (*slang*) head ▶ **nutter** *n* (*Brit slang*) insane person ▶ **nutty** *adj* containing or resembling nuts; (*slang*) insane or eccentric ▶ **nutcracker** *n* device for cracking the shells of nuts ▶ **nuthatch** *n* small songbird ▶ **nutmeg** *n* spice made from the seed of a tropical tree

**nutria** *n* fur of the coypu

**nutrient** *n* substance that provides nourishment

**nutriment** *n* food or nourishment required by all living things to grow and stay healthy

**nutrition** *n* process of taking in and absorbing nutrients; process of being nourished ▶ **nutritional** *adj* ▶ **nutritious, nutritive** *adj* nourishing

**nuzzle** *v* push or rub gently with the nose or snout

**NW** northwest(ern)

**nylon** *n* synthetic material used for clothing etc. ▷ *pl* stockings made of nylon

**nymph** *n* mythical spirit of nature, represented as a beautiful young woman; larva of certain insects, resembling the adult form

**nymphet** *n* sexually precocious young girl

**nymphomaniac** *n* woman with an abnormally intense sexual desire

**NZ** New Zealand

**NZE** New Zealand English

**NZRFU** New Zealand Rugby Football Union

**NZSE40 Index** New Zealand Share Price 40 Index

**O** (*chem*) oxygen; old; same as **nought** sense 1

**oaf** *n* stupid or clumsy person ▶ **oafish** *adj*

**oak** *n* deciduous forest tree; its wood, used for furniture ▶ **oaken** *adj* ▶ **oak apple** brownish lump found on oak trees

**oakum** *n* fibre obtained by unravelling old rope

**OAP** (in Britain) old-age pensioner

**oar** *n* pole with a broad blade, used for rowing a boat

**oasis** *n, pl* **-ses** fertile area in a desert

**oast** *n* (*chiefly Brit*) oven for drying hops

**oat** *n* hard cereal grown as food ▷ *pl* grain of this cereal **sow one's wild oats** have many sexual relationships when young ▶ **oatmeal** *adj* pale brownish-cream

**oath** *n* solemn promise, esp. to be truthful in court; swearword

**obbligato** [ob-lig-**gah**-toe] *n, pl* **-tos** (*Music*) essential part or accompaniment

**obdurate** *adj* hardhearted or stubborn ▶ **obduracy** *n*

**OBE** (in Britain) Officer of the Order of the British Empire

**obedient** *adj* obeying or willing to obey ▶ **obedience** *n* ▶ **obediently** *adv*

**obeisance** [oh-**bay**-sanss] *n* attitude of respect; bow or curtsy

**obelisk** [**ob**-bill-isk] *n* four-sided stone column tapering to a pyramid at the top

O

**obese** [oh-**beess**] *adj* very fat
▶ **obesity** *n*

**obey** *v* carry out instructions or
orders

**obfuscate** *v* make (something)
confusing

**obituary** *n, pl* **-aries** announcement
of someone's death, esp. in a
newspaper ▶ **obituarist** *n*

**object**¹ *n* physical thing; focus
of thoughts or action; aim or
purpose; (Grammar) word that
a verb or preposition affects **no
object** not a hindrance

**object**² *v* express disapproval
▶ **objection** *n* ▶ **objectionable** *adj*
unpleasant ▶ **objector** *n*

**objective** *n* aim or purpose ▷ *adj*
not biased; existing in the real
world outside the human mind
▶ **objectively** *adv* ▶ **objectivity** *n*

**objet d'art** [ob-zhay **dahr**] *n,
pl* **objets d'art** small object of
artistic value

**oblation** *n* religious offering

**oblige** *v* compel (someone) morally
or by law to do something; do a
favour for (someone) ▶ **obliging**
*adj* ready to help other people
▶ **obligingly** *adv* ▶ **obligated**
*adj* obliged to do something
▶ **obligation** *n* duty ▶ **obligatory**
*adj* required by a rule or law

**oblique** [oh-**bleak**] *adj* slanting;
indirect ▷ *n* the symbol (/)
▶ **obliquely** *adv* ▶ **oblique angle**
angle that is not a right angle

**obliterate** *v* wipe out, destroy
▶ **obliteration** *n*

**oblivious** *adj* unaware ▶ **oblivion**
*n* state of being forgotten; state of
being unaware or unconscious

**oblong** *adj* having two long sides,
two short sides, and four right
angles ▷ *n* oblong figure

**obloquy** [ob-**lock-wee**] *n, pl* **-quies**
verbal abuse; discredit

**obnoxious** *adj* offensive

**oboe** *n* double-reeded woodwind
instrument ▶ **oboist** *n*

**obscene** *adj* portraying sex
offensively; disgusting ▶ **obscenity** *n*

**obscure** *adj* not well known; hard
to understand; indistinct ▷ *v* make
(something) obscure ▶ **obscurity** *n*

**obsequies** [**ob-sick-weez**] *pl n*
funeral rites

**obsequious** [ob-**seek**-wee-uss]
*adj* overattentive in order to gain
favour ▶ **obsequiousness** *n*

**observe** *v* see or notice; watch
(someone or something) carefully;
remark; act according to (a law or
custom) ▶ **observation** *n* action
or habit of observing; remark
▶ **observable** *adj* ▶ **observance**
*n* observing of a custom
▶ **observant** *adj* quick to notice
things ▶ **observatory** *n* building
equipped for studying the weather
and the stars

**observer** *n* person who observes,
esp. one who watches someone or
something carefully

**obsess** *v* preoccupy (someone)
compulsively ▶ **obsessed** *adj*
▶ **obsessive** *adj* ▶ **obsession** *n*

> **SPELLING TIP**
> Some people get carried away
> with doubling ss and write
> *obssession* instead of **obsession**

**obsidian** *n* dark glassy volcanic rock

**obsolete** *adj* no longer in use
▶ **obsolescent** *adj* becoming
obsolete ▶ **obsolescence** *n*

**obstacle** *n* something that makes
progress difficult

**obstetrics** *n* branch of medicine
concerned with pregnancy
and childbirth ▶ **obstetric** *adj*
▶ **obstetrician** *n*

**obstinate** *adj* stubborn;
difficult to remove or change
▶ **obstinately** *adv* ▶ **obstinacy** *n*

**obstreperous** adj unruly, noisy

**obstruct** v block with an obstacle
▶ **obstruction** n ▶ **obstructive** adj

**obtain** v acquire intentionally; be customary ▶ **obtainable** adj

**obtrude** v push oneself or one's ideas on others ▶ **obtrusive** adj unpleasantly noticeable
▶ **obtrusively** adv

**obtuse** adj mentally slow; (Maths) (of an angle) between 90° and 180°; not pointed ▶ **obtuseness** n

**obverse** n opposite way of looking at an idea; main side of a coin or medal

**obviate** v make unnecessary

**obvious** adj easy to see or understand, evident
▶ **obviously** adv

**ocarina** n small oval wind instrument

**occasion** n time at which a particular thing happens; reason e.g. *no occasion for complaint*; special event ▷ v cause ▶ **occasional** adj happening sometimes
▶ **occasionally** adv

> **SPELLING TIP**
> *Occassion*, *ocasion*, and *ocassion* are common misspellings of **occasion**. The correct version has two cs and one s

**Occident** n (lit) the West
▶ **Occidental** adj

**occiput** [**ox**-sip-put] n back of the head

**occlude** v obstruct; close off
▶ **occlusion** n ▶ **occluded front** (Meteorol) front formed when a cold front overtakes a warm front and warm air rises

**occult** adj relating to the supernatural **the occult** knowledge or study of the supernatural

**occupant** n person occupying a specified place ▶ **occupancy** n (length of) a person's stay in a specified place

**occupation** n profession; activity that occupies one's time; control of a country by a foreign military power; being occupied ▶ **occupational** adj ▶ **occupational therapy** purposeful activities, designed to aid recovery from illness etc.

**occupy** v **-pying, -pied** live or work in (a building); take up the attention of (someone); take up (space or time); take possession of (a place) by force ▶ **occupier** n

**occur** v **-curring, -curred** happen; exist **occur to** come to the mind of ▶ **occurrence** n something that occurs; fact of occurring

> **SPELLING TIP**
> Note that **occurrence** has a double c and a double r, and in the last syllable an e rather than an a

**ocean** n vast area of sea between continents ▶ **oceanic** adj
▶ **oceanography** n scientific study of the oceans ▶ **ocean-going** adj able to sail on the open sea

**ocelot** [**oss**-ill-lot] n American wild cat with a spotted coat

**oche** [**ok**-kee] n (Darts) mark on the floor behind which a player must stand

**ochre** [**oak**-er] adj, n brownish-yellow (earth)

**o'clock** adv used after a number to specify an hour

**Oct** October

**octagon** n geometric figure with eight sides ▶ **octagonal** adj

**octahedron** [ok-ta-**heed**-ron] n, pl **-drons** or **-dra** three-dimensional geometric figure with eight faces

**octane** n hydrocarbon found in petrol ▶ **octane rating** measure of petrol quality

**octave** n (Music) (interval between the first and) eighth note of a scale

**octet** n group of eight performers; music for such a group

**October** n tenth month of the year

**octogenarian** n person aged between eighty and eighty-nine

**octopus** n, pl-**puses** sea creature with a soft body and eight tentacles

**ocular** adj relating to the eyes or sight

**OD** (informal) n overdose ▷ v **OD'ing, OD'd** take an overdose

**odd** adj unusual; occasional; not divisible by two; not part of a set ▶ **odds** pl n (ratio showing) the probability of something happening **at odds** in conflict ▶ **odds and ends** small miscellaneous items ▶ **oddity** n odd person or thing ▶ **oddness** n quality of being odd ▶ **oddments** pl n things left over

**ode** n lyric poem, usu. addressed to a particular subject

**odium** [oh-dee-um] n widespread dislike ▶ **odious** adj offensive

**odour** n particular smell ▶ **odorous** adj ▶ **odourless** adj

**odyssey** [odd-iss-ee] n long eventful journey

**OE** (NZ informal) overseas experience e.g. he's away on his OE.

**OECD** Organization for Economic Cooperation and Development

**oedema** [id-deem-a] n, pl-**mata** (Med) abnormal swelling

**oesophagus** [ee-soff-a-guss] n, pl-**gi** passage between the mouth and stomach

**oestrogen** [ee-stra-jen] n female hormone that controls the reproductive cycle

**of** prep belonging to; consisting of; connected with; characteristic of

**off** prep away from ▷ adv away ▷ adj not operating; cancelled; (of food) gone bad ▷ n (Cricket) side of

the field to which the batsman's feet point ▶ **off colour** slightly ill ▶ **offline** adj not connected to the internet ▶ **offline** adj not connected to the internet ▶ **off-message** adj (esp. of a politician) not following the official Party line ▶ **off-road** adj (of a motor vehicle) designed for use away from public roads

> **USAGE NOTE**
> Avoid using of after off: He got off the bus (not off of). The use of off to mean from is very informal: They bought milk from (rather than off) a farmer

**offal** n edible organs of an animal, such as liver or kidneys ▶ **offal pit, offal hole** (NZ) place on a farm for the disposal of animal offal

**offcut** n piece remaining after the required parts have been cut out

**offend** v hurt the feelings of, insult; commit a crime ▶ **offence** n (cause of) hurt feelings or annoyance; illegal act ▶ **offensive** adj disagreeable; insulting; aggressive ▷ n position or action of attack

**offender** n person who commits a crime

**offer** v present (something) for acceptance or rejection; provide; be willing (to do something); propose as payment ▷ n instance of offering something ▶ **offering** n thing offered ▶ **offertory** n (Christianity) offering of the bread and wine for Communion

**offhand** adj casual, curt ▷ adv without preparation

**office** n room or building where people work at desks; department of a commercial organization; formal position of responsibility; place where tickets or information can be obtained

**officer** n person in authority in the armed services; member of the police force; person with special responsibility in an organization

**official** *adj* of a position of authority; approved or arranged by someone in authority ▷ *n* person who holds a position of authority ▶ **officially** *adv* ▶ **officialdom** *n* officials collectively ▶ **Official Receiver** (*Brit*) person who deals with the affairs of a bankrupt company

**officiate** *v* act in an official role

**officious** *adj* interfering unnecessarily

**offing** *n* area of the sea visible from the shore **in the offing** (*Brit, Aust & NZ*) likely to happen soon

**off-licence** *n* (*Brit*) shop licensed to sell alcohol for drinking elsewhere

**offset** *v* cancel out, compensate for

**offshoot** *n* something developed from something else

**offside** *adj, adv* (*Sport*) (positioned) illegally ahead of the ball

**offspring** *n, pl* **offspring** child

**often** *adv* frequently, much of the time ▶ **oft** *adv* (*poetic*) often

**ogle** *v* stare at (someone) lustfully

**ogre** *n* giant that eats human flesh; monstrous or cruel person

**oh** *interj* exclamation of surprise, pain, etc.

**ohm** *n* unit of electrical resistance

**OHMS** (*Brit*) On Her *or* His Majesty's Service

**oil** *n* viscous liquid, insoluble in water and usu. flammable; same as **petroleum**; petroleum derivative, used as a fuel or lubricant ▷ *pl* oil-based paints used in art ▷ *v* lubricate (a machine) with oil ▶ **oily** *adj* ▶ **oilfield** *n* area containing oil reserves ▶ **oil rig** platform constructed for drilling oil wells ▶ **oilskin** *n* (garment made from) waterproof material

**ointment** *n* greasy substance used for healing skin or as a cosmetic

**O.K., okay** (*informal*) *interj* expression of approval ▷ *v* approve (something) ▷ *n* approval

**okapi** [ok-**kah**-pee] *n* African animal related to the giraffe but with a shorter neck

**okra** *n* tropical plant with edible green pods

**old** *adj* having lived or existed for a long time; of a specified age e.g. *two years old*; former ▶ **olden** *adj* old e.g. *in the olden days* ▶ **oldie** *n* (*informal*) old but popular song or film ▶ **old-fashioned** *adj* no longer commonly used or valued ▶ **old guard** group of people in an organization who have traditional values ▶ **old hat** boring because so familiar ▶ **old maid** elderly unmarried woman ▶ **old master** European painter or painting from the period 1500–1800 ▶ **Old Nick** (*Brit, Aust & NZ informal*) the Devil ▶ **old school tie** system of mutual help between former pupils of public schools ▶ **Old Testament** part of the Bible recording Hebrew history ▶ **Old World** world as it was known before the discovery of the Americas

**oleaginous** [ol-lee-**aj**-in-uss] *adj* oily, producing oil

**oleander** [ol-lee-**ann**-der] *n* Mediterranean flowering evergreen shrub

**olfactory** *adj* relating to the sense of smell

**oligarchy** [**ol**-lee-gark-ee] *n, pl* **-chies** government by a small group of people; state governed this way ▶ **oligarchic, oligarchical** *adj*

**olive** *n* small green or black fruit used as food or pressed for its oil; tree on which this fruit grows ▷ *adj* greyish-green ▶ **olive branch** peace offering

**o**

**Olympian** *adj* of Mount Olympus or the classical Greek gods; majestic or godlike

**Olympic Games** *pl n* four-yearly international sports competition

**ombudsman** *n* official who investigates complaints against government organizations

**omelette** *n* dish of eggs beaten and fried

> **SPELLING TIP**
> You don't hear it in the pronunciation, but there is an *e* after the *m* in **omelette**

**omen** *n* happening or object thought to foretell success or misfortune ▶ **ominous** *adj* worrying, seeming to foretell misfortune

**omit** *v* **omitting, omitted** leave out; neglect (to do something) ▶ **omission** *n*

**omnibus** *n* several books or TV or radio programmes made into one; (*old-fashioned*) bus

**omnipotent** *adj* having unlimited power ▶ **omnipotence** *n*

**omnipresent** *adj* present everywhere ▶ **omnipresence** *n*

**omniscient** [om-**niss**-ee-ent] *adj* knowing everything ▶ **omniscience** *n*

**omnivorous** [om-**niv**-vor-uss] *adj* eating food obtained from both animals and plants ▶ **omnivore** *n* omnivorous animal

**on** *prep* indicating position above, attachment, closeness, etc. e.g. *lying on the ground; a puppet on a string; on the coast* ▷ *adv* in operation; continuing; forwards ▷ *adj* operating; taking place ▷ *n* (*Cricket*) side of the field on which the batsman stands ▶ **on line, online** *adj* relating to the internet e.g. *online shopping* ▷ *adv* while connected to the internet

▶ **on-message** *adj* (esp. of a politician) following the official Party line

**once** *adv* on one occasion; formerly ▷ *conj* as soon as ▶ **at once** immediately; simultaneously ▶ **once-over** *n* (*informal*) quick examination

**oncogene** [on-koh-jean] *n* gene that can cause cancer when abnormally activated

**oncoming** *adj* approaching from the front

**one** *adj* single, lone ▷ *n* number or figure 1; single unit ▷ *pron* any person ▶ **oneness** *n* unity ▶ **oneself** *pron* reflexive form of **one** ▶ **one-armed bandit** fruit machine operated by a lever on one side ▶ **one-liner** *n* witty remark ▶ **one-night stand** sexual encounter lasting one night ▶ **one-sided** *adj* considering only one point of view ▶ **one-way** *adj* allowing movement in one direction only

> **USAGE NOTE**
> Avoid overuse of the pronoun *one* as a substitute for *I*. Many listeners find it affected

**onerous** [**own**-er-uss] *adj* (of a task) difficult to carry out

**ongoing** *adj* in progress, continuing

**onion** *n* strongly flavoured edible bulb

**onlooker** *n* person who watches without taking part

**only** *adj* alone of its kind ▷ *adv* exclusively; merely; no more than ▷ *conj* but

> **USAGE NOTE**
> In formal use *only* is placed directly before the words it modifies: *The club opens only on Thursdays* but in everyday use this becomes: *The club only opens on Thursdays*

**onomatopoeia** [on-a-mat-a-**pee**-a] n use of a word which imitates the sound it represents, such as *hiss* ▶ **onomatopoeic** adj

**onset** n beginning

**onslaught** n violent attack

**onto** prep to a position on; aware of e.g. *she's onto us*

**ontology** n branch of philosophy concerned with existence ▶ **ontological** adj

**onus** [**own**-uss] n, pl **onuses** responsibility or burden

**onward** adj directed or moving forward ▷ adv (also **onwards**) ahead, forward

**onyx** n type of quartz with coloured layers

**oodles** pl n (informal) great quantities

**ooze¹** v flow slowly ▷ n sluggish flow ▶ **oozy** adj

**ooze²** n soft mud at the bottom of a lake or river

**opal** n iridescent precious stone ▶ **opalescent** adj iridescent like an opal

**opaque** adj not able to be seen through; not transparent ▶ **opacity** n

**op. cit.** [**op sit**] in the work cited

**OPEC** Organization of Petroleum-Exporting Countries

**open** adj not closed; not covered; unfolded; ready for business; free from obstruction, accessible; frank ▷ v (cause to) become open; begin ▷ n (Sport) competition which all may enter **in the open** outdoors ▶ **openly** adv without concealment ▶ **opening** n opportunity; hole ▷ adj first ▶ **opencast mining** mining at the surface and not underground ▶ **open day** day on which a school or college is open to the public ▶ **open-handed** adj generous

▶ **open-hearted** adj generous; frank ▶ **open-heart surgery** surgery on the heart during which the blood circulation is maintained by machine ▶ **open house** hospitality to visitors at any time ▶ **open letter** letter to an individual that the writer makes public in a newspaper or magazine ▶ **open-minded** adj receptive to new ideas ▶ **open-plan** adj (of a house or office) having few interior walls ▶ **open prison** prison with minimal security ▶ **open source** (Computing) intellectual property, esp computer source code, that is made freely available to the public by its creators ▶ **open-standard** adj (of computer programs, codes, etc) freely available to all users ▶ **open verdict** coroner's verdict not stating the cause of death

**opera¹** n drama in which the text is sung to an orchestral accompaniment ▶ **operatic** adj ▶ **operetta** n light-hearted comic opera

**opera²** n a plural of **opus**

**operate** v (cause to) work; direct; perform an operation ▶ **operator** n ▶ **operation** n method or procedure of working; medical procedure in which the body is worked on to repair a damaged part ▶ **operational** adj in working order; relating to an operation ▶ **operative** adj working ▷ n worker with a special skill

**ophthalmic** adj relating to the eye ▶ **ophthalmology** n study of the eye and its diseases ▶ **ophthalmologist** n

**opiate** n narcotic drug containing opium

**opinion** n personal belief or judgment ▶ **opinionated** adj having strong opinions ▶ **opine** v

**o**

(*old-fashioned*) express an opinion ▸ **opinion poll** see **poll**

**opium** *n* addictive narcotic drug made from poppy seeds

**opossum** *n* small marsupial of America or Australasia

**opponent** *n* person one is working against in a contest, battle, or argument

**opportunity** *n, pl* **-ties** favourable time or condition; good chance ▸ **opportunity shop** (*Aust & NZ*) shop selling second-hand clothes, sometimes for charity (also **op-shop**) ▸ **opportune** *adj* happening at a suitable time ▸ **opportunist** *n, adj* (person) doing whatever is advantageous without regard for principles ▸ **opportunism** *n*

> **SPELLING TIP**
> Lots of people forget that **opportunity**, which is a very common word, has two ps

**oppose** *v* work against **be opposed to** disagree with or disapprove of ▸ **opposition** *n* obstruction or hostility; group opposing another; political party not in power

**opposite** *adj* situated on the other side; facing; completely different ▷ *n* person or thing that is opposite ▷ *prep* facing ▷ *adv* on the other side

**oppress** *v* control by cruelty or force; depress ▸ **oppression** *n* ▸ **oppressor** *n* ▸ **oppressive** *adj* tyrannical; (of weather) hot and humid ▸ **oppressively** *adv*

**opprobrium** [op-**probe**-ree-um] *n* state of being criticized severely for wrong one has done

**opt** *v* show a preference, choose ▸ **opt out** *v* choose not to be part (of)

**optic** *adj* relating to the eyes or sight ▸ **optics** *n* science of sight and light ▸ **optical** *adj* ▸ **optical character reader** device that electronically reads and stores text ▸ **optical fibre** fine glass-fibre tube used to transmit information

**optician** *n* (also **ophthalmic optician**) person qualified to prescribe glasses; (also **dispensing optician**) person who supplies and fits glasses

**optimism** *n* tendency to take the most hopeful view ▸ **optimist** *n* ▸ **optimistic** *adj* ▸ **optimistically** *adv*

**optimum** *n, pl* **-ma** *or* **-mums** best possible conditions ▷ *adj* most favourable ▸ **optimal** *adj* ▸ **optimize** *v* make the most of

**option** *n* choice; thing chosen; right to buy or sell something at a specified price within a given time ▸ **optional** *adj* possible but not compulsory

**optometrist** *n* person qualified to prescribe glasses ▸ **optometry** *n*

**opulent** [**op**-pew-lent] *adj* having or indicating wealth ▸ **opulence** *n*

**opus** *n, pl* **opuses** *or* **opera** artistic creation, esp. a musical work

**or** *conj* used to join alternatives e.g. *tea or coffee*

**oracle** *n* shrine of an ancient god; prophecy, often obscure, revealed at a shrine; person believed to make infallible predictions ▸ **oracular** *adj*

**oral** *adj* spoken; (of a drug) to be taken by mouth ▷ *n* spoken examination ▸ **orally** *adv*

**orange** *n* reddish-yellow citrus fruit ▷ *adj* reddish-yellow ▸ **orangeade** *n* (*Brit*) orange-flavoured, usu. fizzy drink ▸ **orangery** *n* greenhouse for growing orange trees

**orang-utan, orang-utang** *n* large reddish-brown ape with long arms

**orator** [**or**-rat-tor] *n* skilful public speaker ▸ **oration** *n* formal speech

**oratorio** [or-rat-**tor**-ee-oh] *n, pl*
**-rios** musical composition for choir
and orchestra, usu. with a religious
theme

**oratory¹** [**or**-rat-tree] *n* art of
making speeches ▶ **oratorical** *adj*

**oratory²** *n, pl* **-ries** small private
chapel

**orb** *n* ceremonial decorated sphere
with a cross on top, carried by a
monarch

**orbit** *n* curved path of a planet,
satellite, or spacecraft around
another body; sphere of influence
▷ *v* **orbiting, orbited** move in an
orbit around; put (a satellite or
spacecraft) into orbit ▶ **orbital** *adj*

**orca** *n* (*Zool*) same as **killer whale**

**orchard** *n* area where fruit trees
are grown

**orchestra** *n* large group of
musicians, esp. playing a variety
of instruments; (also **orchestra
pit**) area of a theatre in front of the
stage, reserved for the musicians
▶ **orchestral** *adj* ▶ **orchestrate**
*v* arrange (music) for orchestra;
organize (something) to produce a
particular result ▶ **orchestration** *n*

**orchid** *n* plant with flowers that
have unusual lip-shaped petals

**ordain** *v* make (someone) a
member of the clergy; order or
establish with authority

**ordeal** *n* painful or difficult
experience

**order** *n* instruction to be carried
out; methodical arrangement
or sequence; established social
system; condition of a law-abiding
society; request for goods to be
supplied; kind, sort; religious
society of monks or nuns ▷ *v*
give an instruction to; request
(something) to be supplied
**in order** so that it is possible
▶ **orderly** *adj* well-organized; well-

behaved ▷ *n, pl* **-lies** male hospital
attendant ▶ **orderliness** *n*

**ordinal number** *n* number
showing a position in a series e.g.
*first; second*

**ordinance** *n* official rule or order

**ordinary** *adj* usual or normal; dull
or commonplace ▶ **ordinarily** *adv*

**ordination** *n* act of making
someone a member of the clergy

**ordnance** *n* weapons and military
supplies ▶ **Ordnance Survey**
official organization making maps
of Britain

**ordure** *n* excrement

**ore** *n* (rock containing) a mineral
which yields metal

**oregano** [or-rig-**gah**-no] *n* sweet-
smelling herb used in cooking

**organ** *n* part of an animal or plant
that has a particular function,
such as the heart or lungs; musical
keyboard instrument in which
notes are produced by forcing air
through pipes; means of conveying
information, esp. a newspaper
▶ **organist** *n* organ player

**organdie** *n* fine cotton fabric

**organic** *adj* of or produced from
animals or plants; grown without
artificial fertilizers or pesticides;
(*Chem*) relating to compounds of
carbon; organized systematically
▶ **organically** *adv* ▶ **organism** *n*
any living animal or plant

**organize** *v* make arrangements
for; arrange systematically
▶ **organization** *n* group of
people working together; act of
organizing ▶ **organizational** *adj*
▶ **organizer** *n*

**orgasm** *n* most intense point of
sexual pleasure ▶ **orgasmic** *adj*

**orgy** *n, pl* **-gies** party involving
promiscuous sexual activity;
unrestrained indulgence e.g. *an
orgy of destruction* ▶ **orgiastic** *adj*

O

**oriel window** *n* upper window built out from a wall

**Orient** *n* **the Orient** (*lit*) East Asia ▸ **Oriental** *adj* ▸ **Orientalist** *n* specialist in the languages and history of the Far East

**orient, orientate** *v* position (oneself) according to one's surroundings; position (a map) in relation to the points of the compass ▸ **orientation** *n* ▸ **orienteering** *n* sport in which competitors hike over a course using a compass and map

**orifice** [or-rif-fiss] *n* opening or hole

**origami** [or-rig-**gah**-mee] *n* Japanese decorative art of paper folding

**origin** *n* point from which something develops; ancestry ▸ **original** *adj* first or earliest; new, not copied or based on something else; able to think up new ideas ▹ *n* first version, from which others are copied ▸ **original sin** human imperfection and mortality as a result of Adam's disobedience ▸ **originality** *n* ▸ **originally** *adv* ▸ **originate** *v* come or bring into existence ▸ **origination** *n* ▸ **originator** *n*

**oriole** *n* tropical or American songbird

**ormolu** *n* gold-coloured alloy used for decoration

**ornament** *n* decorative object ▹ *v* decorate ▸ **ornamental** *adj* ▸ **ornamentation** *n*

**ornate** *adj* highly decorated, elaborate

**ornithology** *n* study of birds ▸ **ornithological** *adj* ▸ **ornithologist** *n*

**orphan** *n* child whose parents are dead ▸ **orphanage** *n* children's home for orphans ▸ **orphaned** *adj* having no living parents

**orrery** *n, pl* **-ries** mechanical model of the solar system

**orris** *n* kind of iris; (also **orris root**) fragrant root used for perfume

**orthodontics** *n* branch of dentistry concerned with correcting irregular teeth ▸ **orthodontist** *n*

**orthodox** *adj* conforming to established views ▸ **orthodoxy** *n* ▸ **Orthodox Church** dominant Christian Church in Eastern Europe

**orthography** *n* correct spelling

**orthopaedics** *n* branch of medicine concerned with disorders of the bones or joints ▸ **orthopaedic** *adj*

**oryx** *n* large African antelope

**Oscar** *n* award in the form of a statuette given for achievements in films

**oscillate** [oss-ill-late] *v* swing back and forth ▸ **oscillation** *n* ▸ **oscillator** *n* ▸ **oscilloscope** [oss-**sill**-oh-scope] *n* instrument that shows the shape of a wave on a cathode-ray tube

**osier** [oh-zee-er] *n* willow tree

**osmium** *n* (*Chem*) heaviest known metallic element

**osmosis** *n* movement of a liquid through a membrane from a lower to a higher concentration; process of subtle influence ▸ **osmotic** *adj*

**osprey** *n* large fish-eating bird of prey

**ossify** *v* **-fying, -fied** (cause to) become bone, harden; become inflexible ▸ **ossification** *n*

**ostensible** *adj* apparent, seeming ▸ **ostensibly** *adv*

**ostentation** *n* pretentious display ▸ **ostentatious** *adj* ▸ **ostentatiously** *adv*

**osteopathy** *n* medical treatment involving manipulation of the joints ▸ **osteopath** *n*

**osteoporosis** n brittleness of the bones, caused by lack of calcium

**ostracize** v exclude (a person) from a group ▶ **ostracism** n

**ostrich** n large African bird that runs fast but cannot fly

**OT** Old Testament

**other** adj remaining in a group of which one or some have been specified; different from the ones specified or understood; additional ▶ n other person or thing ▶ **otherwise** conj or else, if not ▷ adv differently, in another way ▶ **otherworldly** adj concerned with spiritual rather than practical matters

**otiose** [oh-tee-oze] adj not useful e.g. otiose language

**otter** n small brown freshwater mammal that eats fish

**ottoman** n, pl -**mans** storage chest with a padded lid for use as a seat ▶ **Ottoman** n, adj (Hist) (member) of the former Turkish empire

**oubliette** [oo-blee-ett] n dungeon entered only by a trapdoor

**ouch** interj exclamation of sudden pain

**ought** v used to express obligation e.g. you ought to pay; used to express advisability e.g. you ought to diet; used to express probability e.g. you ought to know by then

> **USAGE NOTE**
> In standard English did and had are not used with ought: ought not to (not didn't/hadn't ought to)

**Ouija board**® n lettered board on which supposed messages from the dead are spelt out

**ounce** n unit of weight equal to one sixteenth of a pound (28.4 grams)

**our** adj belonging to us ▶ **ours** pron thing(s) belonging to us ▶ **ourselves** pron emphatic and reflexive form of **we, us**

**ousel** n see **dipper**

**oust** v force (someone) out, expel

**out** adv, adj denoting movement or distance away from, a state of being used up or extinguished, public availability, etc. e.g. oil was pouring out; turn the light out; her new book is out ▷ v (informal) name (a public figure) as being homosexual **out of** at or to a point outside ▶ **out-of-date** adj old-fashioned ▶ **outer** adj on the outside ▶ **outermost** adj furthest out ▶ **outer space** space beyond the earth's atmosphere ▶ **outing** n leisure trip ▶ **outward** adj apparent ▷ adv (also **outwards**) away from somewhere ▶ **outwardly** adv

**out-** prefix surpassing e.g. outlive; outdistance

**outback** n remote bush country of Australia

**outbid** v offer a higher price than

**outboard motor** n engine externally attached to the stern of a boat

**outbox** n (on a computer) folder in a mailbox in which outgoing messages are stored and displayed

**outbreak** n sudden occurrence (of something unpleasant)

**outburst** n sudden expression of emotion

**outcast** n person rejected by a particular group

**outclass** v surpass in quality

**outcome** n result

**outcrop** n part of a rock formation that sticks out of the earth

**outcry** n, pl -**cries** vehement or widespread protest

**outdated** adj old-fashioned

**outdo** v surpass in performance

**outdoors** adv in(to) the open air ▷ n the open air ▶ **outdoor** adj

**outface** v subdue or disconcert (someone) by staring

**outfield** n (Cricket) area far from the pitch

**outfit** n matching set of clothes; (informal) group of people working together ▶ **outfitter** n supplier of men's clothes

**outflank** v get round the side of (an enemy army); outdo (someone)

**outgoing** adj leaving; sociable ▶ **outgoings** pl n expenses

**outgrow** v become too large or too old for ▶ **outgrowth** n natural development

**outhouse** n building near a main building

**outlandish** adj extremely unconventional

**outlaw** n (Hist) criminal deprived of legal protection, bandit ▷ v make illegal; (Hist) make (someone) an outlaw

**outlay** n expenditure

**outlet** n means of expressing emotion; market for a product; place where a product is sold; opening or way out

**outline** n short general explanation; line defining the shape of something ▷ v summarize; show the general shape of

**outlook** n attitude; probable outcome

**outlying** adj distant from the main area

**outmanoeuvre** v get an advantage over

**outmoded** adj no longer fashionable or accepted

**outnumber** v exceed in number

**outpatient** n patient who does not stay in hospital overnight

**outpost** n outlying settlement

**outpouring** n passionate outburst

**output** n amount produced; power, voltage, or current delivered by an electrical circuit; (Computing) data produced ▷ v (Computing) produce (data) at the end of a process

**outrage** n great moral indignation; gross violation of morality ▷ v offend morally ▶ **outrageous** adj shocking; offensive ▶ **outrageously** adv

**outré** [oo-tray] adj shockingly eccentric

**outrider** n motorcyclist acting as an escort

**outrigger** n stabilizing frame projecting from a boat

**outright** adj, adv absolute(ly); open(ly) and direct(ly)

**outrun** v run faster than; exceed

**outset** n beginning

**outshine** v surpass (someone) in excellence

**outside** prep, adj, adv indicating movement to or position on the exterior ▷ adj unlikely e.g. an outside chance; coming from outside ▷ n external area or surface ▶ **outsider** n person outside a specific group; contestant thought unlikely to win

> **USAGE NOTE**
> Outside is not followed by of in standard English

**outsize, outsized** adj larger than normal

**outskirts** pl n outer areas, esp. of a town

**outsmart** v (informal) outwit

**outspan** v (S Afr) relax

**outspoken** adj tending to say what one thinks; said openly

**outstanding** adj excellent; still to be dealt with or paid

**outstrip** v surpass; go faster than

**outtake** n unreleased take from a recording session, film, or TV programme

**outweigh** v be more important, significant, or influential than

**outwit** v -witting, -witted get the better of (someone) by cunning

**ouzel** [ooze-el] *n* see **dipper**

**ova** *n* plural of **ovum**

**oval** *adj* egg-shaped ▷ *n* anything that is oval in shape

**ovary** *n, pl* -**ries** female egg-producing organ ▶ **ovarian** *adj*

**ovation** *n* enthusiastic round of applause

**oven** *n* heated compartment or container for cooking or for drying or firing ceramics

**over** *prep, adv* indicating position on the top of, movement to the other side of, amount greater than, etc. e.g. *a room over the garage; climbing over the fence; over fifty pounds* ▷ *adj* finished ▷ *n* (Cricket) series of six balls bowled from one end ▶ **overly** *adv* excessively

**over-** *prefix* too much e.g. *overeat;* above e.g. *overlord;* on top e.g. *overshoe*

**overall** *adj, adv* in total ▷ *n* coat-shaped protective garment ▷ *pl* protective garment consisting of trousers with a jacket or bib and braces attached

**overarm** *adj, adv* (thrown) with the arm above the shoulder

**overawe** *v* affect (someone) with an overpowering sense of awe

**overbalance** *v* lose balance

**overbearing** *adj* unpleasantly forceful

**overblown** *adj* excessive

**overboard** *adv* from a boat into the water **go overboard** go to extremes, esp. in enthusiasm

**overcast** *adj* (of the sky) covered by clouds

**overcoat** *n* heavy coat

**overcome** *v* gain control over after an effort; (of an emotion) affect strongly

**overcrowded** *adj* containing more people or things than is desirable

**overdo** *v* do to excess; exaggerate (something) **overdo it** do something to a greater degree than is advisable

**overdose** *n* excessive dose of a drug ▷ *v* take an overdose

**overdraft** *n* overdrawing; amount overdrawn

**overdraw** *v* withdraw more money than is in (one's bank account)

**overdrawn** *adj* having overdrawn one's account; (of an account) in debit

**overdrive** *n* very high gear in a motor vehicle

**overdue** *adj* still due after the time allowed

**overgrown** *adj* thickly covered with plants and weeds

**overhaul** *v* examine and repair ▷ *n* examination and repair

**overhead** *adv, adj* above one's head ▶ **overheads** *pl n* general cost of maintaining a business

**overhear** *v* hear (a speaker or remark) unintentionally or without the speaker's knowledge

**overjoyed** *adj* extremely pleased

**overkill** *n* treatment that is greater than required

**overland** *adj, adv* by land

**overlap** *v* share part of the same space or period of time (as) ▷ *n* area overlapping

**overleaf** *adv* on the back of the current page

**overlook** *v* fail to notice; ignore; look at from above

**overnight** *adj, adv* (taking place) during one night; (happening) very quickly

**overpower** *v* subdue or overcome (someone)

**overreach** *v* **overreach oneself** fail by trying to be too clever

**override** *v* overrule; replace

o

**overrule** v reverse the decision of (a person with less power); reverse (someone else's decision)

**overrun** v spread over (a place) rapidly; extend beyond a set limit

**overseas** adv, adj to, of, or from a distant country

**oversee** v watch over from a position of authority ▶ **overseer** n

**overshadow** v reduce the significance of (a person or thing) by comparison; sadden the atmosphere of

**oversight** n mistake caused by not noticing something

**overspill** n (Brit) rehousing of people from crowded cities into smaller towns

**overstay** v **overstay one's welcome** stay longer than one's host or hostess would like ▶ **overstayer** n (NZ) person who remains in New Zealand after their permit has expired

**overt** adj open, not hidden ▶ **overtly** adv

**overtake** v move past (a vehicle or person) travelling in the same direction

**overthrow** v defeat and replace ▷ n downfall, destruction

**overtime** n, adv (paid work done) in addition to one's normal working hours

**overtone** n additional meaning

**overture** n (Music) orchestral introduction ▷ pl opening moves in a new relationship

**overturn** v turn upside down; overrule (a legal decision); overthrow (a government)

**overweight** adj weighing more than is healthy

**overwhelm** v overpower, esp. emotionally; defeat by force ▶ **overwhelming** adj ▶ **overwhelmingly** adv

**overwrought** adj nervous and agitated

**ovoid** [oh-void] adj egg-shaped

**ovulate** [ov-yew-late] v produce or release an egg cell from an ovary ▶ **ovulation** n

**ovum** [oh-vum] n, pl **ova** unfertilized egg cell

**owe** v be obliged to pay (a sum of money) to (a person) **owing to** as a result of

**owl** n night bird of prey ▶ **owlish** adj

**own** adj used to emphasize possession e.g. my own idea ▷ v possess ▶ **owner** n ▶ **ownership** n ▶ **own up** v confess

**ox** n, pl **oxen** castrated bull

**Oxbridge** n (Brit) universities of Oxford and Cambridge considered together

**Oxfam** Oxford Committee for Famine Relief

**oxide** n compound of oxygen and one other element ▶ **oxidize** v combine chemically with oxygen, as in burning or rusting

**oxygen** n (Chem) gaseous element essential to life and combustion ▶ **oxygenate** v add oxygen to

**oxymoron** [ox-see-**more**-on] n figure of speech that combines two apparently contradictory ideas e.g. cruel kindness

**oyez** interj (Hist) shouted three times by a public crier, listen

**oyster** n edible shellfish ▶ **oystercatcher** n wading bird with black-and-white feathers

**Oz** n (slang) Australia

**oz.** ounce

**ozone** n strong-smelling form of oxygen ▶ **ozone layer** layer of ozone in the upper atmosphere that filters out ultraviolet radiation

# Pp

**P** parking

**p** (*Brit, Aust & NZ*) penny; (*Brit*) pence

**p.** (*pl* **pp**) page

**PA** personal assistant; public-address system

**pa** *n* (*NZ*) (formerly) a fortified Māori settlement

**p.a.** per annum: each year

**pace** *n* single step in walking; length of a step; rate of progress ▷ *v* walk up and down, esp. in anxiety; (foll by *out*) cross or measure with steps ▶ **pacemaker** *n* electronic device surgically implanted in a person with heart disease to regulate the heartbeat; person who, by taking the lead early in a race, sets the pace for the rest of the competitors

**pachyderm** [**pak**-ee-durm] *n* thick-skinned animal such as an elephant

**pacifist** *n* person who refuses on principle to take part in war ▶ **pacifism** *n*

**pacify** *v* **-fying, -fied** soothe, calm ▶ **pacification** *n*

**pack** *v* put (clothes etc.) together in a suitcase or bag; put (goods) into containers or parcels; fill with people or things ▷ *n* bag carried on a person's or animal's back; (*chiefly US*) same as **packet**; set of playing cards; group of dogs or wolves that hunt together ▶ **pack ice** mass of floating ice in the sea ▶ **pack in** *v* (*informal*) stop doing ▶ **pack off** *v* (*informal*) send away

**package** *n* small parcel; (also **package deal**) deal in which separate items are presented together as a unit ▷ *v* put into a package ▶ **packaging** *n* ▶ **package holiday** holiday in which everything is arranged by one company for a fixed price

**packet** *n* small container (and contents); small parcel; (*slang*) large sum of money

**packhorse** *n* horse used for carrying goods

**pact** *n* formal agreement

**pad** *n* piece of soft material used for protection, support, absorption of liquid, etc.; number of sheets of paper fastened at the edge; fleshy underpart of an animal's paw; place for launching rockets; (*slang*) home ▷ *v* **padding, padded** protect or fill with soft material; walk with soft steps ▶ **padding** *n* soft material used to pad something; unnecessary words put into a speech or written work to make it longer

**paddle**[1] *n* short oar with a broad blade at one or each end ▷ *v* move (a canoe etc.) with a paddle ▶ **paddle steamer** ship propelled by paddle wheels ▶ **paddle wheel** wheel with crosswise blades that strike the water successively to propel a ship

**paddle**[2] *v* walk barefoot in shallow water

**paddock** *n* small field or enclosure for horses

**paddy** *n* (*Brit informal*) fit of temper

**paddy field** *n* field where rice is grown (also **paddy**)

**pademelon, paddymelon** [**pad**-ee-mel-an] *n* small Australian wallaby

**padlock** *n* detachable lock with a hinged hoop fastened over a ring on the object to be secured

**P**

**padre** [**pah**-dray] n chaplain to the armed forces

**paean** [**pee**-an] n song of triumph or thanksgiving

**paediatrics** n branch of medicine concerned with diseases of children ▸ **paediatrician** n

**paedophilia** n condition of being sexually attracted to children ▸ **paedophile** n person who is sexually attracted to children

**paella** [pie-**ell**-a] n Spanish dish of rice, chicken, shellfish, and vegetables

**pagan** n, adj (person) not belonging to one of the world's main religions

**page**¹ n (one side of) a sheet of paper forming a book etc.; screenful of information from a website or teletext service

**page**² n (also **pageboy**) small boy who attends a bride at her wedding; (Hist) boy in training for knighthood ▷ v summon (someone) by bleeper or loudspeaker, in order to pass on a message

**pageant** n parade or display of people in costume, usu. illustrating a scene from history ▸ **pageantry** n

**pagination** n numbering of the pages of a book etc.

**pagoda** n pyramid-shaped Asian temple or tower

**paid** v past of **pay**; **put paid to** (informal) end or destroy

**pail** n (contents of a) bucket

**pain** n physical or mental suffering ▷ pl trouble, effort **on pain of** subject to the penalty of ▸ **painful** adj ▸ **painfully** adv ▸ **painless** adj ▸ **painlessly** adv ▸ **painkiller** n drug that relieves pain

**painstaking** adj extremely thorough and careful

**paint** n coloured substance, spread on a surface with a brush or roller ▷ v colour or coat with paint; use paint to make a picture of ▸ **painter** n ▸ **painting** n

**painter** n rope at the front of a boat, for tying it up

**pair** n set of two things matched for use together ▷ v group or be grouped in twos

> **USAGE NOTE**
> *Pair* is followed by a singular verb if it refers to a unit: *A pair of shoes was on the floor*, and by a plural verb if it refers to two individuals: *That pair are good friends*

**paisley pattern** n pattern of small curving shapes, used in fabric

**Pakeha** [**pah**-kee-ha] n (NZ) New Zealander who is not of Māori descent

**Pakistani** n, adj (person) from Pakistan

**pal** n (informal) friend

**palace** n residence of a king, bishop, etc.; large grand building

**palaeography** [pal-ee-**og**-ra-fee] n study of ancient manuscripts

**Palaeolithic** [pal-ee-oh-**lith**-ik] adj of the Old Stone Age

**palaeontology** [pal-ee-on-**tol**-a-jee] n study of past geological periods and fossils

**Palagi** [pa-**lang**-gee] n, pl -**gis** (NZ) Samoan name for a Pakeha

**palatable** adj pleasant to taste

**palate** n roof of the mouth; sense of taste

**palatial** adj like a palace, magnificent

**palaver** [pal-**lah**-ver] n time-wasting fuss

**pale**¹ adj light, whitish; whitish in the face, esp. through illness or shock ▷ v become pale

**pale**² n wooden or metal post used in fences **beyond the pale** outside the limits of social convention

**palette** n artist's flat board for mixing colours on

**palindrome** n word or phrase that reads the same backwards as forwards

**paling** n wooden or metal post used in fences

**palisade** n fence made of wooden posts driven into the ground

**pall**¹ n cloth spread over a coffin; dark cloud (of smoke); depressing oppressive atmosphere ▶ **pallbearer** n person who helps to carry the coffin at a funeral

**pall**² v become boring

**palladium** n (Chem) silvery-white element of the platinum metal group

**pallet**¹ n portable platform for storing and moving goods

**pallet**² n straw-filled mattress or bed

**palliate** v lessen the severity of (something) without curing it

**palliative** adj giving temporary or partial relief ▷ n something, for example a drug, that palliates

**pallid** adj pale, esp. because ill or weak ▶ **pallor** n

**pally** adj -lier, -liest (informal) on friendly terms

**palm**¹ n inner surface of the hand ▶ **palm off** v get rid of (an unwanted thing or person), esp. by deceit

**palm**² n tropical tree with long pointed leaves growing out of the top of a straight trunk ▶ **Palm Sunday** Sunday before Easter

**palmistry** n fortune-telling from lines on the palm of the hand ▶ **palmist** n

**palmtop** adj (of a computer) small enough to be held in the hand ▷ n computer small enough to be held in the hand

**palomino** n, pl -nos gold-coloured horse with a white mane and tail

**palpable** adj obvious e.g. a palpable hit; so intense as to seem capable of being touched e.g. the tension is almost palpable ▶ **palpably** adv

**palpate** v (Med) examine (an area of the body) by touching

**palpitate** v (of the heart) beat rapidly; flutter or tremble ▶ **palpitation** n

**palsy** [**pawl**-zee] n paralysis ▶ **palsied** adj affected with palsy

**paltry** adj -trier, -triest insignificant

**pampas** pl n vast grassy plains in S America ▶ **pampas grass** tall grass with feathery ornamental flower branches

**pamper** v treat (someone) with great indulgence, spoil

**pamphlet** n thin paper-covered booklet ▶ **pamphleteer** n writer of pamphlets

**pan**¹ n wide long-handled metal container used in cooking; bowl of a toilet ▷ v **panning, panned** sift gravel from (a river) in a pan to search for gold; (informal) criticize harshly ▶ **pan out** v result

**pan**² v **panning, panned** (of a film camera) be moved slowly so as to cover a whole scene or follow a moving object

**pan-** combining form all e.g. pan-American

**panacea** [pan-a-**see**-a] n remedy for all diseases or problems

**panache** [pan-**ash**] n confident elegant style

**panama hat** n straw hat

**panatella** n long slender cigar

**pancake** n thin flat circle of fried batter

**panchromatic** adj (Photog) sensitive to light of all colours

**pancreas** [**pang**-kree-ass] n large gland behind the stomach that produces insulin and helps digestion ▶ **pancreatic** adj

P

**panda** n large black-and-white bearlike mammal from China ▶ **panda car** (Brit) police patrol car

**pandemic** n, adj (a disease) occurring over a wide area

**pandemonium** n wild confusion, uproar

**pander**¹ v (foll by to) indulge (a person in his or her desires)

**pander**² n (old-fashioned) person who procures a sexual partner for someone

**p & p** postage and packing

**pane** n sheet of glass in a window or door

**panegyric** [pan-ih-**jir**-ik] n formal speech or piece of writing in praise of someone or something

**panel** n flat distinct section of a larger surface, for example in a door; group of people as a team in a quiz etc.; list of jurors, doctors, etc.; board or surface containing switches and controls to operate equipment ▷ v **-elling, -elled** cover or decorate with panels ▶ **panelling** n panels collectively, esp. on a wall ▶ **panellist** n member of a panel ▶ **panel beater** person who repairs damage to car bodies

**pang** n sudden sharp feeling of pain or sadness

**pangolin** n animal of tropical countries with a scaly body and a long snout for eating ants and termites (also **scaly anteater**)

**panic** n sudden overwhelming fear, often affecting a whole group of people ▷ v **-icking, -icked** feel or cause to feel panic ▶ **panicky** adj ▶ **panic-stricken** adj

**panini** [pa-**nee**-nee] n, pl **-ni** or **-nis** type of Italian sandwich, usu. served grilled

**pannier** n bag fixed on the back of a cycle; basket carried by a beast of burden

**panoply** n magnificent array

**panorama** n wide unbroken view of a scene ▶ **panoramic** adj

**pansy** n, pl **-sies** small garden flower with velvety purple, yellow, or white petals; (offens) effeminate or homosexual man

**pant** v breathe quickly and noisily during or after exertion

**pantaloons** pl n baggy trousers gathered at the ankles

**pantechnicon** n large van for furniture removals

**pantheism** n belief that God is present in everything ▶ **pantheist** n ▶ **pantheistic** adj

**pantheon** n (in ancient Greece and Rome) temple built to honour all the gods

**panther** n leopard, esp. a black one

**panties** pl n women's underpants

**pantile** n roofing tile with an S-shaped cross section

**pantomime** n play based on a fairy tale, performed at Christmas time

**pantry** n, pl **-tries** small room or cupboard for storing food

**pants** pl n undergarment for the lower part of the body; (US, Canadian, Aust & NZ) trousers

**pap** n soft food for babies or invalids; worthless entertainment or information

**papacy** [**pay**-pa-see] n, pl **-cies** position or term of office of a pope ▶ **papal** adj of the pope

**paparazzo** [pap-a-**rat**-so] n, pl **-razzi** photographer specializing in candid photographs of famous people

**papaya** [pa-**pie**-ya] n large sweet West Indian fruit

**paper** n material made in sheets from wood pulp or other fibres; printed sheet of this; newspaper; set of examination questions; article or essay ▷ pl personal documents ▷ v cover (walls) with wallpaper ▶ **paperback** n book with covers made of flexible card ▶ **paperweight** n heavy decorative object placed on top of loose papers ▶ **paperwork** n clerical work, such as writing reports and letters

**papier-mâché** [**pap**-yay **mash**-ay] n material made from paper mixed with paste and moulded when moist

**papist** n, adj (offens) Roman Catholic

**papoose** n Native American child

**paprika** n mild powdered seasoning made from red peppers

**papyrus** [pap-**ire**-uss] n, pl **-ri** or **-ruses** tall water plant; (manuscript written on) a kind of paper made from this plant

**par** n usual or average condition e.g. feeling under par; (Golf) expected standard score; face value of stocks and shares **on a par with** equal to

**parable** n story that illustrates a religious teaching

**parabola** [par-**ab**-bol-a] n regular curve resembling the course of an object thrown forward and up ▶ **parabolic** adj

**paracetamol** n mild pain-relieving drug

**parachute** n large fabric canopy that slows the descent of a person or object from an aircraft ▷ v land or drop by parachute ▶ **parachutist** n

**parade** n procession or march; street or promenade ▷ v display or flaunt; march in procession

**paradigm** [**par**-a-dime] n example or model

**paradise** n heaven; place or situation that is near-perfect

**paradox** n statement that seems self-contradictory but

may be true ▶ **paradoxical** adj ▶ **paradoxically** adv

**paraffin** n (Brit & SAfr) liquid mixture distilled from petroleum and used as a fuel or solvent

| **SPELLING TIP**
| Remember that **paraffin** has a
| single r and double f

**paragliding** n cross-country gliding wearing a parachute shaped like wings

**paragon** n model of perfection

**paragraph** n section of a piece of writing starting on a new line

**parakeet** n small long-tailed parrot

**parallax** n apparent change in an object's position due to a change in the observer's position

**parallel** adj separated by an equal distance at every point; exactly corresponding ▷ n line separated from another by an equal distance at every point; thing with similar features to another; line of latitude ▷ v correspond to

**parallelogram** n four-sided geometric figure with opposite sides parallel

**paralysis** n inability to move or feel, because of damage to the nervous system ▶ **paralyse** v affect with paralysis; make temporarily unable to move or take action ▶ **paralytic** n, adj (person) affected with paralysis

**paramedic** n person working in support of the medical profession ▶ **paramedical** adj

**parameter** [par-**am**-it-er] n limiting factor, boundary

**paramilitary** adj organized on military lines

**paramount** adj of the greatest importance

**paramour** n (old-fashioned) lover, esp. of a person married to someone else

P

**paranoia** n mental illness causing delusions of grandeur or persecution; (*informal*) intense fear or suspicion ▶ **paranoid, paranoiac** adj, n

**paranormal** adj beyond scientific explanation

**parapet** n low wall or railing along the edge of a balcony or roof

**paraphernalia** n personal belongings or bits of equipment

**paraphrase** v put (a statement or text) into other words

**paraplegia** [par-a-**pleej**-ya] n paralysis of the lower half of the body ▶ **paraplegic** adj, n

**parapsychology** n study of mental phenomena such as telepathy

**Paraquat**® n extremely poisonous weedkiller

**parasite** n animal or plant living in or on another; person who lives at the expense of others ▶ **parasitic** adj

**parasol** n umbrella-like sunshade

**paratrooper** n soldier trained to be dropped by parachute into a battle area ▶ **paratroops** pl n

**parboil** v boil until partly cooked

**parcel** n something wrapped up, package ▷ v -**celling, -celled** (often foll by *up*) wrap up ▶ **parcel out** v divide into parts

**parch** v make very hot and dry; make thirsty

**parchment** n thick smooth writing material made from animal skin

**pardon** v forgive, excuse ▷ n forgiveness; official release from punishment for a crime ▶ **pardonable** adj

**pare** v cut off the skin or top layer of; (often foll by *down*) reduce in size or amount ▶ **paring** n piece pared off

**parent** n father or mother ▶ **parental** adj ▶ **parenthood** n

▶ **parentage** n ancestry or family
▶ **parenting** n activity of bringing up children

**parenthesis** [par-**en**-thiss-iss] n, pl **-ses** word or sentence inserted into a passage, marked off by brackets or dashes ▷ pl round brackets, ( ) ▶ **parenthetical** adj

**pariah** [par-**rye**-a] n social outcast

**parietal** [par-**rye**-it-al] adj of the walls of a body cavity such as the skull

**parish** n area that has its own church and a priest or pastor ▶ **parishioner** n inhabitant of a parish

**parity** n equality or equivalence

**park** n area of open land for recreational use by the public; area containing a number of related enterprises e.g. *a business park*; (*Brit*) area of private land around a large country house ▷ v stop and leave (a vehicle) temporarily

**parka** n large waterproof jacket with a hood

**Parkinson's disease** n progressive disorder of the central nervous system which causes impaired muscular coordination and tremor (also **Parkinsonism**)

**parky** adj **parkier, parkiest** (*Brit informal*) (of the weather) chilly

**parlance** n particular way of speaking, idiom

**parley** n meeting between leaders or representatives of opposing forces to discuss terms ▷ v have a parley

**parliament** n law-making assembly of a country ▶ **parliamentary** adj

**parlour** n (*old-fashioned*) living room for receiving visitors

**parlous** adj (*old-fashioned*) dire; dangerously bad

**Parmesan** n hard strong-flavoured Italian cheese, used grated on pasta dishes and soups

**parochial** *adj* narrow in outlook; of a parish ▶ **parochialism** *n*

**parody** *n, pl* **-dies** exaggerated and amusing imitation of someone else's style ▷ *v* **-dying, -died** make a parody of

**parole** *n* early freeing of a prisoner on condition that he or she behaves well ▷ *v* put on parole **on parole** (of a prisoner) released on condition that he or she behaves well

**paroxysm** *n* uncontrollable outburst of rage, delight, etc.; spasm or convulsion of coughing, pain, etc.

**parquet** [**par**-kay] *n* floor covering made of wooden blocks arranged in a geometric pattern ▶ **parquetry** *n*

**parricide** *n* crime of killing either of one's parents; person who does this

**parrot** *n* tropical bird with a short hooked beak and an ability to imitate human speech ▷ *v* **-roting, -roted** repeat (someone else's words) without thinking

**parry** *v* **-rying, -ried** ward off (an attack); cleverly avoid (an awkward question)

**parse** [**parz**] *v* analyse (a sentence) in terms of grammar

**parsimony** *n* extreme caution in spending money ▶ **parsimonious** *adj*

**parsley** *n* herb used for seasoning and decorating food

**parsnip** *n* long tapering cream-coloured root vegetable

**parson** *n* Anglican parish priest; any member of the clergy ▶ **parsonage** *n* parson's house

**part** *n* one of the pieces that make up a whole; one of several equal divisions; actor's role; (often pl) region, area; component of a vehicle or machine ▷ *v* divide or separate; (of people) leave each other **take someone's part** support someone in an argument etc. **take (something) in good part** respond to (teasing or criticism) with good humour ▶ **parting** *n* occasion when one person leaves another; line of scalp between sections of hair combed in opposite directions; dividing or separating ▶ **partly** *adv* not completely ▶ **part of speech** particular grammatical class of words, such as noun or verb ▶ **part-time** *adj* occupying or working less than the full working week ▶ **part with** *v* give away, hand over

**partake** *v* **-taking, -took, -taken** (foll by *of*) take (food or drink); (foll by *in*) take part in

**partial** *adj* not complete; prejudiced **partial to** having a liking for ▶ **partiality** *n* ▶ **partially** *adv*

**participate** *v* become actively involved ▶ **participant** *n* ▶ **participation** *n*

**participle** *n* form of a verb used in compound tenses or as an adjective e.g. *worried*; *worrying*

**particle** *n* extremely small piece or amount; (*Physics*) minute piece of matter, such as a proton or electron

**particular** *adj* relating to one person or thing, not general; exceptional or special; very exact; difficult to please, fastidious ▷ *n* item of information, detail ▶ **particularly** *adv* ▶ **particularize** *v* give details about

**partisan** *n* strong supporter of a party or group; guerrilla, member of a resistance movement ▷ *adj* prejudiced or one-sided

**partition** *n* screen or thin wall that divides a room; division of a country into independent parts ▷ *v* divide with a partition

**partner** *n* either member of a couple in a relationship or activity; member of a business partnership ▷ *v* be the partner of ▶ **partnership** *n* joint business venture between two or more people

**partridge** *n* game bird of the grouse family

**parturition** *n* act of giving birth

**party** *n*, *pl* **-ties** social gathering for pleasure; group of people travelling or working together; political organization whose members have common aims and beliefs; person or people forming one side in a lawsuit or dispute ▶ **party line** official view of a political party; telephone line shared by two or more subscribers ▶ **party wall** common wall separating adjoining buildings

**parvenu** [**par**-ven-new] *n* person newly risen to a position of power or wealth

**pascal** *n* unit of pressure

**pash** (*Aust & NZ slang*) *v* kiss and cuddle ▷ *n* act of kissing and cuddling

**pashmina** [pash-**mee**-na] *n* shawl or scarf made from fine soft goat's wool

**paspalum** [pass-**pale**-um] *n* (*Aust & NZ*) type of grass with wide leaves

**pass** *v* go by, past, or through; be successful in (a test or examination); spend (time) or (of time) go by; give, hand; be inherited by; (*Sport*) hit, kick, or throw (the ball) to another player; (of a law-making body) agree to (a law); exceed ▷ *n* successful result in a test or examination; permit or licence **make a pass at** (*informal*) make sexual advances to ▶ **passable** *adj* (just) acceptable; (of a road) capable of being travelled along

▶ **passing** *adj* brief or transitory; cursory or casual ▶ **pass away** *v* die ▶ **pass out** *v* (*informal*) faint ▶ **pass up** *v* (*informal*) fail to take advantage of (something)

**passage** *n* channel or opening providing a way through; hall or corridor; section of a book etc.; journey by sea; right or freedom to pass ▶ **passageway** *n* passage or corridor

**passbook** *n* book issued by a bank or building society for keeping a record of deposits and withdrawals; (*SAfr*) formerly, an official identity document

**passé** [**pas**-say] *adj* old-fashioned

**passenger** *n* person travelling in a vehicle driven by someone else; member of a team who does not pull his or her weight

**passer-by** *n*, *pl* **passers-by** person who is walking past something or someone

**passim** *adv* (*Latin*) everywhere, throughout

**passion** *n* intense sexual love; any strong emotion; great enthusiasm; (**P-**) (*Christianity*) the suffering of Christ ▶ **passionate** *adj* ▶ **passionflower** *n* tropical American plant ▶ **passion fruit** edible fruit of the passionflower ▶ **Passion play** play about Christ's suffering

**passive** *adj* not playing an active part; submissive and receptive to outside forces; (*Grammar*) (of a verb) in a form indicating that the subject receives the action, e.g. *was jeered* in *he was jeered by the crowd* ▶ **passivity** *n* ▶ **passive resistance** resistance to a government, law, etc. by nonviolent acts ▶ **passive smoking** inhalation of smoke from others' cigarettes by a nonsmoker

**Passover** n Jewish festival commemorating the sparing of the Jews in Egypt

**passport** n official document of nationality granting permission to travel abroad

**password** n secret word or phrase that allows access

**past** adj of the time before the present; ended, gone by; (*Grammar*) (of a verb tense) indicating that the action specified took place earlier ▷ n period of time before the present; person's earlier life, esp. a disreputable period; (*Grammar*) past tense ▷ adv by, along ▷ prep beyond **past it** (*informal*) unable to do the things one could do when younger ▶ **past master** person with great talent or experience in a particular subject

**pasta** n type of food, such as spaghetti, that is made in different shapes from flour and water

**paste** n moist soft mixture, such as toothpaste; adhesive, esp. for paper; (*Brit*) pastry dough; shiny glass used to make imitation jewellery ▷ v fasten with paste ▶ **pasting** n (*informal*) heavy defeat; strong criticism ▶ **pasteboard** n stiff thick paper

**pastel** n coloured chalk crayon for drawing; picture drawn in pastels; pale delicate colour ▷ adj pale and delicate in colour

**pasteurize** v sterilize by heating ▶ **pasteurization** n

**pastiche** [pass-**teesh**] n work of art that mixes styles or copies the style of another artist

**pastille** n small fruit-flavoured and sometimes medicated sweet

**pastime** n activity that makes time pass pleasantly

**pastor** n member of the clergy in charge of a congregation

▶ **pastoral** adj of or depicting country life; of a clergyman or his duties

**pastrami** n highly seasoned smoked beef

**pastry** n, pl **-ries** baking dough made of flour, fat, and water; cake or pie

**pasture** n grassy land for farm animals to graze on

**pasty**[1] [**pay**-stee] adj **pastier, pastiest** (of a complexion) pale and unhealthy

**pasty**[2] [**pass**-tee] n, pl **pasties** round of pastry folded over a savoury filling

**pat**[1] v **patting, patted** tap lightly ▷ n gentle tap or stroke; small shaped mass of butter etc.

**pat**[2] adj quick, ready, or glib **off pat** learned thoroughly

**patch** n piece of material sewn on a garment; small contrasting section; plot of ground; protective pad for the eye ▷ v mend with a patch ▶ **patchy** adj of uneven quality or intensity ▶ **patch up** v repair clumsily; make up (a quarrel) ▶ **patchwork** n needlework made of pieces of different materials sewn together

**pate** n (*old-fashioned*) head

**pâté** [**pat**-ay] n spread of finely minced liver etc.

**patella** n, pl **-lae** kneecap

**patent** n document giving the exclusive right to make or sell an invention ▷ adj open to public inspection e.g. *letters patent*; obvious; protected by a patent ▷ v obtain a patent for ▶ **patently** adv obviously ▶ **patent leather** leather processed to give a hard glossy surface

**paternal** adj fatherly; related through one's father ▶ **paternity** n fact or state of being a father ▶ **paternalism** n authority

P

exercised in a way that limits individual responsibility ▸ **paternalistic** adj

**path** n surfaced walk or track; course of action ▸ **pathname** n (*Computing*) file name listing the sequence of directories leading to a particular file or directory

**pathetic** adj causing feelings of pity or sadness; distressingly inadequate ▸ **pathetically** adv

**pathogen** n thing that causes disease ▸ **pathogenic** adj

**pathology** n scientific study of diseases ▸ **pathological** adj of pathology; (*informal*) compulsively motivated ▸ **pathologist** n

**pathos** n power of arousing pity or sadness

**patient** adj enduring difficulties or delays calmly ▷ n person receiving medical treatment ▸ **patience** n quality of being patient; card game for one

**patina** n fine layer on a surface; sheen of age on woodwork

**patio** n, pl **-tios** paved area adjoining a house

**patois** [pat-wah] n, pl **patois** [**pat**-wahz] regional dialect, esp. of French

**patriarch** n male head of a family or tribe; highest-ranking bishop in Orthodox Churches ▸ **patriarchal** adj ▸ **patriarchy** n, pl **-chies** society in which men have most of the power

**patrician** n member of the nobility ▷ adj of noble birth

**patricide** n crime of killing one's father; person who does this

**patrimony** n, pl **-nies** property inherited from ancestors

**patriot** n person who loves his or her country and supports its interests ▸ **patriotic** adj ▸ **patriotism** n

**patrol** n regular circuit by a guard; person or small group patrolling; unit of Scouts or Guides ▷ v **-trolling, -trolled** go round on guard, or reconnoitring

**patron** n person who gives financial support to charities, artists, etc.; regular customer of a shop, pub, etc. ▸ **patronage** n support given by a patron ▸ **patronize** v treat in a condescending way; be a patron of ▸ **patron saint** saint regarded as the guardian of a country or group

**patronymic** n name derived from one's father or a male ancestor

**patter**[1] v make repeated soft tapping sounds ▷ n quick succession of taps

**patter**[2] n glib rapid speech

**pattern** n arrangement of repeated parts or decorative designs; regular way that something is done; diagram or shape used as a guide to make something ▸ **patterned** adj decorated with a pattern

**patty** n, pl **-ties** small flattened cake of minced food

**paucity** n scarcity; smallness of amount or number

**paunch** n protruding belly

**pauper** n very poor person

**pause** v stop for a time ▷ n stop or rest in speech or action

**pave** v form (a surface) with stone or brick ▸ **pavement** n paved path for pedestrians

**pavilion** n building on a playing field etc.; building for housing an exhibition etc.

**paw** n animal's foot with claws and pads ▷ v scrape with the paw or hoof; (*informal*) touch in a rough or overfamiliar way

**pawn**[1] v deposit (an article) as security for money borrowed **in pawn** deposited as security with a pawnbroker ▸ **pawnbroker**

*n* lender of money on goods deposited

**pawn²** *n* chessman of the lowest value; person manipulated by someone else

**pay** *v* **paying, paid** give money etc. in return for goods or services; settle a debt or obligation; compensate (for); give; be profitable to ▷ *n* wages or salary ▶ **payment** *n* act of paying; money paid ▶ **payable** *adj* due to be paid ▶ **payee** *n* person to whom money is paid or due ▶ **payday** *n* day on which wages or salary is paid ▶ **paying guest** lodger or boarder ▶ **pay off** *v* pay (debt) in full; turn out successfully ▶ **pay out** *v* spend; release (a rope) bit by bit ▶ **payroll** *n* list of employees who receive regular pay ▶ **paywall** *n* system preventing access to part of a website unless a fee is paid

**PAYE** pay as you earn: system by which income tax is paid by an employer straight to the government

**payload** *n* passengers or cargo of an aircraft; explosive power of a missile etc.

**payola** *n* (*chiefly US informal*) bribe to get special treatment, esp. to promote a commercial product

**PC** personal computer; (in Britain) Police Constable; politically correct; (in Britain) Privy Councillor

**pc** per cent

**PDA** personal digital assistant: a handheld computer used for personal information such as contact details

**PDF** (*Computing*) portable document format: a format in which documents may be viewed

**PE** physical education

**pea** *n* climbing plant with seeds growing in pods; its seed, eaten as a vegetable

**peace** *n* calm, quietness; absence of anxiety; freedom from war; harmony between people ▶ **peaceable** *adj* inclined towards peace ▶ **peaceably** *adv* ▶ **peaceful** *adj* ▶ **peacefully** *adv*

**peach** *n* soft juicy fruit with a stone and a downy skin; (*informal*) very pleasing person or thing ▷ *adj* pinkish-orange

**peacock** *n* large male bird with a brilliantly coloured fanlike tail ▶ **peahen** *n fem*

**peak** *n* pointed top, esp. of a mountain; point of greatest development etc.; projecting piece on the front of a cap ▷ *v* form or reach a peak ▷ *adj* of or at the point of greatest demand ▶ **peaked** *adj* ▶ **peaky** *adj* pale and sickly

**peal** *n* long loud echoing sound, esp. of bells or thunder ▷ *v* sound with a peal or peals

**peanut** *n* pea-shaped nut that ripens underground ▷ *pl* (*informal*) trifling amount of money

**pear** *n* sweet juicy fruit with a narrow top and rounded base

**pearl** *n* hard round shiny object found inside some oyster shells and used as a jewel ▶ **pearly** *adj*

**peasant** *n* person working on the land, esp. in poorer countries or in the past ▶ **peasantry** *n* peasants collectively

**peat** *n* decayed vegetable material found in bogs, used as fertilizer or fuel

**pebble** *n* small roundish stone ▶ **pebbly** *adj* ▶ **pebble dash** coating for exterior walls consisting of small stones set in plaster

**pecan** [**pee**-kan] *n* edible nut of a N American tree

**peccadillo** *n*, *pl* **-loes** *or* **-los** trivial misdeed

**peck** *v* strike or pick up with the beak; (*informal*) kiss quickly ▷ *n*

**p**

pecking movement ▸ **peckish** adj
(informal) slightly hungry ▸ **peck at**
v nibble, eat reluctantly

**pecs** pl n (informal) pectoral muscles

**pectin** n substance in fruit that
makes jam set

**pectoral** adj of the chest or thorax
▷ n pectoral muscle or fin

**peculiar** adj strange; distinct,
special; belonging exclusively to
▸ **peculiarity** n, pl **-ties** oddity,
eccentricity; distinguishing trait

**pecuniary** adj relating to, or
consisting of, money

**pedagogue** n schoolteacher, esp. a
pedantic one

**pedal** n foot-operated lever used
to control a vehicle or machine,
or to modify the tone of a musical
instrument ▷ v **-alling, -alled**
propel (a bicycle) by using its
pedals

**pedant** n person who is excessively
concerned with details and rules,
esp. in academic work ▸ **pedantic**
adj ▸ **pedantry** n

**peddle** v sell (goods) from door
to door

**peddler** n person who sells illegal
drugs

**pederast** n man who has
homosexual relations with boys
▸ **pederasty** n

**pedestal** n base supporting a
column, statue, etc.

**pedestrian** n person who walks
▷ adj dull, uninspiring ▸ **pedestrian
crossing** place marked where
pedestrians may cross a road
▸ **pedestrian precinct** (Brit)
(shopping) area for pedestrians only

**pedicure** n medical or cosmetic
treatment of the feet

**pedigree** n register of ancestors,
esp. of a purebred animal

**pediment** n triangular part
over a door etc.

**pedlar** n person who sells goods
from door to door

**pee** (informal) ▷ v **peeing, peed**
urinate ▷ n urine; act of urinating

**peek** v, n peep or glance

**peel** v remove the skin or rind of
(a vegetable or fruit); (of skin or a
surface) come off in flakes ▷ n rind
or skin ▸ **peelings** pl n

**peep**¹ v look slyly or quickly ▷ n
quick or furtive look ▸ **Peeping
Tom** man who furtively watches
women undressing

**peep**² v make a small shrill noise
▷ n small shrill noise

**peer**¹ n (fem **peeress**) (in Britain)
member of the nobility; person
of the same status, age, etc.
▸ **peerage** n (Brit) whole body of
peers; rank of a peer ▸ **peerless** adj
unequalled, unsurpassed ▸ **peer
group** group of people of similar
age, status, etc. ▸ **peer pressure**
influence from one's peer group

**peer**² v look closely and intently

**peeved** adj (informal) annoyed

**peevish** adj fretful or irritable
▸ **peevishly** adv

**peewee** n black-and-white
Australian bird

**peewit** n same as **lapwing**

**peg** n pin or clip for joining, fastening,
marking, etc.; hook or knob for
hanging things on ▷ v **pegging,
pegged** fasten with pegs; stabilize
(prices) **off the peg** (of clothes)
ready-to-wear, not tailor-made

**peggy square** n (NZ) small hand-
knitted square

**peignoir** [**pay**-nwahr] n woman's
light dressing gown

**pejorative** [pij-**jor**-a-tiv] adj (of
words etc.) with an insulting or
critical meaning

**Pekingese, Pekinese** n, pl
**-ese** small dog with a short
wrinkled muzzle

**pelargonium** n plant with red, white, purple, or pink flowers

**pelican** n large water bird with a pouch beneath its bill for storing fish ▶ **pelican crossing** (in Britain) road crossing with pedestrian-operated traffic lights

**pellagra** n disease caused by lack of vitamin B

**pellet** n small ball of something

**pell-mell** adv in utter confusion, headlong

**pellucid** adj very clear

**pelmet** n ornamental drapery or board, concealing a curtain rail

**pelt**¹ v throw missiles at; run fast, rush; rain heavily **at full pelt** at top speed

**pelt**² n skin of a fur-bearing animal

**pelvis** n framework of bones at the base of the spine, to which the hips are attached ▶ **pelvic** adj

**pen**¹ n instrument for writing in ink ▷ v **penning, penned** write or compose ▶ **pen friend** friend with whom a person corresponds without meeting ▶ **penknife** n small knife with blade(s) that fold into the handle ▶ **pen name** name used by a writer instead of his or her real name

**pen**² n small enclosure for domestic animals ▷ v **penning, penned** put or keep in a pen

**pen**³ n female swan

**penal** [pee-nal] adj of or used in punishment ▶ **penalize** v impose a penalty on; handicap, hinder

**penalty** n, pl **-ties** punishment for a crime or offence; (Sport) handicap or disadvantage imposed for breaking a rule

**penance** n voluntary self-punishment to make amends for wrongdoing

**pence** n (Brit) a plural of **penny**

**penchant** [pon-shon] n inclination or liking

**pencil** n thin cylindrical instrument containing graphite, for writing or drawing ▷ v **-cilling, -cilled** draw, write, or mark with a pencil

**pendant** n ornament worn on a chain round the neck

**pendent** adj hanging

**pending** prep while waiting for ▷ adj not yet decided or settled

**pendulous** adj hanging, swinging

**pendulum** n suspended weight swinging to and fro, esp. as a regulator for a clock

**penetrate** v find or force a way into or through; arrive at the meaning of ▶ **penetrable** adj capable of being penetrated ▶ **penetrating** adj (of a sound) loud and unpleasant; quick to understand ▶ **penetration** n

**penguin** n flightless black-and-white sea bird of the southern hemisphere

**penicillin** n antibiotic drug effective against a wide range of diseases and infections

**peninsula** n strip of land nearly surrounded by water ▶ **peninsular** adj

**penis** n organ of copulation and urination in male mammals

**penitent** adj feeling sorry for having done wrong ▷ n someone who is penitent ▶ **penitence** n ▶ **penitentiary** n, pl **-ries** (US) prison ▷ adj (also **penitential**) relating to penance

**pennant** n long narrow flag

**penny** n, pl **pence** or **pennies** British bronze coin worth one hundredth of a pound; former British and Australian coin worth one twelfth of a shilling ▶ **penniless** adj very poor

**pension**¹ n regular payment to people above a certain age, retired employees, widows, etc.

P

▶ **pensionable** adj ▶ **pensioner** n person receiving a pension ▶ **pension off** v force (someone) to retire from a job and pay him or her a pension

**pension²** [pon-syon] n boarding house in Europe

**pensive** adj deeply thoughtful, often with a tinge of sadness

**pentagon** n geometric figure with five sides; (**P-**) headquarters of the US military ▶ **pentagonal** adj

**pentameter** [pen-**tam**-it-er] n line of poetry with five metrical feet

**Pentateuch** [**pent**-a-tyuke] n first five books of the Old Testament

**Pentecost** n Christian festival celebrating the descent of the Holy Spirit to the apostles, Whitsuntide

**penthouse** n flat built on the roof or top floor of a building

**pent-up** adj (of an emotion) not released, repressed

**penultimate** adj second last

**penumbra** n, pl **-brae** or **-bras** (in an eclipse) the partially shadowed region which surrounds the full shadow; partial shadow

**penury** n extreme poverty ▶ **penurious** adj

**peony** n, pl **-nies** garden plant with showy red, pink, or white flowers

**people** pl n persons generally; the community; one's family ▷ n race or nation ▷ v provide with inhabitants ▶ **people mover** (Brit, Aust & NZ) same as **multipurpose vehicle**

**pep** n (informal) high spirits, energy, or enthusiasm ▶ **pep talk** (informal) talk designed to increase confidence and enthusiasm ▶ **pep up** v **pepping, pepped** stimulate, invigorate

**pepper** n sharp hot condiment made from the fruit of an East Indian climbing plant; colourful tropical fruit used as a vegetable, capsicum ▷ v season with pepper; sprinkle, dot; pelt with missiles ▶ **peppery** adj tasting of pepper; irritable ▶ **peppercorn** n dried berry of the pepper plant ▶ **peppercorn rent** (chiefly Brit) low or nominal rent ▶ **pepper spray** aerosol spray causing temporary blindness and breathing difficulty, used esp. for self-defence

**peppermint** n plant that yields an oil with a strong sharp flavour; sweet flavoured with this

**peptic** adj relating to digestion or the digestive juices

**per** prep for each **as per** in accordance with

**perambulate** v (old-fashioned) walk through or about (a place) ▶ **perambulation** n ▶ **perambulator** n pram

**per annum** adv (Latin) in each year

**per capita** adj, adv (Latin) of or for each person

**perceive** v become aware of (something) through the senses; understand

**per cent** adv in each hundred ▶ **percentage** n proportion or rate per hundred

**perceptible** adj discernible, recognizable

**perception** n act of perceiving; intuitive judgment ▶ **perceptive** adj

**perch¹** n resting place for a bird ▷ v alight, rest, or place on or as if on a perch

**perch²** n any of various edible fishes

**perchance** adv (old-fashioned) perhaps

**percipient** adj quick to notice things, observant

**percolate** v pass or filter through small holes; spread gradually; make (coffee) or (of

coffee) be made in a percolator
▸ **percolation** n ▸ **percolator** n
coffee pot in which boiling water
is forced through a tube and filters
down through coffee

**percussion** n striking of one thing
against another ▸ **percussion
instrument** musical instrument
played by being struck, such as
drums or cymbals

**perdition** n (*Christianity*) spiritual
ruin

**peregrination** n (*obs*) travels,
roaming

**peregrine falcon** n falcon with
dark upper parts and a light
underside

**peremptory** adj authoritative,
imperious

**perennial** adj lasting through many
years ▷ n plant lasting more than
two years ▸ **perennially** adv

**perfect** adj having all the essential
elements; faultless; correct,
precise; utter or absolute; excellent
▷ n (*Grammar*) perfect tense ▷ v
improve; make fully correct
▸ **perfectly** adv ▸ **perfection**
n state of being perfect
▸ **perfectionist** n person who
demands the highest standards of
excellence ▸ **perfectionism** n

**perfidious** adj (*lit*) treacherous,
disloyal ▸ **perfidy** n

**perforate** v make holes in
▸ **perforation** n

**perforce** (*old-fashioned*) adv of
necessity

**perform** v carry out (an action);
act, sing, or present a play before
an audience; fulfil (a request etc.)
▸ **performance** n ▸ **performer** n

**perfume** n liquid cosmetic worn
for its pleasant smell; fragrance
▷ v give a pleasant smell to
▸ **perfumery** n perfumes
in general

**perfunctory** adj done only as
a matter of routine, superficial
▸ **perfunctorily** adv

**pergola** n arch or framework of
trellis supporting climbing plants

**perhaps** adv possibly, maybe

**pericardium** n, pl **-dia** membrane
enclosing the heart

**perihelion** n, pl **-lia** point in the
orbit of a planet or comet that is
nearest to the sun

**peril** n great danger ▸ **perilous** adj
▸ **perilously** adv

**perimeter** [per-**rim**-it-er] n (length
of) the outer edge of an area

**perinatal** adj of or in the weeks
shortly before or after birth

**period** n particular portion of time;
single occurrence of menstruation;
division of time at school etc. when
a particular subject is taught;
(*US*) full stop ▷ adj (of furniture,
dress, a play, etc.) dating from
or in the style of an earlier time
▸ **periodic** adj recurring at intervals
▸ **periodic table** (*Chem*) chart of
the elements, arranged to show
their relationship to each other
▸ **periodical** n magazine issued at
regular intervals ▷ adj periodic

**peripatetic** [per-rip-a-**tet**-ik] adj
travelling about from place to place

**periphery** [per-**if**-er-ee] n, pl **-eries**
boundary or edge; fringes of a field
of activity ▸ **peripheral** [per-**if**-er-
al] adj unimportant, not central; of
or on the periphery

**periscope** n instrument used, esp.
in submarines, to give a view of
objects on a different level

**perish** v be destroyed or die; decay,
rot ▸ **perishable** adj liable to rot
quickly ▸ **perishing** adj (*informal*)
very cold

**peritoneum** [per-rit-toe-**nee**-um]
n, pl **-nea** or **-neums** membrane
lining the internal surface of the

**P**

abdomen ▶ **peritonitis** [per-rit-tone-**ite**-iss] n inflammation of the peritoneum

**periwinkle**[1] n small edible shellfish, the winkle

**periwinkle**[2] n plant with trailing stems and blue flowers

**perjury** n, pl **-juries** act or crime of lying while under oath in a court **perjure oneself** commit perjury

**perk** n (informal) incidental benefit gained from a job, such as a company car

**perk up** v cheer up ▶ **perky** adj lively or cheerful

**perlemoen** n (S Afr) edible sea creature with a shell lined with mother of pearl

**perm** n long-lasting curly hairstyle produced by treating the hair with chemicals ▷ v give (hair) a perm

**permafrost** n permanently frozen ground

**permanent** adj lasting forever ▶ **permanence** n ▶ **permanently** adv

**permeate** v pervade or pass through the whole of (something) ▶ **permeable** adj able to be permeated, esp. by liquid

**permit** v **-mitting, -mitted** give permission, allow ▷ n document giving permission to do something ▶ **permission** n authorization to do something ▶ **permissible** adj ▶ **permissive** adj (excessively) tolerant, esp. in sexual matters

**permutation** n any of the ways a number of things can be arranged or combined

**pernicious** adj wicked; extremely harmful, deadly

**pernickety** adj (informal) (excessively) fussy about details

**peroration** n concluding part of a speech, usu. summing up the main points

**peroxide** n hydrogen peroxide used as a hair bleach; oxide containing a high proportion of oxygen

**perp** n (US & Canadian informal) person who has committed a crime

**perpendicular** adj at right angles to a line or surface; upright or vertical ▷ n line or plane at right angles to another

**perpetrate** v commit or be responsible for (a wrongdoing) ▶ **perpetration** n ▶ **perpetrator** n

**perpetual** adj lasting forever; continually repeated ▶ **perpetually** adv ▶ **perpetuate** v cause to continue or be remembered ▶ **perpetuation** n **in perpetuity** forever

**perplex** v puzzle, bewilder ▶ **perplexity** n, pl **-ties**

**perquisite** n (formal) same as **perk**

**perry** n, pl **-ries** alcoholic drink made from fermented pears

**per se** [per **say**] adv (Latin) in itself

**persecute** v treat cruelly because of race, religion, etc.; subject to persistent harassment ▶ **persecution** n ▶ **persecutor** n

**persevere** v keep making an effort despite difficulties ▶ **perseverance** n

**Persian** adj of ancient Persia or modern Iran, their people, or their languages ▷ n person from modern Iran, Iranian ▶ **Persian carpet, Persian rug** hand-made carpet or rug with flowing or geometric designs in rich colours ▶ **Persian cat** long-haired domestic cat

**persimmon** n sweet red tropical fruit

**persist** v continue to be or happen, last; continue in spite of obstacles or objections ▶ **persistent** adj ▶ **persistently** adv ▶ **persistence** n

**person** n human being; body of a human being; (Grammar) form of pronouns and verbs that shows if a person is speaking, spoken to, or spoken of **in person** actually present

**persona** [per-**soh**-na] n, pl **-nae** [-nee] someone's personality as presented to others

**personable** adj pleasant in appearance and personality

**personage** n important person

**personal** adj individual or private; of the body e.g. personal hygiene; (of a remark etc.) offensive ▶ **personally** adv directly, not by delegation to others; in one's own opinion ▶ **personal computer** small computer used for word processing or computer games ▶ **personal pronoun** pronoun like I or she that stands for a definite person ▶ **personal stereo** very small portable cassette player with headphones

**personality** n, pl **-ties** person's distinctive characteristics; celebrity ▷ pl personal remarks e.g. the discussion degenerated into personalities

**personify** v **-fying, -fied** give human characteristics to; be an example of, typify ▶ **personification** n

**personnel** n people employed in an organization; department in an organization that appoints or keeps records of employees

**perspective** n view of the relative importance of situations or facts; method of drawing that gives the effect of solidity and relative distances and sizes

**Perspex**® n transparent acrylic substitute for glass

**perspicacious** adj having quick mental insight ▶ **perspicacity** n

**perspire** v sweat ▶ **perspiration** n

**persuade** v make (someone) do something by argument, charm,

etc.; convince ▶ **persuasion** n act of persuading; way of thinking or belief ▶ **persuasive** adj

**pert** adj saucy and cheeky

**pertain** v belong or be relevant (to)

**pertinacious** adj (formal) very persistent and determined ▶ **pertinacity** n

**pertinent** adj relevant ▶ **pertinence** n

**perturb** v disturb greatly ▶ **perturbation** n

**peruse** v read in a careful or leisurely manner ▶ **perusal** n

**pervade** v spread right through (something) ▶ **pervasive** adj

**perverse** adj deliberately doing something different from what is thought normal or proper ▶ **perversely** adv ▶ **perversity** n

**pervert** v use or alter for a wrong purpose; lead into abnormal (sexual) behaviour ▷ n person who practises sexual perversion ▶ **perversion** n sexual act or desire considered abnormal; act of perverting

**pervious** adj able to be penetrated, permeable

**peseta** [pa-**say**-ta] n former monetary unit of Spain

**pessary** n, pl **-ries** appliance worn in the vagina, either to prevent conception or to support the womb; vaginal suppository

**pessimism** n tendency to expect the worst in all things ▶ **pessimist** n ▶ **pessimistic** adj ▶ **pessimistically** adv

**pest** n annoying person; insect or animal that damages crops ▶ **pesticide** n chemical for killing insect pests

**pester** v annoy or nag continually

**pestilence** n deadly epidemic disease ▶ **pestilent** adj annoying, troublesome; deadly ▶ **pestilential** adj

P

**pestle** n club-shaped implement for grinding things to powder in a mortar

**pet** n animal kept for pleasure and companionship; person favoured or indulged ▷ adj particularly cherished ▷ v **petting, petted** treat as a pet; pat or stroke affectionately; (old-fashioned) kiss and caress erotically

**petal** n one of the brightly coloured outer parts of a flower ▶ **petalled** adj

**petard** n **hoist with one's own petard** being the victim of one's own schemes

**peter out** v gradually come to an end

**petite** adj (of a woman) small and dainty

**petition** n formal request, esp. one signed by many people and presented to parliament ▷ v present a petition to ▶ **petitioner** n

**petrel** n sea bird with a hooked bill and tubular nostrils

**petrify** v **-fying, -fied** frighten severely; turn to stone ▶ **petrification** n

**petrochemical** n substance, such as acetone, obtained from petroleum

**petrol** n flammable liquid obtained from petroleum, used as fuel in internal-combustion engines ▶ **petrol bomb** home-made incendiary device consisting of a bottle filled with petrol

**petroleum** n thick dark oil found underground

**petticoat** n woman's skirt-shaped undergarment

**pettifogging** adj excessively concerned with unimportant detail

**petty** adj **-tier, -tiest** unimportant, trivial; small-minded; on a small scale e.g. petty crime ▶ **pettiness** n ▶ **petty cash** cash kept by a firm to pay minor expenses ▶ **petty officer** noncommissioned officer in the navy

**petulant** adj childishly irritable or peevish ▶ **petulance** n ▶ **petulantly** adv

**petunia** n garden plant with funnel-shaped flowers

**pew** n fixed benchlike seat in a church; (informal) chair, seat

**pewter** n greyish metal made of tin and lead

**pH** (Chem) n measure of the acidity of a solution

**phalanger** n long-tailed Australian tree-dwelling marsupial

**phalanx** n, pl **phalanxes** or **phalanges** closely grouped mass of people

**phallus** n, pl **-luses** or **-li** penis, esp. as a symbol of reproductive power in primitive rites ▶ **phallic** adj

**phantasm** n unreal vision, illusion ▶ **phantasmal** adj

**phantasmagoria** n shifting medley of dreamlike figures

**phantom** n ghost; unreal vision

**Pharaoh** [fare-oh] n title of the ancient Egyptian kings

**pharmaceutical** adj of pharmacy

**pharmacology** n study of drugs ▶ **pharmacological** adj ▶ **pharmacologist** n

**pharmacopoeia** [far-ma-koh-pee-a] n book with a list of and directions for the use of drugs

**pharmacy** n, pl **-cies** preparation and dispensing of drugs and medicines; pharmacist's shop ▶ **pharmacist** n person qualified to prepare and sell drugs and medicines

**pharynx** [far-rinks] n, pl **pharynges** or **pharynxes** cavity forming the back part of the mouth

▶ **pharyngitis** [far-rin-**jite**-iss] *n* inflammation of the pharynx

**phase** *n* any distinct or characteristic stage in a development or chain of events ▷ *v* arrange or carry out in stages or to coincide with something else ▶ **phase in, phase out** *v* introduce or discontinue gradually

**PhD** Doctor of Philosophy

**pheasant** *n* game bird with bright plumage

**phenobarbitone** *n* drug inducing sleep or relaxation

**phenol** *n* chemical used in disinfectants and antiseptics

**phenomenon** *n*, *pl* -**ena** anything appearing or observed; remarkable person or thing ▶ **phenomenal** *adj* extraordinary, outstanding ▶ **phenomenally** *adv*

**phial** *n* small bottle for medicine etc.

**philadelphus** *n* shrub with sweet-scented flowers

**philanderer** *n* man who flirts or has many casual love affairs ▶ **philandering** *adj*, *n*

**philanthropy** *n* practice of helping people less well-off than oneself ▶ **philanthropic** *adj* ▶ **philanthropist** *n*

**philately** [fill-**lat**-a-lee] *n* stamp collecting ▶ **philatelist** *n*

**philharmonic** *adj* (in names of orchestras etc.) music-loving

**philistine** *adj*, *n* boorishly uncultivated (person) ▶ **philistinism** *n*

**philology** *n* science of the structure and development of languages ▶ **philological** *adj* ▶ **philologist** *n*

**philosopher** *n* person who studies philosophy

**philosophy** *n*, *pl* -**phies** study of the meaning of life, knowledge, thought, etc.; theory or set of ideas held by a particular philosopher; person's outlook on life ▶ **philosophical, philosophic** *adj* of philosophy; calm in the face of difficulties or disappointments ▶ **philosophically** *adv* ▶ **philosophize** *v* discuss in a philosophical manner

**philtre** *n* magic drink supposed to arouse love in the person who drinks it

**phishing** [**fish**-ing] *n* practice of tricking computer users into revealing their financial data in order to defraud them

**phlebitis** [fleb-**bite**-iss] *n* inflammation of a vein

**phlegm** [**flem**] *n* thick yellowish substance formed in the nose and throat during a cold

**phlegmatic** [fleg-**mat**-ik] *adj* not easily excited, unemotional ▶ **phlegmatically** *adv*

**phlox** *n*, *pl* **phlox** or **phloxes** flowering garden plant

**phobia** *n* intense and unreasoning fear or dislike

**phoenix** *n* legendary bird said to set fire to itself and rise anew from its ashes

**phone** *n*, *v* telephone ▶ **phonecard** *n* card used to operate certain public telephones ▶ **phone in** make a telephone call to deliver information (esp to a broadcasting studio or place of work); (*informal*) deliver (a performance) in a perfunctory manner ▶ **phone-in** *n* (*Brit, Aust & SAfr*) broadcast in which telephone comments or questions from the public are transmitted live

**phonetic** *adj* of speech sounds; (of spelling) written as it is sounded ▶ **phonetics** *n* science of speech sounds ▶ **phonetically** *adv*

**phoney, phony** (*informal*) *adj* **phonier, phoniest** not genuine;

**p**

insincere ▷ *n*, *pl* **phoneys** or **phonies** phoney person or thing

**phonograph** *n* (*US*, *old-fashioned*) record player

**phosphorescence** *n* faint glow in the dark ▶ **phosphorescent** *adj*

**phosphorus** *n* (*Chem*) toxic flammable nonmetallic element which appears luminous in the dark ▶ **phosphate** *n* compound of phosphorus; fertilizer containing phosphorus

**photo** *n*, *pl* **photos** short for **photograph** ▶ **photo finish** finish of a race in which the contestants are so close that a photograph is needed to decide the result ▶ **Photoshop®** *n* software application for managing and editing digital images ▷ *v* (*informal*) alter (a digital image) using Photoshop or a similar application

**photocopy** *n*, *pl* **-copies** photographic reproduction ▷ *v* **-copying, -copied** make a photocopy of ▶ **photocopier** *n*

**photoelectric** *adj* using or worked by electricity produced by the action of light

**photogenic** *adj* always looking attractive in photographs

**photograph** *n* picture made by the chemical action of light on sensitive film ▷ *v* take a photograph of ▶ **photographic** *adj* ▶ **photography** *n* art of taking photographs

**photographer** *n* person who takes photographs, esp. professionally

**photostat** *n* copy made by photocopying machine

**photosynthesis** *n* process by which a green plant uses sunlight to build up carbohydrate reserves

**phrase** *n* group of words forming a unit of meaning, esp. within

a sentence; short effective expression ▷ *v* express in words ▶ **phrasal verb** phrase consisting of a verb and an adverb or preposition, with a meaning different from the parts, such as *take in* meaning *deceive*

**phraseology** *n*, *pl* **-gies** way in which words are used

**physical** *adj* of the body, as contrasted with the mind or spirit; of material things or nature; of physics ▶ **physically** *adv* ▶ **physical education** training and practice in sports and gymnastics

**physician** *n* doctor of medicine

**physics** *n* science of the properties of matter and energy ▶ **physicist** *n* person skilled in or studying physics

**physiognomy** [fiz-ee-**on**-om-ee] *n* face

**physiology** *n* science of the normal function of living things ▶ **physiological** *adj* ▶ **physiologist** *n*

**physiotherapy** *n* treatment of disease or injury by physical means such as massage, rather than by drugs ▶ **physiotherapist** *n*

**physique** *n* person's bodily build and muscular development

**pi** *n* (*Maths*) ratio of a circle's circumference to its diameter

**pianissimo** *adv* (*Music*) very quietly

**piano** *adv* (*Music*) quietly

**Pianola®** *n* mechanically played piano

**piazza** *n* square or marketplace, esp. in Italy

**pic** *n*, *pl* **pics** or **pix** (*informal*) photograph or illustration

**picador** *n* mounted bullfighter with a lance

**picaresque** *adj* denoting a type of fiction in which the hero, a rogue, has a series of adventures

**piccalilli** n pickle of vegetables in mustard sauce

**piccolo** n, pl **-los** small flute

**pick**[1] v choose; remove (flowers or fruit) from a plant; take hold of and move with the fingers; provoke (a fight etc.) deliberately; open (a lock) by means other than a key ▷ n choice; best part ▶ **pick-me-up** n (informal) stimulating drink, tonic ▶ **pick on** v continually treat unfairly ▶ **pick out** v recognize, distinguish ▶ **pick up** v raise, lift; collect; improve, get better; become acquainted with for a sexual purpose ▶ **pick-up** n small truck; casual acquaintance made for a sexual purpose

**pick**[2] n tool with a curved iron crossbar and wooden shaft, for breaking up hard ground or rocks

**pickaxe** n large pick

**picket** n person or group standing outside a workplace to deter would-be workers during a strike; sentry or sentries posted to give warning of an attack; pointed stick used as part of a fence ▷ v form a picket outside (a workplace) ▶ **picket line** line of people acting as pickets

**pickings** pl n money easily acquired

**pickle** n food preserved in vinegar or salt water; (informal) awkward situation ▷ v preserve in vinegar or salt water ▶ **pickled** adj (of food) preserved; (informal) drunk

**pickpocket** n thief who steals from someone's pocket

**picnic** n informal meal out of doors ▷ v **-nicking, -nicked** have a picnic

**Pict** n member of an ancient race of N Britain ▶ **Pictish** adj

**pictorial** adj of or in painting or pictures

**picture** n drawing or painting; photograph; mental image; beautiful or picturesque object; image on a TV screen ▷ pl cinema ▷ v visualize, imagine; represent in a picture ▶ **picturesque** adj (of a place or view) pleasant to look at; (of language) forceful, vivid ▶ **picture window** large window made of a single sheet of glass

**piddle** v (informal) urinate

**pidgin** n language, not a mother tongue, made up of elements of two or more other languages

**pie** n dish of meat, fruit, etc. baked in pastry ▶ **pie chart** circular diagram with sectors representing quantities

**piebald** n, adj (horse) with irregular black-and-white markings

**piece** n separate bit or part; instance e.g. *a piece of luck*; example; specimen; literary or musical composition; coin; small object used in draughts, chess, etc. ▶ **piece together** v assemble bit by bit

**pièce de résistance** [pyess de ray-**ziss**-tonss] n (French) most impressive item

**piecemeal** adv bit by bit

**piecework** n work paid for according to the quantity produced

**pied** adj having markings of two or more colours

**pied-à-terre** [pyay da **tair**] n, pl **pieds-à-terre** [pyay da **tair**] small flat or house for occasional use

**pier** n platform on stilts sticking out into the sea; pillar, esp. one supporting a bridge

**pierce** v make a hole in or through with a sharp instrument; make a way through ▶ **piercing** adj (of a sound) shrill and high-pitched

**Pierrot** [**pier**-roe] n pantomime clown with a whitened face

**piety** n, pl **-ties** deep devotion to God and religion

**p**

**piffle** n (*informal*) nonsense
**pig** n animal kept and killed for pork, ham, and bacon; (*informal*) greedy, dirty, or rude person; (*offens slang*) policeman ▶ **piggish, piggy** adj (*informal*) dirty; greedy; stubborn ▶ **piggery** n place for keeping and breeding pigs ▶ **pig-headed** adj obstinate ▶ **pig iron** crude iron produced in a blast furnace ▶ **pigsty** n pen for pigs; (*Brit, Aust & NZ*) dirty or untidy place
**pigeon**[1] n bird with a heavy body and short legs, sometimes trained to carry messages ▶ **pigeonhole** n compartment for papers in a desk etc. ▷ v classify; put aside and do nothing about ▶ **pigeon-toed** adj with the feet or toes turned inwards
**pigeon**[2] n (*informal*) concern or responsibility
**piggyback** n ride on someone's shoulders ▷ adv carried on someone's shoulders
**pigment** n colouring matter, paint or dye ▶ **pigmentation** n
**Pigmy** n, pl **-mies** same as **Pygmy**
**pigtail** n plait of hair hanging from the back or either side of the head
**pike**[1] n large predatory freshwater fish
**pike**[2] n (*Hist*) long-handled spear
**pikelet** n (*Aust & NZ*) small thick pancake
**piker** n (*Aust & NZ slang*) shirker
**pikey** n (*Brit offens slang*) vagrant; person considered to be lower class
**pilaster** n square column, usu. set in a wall
**pilau, pilaf, pilaff** n Middle Eastern dish of meat, fish, or poultry boiled with rice, spices, etc.
**pilchard** n small edible sea fish of the herring family
**pile**[1] n number of things lying on top of each other; (*informal*) large amount; large building ▷ v collect into a pile; (foll by *in* or *out*) move in a group ▶ **pile-up** n (*informal*) traffic accident involving several vehicles
**pile**[2] n beam driven into the ground, esp. as a foundation for building
**pile**[3] n fibres of a carpet or a fabric, esp. velvet, that stand up from the weave
**piles** pl n swollen veins in the rectum, haemorrhoids
**pilfer** v steal in small quantities
**pilgrim** n person who journeys to a holy place ▶ **pilgrimage** n
**pill** n small ball of medicine swallowed whole **the pill** pill taken by a woman to prevent pregnancy
**pillage** v steal property by violence in war ▷ n violent seizure of goods, esp. in war
**pillar** n upright post, usu. supporting a roof; strong supporter ▶ **pillar box** (in Britain) red pillar-shaped letter box in the street
**pillion** n seat for a passenger behind the rider of a motorcycle
**pillory** n, pl **-ries** (*Hist*) frame with holes for the head and hands in which an offender was locked and exposed to public abuse ▷ v **-rying, -ried** ridicule publicly
**pillow** n stuffed cloth bag for supporting the head in bed ▷ v rest as if on a pillow ▶ **pillowcase, pillowslip** n removable cover for a pillow
**pilot** n person qualified to fly an aircraft or spacecraft; person employed to steer a ship entering or leaving a harbour ▷ adj experimental and preliminary ▷ v act as the pilot of; guide, steer ▶ **pilot light** small flame lighting the main one in a gas appliance
**pimento** n, pl **-tos** mild-tasting red pepper

**pimp** n man who gets customers for a prostitute in return for a share of his or her earnings ▷ v act as a pimp ▶ **pimp up, pimp out** v decorate (someone or something) with flashy accessories

**pimpernel** n wild plant with small star-shaped flowers

**pimple** n small pus-filled spot on the skin ▶ **pimply** adj

**PIN** personal identification number: number used with a credit or debit card to withdraw money, confirm a purchase, etc. ▶ **PIN pad** small pad into which a customer keys his or her PIN to confirm a purchase

**pin** n short thin piece of stiff wire with a point and head, for fastening things; wooden or metal peg or stake ▷ v **pinning, pinned** fasten with a pin; seize and hold fast ▶ **pin down** v force (someone) to make a decision, take action, etc.; define clearly ▶ **pin money** small amount earned to buy small luxuries ▶ **pin-up** n picture of a sexually attractive person, esp. (partly) naked

**pinafore** n apron; dress with a bib top

**pinball** n electrically operated table game in which a small ball is shot through various hazards

**pince-nez** [panss-**nay**] n, pl **pince-nez** glasses kept in place only by a clip on the bridge of the nose

**pincers** pl n tool consisting of two hinged arms, for gripping; claws of a lobster etc.

**pinch** v squeeze between finger and thumb; cause pain by being too tight; (informal) steal ▷ n act of pinching; as much as can be taken up between the finger and thumb **at a pinch** if absolutely necessary **feel the pinch** have to economize

**pinchbeck** n alloy of zinc and copper, used as imitation gold

**pine¹** n evergreen coniferous tree; its wood ▶ **pine cone** woody seed case of the pine tree ▶ **pine marten** wild mammal of the coniferous forests of Europe and Asia

**pine²** v (foll by for) feel great longing (for); become thin and ill through grief etc.

**pineal gland** n small cone-shaped gland at the base of the brain

**pineapple** n large tropical fruit with juicy yellow flesh and a hard skin

**ping** v, n (make) a short high-pitched sound

**Ping-Pong®** n table tennis

**pinion¹** n bird's wing ▷ v immobilize (someone) by tying or holding his or her arms

**pinion²** n small cogwheel

**pink** n pale reddish colour; fragrant garden plant ▷ adj of the colour pink ▷ v (of an engine) make a metallic noise because not working properly, knock **in the pink** in good health

**pinking shears** pl n scissors with a serrated blade or blades that give a wavy edge to material to prevent fraying

**pinnacle** n highest point of fame or success; mountain peak; small slender spire

**pinotage** [pin-no-**tajj**] n blended red wine of S Africa

**pinpoint** v locate or identify exactly

**pinstripe** n very narrow stripe in fabric; the fabric itself

**pint** n liquid measure, 1/8 gallon (.568 litre)

**pioneer** n explorer or early settler of a new country; originator or developer of something new ▷ v be the pioneer or leader of

**pious** adj deeply religious, devout

**pip¹** n small seed in a fruit

p

**pip²** n high-pitched sound used as a time signal on radio; (*informal*) star on a junior army officer's shoulder showing rank

**pip³** n **give someone the pip** (*Brit, NZ & S Afr slang*) annoy

**pipe** n tube for conveying liquid or gas; tube with a small bowl at the end for smoking tobacco; tubular musical instrument ▷ pl bagpipes ▷ v play on a pipe; utter in a shrill tone; convey by pipe; decorate with piping ▶ **piper** n player on a pipe or bagpipes ▶ **piping** n system of pipes; decoration of icing on a cake etc.; fancy edging on clothes etc. ▶ **piped music** recorded music played as background music in public places ▶ **pipe down** v (*informal*) stop talking ▶ **pipe dream** fanciful impossible plan ▶ **pipeline** n long pipe for transporting oil, water, etc.; means of communication **in the pipeline** in preparation ▶ **pipe up** v speak suddenly or shrilly

**pipette** n slender glass tube used to transfer or measure fluids

**pipi** n (*Aust & NZ*) edible mollusc often used as bait

**pipit** n small brownish songbird

**pippin** n type of eating apple

**piquant** [pee-kant] adj having a pleasant spicy taste; mentally stimulating ▶ **piquancy** n

**pique** [peek] n feeling of hurt pride, baffled curiosity, or resentment ▷ v hurt the pride of; arouse (curiosity)

**piqué** [pee-kay] n stiff ribbed cotton fabric

**piquet** [pik-**ket**] n card game for two

**piranha** n small fierce freshwater fish of tropical America

**pirate** n sea robber; person who illegally publishes or sells work owned by someone else; person or company that broadcasts illegally ▷ v sell or reproduce (artistic work etc.) illegally ▶ **piracy** n ▶ **piratical** adj

**pirouette** v, n (make) a spinning turn balanced on the toes of one foot

**piss** (*vulgar slang*) v urinate ▷ n act of urinating; urine

**pistachio** n, pl **-chios** edible nut of a Mediterranean tree

**piste** [peest] n ski slope

**pistil** n seed-bearing part of a flower

**pistol** n short-barrelled handgun

**piston** n cylindrical part in an engine that slides to and fro in a cylinder

**pit** n deep hole in the ground; coal mine; dent or depression; servicing and refuelling area on a motor-racing track; same as **orchestra** ▷ v **pitting, pitted** mark with small dents or scars **pit one's wits against** compete against in a test or contest ▶ **pit bull terrier** strong muscular terrier with a short coat

**pitch¹** v throw, hurl; set up (a tent); fall headlong; (of a ship or plane) move with the front and back going up and down alternately; set the level or tone of ▷ n area marked out for playing sport; degree or angle of slope; degree of highness or lowness of a (musical) sound; place where a street or market trader regularly sells; (*informal*) persuasive sales talk ▶ **pitch in** v join in enthusiastically ▶ **pitch into** v (*informal*) attack

**pitch²** n dark sticky substance obtained from tar ▶ **pitch-black, pitch-dark** adj very dark

**pitchblende** n mineral composed largely of uranium oxide, yielding radium

**pitcher** n large jug with a narrow neck

**pitchfork** n large long-handled fork for lifting hay ▷ v thrust abruptly or violently

**pitfall** n hidden difficulty or danger

**pith** n soft white lining of the rind of oranges etc.; essential part; soft tissue in the stems of certain plants ▶ **pithy** adj short and full of meaning

**piton** [peet-on] n metal spike used in climbing to secure a rope

**pittance** n very small amount of money

**pituitary** n, pl **-taries** gland at the base of the brain that helps to control growth (also **pituitary gland**)

**pity** n, pl **pities** sympathy or sorrow for others' suffering; regrettable fact ▷ v **pitying, pitied** feel pity for ▶ **piteous, pitiable** adj arousing pity ▶ **pitiful** adj arousing pity; woeful, contemptible ▶ **pitifully** adv ▶ **pitiless** adj feeling no pity or mercy ▶ **pitilessly** adv

**pivot** n central shaft on which something turns ▷ v provide with or turn on a pivot ▶ **pivotal** adj of crucial importance

**pix** n (informal) a plural of **pic**

**pixel** n smallest constituent unit of an image, as on a computer screen

**pixie** n (in folklore) fairy

**pizza** n flat disc of dough covered with a wide variety of savoury toppings and baked

**pizzazz** n (informal) attractive combination of energy and style

**pizzicato** [pit-see-kah-toe] adj (Music) played by plucking the string of a violin etc. with the finger

**placard** n notice that is carried or displayed in public

**placate** v make (someone) stop feeling angry or upset ▶ **placatory** adj

**place** n particular part of an area or space; particular town, building, etc.; position or point reached; seat or space; duty or right; position of employment; usual position ▷ v put in a particular place; identify, put in context; make (an order, bet, etc.) **be placed** (of a competitor in a race) be among the first three **take place** happen, occur

**placebo** [plas-**see**-bo] n, pl **-bos** or **-boes** sugar pill etc. given to an unsuspecting patient instead of an active drug

**placenta** [plass-**ent**-a] n, pl **-tas** or **-tae** organ formed in the womb during pregnancy, providing nutrients for the fetus ▶ **placental** adj

**placid** adj not easily excited or upset, calm ▶ **placidity** n

**plagiarize** [**play**-jer-ize] v steal ideas, passages, etc. from (someone else's work) and present them as one's own ▶ **plagiarism** n

**plague** n fast-spreading fatal disease; (Hist) bubonic plague; widespread infestation ▷ v **plaguing, plagued** trouble or annoy continually

**plaice** n edible European flatfish

**plaid** n long piece of tartan cloth worn as part of Highland dress; tartan cloth or pattern

**plain** adj easy to see or understand; expressed honestly and clearly; without decoration or pattern; not beautiful; simple, ordinary ▷ n large stretch of level country ▶ **plainly** adv ▶ **plainness** n ▶ **plain clothes** ordinary clothes, as opposed to uniform ▶ **plain sailing** easy progress ▶ **plain speaking** saying exactly what one thinks

**plainsong** n unaccompanied singing, esp. in a medieval church

**plaintiff** n person who sues in a court of law

**p**

**plaintive** *adj* sad, mournful
▶ **plaintively** *adv*

**plait** [platt] *n* intertwined length of hair ▷ *v* intertwine separate strands in a pattern

**plan** *n* way thought out to do or achieve something; diagram showing the layout or design of something ▷ *v* **planning, planned** arrange beforehand; make a diagram of ▶ **planner** *n*

**plane¹** *n* aeroplane; (*Maths*) flat surface; level of attainment etc. ▷ *adj* perfectly flat or level ▷ *v* glide or skim

**plane²** *n* tool for smoothing wood ▷ *v* smooth (wood) with a plane

**plane³** *n* tree with broad leaves

**planet** *n* large body in space that revolves round the sun or another star ▶ **planetary** *adj*

**planetarium** *n, pl* **-iums** *or* **-ia** building where the movements of the stars, planets, etc. are shown by projecting lights on the inside of a dome

**plangent** *adj* (of sounds) mournful and resounding

**plank** *n* long flat piece of sawn timber

**plankton** *n* minute animals and plants floating in the surface water of a sea or lake

**plant** *n* living organism that grows in the ground and has no power to move; equipment or machinery used in industrial processes; factory or other industrial premises ▷ *v* put in the ground to grow; place firmly in position; (*informal*) put (a person) secretly in an organization to spy; (*informal*) hide (stolen goods etc.) on a person to make him or her seem guilty ▶ **planter** *n* owner of a plantation

**plantain¹** *n* low-growing wild plant with broad leaves

**plantain²** *n* tropical fruit like a green banana

**plantation** *n* estate for the cultivation of tea, tobacco, etc.; wood of cultivated trees

**plaque** *n* inscribed commemorative stone or metal plate; filmy deposit on teeth that causes decay

**plasma** *n* clear liquid part of blood

**plasma screen** *n* type of flat screen on a television or visual display unit

**plaster** *n* mixture of lime, sand, etc. for coating walls; adhesive strip of material for dressing cuts etc. ▷ *v* cover with plaster; coat thickly ▶ **plastered** *adj* (*slang*) drunk ▶ **plaster of Paris** white powder which dries to form a hard solid when mixed with water, used for sculptures and casts for broken limbs

**plastic** *n* synthetic material that can be moulded when soft but sets in a hard long-lasting shape; credit cards etc. as opposed to cash ▷ *adj* made of plastic; easily moulded, pliant ▶ **plasticity** *n* ability to be moulded ▶ **plastic bullet** solid PVC cylinder fired by police in riot control ▶ **plastic surgery** repair or reconstruction of missing or malformed parts of the body

**Plasticine**® *n* soft coloured modelling material used esp. by children

**plate** *n* shallow dish for holding food; flat thin sheet of metal, glass, etc.; thin coating of metal on another metal; dishes or cutlery made of gold or silver; illustration, usu. on fine quality paper, in a book; (*informal*) set of false teeth ▷ *v* cover with a thin coating of gold, silver, or other metal ▶ **plateful** *n* ▶ **plate glass** glass in thin sheets, used for mirrors and windows ▶ **plate**

**tectonics** study of the structure of the earth's crust, esp. the movement of layers of rocks

**plateau** n, pl **-teaus** or **-teaux** area of level high land; stage when there is no change or development

**platen** n roller of a typewriter, against which the paper is held

**platform** n raised floor; raised area in a station from which passengers board trains; structure in the sea which holds machinery, stores, etc. for drilling an oil well; programme of a political party

**platinum** n (Chem) valuable silvery-white metal ▶ **platinum blonde** woman with silvery-blonde hair

**platitude** n remark that is true but not interesting or original ▶ **platitudinous** adj

**platonic** adj (of a relationship) friendly or affectionate but not sexual

**platoon** n smaller unit within a company of soldiers

**platteland** n (SAfr) rural district

**platter** n large dish

**platypus** n Australian egg-laying amphibious mammal, with dense fur, webbed feet, and a ducklike bill (also **duck-billed platypus**)

**plaudits** pl n expressions of approval

**plausible** adj apparently true or reasonable; persuasive but insincere ▶ **plausibly** adv ▶ **plausibility** n

**play** v occupy oneself in (a game or recreation); compete against in a game or sport; behave carelessly; act (a part) on the stage; perform on (a musical instrument); cause (a radio, record player, etc.) to give out sound; move lightly or irregularly, flicker ▷ n story performed on stage or broadcast; activities children take part in for amusement; playing of a game; conduct e.g. fair play;

(scope for) freedom of movement ▶ **playful** adj lively ▶ **play back** v listen to or watch (something recorded) ▶ **playcentre** n (NZ & SAfr) centre for preschool children run by parents ▶ **play down** v minimize the importance of ▶ **playgroup** n regular meeting of very young children for supervised play ▶ **playhouse** n theatre ▶ **playing card** one of a set of 52 cards used in card games ▶ **playing field** extensive piece of ground for sport ▶ **play-lunch** n (Aust & NZ) child's mid-morning snack at school ▶ **play off** v set (two people) against each other for one's own ends ▶ **play on** v exploit or encourage (someone's sympathy or weakness) ▶ **playschool** n nursery group for young children ▶ **PlayStation®** n type of video games console ▶ **plaything** n toy; person regarded or treated as a toy ▶ **play up** v give prominence to; cause trouble ▶ **playwright** n author of plays

**playboy** n rich man who lives only for pleasure

**player** n person who plays a game or sport; actor or actress; person who plays a musical instrument

**plaza** n open space or square; modern shopping complex

**PLC, plc** (in Britain) Public Limited Company

**plea** n serious or urgent request, entreaty; statement of a prisoner or defendant; excuse

**plead** v ask urgently or with deep feeling; give as an excuse; (Law) declare oneself to be guilty or innocent of a charge made against one

**pleasant** adj pleasing, enjoyable ▶ **pleasantly** adv ▶ **pleasantry** n, pl **-tries** polite or joking remark

p

**please** v give pleasure or satisfaction to ▷ adv polite word of request **please oneself** do as one likes ▸ **pleased** adj ▸ **pleasing** adj

**pleasure** n feeling of happiness and satisfaction; something that causes this ▸ **pleasurable** adj giving pleasure ▸ **pleasurably** adv

**pleat** n fold made by doubling material back on itself ▷ v arrange (material) in pleats

**plebeian** [pleb-**ee**-an] adj of the lower social classes; vulgar or rough ▷ n (also **pleb**) member of the lower social classes

**plebiscite** [**pleb**-iss-ite] n decision by direct voting of the people of a country

**plectrum** n, pl **-trums** or **-tra** small implement for plucking the strings of a guitar etc.

**pledge** n solemn promise; something valuable given as a guarantee that a promise will be kept or a debt paid ▷ v promise solemnly; bind by or as if by a pledge

**plenary** adj (of a meeting) attended by all members

**plenipotentiary** adj having full powers ▷ n, pl **-aries** diplomat or representative having full powers

**plenitude** n completeness, abundance

**plenteous** adj plentiful

**plenty** n large amount or number; quite enough ▸ **plentiful** adj existing in large amounts or numbers ▸ **plentifully** adv

**pleonasm** n use of more words than necessary

**plethora** n excess

**pleurisy** n inflammation of the membrane covering the lungs

**pliable** adj easily bent; easily influenced ▸ **pliability** n

**pliant** adj pliable ▸ **pliancy** n

**pliers** pl n tool with hinged arms and jaws for gripping

**plight**[1] n difficult or dangerous situation

**plight**[2] v **plight one's troth** (old-fashioned) promise to marry

**Plimsoll line** n mark on a ship showing the level water should reach when the ship is fully loaded

**plimsolls** pl n (Brit) rubber-soled canvas shoes

**plinth** n slab forming the base of a statue, column, etc.

**PLO** Palestine Liberation Organization

**plod** v **plodding, plodded** walk with slow heavy steps; work slowly but determinedly ▸ **plodder** n

**plonk**[1] v put (something) down heavily and carelessly

**plonk**[2] n (informal) cheap inferior wine

**plop** n sound of an object falling into water without a splash ▷ v **plopping, plopped** make this sound

**plot**[1] n secret plan to do something illegal or wrong; story of a film, novel, etc. ▷ v **plotting, plotted** plan secretly, conspire; mark the position or course of (a ship or aircraft) on a map; mark and join up (points on a graph)

**plot**[2] n small piece of land

**plough** n agricultural tool for turning over soil ▷ v turn over (earth) with a plough; move or work through slowly and laboriously ▸ **ploughman** n ▸ **ploughshare** n blade of a plough

**plover** n shore bird with a straight bill and long pointed wings

**ploy** n manoeuvre designed to gain an advantage

**pluck** v pull or pick off; pull out the feathers of (a bird for cooking); sound the strings of (a guitar etc.) with the fingers or a plectrum

▷ *n* courage ▶ **plucky** *adj* brave ▶ **pluckily** *adv* ▶ **pluck up** *v* summon up (courage)

**plug** *n* thing fitting into and filling a hole; device connecting an appliance to an electricity supply; (*informal*) favourable mention of a product etc., to encourage people to buy it ▷ *v* **plugging, plugged** block or seal (a hole or gap) with a plug; (*informal*) advertise (a product etc.) by constant repetition ▶ **plug away** *v* (*informal*) work steadily ▶ **plug in** *v* connect (an electrical appliance) to a power source by pushing a plug into a socket

**plum** *n* oval usu. dark red fruit with a stone in the middle ▷ *adj* dark purplish-red; very desirable

**plumage** *n* bird's feathers

**plumb** *v* understand (something obscure); test with a plumb line ▷ *adv* exactly **plumb the depths of** experience the worst extremes of (an unpleasant quality or emotion) ▶ **plumbing** *n* pipes and fixtures used in water and drainage systems ▶ **plumb in** *v* connect (an appliance such as a washing machine) to a water supply ▶ **plumb line** string with a weight at the end, used to test the depth of water or to test whether something is vertical

**plumber** *n* person who fits and repairs pipes and fixtures for water and drainage systems

**plume** *n* feather, esp. one worn as an ornament

**plummet** *v* -**meting, -meted** plunge downward

**plump**¹ *adj* moderately or attractively fat ▶ **plumpness** *n* ▶ **plump up** *v* make (a pillow, cushion, etc) fuller or rounded

**plump**² *v* sit or fall heavily and suddenly ▶ **plump for** *v* choose, vote for

**plunder** *v* take by force, esp. in time of war ▷ *n* things plundered, spoils

**plunge** *v* put or throw forcibly or suddenly (into); descend steeply ▷ *n* plunging, dive **take the plunge** (*informal*) embark on a risky enterprise ▶ **plunger** *n* rubber suction cup used to clear blocked pipes ▶ **plunge into** *v* become deeply involved in

**plunket baby** *n* (*NZ*) baby brought up on the diet recommended by the Plunket Society ▶ **plunket nurse** (*NZ*) nurse working for the Plunket Society

**pluperfect** *n, adj* (*Grammar*) (tense) expressing an action completed before a past time, e.g. *had gone* in *his wife had gone already*

**plural** *adj* of or consisting of more than one ▷ *n* word indicating more than one

**pluralism** *n* existence and toleration of a variety of peoples, opinions, etc. in a society ▶ **pluralist** *n* ▶ **pluralistic** *adj*

**plus** *prep, adj* indicating addition ▷ *adj* more than zero; positive; advantageous ▷ *n* sign (+) denoting addition; advantage

> **USAGE NOTE**
> Avoid using *plus* to mean 'additionally' except in very informal contexts

**plus fours** *pl n* trousers gathered in just below the knee

**plush** *n* fabric with long velvety pile ▷ *adj* (also **plushy**) luxurious

**plus-one** *n* (*informal*) person who accompanies an invited person to a social function

**Pluto** *n* Greek god of the underworld; farthest planet from the sun

**plutocrat** *n* person who is powerful because of being very rich ▶ **plutocratic** *adj*

**plutonium** n (Chem) radioactive metallic element used esp. in nuclear reactors and weapons

**ply¹** v **plying, plied** work at (a job or trade); use (a tool); (of a ship) travel regularly along or between ▶ **ply with** v supply with or subject to persistently

**ply²** n thickness of wool, fabric, etc.

**plywood** n board made of thin layers of wood glued together

**PM** prime minister

**p.m.** after noon; postmortem

**PMS** premenstrual syndrome

**PMT** premenstrual tension

**pneumatic** adj worked by or inflated with wind or air

**pneumonia** n inflammation of the lungs

**PO** (Brit) postal order; Post Office

**poach¹** v catch (animals) illegally on someone else's land; encroach on or steal something belonging to someone else

**poach²** v simmer (food) gently in liquid

**poacher** n person who catches animals illegally on someone else's land

**POC** proof of concept

**pocket** n small bag sewn into clothing for carrying things; pouchlike container, esp. for catching balls at the edge of a snooker table; isolated or distinct group or area ▷ v **pocketing, pocketed** put into one's pocket; take secretly or dishonestly ▷ adj small **out of pocket** having made a loss ▶ **pocket money** small regular allowance given to children by parents; money for small personal expenses

**pockmarked** adj (of the skin) marked with hollow scars where diseased spots have been

**pod** n long narrow seed case of peas, beans, etc.

**podcast** n audio file similar to a radio broadcast which can be downloaded to a computer, iPod™, etc. ▷ v create such files and make them available for downloading

**podgy** adj **podgier, podgiest** short and fat

**podiatrist** [poe-die-a-trist] n same as **chiropodist** ▶ **podiatry** n

**podium** n, pl **-diums** or **-dia** small raised platform for a conductor or speaker

**poem** n imaginative piece of writing in rhythmic lines

**poep** n (SAfr slang) emission of gas from the anus

**poesy** n (obs) poetry

**poet** n writer of poems ▶ **poetry** n poems; art of writing poems; beautiful or pleasing quality ▶ **poetic, poetical** adj of or like poetry ▶ **poetically** adv ▶ **poetic justice** suitable reward or punishment for someone's past actions ▶ **poet laureate** poet appointed by the British sovereign to write poems on important occasions

**pogrom** n organized persecution and massacre

**poignant** adj sharply painful to the feelings ▶ **poignancy** n

**poinsettia** n Central American shrub widely grown for its clusters of scarlet leaves, which resemble petals

**point** n main idea in a discussion, argument, etc.; aim or purpose; detail or item; characteristic; particular position, stage, or time; dot indicating decimals; sharp end; unit for recording a value or score; one of the direction marks of a compass; electrical socket ▷ v show the direction or position of something or draw attention to it by extending a finger or other pointed object towards it; direct or face towards **on the point of** very shortly going to ▸ **pointed** adj having a sharp end; (of a remark) obviously directed at a particular person ▸ **pointedly** adv ▸ **pointer** n helpful hint; indicator on a measuring instrument; breed of gun dog ▸ **pointless** adj meaningless, irrelevant ▸ **point-blank** adj fired at a very close target; (of a remark or question) direct, blunt ▹ adv directly or bluntly ▸ **point duty** control of traffic by a policeman at a road junction ▸ **point of view** way of considering something ▸ **point-to-point** n (Brit) horse race across open country

**poise** n calm dignified manner ▸ **poised** adj absolutely ready; behaving with or showing poise

**poison** n substance that kills or injures when swallowed or absorbed ▹ v give poison to; have a harmful or evil effect on, spoil ▸ **poisoner** n ▸ **poisonous** adj ▸ **poison-pen letter** malicious anonymous letter

**poke** v jab or prod with one's finger, a stick, etc.; thrust forward or out ▹ v poking ▸ **poky** adj small and cramped

**poker**[1] n metal rod for stirring a fire

**poker**[2] n card game in which players bet on the hands dealt ▸ **poker-faced** adj expressionless

**polar** adj of or near either of the earth's poles ▸ **polar bear** white bear that lives in the regions around the North Pole

**polarize** v form or cause to form into groups with directly opposite views; (Physics) restrict (light waves) to certain directions of vibration ▸ **polarization** n

**Polaroid**® n plastic which polarizes light and so reduces glare; camera that develops a print very quickly inside itself

**polder** n land reclaimed from the sea, esp. in the Netherlands

**pole**[1] n long rounded piece of wood ▸ **pole dancing** entertainment in which a woman dances erotically using a vertical fixed pole

**pole**[2] n point furthest north or south on the earth's axis of rotation; either of the opposite ends of a magnet or electric cell ▸ **Pole Star** star nearest to the North Pole in the northern hemisphere

**poleaxe** v hit with a heavy blow

**polecat** n small animal of the weasel family

**polemic** [pol-em-ik] n fierce attack on or defence of a particular opinion, belief, etc. ▸ **polemical** adj

**police** n organized force in a state which keeps law and order ▹ v control or watch over with police or a similar body ▸ **policeman, policewoman** n member of a police force

**policy**[1] n, pl -**cies** plan of action adopted by a person, group, or state

**policy**[2] n, pl -**cies** document containing an insurance contract

**polio** n disease affecting the spinal cord, which often causes paralysis (also **poliomyelitis**)

**polish** v make smooth and shiny by rubbing; make more nearly perfect ▹ n substance used for polishing; pleasing elegant style ▸ **polished** adj accomplished; done or performed well or professionally ▸ **polish off** v (informal) finish completely, dispose of

**Polish** adj of Poland, its people, or their language ▹ n official language of Poland

p

**polite** adj showing consideration for others in one's manners, speech, etc.; socially correct or refined ▶ **politely** adv ▶ **politeness** n

**politic** adj wise and likely to prove advantageous

**politics** n winning and using of power to govern society; (study of) the art of government; person's beliefs about how a country should be governed ▶ **political** adj of the state, government, or public administration ▶ **politically** adv ▶ **politically correct** (of language) intended to avoid any implied prejudice ▶ **political prisoner** person imprisoned because of his or her political beliefs ▶ **politician** n person actively engaged in politics, esp. a member of parliament

**polka** n lively 19th-century dance; music for this ▶ **polka dots** pattern of bold spots on fabric

**poll** n (also **opinion poll**) questioning of a random sample of people to find out general opinion; voting; number of votes recorded ▷ v receive (votes); question in an opinion poll ▶ **pollster** n person who conducts opinion polls ▶ **polling station** building where people vote in an election

**pollarded** adj (of a tree) growing very bushy because its top branches have been cut short

**pollen** n fine dust produced by flowers to fertilize other flowers ▶ **pollinate** v fertilize with pollen ▶ **pollen count** measure of the amount of pollen in the air, esp. as a warning to people with hay fever

**pollute** v contaminate with something poisonous or harmful ▶ **pollution** n ▶ **pollutant** n something that pollutes

**polly** n, pl **-lies** (Aust informal) politician

**polo** n game like hockey played by teams of players on horseback ▶ **polo neck** sweater with tight turned-over collar

**polonaise** n old stately dance; music for this

**polonium** n (Chem) radioactive element that occurs in trace amounts in uranium ores

**poltergeist** n spirit believed to move furniture and throw objects around

**poltroon** n (obs) utter coward

**poly-** combining form many, much

**polyandry** n practice of having more than one husband at the same time

**polyanthus** n garden primrose

**polychromatic** adj many-coloured

**polyester** n synthetic material used to make plastics and textile fibres

**polygamy** [pol-ig-a-mee] n practice of having more than one husband or wife at the same time ▶ **polygamous** adj ▶ **polygamist** n

**polyglot** n, adj (person) able to speak or write several languages

**polygon** n geometrical figure with three or more angles and sides ▶ **polygonal** adj

**polyhedron** n, pl **-drons** or **-dra** solid figure with four or more sides

**polymer** n chemical compound with large molecules made of simple molecules of the same kind ▶ **polymerize** v form into polymers ▶ **polymerization** n

**polyp** n small simple sea creature with a hollow cylindrical body; small growth on a mucous membrane

**polyphonic** adj (Music) consisting of several melodies played simultaneously

**polystyrene** n synthetic material used esp. as white rigid foam for packing and insulation

**polytechnic** n (in New Zealand and formerly in Britain) college offering courses in many subjects at and below degree level

**polytheism** n belief in many gods ▶ **polytheistic** adj

**polythene** n light plastic used for bags etc.

**polyunsaturated** adj of a group of fats that do not form cholesterol in the blood

**polyurethane** n synthetic material used esp. in paints

**pom** n (Aust & NZ slang) person from England (also **pommy**)

**pomander** n (container for) a mixture of sweet-smelling petals, herbs, etc.

**pomegranate** n round tropical fruit with a thick rind containing many seeds in a red pulp

**Pomeranian** n small dog with long straight hair

**pommel** n raised part on the front of a saddle; knob at the top of a sword hilt

**pomp** n stately display or ceremony

**pompom** n decorative ball of tufted wool, silk, etc.

**pompous** adj foolishly serious and grand, self-important ▶ **pompously** adv ▶ **pomposity** n

**ponce** n (offens) effeminate man; pimp ▶ **ponce around** v (Brit, Aust & NZ) behave in a ridiculous or posturing way

**poncho** n, pl **-chos** loose circular cloak with a hole for the head

**pond** n small area of still water

**ponder** v think thoroughly or deeply (about)

**ponderous** adj serious and dull; heavy and unwieldy; (of movement) slow and clumsy ▶ **ponderously** adv

**pong** v, n (informal) (give off) a strong unpleasant smell

**pontiff** n the Pope ▶ **pontificate** v state one's opinions as if they were the only possible correct ones ▷ n period of office of a Pope

**pontoon¹** n floating platform supporting a temporary bridge

**pontoon²** n gambling card game

**pony** n, pl **ponies** small horse ▶ **ponytail** n long hair tied in one bunch at the back of the head

**Ponzi scheme** n fraudulent investment operation that pays quick returns to initial contributors using money from subsequent contributors rather than profit

**poodle** n dog with curly hair often clipped fancifully

**poof, poofter** n (Brit, Aust & NZ offens) homosexual man

**pool¹** n small body of still water; puddle of spilt liquid; swimming pool

**pool²** n shared fund or group of workers or resources; game similar to snooker ▷ pl (Brit) short for **football pools** ▷ v put in a common fund

**poop** n raised part at the back of a sailing ship

**poor** adj having little money and few possessions; less, smaller, or weaker than is needed or expected; inferior; unlucky, pitiable ▶ **poorly** adv in a poor manner ▷ adj not in good health

**pop¹** v **popping, popped** make or cause to make a small explosive sound; (informal) (often foll by in or out) go, put, or come unexpectedly or suddenly ▷ n small explosive sound; (Brit) nonalcoholic fizzy drink ▶ **popcorn** n grains of maize heated until they puff up and burst ▶ **pop-up** n (Computing) image that appears above the open window on a computer screen

**pop²** n music of general appeal, esp. to young people

**p**

**pop³** n (informal) father

**Pope** n head of the Roman Catholic Church ▶ **popish** adj (offens) Roman Catholic

**poplar** n tall slender tree

**poplin** n ribbed cotton material

**poppadom** n thin round crisp Indian bread

**poppy** n, pl **-pies** plant with a large red flower

**populace** n the ordinary people

**popular** adj widely liked and admired; of or for the public in general ▶ **popularly** adv ▶ **popularity** n ▶ **popularize** v make popular; make (something technical or specialist) easily understood

**populate** v live in, inhabit; fill with inhabitants ▶ **populous** adj densely populated

**population** n all the people who live in a particular place; the number of people living in a particular place

**populist** n, adj (person) appealing to the interests or prejudices of ordinary people ▶ **populism** n

**porbeagle** n kind of shark

**porcelain** n fine china; objects made of it

**porch** n covered approach to the entrance of a building

**porcine** adj of or like a pig

**porcupine** n animal covered with long pointed quills

**pore** n tiny opening in the skin or in the surface of a plant

**pork** n pig meat ▶ **porker** n pig raised for food

**porn, porno** n, adj (informal) short for **pornography, pornographic**

**pornography** n writing, films, or pictures designed to be sexually exciting ▶ **pornographer** n producer of pornography ▶ **pornographic** adj

**porous** adj allowing liquid to pass through gradually ▶ **porosity** n

**porphyry** [por-fir-ee] n reddish rock with large crystals in it

**porpoise** n fishlike sea mammal

**porridge** n breakfast food made of oatmeal cooked in water or milk; (chiefly Brit slang) term in prison

**port¹** n (town with) a harbour

**port²** n left side of a ship or aircraft when facing the front of it

**port³** n strong sweet wine, usu. red

**port⁴** n opening in the side of a ship; porthole

**portable** adj easily carried ▶ **portability** n

**portal** n large imposing doorway or gate; (Computing) internet site providing links to other sites

**portcullis** n grating suspended above a castle gateway, that can be lowered to block the entrance

**portend** v be a sign of

**portent** n sign of a future event ▶ **portentous** adj of great or ominous significance; pompous, self-important

**porter¹** n man who carries luggage; hospital worker who transfers patients between rooms etc.

**porter²** n doorman or gatekeeper of a building

**portfolio** n, pl **-os** (flat case for carrying) examples of an artist's work; area of responsibility of a government minister; list of investments held by an investor

**porthole** n small round window in a ship or aircraft

**portico** n, pl **-coes** or **-cos** porch or covered walkway with columns supporting the roof

**portion** n part or share; helping of food for one person; destiny or fate ▶ **portion out** v divide into shares

**portly** adj **-lier, -liest** rather fat

**portmanteau** n, pl **-teaus** or **-teaux** (old-fashioned) large suitcase that opens into two compartments ▷ adj combining aspects of different things

**portrait** n picture of a person; lifelike description

**portray** v describe or represent by artistic means, as in writing or film ▶ **portrayal** n

**Portuguese** adj of Portugal, its people, or their language ▷ n person from Portugal; language of Portugal and Brazil ▶ **Portuguese man-of-war** sea creature resembling a jellyfish, with stinging tentacles

**pose** v place in or take up a particular position to be photographed or drawn; raise (a problem); ask (a question) ▷ n position while posing; behaviour adopted for effect **pose as** pretend to be ▶ **poser** n puzzling question; poseur ▶ **poseur** n person who behaves in an affected way to impress others

**posh** adj (informal) smart, luxurious; affectedly upper-class

**posit** [**pozz**-it] v lay down as a basis for argument

**position** n place; usual or expected place; way in which something is placed or arranged; attitude, point of view; social standing; job ▷ v place

**positive** adj feeling no doubts, certain; confident, hopeful; helpful, providing encouragement; absolute, downright; (Maths) greater than zero; (of an electrical charge) having a deficiency of electrons ▶ **positively** adv ▶ **positive discrimination** provision of special opportunities for a disadvantaged group

**positron** n (Physics) particle with same mass as an electron but a positive charge

**posse** [**poss**-ee] n (US) group of men organized to maintain law and order; (Brit & Aust informal) group of friends or associates

**possess** v have as one's property; (of a feeling, belief, etc.) have complete control of, dominate ▶ **possessor** n ▶ **possession** n state of possessing, ownership ▷ pl things a person possesses ▶ **possessive** adj wanting all the attention or love of another person; (of a word) indicating the person or thing that something belongs to ▶ **possessiveness** n

**possible** adj able to exist, happen, or be done; worthy of consideration ▷ n person or thing that might be suitable or chosen ▶ **possibility** n, pl **-ties** ▶ **possibly** adv perhaps, not necessarily

**possum** n same as **opossum**; (Aust & NZ) same as **phalanger**; **play possum** pretend to be dead or asleep to deceive an opponent

**post**[1] n official system of delivering letters and parcels; (single collection or delivery of) letters and parcels sent by this system ▷ v send by post **keep someone posted** supply someone regularly with the latest information ▶ **postage** n charge for sending a letter or parcel by post ▶ **postal** adj ▶ **postal order** (Brit) written money order sent by post and cashed at a post office by the person who receives it ▶ **postbag** n postman's bag; post received by a magazine, famous person, etc. ▶ **postcode** n system of letters and numbers used to aid the sorting of mail ▶ **postie** n (Scot, Aust & NZ informal) postman ▶ **postman, postwoman** n person who collects and delivers post ▶ **postmark** n official mark stamped on letters showing place

**P**

and date of posting ▸ **postmaster, postmistress** n (in some countries) official in charge of a post office ▸ **post office** place where postal business is conducted ▸ **post shop** (NZ) shop providing postal services

**post²** n length of wood, concrete, etc. fixed upright to support or mark something ▷ v put up (a notice) in a public place

**post³** n job; position to which someone, esp. a soldier, is assigned for duty; military establishment ▷ v send (a person) to a new place to work; put (a guard etc.) on duty

**post-** prefix after, later than e.g. postwar

**postcard** n card for sending a message by post without an envelope

**postdate** v write a date on (a cheque) that is later than the actual date

**poster** n large picture or notice stuck on a wall

**posterior** n buttocks ▷ adj behind, at the back of

**posterity** n future generations, descendants

**postern** n small back door or gate

**postgraduate** n person with a degree who is studying for a more advanced qualification

**posthaste** adv with great speed

**posthumous** [**poss**-tume-uss] adj occurring after one's death ▸ **posthumously** adv

**postilion, postillion** n (Hist) person riding one of a pair of horses drawing a carriage

**postmortem** n medical examination of a body to establish the cause of death

**postnatal** adj occurring after childbirth

**postpone** v put off to a later time ▸ **postponement** n

**postscript** n passage added at the end of a letter

**postulant** n candidate for admission to a religious order

**postulate** v assume to be true as the basis of an argument or theory

**posture** n position or way in which someone stands, walks, etc. ▷ v behave in an exaggerated way to get attention

**posy** n, pl **-sies** small bunch of flowers

**pot¹** n deep round container; teapot ▷ pl (informal) large amount ▷ v **potting, potted** plant in a pot; (Snooker) hit (a ball) into a pocket ▸ **potted** adj grown in a pot; (of meat or fish) cooked or preserved in a pot; (informal) abridged ▸ **pot shot** shot taken without aiming carefully ▸ **potting shed** shed where plants are potted

**pot²** n (slang) cannabis

**potable** [**pote**-a-bl] adj drinkable

**potash** n white powdery substance obtained from ashes and used as fertilizer

**potassium** n (Chem) silvery metallic element

**potato** n, pl **-toes** roundish starchy vegetable that grows underground

**poteen** n (in Ireland) illegally made alcoholic drink

**potent** adj having great power or influence; (of a male) capable of having sexual intercourse ▸ **potency** n

**potentate** n ruler or monarch

**potential** adj possible but not yet actual ▷ n ability or talent not yet fully used; (Electricity) level of electric pressure ▸ **potentially** adv ▸ **potentiality** n, pl **-ties**

**pothole** n hole in the surface of a road; deep hole in a limestone area ▸ **potholing** n sport of exploring underground caves ▸ **potholer** n

**potion** n dose of medicine or poison

**potjie** n (S Afr) three-legged iron pot used for cooking over a wood fire

**potluck** n **take potluck** accept whatever happens to be available

**potoroo** n, pl **-roos** Australian leaping rodent

**potpourri** [po-**poor**-ee] n fragrant mixture of dried flower petals; assortment or medley

**pottage** n (old-fashioned) thick soup or stew

**potter**[1] n person who makes pottery

**potter**[2] v be busy in a pleasant but aimless way

**pottery** n, pl **-ries** articles made from baked clay; place where they are made

**potty**[1] adj **-tier, -tiest** (informal) crazy or silly

**potty**[2] n, pl **-ties** bowl used by a small child as a toilet

**pouch** n small bag; baglike pocket of skin on an animal

**pouf, pouffe** [**poof**] n large solid cushion used as a seat

**poulterer** n (Brit) person who sells poultry

**poultice** [**pole**-tiss] n moist dressing, often heated, applied to inflamed skin

**poultry** n domestic fowls

**pounce** v spring upon suddenly to attack or capture ▷ n pouncing

**pound**[1] n monetary unit of Britain and some other countries; unit of weight equal to 0.454 kg

**pound**[2] v hit heavily and repeatedly; crush to pieces or powder; (of the heart) throb heavily; run heavily

**pound**[3] n enclosure for stray animals or officially removed vehicles

**pour** v flow or cause to flow out in a stream; rain heavily; come or go in large numbers

**pout** v thrust out one's lips, look sulky ▷ n pouting look

**poverty** n state of being without enough food or money; lack of, scarcity

**POW** prisoner of war

**powder** n substance in the form of tiny loose particles; medicine or cosmetic in this form ▷ v apply powder to ▸ **powdered** adj in the form of a powder e.g. powdered milk ▸ **powdery** adj ▸ **powder room** (old-fashioned) ladies' toilet

**power** n ability to do or act; strength; position of authority or control; (Maths) product from continuous multiplication of a number by itself; (Physics) rate at which work is done; electricity supply; particular form of energy e.g. nuclear power ▸ **powered** adj having or operated by mechanical or electrical power ▸ **powerful** adj ▸ **powerless** adj ▸ **power cut** temporary interruption in the supply of electricity ▸ **power point** socket on a wall for plugging in electrical appliances ▸ **power station** installation for generating and distributing electric power

**powwow** n (informal) talk or conference

**pox** n disease in which skin pustules form; (informal) syphilis

**pp** (in signing a document) for and on behalf of

**pp.** pages

**PPTA** (in New Zealand) Post Primary Teachers Association

**PR** proportional representation; public relations

**practicable** adj capable of being done successfully; usable ▸ **practicability** n

**practical** adj involving experience or actual use rather than theory; sensible, useful, and effective;

P

good at making or doing things; in effect though not in name ▷ *n* examination in which something has to be done or made ▶ **practically** *adv* ▶ **practical joke** trick intended to make someone look foolish

**practice** *n* something done regularly or habitually; repetition of something so as to gain skill; doctor's or lawyer's place of work **in practice** in reality: referring to what actually happens as distinct from what is supposed to happen **put into practice** carry out, do

> **SPELLING TIP**
> Note the *-ice* ending for the noun, with *-ise* for the verb (*practise*)

**practise** *v* do repeatedly so as to gain skill; take part in, follow (a religion etc.); work at e.g. *practise medicine*; do habitually

**practitioner** *n* person who practises a profession

**pragmatic** *adj* concerned with practical consequences rather than theory ▶ **pragmatism** *n* ▶ **pragmatist** *n*

**prairie** *n* large treeless area of grassland, esp. in N America and Canada ▶ **prairie dog** rodent that lives in burrows in the N American prairies

**praise** *v* express approval or admiration of (someone or something); express honour and thanks to (one's God) ▷ *n* something said or written to show approval or admiration **sing someone's praises** praise someone highly ▶ **praiseworthy** *adj*

**praline** [**prah**-leen] *n* sweet made of nuts and caramelized sugar

**pram** *n* four-wheeled carriage for a baby, pushed by hand

**prance** *v* walk with exaggerated bouncing steps

**prang** *v, n* (*slang*) (have) a crash in a car or aircraft

**prank** *n* mischievous trick

**prat** *n* (*Brit, Aust & NZ informal*) stupid person

**prattle** *v* chatter in a childish or foolish way ▷ *n* childish or foolish talk

**prawn** *n* edible shellfish like a large shrimp

**praxis** *n* practice as opposed to theory

**pray** *v* say prayers; ask earnestly, entreat

**prayer** *n* thanks or appeal addressed to one's God; set form of words used in praying; earnest request

**pre-** *prefix* before, beforehand e.g. *prenatal; prerecorded; preshrunk*

**preach** *v* give a talk on a religious theme as part of a church service; speak in support of (an idea, principle, etc.)

**preacher** *n* person who preaches, esp. in church

**preamble** *n* introductory part to something said or written

**prearranged** *adj* arranged beforehand

**prebendary** *n, pl* **-daries** clergyman who is a member of the chapter of a cathedral

**precarious** *adj* insecure, unsafe, likely to fall or collapse ▶ **precariously** *adv*

**precaution** *n* action taken in advance to prevent something bad happening ▶ **precautionary** *adj*

**precede** *v* go or be before ▶ **precedence** [**press**-ee-denss] *n* formal order of rank or position **take precedence over** be more important than ▶ **precedent** *n* previous case or occurrence regarded as an example to be followed

**precentor** n person who leads the singing in a church

**precept** n rule of behaviour
▶ **preceptive** adj

**precinct** n (Brit, Aust & S Afr) area in a town closed to traffic; (Brit, Aust & S Afr) enclosed area round a building; (US) administrative area of a city ▷ pl surrounding region

**precious** adj of great value and importance; loved and treasured; (of behaviour) affected, unnatural
▶ **precious metal** gold, silver, or platinum ▶ **precious stone** rare mineral, such as a ruby, valued as a gem

**precipice** n very steep face of cliff or rockface ▶ **precipitous** adj sheer

**precipitate** v cause to happen suddenly; (Chem) cause to be deposited in solid form from a solution; throw headlong ▷ adj done rashly or hastily ▷ n (Chem) substance precipitated from a solution ▶ **precipitately** adv
▶ **precipitation** n precipitating; rain, snow, etc.

**précis** [pray-see] n, pl **précis** short written summary of a longer piece ▷ v make a précis of

**precise** adj exact, accurate in every detail; strict in observing rules or standards ▶ **precisely** adv
▶ **precision** n

**preclude** v make impossible to happen

**precocious** adj having developed or matured early or too soon
▶ **precocity** n

**precognition** n alleged ability to foretell the future

**preconceived** adj (of an idea) formed without real experience or reliable information
▶ **preconception** n

**precondition** n something that must happen or exist before something else can

**precursor** n something that precedes and is a signal of something else; predecessor

**predate** v occur at an earlier date than; write a date on (a document) that is earlier than the actual date

**predatory** [pred-a-tree] adj habitually hunting and killing other animals for food ▶ **predator** n predatory animal

**predecease** v die before (someone else)

**predecessor** n person who precedes another in an office or position; ancestor

**predestination** n (Theology) belief that future events have already been decided by God or fate
▶ **predestined** adj

**predetermined** adj decided in advance

**predicament** n embarrassing or difficult situation

**predicate** n (Grammar) part of a sentence in which something is said about the subject, e.g. went home in I went home ▷ v declare or assert

**predict** v tell about in advance, prophesy ▶ **predictable** adj
▶ **prediction** n ▶ **predictive** adj relating to or able to make predictions; (of a word processer or mobile phone) able to complete words after only part of a word has been keyed

**predilection** n (formal) preference or liking

**predispose** v influence (someone) in favour of something; make (someone) susceptible to something ▶ **predisposition** n

**predominate** v be the main or controlling

P

element ▶ **predominance** n
▶ **predominant** adj
▶ **predominantly** adv

**pre-eminent** adj excelling all others, outstanding ▶ **pre-eminence** n

**pre-empt** v prevent an action by doing something which makes it pointless or impossible ▶ **pre-emption** n ▶ **pre-emptive** adj

**preen** v (of a bird) clean or trim (feathers) with the beak **preen oneself** smarten oneself; show self-satisfaction

**prefab** n prefabricated house

**prefabricated** adj (of a building) manufactured in shaped sections for rapid assembly on site

**preface** [**pref**-iss] n introduction to a book ▷ v serve as an introduction to (a book, speech, etc.) ▶ **prefatory** adj

**prefect** n senior pupil in a school, with limited power over others; senior administrative officer in some countries ▶ **prefecture** n office or area of authority of a prefect

**prefer** v -ferring, -ferred like better; (Law) bring (charges) before a court ▶ **preferable** adj more desirable ▶ **preferably** adv ▶ **preference** n ▶ **preferential** adj showing preference ▶ **preferment** n promotion or advancement

**prefigure** v represent or suggest in advance

**prefix** n letter or group of letters put at the beginning of a word to make a new word, such as un- in unhappy ▷ v put as an introduction or prefix (to)

**pregnant** adj carrying a fetus in the womb; full of meaning or significance e.g. a pregnant pause ▶ **pregnancy** n, pl -cies

**prehensile** adj capable of grasping

**prehistoric** adj of the period before written history begins ▶ **prehistory** n

**prejudice** n unreasonable or unfair dislike or preference ▷ v cause (someone) to have a prejudice; harm, cause disadvantage to ▶ **prejudicial** adj disadvantageous, harmful

> **SPELLING TIP**
> There are examples in the Bank of English of **prejudice** being misspelt as predjudice, with an extra d. Although d often combines with g in English, it is not necessary before j except in words beginning with the prefix ad-

**prelate** [**prel**-it] n bishop or other churchman of high rank

**preliminary** adj happening before and in preparation, introductory ▷ n, pl -naries preliminary remark, contest, etc.

**prelude** n introductory movement in music; event preceding and introducing something else

**premarital** adj occurring before marriage

**premature** adj happening or done before the normal or expected time; (of a baby) born before the end of the normal period of pregnancy ▶ **prematurely** adv

**premeditated** adj planned in advance ▶ **premeditation** n

**premenstrual** adj occurring or experienced before a menstrual period e.g. premenstrual tension

**premier** n prime minister ▷ adj chief, leading ▶ **premiership** n

**première** n first performance or showing of a play, film, etc.

**premise, premiss** n statement assumed to be true and used as the basis of reasoning

**premises** *pl n* house or other building and its land

**premium** *n* additional sum of money, as on a wage or charge; (regular) sum paid for insurance **at a premium** in great demand because scarce ▶ **premium bonds** (in Britain) savings certificates issued by the government, on which no interest is paid but cash prizes can be won

**premonition** *n* feeling that something unpleasant is going to happen; foreboding ▶ **premonitory** *adj*

**prenatal** *adj* before birth, during pregnancy

**preoccupy** *v* **-pying, -pied** fill the thoughts or attention of (someone) to the exclusion of other things ▶ **preoccupation** *n*

**preordained** *adj* decreed or determined in advance

**prep.** preparatory; preposition

**prepacked** *adj* sold already wrapped

**prepaid** *adj* paid for in advance

**prepare** *v* make or get ready ▶ **prepared** *adj* willing; ready ▶ **preparation** *n* preparing; something done in readiness for something else; mixture prepared for use as a cosmetic, medicine, etc. ▶ **preparatory** [prip-**par**-a-tree] *adj* preparing for ▶ **preparatory school** (*Brit & SAfr*) private school for children between 7 and 13

**preponderance** *n* greater force, amount, or influence ▶ **preponderant** *adj*

**preposition** *n* word used before a noun or pronoun to show its relationship with other words, such as *by* in *go by bus* ▶ **prepositional** *adj*

**prepossessing** *adj* making a favourable impression, attractive

**preposterous** *adj* utterly absurd

**prep school** *n* short for **preparatory school**

**prepuce** [**pree**-pyewss] *n* retractable fold of skin covering the tip of the penis, foreskin

**prerecorded** *adj* recorded in advance to be played or broadcast later

**prerequisite** *n, adj* (something) required before something else is possible

**prerogative** *n* special power or privilege

> **SPELLING TIP**
> The way **prerogative** is often pronounced is presumably the reason why *perogative* is a common way of misspelling it

**presage** [**press**-ij] *v* be a sign or warning of

**Presbyterian** *n, adj* (member) of a Protestant church governed by lay elders ▶ **Presbyterianism** *n*

**presbytery** *n, pl* **-teries** (*Presbyterian Church*) local church court; (*RC Church*) priest's house

**prescience** [**press**-ee-enss] *n* knowledge of events before they happen ▶ **prescient** *adj*

**prescribe** *v* recommend the use of (a medicine); lay down as a rule ▶ **prescription** *n* written instructions from a doctor for the making up and use of a medicine ▶ **prescriptive** *adj* laying down rules

**presence** *n* fact of being in a specified place; impressive dignified appearance ▶ **presence of mind** ability to act sensibly in a crisis

**present¹** *adj* being in a specified place; existing or happening now; (*Grammar*) (of a verb tense) indicating that the action specified is taking place now ▷ *n* present

**P**

time or tense ▸ **presently** adv
soon; (US & Scot) now

**present²** n something given
to bring pleasure to another
person ▷ v introduce formally or
publicly; introduce and compere
(a TV or radio show); cause e.g.
*present a difficulty*; give, award
▸ **presentation** n ▸ **presentable**
adj attractive, neat, fit for people
to see ▸ **presenter** n person
introducing a TV or radio show

**presentiment** [priz-**zen**-tim-ent]
n sense of something unpleasant
about to happen

**preserve** v keep from being
damaged, changed, or ended;
treat (food) to prevent it
decaying ▷ n area of interest
restricted to a particular person
or group; fruit preserved by
cooking in sugar; area where
game is kept for private hunting
or fishing ▸ **preservation** n
▸ **preservative** n chemical that
prevents decay

**preshrunk** adj (of fabric or a
garment) having been shrunk
during manufacture so that further
shrinkage will not occur when
washed

**preside** v be in charge, esp. of a
meeting

**president** n head of state in many
countries; head of a society,
institution, etc. ▸ **presidential** adj
▸ **presidency** n, pl **-cies**

**press¹** v apply force or weight to;
squeeze; smooth by applying
pressure or heat; urge insistently;
crowd, push ▷ n printing machine
**pressed for** short of ▸ **pressing**
adj urgent ▸ **press box** room
at a sports ground reserved for
reporters ▸ **press conference**
interview for reporters given
by a celebrity

**press²** v **press into service** force to
be involved or used ▸ **press gang**
(Hist) group of men used to capture
men and boys and force them to
join the navy

**pressure** n force produced
by pressing; urgent claims or
demands; (Physics) force applied
to a surface per unit of area
▸ **pressure cooker** airtight pot
which cooks food quickly by steam
under pressure ▸ **pressure group**
group that tries to influence
policies, public opinion, etc.

**prestidigitation** n skilful quickness
with the hands, conjuring

**prestige** n high status or respect
resulting from success or
achievements ▸ **prestigious** adj

**presto** adv (Music) very quickly

**prestressed** adj (of concrete)
containing stretched steel wires to
strengthen it

**presume** v suppose to be the case;
dare (to) ▸ **presumably** adv one
supposes (that) ▸ **presumption**
n bold insolent behaviour; strong
probability ▸ **presumptive**
adj assumed to be true or valid
until the contrary is proved
▸ **presumptuous** adj doing things
one has no right to do

**presuppose** v need as a previous
condition in order to be true
▸ **presupposition** n

**pretend** v claim or give the
appearance of (something untrue)
to deceive or in play ▸ **pretender**
n person who makes a false or
disputed claim to a position of
power ▸ **pretence** n behaviour
intended to deceive, pretending
▸ **pretentious** adj making
(unjustified) claims to special merit
or importance ▸ **pretension** n

**preternatural** adj beyond what is
natural, supernatural

**pretext** n false reason given to hide the real one

**pretty** adj **-tier, -tiest** pleasing to look at ▷ adv fairly, moderately e.g. I'm pretty certain ▶ **prettily** adv ▶ **prettiness** n

**pretzel** n brittle salted biscuit

**prevail** v gain mastery; be generally established ▶ **prevailing** adj widespread; predominant ▶ **prevalence** n ▶ **prevalent** adj widespread, common

**prevaricate** v avoid giving a direct or truthful answer ▶ **prevarication** n

**prevent** v keep from happening or doing ▶ **preventable** adj ▶ **prevention** n ▶ **preventive** adj, n

**preview** n advance showing of a film or exhibition before it is shown to the public

**previous** adj coming or happening before ▶ **previously** adv

**prey** n animal hunted and killed for food by another animal; victim **bird of prey** bird that kills and eats other birds or animals ▶ **prey on** v hunt and kill for food; worry, obsess

**price** n amount of money for which a thing is bought or sold; unpleasant thing that must be endured to get something desirable ▷ v fix or ask the price of ▶ **priceless** adj very valuable; (informal) very funny ▶ **pricey** adj **pricier, priciest** (informal) expensive

**prick** v pierce lightly with a sharp point; cause to feel mental pain; (of an animal) make (the ears) stand erect ▷ n sudden sharp pain caused by pricking; mark made by pricking; remorse **prick up one's ears** listen intently

**prickle** n thorn or spike on a plant ▷ v have a tingling or pricking sensation ▶ **prickly** adj ▶ **prickly**

**heat** itchy rash occurring in hot moist weather

**pride** n feeling of pleasure and satisfaction when one has done well; too high an opinion of oneself; sense of dignity and self-respect; something that causes one to feel pride; group of lions **pride of place** most important position **pride oneself on** feel pride about

**priest** n (in the Christian church) a person who can administer the sacraments and preach; (in some other religions) an official who performs religious ceremonies ▶ **priestess** n fem ▶ **priesthood** n ▶ **priestly** adj

**prig** n self-righteous person who acts as if superior to others ▶ **priggish** adj ▶ **priggishness** n

**prim** adj **primmer, primmest** formal, proper, and rather prudish ▶ **primly** adv

**prima ballerina** n leading female ballet dancer

**primacy** n, pl **-cies** state of being first in rank, grade, etc.; office of an archbishop

**prima donna** n leading female opera singer; (informal) temperamental person

**primaeval** adj same as **primeval**

**prima facie** [**prime**-a **fay**-shee] adv (Latin) as it seems at first

**primal** adj of basic causes or origins

**primary** adj chief, most important; being the first stage, elementary ▶ **primarily** adv ▶ **primary colours** (in physics) red, green, and blue or (in art) red, yellow, and blue, from which all other colours can be produced by mixing ▶ **primary school** school for children from five to eleven years or (in New Zealand) from five to thirteen years

**primate¹** n member of an order of mammals including monkeys and humans

**primate²** n archbishop

**prime** adj main, most important; of the highest quality ▷ n time when someone is at his or her best or most vigorous ▷ v give (someone) information in advance to prepare them for something; prepare (a surface) for painting; prepare (a gun, pump, etc.) for use ▶ **primer** n special paint applied to bare wood etc. before the main paint ▶ **Prime Minister** leader of a government ▶ **prime number** number that can be divided exactly only by itself and one

**primer** n beginners' school book or manual

**primeval** [prime-**ee**-val] adj of the earliest age of the world

**primitive** adj of an early simple stage of development; basic, crude

**primogeniture** n system under which the eldest son inherits all his parents' property

**primordial** adj existing at or from the beginning

**primrose** n pale yellow spring flower

**primula** n type of primrose with brightly coloured flowers

**Primus**® n portable cooking stove used esp. by campers

**prince** n male member of a royal family, esp. the son of the king or queen; male ruler of a small country ▶ **princely** adj of or like a prince; generous, lavish, or magnificent ▶ **prince consort** husband of a reigning queen ▶ **Prince of Wales** eldest son of the British sovereign ▶ **princess** n female member of a royal family, esp. the daughter of the king or queen ▶ **Princess Royal** title

sometimes given to the eldest daughter of the British sovereign

**principal** adj main, most important ▷ n head of a school or college; person taking a leading part in something; sum of money lent on which interest is paid ▶ **principally** adv ▶ **principal boy** (Brit) leading male role in pantomime, played by a woman

**USAGE NOTE**
Do not confuse principal and principle

**principality** n, pl **-ties** territory ruled by a prince

**principle** n moral rule guiding behaviour; general or basic truth; scientific law concerning the working of something **in principle** in theory but not always in practice **on principle** because of one's beliefs

**print** v reproduce (a newspaper, book, etc.) in large quantities by mechanical or electronic means; reproduce (text or pictures) by pressing ink onto paper etc.; write in letters that are not joined up; stamp (fabric) with a design; (Photog) produce (pictures) from negatives ▷ n printed words etc.; printed copy of a painting; printed lettering; photograph; printed fabric; mark left on a surface by something that has pressed against it **out of print** no longer available from a publisher ▶ **printer** n person or company engaged in printing; machine that prints ▶ **printing** n ▶ **printed circuit** electronic circuit with wiring printed on an insulating base ▶ **print-out** n printed information from a computer

**prior¹** adj earlier **prior to** before

**prior²** n head monk in a priory ▶ **prioress** n deputy head nun in a convent ▸ **priory** n, pl **-ries** place where certain orders of monks or nuns live

**priority** n, pl **-ties** most important thing that must be dealt with first; right to be or go before others

**prise** v force open by levering

**prism** n transparent block usu. with triangular ends and rectangular sides, used to disperse light into a spectrum or refract it in optical instruments ▸ **prismatic** adj of or shaped like a prism; (of colour) as if produced by refraction through a prism, rainbow-like

**prison** n building where criminals and accused people are held

**prisoner** n person held captive ▸ **prisoner of war** serviceman captured by an enemy in wartime

**prissy** adj **-sier, -siest** prim, correct, and easily shocked ▸ **prissily** adv

**pristine** adj clean, new, and unused

**private** adj for the use of one person or group only; secret; personal, unconnected with one's work; owned or paid for by individuals rather than by the government; quiet, not likely to be disturbed ▹ n soldier of the lowest rank ▸ **privately** adv ▸ **privacy** n

**privateer** n (Hist) privately owned armed vessel authorized by the government to take part in a war; captain of such a ship

**privation** n loss or lack of the necessities of life

**privatize** v sell (a publicly owned company) to individuals or a private company ▸ **privatization** n

**privet** n bushy evergreen shrub used for hedges

**privilege** n advantage or favour that only some people have ▸ **privileged** adj enjoying a special right or immunity

**privy** adj sharing knowledge of something secret ▹ n, pl **privies** (obs) toilet, esp. an outside one ▸ **Privy Council** private council of the British monarch

**prize**[1] n reward given for success in a competition etc. ▹ adj winning or likely to win a prize ▸ **prizefighter** n boxer who fights for money

**prize**[2] v value highly

**prize**[3] v same as **prise**

**pro**[1] adv, prep in favour of ▸ **pros and cons** arguments for and against

**pro**[2] n, pl **pros** (informal) professional; prostitute

**pro-** prefix in favour of e.g. pro-Russian; instead of e.g. pronoun

**probable** adj likely to happen or be true ▸ **probability** n, pl **-ties**

**probably** adv in all likelihood

**probate** n process of proving the validity of a will; certificate stating that a will is genuine

**probation** n system of dealing with law-breakers, esp. juvenile ones, by placing them under supervision; period when someone is assessed for suitability for a job etc. ▸ **probationer** n person on probation

**probe** v search into or examine closely ▹ n surgical instrument used to examine a wound, cavity, etc.

**probiotic** adj, n (of) a bacterium that protects the body from harmful bacteria e.g. probiotic yogurts

**probity** n honesty, integrity

**problem** n something difficult to deal with or solve; question

or puzzle set for solution
▸ **problematic, problematical** *adj*

**proboscis** [pro-**boss**-iss] *n* long trunk or snout; elongated mouth of some insects

**procedure** *n* way of doing something, esp. the correct or usual one ▸ **procedural** *adj*

**proceed** *v* start or continue doing; (*formal*) walk, go; start a legal action; arise from ▸ **proceeds** *pl n* money obtained from an event or activity ▸ **proceedings** *pl n* organized or related series of events; minutes of a meeting; legal action

**process** *n* series of actions or changes; method of doing or producing something ▷ *v* handle or prepare by a special method of manufacture ▸ **processed** *adj* (of food) treated to prevent it decaying ▸ **processor** *n*

**procession** *n* line of people or vehicles moving forward together in order

**proclaim** *v* declare publicly ▸ **proclamation** *n*

**proclivity** *n, pl* **-ties** inclination, tendency

**procrastinate** *v* put off taking action, delay ▸ **procrastination** *n*

**procreate** *v* (*formal*) produce offspring ▸ **procreation** *n*

**procurator fiscal** *n* (in Scotland) law officer who acts as public prosecutor and coroner

**procure** *v* get, provide; obtain (people) to act as prostitutes ▸ **procurement** *n* ▸ **procurer, procuress** *n* person who obtains people to act as prostitutes

**prod** *v* **prodding, prodded** poke with something pointed; goad (someone) to take action ▷ *n* prodding

**prodigal** *adj* recklessly extravagant, wasteful ▸ **prodigality** *n*

**prodigy** *n, pl* **-gies** person with some marvellous talent; wonderful thing ▸ **prodigious** *adj* very large, immense; wonderful ▸ **prodigiously** *adv*

**produce** *v* bring into existence; present to view, show; make, manufacture; present on stage, film, or television ▷ *n* food grown for sale ▸ **producer** *n* person with control over the making of a film, record, etc.; person or company that produces something

**product** *n* something produced; number resulting from multiplication ▸ **production** *n* producing; things produced; presentation of a play, opera, etc. ▸ **productive** *adj* producing large quantities; useful, profitable ▸ **productivity** *n*

**profane** *adj* showing disrespect for religion or holy things; (of language) coarse, blasphemous ▷ *v* treat (something sacred) irreverently, desecrate ▸ **profanation** *n* act of profaning ▸ **profanity** *n, pl* **-ties** profane talk or behaviour, blasphemy

**profess** *v* state or claim (something as true), sometimes falsely; have as one's belief or religion ▸ **professed** *adj* supposed

**profession** *n* type of work, such as being a doctor, that needs special training; all the people employed in a profession e.g. *the legal profession*; declaration of a belief or feeling ▸ **professional** *adj* working in a profession; taking part in an activity, such as sport or music, for money; very competent ▷ *n* person who works in a profession; person paid to take part in sport, music, etc. ▸ **professionally** *adv* ▸ **professionalism** *n*

**professor** n teacher of the highest rank in a university ▶ **professorial** adj ▶ **professorship** n

**proffer** v offer

**proficient** adj skilled, expert ▶ **proficiency** n

**profile** n outline, esp. of the face, as seen from the side; brief biographical sketch ▶ **profiling** n practice of categorizing and predicting the behaviour of people according to certain characteristics e.g. racial profiling

**profit** n money gained; benefit obtained ▷ v gain or benefit ▶ **profitable** adj making profit ▶ **profitably** adv ▶ **profitability** n ▶ **profiteer** n person who makes excessive profits at the expense of the public ▶ **profiteering** n

**profligate** adj recklessly extravagant; shamelessly immoral ▷ n profligate person ▶ **profligacy** n

**pro forma** adj (Latin) prescribing a set form

**profound** adj showing or needing great knowledge; strongly felt, intense ▶ **profundity** n, pl **-ties**

**profuse** adj plentiful ▶ **profusion** n

**progeny** [**proj**-in-ee] n, pl **-nies** children ▶ **progenitor** [pro-**jen**-it-er] n ancestor

**progesterone** n hormone which prepares the womb for pregnancy and prevents further ovulation

**prognosis** n, pl **-noses** doctor's forecast about the progress of an illness; any forecast

**prognostication** n forecast or prediction

**program** n sequence of coded instructions for a computer ▷ v **-gramming, -grammed** arrange (data) so that it can be processed by a computer; feed a program into (a computer) ▶ **programmer** n ▶ **programmable** adj

**programme** n planned series of events; broadcast on radio or television; list of items or performers in an entertainment

**progress** n improvement, development; movement forward ▷ v become more advanced or skilful; move forward **in progress** taking place ▶ **progression** n ▶ **progressive** adj favouring political or social reform; happening gradually ▶ **progressively** adv

**prohibit** v forbid or prevent from happening ▶ **prohibition** n act of forbidding; ban on the sale or drinking of alcohol ▶ **prohibitive** adj (of prices) too high to be affordable ▶ **prohibitively** adv

**project** n planned scheme to do or examine something over a period ▷ v make a forecast based on known data; make (a film or slide) appear on a screen; communicate (an impression); stick out beyond a surface or edge ▶ **projector** n apparatus for projecting photographic images, films, or slides on a screen ▶ **projection** n ▶ **projectionist** n person who operates a projector

**projectile** n object thrown as a weapon or fired from a gun

**prolapse** n slipping down of an internal organ of the body from its normal position

**prole** adj, n (chiefly Brit slang) proletarian

**proletariat** [pro-lit-**air**-ee-at] n working class ▶ **proletarian** adj, n

**proliferate** v grow or reproduce rapidly ▶ **proliferation** n

**prolific** adj very productive ▶ **prolifically** adv

**prolix** adj (of speech or a piece of writing) overlong and boring

**prologue** n introduction to a play or book

P

**prolong** v make (something) last longer ▸ **prolongation** n

**prom** n short for **promenade, promenade concert**

**promenade** n (chiefly Brit) paved walkway along the seafront at a holiday resort ▷ v, n (old-fashioned) (take) a leisurely walk ▸ **promenade concert** (Brit) concert at which part of the audience stands rather than sits

**prominent** adj very noticeable; famous, widely known ▸ **prominently** adv ▸ **prominence** n

**promiscuous** adj having many casual sexual relationships ▸ **promiscuity** n

**promise** v say that one will definitely do or not do something; show signs of, seem likely ▷ n undertaking to do or not to do something; indication of future success ▸ **promising** adj likely to succeed or turn out well

**promo** n, pl **-mos** (informal) short film to promote a product

**promontory** n, pl **-ries** point of high land jutting out into the sea

**promote** v help to make (something) happen or increase; raise to a higher rank or position; encourage the sale of by advertising ▸ **promoter** n person who organizes or finances an event etc. ▸ **promotion** n ▸ **promotional** adj

**prompt** v cause (an action); remind (an actor or speaker) of words that he or she has forgotten ▷ adj done without delay ▷ adv exactly e.g. six o'clock prompt ▸ **promptly** adv immediately, without delay ▸ **promptness** n ▸ **prompter, prompt** n person offstage who prompts actors

**promulgate** v put (a law etc.) into effect by announcing it

officially; make widely known ▸ **promulgation** n

**prone** adj (foll by to) likely to do or be affected by (something); lying face downwards

**prong** n one spike of a fork or similar instrument ▸ **pronged** adj

**pronoun** n word, such as she or it, used to replace a noun

**pronounce** v form the sounds of (words or letters), esp. clearly or in a particular way; declare formally or officially ▸ **pronounceable** adj ▸ **pronounced** adj very noticeable ▸ **pronouncement** n formal announcement ▸ **pronunciation** n way in which a word or language is pronounced

> **USAGE NOTE**
> Note the difference in spelling between pronounce and pronunciation. The pronunciation also changes from 'nown' to 'nun'

**pronto** adv (informal) at once

**proof** n evidence that shows that something is true or has happened; copy of something printed, such as the pages of a book, for checking before final production ▷ adj able to withstand e.g. proof against criticism; denoting the strength of an alcoholic drink e.g. seventy proof ▸ **proofread** v read and correct (printer's proofs) ▸ **proofreader** n

**prop¹** v **propping, propped** support (something) so that it stays upright or in place ▷ n pole, beam, etc. used as a support

**prop²** n movable object used on the set of a film or play

**prop³** n (informal) propeller

**propaganda** n (organized promotion of) information to assist or damage the cause of a government or movement ▸ **propagandist** n

**propagate** v spread (information and ideas); reproduce, breed, or grow ▸ **propagation** n

**propane** n flammable gas found in petroleum and used as a fuel

**propel** v **-pelling, -pelled** cause to move forward ▸ **propellant** n something that provides or causes propulsion; gas used in an aerosol spray ▸ **propulsion** n method by which something is propelled; act of propelling or state of being propelled

**propeller** n revolving shaft with blades for driving a ship or aircraft

**propensity** n, pl **-ties** natural tendency

**proper** adj real or genuine; suited to a particular purpose; correct in behaviour; excessively moral; (Brit, Aust & NZ informal) complete ▸ **properly** adv

**property** n, pl **-ties** something owned; possessions collectively; land or buildings owned by somebody; quality or attribute

**prophet** n person supposedly chosen by God to spread His word; person who predicts the future ▸ **prophetic** adj ▸ **prophetically** adv ▸ **prophecy** n, pl **-cies** prediction; message revealing God's will ▸ **prophesy** v **-sying, -sied** foretell

> **SPELLING TIP**
> Note the difference in spelling between the noun (**prophecy**) and the verb (**prophesy**)

**prophylactic** n, adj (drug) used to prevent disease

**propitiate** v appease, win the favour of ▸ **propitiation** n ▸ **propitious** adj favourable or auspicious

**proponent** n person who argues in favour of something

**proportion** n relative size or extent; correct relation between connected parts; part considered with respect to the whole ▷ pl dimensions or size ▷ v adjust in relative amount or size **in proportion** comparable in size, rate of increase, etc.; without exaggerating ▸ **proportional, proportionate** adj being in proportion ▸ **proportionally, proportionately** adv

**propose** v put forward for consideration; nominate; intend or plan (to do); make an offer of marriage ▸ **proposal** n ▸ **proposition** n offer; statement or assertion; (Maths) theorem; (informal) thing to be dealt with ▷ v (informal) ask (someone) to have sexual intercourse

**propound** v put forward for consideration

**proprietor** n owner of a business establishment ▸ **proprietress** n fem ▸ **proprietary** adj made and distributed under a trade name; denoting or suggesting ownership

**propriety** n, pl **-ties** correct conduct

**propulsion** n see **propel**

**pro rata** adv, adj (Latin) in proportion

**prorogue** v suspend (parliament) without dissolving it ▸ **prorogation** n

**prosaic** [pro-**zay**-ik] adj lacking imagination, dull ▸ **prosaically** adv

**proscenium** n, pl **-nia** or **-niums** arch in a theatre separating the stage from the auditorium

**proscribe** v prohibit, outlaw ▸ **proscription** n ▸ **proscriptive** adj

**prose** n ordinary speech or writing as opposed to poetry

**prosecute** v bring a criminal charge against; continue to do ▸ **prosecution** n ▸ **prosecutor** n

P

**proselyte** [**pross**-ill-ite] n recent convert

**proselytize** [**pross**-ill-it-ize] v attempt to convert

**prospect** n something anticipated; (old-fashioned) view from a place ▷ pl probability of future success ▷ v explore, esp. for gold ▶ **prospective** adj future; expected ▶ **prospector** n ▶ **prospectus** n booklet giving details of a university, company, etc.

**prosper** v be successful ▶ **prosperity** n success and wealth ▶ **prosperous** adj

**prostate** n gland in male mammals that surrounds the neck of the bladder

**prosthesis** [pross-**theess**-iss] n, pl -**ses** [-seez] artificial body part, such as a limb or breast ▶ **prosthetic** adj

**prostitute** n person who offers sexual intercourse in return for payment ▷ v make a prostitute of; offer (oneself or one's talents) for unworthy purposes ▶ **prostitution** n

**prostrate** adj lying face downwards; physically or emotionally exhausted ▷ v lie face downwards; exhaust physically or emotionally ▶ **prostration** n

**protagonist** n supporter of a cause; leading character in a play or a story

**protea** [pro-tee-a] n African shrub with showy flowers

**protean** [pro-**tee**-an] adj constantly changing

**protect** v defend from trouble, harm, or loss ▶ **protection** n ▶ **protectionism** n policy of protecting industries by taxing competing imports ▶ **protectionist** n, adj ▶ **protective** adj giving protection

e.g. protective clothing; tending or wishing to protect someone ▶ **protector** n person or thing that protects; regent ▶ **protectorate** n territory largely controlled by a stronger state; (period of) rule of a regent

**protégé, (**fem**) protégée** [pro-ti-zhay] n person who is protected and helped by another

**protein** n any of a group of complex organic compounds that are essential for life

**pro tempore** adv, adj for the time being (also **pro tem**)

**protest** n declaration or demonstration of objection ▷ v object, disagree; assert formally ▶ **protestation** n strong declaration

**Protestant** n follower of any of the Christian churches that split from the Roman Catholic Church in the sixteenth century ▷ adj of or relating to such a church ▶ **Protestantism** n

**proto-** combining form first e.g. protohuman

**protocol** n rules of behaviour for formal occasions; (Computing) set of rules for transfer of data, esp. between different systems

**proton** n positively charged particle in the nucleus of an atom

**protoplasm** n substance forming the living contents of a cell

**prototype** n original or model to be copied or developed

**protozoan** [pro-toe-**zoe**-an] n, pl -**zoa** microscopic one-celled creature

**protracted** adj lengthened or extended

**protractor** n instrument for measuring angles

**protrude** v stick out, project ▶ **protrusion** n

**protuberant** *adj* swelling out, bulging ▶ **protuberance** *n*

**proud** *adj* feeling pleasure and satisfaction; feeling honoured; thinking oneself superior to other people; dignified ▶ **proudly** *adv*

**prove** *v* **proving, proved, proved** or **proven** establish the validity of; demonstrate, test; be found to be ▶ **proven** *adj* known from experience to work

**provenance** [prov-in-anss] *n* place of origin

**provender** *n* (*old-fashioned*) fodder

**proverb** *n* short saying that expresses a truth or gives a warning ▶ **proverbial** *adj*

**provide** *v* make available **provided that, providing** on condition that ▶ **provider** *n* ▶ **provide for** *v* take precautions (against); support financially

> **USAGE NOTE**
> The usage is either *providing* on its own or *provided that* (not *providing that*)

**providence** *n* God or nature seen as a protective force that arranges people's lives ▶ **provident** *adj* thrifty; showing foresight ▶ **providential** *adj* lucky

**province** *n* area governed as a unit of a country or empire; area of learning, activity, etc. ▷ *pl* parts of a country outside the capital ▶ **provincial** *adj* of a province or the provinces; unsophisticated and narrow-minded ▷ *n* unsophisticated person; person from a province or the provinces ▶ **provincialism** *n* narrow-mindedness and lack of sophistication

**provision** *n* act of supplying something; something supplied; (*Law*) condition incorporated in a document ▷ *pl* food ▷ *v* supply with

food ▶ **provisional** *adj* temporary or conditional ▶ **provisionally** *adv*

**proviso** [pro-**vize**-oh] *n*, *pl* **-sos** or **-soes** condition, stipulation

**provoke** *v* deliberately anger; cause (an adverse reaction) ▶ **provocation** *n* ▶ **provocative** *adj*

**provost** *n* head of certain university colleges in Britain; chief councillor of a Scottish town

**prow** *n* bow of a vessel

**prowess** *n* superior skill or ability; bravery, fearlessness

**prowl** *v* move stealthily around a place as if in search of prey or plunder ▷ *n* prowling

**prowler** *n* person who moves stealthily around a place as if in search of prey or plunder

**proximity** *n* nearness in space, time, or in a series ▶ **proximate** *adj*

**proxy** *n*, *pl* **proxies** person authorized to act on behalf of someone else; authority to act on behalf of someone else

**prude** *n* person who is excessively modest, prim, or proper ▶ **prudish** *adj* ▶ **prudery** *n*

**prudent** *adj* cautious, discreet, and sensible ▶ **prudence** *n* ▶ **prudential** *adj* (*old-fashioned*) prudent

**prune**[1] *n* dried plum

**prune**[2] *v* cut off dead parts or excessive branches from (a tree or plant); shorten, reduce

**prurient** *adj* excessively interested in sexual matters ▶ **prurience** *n*

**pry** *v* **prying, pried** make an impertinent or uninvited inquiry into a private matter

**PS** postscript

**PSA** (in New Zealand) Public Service Association

**psalm** *n* sacred song ▶ **psalmist** *n* writer of psalms

P

**Psalter** n book containing (a version of) psalms from the Bible ▶ **psaltery** n, pl **-ries** ancient instrument played by plucking strings

**PSBR** (in Britain) public sector borrowing requirement

**psephology** [sef-**fol**-a-jee] n statistical study of elections

**pseud** n (informal) pretentious person

**pseudo-** combining form false, pretending, or unauthentic e.g. pseudoclassical

**pseudonym** n fictitious name adopted esp. by an author ▶ **pseudonymous** adj

**psittacosis** n disease of parrots that can be transmitted to humans

**psoriasis** [so-**rye**-a-siss] n skin disease with reddish spots and patches covered with silvery scales

**psyche** [**sye**-kee] n human mind or soul

**psychedelic** adj denoting a drug that causes hallucinations; having vivid colours and complex patterns similar to those experienced during hallucinations

> **SPELLING TIP**
> The main problem with **psychedelic** is which vowel follows the ch; it should be e

**psychiatry** n branch of medicine concerned with mental disorders ▶ **psychiatric** adj ▶ **psychiatrist** n

**psychic** adj (also **psychical**) having mental powers which cannot be explained by natural laws; relating to the mind ▷ n person with psychic powers

**psycho** n, pl **-chos** (informal) psychopath

**psychoanalysis** n method of treating mental and emotional disorders by discussion and analysis of one's thoughts and feelings ▶ **psychoanalyse** v ▶ **psychoanalyst** n

**psychology** n, pl **-gies** study of human and animal behaviour; (informal) person's mental make-up ▶ **psychologist** n ▶ **psychological** adj of or affecting the mind; of psychology ▶ **psychologically** adv

**psychopath** n person afflicted with a personality disorder causing him or her to commit anti-social or violent acts ▶ **psychopathic** adj

**psychosis** n, pl **-ses** severe mental disorder in which the sufferer's contact with reality becomes distorted ▶ **psychotic** adj

**psychosomatic** adj (of a physical disorder) thought to have psychological causes

**psychotherapy** n treatment of nervous disorders by psychological methods ▶ **psychotherapeutic** adj ▶ **psychotherapist** n

**psych up** v prepare (oneself) mentally for a contest or task

**PT** (old-fashioned) physical training

**pt** part; point

**pt.** pint

**PTA** Parent-Teacher Association

**ptarmigan** [**tar**-mig-an] n bird of the grouse family which turns white in winter

**pterodactyl** [terr-roe-**dak**-til] n extinct flying reptile with batlike wings

**PTO** please turn over

**ptomaine** [**toe**-main] n any of a group of poisonous alkaloids found in decaying matter

**Pty** (Aust, NZ & S Afr) Proprietary

**pub** n building with a bar licensed to sell alcoholic drinks

**puberty** n beginning of sexual maturity ▶ **pubertal** adj

**pubescent** adj reaching or having reached puberty; covered

with fine short hairs or down,
as some plants and animals
▸ **pubescence** n

**pubic** adj of the lower abdomen
e.g. *pubic hair*

**public** adj of or concerning
the people as a whole; for use
by everyone; well-known;
performed or made openly ▸ n
the community, people in general
▸ **publicly** adv ▸ **public house** pub
▸ **public relations** promotion of
a favourable opinion towards an
organization among the public
▸ **public school** private fee-paying
school in Britain ▸ **public-
spirited** adj having or showing an
active interest in the good of the
community

**publican** n (*Brit, Aust & NZ*) person
who owns or runs a pub

**publicity** n process or information
used to arouse public attention;
public interest so aroused
▸ **publicist** n person, esp. a press
agent or journalist, who publicizes
something ▸ **publicize** v bring to
public attention

**publish** v produce and issue
(printed matter) for sale;
announce formally or in public
▸ **publication** n ▸ **publisher** n

**puce** adj purplish-brown

**puck**¹ n small rubber disc used in
ice hockey

**puck**² n mischievous or evil spirit
▸ **puckish** adj

**pucker** v gather into wrinkles ▸ n
wrinkle or crease

**pudding** n dessert, esp. a cooked
one served hot; savoury dish with
pastry or batter e.g. *steak-and-
kidney pudding*; sausage-like mass
of meat e.g. *black pudding*

**puddle** n small pool of water, esp.
of rain

**puerile** adj silly and childish

**puerperal** [pew-**er**-per-al] adj
concerning the period following
childbirth

**puff** n (sound of) a short blast of
breath, wind, etc.; act of inhaling
cigarette smoke ▸ v blow or
breathe in short quick draughts;
take draws at (a cigarette); send
out in small clouds; swell **out of
puff** out of breath ▸ **puffy** adj
▸ **puffball** n ball-shaped fungus
▸ **puff pastry** light flaky pastry

**puffin** n black-and-white sea bird
with a brightly-coloured beak

**pug** n small snub-nosed dog ▸ **pug
nose** short stubby upturned nose

**pugilist** [pew-jil-ist] n boxer
▸ **pugilism** n ▸ **pugilistic** adj

**pugnacious** adj ready and eager to
fight ▸ **pugnacity** n

**puissance** [pwee-sonce] n
showjumping competition that
tests a horse's ability to jump large
obstacles

**puke** (*slang*) v vomit ▸ n act of
vomiting; vomited matter

**pulchritude** n (*lit*) beauty

**pull** v exert force on (an object) to
move it towards the source of the
force; strain or stretch; remove or
extract; attract ▸ n act of pulling;
force used in pulling; act of taking
in drink or smoke; (*informal*) power,
influence ▸ **pull in** v (of a vehicle
or driver) draw in to the side of the
road or stop; reach a destination;
attract in large numbers; (*Brit,
Aust & NZ slang*) arrest ▸ **pull off** v
(*informal*) succeed in performing
▸ **pull out** v (of a vehicle or driver)
move away from the side of the
road or move out to overtake; (of a
train) depart; withdraw; remove by
pulling ▸ **pull up** v (of a vehicle or
driver) stop; remove by the roots;
reprimand

**pullet** n young hen

P

**pulley** n wheel with a grooved rim in which a belt, chain, or piece of rope runs in order to lift weights by a downward pull

**Pullman** n, pl **-mans** luxurious railway coach

**pullover** n sweater that is pulled on over the head

**pulmonary** adj of the lungs

**pulp** n soft wet substance made from crushed or beaten matter; flesh of a fruit; poor-quality books and magazines ▷ v reduce to pulp

**pulpit** n raised platform for a preacher

**pulsar** n small dense star which emits regular bursts of radio waves

**pulse¹** n regular beating of blood through the arteries at each heartbeat; any regular beat or vibration ▶ **pulsate** v throb, quiver ▶ **pulsation** n

**pulse²** n edible seed of a pod-bearing plant such as a bean or pea

**pulverize** v reduce to fine pieces; destroy completely

**puma** n large American wild cat with a greyish-brown coat

**pumice** [pumm-iss] n light porous stone used for scouring

**pummel** v **-melling, -melled** strike repeatedly with or as if with the fists

**pump¹** n machine used to force a liquid or gas to move in a particular direction ▷ v raise or drive with a pump; supply in large amounts; operate or work in the manner of a pump; extract information from

**pump²** n light flat-soled shoe

**pumpkin** n large round fruit with an orange rind, soft flesh, and many seeds, eaten as a vegetable

**pun** n use of words to exploit double meanings for humorous effect ▷ v **punning, punned** make puns

**punch¹** v strike at with a clenched fist ▷ n blow with a clenched fist; (informal) effectiveness or vigour ▶ **punchy** adj forceful ▶ **punch-drunk** adj dazed by or as if by repeated blows to the head

**punch²** n tool or machine for shaping, piercing, or engraving ▷ v pierce, cut, stamp, shape, or drive with a punch

**punch³** n drink made from a mixture of wine, spirits, fruit, sugar, and spices

**punctilious** adj paying great attention to correctness in etiquette; careful about small details

**punctual** adj arriving or taking place at the correct time ▶ **punctuality** n ▶ **punctually** adv

**punctuate** v put punctuation marks in; interrupt at frequent intervals ▶ **punctuation** n (use of) marks such as commas, colons, etc. in writing, to assist in making the sense clear

**puncture** n small hole made by a sharp object, esp. in a tyre ▷ v pierce a hole in

**pundit** n expert who speaks publicly on a subject

**pungent** adj having a strong sharp bitter flavour ▶ **pungency** n

**punish** v cause (someone) to suffer or undergo a penalty for some wrongdoing ▶ **punishing** adj harsh or difficult ▶ **punishment** n ▶ **punitive** [pew-nit-tiv] adj relating to punishment

**punk** n anti-Establishment youth movement and style of rock music of the late 1970s; follower of this music; worthless person

**punnet** n small basket for fruit

**punt¹** n open flat-bottomed boat propelled by a pole ▷ v travel in a punt

**P**

**punt²** (*Sport*) *n* kick of a ball before it touches the ground when dropped from the hands ▷ *v* kick (a ball) in this way

**punt³** *n* former monetary unit of the Irish Republic

**punter** *n* person who bets; (*Brit, Aust & NZ*) any member of the public

**puny** *adj* **-nier, -niest** small and feeble

**pup** *n* young of certain animals, such as dogs and seals

**pupa** *n, pl* **-pae** or **-pas** insect at the stage of development between a larva and an adult

**pupil¹** *n* person who is taught by a teacher

**pupil²** *n* round dark opening in the centre of the eye

**puppet** *n* small doll or figure moved by strings or by the operator's hand; person or country controlled by another ▶ **puppeteer** *n*

**puppy** *n, pl* **-pies** young dog

**purchase** *v* obtain by payment ▷ *n* thing that is bought; act of buying; leverage, grip ▶ **purchaser** *n*

**purdah** *n* Muslim and Hindu custom of keeping women in seclusion, with clothing that conceals them completely when they go out

**pure** *adj* unmixed, untainted; innocent; complete e.g. *pure delight*; concerned with theory only e.g. *pure mathematics* ▶ **purely** *adv* ▶ **purity** *n* ▶ **purify** *v* **-fying, -fied** make or become pure ▶ **purification** *n* ▶ **purist** *n* person concerned with strict obedience to the traditions of a subject

**purée** [**pure**-ray] *n* pulp of cooked food ▷ *v* **-réeing, -réed** make into a purée

**purgatory** *n* place or state of temporary suffering; (**P-**) (*RC Church*) place where souls of the dead undergo punishment for their sins before being admitted to Heaven ▶ **purgatorial** *adj*

**purge** *v* rid (a thing or place) of (unwanted things or people) ▷ *n* purging ▶ **purgative** *n, adj* (medicine) designed to cause defecation

**Puritan** *n* (*Hist*) member of the English Protestant group who wanted simpler church ceremonies; (**p-**) person with strict moral and religious principles ▶ **puritanical** *adj* ▶ **puritanism** *n*

**purl** *n* stitch made by knitting a plain stitch backwards ▷ *v* knit in purl

**purlieus** [**per**-lyooz] *pl n* (*lit*) outskirts

**purloin** *v* steal

**purple** *adj, n* (of) a colour between red and blue

**purport** *v* claim (to be or do something) ▷ *n* apparent meaning, significance

**purpose** *n* reason for which something is done or exists; determination; practical advantage or use e.g. *use the time to good purpose* ▶ **purposely** *adv* intentionally (also **on purpose**)

**purr** *v* (of cats) make low vibrant sound, usu. when pleased ▷ *n* this sound

**purse** *n* small bag for money; (*US & NZ*) handbag; financial resources; prize money ▷ *v* draw (one's lips) together into a small round shape ▶ **purser** *n* ship's officer who keeps the accounts

**pursue** *v* chase; follow (a goal); engage in; continue to discuss or ask about (something) ▶ **pursuer** *n* ▶ **pursuit** *n* pursuing; occupation or pastime

P

**SPELLING TIP**
This family of words should be spelt with a u in each of the first two syllables, as in **pursuing** and **pursued**

**purulent** [pure-yoo-lent] *adj* of or containing pus

**purvey** *v* supply (provisions) ▸ **purveyor** *n*

**purview** *n* scope or range of activity or outlook

**pus** *n* yellowish matter produced by infected tissue

**push** *v* move or try to move by steady force; drive or spur (oneself or another person) to do something; (*informal*) sell (drugs) illegally ▷ *n* act of pushing; special effort **the push** (*slang*) dismissal from a job or relationship ▸ **pusher** *n* person who sells illegal drugs ▸ **pushy** *adj* too assertive or ambitious ▸ **pushchair** *n* (*Brit*) folding chair on wheels for a baby

**pusillanimous** *adj* timid and cowardly ▸ **pusillanimity** *n*

**puss, pussy** *n, pl* **pusses** or **pussies** (*informal*) cat

**pussyfoot** *v* (*informal*) behave too cautiously

**pustule** *n* pimple containing pus

**put** *v* **putting, put** cause to be (in a position, state, or place); express; throw (the shot) in the shot put ▷ *n* throw in putting the shot ▸ **put across** *v* express successfully ▸ **put off** *v* postpone; disconcert; repel ▸ **put up** *v* erect; accommodate; nominate ▸ **put-upon** *adj* taken advantage of

**putative** *adj* reputed, supposed

**putrid** *adj* rotten and foul-smelling ▸ **putrefy** *v* **-fying, -fied** rot and produce an offensive smell ▸ **putrefaction** *n* ▸ **putrescent** *adj* rotting

**putsch** *n* sudden violent attempt to remove a government from power

**putt** (*Golf*) *n* stroke on the putting green to roll the ball into or near the hole ▷ *v* strike (the ball) in this way ▸ **putter** ▷ *n* golf club for putting

**putty** *n* adhesive used to fix glass into frames and fill cracks in woodwork

**puzzle** *v* perplex and confuse or be perplexed or confused ▷ *n* problem that cannot be easily solved; toy, game, or question that requires skill or ingenuity to solve ▸ **puzzlement** *n* ▸ **puzzling** *adj*

**PVC** polyvinyl chloride: plastic material used in clothes etc.

**Pygmy** *n, pl* **-mies** member of one of the very short peoples of Equatorial Africa ▷ *adj* (**p-**) very small

**pyjamas** *pl n* loose-fitting trousers and top worn in bed

**pylon** *n* steel tower-like structure supporting electrical cables

**pyramid** *n* solid figure with a flat base and triangular sides sloping upwards to a point; building of this shape, esp. an ancient Egyptian one ▸ **pyramidal** *adj*

**pyre** *n* pile of wood for burning a corpse on

**Pyrex®** *n* heat-resistant glassware

**pyromania** *n* uncontrollable urge to set things on fire ▸ **pyromaniac** *n*

**pyrotechnics** *n* art of making fireworks; firework display ▸ **pyrotechnic** *adj*

**Pyrrhic victory** [pir-ik] *n* victory in which the victor's losses are as great as those of the defeated

**python** *n* large nonpoisonous snake that crushes its prey

**p**

# Qq

**QC** Queen's Counsel
**QED** which was to be shown or proved
**Qld** Queensland
**QM** Quartermaster
**qr.** quarter; quire
**qt.** quart
**qua** [kwah] *prep* in the capacity of
**quack**[1] *v* (of a duck) utter a harsh guttural sound ▷ *n* sound made by a duck
**quack**[2] *n* unqualified person who claims medical knowledge
**quad** *n* see **quadrangle**; (*informal*) quadruplet ▷ *adj* short for **quadraphonic** ▷ **quad bike, quad** vehicle like a small motorcycle with four large wheels, designed for agricultural and sporting uses
**quadrangle** *n* (also **quad**) rectangular courtyard with buildings on all four sides; geometric figure consisting of four points connected by four lines ▷ **quadrangular** *adj*
**quadrant** *n* quarter of a circle; quarter of a circle's circumference; instrument for measuring the altitude of the stars
**quadraphonic** *adj* using four independent channels to reproduce or record sound
**quadratic** (*Maths*) *n* equation in which the variable is raised to the power of two, but nowhere raised to a higher power ▷ *adj* of the second power

**quadrennial** *adj* occurring every four years; lasting four years
**quadri-** *combining form* four e.g. quadrilateral
**quadrilateral** *adj* having four sides ▷ *n* polygon with four sides
**quadrille** *n* square dance for four couples
**quadriplegia** *n* paralysis of all four limbs
**quadruped** [kwod-roo-ped] *n* any animal with four legs
**quadruple** *v* multiply by four ▷ *adj* four times as much or as many; consisting of four parts
**quadruplet** *n* one of four offspring born at one birth
**quaff** [kwoff] *v* drink heartily or in one draught
**quagmire** [kwog-mire] *n* soft wet area of land
**quail**[1] *n* small game bird of the partridge family
**quail**[2] *v* shrink back with fear
**quaint** *adj* attractively unusual, esp. in an old-fashioned style ▷ **quaintly** *adv*
**quake** *v* shake or tremble with or as if with fear ▷ *n* (*informal*) earthquake
**Quaker** *n* member of a Christian sect, the Society of Friends ▷ **Quakerism** *n*
**qualify** *v* **-fying, -fied** provide or be provided with the abilities necessary for a task, office, or duty; moderate or restrict (a statement) ▷ **qualified** *adj* ▷ **qualification** *n* official record of achievement in a course or examination; quality or skill needed for a particular activity; condition that modifies or limits; act of qualifying
**quality** *n, pl* **-ties** degree or standard of excellence; distinguishing characteristic or attribute; basic character or nature

q

of something ▷ *adj* excellent or superior ▸ **qualitative** *adj* of or relating to quality ▸ **quality assurance** system in which the quality of a product or service is compared with that required

**qualm** [kwahm] *n* pang of conscience; sudden sensation of misgiving

**quandary** *n*, *pl* **-ries** difficult situation or dilemma

**quandong** [kwon-dong] *n* small Australian tree with edible fruit and nuts used in preservesAustralian tree with pale timber

**quango** *n*, *pl* **-gos** (*chiefly Brit*) quasi-autonomous nongovernmental organization: any partly independent official body set up by a government

**quanta** *n* plural of **quantum**

**quantify** *v* **-fying, -fied** discover or express the quantity of ▸ **quantifiable** *adj* ▸ **quantification** *n*

**quantity** *n*, *pl* **-ties** specified or definite amount or number; aspect of anything that can be measured, weighed, or counted ▸ **quantitative** *adj* of or relating to quantity ▸ **quantitative easing** practice of increasing the supply of money in order to stimulate economic activity ▸ **quantity surveyor** person who estimates the cost of the materials and labour necessary for a construction job

**quantum** *n*, *pl* **-ta** desired or required amount, esp. a very small one ▸ **quantum leap, quantum jump** (*informal*) sudden large change, increase, or advance ▸ **quantum theory** physics theory based on the idea that energy of electrons is discharged in discrete quanta

**quarantine** *n* period of isolation of people or animals to prevent the spread of disease ▷ *v* isolate in or as if in quarantine

**quark** *n* (*Physics*) subatomic particle thought to be the fundamental unit of matter

**quarrel** *n* angry disagreement; cause of dispute ▷ *v* **-relling, -relled** have a disagreement or dispute ▸ **quarrelsome** *adj*

**quarry**[1] *n*, *pl* **-ries** place where stone is dug from the surface of the earth ▷ *v* **-rying, -ried** extract (stone) from a quarry

**quarry**[2] *n*, *pl* **-ries** person or animal that is being hunted

**quart** *n* unit of liquid measure equal to two pints (1.136 litres)

**quarter** *n* one of four equal parts of something; fourth part of a year; (*informal*) unit of weight equal to 4 ounces; region or district of a town or city; (*US*) 25-cent piece; mercy or pity, as shown towards a defeated opponent ▷ *pl* lodgings ▷ *v* divide into four equal parts; billet or be billeted in lodgings ▸ **quarterly** *adj* occurring, due, or issued at intervals of three months ▷ *n* magazine issued every three months ▷ *adv* once every three months ▸ **quarter day** (*Brit*) any of the four days in the year when certain payments become due ▸ **quarterdeck** *n* (*Naut*) rear part of the upper deck of a ship ▸ **quarterfinal** *n* round before the semifinal in a competition ▸ **quartermaster** *n* military officer responsible for accommodation, food, and equipment

**quartet** *n* group of four performers; music for such a group

**quarto** *n*, *pl* **-tos** book size in which the sheets are folded into four leaves

**quartz** *n* hard glossy mineral

**quasar** [**kway**-zar] *n* extremely distant starlike object that emits powerful radio waves

**quash** *v* annul or make void; subdue forcefully and completely

**quasi-** [**kway**-zie] *combining form* almost but not really e.g. *quasi-religious; a quasi-scholar*

**quatrain** *n* stanza or poem of four lines

**quaver** *v* (of a voice) quiver or tremble ▷ *n* (*Music*) note half the length of a crotchet; tremulous sound or note

**quay** [**kee**] *n* wharf built parallel to the shore

**queasy** *adj* -**sier**, -**siest** having the feeling that one is about to vomit; feeling or causing uneasiness ▶ **queasiness** *n*

**queen** *n* female sovereign who is the official ruler or head of state; wife of a king; woman, place, or thing considered to be the best of her or its kind; (*slang*) effeminate male homosexual; only fertile female in a colony of bees, wasps, or ants; the most powerful piece in chess ▶ **queenly** *adj* ▶ **Queen's Counsel** barrister or advocate appointed Counsel to the Crown

**queer** *adj* not normal or usual; (*Brit*) faint, giddy, or queasy; (*offens*) homosexual ▷ *n* (*offens*) homosexual **queer someone's pitch** (*informal*) spoil someone's chances of something

> **USAGE NOTE**
> Although the term *queer* meaning homosexual is still considered derogatory when used by non-homosexuals, it is now being used by homosexuals of themselves as a positive term: *queer politics, queer cinema*

**quell** *v* suppress; overcome

**quench** *v* satisfy (one's thirst); put out or extinguish

**quern** *n* stone hand mill for grinding corn

**querulous** [**kwer**-yoo-luss] *adj* complaining or whining ▶ **querulously** *adv*

**query** *n, pl* -**ries** question, esp. one raising doubt; question mark ▷ *v* -**rying, -ried** express uncertainty, doubt, or an objection concerning (something)

**quest** *n* long and difficult search ▷ *v* (foll by *for* or *after*) go in search of

**question** *n* form of words addressed to a person in order to obtain an answer; point at issue; difficulty or uncertainty ▷ *v* put a question or questions to (a person); express uncertainty about **in question** under discussion **out of the question** impossible ▶ **questionable** *adj* of disputable value or authority ▶ **questionably** *adv* ▶ **questionnaire** *n* set of questions on a form, used to collect information from people ▶ **question mark** punctuation mark (?) written at the end of questions

> **SPELLING TIP**
> Remember that **questionnaire** has two *n*s

**queue** *n* line of people or vehicles waiting for something ▷ *v* **queuing** or **queueing, queued** (often foll by *up*) form or remain in a line while waiting

**quibble** *v* make trivial objections ▷ *n* trivial objection

**quiche** [**keesh**] *n* savoury flan with an egg custard filling to which vegetables etc. are added

**quick** *adj* speedy, fast; lasting or taking a short time; alert and responsive; easily excited or aroused ▷ *n* area of sensitive

**q**

flesh under a nail ▷ *adv (informal)* in a rapid manner **cut someone to the quick** hurt someone's feelings deeply ▶ **quickly** *adv* ▶ **quicken** *v* make or become faster; make or become more lively ▶ **quicklime** *n* white solid used in the manufacture of glass and steel ▶ **quicksand** *n* deep mass of loose wet sand that sucks anything on top of it into it ▶ **quicksilver** *n* mercury ▶ **quickstep** *n* fast ballroom dance

**quid** *n, pl* **quid** *(Brit slang)* pound (sterling)

**quid pro quo** *n, pl* **quid pro quos** one thing, esp. an advantage or object, given in exchange for another

**quiescent** [kwee-**ess**-ent] *adj* quiet, inactive, or dormant ▶ **quiescence** *n*

**quiet** *adj* with little noise; calm or tranquil; untroubled ▷ *n* quietness ▷ *v* make or become quiet **on the quiet** without other people knowing, secretly ▶ **quietly** *adv* ▶ **quietness** *n* ▶ **quieten** *v* (often foll by *down*) make or become quiet ▶ **quietude** *n* quietness, peace, or tranquillity

**quietism** *n* passivity and calmness of mind towards external events

**quiff** *n* tuft of hair brushed up above the forehead

**quill** *n* pen made from the feather of a bird's wing or tail; stiff hollow spine of a hedgehog or porcupine

**quilt** *n* padded covering for a bed ▶ **quilted** *adj* consisting of two layers of fabric with a layer of soft material between them

**quin** *n* short for **quintuplet**

**quince** *n* acid-tasting pear-shaped fruit

**quinine** *n* bitter drug used as a tonic and formerly to treat malaria

**quinquennial** *adj* occurring every five years; lasting five years

**quinsy** *n* inflammation of the throat or tonsils

**quintessence** *n* most perfect representation of a quality or state ▶ **quintessential** *adj*

**quintet** *n* group of five performers; music for such a group

**quintuplet** *n* one of five offspring born at one birth

**quip** *n* witty saying ▷ *v* **quipping, quipped** make a quip

**quire** *n* set of 24 or 25 sheets of paper

**quirk** *n* peculiarity of character; unexpected twist or turn e.g. *a quirk of fate* ▶ **quirky** *adj*

**quisling** *n* traitor who aids an occupying enemy force

**quit** *v* **quitting, quit** stop (doing something); give up (a job); depart from ▶ **quitter** *n* person who lacks perseverance ▶ **quits** *adj (informal)* on an equal footing

**quite** *adv* somewhat e.g. *she's quite pretty*; absolutely e.g. *you're quite right*; in actuality, truly ▷ *interj* expression of agreement

> **USAGE NOTE**
> Note that because *quite* can mean 'extremely': *quite amazing*, or can express a reservation: *quite friendly*, it should be used carefully

**quiver**[1] *v* shake with a tremulous movement ▷ *n* shaking or trembling

**quiver**[2] *n* case for arrows

**quixotic** [kwik-**sot**-ik] *adj* romantic and unrealistic ▶ **quixotically** *adv*

**quiz** *n, pl* **quizzes** entertainment in which the knowledge of the players is tested by a series of questions ▷ *v* **quizzing, quizzed** investigate by close questioning ▶ **quizzical** *adj* questioning

and mocking e.g. *a quizzical look*
▶ **quizzically** *adv*

**quod** *n (Brit slang)* jail

**quoit** *n* large ring used in the game
of quoits ▷ *pl* game in which quoits
are tossed at a stake in the ground
in attempts to encircle it

**quokka** *n* small Australian wallaby

**quorum** *n* minimum number of
people required to be present at a
meeting before any transactions
can take place

**quota** *n* share that is due from,
due to, or allocated to a group
or person; prescribed number or
quantity allowed, required, or
admitted

**quote** *v* repeat (words) exactly
from (an earlier work, speech, or
conversation); state (a price) for
goods or a job of work ▷ *n (informal)*
quotation ▶ **quotable** *adj*
▶ **quotation** *n* written or spoken
passage repeated exactly in a later
work, speech, or conversation;
act of quoting; estimate of costs
submitted by a contractor to a
prospective client ▶ **quotation
marks** raised commas used in
writing to mark the beginning
and end of a quotation or passage
of speech

**quoth** *v (obs)* said

**quotidian** *adj* daily; commonplace

**quotient** *n* result of the division of
one number or quantity by another

**q.v.** which see: used to refer a reader
to another item in the same book

# Rr

**R** Queen; King; River

**r** radius; ratio; right

**RA** (in Britain) Royal Academy; (in
Britain) Royal Artillery

**RAAF** Royal Australian Air Force

**rabbi** [rab-bye] *n, pl* **-bis** Jewish
spiritual leader ▶ **rabbinical** *adj*

**rabbit** *n* small burrowing mammal
with long ears ▶ **rabbit on** *v*
**rabbiting, rabbited** (*Brit informal*)
talk too much

**rabble** *n* disorderly crowd of noisy
people

**rabid** *adj* fanatical; having rabies
▶ **rabidly** *adv*

**rabies** [ray-beez] *n* usu. fatal viral
disease transmitted by dogs and
certain other animals

**RAC** (in Britain) Royal Automobile
Club

**raccoon** *n* small N American
mammal with a long striped tail

**race¹** *n* contest of speed ▷ *pl*
meeting for horse racing ▷ *v*
compete (with) in a race; run
swiftly; (of an engine) run
faster than normal ▶ **racer** *n*
▶ **racecourse** *n* ▶ **racehorse** *n*
▶ **racetrack** *n*

**race²** *n* group of people of common
ancestry with distinguishing
physical features, such as skin
colour ▶ **racial** *adj* ▶ **racism,
racialism** *n* hostile attitude or
behaviour to members of other
races, based on a belief in the
innate superiority of one's own
race ▶ **racist, racialist** *adj*, *n*

**r**

**raceme** [rass-**eem**] n cluster of flowers along a central stem, as in the foxglove

**rack**[1] n framework for holding particular articles, such as coats or luggage; (*Hist*) instrument of torture that stretched the victim's body ▷ v cause great suffering to **rack one's brains** try very hard to remember

**rack**[2] n **go to rack and ruin** be destroyed

**racket**[1] n noisy disturbance; occupation by which money is made illegally

**racket**[2], **racquet** n bat with strings stretched in an oval frame, used in tennis etc. ▶ **rackets** n ball game played in a paved walled court

**racketeer** n person making illegal profits

**raconteur** [rak-on-**tur**] n skilled storyteller

**racy** adj **racier, raciest** slightly shocking; spirited or lively

**radar** n device for tracking distant objects by bouncing high-frequency radio pulses off them

**radial** adj spreading out from a common central point; of a radius; (also **radial-ply**) (of a tyre) having flexible sides strengthened with radial cords

**radiant** adj looking happy; shining; emitting radiation ▶ **radiance** n

**radiate** v spread out from a centre; emit or be emitted as radiation ▶ **radiator** n (*Brit*) arrangement of pipes containing hot water or steam to heat a room; tubes containing water as cooling apparatus for a car engine; (*Aust & NZ*) electric fire

**radiation** n transmission of energy from one body to another; particles or waves emitted in nuclear decay; process of radiating

**radical** adj fundamental; thorough; advocating fundamental change ▷ n person advocating fundamental (political) change; number expressed as the root of another ▶ **radically** adv ▶ **radicalism** n

**radicle** n small or developing root

**radii** n a plural of **radius**

**radio** n, pl **-dios** use of electromagnetic waves for broadcasting, communication, etc.; device for receiving and amplifying radio signals; sound broadcasting ▷ v transmit (a message) by radio

**radio-** combining form of radio, radiation, or radioactivity

**radioactive** adj emitting radiation as a result of nuclear decay ▶ **radioactivity** n

**radiography** [ray-dee-**og**-ra-fee] n production of an image on a film or plate by radiation ▶ **radiographer** n

**radiology** [ray-dee-**ol**-a-jee] n science of using x-rays in medicine ▶ **radiologist** n

**radiotherapy** n treatment of disease, esp. cancer, by radiation ▶ **radiotherapist** n

**radish** n small hot-flavoured root vegetable eaten raw in salads

**radium** n (*Chem*) radioactive metallic element

**radius** n, pl **radii** or **radiuses** (length of) a straight line from the centre to the circumference of a circle; outer of two bones in the forearm

**radon** [**ray**-don] n (*Chem*) radioactive gaseous element

**RAF** (in Britain) Royal Air Force

**raffia** n prepared palm fibre for weaving mats etc.

**raffish** adj slightly disreputable

**raffle** n lottery with goods as prizes ▷ v offer as a prize in a raffle

r

**raft** n floating platform of logs, planks, etc.

**rafter** n one of the main beams of a roof

**rag**[1] n fragment of cloth; (Brit, Aust & NZ informal) newspaper ▷ pl tattered clothing ▶ **ragged** [rag-gid] adj dressed in shabby or torn clothes; torn; lacking smoothness

**rag**[2] (Brit) v **ragging, ragged** tease ▷ adj, n (of) events organized by students to raise money for charities

**ragamuffin** n ragged dirty child

**rage** n violent anger or passion ▷ v speak or act with fury; proceed violently and without check **all the rage** very popular

**raglan** adj (of a sleeve) joined to a garment by diagonal seams from the neck to the underarm

**ragout** [rag-**goo**] n richly seasoned stew of meat and vegetables

**ragtime** n style of jazz piano music

**raid** n sudden surprise attack or search ▷ v make a raid on ▶ **raider** n

**rail**[1] n horizontal bar, esp. as part of a fence or track; railway ▶ **railing** n fence made of rails supported by posts ▶ **railway** n track of iron rails on which trains run; company operating a railway

**rail**[2] v (foll by at or against) complain bitterly or loudly ▶ **raillery** n teasing or joking

**rail**[3] n small marsh bird

**raiment** n (obs) clothing

**rain** n water falling in drops from the clouds ▷ v fall or pour down as rain; fall rapidly and in large quantities ▶ **rainy** adj ▶ **rainbow** n arch of colours in the sky ▶ **rainbow nation** South African nation ▶ **raincoat** n water-resistant overcoat ▶ **rainfall** n amount of rain ▶ **rainforest** n dense forest in tropical and temperate areas

**raise** v lift up; set upright; increase in amount or intensity; collect or levy; bring up (a family); put forward for consideration

**raisin** n dried grape

**raison d'être** [ray-zon **det**-ra] n, pl **raisons d'être** (French) reason or justification for existence

**Raj** n **the Raj** former British rule in India

**raja, rajah** n (Hist) Indian prince or ruler

**rake**[1] n tool with a long handle and a crosspiece with teeth, used for smoothing earth or gathering leaves, hay, etc. ▷ v gather or smooth with a rake; search (through); sweep (with gunfire) **rake it in** (informal) make a large amount of money ▶ **rake-off** n (slang) share of profits, esp. illegal ▶ **rake up** v revive memories of (a forgotten unpleasant event)

**rake**[2] n dissolute or immoral man ▶ **rakish** adj

**rakish** adj dashing or jaunty

**rally** n, pl -lies large gathering of people for a meeting; marked recovery of strength; (Tennis etc.) lively exchange of strokes; car-driving competition on public roads ▷ v -lying, -lied bring or come together after dispersal or for a common cause; regain health or strength, revive

**RAM** (Computing) random access memory

**ram** n male sheep; hydraulic machine ▷ v **ramming, rammed** strike against with force; force or drive; cram or stuff

**Ramadan** n 9th Muslim month; strict fasting from dawn to dusk observed during this time

**ramble** v walk without a definite route; talk incoherently ▷ n walk, esp. in the country

r

**rambler** *n* person who rambles; climbing rose

**ramekin** [ram-ik-in] *n* small ovenproof dish for a single serving of food

**ramifications** *pl n* consequences resulting from an action

**ramp** *n* slope joining two level surfaces

**rampage** *v* dash about violently **on the rampage** behaving violently or destructively

**rampant** *adj* growing or spreading uncontrollably; (of a heraldic beast) on its hind legs

**rampart** *n* mound or wall for defence

**ramshackle** *adj* tumbledown, rickety, or makeshift

**ran** *v* past tense of **run**

**ranch** *n* large cattle farm in the American West ▶ **rancher** *n*

**rancid** *adj* (of butter, bacon, etc.) stale and having an offensive smell ▶ **rancidity** *n*

**rancour** *n* deep bitter hate ▶ **rancorous** *adj*

**rand** *n* monetary unit of S Africa

**R & D** research and development

**random** *adj* made or done by chance or without plan **at random** haphazardly

**randy** *adj* **randier, randiest** (*informal*) sexually aroused

**rang** *v* past tense of **ring**[1]

**range** *n* limits of effectiveness or variation; distance that a missile or plane can travel; distance of a mark shot at; whole set of related things; chain of mountains; place for shooting practice or rocket testing; kitchen stove ▷ *v* vary between one point and another; cover or extend over; roam ▶ **ranger** *n* official in charge of a nature reserve etc.; (**R-**) member of the senior branch of Guides ▶ **rangefinder** *n* instrument for finding how far away an object is

**rangy** [rain-jee] *adj* **rangier, rangiest** having long slender limbs

**rank**[1] *n* relative place or position; status; social class; row or line ▷ *v* have a specific rank or position; arrange in rows or lines **the ranks** common soldiers ▶ **rank and file** ordinary people or members

**rank**[2] *adj* complete or absolute e.g. *rank favouritism*; smelling offensively strong; growing too thickly

**rankle** *v* continue to cause resentment or bitterness

**ransack** *v* search thoroughly; pillage, plunder

**ransom** *n* money demanded in return for the release of someone who has been kidnapped

**rant** *v* talk in a loud and excited way ▶ **ranter** *n*

**rap** *v* **rapping, rapped** hit with a sharp quick blow; utter (a command) abruptly; perform a rhythmic monologue with musical backing ▷ *n* quick sharp blow; rhythmic monologue performed to music **take the rap** (*slang*) suffer punishment for something whether guilty or not ▶ **rapper** *n*

**rapacious** *adj* greedy or grasping ▶ **rapacity** *n*

**rape**[1] *v* force to submit to sexual intercourse ▷ *n* act of raping; any violation or abuse ▶ **rapist** *n*

**rape**[2] *n* plant with oil-yielding seeds, also used as fodder

**rapid** *adj* quick, swift ▶ **rapids** *pl n* part of a river with a fast turbulent current ▶ **rapidly** *adv* ▶ **rapidity** *n*

**rapier** [ray-pyer] *n* fine-bladed sword

**rapport** [rap-pore] *n* harmony or agreement

**rapprochement** [rap-prosh-mong] *n* re-establishment of

friendly relations, esp. between nations

**rapt** adj engrossed or spellbound ▶ **rapture** n ecstasy ▶ **rapturous** adj

**rare¹** adj uncommon; infrequent; of uncommonly high quality; (of air at high altitudes) having low density, thin ▶ **rarely** adv seldom ▶ **rarity** n

**rare²** adj (of meat) lightly cooked

**rarebit** n see **Welsh rarebit**

**rarefied** [rare-if-ide] adj highly specialized, exalted; (of air) thin

**raring** adj **raring to** enthusiastic, willing, or ready to

**rascal** n rogue; naughty (young) person ▶ **rascally** adj

**rash¹** adj hasty, reckless, or incautious ▶ **rashly** adv

**rash²** n eruption of spots or patches on the skin; outbreak of (unpleasant) occurrences

**rasher** n thin slice of bacon

**rasp** n harsh grating noise; coarse file ▷ v speak in a grating voice; make a scraping noise

**raspberry** n red juicy edible berry; (informal) spluttering noise made with the tongue and lips, to show contempt

**Rastafarian** n, adj (member) of a religion originating in Jamaica and regarding Haile Selassie as God (also **Rasta**)

**rat** n small rodent; (informal) contemptible person, esp. a deserter or informer ▷ v **ratting, ratted** (informal) inform (on); hunt rats ▶ **ratty** adj (Brit & NZ informal) bad-tempered, irritable ▶ **rat race** continual hectic competitive activity

**ratafia** [rat-a-**fee**-a] n liqueur made from fruit; (chiefly Brit) almond-flavoured biscuit

**ratatouille** [rat-a-**twee**] n vegetable casserole of tomatoes, aubergines, etc.

**ratchet** n set of teeth on a bar or wheel allowing motion in one direction only

**rate** n degree of speed or progress; proportion between two things; charge ▷ pl local tax on business ▷ v consider or value; estimate the value of **at any rate** in any case ▶ **rateable** adj able to be rated; (of property) liable to payment of rates ▶ **ratepayer** n

**rather** adv to some extent; more truly or appropriately; more willingly

**ratify** v **-fying, -fied** give formal approval to ▶ **ratification** n

**rating** n valuation or assessment; classification; noncommissioned sailor ▷ pl size of the audience for a TV programme

**ratio** n, pl **-tios** relationship between two numbers or amounts expressed as a proportion

**ration** n fixed allowance of food etc. ▷ v limit to a certain amount per person

**rational** adj reasonable, sensible; capable of reasoning ▶ **rationally** adv ▶ **rationality** n ▶ **rationale** [rash-a-**nahl**] n reason for an action or decision ▶ **rationalism** n philosophy that regards reason as the only basis for beliefs or actions ▶ **rationalist** n ▶ **rationalize** v justify by plausible reasoning; reorganize to improve efficiency or profitability ▶ **rationalization** n

**rattan** n climbing palm with jointed stems used for canes

**rattle** v give out a succession of short sharp sounds; shake briskly causing sharp sounds; (informal) confuse or fluster ▷ n short sharp sound; instrument for making such a sound ▶ **rattlesnake** n poisonous snake with loose horny segments on the tail that make a rattling sound

r

**raucous** adj hoarse or harsh

**raunchy** adj **-chier, -chiest** (slang) earthy, sexy

**ravage** v cause extensive damage to ▸ **ravages** pl n damaging effects

**rave** v talk wildly or with enthusiasm ▹ n large-scale party with electronic dance music ▸ **raving** adj delirious; (informal) exceptional e.g. a raving beauty

**ravel** v **-elling, -elled** tangle or become entangled

**raven** n black bird like a large crow ▹ adj (of hair) shiny black

**ravenous** adj very hungry

**ravine** [rav-**veen**] n narrow steep-sided valley worn by a stream

**ravioli** pl n small squares of pasta with a savoury filling

**ravish** v enrapture; (lit) rape ▸ **ravishing** adj lovely or entrancing

**raw** adj uncooked; not manufactured or refined; inexperienced; chilly ▸ **raw deal** unfair or dishonest treatment ▸ **rawhide** n untanned hide

**ray¹** n single line or narrow beam of light

**ray²** n large sea fish with a flat body and a whiplike tail

**rayon** n (fabric made of) a synthetic fibre

**raze** v destroy (buildings or a town) completely

**razor** n sharp instrument for shaving ▸ **razorbill** n sea bird of the North Atlantic with a stout bill flattened at the sides

**razzle-dazzle, razzmatazz** n (slang) showy activity

**RC** Roman Catholic; Red Cross

**Rd** Road

**re** prep with reference to, concerning

**RE** (in Britain) religious education

**re-** prefix again e.g. re-enter; retrial

**reach** v arrive at; make a movement in order to grasp or touch; succeed in touching; make contact or communication with; extend as far as ▹ n distance that one can reach; range of influence ▹ pl stretch of a river ▸ **reachable** adj

**react** v act in response (to); (foll by against) act in an opposing or contrary manner ▸ **reaction** n physical or emotional response to a stimulus; any action resisting another; opposition to change; chemical or nuclear change, combination, or decomposition ▸ **reactionary** n ▹ adj (person) opposed to change, esp. in politics ▸ **reactance** n (Electricity) resistance to the flow of an alternating current caused by the inductance or capacitance of the circuit ▸ **reactive** adj chemically active ▸ **reactor** n apparatus in which a nuclear reaction is maintained and controlled to produce nuclear energy

**read** v **reading, read** look at and understand or take in (written or printed matter); look at and say aloud; interpret the significance or meaning of; (of an instrument) register; study ▹ n matter suitable for reading e.g. a good read ▸ **readable** adj enjoyable to read; legible ▸ **reading** n

**reader** n person who reads; textbook; (chiefly Brit) senior university lecturer ▸ **readership** n readers of a publication collectively

**readjust** v adapt to a new situation ▸ **readjustment** n

**ready** adj **readier, readiest** prepared for use or action; willing; prompt ▸ **readily** adv ▸ **readiness** n ▸ **ready-made** adj for immediate use by any customer

**reagent** [ree-**age**-ent] n chemical substance that reacts with another, used to detect the presence of the other

**real** adj existing in fact; actual; genuine ▶ **really** adv very; truly ▷ interj exclamation of dismay, doubt, or surprise ▶ **reality** n state of things as they are ▶ **reality TV** television programmes focusing on members of the public living in conditions created especially by the programme makers ▶ **real ale** (chiefly Brit) beer allowed to ferment in the barrel ▶ **real estate** property consisting of land and houses

**USAGE NOTE**
To intensify an adjective, use the adverb form really, not real: He's really strong

**realistic** adj seeing and accepting things as they really are, practical ▶ **realistically** adv ▶ **realism** n ▶ **realist** n

**realize** v become aware or grasp the significance of; achieve (a plan, hopes, etc.); convert into money ▶ **realization** n

**realm** n kingdom; sphere of interest

**ream** n twenty quires of paper, generally 500 sheets ▷ pl (informal) large quantity (of written matter)

**reap** v cut and gather (a harvest); receive as the result of a previous activity ▶ **reaper** n

**reappear** v appear again ▶ **reappearance** n

**rear¹** n back part; part of an army, procession, etc. behind the others **bring up the rear** come last ▶ **rearmost** adj ▶ **rear admiral** high-ranking naval officer ▶ **rearguard** n troops protecting the rear of an army

**rear²** v care for and educate (children); breed (animals); (of a horse) rise on its hind feet

**rearrange** v organize differently, alter ▶ **rearrangement** n

**reason** n cause or motive; faculty of rational thought; sanity ▷ v think logically in forming conclusions **reason with** persuade by logical argument into doing something ▶ **reasonable** adj sensible; not excessive; logical ▶ **reasonably** adv

**reassess** v reconsider the value or importance of

**reassure** v restore confidence to ▶ **reassurance** n

**rebate** n discount or refund

**rebel** v -belling, -belled revolt against the ruling power; reject accepted conventions ▷ n person who rebels ▶ **rebellion** n organized open resistance to authority; rejection of conventions ▶ **rebellious** adj

**rebirth** n revival or renaissance ▶ **reborn** adj active again after a period of inactivity

**rebore, reboring** n boring of a cylinder to restore its true shape

**rebound** v spring back; misfire so as to hurt the perpetrator of a plan or deed ▷ **on the rebound** (informal) while recovering from rejection

**rebuff** v reject or snub ▷ n blunt refusal, snub

**rebuke** v scold sternly ▷ n stern scolding

**rebus** n, pl -buses puzzle consisting of pictures and symbols representing words or syllables

**rebut** v -butting, -butted prove that (a claim) is untrue ▶ **rebuttal** n

**recalcitrant** adj wilfully disobedient ▶ **recalcitrance** n

**recall** v recollect or remember; order to return; annul or cancel ▷ n ability to remember; order to return

**recant** v withdraw (a statement or belief) publicly ▶ **recantation** n

r

**recap** (*informal*) *v* **-capping,**
**-capped** recapitulate ▷ *n*
recapitulation

**recapitulate** *v* state again briefly,
repeat ▶ **recapitulation** *n*

**recapture** *v* experience again;
capture again

**recce** (*chiefly Brit slang*) *v* **-ceing,**
**-ced** *or* **-ceed** reconnoitre ▷ *n*
reconnaissance

**recede** *v* move to a more distant
place; (of the hair) stop growing
at the front

**receipt** *n* written acknowledgment
of money or goods received;
receiving or being received

**receive** *v* take, accept, or get;
experience; greet (guests)
▶ **received** *adj* generally accepted
▶ **receiver** *n* part of telephone
that is held to the ear; equipment
in a telephone, radio, or television
that converts electrical signals
into sound; person appointed by a
court to manage the property of a
bankrupt ▶ **receivership** *n* state of
being administered by a receiver

**recent** *adj* having happened lately;
new ▶ **recently** *adv*

**receptacle** *n* object used to
contain something

**reception** *n* area for receiving
guests, clients, etc.; formal party;
manner of receiving; welcome; (in
broadcasting) quality of signals
received ▶ **receptionist** *n* person
who receives guests, clients, etc.

**receptive** *adj* willing to accept
new ideas, suggestions, etc.
▶ **receptivity** *n*

**recess** *n* niche or alcove; holiday
between sessions of work; secret
hidden place ▶ **recessed** *adj* hidden
or placed in a recess

**recession** *n* period of economic
difficulty when little is being bought
or sold ▶ **recessive** *adj* receding

**recherché** [rish-**air**-shay] *adj*
refined or elegant; known only
to experts

**recidivism** *n* habitual relapse into
crime ▶ **recidivist** *n*

**recipe** *n* directions for cooking a dish;
method for achieving something

**recipient** *n* person who receives
something

**reciprocal** [ris-**sip**-pro-kl] *adj*
mutual; given or done in return
▶ **reciprocally** *adv* ▶ **reciprocate**
*v* give or feel in return; (of a
machine part) move backwards
and forwards ▶ **reciprocation** *n*
▶ **reciprocity** *n*

**recite** *v* repeat (a poem etc.)
aloud to an audience ▶ **recital**
*n* musical performance by a
soloist or soloists; act of reciting
▶ **recitation** *n* recital, usu. from
memory, of poetry or prose
▶ **recitative** [ress-it-a-**teev**] *n*
speechlike style of singing, used
esp. for narrative passages in opera

**reckless** *adj* heedless of danger
▶ **recklessly** *adv* ▶ **recklessness** *n*

**reckon** *v* consider or think; make
calculations, count; expect
▶ **reckoning** *n*

**reclaim** *v* regain possession
of; make fit for cultivation
▶ **reclamation** *n*

**recline** *v* rest in a leaning position
▶ **reclining** *adj*

**recluse** *n* person who avoids other
people ▶ **reclusive** *adj* .

**recognize** *v* identify as (a person
or thing) already known; accept
as true or existing; treat as valid;
notice, show appreciation of
▶ **recognition** *n* ▶ **recognizable**
*adj* ▶ **recognizance** [rik-**og**-nizz-
anss] *n* undertaking before a court
to observe some condition

**recoil** *v* jerk or spring back; draw
back in horror; (of an action) go

wrong so as to hurt the doer ▷ n
backward jerk; recoiling

**recollect** v call back to mind,
remember ▶ **recollection** n

**recommend** v advise or counsel;
praise or commend; make
acceptable ▶ **recommendation** n

> **SPELLING TIP**
>
> Most people who misspell
> these words use single letters
> throughout (*recomend* and
> *recomendation*); they should,
> of course, double the *m*, as in
> **recommendation**

**recompense** v pay or reward;
compensate or make up for
▷ n compensation; reward or
remuneration

**reconcile** v harmonize (conflicting
beliefs etc.); bring back into
friendship; accept or cause to
accept (an unpleasant situation)
▶ **reconciliation** n

**recondite** adj difficult to understand

**recondition** v restore to good
condition or working order

**reconnaissance** [rik-**kon**-iss-anss]
n survey for military or engineering
purposes

> **SPELLING TIP**
>
> The Collins Corpus shows that the
> most common way to misspell
> **reconnaissance** is to miss out an
> *s*, although there are examples
> where an *n* has been missed out
> instead. Remember, there are
> two *n*s in the middle and two *ss*

**reconnoitre** [rek-a-**noy**-ter] v
make a reconnaissance of

**reconsider** v think about again,
consider changing

**reconstitute** v reorganize; restore
(dried food) to its former state by
adding water ▶ **reconstitution** n

**reconstruct** v rebuild;
use evidence to re-create
▶ **reconstruction** n

**record** n [**rek**-ord] document
or other thing that preserves
information; disc with
indentations which a record
player transforms into sound; best
recorded achievement; known
facts about a person's past ▷ v
[rik-**kord**] put in writing; preserve
(sound, TV programmes, etc.) for
reproduction on a playback device;
show or register **off the record**
not for publication ▶ **recorder** n
person or machine that records
sound or images; type of flute, held
vertically; judge in certain courts
▶ **recording** n ▶ **record player**
instrument for reproducing sound
on records

**recount** v tell in detail

**re-count** v count again ▷ n second
or further count, esp. of votes

**recoup** [rik-**koop**] v regain or make
good (a loss); recompense or
compensate

**recourse** n source of help **have
recourse to** turn to a source of
help or course of action

**recover** v become healthy again;
regain a former condition; find
again; get back (a loss or
expense) ▶ **recovery** n
▶ **recoverable** adj

**re-create** v make happen or exist
again

**recreation** n agreeable or
refreshing occupation,
relaxation, or amusement
▶ **recreational** adj

**recrimination** n mutual blame
▶ **recriminatory** adj

**recruit** v enlist (new soldiers,
members, etc.) ▷ n newly enlisted
soldier; new member or supporter
▶ **recruitment** n

**rectangle** n oblong four-sided
figure with four right angles
▶ **rectangular** adj

**r**

**rectify** v **-fying, -fied** put right, correct; (*Chem*) purify by distillation; (*Electricity*) convert (alternating current) into direct current ▶ **rectification** n ▶ **rectifier** n

**rectilinear** adj in a straight line; characterized by straight lines

**rectitude** n moral correctness

**recto** n, pl **-tos** right-hand page of a book

**rector** n clergyman in charge of a parish; head of certain academic institutions ▶ **rectory** n rector's house

**rectum** n, pl **-tums** or **-ta** final section of the large intestine

**recumbent** adj lying down

**recuperate** v recover from illness ▶ **recuperation** n ▶ **recuperative** adj

**recur** v **-curring, -curred** happen again ▶ **recurrence** n repetition ▶ **recurrent** adj

**recycle** v reprocess (used materials) for further use ▶ **recyclable** adj

**red** adj **redder, reddest** of a colour varying from crimson to orange and seen in blood, fire, etc.; flushed in the face from anger, shame, etc. ▷ n red colour; (**R-**) (*informal*) communist **in the red** (*informal*) in debt **see red** (*informal*) be angry ▶ **redness** n ▶ **redden** v make or become red ▶ **reddish** adj ▶ **redback spider** small venomous Australian spider with a red stripe on the back of the abdomen ▶ **red-blooded** adj (*informal*) vigorous or virile ▶ **redbrick** adj (of a university in Britain) founded in the late 19th or early 20th century ▶ **red card** (*Soccer*) piece of red pasteboard shown by a referee to indicate that a player has been sent off ▶ **red carpet** very special welcome for an important guest ▶ **redcoat** n (*Hist*) British soldier ▶ **Red**

**Cross** international organization providing help for victims of war or natural disasters ▶ **redcurrant** n small round edible red berry ▶ **red-handed** adj (*informal*) (caught) in the act of doing something wrong or illegal ▶ **red herring** something which diverts attention from the main issue ▶ **red-hot** adj glowing red; extremely hot; very keen ▶ **Red Indian** (*offens*) Native American ▶ **red light** traffic signal to stop; danger signal ▶ **red meat** dark meat, esp. beef or lamb ▶ **red tape** excessive adherence to official rules

**redeem** v make up for; reinstate (oneself) in someone's good opinion; free from sin; buy back; pay off (a loan or debt) **the Redeemer** Jesus Christ ▶ **redeemable** adj ▶ **redemption** n ▶ **redemptive** adj

**redeploy** v assign to a new position or task ▶ **redeployment** n

**redevelop** v rebuild or renovate (an area or building) ▶ **redevelopment** n

**redolent** adj reminiscent (of); smelling strongly (of)

**redouble** v increase, multiply, or intensify

**redoubt** n small fort defending a hilltop or pass

**redoubtable** adj formidable

**redound** v cause advantage or disadvantage (to)

**redox** n chemical reaction in which one substance is reduced and the other is oxidized

**redress** v make amends for ▷ n compensation or amends

**reduce** v bring down, lower; lessen, weaken; bring by force or necessity to some state or action; slim; simplify; make (a sauce) more concentrated ▶ **reducible** adj ▶ **reduction** n

**redundant** *adj* (of a worker) no longer needed; superfluous **be made redundant** be laid off ▸ **redundancy** *n*

**reed** *n* tall grass that grows in swamps and shallow water; tall straight stem of this plant; (*Music*) vibrating cane or metal strip in certain wind instruments ▸ **reedy** *adj* harsh and thin in tone

**reef**[1] *n* ridge of rock or coral near the surface of the sea; vein of ore

**reef**[2] *n* part of a sail which can be rolled up to reduce its area ▸ *v* take in a reef ▸ **reefer** *n* short thick jacket worn esp. by sailors; (*old-fashioned slang*) hand-rolled cigarette containing cannabis ▸ **reef knot** two simple knots turned opposite ways

**reek** *v* smell strongly ▸ *n* strong unpleasant smell **reek of** give a strong suggestion of

**reel**[1] *n* cylindrical object on which film, tape, thread, or wire is wound; winding apparatus, as of a fishing rod ▸ **reel in** *v* draw in by means of a reel ▸ **reel off** *v* recite or write fluently or quickly

**reel**[2] *v* stagger, sway, or whirl

**reel**[3] *n* lively Scottish dance

**ref** *n* (*informal*) referee in sport

**refectory** *n*, *pl* **-tories** room for meals in a college etc.

**refer** *v* **-ferring, -ferred** (foll by *to*) allude (to); be relevant (to); send (to) for information; submit (to) for decision ▸ **referral** *n* ▸ **reference** *n* act of referring; citation or direction in a book; written testimonial regarding character or capabilities **with reference to** concerning

> **USAGE NOTE**
> Avoid using *refer back*; *refer* includes the sense 'back' in its meaning

**referee** *n* umpire in sports, esp. soccer or boxing; person willing to testify to someone's character etc.; arbitrator ▸ *v* **-eeing, -eed** act as referee of

**referendum** *n*, *pl* **-dums** *or* **-da** direct vote of the electorate on an important question

**refill** *v* fill again ▸ *n* second or subsequent filling; replacement supply of something in a permanent container

**refine** *v* purify; improve ▸ **refined** *adj* cultured or polite; purified ▸ **refinement** *n* improvement or elaboration; fineness of taste or manners; subtlety ▸ **refinery** *n* place where sugar, oil, etc. is refined

**reflation** *n* increase in the supply of money and credit designed to encourage economic activity ▸ **reflate** *v* ▸ **reflationary** *adj*

**reflect** *v* throw back, esp. rays of light, heat, etc.; form an image of; show; consider at length; bring credit or discredit upon ▸ **reflection** *n* act of reflecting; return of rays of heat, light, etc. from a surface; image of an object given back by a mirror etc.; conscious thought or meditation; attribution of discredit or blame ▸ **reflective** *adj* quiet, contemplative; capable of reflecting images ▸ **reflector** *n* polished surface for reflecting light etc.

**reflex** *n* involuntary response to a stimulus or situation ▸ *adj* (of a muscular action) involuntary; reflected; (of an angle) more than 180° ▸ **reflexive** *adj* (*Grammar*) denoting a verb whose subject is the same as its object e.g. *dress oneself*

**reflexology** *n* foot massage as a therapy in alternative medicine

r

**reform** n improvement ▷ v improve; abandon evil practices ▶**reformer** n ▶**reformation** n act or instance of something being reformed; (**R-**) religious movement in 16th-century Europe that resulted in the establishment of the Protestant Churches ▶**reformatory** n (formerly) institution for reforming young offenders

**refract** v change the course of (light etc.) passing from one medium to another ▶**refraction** n ▶**refractive** adj ▶**refractor** n

**refractory** adj unmanageable or rebellious; (Med) resistant to treatment; resistant to heat

**refrain**[1] v **refrain from** keep oneself from doing

**refrain**[2] n frequently repeated part of a song

**refresh** v revive or reinvigorate, as through food, drink, or rest; stimulate (the memory) ▶**refresher** n ▶**refreshing** adj having a reviving effect; pleasantly different or new ▶**refreshment** n something that refreshes, esp. food or drink

**refrigerate** v cool or freeze in order to preserve ▶**refrigeration** n ▶**refrigerator** n full name for **fridge**

**refuge** n (source of) shelter or protection ▶**refugee** n person who seeks refuge, esp. in a foreign country

**refulgent** adj shining, radiant

**refund** v pay back ▷ n return of money; amount returned

**refurbish** v renovate and brighten up

**refuse**[1] v decline, deny, or reject ▶**refusal** n denial of anything demanded or offered

**refuse**[2] n rubbish or useless matter

**refute** v disprove ▶**refutation** n

> **USAGE NOTE**
> *Refute* is not the same as *deny*. It means 'show evidence to disprove something', while *deny* means only 'say something is not true'

**regain** v get back or recover; reach again

**regal** adj of or like a king or queen ▶**regally** adv ▶**regalia** pl n ceremonial emblems of royalty or high office

**regale** v entertain (someone) with stories etc.

**regard** v consider; look at; heed ▷ n respect or esteem; attention; look ▷ pl expression of goodwill **as regards, regarding** in respect of, concerning ▶**regardless** adj heedless ▷ adv in spite of everything

**regatta** n meeting for yacht or boat races

**regenerate** v (cause to) undergo spiritual, moral, or physical renewal; reproduce or re-create ▶**regeneration** n ▶**regenerative** adj

**regent** n ruler of a kingdom during the absence, childhood, or illness of its monarch ▷ adj ruling as a regent e.g. *prince regent* ▶**regency** n status or period of office of a regent

**reggae** n style of Jamaican popular music with a strong beat

**regicide** n killing of a king; person who kills a king

**regime** [ray-**zheem**] n system of government; particular administration

**regimen** n prescribed system of diet etc.

**regiment** n organized body of troops as a unit of the army ▶**regimental** adj

▶ **regimentation** n ▶ **regimented** adj very strictly controlled

**region** n administrative division of a country; area considered as a unit but with no definite boundaries; part of the body ▶ **regional** adj

**register** n (book containing) an official list or record of things; range of a voice or instrument ▷ v enter in a register or set down in writing; show or be shown on a meter or the face ▶ **registration** n ▶ **registration number** numbers and letters displayed on a vehicle to identify it ▶ **registrar** n keeper of official records; senior hospital doctor, junior to a consultant ▶ **register office, registry office** place where births, marriages, and deaths are recorded

**Regius professor** [reej-yuss] n (in Britain) professor appointed by the Crown to a university chair founded by a royal patron

**regress** v revert to a former worse condition ▶ **regression** n act of regressing; (*Psychol*) use of an earlier (inappropriate) mode of behaviour ▶ **regressive** adj

**regret** v **-gretting, -gretted** feel sorry about; express apology or distress ▷ n feeling of repentance, guilt, or sorrow ▶ **regretful** adj ▶ **regrettable** adj

**regular** adj normal, customary, or usual; symmetrical or even; done or occurring according to a rule; periodical; employed continuously in the armed forces ▷ n regular soldier; (*informal*) frequent customer ▶ **regularity** n ▶ **regularize** v ▶ **regularly** adv

**regulate** v control, esp. by rules; adjust slightly ▶ **regulation** n rule; regulating ▶ **regulator** n device that automatically controls pressure, temperature, etc.

**regurgitate** v vomit; (of some birds and animals) bring back (partly digested food) into the mouth; reproduce (ideas, facts, etc.) without understanding them ▶ **regurgitation** n

**rehabilitate** v help (a person) to readjust to society after illness, imprisonment, etc.; restore to a former position or rank; restore the good reputation of ▶ **rehabilitation** n

**rehash** v rework or reuse ▷ n old ideas presented in a new form

**rehearse** v practise (a play, concert, etc.); repeat aloud ▶ **rehearsal** n

**rehouse** v provide with a new (and better) home

**reign** n period of a sovereign's rule ▷ v rule (a country); be supreme

**reimburse** v refund, pay back ▶ **reimbursement** n

**rein** v check or manage with reins; control or limit ▶ **reins** pl n narrow straps attached to a bit to guide a horse; means of control

**reincarnation** n rebirth of a soul in successive bodies; one of a series of such transmigrations ▶ **reincarnate** v

**reindeer** n, pl **-deer** or **-deers** deer of arctic regions with large branched antlers

**reinforce** v strengthen with new support, material, or force; strengthen with additional troops, ships, etc. ▶ **reinforcement** n ▶ **reinforced concrete** concrete strengthened by having steel mesh or bars embedded in it

**reinstate** v restore to a former position ▶ **reinstatement** n

**reiterate** v repeat again and again ▶ **reiteration** n

**reject** v refuse to accept or believe; rebuff (a person); discard as useless

r

▷ *n* person or thing rejected as not up to standard ▶ **rejection** *n*

**rejig** *v* **-jigging, -jigged** re-equip (a factory or plant); rearrange

**rejoice** *v* feel or express great happiness

**rejoin¹** *v* join again

**rejoin²** *v* reply ▶ **rejoinder** *n* answer, retort

**rejuvenate** *v* restore youth or vitality to ▶ **rejuvenation** *n*

**relapse** *v* fall back into bad habits, illness, etc. ▷ *n* return of bad habits, illness, etc.

**relate** *v* establish a relation between; have reference or relation to; have an understanding (of people or ideas); tell (a story) or describe (an event) ▶ **related** *adj*

**relation** *n* connection between things; relative; connection by blood or marriage; act of relating (a story) ▷ *pl* social or political dealings; family ▶ **relationship** *n* dealings and feelings between people or countries; emotional or sexual affair; connection between two things; association by blood or marriage; kinship

**relative** *adj* dependent on relation to something else, not absolute; having reference or relation (to); (*Grammar*) referring to a word or clause earlier in the sentence ▷ *n* person connected by blood or marriage ▶ **relatively** *adv* ▶ **relativity** *n* subject of two theories of Albert Einstein, dealing with relationships of space, time, and motion, and acceleration and gravity; state of being relative

**relax** *v* make or become looser, less tense, or less rigid; ease up from effort or attention, rest; be less strict about; become more friendly ▶ **relaxing** *adj* ▶ **relaxation** *n*

**relay** *n* fresh set of people or animals relieving others; (*Electricity*) device for making or breaking a local circuit; broadcasting station receiving and retransmitting programmes ▷ *v* **-laying, -layed** pass on (a message) ▶ **relay race** race between teams in which each runner races part of the distance

**release** *v* set free; let go or fall; issue (a record, film, etc.) for sale or public showing; emit heat, energy, etc. ▷ *n* setting free; statement to the press; act of issuing for sale or publication; newly issued film, record, etc.

**relegate** *v* put in a less important position; demote (a sports team) to a lower league ▶ **relegation** *n*

**relent** *v* give up a harsh intention, become less severe ▶ **relentless** *adj* unremitting; merciless

**relevant** *adj* to do with the matter in hand ▶ **relevance** *n*

> **SPELLING TIP**
> A common word in English, **relevant** is not always spelt correctly. The final syllable is the problem and sometimes appears incorrectly in the Collins Corpus as *-ent*

**reliable** *adj* able to be trusted, dependable ▶ **reliably** *adv* ▶ **reliability** *n*

**reliance** *n* dependence, confidence, or trust ▶ **reliant** *adj*

**relic** *n* something that has survived from the past; body or possession of a saint, regarded as holy ▷ *pl* remains or traces ▶ **relict** *n* (*obs*) widow

**relief** *n* gladness at the end or removal of pain, distress, etc.; release from monotony or duty; money or food given to victims of disaster, poverty, etc.; freeing of a besieged city etc.; person who replaces another; projection of a carved design from the surface; any vivid effect resulting from contrast e.g. *comic relief* ▸ **relieve** v bring relief to **relieve oneself** urinate or defecate ▸ **relief map** map showing the shape and height of land by shading

**religion** n system of belief in and worship of a supernatural power or god ▸ **religious** adj of religion; pious or devout; scrupulous or conscientious ▸ **religiously** adv

**relinquish** v give up or abandon

**reliquary** n, pl **-quaries** case or shrine for holy relics

**relish** v enjoy, like very much ▷ n liking or enjoyment; appetizing savoury food, such as pickle; zestful quality or flavour

**relocate** v move to a new place to live or work ▸ **relocation** n

**reluctant** adj unwilling or disinclined ▸ **reluctantly** adv ▸ **reluctance** n

**rely** v **-lying, -lied** depend (on); trust

**remain** v continue; stay, be left behind; be left (over); be left to be done, said, etc. ▸ **remains** pl n relics, esp. of ancient buildings; dead body ▸ **remainder** n part which is left; amount left over after subtraction or division ▷ v offer (copies of a poorly selling book) at reduced prices

**remand** v send back into custody or put on bail before trial **on remand** in custody or on bail before trial ▸ **remand centre** (in Britain) place where accused people are detained awaiting trial

**remark** v make a casual comment (on); say; observe or notice ▷ n observation or comment ▸ **remarkable** adj worthy of note or attention; striking or unusual ▸ **remarkably** adv

**remedy** n, pl **-edies** means of curing pain or disease; means of solving a problem ▷ v **-edying, -edied** put right ▸ **remedial** adj intended to correct a specific disability, handicap, etc.

**remember** v retain in or recall to one's memory; keep in mind ▸ **remembrance** n memory; token or souvenir; honouring of the memory of a person or event

**remind** v cause to remember; put in mind (of) ▸ **reminder** n something that recalls the past; note to remind a person of something not done

**reminisce** v talk or write of past times, experiences, etc. ▸ **reminiscence** n remembering; thing recollected ▷ pl memoirs ▸ **reminiscent** adj reminding or suggestive (of)

**remiss** adj negligent or careless

**remission** n reduction in the length of a prison term; easing of intensity, as of an illness

**remit** v [rim-**mitt**] **-mitting, -mitted** send (money) for goods, services, etc., esp. by post; cancel (a punishment or debt); refer (a decision) to a higher authority or later date ▷ n [ree-mitt] area of competence or authority ▸ **remittance** n money sent as payment

**remnant** n small piece, esp. of fabric, left over; surviving trace

**remonstrate** v argue in protest ▸ **remonstrance** n

**remorse** n feeling of sorrow and regret for something one did ▸ **remorseful** adj ▸ **remorseless** adj pitiless; persistent ▸ **remorselessly** adv

**remote** adj far away, distant; aloof; slight or faint ▸ **remotely** adv ▸ **remote control** control of an

**r**

apparatus from a distance by an electrical device

**remould** v (*Brit*) renovate (a worn tyre) ▷ n (*Brit*) renovated tyre

**remove** v take away or off; get rid of; dismiss from office ▷ n degree of difference ▶ **removable** *adj* ▶ **removal** n removing, esp. changing residence

**Remuera tractor** n (*NZ informal*) four-wheel drive vehicle

**remunerate** v reward or pay ▶ **remunerative** *adj*

**remuneration** n reward or payment

**renaissance** n revival or rebirth; (**R-**) revival of learning in the 14th–16th centuries

**renal** [ree-nal] *adj* of the kidneys

**renascent** *adj* becoming active or vigorous again

**rend** v **rending, rent** tear or wrench apart; (of a sound) break (the silence) violently

**render** v cause to become; give or provide (aid, a service, etc.); submit or present (a bill); portray or represent; cover with plaster; melt down (fat)

**rendezvous** [ron-day-voo] n, pl **-vous** appointment; meeting place ▷ v meet as arranged

**rendition** n performance; translation

**renegade** n person who deserts a cause

**renege** [rin-nayg] v go back (on a promise etc.)

**renew** v begin again; make valid again; grow again; restore to a former state; replace (a worn part); restate or reaffirm ▶ **renewable** *adj* able to be renewed; (of energy or an energy source) inexhaustible or capable of being perpetually replenished ▶ **renewables** *pl n* renewable energy sources ▶ **renewal** n

**rennet** n substance for curdling milk to make cheese

**renounce** v give up (a belief, habit, etc.) voluntarily; give up (a title or claim) formally ▶ **renunciation** n

**renovate** v restore to good condition ▶ **renovation** n

**renown** n widespread good reputation

**renowned** *adj* famous

**rent**[1] v give or have use of in return for regular payments ▷ n regular payment for use of land, a building, machine, etc. ▶ **rental** n sum payable as rent

**rent**[2] n tear or fissure ▷ v past of **rend**

**renunciation** n see **renounce**

**reoffend** v commit another offence

**reorganize** v organize in a new and more efficient way ▶ **reorganization** n

**rep**[1] n short for **repertory company**

**rep**[2] n short for **representative**

**repair**[1] v restore to good condition, mend ▷ n act of repairing; repaired part; state or condition e.g. *in good repair* ▶ **reparation** n something done or given as compensation

**repair**[2] v go (to)

**repartee** n interchange of witty retorts; witty retort

**repast** n meal

**repatriate** v send (someone) back to his or her own country ▶ **repatriation** n

**repay** v **repaying, repaid** pay back, refund; do something in return for e.g. *repay hospitality* ▶ **repayable** *adj* ▶ **repayment** n

**repeal** v cancel (a law) officially ▷ n act of repealing

**repeat** v say or do again; happen again, recur ▷ n act or instance of repeating; programme broadcast again ▶ **repeatedly** *adv*

▶ **repeater** n firearm that may be discharged many times without reloading

**repel** v **-pelling, -pelled** be disgusting to; drive back, ward off; resist ▶ **repellent** adj distasteful; resisting water etc. ▷ n something that repels, esp. a chemical to repel insects

**repent** v feel regret for (a deed or omission) ▶ **repentance** n ▶ **repentant** adj

**repercussions** pl n indirect effects, often unpleasant

**repertoire** n stock of plays, songs, etc. that a player or company can give

**repertory** n, pl **-ries** repertoire ▶ **repertory company** permanent theatre company producing a succession of plays

**repetition** n act of repeating; thing repeated ▶ **repetitive, repetitious** adj full of repetition

**rephrase** v express in different words

**repine** v fret or complain

**replace** v substitute for; put back ▶ **replacement** n

**replay** n (also **action replay**) immediate reshowing on TV of an incident in sport, esp. in slow motion; second sports match, esp. one following an earlier draw ▷ v play (a match, recording, etc.) again

**replenish** v fill up again, resupply ▶ **replenishment** n

**replete** adj filled or gorged

**replica** n exact copy ▶ **replicate** v make or be a copy of

**reply** v **-plying, -plied** answer or respond ▷ n, pl **-plies** answer or response

**report** v give an account of; make a report (on); make a formal complaint about; present oneself (to); be responsible (to) ▷ n account or statement; rumour; written statement of a child's progress at school; bang ▶ **reportedly** adv according to rumour ▶ **reporter** n person who gathers news for a newspaper, TV, etc.

**repose** n peace; composure; sleep ▷ v lie or lay at rest

**repository** n, pl **-ries** place where valuables are deposited for safekeeping, store

**repossess** v (of a lender) take back property from a customer who is behind with payments ▶ **repossession** n

**reprehensible** adj open to criticism, unworthy

**represent** v act as a delegate or substitute for; stand for; symbolize; make out to be; portray, as in art ▶ **representation** n ▶ **representative** n person chosen to stand for a group; (travelling) salesperson ▷ adj typical

**repress** v keep (feelings) in check; restrict the freedom of ▶ **repression** n ▶ **repressive** adj

**reprieve** v postpone the execution of (a condemned person); give temporary relief to ▷ n (document granting) postponement or cancellation of a punishment; temporary relief

**reprimand** v blame (someone) officially for a fault ▷ n official blame

**reprint** v print further copies of (a book) ▷ n reprinted copy

**reprisal** n retaliation

**reproach** n, v blame, rebuke ▶ **reproachful** adj ▶ **reproachfully** adv

**reprobate** adj, n depraved or disreputable (person)

**reproduce** v produce a copy of; bring new

r

individuals into existence; re-create ▶ **reproducible** adj ▶ **reproduction** n process of reproducing; facsimile, as of a painting etc.; quality of sound from an audio system ▶ **reproductive** adj

**reprove** v speak severely to (someone) about a fault ▶ **reproof** n severe blaming of someone for a fault

**reptile** n cold-blooded egg-laying vertebrate with horny scales or plates, such as a snake or tortoise ▶ **reptilian** adj

**republic** n form of government in which the people or their elected representatives possess the supreme power; country in which a president is the head of state ▶ **Republican** n, adj (member or supporter) of the Republican Party, the more conservative of the two main political parties in the US ▶ **Republicanism** n

**repudiate** [rip-**pew**-dee-ate] v reject the authority or validity of; disown ▶ **repudiation** n

**repugnant** adj offensive or distasteful ▶ **repugnance** n

**repulse** v be disgusting to; drive (an army) back; rebuff or reject ▷ n driving back; rejection or rebuff ▶ **repulsion** n distaste or aversion; (Physics) force separating two objects ▶ **repulsive** adj loathsome, disgusting

**reputation** n estimation in which a person is held ▶ **reputable** adj of good reputation, respectable ▶ **repute** n reputation ▶ **reputed** adj supposed ▶ **reputedly** adv

**request** v ask ▷ n asking; thing asked for

**Requiem** [**rek**-wee-em] n Mass for the dead; music for this

**require** v want or need; demand ▶ **requirement** n essential condition; specific need or want

**USAGE NOTE**
*Require* suggests a demand imposed by some regulation. *Need* is usually something that comes from a person

**requisite** [**rek**-wizz-it] adj necessary, essential ▷ n essential thing

**requisition** v demand (supplies) ▷ n formal demand, such as for materials or supplies

**requite** v return to someone (the same treatment or feeling as received)

**reredos** [**rear**-doss] n ornamental screen behind an altar

**rescind** v annul or repeal

**rescue** v -cuing, -cued deliver from danger or trouble, save ▷ n rescuing ▶ **rescuer** n

**research** n systematic investigation to discover facts or collect information ▷ v carry out investigations ▶ **researcher** n

**resemble** v be or look like ▶ **resemblance** n

**resent** v feel bitter about ▶ **resentful** adj ▶ **resentment** n

**reservation** n doubt; exception or limitation; seat, room, etc. that has been reserved; area of land reserved for use by a particular group; (also **central reservation**) (Brit) strip of ground separating the two carriageways of a dual carriageway or motorway

**reserve** v set aside, keep for future use; obtain by arranging beforehand, book; retain ▷ n something, esp. money or troops, kept for emergencies; area of land reserved for a particular purpose; (Sport) substitute; concealment of feelings or friendliness ▶ **reserved**

*adj* not showing one's feelings, lacking friendliness; set aside for use by a particular person ▶ **reservist** *n* member of a military reserve

**reservoir** *n* natural or artificial lake storing water for community supplies; store or supply of something

**reshuffle** *n* reorganization ▷ *v* reorganize

**reside** *v* dwell permanently

**resident** *n* person who lives in a place ▷ *adj* living in a place ▶ **residence** *n* home or house ▶ **residential** *adj* (of part of a town) consisting mainly of houses; providing living accommodation

**residue** *n* what is left, remainder ▶ **residual** *adj*

**resign** *v* give up office, a job, etc.; reconcile (oneself) to ▶ **resigned** *adj* content to endure ▶ **resignation** *n* resigning; passive endurance of difficulties

**resilient** *adj* (of a person) recovering quickly from a shock etc.; able to return to normal shape after stretching etc. ▶ **resilience** *n*

**resin** [**rezz**-in] *n* sticky substance from plants, esp. pines; similar synthetic substance ▶ **resinous** *adj*

**resist** *v* withstand or oppose; refrain from despite temptation; be proof against ▶ **resistance** *n* act of resisting; capacity to withstand something; (*Electricity*) opposition offered by a circuit to the passage of a current through it ▶ **resistant** *adj* ▶ **resistible** *adj* ▶ **resistor** *n* component of an electrical circuit producing resistance

**resit** *v* take (an exam) again ▷ *n* exam that has to be taken again

**resolute** *adj* firm in purpose ▶ **resolutely** *adv*

**resolution** *n* firmness of conduct or character; thing resolved upon;

decision of a court or vote of an assembly; act of resolving; ability of a television, microscope, etc. to show fine detail

**resolve** *v* decide with an effort of will; form (a resolution) by a vote; separate the component parts of; make clear, settle ▶ **resolved** *adj* determined

**resonance** *n* echoing, esp. with a deep sound; sound produced in one object by sound waves coming from another object ▶ **resonant** *adj* ▶ **resonate** *v*

**resort** *v* have recourse (to) for help etc. ▷ *n* place for holidays; recourse

**resound** [riz-**zownd**] *v* echo or ring with sound ▶ **resounding** *adj* echoing; clear and emphatic

**resource** *n* thing resorted to for support; ingenuity; means of achieving something ▷ *pl* sources of economic wealth; stock that can be drawn on, funds ▶ **resourceful** *adj* ▶ **resourcefulness** *n*

**respect** *n* consideration; deference or esteem; point or aspect; reference or relation e.g. *with respect to* ▷ *v* treat with esteem; show consideration for ▶ **respecter** *n* ▶ **respectful** *adj* ▶ **respecting** *prep* concerning

**respectable** *adj* worthy of respect; fairly good ▶ **respectably** *adv* ▶ **respectability** *n*

**respective** *adj* relating separately to each of those in question ▶ **respectively** *adv*

**respiration** [ress-per-**ray**-shun] *n* breathing ▶ **respirator** *n* apparatus worn over the mouth and breathed through as protection against dust, poison gas, etc., or to provide artificial respiration ▶ **respiratory** *adj* ▶ **respire** *v* breathe

**r**

**respite** n pause, interval of rest; delay

**resplendent** adj brilliant or splendid; shining ▶ **resplendence** n

**respond** v answer; act in answer to any stimulus; react favourably ▶ **respondent** n (Law) defendant ▶ **response** n answer; reaction to a stimulus ▶ **responsive** adj readily reacting to some influence ▶ **responsiveness** n

**responsible** adj having control and authority; reporting or accountable (to); sensible and dependable; involving responsibility ▶ **responsibly** adv ▶ **responsibility** n, pl **-ties** state of being responsible; person or thing for which one is responsible

**rest¹** n freedom from exertion etc.; repose; pause, esp. in music; object used for support ▷ v take a rest; give a rest (to); be supported; place on a support ▶ **restful** adj ▶ **restless** adj unable to relax or concentrate

**rest²** n what is left; others ▷ v remain, continue to be

**restaurant** n commercial establishment serving meals ▶ **restaurateur** [rest-er-a-**tur**] n person who owns or runs a restaurant

**restitution** n giving back; reparation or compensation

**restive** adj restless or impatient

**restore** v return (a building, painting, etc.) to its original condition; cause to recover health or spirits; give back, return; re-establish ▶ **restoration** n ▶ **restorative** adj restoring ▷ n food or medicine to strengthen etc. ▶ **restorer** n

**restrain** v hold (someone) back from action; control or restrict

▶ **restrained** adj not displaying emotion ▶ **restraint** n control, esp. self-control; restraining ▶ **restraining order** (Aust, NZ, Canadian & US) temporary court order imposing restrictions on a company or a person

**restrict** v confine to certain limits ▶ **restriction** n ▶ **restrictive** adj

**restructure** v organize in a different way

**result** n outcome or consequence; score; number obtained from a calculation; exam mark or grade ▷ v (foll by from) be the outcome or consequence (of); (foll by in) end (in) ▶ **resultant** adj

**resume** v begin again; occupy or take again ▶ **resumption** n

**résumé** [**rezz**-yew-may] n summary; (US & Canadian) outline of someone's educational and professional history, prepared for job applications.

**resurgence** n rising again to vigour ▶ **resurgent** adj

**resurrect** v restore to life; use once more (something discarded etc.), revive ▶ **resurrection** n rising again (esp. from the dead); revival

**resuscitate** [ris-**suss**-it-tate] v restore to consciousness ▶ **resuscitation** n

**SPELLING TIP**

There is a silent c in **resuscitate**, but only one: it comes after the second s

**retail** n selling of goods individually or in small amounts to the public ▷ adv by retail ▷ v sell or be sold retail; recount in detail

**retailer** n person or company that sells goods to the public

**retain** v keep in one's possession; engage the services of ▶ **retainer** n fee to retain someone's services; old-established servant of a family

**retaliate** v repay an injury or wrong in kind ▸ **retaliation** n ▸ **retaliatory** adj

**retard** v delay or slow (progress or development) ▸ **retarded** adj (offens) underdeveloped, esp. mentally ▸ **retardation** n

**retch** v try to vomit

**retention** n retaining; ability to remember; abnormal holding of something, esp. fluid, in the body ▸ **retentive** adj capable of retaining or remembering

**rethink** v consider again, esp. with a view to changing one's tactics

**reticent** adj uncommunicative, reserved ▸ **reticence** n

**retina** n, pl **-nas** or **-nae** light-sensitive membrane at the back of the eye

**retinue** n band of attendants

**retire** v (cause to) give up office or work, esp. through age; go away or withdraw; go to bed ▸ **retired** adj having retired from work etc. ▸ **retirement** n ▸ **retiring** adj shy

**retort**[1] v reply quickly, wittily, or angrily ▷ n quick, witty, or angry reply

**retort**[2] n glass container with a bent neck used for distilling

**retouch** v restore or improve by new touches, esp. of paint

**retrace** v go back over (a route etc.) again

**retract** v withdraw (a statement etc.); draw in or back ▸ **retractable**, **retractile** adj able to be retracted ▸ **retraction** n

**retread** v, n same as **remould**

**retreat** v move back from a position, withdraw ▷ n act of or military signal for retiring or withdrawal; place to which anyone retires, refuge

**retrench** v reduce expenditure, cut back ▸ **retrenchment** n

**retrial** n second trial of a case or defendant in a court of law

**retribution** n punishment or vengeance for evil deeds ▸ **retributive** adj

**retrieve** v fetch back again; restore to a better state; recover (information) from a computer ▸ **retrievable** adj ▸ **retrieval** n ▸ **retriever** n dog trained to retrieve shot game

**retro** adj associated with or revived from the past e.g. retro fashion

**retroactive** adj effective from a date in the past

**retrograde** adj tending towards an earlier worse condition

**retrogressive** adj going back to an earlier worse condition ▸ **retrogression** n

**retrorocket** n small rocket engine used to slow a spacecraft

**retrospect** n **in retrospect** when looking back on the past ▸ **retrospective** adj looking back in time; applying from a date in the past ▷ n exhibition of an artist's life's work

**retroussé** [rit-**troo**-say] adj (of a nose) turned upwards

**retsina** n Greek wine flavoured with resin

**return** v go or come back; give, put, or send back; reply; elect ▷ n returning; (thing) being returned; profit; official report, as of taxable income; return ticket ▸ **returnable** adj ▸ **returning officer** person in charge of an election ▸ **return ticket** ticket allowing a passenger to travel to a place and back

**reunion** n meeting of people who have been apart ▸ **reunite** v bring or come together again after a separation

**reuse** v use again ▸ **reusable** adj

**rev** (*informal*) *n* revolution (of an engine) ▷ *v* **revving, revved** (foll by *up*) increase the speed of revolution of (an engine)

**Rev., Revd.** Reverend

**revalue** *v* adjust the exchange value of (a currency) upwards ▶ **revaluation** *n*

**revamp** *v* renovate or restore

**reveal** *v* make known; expose or show ▶ **revelation** *n*

**reveille** [riv-**val**-ee] *n* morning bugle call to waken soldiers

**revel** *v* -elling, -elled take pleasure (in); make merry ▶ **revels** *pl n* merrymaking ▶ **reveller** *n* ▶ **revelry** *n* festivity

**revenge** *n* retaliation for wrong done ▷ *v* make retaliation for; avenge (oneself or another) ▶ **revengeful** *adj*

**revenue** *n* income, esp. of a state

**reverberate** *v* echo or resound ▶ **reverberation** *n*

**revere** *v* be in awe of and respect greatly ▶ **reverence** *n* awe mingled with respect and esteem ▶ **reverent** *adj* showing reverence ▶ **reverently** *adv* ▶ **reverential** *adj* marked by reverence

**Reverend** *adj* title of respect for a clergyman

**reverie** *n* absent-minded daydream

**revers** [riv-**veer**] *n* turned back part of a garment, such as the lapel

**reverse** *v* turn upside down or the other way round; change completely; move (a vehicle) backwards ▷ *n* opposite; back side; change for the worse; reverse gear ▷ *adj* opposite or contrary ▶ **reversal** *n* ▶ **reversible** *adj* ▶ **reverse gear** mechanism enabling a vehicle to move backwards

**revert** *v* return to a former state; come back to a subject; (of property) return to its former owner ▶ **reversion** *n*

**review** *n* critical assessment of a book, concert, etc.; publication with critical articles; general survey; formal inspection ▷ *v* hold or write a review of; examine, reconsider, or look back on; inspect formally ▶ **reviewer** *n* writer of reviews

**revile** *v* be abusively scornful of

**revise** *v* change or alter; restudy (work) in preparation for an examination ▶ **revision** *n*

**revive** *v* bring or come back to life, vigour, use, etc. ▶ **revival** *n* reviving or renewal; movement seeking to restore religious faith ▶ **revivalism** *n* ▶ **revivalist** *n*

**revoke** *v* cancel (a will, agreement, etc.) ▶ **revocation** *n*

**revolt** *n* uprising against authority ▷ *v* rise in rebellion; cause to feel disgust ▶ **revolting** *adj* disgusting, horrible

**revolution** *n* overthrow of a government by the governed; great change; spinning round; complete rotation ▶ **revolutionary** *adj* advocating or engaged in revolution; radically new or different ▷ *n, pl* **-aries** person advocating or engaged in revolution ▶ **revolutionize** *v* change considerably

**revolve** *v* turn round, rotate ▶ **revolve around** be centred on

**revolver** *n* repeating pistol

**revue** *n* theatrical entertainment with topical sketches and songs

**revulsion** *n* strong disgust

**reward** *n* something given in return for a service; sum of money offered for finding a criminal or missing property ▷ *v* pay or give something to (someone) for a service, information, etc. ▶ **rewarding**

*adj* giving personal satisfaction, worthwhile

**rewind** *v* run (a tape or film) back to an earlier point in order to replay

**rewire** *v* provide (a house, engine, etc.) with new wiring

**rewrite** *v* write again in a different way ▷ *n* something rewritten

**rhapsody** *n, pl* **-dies** freely structured emotional piece of music; expression of ecstatic enthusiasm ▶ **rhapsodic** *adj* ▶ **rhapsodize** *v* speak or write with extravagant enthusiasm

**rhea** [**ree**-a] *n* S American three-toed ostrich

**rhenium** *n* (*Chem*) silvery-white metallic element with a high melting point

**rheostat** *n* instrument for varying the resistance of an electrical circuit

**rhesus** [**ree**-suss] *n* small long-tailed monkey of S Asia ▶ **rhesus factor, Rh factor** antigen commonly found in human blood

**rhetoric** *n* art of effective speaking or writing; artificial or exaggerated language ▶ **rhetorical** *adj* (of a question) not requiring an answer ▶ **rhetorically** *adv*

**rheumatism** *n* painful inflammation of joints or muscles ▶ **rheumatic** *n, adj* (person) affected by rheumatism ▶ **rheumatoid** *adj* of or like rheumatism

**Rh factor** *n* see **rhesus**

**rhinestone** *n* imitation diamond

**rhino** *n* short for **rhinoceros**

**rhinoceros** *n, pl* **-oses** *or* **-os** large thick-skinned animal with one or two horns on its nose

**SPELLING TIP**
The pronunciation of **rhinoceros** probably misleads some people into making the mistake of adding a *u* before the final *s* (*rhinocerous*)

**rhizome** *n* thick underground stem producing new plants

**rhodium** *n* (*Chem*) hard metallic element

**rhododendron** *n* evergreen flowering shrub

**rhombus** *n, pl* **-buses** *or* **-bi** parallelogram with sides of equal length but no right angles, diamond-shaped figure ▶ **rhomboid** *n* parallelogram with adjacent sides of unequal length

**rhubarb** *n* garden plant of which the fleshy stalks are cooked as fruit

**rhyme** *n* sameness of the final sounds at the ends of lines of verse, or in words; word identical in sound to another in its final sounds; verse marked by rhyme ▷ *v* make a rhyme

**rhythm** *n* any regular movement or beat; arrangement of the durations of and stress on the notes of a piece of music, usu. grouped into a regular pattern; (in poetry) arrangement of words to form a regular pattern of stresses ▶ **rhythmic, rhythmical** *adj* ▶ **rhythmically** *adv* ▶ **rhythm and blues** popular music, orig. Black American, influenced by the blues

**SPELLING TIP**
The second letter of **rhythm** is a silent *h*, which people often forget in writing

**rib**[1] *n* one of the curved bones forming the framework of the upper part of the body; cut of meat including the rib(s); curved supporting part, as in the hull of a boat; raised series of rows in knitting ▷ *v* **ribbing, ribbed** provide or mark with ribs; knit to form a rib pattern ▶ **ribbed** *adj* ▶ **ribbing** *n* ▶ **ribcage** *n* bony structure of ribs enclosing the lungs

**rib²** v **ribbing, ribbed** (*informal*) tease or ridicule ▶ **ribbing** n

**ribald** adj humorously or mockingly rude or obscene ▶ **ribaldry** n

**ribbon** n narrow band of fabric used for trimming, tying, etc.; any long strip, for example of inked tape in a typewriter

**riboflavin** [rye-boe-**flay**-vin] n form of vitamin B

**rice** n cereal plant grown on wet ground in warm countries; its seeds as food

**rich** adj owning a lot of money or property, wealthy; abounding; fertile; (of food) containing much fat or sugar; mellow; amusing ▶ **riches** pl n wealth ▶ **richly** adv elaborately; fully ▶ **richness** n

**Richter scale** n scale for measuring the intensity of earthquakes

**rick¹** n stack of hay etc.

**rick²** v, n sprain or wrench

**rickets** n disease of children marked by softening of the bones, bow legs, etc., caused by vitamin D deficiency

**rickety** adj shaky or unstable

**rickshaw** n light two-wheeled man-drawn Asian vehicle

**ricochet** [rik-osh-ay] v (of a bullet) rebound from a solid surface ▷ n such a rebound

**rid** v **ridding, rid** clear or relieve (of) **get rid of** free oneself of (something undesirable) **good riddance** relief at getting rid of something or someone

**ridden** v past participle of **ride** ▷ adj afflicted or affected by the thing specified e.g. *disease-ridden*

**riddle¹** n question made puzzling to test one's ingenuity; puzzling person or thing

**riddle²** v pierce with many holes ▷ n coarse sieve for gravel etc. **riddled with** full of

**ride** v **riding, rode, ridden** sit on and control or propel (a horse, bicycle, etc.); go on horseback or in a vehicle; travel over; be carried on or across; lie at anchor ▷ n journey on a horse etc., or in a vehicle; type of movement experienced in a vehicle ▶ **ride up** v (of a garment) move up from the proper position

**rider** n person who rides; supplementary clause added to a document

**ridge** n long narrow hill; long narrow raised part on a surface; line where two sloping surfaces meet; (*Meteorol*) elongated area of high pressure ▶ **ridged** adj

**ridiculous** adj deserving to be laughed at, absurd ▶ **ridicule** n treatment of a person or thing as ridiculous ▷ v laugh at, make fun of

**Riding** n former administrative district of Yorkshire

**riesling** n type of white wine

**rife** adj widespread or common **rife with** full of

**riff** n (*Jazz, rock*) short repeated melodic figure

**riffle** v flick through (pages etc.) quickly

**riffraff** n rabble, disreputable people

**rifle¹** n firearm with a long barrel

**rifle²** v search and rob; steal

**rift** n break in friendly relations; crack, split, or cleft ▶ **rift valley** long narrow valley resulting from subsidence between faults

**rig** v **rigging, rigged** arrange in a dishonest way; equip, esp. a ship ▷ n apparatus for drilling for oil and gas; way a ship's masts and sails are arranged; (*informal*) outfit of clothes ▶ **rigging** n ship's spars and ropes ▸ **rig up** v set up or build temporarily

**right** adj just; true or correct; proper; in a satisfactory condition; of the side that faces east when the front is turned to the north; of the outer side of a fabric ▷ adv properly; straight or directly; on or to the right side ▷ n claim, title, etc. allowed or due; what is just or due; (**R-**) conservative political party or group ▷ v bring or come back to a normal or correct state; bring or come back to a vertical position **in the right** morally or legally correct ▸ **right away** immediately ▸ **rightly** adv ▸ **rightful** adj ▸ **rightfully** adv ▸ **rightist** n, adj (person) on the political right ▸ **right angle** angle of 90° ▸ **right-handed** adj using or for the right hand ▸ **right-hand man** person's most valuable assistant ▸ **right of way** right of one vehicle to go before another; legal right to pass over someone's land ▸ **right-wing** adj conservative or reactionary; belonging to the more conservative part of a political party

**righteous** [rye-chuss] adj upright, godly, or virtuous; morally justified ▸ **righteousness** n

**rigid** adj inflexible or strict; unyielding or stiff ▸ **rigidly** adv ▸ **rigidity** n

**rigmarole** n long complicated procedure

**rigor mortis** n stiffening of the body after death

**rigour** n harshness, severity, or strictness; hardship ▸ **rigorous** adj harsh, severe, or stern

**rile** v anger or annoy

**rill** n small stream

**rim** n edge or border; outer ring of a wheel ▸ **rimmed** adj

**rime** n (lit) hoarfrost

**rimu** n (NZ) New Zealand tree whose wood is used for building and furniture

**rind** n tough outer coating of fruits, cheese, or bacon

**ring**[1] v **ringing, rang, rung** give out a clear resonant sound, as a bell; cause (a bell) to sound; telephone; resound ▷ n ringing; telephone call ▸ **ring off** v end a telephone call ▸ **ringtone** n tune played by a mobile phone when it receives a call ▸ **ring up** v telephone; record on a cash register

| USAGE NOTE |
| --- |
| The simple past is *rang*: *He rang the bell*. Avoid the use of the past participle *rung* for the simple past |

**ring**[2] n circle of gold etc., esp. for a finger; any circular band, coil, or rim; circle of people; enclosed area, esp. a circle for a circus or a roped-in square for boxing; group operating (illegal) control of a market ▷ v put a ring round; mark (a bird) with a ring; kill (a tree) by cutting the bark round the trunk ▸ **ringer** n (Brit, Aust & NZ slang) person or thing apparently identical to another (also **dead ringer**) ▸ **ringlet** n curly lock of hair ▸ **ringleader** n instigator of a mutiny, riot, etc. ▸ **ring road** (Brit, Aust & S Afr) main road that bypasses a town (centre) ▸ **ringside** n row of seats nearest a boxing or circus ring ▸ **ringtail** n (Aust) possum with a curling tail used to grip branches while climbing ▸ **ringworm** n fungal skin disease in circular patches

**rink** n sheet of ice for skating or curling; floor for roller-skating

**rinkhals** n S African cobra that can spit venom

r

**rinse** v remove soap from (washed clothes, hair, etc.) by applying clean water; wash lightly ▷ n rinsing; liquid to tint hair

**riot** n disorderly unruly disturbance; (Brit, Aust & NZ) loud revelry; profusion; (slang) very amusing person or thing ▷ v take part in a riot **read the riot act** reprimand severely **run riot** behave without restraint; grow profusely ▶ **riotous** adj unrestrained; unruly or rebellious

**RIP** rest in peace

**rip** v **ripping, ripped** tear violently; tear away; (informal) rush ▷ n split or tear **let rip** speak without restraint ▶ **ripcord** n cord pulled to open a parachute ▶ **rip off** v (slang) cheat by overcharging ▶ **rip-off** n (slang) cheat or swindle ▶ **rip-roaring** adj (informal) boisterous and exciting

**riparian** [rip-**pair**-ee-an] adj of or on the banks of a river

**ripe** adj ready to be reaped, eaten, etc.; matured; ready or suitable ▶ **ripen** v grow ripe; mature

**riposte** [rip-**posst**] n verbal retort; counterattack, esp. in fencing ▷ v make a riposte

**ripple** n slight wave or ruffling of a surface; sound like ripples of water ▷ v flow or form into little waves (on); (of sounds) rise and fall gently

**rise** v **rising, rose, risen** get up from a lying, sitting, or kneeling position; move upwards; (of the sun or moon) appear above the horizon; reach a higher level; (of an amount or price) increase; rebel; (of a court) adjourn ▷ n rising; upward slope; increase, esp. of wages **give rise to** cause ▶ **riser** n person who rises, esp. from bed; vertical part of a step ▶ **rising** n revolt ▷ adj increasing in rank or maturity

**risible** [**riz**-zib-bl] adj causing laughter, ridiculous

**risk** n chance of disaster or loss; person or thing considered as a potential hazard ▷ v act in spite of the possibility of (injury or loss); expose to danger or loss ▶ **risky** adj full of risk, dangerous

**risotto** n, pl -**tos** dish of rice cooked in stock with vegetables, meat, etc.

**risqué** [**risk**-ay] adj bordering on indecency

**rissole** n cake of minced meat, coated with breadcrumbs and fried

**rite** n formal custom, esp. religious

**ritual** n prescribed order of rites; regular repeated action or behaviour ▷ adj concerning rites ▶ **ritually** adv ▶ **ritualistic** adj like a ritual

**ritzy** adj **ritzier, ritziest** (slang) luxurious or elegant

**rival** n person or thing that competes with or equals another for favour, success, etc. ▷ adj in the position of a rival ▷ v -**valling, -valled** (try to) equal ▶ **rivalry** n keen competition

**riven** adj split apart

**river** n large natural stream of water; plentiful flow

**rivet** [**riv**-vit] n bolt for fastening metal plates, the end being put through holes and then beaten flat ▷ v **riveting, riveted** fasten with rivets; cause to be fixed, as in fascination ▶ **riveting** adj very interesting and exciting

**rivulet** n small stream

**RME** (in Scotland) religious and moral education

**RN** (in Britain) Royal Navy

**RNA** ribonucleic acid: substance in living cells essential for the synthesis of protein

**RNZ** Radio New Zealand

**RNZAF** Royal New Zealand Air Force

**RNZN** Royal New Zealand Navy

**roach** n Eurasian freshwater fish

**road** n way prepared for passengers, vehicles, etc.; route in a town or city with houses along it; way or course e.g. *the road to fame* **on the road** travelling ▸ **roadblock** n barricade across a road to stop traffic for inspection etc. ▸ **road hog** (*informal*) selfish aggressive driver ▸ **roadhouse** n (*Brit, Aust & S Afr*) pub or restaurant on a country road ▸ **road map** map for drivers; plan or guide for future actions ▸ **roadie** n (*Brit, Aust & NZ informal*) person who transports and sets up equipment for a band ▸ **roadside** n, adj ▸ **road test** test of a vehicle etc. in actual use ▸ **roadway** n the part of a road used by vehicles ▸ **roadworks** pl n repairs to a road, esp. blocking part of the road ▸ **roadworthy** adj (of a vehicle) mechanically sound

**roam** v wander about

**roan** adj (of a horse) having a brown or black coat sprinkled with white hairs ▷ n roan horse

**roar** v make or utter a loud deep hoarse sound like that of a lion; shout (something) as in anger; laugh loudly ▷ n such a sound **a roaring trade** (*informal*) brisk and profitable business **roaring drunk** noisily drunk

**roast** v cook by dry heat, as in an oven; make or be very hot ▷ n roasted joint of meat ▷ adj roasted ▸ **roasting** (*informal*) adj extremely hot ▷ n severe criticism or scolding

**rob** v **robbing, robbed** steal from; deprive ▸ **robber** n ▸ **robbery** n

**robe** n long loose outer garment ▷ v put a robe on

**robin** n small brown bird with a red breast

**robot** n automated machine, esp. one performing functions in a human manner; person of machine-like efficiency; (*S Afr*) set of coloured lights at a junction to control the traffic flow ▸ **robotic** adj ▸ **robotics** n science of designing and using robots

**robust** adj very strong and healthy ▸ **robustly** adv ▸ **robustness** n

**roc** n monstrous bird of Arabian mythology

**rock¹** n hard mineral substance that makes up part of the earth's crust, stone; large rugged mass of stone; (*Brit*) hard sweet in sticks **on the rocks** (of a marriage) about to end; (of an alcoholic drink) served with ice ▸ **rocky** adj having many rocks ▸ **rockery** n mound of stones in a garden for rock plants ▸ **rock bottom** lowest possible level ▸ **rock cake** small fruit cake with a rough surface

**rock²** v (cause to) sway to and fro; (*slang*) be very good ▷ n (also **rock music**) style of pop music with a heavy beat ▸ **rocky** adj shaky or unstable ▸ **rock and roll, rock'n'roll** style of pop music blending rhythm and blues and country music ▸ **rocking chair** chair allowing the sitter to rock backwards and forwards

**rocker** n rocking chair; curved piece of wood etc. on which something may rock **off one's rocker** (*informal*) insane

**rocket** n self-propelling device powered by the burning of explosive contents (used as a firework, weapon, etc.); vehicle propelled by a rocket engine, as a weapon or carrying a spacecraft ▷ v **-eting, -eted** move fast, esp. upwards, like a rocket

r

**rock melon** n (US, Aust & NZ) kind of melon with sweet orange flesh

**rococo** [rok-**koe**-koe] adj (of furniture, architecture, etc.) having much elaborate decoration in an early 18th-century style

**rod** n slender straight bar, stick; cane

**rode** v past tense of **ride**

**rodent** n animal with teeth specialized for gnawing, such as a rat, mouse, or squirrel

**rodeo** n, pl -**deos** display of skill by cowboys, such as bareback riding

**roe¹** n mass of eggs in a fish, sometimes eaten as food

**roe²** n small species of deer

**roentgen** [**ront**-gan] n unit measuring a radiation dose

**rogue** n dishonest or unprincipled person; mischief-loving person ▷ adj (of a wild beast) having a savage temper and living apart from the herd ▶ **roguish** adj

**roister** v make merry noisily or boisterously

**role, rôle** n task or function; actor's part

**roll** v move by turning over and over; move or sweep along; wind round; undulate; smooth out with a roller; (of a ship or aircraft) turn from side to side about a line from nose to tail ▷ n act of rolling over or from side to side; piece of paper etc. rolled up; small round individually baked piece of bread; list or register; continuous sound, as of drums, thunder, etc.; swaying unsteady movement or gait ▶ **roll call** calling out of a list of names, as in a school or the army, to check who is present ▶ **rolled gold** metal coated with a thin layer of gold ▶ **rolling pin** cylindrical roller for flattening pastry ▶ **rolling stock** locomotives and coaches of a railway ▶ **rolling stone** restless wandering person ▶ **roll-on/roll-off** adj (Brit, Aust & NZ) denoting a ship allowing vehicles to be driven straight on and off ▶ **roll-top** adj (of a desk) having a flexible lid sliding in grooves ▶ **roll up** v (informal) appear or arrive ▶ **roll-up** n (Brit informal) cigarette made by the smoker from loose tobacco and cigarette paper

**roller** n rotating cylinder used for smoothing or supporting a thing to be moved, spreading paint, etc.; long wave of the sea ▶ **Rollerblade**® n roller skate with the wheels set in one straight line ▶ **roller coaster** (at a funfair) narrow railway with steep slopes ▶ **roller skate** skate with wheels

**rollicking** adj boisterously carefree

**roly-poly** adj round or plump

**ROM** (Computing) read only memory

**Roman** adj of Rome or the Roman Catholic Church ▶ **Roman Catholic** (member) of that section of the Christian Church that acknowledges the supremacy of the Pope ▶ **Roman numerals** the letters I, V, X, L, C, D, M, used to represent numbers ▶ **roman type** plain upright letters in printing

**Romance** adj (of a language) developed from Latin, such as French or Spanish

**romance** n love affair; mysterious or exciting quality; novel or film dealing with love, esp. sentimentally; story with scenes remote from ordinary life

**romantic** adj of or dealing with love; idealistic but impractical; (of literature, music, etc.) displaying passion and imagination rather than order and form ▷ *n* romantic person or artist ▸ **romantically** *adv* ▸ **romanticism** *n* ▸ **romanticize** *v* describe or regard in an idealized and unrealistic way

**Romany** *n, pl* **-nies** ▷ *adj* Gypsy

**romp** *v* play wildly and joyfully ▷ *n* boisterous activity **romp home** win easily ▸ **rompers** *pl n* child's overalls

**rondavel** *n* (*S Afr*) circular building, often thatched

**rondo** *n, pl* **-dos** piece of music with a leading theme continually returned to

**roo** *n* (*Aust informal*) kangaroo

**rood** *n* (*Christianity*) the Cross; crucifix ▸ **rood screen** (in a church) screen separating the nave from the choir

**roof** *n, pl* **roofs** outside upper covering of a building, car, etc. ▷ *v* put a roof on

**rooibos** [roy-boss] *n* (*S Afr*) tea prepared from the dried leaves of an African plant

**rook**¹ *n* Eurasian bird of the crow family ▸ **rookery** *n, pl* **-eries** colony of rooks, penguins, or seals

**rook**² *n* chess piece shaped like a castle

**rookie** *n* (*informal*) new recruit

**room** *n* enclosed area in a building; unoccupied space; scope or opportunity ▷ *pl* lodgings ▸ **roomy** *adj* spacious

**roost** *n* perch for fowls ▷ *v* perch

**rooster** *n* domestic cock

**root**¹ *n* part of a plant that grows down into the earth obtaining nourishment; plant with an edible root, such as a carrot; part of a tooth, hair, etc. below the skin; source or origin; form of a word from which other words and forms are derived; (*Maths*) factor of a quantity which, when multiplied

by itself the number of times indicated, gives the quantity ▷ *pl* person's sense of belonging ▷ *v* establish a root and start to grow ▸ **rootless** *adj* having no sense of belonging ▸ **root for** *v* (*informal*) cheer on ▸ **root out** *v* get rid of completely

**root**² *v* dig or burrow

**rope** *n* thick cord **know the ropes** be thoroughly familiar with an activity ▸ **rope in** *v* persuade to join in

**ropey, ropy** *adj* **ropier, ropiest** (*Brit informal*) inferior or inadequate; not well

**rorqual** *n* toothless whale with a dorsal fin

**rort** (*Aust informal*) *n* dishonest scheme ▷ *v* take unfair advantage of something

**rosary** *n, pl* **-saries** series of prayers; string of beads for counting these prayers

**rose**¹ *n* shrub or climbing plant with prickly stems and fragrant flowers; flower of this plant; perforated flat nozzle for a hose; pink colour ▷ *adj* pink ▸ **roseate** [roe-zee-ate] *adj* rose-coloured ▸ **rose window** circular window with spokes branching from the centre ▸ **rosewood** *n* fragrant wood used to make furniture

**rose**² *v* past tense of **rise**

**rosé** [roe-zay] *n* pink wine

**rosehip** *n* berry-like fruit of a rose plant

**rosella** *n* type of Australian parrot

**rosemary** *n* fragrant flowering shrub; its leaves as a herb

**rosette** *n* rose-shaped ornament, esp. a circular bunch of ribbons

**rosin** [rozz-in] *n* resin used for treating the bows of violins etc.

**roster** *n* list of people and their turns of duty

r

**rostrum** *n, pl* **-trums** *or* **-tra**
platform or stage

**rosy** *adj* **rosier, rosiest** pink-
coloured; hopeful or promising

**rot** *v* **rotting, rotted** decompose
or decay; slowly deteriorate
physically or mentally ▷ *n* decay;
(*informal*) nonsense

**rota** *n* list of people who take it in
turn to do a particular task

**rotary** *adj* revolving; operated by
rotation

**rotate** *v* (cause to) move round
a centre or on a pivot; (cause to)
follow a set sequence ▶ **rotation** *n*

**rote** *n* mechanical repetition **by
rote** by memory

**rotisserie** *n* rotating spit for
cooking meat

**rotor** *n* revolving portion of a
dynamo, motor, or turbine;
rotating device with long blades
that provides thrust to lift a
helicopter

**rotten** *adj* decaying; (*informal*) very
bad; corrupt

**rotter** *n* (*chiefly Brit slang*)
despicable person

**Rottweiler** [rot-vile-er] *n* large
sturdy dog with a smooth black
and tan coat and usu. a docked tail

**rotund** [roe-**tund**] *adj* round and
plump; sonorous ▶ **rotundity** *n*

**rotunda** *n* circular building or
room, esp. with a dome

**rouble** [roo-bl] *n* monetary unit of
Russia, Belarus, and Tajikistan

**roué** [roo-ay] *n* man given to
immoral living

**rouge** *n* red cosmetic used to colour
the cheeks

**rough** *adj* uneven or irregular;
not careful or gentle; difficult
or unpleasant; approximate;
violent, stormy, or boisterous;
in preliminary form; lacking
refinement ▷ *v* make rough ▷ *n*

rough state or area **rough it**
live without the usual comforts
etc. ▶ **roughen** *v* ▶ **roughly** *adv*
▶ **roughness** *n* ▶ **roughage** *n*
indigestible constituents of food
which aid digestion ▶ **rough-and-
ready** *adj* hastily prepared but
adequate ▶ **rough-and-tumble**
*n* playful fight ▶ **rough-hewn** *adj*
roughly shaped ▶ **roughhouse** *n*
(*chiefly US slang*) fight ▶ **rough out**
*v* prepare (a sketch or report) in
preliminary form

**roughcast** *n* mixture of plaster and
small stones for outside walls ▷ *v*
coat with this

**roughshod** *adv* **ride roughshod
over** act with total disregard for

**roulette** *n* gambling game played
with a revolving wheel and a ball

**round** *adj* spherical, cylindrical,
circular, or curved ▷ *adv*, *prep*
indicating an encircling
movement, presence on all sides,
etc. e.g. *tied round the waist; books
scattered round the room* ▷ *v* move
round ▷ *n* customary course,
as of a milkman; game (of golf);
stage in a competition; one of
several periods in a boxing match
etc.; number of drinks bought
at one time; bullet or shell for a
gun ▶ **roundly** *adv* thoroughly
▶ **rounders** *n* bat-and-ball team
game ▶ **round robin** petition
signed with names in a circle to
conceal the order; tournament in
which each player plays against
every other player ▶ **round-the-
clock** *adj* throughout the day and
night ▶ **round trip** journey out and
back again ▶ **round up** *v* gather
(people or animals) together
▶ **roundup** *n*

**roundabout** *n* road junction
at which traffic passes round a
central island; revolving circular

platform on which people ride for amusement ▷ *adj* not straightforward

**roundel** *n* small disc

**roundelay** *n* simple song with a refrain

**Roundhead** *n* (*Hist*) supporter of Parliament against Charles I in the English Civil War

**rouse¹** [rhymes with **cows**] *v* wake up; provoke or excite ▶ **rousing** *adj* lively, vigorous

**rouse²** [rhymes with **mouse**] *v* (foll by *on*) (*Aust*) scold or rebuke

**rouseabout** *n* (*Aust & NZ*) labourer in a shearing shed

**roustabout** *n* labourer on an oil rig

**rout** *n* overwhelming defeat; disorderly retreat ▷ *v* defeat and put to flight

**route** *n* roads taken to reach a destination; chosen way ▶ **route march** long military training march

**routine** *n* usual or regular method of procedure; set sequence ▷ *adj* ordinary or regular

**roux** [**roo**] *n* fat and flour cooked together as a basis for sauces

**rove** *v* wander

**rover** *n* wanderer, traveller

**row¹** [rhymes with **go**] *n* straight line of people or things **in a row** in succession

**row²** [rhymes with **go**] *v* propel (a boat) by oars ▷ *n* spell of rowing ▶ **rowing boat** boat propelled by oars

**row³** [rhymes with **now**] (*informal*) *n* dispute; disturbance; reprimand ▷ *v* quarrel noisily

**rowan** *n* tree producing bright red berries, mountain ash

**rowdy** *adj* **-dier, -diest** disorderly, noisy, and rough ▷ *n, pl* **-dies** person like this

**rowel** [rhymes with **towel**] *n* small spiked wheel on a spur

**rowlock** [**rol**-luk] *n* device on a boat that holds an oar in place

**royal** *adj* of, befitting, or supported by a king or queen; splendid ▷ *n* (*informal*) member of a royal family ▶ **royally** *adv* ▶ **royalist** *n* supporter of monarchy ▶ **royalty** *n* royal people; rank or power of a monarch; (*pl* **-ties**) payment to an author, musician, inventor, etc. ▶ **royal blue** deep blue

**RPI** (in Britain) retail price index: measure of change in the average level of prices

**rpm** revolutions per minute

**RSA** Republic of South Africa; (in New Zealand) Returned Services Association

**RSI** repetitive strain injury

**RSPCA** (in Britain) Royal Society for the Prevention of Cruelty to Animals

**RSS** Really Simple Syndication: a way of allowing web users to receive updates on their browsers from selected websites

**RSVP** please reply

**rub** *v* **rubbing, rubbed** apply pressure and friction to (something) with a circular or backwards-and-forwards movement; clean, polish, or dry by rubbing; chafe or fray through rubbing ▷ *n* act of rubbing **rub it in** emphasize an unpleasant fact ▶ **rub out** *v* remove with a rubber

**rubato** *adv, n* (*Music*) (with) expressive flexibility of tempo

**rubber¹** *n* strong waterproof elastic material, orig. made from the dried sap of a tropical tree, now usu. synthetic; piece of rubber used for erasing writing ▷ *adj* made of or producing rubber ▶ **rubbery** *adj* ▶ **rubberneck** *v* stare with unthinking curiosity ▶ **rubber stamp** device for imprinting the

r

date, a name, etc.; automatic
authorization

**rubber²** n match consisting of three
games of bridge, whist, etc.; series
of matches

**rubbish** n waste matter;
anything worthless; nonsense
▸ **rubbishy** adj

**rubble** n fragments of broken
stone, brick, etc.

**rubella** n same as **German
measles**

**rubicund** adj ruddy

**rubidium** n (Chem) soft highly
reactive radioactive element

**rubric** n heading or explanation
inserted in a text

**ruby** n, pl **-bies** red precious
gemstone ▷ adj deep red

**ruck¹** n rough crowd of common
people; (Rugby) loose scrummage

**ruck²** n, v wrinkle or crease

**rucksack** n (Brit, Aust & S Afr) large
pack carried on the back

**ructions** pl n (informal) noisy uproar

**rudder** n vertical hinged piece at
the stern of a boat or at the rear of
an aircraft, for steering

**ruddy** adj **-dier, -diest** of a fresh
healthy red colour

**rude** adj impolite or insulting;
coarse, vulgar, or obscene;
unexpected and unpleasant;
roughly made; robust ▸ **rudely** adv
▸ **rudeness** n

**rudiments** pl n simplest and
most basic stages of a subject
▸ **rudimentary** adj basic,
elementary

**rue¹** v **ruing, rued** feel regret for
▸ **rueful** adj regretful or sorry
▸ **ruefully** adv

**rue²** n plant with evergreen bitter
leaves

**ruff** n starched and frilled collar;
natural collar of feathers, fur, etc.
on certain birds and animals

**ruffian** n violent lawless person

**ruffle** v disturb the calm of; annoy,
irritate ▷ n frill or pleat

**rug** n small carpet; thick woollen
blanket ▸ **rug up** (Aust & NZ) put on
warm clothing

**rugby** n form of football played with
an oval ball which may be handled
by the players

**rugged** [rug-gid] adj rocky or steep;
uneven and jagged; strong-
featured; tough and sturdy

**rugger** n (chiefly Brit informal) rugby

**ruin** v destroy or spoil completely;
impoverish ▷ n destruction or
decay; loss of wealth, position,
etc.; broken-down unused building
▸ **ruination** n act of ruining; state
of being ruined; cause of ruin
▸ **ruinous** adj causing ruin; more
expensive than can be afforded
▸ **ruinously** adv

**rule** n statement of what is
allowed, for example in a game
or procedure; what is usual;
government, authority, or control;
measuring device with a straight
edge ▷ v govern; be pre-eminent;
give a formal decision; mark with
straight line(s); restrain **as a rule**
usually ▸ **ruler** n person who
governs; measuring device with
a straight edge ▸ **ruling** n formal
decision ▸ **rule of thumb** practical
but imprecise approach ▸ **rule out**
v dismiss from consideration

**rum¹** n alcoholic drink distilled from
sugar cane

**rum²** adj (Brit informal) odd, strange

**rumba** n lively ballroom dance of
Cuban origin

**rumble** v make a low continuous
noise; (Brit informal) discover the
(disreputable) truth about ▷ n deep
resonant sound

**rumbustious** adj boisterous
or unruly

r

**ruminate** *v* chew the cud; ponder or meditate ▶ **ruminant** *adj*, *n* cud-chewing (animal, such as a cow, sheep, or deer) ▶ **rumination** *n* quiet meditation and reflection ▶ **ruminative** *adj*

**rummage** *v* search untidily and at length ▷ *n* untidy search through a collection of things

**rummy** *n* card game in which players try to collect sets or sequences

**rumour** *n* unproved statement; gossip or common talk ▶ **rumoured** *adj* suggested by rumour

**rump** *n* buttocks; rear of an animal

**rumple** *v* make untidy, crumpled, or dishevelled

**rumpus** *n*, *pl* **-puses** noisy commotion

**run** *v* **running, ran, run** move with a more rapid gait than walking; compete in a race, election, etc.; travel according to schedule; function; manage; continue in a particular direction or for a specified period; expose oneself to (a risk); flow; spread; (of stitches) unravel ▷ *n* act or spell of running; ride in a car; continuous period; series of unravelled stitches, ladder ▶ **run away** *v* make one's escape, flee ▶ **run down** *v* be rude about; reduce in number or size; stop working ▶ **rundown** *n* ▶ **run-down** *adj* exhausted ▶ **run into** *v* meet ▶ **run-of-the-mill** *adj* ordinary ▶ **run out** *v* be completely used up ▶ **run over** *v* knock down (a person) with a moving vehicle ▶ **run up** *v* incur (a debt)

**rune** *n* any character of the earliest Germanic alphabet ▶ **runic** *adj*

**rung¹** *n* crossbar on a ladder

**rung²** *v* past participle of **ring¹**

**runnel** *n* small brook

**runner** *n* competitor in a race; messenger; part underneath an ice skate etc., on which it slides; slender horizontal stem of a plant, such as a strawberry, running along the ground and forming new roots at intervals; long strip of carpet or decorative cloth ▶ **runner-up** *n* person who comes second in a competition

**running** *adj* continuous; consecutive; (of water) flowing ▷ *n* act of moving or flowing quickly; management of a business etc. **in the running, out of the running** having or not having a good chance in a competition

**runny** *adj* **-nier, -niest** tending to flow; exuding moisture

**runt** *n* smallest animal in a litter; (*derogatory*) undersized person

**runway** *n* hard level roadway where aircraft take off and land

**rupee** *n* monetary unit of India and Pakistan

**rupture** *n* breaking, breach; hernia ▷ *v* break, burst, or sever

**rural** *adj* in or of the countryside

**ruse** [rooz] *n* stratagem or trick

**rush¹** *v* move or do very quickly; force (someone) to act hastily; make a sudden attack upon (a person or place) ▷ *n* sudden quick or violent movement ▷ *pl* first unedited prints of a scene for a film ▷ *adj* done with speed, hasty ▶ **rush hour** period at the beginning and end of the working day, when many people are travelling to or from work

**rush²** *n* marsh plant with a slender pithy stem ▶ **rushy** *adj* full of rushes

**rusk** *n* hard brown crisp biscuit, used esp. for feeding babies

**russet** *adj* reddish-brown ▷ *n* apple with rough reddish-brown skin

**r**

**Russian** adj of Russia ▷ n person from Russia; official language of Russia and, formerly, of the Soviet Union ▶ **Russian roulette** act of bravado in which a person spins the cylinder of a revolver loaded with only one cartridge and presses the trigger with the barrel against his or her own head

**rust** n reddish-brown coating formed on iron etc. that has been exposed to moisture; disease of plants which produces rust-coloured spots ▷ adj reddish-brown ▷ v become coated with rust ▶ **rusty** adj coated with rust; of a rust colour; out of practice

**rustic** adj of or resembling country people; rural; crude, awkward, or uncouth; (of furniture) made of untrimmed branches ▷ n person from the country

**rustle¹** v, n (make) a low whispering sound

**rustle²** v (US) steal (cattle) ▶ **rustler** n (US) cattle thief ▶ **rustle up** v prepare at short notice

**rut¹** n furrow made by wheels; dull settled habits or way of living

**rut²** n recurrent period of sexual excitability in male deer ▷ v **rutting, rutted** be in a period of sexual excitability

**ruthenium** n (Chem) rare hard brittle white element

**ruthless** adj pitiless, merciless ▶ **ruthlessly** adv ▶ **ruthlessness** n

**rye** n kind of grain used for fodder and bread; (US) whiskey made from rye

**rye-grass** n any of several grasses cultivated for fodder

# Ss

**S** South(ern)

**s** second(s)

**SA** Salvation Army; South Africa; South Australia

**SAA** South African Airways

**Sabbath** n day of worship and rest: Saturday for Jews, Sunday for Christians ▶ **sabbatical** adj, n (denoting) leave for study

**SABC** South African Broadcasting Corporation

**sable** n dark fur from a small weasel-like Arctic animal ▷ adj black

**sabot** [sab-oh] n wooden shoe traditionally worn by peasants in France

**sabotage** n intentional damage done to machinery, systems, etc. ▷ v damage intentionally ▶ **saboteur** n person who commits sabotage

**sabre** n curved cavalry sword

**sac** n pouchlike structure in an animal or plant

**saccharin** n artificial sweetener ▶ **saccharine** adj excessively sweet

**sacerdotal** adj of priests

**sachet** n small envelope or bag containing a single portion

**sack¹** n large bag made of coarse material; (informal) dismissal; (slang) bed ▷ v (informal) dismiss ▶ **sackcloth** n coarse fabric used for sacks, formerly worn as a penance

**sack²** n plundering of a captured town ▷ v plunder (a captured town)

**sacrament** n ceremony of the Christian Church, esp. Communion ▶ **sacramental** adj

**sacred** adj holy; connected with religion; set apart, reserved

**sacrifice** n giving something up; thing given up; making of an offering to a god; thing offered ▷ v offer as a sacrifice; give (something) up ▶ **sacrificial** adj

**sacrilege** n misuse or desecration of something sacred ▶ **sacrilegious** adj

> **SPELLING TIP**
> One could be forgiven for thinking that **sacrilegious** had something to do with the word 'religious', which might explain why the most common misspelling of the word in the Collins Corpus is *sacreligious*

**sacristan** n person in charge of the contents of a church ▶ **sacristy** n, pl **-ties** room in a church where sacred objects are kept

**sacrosanct** adj regarded as sacred, inviolable

**sacrum** [say-krum] n, pl **-cra** wedge-shaped bone at the base of the spine

**sad** adj **sadder, saddest** sorrowful, unhappy; deplorably bad ▶ **sadden** v make sad ▶ **saddo** n, pl **-dos** or **-does** (Brit informal) socially inadequate or pathetic person ▶ **sadly** adv ▶ **sadness** n

**saddle** n rider's seat on a horse or bicycle; joint of meat ▷ v put a saddle on (a horse); burden (with a responsibility) ▶ **saddler** n maker or seller of saddles

**sadism** [say-dizz-um] n gaining of (sexual) pleasure from inflicting pain ▶ **sadist** n ▶ **sadistic** adj ▶ **sadistically** adv

**sadomasochism** n combination of sadism and masochism ▶ **sadomasochist** n

**s.a.e.** (Brit, Aust & NZ) stamped addressed envelope

**safari** n, pl **-ris** expedition to hunt or observe wild animals, esp. in Africa ▶ **safari park** park where lions, elephants, etc. are kept uncaged so that people can see them from cars

**safe** adj secure, protected; uninjured, out of danger; not involving risk ▷ n strong lockable container ▶ **safely** adv ▶ **safe-conduct** n permit allowing travel through a dangerous area ▶ **safekeeping** n protection

**safeguard** v protect ▷ n protection

**safety** n, pl **-ties** state of being safe ▶ **safety net** net to catch performers on a trapeze or high wire if they fall ▶ **safety pin** pin with a spring fastening and a guard over the point when closed ▶ **safety valve** valve that allows steam etc. to escape if pressure becomes excessive

**saffron** n orange-coloured spice obtained from a crocus, used for flavouring and colouring ▷ adj orange

**sag** v **sagging, sagged** sink in the middle; tire; (of clothes) hang loosely ▷ n droop

**saga** [sah-ga] n legend of Norse heroes; any long story or series of events

**sagacious** adj wise ▶ **sagacity** n

**sage**[1] n very wise man ▷ adj (lit) wise ▶ **sagely** adv

**sage**[2] n aromatic herb with grey-green leaves

**sago** n starchy cereal from the powdered pith of the sago palm tree

**said** v past of **say**

**sail** n sheet of fabric stretched to catch the wind for propelling a sailing boat; arm of a windmill ▷ v travel by water; begin a voyage; move smoothly ▶ **sailor** n member

**S**

of a ship's crew ▶ **sailboard** n board with a mast and single sail, used for windsurfing

**saint** n (Christianity) person venerated after death as specially holy; exceptionally good person ▶ **saintly** adj ▶ **saintliness** n

**sake**¹ n benefit; purpose **for the sake of** for the purpose of; to please or benefit (someone)

**sake**², **saki** [**sah**-kee] n Japanese alcoholic drink made from fermented rice

**salaam** [sal-**ahm**] n low bow of greeting among Muslims

**salacious** adj excessively concerned with sex

**salad** n dish of raw vegetables, eaten as a meal or part of a meal

**salamander** n amphibian which looks like a lizard

**salami** n highly spiced sausage

**salary** n, pl **-ries** fixed regular payment, usu. monthly, to an employee ▶ **salaried** adj

**sale** n exchange of goods for money; selling of goods at unusually low prices; auction ▶ **saleable** adj fit or likely to be sold ▶ **salesman, saleswoman, salesperson** n person who sells goods ▶ **salesmanship** n skill in selling

**salient** [**say**-lee-ent] adj prominent, noticeable ▷ n (Mil) projecting part of a front line

**saline** [**say**-line] adj containing salt ▶ **salinity** n

**saliva** n liquid that forms in the mouth, spittle ▶ **salivary** adj ▶ **salivate** v produce saliva

**sallee** n (Aust) (also **snow gum**) SE Australian eucalyptus with a pale grey barkacacia tree

**sallow** adj of an unhealthy pale or yellowish colour

**sally** n, pl **-lies** witty remark; sudden brief attack by troops ▷ v **-lying, -lied** (foll by forth) rush out; go out

**salmon** n large fish with orange-pink flesh valued as food ▷ adj orange-pink

**salmonella** n, pl **-lae** bacterium causing food poisoning

**salon** n commercial premises of a hairdresser, beautician, etc.; elegant reception room for guests

**saloon** n two-door or four-door car with body closed off from rear luggage area; large public room, as on a ship; (US) bar serving alcoholic drinks ▶ **saloon bar** more expensive bar in a pub

**salt** n white crystalline substance used to season food; chemical compound of acid and metal ▷ v season or preserve with salt **old salt** experienced sailor **with a pinch of salt** allowing for exaggeration **worth one's salt** efficient ▶ **salty** adj ▶ **saltbush** n shrub that grows in alkaline desert regions ▶ **salt cellar** small container for salt at table

**saltire** n (Heraldry) diagonal cross on a shield

**saltpetre** n compound used in gunpowder and as a preservative

**salubrious** adj favourable to health

**Saluki** n tall hound with a silky coat

**salutary** adj producing a beneficial result

**salute** n motion of the arm as a formal military sign of respect; firing of guns as a military greeting of honour ▷ v greet with a salute; make a salute; acknowledge with praise ▶ **salutation** n greeting by words or actions

**salvage** n saving of a ship or other property from destruction; property so saved ▷ v save from destruction or waste

**salvation** n fact or state of being saved from harm or the consequences of sin

**salve** n healing or soothing ointment ▷ v soothe or appease

**salver** n (silver) tray on which something is presented

**salvia** n plant with blue or red flowers

**salvo** n, pl **-vos** or **-voes** simultaneous discharge of guns etc.; burst of applause or questions

**sal volatile** [sal vol-**at**-ill-ee] n preparation of ammonia, used to revive a person who feels faint

**SAM** surface-to-air missile

**Samaritan** n person who helps people in distress

**samba** n lively Brazilian dance

**same** adj identical, not different, unchanged; just mentioned ▷ **sameness** n

**samovar** n Russian tea urn

**Samoyed** n dog with a thick white coat and tightly curled tail

**sampan** n small boat with oars used in China

**samphire** n plant found on rocks by the seashore

**sample** n part taken as representative of a whole; (Music) short extract from an existing recording mixed into a backing track to produce a new recording ▷ v take and test a sample of; (Music) take a short extract from (one recording) and mix it into a backing track; record (a sound) and feed it into a computerized synthesizer so that it can be reproduced at any pitch ▷ **sampler** n piece of embroidery showing the embroiderer's skill; (Music) piece of electronic equipment used for sampling ▷ **sampling** n

**samurai** n, pl **-rai** member of an ancient Japanese warrior caste

**sanatorium** n, pl **-riums** or **-ria** institution for invalids or convalescents; room for sick pupils at a boarding school

**sanctify** v **-fying, -fied** make holy

**sanctimonious** adj pretending to be religious and virtuous

**sanction** n permission, authorization; coercive measure or penalty ▷ v allow, authorize

**sanctity** n sacredness, inviolability

**sanctuary** n, pl **-aries** holy place; part of a church nearest the altar; place of safety for a fugitive; place where animals or birds can live undisturbed

**sanctum** n, pl **-tums** or **-ta** sacred place; person's private room

**sand** n substance consisting of small grains of rock, esp. on a beach or in a desert ▷ pl stretches of sand forming a beach or desert ▷ v smooth with sandpaper ▷ **sandy** adj covered with sand; (of hair) reddish-fair ▷ **sandbag** n bag filled with sand, used as protection against gunfire or flood water ▷ **sandblast** v, n (clean with) a jet of sand blown from a nozzle under pressure ▷ **sandpaper** n paper coated with sand for smoothing a surface ▷ **sandpiper** n shore bird with a long bill and slender legs ▷ **sandstone** n rock composed of sand ▷ **sandstorm** n desert wind that whips up clouds of sand

**sandal** n light shoe consisting of a sole attached by straps

**sandalwood** n sweet-scented wood

**sander** n power tool for smoothing surfaces

**S & M** sadomasochism

**sandwich** n two slices of bread with a layer of food between ▷ v insert between two other things ▷ **sandwich board** pair of boards hung over a person's shoulders to display advertisements in front and behind

**sane** adj of sound mind; sensible, rational ▶ **sanity** n

**sang** v past tense of **sing**

**sang-froid** [sahng-**frwah**] n composure and calmness in a difficult situation

**sangoma** n (S Afr) witch doctor or herbalist

**sanguinary** adj accompanied by bloodshed; bloodthirsty

**sanguine** adj cheerful, optimistic

**sanitary** adj promoting health by getting rid of dirt and germs ▶ **sanitation** n sanitary measures, esp. drainage or sewerage

**sank** v past tense of **sink**

**Sanskrit** n ancient language of India

**sap¹** n moisture that circulates in plants; (informal) gullible person

**sap²** v **sapping, sapped** undermine; weaken ▶ **sapper** n soldier in an engineering unit

**SAP** South African Police

**sapient** [**say**-pee-ent] adj (lit) wise, shrewd

**sapling** n young tree

**sapphire** n blue precious stone ▷ adj deep blue

**sarabande, saraband** n slow stately Spanish dance

**Saracen** n (Hist) Arab or Muslim who opposed the Crusades

**sarcasm** n (use of) bitter or wounding ironic language ▶ **sarcastic** adj ▶ **sarcastically** adv

**sarcophagus** n, pl **-gi** or **-guses** stone coffin

**sardine** n small fish of the herring family, usu. preserved tightly packed in tins

**sardonic** adj mocking or scornful ▶ **sardonically** adv

**sargassum, sargasso** n type of floating seaweed

**sari, saree** n long piece of cloth draped around the body and over one shoulder, worn by Hindu women

**sarmie** n (S Afr slang) sandwich

**sarong** n long piece of cloth tucked around the waist or under the armpits, worn esp. in Malaysia

**sarsaparilla** n soft drink, orig. made from the root of a tropical American plant

**sartorial** adj of men's clothes or tailoring

**SARU** South African Rugby Union

**SAS** (in Britain) Special Air Service

**sash¹** n decorative strip of cloth worn round the waist or over one shoulder

**sash²** n wooden frame containing the panes of a window ▶ **sash window** window consisting of two sashes that can be opened by sliding one over the other

**sassafras** n American tree with aromatic bark used medicinally

**Sassenach** n (Scot) English person

**sat** v past of **sit**

**Satan** n the Devil **the Great Satan** radical Islamic term for the United States ▶ **satanic** adj of Satan; supremely evil ▶ **Satanism** n worship of Satan

**satay, saté** [sat-ay] n Indonesian and Malaysian dish consisting of pieces of chicken, pork, etc., grilled on skewers and served with peanut sauce

**satchel** n bag, usu. with a shoulder strap, for carrying books

**sate** v satisfy (a desire or appetite) fully

**satellite** n man-made device orbiting in space; heavenly body that orbits another; country that is dependent on a more powerful one ▷ adj of or used in the transmission of television signals from a satellite to the home

**satiate** [say-she-ate] v provide with more than enough, so as to disgust ▸ **satiety** [sat-**tie**-a-tee] n feeling of having had too much

**satin** n silky fabric with a glossy surface on one side ▸ **satiny** adj of or like satin ▸ **satinwood** n tropical tree yielding hard wood

**satire** n use of ridicule to expose vice or folly; poem or other work that does this ▸ **satirical** adj ▸ **satirist** n ▸ **satirize** v ridicule by means of satire

**satisfy** v **-fying, -fied** please, content; provide amply for (a need or desire); convince, persuade ▸ **satisfaction** n ▸ **satisfactory** adj

**satnav** n (Motoring informal) satellite navigation

**satsuma** n kind of small orange

**saturate** v soak thoroughly; cause to absorb the maximum amount of something ▸ **saturation** n

**Saturday** n seventh day of the week

**Saturn** n Roman god of agriculture; sixth planet from the sun ▸ **saturnine** adj gloomy in temperament or appearance ▸ **saturnalia** n wild party or orgy

**satyr** n woodland god, part man, part goat; lustful man

**sauce** n liquid added to food to enhance flavour; (chiefly Brit informal) impudence ▸ **saucy** adj impudent; pert, jaunty ▸ **saucily** adv ▸ **saucepan** n cooking pot with a long handle

**saucer** n small round dish put under a cup

**sauerkraut** n shredded cabbage fermented in brine

**sauna** n Finnish-style steam bath

**saunter** v walk in a leisurely manner, stroll ▸ n leisurely walk

**sausage** n minced meat in an edible tube-shaped skin ▸ **sausage roll** skinless sausage covered in pastry

**sauté** [so-tay] v **-téing** or **-téeing, -téed** fry quickly in a little fat

**savage** adj wild, untamed; cruel and violent; uncivilized, primitive ▸ n uncivilized person ▸ v attack ferociously ▸ **savagely** adv ▸ **savagery** n

**savannah, savanna** n extensive open grassy plain in Africa

**savant** n learned person

**save** v rescue or preserve from harm, protect; keep for the future; set aside (money); (Sport) prevent the scoring of (a goal) ▸ n (Sport) act of preventing a goal ▸ **saver** n ▸ **saving** n economy ▸ pl money put by for future use

**saveloy** n (Brit, Aust & NZ) spicy smoked sausage

**saviour** n person who rescues another; (**S-**) Christ

**savoir-faire** [sav-wahr-**fair**] n (French) ability to do and say the right thing in any situation

**savory** n aromatic herb used in cooking

**savour** v enjoy, relish; (foll by of) have a flavour or suggestion of ▸ n characteristic taste or odour; slight but distinctive quality ▸ **savoury** adj salty or spicy ▸ n, pl **-vouries** savoury dish served before or after a meal

**savoy** n variety of cabbage

**savvy** (slang) v **-vying, -vied** understand ▸ n understanding, intelligence

**saw**[1] n cutting tool with a toothed metal blade ▸ v **sawing, sawed, sawed** or **sawn** cut with a saw; move (something) back and forth ▸ **sawyer** n person who saws timber for a living ▸ **sawdust** n fine wood fragments made in sawing ▸ **sawfish** n fish with a long

**S**

toothed snout ▶ **sawmill** n mill where timber is sawn into planks

**saw²** v past tense of **see¹**

**saw³** n wise saying, proverb

**sax** n (informal) short for **saxophone**

**saxifrage** n alpine rock plant with small flowers

**Saxon** n member of the W Germanic people who settled widely in Europe in the early Middle Ages ▷ adj of the Saxons

**saxophone** n brass wind instrument with keys and a curved body ▶ **saxophonist** n

**say** v **saying, said** speak or utter; express (an idea) in words; give as one's opinion; suppose as an example or possibility ▷ n right or chance to speak; share in a decision ▶ **saying** n maxim, proverb

**scab** n crust formed over a wound; (offens) blackleg ▶ **scabby** adj covered with scabs; (informal) despicable

**scabbard** n sheath for a sword or dagger

**scabies** [**skay**-beez] n itchy skin disease

**scabrous** [**skay**-bruss] adj rough and scaly; indecent

**scaffold** n temporary platform for workmen; gallows ▶ **scaffolding** n (materials for building) scaffolds

**scalar** n, adj (variable quantity) having magnitude but no direction

**scald** v burn with hot liquid or steam; sterilize with boiling water; heat (liquid) almost to boiling point ▷ n injury by scalding

**scale¹** n one of the thin overlapping plates covering fishes and reptiles; thin flake; coating which forms in kettles etc. due to hard water; tartar formed on the teeth ▷ v remove scales from; come off in scales ▶ **scaly** adj

**scale²** n (often pl) weighing instrument

**scale³** n graduated table or sequence of marks at regular intervals, used as a reference in making measurements; ratio of size between a thing and a representation of it; relative degree or extent; fixed series of notes in music ▷ v climb ▶ **scale up** v increase proportionately in size ▶ **scale down** v decrease proportionately in size

**scalene** adj (of a triangle) with three unequal sides

**scallop** n edible shellfish with two fan-shaped shells; one of a series of small curves along an edge ▶ **scalloped** adj decorated with small curves along the edge

**scallywag** n (informal) scamp, rascal

**scalp** n skin and hair on top of the head ▷ v cut off the scalp of

**scalpel** n small surgical knife

**scam** n (informal) dishonest scheme

**scamp** n mischievous child

**scamper** v run about hurriedly or in play ▷ n scampering

**scampi** pl n large prawns

**scan** v **scanning, scanned** scrutinize carefully; glance over quickly; examine or search (an area) by passing a radar or sonar beam over it; (of verse) conform to metrical rules ▷ n scanning ▶ **scanner** n electronic device used for scanning ▶ **scansion** n metrical scanning of verse

**scandal** n disgraceful action or event; malicious gossip ▶ **scandalize** v shock by scandal ▶ **scandalous** adj

**Scandinavian** n, adj (inhabitant or language) of Scandinavia (Norway, Denmark, Sweden, Finland, and Iceland)

**scandium** n (Chem) rare silvery-white metallic element

**scant** adj barely sufficient, meagre

**scanty** adj **scantier, scantiest** barely sufficient or not sufficient ▸ **scantily** adv

**scapegoat** n person made to bear the blame for others

**scapula** n, pl **-lae** or **-las** shoulder blade ▸ **scapular** adj

**scar** n mark left by a healed wound; permanent emotional damage left by an unpleasant experience ▷ v **scarring, scarred** mark or become marked with a scar

**scarab** n sacred beetle of ancient Egypt

**scarce** adj insufficient to meet demand; not common, rarely found **make oneself scarce** (informal) go away ▸ **scarcely** adv hardly at all; definitely or probably not ▸ **scarcity** n

**scare** v frighten or be frightened ▷ n fright, sudden panic ▸ **scary** adj (informal) frightening ▸ **scarecrow** n figure dressed in old clothes, set up to scare birds away from crops; raggedly dressed person ▸ **scaremonger** n person who spreads alarming rumours

**scarf**¹ n, pl **scarves** or **scarfs** piece of material worn round the neck, head, or shoulders

**scarf**² n joint between two pieces of timber made by notching the ends and fastening them together ▷ v join in this way

**scarify** v **-fying, -fied** scratch or cut slightly all over; break up and loosen (topsoil); criticize mercilessly ▸ **scarification** n

**scarlatina** n scarlet fever

**scarlet** adj, n brilliant red ▸ **scarlet fever** infectious fever with a scarlet rash

**scarp** n steep slope

**scarper** v (Brit slang) run away

**scat**¹ v **scatting, scatted** (informal) go away

**scat**² n jazz singing using improvised vocal sounds instead of words

**scathing** adj harshly critical

**scatological** adj preoccupied with obscenity, esp. with references to excrement ▸ **scatology** n

**scatter** v throw about in various directions; disperse ▸ **scatterbrain** n empty-headed person

**scatty** adj **-tier, -tiest** (informal) empty-headed

**scavenge** v search for (anything usable) among discarded material

**scavenger** n person who scavenges; animal that feeds on decaying matter

**scenario** n, pl **-rios** summary of the plot of a play or film; imagined sequence of future events

**scene** n place of action of a real or imaginary event; subdivision of a play or film in which the action is continuous; view of a place; display of emotion; (informal) specific activity or interest e.g. the fashion scene **behind the scenes** backstage; in secret ▸ **scenery** n natural features of a landscape; painted backcloths or screens used on stage to represent the scene of action ▸ **scenic** adj picturesque

**scent** n pleasant smell; smell left in passing, by which an animal can be traced; series of clues; perfume ▷ v detect by smell; suspect; fill with fragrance

**sceptic** [**skep**-tik] n person who habitually doubts generally accepted beliefs ▸ **sceptical** adj ▸ **sceptically** adv ▸ **scepticism** n

**sceptre** n ornamental rod symbolizing royal power

S

**schedule** n plan of procedure for a project; list; timetable ▷ v plan to occur at a certain time

**schema** n, pl **-mata** overall plan or diagram ▶ **schematic** adj presented as a plan or diagram

**scheme** n systematic plan; secret plot ▷ v plan in an underhand manner ▶ **scheming** adj, n

**scherzo** [skairt-so] n, pl **-zos** or **-zi** brisk lively piece of music

**schism** [skizz-um] n (group resulting from) division in an organization ▶ **schismatic** adj, n

**schist** [shist] n crystalline rock which splits into layers

**schizoid** adj abnormally introverted; (offens) contradictory ▷ n (offens) schizoid person

**schizophrenia** n mental disorder involving deterioration of or confusion about the personality; (informal) contradictory behaviour or attitudes ▶ **schizophrenic** adj, n

**schmaltz** n excessive sentimentality ▶ **schmaltzy** adj

**schnapps** n strong alcoholic spirit

**schnitzel** n thin slice of meat, esp. veal

**scholar** n learned person; student receiving a scholarship; pupil ▶ **scholarly** adj learned ▶ **scholarship** n learning; financial aid given to a student because of academic merit ▶ **scholastic** adj of schools or scholars

**school¹** n place where children are taught or instruction is given in a subject; group of artists, thinkers, etc. with shared principles or methods ▷ v educate or train ▶ **schoolie** (Aust) schoolteacher or high-school student ▶ **schoolies week** (Aust informal) week of post-exam celebrations for students who have just completed their final year of high school

**school²** n shoal of fish, whales, etc.

**schooner** n sailing ship rigged fore-and-aft; large glass

**sciatica** n severe pain in the large nerve in the back of the leg ▶ **sciatic** adj of the hip; of or afflicted with sciatica

**science** n systematic study and knowledge of natural or physical phenomena ▶ **scientific** adj of science; systematic ▶ **scientifically** adv ▶ **scientist** n person who studies or practises a science ▶ **science fiction** stories making imaginative use of scientific knowledge ▶ **science park** area where scientific research and commercial development are carried on in cooperation

**sci-fi** n short for **science fiction**

**scimitar** n curved oriental sword

**scintillate** v give off sparks

**scintillating** adj very lively and amusing

**scion** [sy-on] n descendant or heir; shoot of a plant for grafting

**scissors** pl n cutting instrument with two crossed pivoted blades

**sclerosis** n, pl **-ses** abnormal hardening of body tissues

**scoff¹** v express derision

**scoff²** v (informal) eat rapidly

**scold** v find fault with, reprimand ▷ n person who scolds ▶ **scolding** n

**sconce** n bracket on a wall for holding candles or lights

**scone** n small plain cake baked in an oven or on a griddle

**scoop** n shovel-like tool for ladling or hollowing out; news story reported in one newspaper before all its rivals ▷ v take up or hollow out with or as if with a scoop; beat (rival newspapers) in reporting a news item

**scoot** v (slang) leave or move quickly

**scooter** *n* child's vehicle propelled by pushing on the ground with one foot; light motorcycle

**scope** *n* opportunity for using abilities; range of activity

**scorch** *v* burn on the surface; parch or shrivel from heat ▷ *n* slight burn ▶ **scorcher** *n* (*informal*) very hot day

**score** *n* points gained in a game or competition; twenty; written version of a piece of music showing parts for each musician; mark or cut; grievance e.g. *settle old scores* ▷ *pl* lots ▷ *v* gain (points) in a game; keep a record of points; mark or cut; (foll by *out*) cross out; arrange music (for); achieve a success

**scorn** *n* open contempt ▷ *v* despise; reject with contempt ▶ **scornful** *adj* ▶ **scornfully** *adv*

**scorpion** *n* small lobster-shaped animal with a sting at the end of a jointed tail

**Scot** *n* person from Scotland ▶ **Scottish** *adj* of Scotland, its people, or their languages ▶ **Scotch** *n* whisky distilled in Scotland ▶ **Scotch broth** thick soup of beef or lamb and vegetables ▶ **Scots** *adj* Scottish ▶ **Scotsman, Scotswoman** *n*

> **USAGE NOTE**
> *Scotch* is used only in certain fixed expressions like *Scotch broth*. The use of *Scotch* for *Scots* or *Scottish* is otherwise felt to be incorrect, esp. when applied to people

**scotch** *v* put an end to

**scot-free** *adj* without harm or punishment

**scoundrel** *n* (*old-fashioned*) cheat or deceiver

**scour¹** *v* clean or polish by rubbing with something rough; clear or flush out ▶ **scourer** *n* small rough nylon pad used for cleaning pots and pans

**scour²** *v* search thoroughly and energetically

**scourge** *n* person or thing causing severe suffering; whip ▷ *v* cause severe suffering to; whip

**scout** *n* person sent out to reconnoitre; (**S-**) member of the Scout Association, an organization for young people which aims to develop character and promotes outdoor activities ▷ *v* act as a scout; reconnoitre

**scowl** *v*, *n* (have) an angry or sullen expression

**scrabble** *v* scrape at with the hands, feet, or claws

**scrag** *n* thin end of a neck of mutton ▶ **scraggy** *adj* thin, bony

**scram** *v* **scramming, scrammed** (*informal*) go away quickly

**scramble** *v* climb or crawl hastily or awkwardly; struggle with others (for); mix up; cook (eggs beaten up with milk); (of an aircraft or aircrew) take off hurriedly in an emergency; make (transmitted speech) unintelligible by the use of an electronic device ▷ *n* scrambling; rough climb; disorderly struggle; motorcycle race over rough ground ▶ **scrambler** *n* electronic device that makes transmitted speech unintelligible

**scrap¹** *n* small piece; waste metal collected for reprocessing ▷ *pl* leftover food ▷ *v* **scrapping, scrapped** discard as useless ▶ **scrappy** *adj* fragmentary, disjointed ▶ **scrapbook** *n* book with blank pages in which newspaper cuttings or pictures are stuck

**scrap²** *n*, *v* **scrapping, scrapped** (*informal*) fight or quarrel

**scrape** *v* rub with something rough or sharp; clean or smooth thus;

rub with a harsh noise; economize ▷ *n* act or sound of scraping; mark or wound caused by scraping; (*informal*) awkward situation ▶ **scraper** *n* ▶ **scrape through** *v* succeed in or obtain with difficulty

**scratch** *v* mark or cut with claws, nails, or anything rough or sharp; scrape (skin) with nails or claws to relieve itching; withdraw from a race or competition ▷ *n* wound, mark, or sound made by scratching ▷ *adj* put together at short notice **from scratch** from the very beginning **up to scratch** up to standard ▶ **scratchy** *adj* ▶ **scratchcard** *n* ticket that reveals whether or not the holder has won a prize when the surface is removed by scratching

**scrawl** *v* write carelessly or hastily ▷ *n* scribbled writing

**scrawny** *adj* **scrawnier, scrawniest** thin and bony

**scream** *v* utter a piercing cry, esp. of fear or pain; utter with a scream ▷ *n* shrill piercing cry; (*informal*) very funny person or thing

**scree** *n* slope of loose shifting stones

**screech** *v, n* (utter) a shrill cry

**screed** *n* long tedious piece of writing

**screen** *n* surface of a television set, VDU, etc., on which an image is formed; white surface on which films or slides are projected; movable structure used to shelter, divide, or conceal something ▷ *v* shelter or conceal with or as if with a screen; examine (a person or group) to determine suitability for a task or to detect the presence of disease or weapons; show (a film) **the screen** cinema generally ▶ **screen saver** (*Computing*) software that changing images on a monitor when the computer is operative but idle ▶ **screenshot** *n* (*Computing*) copied image of a computer screen at a particular moment

**screw** *n* metal pin with a spiral ridge along its length, twisted into materials to fasten them together; (*slang*) prison guard ▷ *v* turn (a screw); twist; fasten with screw(s); (*informal*) extort ▶ **screwy** *adj* (*informal*) crazy or eccentric ▶ **screwdriver** *n* tool for turning screws ▶ **screw up** *v* (*informal*) bungle; distort

**scribble** *v* write hastily or illegibly; make meaningless or illegible marks ▷ *n* something scribbled

**scribe** *n* person who copied manuscripts before the invention of printing; (*Bible*) scholar of the Jewish Law

**scrimmage** *n* rough or disorderly struggle

**scrimp** *v* be very economical

**scrip** *n* certificate representing a claim to stocks or shares

**script** *n* text of a film, play, or TV programme; particular system of writing e.g. *Arabic script*; handwriting

**scripture** *n* sacred writings of a religion ▶ **scriptural** *adj*

**scrofula** *n* tuberculosis of the lymphatic glands ▶ **scrofulous** *adj*

**scroggin** *n* (NZ) mixture of nuts and dried fruits

**scroll** *n* roll of parchment or paper; ornamental carving shaped like a scroll ▷ *v* move (text) up or down on a VDU screen

**scrotum** *n, pl* **-ta** *or* **-tums** pouch of skin containing the testicles

**scrounge** *v* (*informal*) get by cadging or begging ▶ **scrounger** *n*

**scrub¹** *v* **scrubbing, scrubbed** clean by rubbing, often with a hard brush and water; (*informal*) delete or cancel ▷ *n* act or instance of scrubbing ▷ *pl* (*Med*) hygienic clothing worn by operating theatre staff

**scrub²** *n* stunted trees; area of land covered with scrub ▶ **scrubby** *adj* covered with scrub; stunted; (*informal*) shabby

**scruff¹** *n* nape (of the neck)

**scruff²** *n* (*informal*) untidy person ▶ **scruffy** *adj* unkempt or shabby

**scrum, scrummage** *n* (*Rugby*) restarting of play in which opposing packs of forwards push against each other to gain possession of the ball; disorderly struggle

**scrumptious** *adj* (*informal*) delicious

**scrunch** *v* crumple or crunch or be crumpled or crunched ▷ *n* act or sound of scrunching

**scruple** *n* doubt produced by one's conscience or morals ▷ *v* have doubts on moral grounds ▶ **scrupulous** *adj* very conscientious; very careful or precise ▶ **scrupulously** *adv*

**scrutiny** *n, pl* **-nies** close examination ▶ **scrutinize** *v* examine closely

**scuba diving** *n* sport of swimming under water using cylinders containing compressed air attached to breathing apparatus

**scud** *v* **scudding, scudded** move along swiftly

**scuff** *v* drag (the feet) while walking; scrape (one's shoes) by doing so ▷ *n* mark caused by scuffing

**scuffle** *v* fight in a disorderly manner ▷ *n* disorderly struggle; scuffling sound

**scull** *n* small oar ▷ *v* row (a boat) using sculls

**scullery** *n, pl* **-leries** small room where washing-up and other kitchen work is done

**sculpture** *n* art of making figures or designs in wood, stone, etc.; product of this art ▷ *v* (also **sculpt**) represent in sculpture ▶ **sculptor, sculptress** *n* ▶ **sculptural** *adj*

**scum** *n* impure or waste matter on the surface of a liquid; worthless people ▶ **scummy** *adj*

**scungy** *adj* **-ier, -iest** (*Aust & NZ informal*) sordid or dirty

**scupper** *v* (*informal*) defeat or ruin

**scurf** *n* flaky skin on the scalp

**scurrilous** *adj* untrue and defamatory

**scurry** *v* **-rying, -ried** move hastily ▷ *n* act or sound of scurrying

**scurvy** *n* disease caused by lack of vitamin C

**scut** *n* short tail of the hare, rabbit, or deer

**scuttle¹** *n* fireside container for coal

**scuttle²** *v* run with short quick steps ▷ *n* hurried run

**scuttle³** *v* make a hole in (a ship) to sink it

**scythe** *n* long-handled tool with a curved blade for cutting grass ▷ *v* cut with a scythe

**SE** southeast(ern)

**sea** *n* mass of salt water covering three quarters of the earth's surface; particular area of this; vast expanse **at sea** in a ship on the ocean; confused or bewildered ▶ **sea anemone** sea animal with suckers like petals ▶ **seaboard** *n* coast ▶ **sea dog** experienced sailor ▶ **seafaring** *adj* working or travelling by sea ▶ **seafood** *n* edible saltwater fish or shellfish ▶ **seagull** *n* gull ▶ **sea horse** small sea fish with a plated body and horselike head ▶ **sea level** average level of the sea's surface in relation

**S**

to the land ▶ **sea lion** kind of large seal ▶ **seaman** n sailor ▶ **seaplane** n aircraft designed to take off from and land on water ▶ **seasick** adj suffering from nausea caused by the motion of a ship ▶ **seasickness** n ▶ **seaside** n area, esp. a holiday resort, on the coast ▶ **sea urchin** sea animal with a round spiky shell ▶ **seaweed** n plant growing in the sea ▶ **seaworthy** adj (of a ship) in fit condition for a sea voyage

**seal**¹ n piece of wax, lead, etc. with a special design impressed upon it, attached to a letter or document as a mark of authentication; device or material used to close an opening tightly ▷ v close with or as if with a seal; make airtight or watertight; affix a seal to or stamp with a seal; decide (one's fate) irrevocably ▶ **sealant** n any substance used for sealing ▶ **seal off** v enclose or isolate (a place) completely

**seal**² n amphibious mammal with flippers as limbs ▶ **sealskin** n

**seam** n line where two edges are joined, as by stitching; thin layer of coal or ore ▷ v mark with furrows or wrinkles ▶ **seamless** adj

**seamstress** n woman who sews, esp. professionally

**seamy** adj sordid

**seance** [**say**-anss] n meeting at which spiritualists attempt to communicate with the dead

**sear** v scorch, burn the surface of ▶ **searing** adj (of pain) very sharp; highly critical

**search** v examine closely in order to find something ▷ n searching ▶ **searching** adj keen or thorough ▶ **search engine** (Computing) internet service enabling users to search for items of interest ▶ **searchlight** n powerful light

with a beam that can be shone in any direction

**season** n one of four divisions of the year, each of which has characteristic weather conditions; period during which a thing happens or is plentiful; fitting or proper time ▷ v flavour with salt, herbs, etc.; dry (timber) till ready for use ▶ **seasonable** adj appropriate for the season; timely or opportune ▶ **seasonal** adj depending on or varying with the seasons ▶ **seasoned** adj experienced ▶ **seasoning** n salt, herbs, etc. added to food to enhance flavour ▶ **season ticket** ticket for a series of journeys or events within a specified period

**seat** n thing designed or used for sitting on; place to sit in a theatre, esp. one that requires a ticket; buttocks; (Brit) country house; membership of a legislative or administrative body ▷ v cause to sit; provide seating for ▶ **seat belt** belt worn in a car or aircraft to prevent a person being thrown forward in a crash

**sebaceous** adj of, like, or secreting fat or oil

**secateurs** pl n small pruning shears

**secede** v withdraw formally from a political alliance or federation ▶ **secession** n

**seclude** v keep (a person) from contact with others ▶ **secluded** adj private, sheltered ▶ **seclusion** n

**second**¹ adj coming directly after the first; alternate, additional; inferior ▷ n person or thing coming second; attendant in a duel or boxing match ▷ pl inferior goods ▷ v express formal support for (a motion proposed in a meeting) ▶ **secondly** adv ▶ **second-class** adj

inferior; cheaper, slower, or less comfortable than first-class
▸ **second-hand** *adj* bought after use by another ▸ **second nature** something so habitual that it seems part of one's character ▸ **second sight** supposed ability to predict events ▸ **second thoughts** revised opinion on a matter already considered ▸ **second wind** renewed ability to continue effort

**second²** *n* sixtieth part of a minute of an angle or time; moment

**second³** [si-**kond**] *v* transfer (a person) temporarily to another job ▸ **secondment** *n*

**secondary** *adj* of less importance; coming after or derived from what is primary or first; relating to the education of people between the ages of 11 and 18 or, in New Zealand, between 13 and 18

**secret** *adj* kept from the knowledge of others ▹ *n* something kept secret; mystery; underlying explanation e.g. *the secret of my success* **in secret** without other people knowing ▸ **secretly** *adv* ▸ **secrecy** *n* ▸ **secretive** *adj* inclined to keep things secret ▸ **secretiveness** *n*

**secretariat** *n* administrative office or staff of a legislative body

**secretary** *n*, *pl* **-ries** person who deals with correspondence and general clerical work; (**S-**) head of a state department e.g. *Home Secretary* ▸ **secretarial** *adj* ▸ **Secretary of State** head of a major government department

**secrete¹** *v* (of an organ, gland, etc.) produce and release (a substance) ▸ **secretion** *n* ▸ **secretory** [sek-**reet**-or-ee] *adj*

**secrete²** *v* hide or conceal

**sect** *n* subdivision of a religious or political group, esp. one with

extreme beliefs ▸ **sectarian** *adj* of a sect or religious group; narrow-minded

**section** *n* part cut off; part or subdivision of something; distinct part of a country or community; cutting; drawing of something as if cut through ▹ *v* cut or divide into sections ▸ **sectional** *adj*

**sector** *n* part or subdivision; part of a circle enclosed by two radii and the arc which they cut off

**secular** *adj* worldly, as opposed to sacred; not connected with religion or the church

**secure** *adj* free from danger; free from anxiety; firmly fixed; reliable ▹ *v* obtain; make safe; make firm; guarantee payment of (a loan) by giving something as security ▸ **securely** *adv* ▸ **security** *n*, *pl* **-ties** precautions against theft, espionage, or other danger; state of being secure; certificate of ownership of a share, stock, or bond; something given or pledged to guarantee payment of a loan

**sedan** *n* (*US*, *Aust* & *NZ*) two-door or four-door car with the body closed off from the rear luggage area ▸ **sedan chair** (*Hist*) enclosed chair for one person, carried on poles by two bearers

**sedate¹** *adj* calm and dignified; slow or unhurried ▸ **sedately** *adv*

**sedate²** *v* give a sedative drug to ▸ **sedation** *n* ▸ **sedative** *adj* having a soothing or calming effect ▹ *n* sedative drug

**sedentary** *adj* done sitting down, involving little exercise

**sedge** *n* coarse grasslike plant growing on wet ground

**sediment** *n* matter which settles to the bottom of a liquid; material deposited by water, ice, or wind ▸ **sedimentary** *adj*

**S**

**sedition** n speech or action encouraging rebellion against the government ▸ **seditious** adj

**seduce** v persuade into sexual intercourse; tempt into wrongdoing ▸ **seducer, seductress** n ▸ **seduction** n ▸ **seductive** adj

**sedulous** adj diligent or persevering ▸ **sedulously** adv

**see**[1] v **seeing, saw, seen** perceive with the eyes or mind; understand; watch; find out; make sure (of something); consider or decide; have experience of; meet or visit; accompany ▸ **seeing** conj (often foll by as or at) in view of the fact that

**see**[2] n diocese of a bishop

**seed** n mature fertilized grain of a plant; such grains used for sowing; origin; (obs) offspring; (Sport) player ranked according to his or her ability ▷ v sow with seed; remove seeds from; arrange (the draw of a sports tournament) so that the outstanding competitors will not meet in the early rounds **go to seed, run to seed** (of plants) produce or shed seeds after flowering; lose vigour or usefulness ▸ **seedling** n young plant raised from a seed ▸ **seedy** adj shabby

**seek** v **seeking, sought** try to find or obtain; try (to do something)

**seem** v appear to be ▸ **seeming** adj apparent but not real ▸ **seemingly** adv

**seemly** adj proper or fitting

**seen** v past participle of **see**[1]

**seep** v trickle through slowly, ooze ▸ **seepage** n

**seer** n prophet

**seersucker** n light cotton fabric with a slightly crinkled surface

**seesaw** n plank balanced in the middle so that two people seated on either end ride up and down alternately ▷ v move up and down

**seethe** v **seething, seethed** be very agitated; (of a liquid) boil or foam

**segment** n one of several sections into which something may be divided ▷ v divide into segments ▸ **segmentation** n

**segregate** v set apart ▸ **segregation** n

**seine** [sane] n large fishing net that hangs vertically from floats

**seismic** adj relating to earthquakes ▸ **seismology** n study of earthquakes ▸ **seismological** adj ▸ **seismologist** n ▸ **seismograph, seismometer** n instrument that records the strength of earthquakes

**seize** v take hold of forcibly or quickly; take immediate advantage of; (usu. foll by up) (of mechanical parts) stick tightly through overheating ▸ **seizure** n sudden violent attack of an illness; seizing or being seized

**seldom** adv not often, rarely

**select** v pick out or choose ▷ adj chosen in preference to others; restricted to a particular group, exclusive ▸ **selection** n selecting; things that have been selected; range from which something may be selected ▸ **selective** adj chosen or choosing carefully ▸ **selectively** adv ▸ **selectivity** n ▸ **selector** n

**selenium** n (Chem) nonmetallic element with photoelectric properties

**self** n, pl **selves** distinct individuality or identity of a person or thing; one's basic nature; one's own welfare or interests ▸ **selfish** adj caring too much about oneself and not enough about others

▸ **selfishly** adv ▸ **selfishness** n
▸ **selfless** adj unselfish ▸ **selfie**
n photograph taken by pointing
camera at oneself ▸ **selfie
stick** extendable rod to which a
camera may be attached to take a
photograph of oneself

**self-** prefix denoting of oneself or itself;
denoting by, to, in, due to, for, or from
the self; denoting automatic(ally)
▸ **self-assured** adj confident ▸ **self-
catering** adj (of accommodation)
for people who provide their own
food ▸ **self-coloured** adj having only
a single colour ▸ **self-conscious** adj
embarrassed at being the object of
others' attention ▸ **self-contained**
adj containing everything needed,
complete; (of a flat) having its own
facilities ▸ **self-determination** n the
right of a nation to decide its own
form of government ▸ **self-evident**
adj obvious without proof ▸ **self-
help** n use of one's own abilities to
solve problems; practice of solving
one's problems within a group of
people with similar problems ▸ **self-
interest** n one's own advantage
▸ **self-made** adj having achieved
wealth or status by one's own efforts
▸ **self-possessed** adj having control
of one's emotions, calm ▸ **self-
raising** adj (of flour) containing a
raising agent ▸ **self-righteous** adj
thinking oneself more virtuous than
others ▸ **selfsame** adj the very same
▸ **self-seeking** adj, n seeking to
promote only one's own interests
▸ **self-service** adj denoting a shop,
café, or garage where customers
serve themselves and then pay a
cashier ▸ **self-styled** adj using a title
or name that one has taken without
right ▸ **self-sufficient** adj able to
provide for oneself without help
▸ **self-willed** adj stubbornly
determined to get one's own way

**sell** v **selling, sold** exchange
(something) for money; stock, deal
in; (of goods) be sold; (foll by for)
have a specified price; (informal)
persuade (someone) to accept
(something) ▷ n manner of selling
▸ **seller** n ▸ **sell-by date** (Brit)
date on packaged food after which
it should not be sold ▸ **sell out** v
dispose of (something) completely
by selling; (informal) betray
▸ **sellout** n performance of a show
etc. for which all the tickets are
sold; (informal) betrayal

**Sellotape**® n type of adhesive tape
▷ v stick with Sellotape

**selvage, selvedge** n edge of cloth,
woven so as to prevent unravelling

**selves** n plural of **self**

**semantic** adj relating to the
meaning of words ▸ **semantics** n
study of linguistic meaning

**semantic Web** n proposed
development of the World Wide Web
in which computers can interpret
and act on natural language

**semaphore** n system of signalling
by holding two flags in different
positions to represent letters of
the alphabet

**semblance** n outward or
superficial appearance

**semen** n sperm-carrying fluid
produced by male animals

**semester** n either of two divisions
of the academic year

**semi** n (Brit & S Afr informal)
semidetached house

**semi-** prefix indicating half e.g.
semicircle; indicating partly or
almost e.g. semiprofessional

**semibreve** n musical note four
beats long

**semicolon** n the punctuation mark (;)

**semiconductor** n substance with
an electrical conductivity that
increases with temperature

S

**semidetached** *adj* (of a house) joined to another on one side

**semifinal** *n* match or round before the final ▷ **semifinalist** *n*

**seminal** *adj* original and influential; capable of developing; of semen or seed

**seminar** *n* meeting of a group of students for discussion

**seminary** *n, pl* -**ries** college for priests

**semiprecious** *adj* (of gemstones) having less value than precious stones

**semiquaver** *n* musical note half the length of a quaver

**Semite** *n* member of the group of peoples including Jews and Arabs

**Semitic** *adj* of the group of peoples including Jews and Arabs

**semitone** *n* smallest interval between two notes in Western music

**semitrailer** *n* (*Aust*) large truck in two separate sections joined by a pivoted bar (also **semi**)

**semolina** *n* hard grains of wheat left after the milling of flour, used to make puddings and pasta

**Senate** *n* upper house of some parliaments; governing body of some universities ▷ **senator** *n* member of a Senate ▷ **senatorial** *adj*

**send** *v* **sending, sent** cause (a person or thing) to go to or be taken or transmitted to a place; bring into a specified state or condition ▷ **sendoff** *n* demonstration of good wishes at a person's departure ▷ **send up** *v* (*informal*) make fun of by imitating ▷ **send-up** *n* (*informal*) imitation

**senile** *adj* mentally or physically weak because of old age ▷ **senility** *n*

**senior** *adj* superior in rank or standing; older; of or for older pupils ▷ *n* senior person ▷ **seniority** *n*

**senna** *n* tropical plant; its dried leaves or pods used as a laxative

**señor** [sen-**nyor**] *n, pl* -**ores** Spanish term of address equivalent to *sir* or *Mr* ▷ **señora** [sen-**nyor**-a] *n* Spanish term of address equivalent to *madam* or *Mrs* ▷ **señorita** [sen-nyor-**ee**-ta] *n* Spanish term of address equivalent to *madam* or *Miss*

**sensation** *n* ability to feel things physically; physical feeling; general feeling or awareness; state of excitement; exciting person or thing ▷ **sensational** *adj* causing intense shock, anger, or excitement; (*informal*) very good ▷ **sensationalism** *n* deliberate use of sensational language or subject matter ▷ **sensationalist** *adj, n*

**sense** *n* any of the faculties of perception or feeling (sight, hearing, touch, taste, or smell); ability to perceive; feeling perceived through one of the senses; awareness; (sometimes *pl*) sound practical judgment or intelligence; specific meaning ▷ *v* perceive ▷ **senseless** *adj*

**sensible** *adj* having or showing good sense; practical e.g. *sensible shoes*; (foll by *of*) aware ▷ **sensibly** *adv* ▷ **sensibility** *n* ability to experience deep feelings

**sensitive** *adj* easily hurt or offended; responsive to external stimuli; (of a subject) liable to arouse controversy or strong feelings; (of an instrument) responsive to slight changes ▷ **sensitively** *adv* ▷ **sensitivity** *n* ▷ **sensitize** *v* make sensitive

**sensor** *n* device that detects or measures the presence of something, such as radiation

**sensory** adj of the senses or sensation

**sensual** adj giving pleasure to the body and senses rather than the mind; having a strong liking for physical pleasures ▶ **sensually** adv ▶ **sensuality** n ▶ **sensualist** n

**sensuous** adj pleasing to the senses ▶ **sensuously** adv

**sent** v past of **send**

**sentence** n sequence of words capable of standing alone as a statement, question, or command; punishment passed on a criminal ▷ v pass sentence on (a convicted person)

**sententious** adj trying to sound wise; pompously moralizing

**sentient** [**sen**-tee-ent] adj capable of feeling ▶ **sentience** n

**sentiment** n thought, opinion, or attitude; feeling expressed in words; exaggerated or mawkish emotion ▶ **sentimental** adj excessively romantic or nostalgic ▶ **sentimentalism** n ▶ **sentimentality** n ▶ **sentimentalize** v make sentimental

**sentinel** n sentry

**sentry** n, pl **-tries** soldier on watch

**sepal** n leaflike division of the calyx of a flower

**separate** v act as a barrier between; distinguish between; divide up into parts; (of a couple) stop living together ▷ adj not the same, different; set apart; not shared, individual ▶ **separately** adv ▶ **separation** n separating or being separated; (Law) living apart of a married couple without divorce ▶ **separable** adj ▶ **separatist** n person who advocates the separation of a group from an organization or country ▶ **separatism** n

**SPELLING TIP**
There are 101 examples of *seperate* in the Collins Corpus, which makes it the most popular misspelling of **separate**

**sepia** adj, n reddish-brown (pigment)

**sepoy** n (formerly) Indian soldier in the service of the British

**sepsis** n poisoning caused by pus-forming bacteria

**Sept** September

**September** n ninth month of the year

**septet** n group of seven performers; music for such a group

**septic** adj (of a wound) infected; of or caused by harmful bacteria ▶ **septic tank** tank in which sewage is decomposed by the action of bacteria

**septicaemia** [sep-tis-**see**-mee-a] n infection of the blood

**septuagenarian** n person aged between seventy and seventy-nine

**sepulchre** [**sep**-pull-ker] n tomb or burial vault ▶ **sepulchral** [sip-**pulk**-ral] adj gloomy

**sequel** n novel, play, or film that continues the story of an earlier one; consequence

**sequence** n arrangement of two or more things in successive order; the successive order of two or more things; section of a film showing a single uninterrupted episode ▶ **sequential** adj

**sequester** v seclude; sequestrate

**sequestrate** v confiscate (property) until its owner's debts are paid or a court order is complied with ▶ **sequestration** n

**sequin** n small ornamental metal disc on a garment ▶ **sequined** adj

**sequoia** n giant Californian coniferous tree

S

**seraglio** [sir-**ah**-lee-oh] n, pl **-raglios** harem of a Muslim palace; Turkish sultan's palace

**seraph** n, pl **-aphs** or **-aphim** member of the highest order of angels ▸ **seraphic** adj

**Serbian, Serb** adj of Serbia ⊳ n person from Serbia ▸ **Serbo-Croat, Serbo-Croatian** adj, n (of) the chief official language of Serbia and Croatia

**serenade** n music played or sung to a woman by a lover ⊳ v sing or play a serenade to (someone)

**serendipity** n gift of making fortunate discoveries by accident

**serene** adj calm, peaceful ▸ **serenely** adv ▸ **serenity** n

**serf** n medieval farm labourer who could not leave the land he worked on ▸ **serfdom** n

**serge** n strong woollen fabric

**sergeant** n noncommissioned officer in the army; police officer ranking between constable and inspector ▸ **sergeant at arms** parliamentary or court officer with ceremonial duties ▸ **sergeant major** highest rank of noncommissioned officer in the army

**serial** n story or play produced in successive instalments ⊳ adj of or forming a series; published or presented as a serial ▸ **serialize** v publish or present as a serial ▸ **serial killer** person who commits a series of murders

**series** n, pl **-ries** group or succession of related things, usu. arranged in order; set of radio or TV programmes about the same subject or characters

**serious** adj giving cause for concern; concerned with important matters; not cheerful, grave; sincere, not joking ▸ **seriously** adv ▸ **seriousness** n

**sermon** n speech on a religious or moral subject by a clergyman in a church service; long moralizing speech ▸ **sermonize** v make a long moralizing speech

**serotonin** [ser-a-**tone**-in] n chemical compound that occurs in the brain, thought to be beneficial to mental health

**serpent** n (lit) snake ▸ **serpentine** adj twisting like a snake

**serrated** adj having a notched or sawlike edge

**serried** adj in close formation

**serum** [**seer**-um] n watery fluid left after blood has clotted; this fluid from the blood of immunized animals used for inoculation or vaccination

**servant** n person employed to do household work for another

**serve** v work for (a person, community, or cause); perform official duties; attend to (customers); provide (someone) with (food or drink); provide with a service; be a member of the armed forces; spend (time) in prison; be useful or suitable; (Tennis etc.) put (the ball) into play ⊳ n (Tennis etc.) act of serving the ball

**server** n player who serves in racket games; (Computing) computer or program that supplies data to other machines on a network

**service** n system that provides something needed by the public; department of public employment and its employees; availability for use; overhaul of a machine or vehicle; formal religious ceremony; (Tennis etc.) act, manner, or right of serving the ball ⊳ pl armed forces ⊳ v overhaul (a machine or vehicle) ▸ **serviceable** adj useful or helpful; able or ready to be used ▸ **service area** area beside a motorway with garage, restaurant, and toilet facilities ▸ **serviceman,**

**S**

**servicewoman** n member of the armed forces ▶ **service road** narrow road giving access to houses and shops ▶ **service station** garage selling fuel for motor vehicles

**serviette** n table napkin

**servile** adj too eager to obey people, fawning; suitable for a slave ▶ **servility** n

**servitude** n bondage or slavery

**servo** n (Aust informal) service station

**sesame** [sess-am-ee] n plant cultivated for its seeds and oil, which are used in cooking

**session** n period spent in an activity; meeting of a court, parliament, or council; series or period of such meetings; academic term or year

**set¹** v **setting, set** put in a specified position or state; make ready; make or become firm or rigid; establish, arrange; prescribe, assign; (of the sun) go down ▷ n scenery used in a play or film ▷ adj fixed or established beforehand; rigid or inflexible; determined (to do something) ▶ **setback** n anything that delays progress ▶ **set square** flat right-angled triangular instrument used for drawing angles ▶ **set-top box** device which enables digital television broadcasts to be viewed on a standard television set ▶ **set up** v arrange or establish ▶ **setup** n way in which anything is organized or arranged

**set²** n number of things or people grouped or belonging together; (Maths) group of numbers or objects that satisfy a given condition or share a property; television or radio receiver; (Sport) group of games in a match

**sett, set** n badger's burrow

**settee** n couch

**setter** n long-haired gun dog

**setting** n background or surroundings; time and place where a film, book, etc. is supposed to have taken place; music written for the words of a text; decorative metalwork in which a gem is set; plates and cutlery for a single place at table; position or level to which the controls of a machine can be adjusted

**settle¹** v arrange or put in order; come to rest; establish or become established as a resident; make quiet, calm, or stable; pay (a bill); bestow (property) legally ▶ **settlement** n act of settling; place newly colonized; subsidence (of a building); property bestowed legally ▶ **settler** n colonist

**settle²** n long wooden bench with high back and arms

**seven** adj, n one more than six ▶ **seventh** adj, n (of) number seven in a series ▶ **seventeen** adj, n ten and seven ▶ **seventeenth** adj, n ▶ **seventy** adj, n ten times seven ▶ **seventieth** adj, n

**sever** v cut through or off; break off (a relationship) ▶ **severance** n ▶ **severance pay** compensation paid by a firm to an employee who leaves because the job he or she was appointed to do no longer exists

**several** adj some, a few; various, separate ▶ **severally** adv separately

**severe** adj strict or harsh; very intense or unpleasant; strictly restrained in appearance ▶ **severely** adv ▶ **severity** n

**sew** v **sewing, sewed, sewn** or **sewed** join with thread repeatedly passed through with a needle; make or fasten by sewing

**sewage** n waste matter or excrement carried away in sewers

**sewer** n drain to remove waste water and sewage ▶ **sewerage** n system of sewers

**sewn** v a past participle of **sew**

**sex** n state of being male or female; male or female category; sexual intercourse; sexual feelings or behaviour ▷ v find out the sex of ▶ **sexy** adj sexually exciting or attractive; (informal) exciting or trendy ▶ **sexism** n discrimination on the basis of a person's sex ▶ **sexist** adj, n ▶ **sexual** adj ▶ **sexually** adv ▶ **sexuality** n ▶ **sexual intercourse** sexual act in which the male's penis is inserted into the female's vagina ▶ **sex up** v (informal) make (something) more exciting

**sexagenarian** n person aged between sixty and sixty-nine

**sextant** n navigator's instrument for measuring angles, as between the sun and horizon, to calculate one's position

**sextet** n group of six performers; music for such a group

**sexton** n official in charge of a church and churchyard

**SF** science fiction

**Sgt.** Sergeant

**shabby** adj **-bier, -biest** worn or dilapidated in appearance; mean or unworthy e.g. shabby treatment ▶ **shabbily** adv ▶ **shabbiness** n

**shack** n rough hut ▶ **shack up with** v (slang) live with (one's lover)

**shackle** n one of a pair of metal rings joined by a chain, for securing a person's wrists or ankles ▷ v fasten with shackles

**shad** n herring-like fish

**shade** n relative darkness; place sheltered from sun; screen or cover used to protect from a direct source of light; depth of colour; slight amount; (lit) ghost ▷ pl (informal) sunglasses ▷ v screen from light; darken; represent (darker areas) in drawing; change slightly or by degrees ▶ **shady** adj situated in or giving shade; of doubtful honesty or legality

**shadow** n dark shape cast on a surface when something stands between a light and the surface; patch of shade; slight trace; threatening influence; inseparable companion ▷ v cast a shadow over; follow secretly ▶ **shadowy** adj ▶ **shadow-boxing** n boxing against an imaginary opponent for practice ▶ **Shadow Cabinet** members of the main opposition party in Parliament who would be ministers if their party were in power

**shaft** n long narrow straight handle of a tool or weapon; ray of light; revolving rod that transmits power in a machine; vertical passageway, as for a lift or a mine; one of the bars between which an animal is harnessed to a vehicle

**shag**¹ n coarse shredded tobacco ▷ adj (of a carpet) having a long pile ▶ **shaggy** adj covered with rough hair or wool; tousled; unkempt ▶ **shaggy-dog story** long anecdote with a humorous twist at the end

**shag**² n kind of cormorant

**shagreen** n sharkskin; rough grainy untanned leather

**shah** n formerly, ruler of Iran

**shake** v shaking, shook, shaken move quickly up and down or back and forth; make unsteady; tremble; grasp (someone's hand) in greeting or agreement; shock or upset ▷ n shaking; vibration; (informal) short period of time ▶ **shaky** adj unsteady; uncertain or questionable ▶ **shakily** adv

**shale** n flaky sedimentary rock

**shall** v, *past tense* **should** used as an auxiliary to make the future tense or to indicate intention, obligation, or inevitability

> **USAGE NOTE**
> The use of *shall* with *I* and *we* is a matter of preference, not rule

**shallot** n kind of small onion

**shallow** adj not deep; lacking depth of character or intellect ▶ **shallows** pl n area of shallow water ▶ **shallowness** n

**sham** n thing or person that is not genuine ▷ adj not genuine ▷ v **shamming, shammed** fake, feign

**shamble** v walk in a shuffling awkward way

**shambles** n disorderly event or place

**shame** n painful emotion caused by awareness of having done something dishonourable or foolish; capacity to feel shame; cause of shame; cause for regret ▷ v cause to feel shame; disgrace; compel by shame ▷ *interj* (S *Afr informal*) exclamation of sympathy or endearment ▶ **shameful** adj causing or deserving shame ▶ **shamefully** adv ▶ **shameless** adj with no sense of shame ▶ **shamefaced** adj looking ashamed

**shammy** n, pl -**mies** (*informal*) piece of chamois leather

**shampoo** n liquid soap for washing hair, carpets, or upholstery; process of shampooing ▷ v wash with shampoo

**shamrock** n clover leaf, esp. as the Irish emblem

**shandy** n, pl -**dies** drink made of beer and lemonade

**shanghai** v -**haiing, -haied** force or trick (someone) into doing something ▷ n (*Aust & NZ*) catapult

**shank** n lower leg; shaft or stem

**shan't** shall not

**shantung** n soft Chinese silk with a knobbly surface

**shanty**[1] n, pl -**ties** shack or crude dwelling ▶ **shantytown** n slum consisting of shanties

**shanty**[2] n, pl -**ties** sailor's traditional song

**shape** n outward form of an object; way in which something is organized; pattern or mould; condition or state ▷ v form or mould; devise or develop ▶ **shapeless** adj ▶ **shapely** adj having an attractive shape

**shard** n broken piece of pottery or glass

**share**[1] n part of something that belongs to or is contributed by a person; one of the equal parts into which the capital stock of a public company is divided ▷ v give or take a share of (something); join with others in doing or using (something) ▶ **shareholder** n ▶ **sharemilker** n (*NZ*) person who works on a dairy farm belonging to someone else

**share**[2] n blade of a plough

**shark** n large usu. predatory sea fish; person who cheats others

**shark biscuit** n (*Aust facetious*) bodyboard; young or inexperienced surfer

**sharkskin** n stiff glossy fabric

**sharp** adj having a keen cutting edge or fine point; not gradual; clearly defined; mentally acute; shrill; bitter or sour in taste; (*Music*) above the true pitch ▷ adv promptly; (*Music*) too high in pitch ▷ n (*Music*) symbol raising a note one semitone above natural pitch ▶ **sharply** adv ▶ **sharpness** n ▶ **sharpen** v make or become sharp or sharper ▶ **sharpener** n ▶ **sharpshooter** n marksman

S

**shatter** v break into pieces; destroy completely ▸ **shattered** adj (informal) completely exhausted; badly upset

**shave** v **shaving, shaved, shaved** or **shaven** remove (hair) from (the face, head, or body) with a razor or shaver; pare away; touch lightly in passing ▷ n shaving **close shave** (informal) narrow escape ▸ **shaver** n electric razor ▸ **shavings** pl n parings

**shawl** n piece of cloth worn over a woman's head or shoulders or wrapped around a baby

**she** pron referring to female person or animal previously mentioned; referring to something regarded as female, such as a car, ship, or nation

**sheaf** n, pl **sheaves** bundle of papers; tied bundle of reaped corn

**shear** v **shearing, sheared, sheared** or **shorn** clip hair or wool from; cut through ▸ **shears** pl n large scissors or a cutting tool shaped like these ▸ **shearer** n ▸ **shearing shed** (Aust & NZ) farm building with equipment for shearing sheep

**shearwater** n medium-sized sea bird

**sheath** n close-fitting cover, esp. for a knife or sword; (Brit, Aust & NZ) condom ▸ **sheathe** v put into a sheath

**shebeen** n (Scot, Irish & S Afr) place where alcohol is sold illegally

**shed¹** n building used for storage or shelter or as a workshop

**shed²** v **shedding, shed** pour forth (tears); cast off (skin, hair, or leaves)

**sheen** n glistening brightness on the surface of something

**sheep** n, pl **sheep** ruminant animal bred for wool and meat ▸ **sheep-dip** n liquid disinfectant in which

sheep are immersed ▸ **sheepdog** n dog used for herding sheep ▸ **sheepskin** n skin of a sheep with the fleece still on, used for clothing or rugs

**sheepish** adj embarrassed because of feeling foolish ▸ **sheepishly** adv

**sheer¹** adj absolute, complete e.g. sheer folly; perpendicular, steep; (of material) so fine as to be transparent

**sheer²** v change course suddenly

**sheet¹** n large piece of cloth used as an inner bed cover; broad thin piece of any material; large expanse

**sheet²** n rope for controlling the position of a sail ▸ **sheet anchor** strong anchor for use in an emergency; person or thing relied on

**sheikh, sheik** [shake] n Arab chief ▸ **sheikhdom, sheikdom** n

**sheila** n (Aust & NZ slang) girl or woman

**shekel** n monetary unit of Israel ▷ pl (informal) money

**shelf** n, pl **shelves** board fixed horizontally for holding things; ledge ▸ **shelf life** time a packaged product will remain fresh

**shell** n hard outer covering of an egg, nut, or certain animals; external frame of something; explosive projectile fired from a large gun ▷ v take the shell from; fire at with artillery shells ▸ **shellfish** n sea-living animal, esp. one that can be eaten, with a shell ▸ **shell out** v (informal) pay out or hand over (money) ▸ **shell shock** nervous disorder caused by exposure to battle conditions ▸ **shell suit** (Brit) lightweight tracksuit made of a waterproof nylon layer over a cotton layer

**shellac** n resin used in varnishes ▷ v **-lacking, -lacked** coat with shellac

**shelter** n structure providing protection from danger or the weather; protection ▷ v give shelter to; take shelter

**shelve¹** v put aside or postpone; provide with shelves ▶ **shelving** n (material for) shelves

**shelve²** v slope

**shenanigans** pl n (informal) mischief or nonsense; trickery

**shepherd** n person who tends sheep ▷ v guide or watch over (people) ▶ **shepherdess** n fem ▶ **shepherd's pie** baked dish of mince covered with mashed potato

**sherbet** n (Brit, Aust & NZ) fruit-flavoured fizzy powder; (US, Canadian & SAfr) flavoured water ice

**sheriff** n (in the US) chief law enforcement officer of a county; (in England and Wales) chief executive officer of the Crown in a county; (in Scotland) chief judge of a district; (in Australia) officer of the Supreme Court

**Sherpa** n member of a people of Tibet and Nepal

**sherry** n, pl -ries pale or dark brown fortified wine

**shibboleth** n slogan or principle, usu. considered outworn, characteristic of a particular group

**shield** n piece of armour carried on the arm to protect the body from blows or missiles; anything that protects; sports trophy in the shape of a shield ▷ v protect

**shift** v move; transfer (blame or responsibility); remove or be removed ▷ n shifting; group of workers who work during a specified period; period of time during which they work; loose-fitting straight underskirt or dress ▶ **shiftless** adj lacking in ambition or initiative ▶ **shifty** adj evasive or untrustworthy ▶ **shiftiness** n

**shillelagh** [shil-**lay**-lee] n (in Ireland) a cudgel

**shilling** n former British coin, replaced by the 5p piece; former Australian coin, worth one twentieth of a pound

**shillyshally** v -lying, -lied (informal) be indecisive

**shimmer** v, n (shine with) a faint unsteady light

**shin** n front of the lower leg ▷ v **shinning, shinned** climb by using the hands or arms and legs ▶ **shinbone** n tibia

**shindig** n (informal) noisy party; brawl

**shine** v **shining, shone** give out or reflect light; aim (a light); polish; excel ▷ n brightness or lustre **take a shine to** (informal) take a liking to (someone) ▶ **shiny** adj -nier, -niest ▶ **shiner** n (informal) black eye

**shingle¹** n wooden roof tile ▷ v cover (a roof) with shingles

**shingle²** n coarse gravel found on beaches ▶ **shingle slide** (NZ) loose stones on a steep slope

**shingles** n disease causing a rash of small blisters along a nerve

**Shinto** n Japanese religion in which ancestors and nature spirits are worshipped ▶ **Shintoism** n

**shinty** n game like hockey

**ship** n large seagoing vessel ▷ v **shipping, shipped** send or transport by carrier, esp. a ship; bring or go aboard a ship ▶ **shipment** n act of shipping cargo; consignment of goods shipped ▶ **shipping** n freight transport business; ships collectively ▶ **shipshape** adj orderly or neat ▶ **shipwreck** n destruction of a ship through storm or collision ▷ v cause to undergo shipwreck ▶ **shipyard** n place where ships are built

**S**

**shire** n (Brit) county; (Aust) rural area with an elected council

**shire horse** n large powerful breed of horse

**shirk** v avoid (duty or work) ▷ **shirker** n

**shirt** n garment for the upper part of the body

**shirty** adj **-tier, -tiest** (chiefly Brit slang) bad-tempered or annoyed

**shish kebab** n meat and vegetable dish cooked on a skewer

**shiver**[1] v tremble, as from cold or fear ▷ n shivering

**shiver**[2] v splinter into pieces

**shoal**[1] n large number of fish swimming together

**shoal**[2] n stretch of shallow water; sandbank

**shock**[1] v horrify, disgust, or astonish ▷ n sudden violent emotional disturbance; sudden violent blow or impact; something causing this; state of bodily collapse caused by physical or mental shock; pain and muscular spasm caused by an electric current passing through the body ▷ **shocker** n ▷ **shocking** adj causing horror, disgust, or astonishment; (informal) very bad

**shock**[2] n bushy mass (of hair)

**shod** v past of **shoe**

**shoddy** adj **-dier, -diest** made or done badly

**shoe** n outer covering for the foot, ending below the ankle; horseshoe ▷ v **shoeing, shod** fit with a shoe or shoes ▷ **shoehorn** n smooth curved implement inserted at the heel of a shoe to ease the foot into it ▷ **shoestring** n **on a shoestring** using a very small amount of money

**shone** v past of **shine**

**shonky** adj **-kier, -kiest** (Aust & NZ informal) unreliable or unsound

**shoo** interj go away! ▷ v drive away as by saying 'shoo'

**shook** v past tense of **shake**

**shoot** v **shooting, shot** hit, wound, or kill with a missile fired from a weapon; fire (a missile from) a weapon; hunt; send out or move rapidly; (of a plant) sprout; photograph or film; (Sport) take a shot at goal ▷ n new branch or sprout of a plant; hunting expedition ▷ **shooting star** meteor ▷ **shooting stick** stick with a spike at one end and a folding seat at the other

**shop** n place for sale of goods and services; workshop ▷ v **shopping, shopped** visit a shop or shops to buy goods; (Brit, Aust & NZ slang) inform against (someone) **talk shop** discuss one's work, esp. on a social occasion ▷ **shop around** v visit various shops to compare goods and prices ▷ **shop floor** production area of a factory; workers in a factory ▷ **shoplifter** n person who steals from a shop ▷ **shop-soiled** adj soiled or faded from being displayed in a shop ▷ **shop steward** (in some countries) trade-union official elected to represent his or her fellow workers

**shore**[1] n edge of a sea or lake

**shore**[2] v (foll by up) prop or support

**shorn** v a past participle of **shear**

**short** adj not long; not tall; not lasting long, brief; deficient e.g. short of cash; abrupt, rude; (of a drink) consisting chiefly of a spirit; (of pastry) crumbly ▷ adv abruptly ▷ n drink of spirits; short film; (informal) short circuit ▷ pl short trousers ▷ **shortage** n deficiency ▷ **shorten** v make or become shorter ▷ **shortly** adv soon; rudely ▷ **shortbread, shortcake** n crumbly biscuit made with butter ▷ **short-change**

*v* give (someone) less than the correct amount of change; (*slang*) swindle ▸ **short circuit** faulty or accidental connection in a circuit, which deflects current through a path of low resistance ▸ **shortcoming** *n* failing or defect ▸ **short cut** quicker route or method ▸ **shortfall** *n* deficit ▸ **shorthand** *n* system of rapid writing using symbols to represent words ▸ **short-handed** *adj* not having enough workers ▸ **short list** selected list of candidates for a job or prize, from which the final choice will be made ▸ **short-list** *v* put on a short list ▸ **short shrift** brief and unsympathetic treatment ▸ **short-sighted** *adj* unable to see distant things clearly; lacking in foresight ▸ **short wave** radio wave with a wavelength of less than 60 metres

**shot¹** *n* shooting; small lead pellets used in a shotgun; person with specified skill in shooting; (*slang*) attempt; (*Sport*) act or instance of hitting, kicking, or throwing the ball; photograph; uninterrupted film sequence; (*informal*) injection ▸ **shotgun** *n* gun for firing a charge of shot at short range

**shot²** *v* past of **shoot** ▷ *adj* woven to show changing colours

**shot put** *n* athletic event in which contestants hurl a heavy metal ball as far as possible ▸ **shot-putter** *n*

**should** *v* past tense of **shall** used as an auxiliary to make the subjunctive mood or to indicate obligation or possibility

**shoulder** *n* part of the body to which an arm, foreleg, or wing is attached; cut of meat including the upper foreleg; side of a road ▷ *v* bear (a burden or responsibility); push with one's shoulder; put on

one's shoulder ▸ **shoulder blade** large flat triangular bone at the shoulder

**shouldn't** should not

**shout** *n* loud cry; (*informal*) person's turn to buy a round of drinks ▷ *v* cry out loudly; (*Aust & NZ informal*) treat (someone) to (something, such as a drink) ▸ **shout down** *v* silence (someone) by shouting

**shove** *v* push roughly; (*informal*) put ▷ *n* rough push ▸ **shove off** *v* (*informal*) go away

**shovel** *n* tool for lifting or moving loose material ▷ *v* **-elling, -elled** lift or move as with a shovel

**show** *v* **showing, showed, shown** or **showed** make, be, or become noticeable or visible; exhibit or display; indicate; instruct by demonstration; prove; guide; reveal or display (an emotion) ▷ *n* public exhibition; theatrical or other entertainment; mere display or pretence ▸ **showy** *adj* gaudy; ostentatious ▸ **showily** *adv* ▸ **show business** the entertainment industry ▸ **showcase** *n* situation in which something is displayed to best advantage; glass case used to display objects ▸ **showdown** *n* confrontation that settles a dispute ▸ **showjumping** *n* competitive sport of riding horses to demonstrate skill in jumping ▸ **showman** *n* man skilled at presenting anything spectacularly ▸ **showmanship** *n* ▸ **show off** *v* exhibit to invite admiration; (*informal*) behave flamboyantly in order to attract attention ▸ **show-off** *n* (*informal*) person who shows off ▸ **showpiece** *n* excellent specimen shown for display or as an example ▸ **showroom** *n* room in which goods for sale are on

**S**

display ▸ **show up** v reveal or be revealed clearly; expose the faults or defects of; (*informal*) embarrass; (*informal*) arrive

**shower** n kind of bath in which a person stands while being sprayed with water; wash in this; short period of rain, hail, or snow; sudden abundant fall of objects ▷ v wash in a shower; bestow (things) or present (someone) with things liberally ▸ **showery** adj

**shown** v a past participle of **show**

**shrank** v a past tense of **shrink**

**shrapnel** n artillery shell filled with pellets which scatter on explosion; fragments from this

**shred** n long narrow strip torn from something; small amount ▷ v **shredding, shredded** or **shred** tear to shreds

**shrew** n small mouselike animal; bad-tempered nagging woman ▸ **shrewish** adj

**shrewd** adj clever and perceptive ▸ **shrewdly** adv ▸ **shrewdness** n

**shriek** n shrill cry ▷ v utter (with) a shriek

**shrike** n songbird with a heavy hooked bill

**shrill** adj (of a sound) sharp and high-pitched ▸ **shrillness** n ▸ **shrilly** adv

**shrimp** n small edible shellfish; (*informal*) small person ▸ **shrimping** n fishing for shrimps

**shrine** n place of worship associated with a sacred person or object

**shrink** v **shrinking, shrank** or **shrunk, shrunk** or **shrunken** become or make smaller; recoil or withdraw ▷ n (*slang*) psychiatrist ▸ **shrinkage** n decrease in size, value, or weight

**shrivel** v **-elling, -elled** shrink and wither

**shroud** n piece of cloth used to wrap a dead body; anything which conceals ▷ v conceal

**Shrove Tuesday** n day before Ash Wednesday

**shrub** n woody plant smaller than a tree ▸ **shrubbery** n, pl **-beries** area planted with shrubs

**shrug** v **shrugging, shrugged** raise and then drop (the shoulders) as a sign of indifference, ignorance, or doubt ▷ n shrugging ▸ **shrug off** v dismiss as unimportant

**shrunk** v a past of **shrink**

**shrunken** v a past participle of **shrink**

**shudder** v shake or tremble violently, esp. with horror ▷ n shaking or trembling

**shuffle** v walk without lifting the feet; jumble together; rearrange ▷ n shuffling; rearrangement

**shun** v **shunning, shunned** avoid

**shunt** v move (objects or people) to a different position; move (a train) from one track to another

**shush** interj be quiet!

**shut** v **shutting, shut** bring together or fold, close; prevent access to; (of a shop etc.) stop operating for the day ▸ **shutter** n hinged doorlike cover for closing off a window; device in a camera letting in the light required to expose a film ▸ **shut down** v close or stop (a factory, machine, or business) ▸ **shutdown** n

**shuttle** n vehicle going to and fro over a short distance; instrument which passes the weft thread between the warp threads in weaving ▷ v travel by or as if by shuttle

**shuttlecock** n small light cone with feathers stuck in one end, struck to and fro in badminton

**shy¹** adj not at ease in company; timid; (foll by of) cautious or wary

▷ *v* **shying, shied** start back in fear; (foll by *away from*) avoid (doing something) through fear or lack of confidence ▶ **shyly** *adv* ▶ **shyness** *n*

**shy²** *v* **shying, shied** throw ▷ *n, pl* **shies** throw

**SI** (*French*) Système International (d'Unités): international metric system of units of measurement

**Siamese** *adj* of Siam, former name of Thailand ▶ **Siamese cat** breed of cat with cream fur, dark ears and face, and blue eyes ▶ **Siamese twins** twins born joined to each other at some part of the body

**sibilant** *adj* hissing ▷ *n* consonant pronounced with a hissing sound

**sibling** *n* brother or sister

**sibyl** *n* (in ancient Greece and Rome) prophetess

**sic** (*Latin*) *adv* thus: used to indicate that an odd spelling or reading is in fact accurate

**sick** *adj* vomiting or likely to vomit; physically or mentally unwell; (*informal*) amused or fascinated by something sadistic or morbid; (foll by *of*) (*informal*) disgusted (by) or weary (of) ▶ **sickness** *n* ▶ **sicken** *v* make nauseated or disgusted; become ill ▶ **sickly** *adj* unhealthy, weak; causing revulsion or nausea ▶ **sick bay** place for sick people, such as that on a ship

**sickle** *n* tool with a curved blade for cutting grass or grain

**side** *n* line or surface that borders anything; either of two halves into which something can be divided; either surface of a flat object; area immediately next to a person or thing; aspect or part; one of two opposing groups or teams ▷ *adj* at or on the side; subordinate **on the side** as an extra; unofficially ▶ **siding** *n* short stretch of railway track on which trains or wagons

are shunted from the main line ▶ **sidebar** *n* short article placed alongside a longer one on a website ▶ **sideboard** *n* piece of furniture for holding plates, cutlery, etc. in a dining room ▶ **sideburns, sideboards** *pl n* man's side whiskers ▶ **side effect** additional undesirable effect ▶ **sidekick** *n* (*informal*) close friend or associate ▶ **sidelight** *n* either of two small lights on the front of a vehicle ▶ **sideline** *n* subsidiary interest or source of income; (*Sport*) line marking the boundary of a playing area ▶ **sidelong** *adj* sideways ▷ *adv* obliquely ▶ **side-saddle** *n* saddle designed to allow a woman rider to sit with both legs on the same side of the horse ▶ **sidestep** *v* dodge (an issue); avoid by stepping sideways ▶ **sidetrack** *v* divert from the main topic ▶ **sidewalk** *n* (*US*) paved path for pedestrians, at the side of a road ▶ **sideways** *adv* to or from the side; obliquely ▶ **side with** *v* support (one side in a dispute)

**sidereal** [side-**eer**-ee-al] *adj* of or determined with reference to the stars

**sidle** *v* walk in a furtive manner

**SIDS** sudden infant death syndrome: cot death

**siege** *n* surrounding and blockading of a place

**sienna** *n* reddish- or yellowish-brown pigment made from natural earth

**sierra** *n* range of mountains in Spain or America with jagged peaks

**siesta** *n* afternoon nap, taken in hot countries

**sieve** [siv] *n* utensil with mesh through which a substance is sifted or strained ▷ *v* sift or strain through a sieve

**sift** *v* remove the coarser particles from a substance with a sieve;

**S**

examine (information or evidence) to select what is important

**sigh** n long audible breath expressing sadness, tiredness, relief, or longing ▷ v utter a sigh

**sight** n ability to see; instance of seeing; range of vision; device for guiding the eye while using a gun or optical instrument; thing worth seeing; (*informal*) a lot ▷ v catch sight of ▸ **sightless** adj blind ▸ **sight-read** v play or sing printed music without previous preparation ▸ **sightseeing** n visiting places of interest ▸ **sightseer** n

**sign** n indication of something not immediately or outwardly observable; gesture, mark, or symbol conveying a meaning; notice displayed to advertise, inform, or warn; omen ▷ v write (one's name) on (a document or letter) to show its authenticity or one's agreement; communicate using sign language; make a sign or gesture ▸ **sign language** system of communication by gestures, as used by deaf people (also **signing**) ▸ **sign on** v register as unemployed; sign a document committing oneself to a job, course, etc. ▸ **signpost** n post bearing a sign that shows the way

**signal** n sign or gesture to convey information; sequence of electrical impulses or radio waves transmitted or received ▷ adj (*formal*) very important ▷ v -**nalling, -nalled** convey (information) by signal ▸ **signally** adv ▸ **signal box** building from which railway signals are operated ▸ **signalman** n railwayman in charge of signals and points

**signatory** n, pl -**ries** one of the parties who sign a document

**signature** n person's name written by himself or herself in signing something; sign at the start of a piece of music to show the key or tempo ▸ **signature tune** tune used to introduce a particular television or radio programme

**signet** n small seal used to authenticate documents ▸ **signet ring** finger ring bearing a signet

**significant** adj important; having or expressing a meaning ▸ **significantly** adv ▸ **significance** n

**signify** v -**fying, -fied** indicate or suggest; be a symbol or sign for; be important ▸ **signification** n

**signor** [see-**nyor**] n Italian term of address equivalent to *sir* or *Mr* ▸ **signora** [see-**nyor**-a] n Italian term of address equivalent to *madam* or *Mrs* ▸ **signorina** [see-nyor-**ee**-na] n Italian term of address equivalent to *madam* or *Miss*

**Sikh** [**seek**] n member of an Indian religion having only one God

**silage** [**sile**-ij] n fodder crop harvested while green and partially fermented in a silo or plastic bags

**silence** n absence of noise or speech ▷ v make silent; put a stop to ▸ **silent** adj ▸ **silently** adv ▸ **silencer** n device to reduce the noise of an engine exhaust or gun

**silhouette** n outline of a dark shape seen against a light background ▷ v show in silhouette

**silica** n hard glossy mineral found as quartz and in sandstone ▸ **silicosis** n lung disease caused by inhaling silica dust

**silicon** n (*Chem*) brittle nonmetallic element widely used in chemistry and industry ▸ **silicon chip** tiny wafer of silicon processed to form an integrated circuit

S

**silicone** n tough synthetic substance made from silicon and used in lubricants, paints, and resins

**silk** n fibre made by the larva (**silkworm**) of a certain moth; thread or fabric made from this ▶ **silky, silken** adj of or like silk

**sill** n ledge at the bottom of a window or door

**silly** adj **-lier, -liest** foolish ▶ **silliness** n

**silo** n, pl **-los** pit or airtight tower for storing silage or grains; underground structure in which nuclear missiles are kept ready for launching

**silt** n mud deposited by moving water ▷ v (foll by up) fill or be choked with silt

**silvan** adj same as **sylvan**

**silver** n white precious metal; coins or articles made of silver ▷ adj made of or of the colour of silver ▶ **silverbeet** n (Aust & NZ) leafy green vegetable with white stalks ▶ **silver birch** tree with silvery-white bark ▶ **silver fern** (NZ) sporting symbol of New Zealand ▶ **silverfish** n small wingless silver-coloured insect ▶ **silverside** n cut of beef from below the rump and above the leg ▶ **silver wedding** twenty-fifth wedding anniversary

**sim** n computer game that simulates an activity such as flying or playing a sport

**simian** adj, n (of or like) a monkey or ape

**similar** adj alike but not identical ▶ **similarity** n ▶ **similarly** adv

**simile** [sim-ill-ee] n figure of speech comparing one thing to another, using 'as' or 'like' e.g. as blind as a bat

**similitude** n similarity, likeness

**simmer** v cook gently at just below boiling point; be in a state of suppressed rage ▶ **simmer down** v (informal) calm down

**simnel cake** n (Brit) fruit cake with marzipan

**simper** v smile in a silly or affected way; utter (something) with a simper ▷ n simpering smile

**simple** adj easy to understand or do; plain or unpretentious; not combined or complex; sincere or frank; feeble-minded ▶ **simply** adv ▶ **simplicity** n ▶ **simplify** v make less complicated ▶ **simplification** n ▶ **simplistic** adj too simple or naive ▶ **simpleton** n foolish or half-witted person

**simulate** v make a pretence of; imitate the conditions of (a particular situation); have the appearance of ▶ **simulation** n ▶ **simulator** n

**simultaneous** adj occurring at the same time ▶ **simultaneously** adv

**sin¹** n breaking of a religious or moral law; offence against a principle or standard ▷ v **sinning, sinned** commit a sin ▶ **sinful** adj guilty of sin; being a sin ▶ **sinfully** adv ▶ **sinner** n

**sin²** (Maths) sine

**since** prep during the period of time after ▷ conj from the time when; for the reason that ▷ adv from that time

**sincere** adj without pretence or deceit ▶ **sincerely** adv ▶ **sincerity** n

**sine** n (in trigonometry) ratio of the length of the opposite side to that of the hypotenuse in a right-angled triangle

**sinecure** [sin-ee-cure] n paid job with minimal duties

**sine die** [sin-ay dee-ay] adv (Latin) with no date fixed for future action

**sine qua non** [sin-ay kwah non] n (Latin) essential requirement

S

**sinew** n tough fibrous tissue
joining muscle to bone; muscles or
strength ▶ **sinewy** adj
**sing** v **singing, sang, sung** make
musical sounds with the voice;
perform (a song); make a humming
or whistling sound ▶ **singing
telegram** service in which a
messenger presents greetings to
a person by singing ▶ **singsong** n
informal singing session ▷ adj (of
the voice) repeatedly rising and
falling in pitch

**USAGE NOTE**
The simple past of *sing* is *sang*:
*He sang the chorus*. Avoid the use
of the past participle *sung* for the
simple past

**singe** v **singeing, singed** burn the
surface of ▷ n superficial burn
**singer** n person who sings, esp.
professionally
**single** adj one only; distinct
from others of the same kind;
unmarried; designed for one user;
formed of only one part; (of a ticket)
valid for an outward journey only
▷ n single thing; thing intended for
one person; record with one short
song or tune on each side; single
ticket ▷ pl game between two
players ▷ v (foll by out) pick out from
others ▶ **singly** adv ▶ **single file** (of
people or things) arranged in one
line ▶ **single-handed** adj without
assistance ▶ **single-minded** adj
having one aim only ▶ **single
parent** parent bringing up a child
or children alone
**singlet** n sleeveless vest
**singular** adj (of a word or form)
denoting one person or thing;
remarkable, unusual ▷ n singular
form of a word ▶ **singularity** n
▶ **singularly** adv
**sinister** adj threatening or
suggesting evil or harm

**sink** v **sinking, sank, sunk** or
**sunken** submerge (in liquid);
descend or cause to descend;
decline in value or amount;
become weaker in health; dig
or drill (a hole or shaft); invest
(money); (*Golf, snooker*) hit (a ball)
into a hole or pocket ▷ n fixed basin
with a water supply and drainage
pipe ▶ **sinker** n weight for a fishing
line ▶ **sink in** v penetrate the mind
▶ **sinking fund** money set aside
regularly to repay a long-term debt
**Sino-** combining form Chinese
**sinuous** adj curving; lithe
▶ **sinuously** adv
**sinus** [**sine**-uss] n hollow space in a
bone, esp. an air passage opening
into the nose
**sip** v **sipping, sipped** drink in small
mouthfuls ▷ n amount sipped
**siphon** n bent tube which uses
air pressure to draw liquid from
a container ▷ v draw off thus;
redirect (resources)
**sir** n polite term of address for
a man; (**S-**) title of a knight or
baronet
**sire** n male parent of a horse or
other domestic animal; respectful
term of address to a king ▷ v father
**siren** n device making a loud wailing
noise as a warning; dangerously
alluring woman
**sirloin** n prime cut of loin of beef
**sirocco** n, pl -**cos** hot wind blowing
from N Africa into S Europe
**sis** interj (*S Afr informal*) exclamation
of disgust
**sisal** [**size**-al] n (fibre of) plant used
in making ropes
**siskin** n yellow-and-black finch
**sissy** adj, n, pl -**sies** weak or
cowardly (person)
**sister** n girl or woman with the
same parents as another person;
female fellow-member of a group;

senior nurse; nun ▷ *adj* closely related, similar ▶ **sisterhood** *n* state of being a sister; group of women united by common aims or beliefs ▶ **sisterly** *adj* ▶ **sister-in-law** *n*, *pl* **sisters-in-law** sister of one's husband or wife; wife of one's sibling

**sit** *v* **sitting, sat** rest one's body upright on the buttocks; cause to sit; perch; occupy an official position; (of an official body) hold a session; take (an examination) ▶ **sitting room** room in a house where people sit and relax ▶ **sit-in** *n* protest in which demonstrators occupy a place and refuse to move

**sitar** *n* Indian stringed musical instrument

**sitcom** *n* (*informal*) situation comedy

**site** *n* place where something is, was, or is intended to be located; same as **website** ▷ *v* provide with a site

**situate** *v* place

**situation** *n* state of affairs; location and surroundings; position of employment ▶ **situation comedy** radio or television series involving the same characters in various situations

**six** *adj*, *n* one more than five ▶ **sixth** *adj*, *n* (of) number six in a series ▶ **sixteen** *adj*, *n* six and ten ▶ **sixteenth** *adj*, *n* ▶ **sixty** *adj*, *n* six times ten ▶ **sixtieth** *adj*, *n*

**size¹** *n* dimensions, bigness; one of a series of standard measurements of goods ▷ *v* arrange according to size ▶ **sizeable, sizable** *adj* quite large ▶ **size up** *v* (*informal*) assess

**size²** *n* gluey substance used as a protective coating

**sizzle** *v* make a hissing sound like frying fat

**skanky** *adj* (*slang*) dirty or unattractive; promiscuous

**skate¹** *n* boot with a steel blade or sets of wheels attached to the sole for gliding over ice or a hard surface ▷ *v* glide on or as if on skates ▶ **skateboard** *n* board mounted on small wheels for riding on while standing up ▶ **skateboarding** *n* ▶ **skate over, skate round** *v* avoid discussing or dealing with (a matter) fully

**skate²** *n* large marine flatfish

**skedaddle** *v* (*informal*) run off

**skein** [skayn] *n* yarn wound in a loose coil; flock of geese in flight

**skeleton** *n* framework of bones inside a person's or animal's body; essential framework of a structure; small steel-frame racing sledge ▷ *adj* reduced to a minimum ▶ **skeletal** *adj* ▶ **skeleton key** key which can open many different locks

**sketch** *n* rough drawing; brief description; short humorous play ▷ *v* make a sketch (of) ▶ **sketchy** *adj* incomplete or inadequate

**skew** *v* make slanting or crooked ▷ *adj* slanting or crooked ▶ **skew-whiff** *adj* (*Brit informal*) slanting or crooked

**skewer** *n* pin to hold meat together during cooking ▷ *v* fasten with a skewer

**ski** *n* one of a pair of long runners fastened to boots for gliding over snow or water ▷ *v* **skiing, skied** or **ski'd** travel on skis ▶ **skier** *n*

**skid** *v* **skidding, skidded** (of a moving vehicle) slide sideways uncontrollably ▷ *n* skidding

**skiff** *n* small boat

**skill** *n* special ability or expertise; something requiring special training or expertise ▶ **skilful** *adj* having or showing skill ▶ **skilfully** *adv* ▶ **skilled** *adj*

▎**SPELLING TIP**
▎When you make an adjective

**S**

from **skill**, you should drop an l to make **skilful**. American English keeps the double l in this case

**skillet** n small frying pan or shallow cooking pot

**skim** v **skimming, skimmed** remove floating matter from the surface of (a liquid); glide smoothly over; read quickly ▶ **skimmed milk, skim milk** milk from which the cream has been removed

**skimp** v not invest enough time, money, material, etc. ▶ **skimpy** adj scanty or insufficient

**skin** n outer covering of the body; complexion; outer layer or covering; film on a liquid; animal skin used as a material or container ▶ v **skinning, skinned** remove the skin of ▶ **skinless** adj ▶ **skinny** adj thin ▶ **skin-deep** adj superficial ▶ **skin diving** underwater swimming using flippers and light breathing apparatus ▶ **skin-diver** n ▶ **skinflint** n miser ▶ **skinhead** n youth with very short hair

**skint** adj (Brit slang) having no money

**skip**¹ v **skipping, skipped** leap lightly from one foot to the other; jump over a rope as it is swung under one; (informal) pass over, omit ▶ n skipping

**skip**² n large open container for builders' rubbish

**skipper** n, v captain

**skirl** n sound of bagpipes

**skirmish** n brief or minor fight or argument ▶ v take part in a skirmish

**skirt** n woman's garment hanging from the waist; part of a dress or coat below the waist; cut of beef from the flank ▶ v border; go round; avoid dealing with (an issue) ▶ **skirting board** narrow board round the bottom of an interior wall

**skit** n brief satirical sketch

**skite** v, n (Aust & NZ) boast

**skittish** adj playful or lively

**skittle** n bottle-shaped object used as a target in some games ▶ pl game in which players try to knock over skittles by rolling a ball at them

**skive** v (Brit informal) evade work or responsibility

**skivvy** n, pl **-vies** (Brit) female servant who does menial work

**skua** n large predatory gull

**skulduggery** n (informal) trickery

**skulk** v move stealthily; lurk

**skull** n bony framework of the head ▶ **skullcap** n close-fitting brimless cap

**skunk** n small black-and-white N American mammal which emits a foul-smelling fluid when attacked; (slang) despicable person

**sky** n, pl **skies** upper atmosphere as seen from the earth ▶ **skydiving** n sport of jumping from an aircraft and performing manoeuvres before opening one's parachute ▶ **skylark** n lark that sings while soaring at a great height ▶ **skylight** n window in a roof or ceiling ▶ **skyscraper** n very tall building

**Skype**® n software application that allows users to make voice and video calls over the Internet

**slab** n broad flat piece

**slack** adj not tight; negligent; not busy ▶ n slack part ▶ pl informal trousers ▶ v neglect one's work or duty ▶ **slackness** n ▶ **slacken** v make or become slack ▶ **slacker** n lazy person

**slag** n waste left after metal is smelted ▶ v **slagging, slagged** (foll by off) (Brit, Aust & NZ slang) criticize

S

**slain** v past participle of **slay**

**slake** v satisfy (thirst or desire); combine (quicklime) with water

**slalom** n skiing or canoeing race over a winding course

**slam** v **slamming, slammed** shut, put down, or hit violently and noisily; (informal) criticize harshly ▷ n act or sound of slamming **grand slam** see **grand**

**slander** n false and malicious statement about a person; crime of making such a statement ▷ v utter slander about ▶ **slanderous** adj

**slang** n very informal language ▶ **slangy** adj ▶ **slanging match** abusive argument

**slant** v lean at an angle, slope; present (information) in a biased way ▷ n slope; point of view, esp. a biased one ▶ **slanting** adj

**slap** n blow with the open hand or a flat object ▷ v **slapping, slapped** strike with the open hand or a flat object; (informal) place forcefully or carelessly ▶ **slapdash** adj careless and hasty ▶ **slaphappy** adj (informal) cheerfully careless ▶ **slapstick** n boisterous knockabout comedy ▶ **slap-up** adj (of a meal) large and luxurious

**slash** v cut with a sweeping stroke; gash; reduce drastically ▷ n sweeping stroke; gash

**slat** n narrow strip of wood or metal

**slate**[1] n rock which splits easily into thin layers; piece of this for covering a roof or, formerly, for writing on

**slate**[2] v (informal) criticize harshly

**slattern** n (old-fashioned) slovenly woman ▶ **slatternly** adj

**slaughter** v kill (animals) for food; kill (people) savagely or indiscriminately ▷ n slaughtering ▶ **slaughterhouse** n place where animals are killed for food

**Slav** n member of any of the peoples of E Europe or the former Soviet Union who speak a Slavonic language ▶ **Slavonic** n language group including Russian, Polish, and Czech ▷ adj of this language group

**slave** n person owned by another for whom he or she has to work; person dominated by another or by a habit; drudge ▷ v work like a slave ▶ **slaver** n person or ship engaged in the slave trade ▶ **slavery** n state or condition of being a slave; practice of owning slaves ▶ **slavish** adj of or like a slave; imitative ▶ **slave-driver** n person who makes others work very hard

**slaver** [slav-ver] v dribble saliva from the mouth

**slay** v **slaying, slew, slain** kill

**sleazy** adj **-zier, -ziest** run-down or sordid ▶ **sleaze** n

**sledge**[1], **sled** n carriage on runners for sliding on snow; light wooden frame for sliding over snow ▷ v travel by sledge

**sledge**[2], **sledgehammer** n heavy hammer with a long handle

**sleek** adj glossy, smooth, and shiny

**sleep** n state of rest characterized by unconsciousness; period of this ▷ v **sleeping, slept** be in or as if in a state of sleep; have sleeping accommodation for (a specified number) ▶ **sleeper** n railway car fitted for sleeping in; beam supporting the rails of a railway; ring worn in a pierced ear to stop the hole from closing up; person who sleeps ▶ **sleepy** adj ▶ **sleepily** adv ▶ **sleepiness** n ▶ **sleepless** adj ▶ **sleeping bag** padded bag for sleeping in ▶ **sleeping sickness** African disease spread by the tsetse fly ▶ **sleepout** n (NZ) small building for sleeping in ▶ **sleepover** n

S

occasion when a person stays overnight at a friend's house ▸ **sleep with, sleep together** v have sexual intercourse (with)

**sleet** n rain and snow or hail falling together

**sleeve** n part of a garment which covers the arm; tubelike cover; gramophone record cover **up one's sleeve** secretly ready ▸ **sleeveless** adj

**sleigh** n, v sledge

**sleight of hand** [slite] n skilful use of the hands when performing conjuring tricks

**slender** adj slim; small in amount

**slept** v past of **sleep**

**sleuth** [slooth] n detective

**slew¹** v past tense of **slay**

**slew²** v twist or swing round

**slice** n thin flat piece cut from something; share; kitchen tool with a broad flat blade; (Sport) hitting of a ball so that it travels obliquely ▸ v cut into slices; (Sport) hit (a ball) with a slice

**slick** adj persuasive and glib; skilfully devised or carried out; well-made and attractive, but superficial ▸ n patch of oil on water ▸ v make smooth or sleek

**slide** v **sliding, slid** slip smoothly along (a surface); pass unobtrusively ▸ n sliding; piece of glass holding an object to be viewed under a microscope; photographic transparency; surface or structure for sliding on or down; ornamental hair clip ▸ **slide rule** mathematical instrument formerly used for rapid calculations ▸ **sliding scale** variable scale according to which things such as wages alter in response to changes in other factors

**slight** adj small in quantity or extent; not important; slim and delicate ▸ v, n snub ▸ **slightly** adv

**slim** adj **slimmer, slimmest** not heavy or stout, thin; slight ▸ v **slimming, slimmed** make or become slim by diet and exercise ▸ **slimmer** n

**slime** n unpleasant thick slippery substance ▸ **slimy** adj of, like, or covered with slime; ingratiating

**sling¹** n bandage hung from the neck to support an injured hand or arm; rope or strap for lifting something; strap with a string at each end for throwing a stone ▸ v **slinging, slung** throw; carry, hang, or throw with or as if with a sling

**sling²** n sweetened drink with a spirit base e.g. gin sling

**slink** v **slinking, slunk** move furtively or guiltily ▸ **slinky** adj (of clothes) figure-hugging

**slip¹** v **slipping, slipped** lose balance by sliding; move smoothly, easily, or quietly; (foll by on or off) put on or take off easily or quickly; pass out of (the mind) ▸ n slipping; mistake; petticoat **give someone the slip** escape from someone ▸ **slippy** adj (informal) slippery ▸ **slipknot** n knot tied so that it will slip along the rope round which it is made ▸ **slipped disc** painful condition in which one of the discs connecting the bones of the spine becomes displaced ▸ **slip road** narrow road giving access to a motorway ▸ **slipshod** adj (of an action) careless ▸ **slipstream** n stream of air forced backwards by a fast-moving object ▸ **slip up** v make a mistake ▸ **slipway** n launching slope on which ships are built or repaired

**slip²** n small piece (of paper)

**slip³** n clay mixed with water used for decorating pottery

**slipper** n light shoe for indoor wear

**slippery** adj so smooth or wet as to cause slipping or be difficult to hold; (of a person) untrustworthy

**slit** n long narrow cut or opening ▷ v **slitting, slit** make a long straight cut in

**slither** v slide unsteadily

**sliver** [**sliv-ver**] n small thin piece

**slob** n (informal) lazy and untidy person ▶ **slobbish** adj

**slobber** v dribble or drool ▶ **slobbery** adj

**sloe** n sour blue-black fruit

**slog** v **slogging, slogged** work hard and steadily; make one's way with difficulty; hit hard ▷ n long and exhausting work or walk

**slogan** n catchword or phrase used in politics or advertising

**sloop** n small single-masted ship

**slop** v **slopping, slopped** splash or spill ▷ n spilt liquid; liquid food ▷ pl liquid refuse and waste food used to feed animals ▶ **sloppy** adj careless or untidy; gushingly sentimental

**slope** v slant ▷ n sloping surface; degree of inclination ▷ pl hills ▶ **slope off** v (informal) go furtively

**slosh** v splash carelessly; (slang) hit hard ▷ n splashing sound ▶ **sloshed** adj (slang) drunk

**slot** n narrow opening for inserting something; (informal) place in a series or scheme ▷ v **slotting, slotted** make a slot or slots in; fit into a slot ▶ **slot machine** automatic machine worked by placing a coin in a slot

**sloth** [rhymes with **both**] n slow-moving animal of tropical America; laziness ▶ **slothful** adj lazy or idle

**slouch** v sit, stand, or move with a drooping posture ▷ n drooping posture **be no slouch** (informal) be very good or talented

**slough¹** [rhymes with **now**] n bog

**slough²** [**sluff**] v (of a snake) shed (its skin) or (of a skin) be shed ▶ **slough off** v get rid of (something unwanted or unnecessary)

**sloven** n habitually dirty or untidy person ▶ **slovenly** adj dirty or untidy; careless

**Slovene** adj, n (also **Slovenian**) (person) from Slovenia ▷ n language of Slovenia

**slow** adj taking a longer time than is usual or expected; not fast; (of a clock or watch) showing a time earlier than the correct one; stupid ▷ v reduce the speed (of) ▶ **slowly** adv ▶ **slowness** n ▶ **slowcoach** n (informal) person who moves or works slowly

**slowworm** n small legless lizard

**sludge** n thick mud; sewage

**slug¹** n land snail with no shell ▶ **sluggish** adj slow-moving, lacking energy ▶ **sluggishly** adv ▶ **sluggishness** n ▶ **sluggard** n lazy person

**slug²** n bullet; (informal) mouthful of an alcoholic drink

**slug³** v **slugging, slugged** hit hard ▷ n heavy blow

**sluice** n channel carrying off water; sliding gate used to control the flow of water in this; water controlled by a sluice ▷ v pour a stream of water over or through

**slum** n squalid overcrowded house or area ▷ v **slumming, slummed** temporarily and deliberately experience poorer places or conditions than usual

**slumber** v, n (lit) sleep

**slump** v (of prices or demand) decline suddenly; sink or fall heavily ▷ n sudden decline in prices or demand; time of substantial unemployment

**slung** v past of **sling¹**

**slunk** v past of **slink**

S

**slur** v **slurring, slurred** pronounce or utter (words) indistinctly; (*Music*) sing or play (notes) smoothly without a break ▷ n slurring of words; remark intended to discredit someone; (*Music*) slurring of notes; curved line indicating notes to be slurred

**slurp** (*informal*) v eat or drink noisily ▷ n slurping sound

**slurry** n, pl **-ries** muddy liquid mixture

**slush** n watery muddy substance; sloppy sentimental talk or writing ▶ **slushy** adj ▶ **slush fund** fund for financing bribery or corruption

**slut** n (*offens*) dirty or immoral woman ▶ **sluttish** adj

**sly** adj **slyer, slyest** or **slier, sliest** crafty; secretive and cunning; roguish **on the sly** secretly ▶ **slyly** adv ▶ **slyness** n

**smack¹** v slap sharply; open and close (the lips) loudly in enjoyment or anticipation ▷ n sharp slap; loud kiss; slapping sound ▷ adv (*informal*) squarely or directly e.g. *smack in the middle* ▶ **smacker** n (*slang*) loud kiss

**smack²** n slight flavour or trace; (*slang*) heroin ▷ v have a slight flavour or trace (of)

**smack³** n small single-masted fishing boat

**small** adj not large in size, number, or amount; unimportant; mean or petty ▷ n narrow part of the lower back ▷ pl (*informal*) underwear ▶ **smallness** n ▶ **smallholding** n small area of farming land ▶ **small hours** hours just after midnight ▶ **small-minded** adj intolerant, petty ▶ **smallpox** n contagious disease with blisters that leave scars ▶ **small talk** light social conversation ▶ **small-time** adj insignificant or minor

**smarmy** adj **smarmier, smarmiest** (*informal*) unpleasantly suave or flattering

**smart** adj well-kept and neat; astute; witty; fashionable; brisk; (of a system or machine) using computer technology ▷ v feel or cause stinging pain ▷ n stinging pain ▶ **smartly** adv ▶ **smartness** n ▶ **smarten** v make or become smart ▶ **smart aleck** (*informal*) irritatingly clever person ▶ **smartphone** n mobile phone allowing access to the internet

**smash** v break violently and noisily; throw (against) violently; collide forcefully; destroy ▷ n act or sound of smashing; violent collision of vehicles; (*informal*) popular success; (*Sport*) powerful overhead shot ▶ **smasher** n (*informal*) attractive person or thing ▶ **smashing** adj (*informal*) excellent

**smattering** n slight knowledge

**smear** v spread with a greasy or sticky substance; rub so as to produce a dirty mark or smudge; slander ▷ n dirty mark or smudge; slander; (*Med*) sample of a secretion smeared on to a slide for examination under a microscope

**smell** v **smelling, smelt** or **smelled** perceive (a scent or odour) by means of the nose; have or give off a smell; have an unpleasant smell; detect by instinct ▷ n ability to perceive odours by the nose; odour or scent; smelling ▶ **smelly** adj having a nasty smell ▶ **smelling salts** preparation of ammonia used to revive a person who feels faint

**smelt¹** v extract (a metal) from (an ore) by heating

**smelt²** n small fish of the salmon family

**smelt³** v a past of **smell**

**smelter** n industrial plant where smelting is carried out

S

**smile** n turning up of the corners of the mouth to show pleasure, amusement, or friendliness ▷ v give a smile ▸ **smiley** n symbol depicting a smile or other facial expression, used in e-mail ▸ **smile on, smile upon** v regard favourably

**smirch** v, n stain

**smirk** n smug smile ▷ v give a smirk

**smite** v **smiting, smote, smitten** (*old-fashioned*) strike hard; affect severely

**smith** n worker in metal ▸ **smithy** n blacksmith's workshop

**smithereens** pl n shattered fragments

**smitten** v past participle of **smite**

**smock** n loose overall; woman's loose blouselike garment ▷ v gather (material) by sewing in a honeycomb pattern ▸ **smocking** n

**smog** n mixture of smoke and fog

**smoke** n cloudy mass that rises from something burning; act of smoking tobacco ▷ v give off smoke; inhale and expel smoke of (a cigar, cigarette, or pipe); do this habitually; cure (meat, fish, or cheese) by treating with smoke ▸ **smokeless** adj ▸ **smoker** n ▸ **smoky** adj ▸ **smoke screen** something said or done to hide the truth

**smooch** (*informal*) v kiss and cuddle ▷ n smooching

**smooth** adj even in surface, texture, or consistency; without obstructions or difficulties; charming and polite but possibly insincere; free from jolts; not harsh in taste ▷ v make smooth; calm ▸ **smoothie** n (*informal*) charming but possibly insincere man; thick drink made from puréed fresh fruit ▸ **smoothly** adv

**smorgasbord** n buffet meal of assorted dishes

**smote** v past tense of **smite**

**smother** v suffocate or stifle; suppress; cover thickly

**smoulder** v burn slowly with smoke but no flame; (of feelings) exist in a suppressed state

**SMS** short message system: used for sending data to mobile phones

**smudge** v make or become smeared or soiled ▷ n dirty mark; blurred form ▸ **smudgy** adj

**smug** adj **smugger, smuggest** self-satisfied ▸ **smugly** adv ▸ **smugness** n

**smuggle** v import or export (goods) secretly and illegally; take somewhere secretly ▸ **smuggler** n

**smut** n obscene jokes, pictures, etc.; speck of soot or dark mark left by soot ▸ **smutty** adj

**snack** n light quick meal ▸ **snack bar** place where snacks are sold

**snaffle** n jointed bit for a horse ▷ v (*Brit, Aust & NZ slang*) steal

**snag** n difficulty or disadvantage; sharp projecting point; hole in fabric caused by a sharp object ▷ v **snagging, snagged** catch or tear on a point

**snail** n slow-moving mollusc with a spiral shell ▸ **snail mail** (*informal*) conventional post, as opposed to e-mail ▸ **snail's pace** very slow speed

**snake** n long thin scaly limbless reptile ▷ v move in a winding course like a snake **snake in the grass** treacherous person ▸ **snaky** adj twisted or winding

**snap** v **snapping, snapped** break suddenly; (cause to) make a sharp cracking sound; move suddenly; bite (at) suddenly; speak sharply and angrily; take a snapshot of ▷ n act or sound of snapping; (*informal*) snapshot; sudden brief spell of cold weather; card game in which the word 'snap' is called when two similar cards are put down ▷ *adj* made on the spur of the moment ▶ **snappy** *adj* (also **snappish**) irritable; (*slang*) quick; (*slang*) smart and fashionable ▶ **snapdragon** *n* plant with flowers that can open and shut like a mouth ▶ **snapper** *n* food fish of Australia and New Zealand with a pinkish body covered with blue spots ▶ **snapshot** *n* informal photograph ▶ **snap up** *v* take eagerly and quickly

**snare** *n* trap with a noose ▷ *v* catch in or as if in a snare

**snarl**[1] *v* (of an animal) growl with bared teeth; speak or utter fiercely ▷ *n* act or sound of snarling

**snarl**[2] *n* tangled mess ▷ *v* make tangled ▶ **snarl-up** *n* (*informal*) confused situation such as a traffic jam

**snatch** *v* seize or try to seize suddenly; take (food, rest, etc.) hurriedly ▷ *n* snatching; fragment

**snazzy** *adj* **-zier, -ziest** (*informal*) stylish and flashy

**sneak** *v* move furtively; bring, take, or put furtively; (*informal*) tell tales ▷ *n* cowardly or underhand person ▶ **sneaking** *adj* slight but persistent; secret ▶ **sneaky** *adj*

**sneakers** *pl n* canvas shoes with rubber soles

**sneer** *n* contemptuous expression or remark ▷ *v* show contempt by a sneer

**sneeze** *v* expel air from the nose suddenly, involuntarily, and noisily ▷ *n* act or sound of sneezing

**snib** *n* (*Scot & NZ*) catch of a door or window

**snicker** *n*, *v* same as **snigger**

**snide** *adj* critical in an unfair and nasty way

**sniff** *v* inhale through the nose in short audible breaths; smell by

sniffing ▷ *n* act or sound of sniffing ▶ **sniffle** *v* sniff repeatedly, as when suffering from a cold ▷ *n* slight cold ▶ **sniff at** *v* express contempt for ▶ **sniffer dog** police dog trained to detect drugs or explosives by smell

**snifter** *n* (*informal*) small quantity of alcoholic drink

**snigger** *n* sly disrespectful laugh, esp. one partly stifled ▷ *v* utter a snigger

**snip** *v* **snipping, snipped** cut in small quick strokes with scissors or shears ▷ *n* (*informal*) bargain; act or sound of snipping ▶ **snippet** *n* small piece

**snipe** *n* wading bird with a long straight bill ▷ *v* (foll by *at*) shoot at (a person) from cover; make critical remarks about

**sniper** *n* person who shoots at someone from cover

**snitch** (*informal*) *v* act as an informer; steal ▷ *n* informer

**snivel** *v* **-elling, -elled** cry in a whining way

**snob** *n* person who judges others by social rank; person who feels smugly superior in his or her tastes or interests ▶ **snobbery** *n* ▶ **snobbish** *adj*

**snoek** *n* (*S Afr*) edible marine fish

**snog** *v* **snogging, snogged** (*Brit, NZ & S Afr informal*) kiss and cuddle

**snood** *n* pouch, often of net, loosely holding a woman's hair at the back

**snook** *n* **cock a snook at** show contempt for

**snooker** *n* game played on a billiard table ▷ *v* leave (a snooker opponent) in a position such that another ball blocks the target ball; (*informal*) put (someone) in a position where he or she can do nothing

**snoop** (*informal*) *v* pry ▷ *n* snooping ▶ **snooper** ▷ *n*

**snooty** adj **snootier, snootiest** (informal) haughty

**snooze** (informal) v take a brief light sleep ▷ n brief light sleep

**snore** v make snorting sounds while sleeping ▷ n sound of snoring

**snorkel** n tube allowing a swimmer to breathe while face down on the surface of the water ▷ v **-kelling, -kelled** swim using a snorkel

**snort** v exhale noisily through the nostrils; express contempt or anger by snorting ▷ n act or sound of snorting

**snot** n (slang) mucus from the nose

**snout** n animal's projecting nose and jaws

**snow** n frozen vapour falling from the sky in flakes; (slang) cocaine ▷ v fall as or like snow **be snowed under** be overwhelmed, esp. with paperwork ▶ **snowy** adj ▶ **snowball** n snow pressed into a ball for throwing ▷ v increase rapidly ▶ **snowboard** n board on which a person stands to slide across the snow ▶ **snowboarding** n ▶ **snowdrift** n bank of deep snow ▶ **snowdrop** n small white bell-shaped spring flower ▶ **snowflake** n single crystal of snow ▶ **snow gum** same as **sallee** ▶ **snow line** (on a mountain) height above which there is permanent snow ▶ **snowman** n figure shaped out of snow ▶ **snowplough** n vehicle for clearing away snow ▶ **snowshoes** pl n racket-shaped shoes for walking on deep snow

**snub** v **snubbing, snubbed** insult deliberately ▷ n deliberate insult ▷ adj (of a nose) short and blunt ▶ **snub-nosed** adj

**snuff**[1] n powdered tobacco for sniffing up the nostrils

**snuff**[2] v extinguish (a candle) **snuff it** (informal) die

**snuffle** v breathe noisily or with difficulty

**snug** adj **snugger, snuggest** warm and comfortable; comfortably close-fitting ▷ n (in Britain and Ireland) small room in a pub ▶ **snugly** adv

**snuggle** v nestle into a person or thing for warmth or from affection

**so** adv to such an extent; in such a manner; very; also; thereupon ▷ conj in order that; with the result that; therefore ▷ interj exclamation of surprise, triumph, or realization **so that** in order that ▶ **so-and-so** n (informal) person whose name is not specified; unpleasant person or thing ▶ **so-called** adj called (in the speaker's opinion, wrongly) by that name ▶ **so long** goodbye

**soak** v make wet; put or lie in liquid so as to become thoroughly wet; (of liquid) penetrate ▷ n soaking; (slang) drunkard ▶ **soaking** n, adj ▶ **soak up** v absorb

**soap** n compound of alkali and fat, used with water as a cleaning agent; (informal) soap opera ▷ v apply soap to ▶ **soapy** adj ▶ **soap opera** radio or television serial dealing with domestic themes

**soar** v rise or fly upwards; increase suddenly

**sob** v **sobbing, sobbed** weep with convulsive gasps; utter with sobs ▷ n act or sound of sobbing ▶ **sob story** tale of personal distress told to arouse sympathy

**sober** adj not drunk; serious; (of colours) plain and dull ▷ v make or become sober ▶ **soberly** adv ▶ **sobriety** n state of being sober

**sobriquet** [so-brik-ay] n nickname

**soccer** n football played by two teams of eleven kicking a spherical ball

**sociable** adj friendly or companionable; (of an occasion)

S

providing companionship
▶ **sociability** n ▶ **sociably** adv
**social** adj living in a community; of
society or its organization; sociable
▷ n informal gathering ▶ **socially**
adv ▶ **socialite** n member of
fashionable society ▶ **socialize** v
meet others socially ▶ **social
media** websites and applications
that allow users to interact
▶ **social networking site** website
that allows subscribers to interact,
esp. by forming online communities
based around shared interests,
experiences, etc. ▶ **social security**
state provision for the unemployed,
elderly, or sick ▶ **social services**
welfare services provided by local
authorities or the state ▶ **social
work** work which involves helping
or advising people with serious
financial or family problems
**socialism** n political system which
advocates public ownership
of industries, resources, and
transport ▶ **socialist** n, adj
**society** n, pl **-ties** human beings
considered as a group; organized
community; structure and
institutions of such a community;
organized group with common
aims and interests; upper-class or
fashionable people collectively;
companionship
**sociology** n study of human
societies ▶ **sociological** adj
▶ **sociologist** n
**sock¹** n knitted covering for the foot
**sock²** (slang) v hit hard ▷ n hard blow
**socket** n hole or recess into which
something fits
**sod¹** n (piece of) turf
**sod²** n (slang) obnoxious person
**soda** n compound of sodium;
soda water ▶ **soda water** fizzy
drink made from water charged
with carbon dioxide

**sodden** adj soaked
**sodium** n (Chem) silvery-white
metallic element ▶ **sodium
bicarbonate** white soluble
compound used in baking powder
▶ **sodium chloride** common table
salt ▶ **sodium hydroxide** white
alkaline substance used in making
paper and soap
**sodomy** n anal intercourse
▶ **sodomite** n person who
practises sodomy
**sofa** n couch
**soft** adj easy to shape or cut; not
hard, rough, or harsh; (of a breeze
or climate) mild; (too) lenient;
easily influenced or imposed
upon; (of drugs) not liable to cause
addiction ▶ **softly** adv ▶ **soften**
v make or become soft or softer
▶ **soft drink** nonalcoholic drink
▶ **soft furnishings** curtains, rugs,
lampshades, and furniture covers
▶ **soft option** easiest alternative
▶ **soft-pedal** v deliberately avoid
emphasizing something ▶ **soft-
soap** v (informal) flatter ▶ **software**
n computer programs ▶ **softwood**
n wood of a coniferous tree
**soggy** adj **-gier, -giest** soaked;
moist and heavy ▶ **sogginess** n
**soigné,** (fem) **soignée** [swah-nyay]
adj well-groomed, elegant
**soil¹** n top layer of earth; country
or territory
**soil²** v make or become dirty;
disgrace
**soiree** [swah-ray] n evening party
or gathering
**sojourn** [soj-urn] n temporary stay
▷ v stay temporarily
**solace** [sol-iss] n, v comfort in
distress
**solar** adj of the sun; using the
energy of the sun ▶ **solar plexus**
network of nerves at the pit of the
stomach; this part of the stomach

▶ **solar system** the sun and the heavenly bodies that go round it

**solarium** *n, pl* **-lariums** *or* **-laria** place with beds and ultraviolet lights used for acquiring an artificial suntan

**sold** *v* past of **sell**

**solder** *n* soft alloy used to join two metal surfaces ▷ *v* join with solder ▶ **soldering iron** tool for melting and applying solder

**soldier** *n* member of an army ▷ *v* serve in an army ▶ **soldierly** *adj* ▶ **soldier on** *v* persist doggedly

**sole¹** *adj* one and only; not shared, exclusive ▶ **solely** *adv* only, completely; alone ▶ **sole charge school** (*NZ*) country school with only one teacher

**sole²** *n* underside of the foot; underside of a shoe ▷ *v* provide (a shoe) with a sole

**sole³** *n* small edible flatfish

**solecism** [sol-iss-izz-um] *n* minor grammatical mistake; breach of etiquette

**solemn** *adj* serious, deeply sincere; formal ▶ **solemnly** *adv* ▶ **solemnity** *n*

**solenoid** [**sole**-in-oid] *n* coil of wire magnetized by passing a current through it

**sol-fa** *n* system of syllables used as names for the notes of a scale

**solicit** *v*-**iting, -ited** request; (of a prostitute) offer (a person) sex for money ▶ **solicitation** *n*

**solicitor** *n* (*Brit, Aust & NZ*) lawyer who advises clients and prepares documents and cases

**solicitous** *adj* anxious about someone's welfare ▶ **solicitude** *n*

**solid** *adj* (of a substance) keeping its shape; not liquid or gas; not hollow; of the same substance throughout; strong or substantial; sound or reliable; having three dimensions ▷ *n* three-dimensional shape; solid substance ▶ **solidly** *adv* ▶ **solidify** *v* make or become solid or firm ▶ **solidity** *n*

**solidarity** *n* agreement in aims or interests, total unity

**soliloquy** *n, pl* **-quies** speech made by a person while alone, esp. in a play

**solipsism** *n* doctrine that the self is the only thing known to exist ▶ **solipsist** *n*

**solitaire** *n* game for one person played with pegs set in a board; gem set by itself

**solitary** *adj* alone, single; (of a place) lonely ▶ **solitude** *n* state of being alone

**solo** *n, pl* **-los** music for one performer; any act done without assistance ▷ *adj* done alone ▷ *adv* by oneself, alone ▶ **soloist** *n* ▶ **solo parent** (*NZ*) parent bringing up a child or children alone

**solstice** *n* either the shortest (in winter) or longest (in summer) day of the year

**soluble** *adj* able to be dissolved; able to be solved ▶ **solubility** *n*

**solution** *n* answer to a problem; act of solving a problem; liquid with something dissolved in it; process of dissolving

**solve** *v* find the answer to (a problem) ▶ **solvable** *adj*

**solvent** *adj* having enough money to pay one's debts ▷ *n* liquid capable of dissolving other substances ▶ **solvency** *n* ▶ **solvent abuse** deliberate inhaling of intoxicating fumes from certain solvents

**sombre** *adj* dark, gloomy

**sombrero** *n, pl* **-ros** wide-brimmed Mexican hat

**some** *adj* unknown or unspecified; unknown or unspecified quantity

**S**

or number of; considerable number or amount of; (*informal*) remarkable ▷ *pron* certain unknown or unspecified people or things; unknown or unspecified number or quantity ▶ **somebody** *pron* some person ▷ *n* important person ▶ **somehow** *adv* in some unspecified way ▶ **someone** *pron* somebody ▶ **something** *pron* unknown or unspecified thing or amount; impressive or important thing ▶ **sometime** *adv* at some unspecified time ▷ *adj* former ▶ **sometimes** *adv* from time to time, now and then ▶ **somewhat** *adv* to some extent, rather ▶ **somewhere** *adv* in, to, or at some unspecified or unknown place

**somersault** *n* leap or roll in which the trunk and legs are turned over the head ▷ *v* perform a somersault

**somnambulist** *n* person who walks in his or her sleep ▶ **somnambulism** *n*

**somnolent** *adj* drowsy

**son** *n* male offspring ▶ **son-in-law** *n*, *pl* **sons-in-law** husband of one's child

**sonar** *n* device for detecting underwater objects by the reflection of sound waves

**sonata** *n* piece of music in several movements for one instrument with or without piano

**son et lumière** [sawn eh loo-mee-er] *n* (*French*) night-time entertainment with lighting and sound effects, telling the story of the place where it is staged

**song** *n* music for the voice; tuneful sound made by certain birds; singing **for a song** very cheaply ▶ **songster, songstress** *n* singer ▶ **songbird** *n* any bird with a musical call

**sonic** *adj* of or producing sound ▶ **sonic boom** loud bang caused by an aircraft flying faster than the speed of sound

**sonnet** *n* fourteen-line poem with a fixed rhyme scheme

**sonorous** *adj* (of sound) deep or resonant ▶ **sonorously** *adv* ▶ **sonority** *n*

**soon** *adv* in a short time

**sooner** *adv* rather e.g. *I'd sooner go alone* **sooner or later** eventually

**soot** *n* black powder formed by the incomplete burning of an organic substance ▶ **sooty** *adj*

**soothe** *v* make calm; relieve (pain etc.)

**soothsayer** *n* seer or prophet

**sop** *n* concession to pacify someone ▷ *v* **sopping, sopped** mop up or absorb (liquid) ▶ **sopping** *adj* completely soaked ▶ **soppy** *adj* (*informal*) oversentimental

**sophist** *n* person who uses clever but invalid arguments

**sophisticate** *v* make less natural or innocent; make more complex or refined ▷ *n* sophisticated person

**sophisticated** *adj* having or appealing to refined or cultured tastes and habits; complex and refined ▶ **sophistication** *n*

**sophistry, sophism** *n* clever but invalid argument

**sophomore** *n* (*US*) student in second year at college

**soporific** *adj* causing sleep ▷ *n* drug that causes sleep

**soprano** *n*, *pl* **-pranos** (singer with) the highest female or boy's voice; highest pitched of a family of instruments

**sorbet** *n* flavoured water ice

**sorcerer** *n* magician ▶ **sorceress** *n fem* ▶ **sorcery** *n* witchcraft or magic

**sordid** *adj* dirty, squalid; base, vile; selfish and grasping ▶ **sordidly** *adv* ▶ **sordidness** *n*

**S**

**sore** _adj_ painful; causing annoyance; resentful; (of need) urgent ▷ _n_ painful area on the body ▷ _adv (obs)_ greatly ▶ **sorely** _adv_ greatly ▶ **soreness** _n_

**sorghum** _n_ kind of grass cultivated for grain

**sorrel** _n_ bitter-tasting plant

**sorrow** _n_ grief or sadness; cause of sorrow ▷ _v_ grieve ▶ **sorrowful** _adj_ ▶ **sorrowfully** _adv_

**sorry** _adj_ -**rier, -riest** feeling pity or regret; pitiful or wretched

**sort** _n_ group all sharing certain qualities or characteristics; _(informal)_ type of character ▷ _v_ arrange according to kind; mend or fix **out of sorts** slightly unwell or bad-tempered

> **USAGE NOTE**
> Note the singular/plural usage: _this_ (or _that_) _sort of thing; these_ (or _those_) _sorts of thing._ In the second, plural example you can also say _these sorts of things_

**sortie** _n_ relatively short return trip; operational flight made by military aircraft

**SOS** _n_ international code signal of distress; call for help

**so-so** _adj (informal)_ mediocre

**sot** _n_ habitual drunkard

**sotto voce** [sot-toe **voe**-chay] _adv_ in an undertone

**soubriquet** [so-brik-ay] _n_ same as **sobriquet**

**soufflé** [soo-**flay**] _n_ light fluffy dish made with beaten egg whites and other ingredients

**sough** [rhymes with **now**] _v_ (of the wind) make a sighing sound

**sought** [sawt] _v_ past of **seek**

**souk** [sook] _n_ marketplace in Muslim countries, often open-air

**soul** _n_ spiritual and immortal part of a human being; essential part or fundamental nature; deep and

sincere feelings; person regarded as typifying some quality; person; type of Black music combining blues, pop, and gospel ▶ **soulful** _adj_ full of emotion ▶ **soulless** _adj_ lacking human qualities, mechanical; (of a person) lacking sensitivity

**sound**[1] _n_ something heard, noise ▷ _v_ make or cause to make a sound; seem to be as specified; pronounce ▶ **sound barrier** _(informal)_ sudden increase in air resistance against an object as it approaches the speed of sound ▶ **sound bite** short pithy sentence or phrase extracted from a longer speech, esp. by a politician, for use on television or radio ▶ **soundproof** _adj_ not penetrable by sound ▷ _v_ make soundproof ▶ **soundtrack** _n_ recorded sound accompaniment to a film

**sound**[2] _adj_ in good condition; firm, substantial; financially reliable; showing good judgment; ethically correct; (of sleep) deep; thorough ▶ **soundly** _adv_

**sound**[3] _v_ find the depth of (water etc.); examine (the body) by tapping or with a stethoscope; ascertain the views of ▶ **soundings** _pl n_ measurements of depth taken by sounding ▶ **sounding board** person or group used to test a new idea

**sound**[4] _n_ channel or strait

**soup** _n_ liquid food made from meat, vegetables, etc. ▶ **soupy** _adj_ ▶ **soup kitchen** place where food and drink is served to needy people ▶ **souped-up** _adj_ (of an engine) adjusted so as to be more powerful than normal

**soupçon** [soop-**sonn**] _n_ small amount

**sour** _adj_ sharp-tasting; (of milk) gone bad; (of a person's temperament) sullen ▷ v make or become sour ▶ **sourly** adv ▶ **sourness** n

**source** n origin or starting point; person, book, etc. providing information; spring where a river or stream begins

**souse** v plunge (something) into liquid; drench; pickle

**soutane** [soo-**tan**] n Roman Catholic priest's cassock

**south** n direction towards the South Pole, opposite north; area lying in or towards the south ▷ adj to or in the south; (of a wind) from the south ▷ adv in, to, or towards the south ▶ **southerly** adj ▶ **southern** adj ▶ **southerner** n person from the south of a country or area ▶ **southward** adj, adv ▶ **southwards** adv ▶ **southpaw** n (informal) left-handed person, esp. a boxer ▶ **South Pole** southernmost point on the earth's axis

**souvenir** n keepsake, memento

**sou'wester** n seaman's waterproof hat covering the head and back of the neck

**sovereign** n king or queen; former British gold coin worth one pound ▷ adj (of a state) independent; supreme in rank or authority; excellent ▶ **sovereignty** n

**soviet** n formerly, elected council at various levels of government in the USSR ▷ adj (**S-**) of the former USSR

**sow¹** [rhymes with **know**] v **sowing, sowed, sown** or **sowed** scatter or plant (seed) in or on (the ground); implant or introduce

**sow²** [rhymes with **cow**] n female adult pig

**soya** n plant whose edible bean (**soya bean**) is used for food and as a source of oil ▶ **soy sauce** sauce made from fermented soya beans, used in Chinese and Japanese cookery

**sozzled** adj (Brit, Aust & NZ slang) drunk

**spa** n resort with a mineral-water spring

**space** n unlimited expanse in which all objects exist and move; interval; blank portion; unoccupied area; the universe beyond the earth's atmosphere ▷ v place at intervals ▶ **spacious** adj having a large capacity or area ▶ **spacecraft, spaceship** n vehicle for travel beyond the earth's atmosphere ▶ **space shuttle** manned reusable vehicle for repeated space flights ▶ **spacesuit** n sealed pressurized suit worn by an astronaut

**spade¹** n tool for digging ▶ **spadework** n hard preparatory work

**spade²** n playing card of the suit marked with black leaf-shaped symbols

**spaghetti** n pasta in the form of long strings

**spam** v **spamming, spammed** send unsolicited e-mail or text messages to multiple recipients ▷ n unsolicited e-mail or text messages sent in this way

**span** n space between two points; complete extent; distance from thumb to little finger of the expanded hand ▷ v **spanning, spanned** stretch or extend across

**spangle** n small shiny metallic ornament ▷ v decorate with spangles

**Spaniard** n person from Spain

**spaniel** n dog with long ears and silky hair

**Spanish** n official language of Spain and most countries of S and Central America ▷ adj of Spain or its language or people

**spank** v slap with the open hand, on the buttocks or legs ▷ n such a slap ▶ **spanking** n

**spanking** adj (informal) outstandingly fine or smart; quick

**spanner** n tool for gripping and turning a nut or bolt

**spar¹** n pole used as a ship's mast, boom, or yard

**spar²** v **sparring, sparred** box or fight using light blows for practice; argue (with someone)

**spare** adj extra; in reserve; (of a person) thin ▷ n duplicate kept in case of damage or loss ▷ v refrain from punishing or harming; protect (someone) from (something unpleasant); afford to give **to spare** in addition to what is needed ▶ **sparing** adj economical ▶ **spare ribs** pork ribs with most of the meat trimmed off

**spark** n fiery particle thrown out from a fire or caused by friction; flash of light produced by an electrical discharge; trace or hint (of a particular quality) ▷ v give off sparks; initiate ▶ **sparkie** n (NZ informal) electrician ▶ **spark plug** device in an engine that ignites the fuel by producing an electric spark

**sparkle** v glitter with many points of light; be vivacious or witty ▷ n sparkling points of light; vivacity or wit ▶ **sparkler** n hand-held firework that emits sparks ▶ **sparkling** adj (of wine or mineral water) slightly fizzy

**sparrow** n small brownish bird ▶ **sparrowhawk** n small hawk

**sparse** adj thinly scattered ▶ **sparsely** adv ▶ **sparseness** n

**spartan** adj strict and austere

**spasm** n involuntary muscular contraction; sudden burst of activity or feeling ▶ **spasmodic** adj occurring in spasms ▶ **spasmodically** adv

**spastic** n (offens) person with cerebral palsy ▷ adj (offens) suffering from cerebral palsy; affected by spasms

**spat¹** n slight quarrel

**spat²** v past of **spit¹**

**spate** n large number of things happening within a period of time; sudden outpouring or flood

**spatial** adj of or in space

**spats** pl n coverings formerly worn over the ankle and instep

**spatter** v scatter or be scattered in drops over (something) ▷ n spattering sound; something spattered

**spatula** n utensil with a broad flat blade for spreading or stirring

**spawn** n jelly-like mass of eggs of fish, frogs, or molluscs ▷ v (of fish, frogs, or molluscs) lay eggs; generate

**spay** v remove the ovaries from (a female animal)

**spaza shop** n (S Afr slang) small informal shop in a township

**speak** v **speaking, spoke, spoken** say words, talk; communicate or express in words; give a speech or lecture; know how to talk in (a specified language) ▶ **speaker** n person who speaks, esp. at a formal occasion; loudspeaker; (S-) official chairman of a body ▶ **speakerphone** n telephone with a microphone and loudspeaker allowing more than one person to participate in a call

**spear¹** n weapon consisting of a long shaft with a sharp point ▷ v pierce with or as if with a spear ▶ **spearhead** v lead (an attack or campaign) ▷ n leading force in an attack or campaign

**spear²** n slender shoot

**spearmint** n type of mint

**spec** n **on spec** (informal) as a risk or gamble

**special** adj distinguished from others of its kind; for a specific purpose; exceptional; particular ▸ **specially** adv ▸ **specialist** n expert in a particular activity or subject ▸ **speciality** n special interest or skill; product specialized in ▸ **specialize** v be a specialist ▸ **specialization** n

**specie** n coins as distinct from paper money

**species** n, pl -**cies** group of plants or animals that are related closely enough to interbreed naturally

**specific** adj particular, definite ▷ n drug used to treat a particular disease ▷ pl particular details ▸ **specifically** adv ▸ **specification** n detailed description of something to be made or done ▸ **specify** v refer to or state specifically ▸ **specific gravity** ratio of the density of a substance to that of water

**specimen** n individual or part typifying a whole; sample of blood etc. taken for analysis

**specious** [spee-shuss] adj apparently true, but actually false

**speck** n small spot or particle ▸ **speckle** n small spot ▷ v mark with speckles

**specs** pl n (informal) short for **spectacles**

**spectacle** n strange, interesting, or ridiculous sight; impressive public show ▷ pl pair of glasses for correcting faulty vision ▸ **spectacular** adj impressive ▷ n spectacular public show ▸ **spectacularly** adv

**spectator** n person viewing anything, onlooker ▸ **spectate** v watch

**spectre** n ghost; menacing mental image ▸ **spectral** adj

**spectroscope** n instrument for producing or examining spectra

**spectrum** n, pl -**tra** range of different colours, radio waves, etc. in order of their wavelengths; entire range of anything

**speculate** v guess, conjecture; buy property, shares, etc. in the hope of selling them at a profit ▸ **speculation** n ▸ **speculative** adj ▸ **speculator** n

**sped** v a past of **speed**

**speech** n act, power, or manner of speaking; talk given to an audience; language or dialect ▸ **speechless** adj unable to speak because of great emotion

**speed** n swiftness; rate at which something moves or acts; (slang) amphetamine ▷ v **speeding, sped** or **speeded** go quickly; drive faster than the legal limit ▸ **speedy** adj prompt; rapid ▸ **speedily** adv ▸ **speedboat** n light fast motorboat ▸ **speed camera** (Brit, Aust & NZ) camera for photographing vehicles breaking the speed limit ▸ **speed dating** dating method in which each participant engages in a timed chat with all the others in turn ▸ **speedometer** n instrument to show the speed of a vehicle ▸ **speed up** v accelerate ▸ **speedway** n track for motorcycle racing; (US, Canadian & NZ) track for motor racing ▸ **speedwell** n plant with small blue flowers

**speleology** n study and exploration of caves

**spell¹** v **spelling, spelt** or **spelled** give in correct order the letters that form (a word); (of letters) make up (a word); indicate ▸ **spelling** n way a word is spelt; person's ability to spell ▸ **spellchecker** n (Computing) program that highlights wrongly spelled words in a word-processed document ▸ **spell out** v make explicit

**spell²** n formula of words supposed to have magic power; effect of a spell; fascination ▶ **spellbound** adj entranced

**spell³** n period of time of weather or activity; (Scot, Aust & NZ) period of rest

**spelt** v a past of **spell¹**

**spend** v **spending, spent** pay out (money); use or pass (time); use up completely ▶ **spendthrift** n person who spends money wastefully

**sperm** n, pl **sperms** or **sperm** male reproductive cell; semen ▶ **spermicide** n substance that kills sperm ▶ **sperm whale** large toothed whale

**spermaceti** [sper-ma-**set**-ee] n waxy solid obtained from the sperm whale

**spermatozoon** [sper-ma-toe-**zoe**-on] n, pl **-zoa** sperm

**spew** v vomit; send out in a stream

**sphagnum** n moss found in bogs

**sphere** n perfectly round solid object; field of activity ▶ **spherical** adj

**sphincter** n ring of muscle which controls the opening and closing of a hollow organ

**Sphinx** n statue in Egypt with a lion's body and human head; (**s-**) enigmatic person

**spice** n aromatic substance used as flavouring; something that adds zest or interest ▷ v flavour with spices ▶ **spicy** adj flavoured with spices; (informal) slightly scandalous

**spick-and-span** adj neat and clean

**spider** n small eight-legged creature which spins a web to catch insects for food ▶ **spidery** adj

**spiel** n speech made to persuade someone to do something

**spigot** n stopper for, or tap fitted to, a cask

**spike** n sharp point; sharp pointed metal object ▷ pl sports shoes with spikes for greater grip ▷ v put spikes on; pierce or fasten with a spike; add alcohol to (a drink) **spike someone's guns** thwart someone ▶ **spiky** adj

**spill¹** v **spilling, spilt** or **spilled** pour from or as if from a container ▷ n fall; amount spilt **spill the beans** (informal) give away a secret ▶ **spillage** n

**spill²** n thin strip of wood or paper for lighting pipes or fires

**spin** v **spinning, spun** revolve or cause to revolve rapidly; draw out and twist (fibres) into thread; (informal) present information in a way that creates a favourable impression ▷ n revolving motion; continuous spiral descent of an aircraft; (informal) short drive for pleasure; (informal) presenting of information in a way that creates a favourable impression **spin a yarn** tell an improbable story ▶ **spinner** n ▶ **spin doctor** (informal) person who provides a favourable slant to a news item or policy on behalf of a politician or a political party ▶ **spin-dry** v dry (clothes) in a spin-dryer ▶ **spin-dryer** n machine in which washed clothes are spun in a perforated drum to remove excess water ▶ **spin-off** n incidental benefit ▶ **spin out** v prolong

**spina bifida** n condition in which part of the spinal cord protrudes through a gap in the backbone, often causing paralysis

**spinach** n dark green leafy vegetable

**spindle** n rotating rod that acts as an axle; weighted rod rotated for spinning thread by hand ▶ **spindly** adj long, slender, and frail

**spindrift** n spray blown up from the sea

S

**spine** n backbone; edge of a book on which the title is printed; sharp point on an animal or plant ▸ **spinal** adj of the spine ▸ **spineless** adj lacking courage ▸ **spiny** adj covered with spines

**spinet** n small harpsichord

**spinifex** n coarse spiny Australian grass

**spinnaker** n large sail on a racing yacht

**spinney** n (chiefly Brit) small wood

**spinster** n unmarried woman

**spiral** n continuous curve formed by a point winding about a central axis at an ever-increasing distance from it; same as **helix**; steadily accelerating increase or decrease ▷ v **-ralling, -ralled** move in a spiral; increase or decrease with steady acceleration ▷ adj having the form of a spiral

**spire** n pointed part of a steeple

**spirit**[1] n nonphysical aspect of a person concerned with profound thoughts; nonphysical part of a person believed to live on after death; courage and liveliness; essential meaning as opposed to literal interpretation; ghost ▷ pl emotional state ▷ v **-iting, -ited** carry away mysteriously ▸ **spirited** adj lively

**spirit**[2] n liquid obtained by distillation ▸ **spirit level** glass tube containing a bubble in liquid, used to check whether a surface is level

**spiritual** adj relating to the spirit; relating to sacred things ▷ n type of religious folk song originating among Black slaves in America ▸ **spiritually** adv ▸ **spirituality** n

**spiritualism** n belief that the spirits of the dead can communicate with the living ▸ **spiritualist** n

**spit**[1] v **spitting, spat** eject (saliva or food) from the mouth; throw out particles explosively; rain slightly; utter (words) in a violent manner ▷ n saliva ▸ **spitting image** (informal) person who looks very like another ▸ **spittle** n fluid produced in the mouth, saliva ▸ **spittoon** n bowl to spit into

**spit**[2] n sharp rod on which meat is skewered for roasting; long narrow strip of land jutting out into the sea

**spite** n deliberate nastiness ▷ v annoy or hurt from spite **in spite of** in defiance of ▸ **spiteful** adj ▸ **spitefully** adv

**spitfire** n person with a fiery temper

**spiv** n (Brit, Aust & NZ slang) smartly dressed man who makes a living by shady dealings

**splash** v scatter liquid on (something); scatter (liquid) or (of liquid) be scattered in drops; print (a story or photograph) prominently in a newspaper ▷ n splashing sound; patch (of colour or light); extravagant display; small amount of liquid added to a drink ▸ **splash out** v (informal) spend extravagantly

**splatter** v, n splash

**splay** v spread out, with ends spreading in different directions

**spleen** n abdominal organ which filters bacteria from the blood; bad temper ▸ **splenetic** adj spiteful or irritable

**splendid** adj excellent; brilliant in appearance ▸ **splendidly** adv ▸ **splendour** n

**splice** v join by interweaving or overlapping ends **get spliced** (slang) get married

**splint** n rigid support for a broken bone

**splinter** n thin sharp piece broken off, esp. from wood ▷ v break into fragments ▸ **splinter group** group that has broken away from an organization

**split** v **splitting, split** break into separate pieces; separate; share ▷ n crack or division caused by splitting ▷ pl act of sitting with the legs outstretched in opposite directions ▶ **split second** very short period of time

**splotch, splodge** n, v splash, daub

**splurge** v spend money extravagantly ▷ n bout of extravagance

**splutter** v utter with spitting or choking sounds; make hissing spitting sounds ▷ n spluttering

**spoil** v **spoiling, spoilt** or **spoiled** damage; harm the character of (a child) by giving it all it wants; rot, go bad **spoiling for** eager for ▶ **spoils** pl n booty ▶ **spoilsport** n person who spoils the enjoyment of others

**spoke**¹ v past tense of **speak**

**spoke**² n bar joining the hub of a wheel to the rim

**spoken** v past participle of **speak**

**spokesman, spokeswoman, spokesperson** n person chosen to speak on behalf of a group

**spoliation** n plundering

**sponge** n sea animal with a porous absorbent skeleton; skeleton of a sponge, or a substance like it, used for cleaning; type of light cake ▷ v wipe with a sponge; live at the expense of others ▶ **sponger** n (slang) person who sponges on others ▶ **spongy** adj

**sponsor** n person who promotes something; person who agrees to give money to a charity on completion of a specified activity by another; godparent ▷ v act as a sponsor for ▶ **sponsorship** n

**spontaneous** adj not planned or arranged; occurring through

natural processes without outside influence ▶ **spontaneously** adv ▶ **spontaneity** n

**spoof** n mildly satirical parody

**spook** n (informal) ghost ▶ **spooky** adj

**spool** n cylinder round which something can be wound

**spoon** n shallow bowl attached to a handle for eating, stirring, or serving food ▷ v lift with a spoon ▶ **spoonful** n ▶ **spoonbill** n wading bird of warm regions with a long flat bill ▶ **spoon-feed** v feed with a spoon; give (someone) too much help

**spoonerism** n accidental changing over of the initial sounds of a pair of words, such as half-warmed fish for half-formed wish

**spoor** n trail of an animal

**sporadic** adj intermittent, scattered ▶ **sporadically** adv

**spore** n minute reproductive body of some plants

**sporran** n pouch worn in front of a kilt

**sport** n activity for pleasure, competition, or exercise; such activities collectively; enjoyment; playful joking; person who reacts cheerfully ▷ v wear proudly ▶ **sporting** adj of sport; behaving in a fair and decent way **sporting chance** reasonable chance of success ▶ **sporty** adj ▶ **sportive** adj playful ▶ **sports car** fast low-built car, usu. open-topped ▶ **sports jacket** man's casual jacket ▶ **sportsman, sportswoman** n person who plays sports; person who plays fair and is good-humoured when losing ▶ **sportsmanlike** adj ▶ **sportsmanship** n

**spot** n small mark on a surface; pimple; location; (informal) small quantity; (*informal*) awkward situation ▷ v **spotting, spotted** notice; mark with spots; watch for and take note of **on the spot** at the place in question; immediately; in an awkward predicament ▶ **spotless** *adj* absolutely clean ▶ **spotlessly** *adv* ▶ **spotty** *adj* with spots ▶ **spot check** random examination ▶ **spotlight** *n* powerful light illuminating a small area; centre of attention ▶ **spot-on** *adj* (*informal*) absolutely accurate

**spouse** *n* husband or wife

**spout** *v* pour out in a stream or jet; (*slang*) utter (a stream of words) lengthily ▷ *n* projecting tube or lip for pouring liquids; stream or jet of liquid

**sprain** *v* injure (a joint) by a sudden twist ▷ *n* such an injury

**sprang** *v* a past tense of **spring**

**sprat** *n* small sea fish

**sprawl** *v* lie or sit with the limbs spread out; spread out in a straggling manner ▷ *n* part of a city that has spread untidily over a large area

**spray**[1] *n* (device for producing) fine drops of liquid ▷ *v* scatter in fine drops; cover with a spray ▶ **spray gun** device for spraying paint etc.

**spray**[2] *n* branch with buds, leaves, flowers, or berries; ornament like this

**spread** *v* **spreading, spread** open out or be displayed to the fullest extent; extend over a larger expanse; apply as a coating; send or be sent in all directions ▷ *n* spreading; extent; (*informal*) large meal; soft food which can be spread ▶ **spread-eagled** *adj* with arms and legs outstretched ▶ **spreadsheet** *n* computer program for manipulating figures

**spree** *n* session of overindulgence, usu. in drinking or spending money

**sprig** *n* twig or shoot; (*NZ*) stud on the sole of a soccer or rugby boot

**sprightly** *adj* **-lier, -liest** lively and brisk ▶ **sprightliness** *n*

**spring** *v* **springing, sprang** or **sprung, sprung** move suddenly upwards or forwards in a single motion, jump; develop unexpectedly; originate (from); (*informal*) arrange the escape of (someone) from prison ▷ *n* season between winter and summer; jump; coil which can be compressed, stretched, or bent and returns to its original shape when released; natural pool forming the source of a stream; elasticity ▶ **springy** *adj* elastic ▶ **springboard** *n* flexible board used to gain height or momentum in diving or gymnastics ▶ **spring-clean** *v* clean (a house) thoroughly ▶ **spring tide** high tide at new or full moon

**springbok** *n* S African antelope

**springer** *n* small spaniel

**sprinkle** *v* scatter (liquid or powder) in tiny drops or particles over (something) ▶ **sprinkler** *n* ▶ **sprinkling** *n* small quantity or number

**sprint** *n* short race run at top speed; fast run ▷ *v* run a short distance at top speed ▶ **sprinter** *n*

**sprite** *n* elf

**sprocket** *n* wheel with teeth on the rim, that drives or is driven by a chain

**sprout** *v* put forth shoots; begin to grow or develop ▷ *n* shoot; short for **Brussels sprout**

**spruce**[1] *n* kind of fir

**spruce**[2] *adj* neat and smart ▶ **spruce up** *v* make neat and smart

**sprung** v a past of **spring**

**spry** adj **spryer, spryest** or **sprier, spriest** active or nimble

**spud** n (informal) potato

**spume** n, v froth

**spun** v past of **spin**

**spunk** n (informal) courage, spirit ▶ **spunky** adj

**spur** n stimulus or incentive; spiked wheel on the heel of a rider's boot used to urge on a horse; projection ▷ v **spurring, spurred** urge on, incite (someone) **on the spur of the moment** on impulse

**spurge** n plant with milky sap

**spurious** adj not genuine

**spurn** v reject with scorn

**spurt** v gush or cause to gush out in a jet ▷ n short sudden burst of activity or speed; sudden gush

**sputnik** n early Soviet artificial satellite

**sputter** v, n splutter

**sputum** n, pl **-ta** spittle, usu. mixed with mucus

**spy** n, pl **spies** person employed to obtain secret information; person who secretly watches others ▷ v **spying, spied** act as a spy; catch sight of ▶ **spyware** n (Computing) software installed surreptitiously on a computer to collect and transmit data from that computer to another

**Sq.** Square

**squabble** v, n (engage in) a petty or noisy quarrel

**squad** n small group of people working or training together

**squadron** n division of an air force, fleet, or cavalry regiment

**squalid** adj dirty and unpleasant; morally sordid ▶ **squalor** n disgusting dirt and filth

**squall**[1] n sudden strong wind

**squall**[2] v cry noisily, yell ▷ n harsh cry

**squander** v waste (money or resources)

**square** n geometric figure with four equal sides and four right angles; open area in a town in this shape; product of a number multiplied by itself ▷ adj square in shape; denoting a measure of area; straight or level; fair and honest; with all accounts or debts settled ▷ v multiply (a number) by itself; make square; be or cause to be consistent ▷ adv squarely, directly ▶ **squarely** adv in a direct way; in an honest and frank manner ▶ **square dance** formation dance in which the couples form squares ▶ **square meal** substantial meal ▶ **square root** number of which a given number is the square ▶ **square up to** v prepare to confront (a person or problem)

**squash**[1] v crush flat; suppress; push into a confined space; humiliate with a crushing retort ▷ n sweet fruit drink diluted with water; crowd of people in a confined space; game played in an enclosed court with a rubber ball and long-handled rackets ▶ **squashy** adj

**squash**[2] n marrow-like vegetable

**squat** v **squatting, squatted** crouch with the knees bent and the weight on the feet; occupy unused premises to which one has no legal right ▷ n place where squatters live ▷ adj short and broad

**squatter** n illegal occupier of unused premises

**squaw** n (offens) Native American woman

**squawk** n loud harsh cry ▷ v utter a squawk

**squeak** n short shrill cry or sound ▷ v make or utter a squeak ▶ **squeaky** adj

**squeal** n long shrill cry or sound ▷ v make or utter a squeal; (slang) inform on someone to the police

**squeamish** adj easily sickened or shocked

**squeegee** n tool with a rubber blade for clearing water from a surface

**squeeze** v grip or press firmly; crush or press to extract liquid; push into a confined space; hug; obtain (something) by force or great effort ▷ n squeezing; amount extracted by squeezing; hug; crush of people in a confined space; restriction on borrowing

**squelch** v make a wet sucking sound, as by walking through mud ▷ n squelching sound

**squib** n small firework that hisses before exploding

**squid** n sea creature with a long soft body and ten tentacles

**squiggle** n wavy line ▶ **squiggly** adj

**squint** v have eyes which face in different directions; glance sideways ▷ n squinting condition of the eye; (informal) glance ▷ adj crooked

**squire** n country gentleman, usu. the main landowner in a community; (Hist) knight's apprentice

**squirm** v wriggle, writhe; feel embarrassed ▷ n wriggling movement

**squirrel** n small bushy-tailed tree-living animal

**squirt** v force (a liquid) or (of a liquid) be forced out of a narrow opening; squirt liquid at ▷ n jet of liquid; (informal) small or insignificant person

**squish** v, n (make) a soft squelching sound ▶ **squishy** adj

**Sr** Senior; Señor

**SS** Schutzstaffel: Nazi paramilitary security force; steamship

**SSL** (Computing) secure sockets layer: protocol for encrypting and transmitting sensitive data securely over the internet

**St** Saint; Street

**st.** stone (weight)

**stab** v stabbing, stabbed pierce with something pointed; jab (at) ▷ n stabbing; sudden unpleasant sensation; (informal) attempt

**stabilize** v make or become stable ▶ **stabilization** n ▶ **stabilizer** n device for stabilizing a child's bicycle, an aircraft, or a ship

**stable¹** n building in which horses are kept; establishment that breeds and trains racehorses; establishment that manages or trains several entertainers or athletes ▷ v put or keep (a horse) in a stable

**stable²** adj firmly fixed or established; firm in character; (Science) not subject to decay or decomposition ▶ **stability** n

**staccato** [stak-**ah**-toe] adj, adv (Music) with the notes sharply separated ▷ adj consisting of short abrupt sounds

**stack** n ordered pile; large amount; chimney ▷ v pile in a stack; control (aircraft waiting to land) so that they fly at different altitudes

**stadium** n, pl -diums or -dia sports arena with tiered seats for spectators

**staff¹** n people employed in an organization; stick used as a weapon, support, etc. ▷ v supply with personnel

**staff²** n, pl staves set of five horizontal lines on which music is written

**stag** n adult male deer ▶ **stag beetle** beetle with large branched jaws ▶ **stagette** n (informal) young unmarried professional woman ▶ **stag night, stag party** party for men only

**stage** *n* step or period of development; platform in a theatre where actors perform; portion of a journey ▷ *v* put (a play) on stage; organize and carry out (an event) **the stage** theatre as a profession ▶ **stagey** *adj* overtheatrical ▶ **stagecoach** *n* large horse-drawn vehicle formerly used to carry passengers and mail ▶ **stage fright** nervousness felt by a person about to face an audience ▶ **stage whisper** loud whisper intended to be heard by an audience

**stagger** *v* walk unsteadily; astound; set apart to avoid congestion ▷ *n* staggering

**stagnant** *adj* (of water or air) stale from not moving; not growing or developing ▶ **stagnate** *v* be stagnant ▶ **stagnation** *n*

**staid** *adj* sedate, serious, and rather dull

**stain** *v* discolour, mark; colour with a penetrating pigment ▷ *n* discoloration or mark; moral blemish or slur; penetrating liquid used to colour things ▶ **stainless** *adj* ▶ **stainless steel** steel alloy that does not rust

**stairs** *pl n* flight of steps between floors, usu. indoors ▶ **staircase, stairway** *n* flight of stairs with a handrail or banisters

**stake**[1] *n* pointed stick or post driven into the ground as a support or marker ▷ *v* support or mark out with stakes **stake a claim to** claim a right to ▶ **stake out** (*slang*) (of police) keep (a place) under surveillance

**stake**[2] *n* money wagered; interest, usu. financial, held in something ▷ *v* wager, risk; support financially **at stake** being risked ▶ **stakeholder** *n* person who has a concern or interest in something, esp. a business

**stalactite** *n* lime deposit hanging from the roof of a cave

**stalagmite** *n* lime deposit sticking up from the floor of a cave

**stale** *adj* not fresh; lacking energy or ideas through overwork or monotony; uninteresting from overuse ▶ **staleness** *n*

**stalemate** *n* (*Chess*) position in which any of a player's moves would put his king in check, resulting in a draw; deadlock, impasse

**stalk**[1] *n* plant's stem

**stalk**[2] *v* follow or approach stealthily; pursue persistently and, sometimes, attack (a person with whom one is obsessed); walk in a stiff or haughty manner ▶ **stalker** *n* person who follows or stealthily approaches a person or an animal; person who persistently pursues and, sometimes, attacks someone with whom he or she is obsessed ▶ **stalking-horse** *n* pretext

**stall**[1] *n* small stand for the display and sale of goods; compartment in a stable; small room or compartment ▷ *pl* ground-floor seats in a theatre or cinema; row of seats in a church for the choir or clergy ▷ *v* stop (a motor vehicle or engine) or (of a motor vehicle or engine) stop accidentally

**stall**[2] *v* employ delaying tactics

**stallion** *n* uncastrated male horse

**stalwart** [**stawl**-wart] *adj* strong and sturdy; dependable ▷ *n* stalwart person

**stamen** *n* pollen-producing part of a flower

**stamina** *n* enduring energy and strength

**stammer** *v* speak or say with involuntary pauses or repetition of syllables ▷ *n* tendency to stammer

**stamp** *n* (also **postage stamp**) piece of gummed paper stuck to

**S**

an envelope or parcel to show that the postage has been paid; act of stamping; instrument for stamping a pattern or mark; pattern or mark stamped; characteristic feature ▷ *v* bring (one's foot) down forcefully; walk with heavy footsteps; characterize; impress (a pattern or mark) on; stick a postage stamp on ▶ **stamping ground** favourite meeting place ▶ **stamp out** *v* suppress by force

**stampede** *n* sudden rush of frightened animals or of a crowd ▷ *v* (cause to) take part in a stampede

**stance** *n* attitude; manner of standing

**stanch** *v* same as **staunch²**

**stanchion** *n* upright bar used as a support

**stand** *v* **standing, stood** be in, rise to, or place in an upright position; be situated; be in a specified state or position; remain unchanged or valid; tolerate; offer oneself as a candidate; (*informal*) treat to ▷ *n* stall for the sale of goods; structure for spectators at a sports ground; firmly held opinion; (*US & Aust*) witness box; rack or piece of furniture on which things may be placed ▶ **standing** *adj* permanent, lasting ▷ *n* reputation or status; duration ▶ **stand for** *v* represent or mean; (*informal*) tolerate ▶ **stand in** *v* act as a substitute ▶ **stand-in** *n* substitute ▶ **standoffish** *adj* reserved or haughty ▶ **stand up for** *v* support or defend

**standard** *n* level of quality; example against which others are judged or measured; moral principle; distinctive flag; upright pole ▷ *adj* usual, regular, or average; of recognized authority;

accepted as correct ▶ **standardize** *v* cause to conform to a standard ▶ **standardization** *n* ▶ **standard lamp** lamp attached to an upright pole on a base

**standpipe** *n* tap attached to a water main to provide a public water supply

**standpoint** *n* point of view

**standstill** *n* complete halt

**stank** *v* a past tense of **stink**

**stanza** *n* verse of a poem

**staple¹** *n* U-shaped piece of metal used to fasten papers or secure things ▷ *v* fasten with staples ▶ **stapler** *n* small device for fastening papers together

**staple²** *adj* of prime importance, principal ▷ *n* main constituent of anything

**star** *n* hot gaseous mass in space, visible in the night sky as a point of light; star-shaped mark used to indicate excellence; asterisk; celebrity in the entertainment or sports world ▷ *pl* astrological forecast, horoscope ▷ *v* **starring, starred** feature or be featured as a star; mark with a star or stars ▷ *adj* leading, famous ▶ **stardom** *n* status of a star in the entertainment or sports world ▶ **starry** *adj* full of or like stars ▶ **starry-eyed** *adj* full of naive optimism ▶ **starfish** *n* star-shaped sea creature

**starboard** *n* right-hand side of a ship, when facing forward ▷ *adj* of or on this side

**starch** *n* carbohydrate forming the main food element in bread, potatoes, etc., and used mixed with water for stiffening fabric ▷ *v* stiffen (fabric) with starch ▶ **starchy** *adj* containing starch; stiff and formal

**stare** *v* look or gaze fixedly (at) ▷ *n* fixed gaze

**stark** *adj* harsh, unpleasant, and plain; desolate, bare; absolute ▷ *adv* completely

**starling** *n* songbird with glossy black speckled feathers

**start** *v* take the first step, begin; set or be set in motion; make a sudden involuntary movement from fright; establish or set up ▷ *n* first part of something; place or time of starting; advantage or lead in a competitive activity; sudden movement made from fright ▶ **starter** *n* first course of a meal; device for starting a car's engine; person who signals the start of a race ▶ **start-up** *n* recently launched project or business enterprise ▷ *adj* recently launched e.g. *start-up grants*

**startle** *v* slightly surprise or frighten

**starve** *v* die or suffer or cause to die or suffer from hunger; deprive of something needed ▶ **starvation** *n*

**stash** (*informal*) *v* store in a secret place ▷ *n* secret store

**state** *n* condition of a person or thing; sovereign political power or its territory; (**S-**) the government; (*informal*) excited or agitated condition; pomp ▷ *adj* of or concerning the State; involving ceremony ▷ *v* express in words ▶ **stately** *adj* dignified or grand ▶ **statehouse** *n* (*NZ*) publicly-owned house rented to a low-income tenant ▶ **statement** *n* something stated; printed financial account ▶ **stateroom** *n* private cabin on a ship; large room in a palace, used for ceremonial occasions ▶ **statesman, stateswoman** *n* experienced and respected political leader ▶ **statesmanship** *n*

**static** *adj* stationary or inactive; (of a force) acting but producing no movement ▷ *n* crackling sound or speckled picture caused by interference in radio or television reception; (also **static electricity**) electric sparks produced by friction

**statin** *n* (*Med*) drug used to lower cholesterol

**station** *n* place where trains stop for passengers; headquarters or local offices of the police or a fire brigade; building with special equipment for a particular purpose e.g. *power station*; television or radio channel; position in society; large Australian sheep or cattle property ▷ *v* assign (someone) to a particular place ▶ **station wagon** (*US & Aust*) car with a rear door and luggage space behind the rear seats

**stationary** *adj* not moving

> **USAGE NOTE**
> The words **stationary** and **stationery** are completely different in meaning and should not be confused

**stationery** *n* writing materials such as paper and pens ▶ **stationer** *n* dealer in stationery

**statistic** *n* numerical fact collected and classified systematically ▶ **statistics** *n* science of classifying and interpreting numerical information ▶ **statistical** *adj* ▶ **statistically** *adv* ▶ **statistician** *n* person who compiles and studies statistics

**statue** *n* large sculpture of a human or animal figure ▶ **statuary** *n* statues collectively ▶ **statuesque** *adj* (of a woman) tall and well-proportioned ▶ **statuette** *n* small statue

**stature** *n* person's height; reputation of a person or their achievements

**status** *n* social position; prestige; person's legal standing ▶ **status quo** existing state of affairs

**statute** *n* written law ▶ **statutory**
*adj* required or authorized by law
**staunch¹** *adj* loyal, firm
**staunch², stanch** *v* stop (a flow of blood)
**stave** *n* one of the strips of wood forming a barrel; (*Music*) same as **staff²** ▶ **stave in** *v* **staving, stove** burst a hole in ▶ **stave off** *v* **staving, staved** ward off
**stay¹** *v* remain in a place or condition; reside temporarily; endure; (*Scot & SAfr*) live permanently e.g. *where do you stay?* ▷ *n* period of staying in a place; postponement ▶ **staying power** stamina
**stay²** *n* prop or buttress ▷ *pl* corset
**stay³** *n* rope or wire supporting a ship's mast
**STD** sexually transmitted disease; (*Brit, Aust & SAfr*) subscriber trunk dialling; (*NZ*) subscriber toll dialling
**stead** *n* **in someone's stead** in someone's place **stand someone in good stead** be useful to someone
**steadfast** *adj* firm, determined ▶ **steadfastly** *adv*
**steady** *adj* **steadier, steadiest** not shaky or wavering; regular or continuous; sensible and dependable ▷ *v* **steadying, steadied** make steady ▷ *adv* in a steady manner ▶ **steadily** *adv* ▶ **steadiness** *n*
**steak** *n* thick slice of meat, esp. beef; slice of fish
**steal** *v* **stealing, stole, stolen** take unlawfully or without permission; move stealthily
**stealth** *n* secret or underhand behaviour ▷ *adj* (of technology) able to render an aircraft almost invisible to radar; disguised or hidden e.g. *stealth taxes* ▶ **stealthy** *adj* ▶ **stealthily** *adv*
**steam** *n* vapour into which water changes when boiled; power,

energy, or speed ▷ *v* give off steam; (of a vehicle) move by steam power; cook or treat with steam ▶ **steamer** *n* steam-propelled ship; container used to cook food in steam ▶ **steam engine** engine worked by steam ▶ **steamroller** *n* steam-powered vehicle with heavy rollers, used to level road surfaces ▷ *v* use overpowering force to make (someone) do what one wants
**steed** *n* (*lit*) horse
**steel** *n* hard malleable alloy of iron and carbon; steel rod used for sharpening knives; hardness of character or attitude ▷ *v* prepare (oneself) for something unpleasant ▶ **steely** *adj*
**steep¹** *adj* sloping sharply; (*informal*) (of a price) unreasonably high ▶ **steeply** *adv* ▶ **steepness** *n*
**steep²** *v* soak or be soaked in liquid **steeped in** filled with
**steeple** *n* church tower with a spire ▶ **steeplejack** *n* person who repairs steeples and chimneys
**steeplechase** *n* horse race with obstacles to jump; track race with hurdles and a water jump
**steer¹** *v* direct the course of (a vehicle or ship); direct (one's course) ▶ **steerage** *n* cheapest accommodation on a passenger ship ▶ **steering wheel** wheel turned by the driver of a vehicle in order to steer it
**steer²** *n* castrated male ox
**stein** [**stine**] *n* earthenware beer mug
**stellar** *adj* of stars
**stem¹** *n* long thin central part of a plant; long slender part, as of a wineglass; part of a word to which inflections are added ▷ *v* **stemming, stemmed** ▶ **stem from** originate from

**stem²** v **stemming, stemmed** stop (the flow of something)

**stench** n foul smell

**stencil** n thin sheet with cut-out pattern through which ink or paint passes to form the pattern on the surface below; pattern made thus ▷ v **-cilling, -cilled** make (a pattern) with a stencil

**stenographer** n shorthand typist

**stent** n surgical implant used to keep an artery open

**stentorian** adj (of a voice) very loud

**step** v **stepping, stepped** move and set down the foot, as when walking; walk a short distance ▷ n stepping; distance covered by a step; sound made by stepping; foot movement in a dance; one of a sequence of actions taken in order to achieve a goal; degree in a series or scale; flat surface for placing the foot on when going up or down ▷ pl stepladder ▶ **step in** v intervene ▶ **stepladder** n folding portable ladder with supporting frame ▶ **stepping stone** one of a series of stones for stepping on in crossing a stream; means of progress towards a goal ▶ **step up** v increase (something) by stages; take responsibility for something

**step-** prefix denoting a relationship created by the remarriage of a parent e.g. stepmother

**steppes** pl n wide grassy treeless plains in Russia and Ukraine

**stereo** adj short for **stereophonic** ▷ n stereophonic record player; stereophonic sound

**stereophonic** adj using two separate loudspeakers to give the effect of naturally distributed sound

**stereotype** n standardized idea of a type of person or thing ▷ v form a stereotype of

**sterile** adj free from germs; unable to produce offspring or seeds; lacking inspiration or vitality ▶ **sterility** n ▶ **sterilize** v make sterile ▶ **sterilization** n

**sterling** n British money system ▷ adj genuine and reliable

**stern¹** adj severe, strict ▶ **sternly** adv ▶ **sternness** n

**stern²** n rear part of a ship

**sternum** n, pl **-na** or **-nums** same as **breastbone**

**steroid** n organic compound containing a carbon ring system, such as many hormones

**stethoscope** n medical instrument for listening to sounds made inside the body

**Stetson®** n tall broad-brimmed hat, worn mainly by cowboys

**stevedore** n person who loads and unloads ships

**stew** n food cooked slowly in a closed pot; (informal) troubled or worried state ▷ v cook slowly in a closed pot

**steward** n person who looks after passengers on a ship or aircraft; official who helps at a public event such as a race; person who administers another's property ▶ **stewardess** n fem

**stick¹** n long thin piece of wood; such a piece of wood shaped for a special purpose e.g. hockey stick; something like a stick e.g. stick of celery; (slang) verbal abuse, criticism

**stick²** v **sticking, stuck** push (a pointed object) into (something); fasten or be fastened by or as if by pins or glue; (foll by out) extend beyond something else, protrude; (informal) put; remain for a long time ▶ **sticker** n adhesive label or sign ▶ **sticky** adj covered with an adhesive substance; (informal)

S

difficult, unpleasant; (of weather) warm and humid ▶ **stick-in-the-mud** n person who does not like anything new ▶ **stick-up** n (slang) robbery at gunpoint ▶ **stick up for** v (informal) support or defend

**stickleback** n small fish with sharp spines on its back

**stickler** n person who insists on something e.g. stickler for detail

**stiff** adj not easily bent or moved; severe e.g. stiff punishment; unrelaxed or awkward; firm in consistency; strong e.g. a stiff drink ▷ n (slang) corpse ▶ **stiffly** adv ▶ **stiffness** n ▶ **stiffen** v make or become stiff ▶ **stiff-necked** adj haughtily stubborn

**stifle** v suppress; suffocate

**stigma** n, pl **-mas** or **-mata** mark of social disgrace; part of a plant that receives pollen ▶ **stigmata** pl n marks resembling the wounds of the crucified Christ ▶ **stigmatize** v mark as being shameful

**stile** n set of steps allowing people to climb a fence

**stiletto** n, pl **-tos** high narrow heel on a woman's shoe; small slender dagger

**still**[1] adv now or in the future as before; up to this or that time; even or yet e.g. still more insults; quietly or without movement ▷ adj motionless; silent and calm, undisturbed; (of a drink) not fizzy ▷ n photograph from a film scene ▷ v make still ▶ **stillness** n ▶ **stillborn** adj born dead ▶ **still life** painting of inanimate objects

**still**[2] n apparatus for distilling alcoholic drinks

**stilted** adj stiff and formal in manner

**stilts** pl n pair of poles with footrests for walking raised from the ground;

long posts supporting a building above ground level

**stimulus** n, pl **-li** something that rouses a person or thing to activity ▶ **stimulant** n something, such as a drug, that acts as a stimulus ▶ **stimulate** v act as a stimulus (on) ▶ **stimulation** n

**sting** v **stinging, stung** (of certain animals or plants) wound by injecting with poison; feel or cause to feel sharp physical or mental pain; (slang) cheat (someone) by overcharging ▷ n wound or pain caused by or as if by stinging; mental pain; sharp pointed organ of certain animals or plants by which poison can be injected

**stingy** [stin-jee] adj **-gier, -giest** mean or miserly ▶ **stinginess** n

**stink** n strong unpleasant smell; (slang) unpleasant fuss ▷ v **stinking, stank** or **stunk, stunk** give off a strong unpleasant smell; (slang) be very unpleasant

**stint** v (foll by on) be miserly with (something) ▷ n allotted amount of work

**stipend** [sty-pend] n regular allowance or salary, esp. that paid to a clergyman ▶ **stipendiary** adj receiving a stipend

**stipple** v paint, draw, or engrave using dots

**stipulate** v specify as a condition of an agreement ▶ **stipulation** n

**stir** v **stirring, stirred** mix up (a liquid) by moving a spoon etc. around in it; move; excite or stimulate (a person) emotionally ▷ n a stirring; strong reaction, usu. of excitement ▶ **stir-fry** v **-fries, -frying, -fried** cook (food) quickly by stirring it in a pan over a high heat ▷ n, pl **-fries** dish cooked in this way

**stirrup** n metal loop attached to a saddle for supporting a rider's foot

**stitch** n link made by drawing thread through material with a needle; loop of yarn formed round a needle or hook in knitting or crochet; sharp pain in the side ▷ v sew **in stitches** (*informal*) laughing uncontrollably **not a stitch** (*informal*) no clothes at all

**stoat** n small mammal of the weasel family, with brown fur that turns white in winter

**stock** n total amount of goods available for sale in a shop; supply stored for future use; financial shares in, or capital of, a company; liquid produced by boiling meat, fish, bones, or vegetables ▷ pl (*Hist*) instrument of punishment consisting of a wooden frame with holes into which the hands and feet of the victim were locked ▷ adj kept in stock, standard; hackneyed ▷ v keep for sale or future use; supply (a farm) with livestock or (a lake etc.) with fish ▸ **stockist** n dealer who stocks a particular product ▸ **stocky** adj (of a person) broad and sturdy ▸ **stockbroker** n person who buys and sells stocks and shares for customers ▸ **stock car** car modified for a form of racing in which the cars often collide ▸ **stock exchange, stock market** institution for the buying and selling of shares ▸ **stockpile** v store a large quantity of (something) for future use ▷ n accumulated store ▸ **stock-still** adj motionless ▸ **stocktaking** n counting and valuing of the goods in a shop

**stockade** n enclosure or barrier made of stakes

**stocking** n close-fitting covering for the foot and leg

**stodgy** adj **stodgier, stodgiest** (of food) heavy and starchy; (of a person) serious and boring

▸ **stodge** n (*Brit, Aust & NZ*) heavy starchy food

**stoep** [stoop] n (*S Afr*) verandah

**stoic** [stow-ik] n person who suffers hardship without showing his or her feelings ▷ adj (also **stoical**) suffering hardship without showing one's feelings ▸ **stoically** adv ▸ **stoicism** [stow-iss-izz-um] n

**stoke** v feed and tend (a fire or furnace) ▸ **stoker** n

**stole**¹ v past tense of **steal**

**stole**² n long scarf or shawl

**stolen** v past participle of **steal**

**stolid** adj showing little emotion or interest ▸ **stolidly** adv

**stomach** n organ in the body which digests food; front of the body around the waist; desire or inclination ▷ v put up with

**stomp** v (*informal*) tread heavily

**stone** n material of which rocks are made; piece of this; gem; hard central part of a fruit; unit of weight equal to 14 pounds or 6.350 kilograms; hard deposit formed in the kidney or bladder ▷ v throw stones at; remove stones from (a fruit) ▸ **stoned** adj (*slang*) under the influence of alcohol or drugs ▸ **stony** adj of or like stone; unfeeling or hard ▸ **stony-broke** adj (*slang*) completely penniless ▸ **stonily** adv ▸ **Stone Age** prehistoric period when tools were made of stone ▸ **stone-cold** adj completely cold ▸ **stone-deaf** adj completely deaf ▸ **stonewall** v obstruct or hinder discussion ▸ **stoneware** n hard kind of pottery fired at a very high temperature

**stood** v past of **stand**

**stooge** n actor who feeds lines to a comedian or acts as the butt of his jokes; (*slang*) person taken advantage of by a superior

**stool** n chair without arms or back; piece of excrement

**stool pigeon** n informer for the police

**stoop** v bend (the body) forward and downward; carry oneself habitually in this way; degrade oneself ▷ n stooping posture

**stop** v **stopping, stopped** cease or cause to cease from doing (something); bring to or come to a halt; prevent or restrain; withhold; block or plug; stay or rest ▷ n stopping or being stopped; place where something stops; full stop; knob on an organ that is pulled out to allow a set of pipes to sound ▸ **stoppage** n ▸ **stoppage time** same as **injury time** ▸ **stopper** n plug for closing a bottle etc. ▸ **stopcock** n valve to control or stop the flow of fluid in a pipe ▸ **stopgap** n temporary substitute ▸ **stopover** n short break in a journey ▸ **stop press** news item put into a newspaper after printing has been started ▸ **stopwatch** n watch which can be stopped instantly for exact timing of a sporting event

**stop-work, stop-work meeting** n (*Aust*) temporary stoppage of work as a form of protest

**store** v collect and keep (things) for future use; put (furniture etc.) in a warehouse for safekeeping; stock (goods); (*Computing*) enter or retain (data) ▷ n shop; supply kept for future use; storage place, such as a warehouse ▷ pl stock of provisions **in store** about to happen **set great store by** value greatly ▸ **storage** n storing; space for storing ▸ **storage heater** electric device that can accumulate and radiate heat generated by off-peak electricity

**storey** n floor or level of a building

**stork** n large wading bird

**storm** n violent weather with wind, rain, or snow; strongly expressed reaction ▷ v attack or capture (a place) suddenly; shout angrily; rush violently or angrily ▸ **stormy** adj characterized by storms; involving violent emotions

**story** n, pl **-ries** description of a series of events told or written for entertainment; plot of a book or film; news report; (*informal*) lie

**stoup** [stoop] n small basin for holy water

**stout** adj fat; thick and strong; brave and resolute ▷ n strong dark beer ▸ **stoutly** adv

**stove**¹ n apparatus for cooking or heating

**stove**² v a past of **stave**

**stow** v pack or store ▸ **stowaway** n person who hides on a ship or aircraft in order to travel free ▸ **stow away** v hide as a stowaway

**straddle** v have one leg or part on each side of (something)

**strafe** v attack (an enemy) with machine guns from the air

**straggle** v go or spread in a rambling or irregular way ▸ **straggler** n ▸ **straggly** adj

**straight** adj not curved or crooked; level or upright; honest or frank; (of spirits) undiluted; (*slang*) heterosexual ▷ adv in a straight line; immediately; in a level or upright position ▷ n straight part, esp. of a racetrack; (*slang*) heterosexual person **go straight** (*informal*) reform after being a criminal ▸ **straighten** v ▸ **straightaway** adv immediately ▸ **straight face** serious facial expression concealing a desire to laugh ▸ **straightforward** adj honest, frank; (of a task) easy

**strain¹** v cause (something) to be used or tested beyond its limits; make an intense effort; injure by overexertion; sieve ▷ n tension or tiredness; force exerted by straining; injury from overexertion; great demand on strength or resources; melody or theme ▶ **strained** adj not natural, forced; not relaxed, tense ▶ **strainer** n sieve

**strain²** n breed or race; trace or streak

**strait** n narrow channel connecting two areas of sea ▷ pl position of acute difficulty ▶ **straitjacket** n strong jacket with long sleeves used to bind the arms of a violent person ▶ **strait-laced, straight-laced** adj prudish or puritanical

**straitened** adj **in straitened circumstances** not having much money

**strand¹** v run aground; leave in difficulties ▷ n (poetic) shore

**strand²** n single thread of string, wire, etc.

**strange** adj odd or unusual; not familiar; inexperienced (in) or unaccustomed (to) ▶ **strangely** adv ▶ **strangeness** n

**stranger** n person who is not known to a place or is new to a place or experience

**strangle** v kill by squeezing the throat; prevent the development of ▶ **strangler** n ▶ **strangulation** n strangling ▶ **stranglehold** n strangling grip in wrestling; powerful control

**strap** n strip of flexible material for lifting, fastening, or holding in place ▷ v **strapping, strapped** fasten with a strap or straps ▶ **strapping** adj tall and sturdy

**strata** n plural of **stratum**

**stratagem** n clever plan, trick

**strategy** n, pl **-gies** overall plan; art of planning in war ▶ **strategic**

[strat-**ee**-jik] adj advantageous; (of weapons) aimed at an enemy's homeland ▶ **strategically** adv ▶ **strategist** n

**strathspey** n Scottish dance with gliding steps

**stratosphere** n atmospheric layer between about 15 and 50 kilometres above the earth

**stratum** [**strah**-tum] n, pl **strata** layer, esp. of rock; social class ▶ **stratified** adj divided into strata ▶ **stratification** n

**straw** n dried stalks of grain; single stalk of straw; long thin tube used to suck up liquid into the mouth ▶ **straw poll** unofficial poll taken to determine general opinion

**strawberry** n sweet fleshy red fruit with small seeds on the outside ▶ **strawberry mark** red birthmark

**stray** v wander; digress; deviate from certain moral standards ▷ adj having strayed; scattered, random ▷ n stray animal

**streak** n long band of contrasting colour or substance; quality or characteristic; short stretch (of good or bad luck) ▷ v mark with streaks; move rapidly; (informal) run naked in public ▶ **streaker** n ▶ **streaky** adj

**stream** n small river; steady flow, as of liquid, speech, or people; schoolchildren grouped together because of similar ability ▷ v flow steadily; move in unbroken succession; (Computing) send video or audio material over the internet so that the receiving system can play it almost simultaneously; float in the air; group (pupils) in streams ▶ **streamer** n strip of coloured paper that unrolls when tossed; long narrow flag ▶ **streaming** n

**streamline** v make more efficient by simplifying; give (a car, plane,

**S**

etc.) a smooth even shape to offer least resistance to the flow of air or water

**street** n public road, usu. lined with buildings ▶ **streetcar** n (US) tram ▶ **streetwise** adj knowing how to survive in big cities

**strength** n quality of being strong; quality or ability considered an advantage; degree of intensity; total number of people in a group **on the strength of** on the basis of ▶ **strengthen** v

**strenuous** adj requiring great energy or effort ▶ **strenuously** adv

**streptococcus** [strep-toe-**kok**-uss] n, pl **-cocci** bacterium occurring in chains, many species of which cause disease

**stress** n tension or strain; emphasis; stronger sound in saying a word or syllable; (Physics) force producing strain ▷ v emphasize; put stress on (a word or syllable) ▶ **stressed-out** adj (informal) suffering from tension

**stretch** v extend or be extended; be able to be stretched; extend the limbs or body; strain (resources or abilities) to the utmost ▷ n stretching; continuous expanse; period; (informal) term of imprisonment ▶ **stretchy** adj

**stretcher** n frame covered with canvas, on which an injured person is carried

**strew** v **strewing, strewed, strewed** or **strewn** scatter (things) over a surface

**striated** adj having a pattern of scratches or grooves

**stricken** adj seriously affected by disease, grief, pain, etc.

**strict** adj stern or severe; adhering closely to specified rules; complete, absolute ▶ **strictly** adv ▶ **strictness** n

**stricture** n severe criticism

**stride** v **striding, strode, stridden** walk with long steps ▷ n long step; regular pace ▷ pl progress

**strident** adj loud and harsh ▶ **stridently** adv ▶ **stridency** n

**strife** n conflict, quarrelling

**strike** v **striking, struck** cease work as a protest; hit; attack suddenly; ignite (a match) by friction; (of a clock) indicate (a time) by sounding a bell; enter the mind of; afflict; discover (gold, oil, etc.); agree (a bargain) ▷ n stoppage of work as a protest ▶ **striking** adj impressive; noteworthy **strike camp** dismantle and pack up tents **strike home** have the desired effect ▶ **strike off, strike out** v cross out ▶ **strike up** v begin (a conversation or friendship); begin to play music

**striker** n striking worker; attacking player at soccer

**string** n thin cord used for tying; set of objects threaded on a string; series of things or events; stretched wire or cord on a musical instrument that produces sound when vibrated ▷ pl restrictions or conditions; section of an orchestra consisting of stringed instruments ▷ v **stringing, strung** provide with a string or strings; thread on a string **pull strings** use one's influence ▶ **stringed** adj (of a musical instrument) having strings that are plucked or played with a bow ▶ **stringy** adj like string; (of meat) fibrous ▶ **string along** v deceive over a period of time ▶ **string up** v (informal) kill by hanging ▶ **stringybark** n Australian eucalyptus with a fibrous bark

**stringent** [**strin**-jent] adj strictly controlled or enforced ▶ **stringently** adv ▶ **stringency** n

**strip**[1] v **stripping, stripped** take (the covering or clothes) off; take a title or possession away from (someone); dismantle (an engine) ▷ **stripper** n person who performs a striptease ▷ **striptease** n entertainment in which a performer undresses to music

**strip**[2] n long narrow piece; (Brit, Aust & NZ) clothes a sports team plays in ▷ **strip cartoon** sequence of drawings telling a story

**stripe** n long narrow band of contrasting colour or substance; chevron or band worn on a uniform to indicate rank ▷ **striped, stripy, stripey** adj

**stripling** n youth

**strive** v **striving, strove, striven** make a great effort

**strobe** n short for **stroboscope**

**stroboscope** n instrument producing a very bright flashing light

**strode** v past tense of **stride**

**stroke** v touch or caress lightly with the hand ▷ n light touch or caress with the hand; rupture of a blood vessel in the brain; blow; action or occurrence of the kind specified e.g. a stroke of luck; chime of a clock; mark made by a pen or paintbrush; style or method of swimming

**stroll** v walk in a leisurely manner ▷ n leisurely walk

**strong** adj having physical power; not easily broken; great in degree or intensity; having moral force; having a specified number e.g. twenty strong ▷ **strongly** adv ▷ **stronghold** n area of predominance of a particular belief; fortress ▷ **strongroom** n room designed for the safekeeping of valuables

**strontium** n (Chem) silvery-white metallic element

**strop** n leather strap for sharpening razors

**stroppy** adj **-pier, -piest** (slang) angry or awkward

**strove** v past tense of **strive**

**struck** v past of **strike**

**structure** n complex construction; manner or basis of construction or organization ▷ v give a structure to ▷ **structural** adj ▷ **structuralism** n approach to literature, social sciences, etc., which sees changes in the subject as caused and organized by a hidden set of universal rules ▷ **structuralist** n, adj

**strudel** n thin sheet of filled dough rolled up and baked, usu. with an apple filling

**struggle** v work, strive, or make one's way with difficulty; move about violently in an attempt to get free; fight (with someone) ▷ n striving; fight

**strum** v **strumming, strummed** play (a guitar or banjo) by sweeping the thumb or a plectrum across the strings

**strumpet** n (old-fashioned) prostitute

**strung** v past of **string**

**strut** v **strutting, strutted** walk pompously, swagger ▷ n bar supporting a structure

**strychnine** [strik-neen] n very poisonous drug used in small quantities as a stimulant

**stub** n short piece left after use; counterfoil of a cheque or ticket ▷ v **stubbing, stubbed** strike (the toe) painfully against an object; put out (a cigarette) by pressing the end against a surface ▷ **stubby** adj short and broad

**stubble** n short stalks of grain left in a field after reaping; short growth of hair on the chin of a

**S**

man who has not shaved recently
▶ **stubbly** adj

**stubborn** adj refusing to agree or give in; difficult to deal with ▶ **stubbornly** adv ▶ **stubbornness** n

**stucco** n plaster used for coating or decorating walls

**stuck** v past of **stick²** ▶ **stuck-up** adj (informal) conceited or snobbish

**stud¹** n small piece of metal attached to a surface for decoration; disc-like removable fastener for clothes; one of several small round objects fixed to the sole of a football boot to give better grip ▷ v **studding, studded** set with studs

**stud²** n male animal, esp. a stallion, kept for breeding; (also **stud farm**) place where horses are bred; (slang) virile or sexually active man

**student** n person who studies a subject, esp. at university

**studio** n, pl **-dios** workroom of an artist or photographer; room or building in which television or radio programmes, records, or films are made ▶ **studio flat** (Brit) one-room flat with a small kitchen and bathroom

**study** v **studying, studied** be engaged in learning (a subject); investigate by observation and research; scrutinize ▷ n, pl **studies** act or process of studying; room for studying in; book or paper produced as a result of study; sketch done as practice or preparation; musical composition designed to improve playing technique ▶ **studied** adj carefully practised or planned ▶ **studious** adj fond of study; careful and deliberate ▶ **studiously** adv

**stuff** n substance or material; collection of unnamed things ▷ v

pack, cram, or fill completely; fill (food) with a seasoned mixture; fill (an animal's skin) with material to restore the shape of the live animal ▶ **stuffing** n seasoned mixture with which food is stuffed; padding

**stuffy** adj **stuffier, stuffiest** lacking fresh air; (informal) dull or conventional

**stultifying** adj very boring and repetitive

**stumble** v trip and nearly fall; walk in an unsure way; make frequent mistakes in speech ▶ **stumbling** ▶ **stumble across** v discover accidentally ▶ **stumbling block** obstacle or difficulty

**stump** n base of a tree left when the main trunk has been cut down; part of a thing left after a larger part has been removed; (Cricket) one of the three upright sticks forming the wicket ▷ v baffle; (Cricket) dismiss (a batsman) by breaking his wicket with the ball; walk with heavy steps ▶ **stumpy** adj short and thick ▶ **stump up** v (informal) give (the money required)

**stun** v **stunning, stunned** shock or overwhelm; knock senseless ▶ **stunning** adj very attractive or impressive

**stung** v past of **sting**

**stunk** v a past of **stink**

**stunt¹** v prevent or impede the growth of ▶ **stunted** adj

**stunt²** n acrobatic or dangerous action; anything spectacular done to gain publicity

**stupefy** v **-fying, -fied** make insensitive or lethargic; astound ▶ **stupefaction** n

**stupendous** adj very large or impressive ▶ **stupendously** adv

**stupid** adj lacking intelligence; silly; in a stupor ▶ **stupidity** n ▶ **stupidly** adv

**stupor** n dazed or unconscious state

**sturdy** adj **-dier, -diest** healthy and robust; strongly built ▷ **sturdily** adv

**sturgeon** n fish from which caviar is obtained

**stutter** v speak with repetition of initial consonants ▷ n tendency to stutter

**sty** n, pl **sties** pen for pigs

**stye, sty** n, pl **styes** or **sties** inflammation at the base of an eyelash

**style** n shape or design; manner of writing, speaking, or doing something; elegance, refinement; prevailing fashion ▷ v shape or design; name or call ▷ **stylish** adj smart, elegant, and fashionable ▷ **stylishly** adv ▷ **stylist** n hairdresser; person who writes or performs with great attention to style ▷ **stylistic** adj of literary or artistic style ▷ **stylize** v cause to conform to an established stylistic form

**stylus** n needle-like device on a record player that rests in the groove of the record and picks up the sound signals

**stymie** v **-mieing, -mied** hinder or thwart

**styptic** n, adj (drug) used to stop bleeding

**suave** [swahv] adj smooth and sophisticated in manner ▷ **suavely** adv

**sub** n subeditor; submarine; subscription; substitute; (Brit informal) advance payment of wages or salary ▷ v **subbing, subbed** act as a substitute; grant advance payment to

**sub-** prefix indicating under or beneath e.g. submarine; indicating subordinate e.g. sublieutenant; indicating falling short of e.g. subnormal; indicating forming a subdivision e.g. subheading

**subaltern** n British army officer below the rank of captain

**subatomic** adj of or being one of the particles which make up an atom

**subcommittee** n small committee formed from some members of a larger committee

**subconscious** adj happening or existing without one's awareness ▷ n (Psychoanalysis) that part of the mind of which one is not aware but which can influence one's behaviour ▷ **subconsciously** adv

**subcontinent** n large land mass that is a distinct part of a continent

**subcontract** n secondary contract by which the main contractor for a job puts work out to others ▷ v put out (work) on a subcontract ▷ **subcontractor** n

**subcutaneous** [sub-cute-**ayn**-ee-uss] adj under the skin

**subdivide** v divide (a part of something) into smaller parts ▷ **subdivision** n

**subdue** v **-duing, -dued** overcome; make less intense

**subeditor** n person who checks and edits text for a newspaper or magazine

**subject** n person or thing being dealt with or studied; (Grammar) word or phrase that represents the person or thing performing the action of the verb in a sentence; person under the rule of a monarch or government ▷ adj being under the rule of a monarch or government ▷ v (foll by to) cause to undergo **subject to** liable to; conditional upon ▷ **subjection** n ▷ **subjective** adj based on personal feelings ▷ **subjectively** adv

S

**sub judice** [sub **joo**-diss-ee] *adj*
(*Latin*) before a court of law and
therefore prohibited from public
discussion

**subjugate** *v* bring (a group of
people) under one's control
▶ **subjugation** *n*

**subjunctive** (*Grammar*) *n* mood
of verbs used when the content of
the clause is doubted, supposed, or
wished ▷ *adj* in or of that mood

**sublet** *v* **-letting, -let** rent out
(property rented from someone
else)

**sublimate** *v* (*Psychol*) direct the
energy of (a strong desire, esp. a
sexual one) into socially acceptable
activities ▶ **sublimation** *n*

**sublime** *adj* of high moral,
intellectual, or spiritual value;
unparalleled, supreme ▷ *v*
(*Chem*) change from a solid to
a vapour without first melting
▶ **sublimely** *adv*

**subliminal** *adj* relating to mental
processes of which the individual
is not aware

**sub-machine gun** *n* portable
machine gun with a short barrel

**submarine** *n* vessel which can
operate below the surface of the
sea ▷ *adj* below the surface of
the sea

**submerge** *v* put or go below the
surface of water or other liquid
▶ **submersion** *n*

**submit** *v* **-mitting, -mitted**
surrender; put forward for
consideration; be (voluntarily)
subjected to a process or
treatment ▶ **submission** *n*
submitting; something submitted
for consideration; state of being
submissive ▶ **submissive** *adj* meek
and obedient

**subordinate** *adj* of lesser rank
or importance ▷ *n* subordinate

person or thing ▷ *v* make or treat as
subordinate ▶ **subordination** *n*

**suborn** *v* (*formal*) bribe or incite (a
person) to commit a wrongful act

**subpoena** [sub-**pee**-na] *n* writ
requiring a person to appear before
a lawcourt ▷ *v* summon (someone)
with a subpoena

**subprime** *adj* (of a loan) made
to a borrower with a poor credit
rating e.g. *subprime mortgage* ▷ *n*
such a loan

**subscribe** *v* pay (a subscription);
give support or approval (to)
▶ **subscriber** *n* ▶ **subscription** *n*
payment for issues of a publication
over a period; money contributed
to a charity etc.; membership fees
paid to a society

**subsection** *n* division of a section

**subsequent** *adj* occurring after,
succeeding ▶ **subsequently** *adv*

**subservient** *adj* submissive, servile
▶ **subservience** *n*

**subside** *v* become less intense; sink
to a lower level ▶ **subsidence** *n* act
or process of subsiding

**subsidiary** *adj* of lesser importance
▷ *n*, *pl* **-aries** subsidiary person
or thing

**subsidize** *v* help financially
▶ **subsidy** *n*, *pl* **-dies** financial aid

**subsist** *v* manage to live
▶ **subsistence** *n*

**subsonic** *adj* moving at a speed less
than that of sound

**substance** *n* physical composition
of something; solid, powder,
liquid, or paste; essential
meaning of something; solid
or meaningful quality; wealth
▶ **substantial** *adj* of considerable
size or value; (of food or a meal)
sufficient and nourishing; solid or
strong; real ▶ **substantially** *adv*
▶ **substantiate** *v* support (a story)
with evidence ▶ **substantiation** *n*

S

▶ **substantive** n noun ▷ adj of or being the essential element of a thing

**substitute** v take the place of or put in place of another ▷ n person or thing taking the place of (another) ▶ **substitution** n

**subsume** v include (an idea, case, etc.) under a larger classification or group

**subterfuge** n trick used to achieve an objective

**subterranean** adj underground

**subtitle** n secondary title of a book ▷ pl printed translation at the bottom of the picture in a film with foreign dialogue ▷ v provide with a subtitle or subtitles

**subtle** adj not immediately obvious; having or requiring ingenuity ▶ **subtly** adv ▶ **subtlety** n

**subtract** v take (one number) from another ▶ **subtraction** n

**subtropical** adj of the regions bordering on the tropics

**suburb** n residential area on the outskirts of a city ▶ **suburban** adj of or inhabiting a suburb; narrow or unadventurous in outlook ▶ **suburbia** n suburbs and their inhabitants

**subvention** n (formal) subsidy

**subvert** v overthrow the authority of ▶ **subversion** n ▶ **subversive** adj, n

**subway** n passage under a road or railway; underground railway

**succeed** v accomplish an aim; turn out satisfactorily; come next in order after (something); take over a position from (someone) ▶ **success** n achievement of something attempted; attainment of wealth, fame, or position; successful person or thing ▶ **successful** adj having success

▶ **successfully** adv ▶ **succession** n series of people or things following one another in order; act or right by which one person succeeds another in a position ▶ **successive** adj consecutive ▶ **successively** adv ▶ **successor** n person who succeeds someone in a position

> **SPELLING TIP**
> The Collins Corpus evidence shows that people are able to remember the double s at the end of **success** more easily than the double c in the middle

**succinct** adj brief and clear ▶ **succinctly** adv

**succour** v, n help in distress

**succulent** adj juicy and delicious; (of a plant) having thick fleshy leaves ▷ n succulent plant ▶ **succulence** n

**succumb** v (foll by to) give way (to something overpowering); die of (an illness)

**such** adj of the kind specified; so great, so much ▷ pron such things ▶ **such-and-such** adj specific, but not known or named ▶ **suchlike** pron such or similar things

**suck** v draw (liquid or air) into the mouth; take (something) into the mouth and moisten, dissolve, or roll it around with the tongue; (foll by in) draw in by irresistible force ▷ n sucking ▶ **sucker** n (slang) person who is easily deceived or swindled; organ or device which adheres by suction; shoot coming from a plant's root or the base of its main stem ▶ **suckhole** n (Aust slang) sycophant, toady ▶ **suck up to** v (informal) flatter (someone) for one's own profit

**suckle** v feed at the breast ▶ **suckling** n unweaned baby or young animal

S

**sucrose** [soo-kroze] n chemical name for sugar

**suction** n sucking; force produced by drawing air out of a space to make a vacuum that will suck in a substance from another space

**sudden** adj done or occurring quickly and unexpectedly **all of a sudden** quickly and unexpectedly ▸ **suddenly** adv ▸ **suddenness** n ▸ **sudden death** (Sport) period of extra time in which the first competitor to score wins

**sudoku** [soo-**doe**-koo] n logic puzzle involving the insertion of each of the numbers 1 to 9 into each row, column, and individual grid of a larger square made up of 9 3x3 grids

**sudorific** [syoo-dor-**if**-ik] n, adj (drug) causing sweating

**suds** pl n froth of soap and water

**sue** v **suing, sued** start legal proceedings against

**suede** n leather with a velvety finish on one side

**suet** n hard fat obtained from sheep and cattle, used in cooking

**suffer** v undergo or be subjected to; tolerate ▸ **sufferer** n ▸ **suffering** n ▸ **sufferance** n **on sufferance** tolerated with reluctance

**suffice** [suf-**fice**] v be enough for a purpose

**sufficient** adj enough, adequate ▸ **sufficiency** n adequate amount ▸ **sufficiently** adv

**suffix** n letter or letters added to the end of a word to form another word, such as -s and -ness in dogs and softness

**suffocate** v kill or be killed by deprivation of oxygen; feel uncomfortable from heat and lack of air ▸ **suffocation** n

**suffragan** n bishop appointed to assist an archbishop

**suffrage** n right to vote in public elections ▸ **suffragette** n (in Britain in the early 20th century) a woman who campaigned militantly for the right to vote

**suffuse** v spread through or over (something) ▸ **suffusion** n

**sugar** n sweet crystalline carbohydrate found in many plants and used to sweeten food and drinks ▷ v sweeten or cover with sugar ▸ **sugary** adj ▸ **sugar beet** beet grown for the sugar obtained from its roots ▸ **sugar cane** tropical grass grown for the sugar obtained from its canes ▸ **sugar daddy** (slang) elderly man who gives a young woman money and gifts in return for sexual favours ▸ **sugar glider** common Australian phalanger that glides from tree to tree feeding on insects and nectar

**suggest** v put forward (an idea) for consideration; bring to mind by the association of ideas; give a hint of ▸ **suggestible** adj easily influenced ▸ **suggestion** n thing suggested; hint or indication ▸ **suggestive** adj suggesting something indecent; conveying a hint (of) ▸ **suggestively** adv

**suicide** n killing oneself intentionally; person who kills himself intentionally; self-inflicted ruin of one's own prospects or interests ▸ **suicidal** adj liable to commit suicide ▸ **suicidally** adv

**suit** n set of clothes designed to be worn together; outfit worn for a specific purpose; one of the four sets into which a pack of cards is divided; lawsuit ▷ v be appropriate for; be acceptable to ▸ **suitable** adj appropriate or proper ▸ **suitably** adv ▸ **suitability** n ▸ **suitcase** n portable travelling case for clothing

**suite** n set of connected rooms in a hotel; matching set of furniture; set of musical pieces in the same key

**suitor** n (old-fashioned) man who is courting a woman

**sulk** v be silent and sullen because of bad temper ▷ n resentful or sullen mood ▶ **sulky** adj ▶ **sulkily** adv

**sullen** adj unwilling to talk ▶ **sullenly** adv ▶ **sullenness** n

**sully** v **-lying, -lied** ruin (someone's reputation); make dirty

**sulphate** n salt or ester of sulphuric acid

**sulphide** n compound of sulphur with another element

**sulphite** n salt or ester of sulphurous acid

**sulphonamide** [sulf-**on**-a-mide] n any of a class of drugs that prevent the growth of bacteria

**sulphur** n (Chem) pale yellow nonmetallic element ▶ **sulphuric, sulphurous** adj of or containing sulphur

**sultan** n sovereign of a Muslim country ▶ **sultana** n kind of raisin; sultan's wife, mother, or daughter ▶ **sultanate** n territory of a sultan

**sultry** adj **-trier, -triest** (of weather or climate) hot and humid; passionate, sensual

**sum** n result of addition, total; problem in arithmetic; quantity of money ▶ **sum total** complete or final total ▶ **sum up** v **summing, summed** summarize; form a quick opinion of

**summary** n, pl **-ries** brief account giving the main points of something ▷ adj done quickly, without formalities ▶ **summarily** adv ▶ **summarize** v make or be a summary of (something) ▶ **summation** n summary; adding up

**summer** n warmest season of the year, between spring and autumn ▶ **summery** adj ▶ **summerhouse** n small building in a garden ▶ **summertime** n period or season of summer

**summit** n top of a mountain or hill; highest point; conference between heads of state or other high officials

**summon** v order (someone) to come; call upon (someone) to do something; gather (one's courage, strength, etc.) ▶ **summons** n command summoning someone; order requiring someone to appear in court ▷ v order (someone) to appear in court

**sumo** n Japanese style of wrestling

**sump** n container in an internal-combustion engine into which oil can drain; hollow into which liquid drains

**sumptuous** adj lavish, magnificent ▶ **sumptuously** adv

**sun** n star around which the earth and other planets revolve; any star around which planets revolve; heat and light from the sun ▷ v **sunning, sunned** expose (oneself) to the sun's rays ▶ **sunless** adj ▶ **sunny** adj full of or exposed to sunlight; cheerful ▶ **sunbathe** v lie in the sunshine in order to get a suntan ▶ **sunbeam** n ray of sun ▶ **sunburn** n painful reddening of the skin caused by overexposure to the sun ▶ **sunburnt, sunburned** adj ▶ **sundial** n device showing the time by means of a pointer that casts a shadow on a marked dial ▶ **sundown** n sunset ▶ **sunflower** n tall plant with large golden flowers ▶ **sunrise** n daily appearance of the sun above the horizon; time of this ▶ **sunset** n daily disappearance of the sun

S

below the horizon; time of this ▶ **sunshine** n light and warmth from the sun ▶ **sunspot** n dark patch appearing temporarily on the sun's surface; (Aust) small area of skin damage caused by exposure to the sun ▶ **sunstroke** n illness caused by prolonged exposure to intensely hot sunlight ▶ **suntan** n browning of the skin caused by exposure to the sun

**sundae** n ice cream topped with fruit etc.

**Sunday** n first day of the week and the Christian day of worship ▶ **Sunday school** school for teaching children about Christianity

**sundry** adj several, various ▶ **sundries** pl n several things of various sorts **all and sundry** everybody

**sung** v past participle of **sing**

**sunk** v a past participle of **sink**

**sunken** v a past participle of **sink**

**sup** v **supping, supped** take (liquid) by sips ▷ n sip

**super** adj (informal) excellent

**super-** prefix indicating above or over e.g. superimpose; indicating outstanding e.g. superstar; indicating of greater size or extent e.g. supermarket

**superannuation** n regular payment by an employee into a pension fund; pension paid from this ▶ **superannuated** adj discharged with a pension, owing to old age or illness

**superb** adj excellent, impressive, or splendid ▶ **superbly** adv

**superbug** n (informal) bacterium resistant to antibiotics

**supercharged** adj (of an engine) having a supercharger ▶ **supercharger** n device that increases the power of an internal-

combustion engine by forcing extra air into it

**supercilious** adj showing arrogant pride or scorn

**superconductor** n substance which has almost no electrical resistance at very low temperatures ▶ **superconductivity** n

**superficial** adj not careful or thorough; (of a person) without depth of character, shallow; of or on the surface ▶ **superficially** adv ▶ **superficiality** n

**superfluous** [soo-per-flew-uss] adj more than is needed ▶ **superfluity** n

**superfood** n highly nutritious foodstuff

**superhuman** adj beyond normal human ability or experience

**superimpose** v place (something) on or over something else

**superintendent** n senior police officer; supervisor ▶ **superintend** v supervise (a person or activity)

**superior** adj greater in quality, quantity, or merit; higher in position or rank; believing oneself to be better than others ▷ n person of greater rank or status ▶ **superiority** n

**superlative** [soo-per-lat-iv] adj of outstanding quality; (Grammar) denoting the form of an adjective or adverb indicating most ▷ n (Grammar) superlative form of a word

**superman** n man with great physical or mental powers

**supermarket** n large self-service store selling food and household goods

**supermodel** n famous and highly-paid fashion model

**supernatural** adj of or relating to things beyond the laws of nature **the supernatural** supernatural forces, occurrences, and beings collectively

**supernova** *n*, *pl* **-vae** *or* **-vas** star that explodes and briefly becomes exceptionally bright

**supernumerary** *adj* exceeding the required or regular number ▷ *n*, *pl* **-ries** supernumerary person or thing

**superpower** *n* extremely powerful nation

**superscript** *n*, *adj* (character) printed above the line

**supersede** *v* replace, supplant

> **SPELLING TIP**
> Although there is a word 'cede', spelt with a *c*, the word **supersede** must have an *s* in the middle

**supersize, supersized** *adj* larger than standard size

**supersonic** *adj* of or travelling at a speed greater than the speed of sound

**superstition** *n* belief in omens, ghosts, etc.; idea or practice based on this ▶ **superstitious** *adj*

**superstore** *n* large supermarket

**superstructure** *n* structure erected on something else; part of a ship above the main deck

**supertax** *n* extra tax on incomes above a certain level

**supervene** *v* occur as an unexpected development

**supervise** *v* watch over to direct or check ▶ **supervision** *n* ▶ **supervisor** *n* ▶ **supervisory** *adj*

**supine** *adj* lying flat on one's back

**supper** *n* light evening meal

**supplant** *v* take the place of, oust

**supple** *adj* (of a person) moving and bending easily and gracefully; bending easily without damage ▶ **suppleness** *n*

**supplement** *n* thing added to complete something or make up for a lack; magazine inserted into a newspaper; section added to a publication to supply further information ▷ *v* provide or be a supplement to (something) ▶ **supplementary** *adj*

**supplication** *n* humble request ▶ **suppliant** *n* person who makes a humble request

**supply** *v* **-plying, -plied** provide with something required ▷ *n*, *pl* **-plies** supplying; amount available; (*Economics*) willingness and ability to provide goods and services ▷ *pl* food or equipment ▶ **supplier** *n*

**support** *v* bear the weight of; provide the necessities of life for; give practical or emotional help to; take an active interest in (a sports team, political principle, etc.); help to prove (a theory etc.); speak in favour of ▷ *n* supporting; means of support ▶ **supporter** *n* person who supports a team, principle, etc. ▶ **supportive** *adj*

**suppose** *v* presume to be true; consider as a proposal for the sake of discussion ▶ **supposed** *adj* presumed to be true without proof, doubtful **supposed to** expected or required to e.g. *you were supposed to phone me*; permitted to e.g. *we're not supposed to swim here* ▶ **supposedly** *adv* ▶ **supposition** *n* supposing; something supposed

**suppository** *n*, *pl* **-ries** solid medication inserted into the rectum or vagina and left to melt

**suppress** *v* put an end to; prevent publication of (information); restrain (an emotion or response) ▶ **suppression** *n*

**suppurate** *v* (of a wound etc.) produce pus

**supreme** *adj* highest in authority, rank, or degree ▶ **supremely** *adv* extremely ▶ **supremacy** *n* supreme power; state of being supreme ▶ **supremo** n (*informal*) person in overall authority

**surcharge** n additional charge

**surd** n (*Maths*) number that cannot be expressed in whole numbers

**sure** adj free from uncertainty or doubt; reliable; inevitable ▷ adv, interj (*informal*) certainly ▶ **surely** adv it must be true that ▶ **sure-footed** adj unlikely to slip or stumble

**surety** n, pl **-ties** person who takes responsibility, or thing given as a guarantee, for the fulfilment of another's obligation

**surf** n foam caused by waves breaking on the shore ▷ v take part in surfing; move quickly through a medium such as the internet ▶ **surfing** n sport of riding towards the shore on a surfboard on the crest of a wave ▶ **surfer** n ▶ **surfboard** n long smooth board used in surfing

**surface** n outside or top of an object; material covering the surface of an object; superficial appearance ▷ v rise to the surface; put a surface on

**surfeit** n excessive amount

**surge** n sudden powerful increase; strong rolling movement, esp. of the sea ▷ v increase suddenly; move forward strongly

**surgeon** n doctor who specializes in surgery ▶ **surgery** n, pl **-geries** treatment in which the patient's body is cut open in order to treat the affected part; place where, or time when, a doctor, dentist, etc. can be consulted; (*Brit*) occasion when an elected politician can be consulted ▶ **surgical** adj ▶ **surgically** adv

**surly** adj **-lier, -liest** ill-tempered and rude ▶ **surliness** n

**surmise** v, n guess, conjecture

**surmount** v overcome (a problem); be on top of (something) ▶ **surmountable** adj

**surname** n family name

**surpass** v be greater than or superior to

**surplice** n loose white robe worn by clergymen and choristers

**surplus** n amount left over in excess of what is required

**surprise** n unexpected event; amazement and wonder ▷ v cause to feel amazement or wonder; come upon, attack, or catch suddenly and unexpectedly

**surrealism** n movement in art and literature involving the combination of incongruous images, as in a dream ▶ **surreal** adj bizarre ▶ **surrealist** n, adj ▶ **surrealistic** adj

**surrender** v give oneself up; give (something) up to another; yield (to a temptation or influence) ▷ n surrendering

**surreptitious** adj done secretly or stealthily ▶ **surreptitiously** adv

**surrogate** n substitute ▶ **surrogate mother** woman who gives birth to a child on behalf of a couple who cannot have children

**surround** v be, come, or place all around (a person or thing) ▷ n border or edging ▶ **surroundings** pl n area or environment around a person, place, or thing

**surveillance** n close observation

**survey** v view or consider in a general way; make a map of (an area); inspect (a building) to assess its condition and value; find out the incomes, opinions, etc. of (a group of people) ▷ n surveying; report produced by a survey ▶ **surveyor** n

**survive** v continue to live or exist after (a difficult experience); live after the death of (another)

**S**

▶ **survival** n condition of having survived ▶ **survivor** n

**susceptible** adj liable to be influenced or affected by ▶ **susceptibility** n

**sushi** [soo-shee] n Japanese dish of small cakes of cold rice with a topping of raw fish

**suspect** v believe (someone) to be guilty without having any proof; think (something) to be false or questionable; believe (something) to be the case ▷ adj not to be trusted ▷ n person who is suspected

**suspend** v hang from a high place; cause to remain floating or hanging; cause to cease temporarily; remove (someone) temporarily from a job or team ▶ **suspenders** pl n straps for holding up stockings; (US) braces

**suspense** n state of uncertainty while awaiting news, an event, etc.

**suspension** n suspending or being suspended; system of springs and shock absorbers supporting the body of a vehicle; mixture of fine particles of a solid in a fluid ▶ **suspension bridge** bridge hanging from cables attached to towers at each end

**suspicion** n feeling of not trusting a person or thing; belief that something is true without definite proof; slight trace ▶ **suspicious** adj feeling or causing suspicion ▶ **suspiciously** adv

**suss out** v (slang) work out using one's intuition

**sustain** v maintain or prolong; keep up the vitality or strength of; suffer (an injury or loss); support ▶ **sustenance** n food

**suture** [soo-cher] n stitch joining the edges of a wound

**SUV** sport (or sports) utility vehicle: a powerful car with four-wheel drive, designed for road and off-road use

**suzerain** n state or sovereign with limited authority over another self-governing state ▶ **suzerainty** n

**svelte** adj attractively or gracefully slim

**SW** southwest(ern)

**swab** n small piece of cotton wool used to apply medication, clean a wound, etc. ▷ v **swabbing, swabbed** clean (a wound) with a swab; clean (the deck of a ship) with a mop

**swaddle** v wrap (a baby) in swaddling clothes ▶ **swaddling clothes** long strips of cloth formerly wrapped round a newborn baby

**swag** n (slang) stolen property ▶ **swagman** n (Aust Hist) tramp who carries his belongings in a bundle on his back

**swagger** v walk or behave arrogantly ▷ n arrogant walk or manner

**swain** n (poetic) suitor; country youth

**swallow¹** v cause to pass down one's throat; make a gulping movement in the throat, as when nervous; (informal) believe (something) gullibly; refrain from showing (a feeling); engulf or absorb ▷ n swallowing; amount swallowed

**swallow²** n small migratory bird with long pointed wings and a forked tail

**swam** v past tense of **swim**

**swamp** n watery area of land, bog ▷ v cause (a boat) to fill with water and sink; overwhelm ▶ **swampy** adj

**swan** n large usu. white water bird with a long graceful neck ▷ v **swanning, swanned** (informal) wander about idly ▸ **swan song** *n* person's last performance before retirement or death

**swank** (*slang*) *v* show off or boast ▷ *n* showing off or boasting ▸ **swanky** ▷ *adj* (*slang*) expensive and showy, stylish

**swanndri®** [**swan**-dry] *n* (*NZ*) weatherproof woollen shirt or jacket (also **swannie**)

**swap** *v* **swapping, swapped** exchange (something) for something else ▷ *n* exchange

**sward** *n* stretch of short grass

**swarm¹** *n* large group of bees or other insects; large crowd ▷ *v* move in a swarm; (of a place) be crowded or overrun

**swarm²** *v* (foll by *up*) climb (a ladder or rope) by gripping with the hands and feet

**swarthy** *adj* **-thier, -thiest** dark-complexioned

**swashbuckling** *adj* having the exciting behaviour of pirates, esp. those depicted in films ▸ **swashbuckler** *n*

**swastika** *n* symbol in the shape of a cross with the arms bent at right angles, used as the emblem of Nazi Germany

**swat** *v* **swatting, swatted** hit sharply ▷ *n* sharp blow

**swatch** *n* sample of cloth

**swath** [**swawth**] *n* see **swathe**

**swathe** *v* wrap in bandages or layers of cloth ▷ *n* long strip of cloth wrapped around something; (also **swath**) the width of one sweep of a scythe or mower

**sway** *v* swing to and fro or from side to side; waver or cause to waver in opinion ▷ *n* power or influence; swaying motion

**swear** *v* **swearing, swore, sworn** use obscene or blasphemous language; state or promise on oath; state earnestly ▸ **swear by** *v* have complete confidence in ▸ **swear in** *v* cause to take an oath ▸ **swearword** *n* word considered obscene or blasphemous

**sweat** *n* salty liquid given off through the pores of the skin; (*slang*) drudgery or hard labour ▷ *v* have sweat coming through the pores; be anxious ▸ **sweaty** *adj* ▸ **sweatband** *n* strip of cloth tied around the forehead or wrist to absorb sweat ▸ **sweatshirt** *n* long-sleeved cotton jersey ▸ **sweatshop** *n* place where employees work long hours in poor conditions for low pay

**sweater** *n* (woollen) garment for the upper part of the body

**swede** *n* kind of turnip; (**S-**) person from Sweden ▸ **Swedish** *n, adj* (language) of Sweden

**sweep** *v* **sweeping, swept** remove dirt from (a floor) with a broom; move smoothly and quickly; spread rapidly; move majestically; carry away suddenly or forcefully; stretch in a long wide curve ▷ *n* sweeping; sweeping motion; wide expanse; sweepstake; chimney sweep ▸ **sweeping** *adj* wide-ranging; indiscriminate ▸ **sweepstake** *n* lottery in which the stakes of the participants make up the prize

**sweet** *adj* tasting of or like sugar; kind and charming; agreeable to the senses or mind; (of wine) with a high sugar content ▷ *n* shaped piece of food consisting mainly of sugar; dessert ▸ **sweetly** *adv* ▸ **sweetness** *n* ▸ **sweeten** *v* ▸ **sweetener** *n* sweetening agent that does not contain sugar; (*Brit, Aust & NZ slang*) bribe ▸ **sweetbread** *n* animal's pancreas used as food

▶ **sweet corn** type of maize with sweet yellow kernels, eaten as a vegetable ▶ **sweetheart** n lover ▶ **sweetmeat** n (old-fashioned) sweet delicacy such as a small cake ▶ **sweet pea** climbing plant with bright fragrant flowers ▶ **sweet potato** tropical root vegetable with yellow flesh ▶ **sweet-talk** v (informal) coax or flatter ▶ **sweet tooth** strong liking for sweet foods

**swell** v **swelling, swelled, swollen** or **swelled** expand or increase; (of a sound) become gradually louder ▷ n swelling or being swollen; movement of waves in the sea; (old-fashioned slang) fashionable person ▷ adj (US slang) excellent or fine ▶ **swelling** n enlargement of part of the body, caused by injury or infection

**swelter** v feel uncomfortably hot

**sweltering** adj uncomfortably hot

**swept** v past of **sweep**

**swerve** v turn aside from a course sharply or suddenly ▷ n swerving

**swift** adj moving or able to move quickly ▷ n fast-flying bird with pointed wings ▶ **swiftly** adv ▶ **swiftness** n

**swig** n large mouthful of drink ▷ v **swigging, swigged** drink in large mouthfuls

**swill** v drink greedily; rinse (something) in large amounts of water ▷ n sloppy mixture containing waste food, fed to pigs; deep drink

**swim** v **swimming, swam, swum** move along in water by movements of the limbs; be covered or flooded with liquid; reel e.g. her head was swimming ▷ n act or period of swimming ▶ **swimmer** n ▶ **swimmingly** adv successfully and effortlessly ▶ **swimming pool** (building containing) an artificial pond for swimming in

**swindle** v cheat (someone) out of money ▷ n instance of swindling ▶ **swindler** n

**swine** n contemptible person; pig ▶ **swine flu** n influenza which affects pigs, or human influenza caused by a related virus

**swing** v **swinging, swung** move to and fro, sway; move in a curve; (of an opinion or mood) change sharply; hit out with a sweeping motion; (slang) be hanged ▷ n swinging; suspended seat on which a child can swing to and fro; sudden or extreme change ▶ **swing by** v (informal) go somewhere to pay a visit

**swingeing** [swin-jing] adj punishing, severe

**swipe** v strike (at) with a sweeping blow; (slang) steal; pass (a credit card or debit card) through a machine that electronically reads information stored in the card; activate by moving one's finger across (an item on a screen) ▷ n hard blow ▶ **swipe card** credit card or debit card that is passed through a machine that electronically reads information stored in the card

**swirl** v turn with a whirling motion ▷ n whirling motion; twisting shape

**swish** v move with a whistling or hissing sound ▷ n whistling or hissing sound ▷ adj (informal) fashionable, smart

**Swiss** adj of Switzerland or its people ▷ n, pl **Swiss** person from Switzerland ▶ **swiss roll** sponge cake spread with jam or cream and rolled up

**switch** n device for opening and closing an electric circuit; abrupt change; exchange or swap; flexible rod or twig ▷ v change abruptly; exchange or swap ▶ **switchback** n road or railway with many sharp bends or hills ▶ **switchboard**

S

*n* installation in a telephone exchange or office where telephone calls are connected ▶ **switch on, switch off** *v* turn (a device) on *or* off by means of a switch

**swivel** *v* **-elling, -elled** turn on a central point ▷ *n* coupling device that allows an attached object to turn freely

**swizzle stick** *n* small stick used to stir cocktails

**swollen** *v* a past participle of **swell**

**swoon** *v, n* faint

**swoop** *v* sweep down or pounce on suddenly ▷ *n* swooping

**swop** *v* **swopping, swopped** ▷ *n* same as **swap**

**sword** *n* weapon with a long sharp blade ▶ **swordfish** *n* large fish with a very long upper jaw ▶ **swordsman** *n* person skilled in the use of a sword

**swore** *v* past tense of **swear**

**sworn** *v* past participle of **swear** ▷ *adj* bound by or as if by an oath e.g. *sworn enemies*

**swot** (*informal*) *v* **swotting, swotted** study hard ▷ *n* person who studies hard

**swum** *v* past participle of **swim**

**swung** *v* past tense and past participle of **swing**

**sybarite** [sib-bar-ite] *n* lover of luxury ▶ **sybaritic** *adj*

**sycamore** *n* tree with five-pointed leaves and two-winged fruits

**sycophant** *n* person who uses flattery to win favour from people with power or influence ▶ **sycophantic** *adj* ▶ **sycophancy** *n*

**syllable** *n* part of a word pronounced as a unit ▶ **syllabic** *adj*

**syllabub** *n* dessert of beaten cream, sugar, and wine

**syllabus** *n, pl* **-buses** *or* **-bi** list of subjects for a course of study

**syllogism** *n* form of logical reasoning consisting of two premises and a conclusion

**sylph** *n* slender graceful girl or woman; imaginary being supposed to inhabit the air ▶ **sylphlike** *adj*

**sylvan** *adj* (*lit*) relating to woods and trees

**symbiosis** *n* close association of two species living together to their mutual benefit ▶ **symbiotic** *adj*

**symbol** *n* sign or thing that stands for something else ▶ **symbolic** *adj* ▶ **symbolically** *adv* ▶ **symbolism** *n* representation of something by symbols; movement in art and literature using symbols to express abstract and mystical ideas ▶ **symbolist** *n, adj* ▶ **symbolize** *v* be a symbol of; represent with a symbol

**symmetry** *n* state of having two halves that are mirror images of each other ▶ **symmetrical** *adj* ▶ **symmetrically** *adv*

**sympathy** *n, pl* **-thies** compassion for someone's pain or distress; agreement with someone's feelings or interests ▶ **sympathetic** *adj* feeling or showing sympathy; likeable or appealing ▶ **sympathetically** *adv* ▶ **sympathize** *v* feel or express sympathy ▶ **sympathizer** *n*

**symphony** *n, pl* **-nies** composition for orchestra, with several movements ▶ **symphonic** *adj*

**symposium** *n, pl* **-siums** *or* **-sia** conference for discussion of a particular topic

**symptom** *n* sign indicating the presence of an illness; sign that something is wrong ▶ **symptomatic** *adj*

**synagogue** *n* Jewish place of worship and religious instruction

**sync, synch** (*informal*) *n* synchronization ▷ *v* synchronize

**synchromesh** *adj* (of a gearbox) having a device that synchronizes the speeds of gears before they engage

**synchronize** *v* (of two or more people) perform (an action) at the same time; set (watches) to show the same time; match (the soundtrack and action of a film) precisely ▸ **synchronization** *n* ▸ **synchronous** *adj* happening or existing at the same time

**syncopate** *v* (*Music*) stress the weak beats in (a rhythm) instead of the strong ones ▸ **syncopation** *n*

**syncope** [**sing**-kop-ee] *n* (*Med*) a faint

**syndicate** *n* group of people or firms undertaking a joint business project; agency that sells material to several newspapers; association of individuals who control organized crime ▷ *v* publish (material) in several newspapers; form a syndicate ▸ **syndication** *n*

**syndrome** *n* combination of symptoms indicating a particular disease; set of characteristics indicating a particular problem

**synergy** *n* potential ability for people or groups to be more successful working together than on their own

**synod** *n* church council

**synonym** *n* word with the same meaning as another ▸ **synonymous** *adj*

**synopsis** *n, pl* **-ses** summary or outline

**syntax** *n* (*Grammar*) way in which words are arranged to form phrases and sentences ▸ **syntactic** *adj*

**synthesis** *n, pl* **-ses** combination of objects or ideas into a whole; artificial production of a substance

▸ **synthesize** *v* produce by synthesis ▸ **synthesizer** *n* electronic musical instrument producing a range of sounds ▸ **synthetic** *adj* (of a substance) made artificially; not genuine, insincere ▸ **synthetically** *adv*

**syphilis** *n* serious sexually transmitted disease ▸ **syphilitic** *adj*

**syphon** *n, v* same as **siphon**

**Syrian** *adj* of Syria, its people, or their dialect of Arabic ▷ *n* person from Syria

**syringe** *n* device for withdrawing or injecting fluids, consisting of a hollow cylinder, a piston, and a hollow needle ▷ *v* wash out or inject with a syringe

**syrup** *n* solution of sugar in water; thick sweet liquid ▸ **syrupy** *adj*

**system** *n* method or set of methods; scheme of classification or arrangement; network or assembly of parts that form a whole ▸ **systematic** *adj* ▸ **systematically** *adv* ▸ **systematize** *v* organize using a system ▸ **systematization** *n* ▸ **systemic** *adj* affecting the entire animal or body

**systole** [**siss**-tol-ee] *n* regular contraction of the heart as it pumps blood ▸ **systolic** *adj*

S

# Tt

**T** *n* **to a T** in every detail; perfectly

**t** tonne

**t.** ton

**TA** (in Britain) Territorial Army

**ta** *interj* (*informal*) thank you

**TAB** (in New Zealand) Totalisator Agency Board

**tab** *n* small flap or projecting label **keep tabs on** (*informal*) watch closely

**tabard** *n* short sleeveless tunic decorated with a coat of arms, worn in medieval times

**Tabasco®** *n* very hot red pepper sauce

**tabby** *n*, *pl* **-bies** ▷ *adj* (cat) with dark stripes on a lighter background

**tabernacle** *n* portable shrine of the Israelites; Christian place of worship not called a church; (*RC Church*) receptacle for the consecrated Host

**tabla** *n*, *pl* **-bla** or **-blas** one of a pair of Indian drums played with the hands

**table** *n* piece of furniture with a flat top supported by legs; arrangement of information in columns ▷ *v* submit (a motion) for discussion by a meeting; (*US*) suspend discussion of (a proposal) ▶ **table football** *n* game like soccer played on a table with sets of miniature figures on rods allowing them to be moved to hit a ball ▶ **tableland** *n* high plateau ▶ **tablespoon** *n* large spoon for serving food ▶ **table tennis** game like tennis played on a table with small bats and a light ball

**tableau** [**tab**-loh] *n*, *pl* **-leaux** silent motionless group arranged to represent some scene

**table d'hôte** [**tah**-bla **dote**] *n*, *pl* **tables d'hôte** ▷ *adj* (meal) having a set number of dishes at a fixed price

**tablet** *n* pill of compressed medicinal substance; inscribed slab of stone etc.; handheld computer operated by touching a screen

**tabloid** *n* small-sized newspaper with many photographs and a concise, usu. sensational style

**taboo** *n*, *pl* **-boos** prohibition resulting from religious or social conventions ▷ *adj* forbidden by a taboo

**tabular** *adj* arranged in a table ▶ **tabulate** *v* arrange (information) in a table ▶ **tabulation** *n*

**tachograph** *n* device for recording the speed and distance travelled by a motor vehicle

**tachometer** *n* device for measuring speed, esp. that of a revolving shaft

**tacit** [**tass**-it] *adj* implied but not spoken ▶ **tacitly** *adv*

**taciturn** [**tass**-it-turn] *adj* habitually uncommunicative ▶ **taciturnity** *n*

**tack**¹ *n* short nail with a large head; long loose stitch ▷ *v* fasten with tacks; stitch with tacks ▶ **tack on** *v* append

**tack**² *n* course of a ship sailing obliquely into the wind; course of action ▷ *v* sail into the wind on a zigzag course

**tack**³ *n* riding harness for horses

**tackies, takkies** *pl n*, *sing* **tacky** (*SAfr informal*) tennis shoes or plimsolls

**tackle** *v* deal with (a task); confront (an opponent); (*Sport*) attempt to get the ball from (an opposing player) ▷ *n* (*Sport*) act of tackling an opposing player; equipment for a particular activity; set of ropes and pulleys for lifting heavy weights

**tacky**[1] *adj* **tackier, tackiest** slightly sticky

**tacky**[2] *adj* **tackier, tackiest** (*informal*) vulgar and tasteless; shabby

**taco** [**tah**-koh] *n, pl* **tacos** (*Mexican cookery*) tortilla fried until crisp, served with a filling

**tact** *n* skill in avoiding giving offence ▸ **tactful** *adj* ▸ **tactfully** *adv* ▸ **tactless** *adj* ▸ **tactlessly** *adv*

**tactics** *n* art of directing military forces in battle ▸ **tactic** *n* method or plan to achieve an end ▸ **tactical** *adj* ▸ **tactician** *n*

**tactile** *adj* of or having the sense of touch

**tadpole** *n* limbless tailed larva of a frog or toad

**TAFE** (*Aust*) Technical and Further Education

**taffeta** *n* shiny silk or rayon fabric

**tag**[1] *n* label bearing information; pointed end of a cord or lace; trite quotation ▷ *v* **tagging, tagged** attach a tag to ▸ **tag along** *v* accompany someone, esp. if uninvited

**tag**[2] *n* children's game where the person being chased becomes the chaser upon being touched ▷ *v* **tagging, tagged** touch and catch in this game

**tagliatelle** *n* pasta in long narrow strips

**tail** *n* rear part of an animal's body, usu. forming a flexible appendage; rear or last part or parts of something; (*informal*) person employed to follow and spy on another ▷ *pl* (*informal*) tail coat ▷ *adj* at the rear ▷ *v* (*informal*)

follow (someone) secretly **turn tail** run away ▸ **tailless** *adj* ▸ **tails** *adv* with the side of a coin uppermost that does not have a portrait of a head on it ▸ **tailback** *n* (*Brit*) queue of traffic stretching back from an obstruction ▸ **tailboard** *n* removable or hinged rear board on a truck etc. ▸ **tail coat** man's coat with a long back split into two below the waist ▸ **tail off, tail away** *v* diminish gradually ▸ **tailplane** *n* small stabilizing wing at the rear of an aircraft ▸ **tailspin** *n* uncontrolled spinning dive of an aircraft ▸ **tailwind** *n* wind coming from the rear

**tailor** *n* person who makes men's clothes ▷ *v* adapt to suit a purpose ▸ **tailor-made** *adj* made by a tailor; perfect for a purpose

**taint** *v* spoil with a small amount of decay, contamination, or other bad quality ▷ *n* something that taints

**taipan** *n* large poisonous Australian snake

**take** *v* **taking, took, taken** remove from a place; carry or accompany; use; get possession of, esp. dishonestly; capture; require (time, resources, or ability); assume; accept ▷ *n* one of a series of recordings from which the best will be used **take place** happen ▸ **taking** *adj* charming ▸ **takings** *pl n* money received by a shop ▸ **take after** *v* look or behave like (a parent etc.) ▸ **take away** *v* remove or subtract ▸ **takeaway** *n* shop or restaurant selling meals for eating elsewhere; meal bought at a takeaway ▸ **take in** *v* understand; deceive or swindle; make (clothing) smaller ▸ **take off** *v* (of an aircraft) leave the ground; (*informal*) depart; (*informal*) parody ▸ **takeoff** *n* ▸ **takeover** *n* act of taking control

**t**

of a company by buying a large number of its shares ▸ **take up** v occupy or fill (space or time); adopt the study or activity of; shorten (a garment); accept (an offer)

**talc** n talcum powder; soft mineral of magnesium silicate ▸ **talcum powder** powder, usu. scented, used to dry or perfume the body

**tale** n story; malicious piece of gossip

**talent** n natural ability; ancient unit of weight or money ▸ **talented** adj

**talisman** n, pl -**mans** object believed to have magic power ▸ **talismanic** adj

**talk** v express ideas or feelings by means of speech; utter; discuss e.g. let's talk business; reveal information; (be able to) speak in a specified language ▷ n speech or lecture ▸ **talker** n ▸ **talkative** adj fond of talking ▸ **talk back** v answer impudently ▸ **talkback** n (NZ) broadcast in which telephone comments or questions from the public are transmitted live ▸ **talking-to** n (informal) telling-off

**tall** adj higher than average; of a specified height ▸ **tall order** difficult task ▸ **tall story** unlikely and probably untrue tale

**tallboy** n high chest of drawers

**tallow** n hard animal fat used to make candles

**tally** v -lying, -lied (of two things) correspond ▷ n, pl -lies record of a debt or score

**tally-ho** interj huntsman's cry when the quarry is sighted

**Talmud** n body of Jewish law ▸ **Talmudic** adj

**talon** n bird's hooked claw

**tamarind** n tropical tree; its acid fruit

**tamarisk** n evergreen shrub with slender branches and feathery flower clusters

**tambourine** n percussion instrument like a small drum with jingling metal discs attached

**tame** adj (of animals) brought under human control; (of animals) not afraid of people; meek or submissive; uninteresting ▷ v make tame ▸ **tamely** adv

**tamer** n person who tames wild animals

**Tamil** n member of a people of Sri Lanka and S India; their language

**tam-o'-shanter** n brimless wool cap with a bobble in the centre

**tamp** v pack down by repeated taps

**tamper** v (foll by with) interfere

**tampon** n absorbent plug of cotton wool inserted into the vagina during menstruation

**tan¹** n brown coloration of the skin from exposure to sunlight ▷ v **tanning, tanned** (of skin) go brown from exposure to sunlight; convert (a hide) into leather ▷ adj yellowish-brown ▸ **tannery** n place where hides are tanned

**tan²** (maths) tangent

**tandem** n bicycle for two riders, one behind the other **in tandem** together

**tandoori** adj (of food) cooked in an Indian clay oven

**tang** n strong taste or smell; trace or hint ▸ **tangy** adj

**tangata whenua** [tang-ah-tah **fen**-noo-ah] pl n (NZ) original Polynesian settlers in New Zealand

**tangent** n line that touches a curve without intersecting it; (in trigonometry) ratio of the length of the opposite side to that of the adjacent side of a right-angled triangle **go off at a tangent** suddenly take a completely different line of thought or action ▸ **tangential** adj of superficial relevance only; of a tangent ▶ **tangentially** adv

**tangerine** n small orange-like fruit of an Asian citrus tree

**tangible** adj able to be touched; clear and definite ▶ **tangibly** adv

**tangle** n confused mass or situation ▷ v twist together in a tangle; (often foll by with) come into conflict

**tango** n, pl **-gos** S American dance ▷ v dance a tango

**taniwha** [tun-ee-fah] n (NZ) mythical Māori monster that lives in water

**tank** n container for liquids or gases; armoured fighting vehicle moving on tracks ▶ **tanker** n ship or truck for carrying liquid in bulk

**tankard** n large beer-mug, often with a hinged lid

**tannin, tannic acid** n vegetable substance used in tanning

**Tannoy**® n (Brit) type of public-address system

**tansy** n, pl **-sies** yellow-flowered plant

**tantalize** v torment by showing but withholding something desired ▶ **tantalizing** adj ▶ **tantalizingly** adv

**tantalum** n (Chem) hard greyish-white metallic element

**tantamount** adj **tantamount to** equivalent in effect to

**tantrum** n childish outburst of temper

**tap**¹ v **tapping, tapped** knock lightly and usu. repeatedly ▷ n light knock ▶ **tap dancing** style of dancing in which the feet beat out an elaborate rhythm

**tap**² n valve to control the flow of liquid in a pipe or cask ▷ v **tapping, tapped** listen in on (a telephone call) secretly by making an illegal connection; draw off with or as if with a tap **on tap** (informal)

readily available; (of beer etc.) drawn from a cask

**tape** n narrow long strip of material; (recording made on) a cassette containing magnetic tape; string stretched across a race track to mark the finish ▷ v record on magnetic tape; bind or fasten with tape ▶ **tape measure** tape marked off in centimetres or inches for measuring ▶ **tape recorder** device for recording and reproducing sound on magnetic tape ▶ **tapeworm** n long flat parasitic worm living in the intestines of vertebrates

**taper** v become narrower towards one end ▷ n long thin candle ▶ **taper off** v become gradually less

**tapestry** n, pl **-tries** fabric decorated with coloured woven designs

**tapioca** n beadlike starch made from cassava root, used in puddings

**tapir** [tape-er] n piglike mammal of tropical America and SE Asia, with a long snout

**tappet** n short steel rod in an engine, transferring motion from one part to another

**taproot** n main root of a plant, growing straight down

**tar** n thick black liquid distilled from coal etc. ▷ v **tarring, tarred** coat with tar ▶ **tar-seal** n (NZ) tarred road surface

**taramasalata** n creamy pink pâté made from fish roe

**tarantella** n lively Italian dance; music for this

**tarantula** n large hairy spider with a poisonous bite

**tardy** adj **tardier, tardiest** slow or late ▶ **tardily** adv ▶ **tardiness** n

**tare** n type of vetch plant; (Bible) weed

**target** n object or person a missile is aimed at; goal or objective; object of criticism ▷ v **-geting, -geted** aim or direct

> **SPELLING TIP**
> Note that **targeting** and **targeted** have only one t in the middle

**tariff** n tax levied on imports; list of fixed prices

**Tarmac**® n mixture of tar, bitumen, and crushed stones used for roads etc.; (**t-**) airport runway

**tarn** n small mountain lake

**tarnish** v make or become stained or less bright; damage or taint ▷ n discoloration or blemish

**tarot** [tarr-oh] n special pack of cards used mainly in fortune-telling ▶ **tarot card** card in a tarot pack

**tarpaulin** n (sheet of) heavy waterproof fabric

**tarragon** n aromatic herb

**tarry** v **-rying, -ried** (old-fashioned) linger or delay; stay briefly

**tarsus** n, pl **-si** bones of the heel and ankle collectively

**tart**[1] n pie or flan with a sweet filling

**tart**[2] adj sharp or bitter ▶ **tartly** adv ▶ **tartness** n

**tart**[3] n (informal) sexually provocative or promiscuous woman ▶ **tart up** v (informal) dress or decorate in a smart or flashy way

**tartan** n design of straight lines crossing at right angles, esp. one associated with a Scottish clan; cloth with such a pattern

**tartar**[1] n hard deposit on the teeth; deposit formed during the fermentation of wine

**tartar**[2] n fearsome or formidable person

**tartare sauce** n mayonnaise sauce mixed with chopped herbs and capers, served with seafood

**tartrazine** [tar-traz-zeen] n artificial yellow dye used in food etc.

**TAS** Tasmania

**task** n (difficult or unpleasant) piece of work to be done **take to task** criticize or scold ▶ **task force** (military) group formed to carry out a specific task ▶ **taskmaster** n person who enforces hard work

**Tasmanian** n, adj (person) from Tasmania ▶ **Tasmanian devil** small carnivorous Tasmanian marsupial ▶ **Tasmanian tiger** same as **thylacine**

**tassel** n decorative fringed knot of threads

**taste** n sense by which the flavour of a substance is distinguished in the mouth; distinctive flavour; small amount tasted; brief experience of something; liking; ability to appreciate what is beautiful or excellent ▷ v distinguish the taste of (a substance); take a small amount of (something) into the mouth; have a specific taste; experience briefly ▶ **tasteful** adj having or showing good taste ▶ **tastefully** adv ▶ **tasteless** adj bland or insipid; showing bad taste ▶ **tastelessly** adv ▶ **tasty** adj pleasantly flavoured ▶ **taste bud** small organ on the tongue which perceives flavours

**tat** n (Brit) tatty or tasteless article(s)

**tattered** adj ragged or torn **in tatters** in ragged pieces

**tattle** v, n (Brit, Aust & NZ) gossip or chatter

**tattoo**[1] n pattern made on the body by pricking the skin and staining it with indelible inks ▷ v **-tooing, -tooed** make such a pattern on the skin ▶ **tattooist** n

**tattoo**[2] n military display or pageant; drumming or tapping

**tatty** adj **-tier, -tiest** shabby or worn out

t

**taught** v past of **teach**

**taunt** v tease with jeers ▷ n jeering remark

**taupe** adj brownish-grey

**taut** adj drawn tight; showing nervous strain ▸ **tauten** v make or become taut

**tautology** n, pl **-gies** use of words which merely repeat something already stated ▸ **tautological** adj

**tavern** n (old-fashioned) pub

**tawdry** adj **-drier, -driest** cheap, showy, and of poor quality

**tawny** adj **-nier, -niest** yellowish-brown

**tax** n compulsory payment levied by a government on income, property, etc. to raise revenue ▷ v levy a tax on; make heavy demands on ▸ **taxable** adj ▸ **taxation** n levying of taxes ▸ **tax-free** adj (of goods, services and income) not taxed ▸ **taxpayer** n person who pays income tax ▸ **tax relief** reduction in the amount of tax a person or company has to pay ▸ **tax return** statement of personal income for tax purposes

**taxi** n (also **taxicab**) car with a driver that may be hired to take people to any specified destination ▷ v **taxiing, taxied** (of an aircraft) run along the ground before taking off or after landing ▸ **taxi meter** meter in a taxi that registers the fare ▸ **taxi rank** place where taxis wait to be hired

**taxidermy** n art of stuffing and mounting animal skins to give them a lifelike appearance ▸ **taxidermist** n

**taxonomy** n classification of plants and animals into groups ▸ **taxonomic** adj ▸ **taxonomist** n

**TB** tuberculosis

**tba, TBA** to be arranged

**tbc** to be confirmed

**tbs., tbsp.** tablespoon(ful)

**tea** n drink made from infusing the dried leaves of an Asian bush in boiling water; leaves used to make this drink; (Brit, Aust & NZ) main evening meal; (chiefly Brit) light afternoon meal of tea, cakes, etc.; drink like tea, made from other plants ▸ **tea bag** small porous bag of tea leaves ▸ **tea cosy** covering for a teapot to keep the tea warm ▸ **teapot** n container with a lid, spout, and handle for making and serving tea ▸ **teaspoon** n small spoon for stirring tea ▸ **tea towel, tea cloth** towel for drying dishes ▸ **tea tree** tree of Australia and New Zealand that yields an oil used as an antiseptic

**teach** v **teaching, taught** tell or show (someone) how to do something; give lessons in (a subject); cause to learn or understand ▸ **teaching** n

**teacher** n person who teaches, esp. in a school

**teak** n very hard wood of an E Indian tree

**teal** n kind of small duck

**team** n group of people forming one side in a game; group of people or animals working together ▸ **teamster** n (US) commercial vehicle driver ▸ **team up** v make or join a team ▸ **teamwork** n cooperative work by a team

**tear¹, teardrop** n drop of fluid appearing in and falling from the eye **in tears** weeping ▸ **tearful** adj weeping or about to weep ▸ **tear gas** gas that stings the eyes and causes temporary blindness ▸ **tear-jerker** n (informal) excessively sentimental film or book

**tear²** v **tearing, tore, torn** rip a hole in; rip apart; rush ▷ n hole or split ▸ **tearaway** n wild or unruly person

t

**tease** v make fun of (someone) in a provoking or playful way ▷ n person who teases ▸ **teasing** adj, n ▸ **tease out** v remove tangles from (hair etc.) by combing

**teasel, teazel, teazle** n plant with prickly leaves and flowers

**teat** n nipple of a breast or udder; rubber nipple of a feeding bottle

**tech** n (informal) technical college

**techie** (informal) n person who is skilled in the use of technology ▷ adj relating to or skilled in the use of technology

**technetium** [tek-**neesh**-ee-um] n (Chem) artificially produced silvery-grey metallic element

**technical** adj of or specializing in industrial, practical, or mechanical arts and applied sciences; skilled in technical subjects; relating to a particular field; according to the letter of the law; showing technique e.g. technical brilliance ▸ **technically** adv ▸ **technicality** n petty point based on a strict application of rules ▸ **technician** n person skilled in a particular technical field ▸ **technical college** higher educational institution with courses in art and technical subjects

**Technicolor**® n system of colour photography used for the cinema

**technique** n method or skill used for a particular task; technical proficiency

**techno** n type of electronic dance music with a very fast beat

**technocracy** n, pl -cies government by technical experts ▸ **technocrat** n

**technology** n application of practical or mechanical sciences to industry or commerce; scientific methods used in a particular field ▸ **technological** adj ▸ **technologist** n

**tectonics** n study of the earth's crust and the forces affecting it

**teddy** n, pl -dies teddy bear; combined camisole and knickers ▸ **teddy bear** soft toy bear

**tedious** adj causing fatigue or boredom ▸ **tediously** adv ▸ **tedium** n monotony

**tee** n small peg from which a golf ball can be played at the start of each hole; area of a golf course from which the first stroke of a hole is made ▸ **tee off** v make the first stroke of a hole in golf

**teem**¹ v be full of

**teem**² v rain heavily

**teenager** n person aged between 13 and 19 ▸ **teenage** adj

**teens** pl n period of being a teenager

**teepee** n same as **tepee**

**tee-shirt** n same as **T-shirt**

**teeter** v wobble or move unsteadily

**teeth** n plural of **tooth**

**teethe** v (of a baby) grow his or her first teeth ▸ **teething troubles** problems during the early stages of something

**teetotal** adj drinking no alcohol ▸ **teetotaller** n

**TEFL** Teaching of English as a Foreign Language

**Teflon**® n substance used for nonstick coatings on saucepans etc.

**tele-** combining form distance e.g. telecommunications; telephone or television e.g. teleconference

**telecommunications** n communications using telephone, radio, television, etc.

**telegram** n formerly, a message sent by telegraph

**telegraph** n formerly, a system for sending messages over a distance along a cable ▷ v communicate by telegraph ▸ **telegraphic** adj

t

▶ **telegraphist** n ▶ **telegraphy** n science or use of a telegraph

**telekinesis** n movement of objects by thought or willpower

**telemetry** n use of electronic devices to record or measure a distant event and transmit the data to a receiver

**teleology** n belief that all things have a predetermined purpose ▶ **teleological** adj

**telepathy** n direct communication between minds ▶ **telepathic** adj ▶ **telepathically** adv

**telephone** n device for transmitting sound over a distance along wires ▷ v call or talk to (a person) by telephone ▶ **telephony** n ▶ **telephonic** adj ▶ **telephonist** n person operating a telephone switchboard

**telephoto lens** n camera lens producing a magnified image of a distant object

**teleprinter** n (Brit) apparatus like a typewriter for sending and receiving typed messages by wire

**telesales** n selling of a product or service by telephone

**telescope** n optical instrument for magnifying distant objects ▷ v shorten ▶ **telescopic** adj

**television** n system of producing a moving image and accompanying sound on a distant screen; device for receiving broadcast signals and converting them into sound and pictures; content of television programmes ▶ **televise** v broadcast on television ▶ **televisual** adj

**telex** n international communication service using teleprinters; message sent by telex ▷ v transmit by telex

**tell** v **telling, told** make known in words; order or instruct; give an account of; discern or distinguish; have an effect; (informal) reveal secrets ▶ **teller** n narrator; bank cashier; person who counts votes ▶ **telling** adj having a marked effect ▶ **tell off** v reprimand ▶ **telling-off** n ▶ **telltale** n person who reveals secrets ▷ adj revealing

**tellurium** n (Chem) brittle silvery-white nonmetallic element

**telly** n, pl **-lies** (informal) television

**temerity** [tim-**merr**-it-tee] n boldness or audacity

**temp** (Brit informal) n temporary employee, esp. a secretary ▷ v work as a temp

**temp.** temperature; temporary

**temper** n outburst of anger; tendency to become angry; calm mental condition e.g. I lost my temper; frame of mind ▷ v make less extreme; strengthen or toughen (metal)

**tempera** n painting medium for powdered pigments

**temperament** n person's character or disposition ▶ **temperamental** adj having changeable moods; (informal) erratic and unreliable ▶ **temperamentally** adv

**temperate** adj (of climate) not extreme; self-restrained or moderate ▶ **temperance** n moderation; abstinence from alcohol

**temperature** n degree of heat or cold; (informal) abnormally high body temperature

**tempest** n violent storm ▶ **tempestuous** adj violent or stormy

**template** n pattern used to cut out shapes accurately

**temple¹** n building for worship

**temple²** n region on either side of the forehead ▶ **temporal** adj

t

**tempo** n, pl **-pi** or **-pos** rate or pace; speed of a piece of music

**temporal** adj of time; worldly rather than spiritual

**temporary** adj lasting only for a short time ▸ **temporarily** adv

**temporize** v gain time by negotiation or evasiveness; adapt to circumstances

**tempt** v entice (a person) to do something wrong **tempt fate** take foolish or unnecessary risks ▸ **tempter**, (fem) **temptress** n ▸ **temptation** n tempting; tempting thing ▸ **tempting** adj attractive or inviting

**ten** adj, n one more than nine ▸ **tenth** adj, n (of) number ten in a series

**tenable** adj able to be upheld or maintained

**tenacious** adj holding fast; stubborn ▸ **tenaciously** adv ▸ **tenacity** n

**tenant** n person who rents land or a building ▸ **tenancy** n

**tench** n, pl **tench** freshwater game fish of the carp family

**tend¹** v be inclined; go in the direction of ▸ **tendency** n inclination to act in a certain way ▸ **tendentious** adj biased, not impartial

**tend²** v take care of

**tender¹** adj not tough; gentle and affectionate; vulnerable or sensitive ▸ **tenderly** adv ▸ **tenderness** n ▸ **tenderize** v soften (meat) by pounding or treatment with a special substance

**tender²** v offer; make a formal offer to supply goods or services at a stated cost ▷ n such an offer **legal tender** currency that must, by law, be accepted as payment

**tender³** n small boat that brings supplies to a larger ship in a port; carriage for fuel and water attached to a steam locomotive

**tendon** n strong tissue attaching a muscle to a bone

**tendril** n slender stem by which a climbing plant clings

**tenement** n (esp. in Scotland and the US) building divided into several flats

**tenet** [ten-nit] n doctrine or belief

**tenner** n (Brit informal) ten-pound note

**tennis** n game in which players use rackets to hit a ball back and forth over a net

**tenon** n projecting end on a piece of wood fitting into a slot in another

**tenor** n (singer with) the second highest male voice; general meaning ▷ adj (of a voice or instrument) between alto and baritone

**tenpin bowling** n game in which players try to knock over ten skittles by rolling a ball at them

**tense¹** adj emotionally strained; stretched tight ▷ v make or become tense

**tense²** n (Grammar) form of a verb showing the time of action

**tensile** adj of tension

**tension** n hostility or suspense; emotional strain; degree of stretching

**tent** n portable canvas shelter

**tentacle** n flexible organ of many invertebrates, used for grasping, feeding, etc.

**tentative** adj provisional or experimental; cautious or hesitant ▸ **tentatively** adv

**tenterhooks** pl n **on tenterhooks** in anxious suspense

**tenuous** adj slight or flimsy ▸ **tenuously** adv

**tenure** n (period of) the holding of an office or position

**tepee** [**tee**-pee] *n* cone-shaped tent, formerly used by Native Americans

**tepid** *adj* slightly warm; half-hearted

**tequila** *n* Mexican alcoholic drink

**tercentenary** *adj, n, pl* **-naries** (of) a three hundredth anniversary

**term** *n* word or expression; fixed period; period of the year when a school etc. is open or a lawcourt holds sessions ▷ *pl* conditions; mutual relationship ▷ *v* name or designate

**terminal** *adj* (of an illness) ending in death; at or being an end ▷ *n* place where people or vehicles begin or end a journey; point where current enters or leaves an electrical device; keyboard and VDU having input and output links with a computer ▶ **terminally** *adv*

**terminate** *v* bring or come to an end ▶ **termination** *n* bringing to an end; abortion

**terminology** *n* technical terms relating to a subject

**terminus** *n, pl* **-ni** *or* **-nuses** railway or bus station at the end of a line

**termite** *n* white ant-like insect that destroys timber

**tern** *n* gull-like sea bird with a forked tail and pointed wings

**ternary** *adj* consisting of three parts

**Terpsichorean** *adj* of dancing

**terrace** *n* row of houses built as one block; paved area next to a building; level tier cut out of a hill ▷ *pl* (also **terracing**) tiered area in a stadium where spectators stand ▷ *v* form into or provide with a terrace

**terracotta** *adj, n* (made of) brownish-red unglazed pottery ▷ *adj* brownish-red

**terra firma** *n* (*Latin*) dry land or solid ground

**terrain** *n* area of ground, esp. with reference to its physical character

**terrapin** *n* small turtle-like reptile

**terrarium** *n, pl* **-raria** *or* **-rariums** enclosed container for small plants or animals

**terrazzo** *n, pl* **-zos** floor of marble chips set in mortar and polished

**terrestrial** *adj* of the earth; of or living on land

**terrible** *adj* very serious; (*informal*) very bad; causing fear ▶ **terribly** *adv*

**terrier** *n* any of various breeds of small active dog

**terrific** *adj* great or intense; (*informal*) excellent

**terrify** *v* **-fying, -fied** fill with fear ▶ **terrified** *adj* ▶ **terrifying** *adj*

**terrine** [terr-**reen**] *n* earthenware dish with a lid; pâté or similar food

**territory** *n, pl* **-ries** district; area under the control of a particular government; area inhabited and defended by an animal; area of knowledge ▶ **territorial** *adj* ▶ **Territorial Army** (in Britain) reserve army

**terror** *n* great fear; terrifying person or thing; (*Brit, Aust & NZ informal*) troublesome person or thing ▶ **terrorism** *n* use of violence and intimidation to achieve political ends ▶ **terrorist** *n, adj* ▶ **terrorize** *v* force or oppress by fear or violence

**terry** *n* fabric with small loops covering both sides, used esp. for making towels

**terse** *adj* neat and concise; curt ▶ **tersely** *adv*

**tertiary** [**tur**-shar-ee] *adj* third in degree, order, etc.

**Terylene®** *n* synthetic polyester yarn or fabric

**tessellated** *adj* paved or inlaid with a mosaic of small tiles

t

**test** v try out to ascertain the worth, capability, or endurance of; carry out an examination on ▷ n critical examination; Test match ▶ **testing** adj ▶ **test case** lawsuit that establishes a precedent ▶ **Test match** one of a series of international cricket or rugby matches ▶ **test tube** narrow round-bottomed glass tube used in scientific experiments ▶ **test-tube baby** baby conceived outside the mother's body

**testament** n proof or tribute; (Law) will; (T-) one of the two main divisions of the Bible

**testator** [test-**tay**-tor], (fem) **testatrix** [test-**tay**-triks] n maker of a will

**testicle** n either of the two male reproductive glands

**testify** v -**fying**, -**fied** give evidence under oath **testify to** be evidence of

**testimony** n, pl -**nies** declaration of truth or fact; evidence given under oath ▶ **testimonial** n recommendation of the worth of a person or thing; tribute for services or achievement

**testis** n, pl -**tes** testicle

**testosterone** n male sex hormone secreted by the testes

**testy** adj -**tier**, -**tiest** irritable or touchy ▶ **testily** adv ▶ **testiness** n

**tetanus** n acute infectious disease producing muscular spasms and convulsions

**tête-à-tête** n, pl -**têtes** or -**tête** private conversation

**tether** n rope or chain for tying an animal to a spot ▷ v tie up with rope **at the end of one's tether** at the limit of one's endurance

**tetrahedron** [tet-ra-**heed**-ron] n, pl -**drons** or -**dra** solid figure with four faces

**tetralogy** n, pl -**gies** series of four related works

**Teutonic** [tew-**tonn**-ik] adj of or like the (ancient) Germans

**text** n main body of a book as distinct from illustrations etc.; passage of the Bible as the subject of a sermon; novel or play studied for a course; text message ▷ v send a text message to (someone) ▶ **textual** adj ▶ **textbook** n standard book on a particular subject ▷ adj perfect e.g. a textbook landing ▶ **text message** message sent in text form, esp. by means of a mobile phone

**textile** n fabric or cloth, esp. woven

**texture** n structure, feel, or consistency ▶ **textured** adj ▶ **textural** adj

**Thai** adj of Thailand ▷ n (pl **Thais** or **Thai**) person from Thailand; language of Thailand

**thalidomide** [thal-**lid**-oh-mide] n drug formerly used as a sedative, but found to cause abnormalities in developing fetuses

**thallium** n (Chem) highly toxic metallic element

**than** conj, prep used to introduce the second element of a comparison

**thane** n (Hist) Anglo-Saxon or medieval Scottish nobleman

**thank** v express gratitude to; hold responsible ▶ **thanks** pl n words of gratitude ▷ interj (also **thank you**) polite expression of gratitude **thanks to** because of ▶ **thankful** adj grateful ▶ **thankless** adj unrewarding or unappreciated ▶ **Thanksgiving (Day)** autumn public holiday in Canada and the US

**that** adj, pron used to refer to something already mentioned or familiar, or further away ▷ conj used to introduce a clause ▷ pron used to introduce a relative clause

**thatch** n roofing material of reeds or straw ▷ v roof (a house) with reeds or straw

**thaw** v make or become unfrozen; become more relaxed or friendly ▷ n thawing; weather causing snow or ice to melt

**the** adj the definite article, used before a noun

**theatre** n place where plays etc. are performed; hospital operating room; drama and acting in general ▶ **theatrical** adj of the theatre; exaggerated or affected ▶ **theatricals** pl n (amateur) dramatic performances ▶ **theatrically** adv ▶ **theatricality** n

**thee** pron (obs) objective form of **thou**

**theft** n act or an instance of stealing

**their** adj of or associated with them ▶ **theirs** pron (thing or person) belonging to them

> **USAGE NOTE**
> Note the difference between their and there. Their is used for possession: their new baby. There indicates place and has a similar '-ere' spelling pattern to here and where. Also, do not confuse **their** and **theirs**, which do not have apostrophes, with **they're** and **there's**, which do have them (because letters have been missed out where two words have been joined together)

**theism** [**thee**-iz-zum] n belief in a God or gods ▶ **theist** n, adj ▶ **theistic** adj

**them** pron refers to people or things other than the speaker or those addressed ▶ **themselves** pron emphatic and reflexive form of **they, them**

> **USAGE NOTE**
> Them may be used after a singular to avoid the clumsy him or her: If you see a person looking lost, help them

**theme** n main idea or subject being discussed; recurring melodic figure in music ▶ **thematic** adj ▶ **theme park** leisure area in which all the activities and displays are based on a single theme

**then** adv at that time; after that; that being so

**thence** adv (old-fashioned) from that place or time; therefore

**theocracy** n, pl -cies government by a god or priests ▶ **theocratic** adj

**theodolite** [thee-**odd**-oh-lite] n surveying instrument for measuring angles

**theology** n, pl -gies study of religions and religious beliefs ▶ **theologian** n ▶ **theological** adj ▶ **theologically** adv

**theorem** n proposition that can be proved by reasoning

**theory** n, pl -ries set of ideas to explain something; abstract knowledge or reasoning; idea or opinion **in theory** in an ideal or hypothetical situation ▶ **theoretical** adj based on theory rather than practice or fact ▶ **theoretically** adv ▶ **theorist** n ▶ **theorize** v form theories, speculate

**theosophy** n religious or philosophical system claiming to be based on intuitive insight into the divine nature ▶ **theosophical** adj

**therapy** n, pl -pies curing treatment ▶ **therapist** n ▶ **therapeutic** [ther-rap-**pew**-tik] adj curing ▶ **therapeutics** n art of curing

**there** adv in or to that place; in that respect ▶ **thereby** adv by that means ▶ **therefore** adv

t

consequently, that being so
▶ **thereupon** adv immediately
after that

SPELLING TIP

Do not confuse **there**, which is
closely connected in meaning
and in spelling with 'here', and
**their**, which means 'belonging
to them'

**therm** n unit of measurement
of heat

**thermal** adj of heat; hot or warm;
(of clothing) retaining heat ▷ n
rising current of warm air

**thermodynamics** n scientific
study of the relationship between
heat and other forms of energy

**thermometer** n instrument for
measuring temperature

**thermonuclear** adj involving
nuclear fusion

**thermoplastic** adj (of a plastic)
softening when heated and
resetting on cooling

**Thermos®** n vacuum flask

**thermosetting** adj (of a plastic)
remaining hard when heated

**thermostat** n device for
automatically regulating
temperature ▶ **thermostatic** adj
▶ **thermostatically** adv

**thesaurus** [thiss-**sore**-uss] n, pl
**-ruses** book containing lists of
synonyms and related words

**these** adj, pron plural of **this**

**thesis** n, pl **theses** written work
submitted for a degree; opinion
supported by reasoned argument

**Thespian** n actor or actress ▷ adj
of the theatre

**they** pron refers to people or things
other than the speaker or people
addressed; refers to people in
general; (informal) refers to he or she

USAGE NOTE

They may be used after a singular
to avoid the clumsy he or she:

If a person is born gloomy, they
cannot help it

**thiamine** n vitamin found in the
outer coat of rice and other grains

**thick** adj of great or specified extent
from one side to the other; having
a dense consistency; (informal)
stupid or insensitive; (Brit, Aust &
NZ informal) friendly **a bit thick**
(informal) unfair or unreasonable
**the thick** busiest or most intense
part **thick with** full of ▶ **thicken**
v make or become thick or thicker
▶ **thickly** adv ▶ **thickness** n state
of being thick; dimension through
an object; layer ▶ **thickset** adj
stocky in build

**thicket** n dense growth of small
trees

**thief** n, pl **thieves** person
who steals ▶ **thieve** v steal
▶ **thieving** adj

**thigh** n upper part of the human leg

**thimble** n cap used to protect the
end of the finger when sewing

**thin** adj **thinner, thinnest** not
thick; slim or lean; sparse or
meagre; of low density; poor
or unconvincing ▷ v **thinning,
thinned** make or become thin
▶ **thinly** adv ▶ **thinness** n

**thine** pron, adj (obs) (something) of
or associated with you (thou)

**thing** n material object; object,
fact, or idea considered as
a separate entity; (informal)
obsession ▷ pl possessions,
clothes, etc.

**think** v **thinking, thought**
consider, judge, or believe;
make use of the mind; be
considerate enough or remember
to do something ▶ **thinker** n
▶ **thinking** adj, n ▶ **think-tank** n
group of experts studying
specific problems ▶ **think up** v
invent or devise

**third** adj of number three in a series; rated or graded below the second level ▷ n one of three equal parts ▸ **third degree** violent interrogation ▸ **third party** (applying to) a person involved by chance or only incidentally in legal proceedings, an accident, etc. ▸ **Third World** developing countries of Africa, Asia, and Latin America

**thirst** n desire to drink; craving or yearning ▷ v feel thirst ▸ **thirsty** adj ▸ **thirstily** adv

**thirteen** adj, n three plus ten ▸ **thirteenth** adj, n

**thirty** adj, n three times ten ▸ **thirtieth** adj, n

**this** adj, pron used to refer to a thing or person nearby, just mentioned, or about to be mentioned ▷ adj used to refer to the present time e.g. this morning

**thistle** n prickly plant with dense flower heads

**thither** adv (obs) to or towards that place

**thong** n thin strip of leather etc.; skimpy article of underwear or beachwear that covers the genitals while leaving the buttocks bare

**thorax** n, pl **thoraxes** or **thoraces** part of the body between the neck and the abdomen ▸ **thoracic** adj

**thorn** n prickle on a plant; bush with thorns **thorn in one's side, thorn in one's flesh** source of irritation ▸ **thorny** adj

**thorough** adj complete; careful or methodical ▸ **thoroughly** adv ▸ **thoroughness** n ▸ **thoroughbred** n, adj (animal) of pure breed ▸ **thoroughfare** n way through from one place to another

**those** adj, pron plural of **that**

**thou** pron (obs) singular form of **you**

**though** conj despite the fact that ▷ adv nevertheless

**thought** v past of **think** ▷ n thinking; concept or idea; ideas typical of a time or place; consideration; intention or expectation ▸ **thoughtful** adj considerate; showing careful thought; pensive or reflective ▸ **thoughtless** adj inconsiderate

**thousand** adj, n ten hundred; large but unspecified number ▸ **thousandth** adj, n (of) number one thousand in a series

**thrall** n state of being in the power of another person

**thrash** v beat, esp. with a stick or whip; defeat soundly; move about wildly; thresh ▸ **thrashing** n severe beating ▸ **thrash out** v solve by thorough argument

**thread** n fine strand or yarn; unifying theme; spiral ridge on a screw, nut, or bolt ▷ v pass thread through; pick (one's way etc.) ▸ **threadbare** adj (of fabric) with the nap worn off; hackneyed; shabby

**threat** n declaration of intent to harm; dangerous person or thing ▸ **threaten** v make or be a threat to; be a menacing indication of

**three** adj, n one more than two ▸ **threesome** n group of three ▸ **three-dimensional, 3-D** adj having three dimensions

**threnody** n, pl **-dies** lament for the dead

**thresh** v beat (wheat etc.) to separate the grain from the husks and straw ▸ **thresh about** move about wildly

**threshold** n bar forming the bottom of a doorway; entrance; starting point; point at which something begins to take effect

**threw** v past tense of **throw**

t

**thrice** adv (lit) three times

**thrift** n wisdom and caution with money; low-growing plant with pink flowers ▸ **thrifty** adj

**thrill** n sudden feeling of excitement ▷ v (cause to) feel a thrill ▸ **thrilling** adj

**thriller** n book, film, etc. with an atmosphere of mystery or suspense

**thrive** v **thriving, thrived** or **throve, thrived** or **thriven** flourish or prosper; grow well

**throat** n passage from the mouth and nose to the stomach and lungs; front of the neck ▸ **throaty** adj (of the voice) hoarse

**throb** v **throbbing, throbbed** pulsate repeatedly; vibrate rhythmically ▷ n throbbing

**throes** pl n violent pangs or pains **in the throes of** struggling to cope with

**thrombosis** n, pl **-ses** forming of a clot in a blood vessel or the heart

**throne** n ceremonial seat of a monarch or bishop; sovereign power

**throng** n, v crowd

**throstle** n song thrush

**throttle** n device controlling the amount of fuel entering an engine ▷ v strangle

**through** prep from end to end or side to side of; because of; during ▷ adj finished; (of transport) going directly to a place **through and through** completely ▸ **throughout** prep, adv in every part (of) ▸ **throughput** n amount of material processed

**throve** v a past tense of **thrive**

**throw** v **throwing, threw, thrown** hurl through the air; move or put suddenly or carelessly; bring into a specified state, esp. suddenly; give (a party); (informal) baffle or disconcert ▷ n throwing; distance thrown ▸ **throwaway** adj done or said casually; designed to be discarded after use ▸ **throwback** n person or thing that reverts to an earlier type ▸ **throw up** v vomit

**thrush**[1] n brown songbird

**thrush**[2] n fungal disease of the mouth or vagina

**thrust** v **thrusting, thrust** push forcefully ▷ n forceful stab; force or power; intellectual or emotional drive

**thud** n dull heavy sound ▷ v **thudding, thudded** make such a sound

**thug** n violent man, esp. a criminal ▸ **thuggery** n ▸ **thuggish** adj

**thumb** n short thick finger set apart from the others ▷ v touch or handle with the thumb; signal with the thumb for a lift in a vehicle ▸ **thumb through** flick through (a book or magazine)

**thump** n (sound of) a dull heavy blow ▷ v strike heavily

**thunder** n loud noise accompanying lightning ▷ v rumble with thunder; shout; move fast, heavily, and noisily ▸ **thunderous** adj ▸ **thundery** adj ▸ **thunderbolt** n lightning flash; something sudden and unexpected ▸ **thunderclap** n peal of thunder ▸ **thunderstruck** adj amazed

**Thursday** n fifth day of the week

**thus** adv therefore; in this way

**thwack** v, n whack

**thwart** v foil or frustrate ▷ n seat across a boat

**thy** adj (obs) of or associated with you (thou) ▸ **thyself** pron (obs) emphatic form of **thou**

**thylacine** n extinct doglike Tasmanian marsupial

**thyme** [time] n aromatic herb

**thymus** n, pl **-muses** or **-mi** small gland at the base of the neck

**thyroid** *adj*, *n* (of) a gland in the neck controlling body growth

**tiara** *n* semicircular jewelled headdress

**tibia** *n*, *pl* **tibiae** *or* **tibias** inner bone of the lower leg ▶ **tibial** *adj*

**tic** *n* spasmodic muscular twitch

**tick¹** *n* mark (✓) used to check off or indicate the correctness of something; recurrent tapping sound, as of a clock; (*informal*) moment ▷ *v* mark with a tick; make a ticking sound ▶ **tick off** *v* mark with a tick; reprimand ▶ **tick over** *v* (of an engine) idle; function smoothly ▶ **ticktack** *n* (Brit) bookmakers' sign language

**tick²** *n* tiny bloodsucking parasitic animal

**tick³** *n* (*informal*) credit or account

**ticket** *n* card or paper entitling the holder to admission, travel, etc.; label, esp. showing price; official notification of a parking or traffic offence; (*chiefly US & NZ*) declared policy of a political party ▷ *v* **-eting, -eted** attach or issue a ticket to

**ticking** *n* strong material for mattress covers

**tickle** *v* touch or stroke (a person) to produce laughter; itch or tingle; please or amuse ▷ *n* tickling ▶ **ticklish** *adj* sensitive to tickling; requiring care or tact

**tiddler** *n* (*informal*) very small fish

**tiddly¹** *adj* **-dlier, -dliest** tiny

**tiddly²** *adj* **-dlier, -dliest** (*informal*) slightly drunk

**tiddlywinks** *n* game in which players try to flip small plastic discs into a cup

**tide** *n* rise and fall of the sea caused by the gravitational pull of the sun and moon; current caused by this; widespread feeling or tendency ▶ **tidal** *adj* ▶ **tidal wave** large destructive wave ▶ **tide over** *v* help (someone) temporarily

**tidings** *pl n* news

**tidy** *adj* **-dier, -diest** neat and orderly; (*Brit, Aust & NZ informal*) considerable ▷ *v* **-dying, -died** put in order ▶ **tidily** *adv* ▶ **tidiness** *n*

**tie** *v* **tying, tied** fasten or be fastened with string, rope, etc.; make (a knot or bow) in (something); restrict or limit; score the same as another competitor ▷ *n* long narrow piece of material worn knotted round the neck; bond or fastening; drawn game or contest ▶ **tied** *adj* (Brit) (of a cottage etc.) rented to the tenant only as long as he or she is employed by the owner

**tier** *n* one of a set of rows placed one above and behind the other

**tiff** *n* petty quarrel

**tiger** *n* large yellow-and-black striped Asian cat ▶ **tiger snake** *n* highly venomous brown-and-yellow Australian snake ▶ **tigress** *n* female tiger; (*informal*) fierce woman

**tight** *adj* stretched or drawn taut; closely fitting; secure or firm; cramped; (*Brit, Aust & NZ informal*) not generous; (of a match or game) very close; (*informal*) drunk ▶ **tights** *pl n* one-piece clinging garment covering the body from the waist to the feet ▶ **tightly** *adv* ▶ **tighten** *v* make or become tight or tighter ▶ **tightrope** *n* rope stretched taut on which acrobats perform

**tiki** *n* (NZ) small carving of a grotesque person worn as a pendant

**tikka** *adj* (Indian cookery) marinated in spices and dry-roasted e.g. *chicken tikka*

**tilde** *n* mark (~) used in Spanish to indicate that the letter 'n' is to be pronounced in a particular way

**tile** n flat piece of ceramic, plastic, etc. used to cover a roof, floor, or wall ▷ v cover with tiles ▶ **tiled** adj ▶ **tiling** n tiles collectively

**till¹** conj, prep until

**till²** v cultivate (land) ▶ **tillage** n

**till³** n drawer for money, usu. in a cash register

**tiller** n lever to move a rudder of a boat

**tilt** v slant at an angle; (Hist) compete against in a jousting contest ▷ n slope; (Hist) jousting contest; attempt **at full tilt** at full speed or force

**timber** n wood as a building material; trees collectively; wooden beam in the frame of a house, boat, etc. ▶ **timbered** adj ▶ **timber line** limit beyond which trees will not grow

**timbre** [tam-bra] n distinctive quality of sound of a voice or instrument

**time** n past, present, and future as a continuous whole; specific point in time; unspecified interval; instance or occasion; period with specific features; musical tempo; (Brit, Aust & NZ slang) imprisonment ▷ v note the time taken by; choose a time for ▶ **timeless** adj unaffected by time; eternal ▶ **timely** adj at the appropriate time ▶ **time-honoured** adj sanctioned by custom ▶ **time-lag** n period between cause and effect ▶ **timepiece** n watch or clock ▶ **time-poor** adj having little free time ▶ **timeserver** n person who changes his or her views to gain support or favour ▶ **time sharing** system of part ownership of a holiday property for a specified period each year ▶ **timetable** n plan showing the times when something takes place, the departure and arrival times of trains or buses, etc.

**timid** adj easily frightened; shy, not bold ▶ **timidly** adv ▶ **timidity** n ▶ **timorous** adj timid

**timpani** [tim-pan-ee] pl n set of kettledrums ▶ **timpanist** n

**tin** n soft metallic element; (airtight) metal container ▶ **tinned** adj (of food) preserved by being sealed in a tin ▶ **tinny** adj (of sound) thin and metallic ▶ **tinpot** adj (informal) worthless or unimportant

**tincture** n medicinal extract in a solution of alcohol

**tinder** n dry easily-burning material used to start a fire ▶ **tinderbox** n formerly, small box for tinder, esp. one fitted with a flint and steel

**tine** n prong of a fork or antler

**ting** n high metallic sound, as of a small bell

**tinge** n slight tint; trace ▷ v **tingeing, tinged** give a slight tint or trace to

**tingle** v, n (feel) a prickling or stinging sensation

**tinker** n travelling mender of pots and pans; (Scot & Irish derogatory) Gypsy ▷ v fiddle with (an engine etc.) in an attempt to repair it

**tinkle** v ring with a high tinny sound like a small bell ▷ n this sound or action

**tinsel** n decorative metallic strips or threads

**tint** n (pale) shade of a colour; dye for the hair ▷ v give a tint to

**tiny** adj tinier, tiniest very small

**tip¹** n narrow or pointed end of anything; small piece forming an end ▷ v tipping, tipped put a tip on

**tip²** n money given in return for service; helpful hint or warning; piece of inside information ▷ v

**tipping, tipped** give a tip to ▸ **tipster** n person who sells tips about races

**tip³** v **tipping, tipped** tilt or overturn; dump (rubbish) ▷ n rubbish dump ▸ **tipping point** moment or event that marks a decisive change

**tipple** v drink alcohol habitually, esp. in small quantities ▷ n alcoholic drink ▸ **tippler** n

**tipsy** adj **-sier, -siest** slightly drunk

**tiptoe** v **-toeing, -toed** walk quietly with the heels off the ground

**tiptop** adj of the highest quality or condition

**tirade** n long angry speech

**tire** v reduce the energy of, as by exertion; weary or bore ▸ **tired** adj exhausted; hackneyed or stale ▸ **tiring** adj ▸ **tireless** adj energetic and determined ▸ **tiresome** adj boring and irritating

**tissue** n substance of an animal body or plant; piece of thin soft paper used as a handkerchief etc.; interwoven series

**tit¹** n any of various small songbirds

**tit²** n (slang) female breast

**titanic** adj huge or very important

**titanium** n (Chem) strong light metallic element used to make alloys

**titbit** n tasty piece of food; pleasing scrap of scandal

**tit-for-tat** adj done in retaliation

**tithe** n esp. formerly, one tenth of one's income or produce paid to the church as a tax

**Titian** [tish-an] adj (of hair) reddish-gold

**titillate** v excite or stimulate pleasurably ▸ **titillating** adj ▸ **titillation** n

**titivate** v smarten up

**title** n name of a book, film, etc.; name signifying rank or position; formal designation, such as Mrs; (Sport) championship; (Law) legal right of possession ▸ **titled** adj aristocratic ▸ **title deed** legal document of ownership

**titter** v laugh in a suppressed way ▷ n suppressed laugh

**tittle-tattle** n, v gossip

**titular** adj in name only; of a title

**tizzy** n, pl **-zies** (informal) confused or agitated state

**TNT** n trinitrotoluene, a powerful explosive

**to** prep indicating movement towards, equality or comparison, etc. e.g. walking to school; forty miles to the gallon; used to mark the indirect object or infinitive of a verb ▷ adv to a closed position e.g. pull the door to ▸ **to and fro** back and forth

**toad** n animal like a large frog

**toad-in-the-hole** n (Brit) sausages baked in batter

**toadstool** n poisonous fungus like a mushroom

**toady** n, pl **toadies** ingratiating person ▷ v **toadying, toadied** be ingratiating

**toast¹** n sliced bread browned by heat ▷ v brown (bread) by heat; warm or be warmed ▸ **toaster** n electrical device for toasting bread

**toast²** n tribute or proposal of health or success marked by people raising glasses and drinking together; person or thing so honoured ▷ v drink a toast to

**tobacco** n, pl **-cos** or **-coes** plant with large leaves dried for smoking ▸ **tobacconist** n person or shop selling tobacco, cigarettes, etc.

**toboggan** n narrow sledge for sliding over snow ▷ v **-ganing, -ganed** ride a toboggan

**toby jug** n (chiefly Brit) mug in the form of a stout seated man

t

**toccata** [tok-**kah**-ta] *n* rapid piece of music for a keyboard instrument

**today** *n* this day; the present age ▷ *adv* on this day; nowadays

**toddler** *n* child beginning to walk ▶ **toddle** *v* walk with short unsteady steps

**toddy** *n*, *pl* **-dies** sweetened drink of spirits and hot water

**to-do** *n*, *pl* **-dos** (*Brit, Aust & NZ*) fuss or commotion

**toe** *n* digit of the foot; part of a shoe or sock covering the toes ▷ *v* **toeing, toed** touch or kick with the toe **toe the line** conform

**toff** *n* (*Brit slang*) well-dressed or upper-class person

**toffee** *n* chewy sweet made of boiled sugar

**tofu** *n* soft food made from soyabean curd

**tog** *n* unit for measuring the insulating power of duvets

**toga** [**toe**-ga] *n* garment worn by citizens of ancient Rome

**together** *adv* in company; simultaneously ▷ *adj* (*informal*) organized

> **USAGE NOTE**
> Two nouns linked by *together with* do not make a plural subject so the following verb must be singular: *Jones, together with his partner, has had great success*

**toggle** *n* small bar-shaped button inserted through a loop for fastening; switch used to turn a machine or computer function on or off

**toil** *n* hard work ▷ *v* work hard; progress with difficulty

**toilet** *n* (room with) a bowl connected to a drain for receiving and disposing of urine and faeces; washing and dressing ▶ **toiletry** *n*, *pl* **-ries** object or cosmetic used to clean or groom oneself ▶ **toilet water** light perfume

**token** *n* sign or symbol; voucher exchangeable for goods of a specified value; disc used as money in a slot machine ▷ *adj* nominal or slight ▶ **tokenism** *n* policy of making only a token effort, esp. to comply with a law

**told** *v* past of **tell**

**tolerate** *v* allow to exist or happen; endure patiently ▶ **tolerable** *adj* bearable; (*informal*) quite good ▶ **tolerably** *adv* ▶ **tolerance** *n* acceptance of other people's rights to their own opinions or actions; ability to endure something ▶ **tolerant** *adj* ▶ **tolerantly** *adv* ▶ **toleration** *n*

**toll¹** *v* ring (a bell) slowly and regularly, esp. to announce a death ▷ *n* tolling

**toll²** *n* charge for the use of a bridge or road; total loss or damage from a disaster

**tom** *n* male cat

**tomahawk** *n* fighting axe of the Native Americans

**tomato** *n*, *pl* **-toes** red fruit used in salads and as a vegetable

**tomb** *n* grave; monument over a grave ▶ **tombstone** *n* gravestone

**tombola** *n* lottery with tickets drawn from a revolving drum

**tomboy** *n* girl who acts or dresses like a boy

**tome** *n* large heavy book

**tomfoolery** *n* foolish behaviour

**Tommy gun** *n* light sub-machinegun

**tomorrow** *adv*, *n* (on) the day after today; (in) the future

**tom-tom** *n* drum beaten with the hands

**ton** *n* unit of weight equal to 2240 pounds or 1016 kilograms (**long ton**) or, in the US, 2000 pounds or 907

kilograms (**short ton**) ▶ **tonnage** n
weight capacity of a ship

**tone** n sound with reference to its
pitch, volume, etc.; (US) musical
note; (Music) (also **whole tone**)
interval of two semitones; quality
of a sound or colour; general
character; healthy bodily condition
▷ v harmonize (with); give tone
to; give more firmness or strength
to (the body or a part of the body)
▶ **tonal** adj (Music) written in a key
▶ **tonality** n ▶ **toneless** adj ▶ **tone-
deaf** adj unable to perceive subtle
differences in pitch ▶ **tone down** v
make or become more moderate

**tongs** pl n pincers for picking up
(pieces of coal, sugar, etc)

**tongue** n muscular organ in the
mouth, used in speaking and
tasting; language; animal tongue
as food; thin projecting strip; flap
of leather on a shoe

**tonic** n medicine to improve body
tone ▷ adj invigorating ▶ **tonic
water** mineral water containing
quinine

**tonight** adv, n (in or during) the
night or evening of this day

**tonne** [tunn] n unit of weight equal
to 1000 kilograms

**tonsil** n small gland in the throat
▶ **tonsillectomy** n surgical
removal of the tonsils ▶ **tonsillitis**
n inflammation of the tonsils

**tonsure** n shaving of all or the
top of the head as a religious
practice; shaved part of the head
▶ **tonsured** adj

**too** adv also, as well; to excess;
extremely

**took** v past tense of **take**

**tool** n implement used by hand;
person used by another to perform
unpleasant or dishonourable tasks
▶ **toolbar** n (Computing) row or
column of selectable buttons on

a computer screen, each allowing
the user to access a particular
function ▶ **toolie** n (Aust slang)
older adult who gate-crashes the
schoolies week celebrations

**Toorak tractor** n (Aust derogatory)
luxury four-wheel drive or sport
utility vehicle

**toot** n short hooting sound ▷ v
(cause to) make such a sound

**tooth** n, pl **teeth** bonelike
projection in the jaws of most
vertebrates for biting and chewing;
toothlike prong or point **sweet
tooth** strong liking for sweet food
▶ **toothless** adj ▶ **toothpaste**
n paste used to clean the teeth
▶ **toothpick** n small stick for
removing scraps of food from
between the teeth

**top¹** n highest point or part; lid or
cap; highest rank; garment for the
upper part of the body ▷ adj at or
of the top ▷ v **topping, topped**
form a top on; be at the top of;
exceed or surpass ▶ **topping** n
sauce or garnish for food ▶ **topless**
adj (of a costume or woman)
with no covering for the breasts
▶ **topmost** adj highest or best
▶ **top brass** most important
officers or leaders ▶ **top hat** man's
tall cylindrical hat ▶ **top-heavy**
adj unstable through being
overloaded at the top ▶ **top-notch**
adj excellent, first-class ▶ **topsoil** n
surface layer of soil

**top²** n toy which spins on a pointed
base

**topaz** [toe-pazz] n semiprecious
stone in various colours

**topee, topi** [toe-pee] n
lightweight hat worn in tropical
countries

**topiary** [tope-yar-ee] n art of
trimming trees and bushes into
decorative shapes

t

**topic** *n* subject of a conversation, book, etc. ▸ **topical** *adj* relating to current events ▸ **topicality** *n*

**topography** *n*, *pl* **-phies** (science of describing) the surface features of a place ▸ **topographer** *n* ▸ **topographical** *adj*

**topology** *n* geometry of the properties of a shape which are unaffected by continuous distortion ▸ **topological** *adj*

**topple** *v* (cause to) fall over; overthrow (a government etc.)

**topsy-turvy** *adj* upside down; in confusion

**toque** [toke] *n* small round hat

**tor** *n* high rocky hill

**Torah** *n* body of traditional Jewish teaching

**torch** *n* small portable battery-powered lamp; wooden shaft dipped in wax and set alight ▷ *v* (*informal*) deliberately set (a building) on fire

**tore** *v* past tense of **tear²**

**toreador** [torr-ee-a-dor] *n* bullfighter

**torment** *v* cause (someone) great suffering; tease cruelly ▷ *n* great suffering; source of suffering ▸ **tormentor** *n*

**torn** *v* past participle of **tear²**

**tornado** *n*, *pl* **-dos** or **-does** violent whirlwind

**torpedo** *n*, *pl* **-does** self-propelled underwater missile ▷ *v* **-doing, -doed** attack or destroy with or as if with torpedoes

**torpid** *adj* sluggish and inactive ▸ **torpor** *n* torpid state

**torque** [tork] *n* force causing rotation; Celtic necklace or armband of twisted metal

**torrent** *n* rushing stream; rapid flow of questions, abuse, etc.; (*Computing*) file that controls the transfer of data in a BitTorrent system ▸ **torrential** *adj* (of rain) very heavy

**torrid** *adj* very hot and dry; highly emotional

**torsion** *n* twisting of a part by equal forces being applied at both ends but in opposite directions

**torso** *n*, *pl* **-sos** trunk of the human body; statue of a nude human trunk

**tort** *n* (*Law*) civil wrong or injury for which damages may be claimed

**tortilla** *n* thin Mexican pancake

**tortoise** *n* slow-moving land reptile with a dome-shaped shell ▸ **tortoiseshell** *n* mottled brown shell of a turtle, used for making ornaments ▷ *adj* having brown, orange, and black markings

**tortuous** *adj* winding or twisting; not straightforward

**torture** *v* cause (someone) severe pain or mental anguish ▷ *n* severe physical or mental pain; torturing ▸ **torturer** *n*

**Tory** *n*, *pl* **Tories** member of the Conservative Party in Great Britain or Canada ▷ *adj* of Tories ▸ **Toryism** *n*

**toss** *v* throw lightly; fling or be flung about; coat (food) by gentle stirring or mixing; (of a horse) throw (its rider); throw up (a coin) to decide between alternatives by guessing which side will land uppermost ▷ *n* tossing ▸ **toss up** *v* toss a coin ▸ **toss-up** *n* even chance or risk

**tot¹** *n* small child; small drink of spirits

**tot²** *v* **totting, totted** ▸ **tot up** add (numbers) together

**total** *n* whole, esp. a sum of parts ▷ *adj* complete; of or being a total ▷ *v* **-talling, -talled** amount to; add up ▸ **totally** *adv* ▸ **totality** *n* ▸ **totalizator** *n* betting system in which money is paid out in proportion to the winners' stakes

**totalitarian** adj of a dictatorial one-party government
▶ **totalitarianism** n

**tote**[1] v carry (a gun etc.)

**tote**[2]® n short for **totalizator**

**totem** n tribal badge or emblem
▶ **totem pole** post carved or painted with totems by Native Americans

**totter** v move unsteadily; be about to fall

**toucan** n tropical American bird with a large bill

**touch** v come into contact with; tap, feel, or stroke; affect; move emotionally; eat or drink; equal or match; (Brit, Aust & NZ slang) ask for money ▷ n sense by which an object's qualities are perceived when they come into contact with part of the body; gentle tap, push, or caress; small amount; characteristic style; detail ▷ adj of a non-contact version of particular sport e.g. touch rugby ▶ **touch and go** risky or critical ▶ **touched** adj emotionally moved; slightly mad
▶ **touching** adj emotionally moving
▶ **touchy** adj easily offended
▶ **touchless** adj (of a device) able to be controlled without touching a keypad or screen ▶ **touch down** v (of an aircraft) land ▶ **touchline** n side line of the pitch in some games
▶ **touch on** v refer to in passing
▶ **touch-type** v type without looking at the keyboard

**touché** [too-**shay**] interj acknowledgment of the striking home of a remark or witty reply

**touchstone** n standard by which a judgment is made

**tough** adj strong or resilient; difficult to chew or cut; firm and determined; rough and violent; difficult; (informal) unlucky or unfair

▷ n (informal) rough violent person
▶ **toughness** n ▶ **toughen** v make or become tough or tougher

**toupee** [too-**pay**] n small wig

**tour** n journey visiting places of interest along the way; trip to perform or play in different places ▷ v make a tour (of) ▶ **tourism** n tourist travel as an industry
▶ **tourist** n person travelling for pleasure ▶ **touristy** adj (informal often derogatory) full of tourists or tourist attractions

**tour de force** n, pl **tours de force** (French) brilliant achievement

**tournament** n sporting competition with several stages to decide the overall winner; (Hist) contest between knights on horseback

**tourniquet** [**tour**-nick-kay] n something twisted round a limb to stop bleeding

**tousled** adj ruffled and untidy

**tout** [rhymes with **shout**] v seek business in a persistent manner; recommend (a person or thing) ▷ n person who sells tickets for a popular event at inflated prices

**tow**[1] v drag, esp. by means of a rope ▷ n towing ▶ **in tow** following closely behind ▶ **on tow** being towed
▶ **towbar** n metal bar on a car for towing vehicles ▶ **towpath** n path beside a canal or river, originally for horses towing boats

**tow**[2] n fibre of hemp or flax

**towards, toward** prep in the direction of; with regard to; as a contribution to

**towel** n cloth for drying things
▶ **towelling** n material used for making towels

**tower** n tall structure, often forming part of a larger building **tower of strength** person who supports or comforts ▶ **tower over** v be much taller than

**town** n group of buildings larger than a village; central part of this; people of a town ▶ **town hall** large building used for council meetings, etc. ▶ **township** n small town; (in S Africa) urban settlement of Black or Coloured people

**toxaemia** [tox-**seem**-ya] n blood poisoning; high blood pressure in pregnancy

**toxic** adj poisonous; caused by poison ▶ **toxicity** n ▶ **toxicology** n study of poisons ▶ **toxin** n poison of bacterial origin

**toy** n something designed to be played with ▷ adj (of a dog) of a variety much smaller than is normal for that breed ▶ **toy with** v play or fiddle with

**toy-toy** (SAfr) n dance of political protest ▷ v perform this dance

**trace** v track down and find; follow the course of; copy exactly by drawing on a thin sheet of transparent paper set on top of the original ▷ n track left by something; minute quantity; indication ▶ **traceable** adj ▶ **tracer** n projectile which leaves a visible trail ▶ **tracery** n pattern of interlacing lines ▶ **tracing** n traced copy ▶ **trace element** chemical element occurring in very small amounts in soil etc.

**traces** pl n strap by which a horse pulls a vehicle **kick over the traces** escape or defy control

**trachea** [track-**kee**-a] n, pl **tracheae** windpipe

**tracheotomy** [track-ee-**ot**-a-mee] n surgical incision into the trachea

**track** n rough road or path; mark or trail left by the passage of anything; railway line; course for racing; separate section on a record, tape, or CD; course of action or thought; endless band round the wheels of a tank, bulldozer, etc. ▷ v follow the trail or path of ▶ **track down** v hunt for and find ▶ **track event** athletic sport held on a running track ▶ **track record** past accomplishments of a person or organization ▶ **tracksuit** n warm loose-fitting suit worn by athletes etc., esp. during training

**tract¹** n wide area; (Anat) system of organs with a particular function

**tract²** n pamphlet, esp. a religious one

**tractable** adj easy to manage or control

**traction** n pulling, esp. by engine power; (Med) application of a steady pull on an injured limb by weights and pulleys; grip of the wheels of a vehicle on the ground ▶ **traction engine** old-fashioned steam-powered vehicle for pulling heavy loads

**tractor** n motor vehicle with large rear wheels for pulling farm machinery

**trade** n buying, selling, or exchange of goods; person's job or craft; (people engaged in) a particular industry or business ▷ v buy and sell; exchange; engage in trade ▶ **trader** n ▶ **trading** n ▶ **trade-in** n used article given in part payment for a new one ▶ **trademark** n (legally registered) name or symbol used by a firm to distinguish its goods ▶ **trade-off** n exchange made as a compromise ▶ **tradesman** n skilled worker; shopkeeper ▶ **trade union** society of workers formed to protect their interests ▶ **trade wind** wind blowing steadily towards the equator

**tradition** n body of beliefs, customs, etc. handed down

from generation to generation; custom or practice of long standing ▶ **traditional** adj ▶ **traditionally** adv

**traduce** v slander

**traffic** n vehicles coming and going on a road; (illicit) trade ▷ v **-ficking, -ficked** trade, usu. illicitly ▶ **trafficker** n ▶ **traffic lights** set of coloured lights at a junction to control the traffic flow ▶ **traffic warden** (*Brit*) person employed to control the movement and parking of traffic

**tragedy** n, pl **-dies** shocking or sad event; serious play, film, etc. in which the hero is destroyed by a personal failing in adverse circumstances ▶ **tragedian** [traj-**jee**-dee-an], **tragedienne** [traj-jee-dee-**enn**](*fem*) n person who acts in or writes tragedies ▶ **tragic** adj of or like a tragedy ▶ **tragically** adv ▶ **tragicomedy** n play with both tragic and comic elements

**trail** n path, track, or road; tracks left by a person, animal, or object ▷ v drag along the ground; lag behind; follow the tracks of

**trailer** n vehicle designed to be towed by another vehicle; extract from a film or programme used to advertise it

**train** v instruct in a skill; learn the skills needed to do a particular job or activity; prepare for a sports event etc.; aim (a gun etc.); cause (an animal) to perform or (a plant) to grow in a particular way ▷ n line of railway coaches or wagons drawn by an engine; sequence or series; long trailing back section of a dress ▶ **trainer** n person who trains an athlete or sportsman; sports shoe ▶ **trainee** n person being trained

**traipse** v (*informal*) walk wearily

**trait** n characteristic feature

**traitor** n person guilty of treason or treachery ▶ **traitorous** adj

**trajectory** n, pl **-ries** line of flight, esp. of a projectile

**tram** n public transport vehicle powered by an overhead wire and running on rails laid in the road ▶ **tramlines** pl n track for trams

**tramp** v travel on foot, hike; walk heavily ▷ n homeless person who travels on foot; hike; sound of tramping; cargo ship available for hire; (*US, Aust & NZ slang*) promiscuous woman

**trample** v tread on and crush

**trampoline** n tough canvas sheet attached to a frame by springs, used by acrobats etc. ▷ v bounce on a trampoline

**trance** n unconscious or dazed state

**tranche** n portion of something large, esp. a sum of money

**tranquil** adj calm and quiet ▶ **tranquilly** adv ▶ **tranquillity** n

**tranquillize** v make calm ▶ **tranquillizer** n drug which reduces anxiety or tension

**trans-** prefix across, through, or beyond

**transact** v conduct or negotiate (a business deal)

**transaction** n business deal transacted

**transatlantic** adj on, from, or to the other side of the Atlantic

**transceiver** n transmitter and receiver of radio or electronic signals

**transcend** v rise above; be superior to ▶ **transcendence** n ▶ **transcendent** adj ▶ **transcendental** adj based on intuition rather than experience; supernatural or mystical ▶ **transcendentalism** n

t

**transcribe** v write down (something said); record for a later broadcast; arrange (music) for a different instrument ▸ **transcript** n copy

**transducer** n device that converts one form of energy to another

**transept** n either of the two shorter wings of a cross-shaped church

**transfer** v **-ferring, -ferred** move or send from one person or place to another ▷ n transferring; design which can be transferred from one surface to another ▸ **transferable** adj ▸ **transference** n transferring ▸ **transfer station** (NZ) depot where rubbish is sorted for recycling

**transfigure** v change in appearance ▸ **transfiguration** n

**transfix** v astound or stun; pierce through

**transform** v change the shape or character of ▸ **transformation** n ▸ **transformer** n device for changing the voltage of an alternating current

**transfusion** n injection of blood into the blood vessels of a patient ▸ **transfuse** v give a transfusion to; permeate or infuse

**transgress** v break (a moral law) ▸ **transgression** n ▸ **transgressor** n

**transient** adj lasting only for a short time ▸ **transience** n

**transistor** n semiconducting device used to amplify electric currents; portable radio using transistors

**transit** n movement from one place to another ▸ **transition** n change from one state to another ▸ **transitional** adj ▸ **transitive** adj (Grammar) (of a verb) requiring a direct object ▸ **transitory** adj not lasting long

**translate** v turn from one language into another ▸ **translation** n ▸ **translator** n

**transliterate** v convert to the letters of a different alphabet ▸ **transliteration** n

**translucent** adj letting light pass through, but not transparent ▸ **translucency, translucence** n

**transmigrate** v (of a soul) pass into another body ▸ **transmigration** n

**transmit** v **-mitting, -mitted** pass (something) from one person or place to another; send out (signals) by radio waves; broadcast (a radio or television programme) ▸ **transmission** n transmitting; shafts and gears through which power passes from a vehicle's engine to its wheels ▸ **transmittable** adj ▸ **transmitter** n

**transmogrify** v **-fying, -fied** (informal) change completely

**transmute** v change the form or nature of ▸ **transmutation** n

**transom** n horizontal bar across a window; bar separating a door from the window over it

**transparent** adj able to be seen through, clear; easily understood or recognized ▸ **transparently** adv ▸ **transparency** n transparent quality; colour photograph on transparent film that can be viewed by means of a projector

**transpire** v become known; (informal) happen; give off water vapour through pores ▸ **transpiration** n

**transplant** v transfer (an organ or tissue) surgically from one part or body to another; remove and transfer (a plant) to another place ▷ n surgical transplanting; thing transplanted ▸ **transplantation** n

**transport** v convey from one place to another; (*Hist*) exile (a criminal) to a penal colony; enrapture ▷ n business or system of transporting; vehicle used in transport; ecstasy or rapture ▸ **transportation** n ▸ **transporter** n large goods vehicle

**transpose** v interchange two things; put (music) into a different key ▸ **transposition** n

**transsexual, transexual** n person of one sex who believes his or her true identity is of the opposite sex

**transubstantiation** n (*Christianity*) doctrine that the bread and wine consecrated in Communion changes into the substance of Christ's body and blood

**transuranic** [tranz-yoor-**ran**-ik] adj (of an element) having an atomic number greater than that of uranium

**transverse** adj crossing from side to side

**transvestite** n person who seeks sexual pleasure by wearing the clothes of the opposite sex ▸ **transvestism** n

**trap** n device for catching animals; plan for tricking or catching a person; bend in a pipe containing liquid to prevent the escape of gas; stall in which greyhounds are enclosed before a race; two-wheeled carriage; (*Brit, Aust & NZ slang*) mouth ▷ v **trapping, trapped** catch; trick ▸ **trapper** n person who traps animals for their fur ▸ **trapdoor** n door in floor or roof ▸ **trap-door spider** spider that builds a silk-lined hole in the ground closed by a hinged door of earth and silk

**trapeze** n horizontal bar suspended from two ropes, used by circus acrobats

**trapezium** n, pl **-ziums** or **-zia** quadrilateral with two parallel sides of unequal length ▸ **trapezoid** [**trap**-piz-zoid] n quadrilateral with no sides parallel; (*chiefly US*) trapezium

**trappings** pl n accessories that symbolize an office or position

**Trappist** n member of an order of Christian monks who observe strict silence

**trash** n anything worthless; (*US & S Afr*) rubbish ▸ **trashy** adj

**trauma** [**traw**-ma] n emotional shock; injury or wound ▸ **traumatic** adj ▸ **traumatize** v

**travail** n (*lit*) labour or toil

**travel** v **-elling, -elled** go from one place to another, through an area, or for a specified distance ▷ n travelling, esp. as a tourist ▷ pl (account of) travelling ▸ **traveller** n ▸ **travelogue** n film or talk about someone's travels

**traverse** v move over or back and forth over

**travesty** n, pl **-ties** grotesque imitation or mockery

**trawl** n net dragged at deep levels behind a fishing boat ▷ v fish with such a net ▸ **trawler** n trawling boat

**tray** n flat board, usu. with a rim, for carrying things; open receptacle for office correspondence

**treachery** n, pl **-eries** wilful betrayal ▸ **treacherous** adj disloyal; unreliable or dangerous ▸ **treacherously** adv

**treacle** n thick dark syrup produced when sugar is refined ▸ **treacly** adj

**tread** v **treading, trod, trodden** or **trod** set one's foot on; crush by walking on ▷ n way of walking or dancing; upper surface of a step; part of a tyre or shoe that touches the ground ▸ **treadmill** n (*Hist*)

t

cylinder turned by treading on steps projecting from it; dreary routine

**treadle** [tred-dl] *n* lever worked by the foot to turn a wheel

**treason** *n* betrayal of one's sovereign or country; treachery or disloyalty ▶ **treasonable** *adj*

**treasure** *n* collection of wealth, esp. gold or jewels; valued person or thing ▷ *v* prize or cherish ▶ **treasurer** *n* official in charge of funds ▶ **treasure-trove** *n* treasure found with no evidence of ownership ▶ **treasury** *n* storage place for treasure; (**T-**) government department in charge of finance

**treat** *v* deal with or regard in a certain manner; give medical treatment to; subject to a chemical or industrial process; provide (someone) with (something) as a treat ▷ *n* pleasure, entertainment, etc. given or paid for by someone else ▶ **treatment** *n* medical care; way of treating a person or thing

**treatise** [treat-izz] *n* formal piece of writing on a particular subject

**treaty** *n*, *pl* **-ties** signed contract between states

**treble** *adj* triple; (*Music*) high-pitched ▷ *n* (singer with or part for) a soprano voice ▷ *v* increase three times ▶ **trebly** *adv*

**tree** *n* large perennial plant with a woody trunk ▶ **treeless** *adj* ▶ **tree kangaroo** tree-living kangaroo of New Guinea and N Australia ▶ **tree surgery** treatment of damaged trees ▶ **tree surgeon**

**trefoil** [tref-foil] *n* plant, such as clover, with a three-lobed leaf; carved ornament like this

**trek** *n* long difficult journey, esp. on foot; (*SAfr*) migration by ox wagon ▷ *v* **trekking, trekked** make such a journey

**trellis** *n* framework of horizontal and vertical strips of wood

**tremble** *v* shake or quiver; feel fear or anxiety ▷ *n* trembling ▶ **trembling** *adj*

**tremendous** *adj* huge; (*informal*) great in quality or amount ▶ **tremendously** *adv*

**tremolo** *n*, *pl* **-los** (*Music*) quivering effect in singing or playing

**tremor** *n* involuntary shaking; minor earthquake

**tremulous** *adj* trembling, as from fear or excitement

**trench** *n* long narrow ditch, esp. one used as a shelter in war ▶ **trench coat** double-breasted waterproof coat

**trenchant** *adj* incisive; effective

**trencher** *n* (*Hist*) wooden plate for serving food ▶ **trencherman** *n* hearty eater

**trend** *n* general tendency or direction; fashion ▷ *v* be widely discussed on a social media site ▶ **trendy** *adj*, *n* (*informal*) consciously fashionable (person) ▶ **trendiness** *n*

**trepidation** *n* fear or anxiety

**trespass** *v* go onto another's property without permission ▷ *n* trespassing; (*old-fashioned*) sin or wrongdoing ▶ **trespasser** *n* ▶ **trespass on** *v* take unfair advantage of (someone's friendship, patience, etc.)

**tresses** *pl n* long flowing hair

**trestle** *n* board fixed on pairs of spreading legs, used as a support

**trevally** *n*, *pl* **-lies** (*Aust & NZ*) any of various food and game fishes

**trews** *pl n* close-fitting tartan trousers

**tri-** *combining form* three

**triad** *n* group of three; (**T-**) Chinese criminal secret society

**trial** *n* (*Law*) investigation of a case before a judge; trying or testing; thing or person straining endurance or patience ▷ *pl* sporting competition for individuals

**triangle** *n* geometric figure with three sides; triangular percussion instrument; situation involving three people ▸ **triangular** *adj*

**tribe** *n* group of clans or families believed to have a common ancestor ▸ **tribal** *adj* ▸ **tribalism** *n* loyalty to a tribe

**tribulation** *n* great distress

**tribunal** *n* board appointed to inquire into a specific matter; lawcourt

**tribune** *n* people's representative, esp. in ancient Rome

**tributary** *n*, *pl* **-taries** stream or river flowing into a larger one ▷ *adj* (of a stream or river) flowing into a larger one

**tribute** *n* sign of respect or admiration; tax paid by one state to another

**trice** *n* **in a trice** instantly

**triceps** *n* muscle at the back of the upper arm

**trichology** [trick-**ol**-a-jee] *n* study and treatment of hair and its diseases ▸ **trichologist** *n*

**trick** *n* deceitful or cunning action or plan; joke or prank; feat of skill or cunning; mannerism; cards played in one round ▷ *v* cheat or deceive ▸ **trickery** *n* ▸ **trickster** *n* ▸ **tricky** *adj* difficult, needing careful handling; crafty

**trickle** *v* (cause to) flow in a thin stream or drops; move gradually ▷ *n* gradual flow

**tricolour** [**trick**-kol-lor] *n* three-coloured striped flag

**tricycle** *n* three-wheeled cycle

**trident** *n* three-pronged spear

**triennial** *adj* happening every three years

**trifle** *n* insignificant thing or amount; dessert of sponge cake, fruit, custard, and cream ▸ **trifling** *adj* insignificant ▸ **trifle with** *v* toy with

**trigger** *n* small lever releasing a catch on a gun or machine; action that sets off a course of events ▷ *v* (usu. foll by *off*) set (an action or process) in motion ▸ **trigger-happy** *adj* too quick to fire guns

**trigonometry** *n* branch of mathematics dealing with relations of the sides and angles of triangles

**trike** *n* (*informal*) tricycle

**trilateral** *adj* having three sides

**trilby** *n*, *pl* **-bies** man's soft felt hat

**trill** *n* (*Music*) rapid alternation between two notes; shrill warbling sound made by some birds ▷ *v* play or sing a trill

**trillion** *n* one million million, 10¹²; (formerly) one million million million, 10¹⁸

**trilobite** [**trile**-oh-bite] *n* small prehistoric sea animal

**trilogy** *n*, *pl* **-gies** series of three related books, plays, etc.

**trim** *adj* **trimmer, trimmest** neat and smart; slender ▷ *v* **trimming, trimmed** cut or prune into good shape; decorate with lace, ribbons, etc.; adjust the balance of (a ship or aircraft) by shifting the cargo etc. ▷ *n* decoration; upholstery and decorative facings in a car; trim state; haircut that neatens the existing style ▸ **trimming** *n* decoration ▷ *pl* usual accompaniments

**trimaran** [**trime**-a-ran] *n* three-hulled boat

**trinitrotoluene** *n* full name for **TNT**

**trinity** *n*, *pl* **-ties** group of three; (**T-**) (*Christianity*) union of three persons, Father, Son, and Holy Spirit, in one God

**trinket** *n* small or worthless ornament or piece of jewellery

**trio** n, pl **trios** group of three; piece of music for three performers

**trip** n journey to a place and back, esp. for pleasure; stumble; (informal) hallucinogenic drug experience; switch on a mechanism ▷ v **tripping, tripped** (cause to) stumble; (often foll by up) catch (someone) in a mistake; move or tread lightly; (informal) experience the hallucinogenic effects of a drug ▶ **tripper** n tourist

**tripe** n stomach of a cow used as food; (Brit, Aust & NZ informal) nonsense

**triple** adj having three parts; three times as great or as many ▷ v increase three times ▶ **triplet** n one of three babies born at one birth ▶ **triple jump** athletic event in which competitors make a hop, a step, and a jump as a continuous movement

**triplicate** adj triple **in triplicate** in three copies

**tripod** [tripe-pod] n three-legged stand, stool, etc.

**tripos** [tripe-poss] n final examinations for an honours degree at Cambridge University

**triptych** [trip-tick] n painting or carving on three hinged panels, often forming an altarpiece

**trite** adj (of a remark or idea) commonplace and unoriginal

**tritium** n radioactive isotope of hydrogen

**triumph** n (happiness caused by) victory or success ▷ v be victorious or successful; rejoice over a victory ▶ **triumphal** adj celebrating a triumph ▶ **triumphant** adj feeling or showing triumph

**triumvirate** [try-umm-vir-rit] n group of three people in joint control

**trivet** [triv-vit] n metal stand for a pot or kettle

**trivial** adj of little importance ▶ **trivially** adv ▶ **trivia** pl n trivial things or details ▶ **triviality** n ▶ **trivialize** v make (something) seem less important or complex than it is

**trod** v past tense and a past participle of **tread**

**trodden** v a past participle of **tread**

**troglodyte** n cave dweller

**troika** n Russian vehicle drawn by three horses abreast; group of three people in authority

**Trojan** adj of Ancient Troy ▷ n person from ancient Troy; hard-working person; destructive computer program ▶ **Trojan Horse** trap intended to undermine an enemy

**troll** n giant or dwarf in Scandinavian folklore

**trolley** n small wheeled table for food and drink; wheeled cart for moving goods ▶ **trolley bus** bus powered by electricity from an overhead wire but not running on rails

**trollop** n (old-fashioned) promiscuous or slovenly woman

**trombone** n brass musical instrument with a sliding tube ▶ **trombonist** n

**troop** n large group; artillery or cavalry unit; Scout company ▷ pl soldiers ▷ v move in a crowd ▶ **trooper** n cavalry soldier

**trope** n figure of speech

**trophy** n, pl **-phies** cup, shield, etc. given as a prize; memento of success

**tropic** n either of two lines of latitude at 23½°N (**tropic of Cancer**) or 23½°S (**tropic of Capricorn**) ▷ pl part of the earth's surface between these lines

**tropical** adj of or in the tropics; (of climate) very hot

**trot** v **trotting, trotted** (of a horse) move at a medium pace, lifting the feet in diagonal pairs; (of a person) move at a steady brisk pace ▷ n

trotting ▸ **trotter** n pig's foot
▸ **trot out** v repeat (old ideas etc.) without fresh thought

**troth** [rhymes with growth] n (obs) pledge of devotion, esp. a betrothal

**troubadour** [troo-bad-oor] n medieval travelling poet and singer

**trouble** n (cause of) distress or anxiety; disease or malfunctioning; state of disorder or unrest; care or effort ▹ v (cause to) worry; exert oneself; cause inconvenience to ▸ **troubled** adj ▸ **troublesome** adj ▸ **troubleshooter** n person employed to locate and deal with faults or problems

**trough** [troff] n long open container, esp. for animals' food or water; narrow channel between two waves or ridges; (Meteorol) area of low pressure

**trounce** v defeat utterly

**troupe** [troop] n company of performers ▸ **trouper** n

**trousers** pl n two-legged outer garment with legs reaching usu. to the ankles ▸ **trouser** adj of trousers

**trousseau** [troo-so] n, pl -seaux or -seaus bride's collection of clothing etc. for her marriage

**trout** n game fish related to the salmon

**trowel** n hand tool with a wide blade for spreading mortar, lifting plants, etc.

**troy weight, troy** n system of weights used for gold, silver, and jewels

**truant** n pupil who stays away from school without permission **play truant** stay away from school without permission ▸ **truancy** n

**truce** n temporary agreement to stop fighting

**truck¹** n railway goods wagon; large vehicle for transporting loads by road ▸ **trucker** n truck driver

**truck²** n **have no truck with** refuse to be involved with

**truculent** [truck-yew-lent] adj aggressively defiant ▸ **truculence** n

**trudge** v walk heavily or wearily ▹ n long tiring walk

**true** adj truer, truest in accordance with facts; genuine; faithful; exact ▸ **truly** adv ▸ **truism** n self-evident truth ▸ **truth** n state of being true; something true ▸ **truthful** adj honest; exact ▸ **truthfully** adv

**truffle** n edible underground fungus; sweet made with chocolate

**trug** n (Brit) long shallow basket used by gardeners

**trump¹** n, adj (card) of the suit outranking the others ▹ v play a trump card on (another card) ▹ pl n suit outranking the others **turn up trumps** achieve an unexpected success **trumped up** invented or concocted

**trump²** n (lit) (sound of) a trumpet

**trumpet** n valved brass instrument with a flared tube ▹ v **-peting, -peted** proclaim loudly; (of an elephant) cry loudly ▸ **trumpeter** n

**truncate** v cut short

**truncheon** n club formerly carried by a policeman

**trundle** v move heavily on wheels

**trunk** n main stem of a tree; large case or box for clothes etc.; person's body excluding the head and limbs; elephant's long nose; (US) car boot ▹ pl man's swimming shorts ▸ **trunk call** (chiefly Brit) long-distance telephone call ▸ **trunk road** main road

**truss** v tie or bind up ▹ n device for holding a hernia in place; framework supporting a roof, bridge, etc.

**trust** v believe in and rely on; consign to someone's care; expect or hope

▷ *n* confidence in the truth, reliability, etc. of a person or thing; obligation arising from responsibility; arrangement in which one person administers property, money, etc. on another's behalf; property held for another; (*Brit*) self-governing hospital or group of hospitals within the National Health Service; group of companies joined to control a market ▶ **trustee** *n* person holding property on another's behalf ▶ **trustful, trusting** *adj* inclined to trust others ▶ **trustworthy** *adj* reliable or honest ▶ **trusty** *adj* faithful or reliable

**truth** *n* see **true**

**try** *v* **trying, tried** make an effort or attempt; test or sample; put strain on e.g. *he tries my patience*; investigate (a case); examine (a person) in a lawcourt ▷ *n*, *pl* **tries** attempt or effort; (*Rugby*) score gained by touching the ball down over the opponent's goal line **try it on** (*informal*) try to deceive or fool someone ▶ **trying** *adj* (*informal*) difficult or annoying

> **USAGE NOTE**
> The idiom *try to* can be used at any time. The alternative *try and* is less formal and often signals a 'dare': *Just try and stop me!*

**tryst** *n* arrangement to meet

**tsar, czar** [zahr] *n* (*Hist*) Russian emperor

**tsetse fly** [tset-see] *n* bloodsucking African fly whose bite transmits disease, esp. sleeping sickness

**T-shirt** *n* short-sleeved casual shirt or top

**tsp.** teaspoon

**T-square** *n* T-shaped ruler

**tsunami** *n*, *pl* **-mis** *or* **-mi** tidal wave, usu. caused by an earthquake under the sea

**TT** teetotal

**tuatara** *n* large lizard-like New Zealand reptile

**tub** *n* open, usu. round container; bath ▶ **tubby** *adj* (of a person) short and fat

**tuba** [tube-a] *n* valved low-pitched brass instrument

**tube** *n* hollow cylinder; flexible cylinder with a cap to hold pastes **the tube** underground railway, esp. the one in London ▶ **tubing** *n* length of tube; system of tubes ▶ **tubular** [tube-yew-lar] *adj* of or shaped like a tube

**tuber** [tube-er] *n* fleshy underground root of a plant such as a potato ▶ **tuberous** *adj*

**tubercle** [tube-er-kl] *n* small rounded swelling

**tuberculosis** [tube-berk-yew-lohss-iss] *n* infectious disease causing tubercles, esp. in the lungs ▶ **tubercular** *adj* ▶ **tuberculin** *n* extract from a bacillus used to test for tuberculosis

**TUC** (in Britain and S Africa) Trades Union Congress

**tuck** *v* push or fold into a small space; stitch in folds ▷ *n* stitched fold; (*Brit informal*) food ▶ **tuck away** *v* eat (a large amount of food)

**tucker** *n* (*Aust & NZ informal*) food

**Tudor** *adj* of the English royal house ruling from 1485–1603

**Tuesday** *n* third day of the week

**tufa** [tew-fa] *n* porous rock formed as a deposit from springs

**tuffet** *n* small mound or seat

**tuft** *n* bunch of feathers, grass, hair, etc. held or growing together at the base

**tug** *v* **tugging, tugged** pull hard ▷ *n* hard pull; (also **tugboat**) small ship used to tow other vessels ▶ **tug of war** contest in which two teams pull against one another on a rope

**tuition** n instruction, esp. received individually or in a small group

**tulip** n plant with bright cup-shaped flowers

**tulle** [tewl] n fine net fabric of silk etc.

**tumble** v (cause to) fall, esp. awkwardly or violently; roll or twist, esp. in play; rumple ▷ n fall; somersault ▶ **tumbler** n stemless drinking glass; acrobat; spring catch in a lock ▶ **tumbledown** adj dilapidated ▶ **tumble dryer, tumble drier** machine that dries laundry by rotating it in warm air ▶ **tumble to** v (informal) realize, understand

**tumbril, tumbrel** n farm cart used during the French Revolution to take prisoners to the guillotine

**tumescent** [tew-**mess**-ent] adj swollen or becoming swollen

**tummy** n, pl -**mies** (informal) stomach

**tumour** [tew-mer] n abnormal growth in or on the body

**tumult** n uproar or commotion ▶ **tumultuous** [tew-**mull**-tew-uss] adj

**tumulus** n, pl -**li** burial mound

**tun** n large beer cask

**tuna** n large marine food fish

**tundra** n vast treeless Arctic region with permanently frozen subsoil

**tune** n (pleasing) sequence of musical notes; correct musical pitch e.g. she sang out of tune ▷ v adjust (a musical instrument) so that it is in tune; adjust (a machine) to obtain the desired performance ▶ **tuneful** adj ▶ **tunefully** adv ▶ **tuneless** adj ▶ **tuner** n ▶ **tune in** v adjust (a radio or television) to receive (a station or programme)

**tungsten** n (Chem) greyish-white metal

**tunic** n close-fitting jacket forming part of some uniforms; loose knee-length garment

**tunnel** n underground passage ▷ v -**nelling, -nelled** make a tunnel (through)

**tunny** n, pl -**nies** or -**ny** same as **tuna**

**tup** n male sheep

**turban** n Muslim, Hindu, or Sikh man's head covering, made by winding cloth round the head

**turbid** adj muddy, not clear

**turbine** n machine or generator driven by gas, water, etc. turning blades

**turbot** n large European edible flatfish

**turbulence** n confusion, movement, or agitation; atmospheric instability causing gusty air currents ▶ **turbulent** adj

**tureen** n serving dish for soup

**turf** n, pl **turfs** or **turves** short thick even grass; square of this with roots and soil attached ▷ v cover with turf **the turf** racecourse; horse racing ▶ **turf accountant** bookmaker ▶ **turf out** v (informal) throw out

**turgid** [**tur**-jid] adj (of language) pompous; swollen and thick

**turkey** n large bird bred for food

**Turkish** adj of Turkey, its people, or their language ▷ n Turkish language ▶ **Turkish bath** steam bath ▶ **Turkish delight** jelly-like sweet coated with icing sugar

**turmeric** n yellow spice obtained from the root of an Asian plant

**turmoil** n agitation or confusion

**turn** v change the position or direction (of); move around an axis, rotate; (usu. foll by into) change in nature or character; reach or pass in age, time, etc. e.g. she has just turned twenty; shape on a lathe; become sour ▷ *n* turning; opportunity to do something as part of an agreed succession; direction or drift; period or spell; short theatrical performance **good turn, bad turn** helpful *or* unhelpful act ▶ **turner** *n* ▶ **turning** *n* road or path leading off a main route ▶ **turncoat** *n* person who deserts one party or cause to join another ▶ **turn down** *v* reduce the volume or brightness (of); refuse or reject ▶ **turn in** *v* go to bed; hand in ▶ **turning point** moment when a decisive change occurs ▶ **turn off** *v* stop (something) working by using a knob etc. ▶ **turn on** *v* start (something) working by using a knob etc.; become aggressive towards; (*informal*) excite, esp. sexually ▶ **turnout** *n* number of people appearing at a gathering ▶ **turnover** *n* total sales made by a business over a certain period; small pastry; rate at which staff leave and are replaced ▶ **turnpike** *n* (*Brit Hist*) road where a toll is collected at barriers ▶ **turnstile** *n* revolving gate for admitting one person at a time ▶ **turntable** *n* revolving platform ▶ **turn up** *v* arrive or appear; find or be found; increase the volume or brightness (of) ▶ **turn-up** *n* turned-up fold at the bottom of a trouser leg; (*informal*) unexpected event

**turnip** *n* root vegetable with orange or white flesh

**turpentine** *n* (oil made from) the resin of certain trees ▶ **turps** *n* turpentine oil

**turpitude** *n* wickedness

**turquoise** *adj* blue-green ▷ *n* blue-green precious stone

**turret** *n* small tower; revolving gun tower on a warship or tank

**turtle** *n* sea tortoise **turn turtle** capsize ▶ **turtledove** *n* small wild

dove ▶ **turtleneck** *n* (sweater with) a round high close-fitting neck

**tusk** *n* long pointed tooth of an elephant, walrus, etc.

**tussle** *n*, *v* fight or scuffle

**tussock** *n* tuft of grass

**tutelage** [tew-till-lij] *n* instruction or guidance, esp. by a tutor; state of being supervised by a guardian or tutor ▶ **tutelary** [tew-till-lar-ee] *adj*

**tutor** *n* person teaching individuals or small groups ▷ *v* act as a tutor to ▶ **tutorial** *n* period of instruction with a tutor

**tutu** *n* short stiff skirt worn by ballerinas

**tuxedo** *n*, *pl* **-dos** (*US & Aust*) dinner jacket

**TV** television

**twaddle** *n* silly or pretentious talk or writing

**twain** *n* (*obs*) two

**twang** *n* sharp ringing sound; nasal speech ▷ *v* (cause to) make a twang

**tweak** *v* pinch or twist sharply; (*informal*) alter slightly ▷ *n* tweaking

**twee** *adj* (*informal*) too sentimental, sweet, or pretty

**tweed** *n* thick woollen cloth ▷ *pl* suit of tweed ▶ **tweedy** *adj*

**tweet** *n* chirp; short message posted on the Twitter website ▷ *v* chirp; post a short message on the Twitter website

**tweeter** *n* loudspeaker reproducing high-frequency sounds

**tweezers** *pl n* small pincer-like tool

**twelve** *adj*, *n* two more than ten ▶ **twelfth** *adj*, *n* (of) number twelve in a series

**twenty** *adj*, *n* two times ten ▶ **twentieth** *adj*, *n*

**twenty-four-seven, 24/7** *adv* (*informal*) all the time

**twerp** n (*informal*) silly person

**twice** *adv* two times

**twiddle** v fiddle or twirl in an idle way **twiddle one's thumbs** be bored, have nothing to do

**twig**¹ n small branch or shoot

**twig**² v **twigging, twigged** (*informal*) realize or understand

**twilight** n soft dim light just after sunset

**twill** n fabric woven to produce parallel ridges

**twin** n one of a pair, esp. of two children born at one birth ▷ v **twinning, twinned** pair or be paired

**twine** n string or cord ▷ v twist or coil round

**twinge** n sudden sharp pain or emotional pang

**twinkle** v shine brightly but intermittently ▷ n flickering brightness

**twirl** v turn or spin around quickly; twist or wind, esp. idly

**twist** v turn out of the natural position; distort or pervert; wind or twine ▷ n twisting; twisted thing; unexpected development in the plot of a film, book, etc.; bend or curve; distortion ▶**twisted** adj (of a person) cruel or perverted ▶**twister** n (*Brit informal*) swindler

**twit**¹ v **twitting, twitted** poke fun at (someone)

**twit**² n (*informal*) foolish person

**twitch** v move spasmodically; pull sharply ▷ n nervous muscular spasm; sharp pull

**twitter** v (of birds) utter chirping sounds ▷ n act or sound of twittering; (**T-**)® website where people can post short messages about their current thoughts and activities

**two** *adj, n* one more than one ▶**two-edged** adj (of a remark) having both a favourable and an unfavourable interpretation ▶**two-faced** adj deceitful, hypocritical ▶**two-time** v (*informal*) deceive (a lover) by having an affair with someone else

**tycoon** n powerful wealthy businessman

**tyke** n (*Brit, Aust & NZ informal*) small cheeky child

**type** n class or category; (*informal*) person, esp. of a specified kind; block with a raised character used for printing; printed text ▷ v write with a typewriter or word processor; typify; classify ▶**typist** n person who types with a typewriter or word processor ▶**typecast** v continually cast (an actor or actress) in similar roles ▶**typewriter** n machine which prints a character when the appropriate key is pressed

**typhoid fever** n acute infectious feverish disease

**typhoon** n violent tropical storm

**typhus** n infectious feverish disease

**typical** adj true to type, characteristic ▶**typically** adv ▶**typify** v -**fying, -fied** be typical of

**typography** n art or style of printing ▶**typographical** adj ▶**typographer** n

**tyrannosaurus** [tirr-ran-oh-**sore**-uss] n large two-footed flesh-eating dinosaur

**tyrant** n oppressive or cruel ruler; person who exercises authority oppressively ▶**tyrannical** adj like a tyrant, oppressive ▶**tyrannize** v exert power (over) oppressively or cruelly ▶**tyrannous** adj ▶**tyranny** n tyrannical rule

**tyre** n rubber ring, usu. inflated, over the rim of a vehicle's wheel to grip the road

**tyro** n, pl -**ros** novice or beginner

t

# Uu

**ubiquitous** [yew-**bik**-wit-uss] *adj* being or seeming to be everywhere at once ▶ **ubiquity** *n*

**udder** *n* large baglike milk-producing gland of cows, sheep, or goats

**UEFA** Union of European Football Associations

**UFO** unidentified flying object

**ugly** *adj* **uglier, ugliest** of unpleasant appearance; ominous or menacing ▶ **ugliness** *n*

**UHF** ultrahigh frequency

**UHT** (of milk or cream) ultra-heat-treated

**UK** United Kingdom

**ukulele, ukelele** [yew-kal-**lay**-lee] *n* small guitar with four strings

**ulcer** *n* open sore on the surface of the skin or mucous membrane. ▶ **ulcerated** *adj* made or becoming ulcerous ▶ **ulceration** *n* ▶ **ulcerous** *adj* of, like, or characterized by ulcers

**ulna** *n, pl* **-nae** *or* **-nas** inner and longer of the two bones of the human forearm

**ulterior** *adj* (of an aim, reason, etc.) concealed or hidden

**ultimate** *adj* final in a series or process; highest or supreme ▶ **ultimately** *adv*

**ultimatum** [ult-im-**may**-tum] *n* final warning stating that action will be taken unless certain conditions are met

**ultra-** *prefix* beyond a specified extent, range, or limit e.g. *ultrasonic*; extremely e.g. *ultramodern*

**ultrahigh frequency** *n* radio frequency between 300 and 3000 megahertz

**ultramarine** *adj* vivid blue

**ultrasonic** *adj* of or producing sound waves with a higher frequency than the human ear can hear

**ultrasound** *n* ultrasonic waves, used in medical diagnosis and therapy and in echo sounding

**ultraviolet** *adj, n* (of) light beyond the limit of visibility at the violet end of the spectrum

**ululate** [**yewl**-yew-late] *v* howl or wail ▶ **ululation** *n*

**umber** *adj* dark brown to reddish-brown

**umbilical** *adj* of the navel ▶ **umbilical cord** long flexible tube of blood vessels that connects a fetus with the placenta

**umbrage** *n* **take umbrage** feel offended or upset

**umbrella** *n* portable device used for protection against rain, consisting of a folding frame covered in material attached to a central rod; single organization, idea, etc. that contains or covers many different organizations, ideas, etc.

**umpire** *n* official who rules on the playing of a game ▷ *v* act as umpire in (a game)

**umpteen** *adj* (informal) very many ▶ **umpteenth** *n, adj*

**UN** United Nations

**un-** *prefix* not e.g. *unidentified*; denoting reversal of an action e.g. *untie*; denoting removal from e.g. *unthrone*

**unable** *adj* **unable to** lacking the necessary power, ability, or authority to (do something)

**unaccountable** *adj* unable to be explained; (foll by *to*) not answerable to ▶ **unaccountably** *adv*

**unadulterated** *adj* with nothing added, pure

**unanimous** [yew-**nan**-im-uss] *adj* in complete agreement; agreed by all ▶ **unanimity** *n*

**unannounced** *adv* without warning e.g. *he turned up unannounced*

**unarmed** *adj* without weapons

**unassailable** *adj* unable to be attacked or disputed

**unassuming** *adj* modest or unpretentious

**unaware** *adj* not aware or conscious ▶ **unawares** *adv* by surprise e.g. *caught unawares*; without knowing

| **USAGE NOTE**
Note the difference between the adjective *unaware*, usually followed by *of* or *that*, and the adverb *unawares*

**unbalanced** *adj* biased or one-sided; mentally deranged

**unbearable** *adj* not able to be endured ▶ **unbearably** *adv*

**unbeknown** *adv* **unbeknown to** without the knowledge of (a person)

**unbend** *v* (*informal*) become less strict or more informal in one's attitudes or behaviour ▶ **unbending** *adj*

**unbidden** *adj* not ordered or asked

**unborn** *adj* not yet born

**unbosom** *v* relieve (oneself) of (secrets or feelings) by telling someone

**unbridled** *adj* (of feelings or behaviour) not controlled in any way

**unburden** *v* relieve (one's mind or oneself) of a worry by confiding in someone

**uncalled-for** *adj* not fair or justified

**uncanny** *adj* weird or mysterious ▶ **uncannily** *adv*

**unceremonious** *adj* relaxed and informal; abrupt or rude ▶ **unceremoniously** *adv*

**uncertain** *adj* not able to be accurately known or predicted; not able to be depended upon; changeable ▶ **uncertainty** *n*

**un-Christian** *adj* not in accordance with Christian principles

**uncle** *n* brother of one's father or mother; husband of parent's sibling

**unclean** *adj* lacking moral, spiritual, or physical cleanliness

**uncomfortable** *adj* not physically relaxed; anxious or uneasy

**uncommon** *adj* not happening or encountered often; in excess of what is normal ▶ **uncommonly** *adv*

**uncompromising** *adj* not prepared to compromise

**unconcerned** *adj* lacking in concern or involvement ▶ **unconcernedly** *adv*

**unconditional** *adj* without conditions or limitations

**unconscionable** *adj* having no principles, unscrupulous; excessive in amount or degree

**unconscious** *adj* lacking normal awareness through the senses; not aware of one's actions or behaviour ▷ *n* part of the mind containing instincts and ideas that exist without one's awareness ▶ **unconsciously** *adv* ▶ **unconsciousness** *n*

**uncooperative** *adj* not willing to help other people with what they are doing

**uncouth** *adj* lacking in good manners, refinement, or grace

u

**uncover** v reveal or disclose; remove the cover, top, etc., from

**unction** n act of anointing with oil in sacramental ceremonies

**unctuous** adj pretending to be kind and concerned

**undecided** adj not having made up one's mind; (of an issue or problem) not agreed or decided upon

**undeniable** adj unquestionably true ▶ **undeniably** adv

**under** prep, adv indicating movement to or position beneath the underside or base ▷ prep less than; subject to

**under-** prefix below e.g. underground; insufficient or insufficiently e.g. underrate

**underage** adj below the required or standard age

**underarm** adj (Sport) denoting a style of throwing, bowling, or serving in which the hand is swung below shoulder level ▷ adv (Sport) in an underarm style

**undercarriage** n landing gear of an aircraft; framework supporting the body of a vehicle

**underclass** n class consisting of the most disadvantaged people, such as the long-term unemployed

**undercoat** n coat of paint applied before the final coat

**undercover** adj done or acting in secret

**undercurrent** n current that is not apparent at the surface; underlying opinion or emotion

**undercut** v charge less than (a competitor) to obtain trade

**underdog** n person or team in a weak or underprivileged position

**underdone** adj not cooked enough

**underestimate** v make too low an estimate of; not realize the full potential of

**underfoot** adv under the feet

**undergarment** n any piece of underwear

**undergo** v experience, endure, or sustain

**undergraduate** n person studying in a university for a first degree

**underground** adj occurring, situated, used, or going below ground level; secret ▷ n electric passenger railway operated in underground tunnels; movement dedicated to overthrowing a government or occupation forces

**undergrowth** n small trees and bushes growing beneath taller trees in a wood or forest

**underhand** adj sly, deceitful, and secretive

**underlie** v lie or be placed under; be the foundation, cause, or basis of ▶ **underlying** adj fundamental or basic

**underline** v draw a line under; state forcibly, emphasize

**underling** n subordinate

**undermine** v weaken gradually

**underneath** prep, adv under or beneath ▷ adj, n lower (part or surface)

**underpants** pl n man's undergarment for the lower part of the body

**underpass** n section of a road that passes under another road or a railway line

**underpin** v give strength or support to

**underprivileged** adj lacking the rights and advantages of other members of society

**underrate** v not realize the full potential of ▶ **underrated** adj

**underseal** n (chiefly Brit) coating of tar etc. applied to the underside of a motor vehicle to prevent corrosion

u

**underside** n bottom or lower surface

**understand** v know and comprehend the nature or meaning of; realize or grasp (something); assume, infer, or believe ▶ **understandable** adj ▶ **understandably** adv ▶ **understanding** n ability to learn, judge, or make decisions; personal interpretation of a subject; mutual agreement, usu. an informal or private one ▷ adj kind and sympathetic

**understate** v describe or represent (something) in restrained terms; state that (something, such as a number) is less than it is ▶ **understatement** n

**understudy** n actor who studies a part in order to be able to replace the usual actor if necessary ▷ v act as an understudy for

**undertake** v agree or commit oneself to (something) or to do (something); promise ▶ **undertaking** n task or enterprise; agreement to do something

**undertaker** n person whose job is to prepare corpses for burial or cremation and organize funerals

**undertone** n quiet tone of voice; underlying quality or feeling

**undertow** n strong undercurrent flowing in a different direction from the surface current

**underwater** adj, adv (situated, occurring, or for use) below the surface of the sea, a lake, or a river

**underwear** n clothing worn under the outer garments and next to the skin

**underworld** n criminals and their associates; (Greek and Roman myth) regions below the earth's surface regarded as the abode of the dead

**underwrite** v accept financial responsibility for (a commercial project); sign and issue (an insurance policy), thus accepting liability

**underwriter** n person who underwrites (esp. an insurance policy)

**undesirable** adj not desirable or pleasant, objectionable ▷ n objectionable person

**undo** v open, unwrap; reverse the effects of; cause the downfall of ▶ **undone** adj ▶ **undoing** n cause of someone's downfall

**undoubted** adj certain or indisputable ▶ **undoubtedly** adv

**undue** adj greater than is reasonable, excessive ▶ **unduly** adv

**undulate** v move in waves ▶ **undulation** n

**undying** adj never ending, eternal

**unearth** v reveal or discover by searching; dig up out of the earth

**unearthly** adj ghostly or eerie; ridiculous or unreasonable

**uneasy** adj (of a person) anxious or apprehensive; (of a condition) precarious or uncomfortable ▶ **uneasily** adv ▶ **uneasiness** n ▶ **unease** n feeling of anxiety; state of dissatisfaction

**unemployed** adj out of work ▷ pl n **the unemployed** people who are out of work ▶ **unemployment** n

**unequivocal** adj completely clear in meaning ▶ **unequivocally** adv

**unerring** adj never mistaken, consistently accurate

**unexceptionable** adj beyond criticism or objection

**unfailing** adj continuous or reliable ▶ **unfailingly** adv

**unfair** adj not right, fair, or just ▶ **unfairly** adv ▶ **unfairness** n

**unfaithful** adj having sex with someone other than one's regular partner; not true to a promise or vow ▶ **unfaithfulness** n

**unfeeling** adj without sympathy

**unfit** adj unqualified or unsuitable; in poor physical condition

**unflappable** adj (informal) not easily upset ▶ **unflappability** n

**unfold** v open or spread out from a folded state; reveal or be revealed

**unfollow** v cease to receive messages posted by (a blogger or microblogger)

**unforgettable** adj impossible to forget, memorable

**unfortunate** adj unlucky, unsuccessful, or unhappy; regrettable or unsuitable ▶ **unfortunately** adv

**unfounded** adj not based on facts or evidence

**unfrock** v deprive (a priest in holy orders) of his or her priesthood

**ungainly** adj **-lier, -liest** lacking grace when moving

**ungodly** adj (informal) unreasonable or outrageous e.g. an ungodly hour; wicked or sinful

**ungrateful** adj not grateful or thankful

**unguarded** adj not protected; incautious or careless

**unguent** [ung-gwent] n (lit) ointment

**unhand** v (old-fashioned or lit) release from one's grasp

**unhappy** adj sad or depressed; unfortunate or wretched ▶ **unhappily** adv ▶ **unhappiness** n

**unhealthy** adj likely to cause poor health; not fit or well; morbid, unnatural

**unhinge** v derange or unbalance (a person or his or her mind)

**uni** n (informal) short for **university**

**uni-** combining form of, consisting of, or having only one e.g. unicellular

**unicorn** n imaginary horselike creature with one horn growing from its forehead

**uniform** n special identifying set of clothes for the members of an organization, such as soldiers ▷ adj regular and even throughout, unvarying; alike or like ▶ **uniformly** adv ▶ **uniformity** n

**unify** v **-fying, -fied** make or become one ▶ **unification** n

**unilateral** adj made or done by only one person or group ▶ **unilaterally** adv

**unimpeachable** adj completely honest and reliable

**uninterested** adj having or showing no interest in someone or something

**union** n uniting or being united; short for **trade union**; association or confederation of individuals or groups for a common purpose ▶ **unionist** n member or supporter of a trade union ▶ **unionize** v organize (workers) into a trade union ▶ **unionization** n ▶ **Union Jack, Union Flag** national flag of the United Kingdom

**unique** [yoo-**neek**] adj being the only one of a particular type; without equal or like ▶ **uniquely** adv

**USAGE NOTE**
Because of its meaning, avoid using unique with modifiers like very and rather

**unisex** adj designed for use by both sexes

**unison** n complete agreement; (Music) singing or playing of the same notes together at the same time

**unit** n single undivided entity or whole; group or individual regarded as a basic element of a larger whole; fixed quantity

u

etc., used as a standard of measurement; piece of furniture designed to be fitted with other similar pieces ▶ **unit trust** investment trust that issues units for public sale and invests the money in many different businesses

**Unitarian** n person who believes that God is one being and rejects the Trinity ▶ **Unitarianism** n

**unitary** adj consisting of a single undivided whole; of a unit or units

**unite** v make or become an integrated whole; (cause to) enter into an association or alliance

**unity** n state of being one; mutual agreement

**universe** n whole of all existing matter, energy, and space; the world ▶ **universal** adj of or typical of the whole of mankind or of nature; existing everywhere ▶ **universally** adv ▶ **universality** n

**university** n, pl **-ties** institution of higher education with the authority to award degrees

**unkempt** adj (of the hair) not combed; slovenly or untidy

**unknown** adj not known; not famous ▷ n unknown person, quantity, or thing

**unleaded** adj (of petrol) containing less tetraethyl lead, in order to reduce environmental pollution

**unleash** v set loose or cause (something bad)

**unless** conj except under the circumstances that

**unlike** adj dissimilar or different ▷ prep not like or typical of

**unlikely** adj improbable

**unload** v remove (cargo) from (a ship, truck, or plane); remove the ammunition from (a firearm)

**unmanned** adj having no personnel or crew

**unmask** v remove the mask or disguise from; (cause to) appear in true character

**unmentionable** adj unsuitable as a topic of conversation

**unmistakable, unmistakeable** adj not ambiguous, clear ▶ **unmistakably, unmistakeably** adv

**unmitigated** adj not reduced or lessened in severity etc.; total and complete

**unmoved** adj not affected by emotion, indifferent

**unnatural** adj strange and frightening because not usual; not in accordance with accepted standards of behaviour

**unnerve** v cause to lose courage, confidence, or self-control

**unnumbered** adj countless; not counted or given a number

**unorthodox** adj (of ideas, methods, etc.) unconventional and not generally accepted; (of a person) having unusual opinions or methods

**unpack** v remove the contents of (a suitcase, trunk, etc.); take (something) out of a packed container

**unparalleled** adj not equalled, supreme

**unpick** v undo (the stitches) of (a piece of sewing)

**unpleasant** adj not pleasant or agreeable ▶ **unpleasantly** adv ▶ **unpleasantness** n

**unprecedented** adj never having happened before, unparalleled

**unprintable** adj unsuitable for printing for reasons of obscenity or libel

**unprofessional** adj contrary to the accepted code of a profession ▶ **unprofessionally** adv

**u**

**unqualified** adj lacking the necessary qualifications; total or complete

**unravel** v -elling, -elled reduce (something knitted or woven) to separate strands; become unravelled; explain or solve

**unreasonable** adj immoderate or excessive; refusing to listen to reason ▶ **unreasonably** adv

**unremitting** adj never slackening or stopping

**unrequited** adj not returned e.g. unrequited love

**unrest** n rebellious state of discontent

**unrivalled** adj having no equal

**unroll** v open out or unwind (something rolled or coiled) or (of something rolled or coiled) become opened out or unwound

**unruly** adj -lier, -liest difficult to control or organize

**unsavoury** adj distasteful or objectionable

**unscathed** adj not harmed or injured

**unscrupulous** adj prepared to act dishonestly, unprincipled

**unseat** v throw or displace from a seat or saddle; depose from an office or position

**unsettled** adj lacking order or stability; disturbed and restless; constantly changing or moving from place to place

**unsightly** adj unpleasant to look at

**unsocial** adj (also **unsociable**) avoiding the company of other people; falling outside the normal working day e.g. unsocial hours

**unsound** adj unhealthy or unstable; not based on truth or fact

**unspeakable** adj indescribably bad or evil ▶ **unspeakably** adv

**unstable** adj lacking stability or firmness; having abrupt changes of mood or behaviour

**unstinting** adj generous, gladly given e.g. unstinting praise

**unsuitable** adj not right or appropriate for a particular purpose ▶ **unsuitably** adv

**unsuited** adj not appropriate for a particular task or situation

**unsung** adj not acclaimed or honoured e.g. unsung heroes

**unswerving** adj firm, constant, not changing

**unsympathetic** adj not feeling or showing sympathy; unpleasant, not likeable; (foll by to) opposed to

**unthinkable** adj out of the question, inconceivable

**untidy** adj messy and disordered ▶ **untidily** adv ▶ **untidiness** n

**untie** v open or free (something that is tied); free from constraint

**until** conj up to the time that ▷ prep in or throughout the period before **not until** not before (a time or event)

**untimely** adj occurring before the expected or normal time; inappropriate to the occasion or time

**unto** prep (old-fashioned) to

**untold** adj incapable of description; incalculably great in number or quantity

**untouchable** adj above reproach or suspicion; unable to be touched ▷ n (offens) member of the lowest Hindu caste in India

**untoward** adj causing misfortune or annoyance

**untrue** adj incorrect or false; disloyal or unfaithful ▶ **untruth** n statement that is not true, lie

**unusual** adj uncommon or extraordinary ▶ **unusually** adv

**unutterable** *adj* incapable of being expressed in words ▶ **unutterably** *adv*

**unvarnished** *adj* not elaborated upon e.g. *the unvarnished truth*

**unveil** *v* ceremonially remove the cover from (a new picture, plaque, etc.); make public (a secret) ▶ **unveiling** *n*

**unwarranted** *adj* not justified, not necessary

**unwieldy** *adj* too heavy, large, or awkward to be easily handled

**unwind** *v* relax after a busy or tense time; slacken, undo, or unravel

**unwitting** *adj* not intentional; not knowing or conscious ▶ **unwittingly** *adv*

**unwonted** *adj* out of the ordinary

**unworthy** *adj* not deserving or worthy; lacking merit or value **unworthy of** beneath the level considered befitting (to)

**unwrap** *v* remove the wrapping from (something)

**unwritten** *adj* not printed or in writing; operating only through custom

**up** *prep, adv* indicating movement to or position at a higher place ▷ *adv* indicating readiness, intensity or completeness, etc. e.g. *warm up; drink up* ▷ *adj* of a high or higher position; out of bed ▷ *v* **upping, upped** increase or raise **up against** having to cope with **up and** (*informal*) do something suddenly e.g. *he upped and left* **what's up?** (*informal*) what is wrong? ▶ **ups and downs** alternating periods of good and bad luck ▶ **upward** *adj* directed or moving towards a higher place or level ▷ *adv* (also **upwards**) from a lower to a higher place, level, or condition

**upbeat** *adj* (*informal*) cheerful and optimistic ▷ *n* (*Music*) unaccented beat

**upbraid** *v* scold or reproach

**upbringing** *n* education of a person during the formative years

**update** *v* bring up to date

**upend** *v* turn or set (something) on its end

**upfront** *adj* open and frank ▷ *adv, adj* (of money) paid out at the beginning of a business arrangement

**upgrade** *v* promote (a person or job) to a higher rank

**upheaval** *n* strong, sudden, or violent disturbance

**uphill** *adj* sloping or leading upwards; requiring a great deal of effort ▷ *adv* up a slope ▷ *n* (*S Afr*) difficulty

**uphold** *v* maintain or defend against opposition; give moral support to ▶ **upholder** *n*

**upholster** *v* fit (a chair or sofa) with padding, springs, and covering ▶ **upholsterer** *n*

**upholstery** *n* soft covering on a chair or sofa

**upkeep** *n* act, process, or cost of keeping something in good repair

**upland** *adj* of or in an area of high or relatively high ground ▶ **uplands** *pl n* area of high or relatively high ground

**uplift** *v* raise or lift up; raise morally or spiritually ▷ *n* act or process of improving moral, social, or cultural conditions ▶ **uplifting** *adj*

**upload** *v* transfer (data or a program) from one's own computer into the memory of another computer

**upon** *prep* on; up and on

**upper** *adj* higher or highest in physical position, wealth, rank, or status ▷ *n* part of a shoe above

**u**

the sole ▶ **uppermost** adj highest in position, power, or importance ▷ adv in or into the highest place or position ▶ **upper class** highest social class ▶ **upper-class** adj ▶ **upper crust** (Brit, Aust & NZ informal) upper class ▶ **upper hand** position of control

**uppish, uppity** adj (Brit informal) snobbish, arrogant, or presumptuous

**upright** adj vertical or erect; honest or just ▷ adv vertically or in an erect position ▷ n vertical support, such as a post ▶ **uprightness** n

**uprising** n rebellion or revolt

**uproar** n disturbance characterized by loud noise and confusion ▶ **uproarious** adj very funny; (of laughter) loud and boisterous ▶ **uproariously** adv

**uproot** v pull up by, or as if by, the roots; displace (a person or people) from their native or usual surroundings

**upscale** adj expensive and of superior quality

**upset** adj emotionally or physically disturbed or distressed ▷ v tip over; disturb the normal state or stability of; disturb mentally or emotionally; make physically ill ▷ n unexpected defeat or reversal; disturbance or disorder of the emotions, mind, or body ▶ **upsetting** adj

**upshot** n final result or conclusion

**upside down** adj turned over completely; (informal) confused or jumbled ▷ adv in an inverted fashion; in a chaotic manner

**upstage** adj at the back half of the stage ▷ v (informal) draw attention to oneself from (someone else)

**upstairs** adv to or on an upper floor of a building ▷ n upper floor ▷ adj situated on an upper floor

**upstanding** adj of good character

**upstart** n person who has risen suddenly to a position of power and behaves arrogantly

**upstream** adv, adj in or towards the higher part of a stream

**upsurge** n rapid rise or swell

**uptake** n **quick on the uptake, slow on the uptake** (informal) quick or slow to understand or learn

**uptight** adj (informal) nervously tense, irritable, or angry

**up-to-date** adj modern or fashionable

**upturn** n upward trend or improvement ▶ **upturned** adj facing upwards

**uranium** n (Chem) radioactive silvery-white metallic element, used chiefly as a source of nuclear energy

**Uranus** n (Greek myth) god of the sky; seventh planet from the sun

**urban** adj of or living in a city or town; denoting modern pop music of African-American origin, such as hip-hop ▶ **urbanize** v make (a rural area) more industrialized and urban ▶ **urbanization** n

**urbane** adj characterized by courtesy, elegance, and sophistication ▶ **urbanity** n

**urchin** n mischievous child

**Urdu** [**oor**-doo] n language of Pakistan

**urethra** [yew-**reeth**-ra] n canal that carries urine from the bladder out of the body

**urge** n strong impulse, inner drive, or yearning ▷ v plead with or press (a person to do something); advocate earnestly; force or drive onwards

**urgent** adj requiring speedy action or attention ▶ **urgency** n ▶ **urgently** adv

**urine** n pale yellow fluid excreted by the kidneys to the bladder and passed as waste from the body ▸ **urinary** *adj* ▸ **urinate** *v* discharge urine ▸ **urination** *n* ▸ **urinal** *n* sanitary fitting used by men for urination

**URL** uniform resource locator: a standardized address of a location on the internet

**urn** *n* vase used as a container for the ashes of the dead; large metal container with a tap, used for making and holding tea or coffee

**ursine** *adj* of or like a bear

**US, USA** United States (of America)

**us** *pron* objective case of **we**

**USB** Universal Serial Bus: standard for connecting sockets on computers ▸ **USB drive** *n* (*Computing*) small portable data storage device with a USB connection

**use** *v* put into service or action; take advantage of, exploit; consume or expend ▷ *n* using or being used; ability or permission to use; usefulness or advantage; purpose for which something is used ▸ **user** *n* ▸ **user-friendly** *adj* easy to familiarize oneself with, understand, and use ▸ **username** *n* (*Computing*) name entered into a computer for identification purposes ▸ **usable** *adj* able to be used ▸ **usage** *n* regular or constant use; way in which a word is used in a language ▸ **use-by date** (*Aust, NZ & S Afr*) date on packaged food after which it should not be sold ▸ **used** *adj* second-hand ▸ **used to** *adj* accustomed to ▷ *v* used as an auxiliary to express past habitual or accustomed actions e.g. *I used to live there* ▸ **useful** *adj* ▸ **usefully** *adv* ▸ **usefulness** *n* ▸ **useless** *adj* ▸ **uselessly** *adv* ▸ **uselessness** *n*

**usher** *n* official who shows people to their seats, as in a

church ▷ *v* conduct or escort ▸ **usherette** *n* female assistant in a cinema who shows people to their seats

**USSR** (formerly) Union of Soviet Socialist Republics

**usual** *adj* of the most normal, frequent, or regular type ▸ **usually** *adv* most often, in most cases

> **SPELLING TIP**
> The Collins Corpus shows that it's very common to write *usualy*, forgetting the double *l* of **usually**

**usurp** [yewz-**zurp**] *v* seize (a position or power) without authority ▸ **usurpation** *n* ▸ **usurper** *n*

**usury** *n* practice of lending money at an extremely high rate of interest ▸ **usurer** [**yewz**-yoor-er] *n*

**ute** [**yoot**] *n* (*Aust & NZ informal*) utility truck

**utensil** *n* tool or container for practical use e.g. *cooking utensils*

**uterus** [**yew**-ter-russ] *n* womb ▸ **uterine** *adj*

**utilitarian** *adj* useful rather than beautiful; of utilitarianism ▸ **utilitarianism** *n* (*Ethics*) doctrine that the right action is the one that brings about the greatest good for the greatest number of people

**utility** *n* usefulness; (*pl* **-ties**) public service, such as electricity ▷ *adj* designed for use rather than beauty ▸ **utility room** room used for large domestic appliances and equipment ▸ **utility truck** (*Aust & NZ*) small truck with an open body and low sides

**utilize** *v* make practical use of ▸ **utilization** *n*

**utmost** *adj, n* (of) the greatest possible degree or amount e.g. *the utmost point*; *I was doing my utmost to comply*

**u**

**Utopia** [yew-**tope**-ee-a] n any real or imaginary society, place, or state considered to be perfect or ideal ▶ **Utopian** adj

**utter¹** v express (something) in sounds or words ▶ **utterance** n something uttered; act or power of uttering

**utter²** adj total or absolute ▶ **utterly** adv

**uttermost** adj, n same as **utmost**

**U-turn** n turn, made by a vehicle, in the shape of a U, resulting in a reversal of direction; complete change in policy e.g. a humiliating U-turn by the Prime Minister

**UV** ultraviolet

**uvula** [yew-view-la] n small fleshy part of the soft palate that hangs in the back of the throat ▶ **uvular** adj

**uxorious** [ux-or-ee-uss] adj excessively fond of or dependent on one's wife

# Vv

**V** volt

**v.** versus; very

**vacant** adj (of a toilet, room, etc.) unoccupied; without interest or understanding ▶ **vacantly** adv ▶ **vacancy** n, pl **-cies** unfilled job; unoccupied room in a guesthouse; state of being unoccupied

**vacate** v cause (something) to be empty by leaving; give up (a job or position) ▶ **vacation** n time when universities and law courts are closed; (chiefly US) holiday

**vaccinate** v inject with a vaccine ▶ **vaccination** n ▶ **vaccine** n substance designed to cause a mild form of a disease to make a person immune to the disease itself

**vacillate** [vass-ill-late] v keep changing one's mind or opinions ▶ **vacillation** n

**vacuous** adj not expressing intelligent thought ▶ **vacuity** n

**vacuum** n, pl **vacuums** or **vacua** empty space from which all or most air or gas has been removed ▷ v clean with a vacuum cleaner ▶ **vacuum cleaner** electrical appliance which sucks up dust and dirt from carpets and upholstery ▶ **vacuum flask** double-walled flask with a vacuum between the walls that keeps drinks hot or cold ▶ **vacuum-packed** adj contained in packaging from which the air has been removed

**vagabond** n person with no fixed home, esp. a beggar

**V**

**vagary** [**vaig**-a-ree] n, pl -**garies** unpredictable change

**vagina** [vaj-**jine**-a] n (in female mammals) passage from the womb to the external genitals ▶ **vaginal** adj

**vagrant** [**vaig**-rant] n person with no settled home ▷ adj wandering ▶ **vagrancy** n

**vague** adj not clearly explained; unable to be seen or heard clearly; absent-minded ▶ **vaguely** adv

**vain** adj excessively proud, esp. of one's appearance; bound to fail, futile **in vain** unsuccessfully

**vainglorious** adj (lit) boastful

**valance** [**val**-lenss] n piece of drapery round the edge of a bed

**vale** n (lit) valley

**valedictory** [val-lid-**dik**-tree] adj (of a speech, performance, etc.) intended as a farewell ▶ **valediction** n farewell speech

**valence** [**vale**-ence] n molecular bonding between atoms

**valency** n, pl -**cies** power of an atom to make molecular bonds

**valentine** n (person to whom one sends) a romantic card on Saint Valentine's Day, 14 February

**valerian** n herb used as a sedative

**valet** n man's personal male servant

**valetudinarian** [val-lit-yew-din-**air**-ee-an] n person with a long-term illness; person overconcerned about his or her health

**valiant** adj brave or courageous

**valid** adj soundly reasoned; having legal force ▶ **validate** v make valid ▶ **validation** n ▶ **validity** n

**valise** [val-**leez**] n (old-fashioned) small suitcase

**Valium**® n drug used as a tranquillizer

**valley** n low area between hills, often with a river running through it

**valour** n (lit) bravery

**value** n importance, usefulness; monetary worth ▷ pl moral principles ▷ v **valuing, valued** assess the worth or desirability of; have a high regard for ▶ **valuable** adj having great worth ▶ **valuables** pl n valuable personal property ▶ **valuation** n assessment of worth ▶ **valueless** adj ▶ **valuer** n ▶ **value-added tax** (Brit & S Afr) see **VAT** ▶ **value judgment** opinion based on personal belief

**valve** n device to control the movement of fluid through a pipe; (Anat) flap in a part of the body allowing blood to flow in one direction only; (Physics) tube containing a vacuum, allowing current to flow from a cathode to an anode ▶ **valvular** adj

**vamp**¹ n (informal) sexually attractive woman who seduces men

**vamp**² v **vamp up** make (a story, piece of music, etc.) seem new by inventing additional parts

**vampire** n (in folklore) corpse that rises at night to drink the blood of the living ▶ **vampire bat** tropical bat that feeds on blood

**van**¹ n motor vehicle for transporting goods; railway carriage for goods, luggage, or mail

**van**² n short for **vanguard**

**vanadium** n (Chem) metallic element, used in steel

**vandal** n person who deliberately damages property ▶ **vandalism** n ▶ **vandalize** v

**vane** n flat blade on a rotary device such as a weathercock or propeller

**vanguard** n unit of soldiers leading an army; most advanced group or position in a movement or activity

**vanilla** n seed pod of a tropical climbing orchid, used for flavouring

**v**

**vanish** v disappear suddenly or mysteriously; cease to exist

**vanity** n, pl **-ties** (display of) excessive pride

**vanquish** v (lit) defeat (someone) utterly

**vantage** n **vantage point** position that gives one an overall view

**vape** v (informal) inhale vapour from an e-cigarette

**vapid** adj lacking character, dull

**vapour** n moisture suspended in air as steam or mist; gaseous form of something that is liquid or solid at room temperature ▸ **vaporize** v ▸ **vaporizer** n ▸ **vaporous** adj

**variable** adj not always the same, changeable ▷ n (Maths) expression with a range of values ▸ **variability** n

**variant** adj differing from a standard or type ▷ n something that differs from a standard or type **at variance** in disagreement

**variation** n something presented in a slightly different form; difference in level, amount, or quantity; (Music) repetition in different forms of a basic theme

**varicose veins** pl n knotted and swollen veins, esp. in the legs

**variegated** adj having patches or streaks of different colours ▸ **variegation** n

**variety** n, pl **-ties** state of being diverse or various; different things of the same kind; particular sort or kind; light entertainment composed of unrelated acts

**various** adj of several kinds ▸ **variously** adv

**varnish** n solution of oil and resin, put on a surface to make it hard and glossy ▷ v apply varnish to

**varsity** n (informal) university

**vary** v **varying, varied** change; cause differences in ▸ **varied** adj

**vascular** adj (Biol) relating to vessels

**vas deferens** n, pl **vasa deferentia** (Anat) sperm-carrying duct in each testicle

**vase** n ornamental jar, esp. for flowers

**vasectomy** n, pl **-mies** surgical removal of part of the vas deferens, as a contraceptive method

**Vaseline**® n thick oily cream made from petroleum, used in skin care

**vassal** n (Hist) man given land by a lord in return for military service; subordinate person or nation ▸ **vassalage** n

**vast** adj extremely large ▸ **vastly** adv ▸ **vastness** n

**VAT** (Brit & SAfr) value-added tax: tax on the difference between the cost of materials and the selling price

**vat** n large container for liquids

**Vatican** n the Pope's palace

**vaudeville** n variety entertainment of songs and comic turns

**vault¹** n secure room for storing valuables; underground burial chamber ▸ **vaulted** adj having an arched roof

**vault²** v jump over (something) by resting one's hand(s) on it ▷ n such a jump

**vaunt** v describe or display (success or possessions) boastfully ▸ **vaunted** adj

**VC** Vice Chancellor; Victoria Cross

**VCD** video compact disc: an optical disc used to store computer, audio or video data

**VCR** video cassette recorder

**VD** venereal disease

**VDU** visual display unit

**veal** n calf meat

**vector** n (Maths) quantity that has size and direction, such as force; animal, usu. an insect, that carries disease

**veer** v change direction suddenly

**vegan** [vee-gan] n person who eats no meat, fish, eggs, or dairy products ▷ adj suitable for a vegan ▸ **veganism** n

**vegetable** n edible plant; (offens) severely brain-damaged person ▷ adj of or like plants or vegetables

**vegetarian** n person who eats no meat or fish ▷ adj suitable for a vegetarian ▸ **vegetarianism** n

**vegetate** v live a dull boring life with no mental stimulation

**vegetation** n plant life of a given place

**vehement** adj expressing strong feelings ▸ **vehemence** n ▸ **vehemently** adv

**vehicle** n machine, esp. with an engine and wheels, for carrying people or objects; something used to achieve a particular purpose or as a means of expression ▸ **vehicular** adj

**veil** n piece of thin cloth covering the head or face; something that masks the truth e.g. a veil of secrecy ▷ v cover with or as if with a veil **take the veil** become a nun ▸ **veiled** adj disguised

**vein** n tube that takes blood to the heart; line in a leaf or an insect's wing; layer of ore or mineral in rock; streak in marble, wood, or cheese; feature of someone's writing or speech e.g. a vein of humour; mood or style e.g. in a lighter vein ▸ **veined** adj

**Velcro**® n fastening consisting of one piece of fabric with tiny hooked threads and another with a coarse surface that sticks to it

**veld, veldt** n high grassland in southern Africa ▸ **veldskoen, velskoen** n (S Afr) leather ankle boot

**vellum** n fine calfskin parchment; type of strong good-quality paper

**velocity** n, pl **-ties** speed of movement in a given direction

**velour, velours** [vel-**loor**] n fabric similar to velvet

**velvet** n fabric with a thick soft pile ▸ **velvety** adj soft and smooth ▸ **velveteen** n cotton velvet

**venal** adj easily bribed; characterized by bribery

**vend** v sell ▸ **vendor** n ▸ **vending machine** machine that dispenses goods when coins are inserted

**vendetta** n prolonged quarrel between families, esp. one involving revenge killings

**veneer** n thin layer of wood etc. covering a cheaper material; superficial appearance e.g. a veneer of sophistication

**venerable** adj worthy of deep respect ▸ **venerate** v hold (a person) in deep respect ▸ **veneration** n

**venereal disease** [ven-**ear**-ee-al] n disease transmitted sexually

**Venetian** adj of Venice, port in NE Italy ▸ **Venetian blind** window blind made of thin horizontal slats that turn to let in more or less light

**vengeance** n revenge ▸ **vengeful** adj wanting revenge

**venial** [**veen**-ee-al] adj (of a sin or fault) easily forgiven

**venison** n deer meat

**venom** n malice or spite; poison produced by snakes etc. ▸ **venomous** adj

**venous** adj (Anat) of veins

**vent**¹ n outlet releasing fumes or fluid ▷ v express (an emotion) freely **give vent to** release (an emotion) in an outburst

**vent**² n vertical slit in a jacket

**ventilate** v let fresh air into; discuss (ideas or feelings) openly ▸ **ventilation** n ▸ **ventilator** n

**ventral** adj relating to the front of the body

**V**

**ventricle** n (Anat) one of the four cavities of the heart or brain

**ventriloquist** n entertainer who can speak without moving his or her lips, so that a voice seems to come from elsewhere ▸ **ventriloquism** n

**venture** n risky undertaking, esp. in business ▸ v do something risky; dare to express (an opinion); go to an unknown place ▸ **venturesome** adj daring ▸ **venture capitalist** provider of capital for new commercial enterprises

**venue** n place where an organized gathering is held

**Venus** n planet second nearest to the sun; Roman goddess of love ▸ **Venus flytrap**

**veracity** n habitual truthfulness ▸ **veracious** adj

**verandah, veranda** n open porch attached to a house

**verb** n word that expresses the idea of action, happening, or being ▸ **verbal** adj spoken; of a verb ▸ **verbally** adv ▸ **verbalize** v express (something) in words

**verbatim** [verb-**bait**-im] adv, adj word for word

**verbena** n plant with sweet-smelling flowers

**verbiage** n excessive use of words

**verbose** [verb-**bohss**] adj speaking at tedious length ▸ **verbosity** n

**verdant** adj (lit) covered in green vegetation

**verdict** n decision of a jury; opinion formed after examining the facts

**verdigris** [**ver**-dig-riss] n green film on copper, brass, or bronze

**verdure** n (lit) flourishing green vegetation

**verge** n grass border along a road **on the verge of** having almost reached (a point or condition) ▸ **verge on** v be near to (a condition)

**verger** n (C of E) church caretaker

**verify** v -**ifying**, -**ified** check the truth or accuracy of ▸ **verifiable** adj ▸ **verification** n

**verily** adv (obs) in truth

**verisimilitude** n appearance of being real or true

**veritable** adj rightly called, without exaggeration e.g. a veritable feast ▸ **veritably** adv

**verity** n, pl -**ties** true statement or principle

**vermicelli** [ver-me-**chell**-ee] n fine strands of pasta

**vermiform** adj shaped like a worm ▸ **vermiform appendix** (Anat) same as **appendix**

**vermilion** adj orange-red

**vermin** pl n animals, esp. insects and rodents, that spread disease or cause damage ▸ **verminous** adj

**vermouth** [**ver**-muth] n wine flavoured with herbs

**vernacular** [ver-**nak**-yew-lar] n most widely spoken language of a particular people or place

**vernal** adj occurring in spring

**vernier** [**ver**-nee-er] n movable scale on a graduated measuring instrument for taking readings in fractions

**veronica** n plant with small blue, pink, or white flowers

**verruca** [ver-**roo**-ka] n wart, usu. on the foot

**versatile** adj having many skills or uses ▸ **versatility** n

**verse** n group of lines forming part of a song or poem; poetry as distinct from prose; subdivision of a chapter of the Bible ▸ **versed in** knowledgeable about ▸ **versification** n technique of writing in verse

**version** n form of something, such as a piece of writing, with some differences from other forms;

account of an incident from a particular point of view

**verso** n, pl **-sos** left-hand page of a book

**versus** prep in opposition to or in contrast with; (Sport, Law) against

**vertebra** n, pl **vertebrae** one of the bones that form the spine ▸ **vertebral** adj ▸ **vertebrate** n, adj (animal) having a spine

**vertex** n, pl **-texes** or **-tices** (Maths) point on a geometric figure where the sides form an angle; highest point of a triangle

**vertical** adj straight up and down ▸ n vertical direction

**vertigo** n dizziness, usu. when looking down from a high place ▸ **vertiginous** adj

**vervain** n plant with spikes of blue, purple, or white flowers

**verve** n enthusiasm or liveliness

**very** adv more than usually, extremely ▸ adj absolute, exact e.g. the very top; the very man

**vesicle** n (Biol) sac or small cavity, esp. one containing fluid

**vespers** pl n (RC Church) (service of) evening prayer

**vessel** n ship; (lit) container, esp. for liquids; (Biol) tubular structure in animals and plants that carries body fluids, such as blood or sap

**vest** n undergarment worn on the top half of the body; (US & Aust) waistcoat ▸ v (foll by in or with) give (authority) to (someone) ▸ **vested interest** interest someone has in a matter because he or she might benefit from it

**vestibule** n small entrance hall

**vestige** [vest-ij] n small amount or trace ▸ **vestigial** adj

**vestments** pl n priest's robes

**vestry** n, pl **-tries** room in a church used as an office or robing room by the priest or minister

**vet¹** n short for **veterinary surgeon** ▸ v **vetting, vetted** check the suitability of

**vet²** n (US, Aust & NZ) military veteran

**vetch** n climbing plant with a beanlike fruit used as fodder

**veteran** n person with long experience in a particular activity, esp. military service ▸ adj long-serving

**veterinarian** n (US) veterinary surgeon

**veterinary** adj concerning animal health ▸ **veterinary surgeon** medical specialist who treats sick animals

**veto** n, pl **-toes** official power to cancel a proposal ▸ v **-toing, -toed** enforce a veto against

**vex** v frustrate, annoy ▸ **vexation** n something annoying; being annoyed ▸ **vexatious** adj **vexed question** much debated subject

**VHF** very high frequency: radio frequency band between 30 and 300 MHz

**via** prep by way of

**viable** adj able to be put into practice; (Biol) able to live and grow independently ▸ **viability** n

**viaduct** n bridge over a valley

**Viagra®** [vie-**ag**-ra] n drug used to treat impotence in men

**vial** n same as **phial**

**viands** pl n (obs) food

**vibes** pl n (informal) emotional reactions between people; atmosphere of a place; short for **vibraphone**

**vibrant** [**vibe**-rant] adj vigorous in appearance, energetic; (of a voice) resonant; (of a colour) strong and bright

**vibraphone** n musical instrument with metal bars that resonate electronically when hit

**vibrate** v move back and forth rapidly; (cause to) resonate ▸ **vibration** n ▸ **vibrator** n device that produces vibratory motion, used for massage or as a sex aid ▸ **vibratory** adj

**vibrato** n, pl **-tos** (Music) rapid fluctuation in the pitch of a note

**Vic** Victoria

**vicar** n (C of E) member of the clergy in charge of a parish ▸ **vicarage** n vicar's house

**vicarious** [vick-**air**-ee-uss] adj felt indirectly by imagining what another person experiences; delegated ▸ **vicariously** adv

**vice**[1] n immoral or evil habit or action; habit regarded as a weakness in someone's character; criminal immorality, esp. involving sex

**vice**[2] n tool with a pair of jaws for holding an object while working on it

**vice**[3] adj serving in place of

**vice chancellor** n chief executive of a university

**vice president** n officer ranking immediately below the president and serving as his or her deputy ▸ **vice-presidency** n

**viceroy** n governor of a colony who represents the monarch ▸ **viceregal** adj

**vice versa** [**vie**-see **ver**-sa] adv (Latin) conversely, the other way round

**vicinity** [viss-**in**-it-ee] n surrounding area

**vicious** adj cruel and violent ▸ **viciously** adv ▸ **vicious circle, vicious cycle** situation in which an attempt to resolve one problem creates new problems that recreate the original one

**vicissitudes** [viss-**iss**-it-yewds] pl n changes in fortune

**victim** n person or thing harmed or killed ▸ **victimize** v punish unfairly; discriminate against ▸ **victimization** n

**victor** n person who has defeated an opponent, esp. in war or in sport

**Victoria Cross** n (Brit) highest award for bravery in battle

**Victorian** adj of or in the reign of Queen Victoria (1837–1901); characterized by prudery or hypocrisy; of or relating to the Australian state of Victoria

**victory** n winning of a battle or contest ▸ **victorious** adj

**victuals** [**vit**-tals] pl n (old-fashioned) food and drink

**vicuña** [vik-**koo**-nya] n S American animal similar to the llama; fine cloth made from its wool

**video** n, pl **-os** short for **video cassette, video cassette recorder** ▷ v **videoing, videoed** record (a TV programme or event) on video ▷ adj relating to or used in producing television images ▸ **video cassette** n cassette containing video tape ▸ **video cassette recorder** n tape recorder for recording and playing back TV programmes and films ▸ **video tape** n magnetic tape used to record video-frequency signals in TV production; magnetic tape used to record programmes when they are broadcast ▸ **videotape** v record (a TV programme) on video tape ▸ **video tape recorder** n tape recorder for vision signals, used in TV production

**vie** v **vying, vied** compete (with someone)

**Vietnamese** adj of Vietnam, in SE Asia ▷ n (pl **-ese**) native of Vietnam; language of Vietnam

**view** n opinion or belief; everything that can be seen from a given place; picture of this ▷ v think of (something) in a particular way **in view of** taking into consideration **on view** exhibited to the public ▶ **viewer** n person who watches television; hand-held device for looking at photographic slides ▶ **viewfinder** n window on a camera showing what will appear in a photograph

**Viewdata** ® n videotext service linking users to a computer by telephone

**vigil** [**vij**-ill] n night-time period of staying awake to look after a sick person, pray, etc. ▶ **vigilant** adj watchful in case of danger ▶ **vigilance** n

**vigilante** [vij-ill-**ant**-ee] n person, esp. as one of a group, who takes it upon himself or herself to enforce the law

**vignette** [vin-**yet**] n concise description of the typical features of something; small decorative illustration in a book

**vigour** n physical or mental energy ▶ **vigorous** adj ▶ **vigorously** adv

**Viking** n (Hist) seafaring raider and settler from Scandinavia

**vile** adj very wicked; disgusting ▶ **vilely** adv ▶ **vileness** n

**vilify** v **-ifying, -ified** attack the character of ▶ **vilification** n

**villa** n large house with gardens; holiday home, usu. in the Mediterranean

**village** n small group of houses in a country area; rural community ▶ **villager** n

**villain** n wicked person; main wicked character in a play ▶ **villainous** adj ▶ **villainy** n

**villein** [**vill**-an] n (Hist) peasant bound in service to his lord

**vinaigrette** n salad dressing of oil and vinegar

**vindicate** v clear (someone) of guilt; provide justification for ▶ **vindication** n

**vindictive** adj maliciously seeking revenge ▶ **vindictiveness** n ▶ **vindictively** adv

**vine** n climbing plant, esp. one producing grapes ▶ **vineyard** [**vinn**-yard] n plantation of grape vines, esp. for making wine

**vinegar** n acid liquid made from wine, beer, or cider ▶ **vinegary** adj

**vino** [**vee**-noh] n (informal) wine

**vintage** n wine from a particular harvest of grapes ▷ adj best and most typical ▶ **vintage car** car built between 1919 and 1930

**vintner** n dealer in wine

**vinyl** [**vine**-ill] n type of plastic, used in mock leather and records; (collectively) records made from vinyl

**viol** [**vie**-oll] n early stringed instrument preceding the violin

**viola¹** [vee-**oh**-la] n stringed instrument lower in pitch than a violin

**viola²** [**vie**-ol-la] n variety of pansy

**violate** v break (a law or agreement); disturb (someone's privacy); treat (a sacred place) disrespectfully; rape ▶ **violation** n ▶ **violator** n

**violence** n use of physical force, usu. intended to cause injury or destruction; great force or strength in action, feeling, or expression ▶ **violent** adj ▶ **violently** adv

**violet** n plant with bluish-purple flowers ▷ adj bluish-purple

**violin** n small four-stringed musical instrument played with a bow. ▸ **violinist** n

**VIP** very important person

**viper** n poisonous snake

**virago** [vir-**rah**-go] n, pl -**goes** or -**gos** aggressive woman

**viral** adj of or caused by a virus ▷ adv **go viral** spread quickly and widely among internet users

**virgin** n person, esp. a woman, who has not had sexual intercourse ▷ adj not having had sexual intercourse; not yet exploited or explored ▸ **virginal** adj like a virgin ▷ n early keyboard instrument like a small harpsichord ▸ **virginity** n

**virile** adj having the traditional male characteristics of physical strength and a high sex drive ▸ **virility** n

**virology** n study of viruses

**virtual** adj having the effect but not the form of; of or relating to virtual reality ▸ **virtual reality** computer-generated environment that seems real to the user ▸ **virtually** adv practically, almost

**virtue** n moral goodness; positive moral quality; merit **by virtue of** by reason of ▸ **virtuous** adj morally good ▸ **virtuously** adv

**virtuoso** n, pl -**sos** or -**si** person with impressive esp. musical skill ▸ **virtuosity** n

**virulent** [vir-yew-lent] adj very infectious; violently harmful

**virus** n microorganism that causes disease in humans, animals, and plants; (Computing) program that propagates itself, via disks and electronic networks, to cause disruption

**visa** n permission to enter a country, granted by its government and shown by a stamp on one's passport

**visage** [viz-zij] n (lit) face

**vis-à-vis** [veez-ah-**vee**] prep in relation to, regarding

**viscera** [**viss**-er-a] pl n large abdominal organs

**visceral** [**viss**-er-al] adj instinctive; of or relating to the viscera

**viscid** [**viss**-id] adj sticky

**viscose** n synthetic fabric made from cellulose

**viscount** [**vie**-count] n British nobleman ranking between an earl and a baron

**viscountess** [**vie**-count-iss] n woman holding the rank of viscount in her own right; wife or widow of a viscount

**viscous** adj thick and sticky ▸ **viscosity** n

**visible** adj able to be seen; able to be perceived by the mind. ▸ **visibly** adv ▸ **visibility** n range or clarity of vision

**vision** n ability to see; mental image of something; foresight; hallucination ▸ **visionary** adj showing foresight; idealistic but impractical ▷ n visionary person

**visit** v -iting, -ited go or come to see; stay temporarily with; (foll by upon) (lit) afflict ▷ n instance of visiting; official call ▸ **visitor** n ▸ **visitation** n formal visit or inspection; catastrophe seen as divine punishment

**visor** [**vize**-or] n transparent part of a helmet that pulls down over the face; eyeshade, esp. in a car; peak on a cap

**vista** n (beautiful) extensive view

**visual** adj done by or used in seeing; designed to be looked at ▸ **visualize** v form a mental image of ▸ **visualization** n ▸ **visual display unit** device with a screen for displaying data held in a computer

**vital** adj essential or highly important; lively; necessary to maintain life ▸ **vitals** pl n bodily organs necessary to maintain life ▶ **vitally** *adv* ▶ **vitality** *n* physical or mental energy ▶ **vital statistics** statistics of births, deaths, and marriages; (*informal*) woman's bust, waist, and hip measurements

**vitamin** *n* one of a group of substances that are essential in the diet for specific body processes

**vitiate** [**vish**-ee-ate] *v* spoil the effectiveness of

**viticulture** *n* cultivation of grapevines

**vitreous** *adj* like or made from glass

**vitriol** *n* language expressing bitterness and hatred; sulphuric acid ▶ **vitriolic** *adj*

**vituperative** [vite-**tyew**-pra-tiv] *adj* bitterly abusive ▶ **vituperation** *n*

**viva**[1] [**veev**-a] *interj* long live (a person or thing)

**viva**[2] [**vive**-a] *n* (*Brit*) examination in the form of an interview

**vivace** [viv-**vah**-chee] *adv* (*Music*) in a lively manner

**vivacious** *adj* full of energy and enthusiasm ▶ **vivacity** *n*

**viva voce** [**vive**-a **voh**-chee] *adv* by word of mouth ▷ *n* same as **viva**[2]

**vivid** *adj* very bright; conveying images that are true to life ▶ **vividly** *adv* ▶ **vividness** *n*

**vivisection** *n* performing surgical experiments on living animals ▶ **vivisectionist** *n*

**vixen** *n* female fox; (*Brit, Aust & NZ informal*) spiteful woman

**viz.** (introducing specified items) namely

**vizier** [viz-**zeer**] *n* high official in certain Muslim countries

**vizor** *n* same as **visor**

**v-mail** *n* video message sent by e-mail

**vocabulary** *n, pl* **-aries** all the words that a person knows; all the words in a language; specialist terms used in a given subject; list

of words in another language with their translation

**vocal** *adj* relating to the voice; outspoken ▶ **vocals** *pl n* singing part of a piece of pop music ▶ **vocally** *adv* ▶ **vocalist** *n* singer ▶ **vocalize** *v* express with or use the voice ▶ **vocalization** *n* ▶ **vocal cords** membranes in the larynx that vibrate to produce sound

**vocation** *n* profession or trade; occupation that someone feels called to ▶ **vocational** *adj* directed towards a particular profession or trade

**vociferous** *adj* shouting, noisy

**VOD** video on demand: TV system allowing users to watch programmes at a time of their own choosing

**vodka** *n* (*Russian*) spirit distilled from potatoes or grain

**voetsek** *interj* (*S Afr offens*) expression of rejection

**vogue** *n* popular style; period of popularity

**voice** *n* (quality of) sound made when speaking or singing; expression of opinion by a person or group; property of verbs that makes them active or passive ▷ *v* express verbally ▶ **voiceless** *adj* ▶ **voice mail** electronic system for the transfer and storage of telephone messages, which can be dealt with by the user at a later time ▶ **voice-over** *n* film commentary spoken by someone off-camera

**void** *adj* not legally binding; empty ▷ *n* empty space ▷ *v* make invalid; empty

**voile** [**voyl**] *n* light semitransparent fabric

**vol.** volume

**volatile** *adj* liable to sudden change, esp. in behaviour; evaporating quickly ▶ **volatility** *n*

**vol-au-vent** [**voll**-oh-von] *n* small puff-pastry case with a savoury filling

**volcano** *n*, *pl* **-noes** *or* **-nos** mountain with a vent through which lava is ejected ▷ **volcanic** *adj*

**vole** *n* small rodent

**volition** *n* ability to decide things for oneself **of one's own volition** through one's own choice

**volley** *n* simultaneous discharge of ammunition; burst of questions or critical comments; (*Sport*) stroke or kick at a moving ball before it hits the ground ▷ *v* discharge (ammunition) in a volley; hit or kick (a ball) in a volley ▷ **volleyball** *n* team game where a ball is hit with the hands over a high net

**volt** *n* unit of electric potential ▷ **voltage** *n* electric potential difference expressed in volts ▷ **voltmeter** *n* instrument for measuring voltage

**volte-face** [volt-**fass**] *n* reversal of opinion

**voluble** *adj* talking easily and at length ▷ **volubility** *n* ▷ **volubly** *adv*

**volume** *n* size of the space occupied by something; amount; loudness of sound; book, esp. one of a series ▷ **voluminous** *adj* (of clothes) large and roomy; (of writings) extensive ▷ **volumetric** *adj* relating to measurement by volume

**voluntary** *adj* done by choice; done or maintained without payment; (of muscles) controlled by the will ▷ *n*, *pl* **-taries** organ solo in a church service ▷ **voluntarily** *adv*

**volunteer** *n* person who offers voluntarily to do something; person who voluntarily undertakes military service ▷ *v* offer one's services; give

(information) willingly; offer the services of (another person)

**voluptuous** *adj* (of a woman) sexually alluring through fullness of figure; sensually pleasurable ▷ **voluptuary** *n* person devoted to sensual pleasures

**volute** *n* spiral or twisting turn, form, or object

**vomit** *v* **-iting**, **-ited** eject (the contents of the stomach) through the mouth ▷ *n* matter vomited

**voodoo** *n* religion involving ancestor worship and witchcraft, practised in the West Indies, esp. in Haiti.

**voracious** *adj* craving great quantities of food; insatiably eager ▷ **voraciously** *adv* ▷ **voracity** *n*

**vortex** *n*, *pl* **-texes** *or* **-tices** whirlpool

**vote** *n* choice made by a participant in a shared decision, esp. in electing a candidate; right to this choice; total number of votes cast; collective voting power of a given group e.g. *the Black vote* ▷ *v* make a choice by a vote; authorize (something) by vote ▷ **voter** *n*

**votive** *adj* done or given to fulfil a vow

**vouch** *v* **vouch for** give one's personal assurance about; provide evidence for

**voucher** *n* ticket used instead of money to buy specified goods; record of a financial transaction, receipt

**vouchsafe** *v* (*old-fashioned*) give, entrust

**vow** *n* solemn and binding promise ▷ *pl* formal promises made when marrying or entering a religious order ▷ *v* promise solemnly

**vowel** *n* speech sound made without obstructing the flow of breath; letter representing this

**v**

**vox pop** n (Brit) interviews with members of the public on TV or radio

**vox populi** n public opinion

**voyage** n long journey by sea or in space ▷ v make a voyage ▶ **voyager** n

**voyeur** n person who obtains pleasure from watching people undressing or having sex ▶ **voyeurism** n

**vs** versus

**V-sign** n offensive gesture made by sticking up the index and middle fingers with the palm inwards; similar gesture, with the palm outwards, meaning victory or peace

**VSO** (in Britain) Voluntary Service Overseas

**VSOP** (of brandy or port) very superior old pale

**VTOL** vertical takeoff and landing

**VTR** video tape recorder

**vulcanize** v strengthen (rubber) by treating it with sulphur

**vulgar** adj showing lack of good taste, decency, or refinement ▶ **vulgarly** adv ▶ **vulgarity** n ▶ **vulgarian** n vulgar (rich) person ▶ **vulgar fraction** simple fraction

**Vulgate** n fourth-century Latin version of the Bible

**vulnerable** adj liable to be physically or emotionally hurt; exposed to attack ▶ **vulnerability** n

**vulpine** adj of or like a fox

**vulture** n large bird that feeds on the flesh of dead animals

**vulva** n woman's external genitals

**vuvuzela** [voo-voo-**zay**-la] n (S Afr) plastic instrument that is blown to make a trumpeting sound

**vying** v present participle of **vie**

# Ww

**W** watt; West(ern)

**WA** Western Australia

**wacky** adj **wackier, wackiest** (informal) eccentric or funny ▶ **wackiness** n

**wad** n small mass of soft material; roll or bundle, esp. of banknotes ▶ **wadding** n soft material used for padding or stuffing

**waddle** v walk with short swaying steps ▷ n swaying walk

**waddy** n, pl -**dies** heavy wooden club used by Australian Aborigines

**wade** v walk with difficulty through water or mud; proceed with difficulty ▶ **wader** n long-legged water bird ▷ pl angler's long waterproof boots

**wadi** [**wod**-dee] n, pl -**dies** (in N Africa and Arabia) river which is dry except in the wet season

**wafer** n thin crisp biscuit; thin disc of unleavened bread used at Communion; thin slice

**waffle¹** (informal) v speak or write in a vague wordy way ▷ n vague wordy talk or writing

**waffle²** n square crisp pancake with a gridlike pattern

**waft** v drift or carry gently through the air ▷ n something wafted

**Wag** n (informal) wife or girlfriend of a famous sportsman

**wag** v **wagging, wagged** move rapidly from side to side ▷ n wagging movement; (old-fashioned) humorous witty person ▶ **wagtail** n small long-tailed bird

W

**wage** n (often pl) payment for work done, esp. when paid weekly ▷ v engage in (an activity)

**wager** n, v bet on the outcome of something

**waggle** v move with a rapid shaking or wobbling motion

**wagon, waggon** n four-wheeled vehicle for heavy loads; railway freight truck

**wahoo** n food and game fish of tropical seas

**waif** n young person who is, or seems, homeless or neglected

**wail** v cry out in pain or misery ▷ n mournful cry

**wain** n (poetic) farm wagon

**wainscot, wainscoting** n wooden lining of the lower part of the walls of a room

**waist** n part of the body between the ribs and hips; narrow middle part ▶ **waistband** n band of material sewn on to the waist of a garment to strengthen it ▶ **waistcoat** n sleeveless garment which buttons up the front, usu. worn over a shirt and under a jacket ▶ **waistline** n (size of) the waist of a person or garment

**wait** v remain inactive in expectation (of something); be ready (for something); delay or be delayed; serve in a restaurant etc. ▷ n act or period of waiting ▶ **waiter** n man who serves in a restaurant etc. ▶ **waitress** n fem

**Waitangi Day** n February 6th, the national day of New Zealand commemorating the Treaty Of Waitangi in 1840

**waive** v refrain from enforcing (a law, right, etc.)

**waiver** n act or instance of voluntarily giving up a claim, right, etc.

**waka** n (NZ) Māori canoe

**wake¹** v **waking, woke, woken** rouse from sleep or inactivity ▷ n vigil beside a corpse the night before the funeral ▶ **waken** v wake ▶ **wakeful** adj

**wake²** n track left by a moving ship **in the wake of** following, often as a result

**walk** v move on foot with at least one foot always on the ground; pass through or over on foot; escort or accompany on foot ▷ n act or instance of walking; distance walked; manner of walking; place or route for walking **walk of life** social position or profession ▶ **walker** n ▶ **walkabout** n informal walk among the public by royalty etc. ▶ **walkie-talkie** n portable radio transmitter and receiver ▶ **walking stick** stick used as a support when walking ▶ **walk into** v meet with unwittingly ▶ **Walkman®** n small portable cassette player with headphones ▶ **walkout** n strike; act of leaving as a protest ▶ **walkover** n easy victory

**wall** n structure of brick, stone, etc. used to enclose, divide, or support; something having the function or effect of a wall ▷ v enclose or seal with a wall or walls ▶ **wallflower** n fragrant garden plant; (at a dance) woman who remains seated because she has no partner ▶ **wallpaper** n decorative paper to cover interior walls

**wallaby** n, pl **-bies** marsupial like a small kangaroo

**wallaroo** n large stocky Australian kangaroo of rocky regions

**wallet** n small folding case for paper money, documents, etc.

**walleye** n fish with large staring eyes (also **dory**)

**wallop** (informal) v **-loping, -loped** hit hard ▷ n hard blow

▶**walloping** (*informal*) *n* thrashing ▷ *adj* large or great

**wallow** *v* revel in an emotion; roll in liquid or mud ▷ *n* act or instance of wallowing

**wally** *n*, *pl* **-lies** (*Brit slang*) stupid person

**walnut** *n* edible nut with a wrinkled shell; tree it grows on; its wood, used for making furniture

**walrus** *n*, *pl* **-ruses** or **-rus** large sea mammal with long tusks

**waltz** *n* ballroom dance; music for this ▷ *v* dance a waltz; (*informal*) move in a relaxed confident way

**wampum** [**wom**-pum] *n* shells woven together, formerly used by Native Americans for money and ornament

**WAN** wide area network

**wan** [rhymes with **swan**] *adj* **wanner, wannest** pale and sickly looking

**wand** *n* thin rod, esp. one used in performing magic tricks

**wander** *v* move about without a definite destination or aim; go astray, deviate ▷ *n* act or instance of wandering ▶**wanderer** *n* ▶**wanderlust** *n* great desire to travel

**wane** *v* decrease gradually in size or strength; (of the moon) decrease in size **on the wane** decreasing in size, strength, or power

**wangle** *v* (*informal*) get by devious methods

**want** *v* need or long for; desire or wish ▷ *n* act or instance of wanting; thing wanted; lack or absence; state of being in need, poverty ▶**wanted** *adj* sought by the police ▶**wanting** *adj* lacking; not good enough

**wanton** *adj* without motive, provocation, or justification; (*old-fashioned*) (of a woman) sexually unrestrained or immodest

**WAP** Wireless Application Protocol: a system that allows mobile phone users to access the internet and other information services

**wapiti** [**wop**-pit-tee] *n*, *pl* **-tis** large N American deer, now also common in New Zealand

**war** *n* fighting between nations; conflict or contest ▷ *adj* of, like, or caused by war ▷ *v* **warring, warred** conduct a war ▶**warring** *adj* ▶**warlike** *adj* of or relating to war; hostile and eager to have a war ▶**war crime** crime, such as killing, committed during a war in violation of accepted conventions ▶**war criminal** person who has committed war crimes ▶**warfare** *n* fighting or hostilities ▶**warhead** *n* explosive front part of a missile ▶**warmonger** *n* person who encourages war ▶**warship** *n* ship designed and equipped for naval combat

**waratah** *n* Australian shrub with crimson flowers

**warble** *v* sing in a trilling voice

**warbler** *n* any of various small songbirds

**ward** *n* room in a hospital for patients needing a similar kind of care; electoral division of a town; child under the care of a guardian or court ▶**warder** *n* prison officer ▶**wardress** *n fem* ▶**ward off** *v* avert or repel ▶**wardroom** *n* officers' quarters on a warship

**warden** *n* person in charge of a building and its occupants; official responsible for the enforcement of regulations

**wardrobe** *n* cupboard for hanging clothes in; person's collection of clothes; costumes of a theatrical company

**ware** *n* articles of a specified type or material e.g. *silverware* ▷ *pl* goods

W

for sale ▶ **warehouse** n building for storing goods prior to sale or distribution

**warlock** n man who practises black magic

**warm** adj moderately hot; providing warmth; (of a colour) predominantly yellow or red; affectionate; enthusiastic ▷ v make or become warm ▶ **warmly** adv ▶ **warmth** n mild heat; cordiality; intensity of emotion ▶ **warm up** v make or become warmer; do preliminary exercises before a race or more strenuous exercise; make or become more lively ▶ **warm-up** n

**warn** v make aware of possible danger or harm; caution or scold; inform (someone) in advance ▶ **warning** n something that warns; scolding or caution ▶ **warn off** v advise (someone) not to become involved with

**warp** v twist out of shape; pervert ▷ n state of being warped; lengthwise threads on a loom

**warrant** n (document giving) official authorization ▷ v make necessary; guarantee ▶ **warranty** n, pl **-ties** (document giving) a guarantee ▶ **warrant officer** officer in certain armed services with a rank between a commissioned and noncommissioned officer

**warren** n series of burrows in which rabbits live; overcrowded building or part of a town

**warrigal** (Aust) n dingo ▷ adj wild

**warrior** n person who fights in a war

**wart** n small hard growth on the skin ▶ **wart hog** kind of African wild pig

**wary** [**ware**-ree] adj **warier, wariest** watchful or cautious ▶ **warily** adv ▶ **wariness** n

**was** v first and third person singular past tense of **be**

**wash** v clean (oneself, clothes, etc.) with water and usu. soap; be washable; flow or sweep over or against; (informal) be believable or acceptable e.g. that excuse won't wash ▷ n act or process of washing; clothes washed at one time; thin coat of paint; disturbance in the water after a ship has passed by ▶ **washable** adj ▶ **washer** n ring put under a nut or bolt or in a tap as a seal ▶ **washing** n clothes to be washed ▶ **washing-up** n (washing of) dishes and cutlery needing to be cleaned after a meal ▶ **wash away** v carry or be carried off by moving water ▶ **washout** n (informal) complete failure ▶ **wash up** v wash dishes and cutlery after a meal

**wasp** n stinging insect with a slender black-and-yellow striped body ▶ **waspish** adj bad-tempered

**waste** v use pointlessly or thoughtlessly; fail to take advantage of ▷ n act of wasting or state of being wasted; anything wasted; rubbish ▷ pl desert ▷ adj rejected as worthless or surplus to requirements; not cultivated or inhabited ▶ **waste away** (cause to) decline in health or strength ▶ **wastage** n loss by wear or waste; reduction in size of a workforce by not filling vacancies ▶ **wasteful** adj extravagant ▶ **wastefully** adv ▶ **waster, wastrel** n layabout ▶ **wastepaper basket** container for discarded paper

**watch** v look at closely; guard or supervise ▷ n portable timepiece for the wrist or pocket; (period of) watching; sailor's spell of duty ▶ **watchable** adj ▶ **watcher** n ▶ **watchful** adj vigilant or alert ▶ **watchfully** adv ▶ **watchdog**

*n* dog kept to guard property; person or group guarding against inefficiency or illegality ▶ **watch for** *v* be keenly alert to or cautious about ▶ **watchman** *n* man employed to guard a building or property ▶ **watchword** *n* word or phrase that sums up the attitude of a particular group

**water** *n* clear colourless tasteless liquid that falls as rain and forms rivers etc.; body of water, such as a sea or lake; level of the tide; urine ▷ *v* put water on or into; (of the eyes) fill with tears; (of the mouth) salivate ▶ **watery** *adj* ▶ **water buffalo** oxlike Asian animal ▶ **water closet** (*old-fashioned*) (room containing) a toilet flushed by water ▶ **watercolour** *n* paint thinned with water; painting done in this ▶ **watercourse** *n* bed of a stream or river ▶ **watercress** *n* edible plant growing in clear ponds and streams ▶ **water down** *v* dilute, make less strong ▶ **waterfall** *n* place where the waters of a river drop vertically ▶ **waterfront** *n* part of a town alongside a body of water ▶ **water lily** water plant with large floating leaves ▶ **watermark** *n* faint translucent design in a sheet of paper ▶ **watermelon** *n* melon with green skin and red flesh ▶ **water polo** team game played by swimmers with a ball ▶ **waterproof** *adj* not letting water through ▷ *n* waterproof garment ▷ *v* make waterproof ▶ **watershed** *n* important period or factor serving as a dividing line; line separating two river systems ▶ **watersider** *n* (*NZ*) person employed to load and unload ships ▶ **water-skiing** *n* sport of riding over water on skis towed

by a speedboat ▶ **watertight** *adj* not letting water through; with no loopholes or weak points ▶ **water wheel** large wheel which is turned by flowing water to drive machinery

**watt** [**wott**] *n* unit of power ▶ **wattage** *n* electrical power expressed in watts

**wattle** [**wott**-tl] *n* branches woven over sticks to make a fence; Australian acacia with flexible branches formerly used for making fences

**wave** *v* move the hand to and fro as a greeting or signal; move or flap to and fro ▷ *n* moving ridge on water; curve(s) in the hair; prolonged spell of something; gesture of waving; vibration carrying energy through a medium ▶ **wavy** *adj* ▶ **wavelength** *n* distance between the same points of two successive waves

**waver** *v* hesitate or be irresolute; be or become unsteady ▶ **waverer** *n*

**wax¹** *n* solid shiny fatty or oily substance used for sealing, making candles, etc.; similar substance made by bees; waxy secretion of the ear ▷ *v* coat or polish with wax ▶ **waxen** *adj* made of or like wax ▶ **waxy** *adj* ▶ **waxwork** *n* lifelike wax model of a (famous) person ▷ *pl* place exhibiting these

**wax²** *v* increase in size or strength; (of the moon) get gradually larger

**way** *n* manner or method; characteristic manner; route or direction; track or path; distance; room for movement or activity e.g. *you're in the way*; passage or journey ▶ **wayfarer** *n* (*lit*) traveller ▶ **waylay** *v* lie in wait for and accost or attack ▶ **wayside** *adj*, *n* (situated by) the side of a road

**wayward** *adj* erratic, selfish, or stubborn ▶ **waywardness** *n*

**W**

**WC** water closet

**we** *pron* (used as the subject of a verb) the speaker or writer and one or more others; people in general; formal word for 'I' used by writers, editors and monarchs

**weak** *adj* lacking strength; liable to give way; unconvincing; lacking flavour ▸ **weaken** *v* make or become weak ▸ **weakling** *n* feeble person or animal ▸ **weakly** *adv* feebly ▸ **weakness** *n* being weak; failing; self-indulgent liking

**weal** *n* raised mark left on the skin by a blow

**wealth** *n* state of being rich; large amount of money and valuables; great amount or number ▸ **wealthy** *adj*

**wean** *v* accustom (a baby or young mammal) to food other than mother's milk; coax (someone) away from former habits

**weapon** *n* object used in fighting; anything used to get the better of an opponent ▸ **weaponry** *n* weapons collectively

**wear** *v* **wearing, wore, worn** have on the body as clothing or ornament; show as one's expression; (cause to) deteriorate by constant use or action; endure constant use ▷ *n* clothes suitable for a particular time or purpose e.g. *beach wear*; damage caused by use; ability to endure constant use ▸ **wearer** *n* ▸ **wear off** *v* gradually decrease in intensity ▸ **wear on** *v* (of time) pass slowly

**weary** *adj* **-rier, -riest** tired or exhausted; tiring ▷ *v* **-rying, -ried** make or become weary ▸ **wearily** *adv* ▸ **weariness** *n* ▸ **wearisome** *adj* tedious

**weasel** *n* small carnivorous mammal with a long body and short legs

**weather** *n* day-to-day atmospheric conditions of a place ▷ *v* (cause to) be affected by the weather; come safely through **under the weather** (*informal*) slightly ill ▸ **weather-beaten** *adj* worn, damaged, or (of skin) tanned by exposure to the weather ▸ **weathercock, weathervane** *n* device that revolves to show the direction of the wind

**weave** *v* **weaving, wove** or **weaved, woven** or **weaved** make (fabric) by interlacing (yarn) on a loom; compose (a story); move from side to side while going forwards ▸ **weaver** *n*

**web** *n* net spun by a spider; anything intricate or complex e.g. *web of deceit*; skin between the toes of a duck, frog, etc. **the Web** short for **World Wide Web** ▸ **webbed** *adj* ▸ **webbing** *n* strong fabric woven in strips ▸ **Web 2.0** the internet where interactive experience plays a more important role than simply accessing information ▸ **webcam** *n* camera that transmits images over the internet ▸ **webcast** *n* broadcast of an event over the internet ▸ **weblog** *n* person's online journal (also **blog**) ▸ **webmail** *n* system of electronic mail that allows account holders to access their mail via an internet site rather than downloading it onto their computer ▸ **website** *n* group of connected pages on the World Wide Web

**wed** *v* **wedding, wedded** or **wed** marry; unite closely ▸ **wedding** *n* act or ceremony of marriage ▸ **wedlock** *n* marriage

**wedge** *n* piece of material thick at one end and thin at the other ▷ *v* fasten or split with a wedge; squeeze into a narrow space

▸ **wedge-tailed eagle** large brown Australian eagle with a wedge-shaped tail

**Wednesday** n fourth day of the week

**wee** adj (Brit, Aust & NZ informal) small or short

**weed** n plant growing where undesired; (informal) thin ineffectual person ▹ v clear of weeds ▸ **weedy** adj (informal) (of a person) thin and weak ▸ **weed out** v remove or eliminate (what is unwanted)

**weeds** pl n (obs) widow's mourning clothes

**week** n period of seven days, esp. one beginning on a Sunday; hours or days of work in a week ▸ **weekly** adj, adv happening, done, etc. once a week ▹ n, pl **-lies** newspaper or magazine published once a week ▸ **weekday** n any day of the week except Saturday or Sunday ▸ **weekend** n Saturday and Sunday

**weep** v **weeping, wept** shed tears; ooze liquid ▸ **weepy** adj liable to cry ▸ **weeping willow** willow with drooping branches

**weevil** n small beetle which eats grain etc.

**weft** n cross threads in weaving

**weigh** v have a specified weight; measure the weight of; consider carefully; be influential; be burdensome **weigh anchor** raise a ship's anchor or (of a ship) have its anchor raised ▸ **weighbridge** n machine for weighing vehicles by means of a metal plate set into the road

**weight** n heaviness of an object; unit of measurement of weight; object of known mass used for weighing; heavy object; importance or influence ▹ v add weight to; slant (a system) so

that it favours one side rather than another ▸ **weightless** adj ▸ **weightlessness** n

**weighting** n (Brit) extra allowance paid in special circumstances

**weighty** adj **weightier, weightiest** important or serious; very heavy ▸ **weightily** adv

**weir** n river dam

**weird** adj strange or bizarre; unearthly or eerie

> **SPELLING TIP**
> The pronunciation of **weird** possibly leads people to spell it with the vowels the wrong way round. The Collins Corpus shows that *wierd* is a common misspelling

**weirdo** n, pl **-dos** (informal) peculiar person

**welch** v same as **welsh**

**welcome** v **-coming, -comed** greet with pleasure; receive gladly ▹ n kindly greeting ▹ adj received gladly; freely permitted

**weld** v join (pieces of metal or plastic) by softening with heat; unite closely ▹ n welded joint ▸ **welder** n

**welfare** n wellbeing; help given to people in need ▸ **welfare state** system in which the government takes responsibility for the wellbeing of its citizens

**well¹** adv **better, best** satisfactorily; skilfully; completely; intimately; considerably; very likely ▹ adj in good health ▹ interj exclamation of surprise, interrogation, etc.

**well²** n hole sunk into the earth to reach water, oil, or gas; deep open shaft ▹ v flow upwards or outwards

**wellbeing** n state of being well, happy, or prosperous

**well-disposed** adj inclined to be friendly or sympathetic

**well-heeled** adj (informal) wealthy

**W**

**wellies** pl n (Brit & Aust informal) wellingtons

**wellingtons** pl n (Brit & Aust) high waterproof rubber boots

**well-meaning** adj having good intentions

**well-spoken** adj speaking in a polite or articulate way

**well-worn** adj (of a word or phrase) stale from overuse; so much used as to be affected by wear

**Welsh** adj of Wales ▷ n language or people of Wales ▶ **Welsh rarebit, Welsh rabbit** dish of melted cheese on toast

**welsh** v fail to pay a debt or fulfil an obligation

**welt** n raised mark on the skin produced by a blow; raised or strengthened seam

**welter** n jumbled mass

**welterweight** n boxer weighing up to 147lb (professional) or 67kg (amateur)

**wen** n cyst on the scalp

**wench** n (facetious) young woman

**wend** v go or travel

**went** v past tense of **go**

**wept** v past of **weep**

**we're** we are

**were** v form of the past tense of **be** used after we, you, they, or a plural noun; subjunctive of **be**

**weren't** were not

**werewolf** n (in folklore) person who can turn into a wolf

**west** n (direction towards) the part of the horizon where the sun sets; region lying in this direction; (**W-**) western Europe and the US ▷ adj to or in the west; (of a wind) from the west ▷ adv in, to, or towards the west ▶ **westerly** adj ▶ **western** adj of or in the west ▷ n film or story about cowboys in the western US ▶ **westernize** v adapt to the customs and culture

of the West ▶ **westward** adj, adv ▶ **westwards** adv

**wet** adj **wetter, wettest** covered or soaked with water or another liquid; not yet dry; rainy; (Brit informal) (of a person) feeble or foolish ▷ n moisture or rain; (Brit informal) feeble or foolish person ▷ v **wetting, wet** or **wetted** make wet ▶ **wet blanket** (informal) person who has a depressing effect on others ▶ **wetland** n area of marshy land ▶ **wet nurse** woman employed to breast-feed another's child ▶ **wet room** waterproofed room with a drain in the floor, often used as an open-plan shower ▶ **wet suit** close-fitting rubber suit worn by divers etc.

**whack** v strike with a resounding blow ▷ n such a blow; (informal) share; (informal) attempt ▶ **whacked** adj exhausted ▶ **whacking** adj (informal) huge

**whale** n large fish-shaped sea mammal **have a whale of a time** (informal) enjoy oneself very much ▶ **whaler** n ship or person involved in whaling ▶ **whaling** n hunting of whales for food and oil

**wharf** n, pl **wharves** or **wharfs** platform at a harbour for loading and unloading ships ▶ **wharfie** n (Aust) person employed to load and unload ships

**what** pron which thing; that which; request for a statement to be repeated ▷ interj exclamation of anger, surprise, etc. ▷ adv in which way, how much e.g. what do you care? **what for?** why? ▶ **whatever** pron everything or anything that; no matter what ▶ **whatnot** n (informal) similar unspecified things ▶ **whatsoever** adj at all

**wheat** n grain used in making flour, bread, and pasta; plant producing this ▶ **wheaten** adj ▶ **wheatear** n small songbird

**wheedle** v coax or cajole

**wheel** n disc that revolves on an axle; pivoting movement ▷ v push or pull (something with wheels); turn as if on an axis; turn round suddenly **wheeling and dealing** use of shrewd and sometimes unscrupulous methods to achieve success ▶ **wheeler-dealer** n ▶ **wheelbarrow** n shallow box for carrying loads, with a wheel at the front and two handles ▶ **wheelbase** n distance between a vehicle's front and back axles ▶ **wheelchair** n chair mounted on wheels for use by people who cannot walk ▶ **wheel clamp** immobilizing device fixed to one wheel of an illegally parked car

**wheeze** v breathe with a hoarse whistling noise ▷ n wheezing sound; (informal) trick or plan ▶ **wheezy** adj

**whelk** n edible snail-like shellfish

**whelp** n pup or cub; (offens) youth ▷ v (of an animal) give birth

**when** adv at what time? ▷ conj at the time that; although; considering the fact that ▷ pron at which time ▶ **whenever** adv, conj at whatever time

**whence** adv, conj (obs) from what place or source

**where** adv in, at, or to what place? ▷ pron in, at, or to which place ▷ conj in the place at which ▶ **whereabouts** n present position ▷ adv at what place ▶ **whereas** conj but on the other hand ▶ **whereby** pron by which ▶ **wherefore** (obs) adv why ▷ conj consequently ▶ **whereupon** conj at which point ▶ **wherever** conj, adv at whatever place ▶ **wherewithal** n necessary funds, resources, etc.

**USAGE NOTE**

Where includes the idea at so avoid the use of this preposition: where was it? (not where was it at?)

**whet** v **whetting, whetted** sharpen (a tool) **whet someone's appetite** increase someone's desire ▶ **whetstone** n stone for sharpening tools

**whether** conj used to introduce an indirect question or a clause expressing doubt or choice

**whey** [way] n watery liquid that separates from the curd when milk is clotted

**which** adj, pron used to request or refer to a choice from different possibilities ▷ pron used to refer to a thing already mentioned ▶ **whichever** adj, pron any out of several; no matter which

**whiff** n puff of air or odour; trace or hint

**Whig** n member of a British political party of the 18th–19th centuries that sought limited reform

**while** conj at the same time that; whereas ▷ n period of time ▶ **whilst** conj while ▶ **while away** v pass (time) idly but pleasantly

**whim** n sudden fancy ▶ **whimsy** n capricious idea; light or fanciful humour ▶ **whimsical** adj unusual, playful, and fanciful

**whimper** v cry in a soft whining way ▷ n soft plaintive whine

**whin** n (Brit) gorse

**whine** n high-pitched plaintive cry; peevish complaint ▷ v make such a sound ▶ **whining** n, adj

**whinge** (Brit, Aust & NZ informal) v complain ▷ n complaint

**whinny** v **-nying, -nied** neigh softly ▷ n, pl **-nies** soft neigh

**whip** n cord attached to a handle, used for beating animals or people; politician responsible for

W

organizing and disciplining fellow party or caucus members; call made on members of Parliament to attend for important votes; dessert made from beaten cream or egg whites ▷ *v* **whipping, whipped** strike with a whip, strap, or cane; (*informal*) pull, remove, or move quickly; beat (esp. eggs or cream) to a froth; rouse into a particular condition; (*informal*) steal ▶ **whip bird** (*Aust*) bird with a whistle ending in a whipcrack note ▶ **whiplash injury** neck injury caused by a sudden jerk to the head, as in a car crash ▶ **whip-round** *n* (*informal*) collection of money

**whippet** *n* racing dog like a small greyhound

**whirl** *v* spin or revolve; be dizzy or confused ▷ *n* whirling movement; bustling activity; confusion or giddiness ▶ **whirlpool** *n* strong circular current of water ▶ **whirlwind** *n* column of air whirling violently upwards in a spiral ▷ *adj* much quicker than normal

**whirr, whir** *n* prolonged soft buzz ▷ *v* **whirring, whirred** (cause to) make a whirr

**whisk** *v* move or remove quickly; beat (esp. eggs or cream) to a froth ▷ *n* utensil for beating eggs, cream, etc.

**whisker** *n* any of the long stiff hairs on the face of a cat or other mammal ▷ *pl* hair growing on a man's face **by a whisker** (*informal*) only just

**whisky** *n*, *pl* **-kies** spirit distilled from fermented cereals ▶ **whiskey** *n*, *pl* **-keys** Irish or American whisky

**whisper** *v* speak softly, without vibration of the vocal cords; rustle ▷ *n* soft voice; (*informal*) rumour; rustling sound

**whist** *n* card game in which one pair of players tries to win more tricks than another pair

**whistle** *v* produce a shrill sound, esp. by forcing the breath through pursed lips; signal by a whistle ▷ *n* whistling sound; instrument blown to make a whistling sound **blow the whistle on** (*informal*) inform on or put a stop to ▶ **whistling** *n*, *adj*

**whit** *n* **not a whit** not the slightest amount

**white** *adj* of the colour of snow; pale; light in colour; (of coffee) served with milk ▷ *n* colour of snow; clear fluid round the yolk of an egg; white part, esp. of the eyeball; (**W-**) member of the race of people with light-coloured skin ▶ **whiten** *v* make or become white or whiter ▶ **whiteness** *n* ▶ **whitish** *adj* ▶ **white-collar** *adj* denoting professional and clerical workers ▶ **white elephant** useless or unwanted possession ▶ **white flag** signal of surrender or truce ▶ **white goods** large household appliances such as cookers and fridges ▶ **white-hot** *adj* very hot ▶ **white lie** minor unimportant lie ▶ **white paper** report by the government, outlining its policy on a matter

**whitebait** *n* small edible fish

**whitewash** *n* substance for whitening walls ▷ *v* cover with whitewash; conceal or gloss over unpleasant facts

**whither** *adv* (*obs*) to what place

**whiting** *n* edible sea fish

**Whitsun, Whitsuntide** *n* Christian festival celebrating the descent of the Holy Spirit to the apostles, Pentecost

**whittle** *v* cut or carve (wood) with a knife ▶ **whittle down, whittle**

**away** v reduce or wear away gradually

**whizz, whiz** v **whizzing, whizzed** make a loud buzzing sound; (*informal*) move quickly ▷ n, pl **whizzes** loud buzzing sound; (*informal*) person skilful at something ▸ **whizz kid, whiz kid** (*informal*) person who is outstandingly able for his or her age

**who** pron which person; used to refer to a person or people already mentioned ▸ **whoever** pron any person who; no matter who

**whodunnit, whodunit** [hoo-dun-nit] n (*informal*) detective story, play, or film

**whole** adj containing all the elements or parts; uninjured or undamaged ▷ n complete thing or system **on the whole** taking everything into consideration ▸ **wholly** adv ▸ **wholefood** n food that has been processed as little as possible ▸ **wholehearted** adj sincere or enthusiastic ▸ **wholemeal** adj (of flour) made from the whole wheat grain; made from wholemeal flour ▸ **whole number** number that does not contain a fraction

**wholesale** adj, adv dealing by selling goods in large quantities to retailers; on a large scale ▸ **wholesaler** n

**wholesome** adj physically or morally beneficial

**whom** pron objective form of **who**

**whoop** v, n shout or cry to express excitement

**whoopee** interj (*informal*) cry of joy

**whooping cough** n infectious disease marked by convulsive coughing and noisy breathing

**whopper** n (*informal*) anything unusually large; huge lie ▸ **whopping** adj

**whore** [hore] n prostitute

**whorl** n ring of leaves or petals; one turn of a spiral

**whose** pron of whom or of which

**why** adv for what reason ▷ pron because of which

**Wicca** n modern polytheistic religious movement, based on elements of pre-Christian paganism ▸ **Wiccan** n, adj

**wick** n cord through a lamp or candle which carries fuel to the flame

**wicked** adj morally bad; mischievous ▸ **wickedly** adv ▸ **wickedness** n

**wicker** adj made of woven cane ▸ **wickerwork** n

**wicket** n set of three cricket stumps and two bails; ground between the two wickets on a cricket pitch

**wide** adj large from side to side; having a specified width; spacious or extensive; far from the target; opened fully ▷ adv to the full extent; over an extensive area; far from the target ▸ **widely** adv ▸ **widen** v make or become wider ▸ **widespread** adj affecting a wide area or a large number of people

**widgeon** n same as **wigeon**

**widget** n small mechanism or device, the name of which is unknown or temporarily forgotten; (*Computing*) computer program that can be executed from a PC desktop

**widow** n woman whose spouse is dead and who has not remarried ▸ **widowed** adj ▸ **widowhood** n ▸ **widower** n man whose spouse is dead and who has not remarried

**width** n distance from side to side; quality of being wide

**wield** v hold and use (a weapon); have and use (power)

**wife** n, pl **wives** female partner in marriage

W

**Wi-Fi** n system of accessing the internet from computers with wireless connections

**wig** n artificial head of hair

**wigeon** n duck found in marshes

**wiggle** v move jerkily from side to side ▷ n wiggling movement

**wigwam** n Native American's tent

**wiki** (*Computing*) n website that can be edited by anyone ▷ *adj* of the software that allows this

**wild** *adj* (of animals) not tamed or domesticated; (of plants) not cultivated; lacking restraint or control; violent or stormy; (*informal*) excited; (*informal*) furious; random ▶ **wilds** *pl n* desolate or uninhabited place ▶ **wildly** *adv* ▶ **wildness** *n* ▶ **wild-goose chase** search that has little chance of success

**wildcat** n European wild animal like a large domestic cat ▶ **wildcat strike** sudden unofficial strike

**wildebeest** n gnu

**wilderness** n uninhabited uncultivated region

**wildfire** n **spread like wildfire** spread quickly and uncontrollably

**wildlife** n wild animals and plants collectively

**wiles** *pl n* tricks or ploys ▶ **wily** *adj* crafty or sly

**wilful** *adj* headstrong or obstinate; intentional ▶ **wilfully** *adv*

**will¹** *v, past tense* **would** used as an auxiliary to form the future tense or to indicate intention, ability, or expectation

> **USAGE NOTE**
> *Will* is normal for discussing the future. The use of *shall* with *I* and *we* is a matter of preference, not of rule

**will²** n strong determination; desire or wish; directions written for disposal of one's property

after death ▷ v use one's will in an attempt to do (something); wish or desire; leave (property) by a will ▶ **willing** *adj* ready or inclined (to do something); keen and obliging ▶ **willingly** *adv* ▶ **willingness** n ▶ **willpower** n ability to control oneself and one's actions

**will-o'-the-wisp** n elusive person or thing; light sometimes seen over marshes at night

**willow** n tree with thin flexible branches; its wood, used for making cricket bats ▶ **willowy** *adj* slender and graceful

**willy-nilly** *adv* whether desired or not

**willy wagtail** n (*Aust*) black-and-white flycatcher

**willy-willy** n (*Aust*) small tropical dust storm

**wilt** v (cause to) become limp or lose strength

**wimp** n (*informal*) feeble ineffectual person

**wimple** n garment framing the face, worn by medieval women and now by nuns

**win** v **winning, won** come first in (a competition, fight, etc.); gain (a prize) in a competition; get by effort ▷ n victory, esp. in a game ▶ **winner** n ▶ **winning** *adj* gaining victory; charming ▶ **winnings** *pl n* sum won, esp. in gambling ▶ **win over** v gain the support of (someone) ▶ **win-win** *adj* guaranteeing a favourable outcome for all involved e.g. *a win-win situation*

**wince** v draw back, as if in pain ▷ n wincing

**winch** n machine for lifting or hauling using a cable or chain wound round a drum ▷ v lift or haul using a winch

**wind¹** n current of air; hint or suggestion; breath; flatulence;

idle talk ▷ v render short of breath
▶ **windy** adj ▶ **windward** adj, n
(of or in) the direction from which
the wind is blowing ▶ **windfall** n
unexpected good luck; fallen fruit
▶ **wind farm** collection of wind-
driven turbines for generating
electricity ▶ **wind instrument**
musical instrument played by
blowing ▶ **windmill** n machine for
grinding or pumping driven by sails
turned by the wind ▶ **windpipe**
n tube linking the throat and
the lungs ▶ **windscreen** n front
window of a motor vehicle
▶ **windscreen wiper** device that
wipes rain etc. from a windscreen
▶ **windsock** n cloth cone on a
mast at an airfield to indicate wind
direction ▶ **windsurfing** n sport of
riding on water using a surfboard
propelled and steered by a sail

**wind²** v **winding, wound** coil or
wrap around; tighten the spring
of (a clock or watch); move in
a twisting course ▶ **wind up** v
bring to or reach an end; tighten
the spring of (a clock or watch);
(*informal*) make tense or agitated;
(*slang*) tease

**windlass** n winch worked by a
crank

**window** n opening in a wall to let
in light or air; glass pane or panes
fitted in such an opening; display
area behind the window of a shop;
area on a computer screen that
can be manipulated separately
from the rest of the display area;
period of unbooked time in a diary
or schedule ▶ **window-dressing**
n arrangement of goods in a
shop window; attempt to make
something more attractive than
it really is ▶ **window-shopping** n
looking at goods in shop windows
without intending to buy

**wine** n alcoholic drink made from
fermented grapes; similar drink
made from other fruits ▶ **wine and
dine** entertain or be entertained
with fine food and drink

**wing** n one of the limbs or organs
of a bird, insect, or bat that are
used for flying; one of the winglike
supporting parts of an aircraft;
projecting side part of a building;
faction of a political party; part of a
car body surrounding the wheels;
(*Sport*) (player on) either side of the
pitch ▷ pl sides of a stage ▷ v fly;
wound slightly in the wing or arm
▶ **winged** adj ▶ **winger** n (*Sport*)
player positioned on a wing

**wink** v close and open (an eye)
quickly as a signal; twinkle
▷ n winking; smallest amount
of sleep

**winkle** n shellfish with a spiral shell
▶ **winkle out** v (*informal*) extract
or prise out

**winnow** v separate (chaff) from
(grain); examine to select desirable
elements

**winsome** adj charming or winning

**winter** n coldest season ▷ v spend
the winter ▶ **wintry** adj of or like
winter; cold or unfriendly ▶ **winter
sports** open-air sports held on
snow or ice

**wipe** v clean or dry by rubbing; erase
(a tape) ▷ n wiping ▶ **wipe out** v
destroy completely

**wire** n thin flexible strand of metal;
length of this used to carry electric
current; (*obs*) telegram ▷ v equip
with wires ▶ **wiring** n system of
wires ▶ **wiry** adj lean and tough;
like wire ▶ **wire-haired** adj (of a
dog) having a stiff wiry coat

**wireless** adj (of a computer
network) connected by radio
rather than by cables or fibre optics
▷ n (*old-fashioned*) same as **radio**

**W**

**wireless application protocol**
see **WAP**

**wisdom** n good sense and judgment; accumulated knowledge ▶ **wisdom tooth** any of the four large molar teeth that come through usu. after the age of twenty

**wise¹** adj having wisdom ▶ **wisely** adv ▶ **wiseacre** n person who wishes to seem wise

**wise²** n (obs) manner

**-wise** adv suffix indicating direction or manner e.g. clockwise; likewise; with reference to e.g. businesswise

**USAGE NOTE**
Adding -wise to a noun to create the meaning 'in respect of', as in: Defencewise, the team is strong, is generally unacceptable except in very informal usage

**wisecrack** (informal) n clever, sometimes unkind, remark ▷ v make a wisecrack

**wish** v want or desire; feel or express a hope about someone's wellbeing, success, etc. ▷ n expression of a desire; thing desired ▶ **wishful** adj too optimistic ▶ **wishbone** n V-shaped bone above the breastbone of a fowl

**wishy-washy** adj (informal) insipid or bland

**wisp** n light delicate streak; twisted bundle or tuft ▶ **wispy** adj

**wisteria** n climbing shrub with blue or purple flowers

**wistful** adj sadly longing ▶ **wistfully** adv

**wit** n ability to use words or ideas in a clever and amusing way; person with this ability; (sometimes pl) practical intelligence ▶ **witless** adj foolish

**witch** n person, usu. female, who practises (black) magic; ugly or wicked woman ▶ **witchcraft** n use of magic ▶ **witch doctor** (in certain societies) a man appearing to cure or cause injury or disease by magic ▶ **witch-hunt** n campaign against people with unpopular views

**witchetty grub** n wood-boring edible Australian caterpillar

**with** prep indicating presence alongside, possession, means of performance, characteristic manner, etc. e.g. walking with his dog; a man with two cars; hit with a hammer; playing with skill ▶ **within** prep, adv in or inside ▶ **without** prep not accompanied by, using, or having

**withdraw** v -drawing, -drew, -drawn take or move out or away ▶ **withdrawal** n ▶ **withdrawn** adj unsociable

**wither** v wilt or dry up ▶ **withering** adj (of a look or remark) scornful

**withers** pl n ridge between a horse's shoulder blades

**withhold** v -holding, -held refrain from giving

**withstand** v -standing, -stood oppose or resist successfully

**witness** n person who has seen something happen; person giving evidence in court; evidence or testimony ▷ v see at first hand; sign (a document) to certify that it is genuine

**witter** v (chiefly Brit) chatter pointlessly or at unnecessary length

**wittingly** adv intentionally

**witty** adj **wittier, wittiest** clever and amusing ▶ **wittily** adv ▶ **witticism** n witty remark

**wives** n plural of **wife**

**wizard** n magician; person with outstanding skill in a particular field ▶ **wizardry** n

**wizened** [wiz-zend] adj shrivelled or wrinkled

W

**WMD** weapon(s) of mass destruction

**woad** n blue dye obtained from a plant, used by the ancient Britons as a body dye

**wobbegong** n Australian shark with brown-and-white skin

**wobble** v move unsteadily; shake ▷ n wobbling movement or sound ▶ **wobbly** adj

**wodge** n (informal) thick chunk

**woe** n grief ▶ **woeful** adj extremely sad; pitiful ▶ **woefully** adv ▶ **woebegone** adj looking miserable

**wok** n bowl-shaped Chinese cooking pan, used for stir-frying

**woke** v past tense of **wake¹** ▶ **woken** v past participle of **wake¹**

**wold** n high open country

**wolf** n, pl **wolves** wild predatory canine mammal ▷ v eat ravenously **cry wolf** raise a false alarm ▶ **wolf whistle** whistle by a man to show he thinks a woman is attractive

**wolverine** n carnivorous mammal of Arctic regions

**woman** n, pl **women** adult human female; women collectively ▶ **womanhood** n ▶ **womanish** adj effeminate ▶ **womanly** adj having qualities traditionally associated with a woman ▶ **womanizing** n practice of indulging in casual affairs with women ▶ **womanizer** n ▶ **Women's Liberation** movement for the removal of inequalities between women and men (also **women's lib**)

**womb** n hollow organ in female mammals where babies are conceived and develop

**wombat** n small heavily-built burrowing Australian marsupial

**won** v past of **win**

**wonder** v be curious about; be amazed ▷ n wonderful thing; emotion caused by an amazing or unusual thing ▷ adj spectacularly successful e.g. a wonder drug ▶ **wonderful** adj very fine; remarkable ▶ **wonderfully** adv ▶ **wonderment** n ▶ **wondrous** adj (old-fashioned) wonderful

**wonky** adj **-kier, -kiest** (Brit, Aust & NZ informal) shaky or unsteady

**won't** will not

**wont** [rhymes with **don't**] adj accustomed ▷ n custom

**woo** v try to persuade; (old-fashioned) try to gain the love of

**wood** n substance trees are made of, used in carpentry and as fuel; area where trees grow; long-shafted golf club, usu. with wooden head ▶ **wooded** adj covered with trees ▶ **wooden** adj made of wood; without expression ▶ **woody** adj ▶ **woodbine** n honeysuckle ▶ **woodcock** n game bird ▶ **woodcut** n (print made from) an engraved block of wood ▶ **woodland** n forest ▶ **woodlouse** n small insect-like creature with many legs ▶ **woodpecker** n bird which searches tree trunks for insects ▶ **woodwind** adj, n (of) a type of wind instrument made of wood ▶ **woodworm** n insect larva that bores into wood

**woof¹** n cross threads in weaving

**woof²** n barking noise made by a dog ▶ **woofer** n loudspeaker reproducing low-frequency sounds

**wool** n soft hair of sheep, goats, etc.; yarn spun from this ▶ **woollen** adj ▶ **woolly** adj of or like wool; vague or muddled ▷ n knitted woollen garment

**woomera** n notched stick used by Australian Aborigines to aid the propulsion of a spear

**woozy** adj **woozier, wooziest** (informal) weak, dizzy, and confused

**w**

**wop-wops** *pl n* (*NZ informal*) remote rural areas

**word** *n* smallest single meaningful unit of speech or writing; chat or discussion; brief remark; message; promise; command ▷ *v* express in words ▶ **wordy** *adj* using too many words ▶ **wording** *n* choice and arrangement of words ▶ **word processor** keyboard, microprocessor, and VDU for electronic organization and storage of text ▶ **word processing**

**wore** *v* past tense of **wear**

**work** *n* physical or mental effort directed to making or doing something; paid employment; duty or task; something made or done ▷ *pl* factory; total of a writer's or artist's achievements; (*informal*) full treatment; mechanism of a machine ▷ *adj* of or for work ▷ *v* (cause to) do work; be employed; (cause to) operate; (of a plan etc.) be successful; cultivate (land); manipulate, shape, or process; (cause to) reach a specified condition ▶ **work-to-rule** *n* protest in which workers keep strictly to all regulations to reduce the rate of work ▶ **workable** *adj* ▶ **worker** *n* ▶ **workaholic** *n* person obsessed with work ▶ **workhorse** *n* person or thing that does a lot of dull or routine work ▶ **workhouse** *n* (in England, formerly) institution where the poor were given food and lodgings in return for work ▶ **working class** social class consisting of wage earners, esp. manual workers ▶ **working-class** *adj* ▶ **working party** committee investigating a specific problem ▶ **workman** *n* manual worker ▶ **workmanship** *n* skill with which an object is made ▶ **workshop** *n* room or building for a manufacturing process ▶ **workstream** *n* one of the areas into which a company's business is divided ▶ **worktop** *n* surface in a kitchen, used for food preparation

**world** *n* the planet earth; mankind; society of a particular area or period; sphere of existence ▷ *adj* of the whole world ▶ **worldly** *adj* not spiritual; concerned with material things; wise in the ways of the world ▶ **world-weary** *adj* no longer finding pleasure in life ▶ **World Wide Web** global network of linked computer files

**worm** *n* small limbless invertebrate animal; (*informal*) wretched or spineless person; shaft with a spiral thread forming part of a gear system; (*Computing*) type of virus ▷ *pl* illness caused by parasitic worms in the intestines ▷ *v* rid of worms **worm one's way** crawl; insinuate (oneself) ▶ **wormy** *adj* ▶ **worm-eaten** *adj* eaten into by worms ▶ **worm out** *v* extract (information) craftily

**wormwood** *n* bitter plant

**worn** *v* past participle of **wear**

**worry** *v* **-rying, -ried** (cause to) be anxious or uneasy; annoy or bother; (of a dog) chase and try to bite (sheep etc.) ▷ *n, pl* **-ries** (cause of) anxiety or concern ▶ **worried** *adj* ▶ **worrying** *adj, n*

**worse** *adj, adv* comparative of **bad, badly** ▶ **worst** *adj, adv* superlative of **bad, badly** ▷ *n* worst thing ▶ **worsen** *v* make or grow worse

**worship** *v* **-shipping, -shipped** show religious devotion to; love and admire ▷ *n* act or instance of worshipping; (**W-**) title for a mayor or magistrate ▶ **worshipper** *n* ▶ **worshipful** *adj* worshipping

**worsted** [**wooss**-tid] *n* type of woollen yarn or fabric

**worth** *prep* having a value of; meriting or justifying ▷ *n* value or price; excellence; amount to be had for a given sum ▶ **worthless** *adj* ▶ **worthy** *adj* deserving admiration or respect ▷ *n* (*informal*) notable person ▶ **worthily** *adv* ▶ **worthiness** *n* ▶ **worthwhile** *adj* worth the time or effort involved

**would** *v* used as an auxiliary to express a request, describe a habitual past action, or form the past tense or subjunctive mood of **will**[1] ▶ **would-be** *adj* wishing or pretending to be

**wouldn't** would not

**wound**[1] [woond] *n* injury caused by violence; injury to the feelings ▷ *v* inflict a wound on

**wound**[2] [wownd] *v* past of **wind**[2]

**wove** *v* a past tense of **weave** ▶ **woven** *v* a past participle of **weave**

**wow** *interj* exclamation of astonishment ▷ *n* (*informal*) astonishing person or thing

**wowser** *n* (*Aust & NZ slang*) puritanical person; teetotaller

**wpm** words per minute

**wrack** *n* seaweed

**wraith** *n* ghost

**wrangle** *v* argue noisily ▷ *n* noisy argument

**wrap** *v* **wrapping, wrapped** fold (something) round (a person or thing) so as to cover ▷ *n* garment wrapped round the shoulders; sandwich made by wrapping a filling in a tortilla ▶ **wrapper** *n* cover for a product ▶ **wrapping** *n* material used to wrap ▶ **wrap up** *v* fold paper round; put warm clothes on; (*informal*) finish or settle (a matter)

**wrasse** *n* colourful sea fish

**wrath** [roth] *n* intense anger ▶ **wrathful** *adj*

**wreak** *v* **wreak havoc** cause chaos **wreak vengeance on** take revenge on

**wreath** *n* twisted ring or band of flowers or leaves used as a memorial or tribute ▶ **wreathed** *adj* surrounded or encircled

**wreck** *v* destroy ▷ *n* remains of something that has been destroyed or badly damaged, esp. a ship; person in very poor condition ▶ **wrecker** *n* ▶ **wreckage** *n* wrecked remains

**Wren** *n* (*informal*) (in Britain) member of the former Women's Royal Naval Service

**wren** *n* small brown songbird; Australian warbler

**wrench** *v* twist or pull violently; sprain (a joint) ▷ *n* violent twist or pull; sprain; difficult or painful parting; adjustable spanner

**wrest** *v* twist violently; take by force

**wrestle** *v* fight, esp. as a sport, by grappling with and trying to throw down an opponent; struggle hard with ▶ **wrestler** *n* ▶ **wrestling** *n*

**wretch** *n* despicable person; pitiful person

**wretched** [retch-id] *adj* miserable or unhappy; worthless ▶ **wretchedly** *adv* ▶ **wretchedness** *n*

**wrier** *adj* a comparative of **wry** ▶ **wriest** *adj* a superlative of **wry**

**wriggle** *v* move with a twisting action; manoeuvre oneself by devious means ▷ *n* wriggling movement

**wright** *n* maker e.g. *wheelwright*

**wring** *v* **wringing, wrung** twist, esp. to squeeze liquid out of; clasp and twist (the hands); obtain by forceful means

**wrinkle** *n* slight crease, esp. one in the skin due to age ▷ *v* make

**W**

or become slightly creased
▶ **wrinkly** *adj*

**wrist** *n* joint between the hand and
the arm ▶ **wristwatch** *n* watch
worn on the wrist

**writ** *n* written legal command

**write** *v* **writing, wrote, written**
mark paper etc. with symbols
or words; set down in words;
communicate by letter; be the
author or composer of ▶ **writing**
*n* ▶ **writer** *n* author; person
who has written something
specified ▶ **write-off** *n* (*informal*)
something damaged beyond repair
▶ **write-up** *n* published account of
something

**writhe** *v* twist or squirm in or as
if in pain

**wrong** *adj* incorrect or
mistaken; immoral or bad;
not intended or suitable; not
working properly ▷ *adv* in a
wrong manner ▷ *n* something
immoral or unjust ▷ *v* treat
unjustly; malign ▶ **wrongly** *adv*
▶ **wrongful** *adj* ▶ **wrongfully** *adv*
▶ **wrongdoing** *n* immoral or
illegal behaviour ▶ **wrongdoer** *n*

**wrote** *v* past tense of **write**

**wrought** [rawt] *v* (*lit*) past of
**work** ▷ *adj* (of metals) shaped by
hammering or beating ▶ **wrought
iron** pure form of iron used for
decorative work

**wrung** *v* past of **wring**

**wry** *adj* **wrier, wriest** *or* **wryer,
wryest** drily humorous; (of a facial
expression) contorted ▶ **wryly** *adv*

**wt.** weight

**WWW** World Wide Web

**wych-elm** *n* elm with large
rough leaves

# Xx

**X** indicating an error, a choice, or
a kiss; indicating an unknown,
unspecified, or variable factor,
number, person, or thing

**xenon** *n* (*Chem*) colourless
odourless gas found in very small
quantities in the air

**xenophobia** [zen-oh-**fobe**-ee-a] *n*
fear or hatred of people from other
countries

**Xerox®** [**zeer**-ox] *n* machine for
copying printed material; copy
made by a Xerox machine ▷ *v*
copy (a document) using such a
machine

**Xmas** [**eks**-mass] *n* (*informal*)
Christmas

**XML** extensible markup language:
a computer language used in text
formatting

**X-ray, x-ray** *n* stream of radiation
that can pass through some solid
materials; picture made by sending
X-rays through someone's body
to examine internal organs ▷ *v*
photograph, treat, or examine
using X-rays

**xylem** [**zy**-lem] *n* plant tissue that
conducts water and minerals from
the roots to all other parts

**xylophone** [**zile**-oh-fone] *n*
musical instrument made of
a row of wooden bars played
with hammers

**ya** *interj* (*S Afr*) yes

**yabby** *n*, *pl* **-bies** (*Aust*) small freshwater crayfish; marine prawn used as bait

**yacht** [**yott**] *n* large boat with sails or an engine, used for racing or pleasure cruising ▶ **yachting** *n* ▶ **yachtsman, yachtswoman** *n*

**yak**[1] *n* Tibetan ox with long shaggy hair

**yak**[2] *v* **yakking, yakked** (*slang*) talk continuously about unimportant matters

**yakka** *n* (*Aust & NZ informal*) work

**yam** *n* tropical root vegetable

**yank** *v* pull or jerk suddenly ▷ *n* sudden pull or jerk

**Yankee, Yank** *n* (*slang*) person from the United States

**yap** *v* **yapping, yapped** bark with a high-pitched sound; (*informal*) talk continuously ▷ *n* high-pitched bark

**yard**[1] *n* unit of length equal to 36 inches or about 91.4 centimetres ▶ **yardstick** *n* standard against which to judge other people or things

**yard**[2] *n* enclosed area, usu. next to a building and often used for a particular purpose e.g. *builder's yard*

**yarmulke** [**yar**-mull-ka] *n* skullcap worn by Jewish men

**yarn** *n* thread used for knitting or making cloth; (*informal*) long involved story

**yashmak** *n* veil worn by a Muslim woman to cover her face in public

**yaw** *v* (of an aircraft or ship) turn to one side or from side to side while moving

**yawl** *n* two-masted sailing boat

**yawn** *v* open the mouth wide and take in air deeply, often when sleepy or bored; (of an opening) be large and wide ▷ *n* act of yawning ▶ **yawning** *adj*

**yd** yard

**ye** [**yee**] *pron* (*obs*) you

**year** *n* time taken for the earth to make one revolution around the sun, about 365 days; twelve months from January 1 to December 31 ▶ **yearly** *adj*, *adv* (happening) every year or once a year ▶ **yearling** *n* animal between one and two years old

**yearn** *v* want (something) very much ▶ **yearning** *n*, *adj*

**yeast** *n* fungus used to make bread rise and to ferment alcoholic drinks ▶ **yeasty** *adj*

**yebo** *interj* (*S Afr informal*) yes

**yell** *v* shout or scream in a loud or piercing way ▷ *n* loud cry of pain, anger, or fear

**yellow** *n* the colour of gold, a lemon, etc. ▷ *adj* of this colour; (*informal*) cowardly ▷ *v* make or become yellow ▶ **yellow belly** (*Aust*) freshwater food fish with yellow underparts ▶ **yellow fever** serious infectious tropical disease ▶ **yellowhammer** *n* European songbird with a yellow head and body ▶ **Yellow Pages** ® telephone directory which lists businesses under the headings of the type of service they provide

**yelp** *v*, *n* (give) a short sudden cry

**yen**[1] *n*, *pl* **yen** monetary unit of Japan

**yen**[2] *n* (*informal*) longing or desire

**yeoman** [**yo**-man] *n*, *pl* **-men** (*Hist*) farmer owning and farming

**y**

his own land ▶ **yeoman of the guard** member of the ceremonial bodyguard of the British monarchy

**yes** *interj* expresses consent, agreement, or approval; used to answer when one is addressed ▶ **yes man** person who always agrees with their superior

**yesterday** *adv, n* (on) the day before today; (in) the recent past

**yet** *conj* nevertheless, still ▷ *adv* up until then or now; still; now

**yeti** *n* same as **abominable snowman**

**yew** *n* evergreen tree with needle-like leaves and red berries

**Yiddish** *adj, n* (of or in) a language of German origin spoken by many Jews in Europe and elsewhere

**yield** *v* produce or bear; give up control of, surrender; give in ▷ *n* amount produced ▶ **yielding** *adj* submissive; soft or flexible

**YMCA** Young Men's Christian Association

**yob, yobbo** *n* (*slang*) bad-mannered aggressive youth

**yodel** *v* **-delling, -delled** sing with abrupt changes between a normal and a falsetto voice

**yoga** *n* Hindu method of exercise and discipline aiming at spiritual, mental, and physical wellbeing ▶ **yogi** *n* person who practises yoga

**yogurt, yoghurt** *n* slightly sour custard-like food made from milk that has had bacteria added to it, often sweetened and flavoured with fruit

**yoke** *n* wooden bar put across the necks of two animals to hold them together; frame fitting over a person's shoulders for carrying buckets; (*lit*) oppressive force e.g. *the yoke of the tyrant*; fitted part of a garment to which a fuller part is

attached ▷ *v* put a yoke on; unite or link

**yokel** *n* (*offens*) person who lives in the country and is usu. simple and old-fashioned

**yolk** *n* yellow part of an egg that provides food for the developing embryo

**Yom Kippur** *n* annual Jewish religious holiday

**yonder** *adj, adv* (situated) over there

**yonks** *pl n* (*informal*) very long time

**yore** *n* (*lit*) **of yore** a long time ago

**Yorkshire pudding** *n* baked batter made from flour, milk, and eggs

**you** *pron* referring to the person or people addressed; referring to unspecified person or people in general

**young** *adj* in an early stage of life or growth ▷ *pl n* young people in general; offspring, esp. young animals ▶ **youngster** *n* young person

**your** *adj* of, belonging to, or associated with you; of, belonging to, or associated with an unspecified person or people in general ▶ **yours** *pron* something belonging to you ▶ **yourself** *pron*

**youth** *n* time of being young; boy or young man; young people as a group ▶ **youthful** *adj* ▶ **youthfulness** *n* ▶ **youth club** club that provides leisure activities for young people ▶ **youth hostel** inexpensive lodging place for young people travelling cheaply

**YouTube®** *n* website on which subscribers can post video files

**yowl** *v, n* (produce) a loud mournful cry

**yo-yo** *n, pl* **-yos** toy consisting of a spool attached to a string, by which it is repeatedly spun out and reeled in

**yttrium** [it-ree-um] *n* (*Chem*) silvery metallic element used in various alloys

**yucca** *n* tropical plant with spikes of white leaves

**yucky** *adj* **yuckier, yuckiest** (*slang*) disgusting, nasty

**Yugoslav** *n* person from the former Yugoslavia ▷ *adj* of the former Yugoslavia

**Yule** *n* (*lit*) Christmas (season)

**yuppie** *n* young highly-paid professional person, esp. one who has a materialistic way of life ▷ *adj* typical of or reflecting the values of yuppies

**YWCA** Young Women's Christian Association

# Zz

**zany** [zane-ee] *adj* **zanier, zaniest** comical in an endearing way

**zap** *v* **zapping, zapped** (*informal*) kill (by shooting); change TV channels rapidly by remote control ▶ **zapper** *n* (*informal*) remote-control device for TV

**zeal** *n* great enthusiasm or eagerness ▶ **zealot** [zel-lot] *n* fanatic or extreme enthusiast ▶ **zealous** [zel-luss] *adj* extremely eager or enthusiastic ▶ **zealously** *adv*

**zebra** *n* black-and-white striped African animal of the horse family ▶ **zebra crossing** pedestrian crossing marked by black and white stripes on the road

**zebu** [zee-boo] *n* Asian ox with a humped back and long horns

**Zen** *n* Japanese form of Buddhism that concentrates on learning through meditation and intuition

**zenith** *n* highest point of success or power; point in the sky directly above an observer

**zephyr** [zef-fer] *n* soft gentle breeze

**zeppelin** *n* (*Hist*) large cylindrical airship

**zero** *n*, *pl* **-ros** or **-roes** (symbol representing) the number 0; point on a scale of measurement from which the graduations commence; lowest point; nothing, nil ▷ *adj* having no measurable quantity or size ▶ **zero in on** *v* aim at; (*informal*) concentrate on

z

**zest** n enjoyment or excitement; interest, flavour, or charm; peel of an orange or lemon

**zigzag** n line or course having sharp turns in alternating directions ▷ v **-zagging, -zagged** move in a zigzag ▷ adj formed in or proceeding in a zigzag

**zinc** n (Chem) bluish-white metallic element used in alloys and to coat metal

**zing** n (informal) quality in something that makes it lively or interesting

**Zionism** n movement to found and support a Jewish homeland in Israel ▶**Zionist** n, adj

**zip** n fastener with two rows of teeth that are closed or opened by a small clip pulled between them; (informal) energy, vigour; short whizzing sound ▷ v **zipping, zipped** fasten with a zip; move with a sharp whizzing sound

**zircon** n mineral used as a gemstone and in industry

**zirconium** n (Chem) greyish-white metallic element that is resistant to corrosion

**zither** n musical instrument consisting of strings stretched over a flat box and plucked to produce musical notes

**zodiac** n imaginary belt in the sky within which the sun, moon, and planets appear to move, divided into twelve equal areas, called signs of the zodiac, each named after a constellation

**zombie, zombi** n person who appears to be lifeless, apathetic, or totally lacking in independent judgment; corpse brought back to life by witchcraft

**zone** n area with particular features or properties; one of the divisions of the earth's surface according to temperature ▷ v divide into zones ▶**zonal** adj

**zoo** n, pl **zoos** place where live animals are kept for show

**zoology** n study of animals ▶**zoologist** n ▶**zoological** adj ▶**zoological garden** zoo

**zoom** v move or rise very rapidly; make or move with a buzzing or humming sound ▶**zoom lens** lens that can make the details of a picture larger or smaller while keeping the picture in focus

**zucchini** [zoo-**keen**-ee] n, pl **-ni** or **-nis** (US & Aust) courgette

**Zulu** n member of a tall Black people of southern Africa; language of this people

**Zumba**® n system of keep-fit exercises performed to Latin American dance music

**zygote** n fertilized egg cell

# LANGUAGE
# FOR LIFE

**CONTENTS**

# INTRODUCTION

A dictionary can tell you what a word means and when it can be used accurately. It cannot, though, give you guidance on how to write clearly and appropriately in a variety of situations. The *Language for Life* supplement has been written to help you express yourself effectively at work and at home. It includes advice on how to structure your writing, and how to adapt tone, style and content to different forms of communication – from letters and emails to social media.

# BEFORE YOU START WRITING

It is amazing how much more effective your writing will be with a bit of thinking time beforehand. There are three questions which you should be able to answer about any piece of writing, whether it's an email, text, letter or post:

- **Who am I writing to?** This will determine the style and tone that you use. If you are writing an email to a friend, for instance, then you are likely to use less formal language than if you are writing to apply for a job.

- **What do I want to say?** Make sure that all the information you want to communicate is included, and that it is set out as clearly as possible.

- **Why do I want to say it?** In other words, what do you want to happen as a result of your communication? Whether it's for a job application, to ask someone out on a date, or to offer your condolences for a bereavement, what you want to achieve should be clearly stated.

Once you've answered these questions, writing becomes much easier.

Here are some tips for making your writing successful and some common traps to avoid.

## 👍 Tips:

- **Use plain English.** Aim for concise, simple expression which will make your writing easy to read.

- **Plan.** Think about what you want to say, and how you want to say it. Planning will save you time and make your writing more effective. It needn't take a lot of time but, even if you're only writing a tweet or a text, it will pay dividends.

- **Vary the length of your sentences.** Short sentences are powerful. Longer sentences can express more complicated thoughts, but try to keep them to a manageable length or else they become tiring to read! Try to stick to the principle of including one main idea in a sentence, and maybe one related point.

- **Use active rather than passive verbs.** It is usually better to use active verbs because it makes your writing simpler and less stuffy to read:
  *The programme was watched by an audience of 13 million people* (passive)
  *13 million people watched the programme* (active).
  The verb 'watched' is 'active' in the second example because it is linked to the subject – '13 million people'. The sentence is shorter and clearer as a result.

- **Read your work aloud.** If the sentences work well, it will be easy to read. Check that you have commas where there are natural pauses.

- **Think about register and tone.** Are you using the right level of formality ('register')? Does your writing accurately express your attitude to the subject and the reader ('tone')? How you address a best friend will be different from how you write to a potential employer.

- **Always check your writing before sending it – and then check it again!** You'll be surprised how easy it is to overlook mistakes. Computers have introduced new errors – for instance, did you delete the original passage that you copied and pasted later in the document? If you correct one word in a sentence, make sure the rest of it still makes sense.

> *I wish people would read through what they have written before pressing 'send'. It would save me a lot of time and make their applications more successful.*

(HR manager)

## 👎 Traps:

- **Jargon.** Specialist words which are understood by a particular group of people, or overly technical language. Don't talk about 'interfacing' with someone, if you simply mean 'talking' to them.

- **Clichés.** Words or phrases that are used too often, and have little meaning. They will annoy your reader and distract from what you are trying to say. Examples include sayings like, '*A different kettle of fish,*' and '*At the end of the day*'.

- **Long sentences.** Avoid sentences longer than 15–20 words – they can be difficult to read, and can usually be divided into clearer statements. If your sentences work well, they will be easy to read.

- **Repeating words.** Using the same word more than once in a sentence can be clumsy, and there is usually an alternative. For instance, '*The date of the English exam is the same date as the French exam,*' sounds better as '*The English and the French exams are on the same date.*'

- **Long words.** Avoid using long or complex words for the sake of it, if they can be replaced by shorter, clearer ones. For example using 'proffer' when you mean 'give' or 'articulate' when you mean 'say'.

- **Redundancy.** Avoid using ten words where two will do: '*I am meeting Sophie later,*' is clearer than, '*Sophie and I are due to hook up together at some point in the day.*' Also avoid **tautology** – saying the same thing twice: '*10 a.m. in the morning*' is either '*10 a.m.*' or '*10 in the morning.*'

- **Ambiguity.** Many words can be understood in more than one way. So, '*Clarice was really cold*' could mean that Clarice was unfriendly or that she was shivering. Put yourself in the reader's place to make sure that the meaning of your statement is clear.

- **Causing offence.** A simple rule to follow is: *treat everyone equally in your writing, regardless of sex, age, race, sexual orientation, or physical difference.* Be aware of current customs and values, and also consider different cultures. This is especially relevant if you are communicating with people around the world.

These are only a few points to consider before you start writing, but if you refer to them regularly, they will help you express yourself clearly and consistently in all your communications.

# EMAIL

Emails are an important form of written communication in many people's lives. Whether at home or at work, we spend a lot of our time sending and receiving them. Email correspondence can feel more like a conversation than an exchange of letters. The tone is generally less formal, and the time between sending your message and getting a reply can be minutes or even seconds. The fact that it is instant can be good and bad. Good because it can be a very efficient way of corresponding; bad if you write quickly and carelessly.

## Addressing emails

When addressing emails, the general rule of thumb is that the fewer people you email, the better. There are three address fields to consider, and each serves a different purpose:

- **'To'**: this is for the address of the main recipient, or recipients, of the information or request to do something.

- **'Cc'**: if you are simply informing someone of your actions or requests, put those people in the 'Cc' ('Carbon or Courtesy Copy') field.

- **'Bcc'**: if you are copying someone in but you don't want the other addressees to know you should use the 'Bcc' ('Blind Carbon or Courtesy Copy'). This is frequently used for mailing large groups, where you don't want individuals to know who else is receiving the email.

> *Bear in mind that if you send an email to one person you are 95 per cent likely to get a reply; if you send it to 10 people the response rate drops to 5 per cent.*
>
> (Linguistics professor)

## Greeting and ending

Emails on work-related issues or personal business require a formal style. You can never go wrong with 'Dear Mr Blake' or 'Dear Peter'. If the contact is long-standing and you are on a familiar footing then 'Hi Peter' is acceptable. In initial exchanges of formal email you might sign off in the same way that you would in a formal letter with 'Yours sincerely' or 'Yours faithfully'. As your correspondence gets onto a slightly less formal footing then 'Kind regards' or 'Best wishes' is fine.

## Subject line

You can really help your correspondents by being precise in the subject line. For example if you send out a regular set of minutes by email, don't just write 'Launch Meeting Minutes', but add the date so people can quickly find what they are looking for. If your email contains a specific question it is good practice to add 'Q:' followed by the question in the subject line.

## Layout

Use a paragraph per point you wish to make, and put headings above each paragraph if there are more than three. If your email is long and will require the reader to scroll down the screen, consider writing it as a Word document and attaching it to an email – long emails are not easy to read and respond to.

## Content

Always remember that with email, your writing can be forwarded to anyone with a single mouse click. Be careful that what you write is not defamatory, offensive, or detrimental to you or your business.

> *Never forward without reading the whole email: you never know what indiscretions or traps are in there. Never put anything in an email you don't want the world to know.*

(Local authority manager)

- Restrict the email to a single subject. If you want to email the same person or people about other issues, use separate emails. It makes filing and action points much easier to follow.

- Don't reply straight away to an email that irks you. You will not be able to hide your anger and will not make the situation better. Wait until you have calmed down enough to think through your response and compose a measured reply dealing with the points raised.

- Don't assume that the person you are writing to has the same cultural reference points, sense of humour, or values.

> *I know of people who communicate regularly with colleagues in Italy, where capitalization is used to show something is urgent whereas we read it as shouting.*

(Marketing executive)

## Attachments

Email is great for sharing documents, photographs and audio-files in the form of attachments. But sending large files can cause headaches. Most email providers (and certainly most companies) allocate a storage limit to each email address; if an Inbox becomes too full, you cannot receive or send emails. So be considerate when you send anything as an attachment.

## Replying

Sometimes you get an email which contains a series of questions. It is perfectly acceptable to reply to each of these questions by adding your comments (sometimes in a different colour or with your initials in square brackets before your answer) in the body of the original email. This saves you typing out the questions or writing replies that incorporate the original question. For example:

---

From: Asif Iqbal
To: Fiona McManus
SUBJECT: My paintings

Dear Fiona
Thank you very much for your email about the posters I sell. I've put my answers below your questions with [AI] after.

With thanks and all best wishes

Asif
Mobile: 011111 789456
www.asifiqbal.art.gallery.net


Do you have a website?
[AI] Yes. You can see all my work at www.asifiqbal.art.gallery.net
What sizes do the posters come in?
[AI] Anything from A5 to A1. I can also frame them to order – there's a selection of frames on the website.
What range of prices are there?
[AI] Prices start at $AUS 11.95 and can go up to $AUS 75.00
If you don't have a poster I want in stock, can you source it for me?
[AI] Of course, I'd be happy to help in any way. Have a look through the website and if you can't find what you want, just drop me a line and I'll do my best!

---

## Formal email

The rules for writing formal emails are similar to those for formal letters.

- If you are communicating with someone for the first time you should adopt the structure of a formal letter.

- It is usual and proper to use a greeting of some sort when you begin your email. 'Dear' can never be misunderstood and rarely strikes the wrong note. If you are more familiar with the person you are writing to 'Hi' or 'Hello' is fine. If you're writing to close friends then use whichever greeting you are accustomed to in your social circle.

- If you are emailing someone for the first time without being invited to it is always proper to explain at the very start of the email who you are and why you are writing to them.

- Never leave the subject line blank. In most formal or professional correspondence you should aim to keep the email to one subject. Think clearly what the email is about and be as precise as you can. Keep the subject as short as possible as the recipient's inbox will often only display a limited amount of the line.

- If the email is going to be long it is polite to indicate this in the opening few sentences of the email.

- Structure your email so that each point is addressed in a separate paragraph. If you wish, it is entirely acceptable to add a heading to each paragraph. Your reader can then see at a glance the points you are covering.

- In formal emails, texting abbreviations and emoticons should be avoided.

- When you end your email use the same rules as with formal letters, using 'Yours faithfully' or 'Yours sincerely' as appropriate.

*I avoid using multiple sub-clauses and long sentences and use lists or bullet points rather than block text.*

(Marketing manager)

## Informal emails

For emails to friends and family you can be more relaxed in your style and tone.

- 'Hi' or 'Hey' or other informal greetings are appropriate and you can sign off the email with 'See you' or 'lots of love' or other phrases.

- Even when you're writing to a friend remember that email can seem terse and abrupt if there is no greeting or sign-off.

- It is fine to use texting abbreviations and emoticons in informal emails – just make sure the person you're writing to understands them all!

> *I read the email back to myself as though I were reading someone else's email prior to sending.*
>
> (Course co-ordinator)

# WRITING AT WORK

## Email

Emails are the default means of communication for most businesses. Whenever you write an important email at work it needs to be concise, clear and well thought-out. The tone should in almost all cases be formal.

Some research conducted recently across a wide range of professions suggested that on average people get 100 emails per day and have to respond to about 40 per cent of them. Email adds a lot of extra reading and writing to an already busy work day. So the first question you should ask is 'Is email the best way to say what I have to say?' A frequent complaint of people in business is that they are sent or copied in on emails that they really don't need to see.

> *My tip for effective communication in an organization? Don't write. Phone or speak to someone in person.*
>
> (CEO, International Management Consultancy)

Compare the two emails on the following pages which show the difference between good and bad practice in business email writing.

# BAD EMAIL

Ollie
There are problems re the arrangements for the conference dinner. I met with David yesterday to finalize details and here's what we decided: The venue (Carmichael Hall) is booked for Dec 18th 7:00 – 12:00. Send out the invitations to all conference delegates the week starting November 3rd. Find out from the printers when the invitations are being returned to us and get them send out in a timely fashion to the delegates. You'll need to check against th otiginal delegate list. Hallidays need to know final numbers by Dec. 10th., latest. Call them to let them know Liaise with Sujata over the timing of the speeches and let the relevant people know when their slot is.
Can't think of anything else at the moment but it's down to you now.

- The tone is abrupt, ill-tempered and dictatorial without being helpful.

- The email is very sloppily written: there are spelling and grammatical mistakes throughout.

- Information required to carry out the actions is not provided.

- People the recipient needs to liaise with and get information from are not included in the email.

- The email generates more work for both the sender and the addressee.

- The email is one block of text which makes identifying what needs to be done laborious and time-consuming.

# GOOD EMAIL

Subject: Conference dinner action points 25/10
From: "Hill, Lucy" <Lucy.Hill@bigbooks.co.uk>
To: "Ollie Walsh", "Maine, Sujata" <Sujata.Maine@bigbooks.co.uk

Hi Ollie

Thanks again for offering to help with the arrangements for the conference dinner. I do appreciate it.
David and I had a meeting yesterday to finalize the details. I've included Sujata on the email so you can liaise directly with her on a couple of the points.

## Venue
The venue (Carmichael Hall) is booked for December 18th 7:00 – 12:00.
The contact there is Julia Waters.
Her number is 01354 638976.

## Invitations
The invitations are currently with the printers. When they are returned to us (this Friday, 1st November) they will need checking against the original delegate list.
Sujata: could you send the list to Ollie please?
Invitations should go to all conference delegates the week starting November 3rd.

## The caterers
Hallidays, the caterers, will need to know final numbers by Dec. 10th. Please call them to confirm these numbers (01354 222227).

## Speeches
Finally, please could you liaise with Sujata over the timing of the speeches and let the relevant people know when their slot is? The list of speakers is on the shared drive. (K:/conference2015/speakerlist.doc)

Any questions, give me a call. I'm here all this week apart from Thursday afternoon.

Many thanks,

Lucy

- The writer includes all the people required to do something in the 'To' box.

- There is a precise 'Subject' line.

- The paragraphs are set out so that addressing each point is easy.

- All the relevant information is included (dates, contact names and numbers, and file locations).

- The tone is collaborative, helpful and professional.

> *I keep all emails as brief as possible and use short sentences to get across all important points.*
>
> (Food journalist)

## When not to use email

Avoid the temptation to think that email can be used in all situations.
For example, email isn't very good at conveying tone or emotion accurately.
If you want to discuss something sensitive or personal with someone, it might be better to talk with them in person, or write them a note.

## Letters at work

Formal business letters are, like memos, becoming rarer. Some professions – particularly the law – still rely on written correspondence, but for most businesses email is the default mode. When you come to write a formal letter to someone outside your organization you should observe the rules of letter writing (see pages 30–33).

> *I use email for almost all written communication, but I send letters to staff over HR issues: for example, around persistent absence, capability and contract issues.*
>
> (Local government manager)

A lot of letter correspondence within an organization is about HR issues – resignation letters or changes to terms and conditions, for example. These require a signature, are often 'private and confidential' and, like the work contract, may be required for future reference. For these two reasons, formal letters are the appropriate form of writing. Here is an example of a resignation letter.

---

Anna Wozniaki
Account Manager
Upside Down Records
Flintrock
Sussex
B45 8EP
17 June 2015

Dear Anna

Please accept this as formal notice of my resignation from the position of Account Executive, with effect from today 17th June, 2015.

In accordance with my contract of employment I am happy to continue to work until the end of my notice period which by my calculations is the 15th July.

While I believe that I am moving for good reasons, I am sorry to leave, and I thank you for your support during my time with the company, which I have found enjoyable and fulfilling.

Please let me know the arrangements for returning equipment – my company phone and laptop – and handing over outstanding work and responsibilities.

Yours sincerely

*Martin Fry*

Martin Fry

---

- The letter is polite, formal and shows that the writer wants to help to ease the process of his leaving.

- It offers no suggestions about improvements or criticisms of the company – you might be given an opportunity to do that in person at an exit interview.

# PRESENTATIONS

The key to making a successful presentation is to be well-prepared. Make sure that you fill your available time, pitch the information at an appropriate level for your audience, and keep in mind the main points you want to get across.

## Preparation

- Ask yourself why you are writing the presentation: is it to inform, to persuade your audience to accept your view, or to entertain? Structure your talk to fit in with your aim.

- Write the key points of your argument in a logical sequence on prompt cards. Keep the points to the minimum – just enough to remind you what you need to say.

- Rehearse until you are confident that you know exactly what you are going to say. Make sure that you can deliver the important points clearly and confidently; practice looking at an imaginary member of the audience as you speak.

> *You should always aim to entertain – there's nothing worse than having to sit through a dull PowerPoint presentation where the speaker reads exactly what is on the slides.*
>
> (IT Manager)

## Presentation slides

There are two major mistakes that inexperienced speakers make when they use PowerPoint or other presentation slide packages:

- The speaker reads out (often word for word) what is written on the slide.

- There are too many words on the slide for the audience to read and absorb.

Remember these key points about writing presentation slides:

- Presentation slides should summarize the point you want to make so that the audience can remember what you're saying.

- You should give each slide a heading to reflect the aspect of the subject you are talking about at that time in your presentation.

- Restrict each line on the slide to very short phrases or even single words. Do not use more than five or six lines per slide.

Here are some examples of good and bad presentation slides:

**GOOD PRACTICE**

- Use a large, simple font.
- Write only key points on slide.
- Don't use complicated backgrounds.

**BAD PRACTICE**

- Use a complicated font.
- Add far too many words to the slide so that people find it really hard to take in the point of the slide and spend more time reading the slide than they do listening to you.
- Repeat exactly what you have written on the slide — it's very dull for the audience and does not reinforce your point or make it more memorable.

# JOB APPLICATIONS

A covering letter and CV are usually the first things any prospective employer will see of you. If you want to get an interview for a job, it is important that these documents present you in the best possible light. The following sections deal with how to construct and write your covering letter and CV, and provide tips on how to apply for a job online.

## Covering letter

The covering letter should convey confidence, enthusiasm, technical knowledge and demonstrate an understanding of what the job entails. It need not be long and it should not be a rehash of the accompanying CV. A short, clear, well-written covering letter can make all the difference between two candidates.

> *Some people think the covering letter is another CV. It's not. A covering letter is a way of introducing yourself to the employer and of providing a persuasive case for reading the CV and then getting an interview.*
> (HR Director)

The covering letter should alert the employer to the key points of a CV and show the match between the candidate and the job being advertised. In general it will consist of three paragraphs or so:

- **First paragraph.** Introduce yourself, say which job you are applying for and where you saw it. You can also include a general statement of why you want to apply for the job and how you feel about the company.

- **Second paragraph.** Provide information about your skills, strengths, qualifications and experience. Give specific examples of why you are the ideal candidate and don't simply restate your CV.

- **Final paragraph.** Conclude the letter expressing your desire to get the job and requesting an interview. You should also say what the best way to contact you is, and if there are any inconvenient dates. Always thank the employer for considering your application.

## Useful phrases

First of all, identify the job you are applying for:

- I would like to inquire as to whether there are any openings for junior telesales operators in your company.

- I am writing to apply for the post of senior marketing manager.

- I would like to apply for the position of online learning coordinator, as advertised on your website.

- I am writing to apply for the above post, as advertised in the Guardian of 8 August 2015.

Next, give some examples of personal achievements:

- I have gained experience in several major aspects of publishing.

- I co-ordinated the change-over from one accounting system to another.

- I developed designs for a new range of knitwear.

- I have supervised a team of telesales operators on several projects.

- I contributed to the development of our new database software.

Then outline your personal qualities:

- I see myself as systematic and meticulous in my approach to work.

- I am a fair and broad-minded person, with an ability to get on well with people from all walks of life.

- I am hardworking and business minded, and I tend to thrive under pressure.

Explain why you want this job:

- I am now keen to find a post with more responsibility.

- I now wish to find a more permanent full-time position.

- I would like to further my career in the field of production.

- I feel that your company's activities most closely match my own values and interests.

Express your willingness to attend an interview.

Here is an example covering letter:

15 Sandybank Drive
Derby
DX27 9LC
joelmanners@email.com
01245 645201

27 July 2015

Mr H Carson
Personnel Manager
Allied Derby Building Society
HR House
Illingworth Way
DERBY
DX3 9DF

Dear Mr Carson

Customer Services Manager

I am responding to the job advertised in the *Derby Express* and on your website on the 22nd July. I feel the job is just what I have been looking for, and reading the job description, I am sure that I have the right level of experience, aptitude and training. Your company's support and promotion of ethical investment has always impressed and inspired me and I would very much like to contribute to your success. My CV is attached.

For the past three years I have been Senior Customer Services Adviser at Cathedral County Bank, leading a team of seven people. Since I took on the role our positive response rate has risen by 10 per cent and customer satisfaction in the area I look after by 15 per cent. I was voted Employee of the Month three times by my colleagues in the period. While I am very happy in my job, the opportunities for promotion are limited and I do want to take on a more responsible role in my area of expertise.

I would welcome the opportunity to discuss my application further. Email is the best way to contact me and I am available for interview at your convenience. Thank you for taking the time to read my application.

Yours sincerely

*Mr Joel Manners*

Mr Joel Manners

- Avoid just sending a letter or email with 'Please find my CV attached'. Remember that this application is a two-stage process to try to get an interview. Each step in the process (covering letter and CV) has to make the employer want to take the next step.

- Remember the basics:
    - Check all spelling and grammar two or three times.
    - Make sure you have spelled all names correctly.
    - Include all contact details.
    - Include any information that the job advertisement has specifically asked you to provide.

# A speculative job application

- When applying for a job on a speculative basis, try to speak to the person responsible for recruitment in the appropriate department beforehand. This way, you will have a specific person to write to, as well as having established a relationship with them.

34 St Dunstan's Way
Vancouver
V6G 7D7

19 July 2015

Ms D Wallis
Youngs Accountancy and Finance
19 Lockwood Road
Vancouver
V9P 8K1

Dear Ms Wallis

**post of software development co-ordinator**

Thank you very much for taking the time to speak to me yesterday about the possibility of a position as software development co-ordinator with your company.

Please find attached a CV which highlights my prior professional experience, and the qualities which I feel make me suited to this position. You will see that I have a strong interest in, and knowledge of, staff management, and have gained extensive experience in handling large development projects and meeting deadlines.

I see myself as being well-organized and self-motivated, and have excellent communication skills. I am keen to develop my career with Youngs Accountancy and Finance, and so would very much appreciate the opportunity to discuss further my suitability for the post.

Please feel free to contact me, either by email: dgormanl@netserve.com, or by leaving a message on (604) 473 5522. I look forward to speaking to you soon.

Yours sincerely

*D Gorman*

Deborah Gorman

## CV

Your CV exists to give a brief description of who you are, what you have done and what you can do.

> *What a lot of candidates forget is that the purpose of the CV is to get the interview – not the job. So they give way too much detail and don't tailor it to the role they are trying to get.*

(HR Director)

- The language should always be 'active'. Avoid passive statements like 'Turnover growth of 25 per cent was achieved in the period,' say instead, 'I increased turnover for the period by 25 per cent.' Active language simplifies your statements and makes them easier to read.

- Use positive adverbs ('efficiently', 'successfully' 'effectively') so that your CV will convey a positive impression to your prospective employer.

### CV structure

The most common CV format is called 'reverse chronological', meaning you start with your current job and work backwards. If your earliest jobs have little relevance to your current application, you can simply list the job title, company and the dates you worked there. Summarize your education after the employment section, and then add any additional skills and interests that may be of use to support your application.

You can see a sample CV on the next page:

# Helena Shapur

12 Green Lane, Brighton, Sussex BT1 3EY
Email: h.sharpur@email.com
Mobile: 07123 456789

## Personal profile

An enthusiastic, self-motivated professional, highly qualified in the field of online team management. My motivation is to use the web to help make the most of all businesses I work for. I have an in-depth understanding of a wide range of web technologies from Java to Ruby.

## Career summary

### 2009 – present Development Team Leader, GoGetting.com

I joined the online travel company GoGetting.com as a development officer before being promoted in August 2012 to my current position. Since becoming team leader the site has had a threefold increase in unique visitors thanks to an extensive linking program I developed. As a result of the increased traffic, the company has given me extra responsibility to drive the marketing of the site with selected web partners. I manage a team of seven development officers and am in charge of a budget of £250,000.

### 2004 – 2009 Web Developer, Toprank Recruitment

Having learned a lot at my first company and really enjoyed the experience of working in web development, I joined this small recruitment start-up specializing in the catering trade. During the time I helped program the site's search engine and learned ASP, Java and SQL. I was very proud to have seen one key module of the search engine's development through from design to implementation. The module generated five per cent extra revenue for the company while I was there. I learned a lot about effective teamwork in the process.

### 2002–2004 Junior programmer, Oakhampton Systems

This was a perfect job after graduation. I was part of a small graduate intake whose job was to develop and code account and customer databases. I went on site visits to understand what a client needed and understand the way the business works. I taught myself HTML in this period and designed the company's first website.

## Education and qualifications

1998–2001 University of Windsor, BSC Computer Science (2:1)
1991 – 1998 Greenglades School, Windsor
3 A-levels: Mathematics (A), Physics (A), Chemistry (B)
10 GCSEs

## Hobbies and interests

Between leaving school and starting university I worked for six months so that I could spend three months doing charity runs for Famine Relief, whom I continue to work for as a volunteer. I run long-distance competitively, enjoy cinema, computer games and chess.

References available on request

> *One of the worst mistakes a candidate can make is to send employers a 6-page 'novel' about their work experience, school qualifications and hobbies and pastimes – especially if it is written in size-9 font. Many managers skim read CVs so using short paragraphs and an almost report-like style will mean they are less likely to miss a candidate with relevant skills or experience. This is where editing down and making the CV relate to the job description/advert works to the candidate's advantage.*
>
> (HR Director)

## BASIC GRADUATE CV

# CV

| | |
|---|---|
| **Name** | Kate Maxwell |
| **Date of birth** | 29.02.92 |
| **Address** | 19, The Poplars, Bristol B10 2JU |
| **Telephone** | 0117 123 4567 |
| **Email** | katemaxwell@atlantic.net |
| **Nationality** | British |

**Education**

| | |
|---|---|
| 2011–2015 | **BA Hons in Modern Languages, University of Exeter** (final grade 2.1) |
| 2009–2011 | **Clifton Road Secondary School:** 3 'A' levels – French (A) German (A) History (B) |
| 2004–2009 | **Clifton Road Secondary School:** 8 GCSEs including Maths and English |

**Employment history**

| | |
|---|---|
| 2011–2012 | **Sales Assistant, Langs Bookshop, Bristol** I was responsible for training and supervising weekend and holiday staff. |
| 2012–2013 | **English Assistant, Lycée Benoit, Lyons** I taught conversational English to pupils aged 12–18, preparing the older students for both technical and more academic qualifications. I organized an educational trip to the UK for fourth year pupils. |

**Positions of responsibility held**

| | |
|---|---|
| 2012–2013 | **Entertainments Officer for University Student Social Society** I organized and budgeted for entertainment for a student society with over 1000 members. |
| 2011–2014 | **Captain of the university women's netball team** I was in charge of training, organizing and motivating the women's team. |

**Other skills**

Fluent French and German
Extensive knowledge of Microsoft Word, Excel and Access
I hold a clean driving licence

**References**
on request

## Top ten CV tips

1. Adapt your CV to the job or prospective employer.

2. You have 30–60 seconds to attract your reader's attention so lay out your CV clearly – use a plain font like Arial, Trebuchet or Times New Roman – and keep it to the point. It should not be longer than 3 sides.

3. Remember the CV is a means of getting an interview, not getting the job.

4. Avoid gimmicks like thumbnail images or pictures – they distract from the words you are writing about yourself.

5. Focus your description of your current and previous experience on achievements and the contribution you made to the organizations. If possible quantify your achievements – 'my actions led to a saving of £xx' or, 'as a result profits were up by x per cent'.

6. Give examples of your skills and qualities – don't just say 'I am a natural leader', write a brief description of when you showed this attribute.

7. Avoid bullet points when describing your current and previous jobs. It's much better to write short paragraphs because you can give examples.

8. Format the document to make sure that the printed version reflects what you see on screen. Try not to waste paper by leaving just two or three sentences at the top of the last page.

9. Use 'active' verbs such as 'achieve', 'lead', 'manage'.

10. Finally carefully proofread your CV and, if you can, ask someone else to look at it as well.

## How to send your CV

You can still post your CV if you wish but most HR professionals prefer to receive the document as an attachment to an email. This means that they can share the CV with the relevant staff or store it on their computer for future reference.

## Online applications

Sometimes you will be asked to complete an application form online.
Here are some tips to do this effectively:

- As for written job applications, you should write in a formal style.

- The online system will probably dictate the particular text format (the font and size of type) – you should take this into account when you draft your answers.

- It is useful to prepare a draft of the application and then transfer the information to the online form.

- Copy and save your answers regularly into a normal document in case the system crashes or you have to break off your application and start again.

- Just because the application is automatically filed online, it does not mean you should be any less rigorous in the editing and proofreading you do. If you can print the document out before you submit it, get someone you trust to read it over to look for errors and omissions.

# WRITING FORMAL LETTERS

Emails and other digital media are the prevalent forms of communication for most of us today, at work and at home, but there are still occasions when a handwritten or typed letter is more appropriate.

This section lays out the basic structure and the rules which underpin most formal letter writing. The Domestic Correspondence, Social Communication and Job Applications sections within this supplement will look more closely at situations where formal letter writing is used, and give examples of good practice.

As with any written communication, your letter should be in three discernible parts:

- **An introduction.** This is where you introduce yourself, acknowledge any previous correspondence, and briefly state the reason why you are writing. Ideally it should be no longer than a paragraph of three or four sentences.

- **The middle.** This is the section where you expand your argument, provide further details, and raise any questions you have. The middle of the letter should be a series of paragraphs set out in a logical order. Each paragraph should make a clear, separate point. If the letter is long and covers a range of subjects, it may be appropriate to divide the contents by subheadings.

- **The ending, or conclusion.** The final paragraph should set out what you would like to happen as a result of the communication, whether that be a written response, a meeting to discuss the contents of the letter, or a demand for a refund.

Here is an example of a formal letter:

55 Torrance Close
Gorton
NSW 2234

25 August 2011

Mr L Dylan
Terrigan Building Ltd
340 Shorter Street
Terrigan
NSW 2234
Dear Mr Dylan

**Estimate for extension to living room, 55 Torrance Close**

I am writing to thank you for the written estimate which I received this morning. I have queries about a couple of details in your letter which I would like to be resolved before we proceed any further.

First, can you say exactly when you would propose to begin work on the extension? I realize this depends, to some extent, on how quickly you can finish your current project. I need to know which week work would commence in, however, so that I can make arrangements to store the living room furniture.

Second, can you tell me when you propose to fit the additional plumbing, so that I can arrange to stay with friends while there is no running water? Also, are there any other times when you anticipate that I shall be without water or electricity?

Finally, there is no mention of additional costs for materials. Can I assume, therefore, that these are included in the estimate you have provided for the overall cost of the extension?

Assuming I receive satisfactory answers in writing to these queries, I shall be happy to accept your proposal and go ahead with the project as discussed.

Yours sincerely

*Tom Peterson*

Tom Peterson

Points to remember:

- **Your address.** This should be written in the top right corner of the letter. Do not write your name here, and don't put commas after each line.

- **The date.** The date should come under your address, also on the right. It is common practice to write the date as 25 August 2015, instead of 25th August 2015.

- **The recipient's address.** Write this under the date, but on the left side of the page. Again, no punctuation is required.

- **The greeting.** If you are writing to a friend then you will use, 'Dear Luke,' for instance. Otherwise it should be 'Dear Mr Dylan'. Note that if you are writing to a woman and do not know whether she prefers to be addressed as 'Dear Mrs Dylan', or 'Dear Miss Dylan', then you should use 'Dear Ms Dylan'. If you do not know the person's name then use, 'Dear Sir or Madam'.

- **Headings.** If you are using a heading, then it should summarize the subject matter of the letter, and appear between the greeting and the first paragraph. Headings should be written in bold but not capital letters.

- **The ending.** If you have used the name of the person in the greeting, then you should end with 'Yours sincerely'. Otherwise end the letter with 'Yours faithfully'. 'Yours...' should always begin with a capital letter.

- **Punctuation.** It is not necessary to include a comma after the greeting or after the ending. Don't put full stops in initials – write 'Mr L H Dylan' instead of 'Mr L.H. Dylan'.

- **Signature.** Write your signature but include your typewritten name underneath.

- **Further contact details.** If you are including your email address or telephone number as contact details, then these should be included underneath your postal address:

> 55 Torrance Close
> Gorton
> NSW 2234
> tpeterson@email.com
> (02) 4254 6398

Once you have written your letter check that:

- You have explained why you are writing in the first paragraph.

- You have made all the points that you wanted to.

- Each sentence is clear, concise and unambiguous.

- You have not included too much information, or any irrelevant details.

- Your language has been courteous and polite, even if you are writing a letter of complaint.

- Check once more for spelling mistakes – it is surprisingly easy to miss them!

# DOMESTIC CORRESPONDENCE

This section tackles the range of letters and correspondence that relates to you, your home, your finances and your family. The following points about content, style and tone apply equally whether you're writing a letter, an email, filling in an online form, or if you are speaking to someone on the phone:

- Use formal language.

- Include every detail that will make the letter easier to deal with.

- Lay the letter out clearly – breaking it down so that each paragraph contains a single point.

- Be explicit about what you want to happen next and introduce a timescale where appropriate.

- What you are writing may have legal implications, so take care with the details you include and the language you use.

- Provide as many contact details as you can.

- Write 'Yours sincerely' to end the letter if you know the surname of the person you are writing to. Write 'Yours faithfully' if you do not.

> *When I'm writing to a company, I always try and find out a specific person to address the letter to – or else it can just end up getting lost in the system.*
> (Teacher)

In the following section there is a selection of letters that many of us will have to write at some point:

- Insurance claims

- Planning application objection

- Writing to your MP

- Deferring jury service

- School correspondence

- Letters of complaint

## Insurance claims

Most of us find ourselves having to make a claim to an insurance company at some stage in our lives – whether it be as the result of a car accident, burglary, incident on holiday or some other regrettable occurrence.

The claim can be made verbally, online or in a written statement but whichever form it takes, it is important to consider the kind of language you use and the information that you include.

Ms C Hall
32, Lime Road
Saddleworth
Devon
SD2 8LN
christinehall@email.com
17 June 2015

Ms Ying
Claims Assessor
Admirable Insurance Company
Claims Avenue
Spottington
Hants
SP31 4AQ

My policy number: AIC008997/CH56.

Dear Ms Ying,

I am writing to make an insurance claim, resulting from an accident I was involved in on 16 June 2015. My car is covered by a comprehensive insurance policy which I took out with you some time ago. The policy number is included above.

The incident occurred at approximately 3pm at the junction of New Street and London Road in Saddleworth. The other driver, a Mr Steve Wall, turned right out of New Street and drove into the front passenger side of my vehicle, causing extensive damage to the bodywork and the headlights. I have enclosed a picture of the damage, together with a diagram showing the relative positions of the vehicles, and the direction they were travelling in at the time of the accident.

Mr Wall has admitted liability for the accident. His insurance company's details, together with his policy number, are also enclosed.

As a result of the incident, my car is not roadworthy. I need therefore, to arrange to collect a replacement car from one of your suppliers, which I am entitled to according to the terms of my policy. Can you advise me on the nearest garage and confirm my entitlement? Please let me know if there are any other details you require to process my claim, and also give me an indication of how long it will take to arrange the repair of my vehicle.

Yours sincerely

Ms C Hall

Ms C Hall

- The letter contains all the relevant information – such as dates, policy number, details of the incident – that the company is likely to require.

- In spite of the nature of the incident, the language is restrained – emotional language will not make your claim any more likely to succeed.

- The letter politely requests information from the insurance company which will move the claim on.

## Opposing a planning application

Correspondence with a local authority is often in the form of a complaint or an objection. Whether you are contesting a parking fine or opposing a planning application, the information you include should be precise and accurate to back your claims.

Mr C Hopkins
75 Birchtree Row
Lessington
County Durham
D2 8LN
chopkins@email.com

1 December 2015

Mr Anderson
Director of Planning
Lime Borough Council
Acacia Road
Lessington
County Durham
D5 1AA

Dear Mr Anderson,

**Planning application number LBC123456/7A**
**Address of proposed extension: 77 Birchtree Row, Lessington, County Durham, D2 8LN**

I am writing to object to the proposal to build an extension on the above property. There are several reasons for this.

**Design**
The very modern design of the proposed extension is in unsympathetic contrast to the Victorian style of all the houses in the area.

**Privacy**
The two-storey extension will affect the privacy of my property. The plans show a window that will look directly into my garden.

**Natural light**
The extension will block out the natural light I get in my conservatory all-year round.

**Appropriateness of use**
It is clear from the plans that the owner intends to make and sell drum kits from the property. This will have a significant impact on the local noise levels – the neighbourhood at the moment is very quiet.

I am sure that other local residents will be objecting as well, and I trust you will refuse this application on the basis that it most definitely contravenes your planning regulations.

I would be grateful if you could acknowledge this letter, confirm that it has been logged as an objection to the application within the deadline set by the council, and keep me informed as to the outcome. I can be contacted at the above address or via the email address at the top of this letter.

Yours Sincerely,

*Mr C Hopkins*

Mr C Hopkins

---

- The writer has found out the deadline for his objection and complied with it.

- He has found out and addressed the criteria on which the application will be judged.

- The headings highlight the grounds on which he is basing his objection.


## Writing to your MP

When writing to your MP keep the letter to a single subject and make it as concise as possible. Remember to say what you want the MP to do as a result of your letter. At all times be courteous – just because you may disagree with his views, does not mean that you should be anything other than respectful in your writing.

You can see a letter written to an MP on the next page:

Mr R Boscombe
27 Juniper Road
Flickcroft
West Midlands
reg.boscombe@email.com

15 April 2015

Derek Firbanks MP
House of Commons
Westminster
LONDON
SW1A 1AA

Dear Derek Firbanks

I am writing to draw your attention to the imminent closure of the Priory Centre on Sandhurst Road in Flickcroft. I am a parent whose child uses the premises for a theatre group on Saturday mornings. She finds the opportunity to learn about acting and to perform stimulating and great fun. The group also provides invaluable contact with other children from the area and with the community in general.

There are 120 children aged from six to 16 who attend the theatre classes every week – divided into three age bands. Last term my daughter's group staged a production dramatizing the history of the Priory Centre and its place in the local community.

The theatre group is by no means the only one affected. There are some 30 other activities put on for a huge range of people, including for elderly and disabled groups, at weekends and during the week.

The council plans to pass the plans at a meeting in three weeks' time. I, and many others, would be grateful if you could take this matter up with the leader of the council as a matter of urgency. The loss of the centre will create a huge gap in the cultural life of our community.

Please acknowledge this letter as soon as you can and let me know of your progress.

Yours sincerely,

*Mr R Boscombe*

Mr R Boscombe

- The letter starts with a very specific description of the problem.

- The writer includes his full address so that the MP knows the letter is from a constituent.

- The letter is about one issue which makes it easier to deal with.

- Including anecdotes or some personal detail will help the MP to remember the letter.

- The writer refers to others who are opposed to the closure. Including supporting evidence – be it a petition, or the MP's involvement with or voting record on similar issues – will help the cause.

> *When contacting your MP, a short, handwritten or printed letter is most effective. Take the time to edit your letter for brevity and clarity. Try to make a single coherent point.*
>
> (Campaigning website)

## Deferring jury service

A letter requesting you to serve on a jury is a serious matter – in the UK if you ignore it you could be prosecuted. If the dates you have been called for are very disruptive to your plans, or circumstances are such that you can't attend, then you should write asking for a deferment. The grounds for deferment will be laid out in the letter you receive.

Mr J Brown
The Moorings
Chettleworth
LINCOLNSHIRE
AG7 0BC
james.brown@email.com
01285 78945613

3 February 2015

Mr R Ball
Jury Central Summoning Bureau
Derby
DA1 9IO

Dear Mr Ball

Thank you for the letter dated January 30th inviting me to serve on a jury from March 27th. I would like to ask if it would be possible to defer this until sometime next year? My wife has recently had a car accident and suffered a serious injury. I have now had to become a full-time carer for her and as a consequence cannot leave the house for an extended period.

I would be very grateful if you could agree to this request, and if you require me to provide you with any further information, please do not hesitate to contact me.

I look forward to receiving your response.


Yours sincerely,

*Mr James Brown*

Mr James Brown

---

- It is more effective to provide specific details for your request: it decreases the likelihood of having to give more information and speeds up the process.

- Do not demand that your attendance is deferred.

## School correspondence

There are a few occasions when it will be necessary to write, or email, your child's school, to keep a record of important incidents during their career. Below are an example email and letter dealing with two such incidents: when your child has more than a couple of days off school, and to put on record concerns about bullying.

---

To: J Chalfont <jchalfont@derwentwaterschool.ed.uk
From: kevin.bond@email.net

Subject: Charlie Bond's absence 1st – 5th March

Dear Mr Chalfont

I am writing to explain why Charlie was absent from school last week (1st to 5th March). He woke up with a very sore throat on Sunday morning. We went to the doctor on Monday and Charlie was diagnosed with laryngitis. He started to feel better on Friday morning and is able to return to school today.

Charlie is worried, as the exams approach, about keeping on top of his work, so I would be very grateful if you could let him know what he has missed and help him catch up.

If you have any concerns, please do email or phone me on the number below.

Yours sincerely

Mr K Bond
kevin.bond@email.net
Tel: 01234 456789

---

- The letter quickly and clearly summarizes the course of events and includes evidence of the illness by referring to the doctor's diagnosis.

- The parent, having been very clear about the reason for absence, then presents their own concerns and is explicit about what they want the teacher to do. The letter is useful and effective for the parent, teacher and pupil.

Mrs J Trewin
'The Glade'
Farm Road
Kettering
XA7 2WR
janetrewin@email.com
01234 5678913

29 January 2015

Ms L Edge
Long Oak Primary School
West End Lane
Kettering
XA5 9LD

Dear Ms Edge

I am writing to follow up on our conversation on the phone two days ago. I'm afraid that Julia is still very upset when she gets home from school. The name-calling and exclusion from playground games seems to have carried on, in spite of the warning you said you gave the other children concerned. In fact, I fear that it may have made the problem worse.

As you can imagine this is causing Julia great distress and it is certainly affecting her desire to come to school and learn. I am very anxious to get this matter resolved with all possible speed, and request a meeting with you and the head of year at your earliest convenience.

Please telephone or email me as soon as you can to arrange this.

Yours sincerely

*Mrs J Trewin*

Mrs J Trewin

- The letter quickly summarizes the current situation to remind the teacher of the problem.

- The parent suggests a specific course of action and a timetable.

## Letters of complaint

Complaining about faulty goods or services is an unpleasant but common experience. Whatever your complaint, there are several points which you should bear in mind when composing a letter or email to increase your chances of receiving a satisfactory response:

- Make sure you are complaining to the right person. It may seem obvious, but if you have paid for something in cash or by credit card, then it is the seller of the goods or services who you should address your complaint to – not the manufacturer.

- Be aware of your rights under the Sales and Supply of Goods Act, the Trades Descriptions Act and related or equivalent legislation – these decree that goods or services must be found to be 'as described' when sold.

- There are consumer watchdogs and other bodies who can help you if you are given unsatisfactory responses to your complaints. You can also write to your MP or consult a solicitor, but these should be last measures which hopefully won't be necessary.


### Useful phrases

- I am writing to express my dissatisfaction with the service I received from your ...

- At the time of booking it was agreed that ...

- However, on our arrival, we discovered that ...

- I recently bought ...(include colour, model and price) in your shop in ...

- When I tried to use this item, I discovered that ...

- I have contacted you by telephone three times and each time you have promised to visit and put the faults right.

- To date these problems have not been resolved.

- Under the terms of your guarantee, I would like to request a full reimbursement of the amount paid.

- I am withholding payment of the above invoice until I have heard your response to the points outlined above.

- Under the Supply of Goods and Services Act 1982, I am entitled to expect work to be carried out using due care and skill.

- If I do not hear from you within 14 days, I will have no choice but to take the matter further.

- Because of these faults I now consider you to be in breach of contract.

## Letter or email of complaint concerning faulty goods

15 High Street
Corton
LANCS
LA12 3SH
fheadley@email.com

17 August 2015

Mr D Bryant
High Fi
3 The Parade
Soulton
LANCS
LA23 8GG

Dear Mr Bryant,

I am writing to complain about the Soundalive 411 headphones which I bought from your company, High Fi in Soulton, on 14 August.

When I plugged the headphones into my iPhone and listened to music through them, the sound in the left headphone was distorted at even low levels of volume – it was clear to me that they were faulty.

I returned them to your shop, a thirty mile round trip, but the salesperson who I originally dealt with disputed my claim – stating that the item had been sold in a satisfactory state. He suggested that I take up the complaint with you, as the owner of the shop.

The Sale of Goods Act 1979 makes it clear that goods be as described, fit for purpose and of satisfactory quality. I am therefore rejecting the headphones and request that you refund the £89 I paid, as the condition of the goods I received constitutes a breach of contract. I have enclosed a copy of my receipt.

I also require you to confirm whether you will arrange for the headphones to be collected from me at the above address, or will reimburse me for the cost of returning them by post?

I expect to receive a response detailing your proposals to satisfactorily settle my claim within seven days of this date.

Yours sincerely,

*F Headley*

Mr F Headley

- Although the writer has being treated badly by a member of staff, the tone of the letter is formal. Emotive language is likely to produce a defensive response, whereas a detailed and factual description of the problem is more likely to succeed.

- It is quite reasonable to seek compensation for the cost of returning a faulty item.

- Don't send originals of receipts and other documentary evidence with your complaint – especially if you have paid in cash. They may be the only way you have to prove purchase should you need to take the complaint further.

# Letter to a travel agency complaining about a holiday

Mrs B Pritchard
21 Churchward Close
Hintenbury
GLOS
FL34 3HQ
bpritchard@email.com

21 July 2015

Customer Services department
Sunkissed Holidays
14 The Waterglades
Hintenbury
GLOS
FL34 7HH

Dear sir or madam

I am writing to complain about the holiday I booked through your company on 5 May this year (REF: BA12303/Maga003).

The booking stated that I would have a room with a balcony with ocean views, and that I would enjoy '5 star luxury' at the Mirabelle Resort, with 'top class international cuisine', and 'a choice of four swimming pools – two of which are reserved for adult use only.' Furthermore, the booking was on an 'all-inclusive basis, guaranteeing bar snacks, soft drinks and local brands of beers, wines and spirits', as and when I requested them.

The reality of my experience was very different. On arrival at the resort, I was allocated a room at the back of the hotel, with a view over a busy street. The noise from the traffic kept me awake at night.

The 'international cuisine' turned out to be a buffet featuring the same options practically every night – mostly fried food, chips and salad.

One of the swimming pools was closed for maintenance for the duration of my stay, and there was no attempt to keep any of the three remaining pools segregated for adult use.

Finally, the availability of drinks and bar snacks was very limited – peanuts were the only snack at the poolside bar, which also only had wine stocked on two days of the fourteen I was at the hotel.

I complained about each of these issues to your firm's representative at the resort – a Mr Stephens – during my first week's holiday. He said he would 'see what he could do'. I didn't hear back from him, and he failed to turn up for the 'rep meeting' in the second week. The hotel staff were unhelpful and told me they could do nothing to rectify any of the problems.

As a result of these issues, my holiday was ruined. I am therefore writing to you seeking compensation from your firm, which has clearly failed to deliver what was contractually agreed. I request that you reply within seven days, stating your proposal to compensate me.

Yours faithfully

*Mrs B Pritchard*

Mrs B Pritchard

- Use the company's own description of services to compare your experience with.

- Describe each aspect of your complaint concisely; state what you have done about it, and the response that you received from the relevant authority – in this case the holiday rep and the hotel staff.

## Letter of complaint to a noisy neighbour

Mr G Barton
7 Chestnut Mansions
Pibble
Cumbria
PW12 3RR
gbarton@email.com

14 October 2015

Ms R Devlin
8 Chestnut Mansions
Pibble
Cumbria
PW12 3RR

Dear Ms Devlin

I am writing to you to formally register my complaint about the excessive noise that has been generated from your flat since you moved in two months ago.

As you know, I have complained in person to you five times in the past month about extremely loud music being played after 11 pm. You have assured me that you will 'not let it happen again,' only for me and my partner to have our sleep ruined the next weekend.

We have no objection to the occasional party or celebration, but your behaviour is inconsiderate and unreasonable. The interruption to our sleep patterns is affecting our concentration at work, and therefore I am giving you notice that if this happens again, without prior notice and agreement from us, I shall instruct my solicitor to begin legal proceedings to restrain you from excessive noise pollution.

Yours sincerely

*Mr G Barton*

Mr G Barton

- Legal action should only be threatened after attempts to complain less formally have failed. This letter is written after five such attempts.

- Be clear about what you expect to happen as a result of your complaint – how you expect the other party to modify their behaviour in this instance.

- Also spell out what course of action you intend to take should your demands not be met. You must follow through on this course of action, if you don't get a satisfactory response, or you will not be taken seriously in the future.

# SOCIAL COMMUNICATION

> *And none will hear the postman's knock*
> *Without a quickening of the heart.*
> *For who can bear to feel himself forgotten?*

(W.H. Auden)

Although seemingly belonging to a different world – predating mobile phones, texts and tablet devices, all of which convey informal messages instantly and very well – there is still a time and a place for a carefully handwritten note or card, or printed invitation.

Types of correspondence in this category include:

- Thank-you notes
- Letters of condolence
- Invitations

Here are some general points to consider when writing social communications:

## Tone

Apart from invitations, the tone of most social communications is informal and friendly:

- Salutations can range from 'Dear' to 'Hi'.

- Language is usually quite conversational, with shortened sentences and contractions ('I'm', 'won't'); more emotive and less factual than in business correspondence.

- Endings are similarly warm – 'Lots of love'; 'Love'; 'Speak/write soon'; or slightly more formal such as 'Best wishes', 'Kind regards' or 'All the best' if you don't know your correspondent quite so well.

## Format

Just because it is handwritten doesn't mean that a note shouldn't have a structure. It is still usual to have:

- An introductory line or paragraph, stating the purpose of the letter ('I was sorry to hear about your loss'; 'thank you for the birthday card...').

- A middle section expounding on the subject ('She was a wonderful woman...'; 'The party went really well, all things considered').

- An ending ('I shall hope to speak to you at the memorial service'; 'Let's meet up before another year goes by...").

> *One thing I can't stand? The computer-generated Christmas card – it's so impersonal – "Look, I can do a mail merge on my pc!" If you can't be bothered to handwrite a greetings card, don't bother!*
>
> (Publishing assistant)

Here are some examples of different kinds of social correspondence:

## Thank-you note for a dinner party

A thank-you letter can be as varied as a formal letter: the writer's relationship with the recipient will determine the tone and language used.

---

Tuesday

Hi Moz,

I'm just popping this note through your letterbox to thank you so much for dinner on Saturday. Nigel and I had a wonderful evening. It was lovely to meet Sharon and Graham at last – you've talked about them so much over the years – and they were delightful company. I hope Ben has found the champagne cork (sorry about that!)

By the way, please, please send me your recipe for the chocolate mousse – it was exquisite, and Nigel talked of nothing else on Sunday.

You must come to ours for dinner soon.

Love to you both and thanks again,

Lizzie.

---

- Dating and address can be very informal – this is a note between friends, and knowledge of addresses and contact details can be assumed. Note that the writer uses her friend's nickname 'Moz', rather than full name. You wouldn't use this form of address if writing to a colleague, for example.

- The language is casual – contractions like 'you've' and 'I'm' are absolutely fine. "Please, please send me your recipe...' would be out of place in a formal letter, but it works here.

- In social communication you can refer to events without having to be explicit – here there was clearly an 'incident' with a champagne cork which was a shared source of humour.

## Letter of condolence

46 Cork Lane
Lamington
Herts

12 May

Dear Stephen

I am writing to say how sorry I was to hear of your loss, and that I am thinking of you at this difficult time. Although I was aware that Helen was ill, I was nevertheless shocked to hear of her passing.

I know she was never happier than when she had met you, and the two of you made a lovely couple. She seemed to light up the life of everyone who met her.

I shall certainly attend the memorial service next Thursday, but if there is anything I can do in the meantime Stephen, please don't hesitate to call me. I'm sure Jo and Max are a great comfort to you at the moment.

Thinking of you all with love and affection.

Fiona

- The main point of difference with a thank-you letter, is that the writer should be acutely sensitive to the addressee's feelings, rather than trying to express their own emotions. The references made to the deceased in this letter are mainly in the context of her relationship with the bereaved partner, rather than the writer.

- A handwritten note can be more appropriate than a phone call in situations of grief and loss like this. Writing a letter also gives you more time to think about what you want to say, and how you want to say it.

- Note that the letter, although it is informal in address and tone, still has a discernible structure: the introductory sentence explains the purpose of the letter; the middle paragraph expands on the theme with the writer's memories of the deceased; and the final paragraph acknowledges the future by accepting an invitation and offering support.

> It really helped to receive letters of support from friends. Even though I didn't feel like talking to anyone at the time, it was good to know that others appreciated Jim, and that people were thinking of me and the kids.
>
> (Widow)

## Invitations

Invitations are frequently made by email or by text these days, but there are occasions when a written or printed invitation is still the prevalent form of communication.

Occasions that might require an invitation include:

- Birthday parties
- Weddings
- Anniversary parties
- Christenings
- Funerals
- Housewarming parties
- Dinner parties

**A wedding invitation**

> Boris and Isabel Andrews
> request the pleasure of the company of
> Phillip and Sally Bairstow
> at the wedding of their daughter Florence
> to James Chater
> on Saturday July 18 2015
> at St Bart's Church, Eggleton at 2pm.
>
> R.S.V.P.
> Isabel Andrews, The Gildings, Foxton Lane, Biblington, BB13 5TR
> Tel: 01286 5543077.

- The most important feature of an invitation is that it must possess all the necessary information to allow the recipient to respond with an acceptance or a refusal. There is no point sending out wedding invitations to 400 guests without the date on them!

- Social invitations can be informal or formal. Formal invitations – to a wedding or a christening, for example – will usually be printed.

## A birthday invitation

> *YIKES!*
> *I'm (nearly) thirty!*
> *Help me get over it on Saturday 21 May*
> *at the Stag, Riddlesway, Broxton.*
> *There'll be drinking, dancing and a very special*
> *quiz – how can you refuse?*
> *Please RSVP as soon as possible,*
> *so I can sort out some eats for the night.*
> *See you there,*
> *Charlie Bright*
> *cbright@email.com*
> *06785 4459881*

- This invitation could be sent in the form of an email, handwritten note or printed card.

- The tone is humorous and the language (and punctuation) informal, which suits the occasion.

- The font is also deliberately informal.

- Note the promise of a 'very special quiz' to intrigue the reader and hopefully persuade them to attend.

- Even with this casual approach, the host has taken care to include all the information which the recipient will need to decide whether they can attend or not.

### Replying to invitations

- When replying to invitations, match the style and formality of the invite.

- If you have to decline an invitation, it is good practice to sound apologetic, regretful and explain the reason why you cannot attend.

# SOCIAL MEDIA

> *I use email all the time; Twitter, Facebook and blogging – weekly.*
> (Deputy director, charity)

The development of social media has significantly changed the way we communicate with each other. It differs greatly from conventional forms of communication. You are not speaking to a few specific people but with tens, hundreds or even of thousands at once. As well as words, you use pictures, clips and internet links to share information. The best way to describe what you are doing when you use social media, like Facebook, Twitter or a blog, is that you are projecting a representation of yourself to a wide audience. This makes them very powerful and positive communication tools – for everyone from teenage friends to large corporations. The downside is that you have to be careful about what information you share, and how you share it: how you represent yourself. As social media are constantly developing – in terms of their reach and the purposes for which they are being used – the ground rules for successfully using them are changeable. There are, however, definitely some fundamental 'do's' and 'don'ts', which will be considered here along with the basic mechanics. This guide focuses on Facebook and Twitter, because they are currently the most popular forms of social media. There are many others – like Instagram and Linkedin – which have different formats and purposes, but most of the observations made here will still be applicable.

## Social media 'do's'

- **Decide why you're using it.** Is it to keep in touch with friends, be entertained, promote a business or service, or a mixture of all three? Blogging, Twitter and Facebook are used for all the above reasons, and they have different strengths and weaknesses.

- **Try to be consistent.** If you want to attract more followers on Twitter and other media, this is more likely to happen if people grow to trust and like your opinions or tweets.

- **Be positive.** It's a good principle to keep in mind, even if you don't always follow it. Anger and negativity do not generally translate well into social media, but a positive response to a negative issue can be effective and motivating. Consider whether you might say the same thing, or share the same information, if your audience were in the room with you. If the answer is 'no', then think twice about posting. This is true whether your audience is made up of personal or business contacts, particularly true if it contains both.

- **Be clear.** Nouns and facts work better on Facebook and Twitter than adjectives and adverbs – there is less room for misinterpretation of intention or mood if the message is clear and unambiguous. Of course, if you're casually chatting with friends on Instagram or Twitter, then it's a different matter.

- **Check your privacy settings.** This will help you avoid inadvertently sharing private information on Facebook and other media, or being embarrassed by something posted on your wall to a wider audience than you would like.

- **Reread your message, status update or tweet before you post it.** It's very easy to make mistakes in spelling or tone, especially if you're posting from a mobile phone with a very small keyboard. Consider using emoticons if you suspect your message is ambiguous.

## Social media 'don'ts'

- **'Retweet' (RT) too often.** It can be off-putting to followers. Sharing a link to a video or article you've enjoyed is often welcomed, but be sparing to make a greater impact.

- **Post, or tag, pictures of friends or acquaintances on Facebook.** Unless you're sure they won't mind, keep intimate details of shared events for private Facebook messaging.

- **Be rude.** It's very tempting to react angrily to tweets or posts that we strongly disagree with – don't. Arguments can escalate very quickly in the online environment and you will almost certainly say things from behind your computer screen that you would not in real life. A well-reasoned objection, or counter argument, will have more influence than posting an abusive message but serious issues are unlikely to be resolved online. If someone you're following, or you've 'friended' on Facebook, is a continual source of annoyance, then unfollow or block them.

- **Get upset if you are 'unfollowed'.** Twitter is a more impersonal medium than Facebook, and people chop and change whom they follow with great frequency.

- **Mix up your work life and personal life.** This applies particularly on Facebook. Your work colleagues may be amused by a picture of you at last night's party but your boss, who may be a Facebook friend of one of them, might find it less amusing – especially if you call in sick the next day.

- **Post sensitive news which might be better relayed by telephone.**
  It's very easy to say things online that might be difficult to express over
  the phone, but this doesn't necessarily make it the better option.

- **Be repetitive in your posts and tweets.** Many people repeat variations on
  a theme they consider important, hoping to elicit a response, while their
  audience gets fed up with reading the same information over and over again.

- **Ramble.** On Twitter you're usually restricted to 140 characters, which is good
  practice for learning how to express yourself succinctly. Try to keep Facebook
  updates to one or two lines, if possible. If you have a lot to say, you might be
  better off sending an email, or video calling.

- **Forget to punctuate.** Just because messages are short doesn't mean that
  they will make sense without commas, full stops and other punctuation
  marks.

## Glossary of social media terms

» **@.** The @ sign is used in 'tweets' directly before a username to turn it into
a link to that person's profile:@janesmith for example.

» **# (hashtag).** Hashtags are symbols which allow tweets on a subject to
be grouped together and located by a 'hashtag search'. For instance,
by including the expression, '*#spaceshuttle*' in a tweet, the user makes it
possible for other tweeters to search and locate all tweets with this
expression in them.

» **Blocking.** Blocking is preventing someone from reading your tweets,
or Facebook posts, by denying them access to your account.

» **Links.** Webpage references included in Facebook posts and tweets,
which can be clicked on to take the reader to the relevant web article or
image.

» **Retweet (RT).** Resending or forwarding someone's else tweet with or
without a comment of your own.

» **Status update.** The space on your Facebook account where you let your
'friends' know how you are feeling, or what you are thinking about.
Entries should be kept short.

» **Tweeter.** A user of Twitter.

» **Tweet(ing).** The act of posting a 'tweet' to Twitter.

» **Tweets.** Posts on Twitter made up of 140 characters or less.

» **Tweetup.** A physical meeting of tweeters – a 'twitter meet up'.

» **Wall.** The personal page of your Facebook account where 'friends' can post messages, links and other material.

> *I use Twitter all the time and have found it very useful for work. I'm on Facebook but I never use it.*
>
> (Journalist)

## Blogging

A blog – or 'weblog' – is a website where someone writes their thoughts and opinions in the form of a post. Blogs range in content from online diaries to a promotional tool for business. Mostly they are expressions of personal opinions and beliefs, and so tend to be informal and chatty in tone.

Regardless of why you are blogging, some basic rules apply:

- **Think about your reader.** Are you planning to inform them? Entertain them? Persuade them? Whether it is one of the above or all three, you will have to write accordingly, and be consistent in your approach, or the reader's interest will wane.

- **Be sincere and engaging.** A blog is usually quite conversational in style, so it may help to imagine you are chatting with the reader as you write. Share your experiences and tips, particularly if you're writing about a hobby or interest.

- **Keep posts short and interesting.** People tend to 'scan' blogs for words and images of interest – they may not be paying full attention. For this reason, try to keep sentences short and punchy. Include images and links to other web pages that reinforce your opinions or make the page look attractive. Add headings to break up the text, and keep paragraphs short.

> *I use Facebook to keep in touch with friends around the world, and Twitter to keep tabs on the news and celebrities. Skype is great for conference calls.*
>
> (Writer)

## Emoticons and smileys

Emoticons (from 'emotion' and 'icon') and 'smileys' are typed symbols representing expressions of the human face, from happy to sad. They are used as shorthand in text messaging, email, Tweets and other real-time communications to indicate the tone of the message, when the words alone do not make this clear. For instance, 'I am going out with my parents tonight ☺', or 'I am going out with my parents tonight ☹)

These have now been supplemented and even replaced to some degree by graphical images or 'emoji', which can be selected from a menu rather than created by using keyboard characters.

There is some debate about when it is suitable to use these symbols. Some people may not appreciate them, so think of the specific individual to whom you are writing and try to assess the effect they will have on that person before you decide to include them.

In some cases, you may also find that the emoticons you type are automatically converted into images when you send a message, and this can lead to unexpectedly large phone bills.

Here is a selection of the most commonly used emoticons:

| | |
|---|---|
| **:-)** or **:)** | happy |
| **(-:** | smiling back, also smiling |
| **:-()** | smiling with mouth open |
| **8-)** | smiling with glasses |
| **D:-)** | smiling with baseball cap |
| **|-)** | grin |
| **:>** | devilish grin |
| **:^D** | sounds good (agree) |

| | |
|---|---|
| :-)) | cheerful |
| :-))) | really happy |
| :-D | laughing |
| \|-D | belly laugh |
| :'-D | crying with laughter |
| xD | laughing really hard |
| :-& | tongue tied |
| ;-) | winking, just kidding |
| ;-> | conspiratorial wink |
| >:) | evil grin |
| :p | tongue sticking out, playful, just kidding |
| <3 | heart |
| :-❀ | kissing |
| :-X | big kiss |
| :-x | small kiss, peck |

| | |
|---|---|
| **^5** | high five |
| **:-(** | sad |
| **:'-(** | crying |
| **:-C** | very sad |
| **:-@** | screaming |
| **:-O** | shocked or surprised |
| **:-o** | wow |
| **[:-(** | frowning |
| **:/** | frustrated |
| **:-\** | sceptical |
| **:-||** | angry |
| **>:-|** | cross |
| **:-<>** | surprised |
| **:-(*)** | you make me sick |
| **<:-]** | stupid, idiot |

| | |
|---|---|
| **:-S** | confused |
| **%-)** | confused and happy |
| **%-(** | confused and unhappy |
| **:-(o)** | shouting |
| **:-V** | yelling |
| **:-@** | screaming |
| **\|-@!** | swearing |
| | |
| **]-()** | yawning |
| **\|-i** | sleeping |
| **\|-O** | snoring |